LINCOLN CHRISTIAN UNIVERSITY

P9-DIE-360

The Shaping of Modern China

Hudson Taylor's Life and Legacy

2
(1868–1990)

The Shaping of Modern China

Hudson Taylor's Life and Legacy

2
(1868–1990)

A.J. Broomhall

William Carey Library
Pasadena, California
www.WCLBooks.com

PIQUANT
editions

Copyright © 2005 by the Overseas Missionary Fellowship (OMF International)
This edition copyright © 2005 by Piquant Editions Ltd.
PO Box 83, Carlisle, CA3 9GR, United Kingdom
E-mail: info@piquant.net
Website: www.piquant.net

Set ISBN 1-903689-16-3 (EAN 9 781903 689165)
ISBN for Volume 2: 1-903689-18-X

All Rights Reserved.
No part of this publication may be reproduced or transmitted in any form or by
any means, electronic or mechanical, including photocopying or recording in
any information storage or retrieval system, without permission in writing from
the publishers.

Originally published by the Overseas Missionary Fellowship and Hodder and
Stoughton Ltd UK as *Hudson Taylor & China's Open Century,* Volume 5: *Refiner's
Fire* (1985, ISBN 0-340-36866-7), Volume 6: *Assault on the Nine* (1988, ISBN 0-
340-42629-2), Volume 7: *It is not Death to Die!* (1989, ISBN 0-340-50270-3).

British Library Cataloguing in Publication Data
Broomhall, A.J.
    The Shaping of Modern China : Hudson Taylor's life and legacy. – 2nd ed.
    Vol. 2 : 1868 - 1990
    1. Taylor, James Hudson, 1832-1905 2. Catholic Church – Missions – China
    3. Missionaries – China – Bibliography 4. Protestant Churches – Missions –
    China 5. China – Church history
    I. Title
    266' .0092

Unless otherwise stated, Scripture quotations are from the Holy Bible, New
International Version, copyright © 1973, 1978, 1984 by the International
Bible Society. Used by permission of Hodder and Stoughton Ltd. All Rights
Reserved. 'NIV' is a registered trademark of the International Bible Society. UK
trademark number 1448799.

Cover design by Projectluz
Book design by To a Tee, www.2aT.com

Contents of Volume 2

124745

Part VII: It is Not Death to Die

Maps and Illustrations in Volume 2

Part V

REFINER'S FIRE

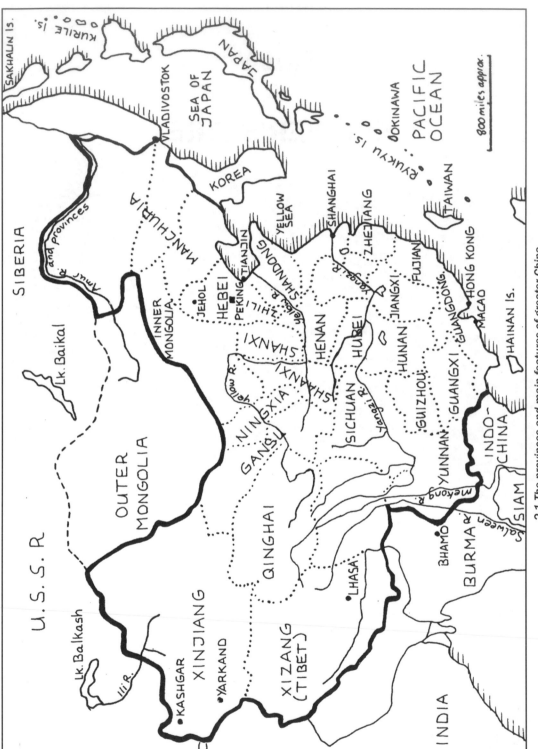

2.1 The provinces and main features of greater China

Preface to Part V

In the detached view of historians, the second Opium War, of 1859–60, was 'followed by about forty years of relatively uneventful relations between the Middle Kingdom and the West'. The word 'relatively' holds the key to such a statement, for the 1870s continued to see crises leading sometimes to the brink of war between China and not only Western nations but Japan as well. As dean of the Imperial Tongwen Academy of Peking, W. A. P. Martin remarked that in twenty-five years only twenty-five riots against foreigners took place. Peace had come at last! Peace and progress, but only after a systematic attempt to crush Christian missions out of existence by mob violence. He spoke too soon. Thirty years after his elevation to this place of honour, Martin himself was to be in danger of his life in the siege of the Peking legations. But that was in the future.

Friction was seldom absent in the period covered by this part of the narrative (1868–75). Orchestrated agitation against foreigners and foreign policies placed the pioneers of penetration into the interior of China in extreme danger time and again. Proclamations for their protection varied in sincerity and effectiveness, and the inability of mandarins to control the scholar-gentry was often demonstrated.

If commerce was to develop and the gospel to be taken deep into China, merchant and missionary must test the unpredictable reactions of the Chinese people. Collaboration in this was unthinkable in the climate of the times. 'Trade' meant the opium traffic as much as it meant tea and silk. Hudson Taylor saw his task as involving the necessity of testing Chinese attitudes; but only as a natural consequence of his prime purpose. The enlightened attitude of Ma Xinyi, Muslim governor of Zhejiang province, had given Taylor the impression that moving upcountry would be more straightforward than proved to be the case. Vehement opposition came as a surprise to everyone, consul, merchant and missionary alike. But the quiet heroism of the pioneers opened the way to better international relations and incidentally to an open door to trade.

Unconcerned about either, the missionary pioneers were intent only on spreading the gospel throughout the empire. Inadvertently they clarified the diplomatic issues, provided the pretext for armed intervention, bore the blame, and in the process vindicated their own integrity. This did not save them from being labelled the tools of the imperialists, prospecting for iron and coal!

Late twentieth-century debate is focused by political views in China on 'the Chinese experience' and 'the missionary experience', in the current jargon. But in the 1870s both were embryonic. In this part of the history we are only just over the threshold of China's humiliation by the West. The later nineteenth- and twentieth-century experience is wholly different. When John King Fairbank[1] used these terms in reference to a span of nearly two centuries (1800–1975) he emphasised our ignorance of the period of history considered in this series about Hudson Taylor.[1]

By offering in this volume historical facts about the individuals concerned, the kind of people they were and their activities, a better contribution to the truth about China and missions may be made than by mere assessment and opinion. 'The Barbarian Question' and 'the Missionary Question' are mid-nineteenth-century terms and are therefore preferred in this context.

Refiner's Fire continues and depends for understanding upon the other parts of this series, *Barbarians at the Gates*, *Over the Treaty Wall*, *If I Had a Thousand Lives* and *Survivors' Pact*. They trace the origins of the Christian Church in China and use available sources to show the real Hudson Taylor in the perspective of contemporary events and personalities. In *Survivors' Pact* the projected China Inland Mission took shape with thirty members. Typhoons at sea and dissension in its ranks failed to destroy it in the experimental phase, and resistance by some mandarins only hardened the resolve of Hudson Taylor and his young men and women. Once again we pick up the threads as if there had been no break in the narrative. But the time has come to stand further back from descriptive detail, to see the broader sweep of events. A year of trial and error, of training and testing of his team, led Hudson Taylor to deploy those he could and to make plans for penetrating deeper into China. Fortunately the future was a closed book. To Chinese and other scholars researching the origins of the extensive Church of today, however, details of the earliest church planting will be important.

Adversity has its value however it is viewed. By testing, proving and purifying it brings out the best—the faith, fortitude and endurance of those undergoing it. In this volume, Hudson Taylor and the novice members of his fledgling Mission meet with adversity far exceeding any they had yet experienced in a spirit of acquiescence in the Refiner's work. If the theme of the series were not Hudson Taylor's humanity but his heart and soul, the problem of what to include would have been greater. Enough is retained to show the kind of man he was.

AJB

Acknowledgments to Part V

Special thanks are due this time to my long-suffering advisers, who waded through much more preliminary typescript than usual. The abundance of source material resulted in a draft which had to be drastically reduced for publication. The mercifully merciless advice of the panel showed clearly where the axe should fall. Some of the deleted material finds a place in the appendices, and the unabridged typescript will remain with the archives for reference.

The understanding comments of reviewers are appreciated, showing as they do a grasp of my declared intentions. In Part VI, which brings us to more recent times, I shall try, briefly, to redress the deliberate economy of assessment and discussion in the earlier volumes. Meanwhile I gratefully acknowledge the encouragement received from the late Bishop Stephen Neill, historian of Christian mission, and other correspondents, and the use of other societies' source books.

AJB

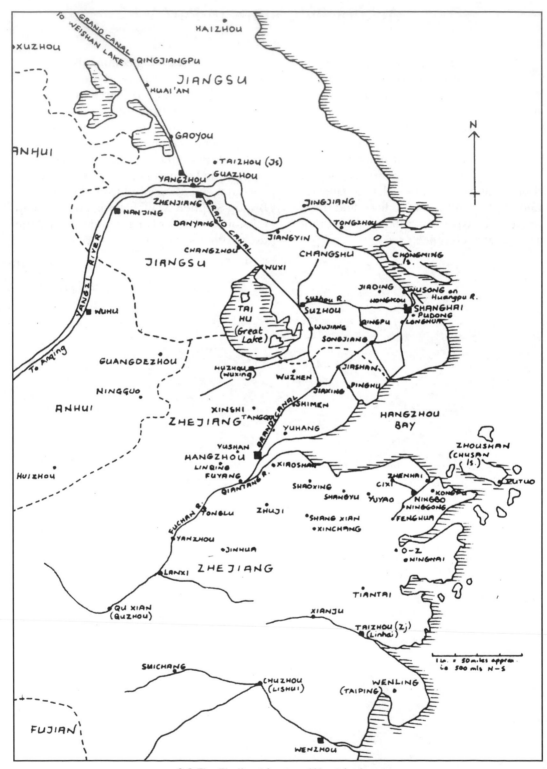

2.2 The Zhejiang front and Yangzi advance

14
Riot (1868)

Millrace of violence (1867–70)

The eventful years 1857–70 were years of unrest and upheaval worldwide, not only in China. Towards the end of 1867 the French had entered Rome (October 30) and Garibaldi had been captured. A British expedition had embarked on the invasion of Etia, leading to the suicide of King Theodore. The French had been driven out of Mexico and 'Emperor' Maximilian shot, and France herself was to suffer ultimate humiliation in the Franco-Prussian war of 1870. Defeat, with the surrender of Napoleon III and his army, led to the republic being proclaimed, Paris being besieged and a communist insurrection taking place in the capital. Paris surrendered in January 1871. Rome and the Papal States, without French protection, were annexed to the new kingdom of Italy, and Germany was proclaimed a united empire. The Age of Bismarck had begun, and William I of Prussia was proclaimed emperor of Germany—at Versailles! The Man of Iron at last began to work for peace, his best hope of preserving supremacy.

In China the 'quiet years' were to be disrupted by a succession of violent incidents. Provocations against merchants and missionaries multiplied, and the consuls welcomed pretexts to justify an assertion of power, to protect their treaty rights. The era of high-handed action by consuls with gunboats at their beck and call was to reach its peak in a series of excesses before being quelled by Sir Rutherford Alcock, the man who had begun it all. In 1848 he had 'declared war on the Chinese empire' after the Qingpu outrage (see 1, pp 131–32f). As minister at Peking in 1868 he had a better understanding of the successive affronts to Chinese pride against which her intellectuals were protesting.

As Hudson Taylor prepared to move 'further on and further in' foreigners were travelling more freely throughout China. T. T. Cooper, agent for the Chamber of Commerce at Calcutta, had conceived the idea in 1862 of entering China from Burma but had had to abandon his plans during the Muslim rebellion in Yunnan. After several years in Shanghai, hearing discussion of a possible Bhamo-Dali trade route, he decided to attempt an overland journey from Shanghai to Calcutta by Captain Blakiston's route (see 1, p 515). In January 1868 he left Hankou in Chinese clothes and travelled up the Yangzi gorges to Chongqing and on to Chengdu and Ya'an. The *North China Herald* of April 11 published his description of Sichuan province and his declared intention of travelling via Batang to Nepal, a route which must take him through Lhasa. At the Tibetan border he, too, was turned back at several points south of Kangding (Tatsienlu) and conceded defeat.[2]

One of Alexander Wylie's promising young Bible Society colporteurs, named Johnson, left Shanghai, also in January 1868, and was last seen at Zhenjiang (Chinkiangy) on the Yangzi, heading for Henan province. His route was almost certainly across the Yangzi to Guazhou, up the Grand Canal through Marco Polo's city of Yangzhou to Qingjiangpu (Tsingkiangpu) (see map 2.2: p 6) as far as the Weishan Lake on the Shandong border. Then he seems to have crossed the neck of Jiangsu province at Xuzhou into the similar neck of Anhui, which shares the Shandong border for a mere twenty-five miles, for 'near the borders' he perished at the hands of banditti, consisting principally if not entirely of disbanded militia. Another report of the murder of a Protestant missionary in Henan province was assumed to refer to the same person as no one else was missing.[3]

In March 1868 Hudson Taylor's young friend R. F. Laughton (see 1, pp 531–32) sent a Chinese employee to rent premises for use as a preaching point in a market town two miles from Yanta in Shandong. Although told specifically to state its purpose, the agent lied to the owners, saying it was for use as a shop. When Laughton came and furnished it as a chapel, the owners protested, offering to refund the down payment. Not knowing the facts, he insisted on staying, whereupon they removed the roof and walled up the door. The consul, Challoner Alabaster, settled the matter by requiring the public dismissal of the employee and the restoration of the house to Laughton, warning Laughton 'in future to acquire any buildings he may need for mission purposes through the consulate'. As a petty incident of little consequence, it had its lessons for missionaries to note. [4]

Jonathan Lees of the LMS and John Innocent of the Methodist New Connexion travelled overland from Tianjin to Jinan (Tsinan) in Shandong in May 1868 to meet W. B. Hodge, a colleague of Innocent's. The journey took them through territory littered with corpses and destruction by the Nianfei and counter-insurgency action.[5]

On May 25, 1868, Robert Hart wrote from Peking to his customs commissioner at Tianjin, G. Hughes, that he had been told at the Zongli Yamen on the previous day of Nianfei rebels having entered Zhili south of Tianjin, between the Grand Canal and the sea: 10,000 in number, they posed a threat to the city. In April a foreign correspondent had written of corpses of men, women and children floating down the Hai He (river) at Tianjin. The court appealed to Zeng Guofan and Li Hongzhang to put an end to the Nianfei scourge, and this time Li succeeded with the aid of Mongol horsemen. A 'peaceful' region, apparently safe to travel in, could become a death trap at any time. At Xian Xian, near the Grand Canal in Zhili, Pére Leboucq had nearly been killed by the Nianfei in February. In May he nearly died at the hands of the imperial troops, and in August from typhoid fever. A proclamation enjoining the populace to protect his mission and orphanage had little effect. On May 18, 1868 (the day Hudson Taylor left Hangzhou and travelled north) both buildings were pillaged by a mob.[6]

Roman Catholic missions in Guangdong had entered during 1867 upon a troubled period of three years. In October 1867 one priest was imprisoned. In August 1868 another was injured in an uprising. In December 1868 another riot led to the destruction of a chapel, the death of seven converts and the wounding of a hundred others and of their priest the Abbé Delavay. Sichuan province saw disturbances of a different nature. Friction between the Catholic community and other people led to clan fights in which the Abbé Mabileau was killed in 1865 and, as Hosea Ballou Morse recorded, 'in the years following, through the action of Christian converts' 105 houses were burned, hundreds of people were wounded (700 according to one of three enquiries) and 173 died. Violent retaliation followed in 1869.

As we come to the scenes of major violence in Taiwan and at Yangzhou and Zhenjiang, engulfing nine of the *Lammermuir* party (see 1, p 700) and the four Taylor children, it should be remembered that these were not isolated incidents.

Pot and kettle (19th century)

The Roman Catholic missionaries' principles and methods of working bore few resemblances to those of the Protestants. Ultimately concerned with the eternal salvation of the Chinese through the atoning death of Christ they worked first to secure their attachment to the Church and afterwards to instruct them. Membership of the Roman Catholic Church was what mattered: to enlist, train and care for its members in the hope that spiritual conversion would result.

The means employed were secondary in importance. Treaty privileges and the French protectorate could be used for the salvation of souls, by protection from persecution, assistance with the magistrates or with litigation, just as much as through schools, orphanages and opium refuges. Sometimes whole villages or clans were enrolled in this way, and the travellers, notably von Richthofen, Younghusband and W. H. Medhurst Jr, remarked on some clean, orderly and industrious Catholic communities they visited,[7] in marked contrast with non-Christian villages.

Mgr Faurie, Vicar-Apostolic of Guizhou, freely used his influence to have antagonists punished, and wrote tongue in cheek if not naively, 'Every one of the individuals who has been punished for reviling our religion has embraced with ardour the true Faith on leaving prison.' Of one in particular whom he had imprisoned and then released he said, 'The same evening he presented himself in chapel to adore the true God.' Alexander Hosie wrote of the handsome palace of the French Bishop in Yunnanfu (Kunming). Pomp, ceremony and prestige could be thought of as glorifying God. But the average foreign priest lived very simply in semi-Chinese style without ever returning to his homeland. Some 'impressed travellers with the radiant strength and beauty of their lives'.

Protestant missionaries believed, however, that Catholicism was failing to give the essentials of the Christian gospel to the Chinese, and therefore disregarded its representatives. Rome, to the average Protestant in the nineteenth century, was anti-Christ, and Catholicism a corruption of the truth. To the Catholics, Protestant missionaries were dangerous heretics leading the people 'from Confucius to confusion'. Chinese cities were 'opened to the gospel' irrespective of a Roman Catholic presence. But anti-foreign and anti-Christian agitation drew little or no distinction between them.[8]

Burlingame, Hart and Martin (1867–70)

The glories of Chinese culture and a wealth of values in the Chinese character appealed to some Western men of insight, while the general run of foreigners were insensitive to them. Lord Elgin, party with the French to the sacking of the Summer Palace in spite of his father's appreciation of the Grecian marbles, claimed of his cooperation with the Peking court after 1860, 'I have been China's friend in all this.'[9] His brother, Sir Frederick Bruce, first resident British envoy in Peking, shared the sentiment. The four Allies, America, Britain, France and Russia, were in fact at one in wanting to restore China to stability. Others gave helpful advice to court and government, but none to the extent of Anson Burlingame, the American minister since 1861.

At 32, Robert Hart was firmly within the counsels of the rulers. H. N. Lay had become Inspector-General of Customs from January 21, 1861, and with the support of the foreign envoys had resisted the Chinese officials who looked upon the customs revenue as 'their legitimate source of emolument'. But after 1863 Lay had become enmeshed in the fiasco known to history as the Lay-Osborne fleet (see 1, p 629), while Hart as acting Inspector-General made his mark in the customs service and from the outset gained the good opinion of all foreign envoys, Chinese officials and foreign merchants alike. Quickly Hart was in control of all the coastal and Yangzi River revenues.

This evangelical Christian, widely acknowledged to be above reproach, was China's true friend and a mandarin for fifty years. Hosea Ballou Morse's intention when he addressed himself to writing about the dynasty was to base his volumes on the life of Sir Robert Hart as a connecting thread.[10] But Hart was too modest to approve and to give him access to his seventy-four-volume diary and letters. Instead Morse had to be content to write his nine-volume history, *The International Relations of the Chinese Empire*. Alicia Bewicke Little, in a satirical passage in her biography of Li Hongzhang, attributed Hart's success and 'the apparent satisfaction of all concerned' to his 'infinite subtlety of mind and adaptability', although his integrity deserved first mention.

W. A. P. Martin also became the personal friend of many leading Chinese officials. As a newly arrived missionary to Ningbo in 1850 he not only moved into the Chinese city but suggested that the whole American Presbyterian mission at Ningbo should transfer from the foreign settlement alongside the consulates and forge closer links with the Chinese people as the CMS and Miss Aldersey were already doing, while living in foreign style. He published his *Evidences of Christianity* in Chinese (*Tian Dao Su Yuan*) in 1854, a book that went through thirty or forty editions and attacked the opium traffic, something only missionaries would do.[11]

His involvement with the United States' envoys began when he offered to serve the Hon W. B. Reed as interpreter in 1858, and with Samuel Wells Williams he helped to negotiate the American treaty. Again in May 1859 he accompanied the Hon John E. Ward to Tianjin, and so became known to more high Chinese officials.[12] At the time of the Peking Convention Martin was in the United States, but he returned in 1862 and after some months in Shanghai began to preach the gospel in Peking, working with William Burns in the small chapel they opened. At the time, Maria Taylor's brother-in law, John Burdon, was chaplain to the British embassy and told Martin that his *Evidences of Christianity* had reached the imperial household. (Would that Robert Morrison could have lived to see this day.) Robert Hart, already a good friend from Ningbo days, was another of Martin's close associates.

Friendly Chinese officials responded to his appreciation of their nation, but when it became known that he was translating Wheaton's *Elements of International Law* with the intention of helping China in her international relations, his future course became predictable.[13] The Grand Secretary Wen Xiang, faced with French intrusions into Annam (Vietnam), welcomed Martin's translation and his

reputation was established. When Prussians captured Danish ships in Chinese waters, the Zongli Yamen found that when they used some sentences, from Martin's book, without revealing their source, 'the Prussian minister acknowledged his mistake without saying a word.' Not only that, with understanding came Chinese approval of *at least some aspects* of Western thinking.

Because funds for all American missions were curtailed by the Civil War, Martin was supplementing his income by teaching in the Tong Wen Guan, a school for interpreters. When, in 1867, with Robert Hart's strong backing he was offered a 'chair' or lectureship in international law and political economy, he leapt at it as yet another entrée for the gospel in influential Chinese circles. On full pay he hurried home to the States, studied his subjects for a year at Yale (where two of his sons were undergraduates), the better to fit himself for the post, and was back in Peking the next summer, 1869. Talented young men from all parts of the empire became his students. One day they might have influence at court or even teach the emperor. His hope was fulfilled when two graduates of the Tong Wen Guan after diplomatic service abroad returned to join the staff and were called to teach the Guang Xü emperor.[14]

Martin was installed on November 26, 1869, as dean of the Tong Wen Guan in the presence of officials of the Zongli Yamen, and over the years his students went on to hold high office both in China and overseas. While most missionaries following the biblical precedent took the gospel to the man in the street, and Hudson Taylor led his young men and women deeper into the interior of an intractably resistant China, Robert Hart and William Martin worked close to the seat of power. Like the apostle Paul who had friends among the high-ranking provincial officials of Ephesus (Acts 19.31), they were far from silent about their Christian message. Whether at the grassroots or the pinnacle of empire, either or more probably each approach held a key to the Chinese church of the future. Previously banned from teaching the gospel in the Tong Wen Guan, Martin was now allowed to do so discreetly. In 1869, he wrote to his mission board, resigning his membership but assuring them that he was no less a missionary than before. Boasting no false modesty, Martin pointed out the strategic value of his position 'One of the highest Mandarins, an Imperial Censor, said in the presence of several others that he had declared when I was not present that "If all missionaries were like Dr Martin he would himself be a Christian".'[15]

Mrs Little introduced Burlingame into her biography of Li Hongzhang largely for 'a touch of comedy'. As a minister in Peking, Burlingame was a success, obtaining by courtesy what others failed to win by bluster. In the spring of 1866 Robert Hart obtained six months' leave in Europe and proposed to Prince Kong that a Chinese delegation should accompany him to study the character of Western people. A Manchu ex-*daotai* promoted to the third rank and serving in the customs under Hart was appointed and by Western standards was well received in European capitals. But at sixty-three his prejudices made him unadaptable. Disgusted by the discomforts of travel and the lack of oriental decorum he encountered, he gave trouble from the start and returned without a good word for his hosts.

Not surprisingly, in November 1867, 'the diplomatic world in Peking was startled by the announcement that Mr Anson Burlingame had been commissioned by the Chinese emperor as his Ambassador-Extraordinary accredited to all the courts of the world.' Burlingame forthwith had conferred on him the red globe of the first civil rank, with one Manchu and one Chinese grandee of second rank as his subordinate envoys extraordinary, together with an entourage of two foreign and thirty Chinese secretaries.

The mission left Shanghai for the States on February 25, 1868. At a banquet given in San Francisco by the governor of California, Anson Burlingame revealed what was in store. Carried away by his enthusiasm and gift of oratory, he appealed to the memory of Ricci, Verbiest, Morrison, Milne, Bridgman and others who had lived and died hoping that the day would soon arrive when this great people (of China) would extend its arms towards the shining banners of Western civilisation. On June 28, 1868—when China in fact was seething with unrest—at a banquet given by the governor of New York, he asserted that China was ready to invite the missionaries to 'plant the shining cross on every hill and in every valley of China and to engage Western engineers to open mines and build railways'. In America great enthusiasm was aroused, 'but his language came as a shock of cold water to those he had left behind in China.' Peking civilities had completely misled him. Riot and murder had begun and the consuls were contemplating force to quell the mood. Incredibly, on July 28, 1868, a 'new' treaty between China and the United States was signed in Washington, reiterating the American Treaty of Tientsin (now Tianjin) with the one exception that the States undertook not to interfere in the development of China. But no power to negotiate a treaty had been granted to Burlingame!

Burlingame moved on triumphantly to Britain in September 1868 to a cool reception by Lord Stanley of the Foreign Office. At Peking the imperial regents were still refusing to grant audiences to foreign envoys, and in the provinces British subjects were being brutally assaulted and denied justice. In Paris he was granted an audience with the Emperor Napoleon III, now nearing his downfall, and proceeded to Stockholm in October and The Hague in November. Returning to London on November 20, Anson Burlingame was received by Queen Victoria on the expressed assurance that it was only the emperor's minority which prevented him from receiving her minister Sir Rutherford Alcock. Two weeks later Disraeli resigned, Gladstone became Prime Minister, Lord Clarendon succeeded Lord Stanley and on December 26 received Burlingame for discussions.[16]

Hawks Pott summarised Lord Clarendon's policy as unfriendly pressure, inconsistent with the independence of China, which should not be applied; Britain's representatives should deal with the central government, not with unenlightened local mandarins; China would be expected to observe the treaties she entered into; and Britain reserved the right to use force to protect life and property.[17] At face value that looked reasonable. But Peking was not remotely comparable with a Western counterpart. The significance of this reversal of policy in China becomes apparent as the Hudson Taylor history proceeds.

In the new year Burlingame met Bismarck in Berlin. W. A. P. Martin recorded, 'His last communication was a telegram, via Siberia, addressed to me for the Tsungli (Zongli) Yamen, reporting a favourable reception at Berlin, adding, "Concluded negotiations with Prussia; strong declaration by Bismarck in favour of China. Now to Russia!"'

The Tsar received him at St Petersburg on February 4, 1869, but the intense cold proved too much. On the 11th he died of pneumonia. H. B. Morse assessed his brief flight of fantasy by saying that Burlingame's contribution to East-West relations was, 'productive finally of good to China and to the world in general; but that in the minds of the rulers of China, its success caused such a revulsion of feeling, and created such confidence in their own judgment . . . as to retard the advance of the empire . . . for some years after.'

The empress dowager, 'vigorous but reactionary', saw to it that Chinese customs and institutions remained as much as possible what they had been under the Qian Long (1736–96) and Kang Xi (1662–1722) emperors, and that the 'wheels of progress' dragged heavily.

So ended with some success the attempt of a sincere friend of China to open the closed minds of Western nations to all the good in the remarkable Chinese. Values the West neither understood nor appreciated would one day be acknowledged. Those like Burlingame who savoured their richness could be pardoned if they became starry-eyed. There was another side of the coin with which Hudson Taylor and the 'Lammermuir party' had become familiar (1, part IV).

1868: A MOOD OF PROTEST

Rebuff at Jinhua
(January–February, 1868)

The success of the Huzhou riot in driving James Williamson, John McCarthy, Hudson Taylor and their battered Chinese companions away from that city in November 1867 left Williamson without a challenging objective (see 1, pp 831–34). The Cordons and Henry Reid, newly arrived in China, had been in Hangzhou for ten days and were beginning to feel at home in their Chinese clothes and the Chinese way of living. Rather than keep them among fellow-foreigners, Hudson Taylor preferred to send them straight into a Chinese environment. Now that Williamson was free to attempt a new city, the Cordons could be with him and Reid could join his fellow-Scotsman Duncan in Nanjing.

After the Qiantang River survey southeastward from Hangzhou (see 1, p 790), McCarthy had lived for a month at the prefectural city of Yanzhou, and Duncan at Lanxi, the commercial centre fifty miles further upstream (see map 2.2: p 6). The Jinhua River, which joined the upper reaches of the Qiantang at Lanxi, was the waterway of an extensive trading area, and Jinhua, 'a beautiful city on very high ground', was its political heart, 130 miles south of Hangzhou, the provincial capital. On January 4, while plans for Williamson were being considered, Miles Knowlton and Carl Kreyer, the Taylors' good American Baptist friends, called at New Lane with a proposition. Knowlton had travelled in the

Jinhua area from his base at Ningbo, and Chinese evangelists had settled in several of the city's country areas. But he was too busy to give them the help they needed. He had come, he said, to urge Hudson Taylor to place missionaries in Jinhua. He had never known trouble on his visits there and believed they would be well received. 'This request coming just when it did, seemed to us like the Macedonian cry,' Maria told the Bergers.

The next day was spent praying about it with the Hangzhou Christians, and on January 6, Hudson Taylor and the heroes of the Xiaoshan and Huzhou outrages, Mr Tsiu and Liu Jinchen, set off with James Williams and Henry Cordon up the Qiantang River.[18] Miles Knowlton had retained a room in a Jinhua home for use on his occasional visits, and the travellers were welcomed when they arrived on the 9th. The very next day they found 'a suitable house, beautifully situated' for themselves, and negotiated its rental for a year. The document was signed that night, the down payment paid, and in the morning they took possession

Nothing could have been easier. Hudson Taylor left the same day with Cordon to return to Hangzhou, leaving James Williamson and his two Chinese companions to carry out repairs. He bagged thirty ducks for the larder on the way home, and arrived on the 15th with presents for Maria's birthday the next day. With no reason to delay, Henry Cordon and his wife and Chinese attendants set off at once to ascend the Qiantang River again and make their home at Jinhua. On arrival at Laud, however, they found one of Williamson's men waiting for them with a message. Things had gone badly wrong at Jinhua on the 22nd. They were to go no further. James Williamson himself appeared the following morning with the now familiar story of violence and eviction. Together they all retreated downstream again.

George Duncan, alone in Nanjing, had already proved himself a successful pioneer. Living simply, with no foreign belongings or luxuries to alienate or tempt the Chinese,

and maturing steadily, his fluency in Nanjing Mandarin made him competent to give Reid, his fellow-Banffshire highlander, a good start in China. So John McCarthy was to escort Reid to Nanjing while Maria and Hudson Taylor stayed with Anne Stevenson at Shaoxing until another confinement was over. Maria would then return to her family at Hangzhou and work on the *Biblical Concordance in Chinese*, while Hudson Taylor made a tour of the southern Zhejiang cities to help the 'Ningbo five', as the earlier cities' members of the Mission were called.

John McCarthy and Reid set off up the Grand Canal and at Suzhou stayed overnight with Charles Schmidt. Then on towards the Yangzi River, passing through the devastated countryside strewn with human bones where 'acre upon acre' lying in ruins impressed Reid with the scale of destruction by the Taiping rebellion. Late on Saturday, January 18, they reached Nanjing and Duncan's cramped quarters still half a poor carpenter's house. McCarthy stayed long enough to help Duncan to rent a house of his own, large enough for two families, with a roomy reception hall for use as a chapel, and by February 2 was back in Hangzhou.

The people of Nanjing, some half million in all, were friendly. But before long Duncan discovered that his new home was too near the magistrate's *yamen* for that dignitary's approval, and had to give it up. Back in the carpenter's shop, Duncan and Reid made the most of their slender foothold. At least there were two pioneers extending the Mission's deployment up the Yangzi valley and established in an ancient capital of the empire.

Hudson Taylor and Maria had left for Shaoxing on the 17th and, glad of a reason for living in a Chinese home, 'rented nice rooms in a quiet house' for themselves while waiting for the Stevenson baby to be born. They were working on a *Report of the Hangzhou Branch of the China Inland Mission* and the third edition of *China: Its Spiritual Need and Claims*, with a new ten-page appendix on the pros and cons of living like the Chinese in Chinese clothes. As always, Maria wrote to Hudson's dictation as he paced the room.

Then on Chinese New Year's Day when the city was filled with noise and merry making, Anne Stevenson went into labour and the two of them took turns to be with her. The weather was cold and the charcoal burner must have been in use to heat the room, for in a classic instance of poisoning by odourless carbon monoxide fumes they came close to fatal asphyxiation. Instead of the customary free ventilation of Chinese rooms, the Stevensons had put up a ceiling and papered over the cracks in their walls. By the time the baby was born, at 3.25 a.m., Maria had a splitting headache but managed to wash and dress her before feeling faint and having to leave the room. Hudson Taylor, attending to Stevenson, became so faint that he had to stop. Maria returned and took over with her head throbbing so hard that, as she wrote, 'I thought I heard the rice pounders at work.' Nearly fainting again she staggered and Hudson put her to bed, to wake in the morning with her head aching violently and 'feeling so ill'. If the labour had been prolonged and the fumes had been undetected (accumulating from the ceiling downwards) all four could have died.[19]

Recovering, they completed the revision of China, and Hudson Taylor left to tour the southern cities. Early in the morning after he had gone, Maria was woken by John Stevenson's hammering at her bedroom door. James Williamson had arrived, forced out of Jinhua. She listened to his story and sent him posthaste to catch up with Hudson Taylor before he left Ningbo. On the same day, the *North China Herald*[20] reported that the British consul had been insulted in the streets of the treaty port of Jiujiang (Kiukiang) on the Yangzi. Security in China was a finely balanced thing.

Williamson's report had familiar overtones. Everything had gone favourably at Jinhua until January 14 when the landlord, a subordinate of the magistrate, had come saying he was in trouble, accused of helping the barbarians. Soon he was

2.3 Slowly upstream, towed by 'trackers'

summoned to the *yamen* and threatened with punishment. The mandarin let him go but then sent for him again, together with the two middlemen who had arranged the deal, and an elderly Christian member of the Ningbo Baptist congregation. The house the foreigner had rented was too close to the *yamen*! They must turn him out, to find another further away.

James Williamson had agreed to move, but the mandarin was not satisfied. He recalled one of the middlemen and ordered that he be flogged with 'four thousand blows'. (Williamson misunderstood and should have said 400.) After 'three thousand' had been administered, the man was thrown into prison. No one had dared to come near Williamson or do anything for him. His companions were in grave danger again. Williamson went to see the middleman in prison, locked 'in a den with a number of criminals . . . like so many wild beasts in a cage', the backs of his legs 'fearfully bruised and swollen', and realised how serious the situation was.

The next morning the landlord and the other middleman were summoned again to the *yamen*, and the wife and mother of the first man were threatening suicide and blaming Williamson for bringing this trouble on them. 'In order to save the people from further ill-usage,' he reported, 'we left the house and proceeded to meet the party coming up, and returned with them to Hangzhou.' There he had reported events to the provincial governor's deputy before hurrying on to tell the Taylors.

With so many young couples of several missions within travelling distance, the Taylors' movements were often governed by confinements rather than by Mission business. Since Dr John Parker had left Ningbo and returned to Scotland in October 1867, no one else with the medical knowledge and experience was available. Maria returned to Hangzhou for the birth of the Inslees' baby, and Hudson Taylor cut short his travels for the confinement of another American Presbyterian, Sarah Dodds, at the end of February. This was to be the pattern year after year.

The only record of his dealings with the consulate at Ningbo on the Jinhua matter is a reference to his taking it up with the magistrate and his superiors. But there was much coming and going. On February 10, James Williamson was back at Hangzhou with a batch of letters from Ningbo, and on the 12th was off again with a new colporteur, bearing a document

2.4 Faster downstream—taking a rapid (notice the main inter-city road, paved with granite slabs)

from Governor Ma's deputy to the Jinhua magistrate. Liu Anchen arrived next from Ningbo and followed Williamson to Jinhua. Then the colporteur returned with the news that the document had been delivered to the magistrate but no action had been taken. Williamson was still in Jinhua, unmolested and waiting to see results. By March 10 the picture was clear. Nothing had happened and nothing would happen. Once again the barbarian had been thwarted. The mandarins were seeing how far they could go. This time even the governor's deputy appeared to be playing safe by putting no pressure on the Jinhua magistrate.

The American Baptists tried again and failed to secure a foothold in Jinhua, but

seven years later in 1875, when the CIM tried once more they succeeded in renting the very same house as before and were still at work there twenty years later.[21]

Southern tour (February 1868)

When he reached Ningbo on January 29 and made his way to Bridge Street, Hudson Taylor was back at his first bachelor quarters and his first home with Maria after their marriage. Here Martha Meadows had died tragically and alone, and James Meadows had built up the congregation and proved himself as a missionary. Now with his new wife, Elizabeth Rose, it was still his home. Hudson Taylor had been there only a few hours when Williamson arrived after dark. Yet another attempt to occupy a new city had been defeated.

Two nights later they were woken by the sound of knocking at the outer gates. To their astonishment, George and Annie Crombie were standing outside with a coffin. Convulsions had quickly led to their son's death at Fenghua. Their first child had died at birth. The heartbroken parents were taken in and yet another burial at the foreign cemetery followed the next day. James and Elizabeth Meadows had lost their first not many weeks before, and Hudson Taylor had been through this grief three times already—at this same house, in London and at Hangzhou.

James Meadows, the Crombies and he then travelled together to Fenghua. Life had to go on. After consultations with the Christians, the first church in the city was organised with Wang Guo-yao and Fan Qiseng as deacons and George Crombie as the pastor (see 1, p 782). With only sixteen members it was a token of things to come, but if ten members tithing their income could support one church worker, sixteen were not to be underestimated. On the 10th he set off over the hills for Jackson's city of Taizhou, passing through Ninghai, a city Crombie was soon to occupy as well as Fenghua. Instead of taking the direct route, Hudson Taylor made a fifteen-mile detour to see Tiantai. The slender youth of Shanghai days had become a stocky man capable of sustained physical exertion for long periods. He told Mr Berger,

> All along the way one comes to a town or village every two or three miles—many of them towns of considerable size, where multitudes are born and live, and die, never leaving their native place. The thought forces itself upon one with painful intensity; and as you pass through town after town seeing others in the distance ... it becomes more and more oppressive. When and how are these poor souls to be reached with the Gospel message?

At Taizhou, Hudson Taylor spent a few days with Jackson, 'days which I have much enjoyed. He has made progress in the language recently, and lives in thorough Chinese style.' That the people all looked upon him as their friend was testimonial enough. This weak, vacillating man seemed at last to be maturing. Hudson Taylor longed to stay with him, to show him how to make more use of his opportunities and to Romanise the Taizhou dialect. But because of his promise to the Dodds he could neither stay nor go on to encourage George Stott at Wenzhou. Had he gone, he would have been with him at another time of stress.

A day at a time (February 1868)

Somewhere on his journey home from the southern district, Hudson Taylor wrote to his mother on February 22:

> This hot weather opens up afresh (though they have never closed) the wounds of six months ago; and the question will sometimes arise as to how my darling little ones and dear Maria, will weather the summer ... I try to live a day at a time (but) do not always succeed (to get through everything) ... Pray for more faith, more love, more wisdom for me (in) my multitudinous and often embarrassing duties.

Two more couples were due at Shanghai very soon, the J. E. Cardwells and C. H. Judds. 'Where are they to be stationed?' One setback after another created its own new problems.

> Of destitute plans there is no lack [of advice], but of open doors, doors open for the untrained in the language and the ways of the Chinese, there are few. But the Lord will provide. In four or five directions I am called for at the same—time where should I go first? ... As to plans and arrangements, I am obliged to make some, but as often as not I am unable to keep them ... all my powers feel overtaxed; and I know that my head must have a few hours' rest ... A large part of my work at home consists in the settlement of questions which have been too embarrassing or too grave to be decided in my absence ... The more hurried my stay in (Hangzhou), the more intense the pressure while it lasts.

Until the team gained more experience and grasp of the language this state of affairs would continue, but as the men progressed they must be found work and responsibilities of their own.

On February 24 the printer's proofs of the Hangzhou Report arrived from William Gamble, and Maria had just handed them to Emily Blatchley when she heard Jennie call out 'Mr Taylor has come!' 'I rushed downstairs and found him in the (office)!' Maria was to write. Each time he came home from a journey her letters echoed the Song of Solomon, filled with pleasure on hearing his voice again. His journey had done him good. But when they were together, a month's accumulation of news and problems had to be shared.

McCarthy had come home with news of Duncan and Reid at Nanjing and had gone back to Huzhou to search (without success) for any sign of proclamations in their favour. He arrived home the next day. Jinhua was also as unpromising as before. She was worried about the dissident Lewis Nicol and the McLean sisters. The rift between them and the rest of the Mission was growing. But that could wait for discussion at a better time. C. R. Alford, the new Bishop of Victoria, Hong Kong, was in Hangzhou, staying at the CMS with Henry Gretton. Hangzhou itself was the most encouraging place. Wang Lae-djün, the church and the school were flourishing. Mr Yu, the teacher, and the school cook had had a fight, had both drawn blood, and had made peace again. Henry Cordon, a butcher by trade, had supervised the killing and dividing up of the cow.

As for Jennie, more than ever in demand, she was being invited into more homes than she had time for. Always riding the crests herself, she raised the tone of the household and set a standard for the less buoyant. On January 14 she had assured her father of her safety and good health, before saying (in words which tell us more about herself):

> I hope Mr Landels will not beg for (the CIM) ... We shall be supplied, for God cannot fail us. He feeds the ravens because He is the Creator, how much more will He feed us who are His servants, His children? Our funds are low, and we daily look to God but without one fear or anxious thought that He will withhold any good thing from us.

Earlier she had written, '(The Chinese) have the very element of longevity in their unimpulsive characters. Oh that they might be won for Christ as a nation . . . Sanctified by His love what a fine people they would make! Sensible, plodding, stable, how well they stand compared with other nations.' And of the approaching Chinese New Year, 'I want the whole city to ring with the name of Jesus . . . We want them to feel that Christians may have more joy at such seasons than they have ever known as heathens. We do not wish to make foreigners of them.'

So Wang Lae-djün, the pastor, and the church members planned their Christian celebrations. With 165 seated, many more neighbours crowded the doorways. The church was in good heart. Its members were continually bringing others to the chapel. Jennie's school could take no more pupils. Every day she was having to disappoint parents who begged her to accept their children. Gone were the days when almost everything that happened at Hangzhou rested on Hudson Taylor's shoulders.

For five days after he reached home there was relative peace. Then on February 29, Mrs Dodd went into labour and the Meadowses and Crombies and a friend arrived, to stay on and off for a month, and everything began to happen all at once.

Yangzi strategy (March 1868)

Since the New Year, and before, the Taylors and the team with them in Hangzhou had recognised the multiplying signs that their days together were numbered. The Hangzhou church was strong but should not be overshadowed by so large a body of foreign missionaries coming and going. The southern region of Zhejiang had a nucleus of missionaries and Christians from whom the work of evangelism and church-planting was expanding. Anglicans, Presbyterians and Baptists were all making their mark from Ningbo. The Huzhou area was closed to missionaries for the present, but the deep interior of China called. The foothold gained at Nanjing itself should be used in a new advance. The time had come to leave only two or three at Hangzhou and to move 'onward and inward'. Charles Schmidt in Suzhou had asked for members of the CIM to join him there. With Jinhua barred against them, the Cordons and McLean sisters were free to go north. The further they were from Lewis Nicol, the less influenced they would be by his rebellious spirit. The great Yangzi waterway gave access to a chain of unevangelised provinces, and the Grand Canal led northward to several more. The McCarthy's and Jennie Faulding, most closely linked with the Hangzhou Christians, would stay while the rest launched out to tackle new cities.

This was how they were thinking and talking together. Back in October Hudson Taylor had written of the need to advance, adding, '(Before long) some may be permitted to break ground in unoccupied provinces.'[22] Duncan had begun the process, but it was time for others to move up to support him. If necessary Nanjing could serve as a Yangzi base, but Suzhou, Zhenjiang (Chinkiang) or one of the cities on the Grand Canal between them must also be considered. Yangzhou on the canal north of the Yangzi could be a first step towards Henan and, being close to the Yangzi and Zhenjiang, could be his headquarters. Not all his colleagues could see the wisdom of pressing inland. Even William Berger was anxious and pleaded the importance of consolidating what had been begun. But most of the team shared Hudson Taylor's broad vision of expansion.

When Jinhua and Huzhou were proving difficult to hold, John McCarthy had written: '"Let not your heart be troubled"—the voice of Him who opens and no man can shut. Is it a further indication that this province should not be our battlefield?'—even though Charles Schmidt had invited McCarthy to move to Suzhou, a very tempting offer. And a fortnight later quoting, the prophet Habakkuk; 'Though the olive tree should fail, the harvests yield no grain and the flocks be cut off, yet will I rejoice in the Lord':

> And such faith and such faith alone, will carry us through if our mission is to do a work for God in this land; none will need it ... more than yourself, in the midst of change of feeling and sentiments, in those to whom you would naturally look for nothing but support and assistance ... And if our way does appear cloudy and uncertain, and the days of joy seem to be very few and far between, yet if He is with us in the fire ... in His presence is fullness of joy ... If I have ever learned the ABC of this myself, you can thank God for having been the instrument of instruction.

This was the spirit that would win through. McCarthy agreed to oversee the Ningbo church to free James Meadows for pioneering on the Yangzi. James Williamson was game for anything. Maria was of one mind with her husband and would go anywhere with him. Where they went, Emily Blatchley and 'good and kind' and competent Louise Desgraz would go with enthusiasm. And the Rudlands, fully absorbed with the presses and a growing team of Chinese printers, were willing to move with them at any time.

'More easily said than done'
(March 1868)

The plan was one thing. To carry it out was altogether another. During March

the Hangzhou premises were crowded to capacity and overflowing with visitors. Added to the Meadows family, the Crombies from Ningbo and Mary Bausum on a holiday visit, came their old friends Dr and Mrs Lord, and Susan Barnes for good measure. All this while Mary Bowyer was dangerously ill again with 'inflammation of the heart'.

James Meadows left on March 2 for Shanghai, to arrange for the arrival of the Cardwells and Judds and Mary Rudland's sister, Annie Bohannan—and then to visit Suzhou to rent premises and consult with Charles Schmidt (whom Meadows had led to Christ) about members of the CIM coming to work there. On the way back to Hangzhou he would look in at Huzhou too and encourage the converted barber. But on the same day William Gamble wrote to say the ship had made an exceptionally fast voyage of 110 days and the Judds and Cardwells were already with him so Maria, accompanied by Ensing, the Chinese girl she had adopted, and the ever-willing McCarthy, set off for Shanghai, to introduce the new arrivals to living in Chinese style and to the difficulties of travelling with minimal privacy by canal boat. McCarthy would have them then in another houseboat.

Bishop Alford arrived for confirmations at the Anglican Church on March 4, and took the opportunity to see the missionaries and arrangements at New Lane, about which he had heard criticisms. A 'crazy woman' involved Jennie in caring for her until she was shipped home to Huzhou. And the peace at No 1 was further disturbed by undercurrents of more discontent in the Nicol camp. The imminent arrival of the new missionaries meanwhile added to the unrest, and neuralgia made it difficult for Hudson Taylor to work. As Maria told his mother, 'Getting away from Hangzhou is better than medicine to him.' While there, he could seldom relax.

Until the visitors had gone and the Cardwells and Judds were provided for, there could be no hope of packing up and moving northward. So the decision was taken that the Cordons and the McLean sisters would accept the Schmidts' invitation and begin work in Suzhou with his help with one familiar complication. Mrs Cordon would need obstetric help in mid-May. Hudson Taylor's plans must revolve round that event. Taking Jane and Margaret McLean to a new environment was a fresh bid to wean them from the complaining spirit they had acquired from Lewis Nicol. Yet Margaret could say of Hudson and Maria, 'We love you so much that sooner than be a cause of anxiety to you we feel we would rather leave the mission.' Perhaps the companionship of Charles Schmidt and his Chinese wife would change their minds about being Chinese to the Chinese. Schmidt himself wore Chinese clothes and lived as a Chinese.[23]

With the Cardwells and Judds had sailed the elder son of Colonel Fishe of Dublin, another young man wanting to be under no one's control, but soon to discover how helpless he was on his own. Edward Fishe stayed in Shanghai at first, but when Hudson Taylor tried to help him, he too became dependent. Half in and half out of the CIM circle, he owed neither allegiance to the Mission nor loyalty to its leader.

Maria, Ensing and John McCarthy reached Shanghai to find William Gamble going out of his way to make the newcomers welcome. 'An invaluable friend of our mission,' Maria called him. All in favour of missionaries wearing Chinese clothes and following Chinese customs, he 'kindly claimed as a privilege that it (the Cardwells' and Judds' change from foreign dress) should be in his house' rather than after they had boarded the canal boats. What other Shanghai residents might say of him mattered little. Charles Judd also came in for Maria's praise. His spirit was excellent, 'entering into the principle of making cheerfully any sacrifice that might conduce to the good' of the Chinese. He and Elizabeth, his wife, had never met the Taylors and saw relatively little of them during the first few weeks in China. But he could never forget what he did see of Maria's calm courage and good sense. 'She

had no mercy on any fastidiousness about food or other matters.'

When they reached Hangzhou on March 17 and entered No 1 New Lane, the plain utilitarian nature of everything struck them. No money was being wasted.

> They had boards on trestles for tables ... bare tables, no cloths; and it was Chinese food. There were no knives or forks ... bare wooden chairs (just deckchairs for luxury)—nothing else ... Plain Chinese bed-frames (with coconut fibre ropes in place of springs) and upright posts for mosquito curtains ... I did not see much of (Mr Taylor), he was so much away, so very busy ... with mission matters and with patients.

Jennie's comment on their utilitarian standards had been, 'Please don't talk of my "hardships"—it is not even a trial to me to have "to rough it". I only told you about our contrivances . . . to amuse you.'

It was typical of the Taylors that the arrival of reinforcements should be an occasion for celebration. A day on the lake and exploring the hills on the far side gave time to get to know each other. A hidden cave they discovered was to Jennie a good hiding place for Chinese Christians in time of persecution. Hangzhou felt safe for them, and when they returned in pouring rain after dark, shut out of the city, the fact that the gate was opened to them as foreigners encouraged confidence.

The very next day they dispersed. The Crombies carried the Cardwells off to join Josiah Jackson at Taizhou, and James Williamson followed with their baggage, while Susan Barnes took Elizabeth Meadows home to Shaoxing. Maria trembled for the Cardwells, because both were so unadaptable, 'unbending'. It was a matter of the will, harder for some than for others. And Hudson Taylor took Charles Judd to the top of the Hill of the City God to see the temples and look out across the vast city and the lake, each the same size and shape lying side by side (see 1, p 747). What he saw of the Judds he liked. Within a few days of arriving, both Charles and Elizabeth were throwing themselves into work and progressing well with the language, he going daily to the tea-shops with a Chinese Christian to gossip the gospel. This was the right kind of man for the interior, to pioneer the cities of the Yangzi valley for a start. But for the present he must stay behind and learn the ropes with John McCarthy's help.

James Meadows and Henry Cordon were to leave for Suzhou on March 30. Maria with Emily, Annie Bohannan and the children, Mrs Cordon and the McLean sisters would follow on April 3. Hudson Taylor would pack up his office and clinic, leaving some stock for John McCarthy's dispensary, and have the baggage ready to be shipped north when sent for. He would then join the others in Suzhou. After Mrs Cordon's confinement he would return to help Jackson at Taizhou and at last visit Stott at Wenzhou before resuming the Yangzi valley advance. So he hoped, but nothing was plain sailing.

A letter came from William Gamble, too strong a friend for destructive criticism, meaning only to help but adding to the pressure on Hudson Taylor. Knowing only a fraction of what Taylor accomplished or the reasons for all Gamble had heard, he expressed himself frankly. Naming each missionary, he advised on how they should be deployed in widespread expansion.[24]

Ill-informed, critical and contradictory though the letter was, it came as clear confirmation to Hudson Taylor and Maria of their planned deployment. Gamble would be pleased to know that within a few days only the McCarthy's, Judds and Rudlands (for the present) would be left at Hangzhou, with Jennie Faulding and the slowly recovering Mary Bowyer, for whom Hudson Taylor was still anxious. One letter like that could be welcomed.

Another in a very different, bitter spirit about church government came from John Stevenson of all men, and shook Hudson Taylor to the core. His 'neuralgic headaches' had become so bad that Maria was handling all she could of his day-to-day work. Jennie knew they were caused 'solely by (nervous) prostration brought on by anxiety and overwork'. Mental distress frequently resulted in disabling physical symptoms. Knowing that Stevenson's letter would distress him, Maria waited a few days before handing it to Hudson. He replied warmly, from his heart. It was all a misunderstanding, as he would show. He had never written as Stevenson said he had. Whatever could he have misconstrued, to be so offended? 'Have I ever, dear Brother, been other than a sympathizer, a friend, a helper to you . . . as you have been to me . . . ? We always have walked in mutual confidence, as well as in love . . . The Lord use you, beloved Brother, ten-thousand fold.' The rift was healed. But the next day he was 'very poorly', Maria noted. On the eve of the great migration to the greater unknown his emotional stamina did not look equal to the strain.

'The stamp of men we need'

On March 12, Hudson Taylor wrote with some feeling about 'the painful experience we still have', to William Berger, who was faced with problem candidates, among them Tom Barnardo and Robert White of Dublin. Before long White was to brush aside all the Bergers' advice, marry, sail at once at his own charges and once in China to attach himself to Hudson Taylor and create his own adder's brood of predicaments.

> None should come out who do not grasp certain principles so fully that it shall not require 'Mr Taylor' to insist on this or that detail. The first and foremost of these principles is that of becoming all things to all men ... Why is it, that in every part of every province in China, Roman Catholic missionaries are both able and willing to live, while away from the ports scarcely one Protestant missionary is to be found? ... Our mission will prove a failure, so far as any extensive evangelisation of the interior is concerned, unless this principle is even more taken up by its members as a body. Give me a score of men such as Williamson and Duncan and McCarthy and with God's blessing in less than four years' time there will not be a province without its missionary. But let me have a few more persons who

oppose this principle at every turn, and if we are not broken up altogether it will be of God's own special interposition ... We, as a mission differ from all the other missions. As soon as some persons arrive here they find a sufficient answer to every question in, 'the American missionaries do this, or the Church missionaries do that, why can't we?' ... The missionaries of almost all the societies have better houses, finer furniture, more European fare etc. than we have or are likely to have ... But ... there is not one of them settled in the interior among the people. Unless persons are prepared to stand alone—separate from these Societies and those who imitate them they should never join our mission at all ... Let them know, too, beforehand, that if they are hearty, loyal members of this mission, they may expect the sneers and even opposition of good, godly men.

[Two weeks later he was more precise.] I only desire the help of such persons as are fully prepared to work in the interior, in the native costume, and living, as far as possible, in the native style. And that I do not contemplate assisting, in future, any who may cease to labour in this way. China is open to all; but my time and strength are too short, and the work too great to allow of my attempting to work with any who do not agree with me in the main on my plans of action ... Indeed, might not even those engaged be sent out single for two or three years, so as to master the language and pioneer for a time before marrying? Their intended wives also might be expected to make some little progress in the language before marrying, and thus would have a fair chance of future usefulness ... Might we not legitimately say ... 'If these conditions seem too hard, these sacrifices too great to make for perishing China, *do not join* our mission. These are small things to some of the crosses you may expect ... to bear ... China is not to be won for Christ by quiet ease-loving men and women' ... The stamp of men and women we need is such as will put Jesus, China, souls, first and foremost in everything and at every time—even life itself must be secondary; nay more, those more precious than life. Of such men, of such women do not fear to send us too many. They are more precious than rubies.[25]

It was not wishful thinking. In time they were to come by the score.

Defiance in Taiwan (1867–July 1868)

During 1867 the British firm of Dodd and Company leased premises at the market town they called 'Banks' on the Danshui River in the north of Taiwan. By the treaties of 1858 'Danshui' was a treaty port, but

2.5 'Foreign dignity', in frock and crinolines

only at the village of Hebei at the mouth was there a deep-water anchorage. Lighters had to convey freight between Hebei and 'Banks', fourteen miles upstream towards Taibei (now the capital of Taiwan). To a man the people of 'Banks' denied possession to the foreigner and for the present there was nothing he could do.

Major trouble returned to Taiwan early in 1868. The island had been part of the Chinese empire since 1683 when the Dutch were forced out. As early as that they had provided a Gospel in Romanised Chinese, but by 1865 all signs of a Church in Taiwan had evaporated. Dr James Laidlaw Maxwell, a Presbyterian physician, had begun working at Tainan in 1865, a few years after the Roman Catholic Church, and four men were baptised the following year. (One who became a preacher was still active in 1905.) But when Maxwell attempted to rent a house, all negotiations broke down 'an interference notoriously ascribed to the authorities'. In a memorial to Sir Rutherford Alcock, Dr Maxwell described what then occurred. A house was obtained through the Commissioner of Customs. After a few weeks 'the missionaries were stoned while walking peacefully about, the landlord of the house occupied by the Mission was threatened with violence, accusations of the most wicked and disgusting character were freely circulated against us and placards were posted up describing us as Resurrectionists, murderers of the most awful type, and as having then many dead bodies secreted in the house'.

He appealed to the Chinese authorities, as also did Mr Swinhoe, then British consul in Taiwan, to issue a proclamation contradicting the false rumours and warning the people against acts of violence. Promises were made but not kept. Increasingly hostile placards were posted up without interference by the authorities. 'A violent assault was one day made upon the chapel, and the district Mandarin who, after long delay, appeared upon the scene, utterly refused to protect us against the mob, unless on a promise that we should leave the place in three days. We had no recourse but to comply, and so we had to leave Taiwanfoo [ie Taiwan] a place in which, by treaty enactment, we should unquestionably have been allowed to settle.'

Consular protests had no effect in securing their return to Tainan, so they transferred to Dagao (Takao), now Gaoxiong, another treaty port thirty miles further south, and premises were purchased. 'About a fortnight after the opening of the chapel, an assault was made upon it', led by people connected with the *yamen*. Again the acting consul failed to obtain redress and the mandarins failed to seize or punish the guilty parties.

On April 11, 1868, a mission catechist was seized in the street at 'Pithau, a District City of Hang-san' (probably Fengshan) and beaten and robbed, but he escaped and rushed into the *yamen*. The magistrate ordered him to prison. Immediately the mob, incited and led by the *yamen* underlings made for the chapel armed with knives and other weapons and began to plunder and carry off everything that could be removed, including medical and other property of the missionaries.

During the next two days they continued, unmolested, to tear down the building itself, carrying away wood, bricks, tiles and everything that could be used elsewhere. The rioters then proceeded to the house of one of the worshippers, plundered it, beat the man's wife, and drove her and her daughter-in-law into the street. One of the Christian workers was chased for three miles and escaped; the other was caught in his father's house, robbed and beaten. Other worshippers fled to Dagao for protection. Hosea Ballou Morse says that on April 24, 1868, both the Catholic and English Presbyterian churches were destroyed by mobs at Fengshan.

When news of the 'Pithau' or 'Pitow' riot spread, another catechist was accused of poisoning people, seized, by local roughs, murdered with stones and knives, and his heart torn out and eaten by his murderers. By 'sympathetic magic' his courage would become theirs, they believed.[26] The *Chinese Recorder* voiced the indignation felt among foreigners: 'We have no complaint against the people for persecution at their hands, but against the authorities and their subordinates in the *yamen*.' A flood of events was developing, which was to engulf Hudson Taylor and the CIM.

On July 31, Acting-Consul John Gibson sent a dispatch to Sir Rutherford Alcock, the British minister in Peking. The day before, the rebuilt Protestant mission chapel at Pitow had for a second time been destroyed by servants of the mandarin. Clearly strong action was needed to change the *daotai's* ways but the 'extreme pressure by the Acting British Consul' was to take a bizarre form. In the process it passed out of his control to that of a naval lieutenant with an exaggerated sense of occasion.

Responsibility lay further up the chain of command. Sir Rutherford had called upon the Chinese government in Peking to 'compel the local authorities to do justice' in Taiwan. At the same time, as at Danshui later in the year, he thought it 'very desirable that a British gunboat should be on the station to support the consular authority'. Unfortunately, consul and lieutenant overstepped the marks[27] and eventually Alcock had to require

Consul Swinhoe to 'state specifically why he considered it necessary to proceed to this act of war'. For by then the Foreign Office and the Admiralty in London were demanding explanations.

On May 2, 1868, the Foreign Minister, Lord Stanley referred to Sir Rutherford Alcock a letter from the LMS in London suggesting that a proposed revision of the treaty with China should have an added clause, specifically conceding to British missionaries the right to reside and purchase land anywhere in the interior as well as at commercial ports. Sir Rutherford replied, 'It does not seem to me that any new clause of a Treaty is required . . . Article VI of the French Treaty is perfectly clear on that point, and what is acquired as a right for French missionaries, is equally acquired by the most favoured nation clause, for the British, as I have recently had occasion to remind the Foreign Board'—the Zongli Yamen. For the diplomats it was crystal clear. For others, mandarins and British subjects unacquainted with the French text, the absence of this clause in the British treaty accounted for breaches of justice. Hence the LMS's request. But Article 12 of the Peking Convention had said enough (see 1, p 627).

As Hudson Taylor prepared to extend operations to inland China, the minister and his consuls were in no doubt that it was their duty to assist British subjects to obtain premises. They had made it plain to the mandarins of Zhejiang who had issued proclamations to that effect, and Hudson Taylor was equally aware of it—as a result of personal involvement over the years and, recently, of the Xiaoshan, Huzhou and Jinhua outrages and threatened violence at Hangzhou and Wenzhou. The trouble was that while the government of China had had to accept the grim fact of superior foreign force, the Confucian literati still rejected concessions made under duress; and mandarins out of touch with reality, as in Taiwan, shared their views and were ready to act against the barbarian as opportunity offered. Another typhoon was blowing up.

The first gusts had been felt but its nature still could not be foreseen.

Converging currents (1868)

Violent outbursts here and there betrayed the underlying indignation of the scholar-gentry against the foreign presence. The indignation of the consular representatives of the Western powers against violations of the treaties was no less. Undercurrents of intrigue by the most xenophobic mandarins, including some at the highest levels, flowed silently while the outspoken foreign press in the treaty ports and Hong Kong called for stronger action to teach the only lesson they seemed to understand. Tension was growing though little other evidence was apparent.

Most sinister was the groundswell of vicious rumour widely spread, with characteristics betraying a common source. According to Du Halde in 1736, a Chinese book dated 1624 expressed the reaction of dissidents to the favour being shown by the Ming Court to the Roman Catholic Church (see 1, pp 19–20, 761). It charged that the outer barbarians were kidnapping children and using their eyes, livers, hearts and other organs to make medicines.

The superstitions of the general public made them susceptible to tales of this sort. After all, why should foreign men be so solicitous for young children? Other accusations of promiscuous behaviour at Christian meetings of both sexes and of immorality by celibate priests fuelled indignation. Ordinary people could be controlled by the mandarins; the danger lay in the inveterate antagonism of the scholar-gentry to everything foreign. 'Should the literati stir up the passions of the people by playing upon their superstitious fears, few officials had the moral courage as well as the ability to keep the peace for long; for their tenure of office was largely dependent upon the goodwill of the scholarly class.' Official connivance was to be expected. Neither official instigation nor a blind eye to the facts would be surprising, right up to the Zongli Yamen and the Peking court.

With hindsight we see that the advance

of missionaries into the interior was coinciding with China's new mood of protest and with the consuls' impatience. So far the first indications differed little from the attitudes usually encountered. On February 6, 1868, the *North China Herald* reported that William Muirhead of the LMS had 'announced his intention of returning to China to carry out a long cherished scheme of establishing missions in the interior of the country. It has been repeatedly pointed out in our columns, that the interior of China is the place for missionaries to locate themselves, rather than linger in the treaty ports or their immediate vicinity.' Without the support of the press, Hudson Taylor intended to do what was advocated. But the reaction of the press to the protests of the literati when they took action was the measure of the editors' surprise. At Zhenjiang and Yangzhou the depth of Chinese feeling was soon to be demonstrated, and at Tianjin the lengths to which some protesters were prepared to go.

The Suzhou interval (April–May 1868)

Until Charles Schmidt and his Chinese wife went to live in Suzhou in September 1867, the only missionaries to visit the city had preached and passed on. William Muirhead and Griffith John had been among the first. Muirhead in Chinese dress had been dragged along the street by his securely fastened *bianzi* and 'a heavy blow on his head made him think his time was short.'[28] During 1867 an American Episcopal missionary, J. W. Lambuth, and a Chinese colleague, known since his residence in America as C. K. Marshall, rented a room near the Ink Pagoda in which they preached during regular visits from Shanghai. Then on his way to Nanjing in September 1867, just before the Schmidts arrived, George Duncan had commended Suzhou, once beautiful but now dilapidated, to Hudson Taylor's attention. With Charles Schmidt's encouragement James Meadows had rented premises in March, and he and Henry Cordon were going to repair them for the Cordons and McLean twins to occupy as the next new station of the CIM.

With high civil rank as a reward by the Chinese government for his part in the defeat of the Taipings and with many acquaintances among the military mandarins of Suzhou, Schmidt was secure from interference although he gave 'public sermons' in his chapel. His deep understanding of Chinese affairs, his fluency and tact, and his ability as a preacher made this ex-soldier a model missionary. Through William Gamble he had formed links with the American Presbyterian Mission (North) who continued there after he left. But for another foreign family to attempt to put down roots in Suzhou was as much an experiment as at Jinhua.

In Hangzhou on March 30, 1868, Meadows and Cordon were ready to set out. All were aware that this was the start of a new advance towards the unoccupied provinces and, following their usual practice, the household at New Lane spent the day in fasting and prayer before the two men went down to their boat. Maria was to follow four days later with Mrs Cordon and the McLean sisters, but by then Hudson Taylor was 'prostrate' with an unnamed illness. The momentousness of this step was enough to account for his symptoms. So Maria stayed to see him through it. Whooping cough was spreading among the Hangzhou missions, and in any case he was needed to doctor the family of D. D. Green, the American Presbyterian, and Jane McLean, already down with it. On April 10 (the day before the attack at 'Pitow' in Taiwan) he sent Maria off to Suzhou with their four children, Annie Bohannan their nurse, Emily Blatchley and Margaret McLean. The boatmen took advantage of them as women, and the journey, which he made in two days a fortnight later, had already taken them eight days when they reached Wujiang, fifteen miles short of Suzhou. By then Charles Schmidt, waiting for them in Suzhou, had become 'very anxious', fearing that they had run into serious trouble on the way. He came down the Grand Canal, met them at Wujiang and escorted their two boats back in the dark to moor in front of his own house at six in the morning. It had been 'one of the worst nights' Maria had ever spent on a Chinese boat, she said without explanation, and Margaret McLean added, 'Mr Schmidt thought (we should) get there as early as possible, so as to avoid being much observed.'

Like No 1 New Lane, the house Meadows had rented had once been a respectable home, but 'was only a shed when we first saw it', Cordon said. With twelve rooms round the courtyard and three upstairs, it included a guest hall large enough to become a chapel seating over a hundred people. Rough repairs had made it habitable. After lying low all day at the Schmidts, Maria, Margaret McLean, Mrs Cordon and one of the children went after dark in sedan chairs and 'kept very quiet' to avoid creating excitement in the neighbourhood. They were there when Hudson Taylor arrived with Jane McLean on the 25th to find that Maria's friendliness and adaptability had paved the way and, as at Hangzhou, by May 4 he had persuaded the previous Chinese tenants to move out cheerfully.

On the way to Suzhou, Maria had had a search made through the big city of Jiaxing, fifty miles east of Huzhou, for the governor's proclamations favourable to foreigners wishing to live anywhere in the province, without finding any. Schmidt, however, had had copies made for Hudson Taylor of two such proclamations in Suzhou. The provincial boundary area between Hangzhou and Suzhou was apparently still unsafe, but at least the *daotai* at Suzhou seemed favourably disposed. With half a million inhabitants, Suzhou offered scope enough for several teams of missionaries. Hudson Taylor could have been justified in making the city a major objective, but Suzhou was the natural outpost of the missions at Shanghai. Beyond it lay hundreds more such cities with no foreseeable prospect of receiving the gospel unless from his little mission with its Ningbo

and Hangzhou Christians. Two foreign and two Chinese missionaries to each unevangelised province was still his almost unattainable goal. The total of missionaries in China had grown to 'about two hundred and fifty'[29] but the CIM'S thirty-four members still included seven beginners and several more who had made little progress since arriving. Among them were the Nicols, now obsessively rebellious, and at least three following their lead. Progress depended on many things, not least the readiness of the team.

Within ten days of Hudson Taylor's arrival at Suzhou, Emily was writing to Jennie, 'We are sending Wu Sin-sang and Hyiao-foh to Changchow to open a school . . . no preaching to be attempted. Evening and morning prayers with the boys but with the doors shut.' This plan was not even to be talked about in Hangzhou. But within a few days the men returned, unable to secure a footing. After setbacks in other cities as well, the tactics had to be changed to what had succeeded so well in Hangzhou—not even tea-shop evangelism until the missionaries' presence was accepted. As a proving ground, Suzhou had produced this deliberate policy for their advance to the Yangzi as soon as the Cordons' baby was born.

By then the Taylor children all had whooping cough, which kept the parents and Emily in attendance at the Schmidts' day and night. Taking turns they went to the Cordons' house to get some sleep. But the administration of the Mission had to continue. Distributing funds and advising each member, reporting to the Bergers and consulting with them, and answering questions from other missions and the consuls never ceased.

A letter, critical of the report of the Hangchow branch of the CIM had been published by the *North China Daily News*. Writing to Jennie, Hudson Taylor said, 'I shall not think of answering publicly . . . but may do so privately. "The Lord reigneth." If it only has the effect of knitting us more closely together we shall have cause for gratitude to God.' As the clouds thickened, this phrase, 'The Lord reigns' was taken up by the team as a victory sign that whatever might happen, God was in control and all would be well. 'Gossip must ever work mischief,' Maria wrote to Mrs Berger, 'and I fear there has been a great deal of this.' Someone, reputed to be Chaplain Butcher of Shanghai, had already replied in the *Daily News* to the critic, and Maria went on, 'Thus God can raise up advocates for us, when even the need of such advocates is unknown to us. I think (Hudson) is right in refusing to enter the lists against a Christian brother . . . in a worldly newspaper . . . He has written privately to Mr Green.' Like Nehemiah, she added, he could say 'I am doing a great work, so that I cannot come down' to such levels. His report was reviewed in the *North China Herald* also, 'but tho' it finds plenty of fault with "the cant", etc.,' it would do no real harm. It was after all no more than a factual statement of events, receipts and expenses.

Far worse than gibes in the press was the correspondence by Lewis Nicol with William Berger and others. Nearly two years after the voyage of the *Lammermuir* he was building on the same old complaints about stockings and 'dirty Chinese cast-offs' (see 1, p 768). Mr Berger replied to Nicol, 'It seems to me, that . . . if you cannot confide [have confidence] in [Hudson Taylor and Berger] . . . it will be your duty to retire from the Mission.' But on May 9 Emily was writing to Jennie at Hudson Taylor's request to answer more allegations made to the Judds. Nicol had been saying that 'Large stores of English clothing and material for making such, brought out for the use of the mission in China, are stored away . . . (rather to) rot than sell them to anyone out here who would make use of them.' Hudson Taylor had 'changed his mind' after reaching Shanghai, and made them all wear Chinese clothes. It was all nonsense, Emily reminded Jennie. No such foreign clothes or materials ever existed. She herself had been in charge of preparations and Jennie had helped. The facts of the matter 'are open to the light' and ought to be made known. Moving to more pleasant

topics she went on, 'We are thinking of sending someone (perhaps Lanfeng) . . . to (Yangzhou) north of the river', to prospect. Again, this was for the Hangzhou team to pray about, but not for wider circulation. 'Mr Taylor says he hopes I have nearly "shut up" . . . so goodbye dearie—it seems a long time since I saw you.'

On May 5, William Berger wrote to Hudson Taylor, ' It is still with me a grave question whether a brother who avows he has no confidence in you (or me) should continue connected with the Mission.' His advice would have taken about two months to reach Hudson Taylor, who confided to Jennie, 'I do not see how we can keep them in the Mission after a letter, worse than ever he has written before, recently sent to Mr Berger.' The pain of dismissing a colleague, and the prospect of unpleasant repercussions, gnawed at his heart and mind while he still hoped that Nicol would reform.

Harder to face was the effect of subversion on other members of the team, for the Cordons and Barchet were the latest partisans. Stephan Barchet had been attached to the E. C. Lords since his arrival in China, although a member of the CIM since its inception. The influence of Edward Lord, a Baptist by strong conviction, and Stephan's engagement to Mary Bausum, Lord's step-daughter, had changed Stephan's own views. Writing to Thomas Marshall, his Congregational minister in London, he enclosed a copy of a letter he had intended to send to Hudson Taylor but had withheld. In it he expressed 'the desire to be considered a friend, not a member, of the Mission (because) elements of the Mission tend to anarchy . . . If it be thought proper that a Methodist should be pastor of a Presbyterian church or a Presbyterian of a Baptist church I differ in opinion, for if a church is Baptist let it be Baptist.' Meadows, a Methodist, had baptised the Presbyterian Crombie's converts, and Nicol had called in an American Presbyterian to sprinkle the Xiaoshan converts rather than have Hudson Taylor immerse them. Unlike previously, the perpetuation of Western denominations among the Chinese now mattered more to Stephan than their acceptance of each other's secondary differences for the sake of unity in the Chinese church. His colleagues in the CIM, like him, had welcomed the unsectarian principle of the Mission and set no store by each other's denominational differences, although Hudson Taylor intended them to be observed in practice. Regretting Barchet's change of stance, Marshall passed his letter on to William Berger.

That was not all. Stephan continued, 'Further may be mentioned the despotic government of the Mission. So long as a man is fallible, it must be seen how dangerous it is to give the entire control of a mission into the hands of a single individual.' He had nothing against Hudson Taylor's character, he emphasised, and was not saying that he acted despotically, but objected to the principle he himself had previously accepted. Finally, and perhaps the crux of the matter, 'I would prefer not to be associated with men who are . . . under the influence of petty jealousies, and are seldom at peace.' E. C. Lord had resigned from his own mission (the ABMU) and become independent some years before, and Nicol and his sympathizers had been to Ningbo often enough to have sickened Stephan. He resigned in June. When the Bryanston Hall congregation ceased to support him, William Berger offered to do so instead. Before long Stephan married Mary Bausum, went to he States and became a doctor of medicine. They returned to China and forty years later were still good friends of the CIM.

News must have reached Suzhou of William Burns's death from dysentery at Yingkou (Niuchuang) on April 4, 1868. Only fifty-three, by the standards of missionary survivors he might have had twenty more years of service ahead of him. Undoubtedly Hudson Taylor felt his loss deeply. Years later he wrote, 'His holy and reverential life and constant communings with God made fellowship with him satisfying to the deep cravings of my heart.' Burns's unsparing devotion to the Chinese and to the spreading of the gospel had also made him a man after Hudson Taylor's own heart. Seven months after reaching Yingkou he died in a cramped little room like the one he had shared with Hudson Taylor in Swatow, with little more than two chairs, two bookcases, a stove and the bench he used as a bed at night. As death approached he appealed to the Presbyterian Church to take up the torch he would carry no longer. Hugh Waddell and Joseph Hunter, MD, of the Presbyterian Church of Ireland responded and arrived at Yingkou in May 1869. Burns's work was continued for decades to come. In 1869 Donald Matheson was to tell Lord Clarendon that Burns's name was 'honoured wherever foreigners are known in China' (see 1, p xiv).[30] To soldier on without the support of Burns's prayers and wisdom was painful to Hudson Taylor. Another ally had been removed.

At last, on May 12, Mrs Cordon gave birth to a stillborn child. No explanation of this frequent occurrence among missionaries is given.[31] Life in Suzhou went on as usual until the 16th, when a boat was hired to take all but the Cordons and McLean sisters as far as 'to Nankin'. In spite of Duncan's difficulties in finding and keeping good premises, his was the only foothold so far beyond Suzhou. 'Pray that if we attempt to take a house (in Yangzhou) we may succeed,' Emily told Jennie in a letter packed as always with business matters. The options were wide open as good, reliable Li Lanfeng, the printer, went ahead. Meadows and McCarthy had gone to help Jackson at Taizhou, so Hudson Taylor's return to south Zhejiang was postponed again. On Monday night, May 18, he, Maria, Emily Blatchley and the children, still all coughing day and night, set off for the Yangzi valley as China's mood of protest deepened.

The boat-people[32] (May–June 1868)

Little had changed, as far as foreigners could tell, in the attitude of China towards them. There had always been sporadic outbursts of feeling, localised and unrelated. Even this was too much for the

2.6 A Manchu lady

presence in the area. Nothing came of this reconnaissance, and on the 23rd they reached the 'silt-choked, fever-ridden' river port of Zhenjiang. Ruined in the Taiping war and suffocated by army camps, it was slow in recovering. But Zhenjiang impressed Hudson Taylor with its importance. With a population of 150,000, many of them the families of the Manchu garrison, the river and canal traffic it handled was 'very great', 'a place of concourse for natives of most of the provinces of China' and equally strategic for merchant and missionary.[33] The LMS chapel was in a suburb manned by a Chinese evangelist. The city itself had none.

Foreign residents of all kinds seldom exceeded thirty in number, although the city stood strategically where the Grand Canal met the great Yangzi. British, American and French consuls, or at least consular offices staffed by a merchant chargé d'affaires or trainee assistant had been established there. Zhenjiang 'completed the chain of stations between (Hangzhou) and Nankin' and could be a useful business centre for the Mission and a central location for the printing press. From it as the hub, the spokes of the Mission's advance could radiate across the Yangzi and up the Canal to the north, and westward up the Yangzi itself, with quick routes east- and southward to Shanghai, Suzhou and Hangzhou. From Shanghai, steamer services to Ningbo, Taizhou and Wenzhou brought the distant outposts close in terms of time.

But Zhenjiang held a factor unknown to Hudson Taylor at the time. In May 1867 a magistrate of the Chinese city of Shanghai, 'well known for his antagonism to foreigners', had unjustifiably seized and flogged a municipal policeman from the international settlement. The foreign municipal council had protested to the magistrate's superior and, degraded in rank, he had been provocatively transferred to Zhenjiang where the small foreign community also enjoyed treaty rights. There he was waiting for his opportunity to retaliate.

Living on the houseboat, Hudson

consuls and diplomats to tolerate. It must stop. Nationals under their protection must be safe wherever they might be and whatever they might do within the law, while holding passports countersigned by China. In fact they were safe—in the normal course of events. So when Hudson Taylor hired houseboats for his family, including Emily, Annie Bohannan and their Chinese companions, he was acting on the 'treaty of amity'. Nothing would ever be achieved by thinking 'there is a lion in the way' (Proverbs 26.13). On this occasion he provided roomier accommodation than usual, for while he hoped to find a foothold in one of the great Yangzi cities without delay, it might be weeks before they could move into a house of their own. He was right. Leaving Suzhou quietly after dark on May 18, they were still living in the boats six weeks later.

In theory they were heading for Nanjing, expecting that by the time they arrived George Duncan would have found such premises as the mandarins would allow him to retain. But on the way through the cities on the Grand Canal, Wuxi, Changzhou and Danyang, they would assess the prospects, knowing of a Roman Catholic

Taylor began house-hunting, and the second '*Lammermuir* day', May 26, the anniversary of sailing from London, was given up to prayer by the homeless leader of the Mission and his family. Every other member was established in a 'station' with regular work, with Meadows and Williamson standing ready to join Hudson Taylor in spearheading the penetration of the unevangelised provinces. Two days later he found a suitable house in the city only three minutes' walk from the city gate, which opened into the 'concession' occupied by foreigners. He was coming to terms with the landlord when the consul's Chinese secretary told him of a Shanghai missionary who was planning to come to Zhenjiang. Immediately he halted his negotiations in order to consult Consul Lay about going on to Yangzhou, but Lay was absent in Shanghai until the 30th.

Apparently Li Lanfeng, who had gone ahead to Yangzhou, had reported favourably, and Duncan had been unable to rent premises in Nanjing, for Hudson Taylor sent the larger (family) houseboat across the Yangzi, three miles wide at that point, to wait there for him, and joined them after arranging with the consul for new travel passes and a certificate of residence for use at Zhenjiang. After spending Sunday at Guazhou, at the mouth of the Grand Canal on the Yangzi north shore, verifying that good access to Yangzhou existed twelve or fifteen miles overland and by canal, they set off again and soon arrived at the city.

The significance of this otherwise bald statement has to be realised. Hudson Taylor and Maria with their four children, his secretary and the children's nurse—helped only by four Hangzhou Christians, employees, not teachers, Tianxi the destitute boy he had adopted eleven years before, and Ensing, Maria's protégée engaged to marry Lanfeng—had left treaty ports behind and were attempting to occupy a major city barely touched by passing missionaries in recent centuries. Even the Catholic Church had only an orphanage in the care of a Chinese administrator. If

the tolerance of the Muslim governor of Hangzhou, Ma Xinyi, were to be extended by Zeng Guofan, viceroy of the two Hangs, (Jiangxi and Jiangsu), and Governor Ding Richang of Jiangsu, and their prefects, the success at Hangzhou could be repeated here in perfect peace. If not, it was as bold a step as any yet taken since the days of Robert Morrison. Apart from trial and error there was no way of knowing.

This section of the Grand Canal had been completed in AD 605, when the city of Yangzhou was called Jiangdu, the River Capital of the Sui dynasty. Linking the Yangzi with the cities of Yangzhou and Qingjiangpu it was 'the highroad from the south to Pekin and most of the northern provinces'. Curving round the south and east sides of the city, beautifully spanned by numerous arched bridges, it framed an octagonal pagoda and graceful temples and gardens inside the city. Three Nestorian churches had once existed there (see 1, pp 13, 14) and for three of his seventeen years (1275–92) in the service of Kublai Khan, Marco Polo had been governor of Yangzhou (c1280). Scholars and painters had gravitated to it over the centuries, and one of the Qian Long emperor's libraries had been kept in the city until destroyed by the Taipings. The population of 360,000 souls necessitated the division of Yangzhou into two administrative counties (*xian*) under a prefect, the *zhiju*. Such a centre of culture, commerce and government, 'famous for its wealth and the beauty of its women', held a place of honour and pride in the esteem of its people, but most of all its literati. At the same time it was 'notorious . . . for its wickedness'.

Hudson Taylor was aware of this and from the first adopted an exceptionally cautious approach to the city. For the first week he and his family lay low in their boat, not venturing out where they might be seen. While their Chinese companions went house-hunting, they employed their time in writing the thirty page *Brief Account of the Progress of the China Inland Mission (May 1866 to May 1868)* in the form of a letter to supporters, ending with '*Lammermuir* day',

May 26, at' Zhenjiang. Their minds were already at ease.

> The opening up of permanent, stationary work in the interior of China is no easy task ... An unsuccessful attempt to gain an entrance into a locality—even in these provinces where foreigners are best known—renders any subsequent efforts far more difficult. Hence the importance of patiently waiting till we have gained the needful experience, before attempting to enter the more remote and untried provinces. [Thanking his friends and readers for their support already given, he continued] For the future, we look with confidence to Him who has hitherto helped us. Our expenditure this year, has been about £4100, while the income has been about £3,300. But He who gave us the balance in hand at the commencement, which has supplied the deficiency in the income, is well able to supply all the still heavier expenses which we may anticipate during the year on which we are just entering. He knows accurately what our needs will be, and therefore we need not be anxious to forecast them.

There is no evidence that anyone had yet suspected him of soliciting funds through such occasional statements of fact, but in time they would, and he would modify his frankness without loss of income.

After several days, heavy rain began to fall and the houseboat leaked at every roof-seam. Oil cloths and umbrellas inside the 'rooms' helped to keep some things dry, but the occupants could only sit huddled in the driest parts and wait for the rain to stop. By Monday, June 8, only a move to an inn on dry land was sensible. At a commercial 'hotel' inside the city, they took five upstairs rooms for the large sum of two dollars a day without food, for as long as they chose to stay. There was no alternative. After two months spent largely on the boats, their new quarters felt 'very comfortable' but, with all the coming and going of inn life beneath them, 'rather noisy' and lacking in privacy. Hudson Taylor had never before seen so clean and respectable a place, normally occupied by merchants while conducting business deals.

Soon after they had settled in, Mr Peng, the proprietor, had second thoughts and became anxious lest letting his rooms to foreigners should get him into trouble. He had not insisted on a middleman with whom to share the responsibility. So Hudson Taylor undertook to ask the magistrate to assure Mr Peng that all was well. A trial was in progress and the magistrate in court, but his subordinates assured Hudson Taylor that he need not worry. For Mr Peng this was not enough and he went out saying he would see the magistrate himself. When he returned, 'the difference in him was most marked', although he too had failed to see the mandarin. 'Instead of talking about a middleman for himself, he offered to become middleman if we wished it, in any house we might rent.' No hint of objection to their presence, only reassurance, had been encountered. Two weeks after their arrival he reduced the rent, but six harrowing weeks of close confinement were to go by before they could all move out. At first only the Chinese could leave the premises to continue searching for a home of their own. Later Hudson Taylor himself joined in, 'gently feeling our way among the people.' Perhaps thirty suitable premises were found, only to be lost before negotiations could be completed. Each time the literati intervened.

'Smallpox' (June–July 1868)

What Hudson Taylor euphemistically called 'a tedious battle with difficulties' acquired a new dimension on June 15 when Tianxi, always at close quarters with the family, fell ill with fever and a rash alarmingly like the early phase of smallpox. The children had not fully recovered from whooping cough, and the baby had not yet been vaccinated. Early the next morning Hudson Taylor took Maria and little Maria to Zhenjiang to catch the river-steamer to Shanghai.

George Duncan had written proposing marriage to Catherine Brown, a twenty-three-year-old friend in Scotland. She could reach Shanghai in July or even June, so Maria would wait in Shanghai for her.

At eleven the same night she wrote to say that William Gamble had insisted on her staying at his place instead of on a boat as she proposed because of possibly spreading infection; Edward Fishe now wanted to join Hudson Taylor and the CIM.

Elizabeth Meadows and Eliza Nicol had both had stillborn premature babies in Ningbo; and Alexander Wylie and Griffith John had penetrated to Chengdu in Sichuan. Wylie had been stoned and in danger of his life.

After he had seen Maria on to the steamer, Hudson Taylor took his house-hunting in Zhenjiang a stage further. The way was clear for him to complete a deal for the house he had found. Then he returned to Yangzhou. Who should arrive there soon after him but George Duncan, down from Nanjing. He had walked the fifteen miles from Guazhou. All mail for Hudson Taylor had been forwarded to Duncan but he had received nothing, not even money sent by Gamble. Where, was it all? Cheques from William Berger and George Müller would be in it, and available cash was running low. To Hudson Taylor's delight, Duncan was willing to postpone his marriage for some months, until Catherine had acclimatised and learned some Chinese, so he returned to Nanjing on the 30th.

Hudson Taylor was writing almost daily to Maria with a stream of administrative instructions, but on the 27th nothing had yet reached her. On the 23rd he had been working until nearly 3.00 a.m. Negotiations for house after house were breaking down after coming almost to the point of agreement. Another confinement, Mrs Cardwell's this time, seemed to demand either his or Maria's presence in Taizhou at the end of July. How could they cope? A secure base in both Zhenjiang and Yangzhou seemed essentials He posted his letter of June 24 at 'the hulk', moored at the riverbank as a landing stage, only to begin another. 'I expect to pay the deposit (on the Zhenjiang house) in an hour or two and to get the document signed'—at last, a foothold with possession in two weeks' time. The Rudlands should prepare to bring the

printing press and move in. Louise Desgraz was to come with them. Mary Rudland would then be near the Taylors for the last few weeks of her pregnancy.

Consul Lay was about to take the steamer up to Jiujiang (Kiukiang), but just in time Hudson Taylor discovered that although he had procured a dispatch from the *daotai* to the Yangzhou prefect it had been lying at the consulate for a fortnight or more. For lack of it, progress in renting premises at Yangzhou had been held up. As the *China Mail* of Hong Kong was to point out, 'Both natives and foreigners are obliged, when they buy property, to have the sale duly registered by the authorities, but there is no such rule laid down for renting a place.' In fact it was never heard of until the missionaries began to move into the interior; and then it was invented as a powerful weapon to impede their progress.[34] Of the Zhenjiang house, the consul-general at Shanghai, W. H. Medhurst Jr., was also to report to Sir Rutherford Alcock in Peking that Hudson Taylor had rented it, 'taking care to conduct the transaction in a plain and straightforward manner, and to record the lease, after execution and signature, with Mr Assistant Allen.' There the acceptance of a hundred dollars by the owner sealed the contract, but at Yangzhou they still had far to go.

On the 29th a whole package of closely written letters, full of detailed instructions about remittances to the team and other business, reached Maria. 'My brain seemed almost to reel after reading them. May the Lord help me,' she wrote. For baby Maria was ill with measles, and very ill. Two days later she heard from Hudson Taylor again. Tianxi's 'smallpox' had turned out to be measles and all three of the children at Yangzhou had gone down with it. Samuel, just four years old, was desperately ill with its most dangerous complication, broncho-pneumonia. Then back to business. The Yangzhou prefect had promised him a proclamation about getting a house and another about a chapel when he was ready for it. He was said to have ordered fifty copies to be written, but none had been placarded yet.

On the night of July 1, Hudson Taylor began with business matters, so that she could take them in before he told her about Samuel. Then, 'Miss Blatchley and I sat up last night with him. We were very anxious . . . He breathes very frequently and shallowly.' That was the softening blow. In fact his respiration rate had been one hundred per minute. At 4.00 a.m. they thought the immediate danger was over. On the night of the 3rd, Hudson Taylor was 'hoping to get some sleep tonight'. The first, fifth and ninth moons of the Chinese calendar were inauspicious for property deals, 'hence part of our difficulty'. They might have to buy a house, because 'rents are terrible'. At 2.00 a.m. when he ended he still had more letters to write, to catch the 5.00 a.m. mail. With one went a cheque to Charles Schmidt. By Sunday, July 5, he knew about baby Maria and was 'dreading' to receive further news. In a tender, affectionate letter to Maria, longing to be with her, to weep or rejoice together, he wrote, 'Is it not Love who has separated us? . . . Perhaps we should both have been overwhelmed had we seen them both in so precarious a state. And so He did not let you

know of Samuel's danger on Wednesday, nor me of darling little Maria's . . . In Miss B.'s case it will be only a less trial to her than to us, if the treasure is taken from us.'

For five weeks they had lived quietly in Yangzhou and now only lacked the city prefect's promised proclamation to complete a contract for the premises Mr Peng was helping them to rent. At last the way was clear. Hudson Taylor sent to Jennie at Hangzhou for James Williamson to bring two boatloads of furniture and essentials for setting up house and 'all the things in my study (except photographic apparatus, shotguns and ammunition) . . . You will wonder at my sending for so many things at once; the reason is that the water (in the canals) will soon be so low that . . . we may have to wait months before they can come'—an important fact to be borne in mind. All mail was to be addressed to the care of J. M. Canny, the French consul at Zhenjiang. But news of baby Maria left 'little human hope of her recovery . . . I know not whether she is alive or not now. I need not tell you how poorly it has made me.' Indeed, the way he became physically ill under emotional stress was an affliction he was not ashamed to admit to Jennie. She knew him too well.

1868: THE RIOT SEASON

'Red in the morning' (July 1868)

So much ill-informed comment on the happenings at Yangzhou originated immediately after the events and followed from false reports and misinterpretations, even in the House of Lords, that the truth has become distorted. Caution needs to be observed by students of the period. Even the historian Hosea Ballou Morse, normally so reliable, wrote, 'In 1867 [sic] the Rev James Hudson Taylor founded the China Inland Mission for the purpose of forcing the previously unsettled question of the right of residence inland, and of "planting the shining cross on every hill and in every valley of China"', either consciously quoting Anson Burlingame's New York rhetoric or forgetting the origin

of it.[35] If this had been Hudson Taylor's motive, he was not only brave or foolhardy but also silent as to any such motive. On the contrary, he acted on the declared right of residence with support of the treaty, proclamations and 'most favoured nation clause'. He did unostentatiously what the French had done for years with flags flying above their property to proclaim their established residence and enforced rights.

In this attempt to present a more complete and factual account of the Yangzhou riot than has been recorded elsewhere, it is right to emphasise that the information exists in three categories. First-hand contemporary accounts and comments, in letters, reports and an affidavit, are most reliable. For this reason we make generous use of them. Of secondary value are first-hand reminiscences, subject to deceptive memory, and even first-hand reports by consuls and others dependent on collected evidence. Lastly, newspaper reports, pure hearsay and unbridled rhetoric such as the Duke of Somerset's spread false statements which have clouded the issues.

The first hint of trouble had come at Suzhou. With little of the language and with a sense of insecurity, Henry Cordon, instead of cultivating friendship with his Chinese neighbours and acquaintances, kept his front door shut and behaved secretively. Soon suspicions were aroused and his landlord asked him to leave. Charles Schmidt poured oil on the troubled waters, and after Wang Lae-djün came up from Hangzhou to help, peace was restored.

But in Zhenjiang an ominous twist in events began on July 8. Posters appeared in the city alleging that young women and children were being kidnapped by being offered drugged food and stupefied by drugged tobacco smoke. Their eyes, livers, and genital organs were then being made into drugs. Thomas Francis Wade, the hero of the battle of Muddy Flat and subsequently Sir Rutherford Alcock's successor as British minister at Peking, told Consul Lay that the Zhenjiang magistrate who had been dismissed from Shanghai was the instigator of these allegations.[36] Hudson Taylor would not have known of them on Thursday, July 9, as he wrote to Maria from Guazhou, before crossing the Yangzi to Zhenjiang. The promised proclamation paving his way to possession of the Zhenjiang house had been delayed, but the Yangzhou proclamation would remove the last difficulties there. 'We may come to terms about a house at (Yangzhou) today or tomorrow. But we have so often been disappointed that we must not be too sure of anything, save of God's help and presence which He will never withhold.' The three weeks since Maria had gone to Shanghai felt like three months. And 'What shall we render to the Lord for sparing our darling children when in such danger?'

Three days later when he must have known of the inflammatory posters, he added, 'For our Master's sake, may He make us willing to do or suffer all His will. In this spirit we may be spared from some of the trials which might otherwise be needed; and when we do pass through the fire, He will be with us.' They were being prepared by slow degrees for upheavals ahead. He wrote to Jennie, discreetly affectionate as always, about the domestic arrangements in Hangzhou wages, accounts, responsibilities, what to do with No 1 New Lane when most of them moved into No 2; and added about his house-hunting, 'As soon as it seems fixed . . . we are left in the lurch again.' He posted these letters 'at the Hulk' at Zhenjiang and received one from Maria. 'I hope to get a (proclamation) and then all will be well.' But this time instead of applying to the *xian* magistrate he turned to the Zhenjiang city prefect who had applied a proclamation for the LMS chapel. 'If he will give me one, well; if not, I must go to the Consul', whose duty it was to see that the terms of the treaties were observed.

To conduct a simple matter of business was like drawing blood from a stone. In any case the sitting tenants, two brothers and two women, by inference the mother and the elder brother's wife, would not move out until 'this luckless (inauspicious) month is out'. If the Rudlands and Louise Desgraz arrived after that they could take possession. Still nothing happened. When the consul applied to the highest prefect, the *daotai*, he was promised the proclamation in a few days' time 'if all were straightforward'. 'But the *xian* [the ex-Shanghai magistrate] was determined that all should not be straightforward.'[37]

At Hangzhou it was swelteringly hot, 92°F in Jennie's room in June and 97°F with perspiration rolling down her face, as she wrote in July. Where could they go to escape the heat? Work that was usually a pleasure 'becomes a continual effort and one's spiritual life is in great danger of waning . . . Oh dear! This is such weather, everything spoils! Steel rusts, moth and worms eat and mildew covers almost everything.' The

Chinese felt it too. Tempers were on edge. The riot season had come. Jennie had been packing up some of Emily's and Maria's things to send with Louise. Three weeks had passed since the prefect had approved the deal. Only delay, no hostility, had been apparent so far. Hudson Taylor was living on his boat at Zhenjiang. 'My precious sister,' he wrote to Jennie; Cordon's Chinese colleague in Suzhou had been offending people by preaching that 'Confucius had gone to Hell, and that sort of thing.' He was being returned to Hangzhou and 'I think he ought not to be allowed, to preach at present.' Any indiscretion was dangerous. Such ineptitude was inflammatory.

Meanwhile the Yangzhou proclamation was published and Hudson Taylor returned there to complete negotiations for the lease on July 17 'with the permission and aid of the Prefect' and with Innkeeper Peng's help. To attract as little attention as possible he moved some of the family into the new premises on the 20th and the rest a few days later. 'For the first fortnight the curiosity of the people gave us some trouble, but caused no serious anxiety' was Hudson Taylor's calm recollection. Maria was more forthright in a letter to Miss Stacey: 'Excepting the annoyance of inquisitive intruders who would make their way in without invitation, we continued there without disturbance.' And Hudson Taylor said, 'While we had many friendly callers, both from among the officials and towns people to whom we were able to speak privately we had no public services.'[38]

Maria was still in Shanghai, waiting with John McCarthy for Catherine Brown's arrival, and preparing Chinese clothes for her. So busy with Mission business that she was losing sleep, and unwell because pregnant again, Maria confessed her ill-health to her husband on July 23. 'But soldiers must not complain of hardships and I don't mean to complain, only it seems so natural to tell you of such things . . . Weariness is easier to bear than anxiety.' For she was anxious. She mentioned complaints from several of the team. And 'I hardly dare trust' myself to speak of Mr Nicol's letter (to William Berger), for the downright falsehood (of it).' If he would not resign and had to be dismissed, what an 'uproar' it might cause! Even James Meadows was restless and needed to get away from Ningbo. Such heat and humidity so easily brought out the worst in people, as she well knew of herself. Perhaps it would help matters if she, at obvious cost to herself and her own family, were to go down to Ningbo for Mrs Cardwell's confinement. What did Hudson think? But the setback at Zhenjiang was also worrying and too reminiscent of Huzhou and Jinhua, especially as the Rudland and Louise Desgraz had been ready to leave Hangzhou on the 23rd with their staff of printers and their own two boatloads of printing presses and baggage for settling at Zhenjiang. Williamson or Judd were to bring two more loads of household effects for Yangzhou, all before the water levels sank too low in the canals.

On the same day and again on the 29th Mrs Berger was writing to Maria one of the strong, positive letters she habitually wrote to members of the Mission in China. 'There was something about (Annie Bohannan's) spirit which invariably told for good on mine . . . Whenever I think of (good, kind) Miss Desgraz, it is with thankfulness to God for giving you such an one . . . William often wishes there were a hundred more Miss Fauldings associated with you.' In June she had written, for them to receive in August, 'These words are comforting me concerning you at this time—"Underneath are the everlasting arms" . . . they will protect you when attacked, and will preserve you from all real danger. Oh how safe you are!' Now on July 23 she said, 'Truly your safety is in God alone . . . May He graciously keep you from feeling afraid!'[39] When she was writing, the prospects were good at Yangzhou and hopeful again for Zhenjiang with consular help. Accompanying a cheque for £40 for Hudson Taylor from George Müller came a letter quoting Psalm 62, 'Trust in him at all times, ye people, pour out your heart before him. God is a refuge for us.' Why so much about safety and protection? Responses to news of violence at Huzhou and Jinhua perhaps, with awareness of potential dangers never far away, but doubly relevant by the time these letters arrived.

Dysentery, light at first, struck Hudson Taylor on the day he moved into the new house, July 20, but he had to supervise repairs to the premises and at the end of the week to go down to Zhenjiang again. The consul had taken up his problem with the antagonistic magistrate's superiors. There on Sunday the 26th his illness took a turn for the worse. He scribbled a note in pencil to Maria in Shanghai, saying he hoped a proclamation would put things right in Zhenjiang, the very next day. 'But I must return [to Yangzhou). I am so ill. Would you write to Meadows and ask if he can come and help me? Go to Ningpo, darling, if you think well. If our hearts are to be . . . a sacrifice, the will of the Lord be done. Soon we shall never part again.'

Knowing all too well the terrible toll of lives by 'dysentery' in China, Maria left John McCarthy in Shanghai to meet Catherine Brown's ship, well overdue, and sent a message to the Cardwells that she herself could not come for the confinement. Because it was the Lord's Day, which on principle she would not voluntarily secularise by travelling, she rejected the possibility of travelling to Zhenjiang by steamer, and after midnight hired a footboat to take her, the baby and an *amah* by canal instead, although it would take two days and nights. When the rowers tired she even took turns at the oars. Passing through Suzhou she called at the Schmidt's and carried a note from him to Hudson Taylor saying, 'I am sorry you are so ill, and we (are praying) for the Lord to spare your life . . . I think you are wanted in the field more than ever now.' He enclosed Hudson Taylor's midnight cheque with the request please to sign and return it!

Maria reached Yangzhou on the 29th to find him better, and word came soon afterwards of a Ningbo doctor having delivered Mrs Cardwell of her child by forceps. So Maria could not have helped much if she had gone. Moreover James

Meadows, his most experienced colleague, was probably on his way to Yangzhou already, with Williamson, to undertake the next advance up the Yangzi.

On the 28th Anson Burlingame's treaty between the United States and China had extended reciprocity to Chinese in the States. Its Article 4 read: 'It is further agreed that citizens of the United States in China of every religious persuasion, and Chinese subjects in the United States, shall enjoy entire liberty of conscience, and shall be exempt from all disability or persecution on account of their religious faith or worship in either country.'[40] Even by the 'most favoured nation' concession by Peking this added nothing to the lot of any foreigners in China. Two days later the Presbyterian chapel at 'Pitow', Taiwan, was wrecked for the second time.

If Maria and Hudson Taylor and Mrs Berger wrote as if they had premonitions of trouble, so did Jennie and Emily. 'What may be in the future,' Jennie's home letter ran, 'we cannot tell; trials there are sure to be, perhaps dangers and sorrows and hardships which as yet we have not dreamed of, but God is with us and He will keep our hearts in perfect peace.' Immunity from physical harm was not promised to God's envoys. On July 19, Emily underlined, bracketed and annotated 2 Samuel 24.24 in her Bible, 'Neither will I offer burnt offerings unto the Lord my God of that which doth cost me nothing.' News had come of another brother's death, leaving two younger sisters and her father of a once large family. It was neither unexpected nor enough to merit such a heart cry. She knew the danger she herself was in.

Premonitions or not, with August they entered a crescendo of sound and fury.

'The laugh of the tea-houses'[41]
(August 1868)

Jennie and the Judds in Hangzhou had a taste of trouble early on Sunday, August 2, when they heard 'a great deal of noise and confusion downstairs' and found the courtyard and main rooms 'full of rough, bad-looking men . . . between forty and fifty (of them)'. A troop of beggar-banditti, flotsam of the rebellion who lived off the populace by intimidation, had invaded the premises. 'They enter respectable houses (. . . the doors are seldom closed here) and ask for money; should they be refused . . . they do not scruple to pillage the house.' Charles Judd went down to them, calmly said he would talk with them outside and 'firmly but gently led them towards the door'. They followed. Out in the street he explained who he was and preached the gospel to them while they 'listened quietly for a few moments and then went away'! When Jennie's mother heard of the potential danger her precious daughter had been in, characteristically her disapproval of Hudson Taylor's leaving Jennie behind was intensified. Had he not promised to protect her? Her attitude changed when news came of the riots he himself went through. Then she was glad Jennie was not in Yangzhou. [As events follow one upon another, the deceptiveness of hindsight needs to be resisted.]

On the same day, August 2, the Rudlands and Louise Desgraz arrived at Zhenjiang with the printing press and their Chinese companions, expecting to occupy the premises promised for July 8. Instead they found the doors firmly closed against them. The magistrate's proclamation was still being withheld. No record has been found of their consulting Consul Lay or his assistant Clement F. R. Allen, although it is likely that they did so. But knowing that Hudson Taylor had moved into his own place in Yangzhou, and seeing no objections, they crossed the Yangzi and later that day arrived at his door with their two boatloads of equipment and personal possessions.

In the absence of any overt hostility in Yangzhou before August 8, apart from the evident objections to leasing property to foreigners, Hudson Taylor did nothing to send them away. He had room in Yangzhou to house them until the Zhenjiang house was vacated and they could return there. With consul and *daotai* both helping, that could not be many days away. To ask them

to manage on their houseboats or to find lodging at an inn or a temple on Silver Island, a quiet retreat in the Yangzi below Zhenjiang might have been reasonable if Mary Rudland had been in better health and if the cost of housing the printers and servants had not been prohibitive. As it was, the *xian* magistrate at Zhenjiang had seen his opportunity to defy both consul and *daotai*, and made dispersal to Zhenjiang impossible.

Sensing trouble in the magistrate's tactics Hudson Taylor was later to write:

> the (Zhenjiang) landlord's family became frightened, and to avoid sharing the punishment they were led to suppose awaited the elder son (whose name alone, according to Chinese custom, appeared on the deeds of rental), they went to the magistrate and told him that the house had been let to me without their consent or knowledge. Therefore the magistrate sent for the elder son, and upbraiding him for letting his house to a foreigner, told him that one person could not be allowed to override the other three owners of the property, and that he must return the deposit-money to me. This he did not attempt to do; but the way in which the missionary and his Consul had been worsted by the cunning of (the magistrate) became the laugh of the tea-house and restaurant. When the fact of the foreigner and even his consul being flouted at Zhenjiang became known at Yangzhou, it suggested the idea that it would not be difficult to eject us from that city; and while the mass of the people were quite friendly, the literary classes were looking on our arrival with great jealousy, and commencing those efforts which resulted in the attacks on us.

All too soon the details of the Yangzhou property were to become part of Foreign Office dispatches and international history as the scene of high drama. The premises were rambling. A gatehouse on the main street served several neighbouring houses, reached by a shared entrance lane about a hundred yards in length and running due south. At the far end (A) two gates opened from the lane into a complex of courtyards, gardens, rockeries and passageways between scattered buildings, each with only a few rooms, well suited to such a mixed party. Inside the gates lay the courtyards of the Chinese quarters and outer reception hall (B). Beyond them and some open ground a walled pavilion (C) gave on to large rockeries, behind which kitchen buildings (D) and a well house (E) were concealed, backing on to quiet lanes to the south and west. On the east side a latticed wall of ornamental bricks flanked an octagonal gateway (F) into the courtyard of a two-storeyed house. Entered only through the house lay another little garden at the back, surrounded by high walls between it and a vacant plot of ground. The centre of the house itself was no more than another guest hall open to the courtyard, and a stairwell, with two living rooms on each side in which the baggage was stacked. At the top of a rough staircase a trap-door could be lowered, isolating the bedrooms from the ground level of the house. Partitions divided this upper floor into seven rooms, each roughly ten or twelve feet square. Outside the Taylors' bedroom window and his office, a narrow sloping tiled roof formed a porch twelve or fifteen feet above the front courtyard.

For a month after he took possession on July 20, Hudson Taylor had kept several carpenters busy repairing the dilapidations and adapting the place for its intended long-term use. But when the Zhenjiang magistrate's neat ploy to thwart the rental of a house in his city became known, active hostility began at Yangzhou, and the inquisitive intruders became more truculent.

The agitators[42] (August 1–18, 1868)

During the first week of August 'one of the agents or middle-men' who had helped Hudson Taylor to lease the property, informed him that,

there had been a meeting of some

of the literary and military (graduates) at which it was determined to stir up the people by "agitating reports" and thus to eject us from Yangchow. From that time we were frequently annoyed, and sometimes endangered, by the throwing of stones at and into our windows from the vacant ground outside.

Before long, small anonymous handbills were posted up in the city, 'containing absurd charges against us, and threatening us, the landlord and the house-agents'. By kindness, and patiently talking with the people 'we succeeded in avoiding any outbreak'.

Seeing that the handbills were not inflammatory enough, the instigators then placarded the walls in the city with posters

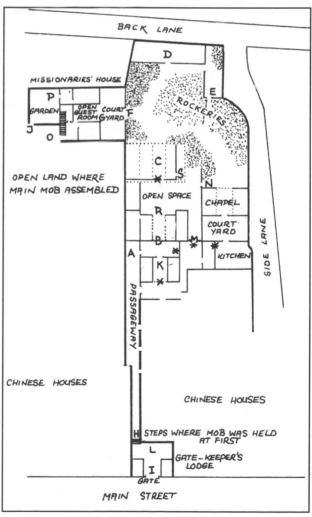

2.7 Scene of the Yangzhou riot

nearly a yard long, calling us 'Brigands of the Religion of Jesus', stating that we scooped out the eyes of the dying, opened foundling hospitals to eat the children, cut open pregnant women (for the purpose of making medicine of the infants), etc. This roused the people so much, that though we were able to prevent a riot by taking our stand at the door of the premises [A in plan], and arguing all day with them as they assembled, I felt it incumbent on me to write to the Prefect, like the apostle Paul in Acts 22 and 23 asking him to intervene. I wrote, enclosing a copy of the anonymous placard, on Friday, August 14, as follows:

J. H. Taylor, Director of the China Inland Mission to His Excellency the Prefect Sun:

Some time ago I had the honour to receive a copy of a proclamation for which I beg to thank you ... I rented a house in the Kiung-Hua-Kuan Street under Your Excellency's jurisdiction, which house is now being repaired. Rude persons and soldiers continually disobeyed your proclamation and day to day came to the house wandering about amusing themselves and acting most indecorously. Some of them insisted on going upstairs and regardless that there were females there entered the rooms and went hither and thither with the greatest boldness and impudence ...

At the present time there are persons spreading unfounded *yaoyen* (incitements) containing many scandals. Moreover these are written in large characters on yellow paper [feigning imperial authority] and placarded about in every direction ... I now enclose a copy of these yaoyen, the only object of my petition being to beg Your Excellency to adopt some method of suppressing them so as to frustrate their insidious purpose ... For matters are in such a state that if they are not stringently prohibited, most assuredly we shall suffer great injury. Therefore I beg beforehand to apprise Your Excellency and again venture to trouble you.

May I request the favour of a reply? With many compliments etc.[43]

The Prefect promised an answer which they received on the following day. It was an evasive reply and even facetious, but ended with, 'I will command the (*xian* magistrate) to put out proclamations in accordance with the (*daotai's*) dispatch prohibiting these things.'[44]

The same day some of the better disposed people forewarned us [in an anonymous letter] that a riot might be expected on the morrow and advised our immediately adopting every precaution to avoid collision with the people. We at once built up as many of the entrances to the house as possible and placing two large chairs across the passage which leads from the street to the house [plan, H] two of us seated ourselves on them and so closed the way. A crowd of from one hundred to two hundred persons was assembled; and from time to time we addressed them, with the effect of preventing any actual breach of the peace. Moreover we did a few days before engage two of the (dibao's) assistants as doorkeepers, who were of some help in soothing the people.

In the evening George Duncan called in on his way from Nanjing to Shanghai to meet his bride. He had to force his way through the crowd at the gates, to find Hudson Taylor 'just up from a sickbed' facing the mob and by the force of personality and 'that remarkable tact which God has given him' holding them at bay. 'Being a fluent speaker of Mandarin, and at the same time a man of great courage and self-possession,' Duncan's arrival was most opportune, Emily observed. 'You can imagine how grateful Mr Taylor felt when he consented to waive his intended journey and stand by us in our peril.'

With the danger increasing, Hudson Taylor proposed to send the women and children to Silver Island. 'With one consent we (women) begged him not to do so,' Maria was to recall. 'For us to have gone away at that juncture would probably have been to increase to those that remained any danger that there might be.' But there was little the women could do to help, so Emily took advantage of a lull to write with characteristic verve to Mrs Berger.

Mr Taylor was boasting of God's care for us to (Mr Peng) of the hotel, who helped us to get this house. The poor man came to us late on Saturday night in great fright. He told us that our present landlord was going to remove his family away from the premises at dawn on account of the expected riot on the morrow. For himself he said he could only depend upon Mr Taylor. Mr Taylor told him *he* depended upon God; and told him to see whether God would not protect us that we were on His business, and He would not have us in danger, and added 'Wait and see, and if God does not preserve us, never trust me again or believe my words.' What an irresistible power is in God's truth! for that heathen man ... went away quite relieved and comforted.

Hudson Taylor's own account continued (in an affidavit required by the consul-general, W. H. Medhurst Jr, and later amplified for the *Occasional Paper*),[45]

When Sunday (16th) came, we found the need of all (our) preparations. From morning till night we had to keep our post at the entrance. It was clear that the attempts to enrage the mob emanated from the respectably dressed persons who from time to time came among them; but our knowledge of what they were saying enabled us at once to answer their remarks. Two or three times there were decided attempts to break into the house; and the windows were frequently assailed with stones and brickbats; but by persuasion, and by avoiding any appearance of fear or attempt at retaliation, we constrained the majority of the mob to admit, however unwillingly, that right was on our side. During this day ... a new placard was freely posted about, more vile and irritating than the previous ones (unfit for publication). It concluded with a notification that on the 1st of the 7th moon, the local examination day (the graduates meet for graduation in Yang-chau on the 1st and 15th of the month), the graduates and the people would assemble on the exercise ground, and thence come to our house and burn it down; when all, natives and foreigners, would be destroyed indiscriminately.

No mention is made in any contemporary record of any thought of notifying the consulate, let alone of asking for help

or protection. 'The great power of our God' was sufficient reality. Whether he intervened with biblical surprises or allowed his people to be 'stoned, sawn in two or put to the sword', as in Hebrews 11, could be left to him. Physical immunity mattered less than the fufilment of God's purposes in allowing these circumstances.

On Monday [Hudson Taylor went on] the crowding was much less but we still had to keep guard at the door. We availed ourselves, however, of the comparative lull to circulate a number of handbills, showing the foolishness of the slanders, and explaining that we could not at once throw the door open, and let the people in to view the premises for themselves, on account of the danger there might be of the falling of scaffolding and of unfinished walls, etc.; that in two or three weeks' time, when the repairs were finished, we would ask them to come again. This seemed to have a beneficial effect, and though there was great crowding all Tuesday (1st of 7th moon, the day on which we were to have been destroyed), and though several attempts were actually made by literary men to stir up the mob, especially by a (graduate) of the name of Koh, no further damage was done than the injuring of some of the window-shutters and the roof by the missiles hurled at the house from the back.

Emily, then 23, was in good form that day, and indeed all through 'this hurricane of trials'.

Today (Tuesday) was placarded as the day for attacking our house and setting it on fire ... Having done all that we can do to fortify ourselves, we know that whatever happens will be by God's permission, for we have put ourselves into His hands. He will not leave us. While I write He is sending thunder and the threatening of rain, which will do more for us, Mr Taylor was saying, than an army of soldiers ... Any attempt to set the place on fire now would be very vain indeed, for the rain is coming down in torrents.

So the day for burning and killing proved to be a damp squib, 'though some of the people were very much excited'. Ten days had passed since word of organised hostility had been received, including four 'almost in a state of siege' which they came to call 'the first disturbance'. 'It has been a hard battle [Emily confessed] to get ourselves established in this city. And now from hour to hour we are crying to God to enable us to hold what through Him we have gained.' The still anonymous agitators had failed to arouse the public to the extremes they urged, but turned to planning more drastic action.

A lull before the storm
(August 19–22, 1868)

Five days had passed since Hudson Taylor's appeal to Prefect Sun. The four days of uproar had in fact been since he promised to intervene. The only *yamen* underlings and soldiers at the scene had been swelling the mobs. On Wednesday, August 19 when one of the literati became conspicuous in the crowd, goading them to violence, though without success, Hudson Taylor addressed the prefect again.

> Matters being most urgent I beg you to excuse the absence of complimentary expressions.
>
> A few days ago I received your reply referring to the light and frivolous disposition of the (Yangzhou) people

2.8 The hairstyle Emily wore, and a child's

and their fondness for making trouble and stating that I was to wait until the (*xian* magistrate) should issue prohibitory proclamations ...

Up to the present I have not seen any steps to repress (these agitators). Therefore the people are the more daring and fearless, daily crowding about the door ...

It is not because I am alarmed that I come again to cry 'danger'. What I feel anxious about is this: Should loss of life ensue, what then will be the consequences? May I beg your serious attention to this question? I came here to propagate religion in accordance with the will of the Emperor as given in the treaty of commerce and amity. Ought I then to be subjected to such insult? I request you to refer to the articles of the treaty which state that British subjects are permitted to buy ground and build chapels in the interior and furthermore are allowed in every place at their own convenience to travel without detention, molestation or hindrance and that in case of need they may with confidence look for protection and aid at any time, etc. It is on this ground that I venture to trouble you again. Yesterday a resident of the city (a graduate) ... of the family name of Koh ... came to the gate making a disturbance and ... with loud shouts threatened ... to collect a mob and come and beat and destroy us using most extravagant language; to this the constable Lin Pian can bear witness. I would therefore respectfully pray Your Excellency to send officers to arrest him and to put a stop to his violence.[46]

To this note the following reply was sent by the Prefect in the afternoon, apparently friendly but frivolously inadequate as before, 'Persons who get up this kind of report and placard generally do it in the dark and without either name or surname. It is not easy for me in a short time to lay hold of them . . . As to the man known to the (constable) who dared to make disturbance at your door I will instantly send for and examine him and issue warning proclamations.'

Thursday, August 20—the day the naval commander issued his ultimatum to the *daotai* at Anping, Taiwan—was another relatively quiet day in Yangzhou. But, as Hudson Taylor stated in his affidavit on August 31, 'Subsequent to the receipt of this I was informed that the Prefect, finding the man Koh was a graduate, did not send for him, but . . . matters continued to look better until August 22nd.'

Catherine Brown had at last reached Shanghai on the 20th, after five and a half months at sea, and fortunately no one brought her on to Yangzhou. But by force of circumstances, unplanned and unwelcome if only for lack of space, there were four missionary men, five women and four children in the house. Chinese colleagues, printers and servants, not the objects of attack on this occasion, numbered nineteen. Taking the prefect's letter at face value, the family became hopeful that 'the disturbance would gradually pass away', and when Hudson Taylor wrote to Jennie on Friday, he plunged straight into business matters, saying surprisingly,

> I have now the hope that ere long the press may be at work again. Our matters at Zhenjiang are looking up and we are hoping after all to get possession of the house. The (*xian* magistrate) has been made to reverse his judgment in the matter. Here we have been in great danger from an excited mob ... For some days ... three or four of us had to sit all day and guard the doors. Now thank God it has passed away, and the excitement is gradually subsiding.

George Duncan even went down to Zhenjiang to see if he could get into the disputed house, returning the next day, Saturday, August 22. While he was away, peace prevailed until two unrelated incidents played into the hands of the plotting literati.

The Saturday night riot (1) (August 22–23, 1868)

After the riots a French priest, presumably Père Sechinger of Zhenjiang, named by Prefect Sun, wrote a brief account of his own part in the events, saying:

> At Yang-tcheou we had a small orphanage,

which in its recent foundation and precarious existence had been the subject of many negotiations, and vexatious difficulties. Towards the end of August 1868 a large mob stirred up by influential literati collected round the orphanage to destroy it. 'What do you want?' cried an old Woman, a heathen, quite unknown to the missionaries. 'We wish to pull down the foreigners' house.' 'There are no foreigners here,' said she, 'they are in another part of the town,' and she showed the mob the Protestant mission house. The crowd went there at once ...

> Next day (the mandarin) went solemnly with a full retinue to our cemetery, where he disinterred twelve corpses to make sure they were not mutilated ... The great man could verily the fact that we disturbed neither the hearts nor the eyes of the dead, yet he issued a notice forbidding people to bring infants to the (church) in future.[47]

In 1872 Hudson Taylor issued a *Summary of the Operations of the China Inland Mission* in which he referred to the Yangzhou riot as being 'occasioned principally by the unwise conduct of (Chinese) in charge of the Roman Catholic orphanage in that city'.[48]

On the same morning, Saturday, 22nd, Captain Sands, the American chargé d'affaires at Zhenjiang, and a Mr Drew visited Yangzhou for a few hours in foreign clothes to see the temples and pagodas. They found the city quiet. But as Hudson Taylor stated in his affidavit:

> Their visit would appear to have suggested another excuse for a riot. In the exercise grounds and tea-houses, and all along the streets, a rumour was industriously circulated that more foreigners had come, and that twenty-four children were missing. I first became aware of danger about four p.m., when one of the servants came running into the house, and asked me to come out at once, as both the inner and outer gates [A and B in plan] had been burst open, and a crowd was already on the premises. Losing no time, I went and found it was indeed so, but succeeded in getting them out, and in stationing two of our number at the end of the entrance lane [at H], as before, while the gates were

repaired by the carpenters then working on the premises.

[Maria supplied more detail.] Finding they had done some damage, he adopted a curious but very effectual method with them. Taking his stand at the place where they had entered, he told them now they were in they might stop in, and tell him who had done the mischief. Of course this made them all most anxious to get out; and as well as they could they slank away, until before long there was not one left. But as evening drew on a real mob began to collect outside our premises ... The mere fact of its being evening instead of daytime, gave affairs a very serious aspect, besides which, the evil intentions of the mob soon made themselves apparent in other ways.[49]

When George Duncan arrived home in the evening he 'found a great crowd of people gathered around the door, (saying) that the foreigners had eaten twenty-four children. As it grew dark the crowd increased until thousands of men surrounded the house trying to break into it and were throwing pieces of bricks and crying at the top of their voices, "Foreign devils!"' 'The (Chinese) say 20,000, but this is probably a number magnified by their fears,' Hudson Taylor told the Bergers. His affidavit continued:

A little later the people began to pelt those sitting at the door—a thing not attempted before; and became more uproarious. (The mob ... were reported to us to have been armed with knives and spears as well as clubs.) We sent messengers at intervals to the prefect; but they neither returned themselves, nor did any help come. The attack became general; some of the shutters of the upstairs rooms of the house were dashed in from behind, part of the garden wall was being pulled down [at J], and it was evident that without help we could not long keep the people out. Mr Duncan and I, therefore, determined to endeavour to make our way through the mob to the Prefect, as there was now no hope of Chinese messengers reaching him. [Before they could go they had to barricade a window 'the shutter of which had given way and fallen down from the incessant

hurling of stones at it'—a measure of the force of the bombardment.] Commending ourselves to the care of our Father, and asking the needed grace, if a violent death were awaiting us (we had previously, in the house, commended those we were leaving behind to God's care), we essayed to set out. We saw at once that it was impossible to pass through the mob in front of the house who now also occupied the rooms [K] at the entrance and the end of the passage [L]; but by passing through a neighbour's house ... we succeeded in eluding the rioters immediately about the door. We had not proceeded far, however, when we were recognised, and the cry was raised, 'The foreign devils are fleeing.'

Happily I knew a by way leading through some fields, by taking which we eluded most of those following us, while our rapid pace soon distanced those who still pursued us, and the thick darkness favoured us much. Moreover, the path we had taken misled many of the people, who thought we were fleeing to the Bast Gate to escape from the city; and, consequently, many persons ran off by a short cut, expecting to meet us there. All this was providential, as it gave us a few minutes at a time when every moment was precious. But when we turned into the main street, we were assaulted with stones, and a mob gathered behind us, increasing at every step. Our rapid strides still kept a clear space between them and us, but we were nearly exhausted, and our legs so hurt with the stones and bricks thrown at us, that we were almost failing, when we reached the door of the *yamen*. But for the protection afforded us by the darkness, we should have scarcely reached it alive.

The gate-keepers were just closing the doors as we approached, alarmed by the yells of the people behind us; but the momentary delay gave time for the crowd to come up and close upon us; the as yet unbarred gates gave way to the pressure, and we were precipitated into the entrance hall. [Duncan said 'The door burst open, letting us fall flat on our faces.'] I am convinced that had the gates been barred, they would not have been opened for us, and we should have been torn in pieces by the enraged mob. Once in the *yamen*, we rushed into the judgment-hall, and cried ... 'Save life! Save life!', a cry which a Chinese mandarin is bound to attend to at any hour of the day or night.

We were taken to the room of the (secretary) and kept waiting for about three-quarters of an hour before we had an audience with the Prefect, all the time hearing the yells of the mob a mile or more off, destroying, for aught we knew, not only the property, but possibly the lives, of those so dear to us. And at last, when we did get an audience, it was almost more than we could bear with composure to be asked as to what we really did with the babies? Whether it was true we had bought them, and how many? What was really the cause of all this rioting? etc.

At last I told His Excellency that the real cause of all this trouble was his own neglect in not taking measures when the matter was small and manageable; that I must now request him first to take steps to repress the riot, and save any of our friends who might still be alive, and afterwards make such inquiries as he might wish, or I would not answer for the result. 'Ah,' said he, 'very true, very true! First quiet the people, and then inquire. Sit still, and I will go to see what can be done.'

He went out, telling us to remain, as the only chance of his effecting anything depended on our keeping out of sight, for by this time the number of rioters amounted to eight or ten thousand ... We were kept in the torture of suspense for two hours, when the Prefect returned with the (governor of the military forces of the city some three thousand men) and told us that all was quiet now; that the military governor himself, the captain of the soldiers who guard the gates, and two (*xian* magistrates) had been to the scene of the disturbance; that they had seized several of those who were plundering the premises, and would have them punished. He then sent for (sedan) chairs for us, and we returned under escort.

On the way back we were told that all the foreigners we had left in the house were killed. We had to cry to God to support us, though we hoped this might prove exaggerated or untrue. [Duncan added, 'As we got nearer the house we smelled a very strange smell ... ', (and Maria: 'his heart sickened as ... he distinguished a smell ... which suggested the thought to his mind that we were being burned',) but 'which we found afterwards were some fur garments burning'.]

When we reached the house, the scene was such as baffles all description. Here, a pile of half-burned reeds showed where one of the attempts to set the house on fire had been made; there, debris of a broken-down wall was to be seen; and strewn about everywhere were the remains of boxes and furniture; scattered papers and letters, 'broken work-boxes, writing desks, dressing-cases, and surgical instrument cases; smouldering remains of valuable books, etc., etc., but no trace of inhabitants within.

They searched and called but could not discover what had become of family and friends.

The Saturday night riot (2)[50] (August 22–23, 1868)

The affidavit only summarised events at the beleaguered house after Duncan and Hudson Taylor had left to go to the *yamen*, but Emily wrote more fully after it was all over.

> The next four or five terrible hours it is difficult to describe. We were separated now; and to personal danger was added the tenfold more painful suspense as to the fate of those away from us. Mr Taylor and Mr Duncan were out in the streets, exposed to the fury of the mob.

[JHT writing] Reid and Rudland (with the servants) kept the doors and entrances as long as possible, determined only to retire from point to point as actually compelled, and hoping to retard the progress of the rioters until help arrived. While they were keeping the people out at the front door [B], a wall that had been built to close up a side door [M] was pulled down, and they had to retire to a nearer point [N]. Now all the teachers' and servants' things were at the mercy of the mob ... Meanwhile the walls (of the house itself) were broken through [at Q and P]. Mr Rudland (and Mr Reid) therefore went to try and keep the people at bay there.

[Emily] We, ladies and children, were alone in the upper storey of the house. It was unsafe to remain in any of the back rooms, on account of the stones and bricks which were being showered in at the windows; so we brought the children into Mrs Taylor's room [above the guest room] and gathered there ourselves to plead with God to protect and save us, and especially to take care of our brothers, who were in the, fore-front of the danger. Sometimes a fresh outburst among the rioters made our hearts chill for a moment, but we preserved our calmness and sustained our courage by ... prayer.

Presently Mr Rudland came up so exhausted that he could hardly stand, and with his clothes all stained with mud. There is a trap-door at the top of the stairs, and we might at least have delayed the rioters for a time ... by letting this down and drawing some heavy boxes upon it. But in doing *so* we might, perhaps, have been shutting up from Mr Reid the only means of escape from the mob. It was an anxious time; any little mistake might sacrifice all our lives in a moment ... We were expecting every moment to see the rioters come up the stairs, when Mr Reid called out from the courtyard below, in a hollow, hoarse voice, as if utterly exhausted, 'Mrs Taylor! Come down if you can. They're setting the house on fire, and I can't help you.'

[Maria] This however could only be done by the window of my room ... We threw mattresses and pillows down in front [at G] as a precaution in case we should fall in the descent, and gathered together some sheets and blankets. [Emily] Mr Rudland got out upon the projecting roof under the window, and let down Mrs Rudland and Ensing (our head printer's young wife married only a few weeks before) to Reid below. [Maria] Six-year-old Freddie (Howard Taylor) was to go next, but as they were passing him through the window he said, 'Let Bertie go first; he's so frightened!' So Herbert was let down and then Howard.

[Emily] Mr Reid hurried them away, and concealed them in the well-house [E] (beneath a little summer house) and then returned for others. But in the meantime, a tall, strong man, naked to the waist, came into the (upstairs) room; and we could see others carrying off boxes from the adjoining rooms. Mrs Taylor went up to the man as he entered, and asked him, 'You see we are all women and children. Are you not ashamed to molest us?' ...

She kept him parleying for a few minutes; but he soon began to lay hands upon us, and search our persons for money, etc. Mrs Taylor had advised me to get a few dollars, in case we should need to escape by boat from the city, and I had tied a small bag with seven or eight dollars in it upon the side-fastening of my dress. The man snatched this from me, and asked for more, threatening to cut my head off if I did not comply ... He next tore off Miss Desgraz's pocket, and took away her hair-ornament; and then being soon satisfied that nothing was concealed about the thin summer clothing we wore, he turned to the boxes and drawers. Mrs Taylor was speaking to him, with her hand raised when he caught, sight of her wedding-ring shining in the candle light, and tore it from her finger ... (Annie Bohannan) escaped with baby (Maria) by going downstairs after a man who was carrying off a box, behind which she screened (her) from the stones and brickbats. She rushed through the fire at the bottom of the stairs, and so got to the front, and took refuge in the well-house.

Mr Reid was again calling to us to hasten, and the smoke was by this time becoming oppressive, while the noise of falling walls and the almost fiendish yelling of the mob warned us that no time must be lost. (Louise Desgraz) was just safely down [by sheet-rope] when the men below cast a heap of burning materials immediately under the window, and cut off escape from us who remained: Mrs Taylor, Mr Rudland, and myself. But just then our attention was directed, not to the means of escape, but to the immediate safety of Mr Rudland. The man who searched us had now turned to him as he stood upon the roof ... caught him by the (hair) and dragged him down upon the tiles ... discovered his watch, and struggled to get possession of it. But Mr Rudland ... threw it out into the darkness ... thinking it just possible that the man might leave us to seek it. This so enraged his assailant that he attempted to thrust Mr Rudland off the roof. But Mrs Taylor and I together caught hold of him and dragged him into the room.

The man (then) snatched an immense brick from the wall which had been partly broken down in the scuffle, and lifted his arm to dash it at Mr Rudland's head. [Rudland] Mrs Taylor put up her hand and stopped the blow; whereupon the man turned to strike her with the brick; but she said to him, 'Would you strike a defenceless woman?' The man, hearing her speak his own language and with such beautiful calmness, was amazed and dropped the brick.

[Emily] Climbing over the wall, (he) made his way across the tiles ... crying to his fellows below, 'Come up, come up!' We were anxious now to make our own escape, (but) [Maria] the man had demolished our sheet contrivance. [Emily] To go down by the staircase was out of the question; at the bottom was a large fire, by the light of which several men were breaking open and ransacking boxes. Not knowing what to do, we returned to the front room, and found that the fire (in the yard) below had been dragged away by Mr Reid ... after being many times obliged to hide ... from his assailants. He said there was not a moment to lose; we must jump down and he would catch us.

[Maria] The only way was to jump from the tiles, though at the risk of breaking our limbs. [Emily] Mrs Taylor went to the edge of the roof, and jumped from it—a height of from twelve to fifteen feet. I saw her fall upon her side, partially caught by Mr Reid; and saw that Mr Reid was ready to receive me. [Maria] But just then he received such a violent blow from a brick on the side of his face, as rendered him ... blind and almost insensible. [Emily] Consequently, I fell upon the stones on my back ... For the instant I felt that I was either dying or stunned; but to lie there was certain death. [Maria] My right leg had somehow been twisted under me in the fall, and it was with difficulty that I regained my feet. I saw Miss Blatchley fall with all her weight on her back by my side ... It seemed to me as if such a fall must break her back. She was momentarily stunned, but the Chinese style of wearing her hair protected the back of her head.

[Emily] Somehow I got upon my feet and then fell again; I got up and fell three or four times before I was able to keep up. Then I saw that Mr Rudland, who had dropped himself from the roof uninjured, was assisting Mrs Taylor. (He) had been attacked by a man with a club, but had escaped with a slight bruise—(and a hernia). [As Emily led Reid away] almost stunned by the blow he had received, and nearly fainting with pain ... the shower of bricks which were flying about us made us exert to the utmost what little strength we had remaining.

[Maria] I found I had received some hurt from which the blood was flowing freely, but the principal pain was from the severe twist of my leg.[51] The night was very dark, and the glare of the fire we were leaving made the darkness seem still more dense. With what haste we could we stumbled over the broken rocks towards the entrance, but finding one of the doors by which we must pass closed and barred, we were brought to a standstill. We waited here [N] while Mr Rudland went to fetch those who were in the well-house, and when we were all together ... made our way as quietly as possible round by an opening where the rioters had knocked down the wall [M], and so got into one of our neighbours' houses by a doorway [Q].

[Emily] We were conducted first to one room, then to another ... as the danger of discovery seemed to increase; and were finally taken to the innermost apartments of (another) house. We sat there in the darkness—such a long, long time it seemed—hoping and fearing as to what had become of Mr Taylor and Mr Duncan. Mr Reid lay groaning with pain; the poor tired children wanted to sleep, and we dared not let them, as we might have to flee again at any moment. Mrs Taylor was almost fainting from loss of blood; and I now found out that my arm was bleeding from a bad cut, and was so painful I could not move it; while many of us were stiff and sore with bruises. [She had in fact sustained a compound fracture of her left elbow.]

[Maria] We were told that our house from which we had just escaped was all on fire, and I fully believed it. Whether we ourselves would live till the morning, or what would become of us we knew not. I felt there was a possibility that Mrs Rudland would be prematurely confined, and that I might have a miscarriage, that very night. But God was our stay, and He forsook us not. This confidence He gave me—that He would surely work good for China out of our deep distress ... One of (the children) said to me, 'Mamma, where shall we sleep tonight, as they have burned up our bed?' ...

From one of our teachers we learned that the Prefect had come with his soldiers, and was driving away the rioters and that the (*xian* magistrate) himself, having discovered where we were, was guarding the house in which we were concealed. But still no word of Mr Taylor. At last, after the sounds of yelling and fighting had subsided, (we heard his) voice. He paused to speak a few words with the (magistrate) and then came in to us; he was not even

wounded seriously, only somewhat lamed by a severe blow from a stone which had struck him in the hollow of the knee, on his way to the *yamen*.

We were now once more all together, and all living; and our first thought was to lift our hearts to God in thanksgiving ... Moreover, we found that our house had not been burned down ... for the neighbours had interfered and helped to put the fires out ... Mr Taylor having called in the (magistrate) to see Mr Reid's condition ... the wounded were removed as soon as possible, and we once more entered the house. It was half past twelve at midnight.

Later Maria found her own Bible, in tatters but 'not a leaf missing', and an untouched bonnet box full of her child Grace's treasures. Exactly a year ago they had watched the life of eight-year-old Grace ebbing away and under cover of darkness had made their secret journey with her body across the lake from Pengshan to Hangzhou. This find was consolation enough. She was rich. More amazing was Emily's discovery: 'The rioters sacked every room but mine in which were all our most important papers and the bulk of our money ($300) . . . The door was standing open; they could not have entered, not a thing was touched.'

Sunday's riot[52] (August 23, 1868)

Knowing that William Berger would receive a flood of enquiries as soon as the news broke in Britain, Hudson Taylor seized his first opportunity to write. His experience of distortions by the Shanghai papers prepared him for the inevitable. As usual they would be repeated in the London press. So a step-by-step statement of the facts would be the best answer. It could not be supplied soon enough. He took up the story where Maria and Emily had stopped, but could not anticipate the form the mis-statements would take, or the magnitude of their repercussions.

A guard of soldiers and some men from the Mandarin's kept watch till dawn; then

2.9 'Mr Reid was was ready to receive me.'

they left us ... The people soon began to re-collect; and again commenced four or five long and anxious hours. We were all nearly worn out, Mr Reid was absolutely helpless ... and others of us stiff and sore from our bruises ... But the people were crowding in front and behind, and something must be done ... Unable to write, I ... sent a Chinese servant over to (Zhenjiang) to inform Mr Allen, of Her Majesty's Consulate, viva voce, of our position. And later in the day, when the (magistrate) told me that it was unsafe to attempt to remove the wounded from the city, I sent another messenger over with a pencilled note ...

The rioters of last night had made a clean sweep of doors, walls, and partitions at the (key points) ... Matters ... looked even worse than the night before ... The premises in front [R] as well as behind were filled with the crowd, leaving no way of escape. A stand was made for a short time at the door [N] which we were still able to close and, leaving my brethren to guard it, I returned to the house ... I succeeded in getting the intruders out, and with the help of the carpenters hastily nailed together some doors and boards, and temporarily closed up the breaches [O, P] ... (But) there was only a six-inch wall in front of the (pavilion) [C], and this (was) easily forced [at S], and the whole front of the building was at their mercy. Once more commending all to our covenant-keeping God ... I (walked through the mob unmolested and) went to the Prefect's for aid. Not a stone was thrown at me on the way. Another long and anxious delay here awaited me. The Prefect had not risen, had not bathed, had not breakfasted. After a time I was told that (he) had sent for the (magistrate) and that he would ... accompany me to the house.

To those I had left behind the time had been one of peculiarly painful suspense ... Now, there was no darkness to favour an escape, and the front of the house was surrounded as well as the back. When the wall of the (pavilion) had been broken through [at S], Messrs Duncan and Rudland took their seats at the octagonal entrance [F] immediately in front of the house, the front garden and rockery being

covered by a crowd which every moment increased. (When) they began to demolish what remained of a fancy wall [each side of F], Mr Rudland took his stand [at G], and assisted Mr Duncan in keeping them out of the house. A few stones were thrown in at the open front of the upstairs rooms, but ... just as anxiety was at its (height) God sent help and the (magistrate) arrived. His soldiers began to disperse the people, and the grounds were gradually cleared; and ... his retainers had the undivided privilege of looting to themselves.

(The magistrate said) that it was not safe for any of the members of our party to leave the city now. He requested me at once to write a letter to the (prefect); to be careful to call the proceedings a disturbance, not a riot, or the people would be more incensed than ever; and to ask him to punish those who had been arrested, and to quiet the people by proclamations. 'Thus,' said he, 'we may restore peace before night, and you will not be under the necessity of leaving the city.' ...

I stated the case as mildly as truth would admit ... (and) sent the letter to the Prefect; but it was opened on the way by the (magistrate) and returned to me as unsuitable. I went to him, and pointed out that the truth must be told. He replied, 'If you persist in sending that letter to the Prefect, I will go back and have nothing more to do with the matter. You may protect yourself as best you can. But I forewarn you that the lives of all your party will probably be sacrificed.'[53]

I saw very well that he wished to get such a letter from me as might be used ... as evidence ... that there had been no serious disturbance; but I felt that ... there was no time to be lost, and that he might really, be ... unable to keep down the mob through another night. At his direction, therefore, and almost at his dictation, another letter was written, omitting mention of the fire and robbery ...

This letter he took away, but told us ... that the only safe plan would be for him to ... remove us, for the present, to (Zhenjiang) ... In the afternoon he engaged four boats, and procured sedan chairs, and coolies for the undestroyed luggage, and sent us to the South Gate.

Forty-eight hours of continuous danger and tension had ended, but not until they were through Guazhou and crossing the Yangzi could they consider themselves safe. Professedly in response to Taylor's appeal, Prefect Sun and the magistrate issued this proclamation the same day, Sunday, August 23:

A Prohibitory Proclamation

The Prefect and Magistrate of (Yangzhou) have received the following communication from the English missionary Mr Taylor. 'The people have been disseminating false reports—that the missionaries keep children in their house and secretly boil and eat them but the people know nothing of the matter and there is really nothing of the sort done. Last night there was a countless crowd of people (round the house) creating a disturbance and I beg that they may be punished and a proclamation be issued to quiet the populace.'

The Prefect and Magistrate therefore declare that the disorderly proceedings of the populace in the missionaries' house were exceedingly rude and ill-mannered and they accordingly issue this prohibitory proclamation for the information of the people forbidding them hereafter to create any disturbance at Mr Taylor's house. If anything of the sort occurs the offenders will be severely punished. Disobey not! The proclamation to be posted in every street.

Every Chinese reading this proclamation would see in its flippancy a snub to the foreigner. It neither denied the rumours, only quoting his comment on them, nor criticised the riots as more than 'rude' disturbances. While calling a halt, it implied a licence to renew the attacks if he should return. Such an attitude to so serious a breach of the peace could not but rebound upon the mandarins.

But written on the same day was another incriminating document which fell into the hands of W. H. Medhurst, consul-general. A letter, purporting to be from one of the literati in Yangzhou to a friend in Shanghai, named several ex-mandarins closely connected with the viceroy, Zeng Guofan, as being implicated in the plot.

From Chiang Huang at (Yangzhou) to a friend at Shanghai.

On 22nd August we had a great commotion ... The cause of this was that when these missionaries first came a rumour got about that the (Roman Catholics) required men's brains for food. The people of the place were filled with fear and suspicion and when on 21st, a foreigner was seen to go out of the South Gate alone with a basket ... ten or more children's corpses were dug up and were found to have been deprived: some of the heart; some of the eyes and some of the brains. This greatly increased the excitement ...

Yen, formerly Viceroy of the Two Kuang (Canton), gave it as his opinion that foreigners were very much afraid of the people and that these had only to collect together and beat the foreigners to get rid of them. (Ex-) Governor Li, Wu Taoutae [ie Daotai] and Pien Taoutae also (used) the same language. Now Yen was a fellow-student of the present Viceroy [Zeng Guofan] (literally of the same year), Li was a pupil of the Viceroy's and Wu an intimate friend of his father's and they are all of one mind. My idea is then that foreigners will be able again to come to Yangzhou and set up a church. They will be killed as they come ... Even if foreigners do write to Nanking the Viceroy will take no notice of their letters as Yen and Li will write him their joint views before they do.

This letter had reached Medhurst without its envelope but otherwise looked genuine.

After the 'typhoon'
(August 24–31, 1868)

On Monday morning, August 24, after a night on the boat under guard by the unfriendly magistrate's men, they set off with an escort of troops down the Grand Canal. Maria's thoughts were far away, on that sad journey across the Hangzhou lake with Grace's body. This time a larger party of them were themselves escaping 'from the jaws of death' she wrote, but still uncertain what they might yet meet.

'We have not had time yet to change our blood-stained clothes,' Emily added to her unfinished letter of the 18th. 'Very earnestly do I desire and plead that (God) will yet take us back to that city for His glory's sake.'[54]

They had not travelled very far before they met the British, American and French vice-consuls, Allen, Sands and Canny. Hudson Taylor's note had reached Allen and they were on their way to investigate. 'After showing us the utmost kindness,' Hudson Taylor said, 'they continued their journey to Yang-chow.' There 'Mr Assistant Allen', after calling on the prefect, went to 'the scene of the disturbance' and 'saw for himself the debris left by the rioters' returning to Zhenjiang the same day. Still on the boat Hudson Taylor was writing to William Berger, 'Thanks be to God, no life has been lost . . . if the loss of our property does not give rise to feelings of joy, it at least appears a very small matter indeed . . . All of us are more or less bruised. Mr Reid has nearly lost his eye and several teeth.' And Maria, to Mary Berger, 'We have had, so to speak, another "typhoon"—not of so long a duration as the literal one we experienced nearly two years ago—but at least equally dangerous to our lives, and in some aspects more terrible while it lasted.' A few days later she had to add, 'We have been surrounded by a very hurricane of trials of various kinds: sorrows, anxieties, perplexities, evil tidings, sufferings and slanders', for by then much more had happened.

Hudson Taylor's tribute to the Zhenjiang foreign community, published in the *Occasional Paper* ran, 'On our arrival in (Zhenjiang), we were received by the foreign residents with the utmost sympathy, and all seemed to vie with each other in their kindness and hospitality. Though most of us were perfect strangers to them, they opened their houses to us and did everything in their power to assist us.' Duncan was taken in at the Customs House, and the Rudlands and Reid by

Captain Sands who gave up all his own accommodation at the US consulate to them. All the Taylor family, including Emily, Louise Desgraz and Annie Bohannan were welcomed at J. M. Cranny's French consulate.[55]

Their reception by the antagonistic magistrate and people of Zhenjiang on the contrary was alarming. In Emily's words:

> Knowing as we did that our (Yangzhou) difficulties were closely connected with, and probably the fruit of those in (Zhenjiang), we were glad to learn, on our arrival here, Monday, August 24, that, in compliance with Mr Allen's demand, a proclamation had just been put out by the (magistrate) about our affairs, which we were led to suppose would be in our favour. But when a copy of it was procured it was found to be a tissue of falsehood and injustice, calculated only to prejudice the people against us and virtually to exclude us from the city.

The prospect of moving into the premises they had rented on June 24 receded again, and they began another, now urgent, search for vacant accommodation, necessarily in the suburb among the other foreigners. By the time it was found, the need had greatly increased. When only hopeful news of Zhenjiang and Yangzhou had reached Hangzhou, Charles Judd and Josiah Jackson had set out with Hudson Taylor's surgical equipment and medicines. Judd recalled years later:

> When we reached (Suzhou), we heard that ... the (Yangzhou) house was burned down and some of them burned to death ... but we at once hastened on ... and found them all at (Zhenjiang) ... Mr and Mrs Taylor occupied one room with a lot of the debris. All the remains of the riot huddled together ... on the ground floor. Others occupied rooms upstairs, not so exposed to damp ... Whenever others were in the same house, if anyone had to occupy a bad room it was always (the Taylors). Whatever difficulty or inconvenience he might ever ask anyone to go into, no one could ever say that Mr T. was unwilling to do the same himself. When I saw them there, Mrs Hudson Taylor was sitting down in the middle of the room amidst all this confusion as

composedly as possible, going on with the composition of a Ningpo Dictionary. She had a wonderful power of concentration. Mr Hudson Taylor lay sick on a bed in the same room ... She struck me as remarkable for her Christian faith and courage. She had a delicate, sweet face, a fragile body but a sweet expressive face of indomitable perseverance and courage.

Ever since leaving Yangzhou, Hudson Taylor had been suffering from his frequent bouts of enteritis, 'a kind of cholera' in intensity. Hearing of it, the consul sent him some chlorodyne which gave him great relief, his own medicines from Hangzhou being still crated. But the greater tribulations were beginning.

And then the press (August 1868)

On receiving Hudson Taylor's hurried note on Sunday, only twenty-four hours before they all arrived from Yangzhou, Clement Allen had immediately sent word to his consul-general, W. H. Medhurst Jr, in Shanghai. But an unnamed correspondent in Zhenjiang gleaned what he could and sent his own account to the secular *Shanghai Recorder*. In it he said, 'They were driven to such extremities that they were forced to throw the children from the upper windows and the ladies were obliged to follow at the risk of their lives. One of them is within a month of her confinement. The outrage was caused by the literary class.'[56]

On the 27th Medhurst sent a dispatch to Sir Rutherford Alcock in Peking.

I regret to have to report the commission of a most serious outrage upon the persons and property of certain British Missionaries resident at Yang-chow-foo*... Reports ... confirmed by a hurried note from Mr Assistant Allen, state that a mob headed by the literati attacked and set on fire the premises in which the missionary families resided; that the onslaught was sudden and severe; that the children and ladies had to be thrown out of the windows to save their lives; one gentleman had his eye knocked out; and that the whole of the party have been more or less injured ... I propose to proceed to (Zhenjiang) at once, and I have requested the Viceroy at

Nanking to depute an official of sufficient standing to meet me there for the purpose of proceeding with myself to (Yangzhou), and holding a formal investigation.[57]

Distortion of the facts had started. The *North China Herald* followed on August 28 with an editorial in characteristic vein, combining truth and hearsay with advice to the minister and consuls. Under the title 'Attack on Missionaries at Yangchow' it described it as:

a very serious attack ... which claims prompt and decided action by the Consular authorities. The literary class are said by the Chinese to have been at the bottom of the whole affair. Six of their Head-men called a sort of guild meeting at the Confucian temple about a fortnight ago, and it was there decided that the foreigners should be expelled from the city. These Head-men are well known and their apprehension may be effected without difficulty ... Some of the ladies and children were badly wounded and the Revd Mr Reid lost one of his eyes. Our correspondent tells us that the ladies, who were on the upper floor with the children, were obliged to throw these out of the window, and then jump after them themselves. One lady was within a month of her confinement, and serious fears are entertained for her life ... We need to point out that, unless prompt and decisive punishment is inflicted for this outrage, there will be no safety for the life of any missionary in this country. The Chinese are gradually coming to believe that Consular action in the provinces is weak and inoperative.

Then followed a long paragraph putting pressure on the British authorities and making comparison with the French who would allow 'little peace for the (Chinese) authorities local or central till it had been thoroughly avenged. The ringleaders should first be made an example of; but, if enquiry bear out our information, the Prefect and subordinate Magistrates should also be degraded.'

Consul Medhurst needed no goading by the Shanghai press. He already knew from Consul Swinhoe of the Taiwan riots and of an ultimatum by the naval commander,

Lord Charles Scott, to the *daotai* at Tainan. He was in close touch with his assistant, Allen, over a contretemps between British merchants and the mandarins at the customs barrier below Zhenjiang, and over the Zhenjiang magistrate's defiance of his own *daotai* and the vice-consul. The Chinese reaction to the replacement of Consul Lay by a Third Assistant had not escaped him. In fact, J. M. Canny, the French consul, told Hudson Taylor

> that the matter would be sure to be taken up by the British Government, as secret orders had been received only a few days before by the Consul at Shanghai, to take the first reasonable opportunity of making an armed demonstration up the Yang-tse-kiang [ie Yangzi River], to overawe the Chinese authorities, and to put a stop to the frequent violations of the Treaty, which threatened the arising of some *casus belli*.[58]

Medhurst himself arrived at Zhenjiang on August 30 and lost no time in verifying from Hudson Taylor and all his party their statements in the affidavit Allen had asked them to prepare; and 'as to our losses as far as ascertained, and taking up this grievance together with the larger losses of some of the (Zhenjiang) merchants from various violations of treaties'. On the 31st he sent another dispatch to Sir Rutherford.

> I arrived here accordingly last night and this morning I interrogated the missionaries most carefully ... The following significant inferences may, I think, be drawn from the accounts so given:
>
> 1. That the attack was entirely unprovoked;
>
> 2. That it was instigated by the literati and gentry generally;
>
> 3. That the outrage was distinctly premeditated and occupied time in being put into execution;
>
> 4. That the local authorities took no pains whatever to prevent or put down the excitement, notwithstanding that they were warned of the possible dmeute [popular rising] and repeatedly and courteously appealed to for protection;

> 5. That when the rage of the mob had been permitted to take its course, and after protection had been tardily accorded, they actually threatened the victims to leave them to their fate unless they recorded it as their opinion that the attack partook of the nature of a simple disturbance, punishable as far as the actors in it were concerned with cangue [the portable neck pillory] and
>
> 6. That since the affair took place the authorities have done nothing towards expressing their disapprobation of the conduct of the ringleaders.

He was proceeding to Yangzhou, he continued, 'to procure the condign punishment of all persons known to have been concerned, to require reasonable compensation to the sufferers' and to demand proclamations strong enough to ensure their future safety. Should he fail to obtain satisfaction from the prefect of Yangzhou, he would 'carry the whole case to His Excellency Tseng Kwo-fan [ie Zeng Guofan] himself'.

> I have communicated (this plan) together with a copy of the affidavit to Her Majesty's senior naval officer who I have no doubt will see the necessity of supporting my action by his presence and co-operation. I trust I shall have your Excellency's approval of my conduct thus far ... The document which ... purports to be a letter written by a man of Yangchow to a friend in Shanghai and apparently was never intended for the eye of a foreigner ... curiously corroborates the statement made by Mr Taylor that the literati were instigators of the attack and influenced the local authorities against the foreigners.[59]

Hudson Taylor's long affidavit, signed by himself, Duncan, Rudland and Reid, and already quoted at length, ended with this paragraph:

> During the whole time that the Mission had been stationed at Yangchow, namely since the 1st June 1868, every member of it has to the best of his and her ability, avoided giving the slightest possible cause of offence to any of the people and has borne with studied patience and endurance any casual insults which may have been offered

from time to time. Even our missionary efforts have not commenced in any public shape but had been entirely confined to personal conversation with visitors to the house. We had no arms or weapons of any kind in our possession from first to last.

A victim of the Chinese protest against foreign intrusion into their country, Hudson Taylor was about to become a convenient pawn in British power politics. On August 31, the refugees moved to two adjoining houses rented at great cost and 'only a stone's throw from the British Consulate' a fact full of unsuspected meaning. Reid, as his face and eye were recovering took Judd off to Nanjing. For Hudson Taylor there was no respite from administrative duties, and in a business letter of August 31 to Jennie Faulding, remitting money for Hangzhou, he remarked, 'A war steamer is expected tomorrow, but I hope that all may be peacefully arranged.' She had personally assumed the financial and administrative responsibility for the school she was running, not knowing that an uncle had bequeathed to her a legacy she would be able to use.

So ended August 1868. Only twenty-four hours later the shouts of rioting mobs reached them again, this time in the Zhenjiang foreign settlement.

The Zhenjiang riot
(September 1–3, 1868)

If the flouting of Vice-Consul Allen and Hudson Taylor at Zhenjiang had been the spark to ignite anti-foreign action in Yangzhou, such resounding success there was all the resentful Zhenjiang magistrate needed to go one better. Starting with his proclamation—'a tissue of falsehood and injustice, calculated only to prejudice the people'—he had gone so far as to say provocatively, 'you are at liberty to follow your own inclinations'. This oblique but obvious hint was quickly taken up by his supporters. Through them he dared to challenge the authority of the *daotai* and to arouse the Manchu garrison against consuls, merchants and missionaries

alike. In Yangzhou the literati were celebrating, as the *North China Herald* reported. 'The mob at Yangchow have been complimented on their recent triumph; congratulatory messages and placards have been freely circulated through the city, and rewards have been promised to the popular leaders . . . If (foreigners) present themselves at the gates they are not to be allowed to enter, and should they by any chance get inside the city walls they are to be instantly set upon and killed . . . (At Zhenjiang) the people have threatened to attack the foreign settlement.'[60] Already this report was more than a week out of date.

On September 1, Consul-General W. H. Medhurst called on Daotai Ying, the Intendant of Circuit over three prefectures of which Yangzhou was one. All along, this friendly mandarin had done his best to get possession of the house in Zhenjiang city for Hudson Taylor. Now he directed the district magistrate 'to rejudge the case and give a verdict in accordance with the facts', that the owner and his family had already approved the contract before the magistrate intervened. He could not but comply. 'But the people having accepted as facts the falsehoods of the (magistrate's) proclamation, determined to resist this new step of the (*daotai*).'

Convinced that 'the power of foreigners had already waned', members of the Manchu garrison and community, including a military mandarin, joined the riotous Chinese in attacking the premises now legally the CIM's. 'Seizing the landlord of the house, they . . . beat him for letting his house to a foreigner. Then they tied his hands behind his back, and passing the rope from his wrists over a beam in the roof hoisted him up and again beat him while suspended, and at last carried him off' to the magistrate's *yamen* where he was imprisoned.

The next morning (Sept 2nd) [Emily Blatchley wrote,] the (*daotai*) returned Mr Medhurst's call, and wished to see Mr Taylor, whom he apologetically declared himself ashamed to meet, seeing that our matters ought to have been settled more than a month ago. He said that not only had foreigners, as such, a right to rent houses in the city, but that, wearing as we did the Chinese costume, we were as one of themselves, and there was the less excuse for opposition ... [Having interviewed Hudson Taylor and inspected the house and rental agreement, he declared that Hudson Taylor was the rightful lessee and ordered the magistrate to see that he was given possession of it.][61]

He finally promised that Mr Taylor should have the house within three days. But at nine o'clock the same night a riotous mob, seven or eight-tenths of whom were Tartars (over whom the *daotai* has no jurisdiction), attacked the *daotai's yamen*, burst open the front doors, and did much damage, keeping up the disturbance till four a.m. His furniture was smashed and he himself accused of traitorous collusion with foreigners.

The whole city by then was in a state of excitement and [Medhurst reported to Sir Rutherford Alcock] rumours are that this Consulate is to be the next point of attack this evening. The *daotai* has sent a message begging me not to ... be put out, and promising that he will endeavour to fulfil his promises ... The anticipated arrival of Her Majesty's Ship *Rinaldo* this evening or tomorrow morning will tend materially to promote this desirable result.

[Emily's account continued] The rioters threatened to come the next night to the foreign settlement and burn down the British Consulate, and so avenge the dishonour done to them in 1840. The Tartar-General, however, was alarmed at the probable consequences of such an event, and stationed double guards at the city gates to prevent his men leaving the city for any such purpose.

When Sir Henry Pottinger had arrived at Zhenjiang with his expeditionary force on July 21, 1840, the Manchu Tartar-General had put up a courageous resistance until, seeing that he was defeated, he immolated himself. Many other Manchus followed suit, until Charles Gutzlaff landed and strenuously intervened to halt the mass suicide (see 1, pp 112–13). This was the injury that the city was determined to

avenge in 1868. September 3 was therefore another day of tension in the foreign community.

Medhurst—man of action[62]
(September 1868)

Consul Medhurst had lost no time in taking up the matter of the Yangzhou riot with Prefect Sun and with Viceroy Zeng Guofan at Nanjing, as his dispatches published in the Parliamentary Blue Books testify. But his hyperbole in Chinese idiom and the literal translation of it into English was to lead to a misapprehension of fact that brought Hudson Taylor under undeserved criticism.

> Consul Medhurst to Sun, Prefect of Yang-chow foo
>
> The British missionaries Taylor and others ... have laid before me a formal complaint in regard to their violent ejectment from your city, and they have earnestly entreated me, as Consul for this district, to redress the many and grievous wrongs which they have sustained, and to secure for them peaceable possession of their late home.

In fact, neither Hudson Taylor nor any colleague at any time asked for such intervention, as was to be made certain after the damage had been done.

Under fifteen headings, Medhurst set out his formal protest.

1. The CIM Premises in Yangzhou had been procured with prefect Sun's knowledge, consent and authorisation and with the approval of HBM Consul at Zhenjiang, duly recorded.

2. From the moment the missionaries entered Yangzhou they had been 'entirely innocent of any offence (and had) borne with exemplary endurance, insults and assaults'.

3. The malicious rumours spread to set mobs against them were not supported by the slightest evidence.

4. The principal authors of the placards and slander were the gentry 'Yen Fuan-shu [sic], Pien Pao-shu, Li Pao-fu and Wen-hsi'.

5. The magistrates evaded Hudson Taylor's courteous requests for intervention, and

6. detained him for two hours during which the house and possessions could have been saved.

7. By fire, plunder and violence, considerable injury had been sustained.

8. The guard had been withdrawn allowing the mob to return to their devastation, and

9. Mr Taylor had been threatened with being left to the mercy of the mob if he did not represent the riot as a simple brawl.[63]

10. Instead of protecting the victims in the *yamen* the authorities had expelled them and issued a false proclamation. So much for the facts.

Consul Medhurst proceeded to demand justice. He was laying these matters before the viceroy and the British Minister Plenipotentiary 'for adjudication and punishment, according to the laws pertaining to such official derelictions of duty'.

11. It was for the rioters to be punished by the Yangzhou authorities, but 'Should any of the culprits be members of the belted gentry, whom it is beyond the power of the Chih-fu [ie yourself the Prefect] to issue a warrant against, I must require him to report their names to His Excellency the Viceroy for degradation and punishment.' Compensation to the tune of two thousand taels must be paid to him, the consul, for distribution to the victims of the riot, Chinese and foreign.

13. Their house must be restored to its original condition.

14. A proclamation must state that all culprits were to be punished; and that British subjects were at liberty to rent premises and reside at Yangzhou; this proclamation was to be engraved on a stone tablet and erected at the place from which the victims were ejected; and

15. they were to be invited by letter or deputy to return there, while any and everyone imprisoned for alleged connection with the missionaries were to be released. These facts and demands, he concluded, he was placing before the prefect 'to avoid any further and disagreeable complications'.[64]

The reply received on September 6 in the name of prefect Sun came from a deputy, none other than the magistrate who had threatened Hudson Taylor with being abandoned to the mob. The prefect himself had gone to confer with Viceroy Zeng Guofan in Nanjing. It said:

On the 22nd August some female children were secretly buried in the Orphanage established by the French missionary, Sechinger (Chiuchien-san), and many corpses were dug up also ... The people went to Mr Taylor's house, and raised a disturbance, which I, with the magistrates and military authorities, effectually put down. No injuries were caused to, nor property stolen from, the missionaries, as may be seen from Mr Taylor's own letter.

The magistrate then quoted a dispatch from Viceroy Zeng, continued with his own equally inept comments, and concluded, 'The affair is settled; there is therefore no necessity for your troubling the Senior Naval Officer to accompany you with an escort as you propose.'[65] Meanwhile Medhurst had written to the viceroy on September 3, and Zeng Guofan's reply to Medhurst's protests also tried to evade the issue.

In Shanghai the editor of the *North China Herald* affected a languid Victorian attitude to events although well aware of their seriousness.

We hardly remember a week in which so little of social interest has been stirring. There is nothing before the Courts, and the Consulate is only saved from oblivion by the opportunity of bestirring itself about the attack on missionaries at (Yangzhou). HMS *Rinaldo* has left for (Zhenjiang), where, we presume, she will form a sort of moral support to Mr Medhurst (and) take him on to Nanking ... The (prefect of Yangzhou) has seized the men who let the house to Mr Taylor and tortured them in order to make them confess that the missionaries did really destroy the children.[66]

Meanwhile in Zhenjiang the Tartar-General had succeeded in keeping his troops under control and the people took their cue from him rather than from the inflammatory magistrate.

On the night of the 4th inst. HMS *Rinaldo* arrived, and on the 5th Mr Medhurst made a demonstration in the city. With a guard of (thirty) marines and blue-jackets he paid a visit to the Tartar-General and demanded the punishment of the military mandarin who had beaten our landlord, and also that a proclamation should be issued forbidding the Tartars from interfering with British subjects who may purchase or rent houses in the city ... This proceeding somewhat quieted the agitation here.

Still the magistrate failed to hand over the rented premises, and scored another victory over the *daotai* by appealing to the viceroy, in whom he had a powerful ally.

1868: GUNBOAT DIPLOMACY

Medhurst makes his point[67]
(September 1868)

From the arrival of HMS *Rinaldo* at Zhenjiang, consular representations to the mandarins took a new tone. Even the disgraced Shanghai magistrate at Zhenjiang played his hand more carefully. But Zeng Guofan shared the view that the power of consuls had waned. In a studied snub he sent as his deputy to investigate the Yangzhou riot a mandarin 'of very, inadequate rank', no higher than *zhixian*, a district magistrate with an opaque white cap-button, inferior to the city prefect (*zhifu*), let alone to the literati responsible for instigating the uprising. Zeng Guofan instructed him to tell the Yangzhou populace that all the trouble had been due to the French Catholics and that no fault was attached to the British missionaries. But this worthy failed to arrive at the agreed rendezvous, and Consul Medhurst proceeded to Yangzhou without him.

Events of such consequence as the crop of outrages—by foreigners as well as Chinese—taking place in 1867–70, had no lack of reporters. The closest eye-witness accounts of the Yangzhou, Zhenjiang and Nanjing affairs are those of Medhurst, Hudson Taylor and those who were with them. A composite account from these sources is therefore the fullest and most dependable. Emily Blatchley, as Hudson Taylor's secretary, was in the right position to put it into words.

Consul Medhurst had been set on going up to Yangzhou with or without an armed escort, to bring Prefect Sun to Nanjing to explain in person to the viceroy why he had not responded when Hudson Taylor first reported threats of violence. *Rinaldo* strengthened Medhurst's hand.

(Mr Medhurst) went on Tuesday the 8th, in a small steamer, with an escort of seventy marines (and blue-jackets) under the command of Captain Bush of the *Rinaldo*, and accompanied by Mr Allen and the French Consul, J. M. Canny, Esquire. A French frigate which had happened to. come down from (Hankou) a few days before ... stayed off (Guazhou) to guard the mouth of the Grand Canal until the return of the expedition. Mr Taylor was unable to go, being laid up at the time with a severe inflammatory attack; but Mr Duncan (accompanied by Mr Jackson), went up with them in our own hired boat.

The guard, Commander Bush (not 'Captain') explained to the Admiralty, was 'composed of nearly the whole of the ship's company, to prevent the possibility of (the consul-general) being insulted by the mob'.

The prefect had been forewarned and was waiting with his retinue at a minor gate of the city when the consul and naval party arrived. His intention to conduct them inconspicuously by back streets to his *yamen* had not reckoned on Medhurst's knowledge of China from childhood, or the presence of Allen and Canny, already familiar with the city. They proceeded to a main gate and marched through busy thoroughfares as conspicuously as possible. Everything seemed perfectly quiet, and without the least sign of hostility apparent they went direct to the prefect's *yamen*, took possession of it, stationed guards at the doors, and demanded an interview with the prefect.

The *North China Herald* reported that '(Consul Medhurst) was received with the utmost respect.' When Prefect Sun arrived back at his *yamen* to find marine guards at his doors and the consul in determined mood, he surprised his visitors by showing 'abject terror', Medhurst told Sir

2.10 The prefect's procession

Rutherford Alcock; and a correspondent of the *North China Herald* wrote:

> It was curious to see the (prefect) during the interview ... He was ghastly with fear, and trembled so that he could hardly hold Mr Medhurst's dispatch in his hand. [And Emily, reporting Duncan's observations:] He was in a terrible state of trepidation, and endeavoured to make out that the whole affair of the night of the 22nd was nothing more than a little excitement and unruliness on the part of the people. But the Consul, after hearing what he had to say, proceeded to take up point by point in such an unanswerable way, that the Prefect was completely silenced. Mr Medhurst then set before him an ultimatum ... [embodying the demands which the xian magistrate as his 'scornful and discourteous deputy' had rejected.]

Some of these the Prefect acceded to; with regard to the others he said he had not the power to act without consulting the Viceroy [and some of the gentry named by Medhurst could not be arrested as they were of higher rank than himself]. It became a question, then, whether to wait where they were until an answer could be received from the Viceroy, or to take the Prefect himself up to Nankin. The latter course was decided upon, the Prefect stipulating that he should be allowed to go in his own boat, and not as a prisoner.

Before leaving, Mr Medhurst and his retinue, accompanied by the Prefect, the two (city magistrates) and the ... commander of the garrison, went to make a personal examination of our desolated premises. Though cleared of debris, swept, and repaired as the place was by the cunning mandarins, still the mended portions of the walls, the absence of partitions, the wall-plaster pricked into an almost regular unevenness by the missiles of bricks and stones which had been hurled, a pile of broken furniture yet remaining, some pieces of partially burned timber, and other traces of fire, these told their own story quite unmistakably.

Allen and Canny had seen it all before repairs had been made, and Medhurst could see for himself the wrenched hinges, the 'piles of broken furniture' and foreign, travellers' trunks. To Medhurst's disgust, the reaction of the mandarins to the detection of their deceit was not to show shame but to sulk. But what impressed him more deeply was the fact that the direct distance between the *yamen* and the house was only half a mile. The sound of rioting by thousands of people must have been heard long before Hudson Taylor arrived to claim protection. With any will to keep the peace, help could have reached them within minutes instead of hours.

In marching from the *yamen* to the mission and afterwards in returning to the boats, Medhurst's party was 'surrounded and followed . . . by a vast concourse of Chinese . . . even when the attendants of the Prefect thrashed the front ranks of the gazers with canes . . . to make them give way'. Yet 'not a single, word of disrespect was heard . . . the inhabitants have always been rather friendly . . . and the strong feeling of antagonism . . . now said to exist can only have been conjured up by the officials and literati'.

Consuls and naval escort passed the night outside the city and in the morning were joined by Prefect Sun in a large mandarin boat for the journey down the Grand Canal to the Yangzi. 'The expedition then returned to (Zhenjiang), the Prefect (in his own boat) being escorted by two of the *Rinaldo*'s cutters. He asked to be allowed to stay the night at (Guazhou) . . . and gave his written promise to be there in the morning, and ready for proceeding to Nankin. Notwithstanding, he made off in the night, leaving his boat there.'

The viceroy's deputy, Zhang Zhixian, was waiting at Zhenjiang for Consul Medhurst, who took him to see Hudson Taylor and his Yangzhou party. Zhang questioned them minutely and examined what evidence of injury was still to be seen after sixteen days. Sir Rutherford in turn told Prince Kong on February 4, 1869, of 'medical evidence of unimpeachable character having satisfied me that the injuries received by Mr Rudland, Mrs Taylor and Miss Blatchley are all of so serious a character as to entail some permanent disability.'[68] Zeng Guofan was later to inform Medhurst that his deputy Zhang had reported no evidence of injuries or bruises. So no charges had been substantiated. As for the pregnant women, neither had given birth, so the allegation that they had jumped could only be based on hearsay.

The inspection completed, Medhurst persuaded the deputy to travel back to Nanjing with him in *Rinaldo* in the morning. Zhang did set out from shore but, pleading alarm at the roughness of the water, returned to safety. With Medhurst on board, *Rinaldo* crossed the Yangzi to Guazhou to pick up Prefect Sun, only to find that 'he too proved false'. Medhurst then steamed on towards Nanjing. The *Times* correspondent who was with him recorded the next episode. Halfway there they overtook a river-boat on which a wildly gesticulating Prefect Sun indicated that he wished to be taken in tow. Blind and deaf to his pleas, they left him behind.[69] The instigators of the Yangzhou riot being none other than Zeng's personal friends, Sun had thought he held the trump card in this game of old state diplomacy. He had calculated on reaching Zeng Guofan before Medhurst, to agree on how to thwart them.

Humiliation at Nanjing[70]
(September 1868)

On Friday morning, September 11, Medhurst proceeded to the viceroy's *yamen* with due ceremony. 'He received me with more than customary state, and seemed inclined to be friendly; but I found it exceedingly difficult to rouse his peculiarly impassive and sluggish nature to . . . the serious importance of my object.' The reason was not far to seek. He had received a minimum of information from the Yangzhou officials and was stalling the consultation until he heard more. 'There seemed to be fair promise of his acting equitably [Medhurst thought], but nothing was immediately decided.'

When Prefect Sun's arrival was announced, Medhurst insisted on being present at an interview with him, but Zeng Guofan would not allow it and Medhurst at length withdrew. In the evening the friendly Daotai Ying of Zhenjiang, also in Nanjing over his own troubles, visited *Rinaldo* with a message from the viceroy and stayed two hours. Zeng was offering a thousand taels in compensation for the Yangzhou losses and injuries. Medhurst rejected the offer as unrealistic and renewed the demands he had submitted to Prefect Sun.

At this juncture Commander Bush, who had been unwell for several days, became dangerously ill with dysentery. Fearing for his life he asked Medhurst to transfer his party to houseboats, and was hurried in his own ship to Shanghai. 'The Consul was, therefore, left with only a small boat [perhaps a launch in which he had come up from Shanghai]. In the eyes of the Chinese who attach such importance to ceremonial trappings and outward insignia, he immediately became 'a person of no moment . . . quite unprotected and helpless'. The effect was electric. The viceroy changed his tone and refused to consider Medhurst's demands. He had just received news of his translation to the viceroyalty of Zhili, he said, the highest in the empire, with its concomitant title of Guardian of the Throne. So he was busy. The implication was clear, Medhurst remarked to Alcock in submitting 'the whole case to your Excellency's superior judgment and authority'.

'I can call to mind, out of my experience of British relations with China, scarcely one instance in which the outrage complained of has been more unprovoked on the part of the sufferers, and in which the evidence of neglect and culpability on the part of the local authorities has been more marked and incontrovertible.' To Zeng Guofan he replied that matters were far from resolved.

Making light of the situation, on the 14th Zeng Guofan rebuked Medhurst's 'breach of faith' in scorning his (inadequate) deputy, Zhang, and instead of himself issuing an edict, said he would order Prefect Sun to issue a proclamation, to invite Hudson Taylor to return, and to release all Chinese 'innocently' under arrest. The ambivalence of his wording was

2.11 A high mandarin's informal sedan chair

characteristic of the proceedings.

Although at such a disadvantage Medhurst was not to be browbeaten. Lacking the physical force, which the mandarin appeared to understand better than reason, he gave defiant words their full weight. On September 18 he acknowledged the viceroy's 'decision', strongly questioned his statements, demanded to inspect any proclamation on the matter before it was issued, rejected the offer of a thousand taels as a charitable gift, and informed Zeng that all relevant papers, including his derisory communication of the 14th, were being forwarded to the British minister in Peking and would no doubt reach the Zongli Yamen. As not only Viceroy of the Two Jiangs but Imperial Commissioner for Foreign Affairs in the Yangzi region,

from Sichuan to Shanghai, Zeng knew that this was fast becoming not a local fracas but an international incident. Yet he put his friends, the gentry of Yangzhou, before diplomacy. Medhurst challenged his defence of them. Zeng's statement that they 'could not possibly from their position and experience have been guilty of inciting the people against the missionaries' was not founded on fact, as investigation would show.

Sir Rutherford Alcock, on receiving Medhurst's first notification, dated August 27, and his report of August 31 with Hudson Taylor's affidavit, informed Lord Stanley at the Foreign Office, adding, 'The Roman Catholic missions in the interior are not exempt from the same sudden outbreaks of popular hostility; and I believe one of the chief occupations of the French Legation here consists in pressing claims for redress, and making reclamations on their behalf.' In ponderously due time (dispatches taking weeks to reach London), Lord Stanley replied on November 20. Of Medhurst's reports he wrote, 'He appears to have acted with great prudence and firmness in the matter; and you will convey to him my approval of his proceedings.'

Consul Medhurst reported to Alcock again after passing through Zhenjiang on his way back to Shanghai. Some face-saving compromise could not be avoided. Ying would lose his office of *daotai* if he said too many home-truths about the Zhenjiang Magistrate. Hudson Taylor was willing to accept a different house in the city as long as it suited his purposes. By this compromise the Chinese authorities would be spared the appearance of defeat over the first house and its suffering owners would escape further involvement. The viceroy's treatment of the delinquent magistrate had been severe, Medhurst wrote, but even the exemplary *daotai* had suffered his displeasure. Towards the guilty Yangzhou gentry who 'were in a position to bring (their weight and wealth) to bear in order to screen themselves from blame', Zeng was being lenient.

It is my belief [Medhurst said] that until the entire Chinese population, official, literary and otherwise, is distinctly informed by Imperial proclamation that British subjects are to be acknowledged and treated in a friendly spirit, and that the compact with the British nation was an Imperial act, it is hopeless to expect that our merchants and missionaries will be regarded as otherwise than objects of contempt and suspicion by the people at large.

The strident press of Hong Kong and Shanghai as ever saw things in a less sober light. In an ill-informed editorial under the title 'Peace or War?' the *China Mail* of September 19 asked:

What is to be the upshot of present events in China? ... Of what use is such consular action as that recorded in the Shanghai papers last to hand? After an insult and outrage, far exceeding any in the recent history of our relations with China, Her Majesty's Consul obtains from the Prefect a declaration that the would-be murderers and assassins are naughty boys, and returns having 'successfully, accomplished the object of his mission'. Away with such puerile nonsense. If indeed another war supervenes, it will have been the work of 'Her majesty's peace mongers'.

As early as September 5 the *North China Herald* was demanding action against the mandarins of Yangzhou. Overlooking the immunity of the literati to corporal punishment, the editorial claimed, 'to spare them . . . might lead to loss of life elsewhere, and eventually perhaps bring about a war . . . The mildest penalty for those men should be a public bambooing and a cangue round their necks at the city gates for three weeks'. On the 11th the *Herald* became unashamedly jingoistic and, surprisingly, took Hudson Taylor's side. 'A file of marines and a gunboat . . . would teach (them) that their literati cannot instigate murderous attacks on foreigners and then laugh in their sleeves at us.'

A week later the editor was strongly urging, in multiple columns about the Yangzhou and Zhenjiang riots, that *Rinaldo* or another warship should return lest

fresh riots occur. 'We now stand as beaten hounds in the eyes of (the viceroy's) subordinates . . . Our minister is surely not going to pocket the snub we have received.' Zeng, China's senior viceroy, should be taken to Peking and charged with dereliction of duty!

On the 25th, when Consul Medhurst was back at Shanghai, Yangzhou was again the major topic for a two-column editorial. Sir Rutherford was surely over-influenced by 'the supine policy dictated from the Foreign Office'—a policy, be it noted, soon to be rejected by the next British government as belligerent. An article of the treaty had been broken! We should insist on satisfaction! Zeng Guofan's volte-face on the departure of *Rinaldo* from Nanjing was 'clear proof of the necessity for coercion . . . So long as force is shown, compliance is ensured.'

Both the *Times* correspondent and the *Herald* reported that when the Zhenjiang *daotai*, on the orders of the viceroy, issued a proclamation (declaring the right of foreigners to reside in the interior of China and that officials must aid them in obtaining houses), a counter-proclamation signed 'the People of Zhenjiang' was promptly issued. It declared that if any foreigners dared to rent premises the house would be burned down and the foreigners and the landlord thrown into the flames. Not only so, any official helping the foreigner would suffer the same fate in the flames of his *yamen*.

Hudson Taylor, who usually drew down censure upon his head, in these circumstances still won the sympathy of the press. The sworn evidence of his party had impressed even their critics. The *Herald* heaped heavy blame for the serious deterioration of diplomatic relations on Commander Bush. Even if 'dangerously ill', why had he not left his ship under his second in command at Nanjing, himself travelling to Shanghai by commercial steamer? But almost in the same breath, *mirabile dictu*, the CIM was applauded for adopting Chinese clothes as 'an imitation of those great Romish pioneers of Christianity, Ricci, Verbiest, Semedo and Valignano'.

When the Admiralty and Foreign Office enquired into the manner of Commander Bush's departure from Nanjing—without question the turning-point in negotiations from imminent success to intolerable humiliation—he was fully vindicated. His condition had been too severe to admit of his being transferred to another ship. But it was the personal deposition of this honoured old officer that not only convinced his superiors but effectively influenced the policy of Lord Clarendon after he succeeded Lord Stanley at the Foreign Office. For Commander Bush had been astounded to learn of the effect of his departure.

> It never entered my head that the presence simply of a small man-of-war could have the slightest effect in influencing the action of the Viceroy of Nanking, one of the most important functionaries in the Chinese empire ... Under no circumstances whatever would I have allowed the ship under my command to be used as a threat to compel a compliance to the Consul's request, however just, without an official communication from the Minister at Peking or from my own Superior Officer.

Disraeli resigned on December 2 and Gladstone formed his government with Lord Clarendon as Foreign Minister, who, coming at once under the influence of Anson Burlingame, in what has been called the 'Clarendon conversion', became convinced of China's good intentions and reversed the instructions being followed by Alcock and his consuls. He instructed them and the Admiralty that Her Majesty's Government desired to deal directly with the central government of China, with Prince Kong and the Zongli Yamen, rather than with viceroys and local authorities as before. Much that had satisfied Lord Stanley now had to be explained, only to be censured. Scapegoats were needed, and in 1888 Hudson Taylor summed up the story of his unprotesting acceptance in 1869 of this role by writing, 'An attempt was made to throw all the blame on the unfortunate

missionaries. This was no small trial to us, but in the meantime we were restored to (Yangzhou), and the Lord comforted us.' There was more to it than that.

'We intend to go forward' (September 1868)

With more than thirty colleagues looking to him for leadership and the distribution of funds, Hudson Taylor could not allow events to disrupt his duties any more than was unavoidable. The preservation of his Mission accounts and records permitted him to take up control after the riots where it had been interrupted. Business friends in Shanghai were sharing the banking, postal and purchasing chores with William Gamble, but more and more he felt the need to have a member of the Mission there to handle the increasing volume of work. With donations in Britain fewer and fewer, William Berger was sending only just as much as usual. At a time of unusual expenses in China, making it go round was difficult. Yet as refugees in the French consulate and then in the two small buildings Hudson Taylor rented in the Zhenjiang suburb, he and Emily kept the office work going.

Meeting the requirements of Medhurst and the mandarins was not least among his difficulties. His colitis, sometimes severe, was sapping his energy. Correspondence with a wide circle of people still ignorant of recent events or prompted by the papers to ask for more news, was more than he could cope with. Well-meaning friends in England were urging William Berger to press for more articles from Hudson Taylor's pen, lest interest in China flag still further. The riot and all that followed supplied that deficiency for months to come. But others influenced by criticisms of the CIM joined in the disaffection.

Maria was constantly in touch with Mrs Berger, her unfailingly faithful confidante. When she wrote on September 7, 'We have been surrounded by a very hurricane of trials', she could add little more. She and the children were having to lie low in cramped conditions, for fear of fomenting unrest. John McCarthy wrote from Hangzhou of problems between the different denominations in the team. The whole five discontented ones—the Nicols, Susan Barnes and the McLean sisters—were 'in committee at Suzhou, without so much as by your leave'. And Lewis Nicol's resentments were leading him into more unfounded allegations. Cardwell was ill and unhappy at Taizhou, zealous in his work but pining to move away. Hudson Taylor agreed to his coming to Nanjing to learn Mandarin.

George Stott was in fresh trouble at Wenzhou since moving his school into more suitable premises.

> The charge ... against me at present [he wrote], is that I am getting up a rebellion; that I invite all the leaders in the plot every night after dark to my house, and instruct them in the art of foreign warfare from foreign books, and harangue them to excite their courage; and that I am in secret correspondence with some foreign magistrates in Ningpo, having the same object in view.

> These handbills have so alarmed the mandarins, that the city gates are now shut immediately after sunset. Then a guard of soldiers is posted at each end of the street leading to my house; and a watchman walks all the distance and reports at both ends, beating all the time he walks a brass gong, which is heard all over the city. For three nights I have been hardly able to sleep for the sound of it.

In his insecurity Stott thought the closing of the city gates, the guard of soldiers and the watchman were part of the threat against him. No letter from Hudson Taylor on the subject has been kept, but he would certainly have pointed out that, on the contrary, they had assuredly been ordered by the mandarin to protect him.

To Hudson Taylor and his team, the deliverance from Yangzhou was clear confirmation of God's hand upon their venture. Three weeks after the Yangzhou riot and ten days after the Zhenjiang mob wrecked even the *daotai's yamen*, Hudson Taylor voiced to William Berger the conclusions he had reached. They were not to be foiled by difficulties.

> We are all now getting over our wounds and bruises ... It is no child's play, and our funds are very low ... But the Lord reigneth. By His grace we intend to go forward and He will not leave us in the lurch.

> 'He'd never have taught us to trust in His name, and thus far have brought us to put us to shame' ...

> We may before the winter possibly be able to attempt some new province. Many of our number are stirred up to press into the interior; and our recent disasters, if such I may call them, only make us the more determined to go on, leaning on the almighty power of our Captain ... I shall have to put away one of the *Lammermuir* party—Nicol—from the Mission. He has done us much harm; and unless restrained by the Lord, if the most unscrupulous lying can do us any harm, he will still cause us much injury.

Three steps were needed. First, to consolidate the work so far begun. He had made provision for it to be carried on in each city so far occupied, and was dealing with its problems. Second, to clear the decks of encumbrances and dangers. For over two years he had dealt patiently with Lewis Nicol and those who sided with him. Suggestions that Nicol should resign if he could not cooperate peacefully had led to nothing. The time had come to grasp the nettle. And lastly, to reconnoitre further afield and place teams where possible. From Wuhan, Griffith John and Alexander Wylie were exploring Sichuan and northward into Shaanxi as far as Hanzhong. Hudson Taylor had his eyes on Henan province, northward up the Grand Canal; on Anhui province further up the Yangzi, on both sides; and on Jiangxi province to the south James Meadows and James Williamson were poised to begin this advance, and Hudson Taylor himself longed to play a part in it.

With fifty or sixty members, the church at Ningbo could manage its own affairs with the help of John McCarthy from Hangzhou, and of George Crombie from Fenghua. In Hangzhou itself, after three years, a congregation of twice that size had Wang Lae-djün as its good pastor, strongly supported by his wife and Jennie

Faulding. Jennie often said when writing home that she would choose to be nowhere else and with no other colleagues than the McCarthys. Last of the *Lammermuir* party—the rest had all scattered—she welcomed the freedom to work with fewer distractions. 'I could not imagine for myself a happier lot.' Running her school, constantly invited to visit Chinese homes all over the city, she felt fulfilled, without a care or fear for the future. One day was much like another. Long might it continue so.

John Stevenson was at last seeing a church of true believers taking shape at Shaoxing. South of Ningbo the little church at Fenghua and its outlying daughter churches were expanding. Three men came from Taiping to Taizhou, a two day walk of forty miles, expressly to hear the gospel. They had with them Luke's Gospel and the Acts, presented to them by a missionary years before, and said there were twenty more men at Taiping who would gladly come as they had. The bush fire was spreading slowly but surely.

Goodbye to Nicol (September 1868)

On September 13, the day Hudson Taylor wrote, 'We intend to go forward', he also wrote to Nicol. He could hope no longer for a change of heart. The letter is a window on both men.[71] William Berger had sent him, he said, a copy of Nicol's 'disgraceful' letter of February 13. Naming missionaries who had testified to the fact that the 'falsehoods and misrepresentations' in the letter had been repeated in conversation with members of his own and other missions 'in the habitual breach and perversion of the truth', the only course left was to 'terminate your connection with the China Inland Mission'. In doing so he was 'acting after conference with and with the concurrence of all the brethren of the *Lammermuir* party and as many of the other brethren of the Mission as I have had opportunity of meeting, since I received the copy of your letter . . . I do not dismiss you because of your denominational views . . . nor yet for your preference for the English costume; nor indeed on any other ground

in whole or in part than that of habitual and deliberate falsehood.' William Berger had sent Nicol a gift of twenty pounds for his current needs, and 'through the kindness of a friend I shall be able to procure a passage to England for you and Mrs Nicol.' Another forty dollars could be made available to him if he needed an outfit for the voyage within the next two or three months.

Believing it to be necessary to have this letter delivered by hand, Hudson Taylor sent it to John McCarthy, apparently asking him to vet it before taking it to Xiaoshan. On September 20 McCarthy replied, 'We hardly knew how much we valued your love, till it was nearly lost to us [in the riot]. May we be bound closer and closer together—for the Lord's sake . . . for the sake of this needy land . . . Thank God, dear brother, and take courage, for if ever you were helped in writing a letter, I believe you were in the one I have just handed to Nicol. What pain it cost you to write that letter I can guess.' To Berger he wrote at length, applauding Hudson Taylor's qualities and defending him against all accusations. His only crime was that of trying to do ten men's work instead of one.

At the time Nicol made no reference to the contents, but William Berger commented, 'Your letter to Nicol . . . was everything that the case required; and how sad was his reply to it.' To the Taylor's grief, by October 5 they had received letters of resignation from Susan Barnes and the McLean sisters. They had hoped that the dismissal would dissolve the alliance and save these three for the Mission, but it was not to be. Maria told Mrs Berger that after 'many prayers that the Lord would remove . . . those who were not really of us', this must be accepted as the answer. 'Perhaps after all these storms the Lord will give us a calm, but all these sorrows and anxieties tell sorely on my beloved Husband's health. If he can get away for a little quiet and change he will (DV) do so, and if possible I shall accompany him.' Jennie was expecting them to visit Hangzhou. Instead 'the advance' claimed priority.

Among Maria's papers is a sad soliloquy. Sooner or later the reckoning had had to be made. 'If (the Lord) has suffered some to come who have caused us untold sorrow, may we not regard this as part of the storms that are to make our young Mission strike its roots into . . . the rock?'

Little information has come to light about the five lost from the Mission. Nicol chose to stay at Xiaoshan, but before long was helping briefly at the hospital in Ningbo. After that nothing more seems to be known. 'Some of them' applied to the LMS, but were not taken into membership. Susan Barnes and Margaret McLean worked at the Union Chapel of the LMS in Shanghai until August 1869, but there the trail runs cold. Jane, too, worked in Shanghai and by 1871 she and Hudson Taylor were on as friendly terms as ever (see p 217f).[72]

Action to advance
(September–November 1868)

September and October were full of diplomatic activity and no foreigner doubted that strong-arm persuasion would be used as soon as possible to resolve the mounting differences between China and the European nations. That Anson Burlingame in Europe was urging peaceful negotiations with a well-intentioned Chinese government stood in marked contrast with the mood on both sides in China, especially in Taiwan and the Yangzi region.

After *Rinaldo* and then Consul Medhurst withdrew from Nanjing it was no time for those who had been thrown out of Yangzhou to attempt to penetrate beyond the city to the north of Jiangsu, on the way to eastern Henan. Yet this was what Hudson Taylor and James Williamson were planning to do. In a little boat on the Grand Canal they could remain out of sight until well clear of Yangzhou, and even a man in poor health could travel in comparative comfort. For a start they would reconnoitre Qingjiangpu, a hundred or more miles beyond Yangzhou. James Williamson hoped eventually to pioneer in Jiangxi province,

but initially he and James Meadows were to secure a footing at Anqing on the Yangzi in Anhui province. Anqing, about two hundred miles above Zhenjiang, would be a forward base for the next advance to Jiujiang, the best starting point into Jiangxi. As the weeks passed they were watching for their opportunity.

Catherine Brown had at last reached China. The prescribed month in a consular centre before British subjects could marry in China would end for George Duncan and her on September 25. On the 17th he and James Meadows left Zhenjiang by steamer for Shanghai to arrange for the wedding and for Meadows to bring his family from Ningbo. The next day Maria set off with Catherine in the Mission's canal boat, to give her a leisurely introduction to this kind of travel. During the same period Hudson Taylor was also away, making preparations for the bride, and for Mary Bowyer to keep her company. Arriving back at Zhenjiang on the same day for Mary Rudland's confinement, Maria and he found it was all over. The riot baby was in perfect health.

All through October the papers were full of rumblings about the riots in Taiwan, inflammatory anti-foreign placards were being posted in Shanghai, and foreigners were being stoned on the streets of Wuhan. HMS *Dove* was ordered back to Zhenjiang as a precaution, and the jingoism in the Shanghai papers approached hysteria. But on Monday, October 26, Hudson Taylor and Williamson started up the Grand Canal. On November 3 he began a letter to the Bergers. 'I am now returning from a journey of exploration as far up as (Qingjiangpu) . . . a large and important town . . . some three miles below where (the Grand Canal) formerly crossed the Yellow River . . . With a view to our ultimately commencing work in K'ai-fung-fu, the capital of Honan, or failing that, in some other city in the province, it seems desirable to have a half-way station.' Oingjiangpu was the farthest point any missionary of any society had so far penetrated from the south (see 1, p 471).

On the same day, Consul Medhurst left Shanghai to return to Nanjing and Zeng Guofan—this time on the flagship HMS *Rodney*, with a squadron of supporting warships. The editor of the *North China Herald* preened himself with the comment, 'We hope, for the sake of the Chinese themselves, that they will yield to what is asked, and not await the seventy-eight guns of the *Rodney*!' Safely home on November 6, Hudson Taylor and Williamson were in time to observe the activity and to be caught up in it dramatically.

Berger takes the strain (1868)

The editorial letters of William Berger in the *Occasional* from the time of the *Lammermuir* party's sailing have been said to form a worthy monument to the memory of this good man. His and his wife Mary's frequent personal letters to the Taylors and each member of the Mission provide material enough for a book in its own right. Without the part they played, the missionaries could hardly have survived as a team. And without their encouragement and advice Hudson Taylor would have found it even harder to keep going. William Berger had given a great deal of thought to problems of church government and wrote long letters on the subject. While still ignorant of developments in China, he said of their differing denominational views, 'We cannot enforce our own views. Indeed we can scarcely say a standard is established in the Word, except for essential doctrines.'

He also thought constantly about how their aim to evangelise the inland provinces could be realised. 'I will tell you my musings concerning your future—namely I fancy you will some day move your headquarters to some desirable city or town very near the (Yangzi), perhaps within easy reach of Hankow; thus you would, I suppose, have easy access to a consul, facility for going to Shanghai and up the river, so as to reach many provinces.' By the time his letter arrived to supply strong confirmation of the step, the home strategist was vindicated and the deployment to the Yangzi had begun. In another letter he mused prophetically

on taking violence and robbery in the right spirit, only to laugh at himself, 'as dear Duncan said, "It is very easy to go to the interior of China in Mr Berger's drawing-room."'

Well-to-do, though not very wealthy, the Bergers devoted their home and most of their time to the Mission's welfare. Capable of contributing very largely to its expenses, they firmly believed that such generosity on their part was neither necessary nor in the will of God. The China Inland Mission and its work in China were the responsibility of a wide circle of Christian friends in most denominations, who were not to be deprived of the blessing of giving in the service of God. In the financial year 1867–68, £3300 had come from the wide circle of donors. Remembering an inflationary factor exceeding twenty we may appreciate this scale of giving. So, when for a variety of reasons the donations the Bergers received for transmission to China fell uncomfortably low, they restrained themselves from the temptation to make up the difference. Instead, they helped when they could in subsidiary ways, as in their offer to pay for the Nicols' passage home.

Their contribution was far more valuable than mere cash. They themselves were wholly immersed in their role of administrators in Britain. After a few years, when the pressure of work became too great, William Berger sacrificed his favourite pastime. He sold the agricultural part of his estate at Saint Hill, East Grinstead, mostly to his own farm manager. Jennie's parents bought and built on another part but lived there less than two years, from 1869–1870. At one time he retired from the management of his factory, but took it up again to allow the added income to give him greater liberty in his Christian activities.

Neither William nor Mary Berger felt competent to write about China or to address meetings. In any case they had neither time nor strength for more than they were doing. Their prayers and strong moral support meant more to the Taylors than any material help. Mary Berger's fine, legible handwriting filled page upon page, overwritten at tight angles in a different colour, of information, comment and love, as genuine as it was effusive, and as prophetic in the truest sense. 'May the knowledge of (God's) great love to us quicken us to endure everything . . . that He permits in the course of our service to Him . . . even though misunderstood, misjudged and unrepresented.' In the letter which would have arrived just before the Yangzhou riot in which she said, 'Underneath are the everlasting arms', she went on, 'They will protect you when attacked, and will preserve you from all real danger. You may . . . quietly stay yourself on Him.'

Jennie had had to stay at Hangzhou, but in Emily they had 'such a treasure'. When news of the murder of Dr Maxwell's Chinese colleague in Taiwan reached Britain, Mary Berger wrote on July 29, ignorant, of course, of events at Yangzhou, 'Truly your safety is in God alone . . . May He . . . graciously keep you from feeling afraid.' And again on September 23, 'We are . . . intensely interested in your movement northward (to Yangzhou) . . . I think the caution you are all using is most commendable.'

William Berger's candid letters were those of a man of affairs in which his affection and confidence constantly came through.

Your life ... is so valuable that every means for its prolongation must be adopted. So I shall ... deliver my message ... You are going beyond your physical powers, and to such an extent that unless you relax I fear the worst. If (you work to excess) during the night as well as the day ... you will assuredly fail and have to give in. Our Father has given us the spirit of a sound mind and holds us accountable for its use ...

[In July] You must not allow the strong language employed by some who have received such limited education unduly to affect you; they are not aware how they wound ... Be of good cheer! Walk holily and humbly with thy God and He cannot fail thee ... No weapon that is formed against thee shall prosper.

[And a few weeks later] Never apologise for your letters; dear Brother, they are always lucid and to the point. I wish I had the same facility of expressing myself ... I shall gladly defray the cost of this third edition (5,000) [of *China: Its Spiritual Need. and Claims*] thus saving trouble as to keeping accurate account of copies we lend or giveaway or put on sale.

As the allegations started by Nicol and relayed by those he spoke to spread to Britain, losing nothing in being relayed, William Berger kept Hudson Taylor informed. Unshaken in his faith in him he waited patiently for the explanation. 'I deeply deplore afflicting you so much, but I see not how to keep (it) back from you . . . If I am wrong kindly say so and I will strive to be more reticent.' The fortnightly mail, taking fifty days in each direction at the fastest, was at best a poor means of communication. Carbon copies, with the stylus, were not yet in general use. Copying each letter consumed too much time. Sometimes a contrite Berger explained that he thought he had mentioned things which Hudson Taylor needed to know, when in fact he had not. And often members of the team made passing references to things the Taylors had omitted. 'The difficulty of acting at such a distance from you and without the power of conferring is very great.' Even the Foreign Office and Minister in Peking had the same problem.

With the transfer to England of the campaign against Hudson Taylor and the Mission, the strain became as much as the Bergers in fickle health could bear. William Berger had not only to present the factual situation in interviews with leading Christians, but to answer troubled questions from correspondents, arising from reports they heard. The confidence of some could not be shaken. Others withdrew support and sympathy. Copies of the plan of No 1 New Lane spoke for the truth more eloquently than anything. Even before she knew that accusations were being sent to friends in England, Emily had sent a room-plan to Mrs Grattan Guinness, who had shown it to others.[73] Well into 1868, when worse attacks of a different nature imposed new stresses, the aspersions on Hudson Taylor's integrity and policies continued.

After news of the riots arrived, the Bergers' sympathy shone from their letters. 'That this outrage will serve for the Gospel I quite hope and think, and shall expect to hear of your being back again in the same house.' That they might be afraid to return to Yangzhou did not enter his head. The motherly Mary Berger said to Maria with penetrating insight:

> Had we not been realising that the work in which you are engaged is God's work, the painful, harrowing tidings which reached us three days since, would have been overwhelming. Our hearts are stirred to their very depths, yet the love and sympathy they can offer are so utterly below your deep need that we turn to Him who alone can be to you all you require. He saw all! He permitted, but He protected too! So far, but no further! ... Perhaps He would show ... that the Christians have confidence in the living God whom they are seeking to make known. [Exactly what the Chinese said.] Perhaps He would teach unconverted Europeans in China that there is a reality in the faith of the missionary ... It may be that by this dreadful outrage He may call the attention of His own dear children all over the world to China—its spiritual need and claims; and such a desire for their souls' salvation may be aroused as never was known before! [Again, exactly what happened.] ... We may well leave it all in His hands ... How could you jump from that height? Yet you were injured.

The newspapers were saying that the children had been thrown from the upper windows. How was it, Mary Berger asked, that in the first letters from Hudson Taylor, Maria, Emily, Duncan and Reid, no mention was made of them? (Lowering them from the upper windows had been the least of the difficulties that night.) And then a tremor of apprehension lest what she was writing should reach Maria when it was hard to relive those experiences. Far from it. Maria read it on December 14 in the very house they had escaped from. 'You are a marvel

to me, beloved friend,' Mary Berger wrote. But in the intervening months what had happened? What of the unborn babe? As far as the Bergers knew, Hudson Taylor had appealed to the consul for help and they could not understand why or know how to defend him. Still they remained unshaken.

They had their own difficulties. Mr Aveline, his secretary, and as devoted as William Berger to the Mission, began to go blind and had to stop work. Criticism of the Mission, stemming both from Nicol and from false accounts of the riot, seemed almost to stop the flow of donations. Then one donor who had said his latest gift would be his last, learned the truth and sent £500, while George Müller asked for the names of five or six more 'thoroughly trustworthy', missionaries to whom to send gifts. George Müller, in channelling to the CIM money entrusted to him for distribution, sent it direct to the individuals. Berger did not know how much was going to China, and Hudson Taylor could not know how to share most equitably the funds at his disposal. When Mr Berger took this up with George Müller he agreed to send his contributions through them.

Editing the *Occasional Paper*, seeing it into print and distributing it issue after issue in his 'spare time' took many hours. Usually content with stating the balance in hand, he sometimes enlarged on how timely donations had arrived in a 'refreshing and encouraging' manner. Occasionally he even referred to future expenses—in a way he soon abandoned, confessing to Hudson Taylor that he wished he could have consulted him first. In August 1868, after the marked inflow of funds, he said in his editorial:

> The number of labourers already in the field connected with this mission ... is now considerable. The amount required to supply their needs and that of the home department will probably not be less than £100 per week, £5200 for the current year ... The questions naturally arise—shall I continue sending out missionaries if in all aspects suitable? Will the needed funds be supplied? And, shall I be overpowering dear Mr Taylor? Then China's *four hundred*

millions ... rise up before me, and seem to cry with a loud voice—'Come over and help us' ... I would now ask you, my dear friends, to share this responsibility and service with me by giving yourselves to prayer, and seeking in every way in your power to make known the deep need of this poor people, so that labourers may be thrust out into this vast field, connected with our Mission and with others ...

By God's help, I hope never to go into debt, and only to enlarge the work as He may put it into the hearts of His people to sympathise and send in the needful supplies from time to time. Towards the end of last month, the balance in my hands was reduced to about £97. I greatly desired to send £300 to Mr Taylor on Mission account, fearing he might be in need, whereupon we made our prayer to God, were kept calm, and were able to believe that He would help us in due time. On August 1st, over £220 was sent in; and on the 13th, over £500, and in all from the 1st to the 24th, [the three weeks of the Yangzhou 'disturbance' and riots] over £950, as though our heavenly Father would say to us, 'If thou canst believe, all things are possible to him that believeth' ... I mention these facts that you may joy with us, even as you so lovingly share our burdens.

A qualified medical man has not yet been raised up to assist Mr Taylor; we therefore continue to pray and wait.

He had noticed an impatience among supporters, with no understanding of the difficulties, to hear of advance into the unevangelised provinces. In spite of publishing many pages of letters about dangerous opposition, he had to remind them that nearly all the team were still novices facing resistance at almost every turn.

The hardest part, assessing candidates (1866–68)

The selection and training of candidates weighed most heavily upon the Bergers in their inexperience. Hearing of how one and another whom they had thought well suited to be missionaries, in new and difficult circumstances had revealed flaws of personality, while the best was drawn out of others, they felt incapable of sound judgment and continually turned to Hudson Taylor for advice.

It is intensely difficult even when men and women have been here long under our eye and roof really to know how they will turn out ... I feel it right now to refer to the disaffection ... to set all upon their guard ... We loved (one in particular) but with us he was excitable, and we thought not likely to prove a wise leader or captain over others [so it was cheering to receive a good account of him.] Still ... be very slow in taking any into your full confidence, rather let them make their own way ... I am declining almost all (candidates) but those of whom we have very much reason to think them desirable persons ... It seems to me ... we should not accept such raw recruits as we have done.

The responsibility of candidate selection was 'so great that unless I was sure God had brought me into the work I should certainly feel led to retire from it—even as you state of yourself in China'. A month later he said, 'I am sure none of the Societies could become so intimately acquainted with their missionaries. On the other hand we may lack perception of character. Our hope is in God.' All too many without education were asking to be sent to China, and had to be disappointed. The rough men of the *Lammermuir* party had yielded too high a proportion of failure to justify sending more of the same type without careful training.

William Berger drafted a letter to all applicants, setting out unequivocally the 'exceptional character' of the CIM, and asking for 'thorough openness' between the candidates and himself. 'The operations being unsectarian . . . are you prepared (to go) avoiding the enforcement of such views as Christians may be allowed to differ upon?' This was an extension of the principle the *Lammermuir* party had agreed to. It required agreement not to press their denominational differences as some Baptist and Presbyterian members already in China had been doing. Hudson Taylor did not question Berger's wording.

Several very suitable women were in touch with the Bergers, but until they heard from Hudson Taylor that single girls could be placed with suitable married couples they could only be asked to wait. Meanwhile Mr Berger was acting on the advice that all unmarried men should be challenged to defer marriage until they had found their feet and learned as much as possible of the language in two or three years. Some responded well.

In contrast, one of the Dublin men of Mrs Gainfort's circle (see 1, p 683), Robert White, was as intent on marrying her daughter Frances as on going to China. 'He seems spellbound.' The girl had a diseased hip, probably tuberculous. And her mother proposed to go with them! 'Impulsive to a degree' and 'a dangerous person' to have in China, Mrs Gainfort created 'a painful scene' when told she should not go. Together they drove the Bergers to distraction. 'We are quite ill with anxiety,' Mr Berger wrote, unable to change the Gainforts' minds. He managed to obtain a signed document from them that they held neither him nor the Mission responsible for any of them, and on arrival in China would all three adopt Chinese dress! Then suddenly Robert married Frances and sailed, without her mother. With the three Dublin students, Tom Barnardo, Charles Fishe and Thomas Harvey, and Jennie's mother and sister Nellie and others, the Bergers saw the Whites off at the East India dock, but warned Hudson Taylor in detail not to admit them to the Mission when they arrived. All too soon his advice proved well founded.

Barnardo, Fishe and Harvey were candidates of whom Mr Berger was more hopeful. Handsome Charles Fishe lived at Saint Hill with them. The others visited them frequently. Thomas P. Harvey, a master-butcher who had turned his attention to medicine in spite of a deficient education, was paying his own way as a student at the London Hospital. He looked 'strong and well', but his father and brother had died of consumption. 'I should say it is in his system. Would this be sufficient reason for refusing him?' William Berger asked Hudson Taylor. With Maria, Emily and Duncan known to have the disease, and with tuberculosis so widespread and little understood, it would be a difficult question to answer. Harvey was overbearing but 'improving in personality, and might sail with Charles Fishe in 1869 without completing his medical course if eventually approved' for the CIM.

Unlike Edward Fishe, who had gone out to China at his own charges without approaching William Berger, Charles Fishe wished to join Hudson Taylor. Serving as the Bergers' secretary for a year, he was their ideal candidate. Without him, Berger feared, his own health would have failed under the pressures on him. Charles was like a son. '(Quiet, and content not to take) a forward place . . . his sterling worth is not seen on the surface, but once known, you will find you have a treasure. There is that in his daily life which produces an influence even when he is silent . . . (He) has been (unknown to himself) my silent comforter. His holy walk, and prayers, and public addresses have . . . helped me beyond explanation . . . He is not easily led, he thinks for himself; yet there is such a spirit of subjection and humility as you find in great minds.'

This paragon was in fact all that the Bergers thought of him, with the one reservation that he was still young and immature. But there was more they had not noticed. Colonel Fishe, his father, wisely withheld permission for him to go abroad until a year older. Yet William Berger wrote in August 1868, 'Except C. Fishe I have no one ready to go.' And in September, 'We hope God is fitting him to bear much responsibility and (to) prove a right hand to you. He is calm and of such general good judgment.' His mother had no doubts about Charles but with reason feared for Edward, should he be left alone to act for himself. Accepting a year's delay was not difficult for Charles. He and Nellie Faulding were attracted to each other.

Another unexpected problem also faced the Bergers. Although a CMS clergyman,

Frederick Gough had come to feel more at home with the CIM, of which his wife (as Mary Jones) had in a sense been a founding member at Ningbo. From the time of the *Lammermuir*'s sailing in 1866, friends of the Mission had met each Saturday to pray in their homes for China. But, wrote William Berger, 'A sphere has been offered Mr G. which I think would perhaps suit him, viz. training (Chinese) youth for becoming evangelists . . . (But) can he also continue his connection with the CIM? He loves to realise the union of true believers and to cooperate with them.' To belong to a transdenominational society would have suited him well, but as a result of their consultations, the Goughs returned to Ningbo in the CMS.

Tom Barnardo (1868)[74]

In spite of the need of experienced doctors being made widely known, none had offered his services to the CIM. Thomas Harvey and Tom Barnardo could not qualify for several more years. The medical student named Evans who had responded to Hudson Taylor's appeals in Dublin seems not to have kept in touch. Barnardo had arrived in London in April 1866, only a few weeks before the sailing of the *Lammermuir*. Though not quite twenty-one, had he been more mature he might have gone to China with the rest. But his father was opposed to his doing so, and Hudson Taylor, seeing 'his youthful assertiveness and somewhat overbearing manner', advised him to take up medicine, allowing him time to mature. So when the Coborn Street houses were given up and Barnardo moved into lodgings nearer to the London Hospital, his intention was to take the entrance examinations without delay.

An evangelist at heart, he could not but be stirred by East London's milling crowds of people. By his own claim, the cholera epidemic of 1866–67—in which, according to *The Times*, 3,909 died in this area alone—opened his eyes to their hopeless degradation. Soon he was preaching in the streets and on Mile End waste and like William Booth at roughly the same time

and place, was being abused and pelted for his pains. The Bergers had doubts about Tom Barnardo's future in the CIM. 'I fear he will not work harmoniously, except he can be allowed to have his own way and go where he likes; and yet he seems desirous to have your counsel, and to follow it as far as he feels led.' Frederick and Mary Gough thought he would never be able to work under anyone.

Then, in December 1867, Barnardo fell seriously ill, but recovered so that William Berger could write, 'Tom Barnardo came to us on Christmas Eve and appears to have China before him as ever. He is still suffering much and has had I think a narrow escape.' Ten days later Tom himself was well enough to write to Hudson Taylor. His exuberant, effusive letter, lavishly larded with quotations from Scripture, like Hudson Taylor's own in his days at Hull, said in essence that he hoped to sail for China in the autumn. Again and again he had weighed up his motives, his 'fixity of purpose' and 'in short my whole heart . . . The leadings of God Chinaward have not slumbered in my breast . . . the taper that God through you first lit in my soul has now really become a fire.' On and on he went in this vein, only turning briefly to report progress in his medical studies. In view of his preoccupation every evening and at weekends with the sea of destitution around him in London's East End, his achievements as a medical student were considerable. But he wanted to cut short his medical course, to bypass the examinations and go to China. He was looking for a successor to take over his work among the children, his Bible classes and the congregation of about ninety members he had brought into being. Yet Barnardo could not reconcile his views on authority and leadership with the policies of the CIM. Unimpeded (or impelled?) by his physical size, 5 feet 3 inches in height, he never would lose his inner urge to lead, command and be second to none. Alert and competent himself, he could afford to be as resolute and 'obstinately persevering' as his thoughtfulness and intelligence directed. Yet he longed at this time to go to China;

as he longed to do all he could for the children of London's slums.

In June William Berger thought Thomas Harvey was wanting 'to be connected' with the CIM. Harvey was sharing in Barnardo's street preaching and had his scalp laid open 'by a missile', painfully enough to deserve mention. As for Barnardo, by the end of July Berger was writing, 'We are somewhat anxious about him.' He had passed the preliminary examination of the Royal College of Surgeons, and there was talk of his going on to take the final examinations of the Royal College and the MD in 1870. But he was neglecting his studies in favour of his wider interests.

Ultimately Tom Barnardo became more and more deeply committed to the East End and never went to China. His close friendship with the Bergers continued, however, and also his correspondence and cooperation with Hudson Taylor.

15
Attack (1868–70)

1868: THE LIMELIGHT

'An anvil, not a hammer'[75]
(May–June 1868)

The Yangzhou riot was as nothing to Hudson Taylor and the Bergers in comparison with the violence of verbal attacks they suffered throughout 1868 and 1869 from fellow-Christians and the secular world. William Jowett's instructions to John Tucker of Madras in 1833 (quoting the advice of Ignatius to Polycarp of Smyrna, 'Stand steady as an anvil when it is struck', and Tucker's own comment, 'Be an anvil not a hammer')[76] had become relevant to their situation. The criticisms directed against the CIM in 1867 were still circulating in 1868, reinforced by Bishop C. R. Alford's airing of them after his arrival in China. In terms of Mission policy alone the climate of opinion was against them in Britain as well as China, owing to difference of outlook.

In *The History of the Church Missionary Society*, Eugene Stock explained the policy of Henry Venn and the CMS on women as missionaries.

> In 1859 the Rev. W. Pennefather, then at Barnet, wrote to the Society offering to train ladies [for service at home and abroad] at an institution he proposed opening. The Committee ... undertook to pay the expenses of any candidate they might send to it. But they still shrank from saying much in print about even the few women the society was employing ... In October of (1863) ... they passed the following resolution: 'that as there are already two Societies in whose principles this Committee have full confidence, whose professed object it is to send out ladies for schools and zenanas in India; this Committee—are not prepared—to take up that branch of missionary operations, except under very special circumstances.[77]

Several offers from ladies to serve with the CMS were therefore declined, the Committee pointing out that wives, sisters and daughters of missionaries were working among Indian women but that the policy of the CMS was not to expand this side of its work. Other major missions shared this outlook. So Hudson Taylor had embarked on an unconventional practice.

When George Smith, first Bishop of Victoria, Hong Kong, retired in 1864, C. R. Alford, the vicar of Holy Trinity, Islington, an active member of the CMS Committee, was appointed to the see of Victoria. But W. A. Russell returned to Ningbo as Secretary for China, 'almost a quasi-bishop' with 'powers of superintendence', and less than five years later (December 15, 1572) he became the first missionary bishop for 'North China', including Ningbo.[78]

That Hudson Taylor should be affected by these events was coincidental. C. R. Alford reached Hong Kong in October 1867 and, with characteristic energy, within a year had visited every Anglican chaplain and missionary on the coast of China, the Yangzi River and at some treaty ports in Japan. At the beginning of March he was in Ningbo and Hangzhou to ordain the new arrivals (in 1867) H. Gretton and J. Bates, and to conduct confirmations. On or about March 4 he 'visited Mr Taylor and Party' and on the 11th wrote at length to his cousin Robert Baxter, who had given them a royal send-off from London in 1866 (see 1, p 701). The form of Alford's letter implied that he had been requested to investigate the reports in circulation about the CIM. After little more than four months in his diocese and only weeks in treaty ports on the mainland so new to him, he could claim no personal knowledge or ability to judge by observation, so he noted the remarks of some missionaries whom he met and reported these. The form and content of his letter followed those of George Moule in 1867.

Doing his best to be fair, but faced with judging a situation from hearsay and a brief social call, Alford commented on their zeal, potential and energy, but added, 'There is a very strong feeling in (the minds of Anglicans and Nonconformists) against the Mission.' He then repeated the familiar allegations of 'the autocracy of Mr Taylor'; of scandalous housing arrangements; of novices engaging in pioneer work, 'prejudicial to the success of missions in general'; and of adoption of Chinese dress 'considered absurdly and calculated to lower the missionaries in the presence of the Chinese.'

'I think there is some truth in these unfriendly criticisms,' he went on to say.

> Perhaps they are sometimes unduly pressed and magnified. But if the Taylor mission is to last and prosper,
>
> 1. Someone or more should be associated with him to bear the responsibility of the movement.
>
> 2. Even Chinese not to say English notions of propriety in reference to the familiar association of young men and women must be respected.
>
> 3. One member, and that a very young member of the missionary body [Hudson Taylor], should respect the judgment; and feelings of the body corporate.
>
> 4. Manifest peculiarities, perhaps absurdities should be avoided.

This well-meaning report reached Robert Baxter in late April or May, when his friend Captain Fishbourne of the Far Eastern fleet (see 1, p 228) became 'greatly incensed against' Hudson Taylor and at first declined to meet William Berger to hear the allegations answered.

At last they dined together and discussed the 'complaints, as outlined' by William Berger to Hudson Taylor:

1. 'The dwelling of the brethren and sisters under the same roof and with partitions of only half-inch board between the bed-rooms.' 'I replied that the (*Occasional*) would show

that the house No 1 has or had two wings and two stairs, the single men being in one wing and the females in the other, and that since obtaining house No 2 the single men had been removed thither.'

In a London drawing-room it all sounded unpardonably primitive. Had William Muirhead been present, as intended, he would have described the construction of not only Chinese houses but Asian homes throughout the tropical and subtropical regions, and the conditions in which foreigners tolerated reduced privacy for the sake of free ventilation from room to room.

2. 'Your intimacy with and kissing the sisters.' 'I explained the long intimacy between your family and yourself with Mr and Mrs Faulding and also spoke of how Miss Blatchley needed your protection, that these two were more like part of your own family and therefore the kiss upon retiring to rest was easily accounted for, that only under peculiar circumstances had you kissed some of the others and lastly that you and Mrs T. had of your own accord thought it wise to desist from the practice, so far back as Jan. or Feb. 1867 . . . I said, "I have a copy of a letter, signed (I believe) by all the single 'sisters' (save one, who was engaged to be married at the time), testifying to the purity of your life and manners and in every respect satisfactory."'

Mr and Mrs Faulding had invited the Bergers for the night, supporting them through this inquisition. Knowing the facts from Jennie as well as the Bergers, they were untroubled. To them the relationship between the Taylors, Jennie and Emily was wholly above board.

3. '(Your position as) "Pastor, medical man, Paymaster and something of Confessor."' This echo of Nicol was easily explained. Robert Baxter seemed satisfied; but to the Bergers' grief, Captain Fishbourne continued to discuss the subject with his acquaintants.

Hearing of the accusations, Dowager Lady Radstock asked for particulars and with Miss Waldegrave wrote to encourage the Bergers. 'The baptism of trial for the Mission in England seems fast drawing on, but we need not fear, so long as we are sincerely desiring to follow holiness and to please the Lord', replied William Berger, closer to the truth than he realised.

'A soft answer' (June 1868)

A few days after their consultation, Robert Baxter sent Mr Berger a copy of Bishop Alford's letter, and William Berger replied with a restrained memorandum, naming neither Lewis Nicol nor those he had misinformed. Nor did he mention those of other societies who supported Hudson Taylor in his policies and practice and had dissociated themselves from the allegations. More than a year had passed and here they were again confronted by the same objections from the same source. The bishop was the latest one to take them up.

The complaint of autocratic direction by Hudson Taylor was not borne out by his correspondence, which showed instead a firmness tempered with friendliness and tolerance. 'Distinct and separate accommodation' had been Hudson Taylor's first concern in renting No 1 New Lane and in hiring boats. Chinese Christians had helped them to find and adapt the premises and, far from it being a scandal, no Chinese, Christian or otherwise, and no other missionaries in possession of the facts had taken exception to the arrangements. After long experience, Hudson Taylor knew exactly how Chinese women travelled, and he always provided for the comforts and privacy of his colleagues by separate covered quarters and usually a separate boat for the women. Any and all missionaries who left the treaty ports and the foreign coastal- and Yangzi River steamers had no choice but to use 'native boats'. This was only one of the skills (and delights) acquired by purposeful travellers. Every one of the early missionary pioneers had worked by 'itineration'. Missionaries who confined their lives and work to the treaty ports and lived in European style while waiting for China to open up would wait a long time. Pressure on Hudson Taylor to disperse his team was as strong as this criticism of his doing so. But the successful occupation of eight cities by these means, in spite of opposition, was already the answer—as the preaching of the gospel with the occupation of every province and hundreds of cities would in a few decades place it beyond challenge. In at least three of those eight cities (Taizhou, Wenzhou and Nanjing) 'no missionary or native assistant had ever been stationed'.

Bishop Alford had accepted the opinion of one school of thought about adapting to Chinese dress and ways. All Mr Berger said in comment was, 'A matter of opinion! Time will show who is wise as to this . . . Let every man be fully persuaded in his own mind.' He could have sent many pages on the subject. As for saying the CIM women looked like prostitutes and vagrants, this was echoing certain elements of the secular press. Both Hudson Taylor and Maria had answered it by detailing the way prostitutes customarily dressed—very different from the dress of Jennie and her friends.

The expression 'a very young member of the missionary body' did Hudson Taylor scant justice, for he was thirty-six and had already been a missionary for fourteen years, longer than any other in Ningbo or Hangzhou with the exception of Dr and Mrs D. B. McCartee (1844, 1852) and E. C. Lord (1847), and of W. A. Russell (1848) and F. F. Gough (1849), both in Britain on prolonged leave of absence. By these standards Hudson Taylor was a veteran. He certainly longed and prayed for a colleague with the vision and ability to share the burden of leadership with him.

Without apology, William Berger had ranged himself firmly alongside his embattled friend—and found himself stoutly backed by loyal supporters.[79]

News of the riot (July–December 1868)

When he was in Ireland in July, William Berger spent an evening with his and Hudson Taylor's friends, including Henry Bewley, the Dublin printer of the *Occasional*, himself an evangelist. The reports about Hangzhou had reached them and many others whom Berger named. He read Bishop Alford's report to them and explained it. 'They were quite satisfied and considered the affair just Satan raging and striving to overthrow (the Mission).' He also met John Houghton of Liverpool, who showed his confidence by sending two hundred pounds from his father and twenty from himself, generous sums at the time. The Grattan Guinnesses also rose to the occasion and declared they would give several weeks, if not months, to working for the CIM before moving to Paris for evangelism on the Continent.

William Pennefather had spoken up for the CIM at the popular Mildmay Conference. 'His confidence in you was unshaken. Dear Lord Radstock has not a moment's question as to your integrity, and he spoke out so . . . frankly. So did Lady Beauchamp and Sir Thomas . . . The Goughs expect to be in China by the end of January . . . I do not think we ought to be discouraged.' When news of the riots became known in Britain, a flood of sympathy and enquiries inundated the Bergers, who wrote:

> Our difficulties are as a feather in the scale compared with yours ... All minds are upon Yang-chau. The public papers, *Times*, *Telegraph* and others, have about a column and a half each upon the subject ... I received a letter from Mr Tarn of the (Religious) Tract Society [Maria's cousin] very strongly reflecting upon your having taken your wife and children and other females to Yang-chau.

The next letter read,

> The excitement, indeed I may almost call it a storm, seems now bursting over us. *The Times* is very severe and incorrect in some things. Whether to reply to the false statements I scarcely know. I should not like to get into a paper war with its correspondent. Perhaps the Lord will put it into the hearts of some of His people to do so and it would come better from them than me.

He wrote all the same.

Criticism of Hudson Taylor over the Yangzhou riot led William Scott of Dundee to write to George Müller for his opinion. But he sent the letter to William Berger to read and forward. In the light of new information from Maria and his own letter to *The Times*, Berger returned it to him, asking him to reconsider what he had said. When he wrote again to George Müller and received a reassuring reply, Scott sent

a donation of fifty pounds in place of the twenty he had intended.

It was an incessant struggle. As criticism mounted on the Yangzhou affair, even the Bergers could not disguise their fears that Hudson Taylor had brought it on himself.

> Many think your party was too large for commencing in a city and the property too much to have had there so early and that it might have been a temptation to the Chinese. Perhaps another time it might be well not to state the amount of property involved as it gives the idea that you urge redress and restitution. For myself I confess I felt it a difficult subject to form a judgment upon ... I do trust the Chinese will not identify the Lord's servants with the British guns or if they do, it may only be from our authorities not allowing any British subjects to be maltreated ... I have stated that I conceive you must have thought it safe or you would not have taken your wife and children and two or three sisters with you.

The first news of the riots had reached them all through the newspapers with their inaccuracies. Letters from China only came later. Mrs Faulding told Jennie:

> On Monday (October 19) your father had been dining in the city, when quite accidentally his eye was struck by the word China in the *Daily News* which was lying close to him. You may imagine what he felt on seeing Mr Taylor and Mr Reid's names in connection with the accounts of the dreadful outrages at Yang-chow ...

> [November 5] Mr Berger felt obliged to send extracts from the letters to the ... *Daily News* and *Revival* ... (and) Mrs Berger wrote ... to all who had relatives at Yang-chow.

> [December 4] Some of our English Papers are as usual blaming the missionaries, foreboding that a war will be the consequence. When I saw the leading article in *The Times* of yesterday, I sent it to Mr Landels requesting he would answer it ... I myself have written to the Editor of the *Daily Telegraph* ...

> [December 18] I trust war will not be the result ... Of course the Mission would be blamed and its enemies would rejoice.

Consul Medhurst's request for a naval squadron had received Sir Rutherford Alcock's approval and armed diplomacy in China was entering upon a new phase.

Who asked for gunboats?
(September–December 1868)

What appeared as isolated incidents involving merchants and missionaries in Taiwan, Huzhou, Zhenjiang and Hangzhou, assumed much greater significance for the men at the diplomatic helm in Peking. When *The Times* of December 1 echoed the Hong Kong and Shanghai newspaper headlines, 'Peace or War?' and wrote of real danger in this direction, it was not mere jingoism. Zeng Guofan, appointed Guardian of the Throne, though still at Nanjing, had humiliated Her Britannic Majesty's consul-general and had shown that a threat of force was necessary to negotiation if he was to talk seriously about the blatant injustices complained of. Furthermore, Prince Kong had failed to 'compel the local authorities to do justice' in Taiwan. A series of provocations had persuaded Lord Stanley (at the Foreign Office in London until December 9) and the minister plenipotentiary in Peking to look for the right moment to make that show of force. China's response would decide which it was to be: peace or war. British prestige was to be restored.

In Taiwan the whole Gaoxiong (ie Dagao) outrage against Catholics and Protestants involving Dr J. L. Maxwell and the death of a catechist had to be investigated. Finally, a proclamation must enjoin respect for Christianity and the rights of British citizens under the treaties of amity! The *daotai* did nothing.[80]

Acting-Consul Gibson's request for a gunboat was granted and the steam-sloop *Icarus*, Commander Lord Charles Scott, proceeded to Taiwan. Thereupon consul and gunboat commander 'grasped the opportunity to demand a settlement of all outstanding grievances' in Taiwan. On August 21 the commander conveyed to the *daotai* at Tainan an ultimatum for the righting of outstanding wrongs. The *daotai* himself held the monopoly of the camphor-trade and was unwilling for the British to trade in camphor. A Mr Pickering of Elfin and Company had been fired on by a company of soldiers and his cargo seized. His Chinese agent's son had been imprisoned. A certain Tinhai had stabbed a Mr Hardy. The murderer of the Presbyterian catechist must be brought to trial.

Then on September 22 Acting-Consul Gibson reported the ambuscades, by sixty or seventy men armed with spears and knives, upon himself and the 'Senior Naval Officer', 'with the object of killing' them. Sir Rutherford Alcock urged Consul Swinhoe to travel at once to the scene. A landing party under a young lieutenant overreacted, seizing the forts at Anping (the port of Tainan) killing twenty-one and wounding as many defending soldiers. On the strength of this act of war the consul and naval commander also went too far, obtaining 40,000 dollars in cash to guarantee satisfaction of their demands, 5,000 dollars as indemnity for the coal and ammunition expended, and 5,000 more, purely as prize money. Their superiors were alarmed. Lord Stanley repudiated them, and also other exactions to indemnify the Catholic and Protestant missions.

Admiral Sir Harry Keppel blamed the consul and complained to Sir Rutherford and the Admiralty of these 'reprehensible actions' and in 1869 of 'the frequency with which consuls requisitioned for gunboats, "inconsistent with strict international law towards the Chinese"'. But where armed diplomacy ended and unlawful coercion began was not apparent, for by then the greater coercion of the great Zeng Guofan, Viceroy of the Two Jiangs at Nanjing, had taken place.[81]

The terms imposed at Tainan were repudiated, but 'in the end all who could be punished were punished, and all who could be compensated were compensated'. It took Lord Clarendon—after the change of government in Britain—to denounce all these 'rash and inexcusable warlike acts'. But as late as December, British and other foreign residents were still being molested by people under the authority of the same *daotai*. Modification of the severe initial demands appeared to have been interpreted as another climb down, another humiliation.

In contrast, in the north of Taiwan, at Danshui and 'Banka', the 'silent pressure' of the presence of a gunboat ensured the return of the merchants. On September 30, 1868, the highest regional mandarin in Taiwan assured Dodd and Company that there would be no impediment to their return to 'Banka', from where they had been evicted. Two representatives of the firm moved in. A mob of five hundred thereupon 'brutally ill-treated them' and seized the premises. The British consul refused to act without the support of gunboats, and 'under their silent pressure, but without the overt exercise of force, he obtained complete satisfaction of his demands'. His superiors approved his action, Lord Clarendon commenting, 'He has succeeded in obtaining redress without employing force.'[82] But the house in 'Banka' had to be given up, and for thirty years no foreigner was allowed to live actually in the town. Instead the merchants 'fired and packed' Formosa tea a mile downstream and a larger, more prosperous town grew up around them. Again on December 6, two Taiwan merchants named Bud and Kerr were mobbed and severely injured. Even so, 'obtaining redress without employing force' won Lord Clarendon's approval.

On the mainland Medhurst's dealings with Zeng Guofan were accompanied by more trouble on the Yangzi. In October some missionaries were 'constantly being stoned' in the streets of Wuchang, so on the 29th Consul G. W. Caine sent a dispatch to the senior naval officer on the Yangzi, Captain Heneage, urgently requesting a gunboat. He sensed that the new mood had been 'brought about I have no doubt by the Yangchow affair'. But Hankou and Wuchang were hundreds of miles further up the great river. With a three- or four-knot current to overcome, HMS *Dove* had

previously taken a month to get there and another gunboat had had to be towed by a more powerful river-steamer. After all the dust of these riots and counteraction had settled, Sir Rutherford Alcock sent a dispatch to Consul Caine, putting his request into perspective but exposing a diplomatic volte face on his own part. With the disturbances of a very serious nature at Taiwan requiring the immediate presence of more than one ship-of-war, and the necessity of so distributing the force available for all exigencies from Singapore to Hakodate, it was 'quite obvious' that the navy could not respond to minor provocations. And then, illogically, 'If the missionaries cannot carry on their labours peaceably and without an appeal to force for their protection, it seems very doubtful how far HM Government will hold themselves justified in resorting to measures of a warlike character for their protection away from the ports.' But in Taiwan, Yangzhou and Wuchang it had been, not missionaries, but 'consuls (who) requisitioned for gunboats'.

This change of stance in January 1869, to putting blame on the missionaries, was new to the situation and part of the political manoeuvring occasioned by Lord Clarendon's return to the Foreign Office in place of Lord Stanley. To the end of 1868 Sir Rutherford had himself been carrying out Lord Stanley's policy, but a sequence of excesses by his subordinates extending into the new year proved too embarrassing for him.

A matter of face[83] (October–November 1868)

Consul Medhurst's report on his rebuff at Nanjing reached Sir Rutherford Alcock at Peking late in September (three months before Lord Clarendon took office). Alcock acted at once. As minister plenipotentiary he was free to take decisions within his brief from Whitehall and must answer to them. He agreed that armed persuasion was needed on the Yangzi and asked 'that grand old man Admiral Sir Harry Keppel' to mount a squadron for the purpose. On October 12 he reported to Lord Stanley that

Viceroy Zeng Guofan had 'turned a deaf ear to all remonstrances' from the moment of HMS *Rinaldo's* departure and he, Alcock, was therefore asking the commander-in-chief to send a force to Zhenjiang to resort if necessary to determined pressure. The Yangzi authorities, he explained, 'have long shown a 'great disposition to treat with neglect all complaints, and either to invite or tacitly connive at popular violence and hostility towards foreigners, to the regret I believe, of the Central Government and, to all appearances, without regard to their instructions'.

Sir Rutherford proposed to blockade the mouths of the vital Grand Canal where it crossed the Yangzi, and even to seize a high official. 'But whatever be the means recent occurrences in Formosa, at Yangchow and at (Zhenjiang), have plainly shown the necessity for decisive action . . . The popular outbreak at (Zhenjiang) [against the *daotai* and consulates] is nothing but an extension of the violent attacks on inoffensive missionaries at Yangchow.' In view of the turn of the political tide as the year ended, his phrase 'inoffensive missionaries' is to be noted. He applauded Medhurst for his firmness and the moderation of his demands, and secured the agreement of Prince Kong and the Zongli Yamen to a full inquiry at Yangzhou. Peking even welcomed action to curb this powerful viceroy who thought little of being out of tune with the Court.[84]

On October 13 the East gate of Shanghai city was placarded with anonymous posters of the familiar type, about children being kidnapped for gruesome purposes. Immediate action by the French consul-general induced the Shanghai *daotai* to have the offensive placards torn down and to substitute a counter-proclamation strongly condemning them. Then the *North China Herald* carried news of the appointment of a new viceroy, to succeed Zeng Guofan as soon as he had settled the Yangzhou and Zhenjiang affairs. The fact that he was Ma Xinyi, the friendly Muslim governor of Zhejiang, boded well for peace on the Yangzi, however much he would be missed at Hangzhou.[85]

The regulation that foreigners must report negotiations for the rental or purchase of premises was peculiar to Zeng Guofan's jurisdiction, the *Herald* maintained, imposed by him to impede the progress of missionaries. The paper also published a three-column protest by an enlightened anonymous 'Spectator' against pressing the Chinese authorities too hard. The fault lay not with Zeng Guofan, he suggested, but strictly with his friends at Yangzhou. Enemies must not be made through insensitive blunders. The wording of an engraved stone tablet about the riots would hold the key to future tranquillity. 'We ought to take care that the guilty only are punished, and do anything rather than awaken the anger of the well-meaning populace, a result that would certainly occur if we compelled them to erect a tablet to their own disgrace.' The tablet should not even refer to the riot. 'Face' mattered supremely. How true this was, would soon be demonstrated.

W. H. Medhurst left Shanghai on November 3 for Zhenjiang. On the sixth a full squadron of three steam-sloops: *Rinaldo*, *Icarus* and *Argus*, and two gunboats, *Dove* and *Slaney*, escorting HMS *Rodney*, flagship of Sir Harry Keppel, arrived there on the way to Nanjing with seven hundred men-at-arms aboard. The issue was no longer the right of missionaries to reside unmolested in inland cities. As the *Times* correspondent put it, 'The case has now grown beyond a mere question of reparation for injuries sustained. Our political prestige has been injured and must be recovered.'[86] The *North China Herald* went further. 'We hope for the sake of the Chinese themselves, that they will yield to what is asked, and not awake the seventy-eight guns of the *Rodney* . . . (Zeng Guofan) may find the British lion unmuzzled, if he waits at Nanking till the *Rodney* gets up.' For this kind of arrogance Britain and the Chinese church are still paying the price.

During October the viceroy had not only cashiered the offending prefect and magistrate of Yangzhou but had degraded by three degrees the Salt Commissioner, a mandarin of higher rank. He himself expected to evade another confrontation with Consul Medhurst by leaving Nanjing to take up his new post as viceroy of Zhili. However, both a memorial from the Zongli Yamen to the emperor on the subject of foreign missions and religious freedom, and the emperor's response were moderate and conciliatory in tone. Both called upon Zeng Guofan to complete the settlement of matters under his jurisdiction before leaving Nanjing to take up his new viceroyalty.

Zeng Guofan had therefore delayed his departure. But great preparations were being made. 'It is expected that (he) will be escorted at least as far as Yangchow . . . by such a following of Mandarins as never before accompanied a viceroy.' Zeng's crowning glory, however, was to be a 'handsome new steamship' of his own in which to travel, the *Tien-chi*, with a foreign captain. The *daotai's* of Shanghai and Zhenjiang and the prefect of Suzhou were being taken up to Nanjing in her, to help in the negotiations.

Leaving HMS *Dove* at Zhenjiang to survey the Grand Canal, the naval squadron proceeded to Nanjing on November 9 and Consul Medhurst marched with an escort and appropriate ceremony to the viceroy's palace. There he presented Zeng with an ultimatum simply reiterating the original demands rejected in September.

Consul Medhurst was not a man to be trifled with. An officer and men boarded the *Tien-chi*, anchored nearby, with a message from Captain Heneage of *Rodney* informing the ship's captain that it was now 'attached' to the squadron. He was not to weigh anchor without orders, on pain of having a prize crew placed in charge. He at once went to inform the viceroy and returned saying that 'the effect of this seizure was electrical'. When Zeng Guofan was told at 6.00 p.m. what had happened, his face had 'changed colour violently'. This blow at his personal prestige was intolerable. 'There was a general explosion

of rage.' But he was helpless. He yielded unconditionally to all Medhurst's terms.

Together Zeng and the viceroy-designate, Ma Xinyi, confirmed the capitulation in a 'conjoint letter' and issued a proclamation that foreigners were not to be opposed; and on the 12th May was entertained on *Rodney*. Leaving one warship to hold the *Tien-chi*, the squadron returned to Zhenjiang the same day, and with his immediate reinstatement at Yangzhou decided upon, Hudson Taylor was invited to dine on *Rodney* on the 14th. The *Times* correspondent's comment voiced the general belief that the court at Peking would be secretly glad that Zeng Guofan had been humiliated. For in Alicia Bewicke Little's view 'Everyone at that time was full of the idea that (Zeng) and Li [Li Hongzhang] together could become masters of Central China.'[87] Too powerful and too influential, he had largely taken to doing as he wished. His antagonism to foreigners was only a case in point, at variance with the current policy of the Zongli Yamen.

Although Yangzhou was the main issue, W. H. Medhurst had also finally settled the two Zhenjiang disputes. The authority of the friendly Ying *daotai* had been established against the opposition of the Manchus and the defiant magistrate, and the parties to exactions and outrages, including torture, against British merchants and their Chinese employees at the customs barrier were brought to book.

The reinstatement (November 1868)

Hudson Taylor had been told to hold himself in readiness to attend a consular court on November 15. This may have been a briefing on the return to Yangzhou, but it appears that a formal hearing of evidence before a high-ranking grain commissioner and the *daotai* of Shanghai took place in Yangzhou city itself on the 17th. While the squadron was at Nanjing, the commander of *Dove* had made soundings of the Grand Canal for sixty miles north from Guazhou, to see how far gunboats could safely go. On the 16th both gunboats, *Dove* and *Slaney* escorted Consul Medhurst to Yangzhou with between three and four hundred marines and sailors and some fieldpieces, and anchored off the East Gate. Duncan, Rudland, Reid and W. G. Stronach, an interpreter in the consular service, travelled independently in the Mission boat. Stronach's father had been the closest friend of Maria's father before his tragic death in 1843 (see 1, p 121). Sentries took command of the gate and the marines were conducted 'to the Temple of Ten Thousand Genii'. A Catholic priest (Sechinger?) described the occasion.

> Mr Medhurst ... and Mr Taylor are taken solemnly through the streets to a large pagoda to accommodate 400 men. Literati with buttons precede the retinue of mandarins. The two ringleaders had been arrested; the others, by joining the procession, gave the necessary satisfaction to foreigners. Two heralds at the head announced to the people in the streets, 'People—take care not to hurt the foreigners, or to call them "foreign devils", but give them the titles of great men.' Mr Taylor is taken back to his house, perfectly repaired at the expense of the mandarins.

But the Yangzhou officials had once again 'taken' the troops through minor streets, so Medhurst and the naval commander mounted a full parade the following day. Marching across the whole breadth of the city by the main streets from the East Gate to the parade ground outside the West Gate, they staged two grand exercises, firing their field guns to impress the populace.

In the presence of the Chinese commissioners the case against the prefect, magistrates and literati was then investigated, as a preliminary to ensuring that all Medhurst's demands were met in full. When Rudland was faced with the murderous plunderer who had twice tried to kill him on the night of the riot, he could not be mistaken. The ringleader Koh was harder to identify, until as Interpreter Stronach informed Medhurst, 'He broke out into a long and incoherent appeal for mercy which had at least the effect of enabling the missionaries to announce, if

possible, more confidently the identity of the man, as his voice and manner irresistibly recalled the impressions of the night of terror.' The leading member of the literati, ex-viceroy Yen of Canton was declared absent; so Medhurst held 6,000 taels against his arrest, and demanded as a formality that the new prefect and magistrate be dismissed if he were not apprehended within two months.

Medhurst had had twenty-seven years of experiences in consular service, some of it as a youth while his famous missionary father was still living. He knew that the real culprits behind the riot would be difficult if not impossible to bring to justice. A proclamation by the viceroys denouncing the previous prefect and magistrate and the leaders of the riot, also announced the impending return of Hudson Taylor and his party: 'Be it known to all that British subjects have liberty to go into the interior without let or hindrance as clearly stated in the Treaty ratified by the Emperor . . . Hereafter should anyone insult, hinder or annoy (British subjects) they shall be immediately seized and severely punished. No mercy shall be shown them. Tremble at this!'[88]

When he had done all he could, Medhurst reported to Alcock on November 20 and 26 that it was not found possible to bring evidence to bear upon the gentry for their complicity in the attacks. It was more than any man's life was worth to testify against them. Alcock protested at this but nothing more could be done.[89] Justice for the Chinese victims of the riot was as much part of Medhurst's demands as for the foreigners. When on the consul's insistence during his September visit to Yangzhou the Taylors' landlord had been released from prison, a pack of 'yamen runners' had been set on him to persecute and ruin him. Mr Peng the innkeeper had also been 'utterly ruined'. Seven or eight yamen runners had dogged his footsteps day and night. 'They lived upon him, smoked opium at his expense, took possession of his house and property . . . Six weeks ago he was a prosperous and independent man;

at present he is an utter beggar . . . simply because he was friendly towards foreigners.'

The inquiry over, the financial losses by the Chinese and missionaries all agreed and reparations settled, Hudson Taylor was formally reinstated at his house on November 18. Consul Medhurst announced that the whole Mission party, including the women, were invited to return, and summarised the indemnities paid to them as 1,128.40 taels for losses by them and their servants, including further repair to the premises; 500 taels in compensation for their injuries; and 197.75 taels to the landlord and carpenter. In all 1,826.15 taels. He had earlier advised Hudson Taylor not to take the women back there until later. With renewed confidence he now asked him to do so at once, knowing full well that Maria's confinement was due at any time. They all returned on November 23, and on the 29th her baby, Charles Edward, was born. On December 1 she wrote to Mary Berger:

> Last Sunday, in the very room from which ... I had ... to take what might have been to my [unborn] infant, not only to myself, a death-leap ... God had given me the desire of my heart ... that if safety to myself and my infant permitted, I would rather it were born in this city, in this house, in this room, than in any other place—your own beautiful spare room ... not excepted.

They gave the baby the Chinese name of Tianbao, 'protected by Heaven', as a testimony to the miracle of his survival. But ever since the riot she herself had been frail and ill. She believed that with her 'chest so weak lately', the sentence of death was upon her. Sir Rutherford Alcock, himself a surgeon, wrote to Consul Medhurst, 'Now that the medical certificate is before me, I see that three of the party, Mrs Taylor, Miss Blatchley and Mr Rudland have suffered permanent and serious injury. Money, unfortunately, can afford no adequate compensation for injuries which cause permanent and disabling effects.' At the time it was thought that Henry Reid's eye had recovered, but in fact he had suffered

the most serious lasting injury, eventually losing the sight of that and probably of both eyes.[90] 'I do not think 500 taels at all adequate,' Sir Rutherford continued, 'and have to instruct you to make a demand of 2,000 taels, to be equally divided among the three already named.' Sir Rutherford also addressed Prince Kong in unambiguous terms, defending the peaceful and good behaviour of the missionaries (including Dr J. L. Maxwell of Tainan), and declined to admonish them to cause no offence, as the Prince had suggested.

An engraved stone tablet was erected at the street entrance to the CIM premises, making no mention of the riot. Forward-looking, it referred only to the right of foreigners to live there in peace and to propagate their religion, a generously face-saving show of wisdom on the consul's part which the people of Yangzhou did not fail to note. When all was over, Hudson Taylor wrote to him saying, 'We feel the more grateful for these measures, because they will facilitate, as we believe, not only our own work in Yangchow, (Zhenjiang) and Nanking, but Christian missions generally throughout the interior of China.' In his *Summary of Operations of the China Inland Mission* (1872) he had more to say.

> It is, perhaps, also due to the members of the Mission to state, that of the indemnity claimed on our behalf by the British Government, more than half was for Chinese whose property had suffered in the disturbance; and that all that was for the missionaries themselves was handed over by them to form a fund for the furtherance of God's work in Yangchau.

In June 1888, Hudson Taylor recalled the events at Yangzhou and Zhenjiang with these observations on the lessons to be learned 'from this and similar experiences'.

> One was to be longer known in a city through itinerant visits before renting houses and attempting to settle in them. Another was not to take much luggage to a newly-opened station ... A third was, not to commence work with too strong a staff, and not to attempt to open contiguous stations simultaneously ... The lessons

learnt there have ... enabled us since peacefully to open many cities in remote parts of China.

There is no command to open mission stations, in the Word of God, and there is no precedent to be found there. The commands to evangelize, to go into all the world to preach the Gospel to every creature, and the examples recorded in the New Testament of the methods of the early workers, might have led us from the first to give itineration a greater prominence than we did. It must be admitted that stations become necessary to some extent; the itinerant work of the Church cannot be carried on without them. It is, however, a grave mistake to make location our first aim ... in proof of which, one notorious fact may be adduced, namely, that the best spiritual work in connection with all missions is to be found in out-stations at a distance, rather than at the station where the missionary resides.[91]

Alexander Michie in his memoir of Sir Rutherford Alcock, *The Englishman in China*, was to write in 1900, 'For the last thirty years Yangchow has been the most peaceable missionary field in the whole empire.' In 1868, however, another major riot, the success of itinerant evangelism and the fundamental value of these foci of the Chinese church a little remote from the foreign missionary, had first to be experienced. With 1870, a new era of the expansion of the CIM was entered upon. Casting the seed, and the net, widespread, with a minimal intrusion of foreignness upon the Chinese, became the aim and practice—while consolidation of the resulting churches in settled situations followed as a matter of course.

Viceroy Zeng Guofan's steamship was released on November 26. He promptly handed his seal of office to Ma Xinyi and left Nanjing. An unnamed source quoted at length in *Li Hung-chang: His Life and Times*[92] described Zeng Guofan's departure. 'On the 15th December the all but Imperial Tseng Kwo-fan left the city which he had so long ruled more like a king than a viceroy . . . All along the road . . . altars, with candles and incense burning, had been erected; and . . . the people again and again bowed down and worshipped him as if he had been a god.'

By December 2, Consul Medhurst and his staff had returned to Shanghai and, not yet having received his minister's demand for higher compensation for the injured, on the 8th he declared the Yangzhou affair ended. A Christian himself, he had treated the missionaries throughout with sympathy and concern. To thank him Hudson Taylor asked William Berger to send as soon as possible the best calf-bound edition of the Bible he could obtain.

Anqing and Anhui next
(December 1868)

The end of the era of opposition to foreigners by literati under the patronage of the old school of viceroys was approaching, but still far from over. Li Hongzhang remained viceroy of Hubei and Hunan, but he was young and well acquainted with foreign ways and power. Under Ma Xinyi as viceroy of Jiangsu, Jiangxi and Anhui, the prospect for peace between the nations was better than it had ever been. The prospect for peaceful penetration by the CIM had therefore suddenly blossomed. With homes assured at last at Zhenjiang for the Rudlands and the printing presses, and at Yangzhou for the Taylors' administrative centre, nothing stood in the way of the advance they had begun in April. The Judds were to come to Yangzhou to understudy the Taylors in planting a local church and to support Maria whenever Hudson Taylor's duties took him away. And other young missionaries were to join them from time to time, beginning with Edward Fishe.[93]

Three weeks after the birth of Charles Edward, weeks spent in distributing the reparations to his landlord and other Chinese in restoring the premises to their former state, Hudson Taylor left Yangzhou again, on November 16. He had hoped to visit every station of the Mission from Nanjing to Wenzhou, but instead was at Nanjing over Christmas to launch the pioneers of Anhui on their way and then to travel alone until March. Meadows and

Williamson were to reconnoitre Anqing on the north shore of the Yangzi. They left Nanjing on December 26, eventually to gain an uncertain footing in the city after months of hard work against determined opposition. Briefly returning to Yangzhou, Hudson Taylor was away again on December 28 to meet Alexander Wylie in Shanghai and learn all he could from him about Sichuan, South Shaanxi and Hubei before he sailed for Britain.

Maria had Louise Desgraz and the Judds with her, but life in Yangzhou was far from plain sailing. In asking the Judds to come to Yangzhou Hudson Taylor had said, 'I do not hide it from you, that it will be exceedingly dangerous, the people threaten to kill the first Europeans that go in, and they have banded themselves together to do it, but God will protect you.' Judd recalled:

> For some weeks after we arrived, the shutters of our house were stoned night after night battered and shattered with stones. We were stoned or mobbed nearly every time we went out on the street. My wife was once delivered marvellously from a mob by two Chinese soldiers coming up just in time and they brought her home. Later on I escaped from a mob of probably 2000 or 3000 people who were stoning me, by going on my pony across a narrow plank over a brook.[94]

All was otherwise well in Yangzhou. The fact that they had been able to open both a boys' and a girls' school indicated confidence among their neighbours. Better still, three Chinese were asking for baptism and several were interested, including Mr Peng the innkeeper. Because Judd needed more exercise but could not afford a pony, Hudson Taylor himself had 'bought a good one' and asked Judd to keep it exercised for him when he himself was away on his travels. Not until long afterwards did Judd discover that Hudson Taylor had never intended to use it himself.

In this one year of difficulty, Jinhua had been lost, Wenzhou, Suzhou, Zhenjiang and Yangzhou had been occupied, and Ninghai and other outstations had been opened in Zhejiang. Qingjiangpu had been reconnoitred and, boldest step of all, Anqing was being attempted. To the friends who believed in him, Hudson Taylor was indomitable, but to Sir Rutherford Alcock and many critics he was only incorrigible, as the coming year was to show.

1869: 'The devil's growl'

The gunboats go too far[95]
(January 1869)

Commander Bush's successful vindication of his action in September 1868 expressed, if it did not initiate, a change of mind in the Foreign Office in London. His indignation that the ship under his command should be used to coerce a viceroy of the Chinese empire, on the word of a consul and not of his own admiral or the minister-plenipotentiary, illuminated the whole scene of gunboat diplomacy. While Lord Stanley's policy in China was not belligerent, he approved of Sir Rutherford Alcock's preference for prompt, decisive action on the right occasions. But even he, on December 1, the day before Disraeli's government fell, pacifically advocated that all cases be dealt with by the minister and

decisions by the Peking government be carried in the *Peking Gazette* for Chinese officials to see. Mellowed from his headstrong early days, Alcock remained formidable. His consuls followed his lead, successfully in W. H. Medhurst's case, leading eventually to his own knighthood, and elevation to minister, but disastrously where misjudgment by inexperienced men led to excess.

The tardiness of communications made consultation between even consuls and minister difficult at any time. Because of *fengshui* the telegraph was not being installed in China. With cables taking at least two weeks between Peking and London, Sir Rutherford could only seek approval if no great urgency existed. Written reports still took two months by the fast 'overland' route. News of the

Anping ultimatum on August 21 and the Yangzhou riots on the 22nd and 23rd reached London in October. Comment came back in December. Sir Rutherford's dispatch to Lord Stanley of September 11 reached him on November 30. His request to the Admiral in October for a show of naval strength on the Yangai would not have been on the Foreign Minister's desk until December. The change of government in Britain on December 9 and Lord Clarendon's 'conversion' through Anson Burlingame's diplomacy, could have no direct effect in China until two months after Lord Clarendon declared his policy on December 28. Events in China during January and February 1869 were still governed by the consuls' understanding of policy as it had been in 1868.

When Lord Clarendon commented to Alcock on January 14, 1869, 'I consider Mr. Medhurst to have acted very rightly,' for limiting his coercion to a show of force without its use, he also rebuked Sir Rutherford for sending a naval squadron to Nanjing and risking war without consulting Her Majesty's Government. Sir Rutherford barely knew by then of a change of Foreign Secretary, let alone of a new policy. The action in October for which he was being rebuked had been in keeping with Lord Stanley's directives. Consultation with Anson Burlingame, Lord Clarendon said, had shown how the whole matter could have been handled through the central government at Peking in a friendly manner. 'Provincial governors are too often in the habit of disregarding the rights of foreigners,' he had protested to Burlingame. But Burlingame had confirmed the wisdom of Lord Stanley's dispatch of December 1 as if the effectiveness of the fiat of Peking could be counted on where men like Zeng Guofan chose to differ. It could not. They were a law to themselves. Distance and delays were too great for proper consultation.

On January 28 another dispatch from Lord Clarendon signalled the end of the era of high-handed action by consuls, gunboats and even Her Majesty's minister-plenipotentiary. In future all such matters must be referred by consuls to the ministers in Peking for reference to the Zongli Yamen, and if necessary to London. But even before this order could reach the consuls, two more outrages had been perpetrated in the name of British prestige.

The first was relatively mild. A certain Rev Wolfe, a missionary at Fuzhou, bought land on Sharp Peak Island on which to build a holiday cottage or 'sanitarium'. When a local Chinese gentleman stirred up the people to prevent him from doing so, he asked the consul to help. The consul called upon the commander of HMS *Janus* to intervene, and on January 20 an armed force overawed the villagers by destroying the instigator's house whereupon terms were signed to permit Wolfe to proceed with erecting his own 'place of coolness'.[96]

The second incident was more serious. By the treaty of 1858 and the Peking Convention two other cities became open ports, the city of Chaozhou, near Chao'an (where William Burns had been arrested), and its deep-water port of Shantou (Swatow) 'with a reputation for piracy and turbulence'. In January 1869 the American consul was stoned at a large village or market town called 'Aotingpow' in the Admiralty reports, 'notorious for its hostility to foreigners'. A few days later, on the 20th, boats from the gunboat HMS *Cockchafer* exercising on the river were stoned from the same place. Men landing to demand an explanation were fired on and ten were wounded.

Consul Challoner Alabaster saw his opportunity to settle at the same time some trade disputes. While Admiral Sir Harry Keppel consulted the viceroy of Canton, the naval commander at Hong Kong lost no time in sailing with four warships to Shantou, landed men on January 29 to attack 'Aotingpow', set fire to the villages the force passed through, and 'by sunset a great part of the town' of from seven to ten thousand inhabitants was destroyed, at the price of six men slightly wounded.

The navy protested at being used so freely and when Lord Clarendon's firm statement of policy reached Peking at the end of February the practice of 'isolated acts of coercion . . . on the initiative of the consul' had to end. The 'vicious circle of irritation and repression' was broken. In response to Sir Rutherford's claim that 'relations with China had never been more satisfactory', Lord Clarendon made the surprising pre-judgment and admission,

> The injudicious proceedings of missionaries in China, the violence engendered by them on the part of the Chinese authorities and people, and the excessive and unauthorised acts of retaliation to which British consular and, at their requisition, the naval authorities had resorted, were indeed sufficient to cause Her Majesty's Government to look forward with apprehension to the intelligence which each succeeding mail might bring.[97]

This state of mind, blaming missionaries but not merchants or others, was to influence public opinion in Britain and add to the Bergers' and Taylors' discomfort. As for the Clarendon policy, Hosea Ballou Morse concluded, 'It is noteworthy that for some years to come, there were almost no acts of violence committed against English mission stations, while those against the Roman Catholic missionaries, under the protection of France, increased in number and gravity.'[98]

If relative peace was restored, it was only relative. Not until the latter half of the 1870s did atrocities cease for a while and foreigners of any nation feel safe. 'Almost no acts of violence against English stations' was cold comfort to young men and women scattered hundreds of miles apart, intent only on peacefully sharing their own knowledge of the gospel with the Chinese around them.

A growl—in the press
(January–March 1869)

For the present the action was over, Yangzhou was quiet and Hudson Taylor was away on his five-month tour of the Zhejiang cities. But the recriminations had begun—in Spurgeon's phrase, the

devil's growl. Hearsay news of the riot had reached London in October through the China papers and the *Times* correspondent's articles in November and December. His news of the Yangzhou settlement followed in the January 21 issue. Criticism of Hudson Taylor had begun on the assumption that he had appealed for consular intervention, quickly exaggerated to asking for gunboats (a canard as alive today as then). W. H. Medhurst's first dispatch had mistakenly supported the myth of an appeal. But as late as mid-January the Bergers were writing of mails having gone astray and vital information being denied them. He dared not draw upon himself the attention of the press until he had facts to go on, but at Mrs Faulding's request William Landels, minister of the fashionable Regent's Park Chapel, had written on December 4 to the Editor of *The Times*:

> So far from 'finding the people as well as the authorities dead against them ... first in one city, then in another', in which they have tried to 'force their way', (the China Inland Mission) have succeeded in opening mission stations in various cities of the interior ... [Miss Faulding] who went out from my church (and) is now in (Hangzhou), is known in every part of the city and has never had a rude word addressed to her. The people invite her to their houses, and press their hospitality on her to an extent which proves often embarrassing.

> Mr Taylor is the last man to seek to involve his country in hostilities with the Chinese on any ground whatsoever. It was not his wish that a gunboat should appear on the scene.[99]

That was true, so far as it went, but Joseph Tarn's objections to Hudson Taylor's taking women and children to Yangzhou were shared by others and the reasons were still not known. Nor why so many had congregated there. In the *Occasional* William Berger bemoaned the missing mail, but fell into the trap of believing newspaper reports of 'the appeal made by Mr Taylor to HBM's Consul'.

'The diplomatic action which has resulted, the peremptory demand for redress and compensation, and the demonstration of force, must not be attributed solely to Mr Taylor's request for protection.' Meanwhile in China, neither Hudson Taylor nor Maria mentioned the subject in their letters, having no inkling that the facts had been misrepresented. By December 18 many were fearing war as a consequence of Sir Rutherford Alcock's sending a naval squadron to Nanjing. What was Hudson Taylor's 'foolhardiness' leading the nation into? Another 'typhoon' was 'bursting over' the Mission.

When Lord Clarendon at last received (in January) the dispatch detailing the strong action taken by Medhurst and the squadron in November, he censured his minister in Peking. In future 'the active interference of H.M. naval forces should only be had recourse to in cases of sudden emergency or of immediate danger to lives and property.' Then followed the withdrawal of powers from Alcock; when once any matter had been referred from the scene of action to him in Peking, it must be referred to the Foreign Office for a decision whether to use force in support of diplomatic pressure![100] But how could the minister in Peking convey in a dispatch all the intricacies of dealing with an international incident involving people like Ci Xi (the empress dowager), Prince Kong and Zeng Guofan? How could he bring home to British statesmen accustomed to European diplomacy the contrasting character of dealings with the Peking court? A new era had begun. The minister's hands were tied. But the era of overbearing action by consuls had to end, and Lord Clarendon had ended it by one clear order.

Strong expressions of opinion on the whole question of consular support for missionaries, both for and against, naturally proliferated as news of Taiwan, Yangzhou, Fuzhou, Hankou and, elsewhere hit the headlines. But the authorities had done a great and lasting disservice to missions and to the church in China by using the Yangzhou episode to serve their own predetermined ends.

As late as February 11, William Berger was writing to Hudson Taylor, 'Will you kindly send me word whether *you* sent for the gunboat . . . ?' At the same time, Jennie was writing to her parents:

> I wonder whether this will be the last time Mr T.'s movements will excite worldwide notice? Perhaps not, for I have often heard him say that it is his impression that in seeking to spread the truth he will lose his life by violent means. He longs to go forward now more than ever and is hoping that the end of this year may find him in (Sichuan).

Mr Medhurst having learned all particulars of the steps taken in Yangchau, said to Mr T., 'Well, I think you have done all that any man could do. There is nothing in your actions here that I would have had otherwise, except it be that I think the ladies should have been moved at an earlier period.' When Mr T. explained that he had nowhere to send them to and that ... it was at (the ladies') request that the thought of removing them was abandoned, then Mr Medhurst said, 'Under those circumstances you were quite justified in the course you have taken.'

A growl—in the Lords[101] (March 1869)

Hudson Taylor and the China Inland Mission had been in the unwelcome limelight of debate, of criticism and of abuse for two years over the Hangzhou allegations, and for six months over the Yangzhou riot. All that had gone before now paled into shadow under the glare of an attack by the Duke of Somerset in the House of Lords on March 9, 1869. In an astonishing and 'most lamentable display of ignorance on the part of some of the members of that noble body' he led the 'anti-missionary sentiment' in a speech beginning by naming the China Inland Mission and asking, 'what right have we to send missionaries to the interior of China?'

To the amazement of many he then described Hong Xiuquan the fanatic Taiping rebel leader and his hordes, linking missionaries with them, and continuing, 'It is most unjust that the English naval power should be used to support them.' When he protested that 'every missionary almost requires a gunboat' the noble lords laughed; but he pressed on, 'The fact is, we are propagating Christianity with gunboats, for the authorities of inland towns know perfectly well that if they get into trouble with the missionary a gunboat will soon come up. They turn the French missionary out of the town, and they knock the English one on the head, so that there is perfect religious equality. We ought, I contend, to recall these inland missionaries.' His unfactual rhetoric became even more vulnerable, however, when he declared surprisingly that nobody was more responsible for this mischief than the London Missionary Society!

When the Foreign Secretary rose to reply, he tried to be fair. 'I cannot help admiring the spirit which animates missionaries, and (their) fearless zeal,' he said. Yet Sir Rutherford Alcock had referred to the riots (in Taiwan and Yangzhou) as proof that 'not only the authorities and influential persons but the whole population of China (were) averse to the spread of the missionary establishment'. As for the LMS, they had asked on February 5 how far they could go in taking up the great opportunities in China without embarrassing her Majesty's Government. The Foreign Secretary had replied, advising them to consult the minister in Peking in specific instances as he was not prepared to apply the provisions of the treaties to hypothetical situations. Finally, he too laid himself open to a devastating riposte by advising that 'the missionaries will do well to follow in the wake of trade when the people have learned to see in it material advantage to themselves, rather than to seek to lead the way'.

The Duke of Somerset was grateful and drew the noose more tightly round his own neck. 'My noble friend (the Earl of Clarendon) is quite right in saying that Christianity can only go in the wake of civilisation and progress.' But present in the House was Dr Magee, Bishop of Peterborough, who had yet to make his maiden speech. He seized this opportunity.[102]

On the spur of the moment Bishop Magee rose to deliver a defence 'which at one bound established his fame as one of the most brilliant debaters of the day'. The advice of both duke and earl was unlikely to be accepted, he began. To leave that part of the world unconverted or to give up the attempt because British commercial interests might be prejudiced was unlikely. The youngest and least zealous missionary would reply, 'There is something more sacred even than that sacred opium trade for which Great Britain once thought it worthwhile to wage war!' That something was obedience to the command of God to seek the conversion of his fellow-man at whatever risk to himself or others. It was hardly generous for one in the safe security of their lordships' House to taunt a man who took his own life in his hand, with imperilling the interests of English trade.' Should he by becoming a missionary lose the rights he would retain as trader? British subjects were equally entitled to protection if they sold Bibles or cotton. But had missionaries always been prevented from becoming 'troublesome', neither the noble duke nor he would have been Christians today. Would the noble earl like to mention what kind of trade the missionary should follow? 'Should he wait till the beneficent influence of firewater or opium had made the people amenable to the Gospel and then preach to men whom the trader had demoralised or intoxicated with his liquor or his vices?'

Little remained to be said. Certainly trader and missionary should be treated alike, Earl Grey agreed, but Britain had abused her superior force, protecting even the abominable coolie trade. She should withhold protection from missionaries, traders and smugglers who penetrated beyond consular protection and incurred hostility. Lord Shaftesbury's comment was no kinder. Those who had raised this fuss were a small independent body of men, 'in no way connected with the great missionary societies' (naming CMS, LMS, Wesleyans and Baptists), acting under no central authority. The great missionary societies should 'be exonerated from the charge which had been justly brought against that small independent body'.

Reaction to the Lords[103] (March 1869)

The Times of March 10 carried a full report of the debate, losing nothing in the telling. 'Parliament is not fond of missionaries,' it said, 'nor is the press, nor is general society. The missionaries are certainly the most independent, perhaps the most wrong-headed of men.' Even so, not until a month later did William Berger feel sufficiently in possession of the facts to write to the editor. By then the need to do so had increased immeasurably.

Some societies naturally needed to justify themselves in the face of accusation. They did so, not realising that dissociating themselves from allegations could further incriminate the CIM. Others consciously pointed the contrast. Both in China and at home some had been cautious to a fault, not to take avoidable risks or to conflict with government policy. On March 31 Donald Matheson spoke for the English Presbyterian Mission. After thirty years as a merchant and partner in Jardine, Matheson, and later 'in missionary operations', he protested to Lord Clarendon against his censure of missionaries, especially in Taiwan. Dr Maxwell had quickly discovered that it was the mandarins who 'entertained an inveterate hatred of all foreigners', but 'as a mission we deprecate the idea of seeking the support of an armed force in carrying on our work, and our missionaries are prepared to meet dangers and opposition in the conflict of Christianity with heathenism'.

Joseph Ridgeway, the outspoken editor of the *Church Missionary Intelligencer*, observed of Lord Stanley's hope that missionaries would 'conduct themselves with circumspection',

> By all the great Societies with whose principles and modes of action we are acquainted this has been done. There has been no startling invasion of the interior; no sudden irruption of a strong body of Europeans into the midst of a heathen

city, with which they have had no previous acquaintance.

Ridgeway's purpose was defensive. While only newspaper reports and Parliamentary Blue Books were available, without the underlying facts, his dissociation of the major societies from Hudson Taylor's 'startling invasion of the interior' and 'sudden irruption by a strong body of Europeans' was to be expected. As late as 1899, when Eugene Stock's *History of the CMS* was published, Hudson Taylor was still being blamed, but with better understanding. Stock recorded of 1869:

> There was no lack of sympathy for the missionaries who suffered, or of approval of the action of the British Consul at Shanghai in going up the river at once in a gunboat, examining into the affair, and demanding reparation from the authorities at Nanking. The attack on the Mission, however, was rather the occasion than the cause of his action ... The English Government had been on the look-out for a convenient opportunity of making a demonstration. It was in the interest, therefore, more of the merchants than of the missionaries that a fleet of seven ships-of-war presently appeared. But of course it suited the anti-missionary public at home to indulge in the usual tirade about 'the Gospel and the Gunboat'; and this was done with the omission of no element of offensiveness by the Duke of Somerset in the House of Lords.

What was true of Britain was also true of the press in China, before and after news of the Lords' debate arrived.

In the *Chinese Recorder* a letter under the pseudonym 'Arthur Challoner', patently the British consul Challoner Alabaster, came to the defence of missionaries in general, who had been ridiculed in the *Saturday Review*, with Hudson Taylor bearing the brunt of 'the uncalled-for attacks which seem to be the fashion . . . This attack—light, yet bitter—the last and happiest production . . . of the reviler . . . will be a matter of surprise to no one.' Directed against the losses sustained by 'the Taylor Mission' it had read,

Would Mr Taylor have done his duty to those who sent him out, had he refused to state (the value of the property destroyed) when called on by the authorities? A concertina and a sedan chair seem extraordinary to the writer at home, but to people out here who know the necessity of chairs, and to missionaries who know the utility of some musical instrument ... it would be an evidence that Mr Taylor's Mission approached apostolic simplicity in its appointments: that one chair only, and a humble musical instrument only, were the extent of its possessions ...

Never was such little justice (done) as against Mr Taylor and his companions. Poor, unfriended, unbacked by a powerful society at home, they had no opportunity, even had they had the inclination, for excess ... For years and years the mission-haters have abused the Protestant missionaries for not going into the interior; and now they do so, the cry is at once that they must be confined to the ports.[104]

Reports of the debate in the House of Lords were the next to reach China and drew the wrath of the *Chinese Recorder*'s editor. 'Hostility to foreigners as such, on the part of certain literati . . . was plainly the animus of the whole affair.' Suppose that the Duke should be the victim of violence after shipwreck on Taiwan, that one of his eyes [like Reid's] should be injured and that the consular authorities should exact prompt reparation—would that be propagating the British system of nobility by gunboat? No more was Mr Taylor propagating Christianity with gunboats! He and his party were assaulted because they were foreigners, to drive them out. As for the duke and earl saying that Christianity should follow 'in the wake of civilisation and progress', they should have recognised that 'If England has any civilisation and progress to bring to China, they are the result of Christianity . . . Christianity is not accustomed to travel in the wake of anything.' His Grace was 'anxious to know what chance we have of reducing these missions, or, at least, of not allowing them to go still further up the country'. 'None, may it please your Grace— not the slightest imaginable chance!' As for sending British missionaries out of China, 'a country where they have as much (legal) right to be as the Duke has to his place in the House of Lords', he shows a disregard for constitutional law.

Lord Clarendon fared no better. In Africa, India, Burma, China, the best response to the missionary's message has been 'away from the marts of trade'. How could he think that 'material advantage to themselves' could be a good basis for Christianity? And was *The Times*, in accusing missionaries of being impudent, uneducated and ignorant of Chinese thought and culture, perhaps ignorant of Wells Williams's masterly *Middle Kingdom* and James Legge's incomparable *Chinese Classics*?—and of the fact that 'no class (of foreigner) makes more rapid advancement, after arrival here, in these regards' than missionaries? Finally, 'All this talk is wide of the case in hand. No want of "learning", no lack of "knowledge of mankind", no rushing in to "controversy" had anything to do with the Yangchow Outrage.'

Such vindication by others spared Hudson Taylor the necessity to set the record straight and eased the suffering that so many slanders inevitably caused. But the circulation of the *Chinese Recorder* was small. It reached few outside China. The damage done by the newspapers and wild rhetoric in Parliament extended throughout the British empire and into the palaces of China's rulers. Li Hongzhang had taken up his post at Wuchang as viceroy of Hubei, Hunan and Anhui when. Griffith John wrote of him:

> Our Viceroy is a very intelligent man, and anti-foreign to the backbone. He knows just as well as I do all that has been said in the House of Lords, and all that has appeared in *The Times* on missionary enterprise. He sees that we are despised and distrusted, and he knows that we are at his mercy. It is certain, too, that the Chinese Government will grant us no privileges willingly. The policy of the Government is, was, and ever will be to oppose the hated foreigner, whether missionary or merchant, in his every attempt to obtain a foothold in the interior.

(As for attacks in the press), the work and the agents have been misrepresented, calumniated, and ridiculed in no measured terms by many of your leading newspapers, and by some of the peers of the realm. Here in China, too, they have been handled rather roughly ... Men who have never put a foot within the door of a missionary's house, chapel, or schoolroom think they have a right to speak authoritatively of him and his labours.

The damage had gone further than Griffith John anticipated. Before long the LMS in London issued instructions that all their missionaries should confine themselves to the treaty ports. Griffith John had been extending his work through the Wuhad complex of three cities, Hankou, Wuchang and Hanyang, and into the provinces. His epic journey through Sichuan and Shaanxi had ended only recently, in September 1868—a journey from which he confessed that he hardly expected to come back alive. He looked forward to establishing a church at Chengdu in Sichuan, where Alexander Wylie had been stoned. At this point the storm in Britain stirred up by the Duke of Somerset and the papers had caused the LMS, and the Wesleyan Methodist Missionary Society also, to shackle their great pioneers in China. Not until twenty years later was the first LMS missionary stationed at Chongqing in Sichuan.

Griffith John protested vigorously against being told to withdraw even from Wuchang. His foothold had been resisted for four months by the literati and only the help of the consul had secured him his treaty right to reside there. To retreat would be to close down everywhere. The LMS premises had been built by contributions from the European community who would have to be consulted. He won his point, over Wuchang only. Wardlaw Thompson, John's biographer, commented on this episode, 'When the spirit of the pioneer is dead, the Christian Society which has to record the fact begins to write its own epitaph.'[105]

Speak or be silent?
(March–September 1869)

Hudson Taylor's silence during this long period as the scapegoat speaks more loudly than the little he wrote. But a letter to his mother, to whom he could always unburden his heart, showed how deeply he was feeling the criticism. Reading it superficially and out of context, some might miss the point and see Hudson Taylor's resolve being undermined, with 'self-pitying isolation' creeping into his correspondence, as has been said. In the same context, Latourette, on the other hand, rightly continued after summarising some of the adversities Hudson Taylor was up against, 'Yet Taylor was undismayed and prayed and planned for the expansion of the Mission.'[106] Isolation he certainly never experienced while enjoying strong friendships with those around him. From Ninghai on his southern tour he confided to his mother on March 13,

Often have I asked you to remember me in prayer; and when I have done so there has been need of it. That need has never been greater than at the present time. Envied by some, despised by many, hated, perhaps, by others; often blamed for things I never heard of, or had anything to do with; an innovator on what have become established rules of missionary practice; an opponent of a strong system of heathen error and superstition; working without precedent in many respects, and with few experienced helpers; often sick in body, as well as perplexed in mind, and embarrassed by circumstances; had not the Lord been specially gracious to me; had not my mind been sustained by the conviction that the work was the Lord's, and that He was with me in—what it is no empty figure to call—the thick of the conflict, I must have fainted and broken down. But the battle is the Lord's. And He will conquer. We may fail, do fail continually, but He never fails ... My own position becomes more and more responsible, and the need of special grace to fill it greater, but I have continually to mourn that I follow at such a distance, and learn so slowly to imitate my precious Master. I cannot tell you how I am buffeted sometimes by temptation.

I never knew how bad a heart I had. Yet I do know that I love God, and love His work, and desire to serve Him only, and in all things ... Never were there more thick clouds about us than at this moment; but never was there more encouragement than at the present time. Nay, might I not say that the very discouragements are themselves encouragements?[107]

He had passed through Ninghai thirteen months ago and prayed that the gospel might soon be preached there. For months the city and surrounding villages had shown a willingness to listen, and five men were asking the evangelist Feng Nenggui for baptism: 'These are very great results, accomplished by God in a new station and in a very short time (but) I incline to think we are on the eve of no slight persecution in China. The power of the Gospel has been little felt heretofore. The foreign element has been the great stumbling block.'

Sir Rutherford Alcock's attitude to missionaries in his communiqués to the Foreign Office had become known through Lord Clarendon's speeches, to the indignation of the whole Protestant missionary body. On the following day in writing to Maria, Hudson Taylor said he thought the (British) government might even compel them to stop wearing Chinese clothes 'or otherwise interfere with our freedom of action'. On June 9 he went further in telling an unnamed colleague to 'wrestle in prayer' and work hard while she could. 'It seems very likely that we shall be recalled from all our stations in the interior in a short time, or that the Chinese will be told that we shall no longer be sustained in our residence there . . . Our position is not, however, more dark than that of the Jews in the time of Esther, nor is God less mighty and gracious.'

In Britain the pressure on the Bergers increased immensely after the Lords' debate on March 9. In his March 20 editorial of the *Occasional Paper* No 17 William Berger said many were urging him to write to the press. And to Hudson Taylor, 'The *Saturday Review* is very bitter, indeed so much so that I think no one will be turned

aside in consequence. Dr Landels kindly offers again to reply to it if I will supply the facts.' William Berger preferred to let it pass, but James van Sommer, Mary Berger's brother, believed it essential 'to correct the erroneous statements . . . propagated in public', so with his help Berger was drafting a letter to *The Times* while he still waited for Hudson Taylor's lost letters to arrive.

When pressure to present the facts overcame his unwillingness, he simply gave the gist of reports from the victims of the riot, stressing that they only notified Vice-Consul Allen late in the events. 'We could have written far more strongly,' he said, 'but we thought it best to act cautiously and as Christians not recriminatingly.' But after he had posted his letter, days passed and it was not published, until during an evening with a friend named Brodie, 'who has a share in *The Times*', they discussed Yangzhou and Brodie offered to unearth and secure the insertion of William Berger's letter. A month later the picture had changed considerably. 'One of the Editors of *The Times* (he who offered to have it inserted) was very pleased with it and sent me a guinea for the Mission.' Correspondence all the more dominated the Bergers' lives, with many commendations of the letter. 'We really have done comparatively little else. Today James (van Sommer) and I have been writing Lords Clarendon and Shaftesbury, the Duke of Somerset and Bishops (of) Peterboro' (Magee) and St David's' enclosing copies of the letter to *The Times*, and to three of them *China: Its Spiritual Need and Claims* and the *Occasional*. R. C. Morgan also reproduced the letter in *Revival*.

Some of Hudson Taylor's missing letters at last turned up on May 1, leaving two earlier ones still to be accounted for. Meanwhile Maria had answered the vital questions and it looked as if the subject of Yangzhou had 'had its day'. People were wanting normal news again.

What Maria had written on February 11 was:

> In the riot we asked the protection of the Chinese Mandarin: my dear Husband did not see it right to neglect this means

of possibly saving our lives. After our lives were safe, and we were in shelter, we asked no restitution, we desired no revenge ... All that my dear Husband did in the way of giving details etc. was at the Consul's request. Perhaps one secret of our matter being taken up so warmly was that it was looked upon as a climax to a series of provocations which the English had received from the Chinese. And the representatives of our government were I believe not sorry to have an opportunity of good ground for settling off a number of 'old accounts'. We felt that it was our God who had so disposed events that our matter should have happened at such a crisis. And is there not a great difference between resisting evil ourselves and defending ourselves by offensive means such as the use of firearms etc. (which some missionaries out here think it right to do) and availing ourselves of the protection which our Government surely pledges itself to afford us when it renders it compulsory on us to take out Passports every year? ... We did not in this instance even ask our Consul to right our wrongs ...

As to the harsh judgings of the world, or the more painful misunderstandings of Christian brethren, I generally feel that the best plan is to go on with our work and leave God to vindicate our cause ... It would be undesirable to print the fact that Mr Medhurst—and through him Sir Rutherford Alcock—took up the matter without application. The new Ministry at home censures those out here for the policy which the late Ministry enjoined upon them ... The fact that my dear Husband had his wife and children with him stamped him in the eyes of respectable people as a respectable man—not one likely to swindle them or be off without sign or trace ... As to the number of persons that were in the house at the time, that was occasioned by circumstances beyond our control.

[And on May 2] I don't think it ever occurred to us that Christian friends at home might be stumbled by our rulers espousing our cause, and requiring for us both restoration and restitution. We fully believed that God could and would

far more than make up to us our losses—perhaps not in kind, but ... in His own way of supplying our need.[108]

Warm letters and generous gifts from George Müller, Philip Gosse, the Howards, Lord Congleton and others did more to encourage the battered Bergers and Taylors. An anonymous contributor to the *Chinese Recorder* by his cogent observations also showed that they had more firm friends in China, taking the offensive against the critics:

> Should it not be rendered illegal for noble Lords, Dukes, or Earls to attempt to speak or legislate upon subjects about which they are profoundly ignorant, without first at least reading the Parliamentary Blue Books printed for their special information? Even a cursory glance at the sworn statement of facts, which forms a part of the Parliamentary Blue Book on the Yangchow riot, would have nipped many of the most plausible speeches against missionaries in the bud.[109]

Not every friend used anonymity to command attention. One in particular rose to the CIM's defence.

Miles Knowlton sums up (May 1869)

Strong intervention to do justice to the maligned missionaries came from the American Miles J. Knowlton, DD, the Taylors' faithful friend since the days of their painful courtship in Ningbo. He as much as anyone in the treaty ports knew what it was to 'itinerate' deep into the countryside. Known as 'Christ-like', his obituary in the *Chinese Recorder* five years later when he succumbed to virulent dysentery, said of him, 'There are no people, we are persuaded . . . who possess the power of gauging character in a more accurate manner than the Chinese . . . He was often designated by them "the Western Confucius", the highest compliment they could possibly pay him . . . They gave him credit for very high moral placidity.'[110]

In a ten-column paper dated May 22, 1869, he examined the reports on the Yangzhou riot, the debate in the House of Lords, editorials and letters to the press and official documents reproduced in the Parliamentary Blue Books and *Morning Star,* emphasising that no one had asked him to do so. It was owed to all missionaries that the facts should be established and that blame should rest only where it belonged. No more than a summary of his arguments can be given here. In China, at least, they satisfied serious questioners and removed the growing necessity for Hudson Taylor to speak out in defence of the truth.

'Ignorance of the facts' was Knowlton's starting-point. 'All the speakers in the debate, and all the editors whose papers I have noticed, appear to take it for granted that the riot arose from the "imprudence" of the missionaries.' How strange, he said, that 'these zealous decriers of missions to the Chinese, have nothing to say, no fault to find with the infamous opium trade.'

1. They had complained of the imprudence of going to Yangzhou so far inland beyond consular jurisdiction, whereas Yangzhou was 'in sight from the (Zhenjiang) British Consulate' and only an hour and a half by pony from the river. What use was a consulate if its writ did not extend so short a distance?

2. The Yangzhou missionaries had passports, the requirement by agreement between governments to permit unlimited travel within the Chinese empire. A passport holder was under the protection of his own government and that of the nation which ratified it. Yet Lord Clarendon had spoken of 'places where no consular authority is at hand'. Merchants and men of science as well as missionaries were constantly travelling far from the consular ports. Was the passport system to be dispensed with?

3. Before going to Yangzhou the missionaries had consulted consular officials 'of different nationalities [American and French] as to the propriety and practicability of residing there'; and they had all agreed that they had the right, and that it was undoubtedly feasible for them to do so.

4. They had obtained an official dispatch from no less than the *daotai* to the Yangzhou mandarin, stating the missionaries' purpose 'and directing them to afford them protection and aid' in exerting their right to rent premises. 'That the Chinese government and the provincial officers do admit this right, is proved by the fact that foreigners do actually possess houses and reside in every province in the empire'—the Roman Catholics.

5. A proclamation by the Yangzhou magistrate in obeying the *daotai's* order had allayed any fears the people might have had, and greatly helped in the rental of premises in a quiet part of the city.

6. Hudson Taylor had been blamed for going to Yangzhou 'in so large a party'. But only he and 'his family' had been there, quietly living in boats and then in an inn for a month during which they found both people and authorities friendly and co-operative. Only when the Rudlands had been prevented from staying at Zhenjiang had they joined the Taylors in Yangzhou, for lack of anywhere else to go. Others were merely visitors passing through, 'one or two having arrived on the very day of the riot ... The *Saturday Review* makes itself merry over the "indemnity for losses extorted from the Chinese."' Far from overcharging, Hudson Taylor's inventory of property stolen and destroyed had fallen short by several hundred dollars. 'The *Saturday Review* misrepresents them as demanding indemnity, but they did not, and the compensation and penalties demanded by Consul Medhurst were most moderate and just.'

7. 'The preaching of Christianity, and especially by declaiming against ancestral worship' had been generally assumed but 'had nothing whatever to do with exciting the disturbance'. No preaching at all had yet taken place. 'Indeed, if a small body of independent men, acting under no central authority, act with so much discretion as facts proved they did, what paragons of . . . prudence must be the missionaries . . . of the great Missionary Societies!'

'How then was the riot caused? . . . By the instigation of the gentry (who) held a secret meeting . . . and deliberately formed their plan for ejecting the foreigners,' emboldened by the withdrawal of the British consul from Zhenjiang and by the Zhenjiang magistrate's success in thwarting Hudson Taylor's attempts to rent premises there. An American Baptist missionary (Horace Jenkins) had only just received rough treatment at Jinhua. 'The contract for a house had been signed but the gentry compelled the owner to sell it instead to them and proceeded to dismantle and move every stick and brick of it'—in spite of the Burlingame treaty of reciprocity![111]

Miles Knowlton then recounted the provocations by handbills and posters and the events of the Yangzhou riot, of Hudson Taylor's repeated petitions to the prefect of Yangzhou, whose failure to act clearly implicated him in conniving with the literati who had raised the mob.

Miles Knowlton had enquired carefully among Chinese and learned that fear lay behind the opposition, fear of unprincipled foreigners coming after the missionaries, 'with sufficient capital to take the trade out of the hands of our native merchants.' 'Is there any act, any course of procedure of the missionaries, to which the blame can be attached? . . . No, no, noble Dukes, Earls and Lords . . . it was not the propagation of Christianity but the persistent reiterated report that the foreigners "boiled and ate babies"! . . . The root of the opposition . . . is not found in any repugnance to Christianity, but in hatred to all foreigners, as such have . . . often been driven from places in the interior . . . At Taiwan . . . gunboats were called in more to vindicate the treaty rights of the merchants, than those of missionaries. The same was substantially the case at Yangchow.' At Shantou and Xiamen (Swatow and Amoy) the serious disturbances had nothing to do with missionaries. Dr Maxwell's protest in the *Chinese Recorder* for April 1869 made the truth about the Taiwan riots abundantly plain. China and the Chinese were exceedingly tolerant of Christianity. Neither they nor the missionaries were culpable. The 'unjust and unrighteous mandarins' and the literati out of office were entirely to blame.

Knowlton finally summarised Consul Medhurst's August 31, 1868, dispatch to Sir Rutherford, reprinted from the Parliamentary Blue Book in the *Morning Star* of February 18, 1869. He applauded his settlement of the whole affair, before offering his own views on how diplomatic relations with the China of the mandarins were best conducted locally, as they had

been, and not by central governments. In a word, missionaries and Hudson Taylor in particular had been made the butt of unjustified blame, the scapegoat for the sins of others.

By September Hudson Taylor was able to write, 'Mr Knowlton's paper on the Yangchau riot has done good here in many quarters and has helped to draw back to their former sympathy some who were a little shaken by some of the false reports which had been industriously circulated. Strange work for some of the Lord's people to be engaged in!'[112]

A few late firecrackers had yet to break the silence, but the Yangzhou issue had run its course for the present and both Hudson Taylor and the Bergers could breathe again. *The Times* was among the last to relent. Someone using the nom de plume 'Veritas', in a letter from Shanghai, dated August 17, described Protestant missionaries as '(enjoying) perfect immunity from all personal danger (with) the inevitable gunboat under the window'. 'The readers of *The Times* will of course understand,' the *Chinese Recorder*'s editor commented, 'that gunboats in China always anchor directly under missionary windows, and are kept here exclusively for the protection of missionaries, who, having "perfect immunity from all personal danger" must always be in need of them.'[113] Taunt and riposte could both have been just for the laugh, but bitterness lay behind the jibe—just another way of baiting the Hudson Taylor bear.

In 1872 when the dust had settled to some extent and Hudson Taylor published a slim report of the years since 1865, he allowed himself this statement:

> We cannot but remark upon the unfair view which was taken of this matter at the time in the public papers at home. We do not remember to have seen it once noticed, that the armed interposition which was made, unsolicited by us, had mainly for its object, and actually resulted in, the settlement of commercial difficulties, the obtaining of pecuniary compensation for mercantile losses, and the restoration of waning British prestige.[114]

The bear's head was still sore—but from new baiting.

'The Missionary Question' again (1869)

Building the next chronological tier upon those already laid we have reached the critical period recognised by Hudson Taylor in his references to the threat of being forced back from the 'interior' to the ghetto settlements of the treaty ports. While Anson Burlingame spoke in glowing terms of China's imagined welcome to messengers of the 'shining cross' (see pp 11–12), the Court and Grand Council of the Chinese government were pressing for greater restrictions, and the British government was inclining in the same direction. In April 1869 the *Scotsman* in an article from China on 'The Late Disturbances in China' had usefully pictured the ruling body in accurate if uncomplimentary terms.

> The Government of Pekin consists of a boy of thirteen years' of age, the Emperor (Tong Zhi), of whom little is known, except that he is not intelligent, and that he has a violent temper; his mother, the Empress Dowager, who is believed to be a shrewd woman; a eunuch, who is the favourite of the Empress Dowager, and has secretly great power; Prince Kong, who is a subtle quick-witted man, fond of dissipation, and has a strong head for liquor. All these are Tartars, and, although they govern through a mixed body of Tartar and Chinese Ministers, they are the heads of the Government.[115]

In his memorial to the throne on the 'barbarian question', the viceroy of Hunan and Hubei, Li Hongzhang, had advocated far-reaching 'restrictions to missionary liberty (through) regulations for the control of Missions', even to the extent of 'placing missionaries under Chinese jurisdiction', with all that those ominous words implied. And it was in 1869 that Wen Xiang, Grand Secretary of the Council (see 1, pp 734, 823), in addressing Sir Rutherford as British Minister said (according to Hawks Pott), 'Do away with your extra-territorial clause [allowing Western justice on Chinese soil] and merchant and missionary may settle anywhere and everywhere; retain it, and we must do our best to confine you and our troubles to the treaty ports.'[116]

The riots and outrages already experienced at the instigation of the literati left little room for the hope that the annulment of extra-territorial privileges would result in a change of attitude. With or without protection by treaty, foreigners threatened the ancient institutions, the merchants by their newfangled machinery, railways, telegraph and tainted merchandise, the missionary by offensive architecture and doctrines which challenged the ancient beliefs and practices. Sir Rutherford therefore resisted the Zongli Yamen's proposals, while advocating to the Foreign Office in London an equivalent shackling of British subjects' movements. Certainly he was in no doubt that (to understate the case) the submission of foreigners to Chinese law would deprive them of the kind of justice they could expect from their own governments.

When news of the debate in the House of Lords (on the Yangzhou riots) and its repercussions in the press had reached Peking, the missionaries there responded

2.12 H. E. Wen Xiang

with characteristic energy. Astonished by what they read, John Burdon and William Collins of the CMS, and John Dudgeon, MD, and Joseph Edkins of the LMS boldly asked Sir Rutherford if they might read his dispatches to Lord Clarendon, which had not been published in the Parliamentary Blue Books, in order to answer them. They knew their man. Sir Rutherford had nothing he was ashamed of. He furnished them with 'copious extracts', and on July 14 they addressed to him a long and closely reasoned letter, expressing their intention that it should be seen also by the Secretary of State for Foreign Affairs.

The 'Missionary Memorandum', as it came to be called, challenged Alcock's claim that missionaries should be confined to the treaty ports before they did more damage to Britain's commercial interests in China. It protested that any hostility by the Chinese was to foreigners, not to missionaries as such. As for commerce being Britain's main object in China, opium was the main commodity! 'Honourable commerce has nothing to fear from Protestant missionaries.' Then Sir Rutherford complained of the revolutionary tendencies of Christianity. True, from the beginning it had been turning the world upside down, but it was in no way seditious or comparable with 'the settlement in Peking of a British Minister, at the point of a bayonet'! Sir Rutherford's thesis could not bear examination.

Alcock replied briefly, promising to forward their letter to Lord Clarendon with comments. A week later John Burdon (Maria's brother-in-law) sent a copy of the joint letter to the *Chinese Recorder* for publication, with his own introduction.

In this he drew attention to the salient points at issue. Writing strongly in support of Hudson Taylor, he went further to resist the move to restrict missionaries to the treaty ports. Lord Clarendon appeared to lean too hard upon Sir Rutherford's 'great experience in China', and had been misled by what he understood him to be saying. 'According to Lord Clarendon, Sir Rutherford "doubted whether any

prospect of success . . . would compensate the dangers (the missionaries) incurred in disregarding not only the laws but the advice of their own government." Thus the British Minister was made to accuse the Protestant missionaries of "disregarding the laws of China!"' And not only Lord Clarendon: the *Pall Mall Gazette* had made 'a ludicrous mistake' by misinterpreting a vague reference by Lord Clarendon in the House to 'a most offensive placard against the Roman Catholic religion (posted on) the walls of Shanghai'. According to the *Gazette*, the Protestants had contrived the offending placard! So what would they not do to revile the religions of China? Foreign Minister and fallible press needed to know the facts:

> When it comes to be understood by Lord Clarendon, as it will be by and by, that the Chinese government is half, 'if not wholly, in sympathy with those local mandarins and native gentry in their opposition to foreigners, and that the authority of the central government over their subordinates and the literati is at best a very questionable thing, it will then be seen that in certain extreme cases, such as that of Yangchow, Sir Rutherford Alcock's action is of more avail toward bringing the problem of foreign intercourse with China to a peaceful solution than all his theorisings about restricting missionaries to the treaty ports.
> J. S. Burdon, Peking, July 23rd, 1869.[117]

In his comments to the LMS directors on the same issue of shackling the missionary, Griffith John was no less explicit.[118] But even after his powerful pleading, the London-based ruling body of the LMS declined to retract their own strong restraints upon their missionaries in China. In loyalty they were reluctantly obeyed while the CIM surged forwards—until the climate of opinion changed and the irrepressible spirit of the pioneer evangelist was given rein to extend its frontiers. Meanwhile, true to his word, Alcock sent the 'Missionary Memorandum' to London where it was published in the Parliamentary Papers of 1870.[119]

After protracted negotiations, Sir Rutherford concluded an Anglo-Chinese

Convention with the Zongli Yamen on October 23, 1869. Alcock's signature should have been final; Prince Kong and four other ministers signed for China, and the emperor's seal was affixed to the treaty. When commercial, not missionary, criticism led the British government to refuse to ratify it, the emperor was deeply insulted and his ministers humiliated beyond redress. As they saw it, British perfidy had yet again been unmasked. That Sir Rutherford had lost face mattered little.

Not only the British were involved, the French were a law unto themselves. But American missionaries and their successive ministers at Peking were by no means silent. In May 1869 the American missionaries of Ningbo petitioned the Hon J. Ross Browne to secure protection for them in the rental of land and buildings. In June Miles Knowlton wrote personally, and in July conveyed to the *Chinese Recorder*[120] the substance of the US minister's reply. To Ross Browne he said:

> The British Government (influenced by the representations, or rather misrepresentations, of Sir Rutherford Alcock) appears disposed to withdraw all protection from residents in the interior, taking in fact a retrograde step. This measure if carried out, will be sure to make those officials and literati who are opposed to foreigners all the more bold and contumacious ... Should that policy result in the driving of the numerous Protestant missionary establishments from the interior ... the result would be to put back the friendly relations of the Chinese with foreigners more than twenty years.

> [The minister replied.] Your memorial and letters are now on the way to Washington, with my most cordial endorsement ... From my first dispatches ... I took up their cause with all my energy. At first I thought it would be better for them not to press too hard against native prejudices, or incur risks by pushing too vigorously into the interior; but I soon gave that up as untenable, and entirely inconsistent with the object in view ... Opposition must be expected and must be overcome. It will never be overcome by standing still or retreating.

The 'Missionary Question' would never cease to be harped upon. In 1871 the Chinese government raised it with renewed vigour. Over a century later it was again under inquiry, this time prompted by the viewpoint of the People's Republic of China. Just as Robert Morrison by sheer force of circumstance became inseparable from his fellow-countrymen of diametrically opposite motives and practice, so each generation of missionary continued to be inextricably implicated in the use of force and the traffic in opium. As the historian George Woodcock put it, 'Always, until the end of the British presence in China, the missionary was beset by a conflict of loyalties. He owed one duty to his religion and the people he was trying to convert, another duty to his country. And there were times when, even against his will, his very presence became an excuse for his country's power to be tightened over the land in which he worked.'[121]

Alford's mission[122] (January–May 1869)

The Bishop of Victoria's prolonged 'visitation' of his scattered diocese had opened his eyes. Complimenting the missions he had visited, he stressed the inadequacy of all that was being done to give the gospel to this huge empire and 'boldly faced the question of founding a new (Anglican) society to remedy the situation'. But his proposition of a new Church Mission for China had a frigid reception in London.

The uproar over the Yangzhou riot, the notorious debate in the Lords, and its repercussions in the press, had needled the big societies into defending their own reputations. 'No startling invasion of the interior; no sudden irruption of a strong body of Europeans' had expressed their defensive attitude. Even if innocent of either a startling invasion or sudden irruption, Hudson Taylor and the CIM were believed to be guilty of both epithets. So they were embarrassing comrades-in-arms. Alford's proposal was condemned (to use Stock's words), 'on the ground that it would be an imitation of the China Inland Mission!' 'The conception is grand,' its opponents declared, 'the execution impracticable, and, if attempted, disastrous', like the charge of the Light Brigade. To send 'numerous missionaries' to China would only mean 'a lowering of the standard, and a mistrust of Native evangelists who would do the work better'. But where were the Chinese evangelists? Sixty-two years after Morrison arrived in China, few converts and fewer trained evangelists even existed. In August 1869 Protestant missionaries in China numbered in all 151 men, 129 women, with 365 Chinese church workers of all kinds, and fewer than 6,000 communicant members in a nation of hundreds of millions. However unwelcome, foreign missionaries in growing numbers would have to share the spadework for a long while to come if the job was to be done and enough Chinese Christians won

to permeate the empire. So Bishop Alford's scheme was never carried out. 'The pioneer work in the interior was to be done by the humble and despised agency which Alford was supposed to be imitating.'

But Eugene Stock was writing thirty years later. At the time Hudson Taylor seemed to stand alone, all but crushed by the difficulty of putting his vision into effect and by disappointment over some of his team.

'Always on the move' (January–May 1869)

While the aftermath of the Yangzhou riot was in motion, it had been 'business as usual' for the Mission and the Taylors—except that for them the usual was the constant cropping up of the unusual. Much was happening and many letters remain to illuminate this difficult year. Its very complexity may best be seen by following Hudson Taylor through it, travelling with him as he led his team, constantly at their beck and call. Within the complexity the pattern is apparent.

Yangzhou was home, at least as the place where the Taylors' personal possessions and mission records were kept. From there frequent journeys were made, across the Yangzi to Zhenjiang on business; upriver to Nanjing and beyond, or down to Shanghai as need demanded; and south by the Grand Canal or coastal steamer to the work centres of the southern region.

In the Yangzi area he now had Meadows and Williamson, two hundred miles to the south-west at Anqing, living on a boat after their arrival there on January 8, and then at an inn. Fifty miles away George and Catherine Duncan and Mary Bowyer were at Nanjing with Elizabeth Meadows and her two children. The rudiments of a congregation and little schools for boys under George, and girls under Mary Bowyer, fully occupied them and their Chinese colleague Li Tianfu.

William and Mary Rudland and their printing staff in the Chinese city of Zhenjiang were making what use they could of the presses, pending the move into their own house in the Chinese city on January 15, and providing a staging-post and business centre for members of the team. Missionaries passing through, renewing passports at the consulate or wanting Hudson Taylor's medical help, stayed with the Rudlands.

Charles and Elizabeth Judd and Louise Desgraz, with Mr Yu's help after he joined them from Hangzhou, supplied the continuity at Yangzhou, inconspicuously giving the gospel to enquiring Chinese no longer afraid to visit them. Edward Fishe, Emily Blatchley, Maria, Annie Bohannan and the children came and went as circumstances directed.

The Cordons and Henry Reid were at Suzhou. Absent for six weeks at a time to preach in the villages, Reid himself had apparently recovered from his riot injuries, except emotionally. Apprehension of violence sapped the enjoyment of his work. Robert and Frances (Gainfort) White lived with the Cordons, although not members of the CIM. In the Yangzi region alone, Hudson Taylor therefore had eighteen missionaries and their children and half a dozen Chinese Christian workers under his care.

The southern field was correspondingly depleted by the move northwards and the resignation of Stephan Barchet, Susan Barnes, the McLean sisters and the Nicols. The John McCarthys, Jennie Faulding, Wang Lae-djün and his wife were building up the Hangzhou congregation, with McCarthy also overseeing the Ningbo church. Midway between the two cities, John and Anne Stevenson were slogging on at Shaoxing with a handful of newly baptised Christians at last to encourage them.

Thirty miles south of Ningbo, George and Anne Crombie with Fan Qiseng and Wang Guoyao served the growing local church and its outposts, now including Ninghai, halfway to Taizhou, a hundred miles southwards. Josiah Jackson and the Cardwells, not one of them either contented or effective, hung on at Taizhou,

still seeing greener grass over the fence in other places, and leaving their post from time to time on one pretext or another.

A hundred miles still further south, George Stott tenaciously ran his little school for boys and preached to any Chinese who visited the chapel. But Stott seemed slow to learn wisdom, and often faced difficulties of his own making. One night death-wails startled him at 2.00 a.m. A child had died of 'croup' in a nearby house. The father called in the *fengshui* expert to discover why it had happened.

> After casting about for some time, (he) pronounced it to be the furnace in my kitchen which had caused the sudden death. A deputation soon waited upon me to request me to pull down the unfortunate thing, as it had an unlucky number of holes in it; but I maintained the innocence of the fire-place, and would not consent to its removal. Then another expert said it was my horse; he was put in a place which was not primarily intended for a horse, and so had upset the equilibrium of the elements ... The poor afflicted father thought I was bent on the destruction of his family, for another child was sick by this time ... Then he went to the city temple; the gods there said he must move away; so he did next morning.[123]

Superstitions made it difficult for Stott, but an unbending attitude could not help. He was lonely and had written to Glasgow to ask Grace Ciggie to marry him.

The medical care of missionaries and others made increasing demands on Hudson Taylor's time. There was a doctor in the international settlement at Ningbo, but his fees excluded most members of the CIM from consulting him. Hudson Taylor was willing to attend them whenever possible, and planned his visits to fit in with confinements; but the abnormal life they lived made calculation of when he would be needed difficult for them. All were young, and pregnancies were frequent. Often severe illness and emergencies tore him away from whatever he was doing. Because of his coming and going, members of other missions, merchants and consular officials, far from Ningbo, Shanghai and Hankou, and other doctors also looked to him for medical attention.

Long business and pastoral letters flowed from his pen, often headed 'on a boat near' wherever he might be. Canal travel was smooth and relatively fast. He was fully at home sitting on his bed-roll in a footboat or lying full length working. Once he arrived at his destinations, he joined in the local activities. Always in demand for doctoring, preaching and discussing problems he, and more often Maria, had to play matchmaker for local church members. Arranged marriages were customary in China and, with Christians so few, they depended on help in finding wives and husbands for each other. When visiting E. C. Lord's or other girls' schools in Ningbo, Hudson Taylor would enquire on their behalf or negotiate for a particular one.

Maria sometimes travelled with him and sometimes joined him at his patient's home to nurse the mother and infant after Hudson's work was done. Emily went with her if she took the children to stay with the McCarthys for a change of company. Emily's secretarial work continued wherever they were. When Hudson Taylor was upcountry he would send the letters he wrote via Maria and Emily to be given serial numbers and copied for filing before being posted.

George and Annie Crombie had already lost two babies. Hudson Taylor's gratitude for their sacrificial spirit when Richard Truelove had forfeited his passage on the *Corea* (see 1, p 607), made him doubly willing to go early to Fenghua and wait for the birth of their third. At the end of January he went first to Hangzhou on the way to Fenghua. Not until June 25 was he to reach home again. Maria, Emily and the family arrived at Hangzhou on February 2 for their first reunion with their many friends since the previous year, and Hudson Taylor invited Wang Lae-djün and all fifty or more church members to a Chinese New Year feast. But no sooner had they reached New Lane than the baby Charles Edward fell ill with bronchitis. After a week he was better and they went on to Ningbo, within call of Fenghua.

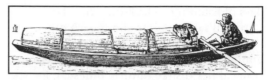

2.13 *Footboats are rowed by leg-power*

Early in January, Stephan Barchet and Mary Bausum, now eighteen, had been married. A week later her mother, Mrs Lord, fell ill with pneumonia and died on the 15th. As Mrs Bausum she had been the staunch friend of Maria and Hudson Taylor through the opposition to their engagement and marriage, and ever since. Her death was the removal of yet another prop in their vulnerable lives, and the loss of one of the hardest working missionaries of any society in China. For Hudson and Maria to move with their family into their first home above the Bridge Street chapel, and from there to visit the Goughs and E. C. Lord and Mary, aroused deep emotions. They had only just left their own daughter Grace's grave and wrestled with Charles Edward's sudden serious bronchitis.

On February 28 all were at Fenghua, and Annie's confinement appears to have been safely over. For on March 13 Hudson Taylor was with Feng Nenggui and Ninghai on the way to Jackson and the Cardwells at Taizhou. He sensed the approach of 'no slight persecution in China' and advised George Crombie, who was with him, not to delay in baptising the five believers he found there. Rumours were flying. To have burned their boats would help them if persecution broke out. News of Sir Rutherford Alcock's attitude and the change of policy by Lord Clarendon and the British government had reached them. 'We need to pray especially that the Gov. may not compel us to put off (Chinese) dress or otherwise interfere with our freedom of action,' he wrote to Maria on Sunday, 14th, after three church services during the day. The Duke of Somerset's attack in the House of Lords and the onslaught in the London newspapers had been during the week just past. It would be May before he knew of them.

He went to Taizhou for a painful few

days of listening to Jackson's and the Cardwell's complaints about each other and other missionaries, their work and limitations. Mrs Cardwell could scarcely conceal her dislike of the Chinese. J. E. Cardwell's ill-health made Hudson Taylor anxious, but it might be simply that he had set his heart on pioneering far up the Yangzi River and nothing less would restore him. Hudson Taylor advised as best he could and kept it to himself for the present.

The quickest postal route to Taizhou or Wenzhou was by Ningbo and coastal steamer, so Maria sent a note to Hudson, saying that the *Chinese Recorder*'s editorial correcting '*The Times*' strictures on us' had cheered her. But Annie Crombie had fever and each of their own children was ill. On the 25th her news was worse. Little Samuel was 'much worse, passing blood every hour or so', with much pain. He was to suffer incessantly from it, but so patiently that they marvelled until he died eleven months later. She was giving him chlorodyne, but was it the right treatment? A Chinese baby in the lower part of the Crombies' house had smallpox and 'Tianbao' (Charles Edward) had come out in a rash. After reading Hudson's medical books she hoped it was a false alarm.

By then Hudson Taylor and Jackson were with Stott at Wenzhou, a large and important city, like Ningbo and Shaoxing in size. From a high hill on the overland journey they had seen the city ten miles away and counted thirty-five towns, villages and hamlets in the fertile plain around it. Taizhou in contrast had given up much of its agricultural land to growing opium poppies. Wenzhou was the farthest point on his journey and so far the least productive. Stott and his servant-companion were the only Christians, and this was the first visit by any other foreigner since they had arrived there. But after a few days with them Hudson Taylor and Jackson had to return.

The Wenzhou dialect was so different from either the Ningbo, which Hudson Taylor used in the south, or the Taizhou colloquial familiar to Jackson, that Wenzhou people could hardly understand them. The value of putting each dialect into roman script had been proved beyond doubt, and Hudson Taylor was working with Jackson to express the Taizhou dialect phonetically in roman letters. Nenggui, a completely uneducated farmer, was reading, writing and teaching his congregation at Ninghai, using the romanised New Testament and other books. Now (in the 1980s) that there are tens of thousands of Christians in each area, these humble beginnings take on new meaning.

Maria in Fenghua was schooling herself not to expect Hudson for another ten days or two weeks, when he arrived, unannounced on April 5. The three weeks they had been parted 'seemed almost like so many months', she told Mary Berger. Samuel was better, but the Crombies' new baby was now ill with bronchitis. From Wenzhou Hudson Taylor had suggested that she invite Jennie for a short holiday to visit their honeymoon beauty spots with them. Travelling with Alosao, the first Hangzhou Christian woman, in the care of John McCarthy in another boat, she reached Fenghua on Tuesday, April 13.

The Crombie baby was 'out of danger'. But early on Wednesday morning it had 'a convulsion of the throat' and died. They all set off for Ningbo and on Thursday Hudson Taylor conducted the funeral in 'the little cemetery where the remains of the Crombies' first two lay', with Maria's first, and Martha Meadows, Dr Parker, Mrs Bausum and so many of their friends. George and Annie left the next day for their outpost, to be surrounded and consoled by converted Chinese friends. 'You would have shed tears of joy at the sight,' they wrote.

Hardly an hour after they left Ningbo a messenger arrived with an urgent letter from Cardwell to say that for the last few days they had been besieged by students attending the civil and military examinations and were 'in constant fear of trouble' and almost worn out. John McCarthy and Mr Tsiu immediately offered to go with Hudson Taylor. The danger would continue for the month of examinations, and Mrs Cardwell and her child, 'great curiosities', would have to be sent to the Crombies. But when Hudson Taylor arrived 'the crisis had passed'. As soon as it became known that a message had been sent to Ningbo 'the abusive mobs (had) ceased to make trouble' and 'a great number of quiet hearers' took their place.

Hudson Taylor had decided to walk the hundred miles back to Ningbo, but that night 'evil-disposed persons' threatened them again, and he was afraid that 'if we leave and trouble should arise (Jackson and Cardwell), wearied out, might be impatient' and make matters worse. On the 26th he could only say to Maria, 'I hope the worst is over', but he did not know when he could come home. 'I do long to be with you, darling, but God has called me away and we must be content . . . Now, my love, my precious one, my own fond darling, rest in Jesus' love, lie in His arms, lean on His bosom.' The letter included a page of detailed business, about handling cheques, and trying to buy plate-glass mirrors at Shanghai and Ningbo for the Yangzhou magistrate, and ended, 'Give my love to Miss Blatchley. Tell her if she loves me to take care of herself . . . My heart yearns for you. Fondest love. JHT.' In the end he stayed the whole month, not leaving for Ningbo until about May 12.

Jennie's holiday had begun, continued and ended strangely. Without having got further than Ningbo, she left on April 21, to return to Hangzhou, sleeping head to foot with Alosao in a footboat. She scarcely knew what to tell her parents in her letters home. 'I have got so accustomed to Chinese life and ways now, that it is difficult to know what to write about.'

For Maria it was hard to wait for possible news of a riot at Taizhou, to keep her five children happy in the Bridge Street garret and to carry on the Mission correspondence in Hudson Taylor's absence. On May 2 she told Mary Berger of a cheering letter from the Judds in Yangzhou. Among several new Christians was Mr Peng the landlord of the inn they had occupied before the riot. 'I think he was much struck by my dear Husband's uprightness towards him in the matter of his indemnification . . . handing over such a large sum without deducting or at least requesting a portion, larger or smaller, as "thanks".' And on the 7th to Hudson, 'I have been writing all day and nearly all last night. Having got off the mail . . . I turn with such different feelings to rest myself in writing to you. I need not weigh my words lest I give offence or cause misunderstanding.'

In long letters to the Bergers, Miss Stacey and others in Britain she was trying to set straight the tangled maze of misstatements about the Yangzhou affair. Meeting the Goughs, the Knowltons and other old friends of bygone days in Ningbo, she had ample opportunity to give them also the facts about the riot. Miles Knowlton's vigorous letter to the *Chinese Recorder* in defence of them was written on May 22. But Maria also had more news of criticisms in the Shanghai papers to share with Hudson.

Back from Taizhou he made a flying visit all the way to Yangzhou and a week later was with Maria in Ningbo again. Writing to his mother about the 'five not very little voices' of his children around him, he commented, 'I have been astonished at the wilful falsehoods circulated by the newspapers and political men, to suit their own ends . . . Well, the Lord reigns. We must keep our eyes fixed on Him.' A passing reference to the baptism, on May 17, of their boatman is all that points to long conversations and daily explanation of Scripture to him as they travelled long distances together. So week succeeded week, and as this chronicle proceeds, enlarging on the major events, the background of similar comings and goings, griefs and delights, needs to be kept in mind.

After all they had been through without a holiday in the past year, and with no urgent demands upon them for the present, they decided to take Emily and the children to the beautiful island of Putuo in the Zhoushan (Chusan) group. With a profusion of rhododendrons, Putuo with its beautiful, long, sandy beach and tranquil temples was popular as a resort of Ningbo and Shanghai residents. For once he would drop work completely and they would enjoy the children together.

'Incurable idiot'[124] (June 1869)

For a full fortnight they seem to have made the most of this holiday. Not a line to anyone hints that any work disturbed their peace. By deduction from references before and afterwards they appear to have enjoyed Putuo from about May 20 until June 5. Then that bliss was over. By June 8, Maria, Emily and the children were with Jennie at Hangzhou and in the lakeside hills. But Hudson Taylor in Ningbo had taken up the threads of work, brought himself up to date on world news and was writing to tell a colleague to 'wrestle mightily' in prayer that they might not all be forced out of their hard won stations in the interior. The Abbé Gilles was flogged to death at Zunyi in Guizhou on June 14. To Maria, Hudson wrote on the 15th, 'My ague is over', and again on the 19th, but from Shanghai.

To his astonishment he found on reaching Shanghai that he was under attack yet again, the butt of merciless slander. Instead of completing the business he had come to do, and going straight on to rejoin Maria at Suzhou, he stayed to find out what was happening. In the *Shanghai Evening Courier* of June 14 he read:

> A report has reached us from Ningpo that the Reverend Mr Taylor of the Inland Mission, recently went on a preaching tour to Pootoo, an island, as is well known, exclusively devoted to the worship of Buddha. The priests who are the sole inhabitants of the island, protested against such an invasion of their privileges, and laid the matter before the *(daotai)*. Instructed by the latter, Mr Bowra, commissioner of customs at Ningpo, appealed to the British Consul, who has summarily ordered Mr Taylor to retire from the island.

The *North China Daily News* repeated the paragraph, and an editorial in the following evening's *Courier* enlarged, on it.

> 'Mr Taylor's Visit to Pootoo'

> Mr Taylor's religion is peripatetic. Today at Hangchow, tomorrow at Soochow, the next day making philtres of babies' eyes

at Yangchau and finally alarming the peaceful seclusion of shaven and placid priests at Pootoo, this restless apostle is as difficult to lay hold of as a flea in a blanket ... It was unnecessary to invoke the aid of the Consul to banish him from the little island where he was last heard of, for his own unquiet disposition would have carried him off speedily enough ...

We are not altogether surprised that Mr Taylor found himself at this particular time at Pootoo. Christians of his stamp, whose every step is dictated by an immediate inspiration of the Holy Spirit, are generally guided to the most pleasant places attainable without too great an appearance of inconsistency (and at the pleasantest season to do so).

On the morning of Hudson Taylor's arrival at Shanghai, a wag in another periodical, the *Shanghai Recorder*, in an equally ill-informed article went one better.

> Giving Mr Taylor full credit for his clerico-surgical character, we imagine that he has forsaken his vocation. In various parts of Great Britain there are to be found institutions (in many of which) the possession of a surgeon who could also officiate as chaplain would be an inestimable advantage. Among the institutions of this kind which present themselves to our memory, one stands out with exceptional clearness—the Hospital for Incurable Idiots. We wish Mr Taylor could obtain admission in some capacity to this excellent asylum. Were he an inmate, much trouble that now occurs would be prevented.

Meanwhile Hudson Taylor called on the editor of the *Courier* to give him the facts, and wrote to Maria, waiting at Suzhou for him.

> A series of articles in the papers here (has stated) that I went to P'u-t'u for purposes of propagandism and had made a disturbance thereby ... You may suppose the anti-missionary papers did not let this pass without comment. 'The pestilent folly (of Mr Taylor) at Pootoo ... it is not to be hoped that an individual who has already by his stupidity produced serious political complications, should be permitted to roam about the country

preparing ill-feeling and ill-treatment for every foreigner who may *be* unfortunate enough to follow his route.'

The editor of the *Evening Courier* tried to extricate himself by a curious bit of duplicity. Complaining of the paragraphs in the *Shanghai Recorder* and *North China Daily News* having led to 'an unusually severe article on Mr Taylor and his Mission in the *Evening Courier* of the 25th', he drew attention to another article in the *Shanghai Recorder* 'so rude as to be almost brutal'. He then proceeded to repeat the facts Hudson Taylor had given him, and to say:

> Going there in search of health, they confined themselves strictly to that pursuit. There was no preaching, no discussion, no distribution of religious books; there was not even a religious conversation with a priest ... There was no tumult, no representation to the (*daotai*), no mediatory message through Mr. Bowra [of the customs] to the Consul, and no order from the latter for Mr Taylor to leave ... No persons, perhaps, were more astonished on perusing your article than Mr Bowra and the Consul at Ningpo ...
> Yours truly, 'Scrutator'

On his own copy of the *Courier* Hudson Taylor made the note, 'Scrutator is the Editor himself. JHT'! The next morning the *North China Daily News* simply published an 'official denial' by W. H. Fittack, HM Consul at Ningbo,

> I deem it right to state that no complaint whatever has been made to H.M.'s Consul at this port, of the nature referred to; that Mr Taylor has not been inhibited as stated; and that the British Consul has not summarily ordered Mr Taylor to retire from the island, on the appeal of Mr Bowra, the Commissioner of Customs, or the appeal of any one else.
>
> As the assertions referred to have no foundation in truth, and as they are of a mischievous character, I consider it my duty to give them my official contradiction and shall feel obliged by your publishing the same.

By then the European mail steamer had sailed and Hudson Taylor had to tell Maria,

'I regret that the statements have gone home a mail before the retractions can do. Nevertheless "the Lord reigneth".' While the troublemaker in Ningbo chuckled over his success, and 'Veritas' sent home to *The Times* his 'gunboat under the window' letter, Hudson Taylor's uncomfortably sensitive nature smarted under the taunts. Petty in themselves, they added to the strain on the camel's back.

Waiting in Suzhou for him to join her, Maria knew how despised he felt and wrote 'I want you.' But the mischief was not easily laid. The missionary *Chinese Recorder* for July cited the falsehood and only retracted it in August with a denial that Hudson Taylor 'had endeavoured to establish a branch of his mission on the island, and had been required by the British Consul to desist'. Miles Knowlton's reply to the attacks in the House of Lords and *The Times* was published in the same issue of the *Chinese Recorder*, a whole year after the misreported events at Yangzhou.[125]

Anqing at last[126] (January–July 1869)

Hardly had the reinstatement at Yangzhou been effected in November 1868 than James Meadows and James Williamson were preparing to advance two hundred miles up the Yangzi to Anqing. Boarding a river junk with Chinese companions on December 26, they arrived on January 8, 1869, and lay low, moored among the many other boats along the bank. Li Hongzhang, a native of Anhui province, (returning from his final, successful campaign against the Nianfei rebels' in the north and on his way to take up office at Wuchang as viceroy of Hubei and Hunan) was staying at Anqing with a huge retinue until after the Chinese New Year in February. Every available house in the city was occupied. So, leaving their Chinese colleagues to prospect for accommodation, Meadows and Williamson went on to Jiujiang, (Kiukiang) one hundred miles further upstream, to arrange for mail to be forwarded and to confer with W. H. Lay, the acting consul at this trading post. There they made the acquaintance of an American Methodist

Episcopal missionary, V. C. Hart and of M. G. Hollingworth, a merchant, the only Protestants in Jiangxi. Both were to become good friends of the CIM. (Josiah Cox, the English Methodist, had already been withdrawn.)

Li Hongzhang was in no hurry to move on and made the most of the celebrations at Anqing until ten days after the New Year (on February 10). As soon as he and his followers had gone, Meadows and Williamson called on the prefect and district magistrate who received them courteously and promised to help them find accommodation. But the sub-prefect to whom they were referred 'seemed anything but pleased, and remarked that our passports said nothing about renting houses. We replied that the treaty did, and showed him a treaty proclamation . . . A day or two after, we sent our servants to engage a room for us at the inn . . . The innkeeper was quite willing, and said it was no matter whether we were foreigners or (Chinese), so long as we paid for our accommodation.' But when they themselves arrived, having sent their baggage ahead, the troubled innkeeper said there was no room for them. 'Some persons had been trying to frighten him. We were now in an awkward position. If we took back our luggage to the boat, it would soon be reported all over the place two "foreign devils" wanted to get into an inn in the city but had been put out . . . We then sent a message to the district magistrate, who immediately sent for the innkeeper and told him to provide a room for us, which he then gladly did, and the same evening even offered to rent us the whole house.'

Two days later the garrison commander sent for their servant. 'Suspecting they might be planning some mischief,' Meadows went with him, to the mandarin's alarm. Asked why he had set men to watch them as if they were thieves or robbers, he claimed with profuse apologies that the provincial governor, a Manchu named Ying Han, had reprimanded him for allowing them to enter the city. Yet only a few days later the prefect and sub-prefect received

them very politely. The governor, they explained, had consulted the viceroy, Ma Xinyi, at Nanjing, and a reply had come that,

> we had a right to preach our doctrine; but there was one thing they did not understand exactly about our passports. When any of the French priests came there, they always brought a letter having the seal of the viceroy, and if we would write our Consul and get such a letter, it would simplify matters ... Mr Meadows then went to (Jiujiang), and stated the matter to Mr Lay ... who told him it was evidently a subterfuge on their part to get rid of us, that our passports and the twelfth article of the treaty were sufficient [1, p 627].

A week after Meadows's return from Jiujiang a proclamation by prefect, sub-prefect and magistrate was displayed outside the inn door saying 'that the religious teachers . . . were there to preach their religion and had passports certifying their respectability and that it was perfectly optional for anyone to connect themselves with the religion but not compulsory. They issued the proclamation to inform the soldiers and people so that they will peaceably pursue their own business, keep the laws, and respect the treaty.'

So far so good, but it said nothing about renting premises. While the mandarins were known to be obstructive, however superficially polite, the townsfolk dared not be friendly. 'It is very trying, wearying work having to deal with unscrupulous officials who, while outwardly professing to be very friendly, may secretly be doing all they can against us,' Williamson wrote.

> Whereas in other places, if we go into a teashop we soon have numbers of persons about us, asking questions, etc., here they will not take the least notice of us. We often give away a few tracts in a teashop, but seldom get into conversation ... Meanwhile, I am staying at the inn, and busy making inquiry about houses. The forenoon is generally spent studying Mandarin with a Nankin teacher, while in the afternoon I mostly go out and pass a little time in a teashop; the reserve and

evident suspicion of the people prevent my doing much in this way ... We must be very careful to guard against doing anything which might cause disturbance, and thus frustrate our efforts.

At last on April 21, while Meadows was visiting his wife and new baby, born at Nanjing, Williamson succeeded in renting a house with three upstairs rooms, breezier and freer from mosquitoes than the ground floor. Well situated on a small hill in the heart of the city near the governor's *yamen,* it showed promise of being healthier and safer than anything they had expected to find. Since December 26 their only home had been their little boat. On Meadows's return they reported their deed of rental to the authorities and the landlord agreed to improvements. At once 'some of the literati, with the neighbours, threatened to burn down the premises'.

Hudson Taylor received the news with the remark, 'I hope no trouble will arise there.' So far every inch of the way was being contested. The natural route to the far western province of Guizhou was up the Yangzi to Wuchang or beyond, and then overland; and further up the Yangzi to Sichuan. But all remained peaceful at Anqing. Mrs Meadows (Elizabeth Rose of the *Lammermuir)* and the children joined them and, undeterred by threats, the Meadows family and Williamson moved into their rented premises on July 9, 1869, the historic date of their 'occupation' of the city and province, the first of 'the eleven'. 'But for the (Yangzhou) affairs, (Anqing) would not have been so easily opened,' Hudson Taylor suggested. He spoke too soon. It was only a matter of time before 'Yangzhou' was repeated at Anqing, without consular intervention.

Undercurrents of danger
(June–October 1869)

Alarm elsewhere had not ended. News of the plundering of the Catholic mission at Zunyi in Guizhou on June 14 and the flogging of the Abbé Gilles so severely that he died from the effects on August 13, must have reached Viceroy Li Hongzhang,

Anhui governor Ying Han and Viceroy Ma Xinyi within two weeks or so. Also in 1869 the French chargé d'affaires, Comte de Rochechourt, while visiting Shanxi province to assess the commercial possibilities and to scotch rumours that all foreigners were soon to be expelled from China, narrowly escaped assassination in Tiayuan, the provincial capital.[127] This too would have been known before the summer had passed.

In August another James Williamson, of the LMS (a younger brother of Alexander Williamson, see 1, p 733), and William Bramwell Hodge of the Methodist New Connexion, left Tianjin in a boat to visit outstations. Soon after midnight of the 25th, while moored in a canal which daily carried merchants with large sums of money and unguarded goods, they were attacked and plundered. When Hodge was woken by the boatmen's shouts and jumped ashore, he saw no sign of Williamson. A gang of armed men attacked him with the flat of their swords, 'unaccountably not using the edges' until he was 'severely bruised from head to foot'. Making his way to the local magistrate's *yamen,* he met the mandarin already coming 'with a company of soldiers'—a highly suspicious fact. They set off in pursuit of the robbers and began to search for James Williamson. His body was found three days later, in the canal twelve miles away.[128] The *North China Daily News* later carried the observation, 'Who ever heard of a mandarin and his followers being up and on the watch between twelve and one o'clock in the morning? Those who have lived long in China know how unlikely, if not impossible, it is for a band of robbers to commit such a deed and remain undetected, if the authority had the will to do it.' Circumstantial evidence was strong that the mandarin was implicated.

September saw the emergence of a dangerous new factor. In Hunan, 'always conservative and anti-foreign', a placard was published which found its way throughout the empire and lay at the root of a deepening animosity. Summarising the history of Christianity in China, it declared that 'pernicious doctrines were daily gaining ground.' Jesus was born during the Han dynasty. Was the world without a divine ruler before that? 'This young serpent must be crushed before it attains its full monster growth!'

In October when a missionary of the American Board attempted to take possession of premises he had leased at 'I-cho' [probably Yi Xian] only seventy miles south-west of Peking, the doors were locked against him. The magistrate had the middleman heavily fined and flogged on his legs and face until the flesh of one thigh was sloughed to a depth of an inch, allegedly for helping a foreigner to obtain premises so near (seven miles) to the imperial tombs. The people of the city had been friendly and willing to have missionaries live among them. When the Zongli Yamen supported the magistrate, the US Minister at Peking chose to take no action. C. A. Stanley (possibly the missionary referred to) concluded that success or failure in any locality, depended upon the liberality or prejudices of the local mandarins and literati. In some instances the risk to the Chinese implicated was greater than that to the foreigner.[129]

Too much for one?
(July–December 1869)

For the last six months of the year Hudson Taylor was like a cork on a choppy sea. Willing to a fault to go to the aid of anyone in need, he still adapted his other work to those claims. After five months on the move, he and Maria were home again in Yangzhou on June 25, but already planning to return to the trouble spots of Taizhou and Wenzhou as soon as they could. Emily and the older three children were with the McCarthys at Hangzhou. 'It is a real trial, and not a small one, to her to be away from us,' Maria told Mrs Berger, 'and we shall much miss her loving attentions and invaluable help.' Since leaving Britain Emily had developed 'a maturity of Christian character' which marked her as one of the Mission's most valuable members.

In contrast with what they had found in the south, there was a good spirit among the missionaries and the handful of Christian Chinese at Yangzhou. The Judds' zeal and Louise Desgraz' stability made them a good team. Looking back only a year to when they were still homeless, cramped together in leaking boats while trying to gain a toehold, they took heart from the contrast. For here they were in their own house with hardly a trace of riot or arson or personal injury, but, instead, their landlord, their loyal carpenter, Mr Peng the innkeeper, their boatman and others who had been no more than pagan bystanders, were 'one in Christ' with them.

For two months they came and went between Yangzhou and Zhenjiang, torn between duty and the illness of one and another. Meadows and Williamson had at last gained possession of the rented premises of their own in Anqing. On July 20 George Duncan succeeded in occupying a house in Qingjiangpu, a hundred miles up the Grand Canal. While Alcock was forging his shackles they were pressing 'onward and inward'.

But Hudson Taylor could join none of them. The Judds were unwell and had to go on holiday while the Taylors did their work. Then urgent news arrived from Emily and McCarthy at Hangzhou. Howard and little Maria were ill with symptoms alarmingly like those from which Grace had died two years ago. What should they do? Take them to Ningbo and by steamer to Shanghai, Hudson Taylor replied. But while letters travelled up and down the Grand Canal between them, how ill were the children? The emergency drove the Taylors to the realisation that this life of homelessness, of travelling and bivouacking, exposed to disease, and staying with other missionaries for short periods was no life for their family. 'It is a serious question with me whether I may not have to send the elder children home before long,' Hudson Taylor confided to his mother. By the time they reached Shanghai the threat of meningitis had passed. John McCarthy put Emily on the river-steamer to Zhenjiang and returned home to Hangzhou.

On August 7 they were all together

again. But on the 22nd Hudson Taylor was wondering if he himself was developing pneumonia, and if Samuel's incessant 'dysentery' was tuberculous enteritis. Hardly had he himself picked up than Maria was 'very ill'. Her pulmonary tuberculosis had shown fewer symptoms recently, but a tormenting suspicion that she and Samuel shared the same lethal disease was growing on him.

September had to be given to another visit to Hangzhou and Ningbo. To travel further to see Stott again was out of the question. Even in the 'state room' of their streamlined footboat, 'little more than a canoe', as Maria described it to Mrs Berger, they continued their unceasing correspondence. 'Carefully packed up together with sundry small boxes and baskets, in a space (less than six feet by four) considerably smaller than your dining room table', she, Hudson and Samuel lived, ate, worked and played for days at a time. 'Comfort is as much a matter of the mind as the body, if not more so,' she concluded. While they were away the Anqing magistrate had sent for Meadows and Williamson and warned them to lie low during the literary examinations, the first hint of the trouble to come.

October brought new anxieties, painful letters to be written to unhappy colleagues, and separation from Maria again when Hudson Taylor returned to Zhenjiang while she stayed in Hangzhou and Ningbo to help in Jennie's preparations for a girls' school, in addition to the one for boys. Month after month the funds of the Mission were at a low ebb. Loss of confidence attributable to the press attacks had followed the accusations of irresponsible behaviour. 'The Mission funds are lower than they ever were before,' he told the team. Some took for granted all he did for them and even complained of neglect, not seeing, or forgetting, that he did as much for each. Occasionally he reminded them of this to make them think. Hudson Taylor wrote (always by hand in his duplicate 'manifold') to James Meadows, his most senior and experienced colleague after six years in China, who had just written thoughtlessly.

(Zhenjiang), October 31, 1869

As to correspondence, I do my best to keep up to it, but there is a limit to one's time and strength ... What can I do beyond trust to your consideration and forbearance? My personal incompetence for the many and onerous responsibilities devolving upon me, is far from being unfelt by me. So far from this, I have very seriously considered the question of attempting to retire from them. And if I am led to work on, it is from the belief that I have neither sought nor pleased myself in the position I now find myself in, and that He who placed me in it can and will work through me all He intends to be done through me in it. And this thought gives me indescribable peace and comfort, under a burden that would otherwise be intolerable ... I have no Mission soap, but I am expecting some of my own in a month or so from England. I might perhaps be able to let you have some of that if you like. Would you wish one quarter or one half (hundredweight)? ... P.S. It just occurs to me to add that some of the members of the Mission may be unaware of the amount of labour involved in helping them. It is real pleasure to do so, but it is none the less onerous. For instance, I have to write to Mr Müller to thank him for your cheque, to Mr Lord asking him kindly to sell it, as he gets a better price than the Shanghai banks will give. Then to enter it in his account, and in my cash account. Then to send the amount to Mr Hart [the American Episcopal V. C. Hart at Jiujiang] with a note requesting him kindly to forward it. Of course I must also advise you of it ... Just now I have seven different portions of Old and New Testament (whole books), and long tracts sent me in several dialects with requests to revise them. This, if possible, is the work of weeks if not months. Yet I am praying for guidance as to whether I may not have to leave tonight for one of our most distant stations on account of a case of sickness.

Tempted as Hudson Taylor might often have been to abandon the role of leader and return to pioneering with a few loyal friends, the very thought was sterile. No one could replace him and few had the determination to persist without him. So far not one in the team, not even McCarthy or

Stevenson, was ready to share his load as an assistant or deputy. He must soldier on. So to Mary Bowyer at Nanjing he next wrote:

> This morning I was called up early and ere long Mrs Rudland presented us with a fine little girl ... I enclose the stamps you wrote for. Some tincture of benzoine shall be sent to Mr Duncan. We increasingly feel the power of the truths we were speaking of together; they are joy and strength every day. There is good work going on at Yangchau. Five were baptised last month ... I enclose the santonine I spoke to Mr Duncan about for Mrs Duncan ... The best thing you can do for Mrs D. if she suffers in her back is to try ten drop doses of Sweet Spirits of Nitre with three drops of Laudanum three or four times a day.
>
> P.S. I must see what I can do about quinine.

And, urgently to John McCarthy, because of another confinement to attend, 'I should have left for Hangchou this evening, but my boatman's (partner) has refused to go. We cannot hire another here, and I should be too late for Mrs Dodd if I wait for Thursday's steamer, or travel by a slow boat. The Lord will doubtless order all for the best.' To George Crombie at Fenghua, 'If you like to send the copy of Ecclesiastes here I will try to finish revising it and have it printed.' And to Cardwell at Taizhou, 'I see no objection to your proposal as to (Jiujiang), if attempted solely as a basis for action as soon as possible in the interior.'

Even so within an hour or two of Mary Rudland's delivery Hudson Taylor was on his way to Hangzhou, leaving Maria to look after her, and travelling fast by footboat. By November 5 he was there and none too soon. He found the McCarthy children and Charles Kreyer very ill. So ill was Kreyer that after recovery he left Hangzhou and his mission. Sarah Dodd's child arrived safely, but serious news arrived from Zhenjiang and Hudson Taylor could not delay more than three days. Jennie wrote home:

> A Romish priest reported that the house we had at (Anqing) (inhabited by Meadows and Williamson) had been pulled to the ground ... He had come down (to Zhenjiang) to put matters into the hands of the French Consul ... Then we heard that the Shanghai papers reported the disturbance and added that the missionaries had this time paid with their lives the penalty of their position, or words to that effect. This is all we know ... I trust that we shall find that much has been made out of little ... Still the Lord reigneth, He has allowed whatever has taken place ... It may be that as a Mission we are to be baptised with His baptism and so made more fruitful. His will be done.

The news was two weeks old already. As he travelled Hudson Taylor reported events to the Bergers. Saying nothing of the alleged loss of life at Anqing, he spoke of being most anxious lest his friends had been injured and needed his help. But as he neared Zhenjiang where the full facts would be known, he unburdened his heart to his old friend George Pearse.

> Some seem to think the whole party were killed ... I know not and can only throw the burden on the Lord ... And now, it may be, He is about to take us through more trying and painful experiences than we have previously experienced. What shall we say? 'Father, glorify Thy name', says the spirit, though the flesh is weak and trembles. He is our strength, and what we cannot do or bear, He can both do and bear in us.

After that, the Anqing affair would have filled his time and thoughts had not new troubles of many kinds descended upon him. December was fraught with tension. Maria and he decided that their four eldest children—Herbert, Howard, Maria and Samuel—must go home to Britain. It held Samuel's only hope of recovery, if indeed he lived through the journey. At great personal grief, Emily undertook to escort and mother them. Maria herself became more and more frail. Serious lapses in morale and conduct among their missionaries tore almost as painfully at their heartstrings; and, ominously, the Bergers' health was failing. The pressures of the Yangzhou riot aftermath had told severely on them. Mary Berger could eat nothing without severe pain. Then William wrote of growing convictions on a subject already theological dynamite in the world of the 'evangelical revival' which provided most of the Mission's support. Andrew Jukes was propagating the revolutionary idea of the 'non-eternity of punishment'. Not only was it the negation of Hudson Taylor's beliefs, so strongly expressed in *China: Its Spiritual Need and Claims*, but it was resisted as unbiblical and therefore heretical by evangelical Christians as a whole. William Berger declared to Hudson Taylor that if his openness to Jukes's arguments became known, the CIM would be doomed. So he had better resign. Hudson Taylor should come home—for other reasons also.

How could he go? He could not be spared from China. How then could the year end on the note of another advance, into yet another province? But it did. This time it was Jiangxi—by the disappointing J. E. Cardwell, in a dramatic change of character.

Silver lining (1869)

To look back very briefly—when he launched the Mission in 1865 Hudson Taylor had no illusions about the difficulties ahead. But knowing what to expect did not make it less hard to bear. Opposition from the Chinese was acceptable. Scorn from cynical foreigners could be tolerated. Opposition from fellow-missionaries was a greater test of resilience. But a sense of personal failure and sinfulness when he was sincerely trying to serve and please God he found to be supremely distressing. In his *cri de coeur* to his mother from Ninghai on March 13, 1869 it was not his health or persecutions or perplexities but his failure to be as Christ-like as he longed to be that distressed him. His brother missionaries and Maria knew his failings well enough. 'Oftentimes I am tempted to think that one so full of sin cannot be a child of God at all.'

Readers unfamiliar with the Pietism of this period (not in the sense of exaggerated or feigned piety but of the historical movement) may be interested to follow the process of thought which had such far-reaching results. Not surprisingly, he had confessed to 'irritability of temper' as

his besetting sin, his 'daily hourly failure'. It was hard to suffer fools gladly. And long separations from Maria subjected him to added tension. During 1869 the *Revival* magazine in Britain carried a series of articles by R. Pearsall Smith, whose influential addresses at Oxford largely gave rise to the Keswick Movement which still draws thousands together annually in several countries around the world. As John McCarthy recalled, his expositions 'had led many of us to think of a much higher (plane) of life and service than we had before thought possible'. Copies of the *Revival*, reaching every CIM station, were creating a desire in many of the Mission to attain to this spiritual goal which for convenience at this point was being called 'holiness' or 'the victorious life'. Before long other terms superseded these to express the answer discovered. In the CIM 'the exchanged life' and 'union with Christ' or just 'union' came to sum up their thinking.[130] William Collingwood, Louise Desgraz' former employer, wrote to her on the subject and in Yangzhou she and the Judds were 'seeking holiness'. In Zhenjiang the Rudlands, at Suzhou the Cordons and in Hangzhou the McCarthys and Jennie Faulding all responded with the same longing as Hudson Taylor himself. Only Maria was unmoved, wondering (as McCarthy put it) 'what we were all groping after . . . (an) experience she had long been living in the enjoyment of . . . I have rarely met as Christ-like a Christian as Mrs Taylor'. In Judd's words, '(It) gave her that beautiful calmness and confidence in God (in which) up to that time she so surpassed her husband.'

The subject has been well documented by the Howard Taylors and in Hudson Taylor's subsequent writings and addresses. Here it is enough to show how his own life came to be revolutionised, in timely preparation for the hardest experiences yet to come his way. J. J. Coulthard, who in time married Hudson Taylor's daughter Maria, recalled in 1905 that Hudson Taylor used to say that when he could bear his distress no longer and was crying to the Lord for help, the words of Scripture, 'He that cometh to me shall never (at any time) hunger, and he that believeth in me shall never thirst' came to him with such power that he knew his search would soon end. 'Cometh' in the sense of 'keeps coming' was the secret. He need never be thirsty again.

Towards the end of August, after his illness at Yangzhou with what he thought to be pneumonia and Maria's subsequent attack of enteritis, he advised Duncan to bring Catherine, his wife, and Mary Bowyer to Zhenjiang because of the Yangzi flooding at Nanjing. They needed boats to move about the city. There at Zhenjiang in the first week of September Hudson Taylor found a letter from John McCarthy waiting for him. They had been in Shanghai together, both dissatisfied with themselves, both on the same search, discussing their spiritual hunger yet unable to help each other. But by August 20 McCarthy was back in Hangzhou surprised by the joy of discovery and quick to share his find with his friend.

> At the time that you were speaking to me, (Holiness) was the subject of all others, which occupied my thoughts ... I have thought of others whom I have met—(Grattan) Guinness for instance ... who seemed able to guide the minds of those with whom they came in contact—*influencing* instead of *being influenced,* really accomplishing that which the Saviour said we should—not only themselves full, but full to overflowing, and overflowing for the good of others. Do you know dear Brother I now think this striving effort, longing, hoping for better days yet to come—is not the true way to happiness, Holiness or Usefulness ... I have been struck with a passage from a book of yours here—'Christ is All'—it said, 'The Saviour welcomed, is all Holiness begun. The Saviour cherished is all Holiness advancing. The Saviour never absent, is Holiness complete ... A channel is now formed, by which Christ's fullness plenteously flows down. The barren branch becomes a portion of the fruitful stem ... The limbs receive close union with the head, and one life reigns throughout the (whole) ... To let my living Saviour work in me His will—my

sanctification—is what I would live for ... Abiding, not striving, nor struggling ...

> I seem as if the first glimmer of the dawn of a glorious day has risen upon me. I hail it with trembling—yet with trust. I seem to have got to the edge only—but of a sea which is boundless. To have sipped only of that which can fully satisfy. Christ literally 'all' seems now to be the power, the only power for service.[131]

The next day he had posted the book, and another letter in which he wrote about believing 'with a true heart in full assurance of faith' that we can boldly 'enter into the holiest' with hearts cleansed from an evil conscience, because of all that Jesus has done for us and now is to us. 'How then to have our faith increased? Only by thinking of all that Jesus is—all he is for us . . . Not a striving to have faith or to increase our faith. But a looking at the faithful One, seems all we need, a resting in the loved One.'

This truth had dawned upon Jennie too, now happier than ever. In Zhenjiang as Hudson Taylor read, the light broke for him also and the next day he wrote to Louise Desgraz at Yangzhou that he had shared McCarthy's letter with all the others. Louise had found the answer before him. 'I have seldom seen so remarkable a change in anyone as has taken place in Miss D . . . Now she is calm and happy.'

> To me it has been the happiest day I have spent for a long time [he said]. The part specially helpful to me is 'How then to have our faith increased, only by thinking of all that Jesus is for us. His life, His death, His work' ... Here I feel is the secret. Not asking how I am to get sap out of the vine into myself, but remembering that Jesus is the vine—the root, stem, branches, twigs, leaves, flowers, fruit—all indeed.[132]

On September 4 Emily Blatchley had written in her journal, 'He too has now received the rest of soul that Jesus gave to me some little time ago.' Instead of 'trying to abide' in Jesus the Vine and asking to be kept so abiding, as if Jesus were the root and we as the branches having to 'get hold and keep hold', he wrote, 'the truth is that He is the whole vine and we are in Him.'

He seems to have paid a quick visit to Yangzhou, his home, for Charles Judd recalled years later:

> Late one evening, I went into his house to welcome him back and at once saw that his heart was full of joy. He walked up and down the room saying 'Oh Mr Judd, God has made me a new man! God has made me a new man! I see that I am a branch in Christ, really united to Him; I have not to make myself a branch, He says that I am one ("Ye are the branches") and I have simply to believe in Him. If I have a thousand dollars in the Bank and ask the clerk at the counter to give me five hundred, putting out my hand to receive them, he cannot refuse them to my hand and say "They are Mr Taylor's", for my hand is part of myself: what is mine is my hand's also, and my hand can take it. I am part of Christ, and what is His I can take.' His faith had now taken hold of the fact of his union—living and actual union with Christ.[133]

He was due to go down to Ningbo again and took Maria with him by canal. It gave them a day at Hangzhou with McCarthy and Jennie, and a chance to share his discoveries with Wang Lae-djün and Mr Tsiu. At Ningbo he called as many missionaries together as he could meet and shared with them and with Frederick Gough 'our oneness with the risen, exalted Saviour . . . the mighty power of absolute and indissoluble union with Him . . . O the years I have struggled to abide in Him . . . to get virtue out of Him . . . practically forgetful of the fullness of Him in whom we are.'

The difficulties of life did not lessen, but he could write to encourage the disconsolate William Berger on October 8 by pointing out that five of the missionaries he, Hudson Taylor, had chosen had been a disappointment, but only two or three of those sent by Berger. Yet he did not despair for now he was trusting that 'the fruit of the vine comes from *abiding*, not *striving*'. God in His wisdom would give him the ability he needed and use him.

Familiar with the *Revival* articles, the Bergers took exception to the overstressing of the passive, receptive aspect of 'holiness'. They replied emphasising the need for active resistance to evil and of effort to obey God, just as Bishop J. C. Ryle in his books was to balance the Keswick Movement's emphases a few years later.

Far from denying the rightness of his friend's cautions, Hudson Taylor and several of his team were finding in their newly discovered truths the answer to their present need. Sharing the apostle Paul's paradoxical experience he could say, 'In all our troubles my joy knew no bounds' (2 Cor. 7.4). 'Now He makes me happy all day long, makes my work light, gives me joy in blessing others . . . I have no fear now of our work being too heavy for Him in Britain or China,' he told the Bergers. Yet funds were lower than ever before, inflammatory placards were being posted again, and in Anqing the riot was only days away. He was ready now for whatever the future might hold. Little could he imagine what that would be.

The Anqing riot[134]
(August–November 1869)

In Anqing the regional literary examinations were about to begin. The magistrate sent for Meadows and Williamson, asked them to suspend public preaching and indirectly urged that they should leave the city, 'hinting at . . . the lawless character of the candidates'.

> We informed him that we had not yet commenced public preaching, and intended to take every precaution ... to avoid coming into collision with these students. [But even so in August] it was rumoured abroad, that by some mysterious influences ... we had brought over to our views 135 persons the first night, and almost as many the second; and that 240 children had been stowed away, eaten, or otherwise disposed of ... The trouble, time and expense ... put it out of the question to leave the city with Mrs Meadows and children and the greater part of our goods for three months ... and we were the more encouraged to stay in the city during the prefectural examinations seeing we were

not so much as insulted during the time of the district examinations.

On November 2, however, an inflammatory placard in large letters was posted on the walls of the Literary Examination Hall, calling on the students and others, to pull the mission house down on the 5th because it was occupied by 'Religious Brigands'.

Meadows and Williamson therefore called on the *daotai*, whose refusal to see them was taken by 'a large number both of literary and military candidates' in the large court of the *yamen* as an excuse for attacking them. 'Williamson's chair was . . . nearly knocked over, with horrid shoutings of, "Kill the Foreign Devils, Beat the Foreign Devils!"' Rushing back into the *daotai's* judgment hall and calling, according to custom, for protection, they were besieged by a mob shouting for their death.

Meanwhile Elizabeth Meadows and the children had been assaulted by another mob at home. The doors she had barricaded with furniture and boxes were battered down, and 'with my Louise in my arms, Sammy screaming at my side, and (the *amah*) crying, my own heart aching, the blood running through my veins with an icy coldness, I watched scores of people plunder the premises.'

> Each one for himself tore open drawers, boxes, and cupboards, carrying off everything in them: now an armful of crockery, now one of clothes, another of books, now and then stopping to break out the windows. Boxes and cupboards as they were emptied were thrown out ...

> I got downstairs somehow, receiving some severe blows by the violent manner in which the men carried the things out. I did not know where to go, but went first to the teachers' room hoping there to be protected ... There was a gentleman in the room whom I had not seen before, and he was helping us, taking all he could from the thieves and stowing them in this room. He made way for me to get into the room and kept the mob out as long as he could, getting his face bruised for his pains.

The mob then plundered this place also, and her person, taking the few dollars she had secreted, and her wedding ring, and even making violent efforts to get Louise from her.

At last the magistrate arrived. A faithful Christian servant then took her hand and led her through the mob to join her husband in the *yamen*. After dark they were given some bedding and money for food and, otherwise completely destitute, were put on board two little river-boats, to go wherever they could.

On the same day the Roman Catholic missions at Anqing and 'Kienteh' were similarly pillaged. According to the *Shanghai Recorder*, 'It is known that the mob made two visits to the China Inland Mission, and destroyed the Roman Catholic Mission in the interval.'[135] While the Meadows family and Williamson painfully made their way to Jiujiang, an English Catholic priest managed to board a steamer and reached Zhenjiang on the 5th, bringing the first news of the riots. No more was heard until Charles Judd was told that 'a foreigner had been killed' at Anqing 'endeavouring to keep the mob from entering the house'.

The night was wintry and bleak. A strong wind blowing upstream met the river current head on and whipped the surface of the Yangzi into angry waves. Nothing could be done but to sit huddled together and endure. Still dishevelled from the riot, they had not even a comb between them, no soap nor towel. 'I took off my chemise to make a napkin for Louise,' Elizabeth wrote. And in this state they reached Jiujiang on November 9 only to find that the friendly American Episcopal V. C. Hart was away until the next day. Preparing to spend another wretched night in the boats, their delight may be imagined when M. G. Hollingworth, the merchant, hearing of their arrival came looking for them. He had his own house full of guests, so he 'did all in his power to make us comfortable' in an empty house, sending 'table, chairs, bedding, coal, and two ladies to inquire into our circumstances . . . one sent me two changes of underclothing and the other a complete suit of outer clothing. He sent us (food) direct from his own table, and came early the next morning to fetch us to breakfast.'

To Williamson, Jiujiang had 'a nice foreign settlement' with thirty foreign residents, 'a small, neatly built church, and a resident chaplain'. When the Harts returned they brought the refugees into their own home, H. N. Lay, the consul, took a statement from them and Hollingworth procured free passages on a steamer to Zhenjiang. On the night of the 11th he and Hart saw them on board. 'The Captain treated us with great kindness' and on reaching the Zhenjiang 'hulk' at midnight on the 12th handed them over to the foreign customs official who made up beds in the customs house for Elizabeth and the children. To reach the Rudland's in the morning was like arriving home, but Elizabeth wrote, 'I felt like Naomi when she said, "Call me not Naomi, call me Marah . . . I went out full and the Lord hath brought me again empty".' Not one relic of their most prized possessions, personal mementoes of home and parents, remained to them.

There Hudson Taylor and Maria joined them.

After Anqing
(November 1869–February 1870)

Knowing from experience what it was like to go through a riot, and to be separated from each other during it, the Taylors' sympathy and encouragement carried weight. As time was to show, this for the present was the best contribution they could make. Hudson Taylor could see beyond the physical and emotional trauma to wider issues. Sir Rutherford Alcock, the minister, happened to be in Shanghai, and hearing from Consul Lay went himself to Anqing to confront the guilty governor and *daotai*. As Hudson Taylor told William Berger:

> From the first I could not but see that the opponents of missions, and especially those opposed to us, might make a trying use of (the Anqing riot) ... Sir R. Alcock has inquired into the matter and the Mandarins, I am told, promised him to repair the house and make good the

losses; but would give no guarantee of exemption from future molestation ... ('They may return but at their own peril.') Messrs. (Meadows and Williamson) are now directed to proceed to Shanghai to give evidence as to their losses. I really do not see that they can refuse to do so, or to receive the compensation, if any be really offered to them. For to refuse this would be to affect the safety of others, and embarrass our officers. Friends at home really cannot understand these things here, and they must give us credit as seeking to please God, and do, as far as we know it, what is right and best. Often our property and not rarely our lives are in jeopardy. We can, in some measure, even rejoice that it is so. But those who neither know, nor can understand, our position must not expect the reasons of all our steps to be apparent to them ...

> If you have another typhoon about the (Anqing) riot do not be cast down, dear Brother, the Lord will strengthen you and us by His own might to bear much more than this. The day may come when we have to look alone to and lean alone on the One sufficient stay. I hope it is so now indeed. When Rome and Jew combined to oppose, God carried His cause through, and He will now carry it through.[136]

That day did come, when even the ambassadors were in fear for their lives.

In March 1870 Hudson Taylor was in the dark as as to what the minister was doing. Alcock did not confide in him as Consul Medhurst did. Li Hongzhang, newly enthroned as viceroy at Wuchang, had 'issued an edict which was popularly interpreted as a condemnation of Christians'.[137] The pillaging of the Catholic premises at Anqing being attributed to Li's action, the French chargé d'affaires proceeded at once to Wuchang with an escort of two gunboats to enforce justice. And the visit of one vessel to Anqing ensured satisfaction being obtained there. Hudson Taylor commented:

> The state of affairs since the riot, up to the time that the French expedition arrived, have been unable as yet to ascertain; but it seems that the visit of Sir Rutherford Alcock was followed by rumours of the

French armed expedition, and the people were very much frightened. Many of them made preparations for leaving the city, but the majority said that there was nothing to fear from the foreigners, who were not like the rebels, for not only would they not touch private property but would also pay a good price for what they wanted ...

There can be no doubt that the French demonstration has been the means of facilitating our return to this city, as well as of bringing down punishment on the rioters ... What is the true disposition of the people towards us, as yet we cannot ascertain.[138]

The direct intervention of Sir Rutherford and the French was not as significant as the attitude and actions of the new viceroy at Nanjing, Ma Xinyi, supported at last by the provincial governor of Anhui, Ying Han. As a Manchu, Ying Han had been true to type at the time of the riot, leaving the prefects to aid and abet the expulsion of the foreigners. So it can be assumed that his role in events after the riot was dictated by the viceroy, Ma Xinyi.

At a time when the great Muslim 'Panthay' rebellion in Yunnan (1855–73), the equally threatening Muslim rebellion in Gansu (1862–76) and the conquest of Kashgar and Urumqi by Yakub Beg (1864–77) had become the Peking court's chief preoccupations, Ma Xinyi might well have taken a less contentious line. Instead he went even further than when the missions had been attacked in Hangzhou. He issued a proclamation in no uncertain terms, commanding mandarins and people to respect the Anqing missionaries and not molest them in any way (Appendix 10). Yet the leniency of the punishments, the association of the culpable prefects with the viceroy instead of demotion in rank, and the frank distinction between missionaries and secular foreigners (to whom no reference was made), confirmed the reputation for wisdom of this enlightened viceroy. None of the people, officials or victims of the riot could object.

Leaving Elizabeth and the children at Zhenjiang for the present, James Meadows and Williamson went back to Anqing on February 23, 1870, to be 'well received by officials and people'. 'The landlord seemed rather disappointed . . . having hoped to pocket the two years' rent which had been paid in advance, and to let it out to other tenants as well. We proceeded to the (*daotai*), who received us with due courtesy and took up some time excusing himself for not having seen us on the day of the riot . . . He was ready to do all in his power to assist us,' and as an extreme mark of courtesy, accompanied them to the outer door of his palatial *yamen*. The occupants of their own house began moving out the next day, and in possession again Meadows dug up the earthen floor of one room and found one hundred and three silver dollars still where he had buried them. He left Elizabeth to decide whether to return, for she had suffered most, and she bravely agreed; but neither of them could shake off the pall of terror their home continually represented to them.

James Williamson's ambition extended far beyond the provincial capital. 'I have long been anxious to live entirely in a boat and travel from place to place, endeavouring to obtain a footing wherever an opportunity might occur. Here such a boat can be hired very cheaply.' The experience of two disturbances, at Jinhua and Anqing, had failed to stifle his urge to pioneer.

Three years later when Hudson Taylor assessed the progress of the Mission during the first few years of its existence, all he wrote of the episode was, 'After months of persevering effort, (Meadows and Williamson) were ejected for a time by the literati, but were able to return, and the work has since proceeded without interruption.'[139] By 1872 far more harrowing events elsewhere had placed Anqing in a different perspective and Hudson Taylor could be excused his brevity. But the province of Anhui had been 'opened' and 'occupied', and soon would have its growing church. Not for twelve more years was any other mission to join the CIM in Anhui. As 1869 ended, J. E. Cardwell arrived at Jiujiang in Jiangxi (a story in its own right) and Hudson Taylor could claim, for what understanding it conveyed, that the extent of the Mission's territory had increased to 200,000 square miles, about the size of France. The whole of Britain boasts less than 95,000. His own travelling as supervisor increased accordingly.

Looking back and far ahead
(1855–1935)

For fourteen years, since 1855, Sir Rutherford Alcock had had to deal from time to time with trouble arising from this incorrigible visionary's penetration into new territories. Only the fulfilment of duty as consul-general and then minister in Peking governed Sir Rutherford's policy and his impartial attitude to Hudson Taylor. Never friendly, as Consul Medhurst and others were, he remained scrupulously fair and impersonal in reporting his objections to missionary 'provocation' of the literati. In contrast Medhurst was warm in his thanks for Hudson Taylor's gift of 'the best Bible available'. By then Medhurst had received Lord Stanley's congratulations and his successor Lord Clarendon's faint praise intended to be read as reproach.[140] So his letter continued:

> That action (at Yangzhou) has certainly not met with the approval at home which I had anticipated for it. But I nevertheless believe that it has had its good effect in a marked degree, and I trust that the policy which has since arisen out of it although based upon somewhat different principles, may in the end secure for all missionaries throughout the country what it was my simple desire to obtain for you, namely, freedom to pursue their avocation without molestation or restraint, so long as they keep within the bounds of reason and discretion.

In November 1869 when the Anqing affair was still an open wound, Medhurst tackled Alcock about the need to settle the still unresolved matter of compensation to the Yangzhou victims, from the indemnities demanded by him from the Chinese government, and sent Hudson Taylor 500 taels as indemnity for personal injuries sustained by the party.

Knowing that Medhurst was under fire from Whitehall for his strong action at Yangzhou and Nanjing, Hudson Taylor did what he could to support him. On January 18 he wrote to James Meadows, 'Mr Medhurst evidently considers the indemnity as claimed by you . . . It is important not to word anything you may write so that it may get into print that the claim was made contrary to your wish. We are placed in a very difficult position, are we not? May God give us wisdom and grace.'[141]

Because critics were accusing the Mission of profiting from the receipt of indemnities, Hudson Taylor was encouraging all who received compensation of any kind at Yangzhou and Anqing to contribute what they received to funds 'for the permanent benefit of the city . . . in trying to remove this slur.' They all did. He and Maria then personally refunded the losses so that they would not suffer more than they had already.

On January 28 Hudson Taylor followed his usual policy of providing factual publicity to counteract falsehoods. Writing from Yangzhou to the editor of the *North China Herald*, he said:

> In conducting the negotiations Mr Medhurst so combined courtesy with firmness, as to secure the necessary redress, without unduly violating the prejudices or irritating the feelings of the people. The demands which he made were so just, and at the same time so moderate, as to commend themselves to the people's own sense of right ... The good discipline too, of our troops, has often been commented on by the Chinese ... the confidence of the people, and the cordiality of the literati ... have been unmistakably indicated during the year. There is, perhaps, no more delicate criterion of the former than the willingness or reluctance of parents to send their children to our schools ... we have had to refuse children from want of accommodation.

> It will be remembered that Mr Medhurst secured for us a stone tablet bearing a proclamation from the Prefect stating

that we were here at the consent and approbation of both local and foreign authorities. By this admirable diplomacy, he not only conclusively set at rest all questions of our right to be here, but also, with a delicate appreciation of the feeling of the (Chinese), placed us in the position of invited guests, when otherwise our mere presence might have galled them as an evidence of their defeat ... Numbers of the literati daily visited us during the examinations (as many have done before and since) and appeared fully prepared to reciprocate courtesies shown to them.[142]

Twenty years later, when Hudson Taylor assessed the lessons learned from the Yangzhou riot and 'similar experiences', the sting had gone from the criticisms of 1868–69 and the reasons for the apparent mistakes of previous days were understood. Apart from others lost by death, disease and retirement, by then the CIM had 285 members in China and supported 117 full-time Chinese colleagues, besides many more voluntary workers. To avoid distortion and wrong interpretation of the facts, and secondary issues such as national prestige overriding the Mission's best interests, the CIM shunned publicity whenever possible. Molestation was to be endured up to the point at which it ought to be reported to the Chinese and foreign authorities and their help requested, but never demanded as of right. Vindication by the Lord was always more satisfying than that obtained by the intervention of officials. 'Take joyfully the spoiling of your goods' and the thought 'Better be had than hard' gave more lasting satisfaction than indemnities wrested from the offenders. Compensation, though never

demanded, could be accepted and used for their benefit. As the first printed form of the Mission's 'Principles and Practice' expressed it in 1884:

> While availing themselves of any *privileges* offered by the British or Chinese Governments, (missionaries) must make no claim for their help or protection. Appeals to our Consuls ... are to be avoided. Should trouble or persecution arise inland, a *friendly representation* may be made to the local Chinese officials, failing redress from whom, those suffering must be satisfied to leave their case in God's hands. *Under no circumstances must any Missionary on his own responsibility make any appeal to the British authorities.* As a last resort, the injunction of the Master can be followed, 'If they persecute you in this city, flee ye into another' ...

> Where prolonged stay in a city is likely to cause trouble ... and where residence cannot be peaceably and safely effected, (it is better to) defer the attempt.[143]

If so long afterwards such counsel needed to be given, certainly at Yangzhou in 1869 the threat was far from over. But no one could foresee that, of all places in China, relations between people, officials and missionaries were to become better in Yangzhou than perhaps in any other city. Yangzhou became the location of the women missionaries' training school. And Anqing, the capital of Anhui, Li Hongzhang's home province, became (according to his biographer, Alicia Bewicke Little), 'best known to English people as the training centre (for men) of the China Inland Mission'.[144]

16
Desolation (1870–71)

1870: 'The dark cloud'

'Don't doctor, work!' (1874)

Dissatisfaction with himself had been partly due to Hudson Taylor's gnawing dissatisfaction with several of his team. Most were turning out well, but some were exasperating. In Meadows, Stevenson, Williamson, Rudland, Duncan, McCarthy and Judd he now had reliable and increasingly valuable men, most of them well matched in their own way by their wives; he also had four dependable single girls, Jennie Faulding, Emily Blatchley, Louise Desgraz and Mary Bowyer. But whatever upheavals came his way, Hudson Taylor was the administrator responsible for keeping in touch with each missionary, good or mediocre, to advise them in their work, to supply them constantly with funds and to maintain their morale in anxious and discouraging times.

No fully qualified doctor had yet come to help him. The smattering of medical knowledge which Edward Fishe, Robert White and Thomas Harvey boasted was not enough to relieve Hudson Taylor of medical responsibility for all his growing team and several in other missions. Soon, while threats to the foreign communities increased, to make up for their lack of the language these inexperienced newcomers tried their hand at doctoring Chinese. Hudson Taylor had to urge greater caution. Quite apart from untoward results of treatment, the wild rumours about foreigners drugging people and stealing their organs could put them in great danger. An experienced surgeon, warmly commended by George Müller, was preparing to leave his practice on the south coast of England and bring his wife and six children to China, when unaccountably he suddenly dropped out of the picture. So while the claims of widely deployed 'workers' constantly called for visits from Hudson Taylor, an almost unbroken sequence of illnesses and obstetric cases had to take priority.

Had it been possible to see more of his team, to talk with them and hold them to even their personal principles, his problems might have been fewer. But without his pastoral oversight, some were temperamentally vulnerable to vitiating influences. John Mara, the Free Methodist whom Hudson Taylor had helped to send to Ningbo, had to be invalided home with delirium tremens. But his own colleague, the once admirable George Crombie, was following the same trend, frock-coated and liking to be called 'Reverend' while drinking and smoking to excess. To William Berger, in the course of a long business letter on the distribution of funds, Hudson Taylor said, 'Those who . . . spend in Port, Claret, Brandy, Cigars, more than is good for them might be increasingly dissatisfied'.

Cardwell, while at Taizhou with Jackson, was 'a cipher', of no value. 'I am afraid that Cardwell has mistaken his calling altogether and that his dislike of the Chinese and everything Chinese, his bad judgment and temper will prevent his ever being of use as a missionary. Still I may be wrong, and China sadly needs missionaries . . . Crombie is a missionary, though of very low stamp.'

Cardwell's health had steadily deteriorated until Hudson Taylor almost despaired. Then, instead of letting Hudson Taylor manage his wife's confinement, Cardwell ran up a bill at the Ningbo hospital which he could not meet. At last he had revealed that his heart was set on pioneering in virgin Jiangxi, not Zhejiang. When Hudson Taylor agreed to his making Jiujiang his base for extensive evangelism in Jiangxi province, he had travelled up the Yangzi by steamer for a fare he could not afford, and by his quick temper so offended the shipping company that they ceased to grant discounts to missionaries. But no sooner had he received a welcome from V. C. Hart in Jiujiang, than Cardwell's health and morale recovered dramatically. He quickly made a reputation for courageous pioneering over great distances, soon had a number of converts as the nucleus of a church, and proved Hudson Taylor wrong.

Before Cardwell and his wife left Taizhou, 'Jackson's city', another chapter of incidents involved the restless Josiah Jackson. 'As to Jackson,' Hudson Taylor confided to William Berger, 'he has some very nice points about him, and has done some work. He speaks well the Ningpo and Taichau dialects and has a considerable knowledge of the Wenchau dialect. He gets on well with the Chinese—perhaps too well sometimes, sacrificing principle. But he is shallow. He smokes and jests and laughs with them until he loses all power to influence them seriously.' Jackson had proposed by letter to a girl in England whom he had never met and Hudson Taylor warned the Bergers, for her own sake on no account to let the lady come to China until she knew what she would be in for. Berger replied, 'Alas! what will be the end of poor Mr Jackson? I do not think I could have taken from him what you have . . . would strongly advise a loving but firm policy from the first, with those who are under your guidance.' Clearly Berger thought that Hudson Taylor was, if anything, too tolerant.

In another letter to Jackson, Hudson Taylor had said, 'You speak of my letter scolding you for leaving Taichau . . . You know, I think, that I am not a scold.' Perhaps he was not being firm enough. Whether it was the same lady or another, in 1873 a Miss Fanny Wilson, equally a stranger, did go to China, persuaded by Hudson Taylor not to say 'Yes' to Jackson until she had seen enough to form a sound opinion of him. She married and for ten years did wonders for him.

Poor Henry Reid was another problem. In spite of damage to his eye, his worst injury in the Yangzhou riot had not been physical but psychological. Still intent on doing his best, he toured the villages round Suzhou for weeks at a time, and later Qingjiangpu, trembling with apprehension that the violence might be repeated. When the Cardwells left Taizhou, the Rudland's took their place. William Rudland's limited education was not up to running the printing press at Zhenjiang and Reid was a suitable substitute. So Rudland found his niche and was still at Taizhou forty years later, building a thriving community of Christians. But Reid added to Hudson Taylor's worries by having a tiff with his Chinese colleague.

When the twenty-two-year-old Edward Fishe had told his parents about the 'Annie' he had met in the Taylor's home in Yangzhou and wanted to marry, he had not said that she was older than he and the uneducated, widowed nursemaid to the Taylor children. Colonel Fishe learned of it through the Bergers and remonstrated with his son, saying he must at least delay long enough to weigh carefully the difficulties he would face from their intellectual and social differences. But he did not forbid the marriage. Edward married her at once, so Hudson Taylor may have planned deliberately to put the excellent Mary (Bell) Rudland in Taizhou with her sister Annie (Bohannan) Fishe, to make a missionary of her. Edward also needed to be held to the essentials, for he too found amateur doctoring an attractive 'bypath meadow'. 'I do not think it at all . . . feasible for you to attempt the cure of opium-smokers,' Hudson Taylor wrote. 'Even had you the requisite knowledge of medicine it would not pay you for the time . . . Consider six or eight hours a day *sacred to the Lord* and His work, and let nothing hinder your giving this time (to language study and practice) till you can preach fluently and intelligibly.' Every hindrance to making Jesus known to the Chinese must be decisively rejected. 'Satisfaction is not to be found in any position or circumstances—it must spring from within or can never be found at all. It is very easy to fancy that we should be happy and useful in any position or circumstances save those we are in.'

Edward's brother Charles was a totally different type of man. Younger, and still youthful when the Bergers (who looked on him as a son) felt they could keep him in Britain no longer, he sailed with Thomas P. Harvey in the *Lammermuir* in July 1869, to arrive at Shanghai on November 9 and go straight to the Taylors and Judds at Yangzhou. On the Bergers' insistence they were to be protected from unsettling influences in Shanghai. To become a missionary he had sacrificed his chosen career in civil engineering and the social standing of his Dublin home circle—and for the present his secret love of 'Nellie' Faulding, Jennie's younger sister. Quiet, discreet, sound in judgment and with Hudson Taylor's magnetic way with children, it was not long before he was asked to become Hudson Taylor's personal secretary, when Emily Blatchley returned to Britain. Of all the team, Charles had more potential as a leader than any other, taciturn Stevenson and amicable McCarthy included.

Thomas Harvey had studied medicine at the London Hospital with Tom Barnardo long enough to have attended more than fifty midwifery cases and to begin surgical operations on cadavers, but was not yet fully qualified as a doctor. He also had 'a tendency to consumption' and an arrogant, overbearing manner when he was not, in contrast, quite charming. The Bergers had warned that he was excitable, 'ardent but easily damped, and as quickly cheered again'. Before long he also had to be told to stop doctoring and get on with the language. But Harvey was a law unto himself and frequently an anxiety to Hudson Taylor, who advised William Berger that in future candidates should complete their medical training or do none at all.

Robert White and his bride, Frances Gainfort, though not members of the CIM, lived at Mission premises as if they were while pleasing themselves. He too played the doctor and had to be warned of the risks. Many Chinese were afraid of this tall, dark stranger in foreign clothes. But by December 1869 White was in Shanghai looking for secular employment. In February 1870 Hudson Taylor wrote, 'Some persons seem really clever in doing the right thing in the worst possible way, or at the most unfortunate time. Really dull or rude persons will seldom be out of hot water in China; and though earnest and clever and pious, will not effect much. In nothing do we fail more, as a Mission, than in lack of tact and politeness.' And again, 'With a very wrong head, (White) has a true heart. I think that as a general rule the man, and certainly the woman, who does not take an interest in children, and who is unable to make children take an interest in himself or herself . . . is a somewhat uncertain boon to a work like ours.' Williamson, the Judds and Jennie were all fond of children, and children and adults liked them. The successful missionaries and potential failures came from varying social backgrounds. It was not the policy of enlisting artisans that was at fault. The medical students were little better. Encouraging the uncultured to be missionaries would have been in doubt if several had not been shaping well. Spiritual maturity or immaturity explained the difference.

Emily and the children
(January–June 1870)

Ever since March 1869 five-year-old Samuel had been suffering from tuberculous enteritis, unable to eat or drink without adding to his abdominal pain. Maria and Hudson Taylor kept him with them, even on their travels, leaving the other children with Emily and their nurse and coming back to them whenever possible. But Herbert, Howard, Maria and the one-year-old Charles Edward were too often ill and upset by the unsettledness of life. The meningitis scare of August and the onset of 'ague' were followed by purulent conjunctivitis affecting each of them in November. By December all the family were ailing. Maria was writing of it being little Maria's 'day for an attack' of malaria, and of Hudson that 'such a little thing knocks him up, and renders him quite unfit for work: as you know, he keeps on long after most people would give up.' In January it was Emily whose 'chest is worse than it has been for a long time', but Maria thought herself better than before.

Only with pangs of grief had they decided to ask Emily to take all except Charles Edward home to England. The prospect of parting with the children was 'the dark cloud which lies before us. Sometimes it seems for a time to take all one's strength and heart away.' To so affectionate a father the tunnel of grief looked endless. Samuel was so ill that he might not survive the journey, but it was his only hope. The long voyage round the Cape would be fatal and via America too expensive, so a French steamer taking two months via Suez was decided on. Hudson Taylor thought he might go with them as far as Suez. An absence of three months could be tolerated and a sea voyage always did him good. But no, he could not leave Maria and the team for so long. He might take Emily and the four children as far as Hong Kong. In the end he could not even do this although, as he later told Jennie, Emily's health was fragile. She would have died but for the change of climate. To trans-ship at Hong Kong would tax her severely, but the missionaries there would help her.

So they began preparing Western clothing for the growing children, and all Emily would need for them on the voyage, including school books. Herbert was nearly nine, and learning Greek. He must keep working at it. Samuel was worse as their departure time was approaching, in March, to avoid winter gales in the China seas and extreme heat in the Indian Ocean and Red Sea. After the new year Hudson Taylor went to Shanghai to arrange for the voyage, to see Consul Medhurst about the Yangzhou property and the reinstatement of the Meadows family and Williamson at Anqing, and to get back to Yangzhou for Emily's twenty-fifth birthday on January 24. But as he told George Müller and E. C. Lord on the 23rd, the day before he arrived home, 'our little invalid became suddenly

and rapidly worse' and 'never rallied fully'. Samuel died on February 4, when he was nearly six, and was buried the next day at Zhenjiang. A few hours after his death, a packet of cheques totalling £250 (a large sum at the time) arrived from George Müller. The grieving parents welcomed it as a token of God's love in the midst of ordeals.

A month later when they were all in Shanghai waiting for the ship, Maria managed a letter to Mary Berger, '(Samuel) was the most patient child, I had ever seen.' Uncomplaining in spite of constant pain from the ulceration of his intestines, he had endeared himself exceptionally to them.

On February 6, George Müller's wife died, and on May 20 the wife of James Wright, his fellow-director of the Bristol orphanage. Sleepless with grief Müller recorded his thoughts in a leaflet entitled *Satisfied with God*. It reached Hudson Taylor in time to console him when his own supreme test came.

Emily felt the approaching separation from the Taylors as intensely as the death of Samuel. 'The thing I dread', tuberculosis which had carried off several of her own family, was already far advanced in her own lungs. But in her own words, she had reached a contented state of wholehearted 'Acquiescence, not submission' to the will of God. Submission only was too grudging. 'I delight to do Thy will, O my God' had become her attitude. Yet the Taylor's help in bearing her illness was hard to forgo. 'Receive her as a daughter,' Maria wrote to Hudson's mother, 'for our sake to begin with, but soon you will continue to do so for her own sake . . . And . . . call her Emily and not Miss Blatchley . . . In leaving us she is leaving home for she has been to us as a daughter and a sister, both in one.'

In mid-February they left Yangzhou and Zhenjiang, travelling by canal boat to Shanghai to be there when Grace Ciggie arrived at last. Time and again, low water levels led to long delays when they ran aground, 'stuck fast for days together at shallow places'. Jennie came from Hangzhou with Mrs Wang Lae-djün to say goodbye to Emily at Suzhou—and without knowing it until long afterwards this was the factor which revolutionised a young man's life. A new believer at Suzhou named Ren was so impressed by her prayerful spirit and accounts of the spiritual life and influence of the New Lane church in Hangzhou, that he 'longed to be in that atmosphere'. After being baptised in November, he went to Hangzhou as a teacher in Jennie's school and, in the course of years, married Wang Lae-djün's daughter. When Lae-djün retired, Ren succeeded him as pastor of the whole Hangzhou circuit of churches—'one of the most gifted and devoted Chinese pastors in China'.

By March 5 the Taylors, Cordons and Emily were in Shanghai, living on their houseboats. Like so many foreigners in her situation, Mrs Cordon could not say precisely when her baby would be born, and for weeks to come travelled with the Taylors wherever they went. In a note to Stephan Barchet, Hudson Taylor wrote hopefully of 'running over to England' in a year or two, to consult with the Bergers and make permanent arrangements for the children. Grace Ciggie arrived and went on to Ningbo. But Hudson was preoccupied with administrative duties.

On the evening of March 22, Maria and he saw Emily and the children aboard the French steamer and he went ashore again. After midnight he began a business letter to the Bergers with, 'At 5.30 a.m. they steam away for Hong Kong and we leave for Su-chair, DV . . . Miss Blatchley will be better than twenty letters, being more intimately acquainted with Mission matters than any other member.'

As soon as they had gone, the Taylors and Mrs Cordon, still 'daily expecting her confinement', started back to Suzhou. 'The moment I can leave her, I must hasten on to Yangchau as Mrs Judd (has dysentery). I feel very uneasy about her—one of our most useful female missionaries.'

On April 9 he was writing from an overcrowded houseboat in Zhenjiang. Elizabeth Judd had been brought there, 'near the point of death', needing to be nursed day and night. 'I found the Judds here, and Mr Meadows and family and Duncan, so we are pretty thick on the ground. Mrs Judd I was quite shocked to see. Her face drawn to one side, her strength gone . . . She is very ill.' In asking Mary Bowyer to come and help, he added, 'There is very little hope of her recovery.' What neither he nor Maria said in their letters, Charles Judd recorded. Although very unfit for travelling at all, Maria had left the boat as soon as she heard of Elizabeth's condition, 'took a (springless) wheel-barrow and came about thirty miles across country', the fastest route. 'She arrived at (Zhenjiang) late in the day, very much worn', but insisted that Charles Judd should get some sleep while she herself sat up with Elizabeth all night long. Mary Bowyer came at once from Nanjing, but even then Maria shared night duty.

The reinstatement of the Meadows family at Anqing 'with the exception of little Sammy whom we have borrowed for a couple of months' (Hudson Taylor said), relieved the overcrowding, and on April 14 Elizabeth Judd was beginning to recover. But Hudson Taylor, still living on the houseboat, had to go up to Yangzhou on business and was away when Maria, sleeping after night duty, was called just in time to receive 'Miss Cordon' into the world.

As soon as Elizabeth Judd was well enough, Hudson Taylor sent her with her husband Charles and Mary Bowyer to Putuo for five weeks of sunbathing, keeping her baby in Maria's care. 'Sometimes the longings for (our) dear absent ones (Grace and Samuel as well as the other children at sea) are indescribable,' he confessed to his mother. Yet his administrative work had to be carried on regardless of all else. The marriage of orphans and others committed to the care of missionaries was one of their responsibilities. To F. C. Lord he wrote, 'You were wishing to get a good husband for Pao-tsie. If we are not too late, we should be glad to propose on behalf of Ah-liang, our head-printer under Mr Rudland . . . superintendent over the other workers.

2.14 Travel by wheelbarrow, even for long distances

Have you any other girls . . . whom you are prepared to betrothe?'

By April the Bergers had disclosed painstaking plans for meeting Emily and the children. Friends at Cannes and Dijon, a German pastor and a man at the harbour in Marseilles were 'on the lookout night and day . . . for the French Mail packet'. The Grattan Guinnesses in Paris would keep them for a brief rest. Then the Bergers would meet them at Dover and bring them home to Saint Hill. Both were there when the travellers landed on the 24th. Until they caught sight of Herbert's Chinese shoes, they could recognise none of them. In Paris Herbert had had what was feared to be 'hydrocephalus'. Mrs Faulding told Jennie, 'I was quite shocked to see dear Emily, she is so altered—no one who has not known her intimately would recognise her, even dear Mr and Mrs Berger did not know her as she stood on the steamer.'

Mrs Berger had more to add for Maria,

'Beloved Miss B. gives me most concern . . . (On June 2) a ring at the bell announced the arrival of a gentleman in his gig . . . It was her father, who could keep away no longer . . . the meeting was most affecting but I left the room immediately . . . She is now walking about with her father in the grounds and round the lake . . . And now farewell, my precious friend. The Lord throw around you His everlasting arms!'— prophetic words again. Maria would never read them, for with June in China they entered upon two months more tense and terrible than they had yet known.

By the end of June when Emily and the children moved to live with Hudson Taylor's sister, Amelia, in Bayswater, they we're 'all much improved in health'. '(Even) Miss B.,' Mary Berger wrote, 'seems to be rallying.' She needed to, for much of her time at Saint Hill had had to be spent briefing the Bergers about China, and working with him on accounts and on the *Occasional*. Business matters she had been commissioned to attend to in London would need all her feeble strength for three more weeks.

The Stott and Ciggie story
(March–August 1870)

After nearly two years constantly in Wenzhou without another western colleague, and never speaking anything but Chinese, George Stott had written to Grace Ciggie. Would she be his wife? For three years she had persevered as the friend of 'fallen women' in the Glasgow Salt Market, maturing and regaining her physical strength. But China was her goal and the Bergers had kept in touch with her. She consulted them about Stott whom she barely knew. They had been together in the Taylor household in Mile End for only three weeks before he went to China. Then she waited while they consulted Hudson Taylor.

At last his reply was received in London and Grace Ciggie came down from Glasgow ready to sail. Try as he might, William Berger had been unable to find a missionary escort for her. All others were travelling by steamer, while careful use of funds still meant the cheaper route by clipper ship for members of the CIM. Grace was game for anything. So a ship was found, the *Kaisow*, with a genial captain and his wife for company. The Bergers fitted up a cabin and the Fauldings saw her off on December 4, 1869, alone among strangers. She was imperturbable.

When the captain said the voyage could take one hundred days at best from the Channel to Shanghai, or two weeks longer even with good winds, she declared that the hundredth day would be her twenty-fifth birthday. Would he please get her there on March 12? In the South China Sea she was still hoping for 'a real storm' and was not disappointed. They reached Wusong on the ninety-ninth day and the captain took her up the Huangpu river to Shanghai by steam-launch on her birthday. He and his wife remained her lifelong friends. She was the last member of the Mission ever to go to or from China by sailing ship.

George Stott arrived at Shanghai. Four and a half years had passed since they had last seen each other at the London docks when Stott and the Stevensons sailed. He carried her off to Ningbo, and put her in the care of the ever-obliging Lords for the month's residence required by consular regulations before their marriage on April 26, 1870. Wenzhou was only one hundred and fifty miles away—three or four days by sea-going junk. But pirates still infested the lonely waters among the many islands down the coast. George wanted to leave at once and take his bride to the humble Chinese home he had prepared for her, but no junk owner would sail without a full convoy and war junk escort. For three weeks they searched before being able to start. And even then, when they reached the Zhoushan Islands their escort would go no further without more war junks for protection. For nine frustrating days they kicked their heels, while a tearful Grace endured her rude initiation into rough travelling conditions in the cramped and crowded junk.

At last after fifteen days they reached 'home'—a bedroom, living-room and study above George's noisy school—only to be besieged day after day by insatiable crowds wanting to see the first foreign woman to visit Wenzhou. Hardly had the excitement died down than the whole of China was electrified by the news that, in June, a massacre of foreigners had taken place at Tianjin in the north.

For three months it was unsafe for George Stott to leave the house, let alone for his wife to show her face. When he had to venture out he was cursed and stoned.

A climate of unrest (1869–70)

Ever since the proclamation of the September 1869 anti-foreign, anti-Christian 'Hunan manifesto', a growing disquiet had been apparent to everyone in touch with the people. The alarms in Wenzhou were only the local expression of a nationwide excitement, an orchestrated surge of antagonism leading directly to the most serious international incident in China between 1860 and 1900.

Unrest was not confined to China. Jealous of Christian progress in Chieng Mai, Thailand, the northern king beheaded two church members and threatened the rest and their missionaries. Dr Daniel McGilvary wrote on September 29, 1869, 'If you never hear from us again, know that we are in heaven, and do not . . . regret the loss of our lives. We are all peaceful and happy.' For four months nothing more was heard of them. But they survived and the king himself fell ill while on a visit to Bangkok and returned home to die.

In Japan William Gamble reported in January 1870 his personal observation of the mass abduction by Japanese government troops of hundreds of Roman Catholic Christians from the valley of Urakami[145] near Nagasaki. Refusing to recant, more than seven hundred were sent by ship into exile and, according to his information, three thousand had already been taken from their homes.

But in China the superstitions and gullibility of the masses were being exploited by the lurid tales about foreigners. The ancient practice of ancestor worship and *fengshui* lent itself to exploitation. In the words of the *Cambridge Modern History*, 'It was impossible to describe the alarm and consternation of the Chinese when at first they believed that native magicians were bewitching them; nor their indignation and anger when they were told that these insidious foes were the agents of foreigners.'

The excitement of the people had been encouraged in the summer of 1869 by the news that Zeng Guofan

> was making preparations for the expulsion of foreigners from China; his removal from Nankin to (Zhili) was considered from the first to be connected with such a plan. Thus one thing after another has increased, deepened and extended the anti-foreign feeling. No sooner was his approach announced than we heard rumours of the intended destruction or expulsion of foreigners. Every month or two these were revived ... Even in (Tianjin) where foreigners had for so many years engaged in business and missionary operations, so great was this fear that it was with much difficulty that buildings could be rented in new localities.

That feeling had been strongly exacerbated by the activities of the so-called French Protectorate. Through the concessions made in the treaties of 1844, 1858 and 1860, all Roman Catholic missionaries and their converts had come under the protection of France. The issue of French passports to priests of other nationalities, the enforcement in the inland provinces of treaty concessions, and the exemption of Catholic Church members from taking part in non-Christian observances and celebrations put the missionaries in a strong position. In 1870 an edition of the Imperial Code, the *Da Qing Lu Li*, was issued with its old articles interdicting Christianity deleted and anti-Christian decrees abrogated. But the return to the Church of properties long since confiscated and put to other uses could not but create deep resentment, as did foreign interference in the natural processes of the Chinese courts of law.

Growing tension everywhere became focused alarmingly on Tianjin when a date was openly cited in other cities for a destructive attack on the French consulate

and missions in Tianjin. On June 14 people were saying in 'Sham-ts'ing', one hundred and fifty miles or more from Tianjin, that attacks would soon begin. In Tianjin itself foreigners first heard these reports a day or two later. 'Some servants in foreign employ . . . removed their bedding etcetera . . . gave the reasons for doing so, and told when the attack would take place.'

Far away in Dengzhou (now Penglai) in the neighbouring province of Shandong, while John Nevius was visiting Hangzhou, ugly rumours of danger to the American Presbyterian missionaries led to their being evacuated to Yantai by British gunboat.[146] The rumours included an intended massacre at Tianjin, long before it took place. Everywhere missionaries recognised the extent of the threat and were asking, as C. A. Stanley of the American Board in Tianjin put it, 'Will missionaries be allowed to stay (in China)?' Their own consuls and ministers might order them out, even if the Chinese did not.

Count–down at Tianjin[147]
(May–June 1870)

There had been foreign residents at Tianjin since 1858, when the British, French and Americans, represented by Lord Elgin, Baron Gros and the Hon W. B. Reed, had captured the Dagu forts and established themselves in the former imperial palace of Huanghailou and adjoining temples for the negotiation of the 'Treaty of Tientsin' (see 1, pp 448–49). These sacred precincts at the junction of the Grand Canal, the Bei He (North River) and the Hai He (the river to the Gulf) had been occupied by the French in 1861 after the capture of Peking. Facing the Chinese walled city, they stood close to the *yamen* of Chonghou, the imperial commissioner for foreign affairs. There the French had built their consulate and the provocative Notre Dame des Victoires, a cathedral due to be destroyed twice and defiantly rebuilt a third time.

In the suburb between the North Gate of the old city and the Hai He, the 'Soeurs de Charité', known also as Sisters of Mercy and Sisters of Saint Vincent de Paul, had an

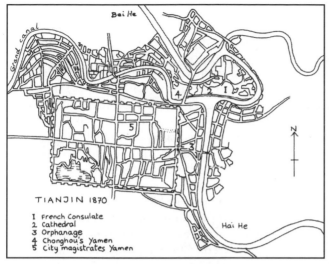

2.15 Map of Tianjin, 1870

TIANJIN 1870

1 French Consulate
2 Cathedral
3 Orphanage
4 Chonghou's Yamen
5 City magistrates Yamen

orphanage staffed in 1870 by five French, one Irish, two Belgian, and two Italian nuns. An international 'settlement' housed the merchant community and Protestant missions, the LMS, American Board and Methodist New Connexion, whose chapels were dotted about the city and suburbs.

Chonghou's influence and prestige, derived directly from the Zongli Yamen, were directed towards foreign relations, but he 'had no place in the provincial administration'. In other words, 'he could bring in the imperial authority, but could not move a policeman.' Among foreigners he was highly respected for 'his benevolence, his pleasing manners, and his perfect courtesy', in Admiral Keppel's words, 'the most finished Chinese gentleman he had ever met, with the exception of the Viceroy of Canton'.

A summary of many subsequent accounts of developments in 1870 epitomised the common understanding of events.

> There can be no doubt that the indiscretion of the poor sisters brought upon them and their Mission this terrible blow. They were accustomed to purchase children, with a view to baptising them and thus saving their souls. Many that were sold to them were sickly; and also an epidemic broke out; and the result was that small coffins were continually coming out of the establishment for burial. This

seemed to the ignorant populace to confirm the belief that the eyes and hearts of children were used in the manufacture of drugs; and one woman who had been employed as cook declared that she had herself witnessed the whole operation and had fled in horror.

Although it was reported that the nuns bought the babies, this was stoutly denied in subsequent inquiries. But they did receive abandoned babies and those that would otherwise be discarded.

A Baron Hubner carefully investigated the facts and the historian H. B. Morse relied on Hubner and first-hand witnesses when he wrote:

> As at Yangchow the final incitement to riot had been the rumour that 'twenty-four children were missing' and therefore presumably kidnapped; so at (Tianjin) the first sign of trouble was manifest in rumours current towards the middle of May, that 'certain children had disappeared, kidnapped by persons in the pay of the missionaries.'

> The practice of kidnapping children and selling them for immoral purposes was known to be common throughout China; and this practice was popularly associated with the horrible mystery hanging over the fate of the children, who disappeared into the orphanage ... Matters were made worse by an epidemic, which visited the orphanage early in June, and caused the death of between thirty and forty children whose bodies were disinterred by crowds of hundreds of Chinese who raided the cemetery daily. This stirred the people to a fiercer rage, and the search for kidnappers became active. On June 6 and later dates, four men were arrested, tried and executed without much formality; and on the 18th another, being arrested and sent for trial, confessed, under torture of course, that he had relations with the cathedral verger (Chinese), to whom he sold his stolen children.

By June even devotees were staying away from both Catholic and Protestant missions, and evading the missionaries when they went out. 'Application was made to the authorities on several occasions . . . by both the English and French Consuls for proclamations to quell the excitement, but no notice was taken of them—they were not answered.' The prefect issued a proclamation against the kidnappers, tacitly endorsing the testimony of the convicted men by its silence about the orphanage and accusing 'other parties' (understood to mean the Catholics) of employing the kidnappers. At once an honorific 'Ten Thousand Name Umbrella' was presented to him by 'a grateful people'. The mandarin hierarchy of Tianjin 'solemnly affirmed the guilt of the Sisters and demanded an inquest', while Commissioner Chonghou pleaded that the matter was outside his jurisdiction.

A mob dominated the inquest and the allegations were declared factual. The local magistrate then demanded an investigation into conditions at the Catholic mission and orphanage. Chonghou arranged for it to be made. On the morning of June 21 the *daotai*, prefect and local magistrate went instate to the cathedral, followed by a large crowd, and confronted the verger with the nineteen-year-old witness who had claimed to sell children to him. His tales were there and then proved to be false. The accusations had been pure invention, to provide a pretext for rabble-rousing. Chonghou claimed he was actually drafting a proclamation in exoneration of the Catholics when the sound of uproar reached him from the direction of the cathedral.

Massacre[148] (June 21, 1870)

Soon after midday fire-gongs were sounded and a mob immediately collected. Witnesses confirmed that instead of carrying fire buckets, the volunteer firemen poured on to the streets armed with weapons, headed for the French consulate, and attacked it. Consul Fontanier at once donned official uniform and made for Chonghou's *yamen* to demand protection.

Commissioner Chonghou's report to

his superiors, the Zongli Yamen, was later confirmed by C. Hannen, the Tianjin Commissioner of Customs, to his own superior officer, Robert Hart. Chonghou had already sent a military mandarin to the scene of the uproar when he was told that M. Fontanier had arrived, demanding to see him. Going to his reception hall, Chonghou was met by a display of fury. The consul, with two pistols in his belt and accompanied by Simon, his consular secretary, wearing a sword, rushed towards him, smashing cups and other objects on a table. Then, 'keeping up an incessant torrent of abuse' he drew a pistol and fired it. 'He was seized,' Chonghou reported, 'and to avoid a personal collision I withdrew.' On returning, Chonghou 'told him that the crowd outside had a very threatening aspect . . . but, reckless of his life, he rushed out of the *yamen*.' Chonghou sent men to escort the consul, and the district magistrate meeting him on the way tried to prevent him from going further, but he fired at the magistrate, hitting one of his attendants. At this the mob surrounded and killed him, 'stripped him of his clothes, mutilated his corpse and threw it into the canal'.

In the short time he was away the consulate had been looted and burned down and everyone in it murdered. At this point a brigadier in the Chinese army named Chen Guorui, a protégé of Zeng Guofan, arrived with a body of men who joined in the destruction and firing of the Catholic cathedral and mission residence. Enquiry later confirmed that a bugle had been sounded at Chen Guorui's quarters at about the same time as the fire-gongs. (More was to be heard of Chen Guorui. He had commanded the garrison which had joined in the riot at Yangzhou, and two years later was to repeat his rabble-rousing there, with Hudson Taylor again as his prime target.)

The mob then made for the orphanage about a mile away, demolishing the 'English chapel' on their route. The orphanage was plundered and burned, the ten nuns were stripped naked before the mob, barbarously stabbed, hacked to death and thrown into the flames. 'Every French man and woman who could be laid hands on was killed, with every accompaniment of outrage and mutilation . . . and between thirty and forty Chinese employed in the mission and orphanage.' Only the charred remains of the Sisters were found afterwards, but the horribly mutilated bodies of most of the other victims were recovered from the river. Among them were the consul and secretary, two priests, four other French men and women, including a merchant and his wife living a mile from the main scene, two Russian men and the wife of one of them. These three Russians were killed amid shouts of 'Kill the French first and then the other foreigners.' But three other Russians were allowed to escape on pleading that they were 'not French but Russian'. A British doctor named Fraser was attacked, but being on horseback at the time, like W. H. Medhurst twenty-five years before (see 1, p 240) escaped at speed. Two Swiss subjects were protected by the mandarins and sent under escort to the British consulate. As the victims' bodies were found they too were delivered to Lay's consulate.

In reporting this to the British chargé d'affaires in Peking (no longer Sir Rutherford Alcock but Thomas Francis Wade, the hero of the Shanghai Battle of Muddy Flat and later, with Harry Parkes, an interpreter to Lord Elgin in the 1860 campaign), Consul Lay declared on July 24 and 25 his conviction that the assault was directed against the French only. Other members of the community strongly challenged this opinion. Certain of reprisals, rich Chinese merchants began leaving Tianjin. Lay warned that 'the Chinese are very determined now, and I am quite certain will take up the gauntlet and fight' if the French attempted reprisals. So the French chargé d'affaires had to beware. If only a small force were to be sent, the Chinese troops would react against the whole foreign community.

On June 21 as the consulate, cathedral and orphanage were burning, Lay's assistant dispatched a courier with a message to the British naval commander at Hong Kong

2.16 The gutted cathedral at Tianjin

and another to Consul W. H. Medhurst at Shanghai. Medhurst received his on June 22, six days later, and the commodore at Hong Kong on July 4 sent on immediately. The news was telegraphed on July 23 from Point de Galle on the southern tip of Ceylon, still the most easterly extent of the cable, and reached London on the 25th. This was the first intimation received in any of the chancelleries of Europe, a week after the outbreak of war between France and the North German Confederation. The first report from Wade in Peking, dispatched on July 6 and telegraphed from Kiahkta on the Manchurian border with Russian Amur reached London on the same day, July 25, more than a month after the massacre. Undoubtedly France would in normal circumstances have taken drastic action, but Napoleon III was in no position to undertake war thousands of miles from home.

The CIM at risk (May–July 1870)

February and March had been busy and fraught with the illness and death of five-year-old Samuel and the departure of Emily and the older children to England. April came in with Elizabeth Judd at death's door. But May was like no other month. 'We had previously known something of trial in one station or another, but now in all, simultaneously, or nearly so, a wide-spread excitement shook the very foundations of native society.'[149] A crescendo of excitement took everyone by surprise.

In writing to George Müller on February 17, Hudson Taylor had said, 'Mr Wade, our new chargé d'affaires at Pekin, is strongly opposed to Christian missions and may cause us much trouble.' In the event Wade did make life difficult but without much effect, and to his own discredit. The first sign of his becoming a thorn in the flesh of Hudson Taylor and other progressive missionaries was his prohibition of the purchase of the Yangzhau and Anqing premises. But the year had begun with few hints of other tensions. On March 19 conditions had still been calm enough for three merchants, including the Meadowses' friend M. G. Hollingworth, to set out from Jiujiang on a 550-mile journey southwards, crossing the Wuyi mountain range (see map 1.1: 1, p 2) to reach Fuzhou without incident on April 16.[150] Yet to William Berger on May 30 Hudson Taylor said, with strong premonitions:

> I increasingly feel that the time is short, very short, and we must not be thinking of pleasing ourselves but of fulfiling the work our loving Master has given us to do ... the work is quiet but the congregations are good ... The weather is now becoming warm and ... might occasion some anxious thoughts—Shall we suffer much from sickness, or lose, any of our number before the season is over?

> [And on June 13] At Yangchau we have had (rumours) again, *owing to a most* unwise attempt of the Roman Catholic missionaries to remove some children from Yangchau to Shanghai. At (Anqing) also rumours have been rife, and Mr Meadows is in trouble about his house; his rascally landlord having taken steps to try and eject him.

Louise Desgraz had been given a third Chinese baby (left on her doorstep) to bring up in the care of Chinese women, and Mary Bowyer had another, being mothered by Catherine Duncan. The one Jennie Faulding had accepted and wisely left in the care of the Chinese had died while she was away from home. The rumours being circulated about the Catholics had suddenly made this fostering of children an increasingly risky practice.

> It appears that there has really been some kidnapping going on, which has been industriously fathered upon the foreigners, notwithstanding proclamations put out

by the mandarins, threatening to punish anyone who should circulate such lies; and the people have shown their belief in the lies by making large white crosses in every street; that the trampling underfoot of the Romanist sign might work evil for the foreigners.[151]

Then on June 14, C. T. Gardner, the acting-consul in Zhenjiang sent this dispatch to Hudson Taylor:

> I have to inform you that the country round about Nanking, (Zhenjiang) and Yangchow is at present in a very excited and riotous state on account of rumours ... Popular excitement has run so high that the authorities have already been constrained to execute several individuals ...

> Under these circumstances I have to warn you to be exceedingly cautious ... not leaving your house after nightfall and (when this is found impracticable) carrying a lantern with your name in Chinese upon it. The authorities at Nanking have had to yield so far to popular prejudice as also to notify that (Chinese) women and children are not to be allowed to go out of doors.

> I need hardly remind you that when the passions of the people are roused the authorities have not always the power even where they have the will to protect you from outrage.

> I have to request you to forward with as little delay as possible a copy of this letter to the various members of your mission.[152]

Soon afterwards, Consul Medhurst sent another dispatch, in even stronger terms, primarily for Duncan and Harvey in Nanjing.

Shanghai, 15th June 1870

Gentlemen,

> ... at the coming examination season you are likely to be in peril of your lives and property ...

> I have addressed the Local Authorities a communication requesting them to afford you all the protection in their power, but you will do well nevertheless to be cautious how far you exasperate, or intensify the ill-feeling against you by too persistently maintaining your position within the

city whilst the excitement prevails ... Chinese mobs have already in similar instances shown themselves capable (of acts of violence) in their blind fury against foreigners. And you must be well aware by this time that ... Her Majesty's Consul cannot undertake to extend protection by forcible measures to persons resident in the interior.[153]

The unsettled state of affairs was not Hudson Taylor's only anxiety during June. Maria's confinement was approaching, and she was as frail as she had ever been. In a note to Louise Desgraz from Zhenjiang on June 14 he explained, 'I am sorry to be away so long . . . and sorry that you should be left alone. But Mrs Taylor cannot be left now safely even for a day; the effect of the last two journeys on her was such that I dare not risk another.' Their friendship was deep, and now, in his note about Maria he went on,

> I have got the very passage for you, and God has so blessed it to my own soul. It is in John 7, vv. 37–39. 'If any man thirst, let him come unto Me and drink.' Who does not thirst? ... No matter how intricate my path, how difficult my service. No matter how great my need, how obstinate my disease. No matter how sad my bereavement, how far my loved ones may be away. No matter how helpless I am; how deep are my soul-yearnings—Jesus can meet all (my need), and more than meet (it).

To James Meadows he wrote on the same day, one of many letters to his missionaries which reflect upon his leadership. 'Matters were in a frightful state in (Nanjing) when I last heard. But two hundred proclamations had been put out by the (viceroy) and it was hoped matters would blow over. (Rumours) are also serious, to say the least, at Yangzhou.' Two days later he told John Stevenson at Shaoxing, 'The people are agitated to a degree . . . but in any case, "The name of the Lord is a strong tower: the righteous flee into it and are safe."' And on June 20 to Duncan and Harvey at Nanjing:

> Please let me have a line, if ever so brief, either from you or Harvey every other day

till the excitement somewhat subsides ... I scarcely know how or what to advise you. I had thought it might be well for you and Mr Harvey to go out of the city with books etc. into the surrounding villages and towns ... In the event of any stir it would be ascertained that you were absent, and your house might not be molested; or if it were, you would escape all personal violence. But I learn that the excitement is even greater in the country than in the city, so that this course is probably not desirable, and might lead to still further misconceptions. [It might be misconstrued as an expedition to collect babies or kidnap people.]

> If the danger of riots seems to increase; the effort, bona fide or otherwise, of the Mandarins to suppress them seem unavailing ... consider whether you should not retire for a time ... To leave unnecessarily would be very undesirable, lest the people in authority should think it a good plan to get rid of us, to keep up chronic excitement against foreigners. On the other hand, to stay and to be injured or killed, at a time when you are powerless to help the native Christians, and can expect little fruit from immediate efforts to spread the Gospel, would be unfortunate, especially as even if you escaped unhurt, there would be a good deal of talk and writing about your obstinacy in remaining after so many warnings.[154]

On the same day he enclosed cuttings from Shanghai newspapers and copies of 'Consular Notifications' with a letter to William Berger, this time about unfounded criticisms being levelled at the CIM.

> Just a hasty line. We are in great perplexity ... Around (Nan-jing) (we are informed by one of the Romanists), rumours have sprung from the missionaries having sent out native agents to baptise beggars and children ... I should leave at once for (Nanjing) were it not for the state of my dear wife, who might need my help at any time—indeed I am not sure that in spite of that I must not run up there to see how matters are; the Lord guide! You can scarcely conceive how destitute of news we are, tho' the place is only (35 miles) from here. Hence our embarrassment. The cellars under the RC building at Nankin are at all times a great mystery to

the (Chinese). And to their minds a prima facie evidence of something suspicious and wrong.[155]

Almost certainly they were wine cellars, adding incidentally to the coolness of the house.

On June 21 (the day of the massacre at Tianjin, though news of it would not arrive until the 29th), Hudson Taylor acknowledged receipt of Medhurst's dispatch saying:

> The latest tidings I received from our Nankin missionaries were favourable. The popular excitement ... appeared on Friday, the 17th inst, to be about over. Throughout its duration our Missionaries received no insult, even in the streets, nor were they treated otherwise than usual ... Some months ago we had arranged for the absence of (Mrs Duncan and Miss Bowyer) from Nankin during the exams, and had maturely deliberated on precautionary measures. (The viceroy's deputy) approved of them, and intimated to Mr Duncan that the Mandarins are fully prepared to protect them while quietly remaining in their houses (the chapel being closed during the exams).[156]

But as so often, it was to Jennie Faulding that Hudson Taylor turned that day:

> Dear Sister, We need your prayers; things look very dark. One difficulty follows another very fast but God reigns, not chance. At Nankin the excitements have been frightful ... Our people have met with no insult ... but had the (RC church) been sacked, they would scarcely have escaped scot-free.

As tensions, difficulties and setbacks increased, this phrase, 'God reigns!' was used more and more as a victory slogan by one after another in the team.

Writing again to encourage Duncan at Nanjing, he reminded him that Ezra and Nehemiah rebuilt the walls of Jerusalem 'in troubled times like these'. 'There has been a strange and erroneous article in the *Shanghai Evening Courier* about (Nanjing) . . . It will be a very great thing, and a most important precedent if you can manage to remain in the city through the [literary] exams—a precedent that will bear more or less on work in every city of the three provinces subject to the (viceroy)'— Ma Xinyi, viceroy of Jiangsu, Jiangxi and Anhui. Another long letter on the 25th gave more careful advice, ending with 'I may come up after Mrs T.'s confinement and relieve you perhaps.'

Anxious to keep the Bergers informed, but still unaware of the massacre at Tianjin, he sent them a long letter on June 27.

> The accounts in the papers have I believe been very incorrect and exaggerated ... It may be of importance to you to know the *Dove* has never left (Zhenjiang), and that no French gunboat has been to (Nanjing) about these matters, and that we have neither desired or needed any help of this kind, or of any other kind. I would advise extreme caution in publishing anything about these matters, as we do not know what use the Authorities may make of them.
>
> The most trying thing that occurred was the sudden illness and death of a child in our (Yangzhou) school in the absence of its mother. Mr C. Fishe guided by a very worthy and capable (Chinese) helper, acted with commendable discretion. The child was sent to two or more native doctors, the disease was at once pronounced incurable by them. The prescription of one of them was secured as an evidence, as well as for use. The medicine was administered and though the case terminated fatally there was abundant evidence that all was done for the child which could have been done for it. Finally they got the constable to bury it he having previously in the presence of numerous witnesses examined the body to see the eyes etc. were there and that there was no scratch on the body in front or behind, and that the fingers and toes and other parts were perfect. The next thing was to get some evidence of the funeral having been conducted by the (constable). Had he been asked to write one, doubtless he would have refused. He was therefore asked by a native teacher for a bill for the expenses that the latter might be able to show to me in evidence that he (the teacher) had had bona fide to pay away these sums. The bill was at once made out, and is an evidence, should

one ever be needed, that the funeral was attended to by him. It has given rise however to no trouble so far; and is not likely to do so.[157]

Maria also wrote to Mrs Berger (with the thermometer 'at times over 90 degrees'):

We have far more to fear from the cool false statements of some of our own countrymen, who probably care nothing about us ... (For instance) one of the Shanghai newspapers stated a short time ago that Mr Taylor had ordered his missionaries away from Nanking, thus leaving the RC missionaries to bear the brunt alone. Now in Nanking what excitement there has been against foreigners has been almost entirely against the RCs; Mr Duncan has been there the whole of the time, and Mr Harvey only absent a few days ...

The 'Interpreter in Charge' here wrote a few days ago to the Commander of the Gunboat stationed at (Zhenjiang) requesting him to send a boat up to (Yangzhou) in order if necessary 'to cover the retreat of the missionaries' ... The judgment of the commander differed from that of the 'Interpreter in Charge' and he wrote a reply accordingly. Now 'the missionaries' had no idea of beating a retreat; and certainly had circumstances compelled them to leave Yangchau they would—after the absurd nonsense that has been current in England about 'Missionaries and Gunboats'—have preferred doing so in some other way than under the 'cover' of a man-of-war boat, but—and here is the danger to us—this correspondence being official, goes home to (the Foreign Office), and I suppose it would be almost impossible to convince those in authority there that we had known nothing whatever of the proposed step until afterwards, that such an idea had never entered our heads, and that when we did hear of it we hardly knew whether to be more annoyed or amused at it.

But God is our refuge and strength and surely we may as confidently trust Him about (rumours) in England or amongst the foreigners in China as about (rumours) in Inland Cities in China.[158]

After news of the Tianjin massacre arrived, Hudson Taylor sent Reid as his messenger to Duncan in Nanjing.

I thought you should know first how serious was the attack on the French, second that as far as we know the English had been unmolested ... Now everyone knows that the Nankin students are under a stronger rein and are more easily governed than those of any other place in China ... (so if) you can safely hold on would say by all means do so, or give me the opportunity of exchanging with you for a time, which I will cheerfully do [Several times he made this offer in replying to nervous missionaries wondering if they should pull out. Relief 'for a time' could do them good.]

You will note that all I have said is based on the assumption that there is no special risk to life in staying, nor of provoking a riot by your presence. Should things so change as to lead you to see that there was seriously increased danger in remaining, it might be worth your thought as to whether you should come down here and personally confer with me ...

By all means hire a boat by the month and do it at once. If matters look in the least threatening, have a trustworthy servant in the boat when you are not in it; that the boat people may not desert you. Do not be too anxious about your things in the case of real danger. Do not leave the house till compelled, if any sudden attack should be made on you when you are in it—for the poorest wall is a great shelter from all but fire and some shelter from that. If the house should be attacked in your absence, I would then make either for the boat or a yamen.[159]

On the 27th he had written, 'I advise you to engage a Hupeh boat by the month. Hupeh men are in general bold and faithful to their employers.' Such a leader deserved the gratitude he received from his colleagues.

After the massacre[160] (July 1870)

As the mob came to the end of their gruesome work at the orphanage in Tianjin, shouts were heard of 'determination to attack' the foreign settlement and merchants' warehouses. If Consul Lay had not acted so swiftly to bring all the foreigners together under the resolute protection of the defence volunteers, and if a heavy thunderstorm had not sent the rioters running for shelter and quenched their fires, the slaughter could have been far worse. It stopped at sixty to seventy Chinese Catholics killed, more, including many Protestants, wounded, and twenty-two foreigners dead, only one unmutilated.

The remaining missionaries retreated to a merchant steamer on the river, but Consul Lay saw danger in any hint of fear, and (Wade reported to Lord Clarendon) 'fully alive to the dangers surrounding him . . . opposed every proposition made him to quit his post, and it is in chief part to his firmness that I attribute the security of the foreign residents.' Chonghou was persuaded to calm the people, but his offer of Chinese troops to guard the settlement 'was declined with thanks'. Lay's certainty that an inadequate use of force by the French 'would be the signal for the rising of the whole of the troops in the city' led him to urge Wade to prevail upon the French chargé d'affaires in Peking to ensure that it did not happen. So an extremely tense peace returned to Tianjin during the succeeding days.

As soon as word of the massacre reached Peking, the foreign envoys realised that 'the interests of all foreign nations and the lives of all foreigners were at stake'. A collective note was addressed to the Zongli Yamen, pointing out that 'foreigners are not everywhere sufficiently protected by local authorities in China'. Justice should be seen to be done or the outrages would be repeated elsewhere. The very next day, June 25, an imperial decree exonerated Chonghou and condemned the prefect and other magistrates with the words, 'their delinquencies admit of no palliation', but no arrests were made until two weeks had passed.

The spectre of war rose visibly before the Court and Council. On the 28th Chonghou was commanded to investigate with the viceroy and then to proceed to France to explain and apologize. Zeng Guofan, the viceroy of Zhili, whose word alone could have done all that was needed, took his time, not arriving from his palace at Baoding until eighteen days after the massacre, a fortnight after receiving his orders. The orphanage was declared innocent of all charges against it, and the people misled by inflammatory placards from elsewhere in the empire an attempt to protect the magistrates. Not until August 7 was the order issued to put the prefect and *xian* magistrate on trial. Brigadier Chen Guorui, 'a military officer of evil reputation' but the protégé of Zeng Guofan, present and leading the attacking mob on June 21, was passed over as of no importance.

On July 5 Wade wrote to Consul Medhurst in Shanghai saying that Peking was entirely peaceful, as if the crisis was limited to Tianjin, but this was far from the case. 'Either as a result of the outbreak in (Tianjin), or . . . as part of the universal and premeditated anti-foreign agitation', H. B. Morse wrote, 'the whole of China seethed with unrest throughout the rest of the year.'

The trouble at Nanjing had begun at about the same time as at Tianjin, with multiplying reports of children missing and the presentation of 'evidence' implicating the Catholic mission in the kidnapping. In spite of strong action by the viceroy, Ma Xinyi, including decapitations, the agitation increased and an attack on the mission became imminent. On the orders of the viceroy, the prefects, magistrates and 'a number of the gentry and literati' of Nanjing visited the priests and sisters. Their report that no foundation existed for accusations, was for the moment enough to restore confidence. Ma Xinyi reported to the Zongli Yamen that he had advised both French and English missionaries 'to move out of the way while the provincial examinations were going on', which in Duncan's case meant lying low in his unpretentious home.

The British naval commander reported to Wade on July 2, 'Both Nankin and Yangchow are in an unsettled state', and on July 16, Wade's dispatch to Lord Clarendon reported alarm at Yantai (Chefoo)—'fear that some attempt was about to be made upon the foreign settlement'. Letters had come from Cantonese in Tianjin before the massacre, to Cantonese at Yantai, inciting them to violence. With no ship or force of men available, the British consul assembled the foreign residents, mounted a guard of volunteers with less than a dozen rifles and a few revolvers, and sent for the *daotai*, who came shortly before midnight. The timing of his visit could have been significant.

After the return of George Moule to Hangzhou in February 1870, Henry Gretton of the CMS opened a 'station' at Shaoxing near the Stevensons. (The word 'station' was used for a complex of premises and activities, 'mission' meaning a unit of missionaries however few.) Following the Tianjin massacre a mob burst into his house, excited by talk of impending mass extermination of foreigners. He turned quietly from directing some carpenters in their work and by his friendliness calmed them so effectively that they withdrew 'half-ashamed, half-reassured'. Stevenson himself was left in peace.

In Hangzhou some ten thousand candidates were attending the literary examinations, and anxiety for the missionaries was great, but no trouble erupted. In fact Jennie's home letter of July 12 showed more concern for her parents than for herself.

> I have just this evening seen the account of the massacre of French Romanists at Tientsin ... I am feeling for you, for I know that you will be anxious about us. There is no sign of dislike to us among the people of (Hangzhou) ... Unless it is God's will no one can harm us, if we are in the circumstances in which He places us ... all must be well even tho' trouble should come. 'Fear not them that kill the body ... the hairs of your head are all numbered.' [She filled a whole page with such quotations from Scripture, to make her point.]

Vigilance committees were formed in Ningbo, as on such occasions in the past, but here too the city rode out the tensions without disturbances. Past history gave the lie to accusations against the missionaries. But the danger was real. Eugene Stock wrote, 'In Zhejiang province] missionaries and converts alike were openly threatened with extermination; but they quietly clung to their posts and looked to the Lord's Almighty Arm for protection.'

Vile placards accused the Stotts in Wenzhou of atrocious crimes. 'Had not some seen barrels in which we salted down babies? . . . Crowds of excited people came daily and wandered all over the place, examining closely every corner to find traces of children's bodies . . . When the excitement became general, I had to call on the Mandarin and request a proclamation, which he gave.'

Stott planned to send his bride away but she protested: she might never get back again so she must stay and trust the Lord. 'We got so used to threatening placards and having the day of our death posted up,' she wrote, 'which passed by as quietly as other days, that we began to feel less anxious.' Yet all through this time one and another Chinese came asking for Gospels to read, the first signs of a sincere response to faithful perseverance.

At Shanghai it was a different story. News of the massacre arrived on June 27. Five foreigners returning to the settlement along the Pudong shore of the Huangpu River were 'roughly handled' and one, a Mr Grant, was later found bleeding and senseless in a creek, with his hands and feet bound. On the 30th, W. H. Medhurst Jr sent a dispatch to the Earl of Clarendon relaying the particulars and reporting that ships and men had been sent to help at Tianjin—only ten old soldiers employed as policemen, a reflection on the knife-edge of danger at Shanghai also. To Wade at Peking he wrote that the Chinese at Shanghai were very disturbed. He himself protested to the *daotai* about inflammatory placards posted in the city. 'The animosity is principally directed against the French; but foreigners generally are looked upon as objects of hatred . . . Last night,' he went on, 'an alarm was given that the French settlement was about to be attacked, and their volunteers turned out at once, but nothing happened.' Admiral Sir Harry Keppel reported to the Admiralty '(the) threatened extermination of all foreigners'. On July 28, the *North China Herald* said, 'The night passed off quietly; and the display of force had a good effect . . . when it showed that we were thoroughly prepared to meet any attack.'

Before the alarms and excursions finally died down, mission chapels, Catholic and Protestant, had been destroyed at Yantai and Dengzhou, Nanjing, Zhenjiang, two cities in Jiangxi, and at Shanghai and Canton. Through June, July, August and beyond, when Hudson Taylor's personal, circumstances were the most harrowing he had ever known, this was 'the climate of unrest' in which he remained the leader of so many threatened young men and women. What had happened at Yangchow in 1868 and, worse still, at Tianjin now, could happen in any of his fourteen stations at any time. On July 4 he wrote to William Berger:

> As matters now are in China it is some comfort to have the dear ones (Emily Blatchley and the children) out of the way ... A little Chinese girl given some time ago to Miss Bowyer, was suddenly taken ill and died about half an hour after I was called to see her ... We had her immediately carried (as a live child might be) out of the city to Mr White's, which is in an isolated position, and then got the constable to ... bury her. Thus public notice was avoided and no one was the wiser. Indeed the whole question of the care of infants, in stations in the interior, is evidently a grave one ... any such young children and infants should be nursed in (Chinese) families and not in *our* premises.

Grim circumstances and the pall of danger on a nationwide scale could not rid him of day-to-day administrative problems. In 1887 he told a small conference of missionaries,

> I received letters almost daily from one and another, saying: 'It seems no use our staying here; there is not a soul in this vast city that will listen to us ... Would it not be better to go somewhere else?' (They) did not know that other cities were just as bad. I was led

to advise that some of the Sisters should be sent to the ports (so that the brethren might feel relieved of anxiety on their behalf), but in every case they should hold the fort themselves. I said, 'You are now placed in a position to help the Chinese as you have never been before. They see that your being a foreigner is now no protection, but increases your danger. Let them see that you are rejoicing in God ... that you do not need any other protection, and that you are not going to run away ... The native Christians, who see that you do not go away, although you might; that you put your trust in God, and are prepared either to suffer or be delivered as He sees best, will learn that there is something in the Gospel worth risking, life for.' What was the result? In almost every place where there were native Christians they grew (in spiritual maturity) as never before.

Life could hardly have been more difficult or the prospects more uncertain, yet greater tests of his fortitude and faith lay only days ahead.

Maria and Noel[161] (July 1870)

In the closing days of June, Maria asked Emily Blatchley in her weekly letters from Zhenjiang to tell Hudson Taylor's parents not to be alarmed, whatever the newspapers were saying, 'but pray that wisdom may be given us'. One slip over a Chinese child could be the pretext to make the Yangzhou riot insignificant. Then news of the massacre arrived. Already Catherine Duncan and Mary Bowyer had been withdrawn from Nanjing, and Louise Desgraz from Yangzhou, so the Zhenjiang house was full when the Rudland's arrived unexpectedly from Hangzhou. During the 'intense excitement' a message had been sent to stop them. They had not received it. The Taylors gave up their room, Maria joining Louise, Hudson Taylor and Henry Reid sleeping in the communal living-room (a passageway to everyone in the house). Work had to continue as though all were well. On July 1, Hudson Taylor wrote to make peace between Edward Fishe and Josiah Jackson in Taizhou.

> We do not know whether we shall be able to hold our own ground at any of our (Yangzi) stations ... (Jackson) has felt annoyed by some of your letters; you have been tried by some of his. He may have been mistaken in some of his steps; you may have erred in some of your judgments ... (He) has had an invitation from Mr Stott ... and you will have exclusive charge and control over the work (at Taichau) ... not of course excluding my own general superintendence ... You are not sent to preach death and sin and judgment, but life and holiness and salvation—not to be a witness against the people, but to be a witness for God to preach the good news—Christ Himself ... You have to win the people's esteem and confidence and love.

And the next day, to E. C. Lord, 'The excitement seems to be on the wane, but any spark may relight it.' Ten days later he was to add, 'That spark may be supplied by the (Tianjin) news.'

Day after day the temperature in the shade was in the nineties and they were in the Chinese city, within the high walls, close and airless. Maria's breathing was 'fast and shallow'. Then:

> After we parted on the night of July fifth my dear wife took a bath ... (and) threw herself down on the bed to rest. [The bedroom was divided by a curtain between her bed and Louise's.] So, with the window open, (she) fell asleep ... It became very cold and windy ... and a sharp attack of English cholera came on (with great abdominal pain) and yet she would not wake me nor wake Miss D. ... When I came in to see her in the morning I was shocked to see the change ...

> By noon of the 7th all the unfavourable symptoms were subsiding ... Williamson was just leaving us for (Anqing) with Sammy Meadows ... (I) told her I thought I would see him to his boat and on my way back buy a little brandy for her.

He satisfied himself that it was all right to leave her, but having bought the brandy, he left Williamson and Sammy to go on and himself returned home.

> When I got back the baby was already born ... I did not like the feel of (Maria's) pulse. As it got dusk she had a little doze, from which she awoke expressing herself refreshed. At this moment Mrs Rudland brought in a candle, I saw the colour leave (Maria's) lips and she turned deadly pale ... I believe that if I had been out of the room, or if we had had no brandy in the house, she would never have recovered.

A severe post-partum haemorrhage was taking place and 'but for instant measures she would not have lasted many minutes'. He was up all night with Maria and the baby, but had to go on with his work the next day. His letter to Henry Cordon at Suzhou on the 8th said, 'It has been reported here that all the Foreign Residents of Suchow have been murdered, but we take little notice of this.' Maria, he said, was very ill. 'I am very anxious about her.'

During the next week she 'seemed to get

weaker instead of stronger but . . . felt sure she would soon be well'. She called the baby 'Noel', simply because, she liked the name. To her it meant 'Peace', and for a week 'he seemed to do famously'.

By the 11th the Chinese were saying, 'It is too hot for business.' Hudson Taylor agreed but had to continue working. Thomas Harvey wrote that day from Nanjing, 'All is quiet here [on the 11th] though the people are still bent on burning down the Roman Catholic establishment.' On the 14th Hudson Taylor had to answer another complaining letter from Edward Fishe and tell him that if he did not wish to bear the responsibility for Taizhou he must either leave, or accept and work under William Rudland's leadership. In confidence he also asked John McCarthy to keep a pastoral eye on all the south Zhejiang missionaries, as he himself could not visit them. This would train McCarthy for leadership. The 15th saw him assuring the US consulate Zhenjiang that he himself saw no immediate danger from the Chinese.

> I ascertained that even at its height the hostility was against the French, who were shamefully blind; and that there was little or no danger to persons of other nationality, unless mistaken for Frenchmen ... My numerous correspondents, native and foreign, keep me well posted up in matters. This is the more needful, as some of our missionaries inland might need timely notice of any event of moment, or their lives might be needlessly sacrificed ... Nothing would sooner induce (the Chinese) to take hostile action, than an impression, however erroneous, that we are afraid of them.

Only the next day, however, Hudson Taylor wrote to Charles Judd at Putuo where his wife was still recuperating. 'No one knows what may be the next news, however. Yesterday I was officially notified that in case of danger we were to take refuge on the gunboat, and that if desired the ladies in the City could move there, the Captain kindly placing his cabin at their service. This will show you the feeling here. I do not think there will be trouble . . . (but you had

better stay at Putuo for another month).' To Charles Fishe at Yangzhou he wrote on the 16th, 'Continue to use all care to avoid trouble. Some seem to look on it as only deferred, not over.' And to Duncan and Harvey, 'Do not relax your vigilance in the least. Alert, but not anxious.' This was the day of crisis at Yantai.

Writing on July 18 to keep the Bergers informed, he reported that outwardly all was peace and quiet.

> The foreign residents here are in some uneasiness as to their safety. I do not think there is much reason to fear. There are probably several gangs of thieves about, and they may try to avail themselves of the unsettled state of affairs. But we shall have more notice before anything very serious is to be apprehended from the people generally ... You will think me very remiss about my accounts ... This is a time of special pressure; and I've not got Miss Blatchley's help. Were she here it would be better both for my dear wife and baby too. Others may be as kind, but few possess her ability ... When shall the Gospel reach the vast neglected districts of this poor Empire?

Even in such circumstances, Maria and he had been planning the house they would like to buy or build in Zhenjiang for a school and work among women, like Jennie's in Hangzhou. Yet the baby had severe 'thrush', an infection of the mouth, with diarrhoea. And the unmistakable signs of terminal tuberculous enteritis convinced Hudson Taylor that in the long run there was no hope for Maria. It was only a matter of time. But he could not believe the end would be soon. Everything failed to arrest Noel's disease and he died on Wednesday evening, July 20, just thirteen days after his birth.

Charles Fishe had come over from Yangzhou to be with them. Of Hudson Taylor he wrote on the 24th, 'He felt it much; she said she did not think it right to allow herself to dwell too much upon it, in her weak state,' But that evening, though her own condition became worse, she chose two hymns to be sung at Noel's funeral. A letter came for Maria from Mrs Berger.

Hudson Taylor replied, 'Could (you) have known that it would arrive, and be read beside the coffin . . . (you) could not have written more suitably.' By the same mail came the news that Emily and the children had reached England safely.

> [July 26] She (Maria) revelled in the enjoyment they would have, and was prepared for the trial of the closing of the little coffin, which had to be done then ... I little thought when I read to her your concluding words, 'And now farewell, my precious Friend. The Lord throw around you His everlasting arms', that they were a final farewell, that she would so soon fare so well, that the Lord was about so truly to throw His arms about her and carry her to His own bosom. 'Even so, Father for so it seemed good in Thy sight,'

The prevailing tensions could not be forgotten, however poignant personal experiences might be. The French consul, J. M. Canny, had asked him for an account of the massacre plot at Ningbo in 1857 (see 1, pp 391–395). He wrote it on July 21. A letter and more generous donations had come from George Müller, by then a warm friend. He read it to Maria 'her infant babe lying in its little coffin near her side, and we together thanked God'. The cheques he forwarded at once, some before and some directly after she herself died.

On Friday the 22nd, 'in the cool of the evening', Noel was buried beside his brother Samuel in the little walled cemetery about a mile from the riverbank. Hudson Taylor took the burial service himself, and afterwards said to the grave-digger, 'I trust I may not have to trouble you again soon.' Then, turning to Charles Fishe he said, 'I think she is needed for the Lord's work; that is a comfort to me and leads me to hope for her.'

They returned via Robert White's house in the cooler suburb, arranged to move Maria there, and reached home again about eight o'clock. 'Maria seemed much as when I left her' and sitting beside her he explained his plan for her. 'Could I have my bath there as often as I like?' she asked. He was very tired and soon fell asleep.

> She asked Miss Desgraz to cover me over, lest I should take cold. I awoke about 9.30 and asked if there was anything I could get her. She said 'No, you must go and get some tea, Mrs Rudland has some waiting for you.' I went into the next room ... and we were chatting together ... when Miss Desgraz who was sitting at the door between the two rooms, heard my name faintly called. I rushed in, and found Maria up and very faint, unable to speak or to get into bed. I lifted her in, withdrew the pillows and bolster and put them under her hips and legs, used stimulants, and heat to the extremities ... I feared she would die ... and asked the Rudland's (and others) to pray God to keep my heart quiet and guide my judgment and He did so. When she felt better the reaction became alarming, violent palpitation came on and it was but too evident the lungs were unequal to the work required of them ... By 12.30 a.m. I persuaded the Rudlands and Reid to go to bed ...

> When she began to come round she said her head was hot ... [He offered to thin out her hair for her but found her head so 'congested' that he cut off all her hair.] When I had (finished) she put her hand up and said 'That's what, you call thinning out, is it? (and smiling) Well I shall have all the comfort, and you all the responsibility as to looks.'

> And she threw her loving arms—so thin— around me, and kissed me in her own loving way for it. We were now able to apply cold to the head to her great comfort and relief. Soon after she dozed, and I left her with Miss Desgraz.

He sent a lock of hair home to his parents and to each of the children, writing on the envelope containing it. 'One half. I dare not risk all by one ship. Take great care of it. J.H.T.' It is very fine, a light brown, almost blonde.

With Reid and the Rudlands he went to pray in another room, and noticed that neither he nor they could pray unreservedly for Maria's recovery. At midnight and 2.00 a.m. he gave her food and medicine, and sat with her till three. Louise would not go and lie down so he asked her to wake him at four. She did, and while he was in the next room Maria woke. The light of dawn upon Saturday, July 23, showed him unmistakably that she was dying. All the household and the young men, Charles Fishe, Harvey and White from the other house gathered round her.

As soon as I felt sufficiently composed, I said to her, 'My darling, are you conscious that you are dying?' She replied with evident surprise, 'Dying! Do you think so? What makes you think so?' I said, 'I can see it, darling ... Your strength is giving way.' ... She continued conscious till about 7.30 ... after which she slept till Jesus took her home, to be 'for ever with the Lord', at 9.20. She suffered no pain. Only felt weary.

[Writing to her cousin William Tam he added,] The Chinese servants and teachers who all respected and loved her, came into her room. She had a message for each, and an earnest exhortation for those who were unsaved to come to Jesus and meet her in heaven. She gave me her dying kisses for her little ones in England, and messages for them. Then language failed her and her last act of consciousness was to put one arm around my neck and one on my head, to look up to heaven with a look of unutterable love and trust. Her lips moved but no sound was uttered ... Then she fell asleep ... Her sleep became lighter and lighter, and it was not easy to say when it ceased and her ransomed spirit entered into the joy of her Lord.

An undated copy of a note in Hudson Taylor's hand to the American Presbyterians in Hangzhou reads, 'Would Mr Dodd gently break these tidings to Miss Faulding and Mr and Mrs McCarthy? Excuse the request and brevity. Mrs Taylor died of consumption of the bowels, baby also of diarrhoea. They are truly blessed! And I too. My heart wells up with joy and gratitude for their unutterable bliss, tho' nigh breaking. "Our Jesus hath done all things well." Yours in Jesus, J. Hudson Taylor.'

Sixteen years later Hudson Taylor mentioned something he had kept to himself:

When I said, 'My darling, do you know you are dying?' She said 'I am so sorry, dear,'

and paused, as if half correcting herself for venturing to feel sorry. I said 'You are not sorry to go to be with Jesus, dear?' I shall never forget the look she gave me, and as looking right into my eyes, she said, 'Oh, no, it is not that; you know, darling, there has not been a cloud between my soul and my Saviour for ten years past; I cannot be sorry to go to Him. But I am sorry to leave you alone at this time.' I knew what she said was perfectly true.

She had made a habit of confessing and receiving forgiveness for any conscious sin. William Rudland also recorded Maria's words and the fact that Hudson Taylor himself went out to buy a Chinese coffin. In such heat it was imperative to lose no time. When Maria's body was laid in it Hudson Taylor took a last look and in Job's words said 'The Lord gave and the Lord has taken away; blessed be the name of the Lord.' Then he 'hurried to his room'. But where could he go? Their own bedroom they had given to the Rudlands. William Rudland closed the coffin.

'My happy one'[162] (July–August 1870)

That same day Hudson Taylor began his letter to the Bergers. 'As I have just re-read (yours). I could not but weep to think that soon I shall have lost the precious letters of Mrs Berger to my dearest earthly treasure . . . Am I too selfish? Forgive me.'

But his grief was quickly submerged in a rapture which did not surprise his friends. By Monday, July 25, he was able to continue a normal business letter, calmly beginning, 'I hasten to fulfil my promise to my happy one that I would thank dear Mrs Berger for her kind letter and for all the love' shown to Emily and the children on their arrival. Towards the end he added, 'dear Miss Blatchley will be able to explain to you better than I can (that we) have little cause to boast as a Mission'. The tribulations of leadership could not but penetrate his mourning. On Wednesday he wrote again, this time about the repercussions from the massacre and apparently 'deliberate machinations' by unfriendly foreigners. More difficulties, right on his doorstep, had coincided with Noel's birth and the deaths first of Noel and then Maria. The request by the well-meaning interpreter-in-charge to the commander of the gunboat 'to cover the retreat of the missionaries' from Yangzhou was a case in point. Misrepresentations in Britain seemed to be 'equally unfounded and perhaps more maliciously circulated' than the equivalent tales in China.

The funeral was on Thursday, July 28, when the great heat yielded a little towards evening. Following Chinese custom, Charles Fishe and Thomas Harvey in white gowns, the dress of mourning, walked ahead of the coffin born by eight Chinese. Behind came Hudson Taylor and all the missionaries, also in white, then the British and American consuls, the foreign officers of the Imperial Maritime Customs, 'and most of the English and American residents here', the merchants. 'They wished to erect a tombstone for her' but, though grateful, Hudson Taylor asked that he might provide it himself. At the graveside he read the burial service and a brief paper about Maria's family, conversion and life in Ningbo, in the Yangzhou riot and since.

Emily Blatchley (hearing from her friends in China) wrote, 'For many days her husband seemed to stand on the threshold (of heaven) with hardly a glance to turn on the desolated earth . . . He himself conducted the funeral with a calm, sustained mind . . . To him death was swallowed up in victory. He realised her joy, her rest. His joy in her joy was unbounded almost.' He himself went down with dysentery the following day, with the onset of fever, and was seriously ill for two months.

He completed his letter to the Bergers on Monday, August 1, probably to catch the mail boat, and at once began another.

> My heart is overwhelmed with gratitude and praise. My eyes overflow with tears of joy mingled with sorrow. When I think of my loss my heart, nigh to breaking, bursts forth in thankful praise to Him who has spared her from such sorrow and has made her so unspeakably happy. My tears are more tears of joy than of sorrow. But most of all I joy in God through our Lord Jesus Christ—in His works, His ways, His providence—in Himself. He is giving me to 'prove (know by trial) what is that good and acceptable and perfect will of God'. And I do rejoice in that will. It is acceptable to me, it is perfect. It is love in action. [He filled a page with Scripture and a hymn, the thoughts that buoyed him up, and continued] Forgive me for rambling on in this way, dear Brother. I feel like a person recovering from a long prostrating illness—yet I am not really weak. I was able to take the service at the Consulate and three Chinese services yesterday.

He was sleepless, 'partly from the great heat and partly from the deep joy in the happiness of my beloved one', but also from his dysentery and fever. He still could not send his statements of account. In fact he was keeping little cash in hand while the country was so disturbed. 'The merchants here and at (Jiujiang) object to cashing dollar bills . . . I have already £sd accounts, dollar accounts, Chinese cash accounts, and now I must keep a tael account.' Nanjing was quiet, he went on, but George and Catherine Duncan had been separated for two months, so Hudson Taylor proposed to take over in Nanjing for a week or two. Not until October when the literary examinations ended would it be safe for Catherine to return there. His illness foiled the plan.

He wrote to George Müller and to his own boys on the same day, August 1, saying, '(Noel) had soft, sweet little eyes, and long silky eyelashes, and a dear little mouth just like Grace's used to be.' He told them about 'Maria's last thought of and messages for (them),' and then 'it may be that God will take away your dear Papa too before very long. But God will always be a Father to you.' News of their mother's death would seem to have been enough for them in one letter. So why did he add that mournful note? The dangers were hourly, and going to Nanjing would increase them. After re-reading Mrs Berger's last letters to Maria on October 16, he wrote of perhaps sending Charles Edward home to join the others, 'which would be better for him, especially were I taken home either by sickness or violence'. Depression may explain the timing of it, though happiness for Maria was the dominant note in the first weeks after her death. The Tianjin massacre and nationwide excitement evoked a different, defiant reaction. He firmly believed that the apprehensions of the consuls and talk of mass extermination of foreigners were unrealistic. A few weeks later it was a different matter. At the time his dysentery, the great killer, was the more likely reason for his remarks. So many expatriates died of it and more of his close friends were soon to be its victims. Only two months previously he had written, 'Shall we suffer much from sickness, or lose any of our number before the season is over?' He could not complain. Indeed, he could say to the Bergers, 'with the disposition the Lord has made of our precious ones I am content, fully content, and grateful for it. But that does not prevent my feeling at times sad, oh, so sad!' How much had happened since May! The euphoria could not last interminably. In Emily's words, 'Then the blank left here turned upon him all its terrible vacancy; he began to realise more what her joy was to cost him.'

'To be the friend of God demanded, even if it repaid, everything he had.'[163]

How many heads?[164]
(August–October 1870)

Nothing stood still in Tianjin or the other treaty ports. Alarm and indignation over the massacre prompted the usual outcry, for retribution from the press and public. Though they worded it differently, even the missionary body called for justice to be seen to be done or the days of a foreign presence in China were numbered. Jonathan Lees of the LMS and William Hall of the Methodist New Connexion made a strong representation to Consul W. H. Lay (July 21). And C. A. Stanley of the American Board (July, November, 1870) closely investigated the circumstances leading to and during the riot. They made their protests public and the leading newspapers published their correspondence.

They ranged themselves alongside not only the Roman Catholics but the French in general in saying that they wanted 'not to be separated from our suffering French brethren in any settlement, and sent their condolences to the survivors.[165] Of the mandarins they wrote, 'The excuses which unhappily served there so well in regard to the outrages at Formosa, Yangchow and elsewhere, fail them now' for their involvement with the fire guild, the troops, led by Chen Guorui, and the rioters had been reliably witnessed. 'We are not crying for war and vengeance,' the missionaries wrote to Lay, 'but we do claim justice.' So they refused Chonghou's premature offer of reparations. But the United States envoy took their claim that 'the path of safety and honour . . . is to stand by our fellow-sufferers in the hour of trial' to mean no less than that a war between France and China must first take place before it would be proper to adjust any claims.[166]

'No money indemnity can satisfy the demand for justice,' the *North China Herald* editorial trumpeted. 'The lives of all the authorities concerned ought to be forfeited . . . If (Chonghou) is allowed to escape, disaster may be expected for every European.'

The universal demand for the punishment of the guilty mandarins was handled adroitly by Prince Kong and the Zongli Yamen.[167] The viceroy, Zeng Guofan, apparently escaped blame as his seat at Baoding was a hundred miles from Tianjin—only a stone's throw to a schemer, however. Chonghou was sent as an envoy to Europe. The prefect and *xian* magistrate suffered exile for incompetence. But eighteen rioters were decapitated (in October) for murder and thirty more banished for a few years. To behead mandarins, as demanded by the Comte de Rochechourt, the French chargé d'affaires, would humiliate the emperor and people, Robert Hart explained to his Customs Commissioner in Tianjin. So common law-breakers must bear the brunt, and Prince Kong had offered fifteen heads, later increased to twenty![168] The foreign representatives rejected this as being in no way satisfactory.

The Comte had been joined at Tianjin in July by his admiral, and threatened to withdraw his legation and call in the navy to maintain the honour of France until on August 4 the news of France and Prussia being at war stole the wind from his sails. From then on the Chinese pleased themselves. Instead, five French men-of-war, three British and one American at Tianjin, with six more at Yantai, cooperated 'for the protection of all foreign interests' while tension in Shanghai continued.

Assassination[169] (August 1870)

Suddenly a new shock wave swept through the nation. At Nanjing the Muslim viceroy, Ma Xinyi, had repeatedly shown his determination to abide by the treaties, however unjust, and to defend the Christians at Hangzhou and, since his promotion, at Anqing, Jiujiang, Zhenjiang, Yangzhou and Nanjing. He had vigorously suppressed all attempts to repeat the Tianjin outrage on the Roman Catholics under his protection. By Hudson Taylor's direction, Duncan and Harvey had lain low while Nanjing was full of examination candidates and their companions, 'fifty thousand strangers', a powder-keg of political violence, rather than to withdraw from the city and risk being unable to return.

On August 22 Ma Xinyi was stabbed in his own *yamen*. Lingering for a day, he succumbed as the news swept through the provinces. The restraining influence in central China had been removed. The *North China Herald* of August 25 reported great excitement in the city. But Duncan wrote, 'Who would have thought that the viceroy who had so many soldiers continually guarding him from danger, should have been laid low by the assassin's hand, whilst we, who seemed so much exposed (should live on in safety)?' He was probably nearer the truth than he knew.

Deep resentment over the removal of Zeng Guofan and his replacement by Ma Xinyi had been felt by the troops from Hunan, Zeng's home province, and resentment was even more widespread over Ma's repression of the Anqing riot and the recent plot against the Catholics in Nanjing. The fact that Zeng Guofan was reappointed to Nanjing in Ma's place is significant; it may be inferred that Zeng's transfer to the inferior viceroyalty of Nanjing was considered to be a disgrace. Both Charlotte Haldane and Alicia Bewicke Little painted a pathetic word-picture of his vainly pleading old age and blindness. 'So the ageing and ailing old warhorse had no choice.' He only lasted two years, and when he died in harness, the empress dowager called him, in a commemorative decree, 'the very backbone of the Throne'.[170] His anti-foreign sentiments were her own.

Universal alarm was (again) felt in foreign circles in China. The defence volunteers rearmed and patrolled the settlements. As the weeks passed, foreigners increasingly felt unsafe. Even before the assassination, an army of forty thousand was reported to be marching eastwards from Shanxi into Zhili, in anticipation of strong French retaliation for the massacre. The Tianjin municipal council (or merchants) considered that the legations should withdraw from the capital before hard winter conditions made it impossible for rescuing troops to reach them. Wade disagreed. While he urged the merchants and missionaries in Tianjin to assess their losses at the time of the massacre, they replied indignantly that they could not even safely appear in the streets to inspect their property.

Meanwhile Hudson Taylor expressed surprise (on August 29) over the excitability of Vice-Consul Gardner.

I saw in (his) letters another evidence of that state of panic in which many foreign communities have been ever since the Tientsin murders. Mr Duncan could scarcely do less, in courtesy, than come down (from Nanjing) and explain [to Gardner?] that all was quiet in Nanjing ... Mr Harvey was unwell and had his things packed for coming down before the arrival of Gardner's letter; so his movement was entirely independent of it ... Mr Duncan has left (again) for Nanking. In Yangchau there has been no excitement whatever about it nor here.[171]

His own information was that the assassination had been a private revenge, an explanation not widely shared.

When Chonghou reached Europe he 'found France prostrate at the feet of Germany, (and) the Emperor gone into captivity'. The powerless government in defeat had no time for Chinese affairs and told Chonghou they wanted no bloodletting, only protection for Frenchmen in China. But although Peking had already assumed it, the court took nothing for granted. On September 9, Robert Hart wrote to his commissioner in Tianjin, 'There is great military activity in this province, and the Chinese are preparing—they say so—to meet France in the field . . . Winter prospects are not agreeable. We'll be safe enough in our houses, but it may not be so pleasant in the streets.'[172]

Knowledge of this made anti-foreign elements throughout the empire the more eager to act. On August 29, J. L. Nevius, again in Dengzhou, reported to the US vice-consul that serious threats to foreigners' lives had been made, should action at Tianjin go against the Chinese. It was being openly stated that foreigners would be murdered on September 16. So they were evacuated by ship. And in October the foreign residents of Canton notified their consul that threats to their security were daily increasing.

Sixes and sevens
(September–October 1870)

From the beginning of this crisis Wade was 'the only one in step'. Full of praise for W. H. Lay's heroism, efficiency and tenacity in an extremely ugly situation, Wade disagreed with Lay's diagnosis of the underlying causes. He repeated to Medhurst in Shanghai his conviction that 'the popular belief that children were received into the orphanage of the Sisters of Mercy for unholy purposes' lay behind the attack, and not a general anti-foreign movement. Why? 'There has not been in or about this city (Peking) the slightest display of hostile feeling towards religious or other foreigners.'[173] According to H. B. Morse, 'the gentry were manifestly filled with the belief' that the orphanage Sisters had bought infants for immoral purposes. Of some inferior literati this may well have been true, but the true intellectuals were more intelligent and clever. As for Wade, as HBM chargé d'affaires he had the ear of Lord Clarendon and, after Clarendon's death in 1870, of Lord Granville.

By September, however, while admitting the insecurity of ministers and others alike at Peking and Tianjin, he gallantly declared himself opposed to withdrawal before the winter. The danger persisted. In December there was still much talk of war, with many dispatches passing to and fro. The *North China Herald* columnists shrugged their shoulders. 'If March finds the foreigners in Peking alive and well, all that can be said is that the luck of the storm passing over enabled the umbrella-less man to get in with a dry skin.'[174] At some point in this climate of danger, the Scottish Presbyterian James Gilmour dressed as a rugged northerner and escaped to the wilds of Mongolia as a missionary far from all diplomats and plots.

On October 18 the Chinese death sentences were carried out like a charade, 'to satisfy the vengeful wrath of foreigners'.[175] Instead of emaciated, tortured prisoners going to the block, the men wore silk, superior coffins were ready for them, each family received 500 taels and a bonus of 100 more from Chonghou on the way to Paris. Their heads were not exposed on the city wall in the usual way, but an aura of martyr-patriot was created for them. For the massacre an indemnity of 250,000 taels was paid, of which 130,000 went to the Roman Catholic Church. The vicar apostolic or bishop refused an indemnity for the murdered victims, but accepted the allocated sum to augment that for reconstruction of buildings destroyed. This included re-erection of the cathedral on its previous, greatly resented site, in Morse's words as 'part of the triple symbol of Roman dominance and French prowess in arms, the church of Notre Dame des Victoires on the site of the imperial temple of Hwanghailow at Tientsin; the cathedral at Canton on the site of what, up to 1857, had been the viceroy's *yamen*; and the (Beitang) cathedral at Peking, erected on land the gift of an emperor [Kang Xi'in, 1693], and dominating with its towers the grounds of the imperial palace'.[176]

Samuel Wells Williams, missionary and US diplomat, author of *The Middle Kingdom*, sympathised with Prince Kong and his colleagues in the Zongli Yamen, saying, 'The whole history of the riot—its causes, growth, culmination, results and repression combine as many of the serious obstacles in the way of harmonising Chinese and European civilisations as anything which ever occurred. In other words, 'the Missionary Question' was as deeply involved as 'the China Question'. Alexander Michie, the Shanghai newspaper editor with no love for missionaries, wrote in his life of Sir Rutherford Alcock, alluding to what would have happened but for France's war in Europe, 'the Chinese government narrowly escaped a signal retribution for its continued guerrilla warfare against foreigners as represented by the missionary vanguard.'[177]

A national embarrassment (September–October 1870)

Wade was not content to trust his own judgment on the Tianjin affair only. Dispatches between London and Peking discussed the part played by Protestant missions and Hudson Taylor in particular. Wade's message to Lord Granville on September 17 contained these words:

> I disapprove, and ... should oppose the establishment of Protestant missions at a distance from the Treaty ports. But when a foreign community has formed itself, its hasty withdrawal is greatly to be deplored. [It crossed *en route* the dispatch from Earl Granville of September 15, saying] ... It is from knowing that missionary zeal might lead to consequences not only fatal to those devoted persons who apply themselves to spread Christianity in China, but

calculated to put in jeopardy the lives and interests of the whole foreign community, that Her Majesty's Government have felt it their duty to discountenance missionary operations which seemed likely to give rise to difficulties with the Chinese Government and people; and Her Majesty's Government trust most sincerely that British missionaries will take warning ... and conduct their operations with the utmost prudence, and with a steady purpose to abstain from exciting suspicion or animosity among the Chinese.[178]

If they thought any of this exchange would alter the intentions or actions of the particular person in mind, they did not know their man. The dispatches were barely on the way when one from Consul Medhurst in Shanghai added fuel to Wade's thoughts. Hudson Taylor's dysentery had dragged on for weeks. The Rudlands had left Zhenjiang to take up the task in Taizhou which they then continued for forty years. Duncan came down from Nanjing to report, and returned. Hudson Taylor found himself 'alone' in the Zhenjiang city house among the single men, ill, 'as weak as a child', and feeling utterly bereft. Painfully conscious of three graves at the foot of the hill outside the city walls, another at Hangzhou, three more of his children far off in Britain, and Charles Edward, not yet two, in the care of the Judds at Yangzhou, the meaning of Maria's death came home to him poignantly. In two of her last letters she had said, 'T'ien-pao (Charles Edward) likes to cuddle and cosset . . . nestling in his Papa's arms . . . playing with his moustache with both his hands, or laying his little head on his shoulder.' All that was over. A week after Ma Xinyi's assassination he brought Elizabeth Judd and 'Charlie', both ill again with dysentery, to the relative safety of Zhenjiang and, with Catherine Duncan to mother his child, took the river-steamer to Shanghai, called on Medhurst, and went on by coaster to Ningbo. There Charles Edward hovered 'between life and death' but recovered enough to complete the journey to the holiday island of Putuo, his best hope of a cure.

Closely in touch with his colleagues

at their locations, Hudson Taylor had information valuable to his friend Medhurst—that all was at present quiet as far as his missionaries were concerned, in Anqing, Jiujiang, Nanjing, Zhenjiang, Yangzhou and Qingjiangpu. All were keeping discreetly within their premises. But anti-French feeling was still strong and liable to erupt into violence in which the rioters might not distinguish between French and British. When he had gone, Medhurst informed Wade, and Wade took the opportunity again to deprecate the residence of British missionaries outside the treaty ports, the treaties with their clear provision for doing so seemingly forgotten, like Bishop Magee's powerful maiden speech in Parliament, about missionaries' rights being in no sense inferior to merchants' rights. The Parliamentary Blue Books contain it all.[179] Medhurst immediately conveyed Wade's message to all members of the CIM through Hudson Taylor, quoting the minister's directive to his consuls, 'Although you are hereby distinctly instructed to refrain from assisting in the acquisition of land or premises away from your Port, it is in my opinion extremely inexpedient that any position now occupied by a British Mission inland shall be, in this period of alarm, precipitately abandoned.'

When this eventually reached Hudson Taylor, he replied (tongue in cheek), 'It is to me personally a matter of gratification to find that the views expressed by HM chargé d'affaires accord with those I have urged on the members of the Mission; and on which we acted during the last summer.'

Oh for MEN! (August–October 1870)

If the first seven months of 1870 had been made difficult by successive crises, Hudson Taylor found the remaining five harder in other ways. Each political crisis had been a vicious turn of the blade in the wounds of death and separation from those most dear to him. That he could fix the eyes of his faith on Maria's joy 'with Christ, which is far better', did not mean that the stresses became fewer or less painful. 'Eye hath not

seen, ear hath not heard, neither hath it entered into the heart of man what God hath prepared for them that love Him,' confirmed the certainty of 'no grief, no pain' in which he rejoiced for her. But as his colleagues returned to their work and the Rudlands moved south to replace Jackson at Taizhou, his own desolation could not but come home to him. Suddenly he was single again, thrown together with the men, instead of sharing with Maria as homemakers to whom the young men and women naturally turned. His dysentery robbed him of sleep and strength. Left alone with his thoughts, he felt bereft yet comforted. Writing from White's bungalow outside the city of Zhenjiang with a panoramic view of the Yangzi, he opened his heart to the Bergers. 'My house was full—now it is still and lonely . . . "I go to prepare a place for you." Is not one part of the preparation the peopling it with those we love?'

News of war in Europe had just reached him. Soon it would be Paris under siege and Napoleon III captured; with a dramatic fall in the receipts of missionary societies as donors' thoughts were full of events on the Continent. The onus of guiding his Mission weighed on Hudson Taylor's shoulders all the more since Maria could no longer share it. Jackson had gone into foreign clothes again. Another Chinese baby in Jennie Faulding's care in Hangzhou had died, still potentially a dangerous thing to happen. Shortly afterwards some parents removed their children from her school, although the teacher was a Chinese. She herself was like her phlegmatic father, but news from China was throwing her mother into a frenzy of anxiety. In February she had written, 'When (the Taylors return) I should not at all like you to be left in China . . . We gave our consent to your going quite with the understanding that we placed you under their care . . . It would not be keeping to their promise to leave you there.' But in August it was, 'When China gets the news of the terrible defeats France has sustained . . . they will feel emboldened to go on with their attacks on Europeans (in

China).' On Jennie's birthday, October 7, her mother wrote:

> Almost all our friends are anxious about you ... Your lives are not safe in China ... and surely life is too valuable to be thus risked. Do let me *beg* of you to return to us ... and then those intensely horrible cruelties—it makes me tremble to think of them—it cannot be right of you to remain if war should have broken out ... Today's paper ... contains a telegram from Hong Kong ... 'Rumours are current of further assassinations ... Troops are massing between (Tianjin) and Pekin, ostensibly to protect foreigners, tho' their real object is considered doubtful.' If you could but know how the thought of your danger is ever uppermost in our minds you would not delay your return a day longer than absolutely necessary ... (The) coffins (of Grace Taylor and the Rudland baby) being on your premises has troubled (us).

In July Jennie had written sympathising with her parents and saying, 'There is no sign of dislike to us . . . in Hangzhou.' To her relief they replied that they were less worried, and Jennie commented, 'There is really no profit in "self-consuming care".' After hearing of Maria's death her thoughts were for Hudson Taylor. 'They were so much to one another, but I believe he will be sustained in spirit. I only fear that his physical strength may fail.' And when Hudson Taylor was making one of his rare visits to Hangzhou, she extended her letter to reassure her parents:

> God will overrule all ... He will bring me home to you at the right time ... Troublous times might come again, what then? Well, dear Mamma, am I not safe in God's keeping? Is it not best for me to be in the path of duty? He who notices the sparrows fall will not forget to care for me ... And if He should appoint it then surely to suffer for Him would not be the worst thing that could happen to me. Would it not rather be an honour?

> [And later] Mr Taylor is going to send down our own boat when he gets to (Zhenjiang) to fetch the two little coffins that they may be placed in the (Zhenjiang) cemetery.[180]

Such strength of purpose that he could count upon, in her and several others, supported Hudson Taylor when sadly many of his team were quailing in the face of threats. George and Grace Stott, the Duncan's, Stevensons and McCarthys, the Rudlands, Judds and Charles Fishe were unshakable. But after the Tianjin matter had been settled, Cardwell, Harvey and even James Meadows returned like Jackson to foreign dress for self-protection. To Hudson Taylor's mind it was a sad departure from trust in God.

In the cooler climate of Putuo Island where he hoped to save Charles Edward's life, in spite of losing sleep from the child's constant need of care, he took up the correspondence he had been unable to do while ill at Zhenjiang. But it was as much as he could manage. 'My head is so tired with night (duty) and exhaustion that I scarcely know what I am doing,' he told the Bergers. 'Mail day comes and finds me sick or behindhand. It needs your love to bear with such inefficiency. You will pray for me that I may not faint under the chastening of the Lord.' They were far away but, after Maria, his closest confidants. He had been accused again of Sabbath breaking, of deviant views on the subject, and had to set out his beliefs in detail for the Bergers to defend him. 'I do not think any member of our Mission save Mr Judd (and possibly Miss Desgraz) would tolerate buying and selling on Sunday.' Another old chestnut had also reappeared, that he had published criticisms of other missions. Again there was no truth in it, but some ghosts were hard to lay.

Jackson had been talking wildly, about someone offering to pay his return fare to England to find a wife. Worse still, Hudson Taylor wrote to Jackson from Putuo, 'It is far from improbable that subscribers to the Mission who do not look on faith in God as a "farce", or looking to Him for guidance as "nonsense", or profession of it as "cant"—to quote words and sentiments attributed to you—may be inclined to object to your continuing a member of the Mission of which these views are the distinctive features.' Even in such a situation when the big stick of authority might well have been used, a quality of firmness without heavy-handed autocracy is apparent in his letters. Referring to the case of Jackson, Hudson Taylor commented to the Bergers, 'I love to think of Jesus as one who upbraids not, and He is our pattern.'

Henry Reid, too nervous to be left in an advance position like Qingjiangpu, had taken over the presses from Rudland. But when Duncan fell ill, he bravely took his place at Nanjing with Thomas Harvey. In October Hudson Taylor, had to ask Reid, 'Have you heard anything of dear Harvey? He cannot surely have been so terrified as to have left China for good, and have said nothing about it to any of us. Ah! for quiet faith in God. I feel greatly troubled about him. I thought he had more love to some of us than to leave us in such suspense.' It transpired that Harvey, without so much as 'by your leave' had gone to Japan and back for a change of scene! At Nanjing Harvey was doing some doctoring, another dangerous practice at this time. 'Medicine is a very sharp knife,' Hudson Taylor wrote, 'and should be well handled or not at all.' At another time he told Reid:

> I was very glad to hear from you, as I always am, though I do not quite understand some parts of one of your letters. Might I suggest to you always to date your letters; to write them on sheets of paper of uniform size and colour; to number the pages—or at least the sheets; to add up and carry forward accounts, numbering consecutive pages, so that one may not have to lay them aside in hopeless despair of ever unravelling the confusion, two or three times before mastering them ... And this while I am longing all the time to know how you are in body and soul.

Then he hoped he had not written too strongly. Reid seemed 'to have no mind . . . The Chinese say (his discourses) are chaff with little grain in them'.

He missed the efficient secretarial help of Emily Blatchley and asked Charles Fishe to join him as personal assistant—and by the way, he wrote to his mother, would she arrange for Emily to have her lungs examined? If seriously ill she must have the help of another governess, to understudy her and get to know and love the children. Only youthful Charles Fishe already appeared to have the makings of a director of the Mission, but he could not yet be appointed over men so much his senior in age and experience.

The greatest disappointment came from an unexpected quarter. His reliable friends Williamson and Meadows had had enough of living under strain, exacerbated by illness, and asked to be withdrawn from Anqing. 'Everyone stands aloof, and we feel that . . . neither rulers or people are to be trusted,' they said. They had already sent Elizabeth Meadows to the relative safety of Jiujiang, though even there some foreigners were attacked. A minor mandarin called on them and warned that their house was not safe. It could have been a ruse to make them leave, but their language teacher heard a report that foreigners in the north had been defeated and 'the people in the city were . . . trying to pluck up courage to attack the two solitary foreigners in (Anqing)'. Ma Xinyi's assassination compounded their fears, and to Hudson Taylor's grief they withdrew to Shanghai, briefly demoralised. He wrote of going himself to replace them, while they rented a house in Shanghai and then gave it up after paying the rent. It looked as if Meadows needed a long leave in England. 'I wish we had a few consistent *men* among us!' Hudson Taylor groaned to Berger. 'You can form no idea of the absurd and unreasoning panic that prevails among some of our communities. And those who leave their work and have nothing else to do are naturally the most easily infected.' Oh for the right kind of men! But in so small a mission he must soldier on, still virtually alone in bearing responsibility as leader.

While at Putuo, he wrote to thank Jennie for her letters of sympathy after Maria's death and Charles Edward's dangerous illness. Beginning formally with 'My dear Sister', he told her about little Charlie's ulcerated mouth and inconsolable misery, saying 'I am almost worn out.' But he had always been able to confide in Jennie, so his letter moved gradually, by way of saying that Emily would have died by then if she had stayed in China, to an unburdening of his own heart about Maria and himself.

> The more I feel how utterly I am bereaved, and how helpless and useless I am rendered, the more I joy in her joy, and in the fact of her being beyond the reach of such sorrow. But I cannot help sometimes feeling, oh! so weary ... My poor heart would have been overwhelmed and broken, had I not been taught more of His fullness and indwelling ... I am not far from her whom I have loved so long and so well, and she is not far from me. Soon we shall be together ... Goodnight. [And then as if calling to mind that Jennie was single.] Jesus is your portion ... Yours affly in Him,

> J. Hudson Taylor.

'How to meet difficulties'
(September–November 1870)

Undated notes for a paper on *How to Meet Difficulties* lie among his documents of this period.[181] The nature of them suggests that he wrote it while at Putuo. Its keynotes read, 'What are difficulties? Circumstances in which our needs are, or appear to be, great in proportion to our resources.' Should difficulties be squarely met or avoided? To determine the will of God is the key to the answer and he expressed his conviction that God's will may be known, and suggested how to find it. The difficulty may be a temptation, or a God-given obstruction to one on the wrong path. But it may be something to be confronted and overcome or to be met with suffering, to our benefit. So 'Fear them not; look them in the face; determine to overcome them in the strength of the Lord.'

Both the Crombies were ill and needed to return to Britain, and the Fenghua church asked for James Williamson to come as their pastor. As another Presbyterian he was well fitted to do so. But when James Meadows wanted to return to Ningbo he had to be told that the Bridge Street church had been successfully indigenous for too long already to be set back by the re-appointment of a foreigner.

Crombie had been arguing his Presbyterian beliefs too forcibly for harmony within a transdenominational society. He might do better to return in a Presbyterian mission, William Berger was warned, unless he became satisfied with the principles of the CIM before returning. Part of the trouble was that all three Crombie children had died and Anne was pregnant again. Unknown to George and Anne, Williamson, Meadows, Hudson Taylor and the Bergers were combining to pay their steamer fare, hoping that the latest baby would live if born at home.

Hudson Taylor was seeing them off at Shanghai in mid-October and spent the night on board ship with them before they sailed early next morning. During the night 'a miscarriage took place and she was in such a dangerous way that it was with difficulty that I was able to leave her to get the change of clothing etc. I had on shore. The (sailing) was kindly delayed for me for half an hour or more by the Captain, who agreed and even wished me to go, as Mrs C could not be moved . . . She gave me great anxiety.' As soon as Anne recovered enough to continue the journey, Hudson Taylor made the most of an 'enforced holiday', stayed in Hong Kong (very likely with James Legge of the LMS, always hospitable to CIM travellers), visited Canton and caught the French mail ship back to Shanghai. An LMS chapel had been burned down in Fushan (Fatshan), and Christians were suffering in several places in Guangdong province, while the long crisis in China lasted. 'The Clarendon policy has done an injury that, I fear, will not soon be recovered from,' he surmised. The complete change of scene had done him good, his love of the sea taking his mind from his grief. When he learned that the next ship to follow him from Hong Kong had been caught in a typhoon and lost without trace, he was impressed that his life was in God's hands.

After Charles Edward's dangerous dysentery at Ningbo and severe 'thrush' at Putuo, Mary Gough had offered to keep him as one of her family. So, trans-shipping at Shanghai, Hudson Taylor went down to Ningbo, planning to visit each station between there and Zhenjiang on his way home to Yangzhou, now only home in that his possessions and precious memories were there. On arrival at Ningbo he found Charlie desperately ill again, this time with croup.[182] He had been black in the face and at midnight Dr John Parker had with difficulty saved his life. To go on with the journey demanded determination. 'My heart aches at the prospect of leaving him again,' he groaned.

In gratitude to Mary Gough he went to great trouble to arrange for his parents, the Fauldings and others to do what they could for her son Tom Jones, now a young man of eighteen taking up medicine. Reunion with the faithful Wang Lae-djün and his wife, and with the McCarthys and Jennie Faulding for nearly two weeks was the tonic he needed. But on arrival at Hangzhou he was called to see one of George Moule's church members who had already 'been left three or four days with her infant partially born'. It was too late to save her life. Two days later he attended Mrs McCarthy in a hazardous confinement, which could also have been fatal if he had not been there.

A letter arrived from his mother. The doctor had examined Emily's lungs and gave her 'no hope'. Her tuberculosis was far advanced. 'My heart felt almost overwhelmed' for a few minutes, he wrote in reply. Was Emily to be taken too? Maria's dying wish had been that the children 'should all be kept as a little family together; and under (Emily's) care'. So now, 'O death, where is thy sting? O grave, where is thy victory?' had new meaning for him.

> Formerly I had thought those taken were to feel this. Now I know those left may also triumph over death ... Often I find myself wondering if it is possible for her who is taken to have more joy in His presence, than He has given to me. If He has taken her to heaven He has also brought heaven to me here for He is heaven ... In His presence is fullness of joy ... 'It is I, be not afraid.' 'I took them.' And my heart

He fills with such deep true unutterable gladness.

Even more disquieting was a note detectable in the Bergers' letters of failing health and even failing resolve. Their invariably kindly, humble letters carried a hint of waning confidence in their own ability to do what was required of them, not only in the selection of candidates. Shock after shock from the international news and then of Maria's death, following all the trauma of the Yangzhou riot aftermath and the defence of Hudson Taylor and the Mission, were more than they could stand. Mary Berger was still suffering pain whenever she took food. William Berger was wilting. On September 23 he wrote, 'I feel my inability . . . my nerves have become so shaken by events.' Letters of sympathy for Hudson Taylor and his team were pouring in and had to be replied to. Mrs Faulding's alarm and concern for Jennie were taxing too. So William Berger confessed, 'I bear burdens too heavy for me. I get weaker year by year.' And as the year ended, 'I am very weakly in body but the Lord knows my need.' How could the Mission continue without the Bergers? There was no one in Britain so far known to Hudson Taylor with the same commitment and liberty to take on the work involved.

All the same, long, affectionate and efficient letters continued to come, dealing with administrative matters, but always so carefully expressed with pages of accounts, especially if any apparent discrepancy should need clarification. Philip Gosse (the naturalist) had sent his greetings and sympathy, but advised, 'Mr Taylor has more and more disappeared from our view . . . Now, seeing that . . . he is manifestly the only mastermind in (the Mission) the recession from communication with the supporters . . . is much to be deprecated. The cream of former *Papers* was his *coup d'oeil* over the Mission, his estimate of work done and his anticipations of progress. Did Mr Gosse know,' Mr. Berger commented, 'what you are asked to bear and pass through, he would not be surprised at your silence.' Still, he was right, a few lines from time to time were essential. Stern business was well balanced by encouragement. 'I see in you what God can do, keeping you in peace and even joy when his billows are going over your soul. (He) has been preparing your soul, dear brother, for stripping it of its chief earthly joy. It has been most marked . . . The furnace has been heated by an all-wise hand, and shall only purify the gold.'

Another struck down (December 1870)

Leaving Hangzhou, Hudson Taylor went next to Suzhou, to be greeted by Henry Cordon with the news that George Duncan was seriously ill at Zhenjiang, incessantly coughing blood. Something about Hudson Taylor impressed Cordon more than this emergency. 'He came to us full of the Spirit. Although he had so lately experienced such deep sorrow, he only spoke of the wisdom and goodness of the Lord.' Hudson Taylor set off at once for Zhenjiang. Starting with the same disadvantages as his companions in the team, and yielding like some of them to the pitfalls of culture shock, criticising and rebelling until he found his feet, Duncan had faced the difficulties and overcome. In pioneering Nanjing he had been wise and not fearless but brave.

Catherine Brown had taken a risk in coming to China to marry a man she scarcely knew, but had all the qualities to make her the right wife for him if they were not 'as unsuited to one another as they well can be'. Unfortunately, as the victim of Victorian mores, like so many of her kind, 'of what marriage involved, she appears to have been in absolute ignorance', while from the first George was rough and demanding. At Nanjing they had quarrelled incessantly and she had been on the point of leaving him, when Hudson Taylor and Maria had gone to the rescue, explaining and advising them over several days. As a result the love and respect of each couple for the other became profound, though the Duncans still found it hard to adapt to each other.

When extreme danger forced Catherine and her companion Mary Bowyer to leave Nanjing for a while, and when Maria was ill and died, Catherine repaid her debt of gratitude in every way she could, mothering Charles Edward and seeing to Hudson Taylor's comfort. For her sake and George's he hurried to help them. There was little he could do. Tuberculosis, the inveterate enemy of so many, with no known cure, had struck the strong Highlander down. He lived, working hard, for only two more years.

The saddest week and hardest year (December 1870)

Perhaps it was too soon, but Yangzhou as 'home' to the Taylors, though they had so seldom lived there, held all Maria's possessions, and Hudson Taylor had to spend a few days disposing of them. Two days before Christmas he wrote, 'Last week was perhaps the saddest I have passed since my dear wife's removal. I was going over many of her things—our betrothal presents, her wedding dress, and many things . . . connected with the birth and death of some of the dear children and with my darling wife herself.' A flood of memories had been inescapable.

He had asked Emily Blatchley to compile material for a memoir of Maria for the children, and then to write it herself. She began but as her health failed had to put it aside. Little survives, but scattered reminiscences and tributes in letters of sympathy confirm the impression of a highly competent, caring and self-effacing wife, mother and missionary colleague. James Williamson recalled her constant attention to the single men's clothes, keeping them laundered and mended. Charles and Elizabeth Judd knew her only from the six weeks they were together in Hangzhou, and then in Zhenjiang after the riots, when Hudson Taylor was down with dysentery. In spite of her injuries Maria had risen to the occasion and struck Judd as being 'the backbone of the Mission at that time'. A false inference has been drawn from his remark that without Maria, Hudson Taylor would have been weak. But throughout the collected correspondence (her own, the Bergers and Hudson Taylor's) the clear impression is given of a consistently unobtrusive but positive personality supporting her husband loyally, and obediently, in his strong leadership, never asserting her own opinions when they occasionally differed from his. It was true, however, that while dysentery disabled him, Maria's quiet strength had inspired her colleagues.

The shattering experience of her death in a year of crisis upon crisis, emphasised the nature of Hudson Taylor's own personality as perhaps nothing else would have done. In Grattan Guinness he had an understanding friend to whom he could open his heart.

> The difficulties and dangers ... and the sickness and sorrows of the past year, I think I may say they have equalled if not exceeded, those of the previous sixteen years of my missionary labour in the aggregate. But be this as it may, the Lord had previously taught me practically, as I never knew it before, our present, real oneness with Christ. And with the exception of the last two months, it has been the happiest and most joyous year of my life.

To William Berger he announced that he was sending the Meadows family home before the summer, and gently held Berger to Mission principles undergoing strain.

> As to appeal, I would suggest we make that to God alone so far as funds are concerned. If the Lord sends still less, and some were to leave us in consequence we might be rather stronger than weaker for the loss. [Then he answered a suggestion that he himself should visit England, to relieve the Bergers and encourage the Mission's supporters.] I need not say how my poor desolate heart often longs to see you all, and how I should like to make some arrangement about family matters, to say nothing of seeing face to face the friends of the Mission. But I think you will see with me that in the present state of matters (in China) I should not be out of the way ... Mrs Faulding has written to Jennie in great trouble urging her to return. There is really no need for it now, so far as immediate danger goes. And

she could not leave her work at present without grave injury to it—and to others ... But I must close. It is 2 a.m. and I rose at 6 a.m. and must not attempt more.

Jennie herself answered her mother's pleas by writing on December 7:

> The panic of the summer has quite passed away ... Fresh missionaries are being sent out by the different societies, but I have not heard of any leaving on the score of 'prudence', not even the most timid ... Now is our opportunity, the people are willing to hear, our opportunity might be short, ought we not then to make the most of it? I have health and am able to work. I will not court danger, but you mustn't want me to come home before God makes it clear to me that I ought ... I hope you will give me your permission to stay ... I think you will.

To Cardwell at Jiujiang, timidly seeking protection in foreign clothes, the symbol of Western power, Hudson Taylor had written after returning to Zhenjiang, to instill some courage, 'As a rule the sooner we, as an inland Mission, can get away from the ports the better . . . Living in the interior of China, and especially in the unoccupied provinces is not, and is not likely to be, an easy task . . . Let us take courage and press forward.'

Looking back over 1870, Hudson Taylor himself said, 'Wave after wave of trial rolled over us; but at the end of the year some of us were constrained to confess, that we had learned more of the loving-kindness of the Lord than in any previous year of our lives. Perhaps, also, more was done during this year than ever before to teach the (Chinese) Christians not to lean upon the arm of foreign protection and support, but upon God alone, on whom, as they had seen, the missionaries themselves had to lean in the hour of trial and danger.'

'The year,' he was content to add, 'was not wholly without some visible sign of progress.' During the less tense periods Stevenson had extended the Shaoxing church to Xinchang beyond Sheng Xian (see map 2.2: p 6) where he had begun work in 1869. Wang Lae-djün had opened a country chapel at his own expense. The Hangzhou evangelists had returned to Lanxi on the Qiantang River, and to other cities. McCarthy had made an evangelistic journey north-east from Hangzhou, Harvey northwards into Anhui from Nanjing, and Rudland and Edward Fishe in two directions from Taizhou. The freehold of the Nanjing house had been successfully purchased, and land outside Zhenjiang on which to build. The invisible signs of progress were not long in making themselves apparent when churches came into being in those cities in which beleaguered young men and women had thought they were achieving nothing.

17
Crucible of Faith (1871–75)

Holding on (January–June 1871)

If the year just ended, 1870, was the hardest in Hudson Taylor's experience so far, the first half of 1871 was in some ways 'harder still'. The new year began well. Someone went so far as to tell Emily Blatchley in a letter that Hudson Taylor was 'never looking better'. He was disciplining himself to go to bed between nine and ten o'clock and to begin the day at six-thirty. After the customary day of fasting and prayer on December 30, things began 'to look up', with conversions and baptisms in most of the Mission's cities, and fewer problems with the team. Whenever he was at Zhenjiang he acted as chaplain to the community and preached at the consulate as well as in the Chinese chapel. In March he organised the congregation as a church, Chinese and missionaries sharing the leadership. But six or seven hours of meetings in a day were too taxing for his strength and the improvement in his health was short-lived. Charles Fishe, as his assistant, was picking up the administrative duties of accounting and routine correspondence, and being called the Secretary in China of the Mission. So Hudson Taylor began to think of making a quick visit of a few months to Britain and back, as the Bergers were urging him to do. To consult with them, renew links with the Mission's supporters, and make arrangements for Emily and his 'three strong, rompy' children, were crying needs.

He had noticed on his visits to his scattered team that the Chinese and foreign evangelists and their congregations followed each other's progress with interest. So he launched a little house journal, the *Monthly Gleaner*, printed on the presses at Zhenjiang, and Fishe took responsibility for producing this. When Hudson Taylor fell ill again and had to cancel a planned visit to Ningbo and the southern area, he very carefully delegated his pastoral duties to John McCarthy. McCarthy was already advising the church leaders of the Hangzhou, Xiaoshan and Ningbo (Bridge Street) congregations. If he were also to visit his missionary colleagues, the Stotts, the Rudlands, Edward Fishe, Williamson and Jackson he could encourage them and help in any way he saw fit. He could be in practice a real though 'not a nominal bishop or overseer'.

> You are really their head as you become their helper and servant. I wish you to feel responsible before the Lord for seeking to help ... really help them, really pray much for them, and, as far as possible, with them; feel and evince a deep interest in all their out-stations and work generally. And above all, don't let them dream you are taking a higher place than their own—leave God to show that in due time.[183]

As a pattern for superintendence as it developed in the years ahead, this basic statement stands as relevant today as then.

After all they had been through, James and Elizabeth Meadows were preparing to return to Britain on leave. They left Zhenjiang for Shanghai on April 7, but were delayed by the premature birth of Elizabeth's baby and continuing ill-health so that they decided to wait and travel with Hudson Taylor. They were still waiting in July. By the time they arrived home, James would have been away for nine years of rebellion, war, riot, threats and recurring dysentery. Knowing of Hudson Taylor's concern for his little Charles Edward, still in the care of Mary Gough though she was ill with a liver abscess, Elizabeth Meadows offered to take him home with them. By then Hudson Taylor's illness and the pain of being parted so far from little

Charlie, his last link with Maria, made him unable to think the question through. If he himself could get away he would be able to have Charlie with him. Outwardly he was composed and cheerful, but John Stevenson had seen evidence of weeping.

By mid-January when he was struggling again with constant pain in his side and chest, he told Jennie and his mother, 'everything is a burden'. But 'matters look encouraging at most of our stations, and the prospects of peace increase. I have midwifery engagements up to the end of June'—including the British and American consuls' wives—but after that he would try to come home. His pain was like the pain that had driven him home in 1860, and as then he feared the worst. It continued for months, but this time without jaundice. Actual gallstone colic was to come later. He preached at the consulate on January 22, and then went down with 'bronchitis' for ten days, nursed by Louise Desgraz. Even so he had to keep up with his correspondence and complete his share of work on the *Monthly Gleaner*.

On the whole China was calm again, but at Anqing and Yangzhou the mutterings of anti-foreign feeling kept being heard. 'We hold our own with great difficulty.' When Thomas Harvey began doctoring again at Nanjing, after saying he would not do so, Hudson Taylor wrote patiently, reasoning at length with him that he was playing with fire. The danger and potential damage could extend far beyond Nanjing to affect the whole work of the Mission, and others too, by limiting them to the treaty ports.

> As you know the Nankin people still believe (that) foreigners ... bewitch people with medicines. And you can scarcely be ignorant that since the return of (Zeng Guofan) ... any medical efforts are open to accidental, not to say intentional misconstruction. Such a case might easily arise as would result in the destruction of all missionary property, Roman Catholic and Protestant, lives might be lost, war ensue. And I cannot but think that no small responsibility would rest on the shoulders of the unintentional but still highly reprehensible author of so much trouble ...

> You have made most commendable progress in the written character. I do not know any member of the Mission who has made such good progress in the same time as you have done; and not many, if any, can write the characters so neatly as you can ... but your ear is as evidently needing help ... Your own servants often misunderstand you, and many (Chinese) have told me that *not* more than half you say is intelligible to a stranger ... Concentrate your efforts on the language and on direct missionary work till you are truly efficient ... I beseech you not to attempt any cutting operations in Nankin. Trifling ones about the eyes, or the removal of tumours, may cost many lives. I would advise you to sell your medicines; they would be worse than useless to you, they would be a temptation. And if it be known that such a supply of medicines has gone to Nankin, who could prevent the report that further bewitching was on the way? The Viceroy himself could not do it.

It was after all only seven months since the Tianjin massacre. Instead Hudson Taylor suggested that Harvey should visit the coast of Jiangsu to find, if possible, a seaside holiday place like Putuo. At the end of March he did go by river and across country from Qingjiangpu, north-eastwards as far north as Haizhou near the Shandong border, an adventurous journey with a Chinese companion. But he found only mile upon mile of tidal swamps. Henry Reid had written proposing marriage to a complete stranger. 'Don't let her out!' was the only advice 'Hudson Taylor could give William Berger. But Reid was doing well at supervising the erection of new school buildings at Zhenjiang, planned with Maria before her death and now a memorial to her. Designed as a home and school for Louise's and Mary Bowyer's work among women and children, it stood outside the city where the air was fresh and the surroundings peaceful. So Hudson Taylor rented rooms nearby for himself.

For a short while in March he was better and gave lessons in Greek to the Zhenjiang household, to their delight. But by the end of the month he was in bed again and so ill that he thought this time death was not far off. He told his father, 'The joy of life has fled', and wrote about committing his children legally to Emily Blatchley if he should die. Perhaps he half wished he could.[184] Far away in England Emily, too, was tearful and lonely, finding the care of his children as much as her failing strength could stand. When his mother and others in China suggested that he should marry her, he replied:

> Poor Freddie [Howard Taylor] ... needs a person of pretty strong nerves and firm deportment to manage him. And Miss Blatchley suffering as she does must often be very unequal to this. I can fully endorse all you have said of her value to me and to the children, and might add much more. The Mission would never have been what it is, but for her ability, diligence, and faithfulness. On at least two occasions, I am convinced, my dear wife owed her life to her kind and vigilant nursing ... Miss Blatchley's present condition is largely the result of her unceasing care of dear little Samuel during the winter of '69–'70. In cold rooms, she was up night after night— sometimes frequently, to save my dear wife whom she loved with a devotion no one else has ever shown. So that if I did not love and value her, I should be ungrateful indeed. But that is quite a different thing from entering into the relationship you so delicately allude to. This has been advised, I do not say urged, by some here, who know her loss to the (Mission), love her and think it would add to my happiness and efficiency. But I have always replied that if there were no other reasons against it, the state of her health was too uncertain to admit the question ... I am, however, rather looking forward to reunion with my own Maria, than to any earthly union ... I can very well foresee that if I do return home my position will be both delicate and trying.

His letters to the children were warmly affectionate, reminding them of his love and friendship while they were with him, and exhorting them to be considerate and good. For Freddie he had this to say,

'There is one thing (God) never does . . . He never undoes what we have done, no matter whether it be right or wrong. And its consequence goes on, and on, and on—but letting Jesus rule in our hearts is the secret of overcoming the bias to do wrong.'

Emily was comfortably established in Bayswater with a sister-in-law of W. G. Lewis of Westbourne Grove, close to Amelia and Benjamin. But the expense was more than Hudson Taylor could justify, and supporters of the Mission might misconstrue his children's being housed in stylish new West End quarters. A seaside town on the south coast would be better for them all. But he was too far away to intervene or to help Benjamin, whose business partnership had had to call in the receivers and come to an end. A deliverance from the wrong kind of company, Hudson Taylor thought. But it meant that Amelia, with eight children of her own, could not help Emily. He himself was needed at home.

Still his illness continued. In editing the April issue of the *Monthly Gleaner*, Charles Fishe wrote, 'Mr. Taylor has been very unwell for the last three months, almost wholly unable to engage in any work.' By mid-May he was writing of having an irregular fever and of months on and off a couch, unable to be up all day. Yet all through these months he continued to carry the day-to-day administration of the Mission, constantly training Charles Fishe to keep it going when he himself would at last be free to leave.

Progress (May–June 1871)

The Mission's work continued to look up. The New Lane church at Hangzhou had fifteen candidates for baptism, about to swell the church membership to sixty-seven. Wang Lae-djün, declining any salary from Mission sources, and trusting God to meet his needs, had opened four country outposts with regular services, and was supervising seven full-time evangelists and colporteurs. He had been up the Qiantang River to Lanxi preaching the gospel in an area where new churches were to result as this evangelism progressed, and on beyond Lanxi to Qü Xian. John McCarthy's continuous training classes were preparing more to join them either locally or far afield as missionaries to other cities. Jennie's friend[331] was among them. Her schools were doing well, financially independent of the Mission, and several older pupils had so far memorised the whole New Testament with the exception of two Gospels. Apart from managing and teaching in the school with Mrs Wang she was still visiting house after house in the city as she had done since her arrival there in 1866. To stay and carry on, as if massacres and uproar elsewhere in China had no relevance in Hangzhou, was in her view the best way to maintain calm, and she was probably not mistaken.

Acting on Hudson Taylor's advice, John McCarthy walked all the way to Taizhou and back, 'preaching along the way' and discovering a personal ability which was to become part of the history of China. At Ningbo, Fenghua, Taizhou and Wenzhou his coming cheered the churches and missionaries, who wrote appreciatively to Hudson Taylor. At Wenzhou and Taizhou such crowds were thronging the premises (a hundred or more day after day to hear the gospel preached) that larger chapels were urgently needed. The response of the people to the foreigners' quiet endurance of threats and stoning was their just reward.

J. E. Cardwell at Jiujiang had acquired a boat and begun evangelistic journeys along the 'endless' rivers and shores of the Poyang Lake. At long last he was realising his ambition and was beginning his major penetration of the province of Jiangxi. After an initial five-day journey he ventured deep into the province for a month. Sailing to the southern extremity of the lake, and up the Gan Jiang River, to the provincial capital of Nanchang, he went on up the Fu He a hundred miles beyond, to a subsidiary city called Fuzhou, in the same latitude as Wenzhou on the coast.

When stones were thrown from an excited crowd he asked bystanders, 'Is this the way to treat a visiting stranger?' and taking his side they stopped the offenders. Another day a man put his hand beside

2.17 Endless waterways in the Poyang Lake region

Cardwell's and said, 'They are the same.' 'Then why do you call me "foreign devil"?' he asked. If their bodies were the same and one was a foreign devil, the man answered, then the Chinese must be native devils and they all laughed. 'You're right,' they said. From then on Cardwell made a point wherever he was of discussing the absurdity of the epithet, 'foreign devil', and heard people change their expressions. At Nanchang literary examinations were in progress and the mandarins sent a gunboat to see him safely on his way, welcoming him back after the unruly students had dispersed.

News of such expeditions, reminiscent of Hudson Taylor's own early adventures before obligations to others tied him down, gave him hope of eventually achieving his ambitions for spreading the gospel throughout China. Only at Anqing and Yangzhou was opposition being maintained and progress slow. Continuing attempts to buy the premises they had rented, expressly to turn them out, kept Hudson Taylor, Meadows at Anqing, and Judd at Yangzhou at their wits' end. To be evicted would make a return well nigh impossible. Yet in both places a church was steadily taking shape as members increased in number and maturity.

Writing to his mother on June 21 Hudson Taylor said, 'Nearly all my things are packed, and I had hoped to be away from (Zhenjiang) by this time. But two cases of confinement which I have engaged to attend have not yet come off, so I am detained—and yet may be for some time . . . I have seemed to realise those thin loving arms almost around me again, as they were when she gave me her parting blessing.'

Feeling drained and exhausted, he was doing all he could to get unco-operative members of his team to pull together. When Reid wrote of going into 'the English costume', Hudson Taylor replied on the 24th,

> No change in your views or action in this matter will in the slightest degree affect my Christian love and esteem for you ... (This question of dress is) one of the topics I propose for conference with Christian friends at home, in its bearing on our work, and on my movements ... [It was a serious matter. If he could not get his colleagues to follow his lead, perhaps he should not continue as leader—or should limit the Mission to those who would?] I wish to develop my own conscientious convictions on this subject; at the same time I do not wish to constrain any to act contrary to their own feelings and wishes ... It must be borne in mind that not merely the feelings and interests of those who would discard the principles and practice of the Mission have to be considered; those who adhere to them, and friends who support them, are not to be forgotten.

Abandoning Chinese clothes, he continued, could embarrass his colleagues who did not and could start another spate of newspaper criticism at the time when more publicity would be most unwelcome. 'We are just now in particularly delicate circumstances politically.' It was impossible to foresee the outcome of any action to disturb the status quo. He did not add that young Reid was probably too out of touch with affairs to realise that a second plot to attack the Mission in Yangzhou, and the concerted attempt in Peking to force all missionaries back to the treaty ports were currently hot issues.

Then came the news, that after a long, long wait for Tom Barnardo to qualify as a doctor and reach China he would not after all be coming. It could not but deepen Hudson Taylor's despondency. Protests from Britain that Hudson Taylor should not be so tied by babies—waiting for confinements—were all very well. No one else could relieve him of the duty and he was unwilling simply to deny his

help to consuls' wives, let alone his own missionaries. So while the Meadows family waited to travel on the same ship as he, he had again to defer his own departure until the pending confinements were over.

The second Yangzhou plot[185]
(April–June 1871)

For months Hudson Taylor had been trying to negotiate the purchase or lease in perpetuity of the Yangzhou premises, using the indemnities received and contributed by each missionary victim. The terms of reinstatement after the riot in 1868 had provided for permanent tenure of the property and had been carved in the stone tablet set up at the gate. But at every turn he had encountered difficulties, until deliberate obstruction could be the only explanation. On January 29 he noted that negotiations in Yangzhou were no further forward than a year ago. Only if all went well could he expect 'to return to England for a short time in August or September'. By April 9 he was more hopeful of success, but doubtful, as others were too, of his own survival. A week later the root cause of his 'fruitless negotiations' suddenly came to light, and rapid developments revealed the seriousness of the situation. A second plot to expel the foreigner from Yangzhou had the backing of two instigators of the Tianjin massacre.

After the murder of Viceroy Ma Xinyi and the investigations into the Tianjin outrage, the aged Zeng Guofan returned to Nanjing as viceroy of the Two Jiangs, the provinces of Jiangxi and Jiangsu, with Anhui—and therefore of Yangzhou and Anqing. From having a protector in Ma Xinyi, Hudson Taylor and the CIM had returned to the state of affairs in 1868 and 1869 when their enemies had been supported by Zeng Guofan. But this time Zeng had returned with the unsavoury reputation of sheltering the literati responsible for the Tianjin massacre, if not of instigating it, while Brigadier Chen Guorui had again been given command of two army camps at Yangzhou, the scene of his earlier crime.

For safety's sake and because of another approaching confinement, Elizabeth Judd had moved to Zhenjiang to be near Hudson Taylor. But Charles Judd, Louise Desgraz, her Chinese language teacher, his mother, wife and children, and a Chinese Scripture reader or 'Bible woman' and about fifteen girl and boy boarders in the Mission remained on the Yangzhou premises.

The actual owner of the property was a retired military mandarin, a Grandee called General Li, who lived in Henan. At various times he had been a Taiping rebel general, a Nianfei rebel leader and an imperial army commander, 'as best suited his purpose for the time being and brought in the largest income'. 'A man of undoubted bravery, he (was) also a man of violent passions and great determination' who kept 'a few private gunboats and some soldiers of his own'.

Hudson Taylor had always negotiated with the owner's uncle, his official representative, a dignitary with the style of Great Father, 'Da Lao Ye', who from the first had been 'most anxious that (Taylor) should retain possession of the premises'.

Summoned (it is said) by Zeng Guofan, (General) Li suddenly appeared in Nankin. There he had an interview with (Zeng Guofan) immediately after which (on April 17) he wrote a most violent letter from Nankin to his uncle at Yang-chow, accusing him of ruining his reputation by letting his property to foreigners, insisting, that by fair means or foul, he must turn them out of the premises on or before (May 4) and insisting, also, that if they were not out of the premises by that time, he, the uncle, should go to the premises, close the first gate and commit suicide within, upon which, said he, 'I will at once come and avenge your death.' He warned the uncle not to attempt to escape, 'for if you do,' he continued, 'I will seize on your wife and children and kill them.'

The uncle and his friends were appalled for, knowing Li's character and reputation and the veneration in which Chinese normally hold their elder relatives, they knew this was no empty threat. The sudden change of tone implied strong influences upon General Li and an intention to do

as he said. The uncle went at once to Judd (on April 19) and told him he 'must immediately get ready to quit' the premises. But to his distress Judd replied that the agreement had been made, the deposit had been paid and the balance of payment was ready for the contract to be signed. 'We could not think of giving it up.'

To appeal to the Yangzhou prefect would be futile, for he was greatly inferior in rank to General Li, and Chen Guorui commanded the troops which the prefect would normally call upon to quell a riot. Chen, since his arrival at Yangzhou, had 'been endeavouring to regain his popularity among the most dangerous class of Chinese, by large distributions of money amongst them. And simultaneously with this, there has been a marked development of anti-foreign feeling amongst the people . . . Before, and up to the time of his interview with (Zeng Guofan) Li and Chen were sworn enemies; suddenly they became fast friends, to all appearance, to the great astonishment of the (people) of Yangchau.' It was the talk of the town that another attempt to drive out or kill the foreigners had brought them together. Judd crossed the Yangzi to consult Hudson Taylor, and they decided that the schools should be disbanded, Louise should come to Zhenjiang, and Judd should hold on at Yangzhou for as long as possible. From then on he was largely alone as the fateful date, May 4, drew nearer.

'(On April 25) Li himself came to Yang-chow from Nankin, and in conjunction with (Chen Guorui) ripened his plans, and they and their soldiery became almost irrepressibly excited.' Charles Judd and the Christians in Yangzhou were then in considerable danger, with nowhere to flee to in the event of an attack. Urgent messages began to pass between all the parties involved, Vice-Consul Gardner himself consulting urgently with the *daotai* of Zhenjiang. May 4 came and went, and the next day one of the Christians pleaded with Judd to appeal to the magistrates for protection. 'I thought of . . . Ezra when he was ashamed to ask the king for a body of soldiers,' Judd replied. 'So we only waited on our God with fasting.' By then Hudson Taylor suspected that Zeng Guofan and the provincial governor were implicated. Only three days remained before the fateful 9th, when murder and destruction were expected. Already Yangzhou was 'full of rowdies' openly boasting of their intentions, and Chen Guorui of his past doings.

Things were getting out of hand. The provincial authorities were alarmed. Expulsion from the city was one thing, but another massacre could call down retribution on their own heads and precipitate a war. Zhang Futai, Governor of Jiangsu, appointed the *daotai* of Zhenjiang to handle the crisis, and the *daotai* immediately notified General Li and the prefect of Yangzhou that they would be held responsible for any disturbance. To Judd's amazement General Li 'became friendly on the governor's orders'. But the facade was transparent and short-lived. Urgently seeking a solution, the *daotai* persuaded a friend named Zhao to buy the Yangzhou premises for whatever General Li would accept, and at Consul Gardner's instance, to lease them to the Mission, initially for five years. There was no time to lose.

General Li still had the whip hand. He arrogantly demanded 4,500 taels—an exorbitant sum—or he would carry out his threat. Early on May 6 his terms were sent to the *daotai*, the consul and Hudson Taylor in Zhenjiang by mounted courier. They must accept the terms or the attack would be made. The messenger could have arrived back on the same day but was hindered. The old uncle and his middleman came to Judd in great distress and would not leave. On the second day the messenger still had not come, and when night fell they were still at the Mission, sick with apprehension. 'They said . . . the next twenty-four hours might find our house the scene of bloody slaughter.' Judd and the Chinese Christians discussed 'how best to dispose of the (Chinese) women and children', but there was nowhere for them to go. When word came at noon on the 8th that the *daotai* (through his friend Zhao) had agreed to

pay the full amount, they were told that the attack would undoubtedly have been made on the 9th.

General Li had won, bought off by a ransom price. But had he? The *daotai* had also won, wresting ownership of the Yangzhou property from Li and paving the way for Hudson Taylor to buy the freehold in due course. At 1.30 a.m. on May 11 Hudson Taylor was writing to his mother while documents for the consul and the *daotai* were being made out in Chinese. 'We have had a very narrow escape from another Yang-chau riot, stirred up by (Chen Guorui) the Tientsin murderer and our landlord. The labour and anxiety are almost more than I can bear.' Later the same day Hudson Taylor attended the American consul's wife in her confinement.

In the *Occasional* of April and of June 1873, Hudson Taylor gave the sequel of this bizarre episode. Just as, after the Yangzhou riot of 1868, the prefect and his family came to a tragic end and the leading agitators were impoverished, so in 1870:

> Many who are friendly to us warned Li and Chen that they would lose their luck (a terrible thought to pagan Chinese) if they molested us ... Within a month of the settlement of these matters, they had a quarrel between themselves ... Both finally reached Nankin, underwent trial by the Viceroy, and have received sentence, confirmed from Pekin, which deprives Li of all rank and title for ever, and reduces Chen to the rank of a major. The latter is further sent to Honan to help in quelling the rebellion there. [Earlier it had been stated that] Li had been beheaded, and Chen degraded and banished from Yang-chau ... The people were awed thereby. But if the sentences were actually pronounced, they were in some way evaded in great measure, as is often the case with the rich in China; for Li is reported to be now living in retirement, in his own native place; and Chen has returned again to Yang-chau, and is leading a private life there, though without his former rank, wealth, or influence.

Most likely Zeng had said what was required of him, and saw to it that his friends came to no greater harm. Knowing the story would soon be learned and reported (erroneously) in the Shanghai papers, Hudson Taylor composed as factual an account of events as was possible and arranged for it to be released anonymously in the *Shanghai Evening Courier*. The whole incident had taken place while he was packing up, preparing to sail for Britain as soon as his last obstetric case was over. There was no knowing what would happen next.

Tilting at a windmill?[186] (June 1871)

True to the precedents he had set, Wade was working for the withdrawal of Hudson Taylor and his mission from the 'interior' to the treaty ports. By the autumn the Foreign Office would be putting more pressure on them through William Berger, but in June the beginnings were simple enough. Writing to George Müller on May 15, Hudson Taylor said enigmatically, 'the Chinese and our own Foreign powers seem growingly inimical to the gospel.' And to William Berger on May 19 he hinted at trouble ahead.

> I learn that Mr Wade has made a representation to the Chinese Foreign Office about our Yangchau affairs. Of its nature I have been unable to learn. He must, I should think, have heard of (Chen Guorui's) boastings of what he was about to do against us and have written in consequence. It may be well for you to know that nothing done has been owing to any report from us, directly or indirectly. Mr Gardner does not know himself what or why (Wade) has so written. The Senior Naval Officer also is said to have been ordered to go to Nankin and make representations to the Viceroy (Zeng Guofan). I do not know their nature either, nor why the Admiral has so directed him.

After the way the Yangzhou riots of 1868 had been inflated into international incidents, Hudson Taylor could be forgiven if he was apprehensive. On June 8 the new consul-general in Shanghai, J. Markham, wrote to C. T. Gardner, his vice-consul in Zhenjiang:

> I have just received a note from Mr Wade and he strongly advocates that Mr Taylor should leave Yangchow, not hurriedly, but in the course of a few months—quietly ... I might run up to Yangchow myself ... Don't let it out that Mr Wade wishes Taylor to remove, but acquaint that gentleman privately with his wishes, and say that although everything is quite quiet and settled now, there is no guarantee that the trouble will not be remembered on some future day ... P.S. Mr Wade bids me caution you 'not to tell any Chinese that we shall support or shall not support the Dynasty in case of Revolution.'
>
> J. M.

Gardner passed Markham's letter on to Hudson Taylor, who (in spite of fever) replied on June 15:

> It is perhaps the best thing for me to write you a private note on the subject, which ... if you think it desirable you can send to Mr Markham, through whom I should be glad to convey my thanks to Mr Wade for his suggestion.
>
> We are most anxious to promote our work with all possible caution; and while, I trust, not unprepared to meet personal danger when inevitable, we seek to avoid everything likely to involve ourselves, and are still more anxious not to involve others, in needless difficulties. We have endeavoured ... to conduct our operations in the interior, in a conciliatory spirit. The recent difficulty at Yangchow was not, I believe, either caused by, or aided and abetted by, the people there, nor by the local officers or the literati, but was entirely confined to Li and Chen, with their partisans, and associates ... The satisfactory conclusion of the recent difficulties has convinced many that we are favoured by Heaven, and that therefore those who attempt to assail us, are likely to be both unsuccessful and unfortunate ... I therefore think that there is now very little danger of troubles arising spontaneously at that city in connection with our work.
>
> Our entire removal from Yangchow would, I fear, give rise to grave difficulties in a number of other stations, and might even seriously affect (Zhenjiang) ... It is undeniable that (Zeng Guofan) could, if he wished it, make trouble (at Yangzhou). Of such trouble we should have ample

notice ... The projected attack on May 9 was known to us by the middle of April.

In two paragraphs he detailed his 'mode of working' in the interior. Much coming and going by the missionaries, often on account of illness, but also in the course of their work, had accustomed the Chinese to their movements. 'Temporary absence being therefore the rule rather than the exception, is deprived of the significance it might otherwise have had.' People would no longer think the foreigners were afraid and running away. The schools at Yangzhou and Nanjing had been closed, and the women in charge transferred to the newly-built school at Zhenjiang. 'Were (these) facts made known to Mr Wade, he would feel satisfied that we have done all that present circumstances render requisite ... Mr Wade is fully alive to the fact that the danger of leaving is sometimes greater than that of remaining so far as National Interests are concerned.'

Christopher Gardner replied the same day:

> Thanks for your letter, in the spirit of which I cordially agree. With Asiatics a bold and determined front to danger is the most prudent course. Sir Harry Parkes and Mr Locke owed their life to their not being afraid [see 1, p 492]. And I believe in the recent trouble at Yangchow, had Mr Judd showed any signs of fear, that the riot would have taken place ... I venture to believe Mr Wade will be perfectly satisfied and will approve the measures of prudence you have taken ...
>
> Believe me, yours with the greatest respect,
>
> Chr. T. Gardner

Consul Markham duly visited Zhenjiang and Yangzhou, but Hudson Taylor was unable in the stormy weather to meet him. Instead he wrote on June 22:

> I believe you saw the only boarders in the Boys' School [at Yangzhou]. Double the number might easily have been admitted, but prudential motives [to avoid suspicion] and want of accommodation, have required the refusal of many applications, some of which were made since the settlement of the recent difficulty with Li and (Chen Guorui) ... A written indenture drawn up and signed by the parents or guardians of each child is required before admitting him into the school ... I need scarcely say that this willingness of the people to entrust to our care ... their own children, on whom they expect to rely in old age, is one of the strongest proofs that we have really gained a position among them, and a considerable measure of their confidence and respect.
>
> It is impossible to view Yangchow as an isolated place. Any removal from it would not only affect other stations of our own Mission ... I submit for your consideration whether it would not also seriously affect foreign relations in this Port, and possibly at (Jiujiang). It would likewise affect the work of other Missions elsewhere ... (At Huzhou) local officers referred to Yangchow as a precedent. A few months ago, a Yangchow man (now magistrate in Shaoxing) took a similar course. And it is not six months since the Prefect in (Taizhou) referred to Yangchow as a precedent authorising the protection and favour of Protestant Missions.

Gardner capped the correspondence four days later with a surprising note:

> Mr Wade had more reason than we knew of for the advice he gave you—facts have come to my knowledge today that render it very advisable gradually to give up your schools at Yangchow, gradually of course. And so to have matters that no lady should reside there. Wade mentioned two or three months. You have that time to make arrangements for disbanding the schools. As for Judd, he is a brave man—my advice is he should stay at Yangchow—he will always get warning enough. The danger will not be to Foreigners alone, but there is a rebellion on foot, and there are reasons to dread that Yangchow will be one of the spots where it will break out ... I will try and see you today.

Hudson Taylor could not but act on such insistence. During July, Charles Judd closed the Yangzhou school and joined his wife at Zhenjiang. Charles Fishe quietly took his place at Yangzhou. Five boys of their own or their parents' volition followed Judd to Zhenjiang and entered the new school there. But letters continued to refer to the likelihood of both Charles and Elizabeth Judd returning to Yangzhou, once the baby was born. Whether Wade was tilting at a windmill of his own imagining or of Prince Kong's contriving, Hudson Taylor could not know. No more was heard of the alleged rebellion, and such diplomatic pressure on Hudson Taylor had if anything the reverse effect, making him more secretive in pursuing his aims. Instead, what came to light was a strong initiative by the Zongli Yamen to curb all missionary activity. Wade used it to restrict Hudson Taylor and the CIM, by directing the attention of the Foreign Minister, Lord Granville, to him.

The 'Zongli Memorandum'
(April–June 1871)

Habitual use of certain terms has endowed historical events and highlights with labels never designed for them. A document emanating from the Zongli Yamen and circulated at first among high-ranking mandarins became known to foreigners and in early 1871 was being referred to as the 'Chinese Circular'. Some continued to use this term to apply to a document issued by the Zongli Yamen to ministers of the foreign powers. Others distinguished between the two and referred to the latter as the 'Zongli Memorandum'. Each was in fact a new twist in the old 'missionary question', too general a term to apply to the specific proposals of 1871.

An editorial note in the *Chinese Recorder* of May 1871 entitled 'A Remarkable Plan for Settling the Missionary Question' reported that, 'The Mandarins of the (Zongli) Yamen at Pekin have been devising a plan to settle for ever the missionary question. They have actually proposed to send all missionary ladies home; to confine each Mission to forty-five converts; to register all baptisms; to compel missionaries, whenever they have business at the Yamens, to appear as natives in the presence of native officials; together with one or two other points.' These

propositions were simply submitted to the foreign ministers for their consideration.

The Memorandum itself was 'dignified and courteous', but radical in its proposals. In addition to the clauses mentioned in the *Recorder*, only the children of Christians were to be admitted to orphanages, women were to be debarred from churches, and members of missionary sisterhoods were not to enter China. 'Excessive and unusual penalties were not to be demanded by foreigners for the murder of missionaries and Chinese Christians.' Passports issued to French missionaries were to limit them to a specific province and prefecture. Officials would regularly inspect mission premises; and local officials were to be consulted and to inspect land before its purchase by foreigners, to ensure against violation of *fengshui*.

Transparently directed at Roman Catholic missions, these proposals threatened Protestant missions also. Even if sincerely intended by the Zongli Yamen to correct abuses, they were open to interpretation at the whim of local mandarins and the public. Although the Memorandum and 'Chinese Circular' were only consultative documents, they were released in the provinces and had immediate repercussions at the grassroots. James Williamson reported from Fenghua in June:

> Rumours have been circulated that a dispatch has been sent out by the Ningbo *daotai* to the district magistrate here, ordering him to inquire about the number of people who had joined the foreign religion, with a view to their apprehension and punishment. The first part seems to have some bearing on the circular of Prince Kong. Such rumours, even if unfounded, are at all times a great hindrance to our work.

Each of the eight articles of the Memorandum affected the prospects of the CIM. No Protestant orphanages had been opened, but the first article would affect schools and the compassionate adoption of foundlings. Women's work, such as the CIM was doing on a growing scale through its single and married women, would be prohibited. The third article would deny missionaries the protection of extra-territoriality and subject them to the capriciousness of local magistrates. And the seventh, binding them to observe the same ceremonies as observed by or 'exacted from the literates', would include kneeling before mandarins, prostrating themselves and knocking their heads on the ground (see ill. 1.63: 1, p 766). As Sir Ernest Satow, a later minister-plenipotentiary, put it, 'The Protestant Powers replied that the abuses complained of did not concern them; while the French Government rejected the whole of the proposals as inadmissible.'[187]

June 3, 1871, saw a great leap forward in communications between West and East, the inauguration of the telegraphic cable link between San Francisco (and therefore London) and Shanghai, and from Singapore (itself an extension from Ceylon) to Hong Kong. But on June 8, T. F. Wade sent a long dispatch to London by slow means. Recorded as reaching London as late as August 15, it included translations of the Memorandum and eight propositions appended to it. According to the *Standard* for December 15, 1871, it drew from a supplement to the *London Gazette* relating to 'the Missionary Question in China' containing verbatim copies of letters between Earl Granville, Foreign Minister, and T. F. Wade, British Minister in Peking.[188] Wade wrote:

> The people at large do not distinguish between Romanist and Protestant, nor between foreigner and foreigner ... The Chinese government would have the missionaries all brought under the same control ... At present they constitute in China an *imperium in imperio*; and it is to be apprehended that ... of this will come an uprising of the people beyond the power of government to control. The responsibility of foreign governments will be great if they do not join China in devising precautionary measures. [Summarising each article, Wade continued circuitously with his own heavily loaded deductions.]

To secure the missionary against the hostility of the lettered class, one of two courses must be pursued—either the missionary must be supported, out and out, by the sword of the protecting powers [an option already excluded by London]; or he must be placed by the protecting powers under restrictions which, whilst leaving him always as much latitude of action as, if simply intent on Christianising China, he is justified in desiring, will yet enable the Chinese government to declare ... that he the missionary, is not authorised by the power protecting him to put forward the pretensions objected to. ... [The missionary must be shackled by his own government and submitted to the will of the mandarins.]

Romanism, in the mouths of non-Christian Chinese is as popularly termed the religion of the French as the religion of the Lord of heaven. A dread of Romish ascendancy, as I have more than once reported ... or that the Romish community will throw itself for support upon the French ... is, in my belief, the suggesting cause of (both Zongli Memorandum and Chinese Circular).

Earl Granville apparently did not see Wade's dispatch until after he had sent a lengthy one of his own, dated August 21. In it he protested that the assertions of the Zongli Memorandum were against missionaries in general without recognition of the fact that not one of the abuses alleged in the Memorandum 'is in any way connected with any British missionary establishment'. There was no wish to secure for missionaries 'any privileges or immunities beyond those granted by treaty to other British subjects'. The treaty of June 1858 had stipulated that 'the Christian religion, as professed by Protestant or Roman Catholics . . . shall alike be entitled to the protection of the Chinese authorities . . . Her Majesty's Government, therefore . . . could not be indifferent to the persecution of Christians for professing the Christian faith.' To prevent women from attending divine worship would be in violation of the treaty, and 'Her Majesty's Government would not countenance any regulation which would cast a slur upon a sister whose blameless life and noble acts of devotion . . . are known throughout the world.'

Missionaries do not forfeit their rights under the treaty, so Her Majesty's Government 'cannot allow the claim that (they) must conform to the laws and customs of China to pass unchallenged'. 'It is impossible to prevent enterprising persons penetrating through a country. Sooner or later they will find their way (even to Sichuan); and the true interest of China is to facilitate rather than to restrict the flow of foreign enterprise.' If British missionaries behaved improperly they should 'be handed over to the nearest Consul for punishment', like other British subjects, as provided in the treaties. Until it could be proved that the minister and consuls were unable to control British subjects in China, Her Majesty's Government must decline to supplement the existing treaties.

When Wade's dispatch arrived, asking for missionaries to be restrained, it therefore received the brief (even curt) reply on August 31 that it had already been answered. But this was not known to Hudson Taylor or others threatened by 'disturbing rumours' based on the Circular, by the Memorandum and by Wade's directives to his consuls—until it was all published in the Parliamentary Blue Books and the press after he reached England. Meanwhile Wade continued to write, focusing his attention on Hudson Taylor by name. 'The Foreign Office believe him,' Hudson Taylor told Meadows.[189]

The suspense made little difference. If the time was short, all the more strenuous efforts must be made 'while it is day'. More and more Chinese evangelists were joining in the work, 'This year witnessed more extensive and important itineration and colportage than any preceding one . . . Such journeys would have been even more numerous, had not sickness to a very serious extent prevented them.'

Winds of change[190] (1871–72)

The wider world of which the Hudson Taylor saga was a part, must again receive a glance to keep perspective. With the end of the Franco-Prussian war, ushering in the era of consolidation by Bismarck of his conquests, Europe entered upon what was a long period of peace. No major war erupted until 1914, long enough for an accumulation of wealth and power to tempt with new thoughts of domination. In Asia the Russian annexation of Kuldja and Ili from Chinese Turkestan, the continuing annexation by France of Indochina and the rapid expansion of Japanese strength and ambitions, further reduced the stability of East Asia.

By a Sino-Japanese treaty at Tianjin on September 13, the Qing dynasty recognised the emergence of Japan from being a tribute-bearing vassal state into national identity, however inferior. But only three months later the seeds of the Sino-Japanese conflict were sown. Since 1372 the Ryukyu Islands had been tributary to China, and since 1451 to Japan also. From the time of the Ming emperor Yong Lo (1403–25) the princes of Ryukyu had received their investiture from China, but after 1609 from the emperor of Japan as well. In December 1871 some Ryukyuan sailors, shipwrecked on the east coast of Taiwan, were killed and eaten by independent aboriginal tribesmen. Japan demanded redress. The percipient Li Hongzhang advised admission of responsibility, but the unstatesmanlike imperial ministers at Peking (in July 1873) told Japan that they claimed no control over the savage tribes in eastern Taiwan. A Japanese force of 6,000 thereupon mustered at Xiamen (Amoy), and landed on the east coast of Taiwan outside Chinese jurisdiction. At that point Peking changed its mind and sent 10,000 troops to Taiwan. China and Japan were heading for a war neither nation wanted nor was ready to undertake. Settlement was effected through skilful diplomacy by T. F. Wade, of which more was to be heard.

Manchu-Chinese obscurantism was slowly yielding to outside influences, but all too slowly. In August 1871 an imperial decree even sanctioned an educational mission to the USA. Robert Hart in his favoured position as inspector-general of the Imperial Maritime Customs was exerting all the influence he could for the good of China, but wisely played his hand as carefully as circumstances demanded. His powerful Chinese opposite number in Canton, successor to the 'Hoppo' of Robert Morrison's day, had the approval of Peking for historic reasons. 'If the Board of Revenue had to choose between him and me, it would throw me over,' Hart wrote to his commissioner, E. C. Bowra, in February 1871. 'For honest collection and truthful report means impecuniosity for the Board.' Graft and corruption appealed even more strongly to those officials than the integrity of Hart, although it was Hart who was strengthening China's government with unprecedented speed.

China must break out of her encrusted ways if she was to survive in a changing world. 'Try to get (the local officials) out of their shells, and put new ideas into their noddles when you get the chance,' was Hart's advice to his Tianjin commissioner. To some extent they were succeeding. 'Steam is taking hold of the official mind,' he could tell Bowra in December 1871, 'and in a few years, if not disgusted by too much pressure, the horse will drink heartily of the water to which he has been led.' (A railway, little more than a tram-line between Shanghai and Wusong, projected in March 1872, was completed in 1876, only to be torn up again when handed over to Chinese control.)

Li Hongzhang was more enlightened than most contemporary mandarins. Closest to Peking in his new position as viceroy of Zhili (after Zeng Guofan's return to Nanjing), he also had most to do with foreigners. He became 'the one man to whom the distracted Manchu Government inevitably had recourse, each time that the crass ignorance of the Princes of the ruling Imperial House had brought the country to the verge of ruin'. Standing physically head and shoulders above his average countryman, he also 'excelled them in mental calibre'.

His relations with foreigners were varied.

When he had ascended the Yangzi River to Wuchang in 1869 as viceroy of Hubei and Hunan, he had pandered to popular feeling by leaving his steamer to complete the journey in a junk—under tow by a steamer and escorted by three others.

When the then British consul of Hankou insisted as Her Britannic Majesty's representative on being admitted by the main entrance to his *yamen*, he complained that the consul visited him too often, giving him a reputation for being mixed up with hated foreigners.

At the time of the Tianjin massacre a British consul wrote, 'I take it for granted that (Li) will not tolerate any outrage on foreigners within his jurisdiction', and this was indeed his reputation. But it was not forgotten that the proclamation by him while he was at Wuchang was blamed for encouraging the literati of Anqing to riot against the Catholic and CIM missions. He it was who memorialised the throne to curb the admission and activities of missionaries, the initiative behind the 'Chinese Circular' and 'Zongli Memorandum'; and he had been quietly building up the navy which was to come into conflict with the Japanese. Keeping the measure of his compatriots, he was bent on reforming and modernising China no less than was Robert Hart, but at his own pace.

The great revolution of 1868 in Japan had overturned the shogun-ate of feudal barons, in favour of the Mikado. January 1869 saw the reception of Western envoys in public audience, and the arrival of the first English missionary, George Ensor of the CMS. (Americans of the Presbyterian and Episcopal Churches were in Nagasaki and Yokohama already.) But proclamations continued to forbid Christianity to the people. Descendants of the old Jesuit converts of Urakami were being persecuted and banished. The British minister to the Yedo court, Sir Harry Parkes pointed out the inexpediency of persecution concurrently with the pursuit of Western civilisation. 'Why!' Japan replied. 'Our employment of Christian teachers in schools and colleges and use of Christian books of education shows that we have nothing against religion of any kind. It was the conspiracy by the Christians, which nearly overthrew the government of a previous century, that is remembered! Public opinion demands control of seditious communities in self-defence.' At the end of 1872, however, in a change of attitude all anti-Christian proclamations were withdrawn and the surviving exiles of Urakami were brought home. The year 1872 was also to see other astonishing developments in Japan, in the army, navy, civil service, schools and colleges, the post office, newspapers, railways, telegraphs and coastal navigation. The contrast between Japan and China could hardly have been more marked.

In China several revolutions had failed or were failing—even the great Muslim revolt of the north-west. The ancient system was being re-established, Christians were again being regarded as suspect or traitorous, and missionaries as 'the outposts of western penetration'. Ironically the slow wheels of history were to bring China back to the same situation a century later. To the literati of 1872, trained in Confucian doctrine and practice which identified politics and religion as inseparables, the 'left-hand, right-hand' relationship between foreign missionaries and their governments was indubitable. Persuasion such as Parkes had used in Japan might have had its influence, but T. F. Wade was not Parkes. Rejecting the Zongli Memorandum in a point by point rejoinder to the minister, Wen Xiang, in June 1871, he simultaneously sought to curb the progressive missionary enterprise—until he failed to win Lord Granville's support. Paradoxically, within five years he himself was to play a major part in the removal of restrictions upon missions.

In 1872, W. H. Medhurst Jr, the Shanghai consul-general before Markham, was to publish a book entitled *The Foreigner in Far Cathay*. In it he set out his opinions on foreigners being 'disguised' in Chinese dress, of which he disapproved, and on missionaries, whose champion he chose to be. We cannot but surmise that he was answering Wade indirectly and supporting Hudson Taylor whom he admired. 'I have no sympathy with those who, for want of consideration or from mere prejudice, think lightly of the work and character of the missionary.' Comparisons of Catholic and Protestant were impossible, he insisted, so different were they in organisation, method and even definition of 'convert'. Each kind was doing good work. Of the Roman Catholics he said:

> Their system is to penetrate deeply into the interior the moment they arrive, to dissociate themselves entirely from the mercantile classes of foreigners, and to work disguised as natives, unobtrusively and unremittingly, at the various stations which have been occupied by them for years, in some cases for centuries. Their devotion is as remarkable as their success has been astonishing, and I am one of those who believe that they have been the means of accomplishing ... a vast amount of good ... I have been often struck by the quiet and respectability which prevails amongst (the Christian families) as compared to the heathen around them.

It was unfortunate that the French government had exacted toleration of Christianity as a treaty right, which had led the Church into claiming property, privileges and judicial rights in such a way as to arouse antagonism to the point of massacre, 'a foretaste, it is to be feared, of what we may yet have to mourn in the future'. How right he was!

From intimate personal knowledge, he denied that Protestant missionaries showed partiality for the use of force or coercive measures, and insisted that they were entitled to full protection and the maintenance of their rights. But 'to erect pretentious edifices after the foreign style of architecture', with steeples and towers in Chinese cities, could only create ill-will. He knew that Chinese shrank from entering foreign buildings, while they would willingly enter Chinese houses occupied by friendly foreigners.

As for the merchants, Medhurst was equally frank. The term 'merchant', so long and so constantly associated with traffic in opium, was almost the synonym in Britain, he wrote, for 'adventurer' or 'smuggler'. On opium the merchant lived in affluence, scorning the Chinese around him.

It was a courageous essay. The merchants were powerful in Britain as in China. He could have prejudiced his prospects as career diplomat. But Medhurst was as courageous morally as physically. His integrity was recognised in his knighthood and appointment as HBM Ambassador to Peking in due course. Hudson Taylor did not need to vindicate himself.

Sister missions (1871–72)

With the new liberties obtained through the treaties of 1858–60, Catholic and Protestant missionaries were pressing out in ways impossible in China for centuries. Although the papacy had fallen on hard times, the Roman Church retained its missionary momentum. The limiting factor for the CMS was still what Joseph Ridgeway had called in the *Church Mission Intelligencer*, 'a Babel-like determination to build up the Church at home, instead of "replenishing the earth"'. With its goal of taking the gospel to hundreds of millions of Chinese, the personnel and funds released for the purpose were still pitiably inadequate. Reinforcements were barely enough to replace casualties. Advance such as the infant CIM had made was still being achieved at a high cost in health and lives in all societies.

The story of the CMS in Hangzhou and Shaoxing was typical. In early 1870 when George Moule returned from home and Henry Gretton 'opened a station' at Shaoxing alongside Stevenson and two American missions, he was joined by J. D. Valentine and his wife in November, on their return in renewed health. But Gretton had to retire ill, and the Palmers took his place in the autumn of 1871, only to withdraw to Britain themselves in shattered health in 1873. Arthur Moule returned to Ningbo in December 1871 with Dr and Mrs James Galt of the Edinburgh Medical Missionary Society, who joined George

Moule in Hangzhou. Galt opened a hospital for opium addicts with the funds the CMS had offered to Hudson Taylor in 1863 (see 1, p 586 & note 808)[191]. But W. A. Russell left Ningbo again in the spring of 1870 to be consecrated in Britain as 'bishop in North China'. Continuity and progress were always difficult to attain. Chaplains and missionaries north of the twenty-eighth parallel of latitude (through Wenzhou) came under Russell, and the remainder to the south under Alford. So Alford resigned in protest, and Hudson Taylor's friend and brother-in-law John Burdon, chaplain in Peking, became the third bishop of Victoria, Hong Kong.[192]

In Shandong the Baptist Missionary Society had lost missionary after missionary. 'Disaster overtook most of them' and of twelve colleagues only the young Timothy Richard survived to continue working alone. Latourette's tribute to him read, 'This lone representative, Timothy Richard, was, however, one of the greatest missionaries whom any branch of the Church, whether Roman Catholic, Russian Orthodox or Protestant, has sent to China.' The *Chinese Recorder* voiced the sympathy of the missionary community with the BMS, saying, 'When will this afflicted Mission see better days?'[193]

Of the Presbyterian, John Livingston Nevius, W. A. P. Martin was to write in his *Cycle of Cathay*, 'He was the first missionary to establish himself at (Hangzhou), the capital of the province, unless Bishop Burdon may contest that honour, and one of the first to break soil in the province of (Shandong).[194]' With Helen his wife, Nevius had pioneered and lived in Hangzhou in 1859, at he same time as John Burdon. By 1869 he resolved to set up an institution there 'for the instruction of candidates for the ministry', with Samuel Dodd but found the foreign influences in Hangzhou too strong for this to be the right venue. Then in 1870, Nevius, 'patient, kind and deferential to the opinions of others', was elected moderator of the Presbyterian Synod of China and returned to Yantai. By 1871 under his leadership, Chinese

Christians were 'fast gaining influence in our ecclesiastical courts'—an early move towards 'the Nevius Plan' for a strong indigenous church, so successfully applied in Korea twenty years later.[195] Slowly but surely, though at a price, the Protestant Church in China was growing and maturing. But it still numbered no more than 7,000 communicants in all.

In 1872 Dr D. B. McCartee, the American Presbyterian veteran in Ningbo, accompanied a Chinese envoy to Japan and negotiated the release of hundreds of victims of the coolie traffic imprisoned on the *Maria Luz*. For this service he received a gold medal from the Chinese government. But he remained in Japan for five years (1872–77) as professor of law and natural science at Tokyo University.

William Muirhead, the first missionary to reside in Suzhou after Charles Schmidt and the Cordons, had a remarkable experience that same year, 1872. Ten years previously, when visiting the headquarters of the Taiping rebels at Nanjing he had heard 'shrieks and groans' coming from a wounded boy up on the city wall. Taking him to Shanghai, he had seen that he was well cared for. In 1872, when Muirhead was trying to rent premises in Suzhou, a young rice merchant offered to help and found him a prime site for a chapel on the city's main thoroughfare. It was the boy he had rescued.[196]

Slowly but surely the gospel was inching forward, taking root where not so long before it had been stubbornly resisted.

1871–72: A 'COUNCIL OF MANAGEMENT'

Priority to the Bergers (1870–71)

Time and again, the prophetic messages of William and Mary Berger to one and another of the Mission team, and particularly to Hudson and Maria Taylor, had proved uncannily timely. William Berger's New Year greeting for 1870 had proved to be such a voice from God.

> Moses prayed 'Show me Thy way.' The Lord replied 'My presence shall go with thee and I will give thee rest' ... Had the Lord shown Moses all the way by which He intended to lead him ... would it not have overpowered or slain (him)? Oh! the Wisdom and Love of God! As we are able to bear it, He shows us His way.'

If for Hudson Taylor the year 1870 had proved to be 'the hardest yet', and in different ways 1871 was harder still, for the Bergers the same was true. Repercussions of the Anqing riot, ill-health, making a home for Emily Blatchley and the 'rompy' children, answering criticisms of the Mission, watching the donations decline, especially when the Franco-Prussian war excited the British nation and a republic in France became the 'all-engrossing subject' all weighed on their minds. Alexander Williamson of Shanghai and Yantai had

been to see them and had unblushingly spoken of his efforts to dissuade Duncan, Reid, Judd and others from wearing Chinese clothes, until William Berger protested. Yet Alexander Williamson was a true friend of the CIM in most respects.

When the Tianjin massacre foreboded ill for the young missionaries far from human protection, they redoubled their faithful praying. And their devotion to the cause was complete. They decided to sell all but forty acres of their estate at Saint Hill, retaining only pasture land and woodland around the house. His bailiff was to farm on his own account. So, while it lasted, the sale of wagons, horses, sheep, cows, pigs and equipment added to the work. Producing the *Occasional Paper* from whatever news arrived from China strained their ingenuity, but knowing Hudson Taylor's difficulties, they restricted their requests to such remarks as, 'Friends at home, I am sure would exceedingly prize reading your lucid statements of affairs.' Berger's factory in Bow shipped thirty-two boxes of supplies, personally ordered and checked by him. And the next note said how 'stunned' they were by news of Maria's and Noel's deaths. If only they could come and be with

Hudson Taylor in his desolation. 'Out of this (your) deepest sorrow and trial . . . shall surely flow some inconceivable blessing . . . Our Father never takes away and leaves us poor.' The assessment of candidates increasingly seemed beyond him. 'After four years . . . I can only say I am sorely discouraged and feel very loathe to have more on trial.' Without doubt the Bergers needed to be relieved of their duties at least for a while.

But William Berger's references to Andrew Jukes, the ultra independent and eccentric preacher and writer, held for Hudson Taylor the surest signs of an approaching end to Berger's place in the Mission. As early as January 1870 he had written, 'Pray . . . that I may be guided into Truth respecting a Doctrine I am examining,' of the 'non-eternity of punishment' of sinners not justified by faith in Christ. As the year closed he returned to the subject. 'At Hackney the dear Brethren have put away several from Communion for teaching the doctrine. Some . . . are personal friends . . . If I receive them will the brethren receive me afterwards?' The stigma among the orthodox of the period could end support of the Mission of which he was a director.

With January 1871 the fall of France was expected at any time and the Bergers' sense of strain increased. Both were in very poor health, Mary 'very weakly' and often in great abdominal pain. But they still had no one able or willing to deputise for them. Mary's brother, James van Sommer, a frequent helper, was tied by his growing family. So William Berger warned, 'The matter of your visiting England . . . as early as you conveniently may be able, grows exceedingly upon me in importance, both as regards my own future and the well-being of the Mission . . . The bare possibility of your visiting us in the autumn or winter of this year is a light to our eyes. Truly we shall rejoice almost without bounds.' Then letters ceased, in expectation of Hudson Taylor's sailing from China during June.

Hudson Taylor wrote, 'I cannot but regret that your mind should be so occupied about (the eternity of future punishment). At one time my own was very much so. It resulted, however, in my being more satisfied with the old view. Mr Jukes's book seems to me the most inconclusive I have seen on the question.' He was praying that William Berger's 'usefulness' would not be 'seriously curtailed' on account of it. And again in June with detailed references to Scripture, 'While God (wishes) that all men should be saved, and offers (salvation) to all freely, He does not decree it.' But it was far too complex a subject to debate by correspondence, and in his state of mind and health. Gardner's letter about rebellion in the wind had just given him more to think about. He spared William Berger the news.

Hudson Taylor's style in writing sometimes bore strong traces of his mother's generation, drummed into him at home. But his spirit and convictions, shining through stilted phraseology, gave a luminescence William Berger's stolidity could not achieve. Urging Hudson Taylor to write for the *Occasional*, to come home to revive the drooping interest of the Missions friends, so easily distracted while no less sincere, he voiced a principle held by Hudson Taylor himself. That God as Father would provide for his children as they obeyed and served him was undoubted. That he would normally do it through his Church was biblical doctrine. That his Church is all too human and prone to neglect its stewardship made it necessary to inform, instruct and exhort his people. Only Hudson Taylor with his knowledge of China and vision for her evangelisation could (of available members of the CIM) convey such a message. In China the resurgence of spiritual morale among the missionaries and churches, and his own obligation to recoup his health and see to the needs of his children, confirmed that the time was ripe for him to go to the Bergers' relief.

Jennie (1871)

The friendship between the Fauldings and Bergers, and William Faulding's help with the Mission's business matters, had led to his buying part of the Saint Hill estate. They took to staying at the Bergers' home farm while sinking a well and building a house in the current architectural vogue, of concrete. 'Is your home like the Bergers?' Jennie asked (see ill. 1.47: 1, p 647). But before they sold their home at 340 Euston Road their circumstances changed. Financial difficulties such as many suffered through the war in France and panic on the Stock Exchange, and William Berger's talk of retiring and perhaps of espousing heterodox interpretations of Scripture, led the Fauldings to abandon their intentions, to put up their Saint Hill property for sale and to stay in London.

Anxiety at home increased Mrs Faulding's anxiety about Jennie as the news went from bad to worse and (Hudson Taylor conjectured) was inflated for political ends. As early as February 1870 she was reminding Jennie that she had talked of going to China for five years initially. In August what upset her was anti-foreign feeling at Shanghai, the French consul at Canton having to take refuge in the British settlement, and the appearance of placards at Hong Kong and other ports predicting extermination of all foreigners. By October it was the threat of war in north China; with the Chinese 'buying and manufacturing large quantities of fire-arms' and the thought of 'those intensely horrible cruelties' at Tianjin that provoked the appeal for Jennie to come home without delay. In December, however, 'the fighting all round Paris and dreadful loss of life,' and the danger of war with Russia unless 'all goes right with Austria and Turkey' distracted her mother's thoughts from China.

Jennie's own letters avoided the subject of returning home and chattered cheerfully on as usual. In the winter, 'we all look so stout with fur and wadding'. 'Mr Taylor got my likeness taken in Suchau and Emily will bring the negative home.' In March 1870 she confessed to having malaria and to taking quinine at frequent intervals, not knowing of the mortal danger of 'blackwater fever' from this practice.

John Eliot Howard, the quinologist and manufacturing chemist, was supplying them all with quinine. 'I have been vaccinating (two Chinese). I got a scab from Mrs Dodd's little baby.' When news of the Tianjin massacre came, 'the Lord reigns, we will not fear' was the steady tenor of her letters. 'It is easy at home to be a professing Christian. I sometimes wonder how many would stand the tests and influences that (Chinese) Christians out here have to encounter. How many are there who are prepared to give up everything for Christ's sake?' At the back of her mind she could have wished her mother would let go of her in that spirit.

When Hudson Taylor wrote of visiting Hangzhou, Jennie told her parents, 'Mr Taylor is thinking of coming here on his way to (Zhenjiang). I hope he will.' But he had to accompany the Crombies to Hong Kong. Then it was, 'I hope he will soon be able to get back again.' In mid-November he arrived at last and stayed with the McCarthys for two weeks. His advice to Jennie about her mother's fears was reflected in her letters.

After he left, he wrote to her (on January 19, 1871), 'My loved Sister . . . It looks as if . . . I shall need to go myself and arrange (for the children). The constant pain in my side and chest reminds me to work while it is day and keep my account balanced.' He said no more, but being with her had disturbed him deeply. With so large a capacity for loving, and with so many women in his team to care for and having now to care for him, having no wife made his relationship with them difficult. His thoughts had naturally turned to Maria. They had loved Emily and Jennie together. Alone, he could love them no less. His mother had encouraged him to think of remarrying, and he had ruled out Emily, so ill and unable to be the support he and the Mission needed. He prayed and thought about it during the next few months, but the difficulties seemed insuperable. He could only struggle on alone.

Jennie was absorbed in her work. In February 1871, in answering her mother's letters she said about one of her schoolgirls with smallpox, 'I, of course, went to her constantly, but having been vaccinated felt little fear . . . The horrors of the Tientsin massacre did indeed make one's blood run cold, and yet are we not ready to think too much of what only affected the body and that for a very short time?' The reputation of her schools, her teachers, house-mothers and of herself ensured no lack of pupils. Several years later Wang Lae-djün was to state that of his congregation in Hangzhou no less than fifty had become Christians through Jennie's influence.

Hudson Taylor's long drawn-out illness had relapsed after a temporary improvement in March, and he remained in no doubt that he must get back to Britain as soon as the confinements still dependent on him were over. Cardwell, for so long a thorn in the flesh, wrote sympathetically from Jiujiang urging him to go. 'We can spare you for a time, but how can we part with you for ever?' Jennie's malaria dragged on too, undermining her strength. But leaving Hangzhou and her schools and many Chinese friends was almost more than she could face. On April 8 as the state of political affairs looked up, Hudson Taylor told the Fauldings that he might be free to leave by the end of July if he lived to do so.

> Under these circumstances I write about your dear daughter. I am not unmindful of the trust you reposed in my precious wife and myself in committing her to our care ... I hear that you have expressed the desire that in the event of my return, she should fulfil the proposal of returning after five years, and she should accompany me. You will be better able to judge, upon reflection whether in my altered circumstances this is desirable or not ... (And) whether it might not be well to leave the matter of her immediate return to her own judgment ...

> I am alone and sick yet not alone. Your dear daughter has been as a Sister to me ... I need not say that her companionship on the voyage would be pleasant to me, and more still helpful with my motherless darling-child; but I believe she deals with God, and were she my own daughter, I should hesitate before requiring her to

come irrespective of the state of her work, and of her conviction of duty ... Kindly reply by return ... (and) to her also by the same mail.

He told Jennie what he had done, and a week later she told her mother what she knew—that he was 'asking you to leave it to me as to whether I shall come too. This I think you will do. God will make my path plain step by step . . . whether I should come or not.' Many of the missionaries' letters referred to the books they were currently reading, and in this one Jennie went on to mention hers—Law's books on the Pentateuch.

In May she had a jubilant letter from Charles Fishe, to confess that in February he had written proposing to her sister Nellie, and the answer had just arrived, with her parents' permission. Then on the 29th, Hudson Taylor told William Berger that the Judds had arrived for Elizabeth's confinement in a few days' time, and that Mrs Gardner's should follow soon after that. Mrs Shepherd, wife of the American consul, was safely through hers, and two more had taken place elsewhere. 'I propose to leave as soon as I can after they can safely be left,' he said. Half his packing was already done, he told his boys in a fatherly letter. 'I have sold the harmonium, to help me complete the building of (the) school, in remembrance of dear Mama . . . I have played on it today, for the last time, some of (her) favourite tunes.'

Instead of going ahead, the Meadows family had decided to wait for Hudson Taylor, but it was also 'manifestly unsafe for Mr Meadows to spend another summer in China'. Having them with him would remove one problem. 'I wrote to Miss Faulding suggesting that . . . any difficulty which might otherwise have been felt as to her return with me would be largely abated . . . (But) I judge that it is not likely that she can leave, even were we delayed till July.'

John McCarthy and Jennie came up to Zhenjiang to consult with Hudson Taylor, and reached a clear plan of action. McCarthy would take over all

Jennie's responsibilities in addition to his supervision of the work in the southern cities, and Jennie would join the Meadows family in Shanghai and sail with them. As to travelling with Jennie, Hudson Taylor was in two minds. She had always been careful not to show her feelings about him. To suggest marriage and be disappointed would only deepen his grief. To reach London and seek her parents' permission first might be the better way. But still his last two obstetric cases showed no sign of action. He handed over all his accounts to Charles, now the official secretary in China of the Mission, and his credits: £1,200 in the bank, nearly $200 in cash, and £748 in dollars of indemnity money subscribed by the victims of the Yangzhou riot to buy the house if possible. But on July 5, with Jennie alone in attendance, Elizabeth Meadows suffered yet another premature birth, of a dead baby. This changed the whole picture. She no longer needed to wait for Hudson Taylor. Now they could sail with Jennie and escape to sea from the great heat. The *Nestor* would leave on July 14 via Suez.

Hudson Taylor would follow as soon as he was free. 'I should much prefer the Cape route,' he wrote, 'but time is precious.' He was at his lowest ebb, 'physically and mentally worth very little,' so he would keep Charles Fishe with him when he travelled to Shanghai and on to Ningbo to collect little Charles Edward. Nine months had passed since he had left him with the Goughs. Then the Duncan's arrived from Nanjing with a sick baby (born in February) for Hudson Taylor to doctor, and at last Consul Gardner's wife was safely delivered with his help. News then came that Jennie was going through a serious exacerbation of malaria and passages on the *Nestor* were very expensive. There was another ship, the *Ajax* and her parents' permission had come to travel with or without Hudson Taylor.

At long last Frederick Hudson Judd was born on Sunday, July 23, destined to become a leading member of the next generation in the CIM. Duncan started the following day with Hudson Taylor's baggage by canal to Shanghai, for him to follow by steamer as soon as Elizabeth Judd could be left. A plaintive note came from Jennie on the 27th (so unlike her, and yet so typical), asking him to pray that she might recover on the voyage. She did not want to reach home 'too much an invalid' lest her mother make it difficult for her to return. And another from Mary Barchet confirmed that Jennie was in 'very poor health'.

Hudson Taylor decided to catch the French mail on August 5 and came down to Shanghai on the 1st. The only other passenger on the Yangzi steamer turned out to be Pére Sechinger, the Catholic priest so closely involved in events following the first Yangzhou riot, and since then head of his mission at Anqing. 'He seemed an earnest and devout man . . . and spoke of the converts in a way that greatly pleased me', Hudson Taylor told Emily Blatchley. To his surprise the Meadowses and Jennie had not gone. He had expected to find that they had left a week ago. It was 'very pleasant' to have fellow-travellers after all. The same day he enquired about all available shipping and 'passages in the French mail', the cheapest dependable accommodation to be had. French shipping was beginning to return to normal after the end of the war in France. His heavy luggage, thirty cases of books and personal possessions (much of it probably Maria's) he sent home by sailing-ship. Then he took a coaster to Ningbo. By August 2 he was with his child at the Goughs, 'so (thin and) grown and altered that I could not have recognised him.' Li Lanfeng, the printer, Ensing's husband, had agreed to go to England with them and was waiting, ready to sail. Like Wang Lae-djün he was to live with Hudson Taylor and be given personal tuition.

Hudson Taylor was in Ningbo just long enough to see a few of his friends before catching the same steamer back to Shanghai. Then followed more partings at Shanghai, from Charles Fishe, McCarthy, Duncan and Reid who had come to see them off, and on the 5th Hudson Taylor, the Meadows family and Jennie were on their way to England, with only Lanfeng and the children in good health.

'The only one' (August–October 1871)

Leaving China on a wave of rumour about missions being banned from 'the interior' demanded faith. On the other hand, if Hudson Taylor personified the troublesome element in missions, a notice in the papers of his departure in poor health might calm the agitation against him. So it turned out, though the wheels of diplomatic action turned slowly. He had provided for the routine distribution of funds through Charles Fishe, and for him to keep the team in touch with each other's work and welfare through the *Monthly Gleaner*. Each had a clear assignment and knew his own sphere, so apart from emergencies everything should continue steadily until he returned. Twenty-five missionaries (with eighteen children) and forty-five Chinese 'workers' in ten cities, with responsibility for the churches in three more, could do good work during the year he expected to be away.[197] Problems needing a decisive answer could be referred to him by cable. William Berger was remitting funds and George Müller still distributing sums from his Scriptural Knowledge Institution's missionary fund from time to time.

Weighing anchor at midday on August 5, the French ship *Volga* came almost immediately into collision with two junks and had to call a tug to help her down the crowded Huangpu River, but otherwise all went well. On going aboard, however, even Hudson Taylor had been appalled. 'The third class accommodation of the *Volga* was very bad and my heart sank when I saw it . . . (until God) inclined their hearts to put us into the second class cabins . . . Miss F. kindly took Charlie with her.' So in comfort on a quiet sea they steamed slowly to Hong Kong, and had two days with James Legge and the CMS and German missionaries before trans-shipping on August 11 to the Messageries Maritimes liner *Ava* for Saigon and Marseilles. 'Lanfeng has very good quarters, and I hope is as comfortable as he can be under present circumstances. We have family prayer together twice a day [in Chinese].' The journey from Singapore to Point de Galle, Ceylon, took two weeks and from there to Aden another nine days, where they took on 'a hundred and twenty Arab firemen for two new steamers at Marseilles,' men accustomed to great heat.

Long weeks together on board ship, with shopping and visits to friends and 'the gardens' at each port, had thrown the travellers together. James Meadows's low state of health and Elizabeth's preoccupation with her children left Hudson Taylor and Jennie with hours in each other's company. With like-minded Jennie to talk and pray with, he revelled in complete relaxation from the pressures of life in China, 'a time of great spiritual joy to me'.

He wrote a long, affectionate, descriptive letter to Emily Blatchley, but had to tell her what was happening. Any doubts about loving Jennie and wanting to marry her had evaporated. He could not reach home and meet Emily without the matter being settled. She had to be told. However painful the news might be, she was too ill ever to return to China as his wife, whereas Jennie, so highly respected by all the Mission, was ideally suited to share his life, impossible although they both knew it was for her to replace Maria.

He had to speak. 'My feelings could no longer be hid,' he confessed to Jennie's parents from the Red Sea. 'I do not so much . . . ask you to give up a daughter . . . as to ask you . . . to make room in your hearts . . . for me also.' It was all that a Victorian suitor would be expected to write, although Jennie was 28 and Hudson Taylor 39.

> You know the affection with which I and my late dear wife watched over her, prayed for her, and desired to do all we could (for her) ... Nor will you deem it unnatural that when I found myself week to week more and more unable to carry on efficiently the work which the Lord has committed to me, my thoughts and prayers respecting the only one possessed at once of the heart for the Lord's service and of that peculiar preparation for sharing my peculiar duties, should unconsciously have been ... intensified ... Each time (I) concluded that there were insuperable difficulties in

the way ... It would be impossible for her to leave (the work in Hangzhou); I found her so fully absorbed in and so happy in it ... that there was no probability at all of (her favouring) any proposal from me.

Rather than travel on the same ship it had seemed 'better not to be too much thrown together, lest it should involve me in further sorrow . . . (so) I do not know whether I more longed or dreaded to find' on arrival in Shanghai, that she had already sailed. When they found themselves together, therefore, he had days of mental turmoil, until 'the expression of my feelings became irrepressible and incapable of further delay.' 'To find my love and my feelings so fully reciprocated as they are', made it possible to talk freely. Jennie's logical habits of mind so closely resembled Maria's that they talked about her, the first true love he could never forget nor put from his thoughts. Jennie knew and had faced it already. She loved Maria too. They would always be able to talk about her unreservedly. There was no need to delay their marriage.

France had declared war against Prussia in July 1810 and after a rapid sequence of defeats, Napoleon III and his army had surrendered on September 2. A republic had been proclaimed two days later, and the German army besieged Paris on September 19. A communist insurrection in Paris at the end of October had been followed by the capitulation of Paris to the Germans on January 28, 1871, and soon afterwards peace talks began with an immense indemnity being demanded by the conquerors. But in May the communists were still destroying the Tuileries, the Louvre and many other public buildings, until French government troops entered Paris and crushed the communists. While Hudson Taylor and his party were at sea, France was restored to peace. On their arrival at Marseilles on September 21 they were able to take a train to Paris, cross to Southampton and reach London in the evening of September 25.

Three obstacles at once (October–December 1871)

Emily was at Barnsley with the Taylor children but sent her congratulations to greet Jennie and Hudson Taylor on their arrival in London. For herself she printed on a card, to keep before her, the words of Jesus, 'EVEN SO, FATHER—or so it seemed good in Thy sight'. It was she, too, who wrote of those painful months for the Mission as 'tunnelling through rock', a picture of determined progress against odds, with no thought of giving up.

They separated, each to their own families, but met again in London before all going together to the Bergers at Saint Hill on October 10. By then, Jennie's parents had plunged them into deep distress by agreeing to their eventual marriage only after she had been at home for a year! Jennie's tearful pleading and Hudson Taylor's persuasion eventually drew from Mrs Faulding the protest that neither of them was physically fit for marriage—her only objection to an early wedding, she said, and nothing would move her. Again, Emily wrote sympathising with Jennie. When Hudson Taylor saw Jennie from time to time he could tell she had been weeping.

He took rooms in Bognor for a fortnight to see if the seaside suited Emily and the children, but Bognor he found depressing and he went to Mildmay 'on the outskirts of London', to consult William Pennefather's curate, Hay Aitken. With his help he rented six rooms at 64 Mildmay Road for 'forty shillings a week with light and attendance' and his mother moved in to make a temporary home for him and Emily, the four children (aged 10, 8, 4 and 2) and Lanfeng. 'It is better perhaps to know well the advantages and disadvantages of a neighbourhood before renting a house,' he said, with Bognor in mind. On October 19 he brought his family up from Bognor to join his mother, and went straight on to Saint Hill.

William Berger had received a notice from Lord Granville, Foreign Minister, through the Rt Hon E. Hammond, urging Hudson Taylor's removal from Yangzhou and revealing serious misunderstandings of the situation there. The tenor of the dispatch suggested that another political storm might be blowing up, so they decided to take time before replying. Hudson Taylor went from Saint Hill to Tottenham, to renew his friendship with the Howards and Miss Stacey, and probably to consult with them about this threat. Then on November 3 he was at the Fauldings' home at Euston, writing business letters to Charles Fishe and others in China, and drafting a letter to William Berger for him to enclose in his reply to Lord Granville on the subject uppermost in their minds. A week later, back at Mildmay Road, he sat down to write a letter to Jennie's parents of which the copy is in her handwriting a gently worded ultimatum pleading for their compliance.

It was never good, he wrote, for Christians to be unable to speak freely to each other, so how much more true of his relationship with them. 'If you will let me love you as a son, and confide in you . . . what a happy relationship will exist . . . after our marriage.' In rejecting his view that he and Jennie would benefit rather than suffer from marrying soon, were they not treating his medical experience of more than twenty years as of no weight? 'We feel it is mistaken kindness on your part, but *very mistaken* and very wrong . . . The whole responsibility rests on us . . . Do not longer withhold your consent.'

There was too much in this contretemps that reminded him of Miss Aldersey's opposition in 1857. Only two days before Maria's death, she had said to him, 'Miss Aldersey's unkindness has caused you so much sorrow and anxiety [through influencing others against him] and me so much weakness. I have never got over it.' Now Hudson Taylor repeated this to the Fauldings and went on, 'I do not want to hear similar language again.' Next week his mother would still be in town and his sister Amelia and William Berger were expected. They could be present if the wedding were to be on Wednesday. Why not agree to it, and all share the joy together?

William Berger and he were treating the content of their reply to the Foreign Office as more important than its date, until the 14th when Berger wrote to say he had posted it. Burdened with his own ill-health and anxieties he underestimated Hudson Taylor's, for he went on to add another hammer-blow. 'In all probability it will be desirable for me to retire altogether, or at least greatly into the background, both on account of my being unable to bear the weight of the Home department as heretofore; and likewise from my religious opinions being so changed from what they were before.' He proposed that they should consult together with George Müller about 'the grave undertaking of reconstructing the Mission'.

Hudson Taylor was suffering 'intense nervous headaches'—'almost worn out with the strain on body and mind' which rivalled the tensions he had endured in China. He could not handle all these problems at once. Getting married was the one most readily overcome. No one had questioned the propriety of his becoming engaged fifteen months after Maria's death. George Müller and his colleague James Wright, whose wives had died in February and May of the same year, 1870, were also about to remarry: Wright on November 16 to Müller's daughter, Lydia, and Müller on November 30 to Miss Sangar, 'mother' of his orphan homes. Death and early remarriage were commonplace in times of high mortality, especially when children had to be provided for. The Fauldings must let him marry without delay. Then he could cope better with the Foreign Office and the Mission's future.

This time Mrs Faulding capitulated, and William Faulding who had stood loyally by his wife while not sharing the strength of her feelings, helped to arrange the wedding. On Tuesday, November 28, Dr William Landels performed the ceremony at Regent's Park Chapel. In the circumstances they dispensed with a honeymoon. On December 30, 1873, two full years later, they found themselves in Fenghua in the absence of other missionaries, and recorded that this was the first time they had been without companions since their marriage. After the wedding Hudson Taylor's mother returned home, and they joined the children at 64 Mildmay Park, while Emily, approving but nonetheless lonely and grieving, had a brief holiday.

In acknowledging a letter of congratulation from Elizabeth Judd, he opened his heart in a way that showed how close their friendship had become.

> The last wish (Maria) expressed to me [between dawn and 7.30 on her last morning?] was that if she were removed, I would marry again ... Seeing the love I have for her is not likely to undergo any change or diminution, I do not want one or two years, or five, to forget her in. You do not know how I love her, nor how seldom for one hour she is absent from my waking thoughts ... And my dear (Jennie) would not wish it otherwise. She has her own place in my heart, which Jesus has given her, a place all the larger because her love is not jealous.

So began his life with Jennie, as romantic as it was sacrificial, of nearly three times as many years as the twelve he had enjoyed with Maria, and as rich. With the obstacle to their marriage surmounted, he returned to work.

Lord Granville takes the point[198] (October–November 1871)

The Foreign Office letter of October 13 to William Berger as Director in Britain of the China Inland Mission was a late response to F. T. Wade's dispatches of June, but a time lapse covered a further exchange of dispatches on the Zongli Memorandum already described. In spite of the disclaimer in Lord Granville's replies to Wade, this courteously worded letter to William Berger strongly hinted that, if not complied with, it could lead to stronger measures later.

> Sir,
>
> ... It would appear that the continued residence of the Reverend Mr Taylor at Yang-chow, notwithstanding the recent attack on his Mission House, is likely to be productive of further difficulty; and that it would be advisable that he should remove from that place ... Lord Granville does not hesitate to appeal to you to withdraw that gentleman from Yang-chow, where by the treaty he has no right to reside, and where his residence may possibly lead to most serious complications ...
>
> Mr Wade has been desired to urge Mr Taylor to leave Yang-chow, and to warn him that if he persists in residing there he will do so at his own peril, and that he must not expect any interference on the part of Her Majesty's Government to ensure his safety, or to obtain redress from the Chinese Government for any injuries he may receive.
>
> I am, Sir, your obedient humble servant,
>
> E. Hammond

Even if a new political storm was blowing up, the rights and wrongs of the Yangzhou situation had to be made plain to the Foreign Minister. He, or at least his junior minister, appeared to have overlooked, firstly, the fact that the Mission's presence in Yangzhou was the result of strong action by Sir Rutherford Alcock and W. H. Medhurst to secure Hudson Taylor's reinstatement, and secondly, that no new attack had been made against the premises since 1868, but only a plot. The actions of the Chinese government and local mandarins supported the presence of the Mission at Yangzhou and only the upheaval caused by the rebellious General Li and Chen Guorui expressed anything to the contrary. Viceroy Zeng Guofan's part in the proceedings was as always shadowy, even when correct to outward appearances. But although Yangzhou was nominally his base, months had passed since Hudson Taylor had lived there. To bring Charles Judd into the matter was unnecessary, beyond a mere mention of his name.

When Hudson Taylor was at Saint Hill on October 20 to consult with the Bergers about a reply, he said in a note to his mother, 'I may have to return to China suddenly, perhaps at once but do not mention this to anyone.' They decided that he should send William Berger a statement which he in turn would forward to the

Foreign Office, and await developments. Yangzhou was under threat, not from any Chinese but solely from the pro-trade, anti-missionary, stance of the minister in Peking, T. F. Wade, without valid reason. *The Times* of October 31 joined in attacking missionaries in general and advocating the necessity of suppressing them, while acknowledging that the British government could only influence British subjects and were powerless against the French Catholics. The new editor of the CMS *Intelligencer* countered this with the retort that merchants whose stock-in-trade was opium could also have 'their warehouses sacked and gutted as readily as if they were nunneries'. Missionary Jonah might be thrown overboard, but it would not ensure that the ship would reach shore. Why not leave Jonah alone?

Hudson Taylor's statement of November 8 was the result of careful thought and made some strong points:

> In deference to Mr Wade's wishes, the work there has been so narrowed up as to be all but abandoned, and that we have not only gone as far in this direction as in the estimation of Mr Markham (our Consul at Shanghai) could be needed, but fully as far as he considered safe, and. even justifiable ...

> There has been no recent riot at Yangchau. Our former landlord there ... did, in April or May last, threaten trouble if his demands were not complied with. Those threats, however, never had sufficient influence on the people to even disturb the price of silver—that most sensitive barometer of political feeling in China ...

> (Mr Markham) inspected our work and expressed himself highly satisfied with what he saw, and gratified at the evident hold we had on the respect of the people. He fully concurred with me in the opinion that our remaining there was very unlikely to become a cause of difficulty or danger, while our leaving the station was almost sure to be so misunderstood as to produce the very evil sought to be avoided ...

> One or two years ago we were apprised that if we continued to reside and work in the interior, it must be at our own risk and peril, but that if prepared for this we were quite at liberty to do so.

> I may further add that the Consular representatives of the United States and France communicated to me their conviction of the danger and impolicy of any further retrograde steps with regard to Yangchau, an opinion shared in by the leading members of the mercantile community of Chinkiang.

Writing with a preoccupied mind only three days before his strong letter to the Fauldings, Hudson Taylor had omitted an important point which he recalled on the 13th and sent as a postscript.

> My dear Mr Berger,

> That you may be the better able to reply to Earl Granville's dispatch about Yangchau, allow me to state what has been done with respect to the station in question. It will doubtless afford satisfaction to His Lordship to be informed (that the *daotai* of Zhenjiang), before purchasing the Yangchau property, asked me whether I intended to keep it permanently, and on the faith that I should do so, purchased it at a price more than double its value to a native ... He secured himself by a written guarantee from me binding me to a heavy loss if I gave up possession of the premises under five years. I believe it would cause great annoyance as well as loss to him were I to leave the station at present.

As soon as the Foreign Office officials verified the date of Wade's dispatch about Hudson Taylor, they would see that they themselves were out of step. William Berger replied to Mr Hammond on November 13:

> It would appear that Earl Granville has been incorrectly informed ... and that the wish of Mr Wade has been already complied with, as far as the circumstances of the case allowed. The present relations of the Station having been personally arranged by Mr Taylor with the (*daotai* of Zhenjiang) could only be safely interfered with by Mr Taylor himself.

> Mr Taylor is now in this country, but purposes returning to China at no very distant period, and will seek by every means in his power to avoid any danger of hostile collision with the Chinese.

Even this was too much for William Berger. On the following day he told Hudson Taylor that he wished 'to retire altogether'. Then for several weeks they waited for the next move from Downing Street, and the wedding took place under this shadow. But they heard no more.

A forward look is justified at this point. Yangzhou not only came to be known as the most peaceful mission centre in China and the home of the women's language school of the China Inland Mission until shortly before the Second World War, but perhaps the most colourful episode in the Mission's continuing presence in that historic city occurred in 1912. General Xu Baosan, commanding the Second Army Corps of the new Republic of China, gave an unprecedented opportunity for CIM missionaries to distribute Christian literature to his troops and deputed his younger brother, the military governor of Yangzhou, to arrange for regular preaching of the gospel to his officers and men. When the resident missionary, A. R. Saunders, left Yangzhou for Britain, General Xu Baosan ordered all members of his own staff and a guard of honour of 5,000 officers and men to escort him to the Grand Canal. By then, of those who had experienced the Yangzhou riot only William Rudland and the Taylor children were still living. Charles Judd also saw the reward of the faith and tenacity he had displayed during the second Yangzhou plot.

The CIM in China[199] (1871–72)

After Hudson Taylor and his party of invalids left China, Charles Fishe took over from Judd in Yangzhou. Combining oversight of the churches in Yangzhou and Qingjiangpu with his secretarial duties, including the distribution of funds remitted from Britain, he edited and printed the *Monthly Gleaner*. Receipts continued low but adequate. Cardwell pursued his ambitious penetration of Jiangxi province from Jiujiang, and had the heartening experience of being sought out by a one-time army officer, a major and commander of a gunboat, who bought a New Testament,

believed what he read, resigned his commission and declared his wish to be a missionary. With an intimate knowledge of the Jiangxi waterways this gentleman, Chen Zhaotong, was a godsend. Together they travelled far and wide. Later they were joined by another converted soldier, Lo Ganfu, a strength to their team, who succeeded in leading three more soldiers and two Daoist priests to Christ. Meanwhile, an ex-officer of Gordon's Ever-Victorious Army, a Colonel Rohde, came to Suzhou wanting to be associated with the CIM, and was preaching with Henry Reid through the Suzhou countryside.

In September 1871 George Duncan, with advanced tuberculosis but feeling stronger, and Thomas Harvey, who at his own expense had erected 'the first Protestant chapel which has ever been built in Nankin', made a long cross-country journey together. Meeting at Wuhu they travelled south-eastwards through Ning-guo and Yanzhou [not Yangzhou] to Hangzhou. When Harvey fell dangerously ill, Duncan, himself febrile and coughing blood, took him to Shanghai where he recovered. Duncan then returned to Nanjing and from there up the Yangzi to the Yuxi River below Wuhu. Penetrating up the Yuxi, through Yuncao to Chao Xian on Lake Chao where 'scarcely a house was left standing' after the Taiping rebellion, he and a Chinese companion crossed the lake westwards and, ascending another river, came to the city of Liizhou, only 120 miles from Anqing. Unacquainted with foreigners, some people called him, 'a Ningbo man', others 'a real foreign devil' and one bent on trouble said, 'The gentry should unite to put him out of the city.' Undeterred by mere words he preached and sold hundreds of Christian books, all he had brought. Duncan had all the makings of a great pioneer.

No record seems to exist of conversations between John Nevius and John McCarthy in Hangzhou, but McCarthy's loyal attachment to Hudson Taylor and faithful implementation of his policies are enough to account for his deep interest in promoting a truly indigenous

Chinese church. Nevius did not publish his principles until 1886–87. In November 1871 the *Monthly Gleaner* carried important notes from McCarthy as 'a member of the China Inland Mission', here abridged. His concept was that of the Pauline 'tent-maker', widely adopted in years to come:

> How is the Gospel to spread in China? ... While by no means undervaluing itinerant labours ... in addition there must be lengthened residence of the preacher among the masses ... Of course not foreign labour ... there must of necessity be a large influx of the (Chinese) element ... That houses should be rented ... is not necessary, nay more, not desirable ... The Foreigner's (house and) chapel are looked upon by the Christians as the Foreigner's. Thus the spirit of self-support which we hope to see grow and mature, is almost strangled at its very birth ... The spirit of the Gospel would certainly lead men to self-support, and thankful effort for Him who has done so much for them ... Is it not unfair to expect them to be bound to our arrangements for them? ... A Chinese tradesman finds no difficulty in getting lodgings in any place he comes to ... Where God has blessed their labours it would not be difficult to arrange for the baptism of converts ... It may be asked, where are they to meet? ... Why not in the house of one of their number? ... If, however, the number increased (they would) get their own meeting-room or chapel ... the point being that the room and all its surroundings would grow out of the felt need on the part of the native (Christian) ... Such converts would be more likely to stand, and in their turn advance the cause of the Redeemer.

McCarthy was writing from personal observation and experience, as Hudson Taylor recognised in his *Summary of the Operations of the CIM*, in 1872.

> In both Ningbo and (Hangzhou) districts he has a large number of (Chinese colporteurs and evangelists). The work of some of these has been itinerant, but settled work is on the increase, and is by far the most effective ... For the harvest we must be content to wait ... It is God's Word that is being preached and sold ... A very industrious man works at his trade all the week, but always gives up his Sundays to God. Wang Lae-djün says that it is a subject of the greatest wonder to the people at his lodgings, when a man so industrious and earnest should be satisfied to 'waste' every seventh day ... (Lo) Ah-ts'ih (was) for a year or two engaged in evangelistic work in the interior, far away from (Hangzhou), and his whole soul was stirred with a deep sense of his countrymen's need, and of the wide opening for (the) Gospel ... When in (Hangzhou) he called the Christians together and [quoting McCarthy] 'explained his plan for the formation of a native missionary society; namely that each (church) member should give something each month' ... and select some man or men to be their representative, supported by them. This money, he said, should not be used for any purpose but the spread of the Gospel; not for the poor (or) a fund from which they could borrow money ... Wang Lae-djün then told them how glad he was to hear of (it) ... The popular belief that they got so much a month for being Christians would be effectually refuted if it were known that, instead ... they themselves gave out money for the spread of the Gospel ... They collected more than sufficient for one man's support for a month and ... intend to send to the other stations of our mission ... inviting (the Christians) either to cooperate, or else to act in the same way independently ...

> When we remember how recently the work at (Hangzhou) was commenced, and how poor the native Christians are in this world's goods, we ... thank God and take courage.

This tale had a sequel. William Rudland's head printer, Tsiang Aliang, had one day said to Rudland, 'My little brother at home (near Fenghua) is feeding the cows and is nearly as stupid as they are. I wish you could use him here in some way.' 'Bring him back with you after the New Year,' Rudland replied. The boy, Tsiang Liangyung, became a Christian, and in 1874 was chosen by the Hangzhou church to be their missionary. He developed into one of the most effective pastors, in charge of the Yushan church in Jiangxi, and his son became a devoted Christian doctor. James Williamson had reported a similar initiative from the Christians in Fenghua and its outstations. They had rented a room in a large village for regular preaching.

A discussion at the Fuzhou Missionary Conference in 1870 on how to establish Chinese churches on a self-supporting basis had been followed by an appeal from Sia Sek-ong of the Methodist Episcopal Church, to his fellow-ministers:

> The trouble is with us. We are afraid to trust God in this matter. But why should we fear? ... (God) knows where our support is to come from; can we not trust Him? ... Will He not feed us who go forth to preach His Gospel, and to suffer for Him? Don't trouble yourselves so much about the people; don't be always looking back to see where your supplies are to come from ... If we were to give as much for Christ as the heathen give to the devil, we would soon be able to support our own pastors. We pay less money as Christians than the heathen do. We must give money, to support the Gospel, and give liberally, or the church can never be established here ... Henceforth let everyone say 'The Saviour is my Saviour, the Gospel is my Gospel, the Church is my Church, the preachers are my preachers', and let us never cease our efforts until the Church of God is firmly established in China.

Today as we see an ever-expanding church in a hostile environment, as rid of foreign restraint as of foreign funds, the insights of a century ago remain for our encouragement.

In December 1871, soon after Hudson Taylor's marriage to Jennie Faulding, disturbingly incomplete accounts began to reach him from China of Charles Fishe being ill, of the missionaries being in financial difficulties, and of Robert White becoming involved in a fracas which could have precipitated another diplomatic storm.

What began with a small abscess in Charles's hip led to complications affecting the whole Mission. Soon he had to be taken to hospital in Shanghai, came close to death and after an operation was still in hospital in March 1872. Hudson Taylor was 'in the dark' as to what was happening.

News travelled slowly, and towards the end of April he heard that Charles was still dangerously ill. During his long illness no one had assumed Charles's responsibilities or acted to keep Hudson Taylor informed.

George Müller had taken to sending his donations through William Berger, instead of direct to the missionaries as before, and although regular remittances were being sent *en bloc* from Britain, they were not distributed in China. As early as December 27, Hudson Taylor was asking how it was that several sums had not been transmitted to John McCarthy, who had suffered a robbery? 'His distress must have been extreme.' Blame undoubtedly lay with Charles, but his illness plunged his foreign and Chinese colleagues into yet greater deprivation, testing their faith in God to supply them by other means. Wang Lae-djün, to show his concern, went so far as to pawn some of his clothes and present the money to John McCarthy towards the expenses of the two boarding schools in Hangzhou. Ample sums for all were inaccessible. As soon as Hudson Taylor knew what was happening he remitted money direct to each missionary, and more to E. C. Lord for distribution.

Robert White was a law to himself. He wore foreign clothes and paid sedan chair carriers at the inflated rates they demanded from foreigners, but Charles Fishe wore Chinese clothes and paid the same amount as Chinese customers. Under White's influence, Charles resumed foreign dress and was promptly charged at the foreign rate. One day when White refused to meet the inflated charge on Charles's behalf, the carriers 'became insolent, whereupon he gave them a sound beating'. On another occasion he gave three men into custody, had the mandarin called, and sat with him in judgment while 'they were condemned, sentenced and flogged then and there.' White claimed independence but still attached himself to the CIM at his own convenience. So when it wass reported to Consul Gardner, Hudson Taylor wrote to Fishe, 'Wade will get to know and will make capital of it, I fear.' It was plain that he must return to China as soon as possible. But with William Berger's retirement imminent and no one yet in sight to replace him, he was needed as urgently in Britain.

Goodbye to the Bergers (December 1871–March 1872)

William and Mary Berger had not spared themselves in representing the Mission in Britain, or in sacrificing their home, Saint Hill, to be its headquarters. His gifts did not include public relations, and as the years had passed since Hudson Taylor's departure in the *Lammermuir*, the *Occasional Paper* alone became inadequate to maintain interest. The continental wars had ended, but great political issues captured attention instead—issues leading to the legalisation of the trades unions, and (in 1872) extension of the franchise to more citizens than ever before, through the secret ballot box.

Because China was seen to be getting the measure of other nations and peace in east Asia could not be counted on, a wait and see attitude spelt inertia among supporters of missions. False reports from China and attacks in the press had made even sympathetic Christians sensitive to criticisms against the CIM. And 'party questions agitating the Brethren' and others, especially on the current issues of 'non-eternity of punishment' and 'universal restoration', were undermining confidence. Hudson Taylor told Charles Fishe, 'Many Churches of England, Baptist, Brethren, etc. are expelling all who hold non-eternity. Some work is quite broken up on account of it. Mr Berger himself greatly fears our work will suffer on his account.' Mary Berger was distressed by his views and had no sympathy for them.

The Christian public needed to have their consciences stirred again, to look away from affairs close at hand and to show concern for the wider world. 'Slipshod stewardship was still handicapping missions', however urgent their appeals. Hudson Taylor believed as strongly as he ever had that the Church would respond to the Holy Spirit's prompting to contribute to missions if it first responded in terms of love and commitment to God himself. His own responsibility was therefore to reawaken those Christians who had responded so strongly before to China's spiritual need and claims. Griffith John, on leave from China, was enrapturing great audiences with his oratory, claiming that the scope he had in the Hankou field was greater even than Spurgeon's in London. The church in Britain needed to be told, and responded when it was.

The Bergers' health had broken and they were spending more weeks on the south coast than at Saint Hill, while Hudson Taylor gave his thoughts to finding successors. In the lodgings at 64 Mildmay Park, over Christmas and the New Year, he faced the immediate prospect of being alone, not only as the leader in Britain as well as China, but in all the daily work of correspondence, public relations and accountancy. He had Emily Blatchley's help again, while Jennie helped her with the children, but both lacked the strength to do much, Emily with phthisis and Jennie still weak from malaria. Emily's 'Even so, Father' had progressed beyond resignation to contentment. 'My one cry is for perfect Christ-like acquiescence in the Father's will. Then . . . I shall have joy, and even undisturbable peace,' she wrote in her diary. So by March she was 'as happy as ever', *en famille* again with Jennie and Hudson Taylor. Without others in the home he did not have to call her 'Miss Blatchley'. She was 'Aimei', 'loved sister', all the time reliving the past while writing her memoir of Maria.

Early in January, he rented a new house on the fringe of fields near the village green and duck-pond of Newington Green, and moved in on January 15. At the other side of the Green, a country lane led away past Henry VIII's old hunting-lodge and Inglesby House, an old residence, through fields as far as Manor House and the Seven Sisters. For twenty more years that district would change only slowly. Emily was the first to use the new address, 6 Pyrland Road, in a letter of January 3. They restarted the almost defunct Saturday prayer meetings, and Hudson Taylor addressed a meeting of the evangelical Week of Prayer, the first of a constant succession of lectures and church meetings, sometimes nightly, from then until October. At Welbeck Street on the 18th he renewed old friendships, and at Portman Square, Tottenham, Hackney all the familiar places, he was welcomed with all the old warmth and no loss of confidence in him. Yet he still felt deflated, needing more time to recover, unequal to the demands on his vitality, but compelled to defer his public appearances no longer. All his old friends wanted to hear him report on the great adventure. Nor could he stay away from London's theatre services, good opportunities to preach the gospel to the unconverted.

William Berger and he spent three days at Bristol with George Müller, discussing the Mission's problems. They found him sympathetic, and left him with a clearer understanding of their difficulties and determined to help them. While he applauded the faith of young missionaries who took responsibility for the expenses of their own work, he saw the danger of fragmentation and of personal domination of a local church. Working as a team, with interchangeability of personnel from city to city according to necessity was preferable, he suggested. No note on his attitude to William Berger's view on 'non-eternity' remains, but the silent comment of all Müller's donations being withheld until after Berger's formal retirement from the Mission led Hudson Taylor to attribute cause and effect, and reinforced his own convictions on the subject.

From Bristol, Hudson Taylor went straight on to Dublin for a strenuous round of meetings and interviews, with Colonel Fishe and John McCarthy's brother William, and others. Still he had 'no strength, nor Jennie', and was glad to get back to Pyrland Road and routine under his own control, however demanding. Copies of his correspondence reveal the impossibility (which he had always pointed out) of directing, let alone leading a team in China, so far away.

Frequent letters to Josiah Jackson tried to hold him to his purpose, keeping him informed of progress towards sending Fanny Wilson to whom he had proposed by letter, out to China. She married him in December 1872 and transformed him (while she lived) into a worthwhile missionary—the reward of Hudson Taylor's long patience. Henry Cordon wrote that his wife's low state necessitated their return home. In view of Cordon's own poor record, Hudson Taylor replied that if they came it must be with a view to not returning to China. So when the Cordons withdrew and Reid irresponsibly followed without consulting his leader or making provision for the property or the work established in Suzhou, Hudson Taylor handed it over to William Muirhead and the LMS. To the troublesome but ailing Thomas Harvey he wrote, 'I am sorry that you and dear Mr Duncan have not got on happily together . . . You must part friends, if you cannot get on together . . . I do not doubt that you have tried him, as much as he has tried you. You cannot correct his failings, you can forgive them; your own, however, you have more serious concern with.'

Cardwell had sent a long account of his epic journey up the waterways of Jiangxi, and of his close encounter with mobs at the capital, Nanchang. Hudson Taylor's acknowledgment went on to say:

> Owing to the touchy state of public feeling here about China, it would not be safe to publish in extension the account of all the treatment you were subjected to. Everything, which so eventuates as to leave hostile collision possible, excites the general public to a degree. They say 'Those missionaries want to embroil us in another Abyssinian war' and much more in that style. We must have as little as possible to do with our Consuls, as they report to Pekin, and Wade who hates missions and missionaries, I fear, will make the most of what can be made to tell against them ... It would seem wise for the present to avoid the (provincial) capital as there are so many other cities open to you.[200]

But the most important overseas letters were to young Charles Fishe, to whom he said, 'I hope nothing will require me to leave England before early in September, and that you will not fail me in this crisis of the Mission.' With Hudson Taylor's strong support Charles was urging Mrs Faulding to allow Nellie out to marry him, but against stronger resistance. As for the fashion-loving Nellie, she longed to get away from the influences of London, 'full of eloquence, politics, anything but Christ' which held her back. Two months had passed since news had come that Charles's health was improving rapidly. How was it that no letter had come from him? Had he relapsed? But to business—Hudson Taylor had had a gravestone made and engraved in memory of Maria and each of her deceased children, and was about to ship it to Zhenjiang. And finally, 'Mrs Faulding is coming round to Nellie's going with us.' More than a year later they were still exhorting her mother even to be willing to let her go.

Editing the fourth edition of *China: Its Spiritual Need and Claims*, his *Summary of the Operations of the China Inland Mission from its Commencement to the Year 1872,* and *Occasional* Nos 29 and 30, absorbed hours of concentration as he prepared a table of the stations and current staff of the Mission, Chinese and foreign, with a map to show how widely they were deployed, in many cases a hundred miles from each other. When Christians knew what was going on they rose to the occasion and joined in. When feeling out of touch, their gifts and even praying seemed to dwindle. Information led to dedication—of their whole lives in many instances. That Hudson Taylor learned this lesson—brought home to him by Philip Gosse—is apparent in his change of practice over the years ahead. If William Berger had been unable to make bricks without straw, no one could. Good reporting from the field of action was imperative. When Hudson Taylor lacked reports hot from the field, he drew upon personal knowledge, and gave vivid pen-portraits of his Chinese colleagues whose example put to shame many a Western Christian.

Twice he spent five days with William Berger, going through the financial accounts from his sailing in 1866 to March 1872, and reviewing all outstanding business. Only one error in accounting emerged, an omission at the time of the Yangzhou riot; and another bizarre episode had been safely weathered, in which the French bank at Shanghai had mislaid and failed to credit the Mission with cheques to the value of £1,106, but found them five months later! On March 16 he returned to London to preach for James Vigeon ('he is doing a good work in London') and then back to Saint Hill for William Berger's formal handover of his audited accounts—which revealed a balance of £336.1s.9d.—and of official records on the 18th. The next day each of them wrote an editorial letter for the *Occasional Paper* No 29, announcing Berger's retirement and Hudson Taylor's assumption of the directorship at home as well as in China. 'Our fellowship together has been a source of unmixed and uninterrupted joy,' Hudson Taylor said in his tribute to his friend, but 'we have, for the past two years, seen unmistakable evidence that the same kind and measure of cooperation was becoming impossible with Mr Berger's failing health and strength'. No one was yet available to take his place, but God would provide in this as in every need.

As for the future, it looked as if Hudson Taylor himself must return to China in the autumn and be back in Britain again after fifteen or sixteen months. With steamers cutting the voyage to a mere six or seven weeks at only £50 per person, by third-class passage on the Messageries Maritimes, travel to and fro had become less time consuming. Experience had shown that, in spite of the difficulties, the unoccupied provinces of China could with determination be entered, and he had every intention of continuing towards that goal. To this end he wrote to George Duncan to lease or purchase premises in Anqing, even if expensive. They must hold on and reach out from there. The loss of William and Mary Berger must not prevent progress.

Alone yet not alone
(March–October 1872)

In James Vigeon, the accountant so committed to going to China until forcibly detained at home in 1866, might have lain the answer to the Mission's need for a representative in Britain. But the silence of the records provides no clue as to why he was not. Instead, from March to September Hudson Taylor carried the full load, often 'weary and in pain', but with no alternative, 'sparing everyone but himself, taking Lanfeng with him to meetings and showing him the Crystal Palace and the historic sights of London, interviewing and advising candidates, trying to acknowledge personally every donation received, and constantly rethinking the administrative problems of the Mission. A period of probation before becoming a full member of the Mission, he thought, might encourage young men and women to make a better start. And labelling some 'associates' could help critics to recognise that the CIM held no responsibility for their actions, as in the case of those who sought Hudson Taylor's help, but went their own way. Still no answer emerged to the most outstanding need, for someone to share the burden.

News came that John Stevenson, who had been ill since October 1871, with malaria and then typhoid fever (one account said cholera), was desperately ill with confluent haemorrhagic smallpox. Vaccination still tended to be unreliable, and the need to repeat it at intervals was not fully realised. Steady, reliable, indefatigable, with strong churches already firmly established in the three cities of Shaoxing, Sheng Xian and Xinchang, to the credit of his Chinese colleagues and himself, his future was full of promise. For nine months he lay ill and out of action, with no medical help beyond what his wife and Chinese friends could give him, while the churches learned to stand on their own feet. But he recovered and, as soon as he was strong enough, visited Sheng Xian.

A scholarly gentleman named Ning, a graduate in the classics and student of Western science, 'a man of ability and considerable standing and influence' but sceptical about Christianity, after meeting Stevenson said to himself, 'Here is a foreigner, a perfect stranger to me, yet so concerned about my welfare that he will pray for me though I do not so much as pray for myself.' Mr Ning began in secret to pray for himself and soon experienced a change of heart which he could not account for. He, his wife and son became strong Christians. 'When I see what he has done, and the persecution that he is exposed to,' John Stevenson wrote, 'I cannot hesitate to say that the age of heroes is not past.'

Hudson Taylor took courage. In June he retraced his steps through the West Country, visiting Bath, Bristol, Barnstaple, Teignmouth, Torquay, Exeter, Yeovil and other towns, some more than once. When the Franco-Prussian war had ended Grattan Guinness's mission to France and Spain, he had returned to Dublin and then to Bath to write his great tome, *The Approaching End of the Age*. Hudson Taylor addressed a meeting in the Guildhall there, and conferred with Guinness whose expansive soul had developed a concern for the whole world, not only for China.

'Grattan Guinness was a man of vision and had become a man of learning. He could inspire and teach, he could move men but he had little understanding of the labour that makes the vision possible.'[201] So even if willing, he was not the administrator needed to direct the CIM in Britain.

Again Hudson Taylor conferred with George Müller, and addressed meetings in the parish church and the historic Bethesda Chapel in Bristol. He met Robert Chapman again at Barnstaple, and other leading Christians who later became the first 'referees' of the China Inland Mission, and was back at Pyrland Road in time for the Mildmay Conference of June 26–28. William Pennefather had invited him to give some of the main conference addresses, beginning with the opening address on the first morning. Sharing the platform with D. L. Moody (on his first visit), Lord Radstock, the Earl of Cavan, and Stevenson

Arthur Blackwood, he faced an audience of hundreds of like-minded Christians, the kind he most wanted to arouse to a concern for China. Rising at the end of the popular missionary hymn, 'Waft, waft ye winds His story', he captured the attention of the conference with his first words, 'My dear friends, the wind will never waft it! If the blessed story of His love is to be taken to the dark places of the earth, it must be taken by men and women like ourselves . . . who wish to obey His great missionary command.' He reported on what had happened in China since he had last addressed the conference and had distributed the first thousand copies of *China: Its Spiritual Need and Claims*. And citing electricity and steam, forces of nature always available but only recently put to use by men, he went on, 'There is a power in us who believe . . . a power that men may wield . . . God's power upon which we may call.' He told them about the dangerous experiences of the past few years in China, and of how the power of God had been displayed in answer to prayer, delivering Chinese idolaters from Satan to serve the living and true God.

Henrietta and Lucy Soltau were staying at 6 Pyrland Road during the conference. According to Henrietta, one day after lunch Hudson Taylor led the household—Jennie, Emily, Henrietta, Lucy and 'one or two gentlemen'—into the sitting-room, to stand round a map of China. 'Now,' he said, 'have you the faith to join with me in laying hold of God for eighteen new men, to go two by two to the unoccupied provinces?' They 'covenanted with him to pray daily for this, till it was accomplished'. Then 'we all joined hands while Mr Taylor prayed.' That his team in China had been reduced to twenty-five, with more leaving soon afterwards, and that the 'crisis' of William Berger's resignation and replacement had not been resolved, were as irrelevant to the task needing to be done as to the power of God in response to believing prayer. Funds were low and donations coming in painfully slowly. With the Mission in some ways at its lowest ebb since its inception, this seemed no time for expansion, yet Hudson Taylor

was in no doubt that the will of God was unchanged—for advance, not retreat.

Two and a half years later they were still praying, little nearer to their goal—except that God's time had come.[202]

'A council of management' for home affairs[203] (July–October 1872)

Hudson Taylor's good friends of Bryanston Hall, Portman Square—Thomas Marshall, John Challice and William Hall—could see that he was bearing too much for one man and reminded him of Jethro's advice to Moses, 'You will only wear yourself out—you must share the load with others. He knew it only too well and had been looking for lieutenants for five years. None had come forward. Nor did Challice and Hall offer more than their support. They were waiting to be asked. In the week after the Mildmay Conference on July 5, Hudson Taylor was spending the evening with Richard Harris Hill, the architect and civil engineer, and Agnes his wife, one of the Soltau sisters, when Hill made a proposition. If Taylor would form a council of friends he could trust, he himself would be willing to serve as its honorary secretary. 'Not seeing any hope of a colleague (to replace Berger), he adopted my suggestion,' Hill noted.

At last there was light at the end of the tunnel. More than once Hudson Taylor had stated his objections to the often cloying effects of committee control in China, and before the *Lammermuir* sailed from London, he and William Berger had opted for the freedom of judgment and action Berger would have as an independent director while the Mission was small. Memories of the failure of the Chinese Evangelisation Society with its large board of management and committee of armchair strategists were too vivid. But William Berger had been a co-founder, committed body and soul to the Mission. Many strong supporters were fit and willing to play a minor role, but until now no one had offered to do more. Perhaps Richard Hill underestimated what would be involved, or having offered to be secretary to a council was carried along in subsequent conversations with

Hudson Taylor to take on more than he had intended. William Berger had managed his factory and farm as well as Mission affairs in Britain, and found them too much. Richard Hill was adding the Mission to his professional practice. His new undertaking was to suffer, for all his good intentions.

At the end of July, Henrietta Soltau, a petite young woman, 'a very nice girl, well educated', with a strong and buoyant spirit, came to Pyrland Road to help for two or three months in any way she could—the beginning of an association which led to her being one of the Mission's most venerated veterans. Consultations between Hill and Hudson Taylor continued, and, realising that at all costs he must leave for China in October, only a few weeks away, he concluded that an advisory council to share the responsibilities in Britain was the right provision to make for his absence. No potential member knew enough of his principles, of the brief history of the Mission, or about China, to replace William Berger as director. So Hudson Taylor would remain as the General Director while the council served the Mission. John Challice and William Hall accepted his invitation to be members, and also the Soltau brothers, George and Henry, and Joseph Weatherley, a family friend of Maria's and trustee of her marriage settlement for the education of her children.

Planning matured while the 'almost overwhelming' pressure of daily duties on Hudson Taylor showed no sign of easing. In a note to his mother on July 20 he even had this to add, 'Mrs Meadows was confined last night of twins at 7 p.m. prematurely. Both died ere midnight.' Again! This had happened to Elizabeth so often, and he felt for her.

Too late to be included in the *Occasional* No 30, a slip was attached announcing that Richard Hill and Henry Soltau had 'agreed to act as Honorary Secretaries during our absence from England'. The Taylors went to the Radstocks the next day, speaking at two meetings, and stayed overnight for long conversations. And then to the Howards and Miss Stacey at Tottenham

for the same purpose. On August 22 the Hills and George Soltau met with Hudson Taylor again, and through this month and September a list of those willing to serve as referees in different parts of the country began to grow. William Pennefather and John Eliot Howard were naturally the first to be included. George Müller's acceptance was received on October 9, the day the Taylors left for China. After a long conversation with Henry Soltau on August 30, Hudson Taylor and Jennie spent another weekend with the Robert Howards at Tottenham. On September 4, John Eliot Howard attended an early morning meeting at 6 Pyrland Road to bid farewell to the Crombies and Lanfeng, escorting Fanny Wilson and a 'Miss Potter' to China. Richard Hill then went with Hudson Taylor to meet the Marquis of Cholmondeley and agree his functions as a referee. And a few days later Hudson Taylor's host at Bath, Colonel Woodfall, also agreed to serve.

Hudson Taylor was preparing boxes for packing up and sailing within a month, but still had a tour of the north to fit in. On the 11th the Judds and Thomas Harvey arrived at Liverpool and came on to London. Elizabeth Judd had become so ill in China that Mary Bowyer at a day or two's notice had joined them to care for her on board ship. Harvey had returned to complete his medical course at his own expense. On the same day Grattan Guinness and Tom Barnardo, two more referees, came to tea—well met, for it had been through Barnardo's friendship and Guinness's *Voice of thy Brother's Blood* that Judd had been directed to China. Barnardo and Guinness, living opposite one another in Bow, were each building up his own great achievements while serving the CIM in his own way.

On September 15, Hudson Taylor preached for William Landels at Regent's Park Chapel in the morning and for William Garrett Lewis at Westbourne Grove in the evening—two more of his new referees. Then, at last, on the 20th he began his farewell visit to Yorkshire on the way to Dundee for a three-day conference, and from there to Kendal. He spent two days with his old friend William Collingwood in Liverpool, left by the 1.00 a.m. train and rejoined his family at 7.30 a.m. on the last day of September 'greatly prospered' and 'not too tired'. Only ten days remained before he would have to catch the French Mail at Marseilles.

On Friday, October 4, Hudson Taylor, Joseph Weatherley, John Challice, George and Henry Soltau and Richard Hill met at 51 Gordon Square, Weatherley's home, 'to inaugurate a Council for the management of the Home affairs of the China Inland Mission'. The Council was to deputise for him in his absence and to advise him when he was in Britain. They clearly understood how it differed from the controlling councils and committees of most other societies, and approved of his principles in this respect. Hudson Taylor then requested and authorised the council, in the event of his decease, to make 'all necessary arrangements for carrying on the work of the Mission'. William Berger's part in the growth of the Mission, and his activities as director in Britain were reviewed as an indication of what the council and secretaries could expect to shoulder, and Hudson Taylor went on to brief them on the complexities of property rental and purchase in China, and (as the minutes read) on the appointment of 'missionary agents'—the term died hard in the thinking of those accustomed to it. Hudson Taylor then handed over the small balance lying at the bank.

On Saturday they met again, as much to pray as to conduct business, with Joseph Weatherley in the chair and Hudson Taylor, Challice, Hall, Hill and Henry Soltau present. One final meeting followed on October 8 at Gordon Square, with Grattan Guinness attending by invitation while the selection and training of candidates was discussed. George Soltau undertook to train and test candidates at his Lamb and Flag Ragged School and City Mission. Hudson Taylor delivered his cash in hand, £21, to the treasurer, and £15 to Emily Blatchley, and at last was free to do his own hurried packing and preparations for departure. Shortly afterwards Theodore Howard, Robert's son, also joined the council. To ease the parting Hudson Taylor's children were in the country at Godalming with his sister Amelia and her big family. He had said goodbye and his heart was heavy. Of all farewells, he confessed, those from his children were the most painful.

Third–class French mail (October–November 1872)

The Crombies had been home from China only two months when Annie wrote in January 1871 from the House Beautiful at Saint Hill to Hudson Taylor, 'I long for the day when we shall start again for China . . . All the kind friends and many comforts of England are not worth a tenth of the privilege of being allowed to bear the burden and heat of the day in China.' But they were not well enough to return until September 1872. By then Lanfeng had been away from his wife and home for more than a year. Travelling third class with the Crombies and Fanny Wilson (through a typhoon in the China Sea) and due the same treatment as other passengers, Lanfeng had found himself exploited by the crew and made to work his passage all the way to China. When Hudson Taylor learned of this, he took it up with the shipping company to recover the fare for Lanfeng.

The Taylors and Emmeline Turner, a new recruit, were seen off at Charing Cross station on October 9 by such a crowd of well-wishers and with so little time for registering their baggage that he could not bid any a proper farewell. Worse still, his father could not get through the barrier to the platform and failed to see him. Nellie and her father missed Hudson Taylor completely, and in the confusion Mrs Faulding left her handbag in the carriage. Hearing too late that he had gone, Major C. H. Malan, a garrison commander at Singapore, sent a hundred pounds for his own use. 'Your visit to me at Singapore on my birthday, August 19, 1871, was one of my brightest days there.'

They had second-class tickets to Marseilles, apparently Richard Hill's parting gift; and after the 'excessive fatigue' of finally clearing up and leaving Pyrland Road, welcomed it as God's special provision for them in the circumstances. The journey of fourteen hours to Paris and twenty-five from there to Marseilles, brought them to the steamer *Tigre* of the Messageries Maritimes. They went aboard to see their third-class cabins: Jennie and Emmeline together with a nine-berth cabin to themselves, and Hudson Taylor sharing with other men in the adjoining cabin. They left their note of introduction and cards for the captain, and spent the night ashore. 'He wrote so cheerfully', Emily told Henrietta Soltau. 'He says Jennie is hardly like herself, she is so well . . . He told me to send his love to you (you hardly deserve it!)' But beneath this exterior Emily was lonely, ill and very sad. 'But it does not tear my heart now as it used to do, for I realise that ties are not made for time (but) for eternity.'

All the routine work had fallen upon her, seeing the *Occasional Paper* through the printers and then distributing them, and dealing with the mail, everything that did not have to wait for the secretaries or treasurer. Finding her so competent and reliable, they soon began to overlook her frail health until she carried more than she could bear. At the same time she had Hudson Taylor's four children to mother, and Tom Jones to keep at his books, working for medical entrance examinations.

Crossing the Mediterranean, Hudson Taylor and Jennie worked on No 31 of the *Occasional Paper*, in a long letter to friends of the Mission introducing the 'Council of Management of the home department'. One part of the council's work was 'so momentous . . . as to call for special remark'—the selection and training of reinforcements. He enlarged on the need for them, on the painfully difficult life they would be called upon to lead, and on their necessary qualifications. 'The work of a true missionary is work indeed; often very monotonous, apparently not very successful, and carried on through

great and varied but unceasing difficulties.' He then introduced the list of referees 'in various parts of the country, whose known sympathy will be helpful to strangers to the mission, and from whom such may learn its character and *bona fide* nature'. Matters which could not at once be made public would be referred to them for advice, should such dire circumstances arise again. He made a careful statement of arrangements for banking and exchange, of how he followed the market fluctuations in order to change sterling into silver taels and Mexican dollars at the most favourable times, and of how this careful stewardship also brought in substantial interest as a by-product of deliberate investment of current funds.

> We shall seek pecuniary aid from God by prayer, as heretofore. He will put it into the hearts of whom He sees fit to use, to act as His channels. When there is money in hand, it will be remitted to China; when there is none, none will be sent; and we shall not draw on home, so there can be no going into debt. Should our faith be tried, as it has been before, He will prove Himself faithful, as He ever has done; nay, should our faith fail, His faithfulness will not; for is it not written, 'If we believe not, He abideth faithful'? ... Pray that (the) principle—of becoming one with the people, of willingly taking the lowest place—may be deeply inwrought in our souls, and expressed in our deportment. With regard to missionaries wearing the native costume, there will always be differences of opinion, and we do not, therefore, make its adoption a *sine qua non of* membership with the mission. But for work in the interior we value it much, seeing year by year more reason to value it.

Most significantly he harked back to his early experiences of years ago when he, with William Burns and others, engaged in itinerant preaching and colportage where residence was impossible. The result had been,

> to convince (him) of (the) comparative inutility (of this type of work). Where interest was excited it could not be

sustained; enquirers had to be left with no one to lead them on ... It became more and more apparent ... that any who might be brought to Christ would need the constant care and teaching of older and more experienced Christians. [Here he stressed fundamental principles.] How could this be done? As we foreigner's could not then reside in the interior, it seemed desirable at first to labour (at Ningbo) until a native church was formed; to spare no pains in thoroughly instructing the converts in the Word of God; to pray that evangelistic and pastoral gifts might be developed among them; and then to encourage them to locate themselves in the interior, visiting them frequently, and aiding them in their work in every possible way.

He then told at length the story of Tsiu Kyuo-kwe and his mother to show how effective the policy had been. This was the way the Mission's work was developing everywhere and would be continued. 'We shall seek by God's help to plant the standard of the cross in new and unoccupied regions, to get as near as possible to the people, and to be as accessible to them as possible, that our lives may commend the gospel.'

The work on the manuscript was finished as they approached Port Said, and it was posted home. After that it was correspondence until they were 'tired of writing'. From Aden he asked that his mother should copy and send him all the Mission's statements of account for the past seven years which he later received and prepared for publication. The long tropical voyage on the Crombies' ship through the Indian Ocean had been too much for Miss Potter, and she had been put ashore at Singapore to recover. When the *Tigre* arrived and most third-class passengers disembarked, Miss Potter joined Emmeline Turner (only to relapse in China and be sent home to die in July 1874).

Approaching China 'in heavy seas', Hudson Taylor quailed at the thought of what lay ahead. 'I should tremble indeed, had we not God to look to.' From Aden he had written, 'Difficulties will be very thick on our arrival but God will perfect that

which concerns us.' At Shanghai he would meet 'the first crush of matters' for to T. F. Wade the Yangzhou affair was still a live issue. If only he could avoid secular business and give himself to spiritual activities! But he could see no remedy while he was the sole leader. A visit to Gutzlaff's grave at Hong Kong must have rallied his spirit, for the memory of Gutzlaff's vision was always an inspiration.

Unknown to them, Henry Reid had passed the *Tigre* in another ship, homeward bound, and George Duncan's health had steadily deteriorated until Catherine had to bring him and their child home on a second ship. Reid's baggage and theirs was on a third vessel which went down with all their worldly possessions. On October 9, the day of the Taylors' departure from London, only nine missionary men, Louise Desgraz and five wives remained in China. Where was the China Inland Mission? The Crombies and Fanny Wilson arrived soon afterwards.

The journey over, Hudson Taylor admitted that he did not enjoy travelling as he had on clipper ships under sail. Little glamour was left. They anchored at the mouth of the Yangzi. Even with Robert Hart's buoys and lightships to mark the channel, it was too dark and thick a night to proceed, so they lay at anchor. 'I can form no conception of what our course (on landing) may be—north, south, east or west—I never felt so fully and utterly cast on the Lord . . . My heart too aches at the remembrance of the past, and at the distance which separates me from so many loved ones.' In the morning, on November 28, the first anniversary of his and Jennie's wedding day, they reached Shanghai.

Taking up the reins
(November–December 1872)

Landing at Shanghai on their first wedding anniversary aroused in Hudson Taylor and Jennie a flood of memories, and a surge of qualms, immediately justified. Before anything else came a visit to the post office to collect their mail. Whom should they meet there but Charles Fishe, looking better and stronger than they had ever known him, but shamefaced in foreign clothes. The pressure of opinion had been too much for him. Being 'a Chinese to the Chinese' was all very well in 'the interior', and out of place among Westerners in an increasingly Westernised international settlement which treated its thousands of Chinese residents as aliens without a say in its government. But Charles was not only wearing them in Shanghai. Unconvinced, it had been easy for him to forget Hudson Taylor's principles and to take the line of least resistance. He was quickly set at ease. Hudson Taylor himself was in foreign clothes and so soon swept up by the need for immediate action as Charles gave him all the news, that he could not get Chinese travelling clothes made before he had to leave Shanghai. Even Jennie and the two girls, Emmeline Turner and Miss Potter, could not complete their shopping before they all set out for Hangzhou by canal boat forty-eight hours later.

The news from Hangzhou was bad. All Chinese who had sold land to foreigners on which to build their foreign homes and churches, were in prison and one of them in chains, with the exception of the New Lane landlords. But no more had been heard of moves to force the CIM out of Yangzhou. The Mission's finances in China were in such a state that Hudson Taylor had to exchange all the foreign currency he had brought with him, regardless of an adverse exchange rate, for no remittances had arrived from Britain. 'Our present supplies will soon be exhausted,' he wrote to the secretaries in London, assuming that they had no funds to send. 'What a comfort it is to know that . . . our Supplier never can be so.' James Williamson, Charles reported, was in a state of nervous exhaustion close to breakdown. Hudson Taylor sent him a message to hand over his work in Fenghua and Ninghai to Crombie and come to Hangzhou ready to be sent home to Britain. News of Reid's irresponsible defection from Suzhou was a greater shock, the first Hudson Taylor had heard of it; and the rapid acceleration of George Duncan's tuberculosis before he sailed for home almost certainly heralded his early death. As painful a reminder of Hudson Taylor's own experiences lay in the news that both the Rudland and Edward Fishe families had lost another child. In the political field reports were hopeful. China seemed to be peaceful again and, on the whole, persecution had ceased.

Preaching to village audiences and at the city of Songjiang on the way to Hangzhou took Hudson Taylor back in thought to his very first journey with Joseph Edkins in December 1854. This time his congregations were drawn by the sight of foreign women in foreign dress, 'the women examining our bonnets and dresses and peeping at our petticoats to their hearts' content', so that they paid no attention to the speaker. Jennie was in her element, happily chatting with them as she revealed more mysteries to the curious women. Emmeline Turner at once caught the spirit of the occasion.

Hurrying on, they were in Hangzhou of happy memories by December 5. Apart from lapses by some Christians, 'on the whole I see very cheering and decided progress here,' Hudson Taylor could tell Richard Hill. Wang Lae-djün, 'a wise as well as a godly man', as pastor in Hangzhou and several outstations, was still supporting and directing a team of evangelists and colporteurs deployed hundreds of miles apart, including some at Lanxi again, the scene of Duncan's and Tsiu's early pioneering, and at Qü Xian, the city they had tried to reach on the first Qiantang River reconnaissance. Better still, two had crossed the provincial border into southern Anhui and occupied Huizhou, one of the cities visited and reported on by Duncan and Harvey on their long journey through southern Anhui in 1871. One of Lae-djün's team was being victimised by extortioners but resisting the demands for money. The Hangzhou schools were in good order, and Emmeline was game to step straight into Jennie's previous post and live among the girls. Miss Potter on the other hand was in a precarious state of health. 'Inflammation of the right lung' had left her an invalid incapable of anything. Jennie was enjoying the bloom of her first pregnancy and delighting in the comfort of getting into Chinese wadded winter clothing at last, snug in the bitter cold.

Before Duncan had had to admit defeat by his illness, he had rented good premises in Anqing as a base for evangelising the province. The Chinese missionaries left in charge had sent word, however, that attempts were being made to wrest this new foothold from the Mission. John McCarthy agreed to go and see what he could do, and left Hangzhou on December 14, little knowing that this step would lead to his becoming one of the internationally famous pioneers of inland China. For the present, Anhui was the province they most wanted to see evangelised in 1873, its northern half from Anqing and its southern half from Wuhu. Jennie took McCarthy's place as servant of the church at Hangzhou, while Hudson Taylor prepared to visit the southern cities immediately after Christmas.

In Hangzhou for a short three weeks, he gave himself to the work he most loved—teaching the Christians and preaching the gospel but also in showing that warm affection which they so prized. He put on a Christmas fellowship-meal for all the church members, and on Christmas Day received £495 in cheques allocated by George Müller from his missionary fund, enough to keep the Mission going. Hours had to be spent on drafting the main contents of

Occasional Paper No 32, an account of all he was learning of recent development, and a biographical essay on Feng Nenggui, the basket-maker responsible for Wang Lae-djün's conversion. So useful had the Mission's *Monthly Gleaner* proved, that another monthly bulletin in Chinese had to be started, for the Chinese missionaries who already outnumbered the foreign.

On December 28 Hudson Taylor set out on his visit to the southern district, calling first at Xiaoshan, the scene of Mr Tsiu's flogging in 1867 and still unproductive. Only two Christians were known to the evangelist who had taken over when Lewis Nicol left. Then on to Shaoxing where Charles Fishe rejoined him. Hudson Taylor had discovered that Charles's sense of disloyalty in forsaking Chinese dress was making him think of resigning from the Mission. Potentially a valuable asset, he needed to be encouraged. Important though adaptation to the Chinese was, dress was not the most important issue where Charles was concerned. His secretarial help was indispensable if Hudson Taylor was not to be bogged down by administrative detail. Would he agree to their travelling together for a few weeks, to act as his personal assistant? Gradually, Hudson Taylor hoped, he could bring about a complete change of outlook and save Charles from giving up. It took him more than six months of close friendship to achieve this, but only a few days to know that beneath Charles's unrest lay his pining for Nellie Faulding. Broadly hinting that he need not wait to marry her if he came home, her mother was refusing to let her go to him.

John Stevenson had recovered from his succession of serious illnesses, but this tall, upright, once handsome man, was now covered with deep pockmarks from the haemorrhagic smallpox that had all but claimed his life. Instead of letting it affect his mind or commitment to the growing churches in Shaoxing, Sheng Xian and Xinchang he now added responsibility for the Ningbo outstations. His and the newly converted gentleman-scholar Ning's single-mindedness were in Hudson Taylor's mind when he wrote affectionately to Emily from Shaoxing, 'My dear, more-than-dear, Sister . . . If I could, I would write you often and long, as I think of you often and much . . . You are *never* forgotten [underlined five times]. I am greatly cheered . . . the time is drawing near for us to attempt one or more new provinces . . . before the year is out.'

Emily was already doing most of what William and Mary Berger had done, correspondence, account-keeping, publishing and distributing the *Occasional*. So this letter had to deal mostly with business matters. Richard Hill's first letter, written on Christmas Day, apologised for letting so many sea-mails go by without writing. His other letters at intervals frankly confessed that he had taken on too much. As a busy architect and civil engineer he had little time to give to Mission affairs.

To Jennie in Hangzhou, Hudson Taylor also wrote frequent love-letters about business and pastoral matters, such as he used to write to Maria. Jungeng, the household servant who had failed them from time to time, had fallen again (see 1, p 813). 'May the Lord bless and forgive Ah-djun [ie Jungeng]. Could you call on him, God is very forbearing with us—we must be like Him. Send Mr Stevenson the four volumes of Chinese classics (Mr Legge's) which I bought in Hong Kong.' James Legge's great achievement in translating the main Chinese classics into English, to create appreciation by foreigners of the Chinese people, was to win him the first professorial chair in Chinese at Oxford after he retired. Hudson Taylor planned to retrieve these books on a later visit, to provide for his own intellectual needs. Then he set off with Charles Fishe for Ningbo.

China peaceful? (1872–73)

The arrest and imprisonment of landowners in Hangzhou who had sold sites to foreigners, was another example of the importance of *fengshui* in the thinking of the people, including the literati. E. B. Inslee of the American Presbyterian Mission (South) and his colleagues, all young and inexperienced, had been sold some property on the Hill of the City God and had proceeded to build foreign-looking houses. To the scholar-gentry these monstrosities, on the hill and at the south end of the city (significant breaches of *fengshui*), offended every sense of priority, towering as they did over the *yamen*s of the high mandarins.[204]

While the imprisonment of the Chinese landowners gave some satisfaction, the safety of all foreigners had been in jeopardy in August 1872, until the intervention of the British and American consuls in Ningbo restored calm and secured the landlords' release. E. C. Lord was American consul at the time. Friendly consultation then led not only to the Presbyterians handing over their property to the mandarins, but to their reinstatement (in 1874) in 'far more commodious' premises at the north end of the city (again of significance in *fengshui*) and generous compensation for the inconvenience caused. An offending schoolhouse on the hill was pulled down to satisfy the geomancers, but geomancy had to compete with market values. The larger building was allowed to stand, 'perhaps the first foreign house ever owned by Chinese in the interior', H. C. Du Bose observed. But most interesting in this episode was the readiness of the Hangzhou mandarins to deal reasonably with the offending missionaries, victims of their own neglect or ignorance of the Chinese outlook. Great advances had been made in a decade.

The sudden death of the aged viceroy, Zeng Guofan, at Nanjing in 1872 had removed one of the greatest figures from the Chinese scene—and a dangerous antagonist of the CIM from the Yangzi valley. But greater events were taking place in Peking, greater than the attempts of the new French envoy to negotiate another treaty, or of the Portuguese to claim jurisdiction over the islands dominating the harbour of Macao.

On April 30, 1872, the boy emperor, Tong Zhi, only son of Yehonala, the Empress Dowager Ci Xi, came of age.[205] Since his accession at the age of five in

1861, after the Jehol plot (see 1, pp 513–15), he had been under the control of his mother and Yong Lu, the imperial Bannerman appointed as his imperial counsellor. 'Passionately devoted to horses and riding' and archery, under Yong Lu's tuition, Tong Zhi was growing up to be a healthy, intelligent and even precocious boy. By the time he was twelve, when by tradition the choice of his future consort and concubines began, Ci Xi had trained him to sit on the Peacock Throne and to repeat what she told him from behind a bamboo screen. But as soon as he was thirteen he began to go his own way, sowing his wild oats in the brothels and opium dens outside the palace, and dismissing those who tried to restrain him.

Coming of age at seventeen, by Chinese reckoning from conception, he had attained the right to make the final choice of his consort and concubines from among the Tartar girls of his own age, or younger, favoured by his regents. Tragically, for he had an unscrupulous mother, he chose the daughter of Chonghou's brother, granddaughter of the Prince of Cheng condemned to death by the bowstring or 'silken cord of self-dispatch' in 1861. Ci Xi's choice for him had been the daughter of Yong Lu's friend Feng Hua. 'To compose the feuds' between Manchu clans, Ci Xi accepted the decision, though Alude (A-lu-de), the young empress, would not be as tractable as Feng Hua's daughter who became the first concubine. The wedding ceremony was to be in October, and the *fengshui* experts, the geomancers and astrologers, ordained that the bride should leave her home at 11.30 p.m. on the 15th and cross the threshold of the imperial palace a few minutes after midnight. In that auspicious half hour her sedan chair of imperial yellow would be borne in solemn silence through the torch-lit streets.

To the amazement of the foreign envoys in Peking, they were asked by Chonghou, recently back from France, to stay indoors and have no part in the celebrations. The ministers to a man were indignant, sensing an international slight and even danger to foreign interests, for what nation on earth does not give prominence to the respect paid by ambassadors of other nations on such occasions! The French envoy reported that 'the two ministers of the (Zongli) Yamen had been received by Mr Wade with an outburst of anger, by General Vlangaly (the Russian envoy) with a sharp lecture, by Mr Low (the American envoy) in a . . . very disagreeable (manner), while at the Spanish legation they encountered a veritable tempest'.

On October 21 the young emperor decreed that the regency of the two dowager empresses, Ci Yd and Ci An, was soon to end. On November 15 an edict was issued declaring, 'His Majesty today assumes control of the government' and on February 23, 1873, a day of yellow bunting and dragon banners at every masthead, Tong Zhi actually assumed control. The very next day the foreign envoys requested an audience, and in April Li Hongzhang, to aid his delicate negotiations over the Taiwan confrontation with the Japanese ambassador, secured for him an audience which was afterwards extended to the representatives of other nations. On June 14, therefore, an imperial decree in condescending tones granted the audience which took place on Sunday, June 29, 1873—not in the palace but in a garden pavilion in the imperial city where the envoys of tributary states were normally received. Eighty years had passed since Lord Macartney had been denied an audience in 1793 for refusing to *ketou* to the emperor, and now 'the defiant vassal state' of Japan had been given precedence over the Western nations, at a time when Japan assumed suzerainty over the Ryukyu Islands and China undertook to keep the savage tribes of Taiwan in order.

Alude from the first took a strong interest in the affairs of state, and with Tong Zhi attempted to establish their independence from his domineering mother, Ci Xi. After twelve years in power, Ci Xi was not willing at the age of thirty-seven to be relegated to comparative obscurity. But when Alude was known to be pregnant, Ci Xi saw herself in danger of being displaced even as dowager empress, for having an heir would in time make Alude the dowager. Meanwhile Tong Zhi returned to his dissolute ways.

While Peking was preoccupied with its own affairs, the Muslim rebellion in south-west China was finally quelled with ruthless slaughter. It had been active for nearly twenty years, mainly in the province of Yunnan. Marco Polo, passing through Yunnan (Cara-jan), in the service of Kublai Khan, had written of encountering Saracens and Nestorians as well as idolaters.[206] Over six centuries later the natural fortress of Dali, walled by mountain ranges with readily defensible passes only on the north and south, was inhabited mainly by Muslims. Known later to the West as Panthays, their appearance was distinctly Han Chinese or Mongol, but often with strongly Arab features as in the north-west.

The first rebellion in 1818 had been followed by others in 1826–28 and 1834–40, but that of 1855 to 1873 was the greatest, with repeated massacres perpetrated by both sides, Chinese and Muslim. At one time the Muslim forces had invested Kunming the provincial capital and controlled most of the province, but with the end of the Taiping rebellion and the release of imperial troops, the Muslims were slowly forced back into the west. The final stand at Dali depended on the defence of Shangguan and Xiaguan, the upper and lower passes, and these were lost by treachery. The traitors themselves were decapitated by the enemy they had helped and on January 19, 1873, according to reports, 30,000 of the 50,000-strong Muslim garrison were put to the sword, with hundreds if not thousands of the common people. On June 10 the fall of Tengyue, near the Burma border, signalled the end of this long rebellion, only less bloodthirsty than the Taiping rebellion itself.[207] So was the south-west 'pacified' and theoretically opened to travel. Twelve years later George Clarke of the CIM described the pathetic lot of Muslim survivors, and after thirty years John McCarthy commented on

the abundance of ruins still in evidence. But with peace in 1873, Hudson Taylor's thoughts returned to his dreams of entering China through Burma.

To rescue Charlie (January 1873)

High winds, snow and sleet made the journey from Shaoxing to Ningbo in a footboat slow and dangerous. Taking three days to cover ninety miles Hudson Taylor and Charles Fishe arrived to find a storm-damaged city under snow and a welcome by the Goughs, who had lost a chimney. But at Bridge Street they found the church members disheartened and lack-lustre, in need of an infusion of faith and teaching through a visit by John Stevenson. They lunched with the Lords and Barchets and caught the steamer to Shanghai, where Hudson Taylor visited 'most of the missionaries' of other missions before boarding the Yangzi steamer for Zhenjiang. 'It does seem so long since I left you, yet I have to go further away,' he wrote to Jennie. However, at Zhenjiang on Saturday, January 11, he had to say, 'Here, it is high time I came . . . In effect Charlie has been out of the Mission for months—or worse.'

As the Zhenjiang city house was empty and unswept they had gone to the Whites. In their comfortable suburban bungalow at the foot of the hill outside, the painful truth came home to Hudson Taylor as the weekend progressed, a revelation more distressing than failure by those members of the team of whom he had never expected much. Instead of living as a Chinese among the Chinese Christians, as intended when left in charge at Zhenjiang by the Judds, Charles had moved in with the independent Whites, an alien among aliens in foreign clothes. By nature receptive to his environment, he had soaked up the Whites' influence.

'The work here is and has been utterly neglected,' Hudson Taylor told Jennie after a cheerless Sunday with a disconsolate remnant of Christians. 'Mr Fishe preaching there sometimes, not even going into the city to (lead the services) . . . The (Christians) have been perplexed and disheartened, and the wonder is that there (are any of them left).' Their survival could be attributed to Louise Desgraz who, responsible for her school, had done what she could to hold them together. One thing was clear, whatever happened Charles must be kept away from the Whites. 'Goodbye, darling,' wrote Hudson Taylor ending his letter to Jennie, 'I must go to my cold, lonely house in the city.' He at least would choose to live among the Chinese. To McCarthy he confided, 'I have had many thoughts which I do not care to put on paper.' He was planning on taking Miss Potter with Jennie to Nanjing, and on keeping Charles under his eye too. For Charles it would clearly be a rescue operation demanding patience and perseverance, but he seemed to be responding.

Moving into the city house paid off at once. The evangelist, inactive in imitation of his missionary colleagues, had 'fallen into gross sin' and had to be suspended. 'We all need helping,' Hudson Taylor commented. How he dealt with this situation held lessons for the Mission. Because of the low morale he must show that he cared. He invited the fourteen church members and 'inquirers' 'to dine with me tomorrow, Sunday, after the morning service . . . They will soon look up, with God's blessing, if they are looked after.' He had twelve good Christians to work with, the nucleus of a potentially thriving church, and enlisted one as a colporteur. The schoolwork was important too. He bought land above Louise's girls' school (the memorial to Maria) to build a boys' school. That would show Zhenjiang was not forgotten.

Sending Charles to Nanjing to get the house ready, on January 22 he himself was on his way to Hangzhou to bring Jennie and Miss Potter back. Nanjing was another difficult place, resistant to the gospel, still a pioneering situation more than five years after Duncan had begun there. Hudson Taylor intended to stay with Jennie until after her baby was born, so what better than to preach the gospel and plant a church, with her and Charles to help. Nanjing was

central to the northern field of the Mission. He would be within easy reach of Zhenjiang and Yangzhou by river-steamer, and with the other Yangzi cities, Wuhu, Anqing and Jiujiang too. To take down the foreign scaffolding and leave established churches in Chinese hands was his dominant thought, moving his foreign missionaries to pioneer new regions, if they were willing to do it.

'If we are well supplied with funds,' he wrote to Emily as he travelled, 'we may make a long stride, DV, this year. If not, we must hold on in faith . . . CTF has been a wet blanket (in Zhenjiang) for some time, I fear—of course without intending it . . . If our native helpers improve as they are doing, we shall soon need very few foreign helpers for our older work. If we have a few men of the right stamp, we shall soon see more than one unoccupied province invaded.'

In another letter to the Bergers he also wrote frankly about arrogance towards the Chinese on the part of some missionaries, and their influence on Charles. 'One of my objects in going (to Nankin) is to be alone with him. I hope . . . to talk over these matters with him alone . . . for I should be so sorry for a young and devoted missionary to be spoiled, as dozens [in various missions] have been, in this way.' The Chinese Christians were developing well, he went on, and 'I hope we may be able to break ground in several new provinces within the next three years.'

He had been away from Jennie for a month when he arrived at Hangzhou on the 28th, and was off again directly after celebrating the Chinese New Year with the church—but this time with her in his big footboat and Miss Potter and her Chinese companion in another.

Attrition (October 1872–May 1873)

Henry Reid's unannounced arrival in London after abandoning Suzhou caused more surprise than he himself received when Hudson Taylor wrote to tell him he should not think of returning to China. Both knew how damaging the Yangzhou riot had been to his emotional balance, and his injured eye was unhealed. When the Council made generous allowance for the shock and injuries he had suffered, refunding his travelling expenses, Hudson Taylor saw further than they and warned that no unauthorised expenditure should be refunded. It would open the door to irresponsibility. But after his return home to Banff, Henry Reid addressed a letter to the friends of the Mission which was published in the *Occasional Paper*. His experiences in China had so shattered his nervous system he said, as 'thoroughly to unfit me for a sphere where courage is so essential. My acquaintance with Mr Taylor has been one of unbroken fellowship, and I cannot resign . . . without testifying to his abounding kindness to us . . . to his holiness of life . . . and more than ordinary self-denial and gentleness.' He could hardly have bowed out more gracefully, but once again the lesson was not lost on Hudson Taylor or the council: zealous people, however attractive, do not necessarily make good missionaries; the assessment of applicants' personalities before they entered the Mission mattered profoundly. Two years later Hudson Taylor wrote that Reid was not only losing the sight of his injured eye but would probably lose that of the other also, by 'sympathetic ophthalmia'.

When George and Catherine Duncan and their child arrived unannounced in London with Mary Bowyer in attendance, ten days after Reid, the shock for the council was even greater, for the tall Highlander was a physical wreck, 'very broken down'. For two weeks the Duncans stayed with the Meadows family, until the doctors sent them to Torquay among friends of the Mission, in a last desperate bid to let the mild climate and sea air do what no other known treatment could do to heal him.

Emily Blatchley felt deeply for him, knowing how hard she had found it to accept the inevitable. His phthisis was only a stage more advanced than her own. On November 25, 1872, she wrote to Henrietta Soltau (herself nursing her very sick father

and sister at Barnstaple). 'He craves for restoration to health.' She could wish him to be submissive to God's will, and better still, to delight in it as she was learning to do.

She had known George Duncan on days of confession, prayer and worship, on the *Lammermuir*, in Hangzhou and since the Yangzhou riot. When he died on February 12, 1873, aged only twenty-nine, it was Emily who wrote for the *Occasional Paper* extolling his faithfulness, his indomitable perseverance, his faith at Nanjing in the Drum Tower days (see 1, p 816) and his courage in staying at Yangzhou when he arrived to find the riot beginning. To 'the comfort afforded by his presence and help, and calm self-possession in the face of danger and death', she could testify from personal experience. His success in pointing Chinese to Christ and tending an infant church at Nanjing where 'there is hardly a corner or street or teashop in the whole place where the gospel has not been proclaimed by (him)', was only secondary to his greatest gift, of being 'essentially a pioneer'. The church at Qingjiangpu was another star in his crown. After his illness had taken a serious turn, he had also added James Meadows's responsibility at Anqing to his own, and had undertaken his longest exploratory journeys in Anhui. At the end, in great pain, 'his patience in suffering (not natural to him), his submission to the will of God, and his thankfulness (showed how) his spirit was ripening'. Dying, he named some of his Chinese friends, and his last words were 'Bless the Lord, O . . . (my soul)!'

Death claimed so many in 1873. Emily's thoughts and the Taylors' were often turned to think about it. Henry Venn died on January 13; William Pennefather on April 30; and on May 11 Richard Hill wrote to say that Lucy Soltau had just died and Henry W. Soltau, their father, was sinking. On March 4 Griffith John's wife died on reaching Singapore, on their way to China. Robert Howard of Tottenham had died, and on May 3 the great missionary explorer of Africa, David Livingstone, died kneeling by his camp-bed. When word came in May that Emily herself was finding it hard to keep going, the impression Hudson Taylor received was that her end must be near. He suffered pangs he could have been spared, for she was still working hard. He had written every month, however busy he was, taking her into his confidence. Had he asked too much of her? She must not economise on food or warmth, but perhaps he had written too late. To lose her would be far too costly a price to pay

'I wish you *definitely* to get (secretarial help) . . . If you break down where will things be?'—seeing the honorary secretaries were not coping. She should ask Catherine Duncan to give a year to helping her. 'She would be happy with you . . . and she loves us and the dear children.' But had he misjudged her strength? In May he wrote 'My own dear Ae-me' [dialect for Aimei] and again, after some stern pages of business, 'I don't like to send you such wretched letters, when you send me such dear, loving, long ones.' Happily married to Jennie, her closest friend, with perhaps only months remaining to Emily for such candour, he knew he was on safe ground in writing 'May God bless you, my own dear Ae-me.'

Teething troubles in London
(October 1872–May 1873)

Apart from carrying a heavy share of routine work, on behalf of the secretaries and council, Emily was finding herself to be Hudson Taylor's mouthpiece, in duty bound to speak out when she learned of their acting in conflict with the Mission's policies. 'You must pray for me, dear, dear Brother. I cannot be blind to the fact that as yet the real responsibility of the work at home rests on me. Mr Challice told me the other day that the Council do depend on me.' As treasurer he had such confidence in her account-keeping that he saw no need of frequent checks on it. 'Mr Challice now sees (since I had a talk with him about it) that we are right in not making collections or asking for money . . . though he did not when you left. I wish all the Council did. I must seek an opportunity of talking with Mr

Weatherley about it. He as good as asked for money yesterday, though he had just said, "We do not ask".' She signed herself 'Your loving Me-me', the Chinese for 'little sister'.

She was writing during the Mildmay Conference of packed audiences overflowing even outside the great hall, though it held three thousand.[208] She herself had been asked to join Charles Judd and Grattan Guinness in addressing a garden meeting with the Earl of Cavan as chairman. His concern for China had been reawakened, he said, by Elizabeth Judd, whom Lady Cavan had invited to their home. After the meeting a Mrs Grace of High Wycombe came up to Emily and promised to give £50 annually to the CIM, and later gave Charles Judd £140 for opening a new station. Grattan Guinness and James Meadows had been touring a number of cities together, speaking about China and calling on young men to commit their lives to Christ, to serve him there. As a result, a young medical student named Arthur William Douthwaite was to attend Guinness's training institute and the London Hospital before sailing with Meadows in February 1874. Douthwaite was to become one of China's notable missionaries, decorated by the emperor.

Guinness moved shortly afterwards to Mile End, and opened the East London Institute for Home and Foreign Missions at Stepney Green, Bow Road, in the poorest part of London, to be among the narrow alleyways and undrained streets with sounds and smells resembling those of distant parts of the earth. He wanted to accustom his student missionaries to life and evangelism in the roughest and most demanding conditions. He himself wrote, 'I selected East London as a training sphere because it contained the largest number of people of any dark and needy district in England'—and because Tom Barnardo was there, but also because of its association with the CIM at Coborn Street. As 'a natural result many of our early students selected China as their sphere and became connected with the China Inland Mission . . . about a hundred . . . some of them numbered among the martyrs . . . It would be impossible to estimate the results for good . . . throughout the world' from Hudson Taylor's making his home in East London.

The Institute had made a tentative beginning when Richard Hill wrote to Hudson Taylor on February 18, 1873, a letter which must have alarmed him by its lack of understanding of what the secretaries had undertaken to do.

> By the time I have sent receipts and a letter to the almost daily batch of donors, I have done about as much as I have time for— and H. Soltau being divided into three parts, with secular calling, 'Lamb and Flag' work and CIM, has of course little time left ... I fear that I may have seemed to aim at what I cannot get through. [He was right. The Bergers had carried more, without an Emily to relieve them of half the load.]

> Mr G. (Guinness) has taken a house in Stepney for a temporary training place for candidates, with a view to Spain, China and other parts of the mission field. He tells me that he will attend to their spiritual training and they will practice mission work in Barnardo's district. Barnardo will reside in the house as major domo—I don't know how far he will have private spiritual influence over them. Some people think he is not old enough for the post, but Mr G. considers him precisely the man for it.[209]

The Institute soon moved into its permanent quarters at Harley House, near Coborn Street, Bow, and became known as Harley College. In the next twenty-one years, Grattan Guinness trained and sent abroad 588 men and women, to every continent, in thirty different societies, including some which he himself founded; and under his son, Dr Harry Guinness, the Institute trained almost as many more.

The first meeting of the London Council after Hudson Taylor's departure in October 1872 had been concerned with the application of a candidate named Frederick Groombridge, one of Charles Haddon Spurgeon's students. 'Having had him under his eye for two years,' Spurgeon gave him 'the highest character', and

George Soltau after seeing him in action at his Clerkenwell mission found him 'very intelligent and spiritually advanced . . . indefatigable in visiting, his heart being entirely taken up with missionary work'. So he was accepted 'without any further hesitation'. A physician who had been a missionary passed him as fit for China; and Groombridge left with another, John Donovan, 'a true Cockney from Limehouse' on December 31, 1872. The council were to learn that appearances can be most deceptive, and references may suffer from an unconscious bias.

Donovan had had an unfavourable 'past history', Grattan Guinness warned, but as his referees considered him a reformed character he, too, was accepted by the council as fit to go. Both signed agreements to work under Hudson Taylor's direction and to wear Chinese dress 'and not to discontinue to do so without first conferring with the Director of the Mission'. Almost from their arrival in China they were to be more trouble than use, finally finding secular employment before returning home. The assessment of candidates would never be easy and would always be more the concern of the Mission abroad than of those entrusted with the decision at home.

Restoring order (February–May 1873)

It was Emily who notified Hudson Taylor of the expected sailing of Groombridge and Donovan from Marseilles on January 5; but her letter reached him on February 23 after they had arrived at Shanghai on the 13th. Fortunately she had wisely repeated the information in a later letter, of December 19, which outstripped the first and reached Hudson Taylor on the 13th. John McCarthy was to have met them but had been delayed. Instead Charles Fishe, still in foreign dress, tracked them down on February 24 when they had already spent ten days listening to Shanghai opinions of Hudson Taylor and his principles. To repair the damage Hudson Taylor took them under his own care at Nanjing, and introduced them to Chinese clothes and Chinese ways; but before long they chose to follow the majority, rejecting his advice and their own promises made in London, in favour of being foreign in appearance and behaviour. Groombridge showed signs of having advanced tuberculosis and Donovan was so uneducated that Hudson Taylor wondered whether he would ever learn the language:

'Nanjing has proved hard ground,' he wrote, 'but we must sow in hope.' By showing 'magic lantern' slides to draw a crowd he was soon preaching the gospel to two hundred who came in spite of persistent opposition by Muslims. The few Christians were encouraged and within a few weeks the hopefulness George Duncan had instilled in them was returning. Li Lanfeng arrived to be their pastor-evangelist, they were organised as a church, and Hudson Taylor was free to give his attention to other cities.

Again he confided in Emily,

We sadly want some real men with enough faith in God to trust Him and do His work, and a good, not an irritable conscience ... one that worries about everything ... Kiss the dear children for me. How I wish I could save you the trouble! [He was hoping to get Herbert and Howard into the City of London School.] A little rough discipline might ... make them strike their roots deeper, give you more hold of their affections, make them men not girls ... Expensive schools beget expensive habits, cheap ones often lead to vulgar habits, so it is very difficult to know ... what to do.

Inflation was affecting all missions, and receipts in Britain were low, but how was it, he asked Richard Hill, that Major Malan's donation of £100 had not been forwarded to China? There was no need to wait for a larger sum to accumulate before transmitting it. In mid-March he had reached the point of having 'not a cent of money in hand', after instructing Tsiu and a colleague to rent premises in Wuhu. The Yangzi advance was as much part of the ongoing commitment of the Mission as feeding its members, and donations had been given specifically for that. To Rudland he wrote, 'I have not a dollar in hand for all the expenses of the Mission. The Lord doubtless will provide; it is specially for

His glory to do so now, as many doubtless thought we were trusting to Mr Berger before.'

Never since the Mission began had such a situation developed. Yet the funds were there, in London. With greater political stability in China he judged the opportunities to be more promising than ever. To Emily, Hudson Taylor had confessed 'I am much crippled just now for want of Mission funds . . . It seems to me that our good friends have forgotten that the main object of all the home operations is the reception and transmission of funds to China. I've been in China nearly four months, and not a penny has been sent.' He had been reduced to using his personal funds for Mission purposes. To her he could say, if the work was to grow, a steady supply would be essential. 'We shall require £250 a month, besides Mr Müller's remittances (which were) uncertain, both as to time and amount.' The secretaries should send fortnightly all they had available. Emily's role was a difficult one, to coach the secretaries into dealing with God, not men, when they had little in hand to transmit, but she succeeded.

Then, at last, gifts including £50 from the Bergers, as friendly as ever, and a transmission of £300 from the secretaries eased the difficulties. But why did Emily rather than Richard Hill send two cheques that did arrive, for £100 and £150, without explanation from either of them? Was each expecting the other to do it? Tactfully he tried to show Hill that the arrangements he had made were falling between two stools, that Emily was carrying too much, that funds received must flow, for they were constantly needed in China. He explained at length what they were used for, and how he did his best to provide each missionary with a remittance at regular intervals. 'I need scarcely say the missionaries themselves know nothing of these calculations . . . They look to the Lord [and receive provision through various channels including Mr Müller's Institute], but so far as I can, I seek to know and supply their need, and so to supply it as to keep them in circumstances of moderate comfort'—by the standards of the CIM.

Richard Hill had misunderstood a request from William Berger to be allowed to know 'the state of the funds' from time to time, as a request to be informed when funds were needed. Berger wrote to Hudson Taylor, 'I did not desire to be informed of the low state of the funds whenever that might arise—far from it . . . I might not be able or willing to carry (the burden).'

The confusion was understandable, and Hudson Taylor replied, 'The only question in my mind was this, Should your enquiry come at a time when our funds were low, how far could we consistently, at the time, give this information?' That, too, was straightened out with the secretaries. A frank answer to a frank question would leave an enquirer with what he had asked for, without in any way being regarded as solicitation. His action then would be his own affair, between himself and the Lord. On May 2, William Berger wrote giving approval of the Yangzhou building fund (to which he had contributed generously) being used for other purposes while building was impossible, but he would prefer it to go to established work rather than to extension in the present circumstances.

Another complication was the fact that Jennie's legacy from her uncle in Australia was coming into her correspondence with her father and others. Joseph Weatherley, Richard Hill and Henry Soltau, as the trustees, were to invest it and remit the interest to her. Instead of welcoming it as a steady source of personal income at a time of perplexity, she wrote, 'I should like to dedicate all my interest for the furtherance of God's work in different ways and . . . to have some of the principal at command for the same purpose. God has all along cared for our personal need, and I shall feel happiest in still looking to Him for the supply of our ordinary wants.' And again to her mother, 'You must not think that because I want £1,000 of the principal of my money sent out here that I shall be reckless with it . . . If it can be used for China wisely

at any time, surely that is not waste, but the best way of putting it out to interest that I know.' The trouble was that such mature thinking looked immature to those who knew little of trusting God as she did from day to day.[210]

Not only the Zhenjiang church had been neglected. Keeping clear of Yangzhou lest he draw T. F. Wade's attention to himself and the Mission's presence there, Hudson Taylor learned from the Chinese that the Yangzhou Christians were also 'in a bad way'. 'They are more to be pitied than blamed, for they have not been fed or watched over as young Christians need.' Edward Fishe, the resident missionary, was not sufficiently able, and his wife, Annie (Bohannan), had been ill for six months. But the critical expiry date of the contract made after the second Yangzhou plot was approaching. Long-term renewal of the lease would make possible a new attempt to establish a strong church. In April, Hudson Taylor told his mother, 'The time for the owners [the *daotai* and his friend] to give us notice if they wished us to leave Yangchau has passed. They have not done so.' It therefore looked as if the plot and Zeng Guofan's attempts to oust him had died with the old viceroy himself. The time had come to act

Meanwhile in Nanjing hardly had funds arrived and that particular problem diminished, than Jennie went into labour, on Saturday morning, April 12. After twenty-four hours she was exhausted and at dawn on Sunday, Hudson Taylor anxiously sent a message asking a Dr Macartney, attached to the Nanjing arsenal, to come and advise him. He spent most of Sunday with them. But Jennie went into convulsions and afterwards did not know her husband. At 1.30 p.m. a stillborn boy was born, and when Dr Macartney left they thought all was well. Not until nightfall did they know there was an unborn twin! She went into labour again on Monday afternoon, 14th, and gave birth to a stillborn girl at 11 p.m. Typically resilient and matter-of-fact, Jennie recovered quickly and told her mother, 'It was a very intensely anxious time for

(Hudson).' She was looking forward to moving to Yangzhou in mid-May, making it their base while putting the church back on its feet, and to working and travelling with him again.

China's hope (1873)

Returning to China with a mental picture of a team in each province and established churches actively reproducing themselves, Hudson Taylor had found his first priority to be rescue operations. Long letters about struggling colleagues and dwindling funds, flagging evangelists and dispirited church members, also carried shafts of confidence. Stripling churches, however few their numbers, he saw as not only good potential but as the source of workers to plant more churches in other towns and cities. To wait for their own local church to be strong was unnecessary. The fact of contributing to the expansion of the Church at large would strengthen the sending church. The absence of several foreign missionaries from China in this respect had its advantages.

In asking John McCarthy in February to take up George Duncan's work in Anhui and carry it into every one of the province's eight prefectures, Hudson Taylor also had the good of Hangzhou in mind. He planned to go there himself but to be busy with administrative work while delegating much of McCarthy's work to Chinese. They would have him and Wang Lae-djün, their pastor, to consult while they found their feet. Complete devolution to the church would follow naturally. Already Wang Lae-djün would not accept a salary: 'he really looks to God for his sustenance.'

> If we can remain in China for a time [he explained in a letter to Emily] the Mission may be put on an entirely new footing, I think. I am striving to make the work more and more native and interior, so as to be workable with as few foreign helpers as possible.
>
> [And to his mother a week later] I am aiming at such organisation of our forces, as will make us able to do more work with fewer foreign missionaries. I think I may eventually attain to one superintendent and two assistant foreign missionaries in a

province, with qualified (Chinese) helpers in each important city, and colporteurs in the less important places. I hope I may be able ere the year closes to commence a college for the more thorough training of our native helpers. Long desired, there is more probability of our attaining this than heretofore.

> [In June he added] Pioneers are trying in several parts of (Anhui) to establish themselves ... The path of patient perseverance in well-doing, of voluntary taking up of the Cross, of forbearance under annoyance, and even persecution, without attempted retaliation is a difficult one; none perfectly pursue it; those whose work involves much of it need our special prayers.
>
> [And in July, 1873, in a statement of classic significance in the strategy of mission] The work ... is steadily growing and spreading—especially in that most important department, *native* help. The helpers themselves need much help, much care and instruction; but they are growing more and more efficient as well as more numerous; and the future hope of China doubtless lies in them. I look on all us foreign missionaries as platform work round a rising building; the sooner it can be dispensed with the better; or rather, the sooner it can be transferred to other places, to serve the same temporary purpose, the better for the work sufficiently forward to dispense with it, and the better for the places yet to be evangelised. As for difficulties and sorrows, their name is legion. Some spring from the nature of the work, some from the nature of the workers. Here Paul and Barnabas cannot see eye to eye; there Peter so acts as to need public rebuke; while elsewhere private exhortation is required.[211]

Hope for China lay in trained Christians, and the missionary scaffolding (not necessarily foreign) being moved elsewhere. This fundamental principle has been repeated, forgotten, and revived again and again in the century since then, until today it is the keystone of missionary strategy.

As early as February, Jennie was telling her parents, 'We want to draw off our strength from the places near the coast with a view to more and more work.' And Hudson Taylor told Richard Hill, 'I do so hope to see some of the destitute provinces evangelised. I long for it by day and pray for it by night. Can He care less for it?'

The most mature Christians were from the longer-established churches in Zhejiang, but the Mandarin-speaking Christians of the Yangzi valley were more recently converted and untaught. His plan was therefore to send a mature Christian, whatever his dialect, with a newer one, to teach and train him while working together.[212] It would be costly, but 'I must ask you . . . and all members of the council to help by believing prayer in the name of Jesus, and we will go forward and trust Him not to fail us.'

To George Müller he could say, 'The work is generally very cheering' and found great pleasure in adding, 'Miss J. McLean, formerly of our Mission, is now working for the Lord here in Shanghai, faithfully . . . looking to Him only for support.' Hudson Taylor had himself contributed to her expenses and would gladly be the channel of donations if George Müller or others wished to help her anonymously. By May Hudson Taylor's notes to Jennie were also about his deployment of Chinese and foreign missionaries. Administration, writing for the *Occasional Paper*, travelling or doctoring, his thoughts were seldom far from this theme.

With John McCarthy's departure to Anqing leaving his family at Zhenjiang, and Mr Tsiu at Wuhu, the development of the 'Yangzi strategy' took a stride forward. To thwart McCarthy when he seemed determined to stay in the property he rented in Anqing, the wily landowner erected another building at the entrance in such a way that access to the Mission house was through a pigsty. With few callers willing to negotiate this obstacle, and with such a landlord, the only course for McCarthy was to move. He found another house and began work. 'McCarthy is about to attempt a great work for God,' Hudson Taylor told Emily, 'greater than he is aware of.' While to Richard Hill he said of the eight prefectures McCarthy hoped to occupy, so far 'he has

2.18 Chinese Christians preaching to a wayside audience (using a visual aid: black for sin; red for the blood of Christ; white for a cleansed heart; gold for eternal glory)

had two (Chinese) pioneers for some time in two of the cities of this province (of Anhui)'.

Mr Tsiu, as one of the most mature and tested members of the team, had a recent convert named Han to train at Wuhu—none other than the proprietor of the inn at which the Meadows family and James Williamson had lived before the Anqing riot. Two others had already been at Huizhou for seven months, and two more were beginning at Guangdezhou, each pair a hundred and more miles apart from the others (see map 2.1: p 2). By June two were added, at Hoyuezhou and Datong, halfway between Anqing and Wuhu, where Mr Tsiu established another bridgehead and Hudson Taylor found him 'surrounded by friendly people'. Tsiu's going from Wuhu left Mr Han and another new Anqing convert to spread the gospel at Wuhu. The seed had taken time to germinate, but when it did George Duncan had been there in Anqing to teach and then baptise them. The churches in Anqing and Wuhu today can look back to these beginnings. McCarthy's work was to visit and encourage all these men, discussing their problems and joining in their work. He himself was a hard worker who gave himself to his task and accomplished it.

Further up the Yangzi beyond Anqing, J. E. Cardwell's ambitious pioneering with Lo Ganfu, the converted soldier, was meeting with both success and opposition. Based at Jiujiang since December 1869 and travelling widely in his 'mission boat' since March 1871, he had visited hundreds of cities, towns and villages and sold thousands of Old and New Testaments, Gospels and Christian books.[213] Between Ningbo and Wenzhou the CIM had nine or ten stations and outstations, but between Jiujiang and the southern city in Rangxi province called Fuzhou, not one outpost of the gospel existed. In September he travelled far to the south of the Poyang Lake and Nanchang, the provincial capital, following the Gan River beyond Ji'an to Wan'an, four hundred miles from Jiujiang, before turning for home again.

With Lo Ganfu and the three other soldiers and two Daoist priests who became Christians through his testimony, Cardwell had a training class of future missionaries. 'It is my heart's desire and daily prayer, that the Lord may send me four or five more such men, so as to form a class of students who shall . . . be fitted to work in the interior . . . Our household now numbers sixteen souls', including three orphan boys whom he was employing someone to teach. Such good letters told also of a Buddhist priest who, on professing to believe, had abandoned his robes and joined the class, but before long proved to be an opium addict out for what he could get! Of seventeen candidates for baptism, seven were soldiers. Forbidden by their mandarin on threat of beheading to attend his teaching, after the first scare they were coming surreptitiously. 'Oh, these officials!' Cardwell wrote. 'When will they cease to be the barriers of all true religious, social, moral, intellectual and political progress?' An anti-Christian riot against the American

Methodist Episcopal Mission twenty-five miles away at Ruichang (Shuichang in the reports) early in 1873, was traced to the local literati, but the Cardwells met with no personal animosity.[214]

Zhejiang had been the nursery of all this growing Church, and continued to provide evangelists, colporteurs, Scripture readers and schoolteachers from its thriving congregations, although the peculiarity of its dialects handicapped the Christians at any distance from their homes. Apart from the American Baptists, and Miles Knowlton in particular, who penetrated the province to the southeast of Ningbo, most other Zhejiang missions still worked on the principle of concentrating on Ningbo, Hangzhou, Shaoxing and a few outstations.[215] Since three other missions had joined him in Shaoxing, John Stevenson was giving more time to the new churches in Sheng Xian and Xinchang in keeping with the CIM's policy to move onwards as others followed them. The Confucian scholar Ning, the 'man of uncommon ability', and his family were being persecuted for their faith and thereby drawing attention to it, so that more conversions resulted. At Taizhou, too, was one of the most progressive churches, keeping William Rudland stretched to seize his opportunities. 'No part of our work gives greater promise at the present time than the country outstations of Taichau,' Hudson Taylor wrote. 'Had we more suitable (Chinese) helpers, their number could be rapidly increased.' At one responsive village a new Christian bought a Buddhist nunnery, threw out its idols and furnished it as a chapel. The fact was widely known and talked about.

Miles Knowlton, looking back over a decade since the end of the Taiping rebellion, reported a fivefold increase in the number of Chinese preachers in the province, from fifteen or twenty to one hundred; and of Christians from four hundred to over fourteen hundred communicants. 'In view of the assertion often made, that the converts are all from the ignorant and un-influential classes, (it should be noted) that over a hundred . . . are literary men; a number of them having literary degrees and several have obtained their degrees since having become Christians.' Knowlton himself, renowned among Chinese for his Confucian excellence of character, baptised sixteen literary men. But his days were numbered. He died of acute dysentery (and his wife and daughter barely survived).[216]

A new phase of the church in China had become discernible—a church becoming strong enough to play the major role in the empire's evangelisation.

2.19 A temple entrance

North or west? (March–August 1873)

When Hudson Taylor told Emily Blatchley in January 1873 about his hopes of making 'a long stride' upcountry, the man he largely set his hopes upon had returned to

Britain with an exhausted wife. Elizabeth Judd, a great spirit in a diminutive body, could not keep pace with her powerful and impatient husband. 'She will never recover while he is in England,' Hudson Taylor dared to say. But after a break of a few months he should be able to return, and Hudson Taylor, was counting on him to take the longest stride. Again it was to Emily rather than the preoccupied secretaries that he explained his plans. With too many irons in the fire and failing to attend to detail, so that Hudson Taylor's accounts with London were becoming impossible to keep, Hill and Soltau could be spared tentative information about immature plans for the future. Emily could be trusted to pray, to comment wisely, and to share her knowledge only with discreet friends. 'Our present thought . . . (when) Judd comes, (is) to send him if possible to pioneer to the west or north in some wholly unoccupied province,' but nothing must come to the ears of the minister at Peking. Even the fact that McCarthy was buying land in Anqing with a view to building must be kept very quiet. 'It is *most important* that this be not made public, as Mr Wade would certainly cause us trouble if he knew it', legal though all the plans were by Chinese and British law.

The two major possibilities for strategic advance were, firstly, northwards up the Grand Canal from Qingjiangpu, across the old bed of the Yellow River and into Henan province and southern Shandong. With this in mind, Hudson Taylor determined to go himself and gain some impressions of that route. Secondly, westwards, beyond Jiujiang to Wuchang and Hankou (now the metropolis of Wuhan), which could form a mission base. Always studying his map, his mind dwelt on the great heartland of Hubei with Henan and Shaanxi to its north, and Hunan to the south, leading on to the southwestern provinces of Guizhou and Yunnan with their aboriginal tribes. Westward beyond Hubei, far up the Yangzi River, was Sichuan, the teeming rice-bowl province bordering Tibet. To go northwards might be limited in scope, but would be

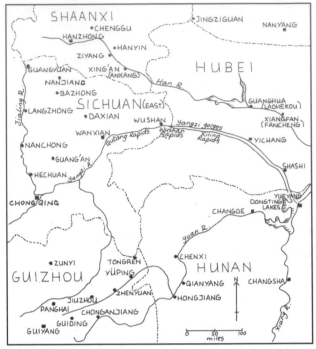

2.20 Key to the west: the upper Yangzi, Han and Yuan rivers

involved in either choice, they must decide for themselves. Judd took his time and had not reached a conclusion when the London Council met on July 27.[217]

Hankou and Wuchang had had missionaries of LMS and Wesleyan Methodist Missionary Society (WMMS) for twelve years already, and of the American Protestant Episcopal Church since 1868. Griffith John of the LMS had been there since 1861 and had baptised 353 adults by 1875. Medical colleagues had joined him for part of this time, and in 1868 Alexander Wylie and Griffith John had made their dangerous journey through Sichuan to Chengdu, north to Hanzhong in Shaanxi and down the Han River to its junction with the Yangzi at Hankou ('mouth of the Han').[218] A great stride for the CIM would be in their wake until new territory was explored and settled work began far beyond Wuhan (see maps 2.1 & 2.20: pp 2 & 204 respectively).

Josiah Cox had been the first Wesleyan to reach Hankou, in 1862 at Griffith John's invitation, and the saintly David Hill and W. Scarborough had arrived in 1865. Scarborough's journey up the Han River to Laohekou (now Guanghua) beyond Xiangfan, was the most ambitious since Griffith John's. In a decade they had baptised a total of 104 adults. Progress was difficult and slow, and there was ample room for more missionaries even in these Wuhan cities, but Hudson Taylor's intention was primarily to use Wuhan as a springboard.

He had other thoughts as well. With Charlie Fishe unready to take up the responsibilities he had relinquished through this long illness, what the Mission in China most needed was an administrator who could set Hudson Taylor free to lead in the fieldwork, the advanced pioneering, evangelism and church planting. He therefore appealed to Henry Soltau to wind up his professional and personal

a natural extension from Yangzhou with communication by canal-boat. To go west, far up the Yangzi, would have the advantage of river-steamers to the base at Wuhan and beyond to the mouth of the Wushan gorges, the gateway of Sichuan. This was the more ambitious choice, the one that said, 'Every province shall be opened to the gospel and at that, soon.'

The claims of the northern option Hudson Taylor set aside for the present. Apart from everything else, it would be more directly under the observation of Wade. To Charles Judd he wrote from Nanjing on March 13, 1873, suggesting that he leave his wife and children to recuperate at home while he returned to China for a year of pioneering in Hunan or Sichuan. Meadows could possibly do it, but with a good command of the Ningbo dialect would be more valuable in Zhejiang.

On May 21 Hudson Taylor wrote again, carefully weighing up the pros and cons on which Judd must base his decision. Even if the whole family came back together, pioneering would involve months of separation from one another. Whether they were prepared for the personal sacrifice commitments at home and to come without delay.

Had I here the co-operation of *one* able, thoroughly reliable, fellow-worker, of faith in God, tact and influence with our missionaries, I should say that in three years' time our work might be doubled in extent and increased manyfold in usefulness. But here I have no one who is sufficiently superior, educationally and mentally and spiritually, to the others to take the position I propose. C. T. Fishe is very nice and gentlemanly, and is superior to any of the others in education, but he has no power in him. McCarthy is by far the most useful of our workers, but I need him in the work, which is his forte, and for the post I propose he is not adapted.

Now, my dear Brother, will you not come out and go into the work with me? There is a sort of lull [in opposition and counter-claims] which is opportune for extending the work into new provinces; we have several converts from provinces which are destitute of missionaries, who may with God's blessing be of great help ... And other things ... lead me to hope that ere long we may be able to take a decided step in advance towards the fufilment of the prayer of some years—the preaching of the gospel in every province of China proper.

Is it not a worthy object, can any sacrifice be too great to hasten its realisation? Is not He whom we serve deserving of all our time, our strength, our powers? If you come you can bring with you others to help in this great work and can exert an influence over many at home, which few could do, as well as one (to) which your position as Hon Sec entitles you to ... China is so large, the work so great and so widespread, that without further help, our onward progress will be greatly retarded.

I do not write in any hasty excitement. I know as much, perhaps, of the difficulty of obtaining what I propose, as most do. I know, too, something of the sacrifice which this step would involve to you. But in view of eternity can we weigh these things? Each of these provinces is as large as an European kingdom. Can we seriously contemplate their populations of 15, 20, 25 millions each, and be willing to leave them to perish?

Two months later he returned to the subject before a reply could have reached him. 'I hope that you and your sister (Henrietta) and Miss Faulding (Nellie) will join us this year.' Again in April he confessed to a strong urge to exhort Soltau to consider the strong case in Scripture for leaving his secular occupations to give his whole time to God's service. Could he not trust the Lord to supply all his needs? 'Our eyes must be upon *the Lord*, not upon His people. His means—not *ours*, not *theirs*, but *His* means are large; and to a faithful steward He will prove a faithful master.'

'I do wish Mr Soltau had faith to cast himself upon God,' Hudson Taylor wrote to Emily. 'I wish you could find time to talk to and pray with him about it.' But Lucy Soltau's and their father's last illnesses preoccupied Henry while the seed-thought germinated, to take dramatic effect a year later. Meanwhile Theodore Howard, a son of Robert Howard, had joined the London Council, taking the chair on January 20, 1873.[219]

On July 18, Hudson Taylor and Jennie set out from Zhenjiang, picked up Groombridge and Donovan at Nanjing, and went on in houseboats up the Yangzi to introduce them to travelling evangelism in China. Calling at each city where Chinese and foreign missionaries of the CIM were based, they visited Mr Tsiu at Datong, and the Chinese holding the fort at Anqing while McCarthy was away. To hold a communion service in the house from which the Meadows family had been ejected in 1869 seemed symbolic of victory against all odds.

Leaving Jennie and Donovan there, Hudson Taylor took Groombridge on to the Cardwells at Jiujiang to put him in the care of an English doctor.[220] His tuberculosis had advanced so alarmingly as to threaten his survival. 'Sometimes I think (he) will not live through the winter,' Hudson Taylor wrote. Before long the poor man resigned, and after a period in Shanghai returned home to die. Both Groombridge and Miss Potter had been passed as fit by the same London doctor, yet now she was not even well enough to go home by ship. When it transpired that Groombridge had followed her to China in order to propose marriage, only to be rejected, a tragic series of mistakes was exposed, which cost much money and effort before they were both back in Britain again. She died in July 1874, and he not long afterwards.

A sidelight is thrown on Hudson Taylor's life by his mention in a letter from Jiujiang that eighty-nine letters were waiting for him there. He dealt with sixty-seven to catch the mail steamer and took the rest on with him, collected Jennie and Donovan at Anqing, returned to Zhenjiang on August 5, and set off the next day for Yangzhou and Qingjiangpu, cheered by the progress he had observed in each place. This time he took Charles Fishe with him, visiting the dried bed of the old Yellow River and preaching to an attentive crowd at Huai'an until his voice failed.[221] Then down to Zhenjiang again only to set off on September 20 for 'the southern stations' of Zhejiang—and two months of 'extreme trial' of the most unexpected nature.

Meanwhile, in London the council was facing another unusual situation. Charles Judd having decided to return to China within a few weeks, though still uncertain about his wife and children, asked that he might take 'a new missionary' with him. No known candidates were ready to go, but Grattan Guinness when consulted answered, Yes, three admirable young men in his training institute had China on their hearts and could be ready in time. They were M. Henry Taylor, Frederick W. Baller and Arthur Wm Douthwaite, the medical student, who was prepared to defer qualifying until after gaining experience in China.

On August 12, Guinness presented each of them for interview, and three days later chaired a subcommittee of the council with Judd present, at which it was decided that Baller, Taylor, Mary Bowyer and the Judds should sail early in September via the United States, to avoid the tropics.

Mrs Grace (who had promised £50 per annum at the Mildmay conference, and had since given Charles Judd £140 for 'a fresh mission station') had then increased it to £300, not knowing of the three men being available. Now she took the Judds' eldest child, Russell, into her own home. Douthwaite was to stay a few months longer and travel with James Meadows. These three were to be among Hudson Taylor's most outstanding pioneers in 'the long stride' to both west and north, Baller as a linguist and sinologue, Henry Taylor as the intrepid spearhead into Henan, and Douthwaite, in company with Hudson Taylor, in Jiangxi and then Shandong, winning the Order of the Double Dragon in the Sino-Japanese war twenty years later (see 1, p 542 & note 735).

'All seems very dark'
(September–November 1873)

While Hudson Taylor was on his Yangzi journey, things were going sadly wrong in the southern area. The timing of his movements was governed by the approaching confinement of Annie Stevenson and of Fanny (Wilson) Jackson. He also needed to have a long talk with the Rudlands. After a spell of success at Taizhou, what looked like spiritual pride had overcome them. He 'is getting very up-ish and conceited . . . Printing his papers and letters (in the *Occasional*) is not doing him any good'—until a surge of threatening behaviour by the anti-foreign, anti-Christian factions in the city had so scared Rudland that in panic he changed into foreign dress to awe them. That garb meant the power of consuls and gunboats behind him, and the threat of reprisals if they should go too far—as if trust in God was a fair-weather safeguard. His Chinese colleagues were dismayed. But worse was to come. Mary Rudland thought she saw one of the younger Chinese missionaries kissing the evangelist's wife. So Mary spoke out. Both men left, insulted, as two others had done previously, and in shame William Rudland wrote offering to resign from the Mission.

Little did Hudson Taylor realise that this was only the prelude to what he already felt was his worst experience 'since Nicol's time'. It had hardly begun. Groombridge had been Nicol all over again in his attitude to Chinese dress, and Edward Fishe was talking of leaving the CIM to join the Robert Whites as an independent missionary. If he did, it would be at the price of separation from his wife, staunchly loyal to Hudson Taylor. 'For myself I shall be far from sorry to lose him,' Hudson Taylor confided to Emily. 'I am pained that (after) long and confidential conversations with him . . . he should have (bought) land to build on, and never breathed a hint of it to me. If (Rudland) leaves in a bad spirit, heaping up all the troubles . . . since and in Nicol's time, he may cause much sorrow.' And poor McCarthy; his wife wanted to give up and go home. 'Now what do all these things indicate? I think, that Satan sees the spreading of the work, dreads it, and is making a strong effort to uproot it. But he will fail. The Lord who is with us, is stronger than he.'

More bad news of Emily's condition had come in several letters. Because of it the Taylor children had been taken to their grandparents, young Tom Jones had at last left Pyrland Road—a welcome guest for his mother's sake, but an intolerable burden for Emily—and Henrietta Soltau, freed from nursing at home, had come to look after Emily. Someone must do Emily's work, so Hudson Taylor wrote asking Henry Soltau and Henrietta to give themselves to it for a year. As the news became worse and worse—Emily on a water-bed, everyone so kind, Emily 'fading', Emily's condition 'precarious', 'I fear, going home', dying—Hudson Taylor felt badly shaken. What could they do from a distance? Could his parents take over her work? 'There is no one able to do the work she has been doing,' he wrote. 'If this work is left undone all my work for all these years may come to nought.' Much as he loved Jennie, he loved Emily too. On the anniversary of Maria's death, July 23, he had written to her, 'I thought that writing to you would be a comfort to me . . . What a happy, happy three years these have been to (Maria).'

With an aching heart he could do nothing more than pray.

Anxieties close at hand demanded no less attention. Passing through Hangzhou, Hudson Taylor learned that students in the city were planning to pull down one of another mission's buildings. 'We need to be very careful.' But Wang Lac-djün's wife was dangerously ill, so while Jennie stayed to nurse her dear friend, Hudson pressed on to Shaoxing to cope with an emergency in Anne Stevenson's pregnancy, three weeks from 'term'. Details are not given, but a placenta praevia seems likely, potentially a matter of life and death to mother and child. While he was there, letters came from Jackson and Rudland reporting that Fanny Jackson had had a spate of fifteen fits at half-hourly intervals. Black in the face, she seemed likely to die each time. But the letter had been two weeks on the way.

If Fanny was still living, her eclampsia was likely to be fatal, but all Hudson Taylor could do was to send Charles Fishe to Taizhou with medicines, telling Jennie to come by fast canal-boat as soon as she could leave Mrs Wang. 'You need not fear being alone for one night' on the way! She reached him on October 4 (in time for her thirtieth birthday)[222] and Anne's baby was born on the 10th. For twenty-four hours Anne seemed unlikely to live, but pulled through. Waiting another day or two until it was safe to leave, the Taylors travelled by fast footboat, raft and then mountain chair, and were at Taizhou on the 15th. On a little scrap of paper (preserved by his mother) he said that Fanny Jackson had given birth to a stillborn child after her convulsions and was recovering, but swollen with oedema and 'water in the chest' as she was, it had been touch and go.

> I feel almost overwhelmed. I have scarcely time to write even a line, I have to think over so many matters, and am so filled with sorrow about dear Miss Blatchley's illness. For the Mission's sake the house at Pyrland Road must be kept on, at least for the present. I don't want the boys to miss getting into the City of London School ... I hope either Mrs Duncan or Miss H. E. Soltau will care for the housekeeping and

dear Miss Blatchley and the children for the present ... Could you not edit the O.P. for us?

How in these circumstances could he himself also produce another issue of the *Occasional*? It was expected of him and he did his best. But the immediate pressure came from a letter announcing the imminent arrival of the Judds' party at Shanghai, with no time to make arrangements to receive them. He would have to go himself. In an agitated letter to Richard Hill, he wrote, 'I cannot possibly meet the party . . . as requested . . . I question whether any circumstances can render it advisable to send a party without giving us a month's more warning . . . Men get dissatisfied and put out before they begin their work if, like Groombridge and Donovan, there is apparent neglect in arrangements for them on arrival.'

Morale was low among the disillusioned Taizhou church members as well as their missionaries. If their teachers failed to live up to their teaching, what hope was there for Christians newly out of a pagan environment? 'The presence of heathenism is very deadening to the soul; and when their hope and zeal run down, we cannot wonder if the (Chinese) do so too.' So Jennie agreed to stay while Hudson made a dash for the Ningbo coaster and by fast walking interspersed with stretches in a mountain chair, arrived in time. On the way he had called in at Ninghai and found another case of sub-Christian living like that at Taizhou. George Crombie had been undermining Jackson's loyalty to their leader again, and his Chinese colleagues were asking for higher 'wages'—as if they were employed to preach the gospel! 'Oh for a baptism of the Holy Ghost . . . the only remedy for our troubles,' Hudson Taylor wrote to Jennie.

Sitting in the mountain chair somewhere between Taizhou and Ningbo, he scribbled another line to his mother. He had stopped a postal courier carrying mail addressed to him in Taizhou, and took delivery there and then. Emily had been to stay with the young Radstocks at Richmond, but was no

better when she returned to Pyrland Road. 'No words can express my sorrow over what I fear will be the end of this attack,' he told his mother. 'It is selfish to sorrow so, for what will be infinite gain for (her). But "Jesus wept" . . . and can sympathise still.' He had thought Emily's tuberculosis 'so far quiescent' that she would live until he and Jennie could get home again and look after her as she had tended his dying Grace. So it was good to know that Joseph Weatherley was getting the boys into the City of London School, and Catherine Duncan was nursing Emily. But he and Jennie were so far away and 'all seems very dark'.

From Ningbo on November 21 he dashed off another line to Jennie, enclosing a cable received from Catherine, dated October 21. 'Emily not expected to live many weeks. She would like you to come. It greatly perplexed and distressed me. But I do not see any reason for going home which we had not before.' If from the secretaries, or if more strongly worded than 'like' it would be different. Judging by the letters received, it was already too late to see her alive, but he could make a quick journey, separate Emily's possessions from his family's, arrange for his children to be cared for together, sort out business problems with the secretaries, and press Mrs Faulding for Nellie's release.

But he was needed in China no less. 'There is nothing feasible and right which

2.21 One kind of mountain chair for short journeys

I would not gladly do for our precious Ae-me—the debt I owe her I can never repay . . . As dear Ae-me says, we must trust (the Lord) implicitly.'

He was thinking of having a permanent Mission agent in Shanghai, with Lanfeng and his wife and the printing press, to handle shipping, postal matters and purchases. Edward Fishe could do that better than church work. It was all put into action in December—the CIM's first business department in Shanghai, an institution which under the management of others was to become renowned through the decades for its scope and efficiency.

When Hudson Taylor next wrote he was in Shanghai in a room with four bedsteads, two chairs and a little table, waiting cheerfully for word of the Judd party's arrival.

They arrived the next day, November 5, a day never to be forgotten by Fred Baller, a born raconteur, on whose fourteen-page reminiscences of their meeting this account depends. A thoroughly Chinese figure, 'the oddest figure I have ever seen', greeted them on landing and invited Baller and Henry Taylor back to his 'hotel' while the Judds and Mary Bowyer went to a friend's home. They found Hudson Taylor such a light-hearted, humorous and saintly person that they had no inkling of what he was going through. While they were with him he wrote again to Emily, 'I have seen very little of the Judds and Mary Bowyer yet, and indeed my heart is so filled with sorrow that I can see nothing . . . I know that He will not forsake me nor leave you.' And to his mother soon afterwards, 'He can spare her and hasten our return . . . if not, we must bow to His blessed will. The words "God my exceeding joy" have been so constantly on my heart lately. He is making me in this heart-breaking trial, to rejoice in Himself, "with joy unspeakable and full of glory". The most painful part of it, perhaps . . . to me and to dear Jennie is (Emily's) desire to see us once more, to resign her charge [the children and Mission matters] into our own hands.'

He launched Baller and Henry Taylor straight into Chinese ways of living, eating, washing and dressing, and took them to Nanjing on November 7. To give time to talk and get to know them, he devoted himself exclusively to them over a period of ten days, introducing them to intensive preaching in the street chapel, before returning alone to Shanghai. 'He stamped us at once . . . with his own stamp.'

> The thing that impressed me [Baller wrote] was that Mr Taylor knew how to make a bargain ... Since then I have often been with him when he has been hiring boats, making contracts, buying land or houses. The Chinese were always loud in his praises on these occasions ... because of the ability with which he conducted the transaction ... He was never in a hurry. He would calmly and deliberately raise points, or go into those raised by the other party ... This lack of hurry was a great power. The average foreigner makes a beeline between the two nearest points, but the Chinese goes round the circle instead of along the diameter. And there can be no doubt that the business capacity Mr Taylor possessed saved the Mission large sums of money ... His abilities would easily have placed him in the front rank had he taken up any line of business.[223]

The respect was mutual. Two real 'MEN' had joined him, and more were soon to follow. He was on the verge of a new era of the Mission, and of China.

Back in Shanghai, he was again in harness. A local resident, David Cranston of the Shanghai and Putong Foundry and Engineering Company, met Hudson Taylor at Jane McLean's house, and wrote a few days later, 'You shall ever be a favourite of mine . . . I should like to sit at your feet and hear all you have learned of the riches that are in Christ Jesus.' The heartaches of life had not silenced him, but were still heavy to bear.

The reasons for staying in China were greater than for going home to Britain, Jennie assured him from Taizhou, far enough from pressures to think dispassionately. She had been trying to exert a good influence (she said), working hard at visiting homes in the city. 'Numbers that I went to came on Sunday.' The chapel was crowded, with some standing. 'Miss Happiness' (see 1, p 744) had been thinking and had a message for Hudson when he needed it. 'It's unbelief that saps our strength and makes everything look dark; and yet He reigns and we are one with Him and He is making everything happen for the very best, and so we ought always to rejoice in Him and rest though it isn't always easy.' She was the right wife for him.

Back in Ningbo again Hudson Taylor was 'so weary' of being separated from her. As for Emily, what could he do? He made a brave attempt to write to her about the cablegram—Emily who might not be alive to read his letter—dating it November 24, 1874, by mistake. 'Dear Ae-me! . . . He has placed me here, you there. For the time being He has separated us . . . I feel bewildered, dear, precious sister . . . I think of how you nursed me in the (guest hall) at Yangchou . . . Of your care of Gracie and Samuel and their sainted mamma—who seems to die again in you, to leave again my precious children bereaved, and me so, so far away. I do pray, "Lord, what wilt Thou have me to do?"'

But Anne Stevenson needed his help again, so he went next to Shaoxing and on to Hangzhou for a Sunday with Wang Lae-djün and the New Lane church before travelling through Sheng Xian, explicitly to meet the scholar Ning and his family. John Stevenson was there. The deep scarring of his face by smallpox was regarded by pagan Chinese as an asset, a sign of death-defying good luck. As Hudson Taylor later recounted in the *Occasional Paper*, at a fellowship meal in the chapel he (Taylor) told the Christians how, on his first overland journey from Taizhou in 1867, he had climbed the hill of their city god 'and saw the whole city at my feet . . . and after preaching to the people (at the temple) till I could do so no longer, I went higher up on the hill, and all alone . . . entreated (the Lord) to have mercy on them and to open the door for the gospel . . . I could have wept with joy to hear the record of what (His) grace had done for one and another.'

Wanted, workers who WORK!
(October–December 1873)

When Hudson Taylor at last reached Taizhou, impatient to be with Jennie again, she had gone. 'Imagine my dismay,' even before reaching the house to learn 'that you had left this morning'—for Ninghai escorted by Rudland. 'I have been kissing you, darling, in mind all last night, nearly, and all today.' Jennie had been as excited, imagining because she had not heard from him for several days that he was ill, alone and needing her. So she had gone to find him. He caught up with her at Ninghai, and they went on to stay overnight with Feng Nenggui at his outstation.

At long last, after Hudson Taylor had been travelling almost incessantly since the beginning of the Yangzi journey on July 17, they reached Fenghua on December 13. Looking back he called it not five months but seven weeks of travelling—reckoning from the day he left Jennie at Taizhou and overlooking their forced marches from the Stevensons to save Fanny Jackson's life, let alone from Zhenjiang to Shaoxing before that. The Fenghua mission house was empty. James Williamson had gone home to Scotland on the verge of a nervous breakdown. But in the time he had been at Fenghua the church had thrived.

This was their chance to work with the church while writing issue No 36 of the *Occasional Paper*, his first opportunity since sending No 35 off in September. In the summer he had hit upon a good source of material, asking Stott, Crombie, Stevenson and others to write year by year reports of the start and progress of their own work, while he himself wrote ten portraits of the Mission's Chinese colleagues. Each issue therefore answered the questions in the minds of friends at home in Britain who looked for evidence of their support being justified. As soon as the *Occasional* was posted, they would go by sea to Wenzhou for their long-deferred visit to George and Grace Stott. So they thought. Before the time came they were off on two more hectic forced marches to save the lives of colleagues.

For the present they were alone together, for the first time since their marriage two years ago, and for Christmas. On Christmas Eve William Rudland sent them the love of the two Taizhou families, his own and the Jackson's. 'Tell (Jennie) that . . . we *are* enjoying rest in (the Lord). My work though hard is a *pleasure,* not task-work, and God does help me to do more than I could before. May God make her as great a blessing to others as He has done to us.' The change from what she had found at Taizhou on first arriving there was profound.

For months, Hudson Taylor had been mulling over the need of colleagues who could be counted on to keep up their standards and drive on at their work, whatever their circumstances. Men and women like the Stotts, McCarthy, John Stevenson and the Judds were the right kind because they were examples to Chinese Christians and to younger missionaries. In praising Emily to his mother in 1870 he had said, 'Though there are others willing to help, some lack ability, others reliability.' It was true of church work, too. In March he had reminded Henry Soltau, concerned with the assessment of candidates, that it was better to weed out the weak ones before they left home than to discover their failings in China.

> The nature of our work here needs to be remembered. It is very trying to the temper and to patience. One must be willing to sow in faith, to work maybe for years ere the fruit appears. Persons who cannot wait are not suited for China. It might sometimes be a test of the earnestness and patience and ability of candidates to suggest a line of self-improving study for six months or a year, with a view to their ultimate efficiency. Many would never be heard of again, but those who were, would be more likely to prove men of the right stamp. Another important thing in missionaries is tact and power of adaptation ... Young men accustomed to please customers in a shop will often be able to adapt themselves to their audiences here better than work-people who are of a rougher mould. And the latter ... do not value direction and are often impertinent to (Chinese) authorities to the great detriment of the work ... New workers should come out on probation ... and are not at liberty to marry for the first two years.

The council in London had worked this out with him in October before he left: 'That candidates should go out on probation for two years, as missionary students, but that no one should be sent out who would not consent to remain for three years in the service of the Mission[224].' On the subject of marriage, Hudson Taylor wrote on December 8, 1873, that 'newly married missionaries lost the first twelve months' through preoccupation with wife and home. In fact, finding themselves in a new environment as part of the socially mixed missionary community did strange things to some, especially if they had more money under their control than they had had before. 'Two out of three men are very different in thought about themselves twelve months after leaving England, from what they were twelve months before,' he told John Challice. Adaptation must start before they were uprooted from the homeland, and certainly on the voyage out. To begin with luxury travel was bad for them. Even third-class conditions could spoil a man or woman.

> If two or three kinds of meat, two or three of vegetables, soup, bread and potatoes *ad lib* and one pint of wine per meal are not enough; or if the privation of a few weeks' loss of privacy, and separation in the case of husbands and wives, who must sleep in separate state rooms, is too appalling, this is such positive luxury and comfort compared with what will be found here, that such persons would do well to stay at home. The only persons wanted here are those who will *rejoice* to work—really to labour—not to dream their lives away; to *deny* themselves; to suffer in order to save. Of such men and women there is room for any number and God *will* support any number—they are His jewels and He values and cares for them.

In October, Richard Hill wrote asking what the council should do about women wishing to join the Mission. 'There are two or three apparently suitable ones who have offered themselves; but none of us seems quite to know your mind about it.' This was the legacy of a change of secretaries without sufficient overlap in office. William Berger had known Hudson Taylor's mind on the subject, and Emily could have told them if they would accept it from her. Back in 1867, Hudson Taylor had asked Berger not to send any more women until there were couples or experienced single women with whom they could live. Since then, no couples in the southern area had been willing or proved suitable to have them, and of the suitable experienced single missionaries, Jennie had married and Mary Bowyer had gone home with the Judds. Hudson Taylor and Jennie had come back with Emmeline Turner, who was shaping well, and with Miss Potter. Only her breakdown in health was forcing her home as soon as fit enough to travel. Louise Desgraz' gifts were of a different nature, though 'but for her the Chinese Christians (of Zhenjiang) would have given up . . . in despair' during their year of neglect under the Fishe brothers. And Catherine Duncan had proved her worth even when handicapped by an unhappy marriage. With the Judds and Mary Bowyer back in China again and Catherine Duncan expected before very long, Hudson Taylor hoped (as always) that more women could come. 'If there are one or two suitable female candidates, who could harmonise with Mrs Duncan, live with her, and work under her, by all means send them if you can. The great difficulty . . . is to find them suitable homes.'

Never had he wished to restrict the part women, married or single, should play. Convinced in 1850 by the rightness of Charles Gutzlaff's principle (see 1, p 146), and confirmed in his belief by the effectiveness of Mrs Lord, Mrs Bausum, Mary Jones, Mary Gough and Maria among Ningbo women the record of the last few years provided absolute proof. Jennie had needed no teaching. From the day of her leaving Shanghai for 'the interior' she had loved to sit and talk with Chinese women and children. Mary Bowyer had quickly followed suit. Not only was the church in Hangzhou a living tribute to their influence; the friendly attitude of the city towards foreigners with a right regard for the Chinese bore witness to their attitude as much as to Hudson Taylor's and McCarthy's. Catherine Duncan had imbibed the same spirit and would show others how to emulate it. Already they could say 'Emmeline Turner gives promise of making a valuable missionary. She has thrown herself heart and soul into the work.' Given people like them, the more women the better. His conviction that they would play a powerful part in the evangelisation of China had never wavered. Now it was stronger than ever.

'Our hearts sing for joy'
(December 1873)

Some miscellaneous notes left by Hudson Taylor include this statement, 'During the latter part of November, December and the first part of January, I asked the Lord to make it specially clear whether He would have us prepare to work in some of the new provinces or not, and also whether we should seek to occupy more stations in (Zhejiang). My mind was assured that we ought to do both.' Tangible confirmation was being given at the same time. On December 5, 1873, Mrs Grace, wrote to Richard Hill saying she was arranging for £800 to be paid to the China Inland Mission in addition to the £300 already contributed for its advance into more provinces. This was enough to give Hudson Taylor confidence that he was not mistaken in his understanding of God's will, and his prayers were being answered. In reporting this development on the 10th, Hill added that James Meadows would be leaving early in January with A. W. Douthwaite, the third of Grattan Guinness's young men. From her Fenghua working 'honeymoon' Jennie wrote to her father on Christmas Day to say that she and Hudson had decided to put the whole of the principal and interest of her uncle's legacy in the care of trustees, to be used at her direction for the work of

God, not only in China. None was to be for personal use, except sometimes to pay for their passages between China and Britain. Her father had exhorted her to think very carefully about how she used the money, and she assured him that over a period of months she had become certain of her duty, 'and I am sure you would be the first to say—Then, do it.'

> We have not used a farthing of Uncle's money for ourselves from the first, and decided not to do so, and my thought has been ... that we should go on looking to God for our own support as before ... We have already been looking to God for support for years, and if we were to use this money for ourselves, we should have to give up taking what He sent us and live on our interest. This we do not think well for two reasons. 1st. We should lose the influence on others of our example; we are asking the members of the Mission to look to God without any definite income, and we wish for their sakes to do the same ourselves. 2nd. I could not expect God's blessing if I let work for eternity be left undone, because I withheld the money when I had it ... No, it is safer to trust in God than in 'uncertain riches' ... 'for where your treasure is there will your heart be also'.

When a copy of Mrs Grace's letter reached China with its insistence 'Remember! FRESH provinces', Hudson Taylor wrote, 'It caused our hearts to sing for joy.' And now like Paul, 'assuredly gathering that the Lord had called us to preach the gospel to the regions beyond', the word was given for Judd to make the long stride to Wuchang. But four prefectures and forty-eight county cities of Zhejiang province still had no known Christians or preachers of the gospel in them. Zhejiang must see advance as well.

1874–75: TORN IN TWO

'A disturbed year for China' (1874)

The Tong Zhi emperor's attainment of his majority and the sumptuous celebrations associated with his wedding had meant a heavy drain on the empire's coffers. No official or eunuch of the court or state government was content without his share. When Prince Kong tried to limit the profiteering by high ministers preparing palaces for the empresses Ci Xi and Ci An on their retirement from the regency, he was even punished by degradation in rank for one day.

The long campaign against the Muslims of the far north-west continued to deplete the empire's wealth, led by Zuo Zongtang (Tso Tsung-t'ang). Even though 'he halted his army, sowed and harvested a crop of grain, and then continued his advance', the costs of an expedition far up the 'panhandle' of Gansu and across Turkestan (now Xinjiang, the New Dominion) were immense (see map 2.1: p 2).

The government's blunder into confrontation with Japan (see p 163) quickly led to a change of direction. A collision between Japanese and Chinese forces could embroil the western nations or greatly embarrass them in their professed friendship with both nations. Sir Harry Parkes in Yedo (Tokyo) and T. F. Wade in Peking did their best to resolve the situation. Robert Hart from his privileged watch-tower chuckled to observe that *fengshui* no longer stood in the way when Li Hanzhang, Li Hongzhang's brother, and Chinese forces in Fujian, opposite Taiwan, needed telegraphy in their emergency. But Wade had an inspiration. Sensing that both governments were looking for a way out, though ignorant of the fact that the Japanese negotiator had come to Peking prepared to reach 'a settlement on almost any terms', Wade devised a formula to save face on both sides. Japan was recognised as justified in avenging the death of Ryukyuan sailors at the hands of Taiwan tribesmen, and withdrew her expeditionary force on payment of an indemnity explained as compensation for the victims' families and payment for roads and buildings constructed by the Japanese.

'Unstinted praise' rewarded Wade. But in accepting this way out, China had

CRUCIBLE OF FAITH   213

to surrender her tributary dependency of the Ryukyu Islands at a time when Britain was annexing Burma, by stages, France was taking Annam, and Japan had her eyes firmly on Korea. Hanoi had been occupied on November 20, 1873, and a Franco-Annamese treaty of alliance was signed in Saigon on March 15, 1874. Alexander Michie characteristically observed that 'the transaction really sealed the fate of China, in advertising to the world that here was a rich empire which was ready to pay, but not ready to fight'.[225]

A bone of contention existed between China and the foreign powers in the existence of a tidal bar of silt where the Huangpu River flowed into the Yangzi near Wusong. In 1874, only thirty years since Captain George Balfour, the first British consul, began turning empty mud flats into a commercial foothold on the mainland (see 1, pp 117ff), Shanghai was handling sixty per cent of all foreign trade with China. For two years, demands that the bar be dredged had been rebuffed by Peking. As Hart told his Tianjin commissioner, 'the question of the Woosung Bar . . . may develop into a *casus* of something very like *belli*'.

Ever since the French concession at Shanghai had been extended in 1863 to include the north gate suburb of the Chinese city, in which Hudson Taylor had experienced his earliest adventures (see 1, pp 259ff and map 1.12: p 164), plans had been made public to move the cemetery of Ningbo residents to another site, to make way for new roads. No objections had been made, but when action was due to begin a riot erupted on Sunday, May 3, 1874. Foreign houses were fired, beginning with the French surveyor's, a score of foreigners and Chinese were injured and seven Chinese rioters were killed when the fire brigade, two hundred men of the Volunteer Defence Corps and one hundred American and French naval ratings helped the *daotai's* troops to restore order. James Meadows and A. W. Douthwaite had arrived from Britain two days earlier and were staying with Edward Fishe at the new premises

in Hongkou (Hongkew). On the way to a meeting in the home of a Mrs Jenkins in the French settlement, Douthwaite and Fishe realised that trouble was afoot and arrived to find American naval casualties having their wounds dressed in Mrs Jenkins's house.[226]

(The rioters) had attacked Miss (Jane) McLean and utterly destroyed her house and furniture [Douthwaite wrote]. She ran into the garden but was knocked down and dragged along by the hair. Mr Weir and a friend named Cranston came upon the scene at this juncture and ran to her assistance. Mr Cranston was knocked down and his head beaten with a stool. They left him for dead (but) a man whom he used to employ picked him up and carried him inside. He soon recovered a little and then tried to walk away. When the rioters saw that he was still alive they rushed at him again and would have killed him but for the man who had befriended him. He begged them to desist, saying that he knew him to be a good man and no Frenchman, so they left him and he was taken to hospital. Mr Weir also received some severe cuts and bruises about the head and arms. Miss McLean got away into the street but was knocked down several times and would certainly have been killed but for some of the Chinese who protected her by pushing her into a teashop and forming a circle round her. They called to the mob that she was not French but was a good woman who kept a school. When she had so far recovered herself as to be able to speak she called out in the Chinese language that she was an English woman. That satisfied them and they went away. By the time I got there her house had entirely disappeared. She bore the ill-treatment she had received in a lovely, joyous, Christ-like manner and refused to put in a claim against the Chinese for damages ...

[Years later Douthwaite commented] My first year was filled with a succession of riots in one of which I lost most of my possessions and narrowly escaped losing my life also.

The grievances of the Chinese were recognised as just, and the French undertook to leave the cemetery undisturbed for all time and kept their promise until two years before the Boxer uprising of 1900. Samuel Wells Williams, who was American chargé d'affaires in Peking in 1874, reported to Washington that all Chinese could be expected to sympathise with those whose ancestral graves were to be violated and to condone their riotous action. Three more riots were to follow in other cities.

The sick and the dying
(January–April 1874)

The events of early 1874 present a picture of the Taylors' hectic life. The Edward Fishes' first child had died in infancy in 1873, and the unvaccinated second child died of smallpox soon after they moved to Shanghai. The toll continued. Some parents wished to send their children home as the Taylors had done, and during his working 'honeymoon' with Jennie at Fenghua, Hudson Taylor was weighing up whom to ask to escort them. He needed an efficient, balanced member of the Mission in London to take over Emily Blatchley's work and responsibility for his own children who were 'like orphans'. Louise Desgraz was ideal. He asked her to meet him in Shanghai and was about to go there on Friday, January 2, when an urgent message came from the Crombies at Ninghai, thirty miles away. Both children were very ill and one apparently dying. Sending Jennie to the Goughs at Ningbo, he 'came at once—no easy journey in the snow.' Persuading the officer on guard to open the city gate to him after dark, he was with the Crombies by midnight. One child was 'in a very precarious state' with whooping cough and the other little better.

On January 7 Hudson Taylor wrote to Jennie that he hoped to be able to leave the Crombies by Monday, 12th, and be in Ningbo on Tuesday. But his note crossed one from her. Fanny Jackson had joined her in Ningbo, she said, and in the night had had convulsions and been semiconscious for two or three hours. Dr John Parker had been sent for. Hudson Taylor came at once, reaching Ningbo on Saturday, January 10.

Annie Stevenson was said to be still very ill at Shaoxing but, Hudson Taylor wrote, 'An hour before my arrival (at Ningbo) an express messenger had arrived from (Taizhou),' saying that William Rudland had smallpox, and two of the children had not been vaccinated. Louise had come on from Shanghai and agreed to escort 'poor Miss Potter' and two or three children to London, and to mother them and the Taylor children at Pyrland Road, but Jennie and he waited only for the carriers to arrive from Ninghai with his medicines and set off for Fenghua again, on the way to Taizhou.

Together they wound up the Mission business they had been working on, and she returned the thirty miles to Ningbo while he continued southwards. [Drawing on two letters,]:

> I went on in (the dark), the wind and rain (and snow), and reached [the Crombies at] Ninghai this afternoon, leaving again with a new sedan and fresh coolies. We have made 30 li [10 miles], (20 li in the dark), and are waiting while rice is cooked, and then go on again. I have promised to walk 20 li if they will go on 20 more ... this will still leave us 110 li tomorrow, a long walk with a heavy burden and some high hills as steep as stairs in some places ... May God help poor Mrs Rudland in her trouble, and if it be His will spare her husband and children ... [Reaching an inn between midnight and 1 a.m. he and the bearers had slept and set off again at 7 a.m. to cover the last 40 miles by 7 p.m.] Well! The Lord reigns, and my heart does rejoice in Him. Sadness cannot rob us of this unchanging source of joy and strength.

Jennie was in Shanghai by Wednesday, 14th, arranging for Miss Potter's journey, when Hudson Taylor was writing to her from Taizhou on the same day, 'Rudland, wife and three children have all had smallpox and are nearly all well again.' He himself had been using his time in Taizhou arranging a long lease for the Mission premises and preaching in the countryside.

With the Rudlands out of danger, his problem was how to shake off the contamination of his own clothing and possessions before going among other fellow-missionaries again, yet he did not seem to be aware that even his letter could carry the infection. Being about eighty miles from Wenzhou, he wanted to visit the Stotts but once again had to disappoint them. Because no Chinese in contact with smallpox considered it necessary to restrict their movements, he felt he would be justified in travelling on the open road for four days to Jinhua (see map 2.2: 2, p 6) and from there by river to 'Guy-tsiu' (ie Ch'ii-chou, now Qü Xian) and Lanxi before going down the Qiantang River to visit Hangzhou and Annie Stevenson at Shaoxing again. He ended his letter by asking Jennie to find suitable wives (in the Ningbo schools) for three Christians at Taizhou.

On Sunday, January 18, he was in the temple which had been converted into a chapel, exposed to a cold wind and uncertain whether Emily would be alive to read what he was writing. He could not see how he could leave China within a few months, and wrote to her, 'The Lord says stay, and I cannot, would not if I could, reverse it.' Jennie told Emily, 'I dream so, so often that your wish has been granted and that we are with you.' When love and duty appeared to conflict, duty came first in the will of God.

But by January 26 Hudson Taylor was in Taizhou again for a few days and writing to Richard Hill. Louise Desgraz would not need any Mission funds for her personal support while in Britain as he would be personally responsible for her.

> You will find her somewhat reserved in manner, and at first sight might fail to duly estimate her sterling worth. For humility, fidelity, truth and conscientiousness, for perseverance in spite of difficulties and discouragements, few equal her. Our work in (Zhenjiang) owed its continued existence to her, and her alone ... But for her, the Christians would have given up in despair.

The Rudlands, Stevensons and McCarthys 'cannot be expected long to hold out

2.22 The granite-flagged 'main road' through a hillside village

without (home leave); and if they did, their families could not'.

He had written to Jennie that the Rudlands were all right and he must change his plans, travelling to Ningbo, Hangzhou and Shanghai to see Louise off to Europe. Two nights later all had changed again. His mountain-chair had come and he was ready to go, when Rudland in distress said that Mary and two of the children had a high fever again. The baby now had unmistakable smallpox. If by the 30th he could not leave, he would send bearers for Jennie. He could not and by then he himself was not well, so he wrote again. 'My anxieties about (Grace Rudland) are far from diminished . . . Come as soon as you can', and he detailed his arrangements for fresh carriers to be at each stage of the one hundred and fifty mile overland journey, and Christians to meet her at some points. 'Little Gracie, now my only anxiety, will be at the height on Saturday night or Sunday.'

Jennie went, and the child survived, but Hudson Taylor himself was ill, so, as soon as they could, they set off for their haven of Fenghua again, hoping to recover and spend a Sunday teaching the Christians at the temple-chapel. Instead, on the way he was unfit to travel or even to leave his bed in 'a very large house more like a barn inhabited by a good many families'. The villagers 'came crowding in to see us,' Jennie wrote. In a large room, a space had been partitioned off on three sides by bamboo matting, but there was no privacy except after dark, because all the children kept peeping through the cracks. 'On Monday morning I made H.'s (mountain chair) as much like a bed as possible and on we went . . . The road was very rough, and we crossed a high series of hills . . . There was so much climbing . . . that the men . . . begged us to stop, an hour before dark.' The rest of the letter is missing.

From February 8 to 20 Hudson Taylor had a nightly fever, and on March 3 was in bed at the garret at Bridge Street, Ningbo, expecting to travel all the way to Hangzhou by boat, because a bed could be made up in it for him. Ten days later he was 'slowly recovering'. 'A severe attack of remittent fever' was his description to George Müller. They were heading for Shanghai, this time to meet the Meadows family and Douthwaite, but without information as to when they would arrive. Then, he hoped, back to Wenzhou at last, and Taizhou again. But on March 30 he was still in bed, seemingly unable to shake off his fever.

They reached Shanghai on April 7 to find a financial crisis on their hands, with Mrs Stevenson's condition such as to need an early return to Britain, but no funds for passages. 'Precious Ae-me,' he wrote to Emily, 'you know I should come if I could', but with funds so low, so many needing his help and such promise of advance to promote into action, 'my way is not open.'

They went up to Zhenjiang to confer with Judd about the advance he was to lead. The Mission houses in the city and suburb were crowded with all who could be there for a day of fasting and prayer on April 14, before the question was settled, to advance north or west? The Whites had packed up and gone home, but Donovan, Baller, Henry Taylor, McCarthy, the Judds and Mary Bowyer (in charge of the school), Jennie and Hudson Taylor were present, and 'local residents', unnamed. Only the Cardwells of the Yangzi team were absent, with a sick child, when the decision was taken to make the long stride to Wuhan and the far west.

Prayer had also been focused on the financial crisis. On April 10, Hudson Taylor's balance for general purposes had been 67 cents. Yet Annie Stevenson must get away before the tropical summer descended on them. The missionaries present, whose own basic needs had been met by George Müller's remittances, contributed 200 dollars towards the family's fares, and Hudson Taylor 'found' the rest. He wrote on the 24th instructing Richard Hill to send £700 of Mrs Grace's big donation, to be used at once for sending the Judds to Wuhan and leasing premises there. On that day Cardwell came down on the Yangzi steamer with his dying child, too late for anything to be done but to comfort him and bury her beside the growing family of Mission graves, where Maria and her children lay. Only two months later Cardwell had to put his very sick wife and two remaining children on a ship for England. The price in disease and death seemed never-ending.

No 6 Pyrland Road (January–July 1874)

Once Henrietta Soltau's father and sister had both died, she was free to rejoin Catherine Duncan in nursing Emily Blatchley. Faithfully they carried on the Mission's routine business on behalf of the secretaries, and the weekly prayer meetings to which few others came, as well as mothering the Taylor children. As Emily became weaker they nursed her on a 'water-bed', a poignant reminder to Catherine Duncan of George's last days, and to Henrietta of her sorrows in Barnstaple. Mary Berger wrote on February 5 that Emily was 'so calm and patient . . . I believe she enjoys real rest in our blessed Lord'. Emily had come a long way in a few years.

Louise Desgraz sailed from Shanghai the next day, February 6, commissioned to take charge of the children and the Mission office, and when she arrived in March the *Occasional Paper* said no more than that Emily was 'patiently suffering the Lord's will'. She too had developed terminal tuberculous enteritis and was going steadily downhill. 'Mrs Duncan has promised not to leave her as long as she lives,' Jennie's mother wrote, 'but is looking *very* jaded with disturbed nights.' And Mary Berger said, 'They became so attached, I cannot say whose love was the stronger of the two.'

Having children in the house had increased their difficulties immeasurably, especially with two boys of thirteen and twelve of whom Miss Stacey wrote, 'I do not remember ever being acquainted with a boy of such energy as Freddie [Howard Taylor]; it is no easy matter to keep pace with the variety and intelligence of his ceaseless questions.' Inevitably Richard Hill declared that Louise and the children would have to be in another house, which he would find for them nearby. And when Joseph Weatherley entered Herbert and Howard at the City of London School (founded 1442) it was to everyone's advantage. The wisdom of Maria's marriage settlement had come to fruition, leading to Howard acquiring high academic distinction in medicine and surgery before following Herbert (1881) and their sister Maria (1884) as a missionary to China in 1888.

One day in 1873 when Freddie had been sent with a message for Grattan Guinness, the door of Harley House was opened by his eleven-year-old daughter Minnie. They stood looking at each other and neither lost the first impression formed on that occasion. Minnie, Geraldine Guinness, also went to China in 1888, and there they became engaged.

But on April 24, 1874, Hudson Taylor was agonising in Zhenjiang over Emily's sufferings and his sure path of duty. 'My own dear Ae-me,' he wrote, 'you know how dearly I love you, and how I long to see you

(and) the dear children. But I dare not doubt that the Lord is doing the best thing for them and for you.' By July Emily was sinking and Miss Potter had died.

Scraping the barrel (January–July 1874)

So much was happening at once, that a coherent account of this period again demands separation of its elements and more retracing of steps. For the two long years in China after marrying Jennie, Hudson Taylor was having to run the Mission on what looked like barely enough funds for survival, let alone for advance. A strong brake was being applied to his abounding enthusiasm and zeal for expansion. Had he possessed the means, who knows how overstretched his depleted team might have become. From time to time large sums dangled before him the promise of future freedom of action, still out of reach. At the same time tangible, though small, advance payments were giving substance to the dream.

Jennie's legacy from her rich uncle in Australia, Francis Hardy Faulding, was one of these, in all about ten to fifteen thousand pounds (at that time).

> My dear wife is left one of five residuary legatees. There are certain persons having annuities out of the estate. Not till after their death can the whole of what will ultimately be divisible be divided ... In the meantime the executors have commenced paying interest ... She feels the whole is the Lord's, and wishes to use it for Him, and has so used it, and not for private purposes ... The whole cannot be realised: half of it, perhaps, may be twenty, thirty or forty years before it can be realised.

The trust she had formed in London was to handle that part of the bequest already distributed, and interest in small sums had begun to reach her at infrequent intervals. To be able to apply them to her colleagues' needs was in her power, such as for fares to Britain or to replace loss by theft. But through Jennie's mother telling the Bergers and others about the legacy, Jennie and Hudson were receiving more advice than they knew how to accept. They had the impression that this highly personal matter had become a threat to the future support of the Mission. Lest misinformation should lead donors to withdraw their support, the Taylors asked the council to publish a statement of their intentions. Instead the council showed that no such danger yet existed, and at last Jennie and Hudson Taylor were left to do as they had intended.

A case in point had involved none other than William Berger, who since his retirement had sent gifts to the Mission from time to time, unpredictably. Since June 1873 he had ceased sending any to Hudson Taylor personally, explaining that if anyone sent him, Berger, £100 as a gift he would feel obliged to return it, seeing that he had no need of it. He was one who had expressed an opinion on how the legacy should be used. But he sent £200 to Richard Hill in May, and again in July, for the Mission, and told Hudson Taylor that he had named the CIM to receive a small legacy in his will.

The generous gifts from Mrs Grace were strictly for advance into a 'fresh province' and could not be used for other immediate purposes. But, month by month, Hudson Taylor was scraping the barrel of available cash. Where was the previously adequate supply for general purposes? In March he had confided to Emily, trusting her to hint tactfully to Richard Hill or Henry Soltau, that 'nearly eleven months have elapsed since I had any (statement of) accounts'. By the end of March when he wanted to distribute funds to all the stations, he had only £5 and $25 in hand. When he arrived in Shanghai on April 7 hoping to find £500 in cheques from Britain, they totalled £25. On the 10th his note to Jennie said, 'The balance in hand was 67 cents! The Lord reigns; here is our joy and confidence.' The Meadows party was expected daily. It was providential that they did not arrive until May 1. Remittances began to come in, as he told his mother in some detail when he could look back in July and see how events had dovetailed together.

Asking Richard Hill on April 23 whether he and the other members of council could carry on beyond the two years they had agreed to serve, if circumstances in China should delay his return, he wrote, 'I never was happier in the work, or freer from care, tho' I have no funds ... P.S. Let me beg that no appeal be made for funds.' It was as though he feared what they might do, even to making public in the *Occasional Paper* his frank, confidential letters to them.

The very next day he wrote in the same vein to the treasurer, John Challice, a letter which he quoted to his mother, editing it for clarity, so that we may draw upon both.[227] No more than £20 or £25 should be spent on a new missionary's outfit, to guard against 'the great risk of young men being spoiled'. And then:

> I am truly sorry that you should be distressed at not having funds to send to me. May I not say 'Be (anxious) for nothing'? ... We should use all care to economise what God does send us; but I do not think that God would have us bear, ourselves, any care about apparent or real lack. After proving God's faithfulness for many years, I can testify that times of want have ever been times of spiritual blessing, or have led to them.

> I do beg that never any appeal for funds be put forward, save to God in prayer. When our work becomes a begging work, it dies. God is faithful; must be so. The Lord is my Shepherd; I shall not want ... Take *no* thought (anxiety) for your life, what ye shall eat ... but seek first (to promote) the kingdom of God, and (to fulfil) His righteousness, and *all these things shall be added unto you* ... It is doubting ... not trusting, that is tempting the Lord ...

> The Lord ... makes our hearts so very glad in Himself alone—not Himself plus a bank balance—that I have *never* known greater freedom from anxiety and care. The other week when I reached Shanghai I was in great and immediate need. The mails were both in, no remittance and ... no balances at home. I cast the burden on the Lord. Next morning I awoke and felt a little inclined to trouble, but the Lord gave me a word, 'I know their sorrows, and I am come down to deliver them ... He said, Certainly I will be with thee' (Exodus 3.7, 8, 12). Before six a.m. I was as sure

help was at hand as when near noon, I received a letter from Mr Müller ... which contained more than £300. My need now is great and urgent, God is greater and more near. And because He is, and is what He is, all is, all will be, all must be well. Oh! my dear brother; the joy of knowing the *living God*, of ... resting on the living God ... I am but His agent; He will look after His own honour, provide for His own servants, supply all our need according to His own riches, you helping by your prayers and work of faith and labour of love.

On May 1, a pencilled scrap of a letter to his mother said the work was going well but:

Pray for funds. We have over 100 agents native and foreign, 170 mouths to feed daily and that number to clothe, not to count the wives and children of the native helpers. I feel no anxiety tho' for a month past I have not had a dollar in hand for the general purposes of the Mission. The Lord will provide. But in the meantime it is impossible for me to return home, or even to go to any distant station here, as I must be on the spot to distribute at once any sums which God may supply.

[And on the same day to Emily] I cannot leave China in the present state of our funds. I have written to Mr Hill, Mr Challice, Mr and Mrs Guinness begging them not to *appeal* for funds. If God try our faith it is to show His faithfulness, and we shall lose the blessing by appeals etc. The work is very cheering. Mr Stevenson has just baptised eight persons and writes of new inquirers and candidates. Lae-djün has recently baptised first fruits in three outstations. New doors are opening before us, and Jehovah Jireh ('The Lord will provide'). Is that not true, my precious Sister, of you and me too?

Yours so affectionately in His deep true love,

J. Hudson Taylor

[And a week later] I have sent all Mr Berger's £170 home to you for housekeeping. [To his mother he continued] We were kept waiting on God till May 5th, when £104.2s. were received from the Sees. ... On the 15th $222.22 reverted to the funds which had been temporarily appropriated in February to an object for which it was no longer needed. And Mr Judd on leaving Nankin for Wuchang was able to hand in $240.71, a surplus of funds given him in December and which had not been required. In these ways, by the sale of some stationery, and by profits on exchange, the most urgent needs of May were met; leaving us all the promises of God to meet the expenses of June, and nothing more.

By May 29 a new setback had occurred. John Challice had sent cheques made payable to 'the Bearer' and no Shanghai bank would cash them. They must be made out to the China Inland Mission.

I asked urgent prayer of some of the brethren for £500 to meet the manifest and unavoidable outlay of that month. Perhaps never in the history of the Mission have we all been so low together. As it proved, the outlay of the month required above £100 more than the sum I had named; and therefore the Lord who meets all our need, supplied it too [detailing the sums received]. The aggregate of these sums comes to about £100 in addition to the money sent from home; so that not only were the current expenses of the month met, but Mrs Cardwell, and her two surviving children were able to return to England ... leaving them with a balance in hand of $3.57 on July 1st.

You will wonder how my dear fellow-workers bear (their own) trials ... I will give you some extracts from the letters of ... June. 'When you said, Pray for £500 for this month's expenses, the sum seemed so insignificant when we referred it to God, that I felt ashamed that we should have to make it a subject for special prayer—though to you and to us, it would be everything so to speak. But God's inexhaustible riches rose up before my mind so vividly, that £500 seemed to me no more than 500 stones of the street. I have not the slightest doubt that He will give you this, and much more, as soon as His time comes. What I have to watch against is impatience at waiting His time.'

[From another] 'Many Thanks for ... the money which I received safely this afternoon. My last cash was spent yesterday morning, and I was waiting on our heavenly

Father today for money to pay my teacher. Blessed be His holy name, He still answers our prayers.'

[Hudson Taylor himself said in a June 11 letter to Emily] I am so thankful for the remittances. The last few months have been the greatest trial of faith since the Mission was formed. My soul has mercifully been kept in much peace, sometimes indeed in great joy, and God has helped us wonderfully. During the long time in which we had no Mission money the Stevensons were helped home, and by a series of providential circumstances ... we have been helped on from day to day.[228]

On July 11, on the way to all the southern stations again, he told his mother, 'Our work is now so extensive, that it cannot be carried on without much difficulty and trial, at less cost than £100 a week . . . We have more than 50 buildings—houses, chapels, and schools—to keep in repair, and four fifths of them to pay rent for . . . The travelling expenses involved in the work in China, now extended to five provinces, are not small . . . Of course, all my own expenses for all purposes, at home and here, are outside of this.'

If ever there existed a recipe for bankruptcy and the destitution of scores of colleagues—Chinese and foreign—as well as of schoolchildren and other dependants, this was it, unless he was not mistaken and the message of Scripture 'Jehovah Jireh: the Lord will provide' was being correctly understood and applied. Events showed that it was, and that '(God's) thoughts are not your thoughts.'

The Zhejiang momentum
(January–July 1874)

Hearing as we do in the late twentieth century of the extensive, lively church in Zhejiang province, the history of its origins captures our attention. Returning again to January 1874 we follow another sequence of events. Hudson Taylor was at the Crombies after his working holiday with Jennie had ended in a forced march to save their alarmingly ill children. By Sunday, January 4, he had dosed them, rigged up

steam-tents to ease their breathing, set them on the road to recovery and soothed the agitated parents. George must have been ashamed to receive such attention, for, back to his pre-furlough behaviour, he had again been setting Josiah Jackson against Hudson Taylor.

After the Sunday services Hudson Taylor turned to letter-writing. His winter travels to save the lives of Annie Stevenson and Fanny Jackson had given him an exciting insight into the teeming density of the population, the state of the churches and individual local Christians in 'the Shaoxing circuit' (of Shaoxing, Sheng Xian, Xinchang and their village outposts), as well as in the Taizhou field and in scattered, sometimes remote, places *en route*. His own conversations with Chinese, as he travelled or stopped at wayside inns, had revealed a spiritual hunger in places beyond the range of the existing team of evangelists. The tone of the articles in the *Occasional Papers* from his pen betrays his enthusiasm as he wrote of 'revival' in the Shaoxing churches, and progress almost everywhere. After telling Jennie about Taiping on market-day (so packed with people for two or three miles of city streets that he could hardly move through them and chose to return along the top of the city wall) he went on:

This morning at the van-tin (foodshop) as we were breakfasting, the people began to ask many questions. Among them a young man showed much earnestness in enquiring of us and in listening to what we said ... I think we shall hear of him again. On our way back to the boat I went into the (temple of the city god) and preached to a little knot of people who gathered around me. Some seemed to hear with pleasure. As we neared the boat we met two men who were seeking us to tell us of a house which we could rent. I sent (my companions) and they took it at 1,000 cash a month, and met two women whose deep earnestness to learn the plan of salvation evidently moved and encourged them. In the boat I had like encouragement. Among a number of others an old man of seventy-two years manifested such a real solicitude as I have never seen exceeded in China. I asked him to come in and sit down. He did so. I began as usual to ask his name. He replied, 'My name is Dzing, but the thing which troubles me is this: the world is all vanity and what is to be done about our sins?' 'Yes,' I replied, 'that is the question, and it is to reply to it that we missionaries have come to China.' 'Our Scholars say that there is no hereafter, that the several elements of the soul (three weng, six pah) are scattered at death—but I cannot think it is so.'

So now, on January 4, after telling his mother about the Crombies' straits and his plans for Louise Desgraz to relieve Emily, he wrote:

> I am now in the act of arranging for the eventual opening up of the whole of this province to the gospel as the Lord gives us men, open doors, and means. Pray for these three things. This province (Zhejiang) contains thirty millions of souls. It is divided into circuits (four): we have workers in each. Prefectures (eleven): we have agents in 6. We alone in 3, with others in 3. (One of these we opened, others came later.) 1 is opened, not by us. 4 are still unopened. County towns (seventy-eight), 4 Prefectures have each 2 (*xian*) cities in their walls. So there are—74 walled cities, 11 of them (prefectures), making 63 (county towns). We opened 10 of these. Others opened 5 of these. 48 (*xian*) county cities remain unopened ... In this province they average nearly 400,000 people in the whole (*xian* or county) ... Others began to work this province in 1842; we in 1857; the CIM in 1866. It shows that there was work for us to do; that we have done some, but there is much (more to be done).[229]

Trekking along the hilly trails had helped him to mull it over. He shared his latest thoughts with Jennie: 'I will try to get Stott to work (Wenzhou) and Jackson (Quzhou) [Cii-tsiu, now Lishui]. Then perhaps Lae-djün and Meadows when he comes might work Hangchau (Jiaxing) and (Huzhou) ... Let us pray much for men, means and open doors ... I do believe that this year will be one of much blessing to us as a Mission.'

By January 26 his thinking had progressed a stage further when he told

2.23 Hudson Taylor's prayer for Chinese missionaries (from a flyleaf of his Bible)

Richard Hill to send two 'suitable' young women with Catherine Duncan, and continued:

> Should the Lord present suitable men for the work, you might send four more with advantage this year ... The work is now greatly extending, and I hope will yet do so ... If the Lord spare me and permit me to labour here a year or two more, I trust there will be no ... county left in this province in which we have not preached Christ either by located or itinerant (evangelists). At present there are many such—fifty, perhaps. [At their own expense, that is—many more than the CIM was supporting financially.]

That last remark 'fifty, perhaps' seems to have been the spark that fired his thoughts through that night. For his first birthday after their marriage, Jennie had given him a new Baxter polyglot Bible, a facsimile in larger type (for his changing eyesight) of his favourite pocket edition. As always, he annotated it with the dates on which he read through each year, systematically day by day. And on a blank page at the end he wrote in pencil:

> Jan. 27th, 1874, T'ai-chau. Asked God for 50 or 100 additional native evangelists and as many foreign superintendents [Gutzlaff's word for the more mature Christian missionary] as may be needed to open up the 4 fu [prefectures] and 48 hien [*xian*, counties] still unoccupied in Cheh-kiang [Zhejiang]. Also for the men to break into the 9 unoccupied provinces [ie the eighteen of the prayer pact made

during the Mildmay Conference]. Asked in the name of Jesus. I thank Thee, Lord Jesus, for the promise where on Thou hast given me to rest. ['He who keeps coming to Me shall never hunger, and he who keeps drinking of Me shall never thirst.'] Give me all needed strength of body, wisdom of mind, grace of soul, to do this Thy so great work. Amen!

[Below this note he added later on] Feb. 1. T'ai-p'ing hien, Sin-ku, opened; Ap. 1 Yu-hang, Hu-chau-fu opened.

The pencilled note to his mother from Ningbo on March 3 when he was recovering from his 'intermittent fever' said, 'We have forty or more stations now'—not only in Zhejiang. And to Emily on March 30, again pencilled in bed because he had not yet recovered his strength, he wrote about the second anniversary meeting of the Chinese missionary society. 'Having 70,000 cash in hand (about $58) they elected one of their number as their evangelist, to be sent at their own expense to some district destitute of the gospel.'[230] The next day, March 31, he wrote in his editorial letter to friends of the Mission, 'There are more than forty stations and one hundred labourers, foreign and native, connected with our work, and about fifty children and adult students are studying the Word of God. Baptisms were being reported from almost' every occupied city and outstation, including Lanxi and Qü Xian far up the Qiantang River, and at last from Yangzhou, Qingjiangpu and even—the latest development—from a second city of the same name, Taizhou in Jiangsu, east of Yangzhou.

An evangelist had also succeeded in getting a footing at Huzhou again, where McCarthy, Yi Zewo and Liu Jinchen had been so badly mauled in November 1867. So far he was unopposed. At Wuhu where Mr Han, the converted Anqing innkeeper, was the evangelist, a native of Hunan province had become a Christian. Hunan was one of the 'fresh provinces' the long stride was to penetrate. What did it matter if they were all 'scraping the barrel' for cash and living more frugally than ever, if such things were happening! The lighter their purses, the more they looked up to their Father who fed the sparrows, and the more they did that, the more happened on the spiritual front.

The momentum in Zhejiang had spilled over to the Yangzi provinces, too. Had circumstances not led unmistakably to the Taylors leaving China for another period in Britain, who could tell what they would be witnessing next? On July 13, Hudson Taylor listed ten places in the southern region he proposed to visit once again before at last sailing for Europe at the end of August, and declared frankly and factually with confidence in his mother's long-proved discretion:

I feel like one almost torn asunder by the claims at home and here. No mission aims at the definite evangelisation of China— or even a single province. All are helping towards it ... in their own way ... A few ... are approximating to the work I hope to see effected, and we are influencing more largely every year older missions to step out and onwards. My plans are now so developing that were I able to remain in China, and had I a few more men of the right stamp, in two or three years we might have (DV) missions founded in every province otherwise unoccupied— nine—in each prefecture of (Anhui); and in each (county of Zhejiang), if funds were adequate. To see the bare possibility of this, and to have to defer it by coming home, is a great trial to me; on the other hand to return may be needful in order to effect it.[231]

As long ago as 1870, the *Missionary Magazine* of the American Baptist Union had published a letter by Miles Justice Knowlton, DD, of Ningbo about the CIM, because it was 'beginning to make some stir in the Western as well as the Eastern world'.

1. They have an excellent spirit self-denying, with singleness of aim; devotional, with a spirit of faith, of love, of humility.

2. Their operations are carried on with great efficiency and economy.

3. They are able and willing to bring themselves into close contact with the people, by living in their houses, using

their dress, and living for the most part on their food ...

4. They are widely scattered, but one or two families in a city.

5: They are having good success; many are doing a great amount of teaching and praying, and souls are added to the church ...

6. They are not generally educated men, but ... showing zeal and aptness to preach and labour for the salvation of souls ...

7. They are willing to 'rough it' ...

My principal fear, from what I saw, is that their health will suffer; but whether it will suffer more than in the case of the missionaries of other Societies, remains to be seen.

I notice that the English Baptist Society is beginning to be influenced considerably by the example of the 'China Inland Mission'. Could not all the old Societies learn some lessons from it? Could they not send some men of piety, good commonsense, energy, and perhaps of some experience, who had not been through the usual college course?[232]

Hudson Taylor had still to descend to greater depths of tribulation, but he was nearer than he thought to the great breakthrough when his 'mad venture' would succeed on a far greater scale. Religious and secular observers alike would soon credit him with having been right all along, and take up his methods to an increasing extent.

The accident[233] (May–June 1874)

In the final days of May, as Hudson Taylor and Charles Judd prepared to travel five hundred miles further up the Yangzi to Wuhan, the Hunanese Christian from Wuhu was baptised with three others at Zhenjiang. Soon afterwards he was joined by another Hunan man. Judd could have no better companions when he ventured into their province. The home of the scurrilous anti-Christian tracts and placards, Hunan gave promise of being as resistant as any province yet penetrated. While the Stevensons arrived in Shanghai, to sail on

June 7—another family to go home as a matter of life and death—the westward advance was beginning.

June 1 found Hudson Taylor and Charles Judd on a little river-steamer, the SS *Hanyang*, travelling as Chinese passengers in quarters unsuitable for Jennie to be with them. 'It was one of McBain's, there were no cabins at all, just a few bunks, it was not much larger than a tug-boat.' 'I was going too,' she told Emily, 'but afterwards concluded that my being in Hankow at a (Chinese) inn might afford food for gossip.' On the same vessel was the Shanghai businessman Thomas Weir, just one month after his adventures with David Cranston in the Shanghai riot. A firm friend of Hudson Taylor, he had used his influence to obtain fifty per cent discounts for members of the CIM on passages between Shanghai and Europe, and for some years secured most favourable terms with the Castle Line for Mission travellers from the United Kingdom too.[234]

By Tuesday, June 2, they had chugged slowly upstream, stopped long enough at Jiujiang for a brief visit to Cardwell and the Christians there, and were due at Wuhan on Wednesday. Then, 'I saw him on the steamer,' Weir wrote. 'He had fallen down a ladder one foot nine inches wide. He was lying on some bales of cargo between decks where he fell . . . in great pain, could not move.'

On arrival at Wuhan, Judd, it seems, found accommodation for them in a Chinese inn, and Hudson Taylor wrote the same day,

Wed. June 3. The steps were very steep, and when on the 2nd or 3rd from the top, my foot slipped and I came down feet first to the bottom [taking the impact on his heels]. The shock was very great, and for a time the agony was intense. After a while I was able to breathe a little and was helped to my bed. (I could not breathe properly for several hours.) ... My spine was very painful ... This afternoon lying still, with my left ankle, which was sprained, elevated, I have no pain, and I can move with much less pain ... I feel very good for nothing today.

The weather was very hot and the mosquitoes in the inn very many and troublesome. Josiah Cox, the Wesleyan, as soon as he knew of their arrival and what had happened, insisted that Hudson Taylor move into his home, while Judd stayed with a missionary with whom he had travelled to China, and looked for premises to rent. 'My back,' Hudson Taylor mistakenly wrote to Jennie, 'is evidently not seriously injured,' and by June 8 he thought his back was 'nearly well'; he could bear some weight on his feet.

Griffith John, Hudson Taylor's old friend of Shanghai days, invited him to move in and stay, although not understanding, yet, why a fourth mission should be added to the LMS, WMMF and Protestant Episcopal Church in the three cities now forming the metropolis of Wuhan. 'I think that the Wesleyan missionaries will be good friends to us,' Hudson Taylor's note to Jennie ran, that same day. 'The London Miss. Socy not quite so warm, perhaps, but they see the need of a place here, if we are to go beyond' which was his intention.

By June 9, Judd had rented a house and left by Chinese steamer to pack up at Nanjing. Young Baller and Henry Taylor were to stay on in Nanjing with Chinese colleagues, while Judd brought his wife and second son, Frederick Hudson, back with him. But on the same day, June 9, a letter from Jennie reached Hudson Taylor. Mary Bowyer had smallpox: 'We have completely isolated her.'

> I left Hankow the same night,' he wrote 'and reached (Zhenjiang) last night ... The populousness of the three places, Wuchang, Hanyang and Hankow, exceeds all I have hitherto seen in China—there must be at least a million souls in them. I propose forming a distinct branch of the Mission—under the superintendency of Mr Judd—for opening up work in these regions.

At Zhenjiang, John Donovan was 'brooding'. He had proposed to Mary Bowyer and been disappointed. Her reason was not long in coming to light, for when Frederick Baller knew that she

had smallpox he could not wait to confess his love for her, or she for him. They had not travelled out to China on the same ship for nothing. She soon recovered from her smallpox, a light attack, and was undisfigured. 'Should she have her health,' Hudson Taylor commented to Richard Hill on June 18, 'they will probably soon be one of the most useful couples we have in the Mission. He is able, and humble; a man of piety and purpose; and his progress in the language is very, very good indeed.' At last the right kind of reinforcement.

In the same letter he wrote of more conversions and more baptisms. China was ripe for the gospel. The Hunan man converted at Wuhu 'seems all on fire for the conversion of his own people'. As for Hudson Taylor himself, apart from the temporary need of a crutch, the accident appeared to be a past event.

> My soul yearns, oh how intently for the evangelisation of these 180 millions of the nine unoccupied provinces. Oh that I had a hundred lives to give or spend for their good ... Better to have pecuniary and other outward trials and perplexities, and blessing in the work itself, souls being saved, and the name of the Lord Jesus being magnified, than any measure of external prosperity without it.

London's greater claims
(May–August 1874)

Nothing was static in the Taylors' lives. (Looking back yet again)—while they were at Zhenjiang for the conference about expanding north or west and, after it, preoccupied with monetary matters and the death of the Cardwell child, James Meadows and A. W. Douthwaite arrived at Shanghai. Edward Fishe welcomed them into the Mission's first business centre, near the Ningbo wharf on the Huangpu River, in 'Hongkew'—little more than a shop-front with rooms behind and above it—and two days later they were involved in the Shanghai riot.[235]

When Meadows learned of Annie Stevenson's urgent need to leave for England, he gladly accepted Hudson

Taylor's request that he step into John Stevenson's shoes at Shaoxing, with oversight of the churches in that 'circuit'. At Shaoxing alone Stevenson had established a church of forty-six communicants. Expecting it to be a temporary post, Meadows was so deeply involved when news came at the end of the year of Stevensons's designation elsewhere, that he was glad to continue there—as he did with only one furlough in the next forty years, until he died.

With their passage money contributed entirely by their fellow-missionaries, John and Anne Stevenson and their five children were in Shanghai by May 29, to sail on June 7, while Hudson Taylor rested on his Yangzi tug-boat before his accident, 'reading and sleeping' and sorting his correspondence files. The financial crisis in China was extreme, but news of remittances from home and £500 of capital from Jennie's legacy being available had changed the picture. The Taylors could leave their colleagues provided for and still have enough for their own fares to Europe. John McCarthy and Donovan with Mr Han of Wuhu were on a pastoral visit up the Grand Canal to the growing church at Qingjiangpu, while Judd was contemplating his approach with the two Hunan Christians to their province, 'one of the most difficult in China'. The intense heat of the summer had begun, and Mrs Cardwell could not face the worst of it in her low state of health, so she sailed for home and her husband stayed to continue his pioneering in Jiangxi.

At last the need for Hudson Taylor to be in London exceeded the need in China. If no more pressing situation developed, as well it might in Yangzhou or Anqing, he could leave. They might be in time to be with Emily after all, though the news of her was bad. She was suffering more than ever and slowly sinking. On July 10 Hudson Taylor set off on another quick tour of the Zhejiang region, intending to do most of his travelling by canal-boat and coastal steamer, to spare his ankle and back. The Rudlands, especially Mary, were not recovering from their succession of illnesses so he must

see them, and the Stotts in their remotest station of Wenzhou, busy with successful work but often persecuted. To catch the French mail-steamer at the end of August was his goal.

On July 13 as he passed through Jiaxing by canal, he recalled his first visit there with Edkins twenty years before. Then a day or two at Hangzhou to encourage Wang Lae-djün and the church, a day or two more with Meadows, settling in at Shaoxing with Douthwaite, and Emmeline Turner at her school. On the 19th Jennie and he met at the Goughs, she having come down by coastal boat. Then with the Crombies at Ninghai on the 22nd, and by the 24th they were looking for the Rudlands at Taizhou, tracing them at last to an old temple in the hills near the mouth of the river. There the sea breezes made the heat tolerable for Mary, at the end of her endurance. Almost eight years had passed since she, as Mary Bell, and William had arrived in China on the typhoon-battered *Lammermuir*.

At once Hudson Taylor told them to be in Shanghai by August 29, ready to leave on the same ship as himself, funds permitting. Another crisis caused by no remittance from London would mean no sailings until it had been weathered. 'I have not a dollar of Mission money in hand now,' he had to admit yet again, 'but our Father has all the gold and silver at His disposal, and if He wish, He can easily provide all and more than we need.' Meanwhile he and Jennie had some money of their own, at God's disposal if he should want them to share it with the rest. The Taizhou church and outreach would be in the good hands of 'some of the best Chinese Christians'. He had intended taking the overland route between Taizhou and Wenzhou in order to see the new believers at these places on the way, including the old man who had gone straight to the point about his sins. But time was running out and the heat was prohibitive. So he and Jennie boarded a coastal boat on July 28 and bucked their way against head winds to Wenzhou for a long weekend with George Stott and Grace (Ciggie).

Returning, they had the choice of ten days on a Chinese junk or longer by sedan chair overland to Ningbo. They chose the junk and almost regretted it. 'It was a question all the time of being either roasted or stewed according as we crawled out of or remained in our little berth. We were twelve days on the way including two . . . at anchor.'

Finally, on the way up to Zhenjiang for a last quick consultation and farewell, Hudson Taylor wrote to Emmeline Turner, on August 20. Telling her his plans, he took the trouble to explain at length how her school accounts had gone wrong through a misplaced decimal point. Then, 'I feel so thankful to the Lord for bringing you out, and for making you such a help and comfort . . . I am persuaded that each year will only deepen the Christian love and confidence we feel towards you'—the kind of letter which won him loyal colleagues.

The Rudlands and their three children arrived in Shanghai, Hudson Taylor returned from Zhenjiang with the four McCarthy children, to escort them to England, and on August 30 they and a merchant friend and his wife from Zhenjiang all sailed as third-class passengers on the French mail-boat, the men and women separated into dormitory cabins. Hudson Taylor made no reference to his back, but he was still dependent on crutches. Either his foot injury had been no mere sprain or he was taking the weight off his spine.

Events soon showed which it was.

The unexpected
(September–November 1874)

The fast voyage of six weeks to Marseilles ended in a way they had not foreseen. Mary Rudland's illness had gone from bad to worse, and Hudson Taylor had developed increasingly severe spinal symptoms. When they reached Marseilles, letters were waiting to say that Emily had died after midnight early on July 25, and Catherine Duncan, worn out after ten months of continuous nursing, had been persuaded to go home to Scotland to recover. By the time they all

reached Paris, Mary Rudland could go no further and Jennie had to break the journey with her. They came on a day later.

The term 'delayed concussion of the spine' sounded well as an explanation of Hudson Taylor's trouble, but was inadequate. By the time he, William Rudland and the seven children reached London on October 14, he was getting about with difficulty even on crutches and by the 28th was forced by pain to keep as much as possible to his room.

The longed-for happy family reunion proved impossible. His son Herbert was with his grandmother getting over scarlet fever, after being nursed by Louise Desgraz. Little Maria and Charles Edward were in quarantine at Pyrland Road, apparently sickening with the same disease. Everyone had 'deserted' Louise to cope as best as she could, except for Douthwaite's fiancée, Lily (Elizabeth) Doig, who called occasionally from outside in the street to know if they needed anything. William Faulding took Jennie and two McCarthy children to his home in Barnet, where Howard Taylor was already staying, and their merchant friends from Zhenjiang took two more. The Rudlands moved into lodgings found by Louise nearby.

Using letter paper with heavy black margins for mourning, Hudson Taylor wrote to his mother on October 22, 'I am almost overwhelmed or you could have heard from me sooner.' No relative had died. The mourning almost certainly was for Emily. But no letters or diaries remain to throw more light on those harrowing days. They had reached home too late, not only to see Emily. On October 23, eight days after arriving, Mary Rudland died.

By normal timing, the news from China would have reached them at the end of October that their faithful friend, Miles Knowlton, had died from dysentery. His wife and daughter had barely escaped with their lives, and were recovering slowly.[236] It was a sad home-coming. Even his sister Amelia and her husband Benjamin could not come to him. They were going through crises of their own.

On November 12 he wrote again to his mother. 'My spine has suffered from the vibration of railways, cabs and omnibuses, etc., since reaching land, now I am forbidden travelling at all and need to spend much time on my back.' Catherine Duncan was in London again and preparing to sail in a week's time, escorting Lily Doig and Nellie Faulding at long last to their fiancés, Arthur Douthwaite and Charles Fishe, in China. Thomas Weir of Shanghai had secured passages for them on a Castle Line ship for only £50 each. On the 28th, one of Jennie's characteristic letters (still with black margins of mourning) exhorted her mother to stop fretting about Nellie. 'The more you give way the more difficult you will find it not to go on doing so . . . Cheer up, Ma dear, I will do all I can to be a comfort to you.' Jennie by then was six weeks from her second confinement. Scarcely a mention of the council or secretaries is to be found. With Hudson Taylor home from China, he was naturally expected to take up the reins of Mission affairs. But it had to be from his bed.

Burma trade route[237] (13 August 1874)

As long ago as the days of the Roman empire, Chinese silks had been carried by camel caravans through Chinese Turkestan to the Caspian Sea and Bosphorus. In the seventh century, Arab dhows traded between the Red Sea and Canton. While Columbus looked for a route to the East Indies by sailing westwards—to find the Americas blocking his route—Vasco da Gama rounded the Cape of Good Hope and made his way across the Indian Ocean to Malaya (see 1, pp 19–20). Sichuan province was one of the great sources of finely woven silk, but the three south-western provinces of Sichuan, Guizhou and Yunnan held more untapped riches which Western nations wished to exploit.

The natural outlet of the huge Sichuan basin was the Yangzi River (see map 2.20: p 204) navigable by steamers from Yibin (Suifu) to Shanghai, an immense distance of sixteen hundred miles, through the fearsome Outang, Wushan and Xiling

gorges and rapids (only blasted clear and made safe since 1950). The plateau of Yunnan at an altitude of 5,000 feet, walled and moated to its north and west by high mountain ranges and the deep gorges of the Salween and Mekong Rivers, also opened naturally to the east through Guizhou and Guangxi provinces to the Yangzi and Red Rivers. Southwards and south-eastwards the fall of land was towards Vietnam, Laos and Burma. But the Irrawaddy River was navigable as far north as Bhamo beyond Mandalay. Exploration of the south-eastern route convinced Archibald R. Colquhoun (1882) that it had strong advantages over the Bhamo route, and the notorious 'Burma Road' of the Second World War followed a route through Lashio. But in 1874 Bhamo was most widely believed to hold the key, for Chinese merchants' pack-trains plied regularly between Bhamo, Tengyue (called Momein), Tengchong and Dali, leading to the provincial capital at Kunming. Half the inhabitants of Burmese Bhamo were Chinese.

Bhamo was the place and this the route Hudson Taylor had wanted to exploit for Mission purposes since 1865, when he made his first proposition to John Stevenson (and consulted William Burns), only to be disappointed by an exacerbation of the Panthay Muslim rebellion in Yunnan. Either before Stevenson left China on June 7, 1874, or soon after Hudson Taylor also reached Britain, they consulted again about making an attempt to enter the western provinces of China through Burma. The passes did not lie above 8,700 feet, nor were the bridges over the roaring rapids of melted Tibetan snows below 2,500 feet. Tengchong lay at 5,500 feet, Dali at 7,000 feet, and Kunming at 6,000 feet, but in the four hundred miles, eight ascents and descents had to be made, an arduous journey but not 'practically insurmountable' as Colquhoun was to describe it, and certainly not to lightly-laden pioneers of the CIM. Excitement and emotional debate over the Burma route were to flourish for a decade.

The British government had dispatched an exploratory expedition under a Colonel E. B. Sladen in 1868, which had been attacked by a Chinese 'Colonel' Li Zhenguo (Li Chen-kuo) close to the border. Li was therefore called 'a brigand and other hard names', although this was a foreign intrusion. So in preparing a second expedition in the year after the massacre of Muslims at Dali, greater precautions were taken. The minister in Peking, T. F. Wade, obtained passports from the Zongli Yamen, and two British consuls with experience in China, Clement F. R. Allen, formerly of Zhenjiang, and Augustus Raymond Margary of Yantai, were appointed in 1874 as interpreters to join the big new expedition under Colonel Horace A. Browne. Margary had joined the consular service at twenty-two in 1867. An explorer named Ney Elias who had studied the new course of the Yellow River, and a surgeon-naturalist, Dr John Anderson, who had been with Sladen in 1866, with collectors, servants and an armed escort of seventeen Sikhs and one hundred and fifty Burmese troops (to see them safely through the tribal territory on the Burmese side of the border), completed the tally of one hundred and ninety-three men.

Allen was sent by sea to Rangoon, but Margary, now twenty-eight, left Shanghai on August 22, 1874, one week before Hudson Taylor left China, travelling with six Chinese up the Yangzi. With introductions from the acting-viceroy of Hunan to all mandarins along his route, Margary sailed from Yueyang above Wuhan across the great Dongting complex of lakes which serves as a flood-reservoir to the Yangzi valley, and up the Yuan River into Guizhou (see map 2.20, p 204). His journey was straightforward even in Yunnan, so recently the scene of rebellion and massacre. In a letter 'he dwelt much on the attention shown him by the acting-governor' of Yunnan. Passing through Dali and Tengchong he came to Manyün (Manwyne to contemporary writers), only fifty miles from Bhamo and half that distance from the China-Burma border. There he was hospitably entertained

for several days by Colonel Li Zhenguo, 'an exceedingly courteous, intelligent and straightforward man; he has done everything to facilitate the advance of the expedition', Margary reported to Wade. But in order to pass through the territory of the warlike Shan and Kachin border tribes he had to wait for an escort of forty Burmese to join him. With them he reached Bhamo on January 17, 1875.

In 1873, while Augustus Margary was on leave in Britain, he had begun 'to think deeply about his soul's salvation' and before returning to China promised to write and tell his mother when he 'found peace'. In Yantai he had taken part in seminars and study of the Bible with his consular colleague Challoner Alabaster (later consul at Wuhan) and with John Nevius and Timothy Richard. During a bout of illness on his journey through Yunnan in November 1874 he read his Bible and gave more thought to his own position. As a result he wrote home from Bhamo to tell his mother of 'his own trust in God and in Christ as his Saviour, and of his desire that prayer should be offered by his Christian friends in England that his journey on government matters to Burmah should end in some way to the opening up of those wide provinces, through which he was passing, to the preaching of the gospel.' His mother told this to John McCarthy, who followed in Margary's footsteps in 1877.

The prospects were good. Colonel Browne completed his preparations and the expedition was to start on February 6. To officials and tribesmen on the Chinese side of the border, ignorant of Peking's approval of this expedition, its size must have looked menacing.

The Huzhou, Suzhou and Ruichang riots (August–November 1874)

Early in August two Chinese evangelists from Hangzhou quietly moved into Huzhou and, after a few days at an inn, to test their reception by the people they rented simple premises in which to preach the gospel, plainly stating their purpose and still without exciting opposition. For two months they were undisturbed and had 'some degree of encouragement', until they began to note the presence of literati among their small audiences. Then on October 12 the neighbourhood *dibao* came in with their landlord and ordered them to leave at once, on pain of having the place pulled down about their ears. The Christians reported this to James Meadows, who, on his way through Hangzhou, consulted the *daotai* about the incident and obtained approval of his going to Huzhou. Together with Arthur Douthwaite, only six months in China, he reached Huzhou on October 31.[238]

After gathering all the facts and making sure that the rental agreement for the Huzhou premises (a little shop with rooms above and behind it) were satisfactory, they called on the city prefect and offered to relinquish them if he would arrange for suitable premises to be provided elsewhere. They told him what he would have known already, that the anti-foreign secret society in Huzhou had threatened to destroy the house and lynch the landlord if the evangelists did not leave. The prefect was very civil, and they returned to the 'chapel' in the evening not suspecting until they arrived how serious the situation had become. In their absence a crowd had broken into the shop-front chapel, overturned the furniture and damaged the living quarters behind, where one of the evangelists was lying ill with typhus.

Leaving Douthwaite to guard the property, and the sick man and his wife if he could, Meadows returned to the prefect's *yamen* to seek official protection. In his absence the chapel and its furniture were destroyed, and after Meadows returned, deceived by the mandarins, he, Douthwaite and the sick evangelist were robbed of almost all they possessed. Promises of restitution were not kept, being only a polite way of quietening the foreigner and gaining time.

Little differed in the pattern of events from the previous riot at Huzhou, and the local literati had again proved their point, that even so near to Shanghai they would not tolerate the intrusion of foreigners. Nor had the inability of the high mandarins to control them altered at all.

Two weeks later, the American Presbyterian Mission at Suzhou, only fifty miles from Shanghai, was attacked during a teaching session for church members. The usual story of a rabble smashing and plundering was repeated, until the late intervention of a magistrate restored a semblance of order. Again one of the minor culprits was sentenced to flogging with 250 blows, considered a light sentence, but the literati were left untouched.[239]

From Jiujiang J. E. Cardwell reported on November 7, 'Two of the American missionaries have just had a severe beating at a city seventy-five *li* [twenty-five miles] from here. The magistrates refused to look at their passports or help them in any way. So they were left to the mercy of the mob, and barely escaped with their lives by swimming a river in darkness.' The city was Ruichang, west of Jiujiang—called Shuichang in the contemporary reports. Early in 1873, H. H. Hall of the American Methodist Episcopal Mission had attempted to open an outstation at Ruichang, only to be driven out by a mob employed by three of the local literati, while the chapel was attacked and its furniture and books destroyed.[240]

On October 29, 1874, V. C. Hart, the good friend of the Meadows and Cardwell families, and two other American missionaries made a courtesy call on the magistrate after renting another building.[241]

They then returned to Jiujiang. The next day, the two Chinese evangelists were driven out by the 'gentry' and threatened with death if they dared to return. Two missionaries and another Chinese Christian therefore took their place and went at once to the *yamen* to see the magistrate, only to be mobbed and insulted in the *yamen* itself. The *yamen* gates were thrown open to let the rabble in, and the Chinese evangelist was twice given 'a most brutal beating'. Driven out of the city, they were stoned as they fled. Both missionaries were hit often on the head, one bleeding profusely. They ran into the canal and struggled to the opposite side, illuminated by lanterns held by the literati to help the mob pelt them as they swam. Wandering about in the dark, wet and cold, it was midnight before they found their boat and could return to Jiujiang.

This was another of the 'forty quiet years' between 1860 and 1900.

1875: 'THE EIGHTEEN'

When weak–strong!
(December 1874–January 1875)

The reports reaching Hudson Taylor as he lay partially paralysed in London, preparing *Occasional Paper* No 39, were daunting. Of Taylor himself, James Williamson, visiting London shortly after his marriage, wrote, 'Almost completely paralysed in his back and lower limbs. A rope fastened above his head enabled him to lift himself with his hands sufficiently to turn from side to side.' William Rudland had taken his motherless children to his own mother at Reading and was there, seriously ill himself, when Jennie wrote to him, 'It seems very unlikely that either we or you will ever see China again.' The CIM was at its lowest ebb since its inception less than ten years before, but its *raison d'être* and its will to win through were unchanged.

Then on Sunday, December 13, a sudden onset of severe 'enteritis' struck Hudson Taylor. Jennie was expecting her baby at any time and avoided infection by keeping away from him. Once again the devoted Louise nursed him until his mother arrived to share the work. But during that week they thought he might die, and together witnessed his signature to a new will in which he left everything to Jennie, making her his sole executrix, 'believing that by so doing, I am consulting both her comfort and the best interests of my dear children, whom I leave with the greatest confidence to her love and care'. By then the children had been scattered to the John Eliot Howards in Tottenham, to the Grattan Guinness family and to Amelia who already had her own nine children and another well on the way.

By Christmas he was beginning to recover his strength when news came that Mr Tsiu had died. After Wang Lae-djün, Tsiu Kyuo-kwe was the one Chinese colleague who could least be spared. His loss was like a death-blow to the CIM itself. Tsiu's flogging at Xiaoshan in 1867 had steeled him to be a fearless preacher, once his natural fear of its repetition had been overcome. He was a spearhead, Wang Lae-djün the shaft of strength and wisdom.

As Hudson Taylor lay in his 'little bed with four posts to the bottom two of which a map of China was pinned'[242], looking at it in terms of millions of people, he thought deeply about the nine provinces still denied the gospel brought by the Protestant Church, though occupied for centuries by Catholic missionaries. The task was becoming no less difficult, the casualties were mounting, the prospects were poor of his recovering to lead the way, and still no gifted leader to support or succeed him had emerged. In spirit he was uncowed. He and the Mission had been praying for two years for those eighteen men needed to launch the new offensive with the gospel. So far only Fred Baller, Henry Taylor and Arthur Douthwaite could be seen as answers to those prayers, but even from bed it was possible to rouse the Church.

The capital gift of £800 from Mrs Grace was already earmarked for pioneering, and in September 1874 Grattan Guinness told the council that she 'had engaged to place £1,000 into his hands for missionary purposes, £500 of which he had agreed with her to hand over' to the CIM.[243] But the financial shortage from which the Mission had been suffering for two long years was a shortage of funds for day-to-day continuance of established work, the unglamorous 'general purposes'. He had no sense of limitation by God only to pray for personnel without making a public appeal for them, as he had in regard to money. The two issues were distinct. On the contrary, he knew that a challenge to unreserved commitment would be of spiritual benefit to the church at large. 'Pray ye therefore the Lord of the harvest that he will send forth labourers into his harvest' and 'Go ye therefore' were two sides of the same coin. So, as the year ended he began to publicise an appeal for eighteen men, of a type not sought by other societies lest he undermine them, in response to prayer. *The Christian* and Spurgeon's *Sword and Trowel* and a number of other Christian periodicals carried the article in which he struck at the heart of the matter. Prayer for China in her need would bring the answer in a way no mere appeal or persuasion could.

APPEAL FOR PRAYER ON BEHALF OF MORE THAN 150 MILLIONS OF CHINESE

There are nine provinces of China, each as large as a European kingdom, averaging a population of seventeen or eighteen millions, but all destitute of the pure Gospel. About a hundred Roman Catholic priests from Europe live in them, but not one Protestant missionary.

Much prayer has been offered on behalf of these nine provinces by some friends of the China Inland Mission; and during the past year nearly £4,000 has been contributed on condition that it be used in these provinces alone. We have some native Christians from these regions, who have been converted in our older stations, and who are most earnestly desiring the evangelisation of their native district. Our present pressing need is of missionaries to lead the way. Will each of your Christian readers at once raise his heart to God, and wait one minute in earnest prayer that God will raise up this year eighteen suitable men, to devote themselves to this work. Warm-hearted young men, who have a good knowledge of business, clerks, or assistants in shops who have come in contact with the public and learned to cover the wants and suit the wishes of purchasers, are well fitted for this work. They should possess strong faith, devoted piety, and burning zeal; be men who will gladly live, labour, suffer, and if need be, die for Christ's sake.[244]

It was a brave and defiant act, made from a paraplegic's bed, with little sign as yet of ever being ambulant again.

On the morning of January 7 his fortitude was to be taxed in quite another way. Jennie was sharing a room with a young candidate, Annie Knight. That morning, as soon as Annie had gone down to breakfast, Jennie quickly prepared for her baby to be born. She had told no one that she was in labour, thinking there was plenty of time. After breakfast all the family, but for Jennie, met for family prayers at Hudson Taylor's bedside and dispersed again. One of the children came in to see Jennie and was sent back with the message, Would Louise please come at once? 'When I reached the bedside the baby was already born,' Louise recalled. 'I ran across (to Mr T.'s room). He could not possibly walk so I wheeled a small sofa by the side of his bed and . . . he rolled himself slowly on to (it), then I wheeled him . . . to Mrs T.'s bedside. Sitting up with great difficulty he did what was absolutely necessary, then threw himself back utterly incapable of doing any more . . . Then I wheeled him back to his bed.' To his mother he wrote, 'Jennie gave birth to a son, Ernest, about nine a.m. . . . She was surprised, we more so.' He was 'a wee little mite', very slow to recover from his precipitate birth, and while not 'retarded' in the modern sense, was handicapped by frailty throughout his subsequent years as a missionary in China. Three weeks later Louise reported to Hudson Taylor's mother that his back was 'paining him a good deal . . . from overworking himself and twisting about in bed'. His bedroom had become the Mission's central office, with John Stevenson and other volunteers spending hours at his bedside writing to his dictation, and the council meeting in the same conditions. The response to the appeal had begun already.

Margary murdered[245]
(January–May 1875)

The council, meeting at No 6 Pyrland Road on December 14, had been startled to hear from the invalid in bed that for ten years he had contemplated sending missionaries into western and southern China via Burma, and now expected his plans to materialise very shortly. Two gentlemen from Burma, one a member of Colonel Slanden's abortive expedition, had been to see him in October, encouraging him to send missionaries soon. Colonel Browne's expedition was about to start, with approval from Peking.

John Stevenson was present at the next meeting of the council on January 25, also held at Hudson Taylor's bedside, when he announced that Stevenson 'would shortly start for Bhamo as his headquarters, and special meetings were to be arranged to bring the matter before the churches'. His wife and children would stay at home. March was set as the time for him to go, and it was hoped that by then he would have a companion.

Augustus Margary had arrived at Bhamo on January 17 with only experience of friendly cooperation by the Chinese to report. On January 26, a Chinese merchant warned the political agent at Bhamo that Colonel Browne would be opposed. Ney Elias and a small party set off by one route on February 6, through Mangmao (Maingmaw), while on February 18 Colonel Browne and the main party crossed the frontier on the Manyün road with Margary. At Mangmao 'on the insistent advice' of Colonel Li Zhenguo, Elias changed his route and, on hearing of how Browne fared, returned to Bhamo.

When Colonel Browne's party entered China he was warned by a Burmese that an ambush lay ahead of him, and between the 18th and 22nd more warnings were given. Margary and his six Chinese companions then went ahead 'to consult with Colonel Li on whose friendliness he relied', and reported that the way was safe. On the 22nd, however, Colonel Browne was hemmed in on three sides by armed men and ordered his Sikhs to fire, covering his retreat to Bhamo where he arrived on February 26. On the way, he was shown letters to Burmese in his force telling them not to be with Browne on February 23, as that night they were to be attacked. On the

25th he learned that Margary and five of the six Chinese had been 'killed on the 21st, by a body of armed Chinese'. Significantly, the only survivor was a Yunnan provincial.

If the resistance had been premeditated, who had been responsible? King Mindon at Mandalay, 'strongly opposed to the further opening of trade routes'? Or the provincial government of Yunnan, no less antagonistic to the British aims, and suspicious of British motives since Colonel Sladen's expedition had unavoidably made terms with the Panthay rebels? In any case, what trade but opium did the British Indian government want to establish through Burma? Colonel Li's mother was Burmese, and only six months previously a rich Burmese caravan bearing tribute to Peking had passed unmolested along this same route. Local Chinese, not Colonel Li who had been at Mangmao, were probably to blame, but ultimately the responsibility had to rest on the provincial government for an armed assault on a British mission bearing documents issued by the Zongli Yamen, and for the murder of a British consul. The acting-viceroy of Yunnan was Zeng Yüying, slaughterer of the Panthay Muslim rebels.

T. F. Wade heard of Margary's death and the repulse of Colonel Browne by a cable from the India Office, London received on March 11. A week later, Wade presented Prince Kong with his demands: a commission of investigation to be conducted in the presence of British officers; a second expedition to be allowed; 150,000 taels to be placed in Wade's hands; and a satisfactory audience of the emperor to be given. A firm riposte could be predicted. The stage was set for another confrontation holding all the ingredients of yet another *casus belli*.

Back in London Hudson Taylor was slowly making progress. 'More power to move about' was followed on January 29 by 'Hudson walked two or three times into the next room . . . with Miss Desgraz' help'. By the end of February he was up briefly every day and in March had his bed moved into his study so that he could sit or lie at will as his back recovered. In February he wrote almost daily to Jennie, away at her parents'. 'Mrs Grace has given £300 for new provinces and £30 for Bibles—promises £50 for passage, £20 for outfit for the first of the eighteen men—and DV £100 in October (bringing the total to £500) . . . thank God.' James Williamson and his bride, 'quiet, gentle, little and tidy', so admirably suited to him, were on the verge of sailing. 'The bustle and packing are now over, and the luggage has gone to the docks.' 'Very little money has come in, the last fourteen days, for general . . . purposes. We must not cease to pray.' Why did many people prefer supporting special projects rather than faithful persistence in hard work? It was understandable, but how could Christians be educated in wise giving without the appearance of asking for funds?

At Pyrland Road again, Jennie told her mother on February 23, 'Many are taking a deep interest in the opening up of work (in west China) via Burmah . . . Today a new friend has sent in £200. Candidates continue to offer themselves' for the nine provinces. Writing to Emmeline Turner, she said, '(Hudson) feels that God has done far more by him while he has been laid low than would have been done, could he have been going round the country as he hoped.'

John Stevenson's farewell meetings were in progress. Both he and his wife were enthusiastic about his venture. But there was no mention of anyone going with him, until March 15, when, surprise upon surprise, the council minutes recorded that Stevenson and Henry Soltau were to sail at the end of the month. Leaving his profession, Soltau was responding to Hudson Taylor's personal challenge. The impact of such dedication upon the Christian public could not but be dramatic. The same minutes recorded that twenty young men had presented themselves in response to the call for eighteen, several of whom were promising.

No one was being naive. Lower Burma was annexed territory, resentful of imperial aggression. Upper Burma remained free, but while a commercial treaty had been reached with King Mindon, he was under suspicion for complicity in Margary's murder. China had demonstrated her objection to any opening of her western borders to foreign trade or anything else foreign. 'The difficulties are to human strength insuperable . . . Is not all Burmah in turmoil? Has not Margary been murdered at Manwyne? Do not the latest tidings tell of Chinese troops massing in Yunnan?'—in anticipation of a punitive strike from Burma.

They sailed from Glasgow on April 6 and reached Rangoon on May 17, to find that the British authorities were still uncertain whether King Mindon or the Chinese were to blame for Margary's death, and would not allow Stevenson and Soltau to proceed. They found a Muslim refugee to teach them the Mandarin dialect of Yunnan, and started on Burmese as well. If December had seen the nadir of the China Inland Mission's early history, with 1875 and Hudson Taylor's rallying call from his bed, a new spirit became discernible among supporters, missionaries and observers alike. Compliments like Miles Knowlton's had been few and far between. Those from men of the type of Consul Medhurst (see pp 116–17) were necessarily veiled. The *Chinese Recorder* tended to overlook the existence of the CIM or to treat it as an afterthought. In 1875 the tide turned, and approval began to colour the comments, as in an editorial in the *Recorder*, 'We cannot but think the Directors of the China Inland Mission have acted wisely in sending Mr Stevenson and Mr Soltau to watch their opportunity of obtaining an entrance into Western China, by way of Burmah.'[246]

'The First of the Nine'
(January–April 1875)

On January 19, Catherine Duncan and her daughter (named Mary Jane Bowyer Duncan, with good reason) reached Shanghai with Nellie Faulding and Elizabeth Doig, and on February 6 Nellie was married to Charles Fishe and Elizabeth to Arthur Douthwaite. The next issue of the *Chinese Recorder* reported the death of

E. C. Lord's wife, his third to fall victim to infections in Ningbo.

April saw Henry Taylor try his wings on a fledgling penetration, from Wuchang through Hubei province into southern Henan, 'the first of the nine', with an evangelist named Zhang, so becoming 'the first of the eighteen' committed to the nine provinces. For fifty-six days they toured the towns and cities of the prefectures of Nanyang and Runing (now Runan). One of Grattan Guinness's students at Harley House, Joseph Adams, went independently to Burma after reading Hudson Taylor's January appeal, joining Stevenson, Henry Soltau and the CIM out here.

Charles Judd was at Wuchang, and in June, with one of the Hunanese Christians named Yao, and another Chinese, entered Hunan, the second of the nine provinces to be tackled. Nine years had passed since the Wesleyan Josiah Cox had visited Changsha, the provincial capital. Griffith John and Alexander Wylie had also travelled in the province. At last, however, premises were found among friendly neighbours and the Chinese Christians began work. Without difficulty they rented a 'house in Yueyang (Yochow) at the outlet of the Dongting lakes into the Yangzi River. But the magistrate 'demanded threateningly', Did they not know of the murder of Margary? Then how did Judd dare to come alone? When he refused them protection, 'a number of ruffians set up the cry, "The mandarin is unwilling to protect him—beat the foreign devil!"' and attacked them. Friendly Chinese defended them until the magistrate sent men in an armed boat to see them off to the next town. The Chinese evangelists returned to Yueyang later in the year.

The Garibaldi spirit (January–April 1875)

Hudson Taylor's condition continued to improve, with setbacks he found hard to tolerate, and the response to his appeal for 'the eighteen' was a tonic to him. When the Mission's referees at Lord Radstock's suggestion wished to meet with him, showing strong interest in all that was happening, Hudson Taylor was unfit to oblige them, but dictated a long review of conditions in China and the prospects of the CIM. 'We hope to do more and not less than the former work, as well as (for the) new regions,' he said, to reassure any who might share William Berger's preference for consolidating the existing gains. 'There is nothing more evident than that the evangelisation of China must be mainly effected by Christian (Chinese); and that (they) can only effectively work in or near their own native districts.'

Elsewhere they were handicapped. They could learn a different dialect, but the tendency was for them to be treated as strangers.

As the number of enquiries from young men and women increased, a general form of letter became necessary, to be incorporated in each personal reply. In a Garibaldian statement he covered the essentials of the Mission's principles and practice, stressing that faith might be tested, and courage too.

> If you want hard work, and little appreciation of it; value God's approbation more than you fear man's disapprobation; are prepared, if need be, to seal your testimony with your blood; and perhaps oftentimes to take joyfully the spoiling of your goods ... you may count on a harvest of souls here, and a crown of glory that fadeth not away, and the Master's 'well done'. You would find in connection with the China Inland Mission that it is no question of 'making the best of both worlds'—the men, the only men who will be happy with us are those who have this world under their feet; and I do venture to say that such men will find such a happiness that they never dreamed of nor thought possible down here. To those who count all things but dross ... for the 'excellence of the knowledge of Christ Jesus our Lord', He does manifest Himself in such sort that they are not inclined to rue their bargain. If after prayerfully considering the matter, you still feel drawn to engage in such work, I shall be only too glad to hear from you again.[247]

No one half-hearted need apply. For

the people of the remoter provinces, unaccustomed to having foreigners among them, resolute men were needed, men who would get on with breaking new ground and working even when they were alone; men who would not keep looking over their shoulders to see what other foreigners thought of them. He had learned through bitter experience. From sixty applications within the year he sent fifteen whom he considered fit and ready to go. One of the first, strange as it seems, was only eighteen years old, but so mature and well grounded in Scripture that Hudson Taylor chose to give him the advantage of an early start in learning the language. He himself had been only three years older when he began in China.

For two months George King served as Hudson Taylor's amanuensis, writing to his dictation from his bed, while they got to know and appreciate each other. Then King sailed unaccompanied on May 15, was shipwrecked by his vessel running on to a reef near Singapore, and arrived at Shanghai in another. Soon the report came back that the Chinese liked him, a compliment that reflected his own attitude to them. On Hudson Taylor's list of members of the CIM, George King was the fifty-fifth to join. He became one of the Mission's famous pioneers, a byword for intrepid travel.

Henrietta Soltau also served as Hudson Taylor's secretary and, like King, absorbed his beliefs and statements so that she too became a lifelong asset to the Mission. Though she sat one day for an hour pleading to be allowed to go to China, he was sure that physically she could never stand the life, and would not send her. Her place was on the home staff. In time she became the trainer of the women candidates.

When George Nicoll of Dundee (to be distinguished from the disappointing Lewis Nicol of Arbroath) read the appeal, he wrote and was invited to London. The Pyrland Road ménage struck him as 'humble' and the prayers of the invalid leader 'child-like'. But family devotions round his bed with only Louise Desgraz, George King and the Taylor family present besides himself, stayed in his memory, with young Freddie, a twelve-year-old, asking questions one after the other, each answered quietly and patiently by his father. Nicoll then spent two weeks at Harley House, being taught by Grattan Guinness and put through his paces as an evangelist among the rough East Enders by Tom Barnardo. Approved and approving, he returned to Scotland to settle his affairs, and was back again to work and train until he sailed in July, another illustrious pioneer.

March and April were difficult months with Louise Desgraz away at first, nursing Hudson Taylor's mother through pneumonia; and then Hudson Taylor, suffering a relapse. But by April 22 he could tell Mrs Gough (Mary Jones) that he was getting up and down stairs and into the garden. She had written on behalf of the Gough children's governess, Miss Bear, who wanted to join the CIM. He said, 'We shall probably see in a few months whether I am likely to be able to return to China again or not.' With or without him, no mention of apprehension appears in the collected papers that the Margary affair might halt this missionary incursion in its tracks, as two government expeditions had been halted. T. F. Wade, minister, was being trifled with at Peking, and becoming impatient. Anything might happen. Much was indeed happening, but not only at the level of international relations. On the eve of the ambitious advance of the CIM into the farthest corners of the empire, great upheavals at dynastic levels boded ill for Christianity in China.

Ci Xi shows her hand[248]
(January–April 1875)

It was common knowledge in Peking in the winter of 1874 that the young emperor Tong Zhi and his chosen friends among the young Manchu noblemen were in the habit of frequenting incognito the brothels and opium dens of the city. The smallpox from which he died could well have been contracted accidentally, but the belief came to be widely held that because he had assumed power and dismissed his regents—the two dowager empresses—he had been eliminated. The custom of refreshing diners by the provision of steaming hot face-cloths at the end of a feast provided the opportunity. It was believed that an infected face-cloth had deliberately been used on him, or some such measure. Before he died on January 13, 1875, he was prevailed upon to issue an edict authorising the dowager empresses, Ci An and Ci Xi, to conduct the affairs of state.

The question of the succession became at once the central issue of the empire. The death of a British consul and the repulse of an expedition from Burma were matters of little moment. Tong Zhi's wife, the empress Alude, was pregnant, and her child, if a son, would automatically be the next emperor. Apart from him, one person was directly qualified to be Tong Zhi's heir, Pulun (son of the adopted son of the Dao Guang emperor's eldest son!). Next in line was the son of Prince Kong, himself Dao Guang's sixth son. But Ci Xi had contrived the marriage of her own younger sister to Prince Chun, Dao Guang's seventh son, who had a four-year-old son named Zaitian (Tsai T'ien). He was ineligible to occupy the Dragon Throne while Pulun and Prince Kong's son were living.

Ci Xi had thought it all through. As soon as her son Tong Zhi died, she summoned court and government in a council of state to determine the succession. The duty of the widowed empress Alude was to be beside her lord's body, so she was excluded. From the start, by sheer strength of personality Ci Xi asserted her own will upon the council. When Prince Kong proposed that the throne remain vacant and a decision be deferred until Tong Zhi's own child was born—the correct procedure—Ci Xi declared an interregnum to be too dangerous at a time of unrest and rebellion. A choice between justice and self-preservation was at once seen to be the prime concern of all present. While her relatives the imperial clansmen remained silent, desperately looking for a way to

thwart her, the appointed career ministers cravenly took her side. Pulun she brushed aside as being the son of an adopted, not a natural, member of the imperial line, although an adopted son or grandson was constitutionally qualified. Prince Kong's son she dismissed from consideration without offering a reason, naming instead her nephew Zaitian. Everyone present knew this to be a breach of dynastic precedent. When the issue was put to the vote, ten princes and clansmen were for one or other of the rightful heirs, but fifteen councillors and ministers voted for Ci Xi's nomination. At her instigation the *Peking Gazette* at once published an edict declaring Zaitian as emperor with the reign title of Guang Xü, 'Continuation of Splendour'.

An appalling miscarriage of justice, precedent and protocol had been perpetrated through stark fear of an unprincipled woman. 'Thousands of memorials poured in from the censorate and the provinces, strongly protesting against . . . a violation of all ancestral custom and the time-honoured laws of succession.' Four years later one of the official censors presented a strongly-worded protest at the graveside of Tong Zhi and there and then committed suicide. Disaster for the empire was assured.

Ci Xi was taking no chances. She had sent urgently to Li Hongzhang, the new viceroy of Zhili, for troops to support her. And Yong Lu, tutor (and father, it was thought) of Tong Zhi, posted his imperial bannermen, the guards regiment, at strategic points in the Forbidden City. With his personal bodyguard of 4,000 reliable men from his own province of Anhui, Li marched the eighty miles from Tianjin in thirty-six hours, timing his arrival for midnight. With all accoutrements muffled and every man holding a chopstick in his mouth to remind him not to speak, the troops marched silently into the Forbidden City, its gates opened to them by Yong Lu's men.

The palace in which Zaitian was sleeping was surrounded to protect him from conspirators, and he was taken from his bed to the imperial palace to be proclaimed emperor in the morning. As his imperial palanquin made its silent journey a dust-storm raged—another ill omen—and a phrase of profound meaning soon circulated through the empire as, for fear of reprisal, the people simply said to one another, 'And the child wept.' When day dawned on the fait accompli, such opponents and political conspirators as had not been arrested in the night knew it was too late.

The little emperor under the domination of Ci Xi was to shed many more tears and to die as Tong Zhi died, almost certainly the victim of her intrigue. And not only he: on March 27, 1875, three months after Tong Zhi's death, Alude with her child unborn died too. When Ci An, the co-regent, also died in 1881 suspicious circumstances were again to point to Ci Xi. 'There is, however, no doubt at all,' Alicia Bewicke Little wrote, 'that she did get (Alude) . . . to commit suicide or die in some way—Chinese people generally say she was made to drink from a poisoned cup.'

Ci Xi never forgot Li Hongzhang's loyalty to her or ceased to admire the éclat of his midnight march. As soon as the situation was stable, he withdrew his men as inconspicuously as they had come. She had exposed for all to see her ruthless determination to have her own way, her unscrupulous character and her steely readiness to bide her time. No wonder, then, that neither Prince Kong nor Wen Xiang, the Grand Secretary, nor the Zongli Yamen had time or inclination to placate outraged foreigners or to find the murderer of a young man, Augustus Margary. If they knew or had an inkling of an answer, it suited them well to keep Wade dangling on prevarications of one kind after another until, enraged, he packed his bags and withdrew his embassy. That meant war at a time when Hudson Taylor's 'eighteen' were poised to defy both mandarins and minister.

With deepening dislike of foreigners and foreign ways, Yehonala, Ci Xi, would one day turn her malice upon them and all Christians in her empire, taking thousands of lives, in an attempt to set history back two hundred and fifty years, to the time of Yong Zheng and Qian Long (see 1, pp 26–28). Through that fire would come again the triumph of the persecuted church.

Postscript to Part V

The last part of this series surveys the fulfilment of Robert Morrison's and Charles Gutzlaff's vision—the gospel taken to the whole of China. In it the final chapter of Hudson Taylor's life is told. In a rapidly expanding Mission his role became increasingly that of administrator, not the stuff of biographical narrative. So this chronicle will sweep through the remaining decades, a counterpoise to the first volume, describing the full flower of his dreams come true.

If the burden of his duties became administrative, it also expanded to include intercontinental travel and the growth of an international membership, losing nothing of the panache, shared at last by colleagues of the right calibre. The drama by which the Empress Dowager Ci Xi sealed the fate of dynastic China extended barely eight years into the twentieth century; and she herself barely outlived the man whose ultimate influence on China was perhaps as great as her own. Dying at the same age as he, (Ci Xi 1835–1908; Hudson Taylor 1832–1905), she carried the ancient mores of dynastic China to the grave with her, unmourned. But the church she had tried to exterminate went on from strength to strength, as it is still doing.

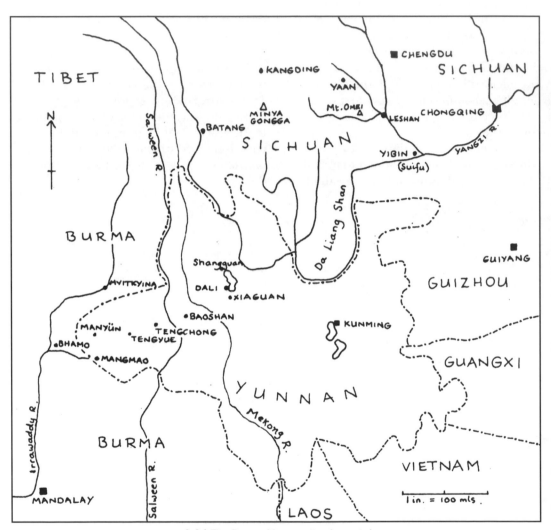

2.24 The Burma-Yunnan 'trade route'

Part VI

ASSAULT ON THE NINE

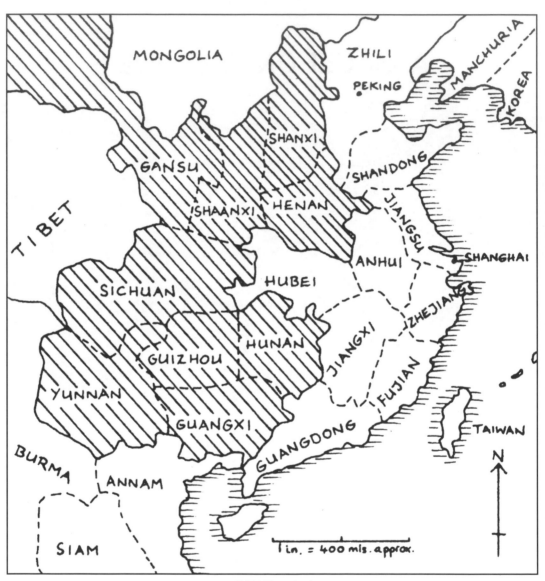

2.25 'The nine'

Preface to Part VI

Anticipating the research to be done for this part of the history, the Postscript of the previous part, *Refiner's Fire*, predicted a sweeping narrative of the final years of the saga. Far from it: what emerged from the archives has merited, in my judgment, retention of much that was to have been passed over. And Messrs Hodder and Stoughton have shown their usual magnanimity. The series is to end with a seventh volume. A digest of the seven must be someone else's work!

The preceding volumes have followed Hudson Taylor's development and early aims in going to China, his formative experiences and setbacks. They showed him as the reluctant founder of an organisation for which he planned no great expansion in size but only in achievement. Its few members, some of whom were of outstanding quality, a bare two dozen Westerners each with a Chinese colleague, were to invade the forbidden interior of China, carrying the gospel of Christ to the remotest provinces and to Manchuria, Mongolia and Tibet. But by 1874 his disappointment with so many of his early recruits, the repeated breakdown of his own health, and the testing of his own resolve and courage to extremes of endurance, brought him and his circle of intimate friends close to the end of hope.

Half paralysed by an accident, and with his supporters' interest in the Mission and in China at its lowest ebb, Hudson Taylor could not escape the oppressing thought that nine vast provinces with one hundred and fifty millions of inhabitants had still to be reached with the gospel (see pp 231–238). At the rate of progress being made by Protestant missions this could not be done in the lifetime of his generation. The coastal provinces of Zhili, Shandong and Jiangsu, Zhejiang, Fujian and Guangdong (see map 2.2: p 6), and three more through which the Yangzi River flowed—Anhui, Jiangxi and Hubei—had a nucleus of missionaries in them, mostly at the treaty ports. Beyond them the nine 'interior' provinces could only be reached with difficulty and danger from natural obstacles and hostile men: Henan, Shanxi, Shaanxi and Gansu in the north; Hunan and Guangxi south of the Yangzi; and Sichuan, Guizhou and Yunnan in the far west. Unlikely ever to return to China himself, he appealed from his bed for eighteen more men, two for each of the nine provinces, once again to leap 'over the treaty wall', defying the danger and resistance from the imperial Chinese government. No assault on mountain peaks has required more dedication or courage.

They began to come. And slowly his strength returned. Then, on February 21, 1875, as the new venture was beginning, Augustus Margary, a British consular interpreter, was murdered on the Burma border. Court intrigues and the dowager empress Ci Xi's seizure of power foiled attempts by the British minister at Peking, Thomas F. Wade, to see justice done. Nothing could be less timely than for 'the eighteen' to attempt to travel, let alone to live in deepest China.

At this point we take up the story. How in these circumstances, with more war clouds over China, could Hudson Taylor's goal be reached? That it was reached is common knowledge. How it was done takes us immediately into what may be judged the most historic eight or ten years of Hudson Taylor's life, and of the China Inland Mission. To Chauncey Goodrich, pioneer of the American Board, Hudson Taylor's success and influence on other missions lay in the magnitude of his vision. In retrospect Goodrich said, 'He extended this Mission till it has become a veritable octopus, stretching out its arms to the most remote borders of China.'[249]

Assault on the Nine builds on what is contained in Parts I to V. Descriptions of life and travelling conditions in China, of customs and beliefs, of dynastic rule and the place of mandarins and the literati in the life of the nation, and much else are again 'taken as read'. We stand back from the detail to see the ever widening picture, and find that even what looked like dry administrative routine is rich with human drama as the frontiers recede. Beginning in the spring of 1875 we find Hudson Taylor, aged forty-three, still dogged by ill-health but confident in his leadership of the young men and women who have caught his own spirit.

As before, my intention is to record events and statements rather than to 'write them up', showing the perspective of secular history and the relevance of contemporary personalities in government, church and other missions. As the CIM expanded from scores to hundreds, the burden of administration increased, but what little I have included has been for the light it throws on the leading figures in the history. A confusing web of names and places may lose its complexity by reference to the Personalia. Assessment and discussion are again reserved for the final volume.

One problem has defied solution after time-consuming research. The nineteenth-century convention of speaking and writing of people as Mr X or Miss Y, without using their initials or 'given' name, was extended to Chinese colleagues. Tracing the achievements of these historic people is made doubly difficult because of surnames being restricted to the 'Old Hundred Names' and spelt with dialect variations. Chinese names, hard for the average reader to pronounce and remember, were simplified for home consumption, so that I have not succeeded in identifying the Chinese pioneers on whose companionship the Westerners' success depended.

Historians of the Chinese church are faced with a daunting problem which I regretfully do little to resolve. We wait expectantly for this gap in the literature of Christianity in China to be filled.

AJB

Acknowledgments to Part VI

The completion of this part has been delayed by factors beyond my control, but the patience and encouragement of readers waiting for it have already put me in their debt. Warm thanks also to David Wavre, Religious Books director of Hodder and Stoughton, for his understanding, and to all who have been inconvenienced by my reclusive existence for so long.

The chief sources have as before been fragile manuscripts and old books, too many to name. Of modern books John Pollock's *Moody without Sankey* and *The Cambridge Seven*, and Ralph Covell's *W.A.P. Martin* have helped me frequently. But Eugene Stock's expansive *History of the Church Missionary Society* (published 1899–1916), rippling with vitality and fact on many themes, continues to inspire.

Relatives of the Cambridge Seven have kindly allowed some 'revelations'. I am particularly grateful to Sir Christopher Beauchamp, Bt, for facts about Sir Montagu's 'fortune'. To those of others about whom I have included less complimentary information in the interests of a full statement, I offer my apologies—my own family among them. When the earlier biographies were written, many contemporaries were still alive and only one-sided accounts were considered appropriate.

Once again, my deepest gratitude to Molly Robertson for more hundreds of pages of meticulous typing, to Val Connolly for all her artwork, and to my faithful advisers for reading it all in the rough and making perspicacious comments.

AJB

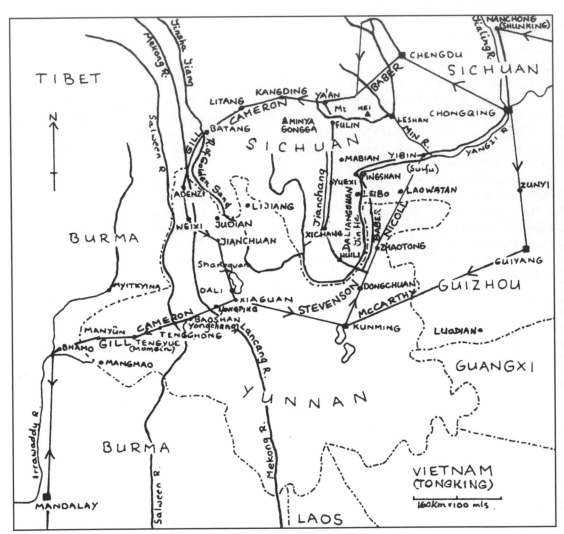

2.26 Treks in the mountains of the west

18

Octopus Mission (1875–79)

PROLOGUE: NO TIME TO 'TEMPT FATE'?

'The Margary affair'
(February–November 1875)

The emperor was dead. An opium-smoker and good-for-nothing, Tong Zhi's passing was no great loss to the empire. But the manner of his dying mattered immeasurably. By her immediate actions his mother the Dowager Empress Ci Xi came under strong suspicion. On coming of age he had assumed power, ending her regency. With the help of Viceroy Li Hongzhang, and her staunch friend the imperial bannerman Yong Lu, a coup d'état had made her regent again, this time of her puppet the infant Guang Xü emperor. When Tong Zhi's child widow Alude and unborn babe, the awaited true heir, also died mysteriously—by poisoning it was believed[250]—little doubt remained that Ci Xi was responsible. Such unscrupulous, cold-blooded scheming boded ill for court and nation.

When Augustus Margary, the young consular interpreter on Colonel Browne's expedition, and five of his Chinese companions were killed at Manyün (Manwyne) no one suggested that it had been at the instigation of the Peking Court (see pp 232–34).[251] On February 21 he left Manyün with some Chinese who had offered to show him the hot springs. They knocked him off his pony and speared him to death. His passport to take that route, to leave and re-enter China by the Burma border, had been issued in the summer of 1874 by the Zongli Yamen, the Peking Foreign Office (see p 233). Responsibility for the murder could never be firmly laid at the door of Zen Yüying, the acting-viceroy of Yunnan, nor of the mandarins of Manyün where he died. But the heads of the murdered men were exposed on the city ramparts like criminals, a tell-tale fact.

Nor could Shan or Kachin tribesmen be confidently blamed for the attack, nor King Mindon of Upper Burma who resented and resisted British penetration through his territory, three hundred miles up the Irrawaddy River beyond his capital at Mandalay. Whether or not the blame could be laid where it belonged, Britain must be seen to obtain satisfaction or such acts would be repeated. T. F. Wade, the minister in Peking, heard on March 11 through the India Office that Margary had been killed on February 21, and at once formulated terms for reparation. He notified London that he had demanded a commission of enquiry, authority for a second expedition to replace the one attacked so treacherously, and 150,000 taels of silver to be deposited with him, Wade, pending conclusion of the matter. He did not add in his cable to London that at the same time he had revived old grievances regarding access to the emperor and tariff concessions and demanded that 'all claims arising out of the action of the (Yunnan) officials' were to be satisfied at once.[252]

The Zongli Yamen accepted in principle Wade's first three demands, demurring only on secondary matters: but when by imperial decree Zen Yüying, as acting-viceroy, ultimately responsible for law and order in his province of Yunnan, was ordered to make the investigation, Wade insisted on someone of higher rank being appointed, and on a British officer being present. Unfortunately Wade's irascible temperament was unsuited to the judicious handling of such affairs, and plunged him into what Alicia Bewicke Little (in *Li Hung-Chang, His Life and Times*) called 'a cat's cradle of negotiations'. He had to consult London, but the telegraphic cable still ended at Shanghai, so he decided to go there to use it. The day after Alude's death on March 28, however, he issued an ultimatum—satisfaction by the 29th or he would withdraw his legation from Peking. His preparations to travel looked like a threat. The American envoy reported to his Secretary of State that Wade, with a full staff of secretaries and attendants, called at the Zongli Yamen where a 'rather stormy and electric' meeting took place.[253] To Wade's embarrassment his demands were accepted. Li Hanzhang, brother of Li Hongzhang and viceroy of Hunan and Hubei, was commissioned to conduct the enquiry, supervised by the Hon T. G. Grosvenor, Secretary of the British Legation, and two consular officials, E. Colborne Baber and A. Davenport, of whom we shall hear more. Even so, Wade left Peking with several secretaries and their families, exciting rumours among the populace of impending hostilities. He stayed in Shanghai from April till July, with brief visits to Hankou and Fuzhou.

Arriving at Wuhan on July 7, Grosvenor reported to Wade that Li Hanzhang denied any knowledge of the attack on Colonel Browne's expedition, and was keeping him waiting. Wade then returned to the north and, fearing (it was said) that Grosvenor and his companion might be held as hostages, at an interview with Li Hongzhang in Tianjin extended his demands upon China. In Grand Secretary Li (see ill. 2.30: p 272) he was faced by one of China's greatest statesmen of all time, who could in no circumstances appear to be ready to meet the demands of the foreigner. Thwarted, Wade stormed out of Tianjin on September 9 'with the most bellicose intentions', reaching Peking on the 14th. But as Henri Cordier, the French observer, said, Wade's warlike tone had little effect on the Chinese.[254] Yet again he presented an ultimatum. If he had struck his flag, the British merchant and missionary communities in Peking and Tianjin would have been left without protection throughout the winter, when the frozen approaches prevented naval intervention. His second departure, on October 11, therefore left the rest of the

diplomatic corps strongly discontented, but on November 5 the imperial mission of enquiry with its British observers set out from Wuhan to ascend the Yangzi gorges to Chongqing.[255] From there they continued up the Yangzi to Yibin (Suifu) at the confluence of the Min River and the upper Yangzi, where they struck out over the mountains via Zhaotong into Yunnan, not reaching Kunming, the provincial capital, until March 6, 1876. So far so good. In November (1875) Thomas Francis Wade became Knight Commander of the Order of the Bath, a dignity probably calculated to help him in his difficult task.

Jackson's folly (May–October 1875)

Brash and impetuous as ever, it was no time for Josiah Jackson in southern Zhejiang, to come into conflict with the mandarins of Lishui (Chu chou) over premises he had rented there, but this he did. Throughout China rumours had spread and grown as news of Margary's death, of Wade being flouted, and of a new threat of war reached the people. A spate of anti-foreign, anti-Christian agitation in the Yangzi valley held the Catholics responsible for another wave of assaults on children, and for the surreptitious cutting off of people's *bianzi*, the work of demons under the priests' control, with strong overtones recalling the Taiping rebellion. Hangzhou, Shaoxing and Ningbo, A. E. Moule reported, were disturbed by the same 'mysterious disappearance' of *bianzi*, 'snipped off by unseen shears'. But when the imperial edict ordering investigation into the murder of Margary set the tone, the provincial magistrates issued strong proclamations to rebuke and quiet the people.

After Jackson's rudeness to the magistrate, Consul Forrest sent a representative to restore peace and good relations at Lishui, and to find other accommodation for him. Wade referred the matter to London, and Lord Derby, Foreign Minister, replied understandingly:[256]

Her Majesty's Government are fully sensible of the benefits which have been derived from the labours of the Missionaries of the

Taylor Mission, and of the self-devotion and courage with which those labours have been pursued. At the same time, they cannot doubt that in this instance and on other occasions the Missionaries have shown an amount of indiscretion which must have created much ill-will ... I have accordingly to instruct you to inform the Taylor Mission that unless (Mr Jackson) and other members of the Mission exercise greater judgment for the future, Her Majesty's government will find themselves reluctantly compelled to withdraw their passports.

For Jackson to play into Wade's hands at such a time of tension was lamentable. As soon as Hudson Taylor in London was informed, he dictated this memorandum to every member of the Mission:

I understand (Lord Derby's letter) may mean not only the presumed offender's passport, but those of all members of the Mission. I cannot but think that His Lordship's judgment is based upon an incomplete acquaintance with the facts; but ... I wish at once to impress upon you all most earnestly:

First, the absolute necessity of desisting from making any representation, private, semi-official or official, of any difficulties in the work to H.M. Consul or consular offices.

Second, if possible to avoid personal (dealings) with mandarins. Communications with mandarins, if essential, must be in writing and worded very courteously, without demands or claims but as a favour. If refused, leave the matter entirely alone ... Anything which may, fairly or unfairly, be termed indiscretion, may be taken as a reason for steps seriously embarrassing to the operations of the Mission, and which might place some, if they continue their work, in a position of antagonism to law and order.

Members must keep informed of the wider scene and behave appropriately. The danger of a national conflagration was never far away.

The church in China[257] (1870–75)

A glance at the state of missions in general and the still struggling Chinese church may help to show how the debilitated 'Taylor Mission' stood in the contemporary scene. Roman Catholic societies were moving reinforcements into China in increasing strength and numbers, sisters as well as priests and male orders. In 1870 about two hundred and fifty priests had been deployed throughout the empire. The Jesuits, concentrating on Jiangsu, Anhui and Zhili, had lost no time in following the victorious forces into territories taken from the Taipings. Immigrants from Hubei occupying land in Anhui left desolate after the Taiping slaughter included Catholic Christians who welcomed priests to live among them. Between then and 1878 a hundred new missionaries swelled the ranks of that society alone. Converts and adherents in Jiangsu and Anhui were reported in 1874–75 to number about eighty-nine thousand.

In contrast, for many years the provinces of Hunan, Hubei, Shaanxi, Shanxi and Shandong had been the sphere of the Franciscans, whose reception was very different. Baron von Richtofen, visiting hostile Hunan, received the impression that the most the missionaries could do, against bitter opposition, was pastoral care of descendants of 'old Christians' of the historic Church. While destruction of property continued, time-honoured tenacity kept the Christians together. In Jiangxi the Lazarists had about twelve thousand adherents in 1875 and ten years later the same number in Zhejiang. The far west was still the field of the Paris Mission (Société des Missions ...trangéres de Paris) with extensive work in Sichuan, Guizhou and Yunnan supervised by five bishops and one hundred and fifty-seven priests in 1872, Chinese and foreign in roughly equal numbers. In Guiyang, the provincial capital, they had two cathedrals and nineteen European priests, as well as several minor establishments with their own clergy. Recovering from near-annihilation at the time of the Muslim rebellion, there were eight thousand Catholics in Yunnan. In Sichuan the adherents were ten times as numerous, and there were missions high in the Tibetan marches, even at Batang. In all of China the number of Catholics had risen from approximately 400,000 in 1870 to 500,000 by 1886, with 2,500 churches and chapels, 30 seminaries, 470 foreign priests and 280 Chinese priests.

By comparison the Protestant achievement looked puny.[258] Of the total of 436 missionaries in 1874, 210 were women in or near the treaty ports. By 1888 there were 489 men, 320 wives, 231 single women and 32,260 Chinese communicants, but the great majority were still in the coastal provinces. Protestant statistics were always confused by inconsistent reporting. Some societies included and others excluded missionary wives as working members. More significantly, the practice of recording baptisms and communicant members of the Churches but not all adherents, as the Catholics did, made true comparison impossible. Two (unnamed) veteran missionaries were still at work after thirty-eight years; twelve had survived twenty-eight years; and ten who arrived in 1854 (including Hudson Taylor, John Nevius and Griffith John) were still active after twenty-one years. In addition there were one hundred in Japan and twenty-five, all American, in Siam, as Thailand was still called. Having served since 1835, the American Baptist William Dean, DD, of Bangkok, was doyen of the missionary community in 'China'—everywhere east of Burma to people of the time.[259]

Of the 'humble and despised' China Inland Mission (CIM), on January 1, 1875, twenty-one were in China and three on their way there, but as many as twelve were on leave in Britain after five or ten gruelling years in action. Even the editor of the *Chinese Recorder*, who should have been better informed, omitted the CIM from his statistical table and entered 'No report from CES'—the Chinese Evangelisation Society which had ceased to exist in 1860. The largely unknown, 'eccentric' China Inland Mission had apparently lost its

leader through ill-health and injury, had no adequate deputy leaders, and outside Zhejiang had been reduced by April to one recent arrival, F.W. Baller, the only one in the Yangzi region. Since February one single woman, Emmeline Turner, remained in China of all those who had so recently shocked staid treaty port society by going upcountry in Chinese dress. The rest were out of sight and apparently out of mind. Sadly true was the fact that five of the *Lammermuir* party had departed, four more and two of the children had died, and Jackson's days in the Mission were numbered.

Even the great Church Missionary Society had in 1872 reached its own 'low water mark' with a 'failing treasury' and 'scanty supply of men'. But by 1875 the tide had turned, candidates were multiplying, a decade of unprecedented advance had begun in Africa and India, not China. Stirred by the death of David Livingstone on May 1, 1873, Church and State had responded. Together the *New York Herald* and London *Daily Telegraph* sent H. M. Stanley on a second expedition into central Africa. His letter from Uganda in April 1875 led to the CMS Victoria Nyanza Mission, and by travelling down the Congo River in 1877 he opened the way for pioneering missions to enter in 1878—led by the Livingstone Inland Mission, founded for the purpose by Grattan Guinness sending two of his Institute men, and followed by the Baptist Missionary Society (BMS).[260]

In China, Hudson Taylor's old friend John Shaw Burdon became Bishop of Victoria, Hong Kong, in March 1874, and in forty years saw the Church in Fuzhou under J. R. Wolfe's supervision double its membership from eight hundred catechumens and communicants to more than sixteen hundred during a time of intense persecution. But few reinforcements came to strengthen the CMS in China, and expansion was restricted to adjacent areas. The same was true in general of other societies, some of which strongly discouraged their members from breaking out of the treaty ports as they longed to do (see pp 284, 290, 350).

Turn of the tide (1875)

In Britain a surprising transformation was taking place. From the lowest of low points in December, when Jennie Taylor had thought them 'unlikely to see China again' and Hudson Taylor with acute enteritis rewrote his will, when with the death of the intrepid Tsiu Kyuo-kwe the Chinese spearhead of advance into the interior had snapped off, and when the Mission appeared to be forgotten by all but an inner circle of faithful friends—a state of affairs described by Eugene Stock as 'pathetic in the extreme'[261]—the fortunes of the CIM changed dramatically.

The stricken man faced with the failure of his hopes was reading through the Bible systematically as usual. On November 29, 1874, he dated and marked Nahum 1.7, 'The LORD is good, a stronghold in the day of trouble; and He knoweth them that trust in Him.' In deep trouble himself, Hudson Taylor took courage. Then on December 6 he read Haggai, chapter 2, and heard God speaking to him. He marked (italics) verse after verse. Verse 4: 'Yet now be strong, O Zerubbabel, saith the LORD; and be strong, O Joshua . . . and be strong, all ye people . . . and work, for I am with you.' Verse 5: 'My spirit remaineth among you, fear ye not.' Verse 8: 'The silver is mine, and the gold is mine, saith the Lord of hosts.' Verse 15: 'And now, I pray you, *consider* from this day . . . from before a stone was laid . . . in the temple of the Lord.' Verse 18: 'Consider now . . . *From the day that the foundation of the LORD's temple was laid.*' Verse 19: ' . . . *from this day will I bless you.*' Verses 21–23: 'I will shake . . . I will overthrow . . . I will destroy the *strength* of the kingdoms of the heathen . . . for I have chosen thee.'

With prophetic insight he believed that the Holy Spirit was applying this passage to China and to himself. Did he see by faith the curbing of dynastic power and the promise of a harvest in China? 'Is the seed yet in the barn?' verse 19 asked. 'Yea, as yet the vine, and the fig tree, and the pomegranate, and the olive tree, hath not brought forth: *from this day I will bless you*'—with confident faith he underlined the words. Events proved him right. Five days later, on December 11, he marked Zechariah 2.8 with the date: 'He that toucheth you toucheth the apple of his eye.' Strength, 'gold', results and protection could be accepted as the Lord's provision if he forged ahead.

But not Hudson Taylor and the CIM alone. Standing back from the events in the foreground to get the perspective of a century on, it is clear that *this was the point at which the tide of all mission to China turned.* For by what now happened, the second of Hudson Taylor's aims, the invigoration of the Church in its duty to evangelise the world, began to be fulfilled. The story of Hudson Taylor's spiritual odyssey on the one hand, and of the Mission on the other, has often been told. But highlights such as the Cambridge Seven have blinded us to this more significant event. Taking place in the shadows of personal weakness and public indifference, a movement began which quickly led to the gospel reaching the far corners of the Chinese empire. A demonstration of the fact of travel and residence in remote provinces being possible and safe threw open the gate for other missions. After a decade of proof to convince the church, the headline event of seven 'sporting hearties' devoting their lives and wealth to the evangelisation of China gave impetus to the movement among the universities which sent thousands more into every continent and country. The dawn of 1875 brought in the age of Protestant missionary expansion, as significant as the advent of William Carey and Robert Morrison; it was the end of what had been, in Stephen Neill's words, 'a time of renewed awareness, and of small and tentative beginnings' in the eighteenth century.[262]

After private prayer for two full years, with only Frederick Baller, M. Henry Taylor and A. W. Douthwaite to show for it, the publication of an 'Appeal for Prayer' for eighteen pioneers struck the strategic moment.[263] As a result of David

Livingstone's death a tide was flowing in the church again, so that 'by his death he effected more than he did by his life'. The theological colleges filled up and candidates of the main societies multiplied. D. L. Moody's first meetings and the 'holiness movement' associated with the presence in the country of another American, Pearsall Smith, and of Evan H. Hopkins and others, led within a few months to Hudson Taylor receiving twenty applications for service in China.[264] Despite himself and to his surprise, the obscurity of the CIM was giving place to prominence. As when he launched the Mission in 1865 after painful years of testing and preparation, he found himself and the CIM the focus of growing popularity and influence.

Still working in bed but conscious of strength returning, getting up for one, then two, then three hours a day, Hudson Taylor directed the attention of awakened Christians to 'the need and claims' of 'the nine provinces' of China still with no Protestant messengers of the gospel. With a variety of volunteer writers, John Stevenson, Henrietta Soltau or George King, a new arrival, sitting at his bedside at No 6 Pyrland Road, he achieved more than if he had been up and about.[265] A class of accepted candidates learned Chinese from him, and the advisory council for Mission affairs in Britain met frequently, also by his bedside. On January 25 they had been startled to be told that John Stevenson was about to sail to Burma in March, 'ere returning to Shaoxing' to pioneer the route into Yunnan which British arms had failed to open for commerce. 'China via Burmah' was a title in the last *Occasional* to be published. Soon 'this mission to West China' was 'giving a wonderful impetus to interest in the whole Mission', and the announcement that Henry Soltau, honorary co-secretary of the CIM, was to leave his profession and go with him, fuelled the excitement (see p 234).[266] After five months on his back, in April Hudson Taylor was on crutches going downstairs to work and up again at night, jubilant over the great developments in the making.

The quality of candidates acceptable to Hudson Taylor was made doubly clear. In the next few years only one stonemason, two carpenters and a housemaid measured up to his new criteria dictated by the sad events of the first ten years of the Mission. He now required an adequate basic education and standard of social behaviour, finding them among fewer artisans but more skilled craftsmen—a jeweller, an 'ornamental carver' and a dressmaker—more shop assistants, students, teachers, nurses and doctors, while he still referred others to the denominational societies and to his friend John Burdon in Hong Kong. By 1900 the one-time stonemason would be the most promising young director in the Mission.

'The Garibaldi spirit' of his reply to enquiries left no doubt that an easy life was the last thing they should expect (pp 235–36). 'Hard work, and little appreciation of it . . . to seal your testimony with your blood . . . to take joyfully the spoiling of your goods' was for men and women 'who have this world under their feet', not those hoping 'to make the most of both worlds'. Nor was it rhetoric. Suffering and death were the price all too many had to pay. Not only that. With his council's approval he was requiring new missionaries to give two years to adaptation and language learning in China before marrying—in the spirit of Emily Blatchley who had heavily underlined part of Galatians 5.24 in her Bible, 'They that are Christ's have crucified the flesh with the affections.'

Full-blooded dedication to their calling must be given, dedication like that of the priests of the Paris Mission whom he respected so highly, quoting T. T. Cooper's *Travels of a Pioneer of Commerce.*

> The young missionary, on entering China, strips himself of his nationality; he shaves his head, and adopts the Chinese costume, and conforms in all respects to the Chinese mode of life. His first two years are spent either at one of the principal mission stations, or at some outstation, in close attendance on an old and experienced Father, under whose care he systematically

studies the language and manners of the people.[267]

The Brighton Convention (June 1875)

The 'holiness movement' was gaining momentum. Instead of only the Mildmay Conference, the summer of 1875 was to see three conferences for the strengthening of spiritual life, for all regardless of denomination who longed to live on a higher plane of obedience to the command of God, 'Be holy, for I the Lord your God am holy' (Leviticus 19.2). Christians aspiring to 'the higher Christian life' were flocking, in hundreds and soon thousands, to hear Scripture expounded. Private conferences were being held at Broadlands (the future home of Lord Mount Temple and the Mountbattens), and later at Mildmay and Keswick.[268]

From May 31 to June 4, H. W. Webb-Peploe was to speak at a Brighton Convention on the theme 'As ye have received Christ Jesus the Lord, so walk in Him', by faith. (The first Keswick Convention was to follow, June 28–July 2, after the Mildmay Conference of June 23–25, such was the spiritual hunger.) In April Lord Radstock had brought Pearsall Smith to meet Hudson Taylor. In the 'Keswick' community of old and young, he would be likely to find some responsive to the spiritual need of China and to the call of God. He decided to attend, using two sticks in place of crutches. It happened that the CIM 'year' was dated from the end of May, and his annual report was due. Hudson Taylor looked through his account books before going to Brighton, and found that since the formation of the Mission in 1865, donations totalling £52,000 had been received. Then he added up his May receipts to date. They came to only £68, 'nearly £235 less than our average expenditure in China for three weeks'. At the daily half-hour of prayer for China in the Mission headquarters at No 6 Pyrland Road, he said to the household, 'Let us remind the Lord of it', and prayed for that amount to be made up. In the evening the postman brought a letter containing a cheque for £235.7s.9d to be entered anonymously as 'From the sale of plate'—to him another gesture of approval from God his Father of the course he was pursuing. Not surprisingly his address at the Convention was on 'Trusting God', that obvious but neglected right of all Christians. When later he wrote an article on the same theme, he ended it on the note, '"Trust in Him at all times", you will never have cause to regret it.' And after a few more weeks he coined the phrase 'Hold God's faithfulness' as an axiom or motto based on Mark 11.22, 'Have faith in God'.[269] To emphasise faith was to miss the point; simple trust in a faithful Father is everything. In this article he also used the words 'All God's giants have been weak men,' strength and self-confidence are all too often a handicap, whereas a sense of weakness and need will tap his limitless resources.

Returning from Brighton on June 4, Hudson Taylor found himself on the station platform with the Russian ex-Minister of Ways and Communications, Count Bobrinsky, who had been at the meetings. They should travel together, the count suggested. 'But I am travelling third class,' Hudson Taylor answered. 'My ticket admits of my doing the same,' the count replied. On the way he drew from his pocket-book a banknote for fifty pounds which he handed to Hudson Taylor as a donation. A foreigner's mistake, thought Hudson Taylor as he pointed it out (the equivalent of £1,500 or £2,000 today?). 'It was five pounds I meant to give, but God must have intended you to have fifty,' the count insisted.

Back at Pyrland Road, Hudson Taylor found the household had met together to pray about a remittance due to be sent to China. The funds in hand were forty-nine pounds eleven shillings short of what they ought if possible to send. He laid the count's banknote on the table before them.

Young men and women living in the climate of such happenings grew to rely on God whatever the circumstances, however far inland they might be. This was preferable to a fixed salary from 'the Mission' or any other source.

The tide was flowing; 'the eighteen' were arriving; advance into 'the nine provinces' had begun; the means were coming in; and 'the Margary affair' was only one more hazard in the long adventure.

1875–77: 'NOT TO TRY BUT TO DO IT'

Expand to consolidate! (Spring 1875)

On his feet again after months in bed, Hudson Taylor was surprising everyone by his energy and the fertility of his ideas. The 'forgotten' mission house in Pyrland Road was milling again with action. The young men and women who came and went recognised a leader in the semi-invalid who talked of such big things he wanted them to do. Some older ones had qualms. Over the years William Berger from time to time had found Hudson Taylor's pace breathtaking. He now cautioned that he should consolidate existing gains before advancing further (see p 235).[270] It was the view commonly expressed by leaders of the great societies. So when he wrote to say it would be wise to call a meeting of the Mission's referees before becoming too deeply committed to occupying nine more provinces, and had expressed his opinion to some of the referees already, Hudson Taylor saw danger ahead. They were influential men who had agreed to commend the Mission when consulted by others, but were not an advisory council. Too easily progress could become bogged down in discussion with half-comprehending well-wishers who, once consulted, would need to be satisfied. In founding the Mission with Hudson Taylor in 1865, even William Berger had rejected the inclusion of a council who could repeat the blunders of the Chinese Evangelisation Society (see 1, pp 501–2). The 'council of management' formed in 1872 to guide affairs in Britain when Mr Berger retired, was primarily to control the transmission of funds and the selection of reinforcements. They could gather round Hudson Taylor's bed informally. But in his state of health to have to defend his actions before an august body of referees, including titled gentlemen, was too much to face.

Instead, he wrote at length a respectful twelve page document of policy and current practice involving a detailed report of progress to date, assuring them that consolidation of the gains already made was no less Mission policy than breaking new ground. 'The evangelisation of China must be mainly effected by Christian (Chinese)', so constant teaching and training of them in the course of field work would be continued. The deliberate transfer of foreign missionaries from established churches would encourage congregations to conduct their own affairs. To demonstrate their progress, from time to time he published translations of sermons preached by men who had so recently been unenlightened pagans. Their grasp of truth and ability to expound it were apparent. Work built muscle, and learning in action was the best kind of school for Chinese and missionaries alike. Both were to advance together. The foreigners were to be the catalysts and examples, the scaffold, not the main frame of the Church. His aim was that they should be far outnumbered by Chinese working Christians. Some with families would have to be salaried or as colleagues have their expenses paid, but a greater and greater proportion would earn their own living or be supported by growing congregations. Mission statistics might well not include such men and women. But 'the conversion, instruction and qualifying of evangelists was a slow process'. Two guiding principles needed to kept in mind. The older work needed time to develop, but to limit a mission to this was to run into soft sand. The sooner work began in every province the better, for great distances and marked dialect and cultural differences meant that each needed its unique methods.

Twenty-eight churches with more than a score of 'outstations' had already been formed under the leadership of seven ordained Chinese pastors, with thirty-three evangelists, twenty-seven colporteurs, six Scripture-readers or 'Bible-women' and two schoolmasters. 'Upwards of fifty' places were occupied by resident Chinese and foreign church workers, and this consolidating work was itself expanding. The nine unevangelised provinces meanwhile cried out for attention. In the south and west were hill tribes for whom he 'yearned'. China was so vast; the task of reaching her myriads so appalling. 'We hope to do *more* and not less for the former work, as well as to attempt to carry the Gospel into the new regions.'

For supporters, in general, Hudson Taylor published an article on the 'Plan of Operation of the CIM', taking its principles from the Acts of the Apostles.

> The early missionaries, appear to have scattered themselves. They visited important centres, usually in twos or threes; stayed there long enough to commence a work, and then trusted much to the keeping of God. (But) they had advantages ... in the godly Jews and proselytes, already acquainted with the Old Testament scriptures ... We may, therefore, anticipate the necessity of a somewhat prolonged residence in our districts, for the purpose of instructing in the word of God those who may be converted ... Those who will be the Chinese workers of the future first need to be ... given time to show what gifts they possess.[271]

His logic was convincing and satisfied his friends. Expansion and consolidation were to proceed hand in hand, the one nourishing the other.

There could be no thought of holding back. In fact the first pioneers of the unoccupied provinces were already in action. By then Henry Taylor had been travelling for two months in Henan with the LMS evangelist Zhang, becoming 'the first of the eighteen' to enter 'the first of the nine' provinces (see pp 234–35).[272] And Charles Judd had braved hostile Hunan province with his companions Yao Shangda and Zhang (Chang), only to be attacked and driven out. George King had reached

China, hoping to pioneer the north-west. Others were either ready to go or in training—George Nicoll of Dundee, James Cameron, like the deceased George Duncan 'a six-foot Highlander', and George Clarke, an emigrant home from Canada.

'James Cameron was a tall, strong, manly yet gentle brother,' Grattan Guinness recorded, a shipwright building 'iron ships', 'who came to us in April 1874 from Jarrow on the Tyne. He was twenty-nine years of age, sensible, vigorous and trustworthy; slow but impressive and intensely earnest as a speaker, and blessed to many souls', a man with 'spiritual perception and a cultivated intelligence'. Cameron was to become known as the 'Livingstone of China'.

Back in 1866 when William Rudland was living with the incomplete *Lammermuir* party at Coborn Street, Bow, he had worked with Miss Annie Macpherson in her Shoreditch night school for street arabs and factory hands. One day he had accosted a youth of fifteen in the street and urged him to attend the night school and Bible classes. The result was pandemonium. The spirited boy took every opportunity to disrupt the classes and incite the other boys, until given an ultimatum, his final chance to mend his ways. He submitted, and was helped to emigrate to Canada, where he worked on the transcontinental railways and as a lumberjack, earning enough to attend college in Canada and the USA during three deep winters. There a copy of *China: Its Spiritual Need and Claims* came into his hands and George Clarke returned to London, to Pyrland Road (see 1, pp 663, 687).[273] Hudson Taylor's advice to him when he sailed to China was, 'Travel, now the opportunity is given; even if you cannot say much, let the people see you; and sell what books you can . . . Do not tell me what you intend to do [lest his letters be intercepted], but tell me what you have done.' And, from long observation of thorny relationships between colleagues in China, 'I have made it a rule in my life that if a man cannot get on with me, I will do my best to get on with him.' These were not empty words: James Meadows could never forget his own journey home from China with Hudson Taylor in a French liner in 1871. Meadows had been put in a hot, stuffy cabin with a dozen strangers and found it and them intolerable. Hudson Taylor was in similar but better circumstances and had Meadows moved in with him, 'at the cost of much discomfort to himself for another five weeks on board. (I) felt inclined to be obstreperous . . . But he managed me so well, quieting and reconciling me to my surroundings, making me believe that he was even better off with my presence than without me.'[274]

Men of the best quality had enlisted. Large gifts had been donated by the dedicated Mrs Grace specifically for 'advance into *fresh* provinces'. While prayer for the eighteen pioneers was being answered and funds provided, advance without delay must override all obstacles. A frank letter from another donor, Mrs Julia Rich of Sandringham House, Margate, revealed another hazard, the harm caused by falsehoods still in circulation.

> Dear Sir ... I hear from a friend who has been in China, that missionaries of your society are frequently reduced to such depths of poverty that they are induced to give up the work and take up with secular pursuits ... and that even their children are sometimes so destitute that the heathen take pity on them ...
>
> For this cause I have not continued my support of your Mission. Will you kindly ... let me know if what I have stated is really the case.[275]

Hudson Taylor was grateful that she had written. It was easy for those who lived as Westerners in China to misjudge others who chose to live simply, close to the mass of Chinese. If they voiced their misgivings, as in the Lewis Nicol episode, great damage could be done. There was no knowing how many were alienated without saying why. So he replied, carefully explaining the facts, here only summarised.

> Dear Madam, I am much obliged for your letter of inquiry ... and shall be glad if you will kindly show your informant this letter, as he has been entirely misled ... I

do not believe that any child or member of the family of anyone connected with our Mission has ever lacked food or raiment for a single hour, though in many cases the supply may not have come *before* it was needed.

No one has been hindered in work by lack of funds; *no one* has ever suffered in health from this cause; *no one* has ever left the Mission on this ground, or has remained dissatisfied on this score, to my knowledge ... One (who resigned) to support a widowed mother (and) one, a probationer, on being recalled to England ... are the only members of the Mission who have engaged in any secular pursuits ... Seven persons have been removed by death. Four of them were consumptive when they went out ... three died of consumption ... the other of smallpox. One died in China of child-birth, and the other two in England...To show you how we compare with others I will only refer to one Mission labouring in the same province as most of our missionaries. The aggregate strength of (that) Mission has been fifteen persons, of whom seven died and three resigned, and one returned ...

The effect of the trials of our faith [periods of stringency] on the Chinese we have found to be only beneficial ... (they) have been stirred up themselves to give of their means to spread the Gospel instead of thinking the rich societies could do it all.[276]

Mrs Rich renewed her support.

Two other incidents also encouraged Hudson Taylor to press on. First, in May 1875 Edward Fishe and his wife (the Annie Bohannan who as the Taylor children's nurse had been through the Yangzhou riot) decided to return to China. 'I'm going whether you come or not,' she declared to her vacillating husband. He became a daring pioneer. And then John McCarthy brought his ailing family home to recuperate after eight and a half years in China, but was so intent on breaking new ground himself that after only three months in England, spent energetically telling all he could about China, he was away again.

That 'wonderful impetus', Burma
(April 1875–May 1876)

The 'Yunnan Outrage', 'respecting the attack on the Indian Expedition to Western China and the Murder of Mr Margary' was common knowledge in Britain. The frustration of Her Majesty's Minister in China, in the heyday of Britain's imperial power and only fifteen years after Lord Elgin's capture of Peking (now Beijing), meant nothing to the news-reading public but a fresh resort to arms unless satisfaction was soon given. At the time, the geographical limitation of travel by Westerners into West China was considered to be Yichang, near the mouth of the Yangzi gorges. (This never applied to the Catholic priests who were escorted in secret by faithful converts or, when the international climate permitted, as dignitaries in style.) To go further up the rapids, was slow and dangerous. The alternative was to brave hostile Hunan to reach Guizhou, the sparsely populated austere mountainous scene of the long Miao rebellion (see 1, pp 285, 566, 569).[277]

In 1868 a French expedition had left Saigon to explore the Mekong, and reached Kunming in Yunnan. T. T. Cooper had travelled from Wuhan as far as Batang only to be turned back, and the next year had tried again from Assam with the same result. Major (later Colonel) Sladen's expedition from Burma into Yunnan in 1868 had failed, as had Colonel Browne's in 1875 with the murder of Margary. So the departure of John Stevenson and Henry Soltau on April 6, 1875, to Burma, with the declared intention of entering Yunnan from Bhamo in the tracks of the two abortive government expeditions, could not fail to excite imagination.

While action to launch as many as eighteen young men into nine possibly resistant provinces at such a time struck some as irresponsible and others as daring faith to be encouraged, to Hudson Taylor both ventures—to Yunnan through Burma, and to the other provinces from the Yangzi—were reasonable. Strong expeditions like Colonel Browne's of one hundred and ninety-three men, mostly armed and intent on promoting the hateful opium trade,[278] could be expected to provoke opposition. Quiet friendliness, demonstrated by simple medical means, could pave the way for two Chinese-speaking preachers of 'virtue' to enter freely. At Bhamo they would be nine hundred miles from Rangoon but only one hundred from the Chinese border and in touch with caravans of Chinese traders. Half the population of Bhamo were Chinese, and five thousand more came over the border each year to trade. Two American Baptist missionaries to the Karen people of Burma had encountered some pack trains in the hills, each of several hundred animals driven by Roman Catholic muleteers who fell on their knees and kissed the missionaries' hands thinking they were priests. As a gateway to China, Bhamo looked promising. As for the young 'eighteen', had not Hudson Taylor himself been demonstrating for over twenty years that foreigners were welcomed almost everywhere, as M. Henry Taylor was finding in Henan? After all, for fifteen years it had been legal under the 'unequal treaties'.

Stevenson and Soltau arrived at Rangoon on May 14, 1875, to find Burma the scene of political unrest. At the time Lower Burma was governed from British India, but Upper Burma was still independent. In 1862 it had been open to commerce, including trade with China, but the British government still suspected King Mindon at Mandalay of having had a hand in thwarting Colonel Browne's expedition. Captain Cooke, the British Resident, had had to withdraw from Bhamo, and all merchants from Mandalay. Colonel Sladen was about to go by gunboat with a diplomatic representative and troops to confront King Mindon, so the Chief Commissioner could not allow Stevenson and Soltau to proceed upcountry. Instead he advised them to call on the Yunnanese son of the late Muslim rebel 'king' of Dali, an exile in Rangoon. Both he and the Rangoon Chinese community received them warmly, provided them with Burmese and Mandarin language teachers, and introduced them to Chinese merchants from Mandalay and Bhamo. 'Natives from Yunnan have come down here to Rangoon just to meet us', Stevenson wrote.[279]

At last the opportunity came to visit Mandalay, and against the advice of many, because of the danger of war both in Burma and China, they left Rangoon on September 9 with a Burmese-speaking American missionary surnamed Rose. The journey from Rangoon to Bhamo by steam launch took twenty-five days, apart from interruptions, and by September 29 they could write that King Mindon had been 'both kind and cordial . . . (He) put no obstacle in the way' of their settling in Bhamo, and gave them a letter instructing the governor of Bhamo to provide a plot of land and facilities to buy building materials and hire workmen.

Word followed them from the Indian government forbidding their journey, but too late. They arrived at Bhamo on October 3, 1875. Professedly friendly, the governor secretly opposed them, and like Adoniram Judson they had to live and work in a *zayat*, a shed by the roadside, until the governor died a few months later. His successor then granted them the site they had chosen, near the city gate through which most Chinese went to and from Yunnan. Soon the confidence of the belligerent Kachin tribesmen was won by John Stevenson's attitude to them, and by Henry Soltau's amateur doctoring. Very unkempt, with menacingly long knives and spears, they even appeared attractive to Stevenson.

> Your letter about the Kak-hyens (Kachin) quite fed my soul [Hudson Taylor wrote in reply to a letter from Soltau]. Oh! I could not but exclaim that I might become a Kak-hyen to win them to Christ. They seem to me to be noble game—men whose changed lives will show what Christ can do, and I asked the Lord for thousands of them, for Christ.

His prayer was answered.

'The Chinese come by crowds,' Stevenson wrote, 'and they have taken the Scriptures into China.' But the British authorities sternly forbade him and Soltau to cross the border. They were still there, busy making friends, when Grosvenor's 'mission of enquiry' at last arrived, having witnessed a 'staged' investigation in Kunming of Margary's murder. But for British obstruction, Stevenson reported, entering China would be as simple for him as crossing into the next county at home. That day was to come. Bhamo was to play a part in the occupation of western Yunnan, and to remain an outpost of the CIM until 1915, the Mission's jubilee.

China's Millions (June–July 1875)

In the last week of May 1875, after the Brighton Convention, Hudson Taylor made a crucial decision to be unconventional again and to initiate an unusual means of informing people about China. Many had become interested and were wanting the facts. Some were critical and needed the facts. By no fault of their own, ignorance handicapped friend and critic alike. The secular press had attractive periodicals illustrated by steel-engravings—the *Illustrated London News*, the *Graphic* and others, the equivalent of today's 'glossy' magazines. No Christian publication had yet emulated them, though some leaflets were illustrated. To catch the eye, to honour the cause, to inform and to challenge was the need. It had to be. The result by today's standards is commonplace.

The *Occasional Paper* of the China Inland Mission was a simple pocket-sized pamphlet of ten to thirty pages. The last issue, in March 1875, had hinted at the hoped-for approach to the West China provinces of Guangxi, Guizhou and Sichuan through Burma and Yunnan, and another issue, No 40, was overdue. The 'wonderful impetus' already given by Stevenson's and Soltau's departure and first letters from Rangoon demanded this new 'leap forward'. But what should it be called? As ever, Jennie Taylor went straight to the point. The CIM existed for China's millions, the phrase Hudson Taylor had used again and again. '*China's Millions* and our Work among them', she suggested, the title that held its own until the end of the year. After that CHINA'S

MILLIONS was enough. For decades the phrase was to be echoed by thousands, falling naturally into Sarah Stock's hymn in 1898, 'China's millions join the strain, Waft it on to India's plain', and outlasting the 'open century'.

Work on it was immediately started, and within a month Volume 1 Number 1 was ready for the press. The magazine was ten inches by seven (later enlarged), a highly topical, eye-catching pace-setter. The front page carried an illuminated title surmounted by the Chinese characters for 'Ebenezer—Hitherto hath the Lord helped us', and 'Jehovah Jireh—the Lord will provide'. Beneath it came an engraving (by favour of the *Graphic*) of Shan people of the Burma-Yunnan border, and the opening words 'The province of Yunnan is attracting much attention at this time, owing to the failure of the British exploratory expedition and the murder of the lamented Margary.' Facts about the Shan preceded an editorial. 'When periodicals are so numerous . . . why commence another? . . . Why is not adeeper interest felt in China by the people of England and . . . the Church? . . . They have never *seen* its glorious hills, its noble ruins . . . nor its crowded cities . . . its countless villages.' If they could, the wonders of China and the Chinese would speak for themselves. *China's Millions* would help to supply the need.

Immediately it plunged into a brief report from Henry Taylor about Henan, the first 'new' province to be entered. Then a Chinese Christian's account of how he had been so struck by John Stevenson's patient persuasion and the sight of foreigners frequently on their knees in prayer, that he asked Jesus to 'receive' him, and went on to become an evangelist.[280] Reports followed from different parts of China. Before extracts from Henry Soltau's letters from Burma, and a final full-page engraving of a scene on the porch of a Chinese roadside eating-house, came Hudson Taylor's main editorial under the title 'China for Christ', with the illuminated text, 'Whatsoever he saith unto you, do it!' He liked to emphasise his point.

2.27 China's Millions: *volume 1, number 1*

It was nine years on the 26th of May since the *Lammermuir* party sailed for China ... We have needed all the time since to gain experience, and to gather round us a staff of (Chinese) workers (to occupy) some fifty stations in five different provinces ... We believe that the time has come for doing more fully what He has commanded us; and by His grace we intend to do it. Not to try, for we see no Scriptural authority for trying. Try is a word constantly in the mouth of unbelievers ... far too often taken up by believers. In our experience, 'to try' has usually meant 'to fail'. (The Lord's) command is not 'Do your best,' but 'DO IT' ... Do the thing commanded ... 'Whatsoever he saith unto you, do it!'

Here lay the secret of Hudson Taylor's own perseverance. It must also be true of the Mission.

The day G. F. Easton, an accepted candidate, ended his seven-year apprenticeship in south London, at last a master-printer, he walked all the way to Pyrland Road. Sharing his sense of achievement, Hudson Taylor asked him to see the first *China's Millions* through the press. Published in June 1875, the magazine has continued its unbroken existence to the present day, nearly one hundred and fifteen years later. With the extension of the Mission beyond China in 1951 it became the *East Asia Millions*. His candidates became salesmen. 'I sold the first six in a newspaper shop in Bow Road near Harley House,' George Clarke recalled. 'I pushed this new paper at Moody and Sankey meetings in London.'[281]

A man for the 'Millions' (May 1875–76)

Before long Hudson Taylor himself would have to return to China. How to deal with candidates, *China's Millions* and the transmission of funds during his absence occupied his thoughts. Part-time honorary secretaries had found the work too demanding. But who could give his whole time to it? For years he had tried to persuade his sister Amelia and her husband Benjamin Broomhall to join him or another society in China. Amelia would gladly have gone, but Benjamin could not see it as the will of God for them and their growing family (see 1, pp 237, 351, 499, 521).[282] His partnership in the New Bond Street business was successful and he was giving his spare time to the early YMCA and as secretary to the Anti-Slavery Society. But while he made a comfortable home for his family, he lived often beyond his means, sometimes finding himself in extreme difficulty, for he was more generous than businesslike. In time the firm failed, the partnership broke up, to Hudson Taylor's relief, and Benjamin set up on his own in Surrey. There too, with his tenth child on the way, he failed to make ends meet and turned to Hudson Taylor for advice, as he had often done in the long years of their friendship. In May 1875, therefore, probably on his way to the Brighton Convention, Hudson Taylor visited Benjamin and Amelia at Godalming. Once again he broached the subject of their devoting themselves exclusively to China where their hearts had been with him for more than twenty years. Aware of Benjamin's limitations, Hudson Taylor respected his abilities and had a place for him. His decision in the last week of May to launch *China's Millions* had confirmed in his own mind the proposition he now made. Would they join him at Pyrland Road for an experimental period, to help with the production and distribution of the magazine and to play host in their home to candidates who came for interviews and training? 'Mr T. thought him the very man for the job,' Louise Desgraz recalled. 'He would be a good judge of what was needed.'

With it he made a 'generous offer'. To avoid misunderstanding, as they were close relatives, he chose personally to provide them with a house and income (see pp 218–19).[283] Benjamin sold up and in July moved into No 5 Pyrland Road with the candidates.

Amelia and her family of ten followed on August 24.

Hudson Taylor's home in No 6 had long since become too full, so rooms were taken next door in No 4 until vacant possession was obtained at the end of August, and a door opened between the two houses. His makeshift office was then exchanged for a more suitable room and things took on a settled appearance. As the Mission continued to grow, No 2 was acquired for Benjamin and family, and other houses for the Mission as the need arose.[284]

'Then Pyrland Road was only partially built . . . it was possible to jump out of the back windows and be almost in open country . . . Many a foolish escapade on the roof and races up and down the builders' ladders' formed the memories of Benjamin's four boys and six girls, despite being under the teaching and firm hand of Miss Wilkin, their governess. In constant contact with the stream of Mission candidates, and under the influence of a crusading father and exceptionally prayerful mother, they could not but be caught up in the concern for China. Five of the ten became missionaries there, and one on the Mission staff in America.

Benjamin had at last found the niche in which his gifts were to be given full scope. He and Amelia came to be regarded as father and mother figures in the CIM, while Hudson Taylor filled the role of beloved leader and administrator.[285] But that lay ahead.

Still more of 'the eighteen' (June–December 1875)

Cameron, Clarke and Nicoll were to sail on August 4, and in October Easton, the printer, and Elizabeth Judd's brother James F. Broumton, a London businessman, were to follow. To those who know the history of their great achievements, each of these names is its own monument.[286] C. G. Moore was another at Rudland Road, a lecturer in theology retained on the home-staff to teach his fellow-candidates. In 1909 he recalled his first interview with Hudson

Taylor, in the days when he was trying to do without the crutches.

> (His study) was largely occupied with packing cases and some rough bookshelves set along one of the walls. Near the window was a writing table littered with letters and papers. In front of the fireplace (unused) was a low, narrow, iron bed-stead neatly covered with a rug. (Nothing else was to be seen in the room that would not have been found in the most barely furnished office.) I hardly think there was a scrap of carpet on the floor, and certainly not a single piece of furniture that suggested the slightest regard for comfort or appearance. Mr Taylor ... lay down on his iron bedstead and eagerly plunged into a conversation which was, for me, one of life's golden hours. Every idea I had hitherto cherished of a 'great man' was completely shattered—the high and imposing airs, and all the trappings were conspicuously absent; but Christ's ideal of greatness was there ... I strongly suspect that, by his unconscious influence, Mr Hudson Taylor did more than any other man of his day to compel Christian people to revise their ideas of 'greatness'.

Hudson Taylor spent long hours talking with the young men about how to cope with life in China, but still had his other work to do, with family life going on around them. George Clarke recalled, 'How well I remember Master Charlie (aged six and a half) putting most difficult questions to his father (and) occasionally Masters Howard and Herbert rolling (in a tussle) under the table.' The way he seemed to go on working day and night impressed James Broumton, as did Hudson Taylor's gratitude for comparatively small donations, and his thankfulness to God when he opened letters and found them. He often prayed, at once, for God's blessing on the donors.

In early June, though still on crutches a year after his accident, Hudson Taylor visited Alexander Wylie (home from China with failing eyesight) and attended the stone-laying ceremony of Tom Barnardo's Ilford cottages. Then in July he took part in a succession of meetings to farewell Cameron, Clarke and Nicoll. In August

he went to Guernsey for a holiday with his family, still working almost all of every day, and by September was 'in full harness' again.[287] But a visit to his parents in Sussex, with all the jolts of hansom cabs over cobblestones and trains starting and stopping, brought his pain back again for five days. At last by Christmas he could claim to be 'feeling (himself) again'. As he looked back over a year so remarkable, so filled with happenings undreamed of in the deep trough of December 1874, he wrote, 'We have had correspondence with more than sixty candidates . . . between 20 and 30 young (men) and 9 or 10 (women) have spent . . . from a few days to several months with us . . . in study and preparation for work in China . . . We lack only four . . . to fulfil our petition for 18 this year.' The four were already in touch with him but not yet accepted. More than eighteen were to be chosen, though some did not sail for China until the new year. During all this time in China the tension between Wade and the imperial negotiators was mounting.

The Eighteen in perspective (13th century–1877)

China had not always been anti-foreign. In the Yuan dynasty (1260–1368) Marco Polo had even been governor of Yangzhou, and many European merchants had lived and moved freely in the empire. Except during the anti-Christian phases (see 1, pp 6–25) Nestorian and, later, Roman priests had been honoured and employed at the seats of government. Even during periods of persecution Catholic missionaries had travelled secretively in almost every province for seven centuries. In 1846 the Abbé Huc and Joseph Gabet had penetrated into Tibet before being deported.

Charles Gutzlaff, so fluent and adapted to Chinese ways that he passed as one of them, was the first Protestant to venture into several coastal provinces. And in 1815 Robert Morrison travelled overland from Peking to Canton in Lord Amhurst's cortége, as a guest of the emperor. Robert Fortune the plant-hunter, W. H. Medhurst, Snr, and others had used disguise to probe the coastal hinterland at great personal risk. But in 1861, after the opium wars when recognition was granted under duress to the conquering nations, still tempting fate Captain Blakiston succeeded in reaching the Tibetan marches with a Lt Colonel Sarel. The future bishop S. I. J. Schereschewsky of the American Episcopal Church travelled part of the way with them. Seven years later (1868) the Frenchman Lieutenant Gamier of the Mekong expedition from Saigon, after failing to reach Dali from Kunming during the Muslim rebellion, withdrew northward to Dongchuan and outflanked the hostilities between Muslim rebels and government forces by an arduous detour across the Jin He, or River of Gold (see map 2.26: p 246) via Huili to Dali and back. Also in 1868 T. T. Cooper ventured through Sichuan as far as Batang and beyond Weixi, West of Lijiang, in the cause of discovery and commerce, only to be turned back.[288] Also in 1868 Major Sladen entered Yunnan from Burma and was forced to withdraw. Four years later, in 1872, Baron Ferdinand von Richthofen tried unsuccessfully to follow Marco Polo's route from Chengdu (his Sindafu) via the Jianchang (Chiench'ang) valley (his Caindu) and its chief city of Xichang (Ningyuan) and over the Jinsha Jiang (River of Golden Sand) to Kunming, Dali and Burma.

Colonel Henry Yule in his long introductory essay to Gill's two volume travelogue, *The River of Golden Sand*, takes pains to make it clear that all these remotest regions had long been 'habitually traversed' and some had been occupied for decades by devoted Catholic missionaries, with enforced interruptions. Where von Richtofen on his way to Xichang was attacked and forced back from the high Da Xiang Ling pass, south of Ya'an, Colborne and (separately) George Nicoll of the CIM were to succeed. The letters of the Abbé Desgodins of Batang were published in 1872, showing him, like so many Catholic priests in faraway places, to be a traveller and observer of note.

Missionaries, often without knowing

it, were to tread in the steps of secular travellers, but were more often to lead the way, crisscrossing territory later to become familiar to foreign railway engineers, merchants and employees of the Chinese Post and Salt Tax offices. They were a disappointment to the geographers, by failing to observe, measure or report on the terrain they traversed, and its products. Colonel Henry Yule wrote appreciatively of their spirit and their relationship with the Chinese, while deploring their neglect as explorers and prospectors. People were their overriding interest. To take the gospel to them mattered most. And anyway, few were trained in map-making or geology, although the use of a pedometer to count footsteps was a common practice among them. Their references to natural resources or other matters of interest to commerce or exploitation were few and far between. Travelling conditions were hard, whether their trail rose and fell thousands of feet or pressed endlessly on through dusty plains.

Josiah Cox's visit to Changsha in anti-foreign Hunan in 1864 had been made entirely by boat 'for the sake of his health',[289] and Paul Bagley entered Sichuan the following year (see 1, p 671). While Cooper and Gamier were exploring the southwest in 1868, Griffith John and Alexander Wylie were braving hostile crowds in Chengdu and escaping with their lives, continuing northward to Hanzhong in Shaanxi and down the Han River back to Wuhan (see map 2.43: p 353).[290] From Wuchang Cox's Wesleyan colleague W. Scarborough visited the cities on the Han River as far as Laohekou (now Guanghua) in 1873, and made many shorter journeys, whereas Griffith John did not pursue his work in Hunan until the 1880s and '90s. His companion of 1868, Alexander Wylie, visited fifteen of China's eighteen provinces over the years, for the British and Foreign Bible Society. Alexander Williamson of the LMS, since 1863 with the National Bible Society of Scotland, also travelled extensively for a few years in the northern provinces before concentrating on the Presbyterian Church in Shandong. His colleague J. McIntyre tried to reach Kaifeng in 1874 but was turned back at the Yellow River (Huang He) close to his goal, unlike another, Oxenham, who succeeded in 1868 in reaching Hankou from Peking. Bible Society colporteurs, a sadly neglected corps of heroes in the published history of the Chinese church, were constantly on the road, paying a high price in suffering (see 1, p 790). But noteworthy because in strong contrast with the China Inland Mission, in reports of most societies published in the *Chinese Recorder* between 1875 and 1877 under the subtitle 'Itinerancy', is the recurring statement that little even of local travel had been or was being undertaken.

Hudson Taylor had appealed for volunteers to penetrate the nine remote provinces which few Westerners had dared to enter, where Catholic missionaries had previously only succeeded by being taken by loyal friends from one Christian home to another, and kept hidden out of sight. Since the treaties of 1858 and 1860 they had emerged under the French protectorate, bought or built imposing residences and asserted the treaty 'rights', assuming the titles and dignity of mandarins. None of these dubious advantages were available to the aspiring Protestant pioneer—no Christian homes or villages, no authority, few friends to guide or advise them. Knowledge, experience and tenuous footholds would have to be won by true trail-blazing.

The assault of 'the eighteen' on the nine provinces unoccupied by Protestant missionaries—for an assault it was, in terms of planning and intensity—had this marked characteristic, that it was deliberately to put down roots, to raise up Christian churches and so to achieve ambitious results, far removed from the haphazard wandering which appearances suggested. Echoing Charles Gutzlaff's policy of sending a mature Christian missionary to lead Chinese evangelists into every province, Hudson Taylor had

declared his aim in 1873 to 'attain to one superintendent and two assistant foreign missionaries in a province, with qualified Christian helpers in each important city, and colporteurs in less important (ones, and) to commence a college for the more thorough training of our Chinese helpers.'[291] By January 1874 he was praying for fifty or a hundred additional Chinese evangelists and his prayer for the eighteen missionary pioneers, begun in 1872, culminated during 1875 in the flood of applicants he was carefully sifting.[292]

First of the nine[293] (1875)

The enterprise of the early pioneers is quickly appreciated by reference to map 2.28, on this page. Conspicuously foreign, even in Chinese dress, they showed great courage, but not more than their Chinese companions needed to be seen in their company. Before the advent of railways, Henan province, 450 miles from north

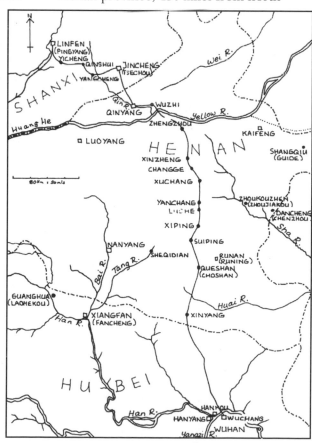

2.28 First of the nine: through Henan to Shanxi

to south and east to west, with an average population of 550 per square mile, depended for communication with other provinces on three rivers and the great imperial trunk road—an unpaved dirt track thronged with horse-drawn carts and mule litters, and loud with the shouts and curses of whip-cracking drivers. Within Henan, roads converged on Luoyang (previously Honanfu), described by von Richtofen as 'the Gate to the North-Western provinces and Central Asia'. There the trunk road began, to pass through Xi'an in Shaanxi, the ancient imperial capital, and over the mountains to Lanzhou in Gansu and on to Suzhou and Yumen, Jade Gate, 1,200 miles away.[294]

Extremes of temperature and an unreliable rainfall inescapably endured by the people, produced strong men inured to hardship, uncouth and easily angered, conservative and anti-foreign in some areas but intelligent, reliable, friendly and welcoming in other places.

On March 30, 1875, M. Henry Taylor, after less than eighteen months of language study, wrote to Hudson Taylor, 'As it is your wish that I should make Henan my future sphere, I turn my eyes towards its 25 millions with much desire.' He found a Christian named Zhang of whom he wrote as 'Chang, my brother' in the LMS church at Wuchang, and leaving Hankou with him on April 3 travelled overland, due north through Hubei (Griffith John's stamping ground) and deep through Henan. Selling copies of Scripture and preaching the gospel in the towns and cities as they went, they worked their way westwards from Runan (Runing) and Queshan (Choshan) as far west as Nanyang. Money and books exhausted, they then headed for home, to arrive at Hankou again fifty-six days later, on May 28. In the autumn after the great heat of summer, they returned, and for eighty-four days (October 24 to January 15, 1876) made a thorough tour of the province as far north as the Huang He, Yellow River.[295] At the prefectural city of Runan the chief innkeeper welcomed them as he had before, and when incited to turn them

out told the magistrate that he had read a Gospel and approved of it. Better still, they found four believers standing firm, the first-fruits of the church of millions in Henan today. Fifty miles further on they discovered a hundred Catholics at Zhoujiakou (now Zhoukouzhen) and at 'Cheng-chou', people who were 'proud, rude, callous and annoying to the last degree'. 'They trampled on our pearls and literally turned to rend us. We prayed for them and left.' They visited the cities of Kweiteh (now Shangqiu), Kaifeng and Luoyang, one hundred and fifty miles apart, and were back in Wuhan on January 15, 1876.[296]

Hunan was the second of the unoccupied provinces to be entered (on June 10, 1875). Charles Judd, Yao Sifu the Hunanese Christian from Jiangxi and another named Zhang, probably Henry Taylor's companion, succeeded in renting premises but were driven out of Yueyang, the gateway to the province, at the mouth of the Dongting lakes.

In the early days of the Taiping rebellion with its quasi-Christian pretensions, Changsha the capital city of Hunan withstood a long siege in 1854 largely through the influence of the scholar-gentry. Ever since, the provincial governor's power had been less than that of the literati, and opposition to foreigners and Christianity remained strong, whatever the attitude of the Peking government. Hunanese soldiers had formed the backbone of the imperial forces which overthrew the Taipings with Charles Gordon's inspiration in 1864, and Hunan's power in the empire continued to be immense.[297]

'Three parts upland and seven parts water', the province and most of its cities were served by waterways fed from the mountain ranges in the west and south. Changsha on the Xiang River dominated the east and south of Hunan, and Changde the western region, on the Yuan River from Guizhou province (see map 2.20: p 204). The Yuan was therefore the natural route to Guiyang and Yunnan, taken by Augustus Margary on the way to Burma, and by the pioneers of the CIM in the period after the Chefoo Convention. Margary had had a taste of the prevailing xenophobia when on two occasions his boat was attacked and finally burned, even though he carried a Peking passport.

Later the same year Yao and Zhang returned to Yueyang, unmolested, but years were to pass before any foreigner could gain a true foothold. The conquest of Hunan is an epic story to which we shall return more than once.

1875–77: 'OUT OF THE LONG RUT AT LAST'

The team complete (1875–76)

With the appeal for prayer published in January 1875 'that God will raise up this year eighteen suitable men', and the flood of men and women who besieged Hudson Taylor with correspondence and interviews, the end of the doldrums had been reached. From the ranks of the Mission itself six had volunteered and made an early start. John Stevenson had ten years' experience to his credit, and John McCarthy and Charles Judd more than eight. Frederick Baller and Henry Taylor had reached China together before the end of 1873, and Thomas Harvey in 1869, though he was at the time studying medicine and did not obtain his diploma as a 'physician, surgeon and apothecary' until October 1875, or sail with his bride to Burma until February 1876.

To Henry Taylor had fallen the honour of leading the way, while Baller 'a most efficient missionary', waited on the Yangzi to receive the next reinforcements from home and initiate them into Chinese life. Henry Soltau from the office of Secretary in London sailed with Stevenson on April 6, 1875, hoping to make Bhamo a little more than a stepping stone to Yunnan. Young George King sailed alone on May 15 to reach Shanghai on July 14 after being shipwrecked. A week after he left London a strenuous round of farewell meetings began, to send off the 'three mighty men', James Cameron, George Nicoll and George Clarke. Fifteen hundred well-wishers thronged the Metropolitan Tabernacle to hear Spurgeon commission them before they left on August 4. Spurgeon gripped Nicoll's hand afterwards and said characteristically, 'May you grow a long "tail" and save many souls.'[298] Baller met them at Shanghai on September 26 and took them up the Yangzi. While Nicoll and Clarke joined the Judds at Wuhan, Cameron spent only three months at Jiujiang with a language teacher before being left alone at Anqing (scene of the 1869 riot) to sink or swim while he soaked up Chinese speech and ways. He learned fast and soon began travelling with a Chinese companion. More unknown young men and women whom Hudson Taylor was training enter the story for the first time in 1876 and '77, soon to be bywords of brave exploration and evangelism. As if in reward for faithfulness in extreme testing, God was lavishing men and money on him for the fufilment of his vision for China.

The day after Cameron's party sailed, G. F. Easton and James Broumton moved into their places at Pyrland Road, to follow in October. A month later J. J. Turner and Charles Budd travelled with John McCarthy to China. Even Benjamin Broomhall, father of ten, was considering whether to go with them. Hudson Taylor needed a mature man at the centre of things in China and thought his brother-in-law could do what was required. But he decided to stay. Joseph Adams had gone independently to Burma from Grattan Guinness's Institute, and in November joined Stevenson, Soltau and the Harveys at Bhamo as a member of the CIM. So within the year these sixteen men were at the scene of action, and five more were preparing to go after the New Year, Francis James, Edward Pearse and George Parker among them. With their departure Jennie wrote on February 29, 1876, 'This makes up the Eighteen.' In addition, but independently, a wealthy young Oxford graduate, Robert J. Landale, went out with Hudson Taylor.[299]

For pioneering, men were wanted but women were not left out. On January 26, 1876, one of the most notable of early pioneers of either sex left with Francis James and Edward Pearse. Elizabeth Wilson, a niece of Hudson Taylor's old friend Miss Stacey, and already known to him for twenty-five years, was now 'a middle-aged lady of energy and means'. When Miss Stacey made a haven for the pale student recovering from 'dissection fever' in 1852 (see 1, p 199) Elizabeth Wilson was there and impressed by his dedication. Caring for elderly parents had kept her from going to China sooner, but once free she delayed no longer. Hudson Taylor introduced her to the council on December 7, 1875, and, as intrepid as any of the men, she played a key role in the occupation of Shaanxi and then Gansu. Five young women followed later in the year to take their own place of honour in history only two years after reaching China.[300] 'Fresh lady candidates keep presenting themselves,' Jennie told Louise Desgraz ambiguously; and soon afterwards added that Hudson was preparing to go back, to care personally for the growing numbers of novice missionaries in need of advice and to see them into the kind of work most suited to each one.

In a review of the year's progress in *China's Millions* for December 1875 Hudson Taylor outlined his thinking about the designation of these pioneers, in a delicate pairing of personalities and denominational preferences.[301] But changing circumstances led, as he constantly found, to changes being made. What mattered was that the nine target provinces were constantly in view, for occupation as soon as possible, not as a distant goal. And not only the nine. Beyond lay 'Tibet, Kokonor, Turkestan and Sungaria' (see map 2.59: p 480). (The English and Canadian Presbyterians were already in Taiwan.) All this while the news from China was of the newly knighted minister Sir Thomas Francis Wade being thwarted, of war-clouds building up, and of Jackson's indiscretions threatening the denial of passports to the whole 'Taylor Mission'. Not only so, with growing

military strength Japan was sending a naval expedition to Korea to obtain concessions by *force majeure*. The breakthrough by 'the eighteen' was to be made while east Asia was as unstable as at any time.

Preparing to be away (1876)

Before he could leave London it remained for Hudson Taylor to provide for his own replacement as administrator in Britain. Since William Berger's resignation, part-time honorary secretaries had not succeeded in accomplishing as much as he had done with Mrs Berger's help. The Mission had grown larger. In January 1876 Richard Hill resigned, proposing George and Henry Soltau's younger brother William for appointment as a salaried full-time administrator. As long as Hudson Taylor was in the country he could manage while he trained William and devolved more work and responsibility on to Benjamin's shoulders. Even when in China he himself would continue to edit *China's Millions*, but its sub-editing and production would have to be done in London. On May 13 he suffered a bereavement as poignant as by the death of any close relative. Miss Stacey, who after his parents had been his closest friend and sympathiser and who had prayed unceasingly for him, died at her home in the village of Tottenham. His human foundations were shaken. For a week he was ill, grief-stricken, though her health had been failing for many weeks. He found it hard to address himself to his work and public engagements. One by one his props were being removed. Then he was himself again. He had to be. In a few days' time one of the big annual events of the Mission would be upon him.

At the tenth anniversary meeting in the great Mildmay Conference Hall on '*Lammermuir* Day', May 26, 1876, (called 'the first of annual meetings') Hudson Taylor restated the 'aims and objects' of the Mission, making the emphasis that if the practicability of working in inland China were demonstrated, the Church of God as a whole in Europe and America would be encouraged to more adequate efforts.[302]

The importance of this objective became increasingly apparent as the advance into the remote provinces took place. The casualties suffered by the Mission, he went on, far from being discouraging, were a source of encouragement.

> It was anticipated, both by ourselves and others, that the hardships of pioneering would tell even more seriously in the way of sickness and death on our members, than on those of other Protestant Missions in China. (Instead) there has been no death or serious illness from violence; and the losses from the ordinary causes have been considerably below the average ... [Citing a review of the thirty years of CMS experience, a society enjoying public confidence,[303] he continued] 'Out of thirty four ordained clergymen sent out only fifteen stayed more than four years ... Of these fifteen, one is dead, one retired, two have been transferred to Japan, and eleven are still at work ... In the case of the American Baptist missionaries labouring in the same district as ourselves, out of ... twenty-one persons, male and female, nine have been removed by death and six by retirement, during the last thirty years. In the ten years of the China Inland Mission (excluding those who have gone out within the last four years) of 39 persons of both sexes, 32 were able to stay more than four years, and 25 are still in connection with the Mission.

Then two unusual statements followed, the first illustrating the slow development of Mission practice in relation to naming specific financial needs, and the second demonstrating that there was no restraint on soliciting donations for other people's good causes. The fact that the Pyrland Road houses were up for sale was reported with the comment: 'It would be a serious inconvenience were we obliged to relinquish them . . . So we have prayerfully concluded to purchase them . . . An immediate outlay of about £1000 is required . . . and we trust God will incline the hearts of His people to send special contributions for this, as a large saving to the Mission in rent will thus be effected.'

At the time a home for missionaries' children was being opened at Coplow House, Tottenham, not by the Mission but as a private venture by Henrietta Soltau and a Miss Minchin, 'a lady of means', 'which will relieve us of much expense and responsibility'. They were open to receive contributions, and the Mission Council would be making grants to them from time to time.

In explanation, the occasion of these statements was exceptional, as the anniversary meeting was attended like a meeting of shareholders by the closest circle of supporters to whom reports were being made in confidence, as was not the case in meetings for the wider public elsewhere. Shortly afterwards, in June, he enclosed a lithographed letter in his own hand to the Mission's friends, with their copy of the *Millions*, saying, 'I feel that you and all who aid us by your prayers, your sympathy and your contributions are partners with us.' Asking them to promote the distribution of *China's Millions*, he mentioned that he had received several hundred pounds 'to cover the cost of publication . . . no small help now that requirements of the work exceed £150 a week', as was apparent from the Mission's annual statement of account. Nevertheless in later years, when this degree of reference to financial needs was criticised as being in breach of the 'no solicitation' principle, it gave place to the stricter interpretation which in contrast was called a 'conspiracy of silence'. It was difficult to steer between the shoals and to let integrity of motive govern the Mission's financial statements.

A highlight of the afternoon meeting was the moment when Hudson Taylor welcomed James Sadler of the LMS in Xiamen (Amoy) as a representative of the society which sent the first Protestant pioneers to China. Hudson Taylor also paid tribute to the Church Missionary Society, the Wesleyan Methodist and Presbyterian societies, and American and European missions. Taking the gospel to the vast empire of China was the task of the whole church and his habit of speaking of the CIM in relation to the rest was winning him their approval. Month by month he was conferring with the London Council about administration during his approaching absence. (We must touch on this because of what happened.) A year of 'temporary assistance' by Benjamin Broomhall had become a long-term appointment. The minutes of February 18, 1876, read that he was in future 'to be attached to the Mission in the same way as the missionaries' and, in August, 'would spend much of his time in holding meetings in the country on behalf of the Missions together with such missionaries as may be at home'. Soon he was 'in Birmingham arranging for meetings' or 'at Bath conferring with ministers'. An administrative structure was taking shape which would remain intact for decades to come, expanded and adapted as necessary.

A statement of the 'Principles and Practice' of the Mission was drawn up, to be signed by each member as a proof of acceptance before going to China, as far as possible to ensure a partnership of like-minded people. All too soon the stark realities of a life too remote from their experience at the time of signing were to show some how superficially they had understood and weighed the cost of such discipleship, and the implications of trusting GOD, not Hudson Taylor, for their means of livelihood.

A week before he left the country on September 8, Hudson Taylor and the council went over the final arrangements for his absence. He intended to be away for only forty weeks, in order to devote time on his return to selecting yet more reinforcements. No new women candidates would be accepted or sent out meanwhile. He had prepared the contents of *China's Millions* for the rest of the year, and to protect Jennie from the criticisms borne by an editor, he restricted her share to sub-editing, with Benjamin selecting news items from recent correspondence. Her work was to be confidential and crucial. As when he was at home, she was also to open Mission letters and reply if she could, or to pass them on to Theodore Howard as council chairman, to William Soltau as

cashier in charge of general office matters and of distribution of *China's Millions*, and to Benjamin if they were concerned with public relations. No members of the council could spare time enough to represent Hudson Taylor in a major role as William Berger had done. Theodore Howard increased the part he played only after a few years. Benjamin and Amelia, young William Soltau and C. G. Moore were each as limited by inexperience of China as the other. So while Jennie could not be in charge, she had to be Emily Blatchley over again, the life and soul of the London headquarters while appearing not to be. At the same time she was mother of the six Taylor children, including her own two, no easy task while Herbert and Howard (fifteen and thirteen) were for ever 'sparring with each other'.

The Mission's accounts were available for inspection by donors, but the account books in which their names were recorded, Hudson Taylor declared, 'are to be considered sacredly private'. If they had survived, much enlightening information would be available to us, but the privacy has been perpetuated. Finally, Jennie, Benjamin and William Soltau would hold themselves ready to attend council meetings when invited to do so, but the responsibility for everything rested upon the honorary 'council of management' as before. It remained to be seen how this loose structure would work out in practice, the best that could be put together with available personnel.

Reconnoitring for bases (1875–76)

In China while T. F. Wade came and went, the young pioneers of the CIM were in action. In the last week of September 1875, when Stevenson and Soltau were in Mandalay to meet King Mindon, Cameron, Clarke and Nicoll were welcomed into the CIM's first transit home at Shanghai, 'opposite the old dock, in an old tumbledown Chinese shanty'.[304] They were put straight into Chinese clothes and the Chinese way of life, and sent six hundred miles up the Yangzi 'by an old junk of a steamer (with a) Chinese captain (taking) one week to Hankow' (Wuhan). This was the right start for them. Frederick Baller and his wife, Mary Bowyer, met the boat at Jiujiang and took James Cameron off for six months' intensive initiation into things Chinese (Baller's forte) there and at Nanjing. Nicoll and Clarke went on to join the Judds at Wuchang, to be trained by them, arriving in time to see Henry Taylor and the evangelist Zhang setting off on their second journey to Henan.

> Soon after arrival we went to the British consul (Challoner Alabaster) to register. He had received a letter from Sir Thomas Wade. [George Soltau in London had negotiated an agreement with the Foreign Office.] Read it slowly for us to copy. It said that if we eighteen men went into the interior we went on our own responsibility and could not look to the British government for protection.[305]

Stevenson and Soltau reached Bhamo at about the same time, October 3, a month before the Grosvenor Mission left Wuhan to see justice done over the Margary affair. And J. J. Turner and Charles Budd arrived at Shanghai with John McCarthy towards the end of 1875 to continue their training by him. Still 'the eighteen' flowed in. Elizabeth Wilson with Francis James and Edward Pearse arrived on March 14, 1876, followed by George Parker and Horace Randle on May 20. While Wade had thundered in Peking and withdrew to Shanghai, and Lord Derby threatened to withhold the CIM's passports, the resurgent Mission, almost indifferent to their misgivings, was getting into place for its great push forward. In fact the first sorties were under way.

When Henry Taylor and Zhang arrived back at Wuhan in mid-January 1876 from their eighty-four day journey, George Clarke (after less than six months in China) was game to go with them on the next expedition. Incessant rain reduced the roads to quagmires and kept them waiting, but in mid-March they were away. Griffith John, who but for his mission's policy would himself have been a travelling pioneer,

had to be content with giving them a send-off from his own home. Joined by the evangelist Yao Sifu[306] and taking barrow-loads of books and tracts, they followed the same route as before (see map 2.28: p 263), northwards through Hubei and into Henan, preaching at place after place as they went. At Runan (in Clarke's diary, Juning) 240 miles from Wuhan, the same friendly innkeeper received them, and they found that the two men, Mu and Wang, who had 'believed' on Henry Taylor's first visit, had been through bitter ostracism and rejection by their families, unshaken. As a result, thirty of Mu's neighbours were interested in a religion that could make him so strong. On April 1 they baptised the two in a country stream, the first members of the Protestant Church in Henan which now numbers hundreds of thousands, even millions.[307] Henry Taylor succeeded in renting a house at the nearby county town of Queshan (Choshan), leaving Mr Mu in charge. So far everything was up to their expectations.

Travelling on, meeting Roman Catholics here and there and a man baptised elsewhere by the LMS, they came to Zhoujiakou (Chou-chic-kou, now Zhoukouzhen). There a minor military mandarin told them that when Henry Taylor was in Kaifeng in December 1875 the literati had bound themselves under an oath to kill him, and waited in groups of ten in the city streets for him to come selling books of the Bible and preaching. Enraged when they found he had moved on to Luoyang, they had torn down his landlord's inn sign and threatened to burn the inn to the ground.[308] Taylor, Yao and Clarke went on, through Guide (Kweiteh, now Shangqiu), but when their wheelbarrow men fell ill, and news arrived of 'disturbances' in Kaifeng against the Catholics, they returned by the way they had come. Yao joined Mu at Queshan, while Taylor and Clarke completed the journey to Wuhan. They had covered eight hundred miles in eighty days.

While they were away, John McCarthy took James Cameron to visit the Anhui stations of Ningguo and Huizhou (see map 2.2: p 6), leaving him for five months (April–August) with the Chinese Christians and no foreign companion. The experience was the making of him as a pioneer, fluent in the language, feeling at home living as a Chinese, and accustomed to travelling with little more than a bed-roll and a minimum of necessities.

The great heat of summer ruled out any major excursions, but in August when it eased a little three teams set out: Baller and Jiang Suoliang (Tsiang Soh-Jang), the Zhenjiang pastor, took George King with them up the Han River; Henry Taylor set off on his fourth Henan journey, again with George Clarke; and Evangelist Zhang went with George Nicoll (joined later by James Cameron) overland through Shashi to Yichang on the Yangzi below the great gorges (see map 2.20: p 204). Yichang was to be their advanced base for penetration into Sichuan province, while whoever held the fort there would evangelise the surrounding Hubei countryside. Without difficulty they rented a house outside the south gate of the city and took possession. George Nicoll had been surprised to find on an evangelistic expedition with Charles Judd that they 'everywhere met with kindness, surpassing by far that shown to street preachers at home' in Britain. The people of Yichang were no less welcoming, although Yichang had been designated a treaty port.

Baller, Jiang Suoliang and King on reaching Fancheng (now Xiangfan) the starting point of two or three good routes to Xi'an, the capital of Shaanxi province, walked straight into trouble. All boats like theirs were being commandeered for troop movements, and they had to change their plans. To hire even a small boat in which to press on up the Han River rapids into Shaanxi they had to pay exorbitantly. They succeeded in entering this third of the nine provinces, but by the time they reached Xing'an (now Ankang) were running out of money and on September 26 had to turn back to Wuhan. The gospel had been preached without hindrance at every stopping place, and George King now knew the ropes for when he could try again. Yet they had only touched the fringe where eight Catholic priests were stationed permanently. By June 1882 when Baller had preached the gospel in thirteen different provinces, by nearly two thousand miles of foot-slogging without meeting a single Christian, his reward was to find fifty or sixty believers worshipping together at Fancheng—just six years after this river journey with George King.[309]

Records of Henry Taylor's and George Clarke's fourth foray into Henan (see map 2.28: p 263) from August until October 25, 1876 are scrappy, and Clarke's diary seems not to have been preserved. A short report on December 12 in the *Shanghai Courier and China Gazette* applauded their 'pluck', but only two other references were published months later.[310] They spent six weeks in their rented house in Queshan before any trouble began. Suddenly an official arrived, had their servant beaten, took away their passport and drove them out. After they had left, a Chinese doctor friend was given 'fifty blows of the bamboo on the hand (and) the doorkeeper [probably the new Christian, Mu, see p 269] received fifty blows on the mouth [with a leather strap]. A friend of Mr Liu [their local language teacher] was recognised on the street and received this brutal usage. All this is the work of a few of standing in the city. The mandarins dared not oppose them.' If such slight association with the foreigners endangered even educated local men, it was right to spare them by withdrawing, although no direct threat to Clarke and Taylor had been made. Renting premises too early had been a tactical mistake. They were seen off by the first official and some soldiers.

Back in Wuhan Henry Taylor wrote to Hudson Taylor for advice. By that time the Chefoo Convention had been signed and prospects were brighter. Good weather could last for another two months, but were there any reasons, Henry Taylor asked, why they should not return to Queshan so soon? Hudson Taylor's reply has not been kept, but on November 24 he told Charles Judd that he was keeping Taylor and Clarke with him at Zhenjiang. Henry Taylor had been shaken by his experience and needed the kind of encouragement Hudson Taylor could give.[311] In January he returned to Wuhan, ready to face Henan again, and bravely went on his fifth Henan journey without a missionary companion. George Clarke was taking Judd's place at Wuhan to free him for a major adventure through Hunan and into Guizhou, by a route which Clarke and others were to take after Judd returned.

Shirking nothing, these men were proving to be what their leader had hoped of them—determined 'not to try but to do it'.

The Chefoo Convention[312]
(March–September 1876)

When the imperial mission of enquiry into the fate of Augustus Margary and his companions reached Kunming on March 6, 1876, the British observers became witnesses of a charade instead of an investigation. 'No witness of the murder was allowed to be produced.'[313] In a patently superficial trial, a subordinate officer and 'thirteen savages kidnapped to do duty as prisoners at the bar' stood accused of these murders. The two consular observers, E. Colborne Baber and Arthur Davenport, reported afterwards that patently none understood the language of the indictment, 'nor did they look in the least like men who were pleading guilty to a capital charge'. It was the Tianjin massacre enquiry over again, pure farce (see pp 140–1). As they could obtain no true investigation, Grosvenor and his party left Kunming on March 25 and travelling via Dali and Tengchong reached Bhamo on May 21.

It was what the minister Sir Thomas Wade had expected. Refusing to accept the Kunming verdict, he demanded of Prince Kong the punishment of Zen Yüying (Tsen), the acting-governor of Yunnan who was ultimately responsible,[314] and returned to Tianjin (Tientsin) and Peking to press his point. There negotiations dragged on, with Li Hongzhang prepared to talk but the

Zongli Yamen repudiating any concessions he might make, on the ground that Li had exceeded his brief. Wade finally struck his flag in June and for the third time withdrew to Shanghai for access to the international telegraphic cable.

From Shanghai he wrote to Lord Derby at the Foreign Office: 'It is currently reported, and generally believed, that the Grand Secretary Li Hung-chang[315] has received an imperial decree directing him to proceed to Chefoo [ie Yantai] to confer with me . . . with more than ordinary powers. (If negotiations should again be broken off) Her Majesty's Government could dictate terms.'

Already in response to a request from Sir Thomas the Foreign Office had informed the Admiralty that a naval squadron was indispensable. Four ships had been ordered to Hong Kong in February and to 'Chinese waters' in March to reinforce his demands. As Hosea Ballou Morse observed, 'Sir T. Wade's buoyant hopefulness was justified.' The Navy was eloquent when statesmanship failed.

When Wade struck his flag, Prince Kong asked Robert Hart whether this time the minister should be taken seriously, and enlisted Hart's help. Hart followed Wade to Shanghai, ostensibly to discuss commercial matters in his capacity of inspector-general of the Imperial Maritime Customs, but actually to bring him back to meet Li Hongzhang at Yantai. Wade agreed, and arrived at Yantai on August 10, where Li Hongzhang joined him a week later, delayed by desperate events at Tianjin. Afraid that Li would be taken hostage by the British, the merchants of Tianjin had tried to dissuade him, and his wife incited a popular rising to persuade him that if he went, the foreign community would be massacred. He was unmoved. A deputation of literati followed him to Yantai, only to return without seeing him, after being convinced by Gustav Detring, one of Hart's commissioners of customs, that this was truly a matter of peace or war, war which must also see retribution for the Tianjin massacre of 1870.[316]

Lord Macartney on his voyage up the coast to Tianjin in 1793 had weathered a storm in a tiny bay with islands at its mouth, that of Yantai. But the lee shore where he anchored was under a bluff, near the fishing village of Chefu. In accounts of the episode, 'Chefoo' became the name in common use, retained by Westerners as the port of Yantai grew and became popular as a health resort.

Six feet four inches in height, Li Hongzhang towered above his own countrymen and most Westerners, dominating them no less with his large and 'brilliant' eyes. His appearance alone commanded respect but being equally astute in mind and wise in action, and a master of prevarication, he was a formidable opponent. Convinced of their integrity, he enlisted Hart, 'as calm as Wade was excitable', and Detring to advise him. As soon as he arrived Li recognised his advantage in the presence at Yantai of the diplomatic representatives of Russia, Germany, America, Spain, France and Austro-Hungary, all of whom had sensed crisis. Anxiously watching Wade's every move they were open to being played off against each other. For Wade had with him the admiral of the China station and another admiral in command of the 'Flying Squadron' poised at Dalian (Dairen, now Luda) on the tip of Liaodong peninsula, just across the straits. No nation wished to be dragged into hostilities (see map 2.45: p 358).

It was Wade's conference, to wring 'satisfaction' of Britain's grievances from an adroitly evasive China, but such an unplanned confluence of observers could not but mean social exchanges between diplomats 'ashore and afloat'. Wise to the acute danger of war, Li Hongzhang seized the initiative, inviting the fifteen most influential individuals to a magnificent feast of alternating Chinese and European courses, and proposed a roast in Western style, that 'as "all within the four seas are brothers", the nations here represented may always dwell in peace and friendship . . . like brothers living together'. This conditioned Sir Thomas and his admirals to his mood

2.29 *Li Hongzhang, viceroy and grand secretary*

as discussion ploughed heavily through the mire of ambiguous aims. But Wade 'was at his best at Chefoo'. After Li Hongzhang adopted Wade's own ploy of threatening to leave Yantai without an agreement, some order was eventually made of it. The 'Flying Squadron' came peacefully to lie 'in beautiful array in Chefoo harbour', and the 'Chefoo Convention' was signed on September 13, in three sections.

The first was a 'Settlement of the Yunnan case', providing for an imperial edict and proclamations in all provinces to ensure safe travel for foreigners, throughout the empire if provided with a passport; for two years British officials were to visit Chinese cities at will, to see that proclamations were posted; trade between Burma and Yunnan, and a second expedition like Colonel Browne's were provided for, to be supervised by British officials stationed at Dali for five years; an indemnity of 200,000 taels was to be paid; and an imperial letter of regret was to be taken by a Chinese mission to London.

The second section on 'Official Relations' provided for the administration of justice at Chinese ports, and that China should treat foreign officials as Chinese representatives were treated abroad.

Under 'Trade', the third section, Yichang, Wuhu, Wenzhou and Beihai (Pakhoi) were to be opened as treaty ports;

a consul was to reside at Chongqing; and six more 'ports of call' on the Yangzi were authorised. For good measure, a British mission was to be ensured safe passage through Tibet, from China to India. Wade feared that if British merchants were so 'enterprising' as to penetrate 1,500 miles up the Yangzi into Sichuan they would be massacred, so he accepted a ban on their residence in Chongqing, but no mention of missionaries was made.

Assessments of the value of the convention were as many as they were contradictory, both at the time and since. Wade succeeded in getting much of what he wanted, yet the *North China Herald* called it 'a mass of meaningless verbiage'. The merchants saw it as an ambiguous substitute for 'the clear and simple provisions of the treaty of Tientsin' (Tianjin) of 1858. The envoys of other nations saw no improvement on the negotiations they had disapproved of in Peking, and all the powers took advantage of China's concessions, while refusing to be bound by Wade's.[317] However, the missionary community hailed the news as being the answer to Valignano's cry 'Oh, Rock, Rock, when wilt thou open, Rock?' (see 1, p 18) not foreseeing the accusation that those who acted on the convention were agents of the foreign powers.

Li Hongzhang had flatly refused to allow his colleague Zen Yüying, acting-governor of Yunnan, to be humiliated, and reported the convention to Peking in novel terms. British protests against punishment of the wrong people, he explained, were to be regarded less as concern for justice and past events than for security in the future. Those convicted by Chinese judicial process would not have been convicted by British law, so 'the memorialists (Li himself) would respectfully pray your gracious Majesties, as an exceptional instance of humanity . . . to deign to accord the request of the British Minister, and as an act of indulgence to consider the possibility of granting remission of their sentences'. Amnesty for all involved! A proclamation would prevent a repetition of the grievance. His

ingenuity had secured a treaty, which went little further than the Treaty of Tientsin while confusing its issues and at little cost to China. W. A. P. Martin even called it 'a triumph for Li Hung-Zhang'.

Travel by foreigners in inland China had been legalised in 1858 and in 1876 was only made less hazardous. But this fact was of no small consequence to the travellers. When all was settled and the civilities followed, Li came aboard Admiral Ryder's flagship with a retinue of two hundred. 'His majestic height, his dignified bearing, his piercing eyes that seemed to see everything at once . . . made an ineffaceable impression'.

China ratified the convention immediately, on September 17, but the British government declined to do so. One clause left a loophole to restrict the import of opium. Nine years later, when further,concessions were extorted from China on July 18, 1885, exempting opium from *likin* tax, Britain at last ratified the whole, on May 6, 1886. Guilt had been exposed. As Samuel Wells Williams maintained, the truth lay bare the Bhamo route was wanted for opium, the insidious evil about which Henry Soltau had written and which Hudson Taylor published in *China's Millions* to throw light on the scandal of its growing grip on Burma as well as China.[318]

The imperial envoy appointed to London and Paris, Guo Songdao, arrived in London on January 21, 1877, and on February 8 in Sir Thomas Wade's presence presented his letters of credence and the one of regret (see p 272). Wade had left China for good. Two years later Guo was replaced by 'Marquis' Zeng, the son of Zeng Guofan, but not before his own province of Hunan had vented its wrath on him by burning down his family home. For a time feeling against the convention was high. Zhang Zhitong (Chang Chih-t'ung), literary chancellor of Sichuan and one of China's most revered scholars, presented a memorial to the throne giving eight cogent reasons why China should go to war with Britain without delay. Too late the die was cast.

'Not too soon and not too late'
(September–October 1876)

The Kunming enquiry failed as James Cameron made his first journey in Anhui. Grosvenor, Baber and Davenport reached Bhamo a week after Joseph Adams and the Harveys arrived there on May 15, 1876. As it happened, the day after Sir Thomas Wade reached Yantai to confront Li Hongzhang, Hudson Taylor named the party of men and women with whom he himself would travel to China. Louise Desgraz and the five young women left on September 5 to join the French Mail at Marseilles, and William Rudland on a different ship. After another painful parting from Jennie and the children, Hudson Taylor followed on the 8th with Robert J. Landale and W. A. Wills (who later joined the BMS). He intended to be back in Britain within a year. The fact of the Chefoo negotiations was known, but whether their outcome would be war or peace hung in the balance. The dispatch of the Flying Squadron to China had looked ominous.

Eugene Stock, who on December 21, 1875, became editor of CMS publications and already respected Hudson Taylor, was to write admiringly of the formation of his team of pioneers during the eighteen months of political uncertainty, so that when agreement was reached they were almost all ready to enter their promised land, the unoccupied provinces.[319] R. J. Landale, 'a gentleman of means and education', was the son of a lawyer of the Supreme Court in Edinburgh, and a graduate of Oxford University who had become interested in China through a visit by C. G. Moore, the theologian candidate. Being able to pay all his own expenses and, apparently on his father's advice, going to see what he was embarking on before committing himself to membership of the CIM, Landale accompanied Hudson Taylor without obligation on either side, but with mutual appreciation and deepening confidence. Hunan, Guizhou and Guangxi were to be the scene of his daring travels.[320]

Seeming disaster marked the beginning of their journey. Hudson and Jennie had been up all night finishing essential work before he set off at 7.00 a.m. At the Gare du Nord, Paris, his most precious document box containing all the work he intended to do on the voyage was left behind. Sent on by the next French mail it reached him a month after he arrived in China, but by then his journey had been the enforced holiday he needed. He had time to write frequently to Jennie, using terms he had been unable to use while Maria's memory remained vivid. The Messageries Maritimes ship, third class, was luxury! Tablecloths and napkins! Linoleum on the cabin floors! How could anyone say it was not good enough? Had the Council understood about keeping funds flowing? 'Ask (them) to remit to China all they can spare.' The heat in the Red Sea, compounded by engine room heat and smells, seemed to emphasize the realisation that nothing ahead would be easy. '"Lo! I come to do Thy will, O God." This is our one duty, one privilege, is it not, darling, "to do Thy will", you . . . in staying at home, I in leaving you. Day by day, one hour at a time, let us do our Master's work.' In the South China Sea Hudson Taylor wrote that the women were to go to Yangzhou, but the publication of their movements must be avoided. Wade and the Foreign Office were still sensitive about the CIM. George Soltau had been negotiating with them since 'Jackson's matter' and 'by undertaking for all our missionaries that they should not appeal to our Consuls for help in any missionary difficulty. On this ground our passports are to be given to us as before. This does not preclude us from getting any help we can from the mandarins.' He thought of first taking Louise and the girls to Hangzhou and from there to Yangzhou. A glimpse of the thriving indigenous church at Hangzhou would set a standard for them at the outset. The Shanghai newspapers published only the passenger lists of foreign river-steamers, so leaving by canal boat or Chinese river-boat would not be noticed. Nothing so leisurely awaited them. Not too soon and not too late, imperial proclamations in the farthest corners of the empire by guaranteeing protection invited entry. The day for which Robert Morrison and Samuel Dyer, Maria's father, had so longed at last had dawned and the teams were ready to go, were well on their way. 'He who holds the Key of David, who opens and no man shuts . . . will open hearts as well as doors,' Hudson Taylor declared.[321]

Learning his limitations[322] (October–December 1876)

Letters waiting for Hudson Taylor at Hong Kong and again at Shanghai when he reached there on October 22, gave him the gist of the situation in China. 'In a word, I find matters better than I expected on the whole,' he told Jennie. For although Catherine (Duncan) Stronach's illness and Henry Taylor's dejection over his expulsion from Henan needed prompt action, good news outweighed the problems. 'An expedition to explore Tibet is to go next year. Yunnan may be opened within five years.' John McCarthy, writing from Zhenjiang to put him in the picture, went out of his way to compliment J. J. Turner on his attitude to the Chinese and growing grasp of the language. 'He is thoroughly at one with your views . . . Easton is fit and anxious to go forward . . . If we can, we ought to go forward now.' (The phrase 'to go forward' was current for 'advance' and became a Mission cliché, still extant.) McCarthy himself would wait for Hudson Taylor but, he added, 'I am hoping that, ere you arrive, there will be men on the way to the three northern provinces.' The imperial proclamations should already have been placarded in every city of the empire, and men should not delay in making the most of them. Easton and Parker were off to Gansu, King and Budd to Shaanxi, and Turner and James to Shanxi with the good Nanjing teacher, Mr Yao (Yao Xianseng), who had 'travelled widely in north China and lived long in Honan'. Nicoll had rented a house in Yichang, and Cameron was joining him from Anhui. A second letter on the heels of McCarthy's first reported the departure of the three teams each with two Chinese colleagues.

Frederick Baller was in Shanghai to meet the ship, and escorted Louise and the young women straight to Yangzhou, while Hudson Taylor and Landale, after two days of consular business obtaining passports, joined McCarthy, 'a great comfort', at Zhenjiang. Hardly had he arrived there than Hudson Taylor went down with 'enteritis', his 'thorn in the flesh', and was unfit to take normal food until mid-November or to leave Zhenjiang until a month later. Forced inactivity gave him the chance to think 'with mounting excitement' over the great things that were beginning to happen.

Ill or not, he had to take what came his way. So soon after her re-marriage in February to William Gavin Stronach of the British consular service, Catherine Duncan was dying in Zhenjiang.[323] Being a consul's wife had made her no less a missionary. As Hudson Taylor 'comforted her last hours', he told Jennie, she 'begged that (her daughter) Millie might be brought up with our children and I acceded to this her dying request, uttered when the power of speech was almost gone'. He himself conducted the funeral, and her husband took Millie home. 'Make them welcome (even) if not convenient, for love of me, darling,' he wrote. And six- or seven-year-old Mary Jane Bowyer Duncan became one of the Taylor family for George Duncan's sake and for another reason. In April the consul's father, John Stronach of the LMS, the closest friend of Maria's father Samuel Dyer, had left China 'to return home for the first time since entering on mission work' thirty-eight years previously. Progress had appeared slow, but in his lifetime immense strides had been and were being made (See 1, p 120).[324]

Administrative problems that needed Hudson Taylor's attention were as varied as they were many. Word came that Fanny Jackson was having eclamptic convulsions as in previous pregnancies. There was nothing he could do to help. 'I cannot get about as I used to do,' he confessed to Rudland. But she survived again, for a few more years. Horace Randle, 'a very dear fellow' who had come to China with George Parker, was having epileptic fits. He had been so long without them that as a candidate it had not occurred to him to mention his past history. Yet he was to be an effective missionary for eighteen years before resigning in 1894.

Christian Chinese needing Christian wives, few of whom were available, looked as always to the mission schools for help. The right to arrange the marriages of pupils was by Chinese custom included in the contract which parents signed when leaving them in school until they reached a marriageable age. Only one, Shao Mianzi, was nearing that time. Sympathizing with the Christian young men and widowers, Hudson Taylor took steps to enlarge the girls' schools under Louise Desgraz' control in Yangzhou and Zhenjiang. And when famine in the north led to hundreds of refugees flocking to the unaffected areas, he authorised the admission of two hundred more at Mission expense.

Josiah Jackson was keeping out of trouble, but problem missionaries occupied their director's thoughts: 'Those who cannot wait to get married' in spite of promising to give two uninterrupted years to gaining the language and experience first; or those who 'have forgotten that they undertook to wear Chinese clothes, and for whom everything and everyone is wrong.' C. G. Moore was rightly wrestling with his own hesitations and objections in London, before coming to China.

> You have referred to the individuality of your theological views ... [Hudson Taylor wrote] but you know our platform and on the doctrines which we all need to hold ... you have, I believe, no difficulty. Other points are of great importance, I admit, but we as a Mission do not attempt to limit ourselves to this or that view. Each member must be responsible to God for what he holds and in his own sphere of labour teaches. And even on the question of (Chinese) dress we only require a candidate to determine whether he will wear it or not, because harmonious action demands all working together to act alike (in any given area). [Moore should get ordained before leaving Britain but not discuss it with the Council 'as they are of diverse views on the subject'.] The native dress proves a real trial to some ... Are you prepared to bear it for Jesus' sake? The work we are attempting to do in the interior cannot be done without it.

He must also be willing to be isolated from fellow-Christians, and to have to change his location from time to time. Too many missionaries had settled down to static institutions.

To Edward Fishe, at last game not only to return to China but as a pioneer, 'The way to permanent residence in the interior may or may not soon open up. But itinerant work is now possible.' Would Fishe join the Judds at Wuchang and alternate with Charles Judd in country travelling, going first to Guizhou? His answer to this fateful question was 'Yes', and he, Annie and the children sailed off to China. Another missionary, who made disparaging remarks about the Messageries Maritimes ships and himself chose to travel by a one-class ship in greater comfort though he had come from a 'working-class' background, roused Hudson Taylor's ire so that he exploded to Jennie, 'It makes me feel angry to hear such wicked and ungrateful remarks.' Henry Taylor, a casualty of heroic reconnoitring in the face of death-threats, still showed the stamina he looked for in everyone—that Hudson Taylor himself had shown from his earliest days in China. To give time and friendship to Henry Taylor was time well spent, while he himself was learning that he could not always be up at the front.

'Like a bombshell scattering us'[325] (October 1876–77)

With the arrival of Hudson Taylor in China an explosion of life and activity in the China Inland Mission took the foreign community by surprise. In the last three months of 1876 and through 1877, 'a most eventful year' because of so much happening at once, most of the eighteen pioneers travelled in most of the nine distant provinces and put down roots in some. Within four months of the signing of the Chefoo Convention, six had been entered. In spite of writing, 'I cannot run about as before', Hudson Taylor himself visited all but four of the Mission locations and outposts, scattered between Wenzhou in southern Zhejiang and Wuhan far up the Yangzi, before returning to Britain. With his recovery from enteritis, in mid-November, the box of documents left in Paris arrived, and from then on he was fully stretched. From time to time too many claims on his strength drew from him such groans as 'I have four times the work I can do'. Between him and John McCarthy was a secret of which even Jennie was in the dark—a scheme which might well have been banned or made too dangerous had it become known. The Convention had flung open the remotest regions of the empire, but for how long? A sense of urgency drove him to encourage more daring enterprises by his half-trained men than would otherwise have been thought wise. But McCarthy was a seasoned traveller in China.

For home consumption he sent a report of progress so far. His zest was apparent. Members of the CIM were on their way into six 'fresh' provinces. Only Guangxi had no one yet assigned to it, and Yunnan (see also maps 2.26 & 2.59: pp 246 & 480 respectively) was barred to Stevenson and Soltau by the British government of India, not by China. An epidemic in Bhamo had carried off a Catholic priest and the hostile Burmese governor, but the latter's successor proved friendly, helped them to secure their building site and gave them a free hand to travel with friendly Kachin chiefs into the hills.[326] The British Resident could not deny them the right when they promised not to cross the frontier.

On November 3 Stevenson and Soltau set off. When John Stevenson had expressed an interest in the Kachins, someone in Rangoon had retorted, 'You should see what sharp spears and knives they carry.' But when they penetrated the jungle and for six weeks slept on earthen floors in the villages and met unfamiliar tribesmen without a qualm, they were not threatened but protected by those weapons. From near Matang they looked across the border into the plain of Longchuan and beyond to

the mountains of Yunnan. 'The (Kachins) I look upon as our best allies,' Stevenson reported, and the Burmese governor 'said publicly that we were at perfect liberty to come and go from the hills as we please and when we please.' Yet, lest they hazard the hopes of the opium 'trade' from India, they were to be fettered by the British for four more years, until 1880. In Shanghai Hudson Taylor asked his friend Walter Medhurst, the consul-general, if he could obtain passports for Stevenson and Soltau such as McCarthy and some others had, valid for the eighteen provinces, so that they would be ready when the ban was lifted.[327] When the chargé d'affaires in Peking consulted India, they were thwarted once again. Yunnan in the far south-west and its twelve million inhabitants would have to wait.

Not so the north-west. The great provinces of Shaanxi and Gansu, with populations of about fifteen and sixteen millions, were accessible, after strenuous journeys across hot dusty plains and cold mountain ranges (see map 2.31: p 279). Shaanxi, the size 'of England and Wales combined, or the State of Nebraska', is broken by hills into three distinct regions. A high tableland in the north, around the city of Yan'an (Yenan) was inhabited by poor cave-dwelling immigrants from many provinces. In the central plain or valley of the great Wei River lies ancient Xi'an,

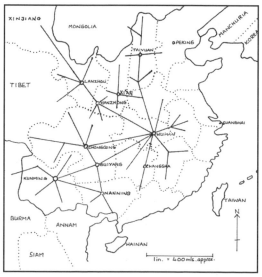

2.30 'Like a bombshell scattering us.'

intermittently the capital of China for a thousand years, home of the Nestorian tablet and, nearby, the vast tomb of Qin Shihuangdi (Chinn Shih Huang Ti) with its army of terracotta figures, and a host of other historical treasures. In the north-eastern segment of the walled Ming city of Xi'an, 50,000 Manchus had their homes.

In the south of Shaanxi, beyond the Qinling (Ts'in-ling) 'mountains' (rising to 11,000 feet, but in reality a tangled, sparsely inhabited mass) are the Hanzhong plain and city, more akin to Sichuan than to the rest of Shaanxi. Access from the Yangzi valley was slow but comfortable, by boat up the Han River with rocky rapids the worst hazard. But to reach the Xi'an plain involved leaving the Han at Xiangfan (Fancheng) or Guanghua (Laohekou) after three weeks' travel from Wuhan, and striking overland east of the Qinling mountains on foot or mounted, for three more weeks of heat, dust and privation.

Gansu lay more weeks and mountain ranges away to the west and north-west. Long and narrow, this province stretched for nine hundred miles between Mongolia and Tibetan Qinghai, from the watered, mountainous south-east through Yumen (Jade Gate) to the deserts of Xinjiang, Chinese Turkestan. Lanzhou, the provincial capital, lay five hundred miles beyond Xi'an (see map 2.59: p 480). The four young men and their four Chinese companions who set out together by river junk from Wuhan on November 8, 1876, to make their first acquaintance with unknown territory, preaching and selling Christian books all along the way, would not return before the end of March. George King and Charles Budd with Zhenjiang Christians named only as Yao and Zhang were to travel widely in Shaanxi, while George F. Easton, and George Parker made for Lanzhou with Zhen, a Zhenjiang man, and the Yangzhou evangelist Zhang. King had only been up the river with Baller. All was new to the rest.[328]

Before they set out, Hudson Taylor had given Easton a piece of advice from his own experience. Learn to recognise official and merchant couriers on the boats and roads and see where they spend the nights. Such inns are dependable. Easton found that the couriers often had rented rooms for their own use in private homes, a useful tip for constant travellers.

Because these first evangelistic journeys are historic in the planting of the great Chinese church, they deserve our close attention. Together they left the Han River above Laohekou at the end of February and hired baggage and riding mules for the mountain journey to Xi'an, preaching and selling books in every town and market they passed through. While the novice missionaries could do little themselves, they listened and learned all the time from the evangelists, and soon were carrying a full share of the work. 'The roads are shockingly bad; we have walked the whole distance, about 22 miles,' Easton wrote. In every place of any size in which they looked, the imperial edict about foreign travellers was in evidence. Here and there 'the officials issued it after our arrival, and were very polite to us'. Xi'an was reached on December 20, and only when their passports had been examined were the foreigners admitted to the city, to preach with good attention each day. There they parted, the Gansu team pressing on to enter the province on December 28, and King, Budd and their companions setting out on a month of travelling and preaching on the Xi'an plain.

Two by two, always one Chinese with one Westerner, and a pack mule loaded with books, the pairs meeting occasionally at prearranged rendezvous, they covered the north-eastern region of Tongguan (see map 2.58: p 466), Chengcheng, Tongchuan and Sanyuan, returning to Xi'an on January 26. After a few days they tackled the cities west of the capital (see map 2.31: p 279), but found at the first (probably Xianyang) that 'some of the literary men had been pasting up printed placards well fitted to inflame the minds of the people against us and our work.' So they wisely withdrew and went to other cities, again separating in pairs to meet at Fengxiang, near Baoji. At Qishan

2.31 *First to the north-west: Shaanxi and Gansu*

Protestant missionaries who have ever visited the place—the capital of a vast and important province, and the highway [the Silk Road] to regions beyond—find two Roman Catholic places of worship with (at least) one resident priest,' exclaimed Hudson Taylor when he read their report. If only the gospel of justification by faith in Christ and his finished work of atonement for sinners who believe was preached, unobscured by Roman accretions! What was wrong with the Church? Christians were asleep. The eighteen were a drop in the bucket. 'I could at once locate fourteen more brethren with great advantage and designate five more [he wrote to Jennie]; and six sisters could also have immediate and useful employment. May the Lord give us grace to be faithful, so that He can entrust us with these twenty-five workers, and with all the funds required for the whole work.'[330]

Expansion of the Mission must be closely related to facilities for absorbing them, not abstractly visionary. Experienced colleagues to train them, and teams for them to join as novices, must be available. They were. Then more must come, and God who sent them would provide for their needs.

In Lanzhou the stock of books and cash in hand were running low. Easton and Parker could not stay more than a week, though well received by the mixed population of migrants from several provinces, including many Peking merchants. They started homeward on the 27th, travelling through Weiyuan and some towns on market day, thronged with eight to ten thousand people, the ideal opportunity for preaching. That their stock of books was exhausted seemed tragic. On February 9 they reached Tianshui (Ts'in-chou), a city made up of six small townships unified by one main three-mile street. Then on through 'mountains very grand and majestic, and scenery really beautiful' to re-enter Shaanxi on February 22 and,

the 'people were kind and the authorities courteous, as we find them at most places'. In this way they worked until the end of February, when they made a quick journey back to Laohckou, reaching Wuhan on March 24 and Zhenjiang, to report to Hudson Taylor, on April 4, five months after setting out. This was evangelism on the grand scale, however fleeting the impact on any single community.

Entering Gansu for the first time on December 28 or 29 by the Pingliang road, Easton, Parker and their friends met with large audiences of well-behaved people to whom not only the gospel but the common terms for God and religious ideas seemed entirely new. But if the number of books they bought gave a clue they seemed interested.[329] Pingliang was almost equally populated by Muslims and men from Hunan, one-time soldiers, but again they gave good attention to the preaching. After three days they started for Lanzhou; on January 5, over the hills to Longde (now in Ningxia) and Huining, where they were almost mobbed for books; past an old bed of the Huang He (Yellow River) and ruins of the Great Wall, to enter Lanzhou on January 20, 1876. 'The very first and only with scarcely a diary comment, to brave the rapids on the upper Han River, past Hanzhong (see map 2.59: p 480), trans-shipping at Laohekou and Wuhan, to reach Zhenjiang and Hudson Taylor on April 9, one year since George Parker left Britain and eighteen months since Easton sailed!

Hudson Taylor himself, arriving at Shanghai in 1854 at the age of twenty-one, with no known friends in China, had begun his active work after a few months spent in learning Chinese, and had travelled, often alone, 'over the treaty wall'. Twenty-three years later he had confidence in his young men and trusted God to see them through these journeys, many hundreds of miles removed from each other and human aid.

The struggle for Henan[331]
(January–May 1877)

Cheered by his weeks with Hudson Taylor, Henry Taylor returned to Wuhan, to wait for a Christian man named Dai, whom they had sent into Henan to assess the attitude of the literati at Queshan. He arrived on January 17 with a good report (which proved to be mistaken) and on the 27th Henry Taylor left without George Clarke (deputizing at Wuchang for Charles Judd) but with a brave Christian named Chu as his companion. On arrival at Queshan they found the rented house occupied by a family installed by the literati, an ominous sign; all their possessions removed by the instigator of the opposition; and the magistrate unwilling to displease these opponents by helping the foreigner. 'All who have called on me have expressed surprise at seeing us back again, and consider us persons of great courage,' Taylor wrote to Clarke. They told him about the beatings inflicted on his friends after he and Clarke left Queshan in October and the ringleader came and offered to return his passport for a ransom of two hundred ounces of silver. 'Of course we refused.' Mr Hu, the Chinese doctor who had had fifty blows on the hand, seemed unafraid to visit them. Although another riot was planned and the day fixed, it had not happened when Henry Taylor wrote to Hudson Taylor,

I hold on my way only by the grace of God,

and the belief that He has called me to open up Honan to the Gospel ... One of the ringleaders came in today and abused us ... We hear this evening that they are determined to kill the foreigner, and that the emperor will promote them for so doing. 'Behold, Lord, their threatenings, and grant unto Thy servants that with all boldness they may speak Thy word.' ... The young scholar [friend of their teacher] who received the fifty blows [on the mouth] last year is doing all he can to get us another house. [And four days later to Elizabeth Judd], All hope of success is gone. The whole city is in excitement ... Let Mr Taylor know ... The rumours are of the worst kind. 'God is our refuge and strength.'

Yet Henry Taylor and Chu were still in Queshan six weeks later, had rented a different house and were about to move in when Taylor reported again:

The opposition is very strong and the mandarin is one with the gentry ... determined to drive us from the place ... I sink beneath the burden. I almost despair of success ... Still, I cannot dishonour my God ... The literati hired a few hundred men who surrounded the house—created a disturbance and threatened the landlord's life; he came terror-stricken to us beseeching us to shield him.

[While Henry Taylor was at the magistrate's *yamen* seeking justice] a messenger came with tidings that our house was surrounded by a mob and that my servant had been beaten very severely—which proved to be the case—so that we have no alternative but to leave ... I would take a long (preaching) journey but I am too weak, being unstrung in body and mind.

Hudson Taylor had advised 'a conciliatory policy' in Henan: 'if they persecute you in one city, flee to another.' To withdraw might have been wiser than to make a brave trial of strength, but who is to criticise such tenacity? On May 12, Taylor and Chu arrived back at Wuhan, 'utterly sad', and inconsolable among all the comings and goings of the other teams. Hudson Taylor sent him as far as he could from the scene of his distress, to the peaceful, thriving church at Qi Man on the Qiantang River in Zhejiang (see map 2.57: p 457). There he could see the second stage of 'occupation', a spontaneous Christian expansion into Jiangxi province led by an indefatigable Captain Yu.

Arthur Douthwaite would be the right man to deal gently with his broken spirit. Less than a year later Henry Taylor and George Clarke left Wuhan again (on Taylor's sixth attempt) with famine relief supplies for Henan, glad to have what Clarke called 'a glorious opportunity of exhibiting the grace of our Lord Jesus Christ'.

Long treks to Shanxi[332]
(October 1876–January 1878)

At the time of Henry Taylor's first expulsion in October 1876, when the two teams were starting for Shaanxi and Gansu—just as Hudson Taylor arrived back in China—the first penetration by the CIM into Shanxi was also made. In 1869 one of Alexander Wylie's colporteurs named Wellman, and Alexander Williamson, with Jonathan Lees of the LMS, had entered Shanxi selling for the Bible Societies, but until 1876 no mission had attempted to settle.

J. J. Turner, after ten months in China, and Francis James, after only seven months, left Zhenjiang on October 18 and Nanjing on the 23rd, on an epic first journey of 1,700 miles with 'the first-rate Nanjing teacher' Yao and a Chinese evangelist and 3,000 Gospels, 1,300 small books and many tracts.

Crossing the Yangzi at Nanjing they hired pack-mules and trekked mile upon mile through countryside and towns still ravaged by the Taiping rebellion of a decade earlier, but suffering again from drought and famine. Hundreds of destitute people were making their way southwards to find food. At Huaiyuan near Bengbu (see map 2.43: p 353) on October 29 they hired a boat, up the Guo River to Bo Xian, and there hired two carts

to take them two hundred miles through Henan. They crossed the Yellow River near Kaifeng, 'a broad and rapid stream', wider than the Yangzi at Zhenjiang, by a large flat-bottomed ferry-boat, a barge carrying two carts, forty mules and horses, some cattle and sixty men, some with loads, rowed (probably) by a dozen standing oarsmen. At a busy town a few miles from the Shanxi border they engaged donkeys to climb the 'almost wall-like ascent' of the Taihang mountains to reach 'Tsechou', now called Jincheng, on the south-eastern uplands of Shanxi.

A mental picture of the province will colour the events we are coming to. Moated throughout its western flank and half its southern border by the south-flowing, silt-laden Yellow River, Shanxi is guarded on the east by the great rampart of the Taihang range. Only here and there could roads of any size break through these walls.

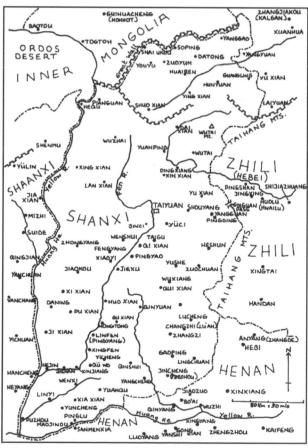

2.32 Long treks to Shanxi

The 'road' of granite steps by which Turner and James entered was in places carved in the solid rock. Baron von Richtofen, a geologist and geographer, estimated that 'some 13,500 square miles of anthracite coalfields with seams varying from twenty to thirty feet in thickness' made Shanxi 'one of the largest and richest coalfields in the world'. Between the western and eastern uplands, flowing southwards from north of Taiyuan, the capital city, lay the Fen River, watering the fertile Great Plain of Taiyuan, a hundred miles long from north to south. Throughout the plain, towns and cities abound, home of most of Shanxi's fifteen million inhabitants at that time, and the ultimate destination of the travellers.

On this journey they had to content themselves with reaching the capital of a prefecture known to them as P'ing-yang, now Linfen, and there to turn southward to Puzhou at the extreme south-western corner of the province. On December 8 they re-crossed the Yellow River at Tongguan (see map 2.58: p 466), headed south-eastwards through western Henan for six hundred and fifty miles to Xiangfan (Fancheng), on December 28, and on January 8, 1877, reached the Mission home in Wuhan. With this appetiser, the longest journey yet made by members of the CIM, they wanted only to refit and confer with Hudson Taylor, who arrived the next day, before setting off again.[333]

'From 1876–1880 Mr Taylor's advent, we used to say, was like a bombshell scattering us,' Elizabeth Wilson was to recall.[334] She was in Wuchang at the time, observing team upon team going, returning, catching Hudson Taylor's spirit, absorbing his pleasure and enthusiasm, and going out again. It was true of the whole period of 1876–80, but most strikingly of the sixty-seven weeks that Hudson Taylor was away from Britain on this occasion (instead of the forty planned). Charles Judd and James Broumton had started out for Hunan and Guizhou on January 2. (We shall come to their story.) Henry Taylor was waiting for Mr Dai and news of Queshan. On the 20th, the day Easton and Parker reached Lanzhou, John McCarthy arrived from a pastoral visit to all the Yangzi stations,[335] ready to go to the rescue of anyone on the great journeys to the north, but also preparing to ascend the Yangzi gorges into Sichuan and, though no one was to know it yet, to attempt to cross Yunnan to Bhamo. Alone on the river-steamer, Hudson Taylor chose to write enigmatically even to Jennie, rather than risk letting the cat out of the bag, 'to request *very* especial prayer for him . . . as he may be in urgent need of it, and to continue *every day* till you hear further. If there be danger . . . McCarthy will be in it . . . No less than six or seven of the unoccupied provinces are being simultaneously attempted, and there can be no such extensive evangelisation unattended with danger.'

The risks had to be taken; the golden opportunity of a lifetime might not last; the literati might reject what Li Hongzhang had done, and repeat Henry Taylor's treatment everywhere.[336]

Hudson Taylor himself undertook to supervise the work in Anhui during McCarthy's absence, so they were conferring together late in the evenings. He was aware of these being momentous days and of being an instrument of God. 'He . . . is giving me very important work to do,' he told Jennie on the day McCarthy left. And in more than one letter he said that news of the old work and the new, of Christians standing firm and idolaters turning to Christ, made his heart 'sing for joy'. Longing to be with her again, he was convinced that he was still needed in China. The only hope of getting away seemed to be if Benjamin and Amelia would come to take his place as advisers to so many young men and women. Perhaps to telegraph for them would be more effective than writing! It was a passing whim, even a lapse of judgment which calm consideration led him to abandon.[337]

If the roads were not impassable through heavy snow and rains, except in Henan and Shanxi where the drought showed no sign of breaking, Turner and James would have got away already. But at last they did, on February 10. After they had gone Hudson Taylor revealed that for the third time since reaching Wuhan he was suffering gallstone colic. Three weeks earlier he had told Jennie, 'I am quite worn out . . . The pressure is too great, so many coming and going', with all that was involved of calculating and consulting, arranging with Chinese merchant firms for cash to be drawn in distant cities, waterproofing and roping baggage, bargaining with boatmen and paying wages. He found a regular dispatch by courier every five days from Wuhan to Chongqing, and on to Guiyang and back. But did she know the hymn 'Jesus, I am resting, resting in the joy of what Thou art' (except that he misquoted it)? A new discovery, it had gripped his mind, echoing and re-echoing inescapably. So when the hubbub ended and he was quietly sailing down the Yangzi in a little houseboat again, he could say that the time in Wuhan had 'greatly benefitted' his health. McCarthy was heading for Sichuan, but in preparing material for the June *China's Millions* Hudson was taking excerpts from T. T. Cooper's *Travels of a Pioneer of Commerce*, to show 'what Rome is doing while we are dreaming'.

Turner and James had only been gone a few days, this time to settle in Shanxi permanently or for as long as possible, when their boat up the Han River struck a rock. Their books were ruined, their personal baggage damaged, and they were set on by pirates, but no lives were lost, so they went on. Hiring a large wheelbarrow to carry the remaining goods and each of them riding it by turns, they hoped to make a quick journey to Tongguan. But the barrow men cheated them repeatedly until they paid them off and hired a trundling ox-cart to pass through the central Henan plains. Crossing the Yellow River at Maojindu (between Sanmenxia and Pinglu) they travelled due north.

> The journey ... has been nearly all through a famine-stricken district ... There has been no rain for two or three years. There is no grass. And the loose sandy soil is dried to

2.33 Full-steam ahead: a long-distance wheelbarrow

> powder, which drives about in clouds ... In some places many have already died of starvation. The beggars are dreadful. They go about in crowds, principally women and children. They surround the passer-by and kneel down and cry for a cash ... These starving people cry in real earnest for a morsel of food ... (or) holding out their basins in mute appeal.[338]

Only close to the rivers was any green vegetation to be seen.

'Passing through Pingyang and fifteen other cities', at last they reached Taiyuan on April 24 and made themselves known, received visitors, and on the 28th set out on an evangelistic itinerary in the great plain for two months. Twenty miles away they found the small town of Jinci with a spring of pure water, and made a good inn their base while they worked to acquire the Shanxi dialect. But towards mid-June their supply of cash was running low and it was time to lay in a new stock of books and Bibles. So, while Francis James moved into Taiyuan, J. J. Turner travelled by the main highway to Peking, and by ship from Tianjin to Shanghai. By then Hudson Taylor was visiting the southern region of Zhejiang and asked Turner to meet him in Wenzhou.[339]

Back in Taiyuan after an absence of two and a half months, first he and then James fell ill with typhoid fever. James hovered between life and death for several days, but by September 24 was strong enough to move to quiet Jinci to recuperate through October and into November. Then, returning to Taiyuan, James seemed well enough for the long journey first by cart to Xiangfan (Fancheng) on the Han River and on by boat to Wuhan. The famine had become so appalling that mobilizing foreign aid had become their first priority. Passing through the worst areas would allow them to observe and describe conditions, and after raising funds to return with others to give what aid they could. So on November 28, 1877, they left Taiyuan—two days

before Timothy Richard arrived on his first visit—and reached Wuhan on January 22, 1878, eleven months and nine days since leaving there. Both of them wrote gruesome accounts of the famine and Turner returned to Shanxi in March with companions and relief funds. James was still too weak.[340]

1876–77: The tentacles reach out

The lure of the west
(December 1876–March 1877)

The lure of the west and south-west was as powerful as that of the north-west and north. Yueyang, gateway to the anti-foreign province of Hunan, had expelled Judd in 1875 (see p 235), and it seemed wise to occupy receptive provinces before challenging the chief source of inflammatory agitation so positively again. Its twenty-five millions must wait a little longer for the gospel. Judd's courage and experience were needed elsewhere for the present. But which provinces were receptive? Sichuan, the brimming rice bowl and market garden of West China with its twenty-seven millions of industrious people, drew like a magnet. Only loyalty to his mission board prevented Griffith John from adding Chongqing or Chengdu to Wuhan as his bases for intensive church planting. So he supported the CIM to the hilt. John McCarthy had an invitation from an influential, enlightened young man to visit his home at Guang'an deep in the heart of the province. He was ready to go. Beyond the well-watered plains (Sichuan means 'Four Rivers'), the mountains climbed westwards above ten thousand feet to the heights of Tibet and the *Manzi*, the 'wild' or 'barbarian' tribes. South and southwestwards mountain ranges flowed in waves to join the plateau province of Yunnan ('South of the Clouds') where puffs of white cirrus hang motionless in the bluest of blue skies as far as the Mekong and Salween chasms that moat the jungles of Burma. Throughout those ranges millions of 'minority people' of scores of different

'tribes' had their fortress homes written off derisively as 'Lolos' by the dominant Han Chinese (see 1, p 4).[341] These were the 'barbarians' progressively forced back into the wilderness by the ever-expanding Han race.

Closer, between Hunan, Sichuan and Yunnan, the sparsely populated, unproductive turmoil of hills and valleys called Guizhou, held its own attractions. Scattered through the hills lived differing ethnic groups of Miao, the rebellious aborigines who had for decades been attacking the encroaching Han Chinese around them. Bordering Yunnan and Sichuan in the west lived about five million 'Lolos'—now called 'Yi', but who call themselves the Nosu—about equally divided between those who accepted Chinese domination and those who struggled to preserve their independence.

The great tableland of Yunnan and Guizhou, averaging five thousand feet above sea level, is tilted towards the east and south so that the main rivers flow out through Hunan to join the Yangzi, through Guangxi by the Red River to Canton, and through Indo-China. The direct route to Yunnan through Wuhan on the Yangzi was naturally up the Yuan River through Hunan and Guiyang, the capital city of Guizhou. Another major route was over the mountains from Chongqing in Sichuan. The perils of the brigand-infested overland routes and of the fierce Yangzi rapids left little to choose between them (see map 2.26: p 246).

Hudson Taylor had been corresponding with a unique figure in Guiyang, a Christian from Jersey named Mesny who had risen to an exalted rank in the imperial Chinese army, officially a mandarin like Charles Schmidt of Suzhou (see p 24).[342] Urging that missionaries be sent there, Mesny promised to assist them. Judd and James Broumton were to respond. In writing about this 'era of pioneers', K. S. Latourette described their exploits as 'biographical rather than institutional'—individual adventures rather than coordinated expeditions. Perhaps he was misled by secondary sources, for the fact that Hudson Taylor planned the nationwide strategy and worked out with each team their destination, approximate itineraries and practical details of stocks of Scriptures, transport, funding and communication, is plainly evident in the manuscripts.[343]

Yichang, springboard for Sichuan[344] (August 1876–May 1877)

On August 28, 1876, George Nicoll left Wuhan by boat with evangelist Zhang, and a 'teacher', that is an educated Chinese with business ability sufficient to draw up contracts, to secure a foothold if they could at Yichang, as a base for entering Sichuan province. By the Chefoo Convention Yichang had been designated a treaty port, but no action had yet been taken and no merchants had moved there, though it was three hundred miles further up the Yangzi from Wuhan, itself six hundred miles from Shanghai. Instead of following the Yangzi for 290 miles round two sides of a triangle, they took the short 150 mile route through the lakes to Shashi. There they made a portage to a larger junk on the Yangzi, and reached Yichang on September 16. An uncle of the teacher, acting as middleman, negotiated the rental of a house in the suburb outside the south gate of the city, and leaving the two Chinese in possession, Nicoll returned to Wuhan. 'May God allow us to keep this place in peace,' he wrote. 'The people do not want foreigners to come.'

James Cameron was to join him. Together with Jiang (Zhang) Suoliang, the Zhenjiang pastor, and two Wuhan Christians surnamed Zhang, they travelled to Shashi. This time they 'soon had a noisy crowd after (them), who were not sparing in missiles harder and more effective than foul names'. They reached Yichang on December 20, the day Easton and Parker arrived at Xi'an. As Chinese as they could be in dress and behaviour, the reception at Yichang was different. 'No one took notice of us in the streets.' Nicoll was to stay, 'to see how things would go', while Cameron travelled in the surrounding country and up the Wushan rapids beyond Zhang his companion's home. In doing so he became the first member of the CIM to enter Sichuan.[345] Of Yichang he remarked, 'The evangelist says the (people) are well pleased to have the foreigners beside them,' a tribute to their adaptation to things Chinese. And on January 2, the day Judd and Broumton left Wuhan for Hunan and Guizhou, Nicoll wrote after walking through the city, 'I only heard the cry "foreign devil" once.' All went well, Cameron came and went, and Nicoll was left in peace to pass on the gospel to visitors and to share Jiang's preaching, so far as his grasp of the language allowed.

The Yichang 'settlement' riot (March 1–5, 1877)

The time had come for John McCarthy to begin his secret journey with the evangelist Yang Cunling (Yang Ts'un-ling),[346] an ex-soldier, as his companion. Coming up the Yangzi from Zhenjiang in December 1876, they left Wuhan on February 2, 1877, 'in stormy, freezing weather' on snow and ice, and also taking the direct route to cut off the great bend of the Yangzi River, spent three or four days at Shashi preaching and selling books without opposition. People were friendly, but businessmen with whom they talked in those gregarious meeting places, the tea-shops, with one voice expressed their anxiety lest the development of Yichang as a port should spoil the trade of Shashi. Then moving on up the Yangzi they joined Cameron and Nicoll at Yichang on February 25.

Intending to stay only a few days while changing to a different type of boat for ascending the rapids, they walked through the city unmolested, arranged for money to be transmitted to Sichuan, and met only with friendliness. But Consul C. King from Jiujiang, a vice-consul and three customs officials all in foreign clothes had arrived to survey and mark out a foreign settlement, and a violent protest was brewing. Already the customs men had been attacked. On March 22 the *North China Herald* reported,

> Some missionaries were also residing in the city ... quietly going in and out among the people for some months. Everything seemed favourable to the consul's mission; but no sooner had negotiations been commenced ... than the old hostility to every encroachment of the hated barbarian immediately manifested itself. The literati as usual were the instigators of the attack ... Inflammatory placards were posted ... reports were diligently circulated that the Foreign Powers intended to take forcible possession ... ejecting the inhabitants, desecrating the ancestral graves, interfering with the fengshui of the city, and bringing endless calamities upon the people.

> (The mandarins and even the *daotai* engaged in defining the territory for the concession) were insulted and maltreated by the mob. And the next step was to give notice to the missionaries, that unless they cleared out in three days, their house would be pulled down, and they would be driven out at the risk of their lives. As the missionaries showed no sign of heeding these warnings, the mob was assembled by beating the gong, and an open attack was made on Saturday, March 3rd.[347]

On March 1, when the gongs had called the people to foregather at the bottom of the street, the landlady had discounted the warnings, John McCarthy noted in his diary. And as to move out would be interpreted as an admission of guilt, 'We decided to remain, come what might, to open the doors (to the public) as usual; and to tell all comers that we had nothing to do with the purchase of land, etc. We had a great rush of people apparently bent on mischief,' but calm and friendly conversation with the gift of pamphlets and the offer of books for

sale convinced most that these foreigners were harmless. The prefect knew what was happening, for who could fail to hear the gongs and uproar, even before McCarthy asked him to intervene, but no one came to disperse the mob.

On March 2, more crowds assembled 'gathering in thousands at the sound of a gong' and a proclamation issued by the prefect and magistrate had no effect. McCarthy told their Christian companions they should leave while they could, for he, Cameron and Nicoll had decided to stay in the hope that doing so would win the approval of right-minded people. Not one would go, and Yang Cunling 'who was nearly killed at Fengyang Fu (on an earlier journey in North Anhui) was the most opposed of any to our moving away'. 'After a hearty prayer meeting we went to bed, commending ourselves to the care of our Heavenly Father.'

They were woken on March 3 by the sound of the gong and 'we were told that they were coming to pull down the house.' The prefect's deputy came in his official sedan chair to remonstrate with a leading member of the literati, but the man's son turned the rabble on him. After breaking up the chair and giving the deputy a beating, they attacked the mission house, smashed down the frontage and swarmed in. To their surprise, calm, unarmed men met them and 'asked what it all meant'. 'Some were for seizing and. beating us; some wished to take (our Chinese companions); but the majority, even in the midst of the uproar, shouted out that no one was to be hurt, and nothing of ours stolen . . . After they had demolished a good part of the place . . . the leaders managed to get them out.'

Very soon another 'surging, screaming' mob broke in, pillaging and destroying, until the magistrate arrived and with difficulty took control. Even so, 'there was yelling and roaring and knocking at the door. The old (mandarin) was green with fright.' Afraid that they would beat him as they had beaten the prefect's deputy, McCarthy agreed to leave the house in his care and move to a boat. The magistrate himself escorted them to the riverside and had them rowed to where the *daotai's* gunboats were moored, sending their remaining possessions after them. McCarthy then went to see Consul King to report the facts, to explain that he had not called on him sooner simply to avoid any misunderstanding, and to insist that he did not want anyone punished on the Mission's account. At last on the 5th the viceroy, Li Hanzhang, arrived and peace was restored. 'A little Yangzhou riot' was Hudson Taylor's comment when he heard.

With so much happening in 1877 it may help us, in relating events to each other, if we glance ahead and later pick up these threads. Nicoll went down to Zhenjiang to report to Hudson Taylor, while McCarthy and Cameron stayed at Yichang in a houseboat provided (at a price) by the mandarins. On March 20 Cameron then accompanied McCarthy, his Sichuan friend Zhang, a teacher, and Yang Cunling up the Wushan gorges, as far as Wushan city in Sichuan. From there he returned to the boat at Yichang until allowed to reoccupy the house in the summer.

In his absence Charles Judd arrived on March 23 at Yichang, nearing the end of his own hazardous journey through Hunan to Guiyang and Chongqing and down the gorges; to his surprise the house was derelict and there was no sign of missionaries. He waited until the 29th before going on to Wuhan (see map 2.48: p 376) and on May 22 returned with Nicoll to make Yichang his own responsibility while Nicoll and Cameron continued their long-interrupted journey to occupy and evangelise the province of Sichuan.[348] Soon these early experiences were forgotten as attitudes changed and foreigners were accepted. Yet time and again, in place after place, the initial price of occupying key cities could be measured in alarms and violence. Yichang proved to be less useful as a supply base and staging post for Sichuan than had been expected, and the work

there was transferred to the Presbyterian Church of Scotland.

Judd's long way to Chongqing[349] (January–March 1877)

Perhaps the most daring and dangerous journey was that taken by Charles Judd and James Broumton, through Hunan, and the lawless border regions of Guizhou to Guiyang. Like all the other journeys it was to be evangelistic, which meant showing themselves openly and looking for audiences and customers for the books they had for sale. But the difference was that Judd was known and had been ejected from Yueyang, the gateway to Hunan; and on the route they planned to take, Augustus Margary (with passports from the Zongli Yamen in Peking) had been roughly handled at more than one place. He, according to Colonel Henry Yule, was 'the first Englishman to accomplish a feat that had been the object of so many ambitions'. So their journey was no light undertaking. Three Chinese companions were to work at Guiyang with Broumton, an evangelist named Chu, the colporteur Yao Shangda and a master craftsman Sen Sifu.

Leaving Wuhan on January 2 in a small houseboat, they stopped to preach at most riverside towns and markets on the way up the Yangzi. At one place boats moored side by side stretched for a mile along the bank, showing how dense the population was, but they could not stay long to give them the gospel. At Yueyang a customs officer politely warned them not to go where there were no officials to protect them, and went into the city to tell the mandarins that they were coming.

It was eighteen months since Judd had been driven out (see p 235), but as they walked through the same city gate and into the streets, the cry was raised, 'Those foreign demons are come again. Kill them, beat them!' But no one injured them. Curses could not stop Judd. The Muslim petty officer in charge of a 'gunboat' (an armed junk with ten or twenty men) came aboard their boat saying he was under orders to escort them, and proved himself a true friend. This mandarin, named Ding Laoye, had twenty small loaves of bread baked for them, and often helped foreign travellers on subsequent occasions. 'We assured him that as we were not officials, but only private persons, we required no such honour.' He answered, 'The people are so fierce that (the mandarins) dare not put out' the imperial proclamation. Still the five missionaries were undeterred from preaching and selling Scriptures; but as a precaution an escort of eight men stayed with them as far as the next city (see maps 2.48 & 2.50: pp 376 & 380 respectively).

Their arrival at Changde at the westernmost end of the Dongting lakes on January 17 had the dramatic effect of bringing a succession of officials in full dress to call on them. 'Greater' civility could not have been shown to us.' Yet something in the atmosphere decided them to move on early the next morning. No proclamations had been posted at Changde, or anywhere that they had touched at in Hunan; and it may safely be assumed that the ostentation of the visiting mandarins was directed not so much towards the foreigners as to the local literati and populace.

Tracking up rapids on the Yuan River for ten miles in unbroken succession, the safety of their boat dependent on the soundness of the plaited bamboo towing cable, they came to a narrow cleft with perpendicular rocks rising more than a hundred feet above the river. 'High up, perhaps 60 or 80 feet from the water . . . there lies a Chinese boat, fast in a cleft,' probably deposited by an exceptional flash-flood, one of the hazards they faced.[350]

Augustus Margary had been protected with great difficulty from mob violence in the town of Pushi, near Chenxi, which Judd's party reached on January 27, but though they walked through the town more than once and preached at the city gate, no antagonism was shown. The fact that they were dressed not in outlandish costume but in civilised Chinese clothes could account for the difference. There they turned up a tributary to Mayang, negotiating rapids time

and again. The boat was holed on a rock, but quickly repaired in the shallows, and on February 3 they crossed the border into Guizhou province—the day after McCarthy started for Sichuan, while Henry Taylor was heading for the fifth time for Queshan, and Easton and Parker were starting back from Lanzhou. At Tongren, Judd wrote, 'We heard some strange tales about the danger of our passing through Chenyuan' (four days further on). Margary's boat had been dragged ashore and burned at this city of Zhenyuan in 1875, but the phenomenon of five men handing out tracts along the mile-long main street created no disturbance. They had found that one of the boat's crew was a Christian from the LMS church in Wuhan, and the skipper was already interested in the gospel. On his own insistence the Christian boatman went all the way to Guiyang and back through Sichuan with Judd. (Now they were in the region of Alfred Bosshardt's and Arnolis Hayman's long captivity and privations at the hands of Mao's Fifth Army on the Long March of 1934–36.)

After Tongren the five had to climb on foot over the mountains, wearing local crampons; for the heavy night mists froze heavily on the rocks and trees, and when their feet could stand no more they hired mountain men with bamboo hammock chairs to carry them. The small city of Yuping had three times been burned down by rebellious Miao tribesmen and Shibing had been destroyed, but those Miao with whom the travellers had dealings were extremely hospitable. On and on they trudged through Chonganjiang and Guiding, until on February 19 they reached Guiyang, the provincial capital.

Thinking that to look at once for 'General' Mesny, the Jersey Christian married to a Chinese, might create difficulties for him, they planned to go to an inn, but Mesny was on the lookout for them.[351] The next day Broumton wrote: 'So here we are, ensconced in a beautiful house, where we are invited to remain as long as we please; our host offers us also a house that he owns in the city, or one in the country (thirty miles distant near a market town). He believes that the people there are ripe for the gospel.'

In keeping with the Mission's strategy, they chose the city property on a hillock close to a busy thoroughfare, a site with tumbledown buildings on it. That mattered little. They moved into two habitable rooms, content to use an abundance of debris to create one tolerable house.

Mesny had told all his mandarin friends that the party was coming, so a stream of high-ranking visitors 'to whom he helps us to give the message of the Gospel' kept them busy. James Broumton had expressed the wish to live among the Chinese at Guiyang, without a fellow-countryman, so that he might more quickly pick up the local dialect. He had his wish. He would be eight hundred miles from his nearest mission colleague; but for the present in Mesny he had an influential friend, and in his colleague Chu, the son of a prefect (so it appears), a useful mentor. John McCarthy was to visit him briefly at the end of May, just before Mesny left, but otherwise it was to be three months before the next travellers (Clarke, Fishe and Landale) joined him. After ten days as Mesny's guest Judd took his leave. To Hudson Taylor he explained: 'We passed through greater danger in Hunan than we were then aware of. There is a secret society in that province, headed by fifteen of the greatest men in China, formed for the purpose of (excluding) any foreigner . . . I have seen their private circular. I shall therefore, DV, return by way of Sichuan.'[352]

Leaving on March 2 he and the Christian boatman reached Chongqing on the fourteenth (the first member of the Mission to arrive there) and at once hired a small boat to descend the gorges to Yichang. The providential presence of the boatman from the rapids of Hunan soon became apparent.[353] On March 17 they were overtaken by three armed men in another boat, one of whom drew his sword saying, 'You are a Romanist and we are determined to exterminate you.' Another boatload of a dozen men with swords and guns then arrived, arrested Judd and took him and his companion back upstream to the village where they had stopped to preach earlier in the day. 'One man with a drawn sword sat close by me (frequently feeling the edge of it), and several others in front each with his own weapon.' Judd's passport and a copy of the imperial edict issued by the governor of Sichuan were shown to the opium smoking headman, but he said, 'I do not want these. Seize his boat.'

The boatman was told that they were to be held until dark and then killed and robbed, and after five hours of threatening flourishes of a sword or musket fire to alarm them, it looked as if 'there was little human hope of escape'. Judd then told his companion to slip away and get the magistrate in the nearest town to protect them. He was intercepted, but fearing that Judd had influential friends within call, their captors changed their tune and took them to another village. In a moment of confusion when another boat collided with theirs, Judd slipped the moorings and with only his boatman and one of the crew rowed hard downstream in the dark for nearly twenty miles, fortunately free from rapids. Where passport and proclamation had failed, Judd concluded, God had delivered them from a very ugly situation. They went on down the Yangzi gorges and reached Yichang five days later, only to find the Mission house in ruins and no one there to greet him. Somewhere in the last Wushan gorge, they had passed McCarthy, Cameron and Yang Cunling, slowly working up against the current.

The whole journey from Wuhan to Guiyang and back again had taken three months, covering two thousand miles, and riverside piracy had posed a greater danger than the schemes of even Hunan's great men.[354] He arrived at Wuhan on March 29 at about the same time as Edward Fishe and his family, who were cheerfully on the way to join James Broumton at Guiyang, and only a few days after King and Budd (March 24) and before Easton and Parker (April 6) ended their own epic journeys.

A shaking of heads (March–April 1877)

Hudson Taylor had been in Wuhan for five weeks, until all the teams of travellers had started out. Their dangerous mission weighed heavily on him, for he believed that missionary progress in China depended largely on its outcome. Already the 'strong base' or 'treaty port' policy of the mainly denominational societies had led to deeply entrenched institutional activity. Schools, hospitals and 'literature' production were proliferating. Failure to prove not only the accessibility of the whole empire, but that every part could be lived in safely, would confirm societies in the current philosophy of static mission being right, and extensive evangelism and church planting being wrong. In his *History of the Church Missionary Society,* Eugene Stock wrote of this dichotomy,

> No forward movement can escape criticism ... Not a few CMS men agreed with the Presbyterian and other missionaries in the maritime provinces in shaking their heads over the CIM itineration. What good could such aimless wanderings effect? How could incessant journeyings over vast areas be called evangelisation? ... The answer was that it was a good thing to familiarise the people with the fact that there were persons who affirmed that they had good tidings to proclaim ... The work, in fact, only proposed to be preparatory; and in that sense, after years showed that its success was unmistakable.[355]

Convinced of its rightness, Stock had touched on only one point to justify it. But there was also far more. Everywhere the travellers' went preaching and 'gossiping the gospel', the seeds of the Church were sown. In some places small communities of Christians soon sprang up. In others fertile soil in the minds and hearts of men and women was made ready for the return of the sowers, who settled where they found a response. A decade later, seeing that it could be done, other missions followed suit and the church in Europe and America began to send reinforcements in their hundreds. This second of Hudson Taylor's declared objectives, awakening the

2.34 Oars out between rapids in a Yangzi gorge

church, was as important as the first, direct evangelism.

Meanwhile criticism was strong, and Hudson Taylor feared that an attack might be made on the CIM at the approaching General Conference of Missions to be held in Shanghai. He decided that his best defence would be to disarm his critics face to face before rather than at the conference, and to lift the whole tone of discussion by emphasis on spiritual issues. In Hankou lived E. Bryant of the LMS, who had expressed his views about Hudson Taylor and threatened 'to expose him' in the press. Late one evening Hudson Taylor (deliberately, his colleagues claimed) went to Bryant's house and said, 'I am in a difficulty, it is too late to cross the (Yangzi) tonight' (for the city gates of Wuchang would be closed before he could get in). 'Could you give me a bed?' 'Certainly, with pleasure,' Bryant could not but reply, and until they retired to bed the two of them enjoyed an animated conversation, courteously steering clear of anything controversial. The next day, after his guest had gone, Bryant confessed that he was ashamed of himself, he 'did not know Mr Taylor was such a good man'.

A well-meaning but ill-informed article in the *Shanghai Courier and China Gazette* had given Hudson Taylor an opportunity to reply, filling in some facts which would surprise many readers. The journeys being made were, he wrote,

> working towards ... more localised efforts than are now possible, (while) besides this work, we have fifty-two stations in five other provinces ... being carried on by *resident* missionaries ... We aim at being an

auxiliary agency (to the great Missionary Societies); and but for the work of our honoured predecessors and ... fellow-labourers from Europe and America, the work we are doing would have been an impossibility.[356]

He reminded readers that colportage and itinerant preaching had played a leading part in the early stages of nearly all the established societies' work. This spadework done by Medhurst, Edkins, Burdon, Aitchison, Nevius, Griffith John and others was not to be forgotten by more recent arrivals. He continued: 'We propose to itinerate constantly at first, and subsequently to carry on localised work only for a time—till (self-supporting) native churches can be left to the ministrations of (Chinese pastors).'

He then summarised the 'Plan of Operations of the China Inland Mission' published in 1875[357] and repeated:

> Again, in the new provinces, itinerant evangelism is the only work at present possible ... and we shall not be slow to avail ourselves of opportunities (for settled work) when they do arise. The evangelisation of China must be mainly effected by native Christians ... We know, too, that many honoured missionaries now in the field would gladly leave their present posts, and go out into the regions beyond, if their various boards were convinced that it were possible and safe to send them. If our men succeed in locating themselves, they will surely be followed by more and abler workers.

David Hill and W. Scarborough of the WMMS at Wuhan were in his mind, as well as Griffith John. And those who would be the Chinese evangelists of the future first needed to be converted and then instructed, trained and given time to show what gifts they possessed.

He had just three months for his diplomacy before the Shanghai conference, and planned to use the time purposefully to make the point that 'the head cannot say to the feet, I have no need of thee', and if the CIM were the feet 'shod with the preparation of the gospel of peace',

they wished only to serve and encourage the head. Instead of travelling by steamer, he hired a little houseboat and, doing his routine correspondence, preparation of *China's Millions* and distribution of funds while he travelled from place to place, he systematically called on every missionary of his own and other missions as he was carried the five hundred miles down the Yangzi to Zhenjiang. To Jennie he had written on February 2 about the coming conference:

> Unless there is a great outpouring of God's Holy Spirit, very much harm may result—very much has already resulted from preliminary discussions about the term for God [the Term Question dividing translators (see 1, p 135)]. In more than one station the missionaries cannot meet for prayer together through it ... Now we are not likely to pass without some blows if some have their wish. But God is an *almighty* Saviour and my hope is in *Him*.[358]

On his little boat he wrote again, on February 16, explaining his journey. 'I do not want an explosion there against the CIM, and a warm feeling on the part of the (Hankou, Jiujiang, Nanjing, Suzhou, Hangzhou, Shaoxing), Shanghai and Ningbo missionaries may prevent it, if attempted by others.' After a weekend with the saintly Methodist David Hill at Wuxue (Wusueh) he was sure of a good beginning, and the next weekend calling on the American Episcopal Mission at Jiujiang forged new friendships. They did not know that he was sleeping in a garret at the CIM house, so open to the weather that one morning he swept up a heap of hailstones on his bedroom floor before beginning his day.

In an open letter published in the *Chinese Recorder*[359] he hailed the prospect of 'spiritual benefits from the gathering together of so many' men and women consecrated to the service of Christ and China. Undoubtedly the Shanghai conference would powerfully affect not only those present but those unable to attend, the Chinese church and missionaries' home churches also. How important then that, as its conveners hoped, it should be 'signally blessed by the Holy Spirit', and what better than that delegates should come to Shanghai already 'filled with the Spirit'. For the CIM he arranged a preliminary conference at Wuhan, not for discussion but as spiritual preparation for the Shanghai conference and for the travellers, inviting members of the other missions to join in.

His calls at riverside towns and cities included those where Chinese Christians were the only missionaries, and one where the CIM missionary after a good start appeared to have lost momentum. The province of Jiangxi, he told Jennie, 'is stiff soil and none but fully *consecrated* men will do much there—cross-loving men are needed. Where are they to be found? . . . Oh! my darling, may God make you one (such) and me another.'[360] They had taken up the bitter cross of being separated for so long, but it was hard to carry. They were pining painfully as the weeks apart multiplied. Stay-at-homes would never succeed in buying up the unique opportunities of the present time.

For one month (March 17 to April 16) he worked at Zhenjiang, thinking constantly of the travellers. The arrival of George Nicoll straight from the Yichang riot, and of Henry Taylor's despairing notes from Queshan drove him to spend hours praying in his own room. In his reminiscences of this period, Nicoll said:

> Mr Taylor was a good deal troubled in spirit at the time ... When his day's work was done he would sit down with a little hand-organ and play and sing (the hymn) ... 'Jesus, I am resting, resting in the joy of what Thou art', over and over again. One day a bundle of letters was brought to him. He stood against the desk to read them. Two were from foreign (missionaries) both telling of serious trouble impending, and two from Chinese, the same.

Hudson Taylor began to whistle the tune of 'Jesus, I am resting' and Nicoll asked 'How can you whistle, with such danger impending to the brethren?' 'Suppose,' he replied, 'I was to sit down here and burden my heart with all these things; that would

not help them, and it would unfit me for the work I have to do. I have just to roll the burden on the Lord.'[361]

An unusual sequence of events was fresh in his thoughts, like a parable or sign from God. At Datong, on his way down the river, he found that a fire destroying a hundred homes had stopped at the Mission house, only burning one of its wooden pillars. At Zhenjiang a similar fire of houses 'all round us' had stopped after igniting only a window frame on the Mission premises. And at Yangzhou, flames had devoured a neighbouring temple but the premises between it and the Mission were spared—a dramatic deliverance, for 'several thousand pounds (weight) of gunpowder' were being stored there.

John Stevenson's wife and children were ill in Scotland, and he himself very run down, so early in April he lodged a protest to the Resident at Bhamo against the restrictions on his freedom of movement, and left Burma to return home for a year. Having in Stevenson a responsible senior member of the Mission in Britain made Hudson Taylor feel less torn between his responsibilities there and in China. He even told Jennie to train Charles Fishe in everything she was doing, so that if he sent for her there would be no delay. What should be done with their children does not appear in these letters. The pressure on him had eased a little.

In a Chinese river-steamer he returned to Wuhan, picking up members of the Mission at each port until on arrival there were seventeen crowded into the little Wuchang Mission house for the conference from April 23 to 26. McCarthy and Cameron were in Sichuan, but Nicoll and the Fishe family were there in Wuchang. Judd had arrived back from his long journey, and King and Budd from theirs. Easton and Parker had come in from Gansu on the eleventh, and George Clarke, Edward Fishe and Robert Landale were preparing to penetrate Hunan, Guizhou and Guangxi directly after the conference.[362] It could not have been better timed.

Sunday was spent in fasting and prayer.[363] From Monday to Thursday six LMS missionaries, six Wesleyans, W. J. Boone Jr of the American Episcopal Church and fourteen from the CIM met in the LMS chapel or at one of the missions. 'Waiting on God', with exposition of Scripture by Griffith John, Hudson Taylor, Boone and others took pride of place. Practical advice by Judd and Hudson Taylor on upcountry travelling and living among the Chinese followed in the afternoons, each of the recent travellers giving accounts of their journeys. The veteran traveller, Griffith John, did not hide his delight. His message to the others he based on 'Tarry ye in Jerusalem until ye be endued with power from on high.' 'We have done very wrong in not waiting upon the Holy Spirit for power and guidance. We have been working like atheists, and I believe we have by this sinned awfully against the Holy Ghost.'[364]

Then on the final day all met for a united communion service. In Charles Judd's *Recollections* is this sentence, 'That time of waiting upon God for this Western movement (into the Western provinces) and the filling of the Spirit for the workers, was the time that Mr Griffith John got such wonderful help.' That (after Hudson Taylor) the most senior person present should be so benefitted, capped everything. Representing the members of the other missions in gratitude for being invited, Griffith John said, 'I thank God for my brethren (the pioneers).' The conference was over, but the next day they met again, and on Sunday, April 29, three hundred or more Chinese Christians and twenty missionaries worshipped together. No one at Wuhan now thought of itineration as 'aimless wandering', or misunderstood what was being done. If the Shanghai conference could even approach this one in quality it would do far more than halt the 'shaking of heads'.

The second General Missionary Conference[365] (May 10–24, 1877)

Seventy years had passed since Robert Morrison came to China, and thirty-four since the first inter-mission conference at Hong Kong which ended so tragically in the death directly afterwards of Morrison's son, John Robert, the chairman, and of Samuel Dyer, the conference secretary, Maria Taylor's father (see 1, p 120). Since then missions to China had multiplied with little coordination, each going its own way, and strong influences were deflecting the emphasis from evangelism and establishing the Churches to a general 'Christianizing' and 'enlightenment' or 'uplift' of the Chinese people. Whoever said, 'When the mind is at sea, a new word provides a raft,' expressed a truth.[366] A proposal in 1874 by the Presbyterian Synod of China, that all Protestant missions should meet at Shanghai, was welcomed as long overdue. But the tone of the conveners' general letter gave rise to misgivings. 'As China opens, our responsibilities increase,' surprisingly continued, 'and as missionaries form perhaps the chief medium through which its (China's) people can receive Western truth and Western thought—and we thus in a large measure possess the power of influencing the future of this Empire—it seems incumbent upon us to adopt every available means to strengthen our position.' 'Christ crucified' was omitted in favour of the production of school books and 'scientific works', for 'such action would greatly aid the elevation of this people and promote the glory of God'. By the date agreed, disharmony over the Chinese term to be used for 'God', the old bone of contention, was threatening to make the conference as dangerous as it was necessary. In some quarters feelings were also running high over the CIM's independent policy of extensive evangelism. A fundamental dichotomy of aims and methods was threatening the unity of the missionary body.

The proponents of the new ideas were men of powerful intellect. Before long the CIM itself was to be penetrated and shaken by their arguments. In the view of those who shared Hudson Taylor's convictions, the differences had to be faced, but in the right spirit. Attendance at the conference was therefore representative of divergent views when it met in Shanghai from May 10 to 24, 1877. Such was the fear of serious clashes of opinion that many stayed away, but several shipping companies reduced their fares for delegates, tempting some delegates to travel even a thousand miles. All told, about one hundred and forty men and women of eighteen missions, three Bible societies, several nationalities and uncounted denominations crammed the available accommodation in what was to become, in Hudson Taylor's words, 'the most important step China missions have yet taken'.[367] Subsequent issues of *China's Millions* devoted twenty-two pages to reporting the best of the proceedings, as well as complete tables of all missionaries by name, location and seniority. An impressive list of sinologues (those versed in the Chinese classics) and translators with well-earned LLD s and DDs was matched by others later to be recognised by the universities; yet the names of unsung heroes of non-academic achievement, even a martyr, are there too—David Hill, Rudolf Lechler, R. W. Stewart, Hudson Taylor, M. Henry Taylor, and others yet to make their mark. A high proportion had been in 'China' (including Siam) for twenty years or longer. As proceedings were to be in English, only one Chinese delegate was present, Dr V. P. Su Vong 'of the Arsenal' (Li Hongzhang's naval and military foundry at Nanjing). He 'urged . . . with great force in excellent English' a point made by Hudson Taylor, 'the paramount necessity' of a medical missionary not neglecting the spiritual aspect of his calling. For the benefit of the Chinese church in Shanghai, delegates also addressed audiences in their chapels, the variety of dialects represented making it simpler to speak in English and be interpreted.

Forty-five dissertations had been requested and were read, including one by Professor James Legge (see Personalia)

on Confucianism. Unknown to him at Oxford, agreement had been reached to steer clear of contention over the 'Term Question' and his essay dealt strongly with the terms for 'God' used by the Sage. For a moment a flash of dissent threatened to inflame the conference, only to be 'hushed at once'. A widely representative committee was appointed to search for common ground, without success, and could only urge 'mutual forbearance'. Following each paper came general discussion, with each speaker restricted to five minutes, signalled by the chairman's bell, The result was 'terse, condensed, sharply defined, forcible and to the point, with little preface and no peroration but the bell'.[368]

The sessions, presided over by Carstairs Douglas LLD , of Amoy, covered a wide range of topics. The agenda reflecting the biblical stance of the majority gave little scope to the advocates of 'the uplift of China by education'. In a 'masterly and powerful' keynote address, the veteran J. V. N. Talmage DD, of Amoy, set the tone without platitudes on 'Preach the Gospel to every creature', followed by Griffith John on 'the Holy Spirit in relation to missionary work' and by the American Episcopal co-chairman R. Nelson DD, on the necessity of 'Entire Consecration'. Alexander Williamson LLD of the National Bible Society of Scotland, one of the conveners, drew rounds of applause as he reviewed 'the Field of Labour in all its Magnitude', emphasizing that preaching should hold priority over colportage; and discussion of James Legge's learned paper on Confucianism brought to their feet the men most fitted to comment—Alexander Wylie, sinologue par excellence, on the effects of Confucian teaching on the moral character of the people; C. W. Mateer on its inculcation of atheism; Williamson on its excellence as a system of self-effort to rectify conduct, so far as it went; and Talmage on its deficiency in not recognizing the fact of sin as man's chief failing. F. F. Gough drew attention to the effect of untruthfulness in Confucius' own teaching and practice on his followers; and Hudson Taylor and others warned against negative attacks on the error of a system, when positive presentation of Christian truth was Christ's commission.[369] Joseph Edkins DD, read a paper on Daoism and Buddhism, showing that, like aphorisms of Confucius, many quotations in each religion, familiar to Chinese audiences, were useful in presenting the gospel. M. T. Yates DD, contributed one on Ancestral Worship, 'the principal religion of the Chinese'. News arrived of a worsening famine in North China, but it made little immediate impact. Harrowing eye-witness accounts of famine conditions were needed to bring home to people's imaginations what was happening.

On May 12 the conference turned to 'the Matter and Manner' of preaching in China, introduced by a master of the art, William Muirhead, who advocated systematic, local itinerant preaching based on an established local church. The subject given to Hudson Taylor, 'Itineration, far and near, as an evangelizing agency', had Wesleyan overtones, a good beginning.[370] But prejudice against the methods he advocated had been increasing. A 'new thing' like this raised conservative eyebrows. So Hudson Taylor explained what was being done, and why.

'Throughout he secured the deepest interest of his audience' as he spoke from 'long experience' of extensive evangelism, 'not as opposed to but as preparing the way for more settled labour'; an activity 'almost indispensable before the gospel would take root and flourish', but 'preliminary and preparatory' to concentrated localised evangelism. This approach he considered to be 'economical of time, and labour, and money to a high degree'. 'All education must be gradual; cramming . . . is not education.' It took time for the meaning of the gospel to dawn on many hearers. 'Time must be given it to strike its roots deep into the inner man.' 'It is my firm belief that during the ten or twenty years which generally elapse between the first visitation of a province and the larger in-gatherings, widespread itineration would . . . gain much time, that whole prefectures, or

even provinces, might in that time hear, and be mentally digesting, the elementary truths . . . As a preparatory work it succeeds.'

Dealing with practical issues, he strongly supported Alexander Williamson (who from 1863–69 had travelled widely through North China, Mongolia and Manchuria for the National Bible Society of Scotland and still represented it at Yantai) in stressing the priority of preaching the gospel, and the limitations of printed Scripture without explanation. What is more, itinerant evangelism was so demanding, so wearing, that robust young men were needed and should launch into it before an unfamiliar climate and conditions had affected their health. 'If the evangelists walk but a few miles a day, spending most of their time preaching, their expenses will be small (for) their comforts will be few . . . As to money, the carriage of silver is both cumbersome and dangerous, but the admirable system of banking that prevails all over China greatly lessens the difficulty. Sums of 100 taels and more can be remitted to any provincial capital of the empire by the ordinary banker's draft.' As for the importance of women missionaries, 'with prudence and care and previous *knowledge of the resources of a district* (a very important matter in some cases) I have found no insuperable difficulty even in overland journeys'.

The conference went on to consider medical missions, 'foot binding' (the cruel custom of painfully deforming the feet of little girls 'to enhance their beauty'), and the work of women for the women of China. When it discussed education and the need for science[371] and other Western knowledge to be taught by Christians before others used it as a weapon for destroying the Christian faith (which none challenged), harmony became threatened as much as by any topic after the 'Term Question'. W. A. P. Martin's and Young J. Allen's papers, by advocating secular literature and the teaching of Western science as more likely than religion to overthrow superstition, were voicing the views of a minority. As 'a product of his age,

Martin identified his Christian faith with Western civilisation', not giving sufficient credence to the fact that Chinese reaction to the impact of 'Western influences' was still one of revulsion.[372] Yet Martin himself was theologically conservative and had no intention of forsaking orthodoxy. He only wished to modify the form of the message, not its content. But the form he proposed came close to obscuring if not changing the content, and was rejected by the conference after Griffith John and Hudson Taylor spoke for the majority.[373]

On another subject there was unity. 'What should be the relation of the Chinese churches to each other, and to the various foreign churches and societies by whom they have been gathered . . . without the surrender of any principles deemed true by any?' The absurd denominational connections of the Chinese church with the divisions of the church in Europe and America, Carstairs Douglas declared, were the only real obstacles. The constant danger existed of making 'a most injurious impression upon the government of China', should Chinese Christians appear subservient in any way to an archbishop or assembly abroad. He could have been speaking in the twentieth century. Many agreed when John Nevius's colleague C. W. Mateer said 'Denominational feeling at home (in Europe and America) ought to be sacrificed for the sake of the unity of the Church (in China).' Quoting Henry Venn, Frederick Gough added, 'the native churches will ultimately choose for themselves', for he could not see the denominations at home being willing to yield.[374] Diehard convention was to bind the church in China until it needed the Communist revolution seventy years later to free them from Western prejudices.

In its appeal to mission boards, colleges and churches of the world to send reinforcements to China the conference, led by Hudson Taylor, declared that China, more extensive and greater in population than any other non-Christian nation, would become one of the great nations of the future. 'Though the oldest nation in the world (they) are as full of vigour and promise as ever. Intellectually they are fit for anything . . . Their enterprise and perseverance are proverbial.' As great colonisers, emigrating in tens of thousands every year ' they will 'ultimately become the dominant race in all these vast countries' of south-east Asia. Thirty-seven years past, it pointed out, there were only three Chinese Protestant Christians in all of China, but the conference knew of twelve or thirteen thousand in 1877. Then followed an historic statement from which flowed events affecting thousands of lives. 'We want China emancipated from the thraldom of sin in this generation. It is possible . . . The Church of God can do it, if she be only faithful to her great commission.'

Twenty years later, when the Student Volunteer Missionary Union's first international conference adopted the watchword, 'The evangelisation of the world in this generation', Robert Wilder explained that its inspiration had come from that sentence in the Shanghai conference appeal. His father had used it and the Volunteers in America had adopted it in 1886.[375] At the 1877 Perth Conference in Scotland, Reginald Radcliffe cried out prophetically, 'Let us pray God to gift 2,500 women at a stroke, and 2,500 men at a stroke, and . . . to scatter them to the ends of the earth . . . I implore you to obey the Lord Jesus: "Go ye therefore and teach all nations."' He lived to see the day.

During the conference when the qualifications needed by missionaries in China were being considered, its chairman, Carstairs Douglas, a man of great intelligence, said, 'Some, alas, seem to be losing hope of getting duly qualified labourers (missionaries), and are asking for under-educated men to supply the urgent need. Let us beware of this fatal error. Let us not encourage the churches of Europe and America to *serve the Lord with that which costs them nothing*. Let us urge them to make sacrifices, to send their best students, their most gifted scholars.' Douglas had generalised, not stating clearly that intellectuals were needed if the attention of Chinese intellectuals was to be won. He appeared to have lost sight of the 'under-educated' giants, Morrison, Medhurst, Edkins, Wylie and others who had great achievements to their credit. Griffith John leapt to his feet in their defence, in defence of the CIM. He had not intended to speak, he said, but Dr Douglas's remarks drove him to do so. Years ago he used to think the same way, but his views had changed. China needed the very best, he agreed, but the best were not only those with the highest education.

> The best agents for this work ... are men possessed of a strong physique, mental vigour, good sound common sense, a fair ... education, a thorough knowledge of the Bible and above all consecration to God ... [Then he became specific, so recently had he personally been moved by such men.] It has been my privilege to come in close contact with not a few missionaries of the China Inland Mission. Though by no means an unqualified approver of all the modes of operation adopted by my friend Mr Hudson Taylor, [he still had strong reservations about the role of women], I cannot but feel that he has been wonderfully guided of God in the choice of his men. Some of them are well educated, having received college or university training; and by far the majority of those among them who have received only a fair English education, are men of real character and great worth. Some of them speak the language with as much correctness, fluency and fullness as any missionaries in China ... I have been struck by their simplicity of aim and preparedness to endure hardships in order to accomplish their missions ... I should rejoice to see hundreds and thousands of such men come out to China ... (Many) appear to be as fit for (pastoral) work as the majority of their more highly educated brethren ... A man is not an *inferior* man because he has not had a college training; whilst a man may be a very inferior missionary in spite of the highest educational advantages ... Let us encourage them and honour them, and never speak of them as offerings presented to the Lord of that which costs the Churches nothing.

Carstairs Douglas had spoken unguardedly, but the conference understood and forgave him. When in his closing, presidential address he said with a breaking voice that some present would not live to meet with the others again, there were those in his audience who realised that for a man of forty-seven to look twenty years older (his hair and long beard snowy white) could have only one meaning. Yet all were surprised when news came that six weeks after reaching Amoy he had died of cholera within a few hours of contracting it.[376]

The conference was over. Instead of ugly clashes, harmony had triumphed. The prospect of closer collaboration sent delegates back to work with their outlook changed. The 'feeling' towards the CIM had been 'very kind', Hudson Taylor told Jennie. Never again would those present make ill-informed criticisms of the Mission. But Elizabeth Wilson discovered, when he was 'almost distracted' by neuralgia from a decaying tooth, that throughout the conference he had again been sleeping on the 'malarial' ground floor, to leave room for someone else upstairs in the overcrowded CIM business premises.[377] When someone remonstrated with him that he was shortening his life by such acts of self-denial and overwork, Hudson Taylor replied, 'Does it not say in God's Word that we ought to lay down our lives for the brethren?'

A tour of the Zhejiang mission centres and a conference at Ningbo for Chinese and foreign Christians together still lay ahead before he could return to Britain.

An age of exploration (circa 1877)

It was the age of expansiveness, of the grand idea, of invention and discovery. The perspective of the China story needs a glimpse of the wider world. Disraeli, Earl of Beaconsfield, persuaded Queen Victoria to take the title 'Empress of India' and, opposed by many, proclaimed it on January 1, 1877. Britain annexed the Transvaal. Russia seized the island of Sakhalin from Japan, to protect the newly built port and naval base of Vladivostok, and declared war on Turkey. In the United States and Canada the Red Indians fought a losing battle against an irresistible tide of men, wagons and railroads pressing relentlessly westwards. The international scramble for colonies and spheres of influence lay ahead (1880–1900), but the mood was already there, waiting to respond to opportunity. Music-hall jingoism was expressing British conceit, while explosive Victorian energy needed only the incentives to launch new enterprises. Missionary attitudes of 'superiority' were the product of the age.

It was also the age of travel, exploration and missionary heroism. To get a balanced understanding of the scale of the CIM's journeys in China requires a glance at contemporary travel elsewhere in the world. David Livingstone had illuminated the vast continent of Africa by his discovery of the Zambezi River, the Victoria Falls and Lake Malawi (1849–59). His challenge to the university at Cambridge in 1857 gave rise to the Universities Mission, but his own return to Africa the same year was to endless difficulties and disappointments, not least Arab and Portuguese obstruction and use of the information he had provided to develop their slave trade. Back in London, he agreed to mount another expedition for the Royal Geographical Society, but only 'as a missionary' (1865), for he must preach Christ wherever he went. Anxiety for his safety prompted H. M. Stanley's search which found him on November 10, 1871, in his base at Ujiji, making Stanley 'the lion of the hour'.

Months again passed without word of Livingstone, so Lieutenant Verney Lovett Cameron, RN, was given command of another expedition penetrating in March 1873 from the east coast in search of him. In October Cameron met Livingstone's faithful bearers carrying his embalmed body to the coast, and went on to recover his papers and maps. Livingstone had died on his knees on May 1, 1873. During the next two years Cameron surveyed Lake Tanganyika (discovered by Speke in 1856), and followed its outlet to the Congo River. The hostility of tribal chiefs prevented his

going down the Congo, so he made for the west coast, reaching Benguela on November 7, 1875, 'the first Englishman to walk right across Africa'.[378]

Belgium assumed sovereignty of the Congo Free State, and with great alacrity Henry Grattan Guinness founded the Livingstone Inland Mission on the same principles as the CIM. Men of Harley House, his Missionary Training Institute (James Cameron's fellow-students), became the first missionaries to the Congo.[379]

'Victorian England reacted with its customary, gigantic vigour'[380] to H. M. Stanley's challenge from Uganda published on November 15. A CMS team assembled under Lieutenant Shergold Smith RN (retired, a student at St John's Hall, Highbury) consisting of Alexander Mackay, an engineer; C. T. Wilson, a curate; T. O'Neill, an architect; John Smith, a doctor; two mechanics, and a builder going at his own expense. Colonel J. A. Grant and Commander V. L. Cameron advised them in their preparations, and by the end of May, 1876, they were at Zanzibar. Within three months the builder was dead. The two mechanics fell ill and returned home. On the doctor's insistence Mackay then followed to the coast but recovered, eventually to become the only one left in Africa. So began the saga of 'Mackay of the Great Lakes' and the Church of Uganda today.[381]

Nearer to China, John G. Paton's life was often threatened by violence and disease in the South Pacific. John Coleridge Patteson was killed on Nukapu, one of the Melanesian islands in 1877. And after ten years in Polynesia James Chalmers and his wife arrived in New Guinea in 1877 to live among cannibals until clubbed to death by another tribe on January 2, 1901, with a fellow-missionary and more than ten tribal Christians. By then the toll of CIM martyrs had reached fifty-nine.

In 1876 Ludwig Ingwer Nommensen of the Rhenish Mission paid his first visit to Lake Toba in the highlands of North Sumatra, homeland of the cannibal Bataks who had killed Samuel Munson and Henry

Lyman of the American Board in 1834. There were fifty-two Batak Christians in all Sumatra. Nommensen 'claimed' the Batak for Christ and within the year 1876 the tally of Christians had risen to 2,056. By 1911 there were 103,505 and after the First World War nearly a million, when enumeration became increasingly of doubtful value. Today the CIM-OMF has members serving the Batak church.

None of this was melodrama but grim reality among primitives. In China it was a wholly different story. Travel was slow and often uncomfortable, but seldom were nights spent in the open. Sophisticated hostility was most to be feared, but where it was absent indifference or curiosity or frank friendliness met the traveller. Courage was still needed, for the unknown could as well be murderous antagonism as a welcome. The unpretentious simplicity of the missionaries' way of life was probably as good a passport or better than any ostentation.

Guizhou and Guangxi at a price[382] (May–November 1877)

The most ambitious journeys in China had begun before the Shanghai Conference. J. J. Turner and Francis James had reached Taiyuan in Shanxi on April 24, 1877 and were 'itinerating' on the Taiyuan plain until their brush with death by typhoid before returning to Wuhan on January 22, 1878. Easton and Parker, King and Budd were back from Shaanxi and Gansu by April 6, but in each case said that neither could work again with the other. The fact that 'Satan (had) been active' troubled Hudson Taylor more by far than all the physical dangers and attrition suffered by his men. Defeat no less than success would be at a spiritual level, not physical. Henry Taylor had arrived 'utterly sad' from Henan on May 12, the day the new partnership of Easton and King left Wuhan together 'in good spirits' to return to Gansu, and Budd set off alone with a Chinese servant to Shaanxi. This time Budd went as far north as Yan'an, the cave-dwelling city which was to become the stronghold of Mao Zedong

and the 8th Route Army before and during World War II. King and Easton reached Xi'an on June 20 and, re-entering Gansu, visited Pingliang and made Tianshui (Tsinchou to them) their headquarters (see map 2.31: p 279). But each of these long, taxing journeys was the second round.

The 'bombshell' that scattered one team after another from Wuhan, before and after the first conference there, sent Cameron and Nicoll on a daring exploration of the Tibetan marches (see map 2.26: p 246) and Marco Polo's Caindu, the Jianchang (Chien-ch'ang) valley beyond the mountain home of the 'independent' Nosu. It also sent George Clarke on a three-stage adventure, firstly through anti-foreign Hunan to Guiyang; then southward from there to survey the last of the nine unoccupied provinces, Guangxi; and finally back again through Sichuan. On this journey he was to conduct Edward Fishe and Robert Landale on their first pioneering venture with the occupation of Guangxi in view. His diary and report in the *Chinese Recorder*, worthy of the Proceedings of the Royal Geographical Society, tell the story.

On May 5, 1877, they sailed from Wuhan up the Yangzi in a small junk, stopping to preach at places on shore until they reached Yueyang on the 10th, the day the Shanghai Conference began and McCarthy started from Chongqing for Burma. Judd's return in March from his similar journey (see pp 287–90) meant that they had benefitted from his experience, and the friendly old Muslim mandarin, Ding Laoye, was ready to escort them from Yueyang across the Dongting Lakes. This time another Muslim, the chief military mandarin, also showed an interest in the gospel. Again they preached at towns and villages, except where the curious crowds became excited or the cry 'Kill the foreigner' was raised. 'What a field for Christ!' Clarke wrote. And when they met an old Christian from Wuchang who had heard Hudson Taylor and William Burns twenty years previously, and another man who had heard about Jesus in Shanghai, the way the gospel was penetrating China was brought home to them.

They reached Changde on May 21 and found they were expected. Not only so, officials and people in most places were civil and even friendly, and in most cities the imperial proclamation had been placarded since Judd passed through. High-ranking mandarins called and shook hands, leaving two soldiers to escort them, and when they moved on up the Yuan River, a highly-placed secretary and a gunboat went with them. 'We were escorted from city to city either by gunboats or soldiers till we arrived at Kweiyang (Guiyang).' Clarke felt like the apostle Paul with the escort of horsemen he had not asked for. At Taoyuan, where Margary had been in trouble, a military mandarin in full dress with his official red umbrella came on board, and when they preached on shore the captain of another gunboat stood by them, helping to sell books. At place after place it was military men who showed the greatest interest and bought books.

On May 29 they were stoned at Chenxi by an excited mob, until a thunderstorm dispersed them, and their boatman pleaded with them not to go on through Zhenyuan in Guizhou where Margary's boat had been burned. But Judd had regretted travelling overland from Tongren, the alternative way, and the main river route with its rapids ought to be tested. 'We were determined to go, and promised to buy him a new boat should his own be burned on our account.' At Yuping, the first city inside Guizhou, the boatman became frantic and threatened to drown himself if they held him to his contract, so at last they relented and hired carriers for the last hundred and fifty or more miles. Zhenyuan apparently provided no excitements for there is no mention of it in Clarke's report.

They reached Guiyang and James Broumton on June 27, their fifty-third day since leaving Wuhan, a journey of 2,790 li. The Chinese mile is normally one third of a standard mile. 'We could obtain little information (about Guangxi) either as to route or people,' Clarke noted, 'excepting

that they were hostile to foreigners, that the Roman Catholics had failed to obtain an entrance into the province, and that no books could be sold there.' Undaunted, after a week's rest he, Edward Fishe and the redoubtable Yao Sifu headed south for Guangxi province on July 4, through Duyiin and desolate tribal country near the provincial border, over poor, muddy tracks with no bridges. 'We found that the *li* were very long, so I put on my pedometer to make a comparison', and used it for the rest of the journey. Very often what was called a *li* proved to be even longer than an English mile.

By common usage, the distances stated in *li* were estimates of difficulty rather than distance. A rough road was 'longer' than a paved one, and a steep descent 'longer' than a climb because harder on the legs. Clarke set his pedometer to read Chinese level *li* and recorded his readings in parallel with the alleged distances from place to place, thus: 78 57; 78 46; 88 75; 33 35, by no means neglecting matters of geographical interest. The object was to assess the feasibility of occupying the far western half of Guangxi province, leaving the east to missions based at Canton.

So they came out of the mountains and made for Qingyuan (now Yishan). 'We had to cross a river. I sent our party forward, and took a handful of books with which to keep the crowd back. After speaking a little I began to sell. The books were eagerly bought . . . the people crowded the boat. I had to sell, and soon they began to pull the books out of the boxes. We crossed the river and still they followed and bought . . . We sold often at double or treble the Wuchang price. *The people would have books!* especially if illustrated . . . Hundreds of books were thus scattered.'

Later they crossed the Red River (see map 2.43: p 353) and after visiting Nanning, and a city near Pingxiang and the Tongking border, turned north-eastwards to Bose (Peh-seh) nowhere seeing signs of the imperial proclamation. Instead, doors were slammed in their faces and everyone seemed to have been warned by soldiers not to take 'the foreign devil' in. The harvest of hostilities at Canton, culminating in the capture of the viceroy and the occupation of his palace by British troops in 1856–57, was still being reaped twenty years later (see 1, pp 365–67, 430). Even Yao Sifu was more than a stranger among his own countrymen, who spoke a vastly different dialect. One day he tried to settle a quarrel between two coolies they had hired. Drawing a knife one cursed him saying, '"You are not in Hunan but Guangxi and I will kill you," and made an attempt. He was quickly thrown down and seized by the throat and the knife was taken away. We were a little anxious about such a fellow.' The Canadian lumberjack had apparently not lost his grip. Western Guangxi was very barren and thinly populated. Finding their way from place to place with the greatest difficulty, at last they met a friendly prefect at Sicheng, who sent a guide for six days' travel to see them over high mountains, 'real lung testers', to Lo-huh (Luodian?), the nearest town in Guizhou. It was good to be among people again who could understand Mandarin Chinese.

Safely back at Guiyang on September 6, after two months on the road, Edward Fishe retired to bed, hoping that he and Clarke could return to his family at Wuhan by going through another part of Guangxi, down the West River to Canton. But for four days he had had a cold and from the 14th grew weaker. The trekking had been tough but not unusual, and in Clarke's words, Fishe was 'one who could bear much and seldom complains'. On the 16th he spoke of writing a report for the *Chinese Recorder*, but two days later he suddenly paused in his breathing and 'to our great surprise we watched him breathe his last'. The weak man of the early days had made good; the vacillator had been vindicated. His was the first death and the first grave in the nine provinces.[383] After the burial 'outside the East Gate', Landale stayed on with Broumton, and Clarke travelled back to Wuhan as Judd had done, via Chongqing, in itself a major achievement. Judd had described the journey, so Clarke confined

himself to saying 'The part of (Sichuan) through which I passed is most densely populated.' This strongly indicated that instead of gliding down the Yangzi, he walked at least to Wanxian before shooting the great rapids. By comparison with his Guizhou and Guangxi travel, this phase of the journey was a holiday on granite-flagged trails, through luxuriant paddy fields, mulberry groves and orchards of fruit and oil-apple, with thronged tea-shops at frequent intervals and good inns. 'Not an hair of our head was hurt, nor any cash stolen by force (over) more than 10,000li.'

But at Wuhan Annie (Bohannan) Fishe, widowed for the second time, was waiting to hear what had happened. George Clarke arrived on November 7, having travelled 3,000 miles in six months, making a total of roughly 5,000 miles through nine provinces since reaching China on September 26, 1875, little over two years before.[384]

Baber, Mesny and Gill
(January–November 1877)

When extracts from E. Colborne Baber's account of his travels were read at the Royal Geographical Society in 1881, Sir Rutherford Alcock's successor as President, Lord Aberdare, called him 'one of the most distinguished' of cadets trained as foreign diplomats in China. He had been chosen to accompany the Hon T. G. Grosvenor as an interpreter 'because of his remarkable knowledge of the Chinese language', spoken and written, and had enhanced his reputation by writing a scintillating, witty account of their journey so full of useful facts that he was seen to be 'thoroughly imbued with the true genius of travel'.[385] Appointed after that expedition to be British Resident at Chongqing for the purpose of promoting trade, with the rank of consul, he penetrated the remotest regions to obtain information, and established the reputation on which he then became Chinese Secretary of Legation in Peking, charged with monitoring the *Peking Gazette* and handling all diplomatic documents in Chinese.

It happened that a freelance explorer, Lieutenant William J. Gill, Royal Engineers, was in Peking to meet Sir Thomas Wade and to obtain passports and the impressive documents which would see him safely on his way to and if possible through Tibet and 'Chinese Turkestan' (Xinjiang, Sinkiang) to Kashgar. From there he hoped to cross Russia. A personal friend of Colborne Baber, and knowing 'not a dozen words' of Chinese, Gill jumped at an invitation to travel together from Shanghai to Chongqing, there to be equipped and sent on his way to Tibet or the far north-west. In Berlin he had discussed the journey with Baron von Richtofen, and in London with T. T. Cooper (see p 7) both of whom had made similar attempts on the Tibetan border with China. As a trained surveyor and geographer Gill's intention was to make detailed scientific observations, such as the

Catholic travellers in most remote regions for all their skill had been unable to make or report in their *Annales de la Propagation de la Foi*.[386]

Baber and Gill left Shanghai on January 23, 1877, with their servants and literate staff, and reached Wuhan, 680 miles up the Yangzi, on the 30th. There they hired a junk and trackers, and arrived at Yichang on March 5, the day after the riot, to find Consul King, his vice-consul, the three European customs officials, a ship's captain, McCarthy, Cameron and Nicoll all licking their wounds. The consul in the company of the high ranking *daotai* had been 'mobbed and insulted' for marking out the projected foreign settlement, taking refuge in a temple from stoning and invective. On March 9, Baber and Gill went on, escorted up the gorges to Chongqing by a 'gunboat' in the form of an armed junk with 'trackers' to tow them against the current, and a detail of soldiers, to arrive on April 8.

Colborne Baber made formal calls on the highest Chongqing mandarins the next day, and received their return calls with due ceremony, so that on the 11th he completed a contract for a furnished mansion worthy of his rank and nation. After nine weeks on their boat they moved in. Not more than a score or so of Westerners, apart as always from missionaries, had ever been to Chongqing, they noted, but Baber had passed through in December 1875 with Captain Grosvenor, and knew the ropes.[387]

Within two weeks Gill was ready to go on to Chengdu, the provincial capital, 'by myself'—meaning without Baber. Travelling in 'knickerbockers' with loads of personal baggage, including a hat box, guns and ammunition, and a large supply of silver distributed through the boxes, he rode in a sedan chair, attended by three coastal Chinese able to speak pidgin-English, a scribe, a quartermaster responsible for finding accommodation and food for the party, and a manager in charge of coolies, chair-bearers and muleteers. Finally, an escort of Chinese braves under an officer communicated with him through his interpreters. 'From first to last I passed for an important official on some secret service, and was invariably treated as such,' he rightly claimed, for who would believe the truthful explanation that he gave (at least to his intermediaries) when asked? The quartermaster rode ahead to engage the best rooms in the best inns at each night-stop, and meals by day. And any but ranking officials knelt and 'banged their heads' on the ground before addressing him.[388]

At Chengdu the senior prefect or *daotai* helped them to find lodgings after they arrived on May 9, in which to leave his main supplies, and while waiting for 'General' Mesny to come from Guiyang, Gill set off again on the 18th to see the source streams of the Min River and the 'wild' Sifan people of Lifan and Songpan, whom the Chinese called *Manzi*, barbarians. For this rougher expedition of three hundred miles, going by Guanxian and back through Mianyang (see map 2.48: p 376) he took two ponies and a sedan chair for himself, as well as a sedan chair for his scribe and ponies for the others. Eight baggage coolies and the chair-bearers, grooms and an escort of four soldiers to clear the road of other travellers completed his cavalcade. But the guard supplied by each mandarin along the route, brought it up to twenty. Word of his coming ensured that the 'Chefoo Proclamation' had been posted where he would have it pointed out to him, even in the rooms assigned to him. By asking innumerable questions and making frequent use of his sextant and aneroid, he amassed a great deal of information, writing it up each evening. At Songpan on June 4 he climbed a hillside to see for himself a family of Sifan, and was back in Chengdu on the 20th to find that 'Mesny', as he called him, as a mark of social status, had arrived.

McCarthy springs his surprise[389]
(March August 1877)

After Colborne Baber and Gill had left Yichang following the riot, John McCarthy, the ex-soldier evangelist Yang Cunling and a 'teacher'[390] completed their preparations

and on March 20 started for Sichuan (see map page 2.48: p 376). With them went Zhang the friend whose home he was to visit, and James Cameron for company through the first gorge and rapids. From Wushan Cameron returned to Yichang (see map 2.20: p 204) and McCarthy completed the three hundred and fifty miles of gorges and rapids to Wanxian, without seeing Charles Judd after his escape.[391]

Leaving his teacher with the boat and baggage, and reducing their 'impedimenta' to what they themselves could carry if need be, McCarthy, Zhang and Yang Cunling struck out overland on foot. Passing through Liangshan and Dazhu, they stayed a week in Zhang's home, twenty-five miles from Guang'an. Zhang's father had been a mandarin at Peking, and so warm was the welcome from family and friends that McCarthy could have stayed for months without exhausting the offers of hospitality made to him, he said. His relaxed friendliness drew the best out of people. No proclamations were seen in such out of the way places, but often he was greeted courteously as 'venerable foreigner', though he was in his prime at thirty-eight. A man from Guizhou made himself known as having met McCarthy in Hangzhou, and enquired after his children. Evidence was multiplying that foreigners *per se* were not the objects of hatred, and that simple knowledge of the gospel was being carried far and wide by Chinese travellers.

Turning northwards they visited Nanchong (Shunking) only six days' walk from Chengdu, and stayed with 'an expectant mandarin' for a few days. There they learned first-hand of the strong anti-Catholic feeling and persecution in the province since the previous year. Yet when he reached Chongqing, travelling down the Jialing River on a rice-boat, they found five newly arrived French priests. 'Persecutions do not prevent them from coming here, but rather seem to send them in greater numbers!' he wrote in his diary.

At Chongqing his secret plan entered its controversial phase. He was to walk from Chongqing to Burma and back. With some obliging consul's aid he had been issued with a passport valid for all eighteen provinces and without an expiry date. But at Chongqing he found Colborne Baber who had made the journey from Chongqing to Kunming and on to Bhamo with T. G. Grosvenor. If Lieutenant Gill had not come up the Yangzi with Baber on a private venture, and gone to Chengdu intending to court danger with 'General' Mesny in Tibet and Xinjiang, John McCarthy might well have been thwarted. As it was, he visited Baber several times, comparing notes, and as he raised no objections, went ahead with his own preparations.

At Chongqing he rented premises for Cameron and Nicoll to use as a base, deposited in them whatever he could do without, and hired a carrier who knew the way from Yibin (Suifu, further up the Yangzi) through the northern tongue of Yunnan province to the capital, Kunming.

This route would have taken him through remote territory around Zhaotong and close to the Jin He (River of Gold), the upper reaches of the Yangzi bordering the Daliangshan, home of the 'independent' Nosu people. But the carrier developed 'a bad leg', the teacher backed out and went home to Anqing, and McCarthy was advised not to linger in anti-Catholic Chongqing any longer than he must. So he and the faithful Yang Cunling left on May 10 to travel on foot through Guizhou instead. They soon fell in with the family of a mandarin and their retainers making the same journey, became their 'honorary medical adviser' and familiar friend, and 'had many opportunities of Christian conversation' with them.

'Wearing the Chinese costume, and having nothing strange or novel with me, we were enabled to move along without any difficulty, through the various towns and cities.' At several places the Société des Missions …trangéres de Paris had stations, for they had been in these south-western provinces for one hundred and twenty years already (see 1, p 28). Indeed, 'all through those districts of (Sichuan) and (Guizhou) through which we passed, their followers

must be reckoned by thousands . . . I met with mandarins and scholars who complained of the protectorate exercised over their converts.' In one town an old man showed him a book Charles Judd had given him, evidence that 'seed-sowing' paid off, even one at a time.

After crossing the border into Guizhou, 'the hills became steeper and steeper and the country more and more wild as we passed on . . . All the way . . . our path was strewn with (wild) roses and blossoming plants, bird song and fragrance.' The Miao freedom fighters (in the neat modern phrase) had devastated such regions as had been occupied, and the surviving inhabitants had taken to growing opium poppies instead of food. One valley eight or nine miles long was entirely given up to opium and fully half the population were addicts. Guard-houses on the heights where a few soldiers watched for rebels or brigands, and 'a few wretched thatched huts, the only vestige that remained of a once flourishing town or village', proclaimed the misery of the province in strong contrast with Sichuan. There every available plot of soil was put to good use, and whitewashed lath and plaster cottages added beauty at every turn of the trail. On May 26 they toiled through 'a well-fortified and almost impregnable mountain pass' and below them in the plain could see Guiyang.

After living on his own as a Chinese since Judd left on March 2, James Broumton to his delight 'heard a knock on the gate, and looking out saw Mr McCarthy'. Mesny had invited Broumton over to his city home every Sunday evening for Christian fellowship and prayer together, but on May 28 he was to leave for Chengdu. He called to say goodbye and handed over a consignment of books and Scripture which he had sent from Wuhan to distribute himself. Broumton confided to his diary that the parting was painful to him; Mesny had been a true friend.

McCarthy stayed two weeks to help Broumton, learning from Mesny about his own route ahead, and preaching the gospel, systematically through the city. The Catholics were strong and numerous, with resident French priests, two cathedrals, and a chapel to the Virgin Mary. 'Being anxious to know personally what the feelings of the people were towards foreigners' in turbulent Yunnan, he decided to walk on following Margary's and (after Kunming) Grosvenor's route but, unlike them, with only Yang Cunling for company and two men to carry a share of Mesny's books. 'Being men of peace we carried no arms . . . but most of the travellers on the road were armed with swords, pistols or guns, firing them off occasionally.' Opium traders travelling 'in companies' or convoys of up to two thousand men presented 'a rather formidable appearance'. But, as McCarthy stated in his address at the Royal Geographical Society on April 28, 1879: 'Several years' experience has only confirmed my deep-rooted conviction that the truest protection for anyone travelling among strangers, is the knowledge on their part of the fact that he can do them no harm. The more he can make this apparent, the better it will be, not only for himself, but also for any that may follow after.'

He had even contracted with his carriers that if they quarrelled with anyone on the way he would dismiss them, and had no trouble. He always looked for the same kind of accommodation in inns or private homes (or, on one occasion, an opium den) as a Chinese traveller would expect in the circumstances. At Kunming, which they reached on July 2, however, he was royally received by a fine old innkeeper with flowing white beard, and ended ten days of enjoyable conversation 'with mutual expressions of regret'.[392] But hostility to the French in Tongking across the southern border made it wise to lie low and refrain from 'doing anything . . . likely to cause excitement, and thus give trouble to the authorities'.

A French priest told him that 'it was well known that the former Governor had given instructions at first to have Mr Margary murdered on his journey to Bhamo, but that these instructions had been

countermanded, and it was decided not to molest him unless he attempted to return.' A Manchu mandarin with whom McCarthy chatted at a stopping-place along the way 'was immensely pleased when he found that I always corrected the people who gave me official titles [such as the priests encouraged] assuring them that I was merely a teacher'—clearly evident anyway from the fact that he was not being carried in a sedan chair. 'We have always found that when we treated the Chinese in a kindly and gentlemanly way, as they ought to be treated, we received the same treatment in return.' Fluency in the language counted for much. And experience had taught him sound lessons. Engaging carriers by the month, and walking all the way eliminated the otherwise frequent source of trouble, hiring horses or men for shorter stages. 'I made it a rule too, always to remain in the first lodging house we came to, irrespective of the comfort or discomfort of the place. By this means one was frequently able to wash and have dinner before many knew we had arrived. Everywhere everyone was friendly'—except two other travellers, from Zhenjiang and Hankou, who were caustic until after a tiring trek McCarthy asked them to come and drink tea with him. 'We parted fast friends.'

Then on and on through July, leaving Xiaguan (near Dali) on August 1. Steep mountains, deep valleys, hot malarial chasms, a swaying chain-bridge over the Lancang (Mekong) River, and to their surprise they came to a city where almost pure Nanjing dialect was spoken and the inns were clean and spacious. Yongchang, as they called it (now Baoshan) had been peopled by immigrants from Nanjing, Yang Cunling's own city, and this was the dialect McCarthy had learned after leaving Hangzhou, so they were received almost as kinsmen.

Tramping on, they passed through an area where terrified people were camping in the hills to escape a plague, and on past hundreds of sealed coffins. By October a thousand had died.[393] Over the Salween River a double chain-bridge and two days of steep climbing brought them to Tengchong and then Tengyue (Momein), a walled city two miles square. Yang Cunling again found a descendant of Nanjing immigrants, who arranged safe conduct for them through the hills. So on August 17 they set out through wild, barren country, past Shan villages walled against marauding Kachins in the hills, fording mountain torrents up to the chin, and sometimes 'wading up to our knees for hours together (where) the only road was a water-course'. They mingled on market day with Shans, Kachins and Lisu tribes-people, and went on in a hollowed-out tree trunk to Manyün, the scene of Margary's murder with his companions and the display of their heads on the 'city' wall.

'Our arrival at Manyün excited a little comment, but as I at once put into circulation among the Chinese some literature which I had reserved for the purpose, and which showed satisfactorily the nature of my mission, the suspiciousness of the people seemed to pass away.' He lodged in an old widow's house, a devoted Buddhist loud in praise of the 'venerable' foreigner who had travelled so far to teach the people to be virtuous. From morning to night 'great numbers of people came to see and talk with the man who had walked across their great country'. And many who had been to Bhamo spoke appreciatively of the medical mission run there by McCarthy's friends. 'I had sent a card to the military mandarin in charge, excusing myself from calling on him on account of my travel-stained condition. He sent a most friendly reply, telling me to be sure and get a proper escort before crossing the hills, and sending kind messages to the members of the China Inland Mission in Bhamo, whose hospitality he had enjoyed when on his way down to Mandalay the year before.'

McCarthy had already arranged for a Kachin chief to see them safely over the border, and assured the mandarin that his practice was 'in everything possible to conform to the customs of the place' he happened to be in. Yang Cunling bought eggs from the mother of the man said to have killed 'poor Mr Margary', and

when people raised the subject (never otherwise) McCarthy 'spoke of it as a thing that was long past, and said that a better understanding now existed between England and China, so that nothing of the kind could occur again'. Staying two nights in Kachin homes he found them 'extremely hospitable', for they had lost nothing by either Major Sladen's nor Colonel Browne's disciplined expeditions. Then in a small boat they completed the journey to Bhamo, on August 26.

Their daily walking distance of between 60 and 120 *li* (theoretically 20–40 miles, including some stretches by boat and sensible rest periods for one or two weeks where they could preach and sell Scripture) had taken them five months, covering a total distance of about 3,000 miles including detours.[394] In so doing he had become the first unofficial Westerner to cross China from east to west. Speaking at the Mission's annual meetings at Mildmay on May 27, 1878, John McCarthy paid tribute to Yang Cunling as an invaluable companion 'without whose assistance I should have been utterly unable to carry

2.35 *Highway travellers passing a warning to robbers*

out this journey'. Unlike some situations in which novices with little of the language referred to the able Christians they travelled with as 'my native assistants', in McCarthy's case the ability and fluency were shared, while he took the risks and Yang Cunling met the objections of anyone biased against foreigners. 'It was not that we were able to overcome difficulties, arising from mandarins or officers trying to oppose our progress, but there was no difficulty in the way at all . . . It was in Burma that I found my first difficulty—not from the Chinese, not from the Shans, not from the Kahchens, nor from the Burmans . . . but from our own authorities.'

High praise from Alcock
(March–August 1877)

Hudson Taylor's disappointment over John Stevenson and Henry Soltau being bottled up at Bhamo was for two reasons: their own promise not to cross through Kachin territory into Yunnan, and the knowledge that the British authorities would have closed Bhamo itself to them and therefore this route into China as soon as they went, promise or none. He himself had refused to give Rutherford Alcock any promise at Shanghai in the early days. On China's part the Chefoo Convention was being implemented. McCarthy said, 'In Yunnan . . . among the common people and the officials it is quite a recognised fact that foreigners have a right to go about in the country. And not merely . . . a *right* to go but it is *expected that they will go*. The only surprise that was ever expressed (in Yunnan) was that no (British) officials were yet appointed.'

The British government of India wanted the Burma route into China for opium, and because the Chefoo Convention left a loophole for a tax on the opium, Britain would not ratify it or let the route be used. Another death would complicate matters unduly. On March 27, 1877, Hudson Taylor warned Jennie in London that nothing about the ban on Stevenson and Soltau must be published, as no one in China must know about it. In fact, the less said

the better about any adverse reception of CIM travellers anywhere. Even on July 26 he wrote in veiled terms lest his letter be intercepted in transit. 'The journeys are important and difficult and dangerous beyond the conception of most. One of our Irish friends is among the southern clouds, gone to visit a Scotchman'—that is, McCarthy is in Yunnan on the way to Stevenson. Stevenson had written saying that without question Bhamo would sooner or later be 'an important station for Yunnan'. The subject must be handled carefully.[395]

When John McCarthy arrived he was in no way bound to stay. If he had been hustled out immediately by Soltau and Adams, in the absence of Stevenson and Harvey, he could have continued the travels he intended, through the most southerly parts of Yunnan and up into Sichuan as far as Chengdu. Stevenson had gone home and the Harveys, shipwrecked on the way from Rangoon to Singapore, had only just exchanged their desert island for a ship to Calcutta.[396] But McCarthy was trapped. Two days after his arrival an official document was handed to him from T. T. Cooper, the political agent down the road. 'British Agency, Bhamo: 28 August 1877. No 71.' The viceroy wished no European British subject to cross the frontier, and the Burmese authorities had been asked to prevent missionaries and others from doing so. This notification, he said, was lest expensive preparations be wasted. Another, No 73, came hot on its heels as Cooper realised what might happen. (No 72 had presumably gone to his superiors.) He would be glad of McCarthy's assurance that he would not cross the frontier. It was given, and for good measure a full account of his journey, for which the viceroy himself sent his thanks.[397]

For six months John McCarthy waited in Bhamo hoping Lord Derby would relent and ratify the Convention. The agreeable placidity that made McCarthy a good missionary and a poor supervisor of others had once again limited his effectiveness. When Hudson Taylor referred in a letter to 'bungling at Bhamo' he probably had in mind this entanglement in the spider's web of officialdom. Writing to William Soltau in London, John McCarthy stated the belief which he later repeated to the Royal Geographical Society: the best way of opening up the route into China was not by armed expeditions but for small parties of unarmed Westerners to travel to and fro on peaceful missions. But if the Indian government were adamant, it was useless for him or Stevenson to knock their heads against a brick wall. 'If I had known as much when on the Kah-khyn (Kachin) hills as I learned on my arrival I would probably not have entered the lions' den . . . I had intended merely to call in to see our friends.' Too late. He gave up waiting and on April 25, 1878, he too arrived in England to be reunited with his family.

In the paper read at the Royal Geographical Society on April 28, 1879, he included observations of a geographical nature, but explained:

> My object in travelling in Western China was purely and simply a missionary one ... while at the same time glad to obtain geographical and general information. The more frequently foreigners can travel among the people without exciting hostility, the sooner will the time come when, without let or hindrance, a more thorough and scientific knowledge of the country will be obtained ... During the whole course of this journey I was not once called upon to produce my passport, nor had I once to appeal to any official for help or protection ... Everywhere I received only civility and kindness. The journey ... is but one of many which, within the last three years, have been taken by the members of the China Inland Mission ... journeys which together represent more than 30,000 miles of travelling ... The spirit of the Chefoo Convention has been loyally carried out by the Chinese officials.[398]

The chairman and president, Sir Rutherford Alcock, declared the journey of more than 2,000 miles actually on foot 'infinitely more productive and fruitful than many' made recently, and attributed McCarthy's success to his wearing Chinese clothes and his fluency in the language. Present at the meeting was the Chinese ambassador Marquis Zeng, son of the late viceroy Zeng Guofan. Speaking through an interpreter of China's long history and great future, he said that,

> The country possessed what would no doubt be a source of future power and wealth—ironstone and coal lying in close proximity over large areas. That had been the element of (Britain's) national development and power; but it was possessed in quadruple extent by China, where there were coalfields extending over thousands of square miles, and ironstone everywhere. With the help of European machinery and all the resources which European civilisation could give, China would develop her coal and iron industry.[399]

It was no secret. Anything missionaries might say in passing about China's natural resources could add little to the public knowledge of the facts proudly proclaimed by China's eminent envoy. Already Baron von Richtofen was writing his *China* (1877–81), full of geological data, and William Gill (promoted Captain) had reported on his explorations in the Royal Geographical Society's Journal. He was also completing his comprehensive two-volume narrative of his travels with 'Mesny' of Guiyang, prefaced with an eighty-page encyclopaedic introductory essay by the scholarly Colonel Henry Yule.

But we have looked ahead to 1879 and must return to two more daring journeys, by Colborne Baber and by Mesny and Gill, and two more by Cameron and Nicoll, separately, to show in marked contrast how they went about it.

Gill's change of plan
(July–November 1877)

With Lieutenant Gill's return to Chengdu and rendezvous with Mesny, an extraordinary companionship was formed. In his two fat volumes of travelogue Gill scarcely mentioned the companion on whom he was largely dependent. Mesny's imperial rank as a high mandarin exceeded even the *daotai* (prefects) of all the cities they passed through. This fourteen-stone (90 kg) warrior in a flowing scarlet warrior cloak, fluent in Chinese and thoroughly at home with the ruling class, commanded the respect of all they met. To anyone familiar with south-west China and this kind of territory, the voice of Mesny constantly supplying information and explanations can be heard in Gill's knowledgeable account of their experiences.

Unfortunately for Lieutenant Gill, relations between Britain and Russia had also deteriorated since Russia declared war on Turkey in 1877, so his Xinjiang expedition had to be abandoned. Tibet was strongly resisting all attempts to penetrate her borders. His choice lay between giving up and returning to Britain from Shanghai, or making for Burma. For an expert geographer the Burma plan offered great possibilities. The route from Chongqing had been travelled and described already. Colborne Baber was about to attempt Marco Polo's route down the Ranchang (Chinn-ch'ang) valley, through Xichang, from which von Richtofen had been repulsed at the outset of his last expedition (see map 2.26: p 246). But the Muslim rebellion in Yunnan had ended, and there was hope that where T. T. Cooper, after all the rigours of the Litang-Batang mountain journey, had been imprisoned and threatened with death at the hands of the outposts of Dali, it would now be possible to get through.

Gill and Mesny decided to take the high road to the Tibetan border and follow it southwards to Dali, there joining the Kunming to Burma road. Colborne Baber, who left Chongqing on July 8, could not have known of this change of plan. Nor could Cameron and Nicoll, about to set off on this identical journey.

So remote from each other are the two styles of travelling—the flamboyant cavalcade of great men with retainers, and the itinerant preacher with 'one man and a mule'—that both deserve attention. But while the geographers took every opportunity to keep detailed journals, the missionaries did their best on the way and

at each night halt to win a hearing for their message and to leave Christian booklets with literate listeners. Their diaries had to be written up by candle-light or a guttering wick in vegetable oil, before they turned in to sleep. The terrain and conditions were the same for mandarins and missionaries. Solitary Cameron would be the next to come this way.

Starting from Chengdu on July 10, with a large train of animals and men, and making good time through Ya'an and Qingqi (Ch'ingch'i), Gill reached Kangding on the 25th. A part-Chinese, part-Tibetan town at 8,850 feet, Kangding lay about 20 miles north of the dazzling peak of Minya Gongga, 24,900 feet, the gateway to the Litang road which went on to Batang almost on the border of Tibet proper. At once the prestige of Mesny and the kindness of the French bishop Monseigneur Chauveau ('Vicaire-Apostolique de Lassa', but calling himself a little more reticently 'Vicar of Tibet') brought them all the advice and assistance they needed. For the eighteen-day climb to Batang they would need to carry all the food their party could need, and have their own riding animals.

The prefect of Kangding presented General Mesny with a mountain pony strong enough to bear his weight up the mountains, always above 10,000 feet but often at 12,000 feet for long stretches, with passes at 14,500 feet before Litang at 13,280 feet and another at 16,570 feet, thirty miles before Batang. Gill bought two good ponies and retained his sedan chair, hiring eight chair-bearers, four more ponies for his staff, and twenty-nine pack-animals for the provisions and his own baggage, not least an inflatable bath-tub of which he made good use, and his hat-box. An escort of soldiers made up the party that climbed steeply westwards to rest for two days at Litang, August 17–19, before braving the Batang road, infested with robbers. Suitably impressed and gratified by a box of cigars, the Litang mandarin sent bands of soldiers 'to scour the hills in all directions' and twelve Tibetan soldiers to swell the escort when they set out again on August 20. The long file of men and animals on the narrow rocky trail kept close together with guards in front, among them and bringing up the rear. *Mirabile dictu*, at every stopping place the 'Margary proclamation' was in evidence. The foreign notables would come to no harm.

Gill was enjoying himself, noting everything he saw and heard, and taking his barometric readings (for altitude) at frequent intervals, even ten or twelve times in a day as the track switch-backed over the wild plateau. Close to their trail the peak of Nenda rose to 20,500 feet like a canine tooth.[400] 'No words can describe the majestic grandeur of that mighty peak,' Gill wrote, 'whose giant mass of eternal snow and ice raises its glorious head seven thousand feet above the wondering traveller'—struggling along with bursting lungs even before the 16,750 foot pass, on jagged rocks so hard on feet and hooves that 'pony after pony succumbed and had to be replaced'. Fifty miles short of Batang the trail turned southwards and on August 25 they entered the 'town' of three hundred families but thirteen thousand lamas in the lamasery, to be welcomed with deep 'head-knocking' *ketous* from officials and soldiers, and by that 'gentleman of great intelligence' the Abbé Desgodins. Driven out of Bonga in 1865, when his premises were sacked, the Abbé had had to be content with Batang for the past twelve years, convinced that eventually he would get to Lhasa. The chief mandarin rose to the occasion, feting the general and Gill as only the Chinese know how. [401]

According to reports, the approach of so large a party had alerted the Tibetans and 'thousands', probably hundreds, were watching the roads to intercept any attempt to cross the border. The track ran only a hundred miles from the Assam border, as Cooper had known when he attempted and failed to enter China from Assam in October 1869. Again the hills were scoured for potential attackers as the cavalcade started off on August 29 'with a small army of escorts', two hundred officers and men. Where the 'road' to Yunnan passed within

five miles of Tibet, they saw a guard of three hundred Tibetans on a nearby hill-slope, and passed unchallenged. Now they were in the territory gashed in roughly parallel chasms by the great rivers of East Asia, the Jinsha Jiangor River of Golden Sand which, joined by the Yalong, a 'River of White Water', forms the Jin He River of Gold, the Yangzi herself, as far as Yibin (Suifu) above Chongqing.

'The great plateau that extends over the whole of central Asia,' Gill explained, 'throws down a huge arm between (the River of Golden Sand) and the (Mekong)', its crest five or six thousand feet above the two rivers. Too often the excessively steep sides of the chasms defied any track to follow the rivers, so the Batang 'road' crossed the River of Golden Sand (two hundred yards wide even here) and followed the ridge from 15,788 feet to Adenzi (Atuntzu, now Deqen) at 11,000 feet.

In so wild a region the only shelter to be found was always of the crudest nature, its entrance 'deep in mud and slime of the blackest' where men and animals crowded into the stable-cum-living-room, and lit a log fire on the central hearth. A notched log gave access to a loft where cornstalks or barley straw might soften the rough rafters, and acrid smoke writhed weakly towards a roof vent and window space, open to wind and rain. So Adenzi, with its few substantial buildings and first evidence of true Chinese influences felt like welcome civilisation again, shocked though Gill was to find that the immorality could be even grosser than at Batang.

T. T. Cooper had been told at Batang to follow the difficult Lancang River trail (the Mekong) to Weixi, fifty miles west of Lijiang, where unfriendly lamas and hostile officials would be sure to send him back, so his repulse and retreat to Batang came as no surprise to them. But Mesny and Gill by following the ridge above the Jinsha Jiang (River of Golden Sand), through Judian and then Jianchuan, had an easier journey, nonetheless involving steep descents of thousands of feet to cross tributaries only to climb as high again. It also gave them an acquaintance with the Lisu and Moso people and their hieroglyphs, leading them on September 27 to the Dali Lake and City. There they were feted by civil and military officials for their exploits. Dali was the capital city of Western Yunnan, as it had been of the ancient Shan kingdom of Nan Zhao and more recently of the so-called Panthay Muslim kingdom. Francis Garnier had approached Dali in early 1868 after crossing over from Huili at the tip of the Daliangshan 'but had to leave in hot haste' when taken for an imperial spy.[402]

After that, the month-long trek to Bhamo held no surprises, never rising above 8,000 feet or dropping below 2,600 feet, to cross the Salween River. On October 7 (Gill recorded) they met a Christian Chinese whose companions, two carriers, were sick, and 'he was naturally very anxious about them, for if either should have died before they reached their homes, the foreigner, it would have been said, would have killed them', or at any rate have been held responsible. This timely reunion of Yang Cunling with General Mesny, to obtain medicine and give news of John McCarthy's safe arrival at Bhamo, Gill did not mention. Where to Yule's displeasure Cooper had disparaged Protestant missionaries, Gill had nothing to say. Colonel Yule himself referred readers to 'many interesting passages' in *China's Millions* adding 'but there is hardly any recognition of geography in it'.[403] But Gill wrote, 'Mr Margary seems to have left a deeply favourable impression wherever he went.' No other house in Manyün was worthy of a general and his foreign friend, so the magistrate gave up his own house to them before seeing them off with an escort of twenty soldiers. Gill rode with a gun-bearer at his stirrup and was fired on once, before the attackers saw the odds and decamped.

On November 1 they reached a tributary of the Irrawaddy where Cooper's boat was waiting with cigars and newspapers to welcome them. Six days in Bhamo as guests of the Resident must have included sociabilities with Henry Soltau and John

2.36 A Nosu man and woman (called Yi by the Chinese)

McCarthy, whom he had met at Yichang after the riot (Stevenson having gone home), but after Gill's privations Cooper's hospitality filled his horizon. Certainly Mesny will have been a frequent guest at the Mission-house in that little market town. On April 24, 1878, T. T. Cooper was assassinated by one of his own sepoy guards.

Gill's glittering technical report won him the Founder's Medal from the Royal Geographical Society and promotion to Captain, Royal Engineers. And Baron von Richtofen when he read it hailed Gill as 'an acute observer' of men and nature (on) 'one of the most successful and useful' journeys recently made.[404] His books remain, a fascinating description of 'the road over the high plateau', to which Yule added in his Foreword, 'More recently, some of the numerous agents of the society called the China Inland Mission have been active in the reconnaissance of these outlying regions.'

Colborne Baber and the Nosu (July–October 1877)

While Gill was visiting Songpan and Mesny was travelling from Guiyang to join him for his central Asian adventure, Colborne Baber in Chongqing was laying plans for his first exploratory investigation of the commercial potential of southern Sichuan. With his experience of Grosvenor's expedition (of 1875–76) behind him he knew what he wanted. For the journey from Kunming to Bhamo the provincial governor had provided an escort of nominally sixty men, but Grosvenor had also enlisted some Sichuan braves as a personal bodyguard. After the pack-train 'with our cumbrous impedimenta galling their reluctant backs (had gone ahead) our vanguard . . . of some ten tall fellows waving immense spear-topped banners, followed by as many . . . armed to the teeth' preceded the mounted diplomats 'attended closely at heel by followers' carrying their rifles and shotguns. Their servants, also mounted, brought up the rear with the sedan chairs, medicine chest, more escorts and more carriers.

Thinking perhaps of John McCarthy, Cameron and Nicoll setting off on foot but still ignorant of how they fared, Baber wrote,

> No traveller in Western China who possesses any sense of self respect should journey without a sedan chair, not necessarily as a conveyance, but for the honour and glory of the thing. Unfurnished with this indispensable token of respectability, he is liable to be thrust aside on the highway, to be kept waiting at ferries, to be relegated to the worst inns' worst room, and generally to be treated with indignity. One may ride on pony-back, but a chair should be in attendance.[405]

Taking his place in a ferry queue was not for the high and mighty foreigner. And Baron von Richtofen's encounter on the pass above Qingqi near Ya'an had been partly due to having no sedan chair, Baber claimed.

So Baber, armed and travelling 'alone', had fifteen coolies to carry the provisions of himself and his attendants when he left Chongqing on July 8. To his surprise, when he reached Chengdu on the twentieth, Gill and Mesny had left only ten days before, making not for Kashgar or Tibet but for Dali and Burma. They could have travelled together down Marco Polo's Caindu, the Jianchang (Chinn-ch'ang) valley, he protested after being the first to make the journey. He visited Mount Emei (Omei),

went on to Ya'an, crossed the Daxiangling pass, where von Richtofen, prospecting for minerals, had fallen foul of the garrison, and entered Qingqi, 'the smallest city in China', a walled market tightly closed in by steep mountain sides.

Crossing the Dadu River to Fulin, and on to Yuexi he came upon 'a glorious hill and valley region, inhabited by Chinese soldier colonists, and those interesting mountaineers the Lolo people'—the Nosu. He was entranced. (The Chinese used *Lolo* almost as they used *Manzi* for a wide variety of minority peoples including Nosu, Shan, Sifan and smaller Tibeto-Burman groups between the Yangzi and Burma.) Baber expatiated on their appearance, the 'horn' into which their hair is gathered and bound above their foreheads, their capacious trousers and heavy tweed cloaks, and their women folk, 'joyous, timid, natural, open-aired, neatly dressed, barefooted, honest girls, devoid of all the prurient mock-modesty of (some women) . . . A sturdy Lolo lord of creation, six foot two high . . . went out and fetched two armfuls of them—about half a dozen (tall, graceful creatures with faces much whiter than their brothers).'

But these were the Nosu on good terms with the Chinese in the Daliangshan, a territory the size of Wales.[406] The only way to meet the defiant Nosu marauders in their own territory, those 'fiercely independent caterans . . . frequent in their raids on the Chinese' (Yule wrote) was by finding a feudal clan chief to guarantee the travellers' security, in exchange for appropriate gifts, bolts of cloth and cones of salt. Baber contented himself with following the borders, southwards to Xichang, eastwards to Huili, crossing the upper Yangzi where it is known as the Jin He, River of Gold or Golden River, and finally northwards along its precipitous eastern flank, to Yibin (Suifu), altogether three hundred miles. Of Yichang (at the time called Ningyuan) he recorded, 'A couple of months before our visit, a French missionary, the only European besides myself who has ever entered the city was driven away by the staves and stones instigated by the Commandant.' But on the viceroy's orders the mandarins in every city posted the proclamation and welcomed Baber, so that it was widely reported that he was an envoy of the emperor to inspect the border regions.

At Huili his route had touched Garnier's and immediately diverged from it again. For on September 18 he crossed the Jin He (Golden River) at Qiaojia (Ch'iao-chic), a raging silt-laden torrent only five hundred feet in width, crushed between steep walls of rock. And instead of gaining the Dongchuan-Zhaotong-Yibin 'road', which he had taken with Grosvenor, he kept as close to the wild river as he could. To 'a Shanghai newspaper' he wrote,

> Thence through the wildest and poorest country imaginable, the great slave-hunting ground from which the Lolo carry off their Chinese bondsmen: a country of shepherds, lonely downs, great snowy mountains, silver mines . . . No European has ever been in that region before myself, not even Jesuit surveyors; the course of the (Yangzi) as laid down in their maps, is a bold assumption, and altogether incorrect . . . It winds about among those grand gorges with the most haughty contempt for the Jesuits' maps.[407]

Baber's accurate sextant readings established the course of the Golden River fifty miles east of the position given previously. He meant 'no European geographer known to me', for later in his 'Travels and Researches' read at the Royal Geographical Society on June 13, 1881, he was to quote at length from the *Annales de la Propagation de la Foi*, 'luminous with ingenuous veracity' by a French priest 'long resident in China', about how he was captured on January 2, 1860, by slave-raiding Nosu and held for forty-eight hours. The inhabitants of the Daliangshan had been driven across the Jin He, the north-flowing reach of the Yangzi, in the reign of Yongzheng (1723–36) and regarded these raids by up to three thousand fighters as collecting rent for their territory forcibly occupied by the Chinese.

When Lord Aberdare hailed Baber

as 'fortunate enough' to have 'visited an entirely new country, and . . . come across a people of whose existence, race and character, hitherto nothing at all had been known' he was misinformed. To the people of China, the Catholic Church and readers of Marco Polo, much was already known. Even Sir Rutherford Alcock commented on Baber's 'discovery of what appeared to be a new language, and of a new people never before visited by any European'. The first entry into the Daliangshan was not in fact until considerably later, though Baber was told by a friendly Nosu shaman 'that under proper securities it may be travelled in safety'. As before, his genius for seeing, surveying and communicating his observations 'with extraordinary vivacity and force' was rightly praised. Of what he saw on the Zhaotong plateau he wrote:

> About twenty miles distant to the north-west, in a cloudy sky, rose a stupendous boss (which resembles a cap of liberty) the culminating point, and the terminal of a snowy ridge some fifteen miles long... The summit falls to the (Yangzi) in a series of terraces ... and abuts on the river with a precipice or precipices which must be 8,000 feet above its water ... I was standing too near those overwhelming heights and depths to be able to judge calmly of their proportions—physically too near the gorges, and mentally too close to the liberty cap ... Later and maturer reflection has brought little result beyond a violent desire to go there again.

The name of that ridge is Taiyang Qiao— the 'Sun-bridge', because 'the setting sun traverses the crown of that portentous causeway'. And beyond it, to the north, the towering precipices of the Longtou Shan, the Dragon's Head, overhang the deep divide of the Meigu He, the River of the Beautiful Maiden.[408]

On October 18 he re-visited a prison in the little town of Pingshan, where he had been in January 1876 on the Grosvenor expedition, and found the same Nosu hostages as he had seen then. And from Yibin (Suifu) he returned to Chongqing by river-boat.

Sichuan 'occupied' (May–October 1877)

At this point a glance back to May, after the Wuchang Conference, reminds us that Hudson Taylor's 'bombshell' had for the second time scattered available pioneers to the four winds. Charles Judd and George Nicoll rejoined James Cameron at Yichang, the springboard for Sichuan, where he had been living on a houseboat since seeing John McCarthy on his way up the Yangzi gorges, following the March 3 riot. At last he had regained possession of the damaged house, and this time his own travels were to expand dramatically while Judd stayed to develop the beginnings of the Yichang church. Chongqing was to be occupied, and the work in Sichuan to begin in earnest.[409]

Yakub Beg, who in 1864 had defied Peking and set up his Muslim kingdom of Kashgaria for thirteen years, had at last met his match. Zuo Zongtang (Tsuo Tsung-t'ang), one of the greatest generals China has ever known, had advanced the whole length of the Great Silk Road and desert trail through Gansu and Xinjiang, and defeating Yakub Beg during the winter of 1876. The far north-west became almost depopulated, with only one in ten surviving. In May 1877, Yakub Beg died (in battle or by poison) and in the autumn Zuo Zongtang retook Kashgar and Yarkand. (But opportunist Russia had occupied Kuldja and the territory of Ili in 1871, and a new confrontation with China had begun. A part was to be restored in 1879 on payment of five million roubles by China, but a final settlement was not reached until 1881.)

So with this background and with three Chinese Christians, Cameron and Nicoll travelled on a public goods-boat towed by 'trackers' up the awesome Yangzi gorges. 'Their stern and solemn grandeur baffles description,' Cameron wrote. 'I had passed through them several times previous to this, yet I could not leave the front of the boat, but had to sit (with Nicoll) drinking in the scene.' Against a swollen current it took them three weeks to reach Wanxian, so they finished the journey by land. As always, whether by boat or by foot it was, in the words of the conference agenda, 'itineration as an evangelistic agency'. 'Far and near', to fellow-passengers and the inhabitants of hamlet, village, market town and city they spoke about 'Christ Jesus crucified for sinners and raised to life again', selling Gospels and explanatory books, always at risk of getting into trouble on account of recent disturbances with Roman Catholics.

June and July they spent based at Chongqing at the house McCarthy had rented on his way to Bhamo. He noted that missionaries of the CIM used it to rest in, coming and going in their work 'without the least trouble, as yet, of any kind',—in the sense of meeting hostility.[410] Preparing to reconnoitre the fringes of Tibet, preaching the gospel as they went, they were ready to start when an unexpected visitor arrived. Charles Leaman, an American Presbyterian from Nanjing, had come with two Chinese Christians of Wesleyan background and 'a large supply of books', on his way to distribute them in Shaanxi and Gansu. On meeting Cameron and Nicoll, just back 'from an inland town', he changed his plan.

They left Chongqing together on August 14, working their way to Chengdu, four hundred miles in twenty-one days, never travelling on Sundays, and always drawing crowds of visitors, and selling all the books they could. Nine days in Chengdu they spent in the same way, while hiring pack-animals and laying in provisions for the arduous climb from Guanxian to Kangding, the shortest route to the gateway of Tibet. They set out on September 13 and reached the foothills on the 19th—the day following Edward Fishe's death at Guiyang. From the outset the animals were unequal to the rough going, and when they came to 'a suspension bridge made of bamboo ropes, 316 paces in length and 7 feet in breadth (with) 10 ropes underneath and five on each side [so Cameron wrote in his diary], we concluded to try the more southerly route . . . less difficult for mules'.

Day by day, in place after place, instead of recording geographical observations or the potential for trade, it was the people and how they listened to the gospel, or the Catholics and how they fared, who took pride of place in their journals. On September 28 they reached Ya'an. The danger of being prevented from going further by officials concerned for the safety of unarmed, unimpressive strangers, led them to 'work' there only until noon on the 29th before moving on. But the next day Nicoll was very ill with 'ague' and Leaman tired out. When the inns were full they were content to lie in rows with fellow-travellers on straw in a loft among the opium-smokers, and shared the common meals of peasant Chinese. It needed stamina. Cameron preached in a market town until his voice gave way, and talked with men who followed him back to the inn. But with Nicoll sometimes too ill even to ride his pony, so that they could not travel, and the pack-mules often failing them, it was October 5 before they reached Qingqi (Ch'ing-ch'i) near the top of the mountain range only seventy miles beyond Ya'an. Qingqi proved to be not only the 'smallest city in China' but apparently the least interested in hearing what they had to say.

Here they faced reality. Their loads were too heavy for the animals to carry in such terrain, one older Christian companion was finding the going too much for his strength, and Nicoll's 'ague' showed no sign of improvement. They at least must return to Chongqing. Leaman offered to go with them. Showing that dogged perseverance which was to carry him on and on for six long years of pioneering, and to earn him the epithet 'the Livingstone of China', Cameron decided to go on without them.

Not one, but two of the most historic reconnaissances of mission history in China were about to begin. Cameron's has often been written about. But Nicoll's unplanned detour with Leaman has been overlooked because it did not receive the publicity given to Cameron. Their itinerary appears not to have been understood at first, for in the map of itineraries published in the *China's Millions* of 1878 it was misplaced. They followed the route almost unknown to Westerners and shunned by Chinese unless heading straight for Dali or Kunming, the route encircling the Nosu homeland, the Daliangshan.

Cameron, 'one man and a mule'[411] (October 1877–January 1878)

The contrast between Gill's 'progress' and Cameron's humble 'itineration' could hardly have been greater, not that Cameron gave it a thought or knew any more of Gill than innkeepers may have told him along the way. Gill had been heading for Xinjiang when he left Chongqing. Just before Qingqi, Cameron had met the *zhentai* (chen-t'ai) or military governor of Qianzhou on his way to Chengdu and had to make way for him and his cavalcade to pass—two hundred pack-animals of possessions, four sedan chairs for his wives, son and himself, and 'many soldiers'. This was how the high and mighty did it, and he did not begrudge General Mesny or Gill their due.

After parting from the rest of his own party he wrote, 'I have a good mule, and also a good coolie as servant . . . My books and tracts, also a few more things, are in saddlebags carried by the mule I hope to ride. The bulk of my silver I carry on my person . . . and find it rather burdensome when I walk.' He rode for five miles and walked twenty when climbing, but on easy stretches rode more. Hoping to spend the Sunday resting, before arriving at Kangding (see map 2.26: p 246), he was asked to move out of his inn to make room for an official who was expected soon. When he met the cavalcade of eighty men later that day, he was glad he had obliged. To be unimportant and free to pass the time of day with anyone without restraints suited him well.

Now he was in semi-Tibetan country where the minority people (called *Manzi* by the dominant Chinese) lived in Tibetan strong houses. Vocabularies which he collected as he travelled showed that these people were (with dialect differences) the same as those of Tibet-proper, as the Abbé Desgodins was to confirm when he 'received (him) very kindly and courteously' at Batang for that rare delight, a meeting of 'strangers in a strange land'.

On October 16 he left Kangding, having 'supplied the city well with tracts' and sold some books, to endure most primitive conditions at the night stops on the arduous way to Litang. Pages of his journal are filled with descriptions of the people, their houses, customs and language. Living at their level and eating their simple barley and oat *tsanba* made them friendly and communicative. In a *Manzi* shack he took down a list of phrases.

> After I had written them down the host requested me to read them over, and was highly pleased with their correctness ... We were soon like old friends ... Supper being over ... our sitting-room became the common bedroom. The females took one side of the room, while the master and his (son) shared the other side with us ... He told me if I ever passed again, to be sure and put up in his house.

People were the reason for his being there, and their geographical environment incidental, revel in it though he did. After crossing the Yalong River at Hekou (the geographical fact failed to impress him):

> We had a huge snow-clad mountain to cross ... It was bitterly cold, and the wind often seemed (to) enter our bones. Both of us have swollen and sore lips, and heavy colds with sore throats. [On the far side a friendly man hailed him from a hut and welcomed them to stay.] He brought each of us a large basin of soup with plenty of beef (and butter, milk and vegetables) in it (and) spent a good part of (Sunday) reading some books I gave him.

At one inhabited place the men looked so evil that Cameron and his man chose to pass on and take what they could find, rather than be robbed (at the least) or never be heard of again. There were nothing but shepherds' tents or watch-fires for mile upon mile as they climbed to 14,500 feet and descended in the dark, missing the 'halt' where they could sleep under cover. On and on they stumbled in good moonlight, until the dogs in another hamlet announced their arrival. But the people were afraid and would not open to them. At last one man relented and plied them with tea by a hot fire until they lay down to sleep. He told them they had come 170 *li* since the morning, but Cameron thought 150 *li* (fifty miles) nearer the mark. By 2.00 p.m. the next day, October 23, they were in Litang, at 13,280 feet 'one of the highest cities in the world', with its gilded lamasery roofs.

Again James Cameron's lengthy and detailed observations on the place, the gilded lamasery, the lamas, the appearance and dress of the men and women, the Shaanxi origin of most of the one hundred Chinese in Litang were what ethnologists and missionaries looked for. Zealous, certainly, for he yearned for Tibet to be open to the messengers of the cross, but not simple. Here at Litang after visiting the lamassery he wrote, 'Oh! When shall 'Christ and Him crucified' be preached to the multitudes who speak (Tibetan)? . . . My hope is in God—I know He will open it in His own time and way. He may not see fit to send me, but He will send his prepared ones; and when His time comes, they will have entrance.'

The Abbé Desgodins of Batang had used very similar expressions of his own patient longings. But Cameron was also scientific, as his meticulous description of the decorations on a lamasery wall revealed.[412]

Cameron's quiet departure seemed to invite disaster. Too high a price was asked for any horse he approved of, and every animal offered to him had a serious defect. So with his one man and a mule he set off on foot. A friendly Shaanxi Chinese overtook him and welcomed them to his home on the first night, where a low kang, a platform of baked earth, served as a bed. With no fire and feeling ill, Cameron lay down 'with a burning skin, almost shivering with cold'. But the next night, after another day's march and with 'two calves for room-fellows' he slept well. At last, on October 29, he managed to buy a good horse, more cheaply than the bad ones in Litang and, still febrile, they climbed up and over a snow-clad pass with their faces and hands scorched by reflected sunlight and the biting wind. So painful were his eyes that he tried to walk with them shut. Untrained and probably unfamiliar with travel books about the dangers and difficulties of such conditions, his intelligence and indomitable spirit saw him through, enabling him to encourage his man and goad the mule over the worst stretches.

On October 31 they had to cross the highest point, sinking a foot deep into the snow, and when the sun was warm, splashing through rivulets on the trail. His own shoes became unwearable, and cheap straw sandals fell to pieces, yet they pressed on. The only alternative was to turn back. 'For more than sixty *li* (nominally twenty miles) we did not see a living soul, and then only one.' Missing the house they had been told of, as it was off the beaten track, they kept going, stopping only to feed the animals and fortify themselves with 'Zanba' (*tsanba*).

Long after dark they reached Batang and could find nowhere to sleep. 'They had no inns (of any kind). Strangers seek quarters in private houses . . . At last a woman took pity on us.' The dangerous journey of more than thirty miles, at risk from snowstorms, injuries and robbers, was over. 'Hitherto hath the Lord helped us', Cameron wrote—only to spend the night tormented by bed bugs, 'my old enemies'.

At first the officials feared that this brave or foolhardy young man was meaning to enter Tibet, only five miles away, and were 'much reassured' to be told he had no such intention. Cameron's aim was to find the extent of Tibetan occupation of the heights above Yunnan. He called on the Abbé Desgodins and enjoyed a long talk with him in Chinese. 'This kind priest gave me much useful information . . . He advised me to call on the mandarin, so that if any disturbance took place he could not say he knew nothing about me.' Two mandarins also entertained him at length, asking what doctrine he taught, an opportunity Cameron welcomed, and promised an escort to see him over the stretch of road that ran close to hostile Tibetans. That

afternoon they sent him a feast of 'ten dishes of meats'. He had nothing he could give them in return.

November 5 saw Cameron on his way to Adenzi (A-tun-tzu) with an alert escort of three and a young literate Tibetan he had engaged as a language informant. 'We passed the place where a man was killed by robbers only two days ago . . . They seemed to expect robbers, but we saw nothing and were not sorry.' 'In (Batang) my face and hands had time to heal, but yesterday evening and today have skinned my face again,' his diary for the 7th reads. Five official couriers joined them, making a party of eleven mounted men to pass the nearest point to Tibet, and they were told of a large body of Tibetans guarding the border. Looking out over Tibet itself, with Tibetan homes in view, Cameron sighed. When would Tibet open her frontier to the gospel? 'It will be open some day!'

Feeling unwell, he welcomed the kindness of *Manzi* people in a well-cultivated valley, who pressed butter, nuts and curd and even a hen on them without haggling for payment. A few 'fathoms' of thread, 'and they went off well pleased . . . and we were very comfortable'. The steep, broken, rocky tracks over the high ridges and deep chasms of the provincial border made progress slow and painful. So it was November 14 when they reached Adenzi in Yunnan. There he succumbed to high fever for two weeks and thought his end had come. What to do with his silver, the Mission's property, worried him as he lay helpless. 'See what a trouble it is to be rich!' he wrote when strong enough to continue his diary. Yet he cannot have had much silver left by this stage in his journey.[413]

On December 3 he thought he would recover if he had more exercise, and nearly changed his mind when on mounting the mule he all but fell off again. He had no strength to control it, and had to have it led, mile upon mile over the snowy mountains and across perilous rope bridges. One night he found himself in a Roman Catholic home near where two foreign priests were living, and avoiding 'controversial matters' they talked about Jesus. But after travelling through the territory of two other ethnic minorities, the Moso and Minjia, he found himself in another Catholic home on the 8th—'the kindest people I have met with on all my journey'.

An official from Adenzi on his way to Weixi caught them up when they were uncertain of the trail and guided them for a day or two, so on the 10th they found themselves among Chinese again, in Weixi where T. T. Cooper had been imprisoned by the Muslim rebels in 1868 and driven back to Batang. Mandarins and people were friendly to Cameron and sent escorts to see him safely through a lawless wilderness. 'What a field for a linguist,' he exclaimed when they met more and more aboriginal people. Like missionaries in a thousand situations he wished he could divide himself up between them. At Jianchuan he preached in Chinese to an attentive crowd, and on December 23 reached Dali, a fully Chinese city with a Catholic bishop in residence. At last he could go from teashop to teashop, sure of an audience and interesting conversations in each.

The rest of the way to Bhamo was plain sailing in comparison. From the time he left Dali on December 28, people he met remembered John McCarthy (1877), and in place after place gospel posters were still where he and his companions had pasted them up. Near Yongping, before crossing the Lancang (Mekong) River, a French priest told him that two other priests had gone towards Bhamo in 1876 and had never been heard of again. When Cameron reached Tengyue (Momein) on January 9 the inns were crowded with travellers waiting for the road ahead to be cleared of robbers. After a hot battle between the militia and a gang of them, fifteen men were brought in and beheaded. While he waited, one of John McCarthy's companions arrived. He had accompanied Yang Cunling from Bhamo to Kunming and was on his way back to Bhamo. They went on together.

With the road cleared of robbers, all Manyün's hostelries were full when they arrived, so McCarthy's man took them to a private home. The woman's son had been so ill in Bhamo that she had gone to him and was despairing of his life when Stevenson and Soltau had first arrived and cured him. At last, on January 18 a convoy of a hundred travellers, with Cameron's party among them, proceeded under an escort of Kachins into the mountains of the Burma border. A night in a Kachin chief's home and another bivouacking in the jungle, and they came to the Shan village of Manmo where Cameron waited for a week. No explanation is given, but a safe surmise is that McCarthy's man had told him of the Indian government's ban on re-entering China, so he sent ahead for advice. Should he retreat while he could? It was too late. T. T. Cooper, the Agent, heard of him and 'asked' him to come to Bhamo. He had no alternative if restrictions by the British were not to be extended.

When Hudson Taylor heard of the success of this and other journeys his admiration and gratitude were profound. He truly loved like sons these men who stopped at nothing for Christ's sake.

Nicoll's journey[414]
(October–November 1877)

George Nicoll's 'ague' left him after Cameron had started from Qingqi, and this altered the whole picture. Instead of heading back to Chongqing by the quickest route down the Min River from Leshan (Rading), Charles Leaman and he could either work their way back through densely populated Sichuan, distributing the excess of books in their 'bulky baggage', or be enterprising and strike southwards, down the Ranchang valley. They chose the second option.

Leaman's account of his travels and observations was published in the *Chinese Recorder* soon after his return to Nanjing. But its emphasis on the cultivated, populated part of Sichuan, barely outlining the southern route and referring only to the 'tribes' in general, shows where his interests lay. Nicoll on the other hand, although an academic and enthusiastic about the Nosu he met, seems to have left so little record of their journey that whoever prepared the map for the 1879 bound volume of *China's Millions* may be forgiven for taking them by the direct route to Leshan and Chongqing. However, Leaman said enough to confirm the impression given by a letter from Nicoll to two trainees in Britain, Samuel R. Clarke (unrelated to George) and J. H. Riley, that he encircled the Daliangshan except for its northern end (see map 2.26: p 246). (He visited Leibo in 1880.)

Leaving Qingqi on October 10 they descended the Daxiangling from 9,360 feet, crossed the Dadu River and the Xiaoxiangling (9,700 feet) on the 23rd, in snow and ice, into the region of 'tame' and 'wild' Nosu, and three days later reached Xichang, 'a busy city and a fine rich valley'. 'We worked in this place with great satisfaction; the people were kind and did not molest us in any way,' Nicoll wrote. As for the Nosu they had encountered on the way, 'I felt quite at home with them, seeing so many things which reminded me of my native (Scotland)', not least 'oatmeal cooked in the same way'.

> These Lolo [ie Nosu) women walk as erect as a soldier ... I longed to see someone among them with a heart burning with love for the Master ... I took a list of their words, so that I could test, as I went along, how far the language was the same; and I found that for over a hundred miles there was no difference ... All the subject Lolos can speak Chinese.[415]

To the west of Xichang lay more unruly territory and the main body of Moso and Minjia people, extending right over the Yalong River and Jinsha Jiang (River of Golden Sand) to where Cameron had met them.

They went on a hundred miles to Huili, 'a larger and finer city,' and eastwards 'over a very difficult road' to cross the Yangzi on November 15, 'a mighty river, two thousand miles from its mouth'. Unknown to them, James Cameron was lying alone and very ill at Adenzi as they climbed 'over very difficult hills' to Dongchuan on the ancient highway between Yunnan and Sichuan. Shortly before Yibin they took to a boat and

reached Chongqing on December 9, 1,600 miles and four months since setting out.

Charles Leaman was a townsman, not cut out for pioneering, so he had suffered from the discomforts of primitive conditions. He returned to Nanjing; and Nicoll confirmed for himself that the Nosu language varied little from place to place along the borders.

As a missionary reconnaissance, with no wish to be the first Westerners to make it, this itinerary was a *tour de force* which established the feasibility of living within reach of the Nosu, and of making contact with the 'independent' inhabitants of the Daliangshan. J. H. Riley was to attempt that, but never put down roots. The Paris Mission had tried and failed to settle in Xichang while the French Protectorate was so unpopular. One and another briefly entered the Daliangshan, from the east, the north and the west, for a few days at a time, and an armed French expedition was to cross over the independent territory in 1908, but not until after the Second World War did missionaries travel and live in the heart of the Nosu homeland until compelled to leave under Mao's new regime at the dramatic end of the Open Century.

Director–at–large[416]
(May–December 1877)

Throughout the Shanghai Conference in May, Hudson Taylor had been run off his feet. Constantly in demand for consultation and advice he had no rest, and racked by facial neuralgia from a decaying tooth, which sometimes drove him 'almost frantic', he was too busy to have it extracted. On May 24th the conference ended, in his view 'the most important step China Missions have yet taken', but he could see no hope of returning to London before August. The Zhejiang missionaries desperately needed a visit. One had become a shameless alcoholic, even attempting to lead a communion service when too intoxicated to stand. He must be replaced. 'Oh! may God make us a holy mission,' Hudson Taylor groaned, 'a united and loving mission, and then we shall be a *successful* mission.' Others were ill and disheartened. Wang Lae-djün, as pastor and in effect bishop of an expanding network of churches, had come to consult him about his problems.

Preparation of 'copy' for *China's Millions* took high priority, for through it he reached not only a broad spectrum of interested Christians in Europe, Colonel Yule among them, but many in China too, consuls, merchants and members of other missions. He asked for a hundred copies of the bound volumes to distribute. Lord Radstock had written decrying so much news of travel and Chinese affairs, wanting in his spirituality more about people to pray for, news of baptisms and ordinations. To Hudson Taylor the pioneering was no less spiritual, as he looked ahead to the churches as yet unborn in each of the provinces being entered. Every issue had its spiritual highlight in his editorials in the series 'China for Christ' of the type Lord Radstock valued. Hudson Taylor was confident. 'It is impossible to meet everyone's view.' 'A paper just suiting Lord R. would not please many. But much may be done to please him.' People must be informed. Factual knowledge made for understanding. If space allowed, he would multiply the articles on Chinese customs, beliefs, culture and history. Illustrations with explanations, of a Chinese wedding, a fortune teller, a gambling house, a street barber, monks, musicians, modes of travel and varieties of scenery made *China's Millions* balanced and attractive. And Hudson Taylor worked all the harder to report evidence of the steady growth of the established congregations. The *Chinese Recorder so* recently supercilious about the CIM, was impressed by the bound volumes. '"China for Christ" is the motto of the untiring editor, and he makes his magazine impress this motto upon his readers by every page.' And later, 'We welcome this elegant periodical, brimful of interesting missionary news . . . The pictures are excellent.'

Achieving that result cost him distress as well as labour, and ceaseless difficulties for Jennie and those who helped her at home. To maintain the standard he did not stop at strong rebukes for them, if proof-reading lapsed or the spelling of Chinese words was inconsistent. Love-letters had to turn to painful business, even if it meant a string of strictures. 'Why do you not send me proofs of the CM early, instead of waiting till they are worked off?' She must remember that work on the forthcoming issues depended on what had gone into print, and mails were so slow to reach him. 'It is such a pity that the January picture was so badly printed and that you have not been more careful.' Again, 'I like the February CM very much and think you have done very well.' Another time a whole page of criticism of the printer's choice of type-face and other shortcomings showed her how fraught he was. She understood. 'I do like our absence from each other for Jesus' sake to cost us something, darling, to be a real sacrifice,' he said. 'I don't think a husband can love his wife too much, but he may be too much influenced by his love.' Their own love was disciplined. Jennie wrote, 'I do not want you to come, darling, before you have finished the work God has for you to do there,' and he agreed, but added, 'Almost sick at heart at our long absence—I hardly know how to finish my note.'

The unstable remaining missionaries of the *Lammermuir* era and their wives in Zhejiang needed more than a visit by Hudson Taylor. On June 8 he took Elizabeth Wilson with him, to stay at Wenzhou while he moved on. Older, mature and sensible, friendly and spiritual, she could restore hope where they were dejected and love where they were at loggerheads. She looked up to him for his unfailing attentiveness, saying 'I always had a sense of being sheltered as by a father, though he was five years younger than myself and generally far off.' They went by coastal steamer to Ningbo and visited all the other missions, in the spirit of the Shanghai conference. He proposed a Ningbo conference in Chinese for members of all the churches, and went on to Shaoxing. James Meadows had again reverted to foreign dress, choosing to be like other missions rather than like the Chinese to whom he was effectively devoting his life. His little daughter sat with her arm round Hudson Taylor's neck while he encouraged her parents. (In time she joined the Mission.)

The Hangzhou church had long since ceased to need foreign help except in teaching, and welcomed their friend as a father-in-God. He invited all members and their immediate families to a fellowship-meal and the Lord's Supper, and during the ten days he was there, June 16–27, he took part in the ordination of the evangelist Jiang Liang-yong (in dialect Tsiang Liang-yung; see p 178) as assistant pastor of the Yuhang congregation he had largely brought into being. They wanted to build a chapel. 'How about this suggestion?' asked Hudson Taylor: Now that they were strong enough, instead of accepting the help of Liang-yong at the expense of the Hangzhou Christians, how about working towards his full support themselves? They agreed. They would start by providing one fifth of his needs, adding one fifth for every additional ten members joining the church.

In Hangzhou itself, with this relief the congregation undertook the full support of Ren Ziqing (Nying Ts-kying, in local dialect), the schoolmaster-evangelist who had first been attracted to Christ by observing Jennie at Suzhou (see pp 121, 155). With Wang Lae-djün away so much visiting his daughter churches, Ren had been deputizing for him. He was ordained assistant pastor, and in time became Lae-djün's son-in-law and successor. The women of Hangzhou were still talking about Jennie, the 'Miss Happiness' who had become one of them from the day she first arrived. The greatest need in this work, Hudson Taylor told her, was more men and women missionaries (thirty more, he said when he passed through Singapore), especially women like her. Then back to Shaoxing, from June 27 to July 4, in temperatures of 90–100 °F in the shade.

His pioneers were never far from his mind while he toured the consolidated results of earlier pioneering. Clarke, Fishe and Landale were arriving at Guiyang (June 28) and John McCarthy at Kunming. James

Cameron and George Nicoll were travelling in Sichuan before their mountain journeys. Also to his joy, Samuel Dyer, Maria's brother, was taking over as China Agent of the British and Foreign Bible Society from Alexander Wylie, forced to retire with failing eyesight. In twenty years the distribution of the Bible Society's million Testaments had been completed by Wylie's great efforts. With greater freedom Samuel Dyer was to achieve even more than Wylie.

When Hudson Taylor and Elizabeth Wilson reached Sheng Man for the weekend of July 7, they found signs of this still being perhaps 'the most successful of all our stations'. Not knowing that the Sunday service would be special in any way, Christians walked three, five and as far as fifteen miles to attend. When a man who had persecuted them was not deterred from heckling by Hudson Taylor's presence, they quietly continued the service, and afterwards he suggested to the *dibao* that a word in the trouble-maker's ear might save them both from repercussions should the man go too far. These poor people excelled in hospitality when their visitors left: the Christians insisted on carrying them in mountain chairs without payment. Throughout this southern tour from June 8 to the last week of September, the only nights not spent in Mission or Chinese Christians' homes were those on junks, along the coast or on the Qiantang River. 'The many new members in all these places was very cheering, and the evident (spiritual) growth observable in the older members impressed me.'

To Louise Desgraz he wrote, 'The work is most cheering—real and progressing. Many new Christians, getting no (material advantages) and hoping for none, on the contrary (are) suffering persecution . . . severely as I have seen.' Because she was being introspective again he had said in another note, 'The world is *unsatisfied*, too large a proportion of the Church is unsatisfied . . . all Christians should be *satisfied*, filled full and overflowing beyond self.' And from Saigon, on his way home in November, 'Forget there is such a person, good or bad, as Louise Desgraz; ignore her will and wishes.' She kept his letters. He was helping each of his growing mission family in the same way.

They travelled to Taizhou, Wenzhou, Lishui (Chūchou) and Jinhua, where they saw the original house from which James Williamson had been evicted in 1868 (see pp 14–15), in use as a preaching hall by a nucleus of eight local Christians. 'We *shall* reap if we faint not!' he reminded Louise. Funds were not coming through to him for distribution, and on August 1 he told Jennie, 'I have only 2 cents in hand and all funds are dry,' except for some reserved for the Crombies' passages home. On September 11 and 12 his subdued excitement was evident as he named November 3 as a possible date for sailing at last (at his own expense), and that eight new Christians from Jiangxi province had come to Qü Xian to be baptised. Beginnings were slow, but altogether the CIM had baptised 755, of whom seventy-five per cent were still in full standing.

Time was running out, and his hope of crossing Jiangxi again, to pack up at. Zhenjiang, had to be abandoned. He travelled down the Qiantang River to Hangzhou and Ningbo and by steamer to Zhenjiang instead. On October 2 he left again with his baggage, depositing it in Shanghai, and hurried back to Ningbo for the conference he had somehow convened, organised and now was to preside over. All meetings were entirely in Chinese, with Chinese and missionary speakers addressing Chinese delegates from the whole of Zhejiang in the church buildings of the CIM American Baptist and Presbyterian churches, the United Methodist Free Church and the CIM, for eleven consecutive days.[417] He thought it 'excellent', immediately effective and a demonstration of how the churches could work together and meet

2.37 Zhejiang and Jiangsu: gateway to new fields

for the Lord's Supper without obtrusive differences. Then he returned to Shanghai and was waiting there when the Wusong railway fiasco reached its climax.[418]

Meanwhile Cameron and Nicoll had set out for the borders of Tibet, George Clarke and Edward Fishe had gone into Guangxi, and Turner and James had been desperately ill in Shanxi. Since Turner came south to consult at Wenzhou, Hudson Taylor himself was 'very taken up' with the rapidly deteriorating famine situation in North China, and to leave China was as painful as it was necessary. But he was needed more in Britain than in China. King, Budd, Easton and Parker had sorted out their differences and were tackling the north-western provinces again. He wrote on October 26:

> 'Be faithful unto death and He *will* give you a crown of life.' Often read the 23rd Psalm and give your Amen to all its statements—in *faith* when you cannot do so in *feeling*. '*The Lord is* my Shepherd.' He *is*, He *is* ... My *cup* runneth over.' *True, true*, for He says so ... Never measure God's promises and statements by your feelings and attainments; accept *all* He says.
>
> Now, farewell, my dear brethren, beloved and prayed constantly for, my joy and crown! May God do for you all and more than all I would if I could for Jesus' sake!

It was only one of scores of such letters he was writing to his widely scattered foreign and Chinese family.

On October 17 he had just sent Jennie a telegram to say 'Coming', when word arrived that Edward Fishe had died. He postponed his sailing to the next French Mail, and sent for the grieving Annie and the children to join him and the Crombies. The Crombie children were so debilitated by chronic dysentery that he wondered whether they would reach Britain alive, for George and Anne were beyond caring properly for them. So he enlisted Emmeline Turner to join the party simply to look after the children.[419] On November 3 his close friend 'Mary Jones' of many memories since 1856 (see 1, pp 348–49) died as 'Ann Maria, wife of Frederick Foster Gough, CMS'. The issue of *China's Millions* which reported the Ningbo conference, carried a meditation by Hudson Taylor on John 17.24: 'Father, I will (I long) that they also, whom thou hast given me, be with me where I am; that they may behold my glory'. If we knew God better we would not be perplexed by his dealings with us. Edward Fishe had been about to take Annie and children deep into the interior, far from the Yangzi, the first wife and family to take such a plunge. Why did God take him? The *love* of Jesus is the answer. 'He does not rob one to enrich another, but does the *best* for all'—the best for the widow, for the orphan, for each of the bereaved, as for the one he takes to be with him in his glory—the best too for China and the Church. 'The happy death of Mrs Gough' was illuminated by the same light.

Travelling third class by the Messageries Maritimes, in Chinese clothes as far as Singapore for the sake of Chinese fellow-passengers, they sailed from Shanghai on November 9. Nothing would be gained, he told Jennie, by her meeting them in Paris. The Crombies' illness and the need to get to work in Britain as soon as possible would overshadow their reunion. His 'forty weeks' away had turned into more than fifteen months. By Aden he could not even face meeting her in public, it must be alone in their own home. But having 'God alone' for so long, without her as an added strength and joy, had been a wonderful experience. 'May the Lord Jesus not be less to you when I am with you again, said his note from Naples. On December 20 he was with her and the children at last.

The 'Millions' in full use (1877–78)

The Britain to which Hudson Taylor returned on December 20, 1877, was a fast changing nation. Yet Britain was being outpaced by other nations. These were exciting times of accelerating invention and discovery, of science and industry. In the last thirty years of the century British steel production (at first the major world supply) was to rise to five million tons. But Germany was to increase hers to seven million and the United States to thirteen million, as world shipping and railways expanded. Lighting by electricity and incandescent bulbs was beginning to replace the hissing gas mantle. The microphone and telephone, the spreading telegraphic network, and at long last comprehensive sanitation through the Public Health Act began to transform living conditions in Britain. And worldwide travel and exploration by Christian missionaries exceeded that achieved by others.

Christmas allowed the Taylor family a brief holiday together after their long separation, a working holiday for Hudson Taylor himself. Herbert, nearing seventeen, and Howard, already fifteen, were no longer the sparring children they had been but thinking adolescents. Maria, nearly twelve, had Millie Duncan as a younger sister, with Charles Edward, nine, and Jennie's two toddlers, Ernest and Amy, for company. But the creaking state of the Mission's administration in Britain cried aloud for attention.

With the honorary office holders as before unable to spare enough time from their professions, and members of the Mission staff in London hobbled by their subsidiary status, Hudson Taylor had no choice but to step straight into work and responsibility. Reorganisation was urgent. The Mission's income had become chronically low and, as Jennie had warned him in a letter received at Aden, some members of the Council were asking for more than the role they had

agreed to play in the Mission's affairs as a 'council of management' in Britain. Their claim was justified in that the selection of new members of the Mission was crucial, difficult and executive rather than advisory. Something so personal could not end with the individuals going abroad. But the principle of management of the Mission by participating leaders, rather than by boardroom directors, remained fundamental. For the moment action on that issue could be deferred, while he himself took the helm. To study the accounts and remit to China all he could send was his first aim.

Wherever he was, whatever his circumstances, creating an effective tool of each monthly issue of *China's Millions* continued to be an unrelenting priority. So easily could the magazine become a mere house-journal of news and anecdote. Every number must have a cutting edge, more than one, carrying its messages of many kinds deep into the awareness of readers. It must report to donors, inform and incite to action, if it was to justify so much thought and work. It was also the conductor's baton. Therefore each main theme must be chosen, and each leading article in the series 'China for Christ' must carry his insights to the Christian public. Christianity in Britain had become too comfortable and the Church turned in upon itself. 'Called to Suffer', the theme of one editorial, tried to restore right thinking. It was not only for the Mission's supporters, but intended for a far wider circulation, for Christian leaders, politicians and sister societies. It was as much his personal part in the evangelisation of China as almost any other role, whether directing the pioneers in their ventures or guiding the emerging churches in their development and witness.

So he crystallised his messages in his own mind and re-echoed them in a hundred and one different ways, never tiring of them himself or missing an opportunity to stress them. His skill as a communicator drew the comments of observers. 'Faith' he certainly mentioned as a biblical subject, but as a by-product and not as often as has been supposed. GOD's *faithfulness* was his recurrent theme: God himself, by his very character unable to default on his sure promises. A Father God, faithful to his own children-by-adoption and bound to meet their needs of guidance, protection or material provision, whether personal or incurred in serving him. 'Trust HIM at all times; you will never have cause to regret it,' was the logical conclusion. 'Hold GOD's faithfulness' expressed the essence of the Greek translated as 'Have faith in God', for the point was not a need to exert faith but God's reliability in response to any faith. 'All God's giants have been weak men,' Hudson Taylor pointed out in this same context: men like David, the secret of their greatness being dependence on GOD. 'Let us see that in theory we hold that God is faithful; that in daily life we *count* (we act) upon it.'[420]

Misconceptions of the aims and methods of the CIM led him also to reiterate year by year the core of his 'Plan of Operation'. Like the apostles, missionaries (Chinese and foreign together) would travel in small teams to strategic centres, stay there or return again for long enough to establish 'a work of God' and, trusting its continuation to the keeping of God, would move on to new regions. 'The necessity of a somewhat prolonged residence . . . for the purpose of instructing in the Word of God those who may be converted' was as much part of the plan as the itineration.

The emphasis on an indigenous Chinese church, in *China's Millions* of 1875–76 and again after the Shanghai conference in 1877, reflected the importance Hudson Taylor attached to the establishment of self-governing, self-supporting churches.[421] 'We propose to itinerate constantly at first, and consequently to carry on localised work *only for* a time [the emphasis in his] till native churches can be left to the ministrations of native labourers', with the help of visiting foreign teachers as long as it was needed and welcomed. Any perpetuation of Western denominational differences would be accidental, as individual missionaries left the mark of personal conviction on their teaching.

Apart from information about China and the progress of the CIM and other missions, all of which occupied many pages, one dominant topic claimed space at frequent intervals: opium. Henry Soltau wrote on the devastating effect of opium on the people of Burma, imposed on them by the British; Cardwell on the same effects in China:

> It is eating out the very vitals of the nation. It is the source of poverty; wretchedness, disease and misery, unparalleled in ... any other country. It debases the debased to the very lowest depths of degradation. It closes the eye to all pity, and the heart to all shame and sympathy. See that poor wretch with the emaciated frame? He has parted with his land, his house, his furniture, his children's and his own clothing and bedding, and either sold his wife or hired her out for prostitution, and all for opium, to satisfy an insatiable appetite ... until it has consumed his life.[422]

The leading article of the December issue of 1877 prepared as Hudson Taylor travelled in southern Zhejiang in September and October, bore the title 'Opium in China', followed by the words 'It is scarcely possible to think of England's responsibility in this matter without feelings of unspeakable humiliation and grief.' Travelling and settled missionaries alike wrote of vast numbers of people, even small children, smoking opium. Of nine viceroys all but three were said to be addicted. The resolution of the General Conference in Shanghai was then set out word for word, denouncing the trade, 'deeply injurious not only to China, but also to India, to Great Britain, and to the other countries engaged in it . . . It is a most formidable obstacle to the cause of Christianity' and should be 'speedily suppressed'. 'That which is morally wrong cannot be politically right.' The conference therefore urged that the (British) Indian Government cease to have anything to do with the production and sale of opium, and that attempts to obstruct the Chinese Government in its lawful efforts to suppress the sale and use of opium, should be opposed. That obstruction currently sprang from the government in Britain itself.

He ran a series of engravings and woodcuts to illustrate the use and effects of opium-smoking. And another series of eight factual articles on the history of the opium traffic, 'dignified' since the opium wars and treaties by the word 'trade'.[423] He quoted Li Hongzhang, Guo Sondao, the ambassador to Britain and France, and other leading Chinese on the inevitability of a Chinese backlash against this British atrocity; Mr Gladstone too; and Sir Rutherford Alcock who cynically blamed the mandarins for being defeated and then signing treaties admitting the curse to China, 'a sign of weakness and . . . of want of courage'! By creating a nation of addicts Britain had driven China to grow her own opium where grain used to be harvested, and by impoverishing a teeming population had deprived her own merchants of an immense potential market for consumer goods.

Through 1878 and subsequently, this championing of the 'anti-opium' cause in *China's Millions* increased in crusading intensity, without diminishing the vigour with which the spiritual need of China and the main work of missions were presented.[424] Nor did such topics prevent the graphic portrayal of a yet more horrifying (only because more urgent) topic: famine.

The Great Famine (1876–77)

Natural disasters were almost commonplace in China. Devastating typhoons struck the southern maritime provinces, bringing floods in their wake. 'China's Sorrow', the Yellow River, from time to time broke her banks and inundated county upon county. Earthquakes, locusts, plague, pestilence and revolutions succeeded one another with frightening frequency. Lingering drought since 1874 had caused hardship for southern Shanxi and the remnants of a population reduced in numbers, health and livelihood by the Muslim rebellion in Shaanxi following the Taiping scourge. As

far north as Linfen (Pingyang) in Shanxi the ruins left by the Taipings in 1853 were a grim reminder of bitter suffering at their hands. Evidence of great forests still remained on the Shanxi hills, stripped bare and eroded, so that from 1871 to 1875 vast areas of southern Zhili were inundated and scoured by floods which swept away the fertile topsoil. Hard on their heels in 1876 came drought and then famine lasting into 1880, extending to the border with Korea. Simultaneously the rains failed over the great area of eastern Shaanxi, most of Henan, southern Shanxi, and Shandong which at that time suffered most.[425]

South of the Yangzi, floods had played havoc with the harvests in central Hunan, Jiangxi and Zhejiang, but excessive rainfall in the southern coastal provinces of Fujian and Guangdong during the spring and summer of 1876 destroyed not only crops and homes but also thousands of people. 'As if this were not enough, a plague of locusts, devouring all they crossed, covered nearly the whole' of Jiangsu, inland Shandong and Zhili as far as north of Tianjin. Floods in five provinces, locusts in three and drought in nine during 1876 were succeeded in 1877 by drought and locusts again in much of the nine northern provinces. By then extreme distress due to the scarcity of food and its high prices had signalled the onset of what was believed to be the greatest famine the world had so far known.[426]

Timothy Richard (in 1874 the only one remaining of twelve members of the Baptist Missionary Society in Shandong) had moved from Yantai to Tsingchou (now Weifang) in 1875, and adopted Chinese clothes and a Chinese way of life. When famine set in he raised enough funds in Shanghai and other ports to begin distributing aid. The problem of orderly distribution to fighting mobs of starving people taxed his ingenuity. They went to all lengths, even of taking him prisoner with three cartloads of relief funds in coins. Then one day he read in 'the feeding of the five thousand', *'He made them sit down.'* In a flash he thought, 'A sitting crowd cannot crush.' Introduced with promises of orderly, fair distribution, the method succeeded. 'The *yamen* people were astonished.'[427] John Nevius joined him and the two of them distributed relief worth Mex. $200,000 in two months, in cooperation with the Chinese authorities. But the fields were unsown and Timothy Richard forecast 'fearful disease and mortality' in the coming spring. Even during the winter of 1876–77 while relief was being administered in Shandong and Zhili, tens of thousands died.

When Hudson Taylor arrived at Wuhan on January 9, 1877, he found Henry Taylor back from his fourth expedition to Henan and first expulsion from Queshan. Joshua Turner and Francis James had arrived the previous day from their 1,700-mile journey through the parts of north Anhui, Henan and southern Shanxi devastated by the Taipings. They had met 'several hundred people, all miserably clad, and looking starved and wretched' heading southward from the spreading famine area. But they described the watered Shanxi valley around Linfen as 'well cultivated' in November 1876.

From then onwards, reports of distress multiplied rapidly. Henry Taylor set off again on January 26, and Turner and James on February 10, into the same regions, with the intention of settling 'permanently'. They walked into famine conditions. People were selling their possessions for cash with which to buy food at exorbitant prices. Then they sold their furniture, clothes, doors and window frames, roof tiles, the timber frames of their homes, and then their wives and children.

Hudson Taylor, preparing for the Wuchang and Shanghai conferences, visiting all the Yangzi Mission centres and coping with 'four times as much work' as he could handle, was thinking hard. What could he do for the destitute? In February he had told Louise Desgraz to expand her boarding schools at Zhenjiang and Yangzhou to take in more girls, the beginning of wider plans. As he travelled he wrote an editorial 'Letter from China' for the *Millions*, on 'Concern for the poor'

and helpless. Psalm 41.1–3 had spoken to him. 'Do not let us spiritualise the text so as to lose its obvious meaning (of not merely sympathy but action). How much of the precious time and strength of our Lord was spent in conferring temporal blessings on the poor, the afflicted and the needy.'[428]

Reaction against a 'social gospel' had not yet clouded the judgment of evangelical Christians. Action 'at the cost of personal self-denial' was the measure of true 'concern'. At his instigation the Wuchang and Ningbo conferences contributed relief funds. And in this spirit he and Jennie were soon to go 'beyond the call of duty'.

'Concern for the poor'   (1877–78)

Hudson Taylor was in Shanghai, waiting for the newly widowed Annie Fishe and her children to join him and sail for home, when two letters came from Arnold Foster of the LMS. They had consulted together about the famine and Foster was raising relief funds in Yantai, Tianjin and Peking as William Muirhead was doing in Shanghai. Foster proposed going at once to the famine areas before returning with eye-witness accounts to arouse concern in Britain and the States. Henry Taylor and George Clarke were to take relief to Henan, and Turner and Francis James (recovering from typhoid fever) to distribute it in Shanxi. When food was available people were too poor to buy it, so even two teams of three men with cash to distribute could save thousands of lives.

The Chinese Government had granted 300,000 taels (£130,000), increased to 400,000 for its own relief measures, but they were 'utterly inadequate', 'a trifle . . . when we remember the corruption that exists among the officials and underlings who dole it out'.[429] Many altruistic mandarins were doing their best. Some gave even a year's salary to supplement their resources. Whatever was done, 'hundreds of thousands will be left to perish'. 'Considering the paucity of men who seem willing to join in the distribution' Foster wrote, he himself was torn between going to raise funds and staying to go inland with what there was.

The Chinese authorities would provide armed escorts for anyone carrying silver into the famine areas. Hudson Taylor wrote, as he sailed on November 9, that he would launch an appeal as soon as he reached home.

Meanwhile the autumn crops had failed again over the whole of the famine area. R. J. Forrest, British consul and (by Muirhead's request) chairman of the newly formed Famine Relief Committee at Tianjin, was to write: 'In November 1877, the aspect of affairs was simply terrible . . . Tien-tsin was inundated with supplies from every available port. The Bund was piled mountain high with grain, the Government storehouses were full. (All possible means of transporting it were commandeered and) the water-courses were crowded with boats, the roads were blocked with carts.'[430]

Disorganised relief measures were exacerbating the calamity.

A hundred thousand refugees had flocked into Tianjin, finding shelter in 'hovels made of mud and millet stalks', but typhus broke out and in the cold weather four to six hundred died each night. A camp for destitute women, its only exit locked, was destroyed by fire in three hours with the loss of 2,700 women. Lumbering wagons, and barges on such waterways as still held water, were robbed of their grain on the way to Hwailu (now Huolu) and the Guguan Pass. Dried up canals did form roads for refugees and relief convoys, but the 4,000 foot escarpment into Shanxi all but defeated such attempts as were made to scale it by cart and mule litter. As Consul Forrest reported:

> The result was visible in the piles of grain in bags, the broken carts and the foundered mules which strewed the road leading up to the plateau.[431]

> [On the one hundred and thirty mile mountain trail over the Guguan Pass] the most frightful disorder reigned supreme ... filled with (an enormous traffic of) officials and traders all intent on getting their convoys over the pass. Fugitives, beggars and thieves absolutely swarmed ...

> Camels, oxen, mules and donkeys ... were

2.38 A springless Peking cart (larger for long distances, with more animals)

killed by the desperate people for the sake of their flesh (while the grain they were meant to be carrying into Shanxi rotted and fed the rats of Tianjin). Night travelling was out of the question. The way was marked by the carcasses or skeletons of men and beasts, and the wolves, dogs and foxes soon put an end to the sufferings of any (sick) wretch who lay down ... in those terrible defiles ... No idea of employing the starving people in making new or improving the old roads ever presented itself to the authorities ... Gangs of desperadoes in the hills (terrorised the travellers) ... In the ruined houses the dead, the dying, and the living were found huddled together ... and the domestic dogs, driven by hunger to feast on the corpses everywhere to be found, were eagerly caught and devoured ... by the starving people. Women and girls were sold in troops to traffickers, who took the opportunity of making money in this abominable manner, and suicide was so common as hardly to excite attention.[432]

The natural southern route of access to Shanxi, from Tongguan in Shaanxi, across the Yellow River and into the central valley basin was undeveloped. The cart-tracks through billows and beds of dust could not sustain any bulk of traffic, even if supplies could pass through the equally terrible famine in Shaanxi. But streams of barely living refugees flowed southwards towards the well-watered Yangzi valley, littering the roadsides with corpses as they fell. Here too women and girls were being transported in exchange for cash or grain, their best hope being to become servant-chattels in southern homes. According to one report by Pere de Marche in May 1877, based on a register kept in the *yamen*, 100,000 women and children had already been sold from the one county of Lingqiu in north Shanxi.[433] This was the route taken in December by Joshua Turner, carrying the emaciated Francis James in a litter to Wuhan, already crowded with refugees.

On November 11, 1877, the imperial *Peking Gazette* published a memorial to the throne in which the viceroy, Zeng Guochuan, brother of Zeng Guofan, said, 'There remains neither the bark of trees, nor the roots of wild herbs, to be eaten,' in southern Shanxi. Autumn sowing had been impossible. No less than three or four million people were starving, but by December the price of grain was still rising. Altogether, in the worst affected provinces, seventy-five million were in 'a state of fearful destitution', Sir Thomas Wade declared in a letter to *The Times*. 'The inhabitants of the United Kingdom and the United States combined hardly number seventy millions,' *The Times* commented.[434] As far away as Xi'an in Shaanxi the price of bread was seventeen times its normal rate, but in Shanxi this was true of unmilled grain brought in by merchants and the government. Before the winter was out parents were eating their own children and neighbours were devouring those who died around them. The worst state of affairs had yet to be reached.

Britain was slow to react to appeals by the Lord Mayor of London, the Archbishop of Canterbury and the leading denominational missionary societies. Early in 1878 *The Christian* published a letter from Hudson Taylor which quickly led to donations being sent for famine relief, but because of the official action he kept his own appeals in a low key. The China Famine Relief Committee, formed in London in February with Arnold Foster as secretary, included Sir Rutherford Alcock, Sir Thomas Wade, Sir George Balfour, Sir Walter Medhurst, Robert Jardine, Professor James Legge and other men of influence. But as reports came from CIM missionaries, Hudson Taylor published them in *China's Millions* and the response grew steadily.[435]

By July he could write for the September issue of *China's Millions:*

> We took early occasion to draw attention to the great need, and in response were able to make our first remittance in September 1877. Since then we have received, including amounts given for orphanage (sic) £6,000. This we have gladly remitted to China for distribution. The (Shanghai Famine) Relief Committee have received about £30,000. The (combined) Missionary Societies have also received about £5,000 more. [For a more realistic impression multiply by, say, fifty.]

He pointed out that some of his donors also contributed to the 'General Relief Fund'.

> Many will eagerly ask, What is the total amount? ... Will it be believed that all that the people of England have given to lessen the sufferings of millions of people under a calamity such as the world has rarely if ever known, is only about £40,000! We think ... of the more than £500,000 contributed for ... the famine in India [Bengal in 1875 and southern India in 1876–77]. (Yet) we derive ... a revenue averaging about £150,000 weekly from the sale of opium in China. (For the five months since the appeals were launched) the sale of opium in China for the same period in other (than) famine years would amount to about £3,300,000. In other words, our revenue from that which is ruining China, would exceed in two days all we have yet given to relieve the suffering Chinese ... Why is this? ... Because the actual state of things is not generally known.

He devoted fourteen pages of this issue of *China's Millions* to the famine, two to the opium scandal and only two to the Mission's normal work.

At first the provincial mandarins resisted offers of help. What base motives had the barbarians this time? It would be better for China to suffer alone than to play into their hands. But when the cooperation of the Relief Committee and distributors (all of them missionaries) was welcomed by no less than the Grand Secretary, Viceroy of Zhili and Guardian of the Throne, Li Hongzhang, together with Zeng Guochuan of Shanxi, officials loyal to them followed suit. Only in Henan did Henry Taylor and George Clarke receive a rebuff when the authorities at Kaifeng refused their funds and assistance, and in Shaanxi where F. W. Baller and J. Markwick received the same treatment.[436]

The price of concern (March–May 1878)

During the last week of March 1878 Hudson Taylor asked Jennie to pray about a new proposition. Only four months after arriving home to end the fifteen-month separation that had at times seemed intolerable, he knew they must part again. The plight of China, especially of her women and children, was preying on his mind. The 'very low' state of the Mission's funds had not changed. Donations were coming in for famine relief rather than for Mission purposes. Even so it was then that he authorised the missionaries in famine and refugee areas to take in two hundred destitute children, giving priority to orphans.[437] He told Louise Desgraz that he was praying for an increase of £5,000 in annual receipts and an additional £2,000 for outfits and passages for new missionaries.

Jennie expressed her confidence in God by saying, 'He wills that we should feel the need of asking, but He *cannot* fail us.' Then Hudson Taylor made his suggestion, that as he himself could not leave Britain yet, she should go, escorting a party of new members and supervising the orphanage scheme in China until he could come and join her. No time could be lost. If women and children were to be saved it must be at once. She was thirty-five and had two infants of barely three and two. The youngest could go with her.[438]

Two years later Jennie wrote to tell the seven children what happened. After praying about it for two weeks she decided on April 12 that she should go, and told her nursemaid, Jane, who offered to stay and work for Amelia if that would help. Amelia was away, but when she heard the news she said, 'If Jennie is called to China, I am called to care for her children', if Jane would stay to help. Apart from her own four boys and six girls, Amelia was running

the Mission transit home and caring for candidates in training. To add Herbert and Howard, Maria and Milly Duncan, Charles Edward and Ernest would not make much difference. Before Jennie left, Amy, her baby, fell ill with whooping cough and had to be left behind too.

On April 16 Hudson Taylor told the council, and the next day Theodore Howard's mother, Hudson's old friend Mrs Robert Howard, called to say she thought it wrong for Jennie to leave her children and husband even for such a cause. As soon as she had gone Jennie went to her bedroom.

> I was feeling deeply how much it would cost me, so ... I asked God to confirm me in going, (saying, '£50 just now would be worth more to me than a fortune at another time; it would be a guarantee of all other needs being met.') I felt like Gideon that my strength in China would be, 'Have not I commanded thee?' and I wanted some fleeces to strengthen my own faith and as answer to those who would have me remain ... I did not doubt that God wanted me to go, but I felt sad ... like Gideon ... the least in his father's house ... the most unlikely one.[439]

The 'fleeces' she put out were two prayers, one for enough money for necessities for the journey 'as we had none to spare', £4 would cover it, and one for a sizeable sum, £50 (at least £2,000 today) for herself and Hudson personally. She told no one, not even him, but at family prayers the next morning she told the children she wanted them to pray with her for two things which she would reveal when the answer was given, 'as His promise that He will bless those I leave behind more than if I stayed with them, and that He will stand by me and help me'. That afternoon a Mr Hams of Jersey, (the friend who had sent Hudson a pair of gloves with a half sovereign inside, in 1852 (see 1, p 185)) called at Pyrland Road and asked, was she going? Yes, getting ready, she replied. He handed her a cheque for £10, the exact amount the Mission allowed for outfitting. 'I thanked God and watched eagerly for the £50 that I was expecting.'

On Monday, April 22, a letter came

from Hudson's parents addressed to her and containing £50. She took it to show him, but as he had someone with him, left it without a word. When she returned he was considering how the Lord would have the money applied, and she said, 'Oh, that money's mine. I have a claim on it that you do not know of.' Then she told him the story of her 'fleeces'. Ten days later she left home, escorting a party of four young men and three women to China, and cheered by a gift the previous day of £1,000 (thought to be from John Challice) for setting up an orphanage.

Among those who saw them off at the station to join the French Mail at Marseilles was William Sharp, a solicitor who had recently joined the London Council. Hudson Taylor's parting exhortation to the new missionaries to make 'gentleness and faithfulness' the hallmark of their service among the Chinese had impressed him. But the Taylors' parting from each other drew from him the confession, 'I felt just as if I were parting with my own wife, and the thought was altogether more than I could bear . . . and yet I suppose that if God *called us* to part, He would enable us to do so with the same calmness that you enjoyed yesterday.' For decades to come he was to be an indefatigable servant of the China Inland Mission.[440]

When they had gone, Hudson Taylor wrote letters of welcome to China, with a good remittance to greet each of the new pioneers on reaching Shanghai. And to Jennie, saying that her mother was proud of her—a transformation from her earlier attitudes. For himself he wrote, 'I, darling, am *grateful* for the grace which has taken you from me.' He began to run a daily fever, 'anything but exhilarating', and confessed, 'I wandered sometimes from empty room to empty room like one who did not know what he wanted,' adding, 'Milly clings a good deal.' His affinity for children had not left him, nor the motherless child's need for love. And later, 'I have more pleasure in you, in your absence, than your presence would afford; for it gives me more joy to see you enabled to put Jesus *first*, and find

in *Him* your present gain.' But to ease his loneliness he asked Herbert, preparing to enter the London Hospital Medical College, to come and share his study and bedroom. Famine relief donations were coming in steadily, and gifts of plate and jewelry. In China's agony they were doing what they could.

The famine at its worst[441] (1878)

After the terrible winter of 1877–78 the hopes of all rested upon spring rains so that something, anything, edible might come to life from the hard soil. Instead blue skies turned to brass as the season advanced. The *Peking Gazette* of March 15 carried a 'memorial' by the High Commissioner for Famine Relief, Yuan Baoheng, and by the governor of Henan. All the previously poor of the province, they testified, had disappeared—dead or dispersed to more fortunate provinces. In their place those who had been well-to-do or even wealthy were in the extremity of distress. Like the poor before them, those who could not move away (taking their valuables, only to be robbed on the roads) were resorting to cannibalism, even of their own kith and kin.[442] Consul R. J. Forrest also reported extensive cannibalism. But now it was no longer the dead and dying whose flesh was taken and skulls opened to extract the brains but, the *Peking Gazette* and *The Times* joined others in reporting that in some regions it had become unsafe to be alone, for some had taken to killing for food. Executions to deter villains had only limited success. Wolves, which had become more and more dangerous in country places, took to attacking men, women and children on city streets. Even after heavy showers in May, the first for three years, and more in July, the distress continued. Too weak to till and sow, many who had seed corn painfully hidden away dared not reveal it. What was sown had to be guarded until it could be harvested. The famine could only grow worse until October.

Hearing that conditions in Shanxi were worse than anywhere, Timothy Richard had left the famine relief in Shandong to his colleagues and travelled through stricken Zhili (Hebei) to Taiyuan, the Shanxi capital. The Peking and Tianjin Missions were supplementing Chinese government relief in their own province of Zhili. On November 30, 1877, when Richard reached Taiyuan with funds from the China Relief Committee and found that Turner and James had left only two days before, he consulted the mandarins, and following their advice began to organise relief work through the local officials of adjoining cities.[443] His courtesy and efficiency immediately impressed them and smoothed the way for all who joined him. He had made a study of etiquette and Confucian conduct.

Joshua Turner and Francis James reached Wuhan on January 22, 1878, from their interrupted 'permanent occupation' of Shanxi, and wrote poignant reports of travelling through 'ragged, homeless herds' of the starving, past corpse after corpse being devoured by dogs or birds. Their desperate appeals for help were among the first to be published. Lurid detail might move some donors who otherwise would read unmoved, as if it were a story.[444] James was too weak to return, but only eight days later, on January 30, Turner left him to regain his strength and, armed with funds contributed in Wuhan, started back to Shanxi. The overland route was too slow and dangerous. By river-steamer to Shanghai, from there by coaster to Tianjin, and inland through the Guguan Pass would take no longer. The Wesleyan Methodist missionary, David Hill, decided to go too, and joined him in Shanghai in mid-February. There a married man, Albert Whiting, an American Presbyterian from Nanjing visiting Shanghai, offered to accompany them, and they sailed together on March 9. Supplied by the Committee at Tianjin with 17,000 taels in silver (about £4,000–5,000) and given a military escort, they reached Taiyuan and joined Timothy Richard on April 2. Zeng Guochuan, the governor, and Commissioner Yuan immediately sent for them, treating them as honoured guests. To their proposal

to go on at once to Linfen (Pingyang), where the famine was most grim, the governor 'objected in a polite way, but very decidedly'. The reason soon emerged. The extreme difficulty of bringing grain into the province, and the inadequacy of government funds with which to meet so vast a crisis, had made it impossible for Zeng and Yuan to provide for every district. Consul Forrest wrote:

> Any distribution made in the districts where the Chinese had started no relief would inevitably lead to an insurrection among the desperate inhabitants, who have hitherto been accustomed in times of distress to join their disaffected neighbours in (Henan) and (Shandong), and carry fire and sword from the Yellow River to the valleys of the Han and (Yangzi). A few foreigners giving help where the mandarins were doing nothing would have excited the people at once, and the pillage of one or two *yamen*s, and the murder of a few (mandarins) would have been the signal for a general conflagration ... It may be fairly stated that while the foreign relief at one time, but for extreme good sense, gave cause for much political uneasiness, it eventually, by the emulation which it excited, prevented an insurrection with which the Chinese government might have found it hard to deal.

By taking over where the governor had begun, they freed him to tackle a new area. He sent a representative with Timothy Richard and Whiting to one city, while another took David Hill and Turner to a second. Within a few days Albert Whiting was desperately ill, and died on April 25, 'carried off by (famine) fever', typhus.[445]

He was not the first or the last to make this sacrifice. Famine fever continued rife in Tianjin and Peking and throughout the famine area, taking the lives of three French Sisters of Charity and several priests; the Methodist W. Nelthorpe J. Hall on May 14, barely sparing his wife; Letitia Campbell of the American Episcopal Church on May 18; and John S. Barradale of the LMS on May 25. His wife had succumbed to the fever in 1877.[446] 'Yuan Baoheng, the Famine Commissioner, followed next,' Consul

Forrest added, 'and a large number of the assistants employed in distributing aid died, or were disabled by typhus . . . (Later) Mr Turner, of the China Inland Mission, and Mr Smith, of the American Board, survived fearful attacks.' But in Turner's case it was dysentery that nearly proved fatal.

Their sacrifice went far towards convincing the literati that not all barbarians were unscrupulous. Some were sincerely devoted to China's welfare. Grand Secretary Li Hongzhang on hearing of Hall's death said to his adviser, the customs commissioner G. Detring, 'that there must be something in a faith which induced the foreign gentlemen to come to China and gratuitously risk their lives, and even forfeit them' for the Chinese.[447] One of the CIM famine relief workers, unnamed, wrote as this toll increased, 'It is probable that others of us will be called away. We must hold ourselves prepared, though of course we shall use every precaution against the fever. If I die . . . I wish to be buried here.' His colleagues used much the same words.

They quickly won confidence by systematic preparations that proved their integrity and the reliability of the people they dealt with.

> Our plan is to take the money in cash to the village temple, and then go round to the families on the list, with one of the headmen, see the house, make some inquiries, compare their statements with the number of mouths entered on the list, then give them a ticket for money which they take immediately to the temple to be cashed. In some instances we strike off the name altogether. This plan is very laborious, but it brings us into contact with the people themselves, and prevents unfairness ... We gave money to one village but the next day the headmen brought back the share of twenty people, saying they had (died) since the lists were made, only a few days ago.

> Today, one representative of each family from seven villages came by appointment to our temple. They gathered in the open space in front of the door and were admitted, two villages at a time, into the temple yard. Mr Richard distributed to one, and I (Turner) to the other. Each person came up to the table when his name was called, and received 800 cash (about three shillings) for each needy member of his family ... In this way the wants of 1,400 or more persons and their families were supplied. In the evening it began to rain, and soon was pouring heavily ... Rain and money to buy seed came together.[448]

Jennie reached Shanghai on June 13 with her seven companions, where she handed them over to Baller, Judd and George Clarke. The women they took to the Mission language school at Yangzhou and the men to Anqing. Adam C. Dorward was to become the intrepid pioneer of Hunan, J. H. Riley of western Sichuan, and Samuel R. Clarke of the minority tribes of Guizhou. Fanny Rossier of Lac Leman, Switzerland, married George Clarke and went to Dali in Yunnan, weeks of travel beyond her pioneer 'sisters' by then in Chongqing and Guiyang.

July was the hottest time of year, and Wuhan proverbial as one of China's 'three furnaces'. Jennie's first job was to get the two hundred famine orphans into existing CIM premises, the CIM schools or into other care in the Yangzi valley region. She conferred with Louise Desgraz at Zhenjiang, went on to Anqing and back to Nanjing. Apart from one or two found here and there, the Yangzi valley turned out to be the wrong place for the purpose. Thousands of women and children were arriving from the north, to be quickly sold and carried off, out of reach. More significantly, the old rumours of exploitation of children by foreigners for sinister and immoral purposes had not died out. It was unsafe to collect children except in the famine areas.[449] Then a letter reached her from Hudson Taylor, written on May 10 soon after she had left him. If orphanages should prove impracticable in the Yangzi region, he suggested, she should consider going to the heart of the famine, to Shanxi.

She had already written to Joshua Turner and Timothy Richard for advice. Was there scope for two or three women to help them? But at Nanjing she contracted cholera. It was widespread. William

Rudland's second wife died of it on June 29, and Fanny Jackson on August 21, within twenty-four hours of her first symptoms. Chauncey Goodrich of Tianjin had married on May 30 and was widowed on September 3. But Jennie recovered quickly and was at Yangzhou when replies arrived from Shanxi. Typically she made little of her narrow escape. 'I spent some time in Nanking.'[450]

Consul Forrest reported on the actions of the Tianjin Relief Committee:

> In June, Mr Richard had begun to interest himself on behalf of some of the poorest orphans of (Taiyuan) and had fixed on a temple in which to locate them, when the Governor (Zeng) informed him that he (himself) would undertake such an institution in the city, and forwarded the rules under which he proposed to conduct it. [Very likely this too was to forestall accusations against the foreigner.] Mr Richard, thereupon, with the Governor's approval, commenced a systematic relief to the orphans, widows and aged, in some scores of the surrounding villages. In September, 1878, seven hundred and forty-four names were enrolled under the superintendency of Mr Turner, and on the 17th January, 1879, the numbers were Orphans, 822; Aged and Widows, 334—Total, 1156. Mr Hill, at Pingyang Fu, had adopted a similar plan with the approval of the officials.

It was August 8 when Jennie heard from Turner and Richard that her 'letter came to them as the answer to many prayers'. The opportunity in Shanxi was unique, they said.[451] On the ninth William Muirhead, as organizing secretary of the China Famine Relief Fund, also wrote saying, 'Children could be obtained without prejudice to the missionary cause' in Shandong and Zhili—only eight years after the Tianjin massacre of orphanage nuns. 'The only safe way at present is to open an orphanage in the famine district.' By then Francis James was recuperating in Yantai and about to marry Marie Huberty, a Belgian who, like him, had joined the Mission in 1876. Jennie enlisted two more of their contemporaries, Celia Horne and Anna Crickmay, and with the ubiquitous Frederick Baller to escort them,

sailed from Shanghai on September 21 to Tianjin.[452] They were waiting there for the honeymoon couple to join them when news came that Joshua Turner was alone and dangerously ill in Shanxi.

In May, David Hill and Turner had been permitted to start famine relief at Linfen (Pingyang) in the south of the province, with an official to vouch for them. And after bringing 51,890 taels of silver from Shanghai to the Committee in Tianjin, an American Presbyterian from Zhili named Jasper McIlvaine had begun distributing 3,000 taels of relief money at Tsechou (now Jincheng) also in the south of Shanxi. Between then and the end of September, Richard, Hill, Turner and McIlvaine had between them identified and provided 100,641 people with about 500 cash each, enough to keep them alive until such harvest as there might be. Then, as Timothy Richard wished to make a fleeting visit to Shandong to get married, Turner took his place for a few weeks, providing for the aged and orphans around Taiyuan. Two weeks later he became so ill with dysentery that by the time David Hill had come to the rescue on September 26 he was hovering between life and death. They needed help without delay.[453]

Baller and the three women set off as soon as the news reached them and, travelling by boat to Baoding, by cart to the foot of the pass and from there by mule-litter, arrived at Taiyuan on October 23. To their surprise the people of these disaster areas were friendly and open, unlike the reticent folk in the Yangzi valley. Francis James and his bride arrived a few days later and the Richards soon after them. Three more men for Shanxi, Parrott, Elliston and Drake, sailed on November 14.

The prospect of 'any number' of

2.39 A common mule litter for the mountains (more stylish for mandarins)

children to care for, as Turner said, led Jennie to rent premises, set up an 'industrial school' for destitute women and begin taking in orphans. On November 22, Hudson Taylor wrote suggesting that she assess the prospects in Linfen also. By December both her refuge and Timothy Richard's school for destitute boys were daily being asked to take in more, but not to the extent expected. Deliberately, the governor's orphanage was admitting most.[454] All the same, with the 1,156 orphans and elderly in the missionaries' care one way or another, their hands were full. Shortly before Christmas two Yantai missionaries of the SPG, C. P. Scott and Albert Capel, joined David Hill at Linfen until May 1879, with 3,000 more taels, and Jennie deferred a move by the CIM in that direction. It later became the Mission's major sphere in Shanxi.

By February 1879 she herself had done what she came to do, and could leave the orphanage and 'industrial school' to Anna Crickmay and Celia Horne under Joshua Turner's care. (In 1881 he married Anna.) Jennie left Taiyuan on the 11th with Frederick Baller and was back in Shanghai on March 5, to meet Hudson Taylor and the reinforcements he was bringing.[455] Autumn rains had brought the prospect of food for all in 1879. But April and May were to see the highest death rate of the whole famine, from malnutrition, typhus, dysentery and, on top of it all, smallpox.

'A turning point' (1879)

The first rains in 1878 had held out some hope of an autumn harvest, but that still lay months ahead. The distress had become worse and worse until October, while speculators' mountains of grain rotted at Tianjin, waiting for the means of transport to improve. In northern Shanxi a third of the population died, according to Timothy Richard's careful estimate. Officials had no way of keeping accurate records. The village headman knew best. In southern Shanxi David Hill and Jasper McIlvaine estimated that three-quarters perished in each relief area. The Peking authorities placed the total at five and a half million in Shanxi, two and a half million in Zhili, one million in Henan and half a million in Shandong by the spring of 1879 when good harvests were expected. Nine and a half million died. To convey the government allocation of grain to Linfen in early 1879 would have cost one and a half million taels, before it could be distributed. By the sale of official titles and honours, 200,000 taels had been assigned for this.

A new horror then claimed more victims. Among those who had survived to enjoy eating again 'a pestilence of dysentery beat out typhus as soon as the harvest was gathered, and the stomachs of the people were inflamed by too great indulgence in unaccustomed foods'. Fields of millet stood unharvested, sagged and decayed. Their owners had died and others were too weak to do the work. Millions with no fields or income were dependent still on outside help. The London relief committees misunderstood news of the first rains and first harvest and closed their books in September 1878, even though in July the Shanghai committee had cabled, 'Available means exhausted. Appeal for prompt transfer of £5,000.' Recovery would depend on outside help for several more months.[456]

Although the aid to China amounted to about £50,000, 'a paltry sum' in the circumstances, of which £8,000 came through the CIM, £10,000 through other societies, and the rest through the London committee, the initial response had not been sustained. In his preface to the 1878 bound volume of *China's Millions* (issued in 1879) Hudson Taylor said:

> Is it not humbling to think that the entire amount raised for the famine relief during 1878, though it has called forth (gratitude) from the most influential official in the empire (Li Hongzhang) and from the Chinese Ambassador in London (Guo Sondao), is actually exceeded by the amount we through our Indian government receive in three days from the sale of opium in China.

When Marquis Zeng succeeded Guo as ambassador in February 1879, he too expressed his gratitude and his wish to meet Hudson Taylor. In most of China a new attitude to missionaries was becoming apparent. They were being received 'kindly' and 'with respect'.[457] Consul Forrest testified of the relief workers:

> The officials treat the missionaries now with the most marked cordiality and assist them in every way in their power ... That obdurate class 'the literati and gentry' are ... confessing that their efforts for the relief of the suffering millions are not only an example to them but has really been the incentive which has produced Chinese action.

> H.E. the Grand Secretary and Viceroy, Li Hong-chang, did me the honour of dining with me yesterday, to celebrate Her Majesty's, birthday ... the first time a viceroy has accepted a consul's invitation to dine with him. He spoke most feelingly and thankfully of the (relief) efforts.[458]

F. H. Balfour, another British official, also wrote: 'The sight of so much self-sacrificing labour and Christ-like self forgetfulness . . . has filled the (Chinese) with astonishment . . . Are these the foreigners we have heard so much about— the malignant, unscrupulous, deceitful foreigners?'

To a very small extent the self-denial of the relief workers was atoning for the immense wrongs done to China. But, Hudson Taylor commented, the desperate spiritual state of the Chinese people was only beginning to dawn on the Western church.

In gratitude China contributed in 1880 to the Irish Relief Fund. The days of uncomprehending prejudice and hostility were passing. Relatively progressive men like Li Hongzhang still had the diehards at Peking and the superstitious to contend with, but with American engineers and equipment the Kaiping mines had begun work in 1877, and the Shanghai Steam Navigation Company merged with the China Merchants Steam Navigation Company.[459] Dr Halliday Macartney, director of Li Hongzhang's arsenal at Nanjing, accompanied Guo Songdao

to London and for thirty years, until December 1905, was 'the able, loyal and trusted adviser of each successive Chinese envoy' to London.[460]

On February 3, 1879, George Clarke, this time with A. G. Parrott as a companion, left Wuhan for Shanxi. They travelled via Queshan where a mandarin apologised for the treatment Henry Taylor and Clarke had previously received, and through Zhengzhou to Jincheng (Tsechou) in Shanxi.[461] Jasper McIlvaine had finished his work and gone, so they took responsibility for several villages which neither he nor the government had been able to help. Going from village to village and house to house, what moved them most deeply was 'the grief of the people that their gods had failed them' while strangers had kept them alive until things began to grow again. 'An old widow would walk several miles . . . merely to present us with a few vegetables as a token of her gratitude.' With returning hope also came revived hatreds: 'several attempts were made to get up a riot and expel us from the city'. So they moved on to Linfen, joining Turner and Elliston. By the summer little relief work remained for them to do, and they were free to spend their days preaching the gospel.

A journey of inspection was made in 1879 by W. C. Hillier of HBM consular service, Shanghai, on behalf of the China Famine Relief Committee with 2,000 taels to distribute to Shanxi.[462] Taking S. B. Drake, another of the newly arrived CIM men, for company, he left Wuhan on January 10. Southern Henan they found to be 'under cultivation as far as eye could see' but the people as 'contemptuous of the foreign devil' as in normal times—sure proof that Hillier was in foreign clothes. 'Mr Drake being in Chinese dress passed unnoticed.' But northern Henan showed all the physical signs of famine, in dismantled homes and government concentrations of refugees.

> Many towns and villages were almost empty ... (we heard) nothing but the echo of our own footsteps as we hurried through ... cities of the dead. We had the curiosity to enter into one of these houses, but the

sight that awaited us there gave us both so terrible a shock that we went into no more ... We gave up talking much about the things we had seen. The misery was too deep to be discussed. Only in some homes were the dead in coffins or bricked in by their families—to foil the certain alternative of being exhumed and eaten by starving neighbours.

At Linfen on February 18 they found Scott and Capel occupying a temple allocated to them by the authorities, and Richard and Turner living with David Hill in 'his own hired house'. Hillier and Drake handed over the funds to Hill and joined in their distribution. The thoroughness and wisdom of the way it was done drew praise from Hillier. Lest any headman should be accused of profiting from the distribution of funds, each was made a payment in full view of all, for the work they had put into drawing up lists and escorting the distributors from place to place.

Hillier left Linfen on February 25 and like Jennie took the road through 'the terrible (Guguan) Pass' to Tianjin. 'I met thousands of mules, donkeys, camels and men streaming through the Pass . . . all laden with grain . . . even little boys nine or ten years old being pressed into the work . . . Thousands of people are thus enabled to earn enough to support themselves.' In his report he dealt in gruesome detail with the deprivations by wolves and the lengths to which cannibalism had descended, before reviewing the measures needed to prevent a repetition of such a famine—reforestation, road-making and eventually a railway even through those mountains. Nowhere in the records studied is there any mention of men being mobilised to widen the roads, improve the gradients and eliminate the bottle-necks while the famine lasted. R. J. Forrest also discussed the major measures needing to be undertaken by the Government. 'Venality and utter corruption' were the greatest problem, Hillier continued. In Shanxi 'even to myself, a "barbarian" in the genuine barbarian dress, perfect civility was shown in and around Linfen, while to Messrs

2.40 'The live eat the dead' (woodcut used to raise famine funds in the provinces with plenty).

Richard, Hill and Scott [those fluent in Chinese] the respect was very marked.' (Not surprisingly a strong church resulted.)

From sixteen or seventeen times the previous market price, the value of grain had returned to five or six times the norm, and then to merely double the old price. The true famine was all but over, at a cost of not less then ten million lives, and probably thirteen million, with the expenditure of 125,487,858 taels by the Tianjin Famine Relief Committee alone.[463] But food was only one factor. Homes and livelihoods had still to be rebuilt. Even as far away as Gansu in 1880, George Easton found himself debarred from a house because in it were refugee women huddled together for warmth, through lack of clothing. He bought and distributed supplies of second-hand clothes.[464]

Other refugees had returned home hearing that harvests were being reaped, only to die because there was little to go round. The armchair critics could complain of *ad hoc* philanthropy being misplaced, money, labour and lives poured into a sieve, where prevention would have been better. But once the disaster had struck, it was cure, not prevention, that was needed. The climate was beyond control, the destruction of forests had gone on for centuries, the venality of officials was beyond the influence of missionaries except in the long term, and *fengshui,* the barrier to the provision of road and rail, could only be circumvented by the Chinese themselves. Li Hongzhang did his conservative best, only to meet strong resistance. He yielded for the time being. Of about thirty missionaries who left their regular work to do famine relief, twelve were young men and women of the CIM.[465] Alexander Wylie of the LMS and Bible Society paid tribute to them at a meeting chaired by Lord Shaftesbury. 'Among the earliest volunteers were members of the China Inland Mission . . . There is one . . . fact of such a noble character that I think it ought to be held up to view, I mean the conduct of the heroic lady Mrs Taylor.' But leading the way and making so great a success of it were Timothy Richard of the BMS and David Hill of the WMMS. Joshua Turner had twice come close to death, and Francis James once. Only Albert Whiting of the American Presbyterian Mission gave his life in Shanxi, the other deaths being in Zhili. But following a severe illness while taking relief to Shaanxi, Markwick progressively lost his sight and had to leave China.

In 1880 the magistrate of Linfen Xian erected a six-foot stone tablet at the temple of the Linfen city god, giving what David Hill called 'the most accurate, vivid and concise' account of the famine Hill had seen.[466] He told of a magistrate in Shandong who donated a whole year's salary, which prompted the leading literati of his city also to make large donations. Their 3,000 taels had been distributed unostentatiously in Linfen Xian. A glowing tribute to Hill, Turner and Richard (in that order) necessarily ended with the words, 'How profound then and how long-continued must have been the influence of the virtue and beneficence of his sacred

Majesty the Emperor, that they should thus be moved by the call of Heaven.'

In his book *The British in the Far East,* the historian George Woodcock described Hudson Taylor's mission (as he called the CIM) as,

a movement of dedicated men and women who would seek 'absolute simplicity in everything' ... Sectarian disputes should be abandoned as unnecessary luxuries, an interdenominational movement, linked to no one Church, should be established, aimed at teaching uncontroversial Protestant Christianity ... (with) a new type of missionary who would be willing to live and travel as an ordinary Chinese might do, and to look and speak like him, except that his speech would be of Christ ... From their initiative sprang a deeper involvement, among missionaries in general, in the massive social problems of China. In this respect the relief work undertaken by British mission workers during the great famines of 1876 to 1878 was a turning point ... It is significant that Timothy Richard, the English Baptist who led the famine relief of 1876, should more than twenty years later have founded the Shansi Provincial University, one of the pioneer institutions of its kind in China.[467]

In 1880 a very highly qualified physician and surgeon, Harold Schofield, joined the CIM and began work at Taiyuan. The medical arm of the Mission had begun in earnest, to lead on to hospitals and leprosaria in several provinces, and many dispensaries.

The year apart (May 1878–April 1879)

We return to Hudson Taylor. Reunion with his family for Christmas 1877 had been a necessary but secondary reason for his return home. The state of the Mission in Britain had compelled it. Hudson Taylor had had to rely on a make-shift staff of inexperienced men under the control of the 'council of management'. During his 'forty week' absence in China, Jennie had provided some stability, but management by part-timers, however devoted, had not been successful. Even the help of John

McCarthy had failed to provide the needed coherence. When William Berger had been director, Hudson Taylor, although far away in China, had seldom felt so out of touch as Berger's successor had left him. With so much happening in China he was needed there above all. In as short a time as possible while in Britain he must reorganize. He must shed much of the routine burden of *China's Millions* as soon as he could find a reliable co-editor; and appoint an executive secretary empowered to get the administrative work done. He must also interview and send to China as many as he could of the twenty-four or more new missionaries he was praying for.

The number of constant friends of the Mission, committed to caring about China, praying and influencing others for the salvation of her dying millions, was still pathetically small. Spasmodic enthusiasm over pioneer journeys, famine or response to the gospel was not enough. So immense a cause needed commitment by many churches, personifying the Church at large, and by many more individuals with the devotion of his own parents and Amelia, of the Howards, Miss Stacey, Lord Radstock, the Beauchamps and others who never lost interest or stopped praying. This meant personally meeting as many as possible who showed initial concern, and addressing all the audiences he could. The knowledge that he was back in Britain led to more than enough opportunities of every kind.

After Jennie left Britain in May 1878 he gave himself increasingly to this work. He made a point of visiting each of his council members in his own home, to listen and to build on his dedication to the cause. He preached at churches of most denominations and at a succession of conferences. According to John Stevenson he always carried 'an 18-province revolver in his pocket', a folding map of China to help people grasp intelligently what was going on, the extent of the famine, and the significance of the great journeys being made. He had a copy of the map with the journeys marked on it bound into each annual volume of *China's Millions*, and at the twelfth anniversary meetings of the CIM he emphasised the importance of all that the map demonstrated.

Factual reports of the Mission's progress took pride of place, but Hudson Taylor's closing address went to the heart of the matter in two points he constantly made. Not surprisingly the first was 'the faithfulness of God', but the second stressed the moral and spiritual danger to young missionaries in a pagan environment, and therefore the need of unfailing prayer for them.[468] Expansion of the Mission's commitments had drawn questioning comments from some. So he reminded his audience that the successful adventure of invading and occupying the nine unevangelised provinces had been financed by funds donated specifically for that purpose, over and above the income for other purposes. But with the already increased liabilities, was the current move to send twenty or thirty *more* men and women prudent,

> with a current income not equal within a thousand or two thousand pounds to the expenses of the Mission? ... Well, we have looked the thing in the face ... and this is (our) conclusion: that with the current income of the Mission we have nothing to do, but with God we have everything to do; that *we* are not going to send out twenty or thirty missionaries, or one, but we are going to ask *God* to send (them); and if He sends (them) He is just as able to supply them as ... those who went previously. [To the incredulous or cynical this may have sounded disingenuous, but of his translucent sincerity those who knew him were in no doubt. As for candid statements of the financial position, this was another annual business meeting of the equivalent of shareholders. Far more important were the purely spiritual issues.] If this is a real work for God it is a real conflict with Satan ... We should not underrate the powers of darkness ... *This is the thing that causes me concern* ... that God *will keep* our young (men and women) in spheres where they will be surrounded by such a mass of moral pollution ... of scepticism and infidelity, as is enough to swamp them, to destroy their faith.[469]

He could have named colleagues he had in mind, and the influence of theologically unstable missionaries, but he spoke prophetically. In the next few years he was to grapple with case after case of defeat and defection.

No General Missionary Conference had been held since the first in Liverpool in 1860. In confidence to Jennie, Hudson Taylor described the second, held at the Mildmay Conference Centre, October 22–25, 1878, as 'stiff, hard, cut and dried', neither well managed nor well attended and, in contrast with the inspiring Shanghai Conference of the previous year, sadly disappointing. But it had highlighted the unity of 'the field which is the world', as India, Africa and the islands of the seas as well as China had been represented. He had shared the platform at two meetings on China with his old friends Bishop John Burdon and Professor James Legge, and with Dr J. L. Maxwell of Taiwan, and reported them verbatim in the *Millions.* His own subject was 'The Progress and Success of Protestant Missions in China'. The annual Mildmay Conference and another in Glasgow claimed him for several addresses, but also to interview men and women wanting to go with him to China. In a stonemason[470] named William Cooper he was to see great hope for the future. The result of a year's work was that fourteen men and fourteen women left in 1878 and four more men in March 1879, followed by two in November.

Economic depression and political excitement over Russian expansionism from Turkey to Turkestan led potential donors to conserve their personal wealth, and missions suffered in consequence. Even when international pressure forced Russia to negotiate with China over Kuldja and Ili, the slow progress was parallelled by low giving and consequent perplexity for Mission leaders. At this time, however, new sources of income emerged. Lord Radstock, not a wealthy man, often sent donations to the Mission from wherever he might be in his travels as an evangelist on the Continent. During 1878 he was in Sweden, well received by the truly Christian queen, and largely responsible for a growing interest in missions to China. A donation came from Jonkoping towards the orphanages, and in mid-January 1879 a gift of £200 to Hudson Taylor from Stockholm. Thomas Berger increased his contribution to £2,000 in the year. And the philanthropist Robert Arthington, to whom Hudson Taylor had appeared 'humble and very intelligent', arranged to meet him and offered £100 if the CIM were to devote a missionary to the tribal Miao of Guizhou, a plan already afoot.[471] Through Wylie's influence the Bible Society of Scotland offered £60 and the BFBS £100 towards the support of colporteurs working with CIM missionaries.

But as the year progressed there seemed to be no answer to the problem of administration in Britain after Hudson Taylor left again. George Soltau resigned and emigrated to Tasmania. Richard Hill proposed the appointment of William Soltau as a salaried secretary. The council minuted that in his representation of the CIM all over Britain, Benjamin Broomhall needed 'authentication' and in March resolved that he and William Soltau should be 'assistant secretaries'.[472] Hudson Taylor was praying for 'organizing capacity' in himself, 'The Lord make me equal to increasing claims.'[473] In August he mentioned to Jennie that William Soltau's heart was not in his work, and that Benjamin although enthusiastic was 'never up to time and cannot economize. I do not now see a wise and prompt editor for *China's Millions,* (so) I must not leave till there is someone . . . who sees things from my standpoint, and on whom I can depend'. The need for administrators in China was as great, with the Mission growing so fast. Yet he himself at forty-six was senior to all other members with the exception of Elizabeth Wilson and Benjamin, and none yet showed the needed ability.

A return of 'ague' in June and July reduced Hudson Taylor to such poor health that the Beauchamps invited him to join them in the south of France and Switzerland. He had to take work with him, and for some days could not climb with the others, from pain in his side, but by early September was up on a glacier on three successive days, and walking seven or eight miles at a time, sometimes alone.[474] 'I am here for work—the work of getting well again,' he wrote. The effect of 'pure air from pure white peaks' was 'indescribable'. One day was doing him a month's good, the result of 'all this pleasure and all this kindness'. Then a day with William Berger in Paris 'to regain his full sympathy', and he was back at his desk and off again by the night train to the Dundee Conference, feeling 'wonderfully well'.

His eldest son, Herbert, was at medical college, and Howard, the second son, would soon be ready to join him although not yet seventeen. So Hudson Taylor arranged with the trustees of Maria's endowment of her children to advance the fees. That settled, he still had to arrange for the Mission before he could leave for China.

For lack of an obvious solution he appears to have aimed at a course of trial and error or a bold venture of faith, like walking on water. In September he deputed more work on the *Millions* to Benjamin, even to writing a major editorial, but someone to take over the chief responsibility was still 'a great unmet need' in December. He hoped to sail in February. January came and he told the council he must go. Invitations to speak at meetings in Holland crystallised his thoughts. He would go there on the way to Marseilles and the French mail boat to China. On February 4 the council minuted that Hudson Taylor would continue as editor, supplying John McCarthy with material and full instructions from China. But 'Mr Broomhall who will take the general direction of this and the rest of the home work' would supply items relating to 'home proceedings'. McCarthy was to take over 'meetings in the country', and Benjamin would deal with candidates until the council invited them to come into residence.

In view of what was to happen, a little more about this arrangement maybe useful. The next day, February 5, another minute read: 'That Mr Broomhall be appointed the General Secretary of the Mission, with the distinct understanding on the part of Mr Taylor and the Council and himself, that he is considered responsible for the general superintendence and conduct of the home work of the Mission, Mr McCarthy and Mr (W.) Soltau agreeing to act under his direction.'[475]

Hudson Taylor told the council that he had asked Theodore Howard in the event of his (Hudson Taylor's) decease, 'to undertake, if only for a time, the position of Director of the Mission . . . He hoped that ultimately there might be found in China . . . some one or more competent to direct the foreign work.'

Again on February 10 they met to carry the arrangements further. Theodore Howard was appointed Director in Britain during Hudson Taylor's absence, with an emphasised reiteration of the principle 'that the *general* function of the council is *to advise* the Director or Directors for the time being'. This definition by the council itself answered those members who had wanted greater control, and went on to endorse the decision of February 5 by stressing that: '(Mr Broomhall's) responsibility was not in any way diminished, nor the relationship of his fellow-workers to himself altered, but that in Mr Howard he would have one to whom he could refer in any circumstances requiring direction . . . It was with this understanding . . . that (Mr Howard) had accepted the position of Director.'

He could not take on more than that.[476] A 'president and premier' administration had been adopted, and after its teething troubles worked well enough for a while. No longer secretary to the Anti-Slavery Association Benjamin now concentrated his energies on China. The total membership of the Mission had been thirty-eight when he first joined the staff in 1875, and was sixty-nine in May 1879. When he retired in 1895 to devote his last sixteen years to the abolition of Britain's scandalous opium trade there were 630 members.[477] After praying for organizing ability, Hudson Taylor had found his way through the impasse but, knowing Benjamin so well since boyhood together, he acted with no little courage. They had very much in common. Their openness to all denominations was a particular asset in a transdenominational missionary society. Benjamin won the label of Baptist by presenting volumes of C. H. Spurgeon's sermons to outgoing missionaries, although he himself was both Anglican and Methodist in sympathy. He had found his niche and within five years was riding the crest of the Mission's heyday, a development impossible for anyone to foresee.

Arrangements for Britain were only part of the picture. Sir Thomas Wade had returned to Peking and the CMS was feeling his prejudice again, following extremes of oppression in Fujian. The new theological college at Fuzhou was burned down on August 30, 1878, but reparations offered by the Chinese Government were diverted by the consul to the purchase of land for a race course, Eugene Stock recorded.[478] Hudson Taylor advised that CIM personnel should avoid passing through Tianjin lest word of their destinations inland should prompt Wade to restrict their movements. He planned that when the famine ended, stations should be opened in southern Shanxi from which to work in resistant Henan and Shaanxi. Later he wrote that Wade was not only taking strong action against the CMS but 'really against all missionary work (outside) foreign concessions'. Anti-French feeling and the war clouds of the Franco-Chinese hostilities in Indo-China in the 1880s were gathering. 'Things look dark for Missions in south China, and the same spirit and persecutions may spread northwards, but the LORD reigneth.'

The endless round of meetings continued, and the Mission's day of prayer was observed on December 31 at Pyrland Road. The varied nature of Hudson Taylor's life still had its medical episodes, even in Britain. An epidemic of 'spasmodic croup' was carrying off many small children in London, but under Hudson Taylor's treatment the Ballers' younger daughter

was recovering. During the well-attended evening prayer meeting her nurse came to the door with the child in her arms, called Mrs Baller (Mary Bowyer) and showed her that the child was 'dead', blue and limp. They called Hudson Taylor. His first efforts to resuscitate her failed, but with mouth to mouth respiration for several minutes the child's colour changed and she began to breathe. Through the night she had occasional convulsions but survived unharmed—to become a member of the Mission in Hunan.[479]

A sidelight on the incident typified Hudson Taylor's attitude to prayer. When he was called to help, a woman in the meeting with strong faith-healing convictions appealed to him to pray for the child. 'Yes, pray,' he answered as he hurried out, 'while I work.' His son Howard's comment in later years when they had been close companions in many situations was, 'He prayed about things as if everything depended upon the praying . . . but he worked also, as if everything depended on his working.'[480]

Back to the fray (February–April 1879)

Hudson Taylor crossed over to Holland on February 24, and spoke at four meetings at The Hague and Amsterdam, although 'almost too tired to think' from the pressure of last things to attend to before leaving London. To Benjamin, in charge without Hudson Taylor to consult, he wrote that he had been caught out, not knowing the language—a collection had been taken! Among many words of advice he said characteristically, 'I should not hesitate to shorten our (weekly) prayer meeting if ever it should seem to drag.'[481] Detailed instructions followed on how to cross Paris by cab, for the party of young men due to join him on the ship: J. J. Coulthard, William J. Hunnex, Henry W. Hunt, T. W. Pigott (paying his own way), William McCarthy and his wife. His hostess insisted until he agreed, on paying for a first class 'sleeper' to Marseilles. But this time through no fault of his own his medicine chest could not be found on the ship, with dire results. It had been crated for him, unlabelled as to contents. From Marseilles he paid a quick visit to William Berger at Cannes, and to George Müller and C. H. Spurgeon at Mentone.

Describing him in his magazine *Sword and Trowel* Spurgeon said:

> Mr Taylor ... is not in outward appearance an individual who would be selected among others as the leader of a gigantic enterprise; in fact, he is lame in gait, and little in stature; but ... his spirit is quiet and meek, yet strong and intense; there is not an atom of self-assertion about him, but a firm confidence in God ... His faith is that of a child-man ... too certain of His presence and help to turn aside ... (He has) about him a firmness which achieves its purposes without noise ... He provokes no hostility, but ... arouses hearty sympathy, though he is evidently independent of it, and would go on with his great work even if no one countenanced him in it ... The word China, China, China is now ringing in our ears in that, special, peculiar, musical, forcible, unique way in which Mr Taylor utters it ... He did not deny the fact (that he was already growing a queue).[482]

He had been ill at Cannes and was worse by Naples, needing the missing medicines. They settled into a routine of Bible study, prayer and Chinese language lessons daily, and he formed a high opinion of all his party. At the end of the journey he described it as 'remarkably pleasant'. But by Singapore he was so ill with dysentery that they feared it might cost him his life to go on, but he went.[483] At Hong Kong he was well enough to take a wrangling sanban boatman ashore to see that his passenger knew not only the right fare but where it was placarded at the town hall for the boatmen's benefit.

A pile of letters awaited him, one telling him that Jennie was in Shanghai, and plunged him into the inevitable problems. E. Tomalin, one of the December batch of reinforcements, had smallpox. He survived and married Louise Desgraz. George Nicoll offered to nurse him but had not been vaccinated. Francis James was talking of resigning over the financial policy. Jackson was in debt and being sued for medical fees which he refused to pay. Thomas Harvey's wife and newborn twins had died, and of three of Grattan Guinness's children taken ill, only Geraldine, aged sixteen, had survived. So it went on. But Jennie was her usual self, a worthy wife:

> I have been ... thinking of them (the difficulties) with something of rejoicing. What a platform there will be for our God to work and triumph upon! And how clearly we shall see His hand! ... In the Master's presence the servant's only responsibility, and his sweetest joy is to obey ... Surely to need much grace, and therefore to have much put upon you, is not a thing to be troubled about. Don't you think that if we set ourselves not to allow any pressure, to rob us of communion (with the Lord) we shall live lives of hourly triumph, the echo of which shall come back to us from all parts of the Mission? Our faith must gain the victory for our brethren and sisters.[484]

On April 22 they reached Shanghai, to be met by the faithful Thomas Weir and taken in his launch to the very door of the new CIM transit home, so small and cramped that Hudson Taylor began weighing up what kind of premises were really needed in Shanghai. It led in time to another of his major innovations. They spent the first day ashore in prayer with fasting, before tackling the problems. To Jennie he seemed very run down, though better than he had been. But his dysentery returned before he had even dealt with all the accumulated mail, and they were strongly advised by Dr Johnson of the LMS to go to Yantai to escape the approaching heat of summer. By then he was in a 'very low' state, and willing to be taken.

19
First-Time Achievements (1879–83)

Bands on the Bund (1879–82)

Shanghai was no longer the settlement on a swamp of twenty-five years before, with ships' clinkers surfacing the paths. Metalled roads, rickshaws plying for hire, young bloods and sailors jostling through packed streets to the races, ladies taking the air on their menfolks' arms, watching the ships unloading in the muddy Huangpu River, or listening in the comfort of their carriages to ships' bands on the Bund—all was as unlike the true China as could be. Shanghai was an entry port expanding constantly. The value of land and buildings in the American, British and French concessions alone, assessed in 1870 at 14 million taels had risen by 1905 to 220 million taels. Not only Shanghai but China and the nineteenth century world were changing fast. Hudson Taylor himself was engineering one of the great transformations, the opening up of inland China. In Korea, Indo-China, Turkestan, as in Africa and elsewhere, the scramble for colonies and spheres of influence had begun. Before long the Western powers and Japan would be 'slicing the melon' of mainland China itself. Foreign issues played so large a part in the nation's affairs that all members of the Grand Council joined in deliberations of the Zongli Yamen, making it in effect a cabinet.[485] The old bone of contention between China and Japan, the suzerainty of the Ryukyu Islands, led both countries in 1879 to ask the advice of General Ulysses Grant, victor of the American Civil War and President, 1865–76. China conceded to Japan in 1881.

With the death of Yakub Beg and China's reoccupation of Kashgaria, the gentlemanly Chonghou of the Tianjin massacre events (see pp 124–26) was sent in 1879 to St Petersburg to settle the controversy over Ili.

The sweeping concessions he made in his treaty so enraged the Peking court that on his return he was condemned to death by decapitation, although a Manchu imperial clansman.[486] The anti-foreign party at court had sensed fraternizing with the barbarians in his actions. But the Western envoys resented what they saw as an attack on civilised diplomacy, and Russia confronted Zuo Zongtang's sixty thousand seasoned troops with ninety thousand of her own in the Kuldja-Ili area.

Through Robert Hart, China invited 'Chinese' Gordon to come and advise them. He had long interviews with the Grand Secretary, Li Hongzhang, his superior in the Taiping war and in Peking, which led him to a startling conclusion.[487] He wrote to Dr Halliday Macartney: 'It struck me that the question is not between Russia and China; it is between the Manchus and the Chinese people; the former are on their trial before the people and they scarcely dare to give in to Russia. The Chinese people wish for war, in hopes of being rid of the Manchus.'

In fact Gordon saw three factions, Li Hongzhang, the Imperial Court and the literati, to whom he was referring as 'the Chinese people'. Because in 1858 and 1860 the capital had been shown to be vulnerable, he advised: 'If you will make war, burn the suburbs of Peking, remove the archives and the emperor from Peking, put them in the centre of the country [as was to happen in 1900], and fight (a guerilla war) for five years. Russia will not be able to hurt you. If you want peace, then give up Ili.'

He had clearly seen 'that if the emperor left Peking for the centre of China, there would be an end of the Manchu dynasty'.[488] Gordon was too blunt in speech for the Chinese, but did what he came to do and they took his advice. China chose peace, but with skilled diplomacy.

In June 1880 Queen Victoria of England addressed 'a personal appeal for clemency (towards Chonghou) to the great empress dowager' and, reading the hidden message in Gordon's advice, to mollify Russia, she extended a reprieve to him. Marquis Zeng then went to St Petersburg with Dr Halliday and concluded 'a bloodless diplomatic triumph' with the return of Ili and other retractions by Russia, for which he was loaded with honours.

Gordon had also pointed out the disadvantage to Peking of having no telegraphic link, even with Shanghai, and steps were quickly taken to rectify this. *Fengshui* had to oblige. In June 1881 the *Rocket of China,* a locomotive, made its first short journey. Modernization had begun its cumbrous course.[489] Further afield, French encroachment in Indo-China heralded the bitter war with China of the 1880s, King Mindon of Upper Burma died and was succeeded by his cruel son Thebaw; General Roberts occupied Kabul; the Zulu war established Britain in yet another conquered territory; and from 1880 to 1885 the Irish question loomed large. While only the Franco-Chinese war was to threaten the CIM explicitly, Hudson Taylor was entering upon a period in some ways more painful than any yet endured. The capacity of the church at home to lose interest was unchanged. The CMS in 1880 adopted an unprecedented 'Scheme of Retrenchment', to withdraw from Peking and parts of North India and drastically to reduce its men in training and sent overseas. The policy was reversed, but it illustrates the climate of support in Britain. As if tested to the hilt for four years and found reliable, Hudson Taylor was then to watch amazed as a golden era unfolded.

Chefoo, 'where the blue air sparkled' (1879)

The rocky northern coast of the Shandong peninsula is studded with little bays and coves, fringed with fine white sand. Stormy and cold in winter when the beaches were stacked with ice floes driven ashore, Yantai was ideal as a holiday and health resort through most of the year. The bay, another lake of Galilee, is framed by hills and by the Bluff and islands shielding it from the open sea (see p 272). The market town of Yantai and the anchorage for junks lay at one end of a long sandspit, and Chefu, a fishing village, at the Bluff end. Across the harbour at Yantai lay a rocky point with perhaps a few fishermen's huts on it which, after the treaties of 1858 and 1860, became Settlement Point, the 'concession' occupied by a consul, foreign traders and missionaries. Holmes settled ashore; Hudson Taylor's good friend Joseph Edkins of the LMS moved there with his bride from Shanghai; and, also in 1860, O. Rao and Bonhoure of the Paris Evangelical Mission. Many others followed, to build up their own work in Yantai and the provincial hinterland beyond. In 1863, Calvin W. Mateer and Hunter Corbett joined Nevius, Corbett to stay on for most of his life.

So it continued. Alexander Williamson made 'Chefoo' his base for the National Bible Society of Scotland in 1863, and Charles Perry Scott for the SPG in 1874. More short-lived BMS missionaries and the indestructible Timothy Richard came and went. Augustus Margary and Challoner Alabaster of the British consular service enjoyed the very ecumenical Bible study sessions until posted elsewhere, Margary to die at Manyün. The Church of Scotland built a marble church; Nevius imported hundreds of saplings to improve the quality of Shandong's fruit orchards; the Chefoo Convention brought the Grand Secretary, Li Hongzhang, the envoys of Britain and several other states, and a fleet of warships in 1876. 'Chefoo' became known as 'the sanatorium of China', a popular naval resort for shore leave, to evade the diseases and heat of southern summers. Yantai was the port and Chinese city; but 'Chefoo' had come to mean a foreign settlement and all its affairs.[490]

Jennie had spent two days at Chefoo in the last week of October 1878, on her way to Shanxi, and had met a customs officer named Ballard and his wife, a missionary. Apart from that, when Dr Johnson urged them to go at once to Chefoo, she and Hudson were heading for the unknown, taking Coulthard and E. Tomalin, a newcomer, with them as secretaries. The north was entirely new to Hudson Taylor and he was prostrate, able to take only milk. They ran into fog and made slow progress. Instead of two days they were likely to take four to cover the distance. The ship's supply of milk ran out and Jennie herself, seasick and not knowing what to do, watched him getting weaker. 'It was one of the saddest days I ever spent. Then at 9.00 p.m. I cried to God to undertake for us, to take away the fog, to teach me what nourishment to get for (him).' Both of them believed that the Lord of heaven and earth who had calmed the storm, controlling wind and waves at a word, still could and often did intervene, in keeping with his command, 'Ask anything in my name.' She woke next morning to find the sun shining, and on going on deck met the 'second mate' who said the fog had lifted soon after 9.00 and they had had a clear night. They reached Chefoo late, but in daylight instead of darkness.

The ship stayed only long enough to disembark them into a *sanban* by which to reach the shore, and in it Hudson Taylor lay while Jennie and Coulthard went to consult Ballard. Chefoo had two 'hotels', too expensive for them, and private homes prepared to take lodgers. The Ballards would not hear of their going elsewhere, took them in and treated them as 'family' from May 8 until December 9 when Hudson Taylor, fully recovered, made an overland journey with Coulthard—right across Shandong and Jiangsu to Yangzhou and the Yangzi stations.

As his health steadily improved, he quickly saw that this was an exceptional place, of great potential for the Mission. Only a week after their arrival he was taken by boat across to the Bluff, to see if at that distance from the settlement young missionaries could learn the language among the Chinese of Chefoo, or premises be rented for a convalescent home. Frederick Baller came up to Chefoo, and on June 24 they went across together and rented a house. Baller and Pigott moved in for four months.

Meanwhile progress was being made in another direction. John Nevius, a good friend since 1855, came to see Hudson Taylor and discussed with him the 'indigenous principles' he was developing in his Shandong work, later to be applied so successfully in Korea. And the British consul at Chefoo proved to be C. T. Gardner of Zhenjiang and the second Yangzhou plot, of 1870. He had a vacant 'cottage' and Ballard a shack and unused warehouse, all of which Hudson Taylor rented. Much as the *Lammermuir* party had used William Gamble's old Chinese theatre in 1866, these makeshift quarters were roughly partitioned and adapted as the first foothold of the CIM.

Elizabeth (otherwise Jane) Judd had been so ill at Wuhan that only return to England held hope of her recovery. Hudson Taylor sent for Charles Judd to bring her and the children to the magic air of Chefoo, 'cool and bracing' instead of the 'stewing, damp heat (they were) accustomed to'. Charles was to be in charge at Chefoo while Hudson Taylor ran the Mission. They arrived on June 28, 1879, when 'the furnace' of Wuhan was so extreme that Griffith John fainted at breakfast after one hot night. James Cameron, Frank Trench and others came to Chefoo for consultation and a rest, and the sixty year-long history of 'Chefoo' as the Mission's life-saving health resort had begun. By August there were four at Chefoo and seventeen in the Judds' bungalow and warehouse on Settlement Point.

Hudson Taylor was deeply immersed in work again, often late at night, so much that Jennie wrote, 'I am dreading the effect of overwork on (him).' He could not do things by halves. Difficulties of many kinds were crowding upon him. Members of the CIM were behaving irresponsibly. Some were being side-tracked by well-meaning missionaries of other persuasions. His old thorn in the flesh at Zhenjiang, Robert White, was at it again, denouncing 'organised' missions and unsettling them.

And, to his great distress, Timothy Richard had been winning adherents to his own viewpoints in Shanxi.

So on July 30, Hudson Taylor sailed for Shanghai in a coastal steamer, to tackle the trouble on the Yangzi, and headed right into a typhoon.[491] Experienced as he was, this time he felt there was little hope as the ship was hurled about by wind and waves. '(At about one a.m.) I asked God to give me the lives of all on board, as He gave Paul.' He felt assured that his prayer was heard, removed his life-belt, turned his mattress over and slept on the drier side. The captain put the ship about and ran before the wind, the barometer began to rise soon after 1.00 a.m. and they survived. Yantai was lashed by the typhoon, the sea wall and jetty partly washed away, small boats wrecked and the British and Chinese gunboats at full steam barely kept off the rocks. Jennie's letter called it 'awfully grand' and went on, 'I did rejoice . . . that you were in such safe keeping. I think some of our friends wondered that I was not more excited and anxious, but when our Father had you in the hollow of His hand, why should I fear? I only wished I were with you. Don't work all night, or talk!' she told him, but knew it was hardly worth saying.

At Zhenjiang he found White very ill, 'a skeleton', and doctored him back to health. But C. G. Moore's young wife was also wasting away, in her case from 'hysteria' (anorexia nervosa). He sent them to Chefoo, where she hovered between life and death, nursed day and night by Jennie and others.[492] At Yangzhou he arranged for a new orphanage to be built, and wished he himself could stay and 'be a missionary again'. But after a month hard at work in the great heat he again became so 'dangerously ill', 'thin and weak' with dysentery, that he himself had to be taken downriver to Shanghai, and returned to Chefoo. He had been planning to travel with Coulthard and Jennie to Shanxi, and in Zhenjiang succeeded in obtaining eighteen-province travel passes. (Trench, Cameron and Pigott had each been given one, but few others were ever issued.)[493] Secretly

he hoped to cross from Shanxi to Gansu and the south-west, even to Bhamo. But here he was, back at Yantai on September 12, recovering but too weak to contemplate another journey.

'Chefoo', concept and tradition[494]
(1879–1986)

Crowding under crude conditions in the warehouse might express the spirit of the CIM, to put values before comfort, but it could only be temporary. With so many missions working in or using Yantai as a base for evangelism there was no thought of the CIM adding to their number. But as a health resort, permanent premises were needed. And what better place could there be for a school for children of the Mission? Premises and sites in the Settlement were at a premium, and some missions had occupied Temple Hill overlooking the Chinese city. Beyond the sparse suburbs, fields stretched out towards the encircling hills for two or three miles eastwards above the long sandy beach and the mule road to Ninghai.

On September 19, Jennie's diary read, 'To Bay, for site'. A field of beans beside a gully with a freshwater stream looked ideal, two miles from the settlement and a few hundred yards from the sands. But how could they find the owner and enquire the price without giving him the whip hand in negotiations? At this point a farmer came up and said to Hudson Taylor and Judd, 'Do you want to buy land? Will you buy mine?' He owned the beanfield. It took little time to agree a fair price. It was theirs for ninety Mexican dollars (£18); and neighbouring owners were willing to sell too.

Hudson Taylor drew up plans for a house with five rooms upstairs, about five down and verandahs. They employed men to quarry stones from the gully, made their own bricks, sunbaked and fired, and bought the timber and fittings of a nearby wreck, *The Christian*—oak beams, Norwegian pine, and teak planking from another wreck for the floors. Cabin fittings provided doors, cupboards and 'a splendid sideboard', with locks and hinges and anything else they wanted at 'two dollars a hundredweight'. Glass for windows came from Shanghai. The completed house cost £562, less than Mex. $3,000, and the worst shortcoming was that the wooden plugs used to fill the ship's bolt-holes tended to come out. This house, known as the 'Judds's house', or the first 'Sanatorium', served its purpose until 1915 when it was demolished to make way for a modern hospital. And the whole expanding complex played a vital role until taken by the Japanese in 1943.

Hudson Taylor took his share of supervision of the work and preaching to the workmen, the best change of occupation and exercise he could wish for. As Jennie noted on November 4, he was up at 2.30 a.m. to do Mission accounts before walking two miles from the Ballards to the site, a camp of matting shelters for masons, carpenters, brickmakers and missionary supervisors. Living and working with the Chinese, the language students were progressing 'famously'. Sundays on half-pay, with two gospel meetings for the men, led to conversions. One, Lao Chao, was head-servant of the Boys' School over forty years later.

Before the first house was ready, the foundations of a second sanatorium were laid, a convalescent home finished in December 1880, when the Taylors moved in. After that a school, intended for the Mission's children, and later a hospital, a dispensary and other facilities for Chinese were projected. As Dixon Hoste, of the Cambridge Seven was to point out, Hudson Taylor was no mere ascetic, but a realist.[495] The first building was needed in a hurry, but the rest were built conventionally, in keeping with the standards of a treaty port, and planned for comfort and convenience.

On December 6, 1879, he told James Meadows that he proposed to open a boarding school, and within a year it materialised, on December 1, 1880. In W. L. Elliston he had the ideal schoolmaster.[496] The Judds' three sons became the first pupils, soon joined by others, until in mid-May 1881 there were sixteen. After many requests it was decided not to limit the school to children of the CIM, nor of other missions only. Eyes had been opened throughout the foreign community in China to the unique suitability of Yantai for this purpose. Consular and merchant families were also welcomed. When thirty had been enrolled and more were applying, Hudson Taylor bought land right down to the seashore. By September 1881 'fifty or sixty scholars', boys and girls, some not resident, were in the school, and accommodation for one hundred and fifty boarders in a 'Protestant Collegiate School' was embarked upon. They were ready for thirty more by October, but Elliston was overworked and suitable teachers were not forthcoming from Britain as had been hoped. They did not need to be members of the Mission. The Taylors' eldest son, Herbert, had left medical school and was due in Shanghai on December 9. He joined the staff as Elliston's assistant. Miss C. B. Downing of the American Presbyterian Mission took charge of the girls and, in a parallel venture, an 'independent' lady, Mrs Sharland, ran a school for Eurasians in the port. Mrs Sharland later joined the CIM. By the end of August 1882 Hudson Taylor was planning a greatly enlarged school complex. The 'Chefoo School' had become popular and successful, and by 1883 fees were meeting all costs. During that year a small hospital, a dispensary and a chapel for the Chinese had also been added to the expanding facilities.

Even before the end of 1879 the *Chinese Recorder*[497] published a proposal by 'Sanitas' that by co-operative effort, costing up to 300 taels from each major society, a missionary sanatorium could be established at Yantai such as the CIM were erecting. 'Chefoo' had become far more than a misnomer for Yantai or only a summer resort. (Here we look far ahead.) As long as China's open century continued, no more vital element of the combined missionary venture existed. Chefoo was 'an important factor in (Western) life in China'. As Hudson Taylor told his parents in March 1880, once visit Chefoo and you will never be satisfied with England again! The schools acquired a reputation for good examination results in the College of Preceptors Examinations for some years, and then the Oxford Local Examinations. 'The best school east of Suez' gave the lives of thirty-four young men in the First World War; and among its alumni included the author Thornton Wilder and H. R. Luce, Editor of the *New York Times* and Editor-in-chief of *Life* and *Time* magazines. But 'Chefoo' was so much the personification of the Boys, Girls and Preparatory schools 'on the shores of an Eastern sea', from 1881 until 1943 (when they marched *en bloc* to internment in Japanese concentration camps) that 'daughter' schools at a score of other places in seven countries of East Asia have been and still are known by the same name. If the only way to give the gospel adequately to China was through men and women giving the best years of their lives, indeed a lifetime spent sacrificially, separations were inevitable if the children were to be properly educated. 'God will bless the chicks more through our sacrifice,' Jennie wrote to her mother. But schools on the field of action from then on meant shorter periods apart.

Constantly on the move (1876–83)

Ill-health had led to Hudson Taylor's recognition of Chefoo as the God-given answer to one of the Mission's greatest needs. Recurring ill-health forced him time and again to retreat there from sorties, some adventurous, into the widely expanding field of the CIM. After being taken to Shanghai dangerously ill and shipped back to Yantai on September 10, 1879, he transferred his official business centre to Chefoo. There he had to stay, sometimes for months on end, often to his great distress for his influence was most felt through personal contacts. The rapid numerical growth of the Mission to more than seventy Europeans and well over one hundred Chinese in sixty-four locations, entailed incessant administrative correspondence and interviews, with the local building developments a welcome diversion. In his preface to the 1878 bound volume of *China's Millions*, after dealing with the great famine and iniquitous opium trade, he enlarged on the importance of Chinese missionaries.

> No greater blessing can be desired for China than that there may be raised up ... a large number of men qualified to do the work of evangelists and pastors ... The sooner a few converts can be gathered in each of the interior provinces, the sooner may we hope to have men in training for Christian work in widely distant parts of the empire.

This led him on to 'the accessibility of the people'. Reviewing the journeys already made, he concluded 'These and other journeys (amount to) about 30,000 miles of travel'—by about twenty pioneers in eighteen months. During the four years of his fifth period in China, this considerable achievement was to be repeated again and again as the foreign community in China watched it wide-eyed. Even to summarise the journals, reports, memoirs and biographies of the pioneers engaged in this great explosion of Mission energy (between 1876 and 1883) would take up many pages, but its importance justifies generous attention. By it Hudson Taylor and the CIM achieved the recognition denied them previously. But more, by such thorough penetration of the empire they were going far towards the fulfilment of the twin aims: 'to carry the good news of the love of God in Christ Jesus to the nation; and to awaken the Christian Church in other lands to China's claim upon it.'

Hudson Taylor himself made two trail-blazing journeys, and some of 'the eighteen' were almost constantly on the move. James Cameron and a newcomer, Adam Dorward, were men after his own heart, equally inspired with a refusal to allow hardship or hostility or disappointment to halt their preaching of the gospel. Some were always on the move within their own provinces. Some preached and sold gospels extensively as they reconnoitred for others to move into the places they identified as strategic. Together they 'made a definite mark in the history of missions in China'.[498] He himself held the reins firmly, very firmly at times when discipline was needed, but very loosely in the case of men and women whom he could trust to plan and work and use scarce funds responsibly. To work out the broad plan with them gave him deep satisfaction. The sheer number of individually adventurous enterprises which he suggested and guided during this period is surprising, for all the activities of the sixty-four 'stations' were also under his personal supervision.

His own travels were as often 'trouble-shooting' as they were to meet, consult and re-inspire his team. In regional conferences such as neither he nor they could easily forget, he explained his strategy, listened carefully, and expounded from Scripture what God had been teaching him. 'Joe' Coulthard, his personal secretary wherever he went, said he 'seemed apparently to value anything one said'.[499] But these four years, exciting and successful in so many ways as he saw Christians multiplying in every province and missionaries taking root in most, demanded even more of Hudson Taylor (at forty-six to fifty years of age) in personal trust in God and endurance of the Refiner's fire than he had needed at any time in the past. The Mission's lowest ebb had been reached in December 1874, but Hudson Taylor's personal low point came eight years later, in 1882.

Although most other societies chose to concentrate their work, notable exceptions existed. At the Annual Meeting of the CIM in London in May 1881, on his return from famine relief, David Hill said, 'I feel almost like a missionary of the China Inland Mission . . . I have been struck with . . . the adaptiveness (and) and aggressiveness of the China Inland Mission.' He felt shackled by 'the plant' of institutions, buildings, established by his own mission. One day he said to George Andrew, 'The policy of Mr Taylor is diffusion, while that of my Society is concentration . . . (My advice to you is) "Itinerate, itinerate",' urging him to read the memoirs of J. J. Weitbrecht, the great itinerant missionary of the early CMS in India, and the biography of William Burns.[500] The reward of his own brave expedition to Shanxi was the conversion of 'Pastor' Hsi. Virgil C. Hart of the American Episcopal Church at Jiujiang travelled almost incessantly in his 'yacht' on the waterways of Jiangxi. Samuel Schereschewsky of the same Church was in Peking when he heard that a certain lady had arrived in Shanghai. He 'walked all the way' to propose to her. As Bishop from 1877 to 1883 his travels took him up and down the great Yangzi River. Alexander Williamson travelled far across Manchuria and north China for the NBS of Scotland. And Griffith John, after his tour in 1868 through Sichuan with Alexander Wylie, made frequent pastoral journeys from Wuhan into the hinterland of Hubei. In 1880 he ventured into anti-foreign Hunan, and again with John Archibald of the NBSS; in 1883 he was rioted out of Longyang.[501]

Apart from his own abortive journey in the typhoon from Yantai to Shanghai and then to Zhenjiang at the end of July 1879, Hudson Taylor and Coulthard, after only seven months in China, travelled overland for three hundred miles in twenty-four days (December 9 to January 2, 1880) by mule litter through Shandong and Jiangsu from Yantai to Qingjiangpu (see map 2.2: p 6) and Yangzhou. No other Westerners had yet made this journey. His hope was to go overland from there to Shanxi as soon as some urgent work had been attended to. Jennie went by ship to join him at Zhenjiang for the purpose, for Tianjin was ice-bound at that time of year. But floods of correspondence, disciplinary problems and the need to spend from February 9 to March 24 at Wuhan dispatching party after party of pioneers to the four winds kept him on a leash. This time 'the bombshell' broke through all precedents and previous restraints. Elizabeth Wilson herself, and other women, brides and single girls, were scattered to the far western provinces. The success of Jennie's Shanxi experiment with Celia Home and Anna Crickmay had decided him on this even more daring innovation.

From then until mid-September he was constantly on the move, only in one place for a few days at a time. Visits to each Yangzi River station in April and May, and a tour of southern Zhejiang, to Hangzhou, Ningbo, Wenzhou and intervening places in June and July carried them by sea-going junk to Taizhou, and from there over the hills to Henry Taylor at Jinhua and in August to Qü Xian on the Qiantang River (see also map 2.60: p 484).[502] These were old haunts. From Jinhua he wrote revealing to Jennie his proposition that from Shanxi they should visit each of the far western pioneers, in Shaanxi, Gansu, Sichuan, Guizhou and Yunnan. From there they could cross into Burma and make a very necessary visit to Britain, or return by way of Yichang. To the last this was his hope, but although some of the most serious problems were developing in Shanxi, one predicament after another prevented his reaching even that province.

As if he was still a young man, he decided at Qü Xian to break new ground, cutting across Jiangxi to the Yangzi (see map 2.57: p 457). They made for Yushan, passed down the Guangxin River through Guangxin itself, now the great city of Shangrao, and through Guixi and the Poyang Lake to Cardwell's home at Dagutang on a hill overlooking the lake near Jiujiang. Hearing that several of the Pearse family were ill at Anqing, they hurried on, too late to do much. Mrs Pearse had been ill with dysentery and the eldest child with whooping cough, but the baby, only just alive when he arrived, died in Hudson Taylor's arms. Years later Mrs Pearse recalled, 'Anyone who knew dear Mr Taylor would understand how truly he entered into our sorrow . . . He seemed to lay aside everything else for the time being to be as a *father* to us.' He was not ashamed to shed tears with them.[503] He could only stay to give advice on how to use the medicines they had. Edward Pearse stayed with his wife and children until they could travel with Jennie to Yantai, while Hudson Taylor went on, taking the little coffin in a packing case as his own personal luggage,

for burial beside his own children and Maria.

Another visit to Ningbo had to be fitted in before he returned to Yantai in September, until February 1881. But then from March until May it was Shanghai, the Yangzi region and Zhejiang all over again. The hottest months he spent working at Chefoo (Yantai), and in November and December he was back on the Yangzi for some historic conferences. Apart from a few weeks in Chefoo during 1882 he travelled extensively again, always hoping to get to Shanxi, but drawn by painful necessity from place to place up and down the Yangzi and through the trouble spot of southern Zhejiang. At last the opportunity to go up to Shanxi arrived, and on November 4, 1882, he left Yantai for Tianjin—only to be thwarted at Baoding. The man he most wanted to meet had left Shanxi and passed him on the road. By the time Drake returned from Yantai, married, it was too late to attempt Shanxi again. After one more conference at Anqing and a final winding up at Chefoo (Yantai), Hudson

2.41 G. F. Easton

Taylor sailed for Britain on February 10, 1883.

By computation with dividers, journey by journey, he himself had travelled fifteen thousand miles since landing on April 22, 1879. The true mileage must have been far in excess of that. Yet in none of the maps which he painstakingly annotated to show the journeys made by others, did he include his own. After 1880 no map of China could bear the routes of more than a few travellers without hopeless confusion. The folding map in *China's Millions* of 1879 had all it could take. James Cameron's 'cat's cradle' had to be shown in isolation, but after that it was not itineraries but footholds, 'stations' occupied in every province, that took pride of place. The distances covered were sometimes accurately recorded, amounting to thousands of miles, but the days, weeks and months on the road more graphically convey the toil and endurance of men and women who walked so that they could talk with fellow-travellers; and were in no hurry to move on, so that they could preach Christ and sell Gospels in every city, market town and village. The travels of Hudson Taylor and his team formed only the framework of their true activities. Men led the way, assessing the safety, but as soon as that appeared to offer reasonable hope of foreign women being unmolested, he also gave them full scope.

Cameron's cat's cradle, the south (January 1878–June 1879)

The tall highlander, James Cameron, was not content to enjoy the pleasant company of Henry Soltau and John McCarthy in Bhamo in January 1878 simply hoping that the British Indian government would relent and allow them to re-enter China. If he could not complete his planned itinerary of Yunnan from the Burma-Dali direction he would try from Guangxi in the south-east. 'I left without loss of time,' he reported very typically, and instead enjoyed three weeks of enforced idleness chugging down the Irrawaddy in the old steam-launch for nine hundred miles to Rangoon. From there to Singapore and Hong Kong was straightforward. Neither uncharted rocks nor typhoons broke his journey. He called on the German and American missionaries in Hong Kong and Canton, enquiring about the extent of their work and his best route ahead, and it seems that in Hong Kong he met John Shaw Burdon, Bishop of Victoria, (Maria Taylor's brother-in-law).

Burdon was suffering the same frustrations imposed from London in 1872 by the division of territory, with W. A. Russell taking 'North China'.[504] Burdon, 'an able and large-minded man' and always an evangelist, saw the Church in Fujian undergoing fiery persecution, and doubling its strength while various American and European missions continued under fierce opposition among the Cantonese and Hakkas of Hong Kong and Guangdong. So he pioneered a virgin field of evangelism at Beihai (Pakhoi) on the most southerly tip of what is now Guangxi province, staffed it with Christian Chinese and at Hong Kong trained theological students for future Church leadership.[505]

2.42 James Cameron

When Cameron arrived, John Burdon provided one of his Chinese students as a companion on the next adventure, and put his Beihai premises at his disposal as a base for penetration through Guangxi to Yunnan and Guizhou. Cameron made his way to Beihai, trans-shipping at Hainan Island,[506] and at once recognised the importance of the little port of '12,000 souls, besides a large floating and moving population'. At that time part of Guangdong province, it was the entry point for western Guangxi and Yunnan. 'Were the Gospel to have decided triumphs in Pakhoi [dialect for Beihai] the knowledge of salvation would spread far and wide,' Cameron wrote, among ethnic and social observations of a highly professional standard which he made as he travelled.[507]

On June 11 he and the student were off on the road to join the great West River near Nanning. Cameron could find few people who understood Mandarin, and the student was still 'too timid to preach much' in his native Cantonese, until they reached the river. There more people were bilingual. But the Nanning literati 'seemed determined on a riot', so after four days of 'much opposition' to their preaching, 'and a great amount of hostile feeling', they headed upriver, preaching at villages with 'unusually good audiences'. At Bose (or Peh-seh) he was told about Clarke and Fishe having been there, and was also generously helped by the local officials. They crossed the Red River on the border of a small tongue of Guizhou, and after little more than thirty miles, through Xingyi, left Guizhou again, to enter Yunnan. Here one of their carriers absconded with his load, taking a long detour over a rocky hill, back to their starting point. But Cameron was not a highlander without some knowledge of following a spoor. He caught him red-handed. 'Although I did not accuse him of trying to run off or even scold him, he was

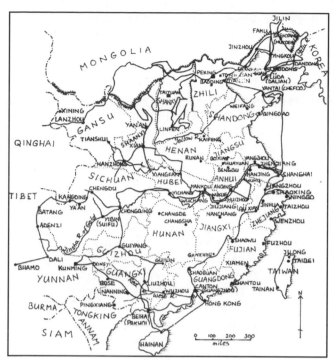

2.43 Cameron's travels: eight years on the go

quite frightened, and at the nearest village the natives wanted to give him a beating, but of course they were not allowed (to).'[508]

They reached Kunming, the provincial capital of Yunnan, on August 17 and found themselves 'in the very inn and room Mr McCarthy had occupied . . . on his way to Bhamo'. The people were 'quiet and very civil' and after his preaching some came to talk with Cameron in his inn, confirming McCarthy's impression that Kunming would be a good mission centre. The Roman Catholics already had an imposing 'foreign-looking edifice' (in Hosie's words 'a handsome palace') in Kunming, and 'evil reports in circulation about them' were so manifestly false, that Cameron defended them, without effect on the critics.[509] Those were still the days when Catholics regarded all Protestants as dangerous heretics and the average Protestant of the time saw Roman Catholics as anti-Christ, propagating a false gospel. At best they disregarded or grudgingly admired each other as brave men and women, but discounted what they taught as inadequate and schismatic. The vicar-apostolic of Yunnan gave to applicants for instruction as his summary of Christian beliefs and duties, 'to believe and hope in God, in one only God in three persons, to love and serve Him, to obey His law, to believe in Jesus Christ, our God and Saviour, to hope in His mercies, and to follow His counsels and to imitate His virtues'.[510]

Leaving Kunming 'about the end of August' and following the ancient road 'to Peking', they reached Guiyang in twenty days, to be welcomed by James Broumton and Robert Landale (see map 2.48: p 376). Cameron was indefatigable. 'As the (Chinese) with us needed rest, and as I wanted to see (George) Nicoll, I set out for (Chongqing) in Sichuan accompanied by Landale . . . a hard journey both ways.' At Chongqing they met the newcomers Riley and Samuel Clarke. Cameron was already known in high places by his epic adventure with 'one man and a mule', and a change of attitude towards the CIM is noticeable from around this time, even in Sir Thomas Wade, the minister. 'The wet season having set in', Cameron's little 'detour' of four hundred miles on foot had to be completed by the main road instead of by another route as intended.

When they reached Guiyang again a new complication faced them. One of Cameron's men from Guangxi had been so ill that he had to be taken home by mountain chair and, where possible, by river. James Broumton went with them, from November 4 to December 11. Their route took them again through Miao tribal territory, his special interest. At Guilin (Kweilin) Cameron wrote 'We might have had trouble, (but) being men of peace, we only spent two or three days', as always preaching and selling books to the 'bold and fearless' people. Then at Liuzhou they parted, Broumton heading back to Guiyang alone. Cameron had to pass through a robber-infested region.

> At one place a woman, and the household effects, had been carried off the night previous. At another ... one or more travellers had been killed, a day or two before. But I saw nothing alarming and reached Pakhoi in safety on Christmas Eve, finding such a bundle of letters—eighteen

months' correspondence—awaiting me. So I was happy indeed, and thankful to my Heavenly Father for journeying and other mercies.[511]

It would seem that Cameron made a good impression at Beihai (Pakhoi) on the consul, W. G. Stronach, for he wrote to Hudson Taylor suggesting that he buy premises and establish a mission base there. But although nearer in miles, the journey from Beihai to Guizhou or Yunnan had proved more difficult than by other routes. Cameron himself was ready to move on. 'As soon after their (Chinese) new year (1879) as men could be engaged to carry my luggage'—the indispensable loads of books—Cameron set out again, overland to Canton. He had been learning Cantonese and could speak now of 'supplementing' his 'slight knowledge' of the dialect with Mandarin. He was always learning. This time he found that by using his daylight hours 'working' in the towns and villages when people were gathered at markets, he could sleep on 'passage boats' at night and wake at the next busy place. In this way he found here and there to his joy and theirs, evangelists and members of several mission churches. 'I expect the whole province will soon be occupied in this way, and that they will extend their operations into those parts of (Guangxi) where the Canton dialect is spoken.' This was in fact the strategy of the southern missions, and determined the policy of the CIM to leave Guangdong, Guangxi and Fujian to them.[512]

On the way Cameron fell ill and for a month was cared for by the Canton missionaries[513] learning of the bitter persecutions 'that tested the genuineness of the work', and the steady expansion of the Church resulting from it. Then on March 18, 1879, he was off again, with a Hakka Christian companion, and found too late that the river-boat he engaged was already carrying two cases of smallpox and two of high fever. In spite of this contagion, at Shaoguan two Methodist missionaries (Selby and Hargreaves) insisted on his joining them for a few days, and delighted him with their daily preaching and discussion of the gospel in the city, in the CIM manner.

April 5 saw him crossing the thousand-foot Meiling Pass into Jiangxi, for a taste of old-fashioned harassment at Nangang by a mandarin who set his *yamen*-runners on to badgering the innkeeper until Cameron obligingly moved on. But at the next city of Ganzhou the innkeeper was beaten for 'harbouring a foreign devil'. This was no journey from one end of the province to the other. It was true 'itineration'. 'I visited all the cities in the eastern part of the province . . . as I thought those cities had less chance of being visited (with the gospel) by others . . . The road was bad for walking.' His reward was to find 'very civil' people who listened attentively to him. From there he crossed the mountains into Fujian and visited the missionaries and church at Shaowu. 'Mutual love to the Lord Jesus soon draws people together and makes Christians feel like old friends instead of acquaintances of yesterday . . . Such (experiences) cheer and encourage wanderers like myself . . . Parting with (them) filled me with sorrow.' He was very human, not immune from loneliness and depression, in his prolonged isolation.

Striking north, back in Jiangxi again, 'We found wheelbarrows in use. I hired

one to carry my baggage and coolie as he had hurt his foot.' It is not difficult to see why Cameron himself was well treated almost everywhere he went. Words flow, and he wrote as if his legs carried him swiftly from place to place, but crossing the 'rapid and dangerous' rivers was not so easy. On the edge of Cardwell's stamping ground at Hekou (now Yanshan) and the Qü Xian outposts of Shangrao (Guangxin) and Yushan where he knew there were Christians, he could not find them (see map 2.57: p 457). But at 'Singkeng' 'I had a hearty welcome from an old farmer and his family. The news soon spread . . . so the Christians gathered . . . We soon sat down to a sumptuous supper and . . . I had the best room given to me. For a long time after I could not sleep for joy . . . In every village . . . on our way to the next city, many had a very intelligent knowledge of the gospel.' Little by little it was taking root.

He reached the Douthwaites at Qu Xian on May 15 and could not bring himself to go on, he 'liked the people and place so much'. 'In my life, parting seems to be the rule, and yet one never feels (able) to get used to it. On the way to Shaoxing I felt very lonely.' Now he was in James Meadows's well-worked territory. He hurried on by night-boat to Hangzhou, and by footboat (see p 99) to Shanghai where he found Robert Landale, his companion on the Guiyang-Chongqing detour, and sailed with him for Yantai. Once there, he confessed, 'I found I was more run down than I was aware of.'[514]

Cameron's cat's cradle,[515] the north-east (June 1879–December 1882)

Before Hudson Taylor left Yantai on July 30, 1879, and headed into the typhoon, he and Cameron had ample time to plan another great itinerary. In 1869 the Irish Presbyterians had responded to William Burns's deathbed appeal for Manchuria to be given the gospel (see p 27). Hugh Waddell and Joseph Hunter MD occupied Yingkou (Niuchuang) and the church they planted had spread and taken root against opposition in Shenyang (Mukden)

2.44 Sketching or preaching, sure of a crowd

and south-eastern Manchuria almost as far north as Harbin.[516] They had not been the first. Alexander Williamson had been through the region in 1866–68, and John Ross of Yantai followed in 1872. However, apart from the natural extension of these churches, vast areas of Manchuria (now the provinces of Laoning, Jilin and Heilongjiang) were without the gospel. First-hand knowledge of the region was needed, as well as of the most northerly parts of Shanxi and Shaanxi provinces, bordering Inner Mongolia.

Cameron accepted this challenge, and the arrangement with the B&FBS, worked out with Alexander Wylie's help in London, offered an opportunity for Cameron to have travelling companions financed by the Bible Society. The plan was for Wylie's successor as Agent in China, Samuel Dyer (Maria's brother), and two Bible Society colporteurs Guang and Wu to go with him in August, taking a large supply of Bible portions and collecting more at various rendezvous. Hudson Taylor, in Zhenjiang by then, obtained passports for them. But this plan fell through, and T. W. Pigott, who had arrived in China with Hudson Taylor only four months previously and was learning Chinese at the Chefoo Bluff, took Dyer's place at short notice.[517] Pigott had no more experience of the Chinese way of life than he had acquired in Yantai, and none of travelling. So Cameron first took him for a trial ten-day circuit of the Shandong promontory to the east of Yantai, all on foot, with books and bedding on pack mules. Each day from September 4 to 13 they walked twenty or thirty miles, preaching the gospel at every resting place except in the bigger towns, where they worked for part or all of a day. On the last day, lightly laden, they capped this achievement by covering one hundred and twenty *li*, about forty miles, reaching Chefoo 'late' in the evening. Pigott had proved himself. He did not realise that Cameron had found it a depressing tour of down-at-heel places with illiterate people slow to understand. His Nanjing Mandarin was

not to blame; it served him well in most of China.

Cameron, Pigott, Guang and Wu arrived at Tianjin by ship on September 30, 1879, and while Pigott and Colporteur Guang took the main bulk of books by steamship to Yingkou, Cameron and Wu began selling and preaching, first in Tianjin itself and from October 10 north-eastwards to Shanhaiguan where the Great Wall runs down into the sea (see map 2.59: p 480). Beyond it lay Manchuria and Shenyang ('Mukden'). They hired a cart and covered long distances on the busy highways. After Jinzhou they turned south and in November reached the United Presbyterian Mission at Yingkou. Pigott had bought a cart and team of animals and was away testing them, on a visit to the churches with James Carson of the Presbyterian Church of Ireland.

Ten days later they 'set out in high spirits' with their companions, travelling southwards down the west coast of the Liaodong peninsula, into a snowstorm that took many lives. Their cart turned over, as was happening frequently, and by the time they had it upright again it was too late to go on. So they shared out what food they had with them between the two colporteurs, the carter and themselves, enough for perhaps one quarter of a meal each, and huddled together in the cart from Thursday until Saturday morning. Cameron and Pigott tried and failed during the storm to reach the nearest town, somehow finding their way back to the cart after becoming lost. But when their companions became distressed they tried again. The air had cleared and the town lay only a few hundred yards away. They found men and animals to help, and returned to find the cart and all its contents forsaken, but still unrifled. Safely reunited at an inn they gave thanks that not even the life of an animal had been lost, but they all had frostbite. So miraculous did their escape strike the townsmen as being, that crowds listened attentively to the gospel as long as they were there. 'They often said we must be good people to have escaped so.'[518]

Wu and the carter had to be shipped

2.45 Cameron's north-eastern journey

Even the mandarins sent a military escort to see them on their way.[519] Thousands of miles apart, in the extremities of the empire, the roots of the Church were striking deeply. No one, without exception, could testify to this as James Cameron could.

They travelled north through Changdu, and a hundred miles on reached Changchun, thronged for Chinese New Year, the perfect opportunity for preaching and selling to people from far and wide. Meeting Mongols as well as Manchus from Heilongjiang, they found convincing evidence that most people were Mandarin-speaking immigrants. 'It would almost seem as if, through becoming rulers of China, the Manchus had lost their own language and country. They will indeed have no country to return to' from the hundreds of garrison towns they occupied throughout China.

On February 16, 1880, they resumed their journey into Jilin and made for the provincial capital, also called Jilin.[520] Here too they drew large crowds and quickly sold two thousand books and tracts. But what was that among '200,000 souls, yet no one to tell them of Jesus!', apart from occasional visits by the Presbyterians? 'They found the French Catholic priests hard at work here, as in almost every other part of the Chinese Empire, far ahead of the Protestants.[521] Officials and people were 'most civil', the climate 'dry and bracing', but supplies were nearly exhausted and on February 23 they had to start back to Peking to restock with books.

Following a different route, through Shuanggang and Yitong, they 're-entered the stockade' (a token line of defence) and on March 4 reached 'the Mongol gate' of Faku (Fahkumen). By then they had used up what was left of their stock so, leaving their companions to rest at Xinmin, Cameron and Pigott made a detour to Yingkou to borrow enough books to see them to Peking. The hard journey took

home to Yantai from the nearest port; Pigott and Guang took the cartload of books to Shenyang (Mukden) by the main roads (see maps 2.43 & 2.45: pp 353 & 357 respectively); and Cameron with a pack mule worked his way up the east coast of the peninsula alone. Pigott fell ill on the way but reached Shenyang on January 17, less than nine months since he arrived in China.

The consul at Yingkou had extracted a promise from Cameron not to enter Korea, for he could have done so without difficulty. He walked through Dongguo to Dandong on the Yalu River, and on to 'the Corean gate' where he stayed for several days, talking and leaving books with Chinese-speaking Koreans. For two days he had travelled through 'neutral' territory, a Chinese buffer-zone, drawn to the 'forbidden land', but having to keep his rendezvous with Pigott at Shenyang (Mukden). Their welcome by the sixty or so Christians of Shenyang, Manchus among them (mostly Ross's converts), and the warmth of their send-off on January 23 foretold a strong Manchurian Church.

2.46 A north China peasant, inured to hard winters

and rough living they had sold more than 20,000 Gospels and other parts of the Bible, distributed thousands of tracts, and preached to tens of thousands of people.[522] Colporteur Guang stayed to work faithfully with Cameron for two years, until December 1881 when their agreement with the Bible Society ended. And Cameron went on into the summer of 1882. Such gargantuan effort must reap its rewards.

Cameron's cat's cradle, the north-west[523] (May 1880–August 1882)

If the reader needs tenacity to follow the records of these travels, the men who made them needed all the resolution they could muster. Few persevered for long. James Cameron did little else for seven years, but by the end had had enough and called a halt. The last year of his north-western journeys needed strength of will. Even with maps to follow, dry records make dry reading, but the sheer scale of his exploits illuminates his achievement.

The working interval at Peking was soon over. On May 20, 1880, they resumed the travelling which for Cameron was not to end until August 1882. They intended no less than to visit, with A. G. Parrott, 'every city in (Shanxi) and the adjoining (province of Shaanxi) together with any neighbouring cities of (Gansu).' The ambitiousness of the plan in almost anyone else's hands would have been unrealistic. As it was, Pigott could only give two months before returning to Yantai. To replenish their stocks during the first itinerary of over a thousand miles, they sent a consignment of books ahead to await them at Kalgan (now Zhangjiakou) north-east of Peking and near the Mongolian border (see maps 2.32 & 2.43: pp 281 & 353 respectively). On the northern arm of the Great Wall where it is doubled for two hundred miles, enclosing many towns and cities, Kalgan was the strategic base held by Chauncey Goodrich of the American Board, for evangelism in Mongolia, but the key to the region of Shanxi between the walls was Guangling. So to Guangling they went, over a high mountain pass, leaving Zhili through Yu Xian.

them sixteen days, and when they resumed the trek to Peking, Pigott's journal re-echoed much of what they had experienced for months already: '26th to 29th progress very slow; the cart perpetually sticking fast in the mud.' Often it had been 'up to the axles', and even 'to the shafts', with their shoulders and brute force needed to get them through. On April 1 'an unruly crowd threw mud and stones at us', but this was exceptional, and on the 12th they 're-entered China Proper' at Shanhaiguan.

American Board missionaries compelled them to spend a few days at Tong Xian (T'ungchou), and at Peking W. H. Collins of the CMS received them royally, by long-standing invitation. Other missions also went out of their way to welcome them, for in eight months of rough travelling

Surviving reports and journals from this point are briefer and almost devoid of dates, but take them westwards across the northern tip of Shanxi, through the Great Wall into what is now Greater Mongolia, following close to the great northern loop of the Yellow River enclosing the Ordos Desert, to Togtoh and Baotou. Returning eastwards they came to the city of Guihuacheng (now known by its original Mongol name, Hohhot).[524] Including a Manchu quarter this large and prosperous city of 10,000 families lay at the eastern end of a fine plain in Mongolia, with four other good-sized places within a hundred miles. They were impressed by its size, activity and intelligent, courteous people. 'There is probably no city north of (Taiyuan) more important for us to occupy than this,' for work among Mongols and Chinese, Cameron reported to Hudson Taylor, who said at the Shanxi conference in July 1886, 'We had determined in 1880 to work that city (Guihuacheng) and the prefectures of Soping and Datong.'[525] But men of the right spirit were hard to find. After trial periods by several members of the Mission, George Clarke of Dali occupied Guihuacheng in 1886 and others settled at Baotou.

Cameron fell ill with fever after returning through the Great Wall at Shahukou, but as soon as he could keep his balance on a mule travelled to Datong where they had arranged to meet the colporteurs and on to Zhangjiakou (Kalgan). Seeing Cameron's condition, Chauncey Goodrich kept him for a month to regain his strength.[526] Then on August 17, 1880, with fresh stocks of books, they crossed the mountains southwards and, denying themselves a visit to the scenic holy mountain of Wutaishan, divided up in pairs and zigzagged from city to city east of Taiyuan, and countless towns and villages between them. Cameron was the last of the team to arrive at Taiyuan, and the first, with the faithful colporteur Guang, to set out again, working their way down the Taiyuan plain until they came to Linfen

(Pingyang).[527] A. G. Parrott joined him briefly on his return journey northward.

The matter-of-fact, deliberate style of Cameron's journal—'We now turned (on October 26, 1880) to the north-east and east (for) two months . . . in this part of (Shanxi), as also several cities in (Henan)'—reveals again the spirit Hudson Taylor loved so strongly in this man for his entire commitment to taking the gospel to every corner of the land. 'We visited altogether twenty-nine cities (and) of course all the market towns and villages . . . along the route.' Up into the hills as far north as Heshun and everywhere down to Lucheng and Changzhi (Lu'an, Lungan) in November, they found the population reduced by famine to one third of what it had been, and wolves more numerous and fearless than ever. 'We saw not only ruined houses but half-ruined cities and villages, and . . . the people seemed to have no heart or hope left.' Steeply up the Hanling range and as steeply down into Henan, they covered the cities north of the Huang He (Yellow River) from Anyang (Zhangde) near the hill border southward to Weihui near Fenqiu and then westward to climb into Shanxi again.

Back at Linfen for the Chinese New Year of 1881, Cameron enjoyed the rare experience of working with the first men to be baptised there, and other new (unnamed) believers who from his description included the famed future Pastor Hsi. But only briefly, for on February 8 he left for Taiyuan again with A. G. Parrott, and on March 14 resumed his partnership with Pigott. Parrott was systematically working through the western hill cities so, after nine or ten months largely given to Shanxi, Cameron crossed the Yellow River into Shaanxi, climbed up to Suide on March 28, and went on to Mizhi, Jia Xian and Shenmu (see map 2.32: p 281). The thoroughness of these journeys, penetrating the remotest regions, surprises anyone investigating them in detail. No inns existed fit for moneyed merchants, but caravanserai for muleteers and camel drivers, with brick beds and coarse corn or millet and steamed bread for daily food, were the luxuries enjoyed after long dusty days. At Shenmu on a main road 'to Peking', Cameron wrote, 'I had a stirring time' contending with drunkards—meaning that they had pestered and molested him and Pigott, taxing all his ingenuity to quieten and get rid of them.

They were close to the Great Wall again, and to the Ordos Desert beyond, crossing and recrossing the ruins of the wall as they moved south-westward along the desert edge for fifty miles to Yulin. 'We were astonished to find that the surrounding sand was almost level with the (city) wall. Some (dunes) were . . . already higher . . . (all formed) within the last twenty years.' After another week Pigott fell ill but Cameron pressed ahead through 'Ordos country' to Jingbian, about sixty miles from the present Ningxia (see map 2.31: p 279) and only three hundred from Lanzhou 'as the crow flies'. Finding a Catholic priest near a 'station' with three more in residence, he felt ashamed. 'The Romanists certainly put Protestants to the blush; for where now is the heathen land they have not occupied or attempted to occupy?' Rejoining Pigott after a week, a sweep to the south brought them to Yan'an, a lethargic place of loess caves, due to be Mao's headquarters sixty years later. But Pigott's two months were up, and they parted company at Qingjian, he to reach Taiyuan by a ten day journey on his own, and Cameron to arrive at the ancient capital of Xi'an, on the same day May 25, 1881.

With no books left and his new stock not yet arrived, he waited 'and found the people quiet except when I preached on the street—then they opposed'. But he met a National Bible Society of Scotland colporteur who spared him a few hundred Gospels, and with this armament he criss-crossed between cities across the plains south-eastwards, then over the Qinling mountains, and at Jingziguan where Shaanxi, Henan and Hubei meet he found a cache of books left by Parrott (see map 2.20: p 204). This fact alone indicates the degree of penetration being achieved.

Instead of gliding peacefully by boat downriver to Xiangyang and Fancheng (Xiangfan) and the comforts of a CIM outpost and Chinese Christians, Cameron struck across country to more cities of Henan on the way to Nanyang. There again, instead of taking a river-boat he chose to turn south-westwards, preaching in market towns and collecting in Fancheng a large consignment of books for the next phase.

He took his load of books by boat to Xing'an (now Ankang), the furthest point on the Han River reached by Baller and King in 1876, and used it as a base for evangelism in accessible towns. At one market town the headman ordered him out, threatening him with a beating; but instead of turning people against him this made them more obliging, for fear of repercussions from the city mandarins. While the boat 'tracked' slowly, up the winding river Cameron walked overland to Hanzhong to collect the first home letters he had seen since March in Taiyuan.

In the two years since George King had begun work in Hanzhong a church of forty or fifty Christians had come into being, nearly all natives of Sichuan. It was August and Cameron deserved a rest, but he denied himself the pleasure of their company. To rendezvous with his boat and supplies he took a mountain short cut to Ziyang and soon regretted it (see map 2.31: p 279). Thrown off balance by striking a jutting rock, his loaded pack-mule crashed head over heels for several hundred feet down the steep hillside. Stone dead, 'the last relic of Manchuria' became quick income to a countryman who bought the carcass for a song and sold its flesh pound by pound in the nearby village. Cameron had become too fond of it to join in the meal put on by his innkeeper.

A difficult detour to Hanyin and back to Xing'an led him on a northward march to Xi'an again on October 8.[528] From there he worked his way north-westwards from city to city, crossed into Gansu and for ten days moved southwards, leaving no big place untouched, as far as Tianshui. George Parker was away, so Cameron stayed only one day and made for Hanzhong again, his books nearly all sold. The three last cities of Shaanxi were soon visited, and then he swallowed up the final seventy miles in two days' forced march. 'I was indeed glad when I had reached the last city, and had disposed of my last Gospel. I felt much the need of rest, and I then thought of taking up settled work . . . I arrived in (Hanzhong) on November 11th, just in time to sit up with poor Mr (George) King as he watched his little boy, who died on the morning of the 12th.'

There was to be no rest. An educated Christian named Ho, the first believer in Hanzhong (see map 2.48: p 376), invited Cameron to go with him to preach the gospel to his clan in Sichuan, at their request. 'A revulsion of feeling' was Cameron's reaction, so weary of travelling had he become. But he could not reject so God-given an assignment. For eight days they trudged the two hundred miles in pouring rain, fording flooded rivers, drying out by charcoal fires at night, preaching and pasting up gospel posters in the towns and villages. On arriving at Nanjiang and at one village after another, crowds of 'relatives' gathered to greet them. Mr Ho rose to the occasion, reminding them of how religious he had been, loyal to their ancestors and going on to tell how he had found no foreign doctrine but the universal answer to people's needs. His own family responded and, led by him, burned their idols and ancestor tablets—the beginning of a new church in northern Sichuan.

Cameron returned to Hanzhong until the end of the year 1881, and then travelled by stages, still preaching where he could, back to Wuhan, Anqing, Zhenjiang and to Shanghai for two months' work before returning to his September 1879 starting point, Yantai, for the summer. Only one province, Hunan, had escaped him, and the outlying dependencies of Tibet, Xinjiang and Taiwan. Finally, 'In August, 1882, I left for England, having finished almost seven years' work in this vast empire.'

At the annual meetings in London, 1883, he paid a glowing tribute to those in other missions who were like brothers and sisters, mothers and fathers to him on many occasions. And to the Chinese, not only Christians. Time and again 'literary men' would sit for hours talking with him at his inn. To encourage them to buy his books he would say, 'Take these home—look them through, and bring them back.' Trustful friendliness won him friends. And mandarins too, 'there were very few who were not friendly and somewhat kindly in their manner . . . I liked to come in contact with them . . . and to speak the gospel to them in their own homes.'[529] Many remarkable things were being done in China by many remarkable men and women, but perhaps none comparable with the 'itinerations' of this calm, courteous Scotsman, preparing the way, always self-effacingly, for others to reap where he had sowed.

The women pioneers (1879)

Hudson Taylor's revolutionary ideas had one explanation among others, namely his early isolation in China as the first 'agent' of the ineffective, incompetent Chinese Evangelisation Society. Forced to make his own observations and choices, he very early saw that Chinese women were largely out of reach of the gospel unless it could be brought to them by Christian women. He pleaded with his sister Amelia to come and do this. In Ningbo, 1856–60, the effectiveness of Mary Gough, Maria and Burella Dyer and of Mary Jones confirmed him in this conviction. After Maria became his wife the value of her work among women could be proved incontrovertibly. But not only among women. Educated Chinese men admired and respected her knowledge and ability.

When the *Lammermuir* party arrived at Hangzhou on November 21, 1866, Maria's strong leadership and example were felt by the young women and also by Hudson Taylor and the men of the party. Her example set the pattern and the pace of evangelism among the women of Hangzhou, which Jennie Faulding and Mary Bowyer at once took up. The church in Hangzhou came into existence as much from their work as from that of the novice pastor, Wang Lae-djün, Hudson Taylor, Judd or McCarthy. Then when the Taylors made their bold advance to Yangzhou, Jennie stayed with the McCarthys and Lae-djün, at twenty-four carrying responsibilities normally borne by mature missionaries. Hudson Taylor wrote to her on June 24, 1868, as he might have written to a young man in an equivalent position:

> You cannot take a pastor's place in name, but you must help Lae-djün to act in matters of receiving and excluding (candidates for baptism) as far as you can. You can speak privately to (them) and can be present at Church meetings and might even, through others, suggest questions to candidates. Then after the meeting you can talk privately with Lae-djün ... so he may have the help he needs, and yet there will be nothing which any can lay hold of and charge as unseemly.[530]

—unseemly, that is, for a woman among men, and for a woman in what was conventionally the preserve of a male missionary. Some critics would leap to rebuke her on either score, but Hudson Taylor saw women as 'the most powerful agency' for carrying the gospel into China's homes.

On May 24, 1870, he had written to Emily Blatchley (see pp 119ff) when she had barely arrived back in Britain with his children. At only twenty-five she was to represent him, unofficially, by quiet influence upon his well-meaning but uncomprehending official representatives For she was not only naturally capable but more closely one in mind and spirit with him and Maria than they. Hudson Taylor's confidence in her was complete, so he wrote (in her own poetic style):

> May He make you so conscious of His indwelling ... that you may realize ... that in Hin the weak is strong, the ignorant wise, the mute eloquent, the incompetent all-sufficient, and that in Christ Jesus there is no male or female, that so far as moved by Him, and acting for Him, you are no longer a girl whose place it is to keep back, retired and silent, but His instrument, called to adorn Him who is your adornment.[531]

Some account of her success has been given in part V in this volume.

Now, in 1874, nine years later, Jennie had also come through an extreme test, that of leaving her children and him, to be the first Western woman to go deep into inland China, at a time of extreme famine, to show the love of Christ in action. In courage and ability she and her companions had proved him right. With plain evidence multiplying that in most of the empire it was safe for foreign men to travel, and in some places to live unmolested, he was convinced that the time had come for what would be 'a great step in advance', the most dangerous innovation yet attempted. The only comparable venture, 330 miles into the 'interior' had been made in Shandong by Mrs Alexander Williamson in western clothes, to Wei Xian in 1875, and via Weifang (Tsingchou) to Jinan in 1876. Travelling with her husband by mule litter, they had dispensed medicines at each stopping place on their journey.[532] Without doubt in their own minds Hudson Taylor and Jennie believed that the will of God was for women to be at the forefront with the men—and even without them.

In Yantai he discussed with Jennie whether the well-proven pioneers, George King, George Clarke, George Nicoll and others, might now marry, as some were 'impatient' to do, intending to take their brides far upcountry with them. To one impatient newcomer pleading his 'special case', Hudson Taylor replied:

> None can be more earnest than myself to see woman's work commenced in the interior of the various provinces; this has long been the consuming desire of my heart ... I truly joy in the joy (of the happily married) and I share in deep sympathy in their loneliness before marriage. But it is required of stewards that they be found *faithful*; and if, without adequate reason, I were to set aside (to the detriment of the work and yourselves) the stipulations agreed upon, I should feel that I was not guided by fidelity to principle so much as caprice of feeling.[533] [And to candidates in general:] Unless you intend your wife to be a true missionary, not merely a wife, homemaker and friend, do not join us.

He failed to hold them to the highest, and they resigned.

Conditions were better than when he took his own family to Yangzhou. Famine relief admittedly was exceptional, and the route to Shanxi was used and guarded by Peking officials. But for two or three years he had been preparing for this moment. For a few months, while the *Lammermuir* women were on furlough in Britain, only one unmarried woman of the CIM, Emmeline Turner, had been left in China. But on the heels of the eighteen men

pioneers, he had sent out seven women in 1876–77, none married, and fourteen more in 1878, of whom twelve were single.[534] Before leaving Britain himself in February 1879, his editorial in *China's Millions* had stressed the importance of women's work:

> The early religious and moral education of the whole rising generation, and the strongest and most constantly operating influence that is brought to bear upon the male part of the population through life, is in the hands of the women; and ... these women can only be effectively reached and instructed by their own sex ... The Lord increase the number of lady workers in China tenfold![535]

At the General Missionary Convention of October 1878 in London, George Smith of the English Presbyterian Mission had claimed that the work done among women made an important contribution towards his society's objective of 'establishing in China a self- supporting, self-ruling, self-propagating Church'. The significance of his speech lay in its divergence from current opinion and practice. For years almost the only place for Western women in China had been in education. But the CIM's *Lammermuir* party had set a new pace, and a decade later there were sixty-three unmarried women missionaries of all societies in China. When the General Conference met at Shanghai in May 1877,[536] it appealed for women as well as men, with poor response except in the CIM.

Griffith John, whose wife had died at Singapore on the way back to China, had married again in 1874, a person whose addition to the missionary body in Wuhan soon resulted in many more Chinese women and whole families joining the Church. Yet he wrote to the directors of LMS in 1875, 'I am not a strong believer in unmarried female agents in China.'[537] Like so many he was watching 'with considerable anxiety and hesitation' the experiment being made by 'another mission'. He could only have meant the CIM. A few months later his words to the directors were even stranger. 'I feel sure you are going to waste a good deal of money and introduce elements of discord into missions.' Yet in April 1877 when the only single woman in the LMS in China was the Goughs' one-time governess, Miss Bear, on a temporary assignment, he could say, 'I thank God for the CIM.' He was coming round.

In pursuing his unconventional course, Hudson Taylor faced a choice. Jennie's adventurous penetration into Shanxi, and her companions' peaceful residence in Taiyuan, while Henan, Shaanxi and Hunan would not tolerate foreign men, could be left as an isolated achievement or developed to whatever extent proved possible. The die was cast. On August 2, 1874, when he reached Shanghai he discussed the proposition with Charles Moore, a godly intellectual, and on the 11th told Jennie his plans for the western provinces. As a first step, married couples would attempt to settle in Shaanxi, Gansu, Sichuan and Guizhou. Later one couple and single men would move into Yunnan. He hoped he and she would be able to go and see these places for themselves after meeting Cameron and Pigott in Taiyuan. They never succeeded in doing so.

George King had married earlier in the summer of 1879 and taken his bride Emily to Wuhan. At twenty-three he had already packed a wide experience of China into four years. Hudson Taylor had confidence in him. But she had only arrived in late November 1878, and had little language or experience. The historic letter was sent. Would they be the first, and to join Easton at Tianshui in Gansu, taking eighteen boxes of books? The answer 'Yes!' arrived without delay, and on September 18, 1879, they were on their way up the Han River rapids, a two- to three-month journey. By the time they arrived at Hanzhong in southern Shaanxi, he had to break the journey for a few months there for his wife's sake. 'Who is this foreigner?' the magistrate enquired. King sent his 'card'. Remarkably, they had met and become friends at Xi'an. The magistrate told him to choose the house he would like to rent, and the contract would be approved.[538]

Hudson Taylor's policy of letting the men plunge in with little of the language had paid rich dividends in fluency. Now he was placing equal confidence in the young women. What if their husbands were to die? They would have Christian Chinese colleagues with them, but how would they stand up to the strain? And what would the critics say then? He chose to be guided by Scripture, 'He that observeth the wind shall not sow; and he that regardeth the clouds shall not reap' (Ecclesiastes 11.4). In the event it was Emily King who died after only two years, from typhoid, a disease common at the coast. By then what mattered more was that women had found their place, had made a start. In time they were to outnumber the men by two to one.

The first women to the west (1879–80)

Emily King was the first foreign woman to go into the far west of China since any in Marco Polo's day. After George Clarke and A. G. Parrott had been driven out of Jincheng (Tsechou) in Shanxi and went to Linfen, Parrott stayed but Clarke moved on to Yantai. He, Cameron and Nicoll had reached China in 1875 shortly after King, and were fully as experienced as he. Hudson Taylor's proposition to Clarke and Nicoll matched their own thoughts, to marry without delay and travel together up the Yangzi gorges to Chongqing. There Clarke would leave the Nicolls and go on with his Swiss bride, Fanny Rossier (one year in China), to join James Broumton at Guiyang. When others took their place they would move on, far into Yunnan.

When they reached Shanghai in early September, Hudson Taylor was there, 'dangerously ill' again but recovering enough to be taken back to Chefoo. The Clarkes and Nicolls were married on September 15 in Shanghai, and on November 3 set out from Wuhan on their hazardous journey. Its dangers they knew, from rocks and currents in the many Yangzi rapids, from possible encounters with river pirates, and from angry mobs in Sichuan whose attacks on Roman Catholics might be turned on them too. A greater hazard, more capable of ending the whole project at the start, was intervention by the consuls or minister, Sir Thomas Wade, if they heard of it. No question of legality could arise, but while being as harmless as doves, they needed the wisdom of serpents. To say nothing in Wuhan about going to Chongqing, when starting for Yichang, would arouse no suspicions.[539]

Yichang was the normal place for transferring to smaller boats for the gorges. In advising them about this, Hudson Taylor also sent Nicoll instructions about reporting his movements. Although a schoolmaster by profession he had been less systematic than others with less education (including Cameron and Clarke). Every journey in new territory was a reconnaissance to benefit colleagues. So places should be named and described or assessed, distances noted, the attitudes and characteristics of the people and officials also; inns should be recommended, and accounts given of the duration and kind of work achieved. He mentioned trades, but not mineral resources or commercial matters of interest to geographers or consuls. They were taking their wives far from medical aid, so he taught them the essentials of treatment for the diseases they were most likely to meet and, presumably, how to help at the birth of a baby.

The courage of those first pioneers deserves more praise than they would have tolerated in their day. K. S. Latourette allowed space in his mine of information to pay this tribute: 'Between 1878 and 1881 he (Hudson Taylor) began to send them alone into the interior provinces, a policy whose success testified both to the courage of the women and to the character of the Chinese.'[540] Indeed Mrs C. W. Mateer testified that women were far safer in China than in New York or London, and Elizabeth Wilson who later spent years in Hanzhong and Gansu only once in her long experience had any anxiety for the young women she was escorting.

Slowly the trackers towed their boats upstream, day after day, until on December 17 George Clarke recorded:

In ascending the rapids we have been exposed to danger. Whilst waiting at one of these for a day and a half ... two boats like our own were crushed (but) we only sustained a little damage. Boats waiting their turn to ascend are exposed to injury from ... the current or swell, and (from) large boats ... between which there is a danger of getting jammed like a nut in a nutcracker. The crashing sound is anything but comforting.

At Wushan we found a boat waiting for us from the *yamen* (displaying) a flag (with) white characters on a red ground, 'To receive and escort the foreign travellers' ... I have not seen the same respect shown before.[541]

The Yichang mandarins had sent word ahead of them. Two days before Christmas, however, 'the most trying of all my travelling experiences' happened when they were wrecked. Their boat was holed on a rock, fortunately close to land. They got their wives ashore and threw or carried to them everything that could be saved. 'The boat was filling fast and going down.' Of eleven boxes of books only four or five were rescued dry, so Christmas Day was spent drying books and possessions, spread out on the rocks. A tent made from masts, oars and mats gave some shelter from the 'piercing cold', but the risk of a foray by looters was their main anxiety. By the 29th the boat had been raised and repaired, and they made another attempt 'into the teeth of a small rapid'. This time the tracking cable and ship's mast snapped, and they were swept downstream. Clarke and Nicoll at the oars caught a back current which brought them to their camp site again. If this accident had happened at a major rapid, boat, goods and lives might well have been lost.

The first foreign women to enter Sichuan reached Chongqing on January 13, 1880, to learn that the Roman Catholics across the river had been attacked. 'Maybe our Father saw fit to detain us,' Mary Ann Nicoll wrote, 'that we might arrive here in safety. Not even a crowd gathered when we landed.' The crowds were soon to come. A month later, after the Clarkes had gone, 'As soon as it was known . . . the women flocked to see her. (At first) we had from 100 to 200 women daily . . . but since the (Chinese New Year, except when it was raining) we have had from 200 to 500 women daily. We receive the men in the front of the house, and the women in the inner hall.'[542] An elderly military mandarin himself came to take them to a feast in his home, and a motherly old lady, 'knowing how weary she (Mary Ann) must be, used sometimes to send her (sedan) chair' to bring her to her own home, put her to bed and quietly fan her till she fell asleep. When she woke she was given a good meal before being taken back to her husband. For two years she saw no other Western woman, and then only in transit.

George and Fanny Clarke stayed only a week at Chongqing before going over the mountains to Guiyang. In seventeen days of travelling only two were dry and sunny, so the trails were dangerously slippery. 'The men often let her (mountain-chair) fall . . . she would rather travel up all the large rapids of the (Yangzi) than take this journey . . . She was such a good traveller though.' On February 5, 1880, they joined James Broumton in Guiyang, and the first Western woman in Guizhou began her strange new life. Eleven weeks later, on April 20, two more arrived, overland all the way from Wuhan.[543]

The first unmarried one (1880)

When Hudson Taylor arrived in Wuhan with Frank Trench on February 9, 1880, he kept his intentions secret. Disapproval of them was so predictable that he avoided contact with members of other missions who might question him. 'None know of our plans.' The fact of young brides having gone to Chongqing and Guiyang would be known, and he had come, as Elizabeth Wilson said of this occasion in particular, like 'a bombshell scattering us' again.[544] But this time young unmarried women were involved. Two struck Hudson Taylor as suitable. Jane Kidd, as playful 'as a kitten' (in Hudson Taylor's phrase) but an effective missionary already; was fluent

enough after one year in China to keep up an animated conversation; she was to go with William McCarthy's widow to join the Clarkes at Guiyang. And 'Miss A. L. Fausset' after nearly two years in the country, 'truly devoted and most unselfish', was to go up the Han River with Elizabeth Wilson to the Kings at Hanzhong (see map 2.20: p 204).

For a week after his arrival at Wuhan Hudson Taylor prepared the travellers for whatever lay before them, combining daily sessions of prayer and study of the Bible with practical advice and business matters. The words Jane Kidd most took to heart were his powerful farewell reminder, 'You have only the great GOD to take care of you!' They summed up his own confidence in the omnipotence and faithfulness of the One they served.[545] He had chosen Frederick Baller as 'the best possible escort' for Ellen McCarthy and Jane Kidd. And Frank Trench, the competent man of independent means who had been proving himself by thorough itineration of the cities of Anhui, was to go with them on his way to Yunnan. An evangelist named Yao, the Bible Society's colporteur Lo, and a Christian woman made up the party.[546]

Instead of the Yangzi route through Chongqing they were to cross Hunan, the hostile province where the people on this route to Guiyang had burned Augustus Margary's boat, and stoned other travellers, yet treated Judd, Broumton and Clarke at different times with respect. The rapids on the Yuan River by comparison were small hazards on 'the first visit of ladies to such a rowdy province'. But five years had passed since Margary and Judd were there, and Hudson Taylor also 'wished to have (Baller's) judgment as to the preparedness of the province for settled work'.

They left Wuhan on February 19 in a houseboat captained by a member of Griffith John's church, reached beautiful Yueyang at the mouth of the Dongting Lake on the 27th and anchored for the weekend to ride out 'a perfect hurricane'. Men and women came aboard to visit them, and the *laoban* (captain) and his wife proved to be as 'ready with a word for the Lord Jesus' as his passengers. 'There was a boldness and frankness about (the people of Hunan), an absence of hollowness, and a reality . . . It was a treat to preach to them.' The women were delighted to see foreign women and 'stroked their hands and stroked their cheeks', saying they were beautiful.[547]

Safely across the lake and working up into the Yuan River the widely travelled Baller said of the well-wooded pastoral scene, 'This province is one of the finest, if not the finest, in China.' Then, moored for the night, men and women went ashore, to be 'received with the greatest kindness'. 'An attentive listener' invited Baller and Trench to explain the gospel to him more fully, and his boys took their hands to lead them to his home. Then they preached for an hour to a roomful of people. So far so good.

The next night some men the worse for drink tried to pick a quarrel and pelted them with clods of earth. But the weekend at Changde was peaceful, with good audiences, and as the river narrowed, fierce rapids several miles in length were safely negotiated. At place after place without exception women flocked to welcome 'the ladies' and listen to the gospel, until they reached Qianyang near the Guizhou border. There 'our old enemies the officials' stirred up the riff-raff to snatch away the books people had bought, and forced the travellers to move on. Even so, people followed in boats asking for more, and 'one decent man' showed that he had read over and over again the books brought from Wuhan by a friend. The steady penetration by the gospel was thrilling to observe. Their boat was battered and tossed about day after day until, badly holed by a rock in one rapid at the provincial border, they kept afloat only 'by dint of hard baling' and plugging the leak while they limped to where they could tie up and effect repairs.

After seven weeks by boat, nine more days spent crossing the high mountains brought them to Guiyang and the Clarkes, on April 22. Jane Kidd had made history, the first single girl to enter the far western provinces of China. Three days earlier, to their surprise they had met James Broumton on his way to a festival of Miao tribesmen of various tribes, so good was his rapport with them. For learning the Miao language, this opportunity for comparing their dialects was too good for him to miss. Trench and Yao came in behind the others a few days later, having begun their colportage of Guizhou at the city of Guiding. As soon as Broumton was free in May they were to make a major assault on Yunnan together, including Kunming the capital.[548] After a few days Baller left with Lo, travelling by Chongqing and the Yangzi gorges to take charge at Wuhan. Faith and courage had been vindicated once again.

Women 'alone' against the current[549] (February–November 1880)

When Jennie Taylor and 'Miss Fausset' arrived at Wuhan on February 20, the day after the Guiyang party left, Hudson Taylor discussed his next plan with them. A new kind of courage was involved. All available missionary escorts and even Chinese Christian companions were away on other ventures, and none could be borrowed from other missions. Griffith John had already provided two colporteurs for Shanxi. But George and Emily King at Hanzhong intended to complete their journey to Gansu after their child was born. Someone must care for the growing number of Christians at Hanzhong (see maps 2.20 & 2.31: pp 204 & 279 respectively).

Elizabeth Wilson had begun life in China at the late age of forty-six, and after four years could make her meaning known in Chinese only with difficulty. But her greying hair was an advantage in a Confucian society that respected age, and her cheerful, outgoing way with Chinese women won her friends. She employed a cook named Zhou, witty and conceited, with shortcomings that made him a doubtful asset. If she and young Miss Fausset were to ascend the Han River with its rapids, they must at least have a reliable Christian escort. The only one who answered to this description was Huang Kezhong, one of Charles Judd's converts, who lived in a shack on his own, because he had leprosy.

2.47 'Eye of a needle': through the Hanzhong city wall

The two women were game to go, and Hudson Taylor had confidence in them. His sense of God's guidance in these circumstances made him willing to add risk to risk, in human terms. Shipwreck could come to anyone, even a Baller or Cameron, but what of the wickedness of men? A good *laoban* with his wife on board, Huang Kezhong as a standby, and 'the great GOD' in full control seemed insurance enough against any calamity. So it was decided. They would go.

A few days later Hudson Taylor and Huang Kezhong went out to hire a boat, and slept on board that night. In the morning 'the ladies' joined them, and noticed at once that Huang's bedding, a wadded *pugai*, stank offensively. Hudson Taylor had slept alongside him without complaining, but now he arranged for it to be exchanged for a clean one. He travelled with them for several hours before going ashore, returning with a basket of eggs and lard. Miss Fausset then recalled that she had commented on vegetable oil having spoiled the flavour of some meat. This was his parting present. He prayed with them and left to return to Wuhan. Elizabeth Wilson felt cared for, supported by his attentiveness on many occasions. Her travelling boxes still bore her name stencilled by him in London.[550]

On May 21 they arrived at Hanzhong, one thousand miles upstream and nearly three months from their starting point. Huang Kezhong had been all they hoped of him, talking to people at every opportunity about Christ, and bringing women and girls

to hear more from the missionaries. The *laoban* took them to visit his own home, and brought his crew to listen when the four Christians had their daily Bible reading and prayer. He tried to keep them hidden in potentially hostile places, and their only alarm was to wake one morning to find their bedding and some clothes missing, stolen by thieves while they slept. But their passports and money were safe. Once a crowd cut the boat's mooring ropes, simply hoping the excitement would bring the foreign women out where they could see them again. Elizabeth Wilson called it 'a straightforward boat journey' with little to report. Miss Fausset had been 'always ready for work', showing 'excellent judgment'. From the moment of arrival they were swept into the work of the 'station'.

There was more than enough to do. George King was exhausted, pressed to the limit of his strength by the demands of his work and by opium addicts clamouring for treatment. On their one street alone they counted two hundred places where opium was on sale. On the 18th he had been threatened with eviction, but the magistrate, the acquaintance from earlier days in Xi'an who had welcomed him to Hanzhong, nipped trouble in the bud. Two days after the women arrived, George Easton turned up. Hearing of King's need of help he had covered the one hundred and fifty miles from Tianshui in three days. By the end of 1880 there were twenty baptised members of the church. And Zhou, the cook, and Huang Kezhong (forced to live in isolation outside the city) had shaped up so well that they were ordained deacons.

Somehow Elizabeth Wilson acquired the reputation of being the first unmarried woman to the 'unoccupied' western provinces, but must yield the honour to Jane Kidd by a difference of one month (April 22–May 21), or share it with Jane and Miss Fausset.

Gansu before the brides arrived (1878–82)

The story of the far north-west of China is the tales of the *Arabian Nights* set in the

Celestial Kingdom. In the days of the Great Silk Road what are now Shaanxi, Sichuan, Gansu, Ningxia and Xinjiang were all administered from Xi'an, or Chang'an as the old capital was called. Mountains and deserts stretched endlessly westwards into Tibet on the southward side and into Mongolia and the Gobi Desert in the north. Intense heat, intense cold and long tracts without water characterised the western half, but in the eastern half grain, fruit and wild animals abounded. People of many origins shared the natural wealth: Chinese from every province, Tibetans, Mongols, aboriginal tribes and Turqis, with a preponderance of Muslims.

Before the great conquest of the Muslim rebellion by Zuo Zongtang (see p 314), Gansu extended 1,500 miles to the Afghan and Russian borders. But in 1877, 1882 or 1884 (as variously stated) the period we have entered with the pioneers of the CIM, this administrative territory was halved, to create Xinjiang and a more manageable Gansu. The capital of Gansu, Lanzhou, stood at 5,000 feet, seventy-two days travel from Wuhan and the same again from Urumqi, capital of Xinjiang. But Tianshui (Tsinchou) at 3,300 feet, halfway between Lanzhou and Xi'an and on one of the main trade routes, commanded the most populated and productive part of the province. Only one hundred and fifty miles from Hanzhong (an excellent staging post on the navigable Han River in southern Shaanxi), Tianshui was the strategic city for occupation by the Mission. That a Hunan military mandarin should provide the premises when the right time came was wonderful but true.

We saw (see p 279f) how G. F. Easton and George Parker first entered Gansu on December 28 or 29, 1876, and reached Lanzhou on January 20, 1877, after travelling for five months, to occupy Tianshui in 1878. The year 1885 was to see missionaries settle in Xining, at 8,000 feet the key to the Tibetans of Qinghai province, and at Ningxia in the north-east among Muslims and Mongols (see maps 2.31 & 2.59: pp 279 & 480 respectively). But in the

first few years not only Parker and Easton but women were to share in the travels over thousands of miles. They took the gospel to towns and cities over wide areas and left Christian books with the people.[551]

While Parker and Budd attempted to gain a foothold in Xi'an, and, after being forced out, worked by boat up and down the Han River for several months, Easton returned to Gansu and travelled the Qinghai border from March 15 to April 19, 1878. Records are vague, and dates confused, as individuals lost count or simply failed to name the month or year in their letters. But in the summer, after visiting Chongqing, Easton was on his way back alone to Gansu when he fell ill with smallpox at Langzhong (Paoning) in north Sichuan. Seeing his employer so ill, Easton's hired carrier decamped with his possessions. So Easton had to retreat all the way back to Chongqing. By November 15 he was well enough to try again, this time with George King, taking twenty-six days to Tianshui, and embarked on more itinerations in Gansu. But King was to marry in 1879 (see p 364), and left the next day for the coast.[552]

It was while Easton was alone for the first half of 1879 without any Christian companion, that he discovered in the Tianshui city and countryside the desperate plight of almost naked refugees from the Shaanxi famine (see p 337f). Debarred from entering some premises, he was told that the occupants had sold their clothes for food. At once he bought secondhand clothing and sacks of corn, distributing them from the inns he stayed in temporarily, while waiting for advice from Hudson Taylor.

Throughout June and July he travelled more extensively, visiting the Qinghai borders and tribal peoples, the city of Xining and the provincial capital of Lanzhou.

> To my surprise, at Sining I found Count Béla Széchényi, a Hungarian nobleman (and two companions) on a scientific journey to Lhassa, and on to India ... Colonel Prejevalsky and eight other

Russians are on their way from Russia via Ili, and are expected in (Lanzhou) and Sining about October; they intend making for Lhassa ... Széchényi intends reaching Lhassa 'dead or alive' ... Five Germans arrived (in Lanzhou) to commence (a) cloth and woollen works, but one of them has since committed suicide.[553]

Therefore the CIM delayed attempts to occupy Lanzhou until excitement over the advent of so many armed foreigners had subsided.

Easton waited until late autumn for the Kings, but hearing from Hudson Taylor that thousands of taels of silver were available for famine relief, went down to Hanzhong and returned with 2,500 secondhand garments on pack mules for the destitute in southeastern Gansu. On February 3, 1880, he reached Tianshui and by the 23rd had verified the need of individuals and issued all he had brought. George King sent five more mule-loads with 1,400 garments for children, and from two rented shops in which he organised his work, Easton distributed clothing and grain within a radius of about twenty miles.

In May 1880 he made the forced march in three days to help George King in distress at Hanzhong (see p 368), and was travelling again after the summer. But in early 1881 his place in Gansu was taken by George Parker, and we find Easton waiting at the coast for his fiancée, Caroline Gardner, to arrive from Britain. Steamers were plying the Yangzi and along the China coast, but all travelling elsewhere had to be by slow river and canal boats, by pony or mule-back, by cart or litter or wheelbarrow, or more often on foot. The wonder then is that some of these men and women covered such great distances, treating months and weeks as we do days or hours, spreading the truth, 'Christ died for sinful men and women', and leaving books, leaflets and posters to reinforce their words.

Finding that his fiancée was not due until April, Easton escorted Robert Landale and his bride and two single girls overland via Jinan, Shandong, to Taiyuan in Shanxi. From there he visited Gansu again, in time

to take Elizabeth Wilson to the bedside of Emily King, dying of typhoid at Hanzhong. And on the way back to Yantai he helped Henry Hunt, ill at Runan in Henan. At last in August he married Caroline at Chefoo. Together they took a new missionary, Hannah Jones, with them to Hanzhong. But the plot thickens, and other threads must be picked up before Hannah Jones is with the Tibetans of Qinghai.[554]

Women on the borders of Tibet (1879–82)

Just when George Parker and Shao Mianzi, the Chinese schoolgirl at Yangzhou (see p 276) fell in love is not mentioned in the documents we have. Hudson Taylor was in London when indignant letters began to reach him from the missionaries responsible for her. She was a fine girl, intelligent and active as a Christian, well suited to be a pastor's wife in a year or two. But Parker was determined to marry her, and nowhere is it suggested that the wish was not mutual. There were, however, strong reasons why George should think again. On July 5, 1878, Hudson Taylor wrote to him as candidly as he ever did, saying that his mother was in tears, pleading that he should change his mind for serious practical reasons. Chinese culture, attitudes and family ties were so widely different from European ones in those days that many marriages between the races foundered over the inability of partners to adapt to each other. Adaptation between two people of the same background and upbringing was difficult enough, but he would be marrying a family, not only a wife. All the social obligations towards her parents and relatives, that a Chinese husband would take for granted, would be more than he could take.

No objection was raised to an inter-racial marriage *per se*. Yet even adaptation was a minor matter beside the fact that Mianzi had entered the mission school soon after the upheavals at Yangzhou in 1868–70. Following custom, a contract had been drawn up between her parents and Charles Judd for the Mission, with Hudson

Taylor's help. Among the usual terms, after educating and caring for her over the years the Mission was to have the right to arrange her marriage. Only so could a Christian girl be saved from betrothal to a pagan, and certain persecution when she refused to perform the ancestral rites. Hudson Taylor's letter to George Parker said:

> When I proposed to the parents to give (the Judds) the right of betrothal (to a Christian husband) they objected, lest she should afterwards be married to an Englishman or taken (abroad). I promised them most solemnly and absolutely that she should only be married to a Chinese Christian and should not be taken away from China ... No amount of subsequently purchased consent would ever satisfy the parents that all we had said was not false, and that the intention from the beginning was not what they had objected to and feared. (To break this undertaking would ruin the Mission's schools.) (I) entreat you to abandon the thought (and to trust God to provide you with) a true helpmeet suited to you.[555]

A many-sided correspondence followed. The contract was the crux. Theodore Howard thought Charles Judd too hard on Parker. Hudson Taylor judged that half a dozen of George's friends were ready to resign if in their opinion he was disciplined or forced to yield. Frederick Baller, in charge at Yangzhou, was receiving daily visits from Mianzi's father, an opium smoker out to make trouble but talking only of the financial loss to his family if he surrendered Mianzi and his rights. Soon all was settled; indeed before Hudson Taylor from a distance could take any further part in it, Mianzi's father himself volunteered an acceptable solution, simply compensation for his expenditure on her since her birth. He willingly signed a document agreeing to the marriage, and absolving George from all claims. On June 10, 1879, Judd informed Hudson Taylor that all had been satisfactorily settled, and eight months later 'Miss Minnie Shao' married into the CIM at HBM Consulate, Yantai, the first Asian member.[556]

They travelled up the Yangzi and Han Rivers to Hanzhong, delaying at Fancheng to be with Emily King through her confinement, before continuing the long journey to Tianshui in December. Elizabeth Wilson went with them from Hanzhong, perched above her baggage on a mule—the first missionary women in Gansu.[557]

She and 'Minnie' took Tianshui by storm, visiting the women in their homes, especially after Minnie's first child 'Johnnie' was born in February 1881, and soon there was 'hardly a lane or courtyard' where they were not known and welcomed. But in May word came that Emily King had typhoid. Elizabeth Wilson started back to Hanzhong immediately with G. F. Easton, but in vain. Emily died, and six months later her child died of dysentery, on November 12, 1881, when James Cameron was there to support George King in his renewed grief.

In February 1882, King took Elizabeth Wilson yet again to Tianshui, this time with twenty-three-year-old Hannah Jones as well, setting George Parker free to leave on the 21st, on a five-month journey through north-eastern Gansu and Ningxia. Pioneering was in his blood. Hardly had he reached home than he swept his wife and Hannah Jones away, to take the gospel to Tibetan women and mandarins' wives on the Qinghai border, while Elizabeth Wilson and A. W. Sambrook from Henan held the fort at Tianshui.[558] Leaving Minnie and Hannah at an inn, Parker himself went on to Labrang (now Xiahe), only inferior to Lhasa, and to Huozhou (or Hezuo) 'the most important Mohammedan centre in China'. Welcomed at each place, he was rebuked for not bringing Arabic Bibles. 'I could have sold a large number of Arabic and Persian Scriptures,' he wrote in his diary, 'but few can read Chinese.' They returned to Tianshui on September 26, completing a distance of one thousand miles in seventy-eight days, roughly the same time and distance as on another of his journeys. He had sold 25 complete Bibles, 183 New Testaments, 685 'quarter testaments' (a Gospel, Acts and some

Epistles) and 5,732 single Gospels, and was asked for more in different languages.

Their return set the intrepid Elizabeth Wilson free to go back to Hanzhong, taking seventeen days in bad weather. Once her mule very nearly went over the precipitous edge of a narrow mountain trail. Another time it bolted, throwing her and its panniers with 'my heavy tin box on top of me,' she wrote, grateful that 'God had provided a soft bed of sand . . . Head and chest were bruised but no bones broken,' and she had 'only' four more days' travel in that state on the same mule. Not least among the qualities shown by these men and women was their willingness to risk injury, illness and the malice of evil men when hundreds of miles apart from each other and distant from any skilled medical help.

For twenty years Hudson Taylor himself had been almost the only doctor in the Mission, in spite of many prayers and pleas to the profession. But at last, in January 1880 Dr W. L. Pruen arrived, and on April 7, 1880, the highly qualified surgeon Harold Schofield left home with his wife to join the CIM in China. Then on August 16, 1882, two more followed him, E. H. Edwards and William Wilson, Elizabeth's nephew.[559]

We shall hear more of George and Minnie Parker but may be forgiven for looking ahead to their old age. He only returned to England twice, in 1890 and 1907, and twice at least they lost all they possessed, by looting in 1900 and 1914. He died in Henan on August 17, 1931, the Mission's doyen of active members, with fifty-five years' service to his credit. Of all surviving active members, his widow Shao Mianzi was then the most senior. Her son, the Chief Electrical Engineer of Greater London's Underground, tramways and trolley-bus services (the latter his innovation) served the Mission on its London Council. And her daughter, Mrs Mason, became as good a missionary as her mother.

1880–83: 'DARING AND SUCCESS'

Trench takes on Yunnan (1880–81)

'This great explosion of Mission energy' showed no sign of slackening. Each of the nine provinces had been crossed and re-crossed in systematic 'seed-sowing'. And more than a token 'occupation' of Taiyuan, Tianshui, Hanzhong, Chongqing and Guiyang meant a strong foothold in all but four of the nine. Henan, Hunan, Guangxi and Yunnan remained to be 'occupied'. Newcomers to the CIM were catching the spirit of the earlier pioneers and joining in the assault. K. S. Latourette referred to 'the daring and success of the Mission'.[560] Hudson Taylor and the China Inland Mission were sweeping ahead on the momentum of one of the great epochs of the Mission's history. It rose to its most conspicuous outcome (the advent of the Cambridge Seven in 1885) but not the apogee of achievement. That had been reached by then.

After Frederick Baller and Frank Trench had delivered Ellen McCarthy and Jane Kidd safely to the care of George and Fanny Clarke at Guiyang, in April 1880 (see pp 366-67), Baller returned via Chongqing to Wuhan and Trench continued his colportage in Guizhou. James Broumton returned from two weeks at the exotic Miao tribal festival (April 16–May 1, 1880) and ten days later he and Trench set out for Yunnan to preach and sell books in as many walled cities and intervening towns and villages as possible. With seven carriers laden heavily with books they trekked for five weeks and a day over the mountains to Kunming, the lakeside capital of Yunnan. 'Resting' on Sundays and at two cities on the way for three or four days of work, they arrived on June 16, to work systematically through the great city until Broumton started back towards the end of the month. 'The handsome palace of the French Bishop', as imposing as the princely status he assumed, indicated the extent and strength of the Church of eighty thousand adherents he ruled. But even ten thousand nominal Catholics in so great a city left ample scope for Broumton and Trench to evangelise among 'quiet attentive people'.[561]

Broumton reached home and his normal work on August 16, 'somewhat fagged after my 1,000-mile walk,' but grateful for protection 'from all evil, sickness or violence. Most travellers in Yunnan carry arms, we had none; but we had the arm of God.' Within a few months he was engaged to marry Ellen McCarthy. Trench and the carrier he had employed at the end of the boat journey through Hunan (not a Christian and of uncertain integrity), proceeded to visit 'every city in south and south-eastern Yunnan'. He was still at it in December, enjoying the mild climate of this part of the plateau, at 3,000 to 5,000 feet on the latitude of Hong Kong. But illness (unspecified) and the need to collect another load of books forced him to withdraw to the Yangzi again, and to Shanghai for treatment.

By April 1, 1881, Trench was ready to start back from Wuhan, intending to join James Broumton, who had married and gone ahead with his wife and others on March 26. In appalling weather they failed to find each other, and Trench duly arrived at Guiyang on May 31, well ahead of the rest, only to suffer a relapse of his symptoms. He worked within reach of Guiyang hoping to recover and to leave for western Yunnan province, but in September he had to capitulate and return to the doctors at Shanghai.[562]

In the *Reports of Her Majesty's Consuls in China*, published as a Parliamentary Blue Book, Challoner Alabaster, the consul at Wuhan, the hub of the CIM's movements, wrote:

> You can travel through China as easily and safely as you can in Europe when and where you leave the main road.

> Apart from this increased care on the part of the mandarins, this improved state of affairs is due to the fact that the natives are becoming more accustomed to the presence of foreigners among them, much of the credit of which belongs to

the members of what is called the China Inland Mission, instituted by the Rev Hudson Taylor MRCS, some dozen years ago.

> Always on the move, the missionaries of this society have travelled throughout the country, taking hardship and privation as the natural incidents of their profession, and, never attempting to force themselves anywhere, they have managed to make friends everywhere, and, while labouring in their special field as ministers of the Gospel, have accustomed the Chinese to the presence of the foreigners among them, and in great measure dispelled the fear of the barbarian which has been the main difficulty with which we have had to contend.

> Not only do the bachelor members of the Mission visit places supposed to be inaccessible to foreigners, but those who are married take their wives with them and settle down with the goodwill of the people in districts far remote from official influence, and get on as comfortably and securely as their brethren of the older Missions under the shadow of a Consular flag and within range of a gun-boat's guns; and, while aiding the foreign merchant by obtaining information regarding the unknown interior of the country and strengthening our relations by increasing our intimacy with the people, this Mission has, at the same time, shown the true way of spreading Christianity in China.[563]

Little did either Alabaster or Hudson Taylor anticipate the hostile innuendoes later to be made, that missionaries deliberately sought information for the merchants. Only ten years previously 'the devil's growl' in the press and the House of Lords had been focused on Hudson Taylor, this 'flea in a blanket', this 'incurable idiot' and his troop of novices. At least that had changed, and more was to happen in the next few years before a flare of undreamed of publicity was to levitate the humble Mission to almost dizzying heights.

Stevenson and Soltau, first from west to east (1879–81)

John Stevenson and Henry Soltau had arrived at Bhamo in October 1875 expressly to open up a route into remote south-western China. Since then the British-Indian government had persistently obstructed them. But in Bhamo, once the antagonistic Burmese governor was replaced, officials and people were only friendly. The clinic was valued, and (in spite of his irascible manner) while Dr Thomas Harvey was there it acquired a reputation extending to Dali and beyond in Yunnan. They survived the cholera that took the life of the governor and Roman Catholic priest, and many visits to the bellicose Kachins in the hills. One night when Stevenson was unwell and stayed at home instead of going as usual to the clinic, a man was killed by a tiger on the road he would have taken, and another mauled. Fire destroyed the house next door but left their thatched house unscathed. But still not one of the many Chinese and Burmese to whom they preached the gospel showed more than a polite interest.[564]

After the ghoulish Thebaw succeeded his father, King Mindon, at Mandalay, atrocities multiplied and relations with the British rapidly deteriorated. On October 3, 1879, a steam launch arrived at Bhamo with a message for Stevenson and Soltau. T. T. Cooper, the Resident, had been murdered by his own sepoy guard, and his successor had been withdrawn as the dangers increased. The British representative in Mandalay was himself withdrawing to Rangoon. 'Leave by this steamer,' ran the message. 'It is the last.'

Stevenson and Soltau 'decided not to leave their posts', and the American Baptist missionaries to the Burmese stayed with them. Not to be always under the Resident's eye was a relief. A month later the dispensary was still in full swing, Soltau reported. Attendances often lapsed at the merest hint of rumours against them, but otherwise all were as friendly as ever. The Kachin chiefs whose homes they visited from time to time were among their best friends, and whenever they chose to go into the hills they had no lack of escorts. Stevenson decided to make a reconnaissance into China as a guest of

the Kachins, knowing that the Chinese merchants and muleteers had spoken well of him in the plains beyond the border.

He left on November 18, 1879, with Kachin escorts, and while Hudson Taylor and J. J. Coulthard were travelling by mule litter from Yantai to Yangzhou, John Stevenson penetrated more than a hundred miles into Yunnan, to the city of Yongchang (now Baoshan), between the Salween and Mekong Rivers, less than a hundred miles from Dali. Not only the medical work but the Gospels and tracts distributed in Bhamo 'had affected a wide area'. Not even the Chinese authorities were surprised to see him, the first European to enter China from Burma since Margary's murder. He returned safely to Bhamo, reassured and planning next time to keep going eastwards.

Hudson Taylor was less sanguine when he heard the news. Sir Thomas Wade had received adverse reports from some consuls about 'unwise' missionaries in their areas, and applications for 'passports' (travel passes) were being denied on flimsy grounds. 'I hope Stevenson's crossing the border may not occasion serious trouble,' he wrote to Benjamin and Amelia on March 12. But apparently any repercussions took only time to be resolved, and work in Bhamo proved too satisfying to forsake, for Stevenson and Soltau did not leave until November 29, 1880, after the monsoon rains. Count Bela Széchényi, after meeting George Easton at Sining and failing to enter Tibet, had been forced like all others before him to opt for Burma instead. But his ill wind blew good to the Mission in Bhamo. He presented his well-proved ponies to Stevenson and Soltau.[565]

A new commercial caravan route through friendly Kachin territory provided the opportunity, but it looked as if the Burmese deputy-governor would forbid them to go. That night an attack was made by Kachins on merchants camped outside the Bhamo city walls, and when the deputy himself came to the Mission next morning prospects looked bleak. But he had simply come to assure them that he would protect the Mission property in their absence.[566]

Travelling in Western clothes, with Kachins carrying loads of books and medicines for their work along the way, they joined a long train of six hundred animals and four hundred men filing out towards the hills. Kachin chiefs and Chinese merchants led the way, Chinese, Shan and Kachin muleteers followed with three pack animals each, guarded by Kachins armed with spears, matchlocks and tasselled machetes ornamented with silver. Over forty chiefs representing one hundred Kachin families formed the escort among whom Stevenson and Soltau brought up the tear.

In tense silence broken by the jingle of harness they marched hour upon hour. An attack by rival chiefs could be expected, as their way of collecting 'road-tax'. But nothing happened until on December 1 at the midday halt half a dozen Kachins tried to make off with the Széchényi ponies and the missionaries' pack-loads. When Soltau stopped them, they 'drew their frightful-looking sword knives and flourished them over my head as if to cut me down, The Lord kept me perfectly calm . . . My composure baffled them, and they seemed afraid to strike'. At this point friendly chiefs came to the rescue and in the fight that followed, 'with the backs and not with the blades' of their short-swords, Stevenson and Soltau were dragged to safety at the far end of the camp. Their animals and possessions were recovered, and after some firing of guns and wild cursing, the rival chiefs settled down together to parley over pipes and alcohol.

It transpired that a Kachin chief had disappeared at the time of Major Sladen's expedition in 1867–68, and although the matter had been amicably settled, this was a plot to have the blood of Englishmen, or failing that to collect a ransom. By nightfall a settlement of just twelve rupees had been agreed and, in celebrating, the chiefs of both sides were 'considerably intoxicated', with 'bullets whizzing about among the trees, so that we became more afraid of our friends than of our enemies'.

This was not the last of such excitements, but on December 4 they emerged from the hills into peaceful Shan territory, and from then on travelled in peace, broken only by calls for medical treatment wherever they went. Passing through Tengyue (Momein), Tengchong, Baoshan and Xiaguan, they reached Dali, the old capital of western Yunnan with its marble and granite temples and bridges, on December 31. Influential men who had met them in Bhamo introduced them to the mandarins, and until January 6, 1881, they were kept busy talking, preaching the gospel and selling books.

The direct route to Kunming took them through beautiful country bedecked with rhododendrons and camellias, and inhabited by 'Lolo' tribal people. But they also travelled through untended agricultural land, mile upon mile, with endless evidence of desolation from the long Muslim rebellion. Kunming, '496 miles from Bhamo', was reached on January 21, but they met with no trace of Trench. Leaving the imperial road to Guiyang, they turned north through Dongchuan to Zhaotong, on February 4.

Soon afterwards 'we were met by two extraordinary objects [Miao tribesmen] . . . leading a goat'—'far wilder-looking than any men or women we have seen among the (Kachins)'. It seems not to have struck them that two apparitions in European dress were far more 'extraordinary objects' on the hills north of Zhaotong. Here 'narrow tracks that skirted dangerous precipices, steep ravines, and narrow ledges cut in the face of the rock' were too narrow for pack-loads to pass and too broken for travellers to stay mounted.

At last they reached Laowatan, '756 miles from Bhamo', sold their animals, shot the rapids of the Heng River, and entered Sichuan on February 14 (see map 2.26: p 246). Seventy-nine days after leaving the Irrawaddy River, '1,000 miles from its mouth, we entered the muddy waters of the (Yangzi) 1,756 miles from its mouth'. And on February 22 they arrived at Chongqing. In more than 1,000 miles of travel they had met no other missionary.

They rested for only a few days. Late one night on their way to Wuhan, when anchored a mile above Wanxian, they were surprised by a messenger from the city magistrate. A friend of General Mesny and of James Broumton with a photograph to prove it, he declared that a boat would attend them in the morning to bring them to breakfast in the *yamen*. Sure enough they became his honoured guests. 'Throwing off all reserve, he chatted with us in the most friendly manner,' before returning them to their boat. Such a far cry from the attitudes of the literati and mandarins of even five years before, fully vindicated the policy of seeing and being seen widely throughout China.

Descending the Yangzi gorges without mishap, they reached Wuhan on March 25, and took their time to complete the journey to Zhenjiang and Shanghai. The first successful attempt by Westerners to cross China from west to east was headline news and they were lionised. But astute readers of *China's Millions* in China, Europe and the States recognised the unsung itinerations of others as being of equal or greater value.

Stevenson was back in Bhamo, via Rangoon, on July 26, 1881. He immediately went down with 'jungle fever' for three weeks but recovered, to hold the fort for two more years, with an evangelist. Free to enter Yunnan at any time, his opportunities in Bhamo were too many to allow him to leave. Soltau returned to Britain to study medicine, becoming fully qualified. He married and brought his bride to Bhamo in November 1883, only to be driven out in 1884 by a revolt and the sacking of the town.[567]

After several failures by government expeditions, their west to east adventure deserved publicity and was reported in the *Proceedings of the Royal Geographical Society, 1880–81*. It had, however, followed in reverse the well-documented route taken by other travellers from east to west. Its lasting value lay rather

in the fact that the mature John Stevenson endorsed John McCarthy's and Broumton's judgment that Kunming would be a valuable centre for the Mission in Yunnan, and McCarthy's and Cameron's that Dali held the key to western Yunnan and the border tribes. The eventual opening of the southern route and railway from Tongking (North Vietnam) ended attempts to develop access from the west, until World War II. But that was far ahead. France had been annexing more and more of 'Indo-China' since 1787, and her invasion of Tongking in 1882 precipitated the Franco-Chinese war of 1884–85.[568]

A firm foothold in Sichuan (1878–81)

Henry Soltau's description of their arrival at Chongqing on February 22 opens a window on life in this 'city set on a hill' with battlements and parapets along the edge of a cliff above a long line of junks at anchor. The man they sent to find the CIM and say where their boat was moored came back with a stranger in Chinese dress.

After his exploratory journey round the Daliangshan in October–November 1877 (see pp 318–19), George Nicoll had written urging two candidates in Britain, Samuel R. Clarke and J. H. Riley, to consider taking the gospel to the Nosu. Hudson Taylor approved, and in October 1878 they had joined Nicoll at Chongqing. Within a year they were pulling their weight in a thriving work in the city and Sichuan countryside.

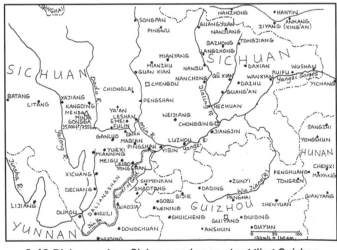

2.48 Rich, populous Sichuan and poor, struggling Guizhou

Surprised to find John Stevenson and Soltau in foreign clothes, and anxious not to draw a crowd on their way through busy streets to the CIM Mission house, young Samuel Clarke hired sedan chairs to hide them in and followed behind them. Fresh from unresponsive Bhamo and their long journey without meeting a Christian, they found the contrast at Chongqing exhilarating. Opposite the entrance to the premises they first saw a mandarin's proclamation:

> The place where the Gospel is preached is a solemn place; everything must be quiet and reverent. Men and children must listen in the outer hall, and women in the inner. Let there be no noise or uproar. All idlers are forbidden to enter and loiter about. There are to be no crowds round the doors. Everything must be done according to order, and if anyone dare disobey, let him be immediately bound and sent for punishment.[569]

Then they were being greeted by more Chinese and Europeans ('pale and thin') than they had expected to see.

George Nicoll was ill, and away for a few days with his wife. But Riley and a colporteur of the National Bible Society of Scotland named Wilson were at home, and four Chinese colleagues. The B&FBS colporteur, Mollman, an older man, made the CIM his base but was also away. Across the central courtyard beyond the big hall used as a chapel, stood the main two-storey building. On the ground floor the formal reception room where literati were entertained was flanked by store rooms and the Chinese staff's own rooms. Above were bedrooms for Riley, Wilson, Mollman and guests. Flanking the courtyard, on the right a noisy school was in full swing, with Samuel Clarke's room beside it, and on the left the communal dining-room and kitchen, with the Nicolls' private quarters. One of the Chinese, from the LMS in Wuhan, was working for the American Bible Society, another, a Wesleyan, for the B&FBS. The senior Sichuanese evangelist had been converted through the American Presbyterians in Canton, and his son worked

with him. Denominational differences were forgotten in their essential unity.

Chinese visitors kept coming in, and frequent meetings drew fifty or sixty at a time. It was in this place that Nicoll's bride had coped week after week with crowds of women callers after her marriage in September 1879. She was still the only foreign woman in the province, so populous that a hundred Christian missionaries deployed among its cities would be none too many. Although the first believers were not baptised until June 1880, 'the large, quiet, orderly congregations on the Lord's day might give a stranger to suppose the station had been opened fifty years'. In that comment by Hudson Taylor we see the sapling start of a church in Sichuan which today is a great tree.[570]

From July 21 to September 19, 1879, Riley and Mollman had travelled, preaching and selling Gospels, to Emei (Omei) city and its sacred mountain, crowned since the Han dynasty in AD 200 with beautiful Buddhist monastery-temples where their books would be read with interest. From there they went to Ebian (Opien) city on the northern flank of the Nosu homeland to reconnoitre, intending to go to Mabian to find a place for Riley and Samuel Clarke to settle. The Ebian magistrate was anxious, however, lest they come to harm from wild Nosu on a foray—'fine stalwart fellows', Riley called them. So they had to be content with hiring one Nosu, called Niko, to return to Chongqing with them. From him they learned more than his language—Niko schemed to take a beggar-boy with him when he returned home, to sell him to the Nosu as a slave.[571]

Samuel Clarke then took a turn with Mollman, making another five hundred mile figure-of-eight tour of cities along minor roads to Chengdu, the provincial capital, and beyond. Starting on October 6 they were not back until November 25, drooping with fatigue from travelling and preaching at every place of any size. At night they had been objects of insatiable curiosity, or were kept talking until late by enquiring people.

In the spring of 1880, from March 8 to May 8, Riley and Samuel Clarke with Niko as interpreter, made a second reconnaissance of the Nosu border. This time the goal was Leibo (Luipo) at the mouth of the Valley of the Beautiful Maiden beneath the towering Dragon's Head and Sun Bridge (see p 313).

By the time they reached the village of Huanglang on April 13, they were running out of silver. While Clarke went back to Chongqing for more, Riley pressed on with Niko and the young Sichuanese evangelist. On the 18th they heard that a man had escaped from a Nosu attack only after they had stripped him naked, but a woman and child had been carried off. Even Niko was sick with apprehension, but Riley insisted on going on, and Leibo was reached on April 24. Two days later fifteen Chinese were caught and killed nearby. Reluctantly Riley wrote, 'As the Lolos in this neighbourhood are so much given to plunder just now, I think this is not the best time to seek an entrance among them.' Ebian had been more promising. He withdrew to Yibin, met Samuel Clarke there, sent Niko home, and waited for a more propitious time. Between these expeditions and others into the province in other directions, they worked among the two or three hundred thousand inhabitants of Chongqing itself.

George Nicoll's protracted ill-health was thought to be due to heart disease, and during a time of political excitement after Stevenson and Soltau had gone, when a consular representative was attacked (on June 3, 1881) and a house destroyed, he took his wife to the coast. He was still recuperating at Chefoo six months later, but recovered enough to return to Chongqing and struggle on, still hampered by ill-health, until sent home.

A Swiss girl first in Yunnan (1881–83)

Ellen McCarthy and Jane Kidd had not been in Guiyang long before James Broumton, back from his thousand mile working tour of Yunnan, carried Ellen off again to marry her at Wuhan early in 1881. George and Fanny Clarke had hesitated to go five hundred miles away from fellow-

missionaries, to Dali, until their first child was born and strong enough to travel. But the child died. Through their grief they saw the hand of God freeing them to occupy a house at Dali rented from the consular 'writer' in Chongqing. In Broumton's absence they could not leave Jane Kidd alone in Guiyang, so Samuel Clarke gallantly came from Chongqing to take charge until the Broumtons returned, and the George Clarkes set off on May 16, 1881.[572]

A Swiss girl therefore became the first foreign woman to enter Yunnan, and the first to die there. 'A prosperous journey' brought them to Kunming on June 7, where they found the people 'not curious or troublesome'. Before the end of June they were in Dali, further from other Westerners than were any other foreigners in China. No mail service existed and communication even by public courier was difficult and expensive. The occupants of the Chongqing writer's house refused to move out, and the Clarkes had to make shift for five months without even a proper room of their own. They had no Chinese Christian with them, and found themselves under suspicion of ulterior motives in coming. 'I don't suppose any station has been opened under such difficulties,' George wrote. His wife found reminders of Switzerland in the snow-capped, 15,000 foot mountains she could see. Like Daniel's three young men in the burning fiery furnace, she wrote, they were content to wait for the Lord's deliverance. The only domestic help they could get was from a woman and her child escaping from her opium-sot husband who had already sold two of their children. He soon tracked her down, to sell her too. 'This is a terrible place; Sodom and Gomorrah could not have been much more wicked . . . Our neighbour was going to kill his wife and child. My husband and three women held him.'[573]

At last they found a house to rent, employed a teacher and opened a small school with seven pupils. In what he called his spare time, during the first year George hand-printed 6,600 'Gospel books' under twelve titles, totalling 48,700 pages with 3,000 maps. His working hours he spent distributing them and trying to get a hearing for the gospel. More months went by, until on May 21, 1882, two sick explorers, hungry and dishevelled, stumbled into Dali and found an inn.

Archibald R. Colquhoun, an Indian government engineering administrator, and his companion Charles Wahab, had started out from Canton on an exploratory survey of southern China, crossing from east to west close to the Tongking and Laotian borders. All that could go wrong did so. Dysentery, fever, the disloyalty of the interpreter, and obstruction by a high mandarin forced them to make a major change of direction without enough money to complete the journey. Wahab was too weak to ride an animal and had to be carried. Even Colquhoun 'reached (Xiaguan) in a famishing condition', but after resting managed to cover the last eight miles to Dali. 'I was too fatigued to walk, and this part of the day's work [clinging to his mule on a very slippery stone causeway] wearied me terribly . . . Torn clothes, broken shoes, unkempt hair and weariness nearly amounting to prostration must have given me a more than usually seedy appearance.'[574]

When planning his journey in England he had consulted John McCarthy and Stevenson, and was carrying a note of introduction from Benjamin Broomhall,

though he had had no intention of passing through Dali. While he cleaned himself up, his interpreter made enquiries and arrived back at the inn with George Clarke. The French priest was away, and these were the first Europeans the Clarkes had seen for more than a year. They insisted on Colquhoun and Wahab moving in with them until well again. 'The very fact of finding a highly-educated lady in this faraway land—where so many missionaries have already met their deaths—speaks volumes for their self-abnegation and zeal . . . ' Colquhoun later wrote. 'I felt unwell and would have been seriously ill' but for the 'unbounded hospitality and generous assistance' provided.

By May 30 he was strong enough to go on, Wahab could ride an animal, and Clarke had been able to lend them some silver for the remaining stages to Bhamo. So they went, only to find themselves in dire straits again until they encountered Pére Vial, a Catholic priest who accompanied them to Bhamo. There the American missionaries supplied 'a good large tub, with plenty of delicious soap' and a breakfast about which they could not stop talking when they met John Stevenson afterwards. 'Mr Stevenson . . . immediately set about sharing everything he had with us. His house, his clothes, his food, and the last half-penny of the small stock in his purse, he placed at our disposal.' Wahab recovered enough to be shipped home to Britain, but died before Colquhoun's two-volume travelogue was published.[575]

During the days spent together in Dali, George Clarke translated for Colquhoun 'A Manuscript Account of the Kwei-chau Miao-tzu', written in about 1730 after their subjugation. Eighty-two different tribes or clans of minority peoples, including the Nosu—'their customs are devilish and their place is termed "the Devil's Net"'—the Zhong Jia, Yao and many kinds of 'Miao', were described.[576] Then George and Fanny were alone again until Arthur Eason, a newcomer to the ranks of CIM pioneers, visited Dali for a few days in the last week of June, 1882. This was the first opportunity

2.49 Courtesy call: the mandarin, Pére Vial, Wahab and Colquhoun

for 'Christian fellowship' they had had since parting from Samuel Clarke in Guiyang on May 16, 1881. They thought they had been away for 'eighteen months'.[577]

Adam Dorward, 'though it be by my life' (1878–83)

The action continues, the pageant moves on, a succession mostly of young men and women taking risks 'beyond the call of duty'. That they were making history, while their leader battled with adversity of other kinds, few could recognise at the time. They all knew Hudson Taylor's master-plan, to put down roots in the nine provinces, and each played his or her part 'for the glory of God'. For some that part was to mean long years without house or home; for others death or bereavement. Where fiction would bring in more variety, stranger reality demands that we stay with these pioneers a little longer, to meet three more.

In 1875 six outstanding men had come to China: Cameron, George Clarke and Nicoll; Broumton, Easton and King. Elizabeth Wilson and George Parker followed the next year. 1878 brought Trench, Riley, Samuel Clarke and Adam Dorward, and 1881 saw George Andrew and Arthur Eason arrive. These last three now come into focus.

Adam C. Dorward stands out, unique in that he took on the most dangerous province and for eight years worked in it, often alone and homeless, until he died. 'As Lhasa to Tibet, so has Hunan been to China.' The hostile literati succeeded in making Hunan the last province to yield to the tenacity of the pioneers.

Dorward had given up good prospects in his uncles' tweed mills to go into training at Harley House. Under Grattan Guinness for three or four years, he shared a room with James Fanstone, the future apostle to Brazil. As Hudson Taylor in his youth had seen remote central Asian Ili as his

goal, Dorward set his heart on Tibet, the greatest challenge he knew. He reached China in June 1878 and after a short introduction to the language chose to live with Chinese, away from fellow-Europeans. Datong in Anhui became his home for a year with an evangelist and a colporteur. While they learned more from his example than his teaching, he became a Chinese to the Chinese with their help. Then, with his base at Anqing (see map 2.57: p 457), he embarked on three ambitious journeys through different parts of Anhui province. For six weeks they moved from city to city (August 6–September 17, 1879) until their stock of books was exhausted. In trying his wings he could not have wished for a better companion than John McCarthy's ex-soldier friend Yang Cunling. They matched each other. 'Endowed with a strong will and firm resolution, (Dorward) was at the same time one of the meekest and least self-assertive of men.'[578]

In December, and January 1880, and again in March with another companion, Dorward 'lived rough' and proved his fitness for a hard life. In eight months he

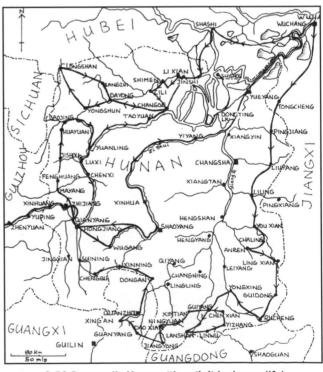

2.50 Dorward's Hunan: 'though it be by my life'

walked 1,200 miles, and travelled 500 by boat. To Hudson Taylor when he met him at Shanghai in June 1880, he seemed 'young and alone' but the right man for dangerous Hunan, so he offered him the honour. Dorward accepted. In the heat of mid-July he walked from Yangzhou to Yantai (see map 2.60: p 484), Hudson Taylor's overland journey of 500 miles in reverse, and after a holiday by the sea was 'very impatient to get off to Hunan'.

> I feel unfit for such glorious work and unworthy of such an honourable position in the Lord's service, but ... if only I can by my efforts, trusting in God's blessing, lead a few of these perishing souls to the knowledge of Christ Jesus, and in any way hasten the opening of that province to the gospel, though it be by my life, I shall be satisfied and my coming to China shall not be in vain.

He could have had funds guaranteed by the Bible Society in return for his work for them, but preferred to do without, in order that he might 'have to look to God for it'.[579]

Judd, Yao and Zhang had made the first attempt on Hunan in 1875. After the Chefoo Convention, Judd and Broumton had crossed through the province to Guiyang, followed by George Clarke, Edward Fishe and Robert Landale, varying the route (see pp 299–300). Baller and Trench had escorted Ellen McCarthy and Jane Kidd from Wuhan in the spring of 1880 spending a month (Feb 27–Mar 31) within Hunan. Meanwhile Bible Society colporteurs and other CIM and LMS missionaries had briefly touched the fringes of the province. So when Dorward, Yao Shangda and another Chinese set foot on Hunan soil on October 27, 1880, to a welcome of 'Beat the foreign devil!', they were not the first to preach the gospel in the province.[580] But they did so on a wholly different scale. They crossed the province from north-east to south-west, and stayed in Changde from November 16 to 29, before working through the western cities again and replenishing their funds at Guiyang, by then nearer than Wuhan.

Returning to Hongjiang, where they had left a cache of books, they then broke new ground, 'covering some two hundred miles of country (between Hongjiang and the Dongting Lake) previously unvisited by any Protestant missionary', and arrived back at Wuhan on April 1, 1881, to be greeted by Hudson Taylor himself. In five and a half months they had sold and distributed 30,000 books and leaflets, including 1,700 to 1,800 Gospels, a good start to eight years of similar work.[581] The *yamen* underlings of some mandarins and literati, suspicious of his motives, had tried to make trouble, but most people they encountered had been neutral or even friendly. At Yuanzhou (now Zhijiang), when some stones were thrown at his boat from a crowd on land, Dorward coolly went ashore and chatted with them. 'He's not a foreigner but an interpreter', they decided, and after a day of book-selling he summed them up as 'exceedingly good'. Where Henry Taylor had failed by stolidly trying to hold his ground at Queshan in Henan, until his own courage cracked, Adam Dorward was using the biblical alternative advised by Hudson Taylor, of tactfully moving on from place to place before opposition could build up.

At Wuhan Hudson Taylor had been seeing James Broumton and his party off on March 26, across Hunan to Guiyang, and was himself about to leave by river-steamer. So instead of resting, Dorward joined him on the boat to report on his travels and at Anqing to enlist Yang Cunling for his next foray into Hunan. By hurrying he hoped to overtake Broumton's party and help them through the dangerous rapids of the Yuan River and the cities that had been most hostile to others. Without help Broumton could be put under intolerable strain— exactly as happened.

Director in action (March–June 1881)

After meeting the surgeon Harold Schofield and his wife at Shanghai on June 30, 1880, Hudson Taylor had made his own long journey through southern Zhejiang and the Guangxin River region of Jiangxi (see p 351). He then returned to Yantai for four months (October 1880–February 1881), and on February 24 was in Shanghai again to meet the French Mail bringing George Andrew and Arthur Eason. Time and again he had written, in letters to Jennie, Theodore Howard, Benjamin and Amelia, 'We need more good men.' He was having ceaseless trouble with some disappointing men and a few gross failures. In Schofield, Andrew, Eason and others in the next five years his prayers and hopes were to be fulfilled.[582]

He firmly believed in establishing a personal friendship, beyond mere personal acquaintance, with each individual. George Andrew never forgot how Hudson Taylor took him by the hand after they had had a long talk together, and 'expressed his thankfulness to God for bringing me to China'. "Remember," he said, "that the work of the Lord is the LORD's work," emphasizing that I was not an agent but an instrument.'

On his part Hudson Taylor was impressed by the quality of both men, Andrew and Eason. In fact, of recent arrivals, he wrote to Benjamin when he reached Anqing with Dorward, 'Six of the seven are treasures indeed. I am at my wits' end to know what to do for six more like them.' The scope for deploying them was so great. Advances in every direction, beyond expectation, were needing to be secured by occupying intermediate 'stations' along the routes, if perilous beginnings were to be consolidated. They were learning that one man, perhaps with more than one woman missionary, in any location, needed to be able to call on the help of another in emergencies. A minimum of three men to two mission centres was proving necessary. Less enterprising men would have to be content with advancing one step at a time. The long stride had succeeded too often to be abandoned now.[583]

He took the bold (but not unprecedented) step of asking Andrew and Eason after only a month in China to join James Broumton, his bride and Charlotte Ken, a nurse who was to join Jane Kidd, on their imminent departure to Guiyang. With little knowledge of the language or of things Chinese, they were to face nine hundred miles of primitive travelling conditions and the possible malice of literati and mobs. J. J. Coulthard took them up the Yangzi to Wuhan and thought them 'sterling missionaries, prepared to endure hardness'. They were to study Chinese in the dialect of Guiyang instead of at Anqing. Frank Trench was also on his way back to Yunnan after treatment in Shanghai. He was to start a week after the Broumton party, to catch them up at the far side of the Dongting Lake and travel with them.[584]

All were ready on March 18 when Hudson Taylor himself arrived at Wuhan to see them off. Finding the Ballers in poor health he sent them to take charge at Chefoo while he and Jennie made their projected journey to Shanxi and the western provinces. This vital business centre of Wuhan had to be reliably manned, and he could only use available men, so he confidently appointed his personal secretary to replace Baller. The position involved handling and transmitting large sums of money, and signing documents in the name of the Mission. 'I was barely twenty-one years old at the time,' Coulthard wrote. 'He felt he had got men from the Lord and that God trusted them . . . If anyone raised a prejudice against them it did not affect him at all.'[585]

Finally Hudson Taylor invited members of other missions to a commissioning service before the Broumtons left, and notes taken by Mrs Bryson of the LMS caught the atmosphere. He applied Psalms 123, 124 and 125 to the travellers. Relying only upon God and his enabling, 'they must not be surprised if their message were to be received with scorn and contempt'. On their difficult and dangerous route through hostile Hunan, quite possibly 'men would rise up against them'. In the many river rapids they would see the wrecks of other boats and might experience disaster themselves. They should remember the psalmist's words, 'The water had overwhelmed us, the stream had gone over our soul', and that their hope was 'in the name of the Lord who made heaven and earth'. They knew that he lived by these precepts himself. From Deuteronomy 4 he showed that obedience and entire consecration to God are prerequisites of success; and from Joshua 1 that undeviating courage with constant dependence on the Word of God were conditions of the promises 'I will not fail thee nor forsake thee,' and 'Then shalt thou have good success.' He urged them to preach and teach gently, not by argument, which alienates the one who is worsted. By Christ-like living and loving while delighting in him, they would 'bring forth fruit in due season'. The stark possibility that those present on this occasion might never meet again, added solemnity to the communion service.

Then Hudson Taylor spoke individually to each traveller. To George Andrew he said after encouraging remarks about his own experience of being unable to speak Chinese at first, 'Your faith will doubtless be tried; sometimes, it may be, your supplies will fail altogether and you may not know where to turn for help. Then, in your extremity, you need fear nothing, for the Lord will be with you . . . and will be your helper.' To Charlotte Kerr he spoke frankly of facing up to loneliness, such as Jesus had experienced, that she might be a comfort to Chinese women as well as to her colleagues.[586]

On March 25 a surprise and 'great excitement' almost eclipsed the elation they already felt as boats were hired to cross Hunan. Stevenson and Soltau arrived with their story of 1,990 adventurous miles from Burma, and of having rented a house in Dali. Hudson Taylor's delight overcame his concern that they had unwisely made the journey dressed as foreigners. Due to start on the 22nd, Broumton's party had been delayed by the officiousness of a mandarin, but on March 26 they were away, heading straight into trouble.

Frank Trench left on April 1 to overtake them. He was to rent premises in Kunming, to occupy Dali if George and Fanny Clarke were not there already, and to go on into

the Shan States of western Yunnan if he could. Adam Dorward arrived on April 1 from his five and a half months' absence, 'very pleased with Hunan . . . the right man for that province', Hudson Taylor told Jennie. 'God is evidently so arranging things as to make the most of my visit . . . So many are now meeting me and so many arrangements are being made.' He and Dorward boarded the steamer on April 4 for Anqing, and by the 7th Dorward and Yang Cunling were on their way back to catch up with the Guiyang party.

Until something came of these bold moves, it was important not to stir up criticism. 'No statement (is) to be published prematurely,' Hudson Taylor instructed London, 'it might defeat us and defer success. But the more prayer the better.' Those in the know held their breath as days lengthened into weeks and no news of the travellers arrived.

Broumton's ordeal[587]
(March 26–June 21, 1881)

The mouth of the Han River gave more shelter to shipping than the shores of the Yangzi, so James Broumton and his wife, Andrew, Eason and Charlotte Kerr had first to cross the great river from the Wuchang side to join their hired houseboat. They found the Han 'completely blocked with boats'. Working their way through the log-jam took time, and an adverse wind forced them to tie up not far from their starting point, the Mission home at Wuchang, again. In spite of dawn starts, day by day, each night fell when they had made a mere twenty miles upstream against strong Yangzi

2.51 Wuhan: where the Han River joins the Yangzi (Hankou (left), Hanyang (right) and distant Wuchang)

currents and headwinds. By April 2 they had only covered a hundred miles. This was gentle training in patience for what lay ahead. The explanation was to come after ten days of high drama.

They pulled into a winding creek and tied up near the small village of Luqikou for a quiet Sunday. Early that afternoon a thunderstorm suddenly broke over them. More and more boats left the Yangzi to shelter in the creek, and when the steep banks were lined with junks packed closely side by side, still more anchored in midstream. Rain fell all through the night. By Monday afternoon the swollen tributary was a raging torrent. Anchors dragged, cables snapped, and boat after boat was swept towards the Yangzi, colliding with others, dragging them loose and turning turtle. In the dark the crashing and cries for help went on and on, but for the present the Broumtons' boat was unaffected, moored to the lee bank of a wide curve. Those on the outer curve were being swept away. Broumton found a shack on shore where the women could shelter with George Andrew for support, and himself returned to guard their baggage with Eason. A heavily laden coal-boat lay alongside, being forced against them by the current. Suddenly, near midnight, with a deafening crash, one side of their hull and cabin caved in. They leapt ashore, assessed the damage and slaved hard to haul their possessions and the ship's fittings to safety up the bank. As Broumton, Eason and Andrew in turn kept guard, along both banks fires were lit by other marooned people and 'threw a lurid glare' on the raging torrent and the devastation ashore.

The storm passed over and repairs began, but twenty large boats and a hundred lives had been lost. With daylight the news spread that foreign women were among the survivors. Threatening crowds 'forced their way in everywhere' to stare interminably. Lost sleep and the strain of keeping calm and courteous hour after hour made the women 'almost ill', until Broumton found 'an old shop', semi-derelict but 'almost a palace . . . we did not mind the dirt.' After dark they took possession, the women hiding in the loft for four days while carpenters made their boat safe to go on up the Yangzi. On the 11th another storm lashed them at anchor in a sheltered cove, halting them for two more days. But at last on the 13th they reached Yueyang at the entrance to the Dongting Lake. There Yang Cunling found them. In four days he and Adam Dorward had come as far as they in nineteen. Together they entered Hunan.

More storms made hazardous the crossing of the lake, and one of Dorward's crew was lost overboard. But at one anchorage a man who had welcomed Baller to his house saw Dorward when they tied up for the night, and invited him in. 'Scarcely a day passes but we are brought through some fresh difficulty,' Broumton wrote on April 26. At last they were safely in the Yuan River and near Changde. This was where Adam Dorward had planned to strike off overland, but the rapids still lay ahead of Broumton's inexperienced party, and Trench, who was to have escorted them, could not be found. Reluctantly Dorward decided not to leave them.

George Andrew then fell ill with smallpox, and Dorward nursed him, isolated at the stem of the river-boat, day and night, week after week. Charlotte Kerr was busy doctoring the women who heard about her from the boatmen, and suffering herself from 'ague'. But the Hunan people were friendly, and even the men who demanded to see the foreign women were content when Ellen Broumton, blonder than Charlotte, consented to show herself. 'Mr Dorward's intense *delight* as to the *wonderfully good behaviour* of the Hunan people' amused the others. In this change from violence to mere curiosity he saw hope, a promise of the province accepting him.

More than a month of travelling and hairbreadth escapes still lay ahead of them. On May 4, the boat's bamboo towline broke on the way up a rapid, and they nearly came to grief. But on May 18, beyond the city of Hongjiang near the Guizhou border, they were holed by a hidden rock and quickly filled with water. The sick man Andrew was carried in a sheet slung from a pole to a house on the mainland. And once more their sodden baggage was landed, at first on an island in midstream. Cunling, Dorward, Eason and Broumton were wet through all day long, salvaging all they could. Slowly they moved their saturated books and personal possessions from the island to the riverbank, only just in time. By the 22nd the river had risen thirty or forty feet, covering the island.

Again, the people of the hamlet of Losiping treated the foreigners well. With charcoal fires and two days of sunshine everything was dried, and in return for her 'doctoring' Charlotte Kerr was given more than they all needed of vegetables and meat. The villagers listened for hours to Cunling's preaching, and welcomed him and Adam Dorward when they returned from Guiyang.[588] 'The whole village turned out to see us start', overland on foot and by mountain chair. At Yuanzhou men tore down the inn windows to get an unimpeded view of the strangers. And Zhenyuan in Guizhou (where Margary's boat was burned) lived up to its reputation for rowdiness. Only when the two women came out of their inn rooms to stand on show before a crowd of men could quiet be restored. By enduring hardships at many points along the way, they left a good impression of the maligned 'foreigner', and helped to destroy prejudice.

Frank Trench had reached Guiyang a full month before, growing more and more anxious about their safety. When he came upon them 'three stages' (about ninety miles) out from Guiyang, it became a triumphal entry of the five men and two women who rejoined Jane Kidd on June 21, almost three eventful months since leaving Wuhan. To meet the first-ever Miao tribal Christian, a woman, on their arrival was reward enough. Now there are tens of thousands of Miao Christians.

When the news reached Hudson Taylor, he too was jubilant.

Curiosity is being appeased; hostility removed [his editorial in the *Millions* read]. The stay of missionary ladies in the heart of Hunan for a fortnight in one place [Losiping], the journey overland to the notorious city of (Yuanzhou), and a night spent onshore there at the inn; the not less rowdy city (of Zhenyuan), visited by ladies, who slept there also, and departed without any insult or danger all point to the conclusion that *China is opening* ... far more rapidly than Christian Missions are prepared to follow up ... Were the Lord to grant us double the number of workers, and double the means, within twelve months we could have them allocated and at work.[589]

Sequels in summary (July 1881–1883)

This story took unexpected turns soon after the long journey ended. After six days Adam Dorward and Yang Cunling walked back to Hongjiang in Hunan, preaching the gospel as they went and spending half a day at friendly Losiping. Frank Trench had reached Guiyang in sixty-one days, unhindered by officials but shown 'bad feeling' by fellow-travellers influenced by current Russian aggression at Ili. When preparing to take Arthur Eason as his companion on a marathon itinerary of western Yunnan, Trench fell ill again with the same complaint as had taken him to Shanghai. Charlotte Kerr's attack of 'ague' became 'severe and all but fatal'. Soon after reaching her place of work she too had to face returning to the coast for treatment. This meant Jane Kidd handing over her school and women's work to Ellen Broumton, and escorting Charlotte with Trench to Chongqing and down the Yangzi, at least another month of travelling.

When they arrived at Chongqing in October 1881, and while Trench and Charlotte Kerr rested before braving the Yangzi rapids, Jane Kidd threw herself into work among the women of Chongqing. The Nicolls were away and Riley had more on his hands than he could manage. 'Suicide (by opium) is terribly common here. Last month we had twenty-six cases, twelve men, twelve women and two girls . . . All, I believe, except four, were brought round,' he wrote to Hudson Taylor as soon as his visitors had gone.[590] Could Miss Kidd not be spared from Guiyang to work in Chongqing? She was 'well understood and has a very winning way of speaking to the women'. Hudson Taylor understood, and probably consulted her. For he told Riley to rent another house for women's work, and sent Jane back to Chongqing, escorted by David Thompson, a new colleague for Samuel Clarke at Chengdu. Within three months she and Riley were married at the Yichang consulate.

George Andrew, convalescent, and Eason settled down to language study at Guiyang, but before long heard from Hudson Taylor. With Trench unable to occupy Kunming and support the Clarkes at Dali, would they do so instead?

> I have, after mature thought, concluded to ask you both to go there ... I should advise your securing accommodation in (an) inn, and not attempting ... to rent a house until you have been there sometime ... and have made some friends in the place. I would suggest ... you go out in turn on missionary journeys (with a Chinese companion) ... There should always be one of you (in Kunming, so that remittances) may not be lost. I would advise your taking as little baggage with you as you can ... Much baggage would be a source of danger as well as expense ... I should be thankful if you will aim at selling Scriptures and preaching the gospel in every city in Yunnan which has not been visited ... and in as many market towns as possible.[591]

On January 20, 1882, within eleven months of reaching China, they left Guiyang and established themselves in Kunming (where they met but were unable to help Colquhoun and Wahab in their plight). They worked through every city of Yunnan east of Dali, and Eason visited George and Fanny Clarke at Dali before himself returning to Wuhan to get married. George Andrew changed places with the Clarkes at Dali, giving them some months in Kunming for 'a wonderful time' of street preaching, and was host to Alexander Hosie at Dali in March 1883.[592]

Hudson Taylor's impressions of Andrew and Eason when they arrived in China had been right. They had quickly shown their mettle and maturity as trail-blazers.

An attic in Hongjiang (July 1881–December 1883)

Adam Dorward and Yang Cunling had walked from Guiyang to Hongjiang in Hunan, preaching the gospel as they went. There they tried and failed to rent even the humblest foothold, but by living inconspicuously at inns and a 'policy of perseverance and conciliation' made friends for the future. Then in a series of cities on a loop northwards through Fenghuang to Baojing near the Sichuan boundary and back to Changde, they had a mixed reception. At some the *yamen* would not even let them through the city gates, but work with few encouragements drew from Dorward the remark, 'If our work is true, "we are labouring together with God"; and that means that success is . . . an absolute certainty.'[593] Yang Cunling had to return home, but after several shorter journeys Dorward set out from Wuhan with another evangelist on December 1, ascending the Zi Shui through Yiyang to Shaoyang and meeting stiff opposition; before circling westwards to reach Hongjiang again on January 1, 1882. This time they succeeded on the 20th in renting an attic under the tiles; this the evangelist occupied while Dorward judiciously withdrew.

In March Dorward went to consult Hudson Taylor in Shanghai. 'How Father loved him!' 'Joe' Coulthard exclaimed (after Dorward's death and his own marriage to Hudson Taylor's daughter Maria). By April 2 he was on his way back to Hunan, making Shashi his base, and set off from there on May 4. June 17 saw him in Hongjiang again, and 'working quietly' he managed to stay unchallenged for three and a half months, breaking the opium addiction of two or three men at a time until forced out by the literati in October. Friendly people presented him with parting gifts of 'pork, ducks, grapes, pears, bamboo shoots, and about a dozen packets of confectionery' and 'at least six or seven appeared interested in the Truth'. The seed of a church in Hunan was germinating. A year later he was writing of his landlord's brother being truly converted, and eleven or twelve cured addicts remaining free.[594]

Although himself expelled, he left two evangelists at Hongjiang, so when they turned up at Wuhan he was deeply disappointed and without waiting set off by boat on December 5, 1882, to regain lost ground. Taking yet another route through the Dongting Lakes to Anxiang and Li Xian in the north, south of Shashi (see map 2.50: p 380) he found friendly people who helped him to engage carriers for an overland journey through Cili to Changde. And on January 1, 1883, as he turned westwards he rejoiced in his diary at the ease and comfort of travelling conditions (that is, without harassment, a far cry from even two years previously) for he was still sleeping on straw or table tops or whatever an innkeeper could offer him. He foresaw 'permanent settlement among the people' but it was never to be his own lot.

This time he was penetrating the far north-western corner of the province. At Yongshun he met two Koreans and took unhurried time to tell them the gospel before making for the remotest city of Longshan, close to the junction of the Hubei, Sichuan and Hunan borders. Even the opium-besotted officials treated him well, and he sold more books than in some larger cities. At Sangzhi and Yongding (now Dayong), however, the presence of a foreign copper-mine prospector in the region had filled the people with suspicion. Here he learned that Griffith John and John Archibald of the National Bible Society of Scotland were in the vicinity, but could not find them. And on February 10 he was back at Wuhan from what had been 'the most encouraging tour he ever took in (Hunan)'. He had walked five hundred miles and sold 1,600 Gospels and booklets.

In May 1882, on his way from Shashi to Changde and Hongjiang, Dorward had opened his heart in a frank letter to Hudson Taylor. In the deafening noise of his inn,

with no privacy in which to pray, he wrote, 'I feel my soul to be very dry and parched, and sometimes I think I shall not be able to continue much longer at this isolated kind of work.' Not only loneliness but the pressure of unrelieved 'heathenism' around him were as much as he could stand. He felt the need of being 'alone with God . . . to spend a few days in a room by myself . . . apart from all noises and distractions (to) pour out my soul to Him, and hear His voice speaking to me.' 'Fellowship with the Lord's people' would be reviving, but 'there is nothing I would like so much as a heart wholly occupied with God—a pure, holy, consecrated heart'. Saintly he certainly was, but another kind of life was not to be. He was still travelling, often alone, six years later.

Before he ventured on his longest and most daring journey, through Jiangxi into eastern and southern Hunan, through north-eastern Guangxi and up to Hongjiang again, from April to July 1883, he learned that Griffith John and Archibald had been 'badly mobbed' at the city of Longyang, south of Changde.[595] A Roman Catholic priest had been forced out of Changde for trying to buy a house, and orders had been issued that he was not to be allowed to land anywhere along his escape route. It happened that his boat was at anchor off Longyang when Griffith John arrived and, ignorant of the priest's presence, tried to go ashore. Mistaking his identity, the people vented on Griffith John and Archibald the venom intended for the priest. Dorward admitted to some trepidation as he left his friends on April 2, 1883. He was not to see them again until he had walked 1,300 miles on the outward journey alone, had sold 7,000 books and 1,500 Gospels, and lived again for five months at Hongjiang, from July 29 until about December 20.[596]

All through these epic years of 1879–83, Hudson Taylor longed to join in the pioneering, the actual travelling in untried areas. He succeeded in making a few exploratory journeys, but recurrent ill-health, and administrative pressures which all but broke his spirit, largely anchored him to the circuit of Yantai, Shanghai, Zhejiang and Wuhan. Hardest to bear was 'the Shansi spirit' of complaint and loss of conviction and purpose. At its heart lay the attitudes to compromises which had been voiced at the Shanghai Conference in 1877, and new theories on how best to 'Christianize' the nation. Mass 'conversion' achieved by muting the gospel until the literati were won over, the proponents maintained, could be brought about by emphasis on the similarities between the Chinese classics and many Christian beliefs, while head-on conflict between the gospel and Chinese cultural practice would harden opinion and opposition. Hudson Taylor found himself cast inescapably in the role of opponent of these views, and champion with others of preaching 'Christ crucified'— a harder battle in some ways than frontline pioneering might have been (1 Corinthians 1.18, 23).

20

Crescendo (1877–87)

1877–85: 'J'ATTAQUE'

The ancestor controversy (1877–85)

The penetration of China was more spiritual than territorial. The whole purpose of long journeys and encounters with danger was to 'rescue the perishing', 'to snatch them as brands from the burning', to challenge Satan's hold on China's millions. None expected to emerge unhurt. Hudson Taylor's constant warning to his members not to neglect their intimate fellowship with God sprang from personal knowledge of the debilitating, destructive effects of close contact with paganism, vice, dissension between Christians—and latterly the Trojan horse of the 'new theology'.

Timothy Richard's increasing propagation of his views had its effect on those whose intellect and convictions were weaker than his own. He protested that the gospel of '"God so loved the world that He gave His only begotten Son that whosoever believeth in Him should not perish but have everlasting life" is only the thought of the most romantic of missionary tyros'. Chinese beliefs and practices, he claimed, also expressed God's truth. 'Moral teaching is another forte of theirs.' Virtuous example is often to be found. 'What then are the myriads of temples, these clouds of incense, their incalculable heaps of paper-money, and these innumerable instances of answered prayer (proof of the living power of their gods) but the evidence of a faith that is all-pervading from the Emperor to the beggar.'[597] Nebulous 'faith' instead of faith in 'our God and Saviour Jesus Christ'? As was to be expected, where he lived and mixed with other missionaries his ideas were most expounded and 'the Shansi spirit' went deepest, deflecting and destroying the biblical faith of some. To Hudson Taylor and the rest of the CIM, Timothy Richard and his friends were on a false trail.

W. A. P. Martin's advocacy of a liberal attitude to ancestor worship fell into the same mould, although he remained theologically conservative. After the General Missionary Conference of May 1877 in Shanghai, W. A. P. Martin had quietly continued to press his views. Confucian philosophies and 'ancestor worship' became major topics of debate among missionaries and Chinese Christians, as among Chinese and Westerners who understood only the philosophical issues. Because some members of the CIM were confused by the arguments to the extent of resigning and fomenting discord, a brief summary of this far-reaching subject is essential, leaving it to be amplified in connection with the General Conference of 1890.

This rite of 'ancestor worship' is as alive today as in the nineteenth century. The practice has two inseparable aspects. One is the commemoration of deceased parents and other forebears—a family event expressing respect and gratitude. The other, animistic in origin, concerns communication with the spirits of the dead and placation of vengeful ones. The first can be a joyful reunion of members of a family, akin to Thanksgiving or Christmas festivities. The second merges imperceptibly with the first, so that candles, flowers, decorations, memorials, bows and declarations become inseparable from outright idolatrous practice.

In valuing the first, dutiful sons and daughters are involved in ancient customs associated with the second. Expressions of respect and veneration merge into prayers of confession and supplication. 'Announcements' become petitions, decorations become offerings, bows become prostrations, awe becomes fear, petition becomes placation, and veneration becomes worship. An attempt to retain the first innocuous, admirable intentions becomes entangled in the practices of the second. From the beginning of Biblical Christianity in China (as distinct from deviant forms) Chinese believers have recognised the differences and renounced the custom rather than compromise. A dogged minority have followed Matteo Ricci and Martin in searching for ways of retaining the customs while denying the idolatry, without success. Failure has always lain in the impossibility of doing so without compromise or the appearance of it. Hope lies in an unmistakable substitute for the pagan practice. The search during the days of the 'open century' concerns us here, but it also is still active.

Based on a belief in the existence of two worlds (the world of light, known by experience, and the world of darkness after death), the practice of 'ancestor worship' attempted to harmonise the two. The dead, it was believed, still depended on the living to provide for them. By burning replicas of all they needed in the after-life, the living could supply them. But neglected ancestors or spirits with no one to care for them took revenge by causing disease, death and calamity. Rituals performed after a death—connected with the burial, with a memorial tablet, with annual sacrifices at the graves and at ancestral halls—were thought necessary to keep the spirits quiet and to protect the living. Ancestral tablets carried the name and dates of birth and death of parents and grandparents, and twice daily the family worshipped by prostrations, incense burning and offerings to the spirits believed to occupy them. Sickness in the family drove them to pray to the ancestors for help, and 'paper money' was burned to appease malevolent spirits. Death set in motion all the rituals to honour the dead person and prevent him from returning to avenge the injuries done to him in his lifetime.

At death one of the three souls of the deceased was believed to be seized by the ruling demons of the world of darkness for torture and punishment by an endless variety of terrors, unless extricated by

the efforts of the living. Of the two other spirits, one stayed with the corpse and the other entered the tablets. This purgatory could be relieved but never ended. A blood relative must maintain the ancestor worship and bear sons to perpetuate the practice. Should an only son become a Christian and repudiate ancestor worship, the whole community would anathematise him, believing that he would consign his ancestors to spiritual destitution as victimised spirits. Deep conviction and moral courage were needed by believers.

Twice every year, in the spring and autumn, festivals at the public cemeteries or private mausoleums brought families together to renovate and decorate the graves, offer sacrifices and present more paper effigies by burning. The family prostrated themselves in the *ketou*, precisely as they did before the temple idols, for the form, manner and intent were the same. What was done to gratify the ancestors was also done to appease the demon-spirits. 'If worshipping at the tombs and before the ancestral tablets is not worship, then the worship of their idols is not worship.' Of the three compelling motives, affection, self-interest and fear, fear was the strongest. Ancestor worship is 'the very last thing they are ready to give up'.[598] It was and is therefore the greatest obstacle to acceptance of the gospel which admits of 'no one else', 'no other name' than 'Jesus' as the 'one mediator between God and men'. The undermining of ancestor worship by twentieth-century atheism has therefore paved the way in one respect for acceptance of the Christian gospel, as the return of the old customs has faced Christians with the need to declare their loyalties. But in the nineteenth century ancestral rites were observed by all, from emperor to pauper.

Where Westerners think of their ancestors historically or as living souls in a world apart, the classical Chinese concept is of the soul or souls of man continuing their existence with enhanced power in the unseen world after death. Such a belief became a fear, fear a cult, and the cult a religion.[599] A 'dear old grandfather' as soon as he died was feared as a *guishen,* a spirit to be dreaded. But filial piety apart from such beliefs resulted in a son's preparation of coffins for his parents years before they needed them as a comfort and reassurance to them. It led also to a general recognition of the sanctity of graves, though fear of the spirits was at least as strong a factor in this. Worship was distinguished from respect and veneration by sacrifices, never made to the living. And sacrifice was intended to establish communication (even communion) with the dead, not a commemorative rite but real dealing with spirits. It became a placation of the departed or of demon impostors.[600]

Christian attitudes to ancestor worship were mentioned in the first book of this series (see 1, pp 19–20 & 22–25). The weakness of the Jewish communities and the Nestorians, that of compromising their beliefs by accepting the ancestral rites, reduced them to bare survival. Matteo Ricci's compromises, allowing participation in the rites if a cross or crucifix were concealed among the objects of worship, not only met with the opposition of the Dominicans and Franciscans but of his fellow-Jesuit successor Longobardi, and ultimately of the Papacy. Mezzabarba's concessions based on loopholes in the papal bull were swept away by the Pope in 1742, and the notorious 'rites controversy' ended to the satisfaction of the Greek Orthodox Church and the Protestants. Robert Morrison, William Milne, Walter Medhurst, Elijah Bridgman, David Abeel, William Boone, all the truly learned divines and also the Sinologists John R. Morrison, Sir John Davis and Samuel Wells Williams agreed.[601] Missionaries of all societies shared the same view until W. A. P. Martin began to return to Ricci's reasoning. A few others followed him, most significantly Timothy Richard, Gilbert Reid and Young J. Allen. But, as the General Missionary Conference demonstrated in 1877 and again in 1890, the overwhelming majority were unmoved.

Writing in 1846–47 when Protestant Chinese Christians numbered fewer than a hundred, Wells Williams said, 'The few Chinese who have embraced the doctrines of the New Testament . . . regard the rites as superstitious and sinful.' Without question it was worship and as such it was idolatry. To distinguish between cultural commemoration and idolatrous worship was impossible, for commemoration was by sacrificial worship. Biblical Christianity had no place for it except 'Come out from among them and be ye separate . . . touch not the unclean thing.' But the price of faithfulness was often persecution and

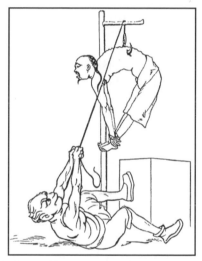

2.52 From a Hanzhong temple: the torments of hell

ostracism, expulsion from the family. They were prepared to pay it. Yet that is not all. A Christian expression of affection and honouring the family's forebears was and is right, just as admiration and emulation of all that is good in Chinese culture and morals was and is to be encouraged, *short of compromise.* This was where Martin and Richard parted company from their colleagues.

Timothy Richard and 'the Shansi spirit' (1879–83)

This period of five years, Hudson Taylor's fifth in China, was so eventful as to need separate handling of each main feature. Every advance was matched by particular difficulties for Hudson Taylor himself. They are pertinent to the advances made.

His recurrent ill-health was enough handicap, but well or ill he had to keep the administrative wheels turning. A 'touch of the oiled feather' (Jennie's phrase) was often enough. But broken wheels were another matter. While the success of venture upon venture, as already described, buoyed him up and led him on to attempt more, all was against forces of resistance which could have stalled the Mission and wrecked it. He personally was tested as he had been at every phase of his lifework and, until men of the right spiritual calibre and natural ability matured in experience, he had to handle the frequent (and often concurrent) adversities largely alone. Such men were at last emerging.

The story of Shanxi cannot be complete without this painful episode. A phrase 'the Shansi spirit', found in a few letters, described a whirlpool of complaints, misunderstandings, derelict spiritual morale and finally resignations from the CIM and BMS. At the vortex was the remarkable personality of Timothy Richard, still young and developing but intellectual, original and inevitably influential. K. S. Latourette, from the high ground of his immense knowledge of Christian missions in China could not only call Richard 'one of the greatest missionaries whom any branch of the Church . . . has sent to China (see p 166),'[602] but, 'like Hudson Taylor, Richard dreamed and planned in terms of all China. He, like Taylor, laid comprehensive plans for preaching the Gospel to every Chinese.' Unlike W. A. P. Martin, however, Richard's 'gospel' was different, a broad concept of the Kingdom of God on earth, 'how by the grace of God we may be able to save the world in this generation from the wicked ones who tyrannise over the poor and needy'. Much depends on what is meant by a word. Precision and definitions mattered immensely in this context. He foresaw 'the danger of the conversion of China from her traditional teaching of the superiority of the moral and intellectual to primary dependence upon physical force'. 'He held that it was possible to find approaches which would win for Christianity the sympathy and cooperation of all the Confucianists, Buddhists, Taoists and secret sects . . . He held that God had been at work in each of these religions, and that pointing out the similarities of each to Christianity, contacts would be established which would win their adherence to the Christian faith.'

He therefore sought out the contemplative sects in each religious discipline, to find and influence those who were seeking higher truth. And to fit himself for this he devoted much of his time to studying the Chinese classics and religious pamphlets. He adapted Chinese dissertations on ethical themes by eliminating pagan concepts and substituting the worship of God. As early as his first year as a novice in China, when a colleague showed Richard an ancestral tablet which a converted Chinese was going to burn, Richard said, 'I suppose you will at the same time burn your parents' photographs.' He did not change. 'Such was his attitude towards ancestor worship, as towards Chinese religions in general' in later years, his biographer W. E. Soothill, professor of Chinese at Oxford, commented.[603]

By the time Richard retired in 1915 he could see immense changes in the Chinese way of life. Partly from his own great influence, the changes also sprang from many other factors, especially the need to match the growing threat of Japanese Westernisation. So Richard lived to see China converted to the Western science and Western education he had worked so hard to convey in lectures to officials and scholars, and by a flood of publications. He had set his sights on the 100,000 literati, saying, 'When these are won to Christ the whole nation will follow.' But what he meant by 'won to Christ' was 'in striking contrast' to what Hudson Taylor and his missionaries meant and taught. Soothill wrote that Richard 'came out of the horror [of the Shandong-Shanxi famine] with the one word "Education" branded into his soul, a word which became the key-note of his life.'[604] Education would enable China to cope with such disasters. Hudson Taylor gave spiritual regeneration a higher priority.

More than a year before Richard went to Shanxi for famine relief, J. J. Turner and Francis James had criss-crossed the province with colporteur-evangelists on the three-month reconnoitring journey of 1,700 miles from Wuhan in 1876. And after 'settling permanently' in the province with Taiyuan as their base, from April to November 1877, Francis James had fallen ill with typhoid, forcing them to withdraw temporarily to Wuhan again. When the famine died down, David Hill, Turner and James intensified their preaching of the orthodox gospel and distribution of Scripture and soon were reinforced by Jennie Taylor, Anna Crickmay, Celia Horne, Elliston, Drake, Pigott, Parrott and for a time James Cameron, George Clarke and their Chinese companions, followed by Robert and Mary Landale, Emily Kingsbury, Agnes Lancaster and Dr and Mrs Schofield. Yet Timothy Richard, who did not come to Shanxi until late November 1877, opposed their methods as counter-productive and strongly advocated his own.

David Hill of the WMMS found himself having to choose between the two. After his first dealings with Timothy Richard in 1878 he wrote to his brother Edward about missionary methods, 'probably in the first place this is better—finding out, making selection of the worthy men of a place and working out from them, though not to sound abroad the gospel differs from my plans in the past, and I am not exactly satisfied yet which is the better to begin with'—a faithful reflection of Richard's influence. But three years later David Hill said at the fifteenth anniversary meeting of the CIM in London, 'I feel almost like a missionary of the China Inland Mission.' Well before he left Shanxi in May 1880, he had rejected Richard's policy.[605]

Timothy Richard had met a kindred spirit in Shandong, the Scottish Presbyterian missionary Mary Martin. After marrying in October 1878, when he had been ten months in Shanxi, they made their home in Taiyuan. Relations between all these people, and the 'Oberlin Band' of the American Board when they also came to Taiyuan in 1881, were cordial. For all were agreeable people, willing to differ amicably. But from the beginning the attractive and persuasive nature of the Richards led to one and another of the CIM missionaries being won over. Mary Martin 'had also been growing away from the stern dogmas in which she had been trained', and replied to her brother's exhortations, 'If you had travelled over the world as I have, and seen the millions (of Chinese) you would, like me, feel it such a joy to be able to lay for ever aside that doctrine we were taught as Bible truth in Scotland'—the Westminster Confession and its biblical authority.[606]

As early as August 15, 1878, Hudson Taylor confided to Lord Radstock, 'The faith of one brother has quite broken down, under the unhelpful influence largely of other missionaries, and we shall have to recall him.' Others were succumbing, and in March 1879 Francis James was talking of resigning from the CIM to look for a regular salary such as other missions provided.[607] By August when George Clarke arrived at Yantai (after three months in Shanxi following his expulsion from Jincheng), even he was 'a faithful reflection of the Shansi state of mind'. On March 6, 1880, Hudson Taylor named in a letter to London those who were unshaken by Richard's arguments.

> (His) presence in Shansi causes me great anxiety for some of his views are so Romish [an allusion to Ricci], and his personal influence so strong that the CIM has no existence, scarcely, or place, or work or claims in the minds of (two of the CIM missionaries). This is not necessarily Mr R's fault; it is rather the inevitable result of a strong and attractive character over weaker minds.

Turner and Drake were so convinced of the rightness of Richard's policy that the persistence of the rest of the CIM Shanxi team in 'Scriptural colportage' and evangelism was driving them to resign. Hudson Taylor commented, 'Richard is driving a good theory to death. He refuses to preach to the masses, is for circulation of moral and theistic tracts, not containing the name or work of Christ, to prepare the way, as he thinks, for the gospel.' By May, Francis James had resigned, and at his request Hudson Taylor wrote to the BMS in London endorsing his application for a transfer of membership and referring them to Timothy Richard for his opinion.[608]

When the Oxford graduate Robert Landale married Mary Jones of Ningbo, step-daughter of Frederick Gough, Hudson Taylor gave them the choice between Wuhan and Taiyuan as their sphere of work. They chose Taiyuan. So did the surgeon Harold Schofield and his wife after four months of language study at Yantai. All four were sufficiently at home with Christian theology and mission strategy to be unaffected by Richard's views.

Until 1881 the CIM avoided separating their work from Richard's, but Chinese Christians could only be confused or harmed by the conflicting teaching of the missionaries. What was to be done? When the admirable J. J. Turner himself arrived at Yantai 'utterly down in body, soul and mind', the price of cooperation had become too high. Hudson Taylor at last advised a parting of the ways. Let Timothy Richard pursue his policy, and the CIM their own. Being first in the field of Shanxi and Taiyuan justified this action, however regrettable it might appear to be. The precedent had been set by the apostle Paul in writing to the Galatian church (1.6–9): and by Jude, 'I . . . appeal to you to join the struggle in defence of the faith which God entrusted to His people once and for all. It is danger from certain people . . . ' (Jude 3, 4 NEB).[609] Quite independently, in Shanghai the Union Church had acquired a minister whose 'liberal' teaching and admission of 'the unconverted and immoral to the Lord's table' incensed members of his congregation. A nucleus of them, including Weir, Cranston and the Hudsons (see p 214), established the Free Christian Church and invited Hudson Taylor to advise them. Edward Pearse served briefly as their first pastor, followed by Judd, Hudson Taylor and other CIM missionaries when available.

A united church was so important to Richard, overriding theology, that he travelled to Yantai to persuade Hudson Taylor. Turner returned to Shanxi with him, resigned from the CIM, and was later followed by two or three others. Timothy Richard played an immense role in China during the next few decades, in touch with some of the highest mandarins of the land. But his role in Taiyuan ended in 1886 when he returned from a disappointing visit to Britain. The Committee of the BMS could not see their way to adopting his scheme for a college in each provincial capital of China. 'He came home in anguish,' his wife told her diary. During his absence, orthodox BMS missionaries came to Taiyuan, and when Richard returned and tried to resume his old methods, his own colleagues protested. As he could not be dissuaded, 'they sent a long letter to the Committee, censuring me in regard to both my theological views and to my methods of work.'[610]

Richard decided to leave Shanxi and moved to Tianjin and then Peking. He petitioned his mission to be allowed to establish a college at Jinan, the capital of Shandong, and on being advised to rejoin his Shandong colleagues in conventional 'church-planting', chose to resign and engage in literary work. He edited *Shi Bao*, *The Times* of North China and, after Alexander Williamson died in 1891, became the director of 'the Society for the Diffusion of Christian and General Knowledge among the Chinese', later called the Christian Literature Society. 'Instead of writing goody-goody tracts . . . We decided to enlighten China on the world's progress and put her in a fair way of saving herself.'[611] In this second phase of his life he earned his great reputation among Chinese and foreigners until his name was familiar to emperor and schoolboy.

In Shanxi the CIM and BMS worked in close harmony through the decades that followed and, returning to their former convictions, the CIM missionaries who had resigned served in other missions for many years. But these were not the only resignations during those momentous years, nor the major problems Hudson Taylor faced.

'My face like a flint' (1879–83)

Like windows into Hudson Taylor's soul, his editorials in *China's Millions* reveal his train of thought. In January 1880 he headed his New Year greetings with the words of Isaiah 50.7, 'The Lord God will help me; therefore I shall not be confounded; therefore have I set my face like a flint, and I know that I shall not be ashamed.' What was good for the Servant Son of God was good for his servants. Adversity was to be expected and endured. More positively—this was the road to success. In *China's Millions* of 1878 he had written, 'Sometimes a longing indescribable comes over me to be with some dear brother and encourage him when depressed.' He himself often needed such encouragement. He had learned to draw upon 'the encouragement of the Scriptures', but being frequently under assault caused him acute suffering. His thorn in the flesh, 'dysentery', dragged him down, magnifying the problems he faced.[612]

He had arrived back in China in April 1879 weak from a life-threatening attack on the voyage. Relapsing in Shanghai he reached Yantai fit only for bed. But his resilience made possible a visit to the Yangzi region, until his anxious companions had to take him back again. Up and down in health as he recovered strength in the invigorating climate of 'Chefoo' and set off again to Zhejiang or Yangzhou or distant Wuhan, he frequently fell ill again. By July 1881 Jennie had been more than three years away from her little children and longed to be with them again. But Hudson was not well enough to be left and parting was too painful to contemplate. She stayed until the autumn.[613]

A fast-growing mission meant more and more administrative correspondence and problems to resolve. The council in London were still learning. Some newly arrived missionaries showed that they should never have come. In the process they damaged relations with Chinese, consuls and fellow-missionaries. Two revealed that they were epileptics who had thought themselves cured, until new stresses proved they were not. Two others showed that they were mentally ill, not only 'unbalanced', and had to go home. Another had 'a morbid conscience' and needed 'careful handling'. One new arrival made no attempt to learn the language and Hudson Taylor sent him back as 'a thoroughly good-for-nothing fellow'.

Henry Taylor, 'broken' by the rough handling and 'deep hate' he had encountered in Henan, tried to find a niche in Zhejiang. Resentment made him incapable of a new start. He quarrelled bitterly with his Chinese colleague at Jinhua, and resigned from the CIM to take up a lucrative post in the Customs service. To dare to invade Satan's domain in the hearts of men was to invite attack, and he fell wounded emotionally and spiritually. So 'pray for those you send, shield them by prayer', Hudson Taylor urged the Mission's friends. The first pioneer to penetrate the first of the nine unevangelised provinces had become the first such casualty. And not only he. His newly comfortable circumstances became a strong inducement to some colleagues in Zhejiang, where loyalty to the Mission's principles had too often been half-hearted. Close proximity to other societies with foreign life styles strengthened the temptation. In March 1882 'nearly all' were affected, and Hudson Taylor almost wished they were not his responsibility.[614]

International tensions in south China and Indo-China threatened the rest of the empire, like a menacing cloud over whatever else was happening. The sudden death of the co-empress regent, Ci An, by the hand of Ci Xi it was believed, signalled the presence of a most unscrupulous person still at the seat of power. In this climate Hudson Taylor was sending out men and women into the remote provinces.

He built up the 'sanatorium' and school complex of premises at Chefoo, and because W. L. Elliston proved such a good master, other missions, merchants and consuls used 'much solicitation and pressure' to persuade Hudson Taylor to open the school to their children also. Simply making Chefoo what it became, with constant staffing problems, demanded much of him. The administrators he needed were slow in coming. One capable individual in Britain was suggested, but Hudson Taylor knew him too well. He would continually be in hot water through inability to stand being reviled as a 'foreign devil'. 'No more hinderers' were wanted; Satan was 'enough already'![615]

The illnesses of one after another, and the deaths of missionaries and their children weighed upon him. Again and again C. G. Moore's wife was 'dying' of self-imposed 'hysterical' starvation (anorexia nervosa), consuming the time, sleep and energy of others, 'a great care'. Her distraught husband, capable and influential, hung around, dissatisfied and unable to work until he could take her home to Britain and join the staff there. Then in May 1881 Emily King died of typhoid in faraway Hanzhong, and soon 'everything at once' seemed to happen. Hudson Taylor's mother suddenly 'fell asleep while sitting in an armchair' in July 1881; Jennie's mother died of cancer in August, and in November Hudson Taylor's father collapsed while giving instructions to some workmen in his garden, and died.[616] Feeling 'orphaned', he and Jennie could see no alternative to parting from each other. One of them must see to family affairs at home. She sailed from Yantai on October 13, 1881. Without her and desperately longing, as his love-letters show, he stayed on until February 6, 1883, for he was needed more in China than in Britain.

Mrs E. C. Lord and the Judd baby were under his medical care that August. But both died. Then he himself went down with 'choleric' (dysentery). Caroline Kerr arrived from Guiyang, still very ill, 'nearly fatally'. News came of John Stevenson with jungle fever in Bhamo, where the Catholic priest had died of it. And in giving birth to her first child, Mary Landale died at Taiyuan. She was like a daughter to Hudson Taylor,

the child of his close friends John and Mary Jones of early Ningbo days (see 1, p 559).[617] A very promising Scotsman named William Macgregor arrived in April 1882 to pioneer in Guangxi after two years with George Clarke at Dali. He set himself to master Chinese rapidly, and was learning every character and the meaning of one chapter of the Chinese New Testament each day. But in October he contracted virulent smallpox and died.

Jessie Murray had written to Jennie in October 1881, telling about a Christian schoolgirl who died in her school at Shaoxing. Towards the end 'it seemed as if she had been . . . to the very door of heaven'. 'Inexpressibly happy,' she had said to those around her bed, 'You must not weep. I have *seen* the Lord! I have *seen* heaven. *It is very, very* good . . . I wish you could come—there is *nothing* to fear.' And Jessie Murray added, 'It is not death to die. How glorious!' 'It is not *death* to *die*' put things into perspective.[618]

All through these five years the Mission's receipts continued painfully low—£1,000 less in 1881 than in previous years—although other British missions reported an increase.[619] But this was not Hudson Taylor's chief concern. Even when funds were in hand in Britain, they were not being regularly remitted to him. With so much on his mind, he extended his habitual hours of prayer and fasted more than usual. What was God saying to him through all this testing? 'What if the presence of men like (X and Y) is the cause of God's favour being withheld?' 'I am in great straits for funds. I am happy about it. The Lord may take away all our troublesome people through it and give us true-hearted ones instead'—those who would look, as most did, to God instead of to 'the Mission' to supply their needs.[620]

On December 23, 1881, he wrote, 'We had to win from Him by daily prayer and trust the funds to make remittances (to individuals). We did not ask in vain, for 4/5 of the last month's income for general purposes was received in China' (instead of from Europe), including sizeable gifts from a consul and the parents of a non-CIM child in the Chefoo school. Some might forget their intentions when they joined the Mission, and take to grumbling. The true spirit was reflected in the missionary's letter comparing herself to King Saul's lame son Mephibosheth, 'fed at the King's table'. As guest of the King she would always be content. Elizabeth Wilson also drew attention to the difference between looking to God and relying on 'the Mission' to supply recurring needs, when she wrote from Hanzhong on November 26, 1880, 'Our confidence must be in God, who has never failed those in the Mission who trusted in Him', implying that the complaints of 'passengers' were self-explanatory.[621]

The trouble was not only over money and men who should never have joined the CIM. A wave of indiscipline swept through the Mission, affecting even some of the best members. Perhaps Hudson Taylor's immobilisation by illness, and by the need to be on hand to distribute funds when they came, gave them an impression of independence from him. One after another did what he thought right or simply wanted to do, without consulting their leader. Others rejected his advice and even his instructions. One of the epileptics, strongly advised by Hudson Taylor and the LMS doctor in Shanghai to defer his marriage, secretly arranged it with the Settlement chaplain and announced a *fait accompli*. Another declined to wait until he and his fiancée had fulfilled their language study and period of adaptation to the climate and the customs of China. When held to their promise they resigned. He joined another mission and went on to win the Order of the Double Dragon for services to the Chinese empire.

'In matters of the heart few accept advice,' Hudson Taylor wrote. Even one or two of the best pioneers married without consulting him. 'I see the importance of being firm, more than ever,' he added. Far from being autocratic, he treated them as friends and expected and usually received loyal cooperation. When it involved taking young brides far upcountry they could not afford to act independently. One of his trusted assistants fell so deeply in love with a newcomer, almost at first sight, that they could neither be together nor separated without emotional stress. He took the poor swain away with him on a long journey to calm down, and made an exception to his own rule by allowing them to marry at the first opportunity after his return. He believed in a minimum of rules, and that they should be servants, not tyrants. But liberal control depended on willing concurrence.[622]

Jackson the incorrigible had incurred large medical bills when his wife was ill and died. Refusing to pay he was sued at the consular court. Hudson Taylor intervened and at long last sent him home to Britain, not to return—unless showing great improvement! On August 26, 1884, the London Council meeting with Hudson Taylor minuted that Jackson's connection with the CIM was to end, after nineteen years of patience.

Truancy was another failing of undisciplined missionaries. Forsaking their work and the employees who depended on them for daily or weekly wages, they sometimes went to a neighbouring 'station' or further afield for a change, or to find a wife. It was understandable; they were unexceptional people. But if this happened, binding rules and regulations would have to be introduced. 'It is reported that CIM missionaries have nothing to do and do nothing,' Hudson Taylor groaned to Benjamin about one district. He had to treat some young men as immature, but how should he deal with one or two senior missionaries with humble origins whose life style in 'fine houses with fine tables' not only suggested no lack of money but set a bad example?

'Prickly' and 'rude' missionaries also needed more than the 'oiled feather' to lubricate their troubled relationships. One undertook the task of business manager at Shanghai, as Mission buyer and travel agent.[623] Inevitably he was asked to make private purchases for individuals inland, and grudgingly obliged, but he seldom rendered an account. Appeals to Hudson Taylor fell as heavy straws on the overladen camel's back. Far worse were those few given to tongue-lashing the Chinese or even striking them. Carriers or tradesmen so treated could well stir up a riot. The consuls protested. At Chongqing it transpired that a visiting missionary of another society, using the CIM premises while dressing and behaving with colonial arrogance, was chiefly to blame. At Consul Baber's urgent request his society withdrew him. But one of the CIM men aped the older man and was slow to reform. When yet another had to be dismissed 'the shock to the Mission' was as great as if ten had to be dismissed later in the Mission's history.[624]

Reports of such incidents reached Sir Thomas Wade's ears in Peking, and through him the Foreign Office in London. They are still on file at the Public Records Office. Wade instructed the consuls to restrict as far as possible the issue of passports. But the risk of passports for travel and residence in China being denied to all CIM missionaries became so grave that Hudson Taylor wrote urgently to everyone. If overbearing behaviour towards Chinese continued, all might be required to register in person at consular ports involving great difficulty, expense and waste of time, let alone danger *en route*. That ended the emergency. Four good men (Elliston, Parrott, Stevenson and Turner) whose passports had been withheld then received them.

It was reasonable that missionaries of different societies should live and work together, or receive each other in transit. But dilemmas arose when some in foreign dress and carrying firearms made themselves at home in CIM premises in the absence of the resident missionary, rather than go to an inn. Evangelists and employees were unaccustomed to being treated impersonally. The problem of returning hospitality with hospitality defied solution for many years. At other times, as different societies moved into cities already occupied to plant churches of their own denomination, rivalry sometimes developed. Except in large cities and business centres,

Hudson Taylor preferred to move away to new territory.

Problem followed problem in the director's mail, and he learned to meet them by 'living one day at a time rather than carry tomorrow's problems today'. 'The Lord God will help me; therefore I shall not be confounded.' On November 14, 1881, the day he received Henry Taylor's resignation, he wrote, 'Almost a storm of business to be done today.' This, after spending the whole voyage from Yantai to Shanghai dictating letters to Parrott. When two other couples resigned in the same fortnight, Hudson Taylor wrote frankly in *China's Millions* about this epidemic; 1881 had been 'a year of trial' unlike any other.[625] J. J. Coulthard, his personal secretary during much of this time, recalled:

> It was his habit to rise before us, very early any time before dawn, and by candle-light read his Bible ... He valued dispatch and prompt execution in correspondence, remittances, etc ... At some of the stations there were a great many difficulties to be met, but he never trusted to anyone's advice, he always prayed about the work; some said he was able to get his own way by his personal magnetism, but he always prayed about everything. His way of living was so simple. He would take such notice of (a little child) and win the mother's heart. Then (he would) read the Bible with (the missionary in difficulties or disaffected), and would give such helpful talks (about the passage), and invariably the difficulties were settled.[626]

But the obverse of the coin held a very different image. Trouble was the exception to the steady, faithful, costly part being played by most of the Mission. The Broumtons and Camerons, the Clarkes and Dorwards and Eastons of the CIM were penetrating ever further into the interior. The seldom-mentioned men and women were building up strong churches in obscure places. Louise Desgraz, who married Edward Tomalin in 1882, was one of these. '(There was) never a leader with more cause for thanks for loyalty than I,' he assured her. Friends of the Mission at home were unruffled by the squalls. The Earl of

Shaftesbury who in ignorance had belittled the CIM (see pp 86-87), as chairman of the annual meeting now said, 'I like this society very much.' And Lord Radstock, enclosing £100, wrote to Jennie, 'The labours (of your dear husband, highly honoured is he) are not only owned of God in China but for the strengthening of the faith of many in England.'[627]

The Seventy (November 1881–82)

A more difficult year lay ahead. The greatest advances seemed always to be accompanied or followed by counter-attacks from the great 'adversary' of 1 Peter 5.8. By this yardstick the 'daring and success' of Hudson Taylor and his pioneers deserved a major onslaught. But they had only begun their invasion of inland China. The missionary community and the churches at home were about to be startled by yet another 'bombshell'. Adversity aroused him. It spurred him to stronger effort. But not defensively. As in the First World War Foch's famous dispatch read, 'My centre is giving way, my right is in retreat, situation excellent. I shall attack!'[628] so now, low income and disarray in the Mission had to be seen as distractions from the prime objective, the gospel to every corner of the empire, and so to every man, woman and child.

While Jennie was on the way home to Europe, Hudson Taylor and Parrott went up the Yangzi to Wuchang, visiting stations *en route*. At Anqing on November 21 he wrote to her, 'God is greatly helping me . . . to rejoice in our adverse circumstances, in our poverty, in the retirements from our mission.' And quoting her, 'All these difficulties are only platforms for the manifestation of His grace and power and love.'[629] Joe Coulthard was in charge as business manager at Wuhan, and Jane Kidd, Adam Dorward, Trench and Pigott, five of the best type, were passing through. Whenever he was among his missionaries, Hudson Taylor seized the opportunity to lift their spirits above the everyday things of life to the spiritual level, by singing, praying and sharing with them the truths he himself was learning daily from his feasting on the Bible. During the week they were together, they spent time doing this each morning and evening, and discussing the working out of the Principles, the shortage of funds, and the inadequacy of their present numbers.

This last subject seemed most urgent. In province after province and city after city more fully committed men and women were needed. In October he had sent home his short editorial for the December *Millions* about 'Western China opening'. 'Were the Lord to grant us double the number of workers and double the means, within twelve months we could have them all located and of work . . . Who will come to the help of the LORD?'[630] The CIM already numbered ninety-six missionaries, twenty-six of whom were wives and mothers with limited freedom for activities among Chinese outside their homes; and in addition about one hundred Chinese colleagues. But the size of the task and the policy of most other societies to base their work on the treaty ports left the CIM little choice but to expand their effort, and therefore their numbers.

The Mission house in Wuchang (the southern city of the three which with Hankou and Hanyang now comprise Wuhan) stood near a little hill crowned by a Yuan dynasty (1280–1368) pagoda. (The approach to the great twentieth century bridge across the Yangzi River now makes use of this Snake Hill, and the pagoda has been rebuilt further to the south.) On Friday afternoon, November 25, Hudson Taylor and Parrott were strolling together on the grassy hilltop, discussing the need to expand the Mission. Financing it was no problem. If God was saying to them, 'Enlarge the place of your tent . . . do not hold back; lengthen your cords, strengthen your stakes. For you will spread out to the right and to the left . . . Do not be afraid,' he would provide for those he sent. Then how many were they talking about? By rough computation fifty-six could already be placed. Allowing for losses by illness and resignation, and for more and more

Christians needing to be taught, as many as seventy would be a realistic number to pray for. They realised that they had been praying only vaguely for reinforcements. In the six years 1876–81 about seventy had come to China. An average of ten or a dozen each year was too few. Seventy more were needed soon. However out of context the thought, 'seventy others also' had been the number Jesus had sent out on one occasion. A cheerful irrelevance? Should they pray for so many now? As they walked, Parrott's foot kicked a string of one hundred brass cash in the grass (see ill. 1.15: 1, p 229). It reminded them that 'all the silver and the gold' was the Lord's. He would meet the cost.

By Sunday they were convinced that God was guiding them. Over tea they consulted Coulthard and Trench, who agreed. Across the table they promised each other to pray for 'seventy more' until they arrived. Dorward was leaving for Hunan again on Tuesday, 29th, and Jane Kidd with her Chinese companion and David Thompson for Chongqing, so Monday evening was given up to prayer. With all the household present, Hudson Taylor prayed specifically for seventy, and one of those present wrote in his journal afterwards, 'I quite believe he prayed the prayer of faith tonight.' To explain to the others how he reached that number, he worked it all out on paper, province by province, city by city—'forty-two men and twenty-eight women for our work, and large reinforcements to all the evangelical societies'.[631] On the Wednesday night someone suggested, how good it would be to meet again to praise the Lord, when the seventy had all come. Why wait? said someone else. To be able to get together was unlikely. So that evening they praised God in advance.

At the time they mentioned no date by which the seventy should come. Interviewing, training, equipping, accommodating and introducing to the language and land of China would limit the number who could be handled at any one time. But the need of them was already pressing. Spread over three years, seventy would not be too many. Later 'within three years' became the goal of their prayers, twice as many per annum as usual. On December 1, Hudson Taylor was on his way down to Zhenjiang and writing to Jennie. He was inviting the Anqing staff and language students to join him at Zhenjiang for a similar informal conference.

> God is faithful and expects us to walk by faith [he wrote]. This month the home remittance was [worth by exchange] taels 300 perhaps; the contributions in China exceeded taels 1,200. At the beginning of the month I did not know what I could do; *He* knew what *He* would do ... [with so little for so many].
>
> We have our definite lines of work; we must not leave them nor get weary of them. If any leave us on account of them, they not we are the losers. If any members of our home Council cannot go along with us, they too will sooner or later need to go. God remains faithful. Do not be cast down, Darling, if you meet with difficulties at home. All things are working together for good, as in due time we shall see. Pray much for me ... Satan is a terrible reality and so is the flesh; but more is He who is with us.[632]

Missionaries of the American Episcopal Church and a customs officer were present as guests at the Zhenjiang conference, December 3–9, where agreement was again unanimous. He wrote to all members of the Mission inviting them to join him and each other in praying for 'seventy' if they felt able to do so. Without the background knowledge all could not be expected to agree at once. Nor did they. Even protests were predictable. If the Mission's income was so low, not keeping pace with the Mission's growth (£8,119 in 1875–76 and £8,692 in 1879–80), how could they nearly double the membership? There was nothing secret about all this. Soon critics within and outside the CIM were questioning and condemning the latest irresponsibility.

At Shanghai Hudson Taylor met his son Herbert, arriving from England to join the teaching staff at Chefoo; he took him to see his mother's grave at Zhenjiang and the scene of the Yangzhou riot. Then he went on to Ningbo and the Zhejiang region. Once again the question of re-baptism had arisen, and he agreed to baptise Pearse and Parrott as 'believers'.[633] At Ningbo on January 7, 1882, he drafted an appeal to the Churches in Great Britain and Ireland,

> 1. To unite with us in fervent, effectual prayer (for) more labourers in connection with every Protestant missionary society on both sides of the Atlantic.

> 2. ... for forty-two additional men and twenty-eight additional women, called and sent out by God ... We are not anxious as to the means for sending them forth or sustaining them ... urging such to count the cost ... to ask themselves whether they will really trust Him for *everything* ... Mere romantic feeling will soon die out in the ... constant discomforts and trials of inland work ... when severe illness arises, and perhaps all the money is gone. Faith in the living God alone gives joy and rest in such circumstances ... He is supplying, and ever has supplied, all our needs; and if not seldom we have fellowship in poverty with Him who for our sakes became poor, shall we not rejoice ... that we have been (like Paul) 'poor yet making many rich'?[634]

He would set no standard by which God should be expected to provide; only the absolute standard of the immutability of His promise.

This appeal was circulated among the active members of the Mission for optional signature, and took months by the slow postal system to be completed. A letter written by Hudson Taylor at Wuchang on November 26, 1881, and published in the March *Millions* naturally made no mention of it.[635] Thanking supporters for donations during the year, he referred to the extreme limitations of income only by saying, 'Though our needs have been many and great, I can again testify that God has supplied all our real needs, though oft times more sparingly than, had we had our choice, might have been done. But for all the trials of faith we can thank and praise Him; doubtless He sees them necessary.'

His letter to the annual meeting at Mildmay on June 6, 1882, also remained

silent on the subject. And Theodore Howard, the director in Britain, made no reference to it in his address. Lord Shaftesbury as chairman in the afternoon this time went further than before in saying of the CIM, 'This is one of the nicest and snuggest little societies I know ... small in magnitude and yet it is very vast in operation ... I would be very sorry if it went beyond the power of the superintendence of Mr Hudson Taylor.'[636] And in the evening Lord Radstock, a sacrificial donor, added, 'Christians in England are not half awake about China. I consider that the income of this Society is a contemptible income ... There is no country where Christians allow themselves so much self-indulgence as in England.' From extensive knowledge of Europe he spoke with authority.

This malaise among Christians had been troubling Lord Radstock. In the May meetings of the previous year, in the Exeter Hall, he had said:

> I believe that our great failure in England arises from what I should call a comfortable religion ... that there are more Christians that are injured by comfort than by anything else. Comfort seems to paralyse work on all sides ... There is a circle of habit which enchains most Christians ... When they get beyond that circle into utter abandonment to God, they have a revelation of Christ's presence and Christ's joy which those who remain within that wall never experience ... It requires faith for a man to go out to China simply with his passage paid ... They will not tell you when they are in need, and if you want to find out ... the only thing is to pray about it, and in your prayer God will direct you.[637]

That was true of material needs, but from the beginning Hudson Taylor had believed that the Church, disabled by comfort, should be challenged to face her obligation to 'preach the gospel to every creature'. To appeal in 1875 for eighteen for the nine unevangelised provinces had been dramatic. So soon afterwards to appeal for seventy would strike a complacent public as irresponsible unless presented with the right support. Even the Mission's referees might balk at this. The individual signatures of those who would have to divide the Mission's income with the newcomers, were worth waiting for. So in June 1882 it was still China's general need and not the specific appeal which was publicised.

At long last, in the February issue of *China's Millions,* 1883, the full text was followed by facsimile signatures of seventy-seven missionaries, beginning with 'J. Hudson Taylor, 1854' and ending with 'H. Hudson Taylor, 1881'—Herbert, at the age his father had been when he first reached China. Some others had objected to enlarging the Mission while the funds were low, and some of naming 'seventy', though promising to pray in general terms.

By then a whole year had passed. And only eight had arrived. For the rest to come within two more years would tax the accommodation and smooth running of the Mission. By the close of the financial year, 1882–83, only a maintenance amount of £10,840 had been received, and one gift of £3,000 towards the advance.[638] Instead of answered prayer in the form expected, resignations and the death of one valued worker after another had to be reported. The whole of 1882 deserved its epithet, 'a year of trial'.

'Our mismanaged mission' (1882)

To mark the twelfth anniversary of the sailing of the *Lammermuir* in 1866, Hudson Taylor stated in 1878,

> Of all who have offered for China, not one of whom we have had reason to believe to be qualified has ever been refused; and funds have never failed to come for the outfit and passage of all who have been accepted, and for the subsequent support of all who have gone forth ... The contributions from year to year have sustained the work adequately, though not without faith being at times considerably exercised. But we have never had to leave an open door un-entered from lack of funds.[639]

The same could have been said of the next four years. Marked progress had been in the face of minimal resources. William Berger, had been a faithful donor, even though never able to contribute really large sums. At the end of 1881 when he finally surrendered his directorship in the starch factory at Bow, he wrote to tell Hudson Taylor that as his income would become one third of what it had been, his ability to help would be correspondingly less.[640] 'Put not your trust in princes' had a firm place in Hudson Taylor's thinking. His dependence on 'God alone' was strengthened. And when his own father's death provided Amelia with the income from five houses in Pyrland Road, secured to her and her children, it may be surmised that Hudson was also a beneficiary.[641] In the summer of 1882 so little Mission money was being forwarded from Britain that he had to stay in Yantai for more than three months, simply to be available to distribute at once whatever might be received. The last three months of the year were as trying. In August 1883 he told the story in full.

> In the months July, August, and September [1882] we had received from home besides special donations, over £2,000 for the general purposes of the Mission; but during October, November, and December only £3,9319s.6d. was received for these general purposes, a sum very far from sufficient for the wants of any one month. In October ... moneys for the expenses of long journeys seemed needed; and when we ... found, instead of the hoped for £700 or £800, or more, only £96. 9s.5d. ... locking the door, (we) knelt down and spread the letter before the LORD, asking Him what was to be done with ... a sum which it was impossible to distribute over seventy stations in which were eighty or ninety missionaries (including the wives), not to speak of about 100 (Chinese) helpers and over 100 (Chinese) children to be boarded and clothed in our schools. Having first ... rolled the burden on the LORD, we then told the need to others of our Mission in Chefoo ... but let no hint even of our circumstances be given outside.

> Soon the answers (to prayer) began to come, in local gifts from kind friends ... and ere long all the needs of the month were met ... We had similar experiences in November, and again in December.[642]

One day, coming across Mary Ann Nicoll in the house in Chefoo, Hudson Taylor asked her, 'What would you do if you had a very large family and nothing to give them to eat?' She knew it was his way of explaining why he spent so much time alone in his room, 'waiting upon God'.

His confidence in the Lord to supply in one way or another was one thing. The reliability of the staff in London to remit funds was another matter. Charles Moore had taken his wife home and succeeded William Soltau as cashier-accountant at Pyrland Road. But his distraction by his wife's condition continued, and there was no improvement in the state of affairs he had gone to remedy. In January 1882 Hudson Taylor was exasperated. Moore was not sending telegraphic remittances as instructed. 'I have written till I am tired and sick of the subject,' Hudson Taylor confessed to Jennie. By April that had improved, but even the Mission treasurer was not answering letters and Hudson Taylor felt in the dark. But for letters from Jennie and one or two others, 'my knowledge of England would be mainly geographical'. Neither Theodore Howard nor Benjamin were intervening to put things right. Jennie's personal legacy was available to pay the ocean passages of ten of the Seventy, about £300, but how did the Mission's finances stand? Were letters going astray or being stolen?

In September he was still starved of information. Theodore Howard occasionally replied but did not answer his questions, and Benjamin did not give enough information about the new men and women he was sending out. Even Jennie seemed too busy, writing briefly about business while Hudson pined for deep communion with her. 'It just seems as if nobody cares for me,' he groaned. 'The constant uncertainty and no tidings from home is a painful contrast to Mr Berger's administration.' At last it transpired that letters were being sent via America and both being delayed and going astray.[643]

He badly needed to go to Shanxi to sort out the deepening troubles between the missionaries, but could not leave the helm. At least Joe Coulthard was coming to take over the accounts, and Douthwaite to act as an assistant editor, dealing with material from sources in China. By October there was barely time to get to Tianjin before ice would close the port to shipping. 'A long, cold winter's journey (overland) is the alternative, all caused by want of compliance with my reasonable directions . . . I have asked again and again for lists of the missing vouchers, but McCarthy sends me no reply.' 'I have no one but you (on earth) to tell some of (these things) to. It is only through God's special care that our mismanaged mission does not come to nought.' He was at 'a complete standstill', unable to travel or to manage the Mission. 'There are two aspects of these things the one, God's purpose in permitting it, the other the incompetence or disobedience of those who ought to be carrying out my instructions.'

When a fortnightly mail boat came with nothing for him, he left for Tianjin and Shanxi—on the occasion when the one he most needed to meet had left his work and gone to Chefoo. 'I am very, very sorry for this. The Mission will come to an end if this lawless running away from work . . . is to go on.' So Hudson Taylor visited the other missions. In Peking 'Dr Edkins, the first missionary that I met in China,' chaired a meeting at which Hudson Taylor explained 'the rise and progress' of the CIM. W. A. P. Martin showed him over his college, and the Hon T. G. Grosvenor (of the Margary investigation), chargé d'affaires at the legation, 'advised me *privately* by all means to "press forward (towards Tibet via Gansu), but *carefully*."' Then the truant and his bride returned bringing a missing transmission of money for immediate distribution and Hudson Taylor 'got them away' to their work again.

Now he could see that he must return to Britain, to get the machinery turning smoothly again, and to have a hand in the selection of the Seventy. On the last day of 1882 he told Jennie that £350 had been telegraphed from London, 'but £750 seems needed'. And paradoxically, 'I can't tell you how happy I am amidst it all.' 'Now we shall see what GOD will do,' spiced every turn of events.

Despair (1882–83)

Looking for the firm ground of God's promises in the quicksands of despondency had become habitual for Hudson Taylor. His survival would have been remarkable, but 'to walk on the water' when he 'was assailed by such depression, loneliness and forebodings, due in part to illness,' surprised those who knew how he was suffering. In his *A History of Christian Missions* in *China*, K. S. Latourette's reliance on secondary sources led to his misunderstanding of the facts when he wrote, 'at last his hopes (of seventy additional missionaries by the close of 1884) were to be frustrated.'[644] His 'depression and foreboding' were at no time due to that. An appeal had not yet been publicised. Signatures were being collected. He was not shaken by such things. Every reference he made to the Seventy assumed fulfilment. It was the spiritual failure and disloyalty in Zhejiang and Shanxi, and 'the utter inadequacy of existing arrangements' in London which shook him to the core. The Howard Taylor biography highlights his spiritual resilience, a lesson in 'overcoming', but the need for resilience is as revealing.

He and Jennie had suffered so much separation for the sake of the gospel, the Mission, the famine and the family, it was almost more than he could bear. At Ningbo early in January he stayed with his old friend, the recently widowed E. C. Lord. A restless companion so prevented him from sleeping that he got up at 1.00 a.m. Looking at his photograph of Jennie and the children by candlelight decided him to write. 'I don't like these nice bedrooms with their sunny sheets,' he confided to her. 'They seem to want you. In rough places I am glad you are not there to share my discomforts.' On the way to Wenzhou in February (trouble-shooting) he called their separation 'a time of great trial; I seem unable to rise above it as I should. The Lord knows my heart and my determination by His grace to make His work the first thing.' And a few days later, the flippancy of some missionaries in southern Zhejiang, lacking spiritual life and power, drove him to say, 'These things almost break my heart . . . Blessed Jesus! . . . make me more like Thyself.'

In mid-March he was in Shanghai, feeling too ill to write, lying on his bed doing nothing, scarcely able to bear the separation any longer, grieving for Robert Landale over the death of his Mary, and for F. F. Gough, her widowed step-father. 'I feel as if my journeying days were almost over; the last journey tired me more than I have ever felt a journey do.' On April 2 he was almost at the end of his tether. Except for Jennie and China he would long to die, he said. 'Sometimes I feel the Lord will soon say Enough, and call me to the only true rest . . . Perhaps I may stay here to see the Seventy out and settled, and then return to England for good. Or, I may never return . . . I must get to Chefoo, I think, and see if I can brace up for a little more work . . . My heart feels ready to break.' Still at Shanghai four days later he wrote that he was still needed in China and she in Britain, so they must go on enduring. He was carrying on his work in spite of how he felt, and these were often asides in business letters to her. 'Cheer up and trust,' he wrote to John Stevenson, adding, 'myself far more'.

On the way to Chefoo he felt that he and she were very unlikely to meet again on earth. And safely there, 'You've got my heart so tight that I must gasp for breath on paper every now and then for sheer relief.' 'The very thought of six or eight months more of this separation seems overwhelming.' But Chefoo held 'a large and happy family' of missionaries, and soon he was buying the land between the beanfield and the sea, and getting estimates for another building, a school for Eurasians and a 'medical college' (to train missionaries) under Douthwaite and others. Adam Dorward was a great cheer to him.

He picked up so well that he could not

understand why Jennie's letters showed she was anxious about him. He had forgotten his depression when he replied, 'I have not been so well for years.'[645] Then he was off to Shanghai again with Parrott, his Corresponding Secretary, to meet 'many and serious difficulties'. 'Most friends are disappointed that at least a quarter of the Seventy are not in China already.' They went on up the Yangzi to Anqing, where he revealed that through these months of suffering he had been feasting on the Song of Solomon.

From June 24 when he arrived until July 1 when he and Parrott had to leave, all who could, met daily from 7.00 to 9.00 each morning and evening to hear him expound the Song of Songs, and Mission principles. 'The Holy Spirit seemed to fill us this morning till several of us felt as if we could not bear any more . . . So long as God gives us such times as these, we will not be cast down, however great the difficulties and trials. We were all melted by the contemplation of His love, and felt how great a dishonour was done to Him by distrust in any of its forms. If you want blessing, make room for it.' They spent the last day in fasting and prayer,[646] and they hugged each other goodbye. Those studies in the Song of Songs were published in *China's Millions* and under the title *Union and Communion,* reprinted time and again.

Briefly feeling well again he went down to Ningbo and neighbouring cities. At last the temptation to follow Henry Taylor into lucrative secular employment was losing its attraction for some who should have been immune to it. 'There is such a lack of sustained spiritual power among us that one fears to be long away or far away from the field.' And yet in September the administrative failures in Britain led him to write, 'If God were not God indeed, the Mission would have been in ruin long ago.' Worse still, a whole packet of letters and documents fell (or were taken) from his own pocket in the road, and were never recovered. One of the Shanxi malcontents arrived in a deplorable spiritual state, making trouble. Another

got married in Peking expecting to 'claim' costs afterwards, and Hudson Taylor feared he would never be able to get away from such entanglements. 'Shall I never get to Shansi?'—to deal with that festering wound—became a recurring theme.[647]

October came. 'I am getting old and feeble, and incapable of much work.' He was fifty but burning out. 'May God . . . help a weary, fast-failing old man—for if not in years, in constitution I am such.' Yet at Tianjin, Tong Xian, Peking and Baoding in November he was riding high and by invitation preaching in other missions' chapels. By the end of these four years in China he had covered 23,800 kilometres, reckoned by map and dividers. Equivalent to 15,000 miles, it was a gross underestimate in terms of actual travelling.

On January 6, 1883, he was in Yangzhou, tempted to pack up and go home, 'but I try not to give way to the tempter', and on the 17th a flimsy letter from Jennie almost broke his resolve. 'I feel as if my heart would break soon if I don't have you yourself. I was almost in a mind just to run off by today's P and O, leaving my foreign clothes at Chefoo, and papers and books . . . Though the tears will come into my eyes every few minutes, I do want to give myself, and you too, darling, for the life of the Chinese and of our fellow-labourers . . . An easy-going non-self-denying life will never be one of power . . . Pray for me, my own heart's love, that neither my faith, nor my patience fail . . . I have been so pressed and wearied. The strain is very great.'[648] Without doubt it was time he went. Coulthard, Parrott, Douthwaite, Baller—younger men could manage in China while he tried to put things right in Britain.

At last another long-delayed transmission from London allowed him to sit up most of the night with Joe Coulthard dispatching remittances. And on January 23 he cabled to say 'Coming'. More and more were afraid that he had gone too far over the Seventy. Didn't low income show it was folly to double the Mission in size? He answered, 'We can afford to be poor with so rich a Father.' A few days before he sailed from Yantai on February 6 to catch the French Mail at Hong Kong, he and some others asked God 'to set a seal on this matter', to lead one wealthy Christian 'to make room for a large blessing for himself and his family' by giving liberally towards the Seventy.[649]

On the French ship in the Saigon River he wrote, 'I am quite clear, thank God, that my love for you has not caused me to hurry home before His time.' His only fear was lest being with Jennie again should weaken their love for God.[650]

Big waves have deep troughs. Though he did not yet know it, he had set a tidal wave in motion. If he still needed encouragement, it was waiting for him at Aden—news that on February 2 an anonymous donor had contributed £3,000, to be thought of as well over £100,000 today. In 1884 it was followed by another £1,000 from the same family. God's seal had been set on the Seventy. Fifty years later it came to light that this donor was the publisher Robert Scott, of Morgan and Scott.[651]

Pause to take bearings (1878–85)

If great things had been happening for missions in China, there was plenty in the outer world to shake complacency. The climate of the day is relevant to the narrower events of Hudson Taylor's story. Queen Victoria might be declared Empress of India (to strong protests by Lord Shaftesbury, prophet of Justice), and the Transvaal be annexed to the British empire, but it took more to satisfy the spirit of conquest. The year 1878 had seen war with Afghanistan and massacre in retaliation, and 1879 the abortive occupation of Kabul. The Zulu war in the same year, with the shock of defeat, the death of Prince Louis Napoleon, and the answering slaughter at Ulundi when 20,000 Zulus were mown down by modern firearms, were a costly price to pay. Clashes with the Boers had followed in 1881, the year the West trembled over the assassination of Tsar Alexander II by a grenade thrown by members of the Peoples' Will, and of President Garfield. Marx and Engels saw the

Russian crisis as ushering in the Commune of their dreams. But Tsar Alexander III reacted energetically. Lenin was a schoolboy when his brother was executed. Britain defeated Egypt and occupied the Nile Valley and the Sudan. Although in 1883 the Mahdi overcame a British force, General Gordon was sent to Khartoum. (His journey to Peking had been in 1880.) Lord Wolseley led an expedition to support him, but it came too late. He was killed on January 26, 1885. The epic story of Gordon happened therefore to coincide with Hudson Taylor's departure from Yantai on February 6, 1883, until he was on his way back to China again. During his time in Britain (in fact, from 1880 to 1885) Parliament was taken up with the intractable Irish question, following the assassination of Lord Cavendish and Mr Burke at the Phoenix Park, Dublin, in 1882.

In East Asia comparable events were taking place. The Empress Dowager Ci An had died mysteriously on April 9, 1881, leaving Ci Xi, the invulnerable Yehonala (in Manchu, Yehe Nara) as the young emperor's sole regent. On March 25, 1882, France had occupied Hanoi, and in May Korea signed a treaty with the United States. Back in 1876, Japan had demanded direct dealings with Korea as an independent state. An anti-Japanese riot in July 1882 increased the tension. When the French Chamber approved the expense, on May 15, 1883, and France sent an expeditionary force to Tongking (North Vietnam today), Annam in the south accepted the French 'protectorate' after a decade of encroachment.

China had had enough. There was rioting at Canton on September 10, 1883. Houses on Shamian 'island', the foreign concession, were burned. But on December 16, France challenged China by taking the border town of 'Sontay' from its Chinese garrison. Throughout southern China attacks were made on foreign property. More than eighteen Protestant chapels were destroyed. Thousands of refugees flocked into Macao and Hong Kong. But trouble was not only in the south. In the south-western provinces and in Shaanxi and Shanxi placards threatened extermination and mandarins became hostile, especially to Catholics. For a fourth time Prince Kong was degraded and dismissed from office as foreign minister, this time for ten years. Instead, Li Hongzhang's star entered its ascendancy. But on July 12, 1884, after a French defeat, an ultimatum was delivered at Peking. In August French ships destroyed the Chinese fleet and docks at Fuzhou, and attacked the forts at Jilong on the northern coast of Taiwan, blockading Taiwan in October. Understandably Chinese turned upon all foreigners and Christians.[652] The Chinese strongman Yüan Shikai had become Resident at Seoul in the spring of 1883. On December 4, 1884, a *coup d'état* and riot at Seoul, followed the next day by a clash between Chinese and Japanese guards, showed the way the wind was blowing. Once more the Grand Secretary Li Hongzhang was called to the rescue. His Sino-Japanese convention on Korea, signed at Tianjin on April 18, 1885, only postponed war.

Missions in China had faced the usual considerable difficulties before the Franco-Chinese war erupted. The CMS in Fuzhou had lost five missionaries, three by death, leaving only a new arrival, John R. Wolfe, to carry on there and at three or four cities with resident evangelists. In 1866 the first two baptisms had been recorded, but in *China's Millions* of January 1885, a page was devoted to celebrating, among other things, the 1884 report of this sister mission. Wolfe's policy of working through Chinese colleagues as far as possible had resulted after eighteen years in 5,414 believing adherents of whom 1,587 were communicants in 120 towns and villages. Seven Chinese clergy, of whom three had died, 107 catechists and about 100 lay workers served nine churches, seventy preaching chapels, a theological college, a medical mission and boarding schools. Yet at the height of this work Wolfe had only seven Western colleagues. Persecution and the martyrdom of one Christian had been the climate in which this growth had taken place. After the bishop W. A. Russell had

died on October 5, 1879, his territorial diocese was divided at the 28th parallel. C. P. Scott of the SPG became Bishop in North China, and G. E. Moule in 'Mid-China'. Bishop Burdon of Hong Kong succeeded in persuading the CMS in 1882 to give China 'a much more prominent position' in its sympathies. And a gift of £72,000 came to the CMS for training and supporting nationals as evangelists in China and Japan.[653] At the annual meeting of the CMS in 1885, Canon Hoare declared, 'All England is ashamed' that the government had failed to relieve Khartoum before Gordon was killed. The audience roared and cheered. Then Hoare went on, 'You did not let me finish my sentence. You sent my dear son to China; are you going to leave him alone there?'

The LMS page in the February *China's Millions* told of chapels filled to overflowing, but of few baptisms. Griffith John, however, reported a church membership at Wuhan and district of 777. The Amoy area, with twenty-two outstations, had 883 members and over 400 more adherents, while in the whole of China this society alone served 2,924 church members. Had Robert Morrison (see 1, pp 42-96) foreseen even these results his joy would have known no bounds. Seventy-seven years after he arrived in China, they demonstrated the continuing difficulty but also the increasing tempo of success. A century later the count is in millions, devoid of denominational labels.

Already a decade of religious liberty in Japan had by 1883 allowed 145 missionaries to enter the country. An influx of 5,000 Japanese into the Protestant Church regrettably resulted in newspaper discussions of the possibility of Japan becoming a Christian country. Immediately a revival of Buddhism and the expenditure of vast sums on temples and colleges created an effective barrier to Christian advance.[654] The vigour of Japan in every sphere threw into contrast the comfortable lassitude of China, wearied by tens of centuries of ponderous progress. China seemed to want nothing but to be left to get on with her old ways. The pressure of expanding forces from West and East made that impossible. The scramble for colonies had begun. Li Hongzhang, Zhang Zhitong (Chang Chiht'ung)—promoted from governor of Shanxi to viceroy of Guangdong and Guangxi and then of Hunan, Hubei and Anhui—and others recognised the need for reform and modernisation and did what they could. But with Ci Xi in power that could only be with extreme caution. If the powerful were hampered, what of the weak and alien?

Harold Schofield, a seed in the ground[655] (1880–83)

The arrival of Harold Schofield and his wife at Shanghai on June 30, 1880, opened a new era in the history of the CIM. Among the predominantly yeomen types making up the Mission were a handful or two of men and women from more educated and well-to-do backgrounds. John Stevenson and Arthur Douthwaite had set aside their professional training to go to China. Robert Landale, an Oxford MA, had been encouraged by his barrister father to go first as a 'traveller', to see for himself before sacrificing his prospects. Trench also moved cautiously at first. They had both done well and returned from home leave as full members of the Mission. Robert Landale had been 'impressed' by the quality of Hudson Taylor and the CIM and was a good companion for the Schofields on the voyage out. But Robert Harold Ainsworth Schofield was a new phenomenon.

He was twenty-nine and already widely experienced. For his wife he jotted down the scholarships he had been awarded.[656] Having qualified MA and BM, Oxon, both in December 1877, he went on to be elected FRCS England in May 1878. With his travelling scholarship he proceeded to Vienna and Prague for specialist studies, and on his return served as 'house-surgeon' for a year and 'house-physician' for six months at St Bartholomew's Hospital, London.

When war broke out between Turkey and Serbia, Schofield offered his services to the Red Cross Society. He was given charge of a hospital at Belgrade for one month, and in a similar capacity for two months in the Turkish army during the war with Russia. On his return, he 'associated himself with the China Inland Mission', and faced the expected protests. Some of his best friends tried to dissuade him, 'on the plea that "there was so much need at home". How I wish [he wrote from China] that they and all who use this argument could just live here for a while, and see and feel the need for themselves; they would then be disposed to ask . . . whether they themselves had a special call to stay at home.' Again 'I cannot for a moment think that home is my sphere, especially as natural inclination is all on that side, as well as prospects of worldly advancement.' As a medical student three years before qualifying, he had read the life of Dr Elmslie of the CMS in Kashmir, and consecrated his life to God, to serve him abroad. Nothing deflected him from this resolve.

Hudson Taylor met them on arrival at Shanghai and found them 'pleasant but distant'. The shock of meeting him in Chinese clothes, described by many as 'unimpressive' on first acquaintance, was enough to account for that. He found he had to move carefully. They agreed first to go to Yantai for language study. He had arranged for them to live as paying guests with the Ballards of the Customs service, two miles from the English speaking CIM community of Chefoo. They would take their time to decide about going into Chinese dress themselves. That would determine where they worked, he explained, for everyone in the CIM away from the treaty ports now regarded this as necessary.[657]

Back in January Hudson Taylor had replied to Benjamin's first letter about Schofield, 'If he be the right man he will be a treasure indeed . . . But has he faith in God? Is he willing to endure (and see his wife endure) the indispensable hardships of a pioneer worker?' He would be useful in Zhejiang in foreign clothes, but ten times as useful in Chinese clothes upcountry. But by January 20 he was putting it more strongly.

Nearly every post suitable for a missionary in foreign dress was filled. The Schofields must be in full sympathy with the principles of the Mission. They satisfied the council that they were and, once settled at Yantai with opportunities for long conversations with Hudson Taylor, they clearly showed that they were with him heart and soul. Afterwards their correspondence revealed their spiritual maturity. 'The secret of it lay, I think,' his wife was to write, 'in a heart and life given up to God and His service, unclouded faith in God as Father and in Jesus as a Saviour from the *present power* of sin . . . He was in fullest sympathy with Mr Taylor's principles and work . . . in perfect confidence that God would supply, not only all spiritual, but every temporal need of the Mission.'[658]

For three or four months the Schofields worked hard at Chinese and fitted in well at Chefoo. They undertook to join Robert Landale in the Taiyuan team, and travelled third class on the coaster to Tianjin—but the captain insisted that they have their meals in the first class saloon. From arrival at Taiyuan late in November they made their mark, getting on well with Timothy Richard. Schofield developed his medical work carefully, at first reserving time for language study. He surprised the others by his progress, soon joining in street preaching. He even kept a diary written in Chinese characters, and would sit for half an hour with his patients, talking about their families and farms. 'He had a large vocabulary which enabled him to speak without hesitation, and thus he made many (Chinese) friends.'[659]

In the first eighteen months he treated over three thousand patients and performed eighteen operations under chloroform. Tragically, Mary Landale died a week after the birth of her firstborn, and Robert had to take his child home to Britain, after helping the Oberlin missionaries look for a city to settle in. T. J. Pigott became a patient after tackling an intruder in the night and receiving 'a number of severe and dangerous wounds (from) a large carving knife'. Only the high collar of a Chinese jacket saved him from having his throat cut.

Harold Schofield wrote in February 1883 appealing to medically qualified men and women to come to China. 'There are already eight American ladies (doctors) . . . One American mission alone has five such ladies in the field.' In his second full year he had treated 6,631 patients including many cases of lacerations by wolves, and performed 292 operations, 47 under chloroform. But in July, 1883, a very ill man with virulent diphtheria was brought in. During the few hours before he died Schofield personally cared for him, and from infected body-lice himself contracted typhus. Timothy Richard heroically nursed and treated Schofield on the instructions he gave until he could no longer speak. He died on August 1, 1883, at the age of thirty-two.[660] The shock to the whole Mission and far beyond was intense. Why? Why he of all promising people? What great developments in China might he not have brought about? 'Tell Mr Taylor and the Council . . . that these three years in China have been by far the happiest in my life,' he had said to his wife. Together they had been praying, she told Hudson Taylor, 'That God would open the hearts of the students at our Universities and Colleges to the needs of the Mission Fields of the world. He longed and prayed so earnestly for the best men in all respects to be sent to China.' And Hudson Taylor added 'I have sometimes thought that in those prayers the greatest work of Harold Schofield was accomplished, and that, having finished the work that God had given him to do, he was then called to his eternal reward.' His widow took their two children home. One was hardly ten weeks old. 'On the morning before he passed away,' she recalled, 'his face was so radiant with a brightness not of earth, and since then I have often thought those lines were a true description of him, "Jesus Himself, how clearly I can trace His living likeness on that dying face." A short time after that he looked up, smiled, and said, "Heaven at last", and seemed as if he had recognised someone.' Some of the most influential lives have been brief, Henry Martyn, Samuel Dyer and Bishop Hannington of Uganda among them.

How Harold Schofield's prayers were answered is the continuing story. On the day Hudson Taylor received news of his death, he also received the first enquiry from a growing flood of men and women of that type. It came from Dixon Edward Hoste, Lieutenant, Royal Artillery, who was to succeed him eventually as General Director.

Medical plans for the CIM (1880–1900)

The vast ocean of physical suffering that was China could not be relieved by a few doctors and amateurs doing their poor best with a few simple remedies. In the 1880s scientific medicine was still in its infancy. The best known treatment of typhus was aconite, quinine and 'cold packs to the torso'. Harold Schofield with his array of qualifications was a child of his times. An hour after examining the dying diphtheria patient he had told his wife at dinner, 'that diphtheria could produce typhus, and typhus diphtheria' (so she understood). In the report on his first year's work he had written of the Shanxi climate, 'even in the winter months the effect of the sun's rays is very powerful and it is unsafe to go out bare-headed'.[661] Preventive medicine was in its infancy. European medical colleges taught what they knew, and much besides but, as an editorial in the *British Medical Journal* (23 November 1985) began, 'A century ago in the United States scientific medicine scarcely existed . . . The foundation of the Johns Hopkins Medical School in 1889 . . . led to a scientific revolution in medical academic circles that was to establish the United States as the world leader in biomedical science in the modern era.'

Medical schools still taught the accumulated practical experience of centuries, surgical, obstetric and medicinal. Much of it could be conveyed to students in a short time. In 1887 Hudson Taylor had considered travelling via the States to find a short medical course for suitable

missionaries, and with the London Council decided to help them financially to obtain a recognised qualification. In 1883 James Cameron, his arduous travelling days over, crossed from Britain to New York and less than a year later was listed, in September 1884, as James Cameron MD (USA). On his return to China he became superintendent of the mission in Shandong and worked as a doctor at Chefoo. A. W. Douthwaite also completed his medical course, at Vanderbilt University, Nebraska, cramming the work of three years into one year, to qualify MD (USA) in nine months. Cameron then married the widow of a Shanxi missionary named Rendall, who had died at Taiyuan after only two years in China, and practiced medicine at Chongqing until he himself died on August 14, 1891. Horace Randle also became MD (USA), and Frank Trench began the study of medicine at Edinburgh in 1884, followed by George King.

Well before then, the long years of being the only available doctor in the mission ended for Hudson Taylor with the arrival in China of W. L. Pruen, LRCP, LRCS (Edinburgh) in January 1880, and Harold Schofield in June. Henry Edwards and William Wilson (Elizabeth Wilson's nephew) arrived together in October 1882. Edwards reached Chongqing on his way to Yunnan, but was recalled to replace Schofield at Taiyuan, and Wilson after failing to gain a footing in Xi'an by medical means set up a hospital at Hanzhong.

William Wilson earned notoriety during his eleven years (1884–95) at Hanzhong by his skilled use of local cotton products for surgical dressings, and of Chinese chemicals by refining and transmuting them. He distilled local spirits to obtain alcohol, and made extracts of botanical drugs. He also converted the zinc linings of packing cases into zinc oxide.[662] After a period at Chefoo, Pruen succeeded Cameron at Chongqing and then pioneered the medical work at Chengdu and Guiyang, while the Chengdu hospital work was taken over by Canadian missions. Two of the Seventy, Wilson and Edwards were followed in November 1884 by a third doctor, Herbert Parry, first of another family to become pillars of the Mission. Most members therefore were within a few hundred miles of medical aid, and Hudson Taylor still helped when he could.

Dr John Kenneth Mackenzie of the LMS here comes into the CIM's orbit as a close friend. Because of his wife's ill-health, he took her from Wuhan (where he had spent four years with Thomas Bryson after reaching China in 1875) and began again at Tianjin. There his medical reputation became known to the great Li Hongzhang. At the annual meetings of the CIM on May 31, 1883, both Bryson and Mackenzie gave major addresses. 'One day there came a courier,' Mackenzie said, 'calling us to go up to the palace of the Viceroy whose wife was at the point of death. The native physicians had said there was no hope . . . Gradually she became better, God blessing the means for her recovery . . . One day the Viceroy said to us, "I believe that Western medicine and surgery can achieve what Chinese cannot. There is a temple there; you can have it for a dispensary."'[663]

The temple was 'close to the busiest and best part of the city,' Mackenzie had told Cameron and Pigott in 1879. The Viceroy handed him a generous amount of silver 'and promised to bear all expenses and pay for all medicines . . . A great wall of opposition seemed broken down . . . The dispensary was crowded with patients daily (and) numbers of the highest classes, from Li's own family downwards, came to be treated . . . He thus is enabled frequently to set the Gospel before them and to remove many mistaken ideas (about the mysterious foreigner) from their minds.'

With funds contributed by Li and other Chinese, a hospital was built in 1880, and Mackenzie began a medical school, training doctors for government service. The importance of this man to the future of relations between China and the West, as well as missions in general, could hardly be exaggerated. When Mackenzie had to take his wife home to Britain, Hudson Taylor offered him the hospitality of the Mission at Pyrland Road and wrote to Jennie on

December 5, 1882, 'Dr Mackenzie is one of the best and most important men in China. Take him in, if he comes, at almost any cost.' But Mackenzie died in 1888 and official support was withdrawn from the hospital.

On August 6,1880, when Hudson Taylor was travelling slowly by boat towards Qü Xian near the Zhejiang-Jiangxi border, he outlined to Theodore Howard the plans he intended to discuss with Douthwaite, the medical student. 'Something as follows' included a central hospital in which to give doctors experience and to train others in basic medicine; an attached opium refuge for addicts, for training missionaries to treat them; an opium refuge in each inland station, at which a range of medicines would be stocked for sale to the public with instructions in their use; and trained Chinese medical assistants with evangelists at each outstation—a rural health service. Initially it would cost £2,500 (at current values) rising to £4,000 for premises and stock. Douthwaite moved to Wenzhou for two years and treated more than four thousand patients in his first year, and then to Chefoo in April 1882, to recover from bronchitis.[664] This was his niche. Ideal as the leader of the community and popular as the doctor, especially after returning from the States with his MD, he established a hospital and a 'fever (isolation) hospital' (in memory of his wife when she died of 'typho-malarial fever') and began teaching. When Korea became open to missionaries by the treaty of 1883 he reconnoitred there in the winter of 1883–84, in response to an invitation from Sir Harry Parkes and at the request of Alexander Williamson of the Bible Society of Scotland. Hard on his heels came the first missionaries of the American Presbyterian Mission (North) and Methodist Episcopal Church, in 1884.[665] The evidence strongly suggests that Dr Douthwaite was the first to enter Korea at this time.

Hudson Taylor also discussed his plan with Harold Schofield, for him to consult Mackenzie on his way through Tianjin. Mackenzie made Schofield thoroughly at home and impressed him with the wisdom of how he ran his dispensary in the temple and had built his new hospital. Both were thoroughly Chinese, with brick *kangs* in place of beds. But after a debacle in Peking in which medical assistants with medicines for sale had feathered their own nests, he 'disapproved in very strong terms of that aspect of the plan'. The temptation it created was too great.[666]

Within twenty years, when there were one hundred and twenty medical missionaries of all societies in China (of whom sixty-one men and two women were British and the rest American and German) the CIM had fourteen fully qualified doctors in seven hospitals with oversight of sixteen branch dispensaries and numerous opium refuges.

1883–85: A WAVE OF POPULARITY

The rising tide in Britain (1883)

When the Marseilles boat train steamed into the Gare de Lyon, Jennie was on the platform to meet Hudson Taylor. The pain of anticipation had felt almost intolerable. Their reunion was beyond words, though they had so much to say. In the cab, trotting through the Paris streets to their favourite hotel, they held hands in silence.

He had reached Marseilles on March 17, 1883, and gone straight to the Bergers at Cannes for the weekend. William Berger had written, 'Kindly let me know more about the CIM and its needs—new missionaries—claims in China—if danger from the present state of France and China.' And later, when sending a cheque for £500, 'My heart is still in the glorious work.' 'Most heartily do I unite in praying for the seventy more workers! But I do not stop at seventy. Surely we shall see greater things than these.' He saw himself as still part of the Mission, more than a supporter, when he wrote, 'And if legitimate and great need should arise I would do more. Keep me *au courant*, SVP.' He had come far from advising caution and consolidation of existing work in China, as he did in 1875.[667]

After eighteen months apart (October 13, 1881–March 23, 1883) the Taylors had only the weekend to themselves. But it could not be all holiday. He needed to be briefed on the state of things in Britain. After the administrative hitches there was a great deal to put right. A note from Benjamin welcomed him with, 'I have no more cherished desire than to help you and to do so to your own satisfaction; if I cannot do this I would rather retire. I have had respect and favour both in the Mission and outside altogether beyond anything I could have expected, and far exceeding anything I have deserved, for I have fallen sadly short of satisfying myself.' Now Jennie could explain. All the staff in London had been stretched to their limit. Anxious friends of the Mission had questioned the wisdom of appealing for seventy more members when funds were barely enough for current expenses, and it had not been easy to answer them. With full steam ahead a ship must expect a bow wave. But at last the 'folly' was vindicated. The April issue of *China's Millions* was in print, announcing the stupendous gift of £3,000. Ample funds could at once be remitted to Coulthard.

Crossing the Channel and reaching London on March 27, Hudson Taylor was delighted with what he found. He had been away four long years. His son Howard had become a young man of twenty and Maria sixteen. Two of Benjamin's and Amelia's family were over twenty and three others over sixteen, maturely in sympathy with the Mission. Maria Taylor and Gertrude and Hudson Broomhall were hoping to be among the Seventy. Others hoped to follow later. But better still, on arrival he noticed 'the new position accorded to the Mission in the esteem of the Christian public'. The half had not been told him. The incessant journeys and industry of the pioneers had caught their imagination. In 1883 twenty more of the Seventy were to be sent, and applicants to go in 1884 were multiplying.

'The eight years of Mr Broomhall's unwearied labours had told especially in the direction which was his forte—that of inspiring confidence and making friends.' It resulted in accumulating invitations to address meetings or to send representatives of the Mission.

Meeting his own old friends, Hudson Taylor was even more encouraged. He came across Lord Radstock at Mildmay and spent an evening with him at Portland Place. He had no truer friend, not even the ageing William Berger, John Eliot Howard or George Müller. 'I pray at least once a day for CIM,' Lord Radstock wrote. 'You are a great help to us . . . by strengthening our faith.'[668] Hudson Taylor spoke at one of Spurgeon's meetings, convened the council twice, spent an afternoon with James Cameron whom he respected so highly, met the Bible Society secretaries one day and attended their committee a few days later, and spoke at Annie Macpherson's Home of Industry where he declared; 'There are three truths, 1st, That there is a God; 2nd, That He has spoken to us in the Bible; 3rd, That He means what He says. Oh, the joy of trusting Him!' In his June editorial in *China's Millions* he went on 'The missionary who realizes these truths . . . knows that he has solid rock under his feet whatever may be his circumstances.'

Then an evening with the Grattan Guinnesses at Harley House, at Tottenham with the Howards, and at a farewell for George Nicoll (returning to China in restored health), and Marcus Wood, a strong new member with his eye on Guangxi. Hudson Taylor preached for the Open Air Mission, addressed the annual meeting of the Anti-Opium Society; agreed to address the Rev John J. Luce's conference at Gloucester, and attended May meetings of the Salvation Army, the LMS, the Bible Society, the Evangelical Alliance, an Anti-Vice Organisation, the Religious Tract Society, the YMCA, and on May 31 the CIM's own annual meetings. Apart from these he spent an afternoon at the Earl of Shaftesbury's home at 24 Grosvenor Square, met George Müller who was to

speak for the CIM, and stayed a night at the home of Mr Stoughton the publisher, a generous donor, and on another occasion with Mr Hodder. So it continued, month after month, superimposed upon routine Mission business and the interviewing and sifting of candidates. Benjamin's life was as full. But still the demands piled higher so that in June Amelia offered her brother a bedroom and study in one of the houses she owned in Pyrland Road, as an escape from interruptions.

All the temptations and sufferings of the past year could at last be seen at their true value. 'Every branch that does bear fruit He trims clean so that it will be even more fruitful.'[669] The 'man of God' must expect the pain of the pruning knife. The presence of the Holy Spirit at the Wuhan and Anqing conferences before he left China had thrilled those present with the joy of the Lord, so that Hudson Taylor could write to Jennie before leaving China, 'I too have done more (I think) for our people here this year than in any former one.' A change of location must not lower their standards. 'May God bless our meeting (each other) and ever keep JESUS first. I feel almost afraid . . . I want you so, and *He* has been so near to me during your absence.' And again from the ship, 'I feel almost afraid, darling, lest I should have less of the manifestation of His presence, which has been so real and vivid in your absence.'[670]

He need not have feared. He was 'filled with the Holy Spirit' as he travelled round Britain. When he spoke at the Gloucester Convention and afterwards in an adjoining room with twelve individuals, John Luce, the convener, recalled, 'I can never forget the overwhelming power of that little meeting in my own soul. I was so moved that I had to ask Mr Taylor to stop; my heart was broken, and I felt, as never before, that I had as yet given up nothing for my Lord . . . Three (of the twelve) went to China as a result.'[671]

From Gloucester he travelled to his friends in Bath and Bristol, where he interviewed candidates and preached twice. Then to Cheltenham for two meetings in the Corn Exchange, and back to London to speak at the Ecclestone Hall near Victoria and the YMCA in Aldersgate Street. Going straight on to Southampton, to a private conference of Canon Wilberforce, Lord Radstock and their friends, only to be asked to return for a week of public conference in August, he returned to address the Mildmay Conference, June 27–30. July saw him back at Gloucester, at Bishops Stortford, at the Keswick Convention, at Kendal and Rochdale. For ten days or so he dealt with mail and interviews in London, meeting Dixon Hoste for the first time, and then off again. Through the past twenty or more years of his friendship with Lord Radstock and his relatives the Beauchamps and the Hon Miss Waldegrave, he had known the Hon Granville Waldegrave, Lord Radstock's eldest son, as a child and growing schoolboy. Since then Granville had been a pillar of the Christian Union at Cambridge and a strong influence on Montagu Beauchamp and others soon to enter this saga.

Granville introduced Hudson Taylor to Lord and Lady Tankerville, who invited him to Chillingham Castle, Northumberland, in mid-August, to speak at a drawing-room meeting for neighbours and to preach in the parish church. And Granville was there when the news arrived of Harold Schofield's death and 'a violent sick-headache' laid Hudson Taylor out on Sunday morning.[672] We feel sure that there is much love (from God) in it,' Hudson Taylor observed prophetically, not yet knowing of Schofield's prayers, 'and somehow or other much blessing to follow.' Then back to London with Granville, via Cliff House, the Grattan Guinness family home. There he gave an address on 'Unfailing springs of the water of Life' (Isaiah 58.11; Revelation 22.17) through which Geraldine Guinness 'received her call' to China. And on to Southampton for the general conference 'for the deepening of spiritual life'. In the last week of the month he 'farewelled' three groups of the Seventy leaving for China, and another group of three a fortnight later.

September was as full of meetings and conferences, while his whole family had the run of the Radstocks' Richmond home for a month while they were away. He met the committee of the Society of Friends on September 6 and helped them to send their first representatives to China, under the wing of the CIM, and went up to Scotland to address conferences at Perth and Dundee. John Stevenson arrived with Henry Soltau on September 15 from Burma and rejoined his family in Scotland after almost eight years of isolation from them and from the rest of the CIM. His coming was most timely.

Returning through Edinburgh and Leicester, Hudson Taylor was joined by Thomas Barnardo for a private conference in Salisbury, in the home of Canon E. N. Thwaites of Fisherton, who had been at the Gloucester Conference. Leading Christians were asking Hudson Taylor to expound Scripture to them. Yet it was not so much what he said as the presence of God in the meetings that drew them.[673]

Mrs Thwaites had been going through a period of 'great (spiritual) darkness', her faith imperilled by her own rebellion against God. 'What most appealed to me,' she admitted, 'was intellectual power and enthusiasm in (parish) work.' As Hudson Taylor spoke, a deep sense of calm came over her—'a fresh revelation of God coming down and meeting human need,' was how she put it. 'I began to yield myself to God.' Her drawing-room was packed at one meeting, 'and the power of the Holy Ghost was so intense'. As a result of this two-day conference fifteen or sixteen offered themselves to God, to serve him abroad. Rosa Minchin was a fifty-two-year-old, accepted to run the Chefoo sanatorium. She was to die within eight months of reaching China. Emily Whitchurch of Downton was bludgeoned to death in the Boxer rising of 1900. Some, when confronted with Jesus who 'emptied Himself and became of no reputation' for their sake, gave up jewellery, symbols of their self-centredness. John Luce was present and wrote that 'People felt they had received so much . . . (they) would give anything'. 'Rings, chains, two watches and a whole jewellery case (were) sent afterwards.' Yet it was not oratory or about the CIM, but with 'beautiful, gentle, loving simplicity' that Hudson Taylor spoke, 'always bringing us to God first', before talking about China or anything else—'always so glad to say a good word for others, for other missions and Christian enterprises'.[674]

In October he had meetings to address on most days, in and around London, in Norwich and at a conference at Leicester where the convener F. B. Meyer was as hungry for God as were his congregation. From November 14 until December 18 Hudson Taylor was away in the north, sometimes 'tired out'. But William Sharp, the new solicitor member of the London Council, was more anxious lest Benjamin's health should break under the strain of his overwork. As executive secretary 'BB' was handling Mission correspondence about the council's affairs, all business with scores of candidates until and after meeting the council, outfitting them and arranging the farewell meetings and the departure of old and new missionaries, and producing the monthly *China's Millions*. All the staff were stretched to the limit by the Mission's growing popularity. Sharp was to say of Hudson Taylor:

> His restful spirit and simplicity of faith were all-inspiring; his entrance into any assembly was to make those present conscious of a peculiar atmosphere of spiritual power.

> When in Council, with some difficult subject ... to which our united wisdom brought no apparent way out, he would ... call us to go on our knees, confessing to God our inability and want of understanding, and asking Him in the fewest and simplest of words to show us His will. Thus the expression of his habitual intimacy with God became a wonderful experience in one's own life.[675]

On his tour of the north Hudson Taylor went first by night train to St Boswells, Roxburgh, just over the Scottish border, as guest of Lord Polwarth. There he found William Hoste, 'the one who was at

Cambridge, not the soldier', engaged as tutor to the family. 'I should not wonder if he should not go to China too. His youngest brother also desires to be a missionary.' Lord Lichfield's son was in the party. God was bringing the claims of China before a new stratum of society, and using Hudson Taylor to influence them.

He was staying with Dr Kalley of Edinburgh, 'very active among students', when word came of the death of John Eliot Howard, FRS, Hudson Taylor's intimate friend and supporter since 1850. 'The shock made me feel quite ill' from Friday until Sunday, he wrote. The Howards wanted Hudson Taylor to conduct the funeral at Tottenham, but although he telegraphed to Dr Andrew Bonar in Glasgow, it was too short notice for him to be released from the many meetings arranged. So he was spared what would have been an ordeal. Benjamin wrote after the funeral of 'an immense concourse . . . between one and two thousand. Among them W. Fowler MP for Cambridge and R. N. Fowler, the present Lord Mayor of London'.[676]

In view of the phenomenal turn in events soon to take place at Edinburgh, it is interesting to notice that during his ten days there, Hudson Taylor preached four Sunday sermons and spoke at two meetings for students, three times for the YMCA and once at the annual meeting of the Edinburgh Medical Missionary Society, preparing the ground for the most memorable meetings among students yet known in Scotland. At Glasgow, too, he and John McCarthy had students' meetings, and interviewed several 'promising men'. Two joined the CIM as a result.

It was the same at Aberdeen—too many meetings and sermons for his own good, but insatiable audiences in the United Presbyterian Church of Scotland and the Free Church, YMCA and college circles, and at Montrose, Dundee, and Dumfries. The very simplicity of his style and subjects made him intelligible to anyone who listened. What they heard they recognised as old truths suddenly become alive and relevant to them as individuals. Or new to them in every way as God's message, demanding a response. Or more profound than rhetoric could make it. Laymen and 'divines', students and professors heard the voice of God and were hungry to hear more. They responded by repentance and deep dedication of their lives and substance.

He was also writing a long article on the Opium Trade, and speaking here and there for the Anti-Opium Society, whom McCarthy thought to be under the influence of opiates! He found time to visit Adam Dorward's mother at Galashiels. Unknown to them, Adam was at that time being driven out of Hongjiang after five months' 'occupation', and the French were driving the Chinese garrison out of Sontay. After Dumfries and Carlisle, back to London for a council meeting as soon as he arrived. To every host and hostess he sent a bound and gilt-embossed annual volume of *China's Millions*. Then away again to Weston-super-Mare. The Earl of Cavan, a friend for many years, had invited him to stay, but as his place was some distance out of town Hudson Taylor simply went for lunch. On the same evening he visited Augustus Margary's mother. The year ended with the customary 'day of prayer', and a letter from the Leeds philanthropist Robert Arthington inviting Hudson Taylor to visit him.

During 1883 twenty more of the Seventy had sailed to China, leaving forty-two to follow in 1884 if the full number were to go within the arbitrary three years.[677] Then 'about the end of 1883' a Cambridge graduate named Stanley Smith, eldest son of a Mayfair surgeon, Henry Smith, FRCS, of John Street, Berkeley Square, wrote to the CIM, and on January 4, 1884, arrived at Pyrland Road for an interview with Hudson Taylor. A friend of William Hoste, of Granville Waldegrave and of Montagu Beauchamp, Stanley Smith was the next link in a remarkable chain being forged for China and the CIM.[678] John R. Mott was to call it 'the germ of a world movement'.

D. L. Moody and the 'Cambridge band' (1867–82)

The seven men who came to be known as the 'Cambridge band' and later as the 'Cambridge Seven' in fact included one, Dixon Hoste, who had not been to Cambridge but to the Royal Military Academy, Woolwich, and was a lieutenant, Royal Artillery. Cecil Polhill-Turner of the same rank in the 2nd Dragoon Guards, the Queen's Bays, had been for a year or more at Jesus College when he was commissioned first to the Bedfordshire Yeomanry in 1880 and then to the Queen's Bays in 1881. The Royal Dragoons were the resplendent heavy cavalry seen in glittering cuirasses in royal processions and the, 'changing of the guard'.[679] Only in 1884–85 did the seven men gradually come together through their links with the CIM. Before that some had been acquainted through mutual friends or relatives. Each was outstanding in his own way, and individually two or three had already become famous as sportsmen in 'a generation which set much store on social position and athletic ability in an aristocratic age', as John Pollock put it.[680] Giving up wealth and prospects to become missionaries, and doing so all together, to bury themselves in China with the little known CIM, was highly sensational. Not until February 1885, on the eve of departure, did all seven combine to be 'farewelled' and to travel together; but by then, in groups of two, three or four, they had taken the country by storm.

Their story is as much the story of the American evangelist D. L. Moody as of themselves or the CIM. They were only children when he first came to Britain in 1867. The eldest by three months was W. W. Cassels (born on March 11, 1858) and the youngest, Arthur Polhill-Turner (February 7, 1863). In 1872 Hudson Taylor had shared the platform at Mildmay with Moody before he was well known in Britain. But in 1875 when Moody filled the Agricultural Hall in North London with 15,000 seated, and Gladstone (shown to his seat by Eugene Stock) said, 'I thank God I have lived to see the day', any or all of the Seven could have been present (see 1, p 803).[681] Moody's mission to Cambridge in 1882 (November 5–12) and following it in the Dome at Brighton, netted some remarkable fish for the future of missions to the world, among them some of the seven. When he returned for eight months in London in 1883–84, many of his most valuable assistants were the maturing converts of his earlier visits.

Up and down the country where Moody had prepared the ground by making new and older Christians hungry to learn more and to know how to serve God, preaching by members of the CIM and by the evolving 'seven' met with enthusiastic response. Hudson Taylor, filled with spiritual power since God's pruning knife had done its work on him in 1882; John Stevenson, John McCarthy and Robert Landale, each refined and brought closer to Christ by sickness or bereavement or other distress in their families, were making a strong if quiet impression.

Stanley Smith, before any formal connection with the CIM, was rousing audiences by infectious devotion to Christ expressed through a remarkable gift of oratory. He had been a practising Christian since 1874. At Repton, his public school, Granville Waldegrave had shepherded him along. And Granville's cousin Montagu Beauchamp, a year older than Stanley, had become his good friend. Then a serious illness had removed Stanley Smith from school for a year before he went up to Cambridge, to rejoin them in 1879. Stanley's father, the godly London surgeon, and Montagu's ultra-Christian home circle gave them more than Repton in common, the inestimable heritage of a childhood steeped in devotion to Christ. They attended meetings of the fledgling Cambridge Intercollegiate Christian Union and helped with meetings for slum children. Both Montagu and Stanley joined the Trinity College rowing club.

Granville had been at St Petersburg with his father for an evangelistic mission among the aristocracy of Russia. When he came back in April 1880 he lost no time in facing Stanley with the need to be more than a dutiful but half-hearted Christian. It touched the right 'nerve'. It was all he needed to bring him back to true dedication. He threw himself into evangelism in Mile End, Stepney and other parts of London, and among soldiers at Aldershot. But others could do that. He saw a greater need far overseas and wanted to go, but vaguely, not knowing where.

One of Stanley Smith's friends at Trinity was William Hoste, from Clifton College, Bristol, a Christian and also a rowing man. Yet another oarsman, better at rugby and 'association' football but unfortunate to miss his 'blue'[682] by breaking a leg, was William Cassels—'William the Silent', two years ahead of Smith and Beauchamp at Repton and therefore less in touch with them, He took his degree in 1880 and was reading for Anglican ordination when a closer friendship with Stanley Smith developed. Also at Trinity were two Etonians, George 'GB' and Charles 'CT' Studd, joined by their elder brother Kynaston 'JEK' when he came up to university after having first gone from Eton into business.

By the autumn of 1881 Stanley Smith was captain of his college boats, and both he and Montagu Beauchamp rowed in the university trial eights. On a holiday in Normandy with Lady Beauchamp, her family[683] and the young Waldegraves, 'SPS' had the disappointment of not being chosen for the 'varsity boat when 'Monty' was selected. Yet back again in England Stanley was called, and in the Lent term confirmed as stroke oar, winning his blue, when Montagu was dropped. He set out to win all his crew for Christ, as C. T. Studd was to attempt for the all-England cricket team. Smith took his degree in 1882 and while he thought about his future and filled in time before starting to teach in the autumn, he went as a holiday tutor to the younger brother of a college friend, the Burroughes of Burlingham Hall, in Norfolk, cousins of the Hostes. There he met an elderly gentleman who on a second visit showed him the difference between living as an average Christian and living altogether

2.53 Tedworth House, England

2.54 Studd's choice in China

possessed, set free from the domination of personal sin and used by the Holy Spirit of God. He learned to take at face value and to act on the truth, 'He died for all, that those who live should live no longer for themselves but for Him who died for them and rose again', and 'Present your bodies a living sacrifice, holy, acceptable unto God'. From then on, this attractive, athletic, handsome young gentleman possessed not only oratory but power to preach and testify for Christ. He stood in the market places and at Speakers' Corner in Hyde Park, well able to hold his audience of 'curious gentry and casual strollers'.

The Studd brothers[684] were unique, not in their luxurious upbringing but in sport and in their outspokenness as Christians. Their father, Edward Studd, a retired jute planter, owned the palatial Tedworth (now Tidworth) House in Wiltshire, kept a stable of about twenty horses and his own race-course, won the Grand National with Salamander, was Master of Hounds, laid out his own first-quality cricket ground, in the days when country-house cricket was at its height, and had his world at his feet. Then Moody and Sankey came in 1875—Sankey to sell organs and Moody to sell hymn books, the cynics said. The papers so abused them that Edward Studd went to see for himself, and came home 'a new man in the

same skin'. 'But it did make one's hair stand on end,' his son 'CT' declared. 'Everyone in the house had a dog's life of it until they were converted.' The three brothers were at Eton, and all three in the cricket XI when they beat both Winchester and Harrow. But the 'dog's life' ended in the thoroughgoing conversion of each boy on one summer's day at home. A visitor took their 'cruel practical joke' against him so well as to earn their respect and a hearing when he talked with each of them on the quiet about the meaning of Christ's death for them. For such leading athletes to begin a Bible study class at Eton could not fail to influence others.

George and Charles went up to Cambridge, 'CT' an 1879 freshman with Stanley Smith, Montagu Beauchamp and William Hoste. 'CT' at once won his cricket blue and went on to play for the university for four years. George captained the XI in 1882, 'CT' in 1883 and Kynaston in 1884, an unbroken family record. In 1882 'CT', in his third year and aged twenty-one, attained national fame when Cambridge 'defeated the unbeaten Australians', and in August played for England in the historic match that created The Ashes.[685] His all-round brilliance ensured his going to Australia to win back The Ashes in 'one long blaze of cricketing glory'. The name of C. T. Studd was on everybody's lips. But while Kynaston was unashamedly a Christian, working to show other men the way to Christ, 'CT' although idolised and influential went little further than inviting them to meetings, a 'proper' Christian but by his own admission 'no obedience, no sacrifice'.

Moody for town, gown and army (1882–83)

Kynaston Studd as an older man dropped naturally into the role of university cricketer and leader of the Christian Union. In February 1882 he organised and sent to D. L. Moody in Scotland an invitation signed by undergraduates, clergymen and dons[686] (including Handley Moule, Principal of Ridley Hall) to conduct a mission to the townsfolk and students of the university. Moody accepted for November 5–12, eight days beginning on a Sunday which happened to be Guy Fawkes Day, celebrated by fireworks and high spirits. 'There never was a place,' said Moody, 'that I approached with greater anxiety than Cambridge.' When 'JEK' later met and heard this broad American of rough un-English speech and manners his heart sank. What fiasco or disaster were they in for? A marked man, he had already personally signed an invitation to every one of the 3,500 undergraduates.

Seventeen hundred undergraduates were counted entering the great Corn Exchange, 'laughing and talking and rushing for seats'. Some started building a pyramid of chairs. A firework exploded against a window outside. Dons and clergy led Moody and Sankey on to the platform to a chorus of 'hoots and cheers'. Sankey's sacred songs were greeted with cries of 'encore!' after each verse. Moody started speaking about Daniel and was heckled with shouts from the rowdies. He kept his temper and his bluff humour. The majority were listening. At the end he asked any who wished to pray to stay behind, and four hundred stayed.

The following morning, Gerald Lander of Trinity, the leader of the uproar, arrived at Moody's hotel with an apology signed by his fellow-culprits. On the Wednesday night in a full gymnasium hall Moody said, 'I feel sure many of you are ready and yearning to know Christ.' And he asked them to climb the central iron staircase 'in full view of all' to the fencing-gallery where he and Sankey would talk with them. Fifty-two went up, among them Gerald Lander. On Thursday night when thirty more climbed that staircase, one who should have joined them crept away to count the awful cost of burning his bridges if he did turn to Christ unconditionally. Arthur Polhill-Turner had not been one of the pyramid builders and hecklers, but felt 'secure in his destiny as a clergyman', the comfortable profession for which he was training at Trinity Hall. At that Thursday meeting and on Friday and Saturday Moody's denunciations of sin,

'always balanced by the wonderful love of God' broke his rebellion.

Back in the Corn Exchange on the final day, the 12th, D. L. Moody faced nearly two thousand university men without a 'shadow of opposition, interruption or inattention'. The lives of too many men of the fast set, the pubs and race-tracks, had been changed before their eyes in college after college. When he asked all 'who had received blessing' during the week to stand, two hundred rose to their feet, Arthur Polhill-Turner among them.

Cecil and Arthur Polhill-Turner were the second and third sons of the late Captain F. C. Polhill, formerly of the 6th Dragoon Guards, Member of Parliament for Bedford, a Justice of the Peace and High Sheriff for the county in 1875. With a wife, three sons and three daughters and all he could desire, life for Captain Polhill and the family at Howbury Hall had been carefree, until Alice his eldest girl exchanged nominal Christianity for true faith in Christ and became 'the talk of the hunting field'. He died in 1881 at only fifty-five.[687]

Cecil had joined his new regiment in Ireland, but was on leave, hunting and shooting, when Arthur arrived home from Cambridge. To Cecil's alarm his brother talked 'of going to preach in China'! What madness was this? How Arthur had come to the idea is not clear; perhaps through Montagu Beauchamp or William Hoste to whom Montagu had lent copies of *China's Spiritual Need and Claims*. Since Moody's mission 'the old life of theatres, dancing, racing and cards' had given place to friendship with maturer Christians, with Kynaston Studd, Beauchamp (no longer half-hearted) and others whose passion in life was becoming 'the gospel to the world'. Of the Seven, Arthur's remark to Cecil in the winter of 1882 appears to have been the first mention of China. Cecil had to admit to himself that Arthur's experience was the genuine article, 'I knew he was right.' His regiment moved to Aldershot, and he went with Arthur to two of Moody's meetings in London. But all through 1883 he knew that becoming a Christian would alienate him from his fellow-officers and perhaps cut short his intense enjoyment of life in the cavalry with its immaculate drill, its polo and camaraderie.

William Hoste's position was strangely similar to Arthur Polhill-Turner's. After the Cambridge Mission, D. L. Moody had gone on to Oxford and then to Brighton. When the Cambridge term ended and William Hoste returned home to Brighton, his brother Dixon was there on leave from his battery at Sandown Fort in the Isle of Wight. The Hostes were a Norfolk family, staunchly Protestant since the early Reformation. Jaques Hooste was sheriff of Bruges in Flanders in 1345, as were six of his family successively during the next seventy years. But persecution drove many of the Dutch nobility to England. A Hooste relative, a girl of eighteen, was burned at the stake. So a later Jaques Hooste moved to England in 1569, was naturalised and granted wings to his coat of arms and crest in recognition of his flight. By 1675 the family were settled in Norfolk. Around 1686 James Hoste, Member of Parliament, bought the Sandringham estate, and it remained their home until 1834. His brother's son, a sporting parson more in the saddle and in debt than in the pulpit, had two sons, among other progeny. William attained the rank of captain, Royal Navy, under Nelson, and for gallantry and a famous victory off Lyssa in the defence of Portugal in the Peninsular War was honoured with a baronetcy. George his brother, a colonel in the Royal Engineers and later knighted for his part at Waterloo in 1815, became Gentleman Usher to Queen Victoria, and in time the grandfather of William and Dixon Edward Hoste. Their father was Major-General Dixon Edward Hoste CB, Royal Artillery, living at Brighton since retiring in 1881.[688]

Uncompromising Christians, the general and his wife had brought up their family of four daughters and six sons with the Bible 'almost from end to end implanted on the mind for life', and to remember the needs of missions, especially the CMS. The family were neatly arranged in two symmetrical groups of five, three boys with 'a sister at the head and another at the tail of each group', Dixon liked to recall. He was the second son, in the middle of the first set. But his personal Christianity was no more than head knowledge and the public school churchmanship instilled at Clifton College. For three years in his regiment he shrugged off all but garrison religion in any form, although he knew at heart that the Bible was true and he was wrong. The price of being a Christian was more than he was prepared to pay. His goal was progressive promotion for dedicated efficiency as a soldier.

So when he found his family attending the Moody mission near his home, he declined his mother's invitation to accompany her and settled down for the evening. But William, straight from the Cambridge and Oxford missions,' said 'Come on, Dick! Put on your wraps and go with me!' Despite himself, Dixon went, and to his surprise met with God. First, Moody talked to God, as if He were there, a friend. Then Moody warned his audience to 'flee from the wrath to come'. 'A deep sense of my sinful and perilous state laid hold of my soul with great power,' Dixon was to record.[689] For two weeks he went regularly to the Dome but resisted in agony while his mother and William and others prayed for him in his struggle. The last night came and he knew it was now or never—what he knew to be right, or short-term indulgence— Christ or career. If Christ, then it must be as completely as he had given himself to soldiering.

He was at the back of the hall. 'I shall never, in this life or the next, forget how, when under conviction of the sin of my ungodly life, I knelt at the back of the hall in Brighton and placed myself, my whole being, unreservedly at the disposal of the Lord Jesus . . . thankfully receiving the salvation offered so freely through the sacrifice on Calvary.' To his amazement peace and a sense of having been forgiven filled him. When Moody called for those who had responded to confess their faith by coming to the front, his family saw to their delight this tall, soldierly figure making his way forward with the look of a man who has won.

Within two weeks Hoste knew that nothing now mattered so much as taking this gospel to 'where Christ is not known . . . I want to give my life to this.' General Hoste would not hear of his resigning his commission until he had taken time to weigh it up more calmly. Dixon decided to say no more until his father raised the subject again. He was disciplining himself to overcome a strong streak of shyness. He returned to his battery at Sandown Fort and on the first evening told his commanding officer and fellow-officers in the Mess that he had become a Christian. To his surprise they took it calmly, impressed by his conviction and fearlessness. 'He was on fire with it all . . . which to this day I reverence,' a brigadier who had been his junior in 1882 was to recall in 1946.

So back he went to the life he so enjoyed, the battery drill, the polo and the friends he had made, for a year and three months until he resigned his commission. His brother William fed him with books, among them some from the CIM, *China's Spiritual Need and Claims* and probably *China's Millions,* for he had once admired the 'simple and direct faith in God for temporal supply and protection, and also the close identification by the missionaries with the Chinese social life'.

In May 1883 General Hoste wrote to say that if Dixon still wished to become a missionary he would no longer stand in the way. By then Dixon had been impressed by the demanding standard of the apostle Peter's injunction, 'If any man speak, let him speak as the oracles of God', that is, 'as one speaking the very words of God'.[690] Set on maintaining the highest standards in his life as a Christian no less than as an officer, he resolved to pray and to 'wait on God' until sure he was being 'led by the Spirit', before he took action, wrote a letter or attempted to preach. If he often appeared cautious, deliberating before taking action, this lay at its root. On July 23 he wrote to Hudson Taylor:

Sir; I have for some time been thinking about offering myself for the China Inland Mission ... My time is just now, in the drill season, very much taken up with my duties ... This must be my apology for asking whether I can see you on Friday or Saturday next. I have the honour to be, Sir, your obedient servant, D. E. Hoste, Lieut. R. A.

Three days later an inspection of troops made him postpone his visit.

With Hudson Taylor away on tour in the north, Benjamin Broomhall acknowledged the letter, and on August 1 (the day Harold Schofield died) Hudson Taylor read it on his return. Years later, when D. E. Hoste was Benjamin's son-in-law and General Director of the Mission in Hudson Taylor's shoes, he wrote (with the humility that required references to himself to be in the third person) that Hudson Taylor,

was careful to set before him the real character of life and work in inland China, telling him quite plainly that it involved isolation, privation, exposure to the hostility of the people, and the contempt of his own countrymen, and also many trials of faith, patience and constancy ... (He) went away deeply impressed with the character of the man ... and with his heart more than ever set on becoming a missionary in China ... more and more impressed with the need of the utmost care and caution lest he should presume to enter so privileged a life and service ... without having been called and appointed thereto by the Lord.

Hudson Taylor had advised him first to mature as a Christian and then to gain experience of evangelism. He accepted the advice, and drew upon his parents' faithful teaching over the years.

One day I was in my room, tilted back in my chair with my open Bible before me. I had begun thoroughly to enjoy the Word of God. As I read I smoked, and raised my head occasionally to blow the tobacco smoke over the open pages before me. All at once the thought came to me—'Is this honouring to God ... ?' I at once stopped smoking, and from that moment have never touched tobacco.

In another jotting the informal DEH comes through: '(the CIM) thoughtful, sober-minded, feet on the ground: this gained my confidence. So much cackling *before* they have their egg! (CIM) show the *real* thing.'

From time to time as he was able he came to Pyrland Road, and became acquainted with those regularly at the Saturday prayer meetings. On one of these occasions as he entered he saw Benjamin's petite daughter Gertrude at the piano and said to himself, 'I shall marry her one day.' She and her brother Hudson left for China among the Seventy on September 24, 1884, while Hoste let God guide him and bring them together in due time.

'Sporting hearties' for the CIM (1883–84)

Meanwhile Stanley Smith, unsure of where God was leading him, considered a variety of possibilities in Britain. Back in 1880 he had applied to himself the words of God addressed to Ezekiel: 'Thou art not sent to a people of strange speech.' But on November 30, 1883, the commission given to Isaiah impressed him: 'I will also give thee for a light to the Gentiles, that thou mayest be my salvation unto the ends of the earth.' His use of Scripture may have been shaky, but 'I got set free,' he said, from the sense of restriction, free to act on a growing estimation of the CIM. A month later, 'about the end of 1883, I wrote to Mr Taylor, telling him I wanted to come out to China.'[691] Five months after Schofield's death, a second man of the type he (Schofield) had had in mind had approached the Mission. On January 4, 1884, a long evening with Hudson Taylor took Smith to the point of saying, 'I hope to labour for God there soon.'

William Cassels was ordained on June 4, 1882, and went as curate to the overflowing working-class church of All Saints, South Lambeth, under Allen Edwards. The pews, the aisles, even the chancel and pulpit steps were packed with people on Sundays, and three thousand children filled six Sunday schools. Edwards and Cassels heard people say in the streets 'There go David and Jonathan,' so one were they in partnership. This training for the future could scarcely have been better as during the next two years he thought more and more about going overseas. His forebears, named Cassels's, had been ship-owners on the Firth of Forth and his grandfather a physician in Kendal and Lancaster. His father had become a merchant in Lisbon and Oporto where he met a West Country mill-owner's daughter whom he married. Of their thirteen children William Wharton was the ninth, and the sixth of seven sons.[692]

His family background with a vicar uncle and Repton schooldays had led on easily to ordination and the intention to join the Church Missionary Society. But when he 'expressed a strong desire for work in inland China' and was told that the CMS had no plans to go there, he turned his attention to the CIM. In February 1884 Stanley Smith took part with Cassels in an evangelistic mission in Clapham, between South Lambeth and the school at Newlands where 'SPS' was teaching. They talked together about China. Then in March Stanley Smith joined in Moody's London campaign, earning Moody's admiration for his zeal and ability in the 'inquiry room'. After the afternoon campaign meeting on March 26, Stanley took his mother to tea with Moody and was invited to come to Massachusetts to help in training converts at Moody's training school. From Moody they went home to 13 John Street, Mayfair, where Hudson Taylor joined them for dinner and discussed Stanley's future. That settled it. He walked part of the way back to Pyrland Road with Hudson Taylor, and the same night wrote, 'decided to go to China with Hudson Taylor . . . and to go, DV, via America to see Moody's training home'.

On February 26, 1884, the day before the two Salisbury Women (Rosa Minchin and Emily Whitchurch), two other women and two men sailed for China, making forty-two of the Seventy, D. E. Hoste had met the CIM council informally, as he was still not sure that it was God's will for him to resign his commission to go to China. But by April

15 he had already acted, as he told Hudson Taylor in characteristic prose:

> I have been with my battery for the last six weeks, having been recalled by telegraph, on 4th of March, and am now come on leave, pending my name appearing in the Gazette, as retired from the army ... My own feeling is now that I should go to China, and if so I would esteem it a most blessed privilege to go under the auspices of the China Inland Mission.

He still distinguished between his own sense of what would be right, and an assurance that this was God's will for him. It depended after all on the CIM's view. On Hudson Taylor's advice he was hoping to gain experience as a counsellor in Moody's inquiry room as Stanley Smith had done.

By then Stanley had had his formal interview with the London council, on April 1, following a public meeting of the CIM in the Mansion House, presided over by the Lord Mayor. His offer to serve in China with the CIM had been 'cordially accepted', and the first of what George Woodcock called the CIM's 'sporting hearties' was a probationer of the Mission, to Dixon Hoste's delight. But,

> It was not SPS at all—to begin with [Hoste was to recall]; Studd came through McCarthy, Beauchamp had known JHT for years, SPS was a percussion cap!—the gun already loaded in many cases. Oh! so attractive! Brilliant fellow. (And why the CIM? So practical. So sane.) We young fellows notice how much they (the CIM) *pray* for the safety of their people, and for the money to *reach* them.

The council as well as Hudson Taylor and the general secretary were kept extremely busy, interviewing and advising many candidates at frequent meetings all through 1884. On August 4 the future pioneer of Tibet, Annie Royle Taylor, 'Lady Probationer, London Hospital' was 'cordially accepted'; the acceptance of Gertrude and Hudson Broomhall, future treasurer in China, both well known to the council, was 'agreed'; and 'Jeanie' Gray (later to marry Herbert Hudson Taylor) was interviewed. The minutes of October 7

record that the Rev W. Cassels was 'cordially accepted', and 'Mr Hoste' accepted subject to his references proving satisfactory. Already Cassels's six brothers had gone overseas, and in agony of heart his mother had pleaded with Hudson Taylor not to take William. To her joy he 'assured her that he held a parent's wishes sacred and would not encourage William if she opposed' his application. But on October 1 a letter from her withdrew her objection lest she should prove 'a bad mother to one of the best of sons'.

Dixon Hoste could have fallen at the council fence, for the vicar of Sandown grudgingly characterised him as shy and reserved, 'not naturally enterprising' and 'not naturally fitted for (missionary) work, but I may be mistaken'. And then, significantly, 'I should have liked him to have remained in the army'. The council understood. They themselves saw humility, sincerity, wise judgment, character, courage and self-sacrifice. More than mere assessment was involved. Now there were three 'sporting hearties' and talk of them sailing with Hudson Taylor in December, with a schoolmaster for Chefoo, Herbert L. Norris, for good measure. For fast growing numbers of raw probationers learning the language in the Yangzi stations needed Hudson Taylor's presence to deploy them appropriately, in terms of the greatest needs for reinforcements, of denominational preferences, of physique and aptitude.

In the spring of 1883, C. T. Studd had returned from Australia with The Ashes, the best all-round cricketer in Britain for the second year running, but spiritually at low ebb, until in November his brother George was hovering between life and death.[693] Fame and wealth no longer meant anything to George. At the gateway of 'eternity' in their London home, No 2 Hyde Park Gardens, 'he only cared about the Bible and the Lord Jesus Christ'. Watching him and waiting on him hour after hour, 'CT' saw the transience, the emptiness of all this world could offer. 'God brought me back' to consecration, as he brought George back to life. And at one of Moody's meetings

'(God) met me again and restored to me the joy of my salvation'. 'My heart was no longer in the game' of cricket. What mattered now was to serve and to lead others to Christ. He took members of his Test team to hear Moody, and thrilled to see them turn to Christ, especially A. J. Webbe, H. E. Steel and the captain, N. Bligh, the future Lord Darnley. But he could not fathom what he was to do with his own life now that he had taken his degree. He decided to read law. The *Daily Telegraph* was to indulge in hyperbole about his sacrificing a brilliant career at the Bar to become a missionary. But he knew that for him the Bar was wrong. He must spend his life for Christ. He read Hannah Pearsall Smith's *The Christian's Secret of a Happy Life*, in a word, abandonment to Christ and 'absolute faith' in Him. 'Christ's love compels us . . . He died for all, that those who live should no longer live for themselves but for Him who died for them and was raised again.' He knelt and prayed in the words of F. R. Havergal's hymn:

Take my life and let it be

Consecrated, Lord, to Thee!

He was ready at last for marching orders and was not kept waiting.

On Saturday, November 1, Stanley Smith called at Hyde Park Gardens on his way to Pyrland Road. Too many claims in Britain had decided Hudson Taylor to ask John McCarthy to deputise briefly for him in China. McCarthy was being 'farewelled' at the weekly prayer meeting, so 'CT' went along with Stanley. Listening to McCarthy tell about his own call by God when Hudson Taylor came to Dublin in 1865 (see 1, pp 680–81), and to Stanley Smith and Robert Landale, 'all (of whom) spoke splendidly', Studd knew without doubt that God was sending him to China. On the way back he told Stanley Smith, and at home broke his news to Kynaston and their mother. They knew him too well not to be alarmed, a Roman candle, impulsive, unpredictable, even unbalanced. Mrs Studd was distraught, for two days imploring him to wait at least a week 'before giving himself to H. Taylor'. When Montagu Beauchamp

called round he found Kynaston in the depths of depression. 'CT' was 'a fanatic'. But 'CT' could not be budged: he went back to Pyrland Road on November 4, was interviewed by members of the council and recommended to 'consider the question . . . more fully and . . . if he still wished to go, to write definitely offering himself'. This he did, and was taken at his word and accepted.

Since Montagu Beauchamp was a child of five, playing with Hudson Taylor's chopsticks and (detached) pigtail, they had often been together and knew each other well. In September 1878 as the guest of Lady Beauchamp and the Hon Miss Waldegrave in the Engadine and on the Pontresina glaciers, Hudson Taylor had shared their concern for the Beauchamp sons. Montagu, the fourth, was eighteen and still at Repton. There and at Cambridge he trailed behind the others, especially Stanley Smith, as a Christian. Hudson Taylor went on praying for him. Late in 1881 Montagu wrote to tell Kynaston Studd that at last he had 'yielded all to Christ', and came up to Trinity 'so full of zeal instead of his coldness and lukewarmness'. When Stanley lapsed into smoking again, it was Montagu's influence on the family holiday of the Beauchamps and Waldegraves in Normandy that rallied his spiritual discipline.

After taking his degree in 1883, Montagu had started on an ordination course at Ridley Hall, but without conviction that he should be ordained. He withdrew and in 1884 went through a spell when his faith was shaken, until his eldest sister helped him back to a 'very deep spiritual experience of reconsecration to God'. In the autumn the talk of his family (at their home, 4 Cromwell Road, opposite the Natural History Museum) was of Stanley Smith's impending departure to China. Lady Beauchamp had often said that it would give her great joy to have a missionary son. When Hilda Beauchamp's engagement to Kynaston Studd drew the two families together, and Montagu saw the Studds' distress over CT's decision to go to China, his own conscience was needled into writing to his mother (to quote Pollock), 'If Charlie Studd was willing to go in spite of his family, ought a man to hold back whose mother would rather encourage than hinder?'[694] One day Stanley and Montagu were in a restaurant opposite Victoria station, talking about China, when Stanley said, 'If you saw two men carrying a log of wood, one end much heavier than the other, which end would you help at—the heavier or the lighter?' Montagu went home and thought about it, and as he prayed became convinced 'that not only was I to go but to induce others to go too'. The mothers of the seven were being drawn in, some despite themselves.

A 'big go' for China (1884)

From the emerging Cambridge Seven we revert to Hudson Taylor in another strenuous year. Two quarto letter books of 1884 in his and Jennie's handwriting have been preserved. One records the source, contents and date of reply to 997 letters from China by October 13, and the other 1,992 personal letters from correspondents in Britain by October 25.[695] On January 1 alone he replied to seventeen from China. General Mission letters were handled by others. In the year, he dealt with about 3,200 personal letters between and during his frequent journeys, meetings and interviews. By January 19 'Benjamin B.' was writing that Hudson was 'prostrate'. Splitting headaches immobilised him. The pace was too great. Already in January he had taken part in fourteen meetings in London, Andover and Southsea.

After five days' rest at old Mrs Robert Howard's home in Tottenham he was on the welcome treadmill again. Farewell meetings for the Salisbury ladies followed in February, with lectures at Harley House and to students of the Presbyterian College, at Spurgeon's Tabernacle and the YMCA, as well as in a variety of churches. Dixon Hoste met the council, and from Glasgow, before he left for China, John McCarthy reported serious consultations with men of the first quality. If office routine had not been McCarthy's forte, personal counselling at a high spiritual level was another matter.

C. T. Studd's dramatic decision was not made until November 1 of that year, 1883, but on February 2, 1884, McCarthy wrote that he was staying at the home of 'a fine young fellow, very wholehearted for God. He has been to China and Burmah (and) seen a vision of a needy world.' He was also very wealthy. Archibald Orr Ewing and his friends, Walter B. Sloan and Campbell White (Lord Overtoun), had talked with John McCarthy the previous day. Orr Ewing and Sloan were not only to go to China together a year after the Seven, but also to become stars in the Mission's crown.[696]

On March 5, Hudson Taylor crossed over to Belfast for a week of meetings arranged by the YMCA, and to reap more 'good, reliable men,' 'valuable candidates'. No one realised that he was not fit enough to stand from 8.00 to 9.40 p.m. and then to perch on a backless bench before his turn to speak. He confessed to Jennie that he was 'too tired to do well . . . a pity . . . for it was a magnificent meeting'. Like a snowball he gathered work as he went. On March 13 he met the theological students, 9.00–10.00 a.m.; working women 2.00–2.30 p.m.; ladies, gentlemen and ministers, 3.00–4.30 p.m.; and 'candidates to China', 4.30–5.30 p.m.[697]

At Nottingham the next day he was disappointed to hear from Benjamin who had personally arranged the meetings that 'some magic lantern business' had been introduced and should be eliminated. Hudson Taylor agreed. They drew the wrong people in the wrong spirit and offended some supporters. To 'exalt the Lord', and to do his will, created the right atmosphere and results. Eugene Stock stated that this emphasis was the CIM's great contribution to the Christian Church at this period.[698] The 'happiest hours' were spent at the Congregational College. Then back to London, and Mrs Robert Howard sent a carriage to bring him and Jennie to her home for the weekend. Then to Reigate and the home of Florence Barclay who was soon to join the Mission. (In 1892 she married Montagu Beauchamp.) 'I do not know anything so encouraging as insuperable difficulties,' Hudson Taylor said to them. 'There is a POWER behind us that can lay low every mountain in its pride.'[699] The philanthropist Robert Arthington, 'emphatically' enthused, reminded Hudson Taylor of his interest in the aboriginal tribes and Tibet.[700] Together Hudson Taylor and Benjamin revised and issued a large illustrated fifth edition of *China's Spiritual Need and Claims.* It sold fast and well. *China's Millions,* an unrelenting labour, was also in greater demand, with news of French action in Indo-China and increasing persecution of Christians in China. But there were many conversions to report, and Cameron's travels were still big news. From Xi'an, George King wrote that for his work in Shaanxi province and Xi'an its capital, 1,500 preachers of the gospel would not be too many. 'Were I in England again, I would gladly live in one room, make the floor my bed, a box my chair' if it would help to get the gospel to those who 'perish for lack of knowledge'. The church at home must care more about the Christless. With the Eastons and then George King and Dr William Wilson hounded out of Xi'an, and the landlords of the inn they used and of the house they rented being beaten and imprisoned, it was still an uphill fight. The danger to their Chinese colleagues had become too great, so they withdrew and King and Wilson went straight back to Xi'an. 'No sorrow seems great, no trial severe, after my having lost my dear wife and boy,' King wrote. Then came the news from George Clarke that his wife had died in Dali on October 7, 1883. 'The last foreign sister she saw was on May 16. I have been burying my sorrow by preaching in the open air.'

May, with a long list of meetings, ended with the CIM's annual meetings, chaired by Robert Scott the publisher when Lord Shaftesbury was detained at the last minute. Of 428 Protestant missionaries in China, 126 were now members of the CIM, 33 of them unmarried women, But 'Scotland has 3,845 ordained ministers' and Glasgow more than in all of China!'[701] Looking out over the audience Hudson Taylor recognised friends who had been praying

for China before he first went out, thirty-one years before. One friend had missed only one of the weekly prayer meetings in nineteen years. The family atmosphere was strong. The year before, both John Eliot Howard and Lord Congleton had been on the platform. Both were 'with the Lord'. It was good to see so many Christians in the audience, but 'one is almost tempted to wish a persecution could come after the work of Moody and Sankey, to scatter us all to some dark parts of the world'.

June 25 saw the Mildmay Conference with Bishop Hannington of Uganda and Professor Drummond of Edinburgh speaking. Then on the 27th Hudson Taylor gave the closing address. The great audience had sung the hymn 'Waft, waft ye winds the story' when he rose to his feet, led in prayer and said, 'It will not do to sing (that). The winds will not waft the story. No! Mothers must give up beloved sons; fathers must give up precious daughters; brothers and sisters must cheerfully yield one another to the Lord's service . . . It is in the path of obedience and self-denying service that God reveals Himself most intimately to His children.' At the Salisbury conference in September, Bishop Hannington said that his own call to be a missionary had come from China, and he 'chose to forget Africa for a while to pray for China'.

By invitation of the Lord Mayor of London, Alderman Robert N. Fowler (who in 1860 had been treasurer of the ill-fated Chinese Evangelisation Society), another CIM meeting was held on July 8, 1884, with the Lord Mayor himself again presiding. He held up Consul Alabaster's report (see page 373), presented to Parliament a few days before, and read out its compliments to the CIM. But three days later the French ultimatum was presented at Peking and war was declared. Public attitudes were volatile. Criticisms of Hudson Taylor increased, for sending out more and more young missionaries including mere girls in these circumstances. Henrietta Soltau heard someone expostulating at the madness of running such risks, and Hudson Taylor's quiet humour in reply, 'I have never found in my Bible that the Lord says the Gospel was not to be taken to China when there was war with France.'[702]

At least three donors had seen how tired Hudson Taylor was and sent gifts to pay for a good holiday. So he, Jennie and Maria were at the Keswick Convention together when Walter B. Sloan went on his knees in the great marquee and put himself at God's disposal, 'for China'. Not yet eighteen, Maria sailed on August 27.

Thanking Miss Arthington in August for a donation, Jennie said, 'The very prosperity that the Lord is giving us just overwhelms him (JHT) with work.' But it was better to be overwhelmed than to let the opportunities go by. D. J. Findlay of Glasgow telegraphed, 'Tent conference fixed for 27th Sept. on your account. Do not disappoint us. Want you for 28th also.' And he wrote 'We want to make our conference a big go for China and of course you are indispensable. We also want McCarthy, Stevenson, Landale, and as big a contingent as possible.' What could he do but go? He enlisted Stanley Smith for the first of six weeks of meetings he was to have, and as soon as he could get away from the Salisbury conference Hudson Taylor and Benjamin joined the others at Glasgow. Instead of being exhausted at the end, he felt 'rested', he told Jennie, so uplifting had the meetings been, reaping the harvest of Moody's campaign of 1882.[703]

October was fuller still. After Glasgow and Greenock came a great meeting on October 2 in the United Presbyterian Synod Hall, the largest in Edinburgh, with the same four stalwarts to support him, reinforced by Trench; and another in the Free Assembly Hall chaired by Lord Polwarth. Frequent applause greeted their reports of 22,000 converts in all of China in the past year; and of £130,000 having been received by the CIM since its inception. Then he himself had a big meeting at Chillingham Castle on the way back to London. A letter followed him from the Earl of Tankerville's staff, thanking him and enclosing a donation.

He had already been to Belfast. Dublin wanted him too. With Smith, Cassels and Hoste already in the Mission he was planning to take them to China by 'the first boat in December'. It meant leaving Jennie behind again, but with such scope for influencing the church in Britain he hoped to be back after only a brief absence.[704] Time was short. Eight others sailed away on October 8, and on the 10th he and Stanley Smith crossed over to Dublin. Hudson Taylor's SOS shows the tempo of life. 'I've got the wrong trousers on. Send my best.' All went well except that few opportunities were given for the still unknown Stanley Smith to speak. However, on the 14th 'we had a wonderful audience tonight. I have seldom seen such a sight.'

A cable arrived at Pyrland Road from China, 'Trouble inland, impossible forward arrivals . . . send no more till way clear.' The *Pall Mall Gazette* of October 13 reported riots at Wenzhou on the 5th and most foreign premises burned, including the Stotts' but excluding the consulate and Customs house. Repercussions of the French attacks on Fuzhou and Taiwan were spreading. Deciding with Benjamin that 'in quietness and in confidence shall be your strength', Jennie sent the cable on by post instead of telegraph. 'I expect, darling, that you are remembering that Maria is due in Shanghai this week'—in the dangerous Taiwan straits as she wrote. The Chinese were fleeing from Ningbo, sure of attack soon. And Hudson Taylor began hearing of 'destruction and damage in different stations'. He prayed about the cable and disregarded it. Seventeen more were *en route* in two ships anyway, Amelia's son and daughter (Hudson and Gertrude) among them. The next group would sail as planned. It included six Glasgow women, the Murray sisters, widely experienced and in their thirties, going at their own expense, and Kate Mackintosh, soon to become a pioneer of 'women only' outposts. 'One of the best parties that ever went to China.' One effect of the attacks on Taiwan was that Eleanor Black, designated to Taiwan, did not go, and the CIM did not work in Taiwan until 1952.[705]

He was back in London in time for the Saturday prayer meeting on October 18 before their departure. The Seventy had been exceeded. 'The room was crammed and thirty or more people were standing in the halls,' Jennie wrote to Maria. It was 'as if the world were moved . . . more power with God was felt than ever before . . . I felt that eternity would show the result.' After the farewell communion service on the day before they joined their ship, the council minuted their opinion that women should carry equal weight with men in deciding 'station' affairs. (The suffragette movement began early in the twentieth century; winning suffrage for women of thirty in 1918 and equal suffrage a decade later.)

Stanley Smith's letters to Hudson Taylor convey the warmth between them, almost as father and son, since being in Glasgow, Edinburgh and Dublin together. 'Enclosed is a photo with love.'[706] From Cambridge where he was busy with many college meetings he wrote of trying to arrange three meetings each night for a team led by Hudson Taylor. 'I have met with such love; and I believe a warm welcome will await you. I have engaged the Alexandra Hall every night from November 12–17 and a friend of mine has offered to defray all expenses.' Robert Landale was busy in the same way at Oxford and 'much encouraged' although his meetings were 'not so large or numerous . . . SPG [the "high church" Society for the Propagation of the Gospel] is more the article for Oxford than CIM or even CMS.'

November (not March) came 'in like a lion' and roared its way through, more eventfully than October. The Saturday prayer meeting on November 1, far more than an institution at any time, was honoured by the presence of Reginald Radcliffe, the veteran evangelist, now throwing in the weight of his effectiveness to help the CIM. Hudson Taylor was with the Kemp and Pigott families for meetings at Rochdale, but John McCarthy was taking leave of the United Kingdom, to sail on November 6. This was the occasion of C. T. Studd's 'resolve' to go to China,

and its immediate effect on Montagu Beauchamp, confirmed after a 'chance' meeting and journey with Stanley Smith on the smoky 'Underground' to Victoria and that memorable cup of tea. Charlie Studd's mother came in distress to talk with Jennie at Pyrland Road and left satisfied. Lady Beauchamp also consoled her, and despite herself she began to find their enthusiasm infectious. Hudson Taylor was away again when Montagu's mother came to see Jennie. Glad that Montagu was going, 'She would like (him) to go out with you that he may drink into your views—a *very* satisfying talk'.[707] In China Hudson Taylor was to honour her wish. They made long journeys together and developed an even closer friendship.

Passing over the Oxford and Cambridge meetings for the moment, it may help understanding to get the perspective of November, December and January from Hudson Taylor's point of view. Illness on his return from Rochdale delayed his joining the team at Oxford, but he played a full part at Cambridge and went on to Ipswich—in the Town Hall, with the mayor and aldermen complete—to Nottingham with Studd and Hoste, to Leicester with Studd and Smith, for two meetings in F. B. Meyer's Melbourne Hall, and for Lord Radstock two meetings at the Eccleston Hall in London with Smith, Studd and Cassels. The Leicester meeting was historic, for early the next morning the minister himself, F. B. Meyer, came round to ask Smith and Studd, 'How can I be like you?' 'The talk we had then was one of the most formative influences on my life,' the future saint and Bible expositor was to claim. In a different key, one of the audience sent a gift of underwear for Hudson Taylor, Smith and Studd; and another promised a Stilton cheese for every new missionary who would accept it.[708] The outcome was hilarious (see pp 442–43).

Not surprisingly, other missions, denominational churches and other countries were not only hearing of but being influenced by what was happening in Britain. The Methodist Bible Christians, and the Friends' Foreign Mission had consulted Hudson Taylor and invited him to address their annual meetings, in May, with the direct outcome that they sent missions to China from each body, under the wing of the CIM.[709] Approaches from Scandinavia led in time to another associate mission of the CIM sending Norwegian candidates to London for training. And a visitor from the United States, also in July, was the first hint of the unplanned future international nature of the Mission. On August 13, Major-General Haig of the Kabyle and Berber Mission, initiated by Hudson Taylor's old friend George Pearse and parent Society of the North Africa Mission, consulted Hudson Taylor on administrative problems. In November the first links with Sweden were forged by a request from a Pastor Holmgren for an article from Hudson Taylor. And in December a Professor Tauxe of Aigle proposed an *Occasional* on China for French Switzerland.[710]

In mid-December Hudson Taylor discussed his plans for administrative reorganisation in China, and worked on three monthly issues of the 1885 *China's Millions* in preparation for leaving Britain on January 20. With such momentum as had built up during the last few months, and with John Stevenson home from Burma, 'filled with the Spirit' in a way he had never experienced before, and proving to have a strong gift for administration, Hudson Taylor could afford to leave for a while. The need for the General Director to be in China had become paramount. Through all the long years of overwork, crying for delegation of duties, a potential lieutenant had been within calling distance. But Stevenson had been dour and withdrawn, until he put himself at God's disposal. Apart from the Franco-Chinese war in the south, the *coup d'état* and anti-Japanese riots in Korea had precipitated a new crisis in the north. Hudson Taylor could delay no longer.

'An expanding circle of action'[711] (November–December 1884)

Some wild things have been written about Hudson Taylor and the so-called 'Cambridge Seven', best answered by the facts. Apart from the biographies of Cassels, Hoste and C. T. Studd, the story of the Seven and their dealings with him has usually taken them as far as China. More light can be thrown on this early period and on their later history, instructive from the way they turned out.

When the first CIM meetings took place in Oxford and Cambridge in November 1884 there was no Cambridge Seven, not even a Cambridge five. As an Oxford graduate Robert Landale had tried to stir up interest in his own university, and Stanley Smith had been well received. But his warning that the climate was unfavourable proved true. News of C. T. Studd's decision to go to China was to create a great stir in the cricketing and university world, but his presence in Oxford from Wednesday, November 5 to Monday 10, could not have been planned. On the heels of deciding on November 1 and meeting the CIM council for the first time on the 4th, he at once joined Smith and Hoste to go there on the 5th. Beauchamp turned up on the 7th. Hudson Taylor's illness kept him back until Saturday the 8th, which was also the earliest day Cassels could manage although billed as a speaker. After the first meeting attendance was poor and the team disheartened, but on the 11th an Oxford donor wrote 'greatly rejoicing' that God 'so marvellously helped' them. They had given of their best. And on the same day Hudson Taylor told the council that he expected 'some of those present to become missionaries'.[712]

Cambridge was entirely different. The lively Christian Union had prepared for six days of activity on behalf of the CIM and other missions. 'Extraordinary interest was aroused' by the news that C. T. Studd, ex-captain of the Cambridge XI and England's most outstanding cricketer of the day, still at the height of his powers, with S. P. Smith, stroke oar of the University Eight, and Montagu Beauchamp who had narrowly missed his place in the same boat, were about to tell the university why they were going to China of all places and in wartime. 'The influence of such a band of men . . . was irresistible,' Eugene Stock said in his *History of the Church Missionary Society*. 'No such event had occurred before; and no event of the century has done so much to arouse the minds of Christian men to see the tremendous claims of the field, and the nobility of the missionary vocation'—strong words, for David Livingstone's appeal to the universities in 1857 had given rise to the Universities Mission to Central Africa.[713]

Concerned not to fish in other societies' waters, Hudson Taylor had asked the CMS to send representatives to take part in the meetings. In thanking him for this 'kind and brotherly invitation' Stock himself lamented that he had four other engagements that could not be shelved. And in his history he said, 'The gift of such a band to the China Inland Mission was a just reward to Mr Hudson Taylor and his colleagues for the genuine unselfishness with which they had always pleaded the cause of China and the World, and not of their own particular organisation.' Prospective CMS men supported the mission and testified from the platform with the team. One of them was Arthur Polhill-Turner, 'two years to the day since his conversion'. As a result more offered their lives to the CMS. Cynical dons and facetious freshmen had their say, but they were merely the losers.

The meetings ran from November 12 to 17, with Dr Handley Moule, Principal of Ridley Hall and later Bishop of Durham presiding at several, and Hudson Taylor speaking at each except on the Friday, 'mail day'. Smith's charm and fluency, Studd's down to earth colloquialisms, Beauchamp's straightforwardness, Hoste's laconic, military directness, and each one's transparent love of Christ and costly sacrifice shook their audiences. Utter consecration, in athletes of the best type, each confirming the reality of the others' experience; challenged the mediocrity of everyone's life. 'Mounting enthusiasm' (so

different from Oxford) and many long personal conversations filled their days. On Sunday afternoon a 'very remarkable' meeting (in Handley Moule's words) was open to townsfolk as well as the university. That evening fifty men stood to declare their willingness to serve God overseas, and the next day when Stanley Smith asked 'all who intended to become missionaries' (not specifying where or how) to stay behind after the last meeting closed, forty-five stayed, Arthur Polhill-Turner among them.

His brother Cecil had faced up to the loss of all he so greatly valued, in the Guards and hunting field, and to his mother's rebuke. His Roman Catholic bachelor uncle, Sir Henry Barron, 'British Resident at the court of the Kingdom of Wurttemberg' had made him his heir. The odds on being disowned were considerable. But after a winter leave spent with him Cecil returned to his regiment 'with a mind fully made up. I had yielded to and trusted in Jesus Christ as my Saviour, Lord and Master', without any reservations. He had shown himself 'too good an officer to be treated with disrespect' when he told the Mess what had happened, and now played polo and cricket 'for Christ'. Many high-ranking officers of the first quality were dedicated Christians. He could be the same. But he went to a 'China missionary meeting, and from that time I made up my mind to engage in the Lord's work in China'. On December 1 a memorable meeting of the CMS in Cambridge fed the enthusiasm aroused by the CIM, and both societies reaped the benefits. Cecil spent three days with Arthur, talking and praying together, so far had they travelled in a short time.

Reginald Radcliffe had recognised the power in the young men around Hudson Taylor and convinced him that before they sailed away, the universities of Scotland should be visited also. Radcliffe consulted Professor Alexander Simpson of Edinburgh and an itinerary of Glasgow, Dundee, Aberdeen and Edinburgh was quickly arranged. After the Eccleston Hall 'farewell' meetings 'CT' and 'SPS' took the night train to Glasgow just as they were—Studd, to his mother's distress, without even a change of clothes. Hudson Taylor asked that a parcel might be sent after him. They were 'in a mortal funk' about meeting unknown students. They need not have feared, though uproar was a Scottish way of life.

From Dundee, where Stanley Smith was left after the meeting to talk with students while Reginald Radcliffe, Robert Landale and Studd went on to Aberdeen; 'SPS' wrote to Hudson Taylor that Mr Radcliffe proposed a repetition of the tour from January 10–22, to Liverpool and other cities in England.[714] 'Could you come? If not, may we go?' It would mean deferring their departure to China until late in January. He agreed, although it would mean separating, Hudson Taylor himself having to go ahead on January 20. He had cancelled the December sailing, although a small army of new missionaries learning the language in China needed his decisions on their deployment.[715]

John Stevenson had played a major part in the preparations in Scotland, and after the Edinburgh meeting called it 'a most remarkable one'. 'SPS' was 'simmering'. A committee of professors and students had taken the Free Assembly Hall holding one thousand, and advertised the occasion very enterprisingly. Students packed the hall, singing and beating time with sticks. Compared with Smith's inspired eloquence, Studd was prosaic, but such sincerity and devotion 'if anything, made the greatest impression'. They cheered him to the echo, and at the same time were 'spellbound'. When the meeting ended a stampede of men crowded around them to say goodbye, showing on their faces that the message had gone deep. A hundred saw them off at the station, when they left for London to be at Kynaston Studd's marriage to Hilda Beauchamp.

The last half of December went in smaller meetings in the South and Midlands. John Stevenson travelled with Hoste and Cassels to the Isle of Wight, the first of a continuous round of meetings which occupied him until March 1885,

many of them in Devonshire. He was famous as the first Westerner to cross China from west to east, as McCarthy had been from east to west. But the taciturn Scot had become a new man, with richer experiences ahead of him at Keswick in 1885. He and 'Benjamin B.' made the most of the flood of requests for speakers. 'We had heaps of money' for it, with costs covered, over and above generous donations. Funds had flowed in, but no more than were needed for the Mission doubling in size. The balance in hand as the year closed was £10. 'Nobody else had such a story to tell about China as we had in those days.' 'JHT was very bright, full of enthusiasm, well and strong, travelling at night, speaking so powerfully, so clearly, always simple and telling . . . overwhelmingly busy, full of hope and courage—fifty-two, in his vigorous prime. Mr Broomhall too. No friction anywhere . . . enthusiasm itself about the Seventy and the Cambridge band.' Where was that 'fast-failing old man' of 1882?

Smith, Studd and Cassels spoke on Christmas Day at the YMCA headquarters in Aldersgate before joining their families' festivities.

Hoste writing to Hudson Taylor on December 30 signed himself affectionately yours in Christ'—gone the remote 'Sir' of early in the year. He arranged for meetings in Brighton in mid-January, with Hudson Taylor the guest of his parents. The Cambridge trio of Smith, Studd and Cassels were there on December 29, before Hoste and Stanley Smith spent the last day of the year at Pyrland Road in fasting and prayer. Neither Montagu Beauchamp nor Arthur Polhill-Turner had yet joined the Mission, and Cecil Polhill-Turner had still to make his first approach.

Then there were seven (January 1885)

After the high points of November and December who could have thought they would be exceeded? The receipts in January alone were more than the income for the financial year 1866–67; and the income for 1885 became double that of the painful period of 1881–82. New donors included a senior administrator of the Bank of England, Hammond Chubb, who later joined the CIM council. With a gift of £200 (several thousands today) old Mrs Grace (see p 256) asked, Why stop at the Seventy? Ask for seven hundred, a thousand. Lord Radstock, never failing to contribute to Hudson Taylor personally when sending larger sums for the Mission, wrote from Calcutta that he had met a leading 'wine and spirit' merchant named Stark, 'a complete man of the world', self-styled a 'sceptic and freethinker' when he boarded the P&O *Chusan*. Two young women had attracted his attention, standing at the ship's rail softly singing together. Afterwards 'Gertie' had passed the time of day on deck with him, drawing from him that he was the only unbeliever in his family. It unsettled him. He began to sit behind a partition where he could hear them having daily 'devotions' together. Nothing of mere formality spoilt it. Every word was real to them. Then, after long talks with Gertie's brother he had turned to Christ and destroyed his 'infidel' books and papers. In Calcutta he could not stop telling other people, and wrote offering his services to the CIM.[716]

Hudson Taylor had agreed to visit William Berger at Cannes, leaving London on January 20. His days until then would be full. A party of six men including his personal secretary W. J. Lewis sailed on January 15. He was to join them at Suez. On January 1, Reginald Radcliffe himself wrote, listing the many cities in Scotland and England in which he was to hold meetings with Stanley Smith and Studd, this time from January 9 to 25.[717] He would like to keep the men until February 9 in Bristol. Hudson Taylor replied by telegram. Manchester and Leeds on January 26 and 28 must be the two men's last. Until January 8 and on each day after the 29th they had farewell meetings to attend until they sailed on February 4.

Cecil and Arthur Polhill-Turner were in close touch with the others. They arranged for Stanley Smith to speak in Bedford on Friday, January 2, and for C. T. Studd to join them on Saturday for a drawing-room reception at Howbury Hall, for thirty-five county neighbours. Sunday they spent together. As a result, as soon as their friends had gone, Cecil sat down and wrote to Hudson Taylor as a stranger, 'Jan 5th, 1884 Dear Sir,' asking for a personal interview. Jennie stamped it 'Received 6 Jan 85'. On the 7th he wrote that he and his brother would come to Pyrland Road at 1.00 p.m. on the 8th (to lunch?), hoping to attend the big farewell meeting afterwards.[718] Their friends would have forewarned them, but the austerity of what they found confirmed the impressions they already had of the CIM and of what lay ahead of them: combat, not comfort; sincerity, not emotion. Hudson Taylor was pleased with what he saw, and invited them to meet the council on the 13th. But he was sure enough of the outcome to have them on the platform with him that evening of the 8th at the Exeter Hall in the Strand.

An audience of three thousand streamed in to give Hudson Taylor twelve new missionaries (over and above the seventy-six of the Seventy) and the 'Cambridge band' of four or five a worthy send-off. Even to some of the five the eleventh hour addition of the Polhill-Turners to the platform party, must have been as great a surprise as to them themselves. But this was what pleased Dixon Hoste, no beating about the bush. The February *China's Millions*, already at the printers, came out with the announcement that Cassels and Hoste were to sail on January 28, and Studd, Smith and Beauchamp to join them at Suez. In the end two parties left on January 15 and 28 but demands on the Seven kept them back to leave together on February 5. At this long meeting on January 8 all were introduced to the audience and probably made a few remarks. The Polhill-Turner brothers explained briefly how they also came to be there, and Stanley Smith gave the final address.

Ones and twos of their type had been 'farewelled' before. Harold Schofield had created a stir, but seven such conspicuous exceptions to the rule presenting themselves together shook the placid waters of the evangelical pond. The twelve others were almost lost in the glare of publicity surrounding the seven. Yet few had any inkling of the effect this galaxy was about to have on Britain and the world scene. The secular press took up the excitement and they became the talk of the town: Studd, Britain's best cricketer; Smith of the Cambridge Eight; Hoste, a Royal Artillery officer; Cassels, a footballer and clergyman; Beauchamp, son of a baronet; Cecil Polhill-Turner, still in the Dragoon Guards; and his brother, of Eton and Cambridge. This was 'news'. None had a 'first' or would claim to be an intellectual, but all had renounced wealth or prospects of advancement or both, for Christ and for China, at a time of war in the East. Directly after the Exeter Hall meeting a Harley Street specialist wrote to Hudson Taylor that he too was 'determined upon giving up the pleasures of the world' and asked for an interview. Only three weeks remained before the seven were to sail. Called 'the Cambridge party' at first, and then a 'Cambridge band', the popular term 'Cambridge Seven' came into use after they had gone.

When Smith and Studd joined Reginald Radcliffe at Liverpool on January 9 they found a crowd of twelve hundred young men ready for 'revival'. Many responded in tears to their call for surrender to Christ, and seventy or more were 'awakened'. Hudson Taylor spent the 12th with Dixon Hoste and his parents at meetings in Brighton; and on the 13th informed the council that he had interviewed and accepted Montagu Beauchamp. It was short notice, Cecil Polhill-Turner was young as a Christian, but with refreshing freedom of action and lack of 'red tape' the council also welcomed the two brothers to proceed to China with their friends, with or without formal identification with the Mission, which could follow 'after a time if on both sides it seemed desirable'. Beauchamp sent in his signed copy of the 'Principles and Practice' that same day, adding in his strong, cultured handwriting, 'I fully agree to the same, and should like to go out to

China with the party leaving London Feb 4th, 1885.' Arthur Polhill-Turner wrote on January 14th to say, '(Cecil) has sent in his [army] Papers and is now like myself at your service.'

Things were moving fast, and the impending separation from their sons was tugging at maternal heartstrings. Mrs Studd had already been asked to dispose of Charles's 'goods and chattels' and had sent a cheque to the CIM,

which I am almost sorry Mr Taylor did not keep ... I am most thankful that Mr Taylor's advice as to his wearing proper clothing has been heeded—dear fellow! He is very erratic and needs to be with older and more consistent Christians! [And to Jennie on January 5] A few lines to ask you to impress on him the necessity of taking what *is necessary to be comfortable*. He seems inclined to take *so very little*, hardly enough to last him, to say nothing about cleanliness in the hot climate ...

After Hudson Taylor had left Britain on January 20, Jennie wrote to him, 'I am afraid Mrs Studd is going too far in carrying out your suggestions . . . They told me that a case was going to (Hanzhong) to be unpacked before he arrived that he might find a room ready prepared with curtains . . . knives and forks, table napkins etc., etc. . . . to him unknown provision'— for 'CT' of all ascetics![719] If they reached him in China he certainly disposed of them at once.

2.55 The 'seven' complete, l to r, back: Smith, Beauchamp, Studd, C. Polhill; front: A. Polhill, Cassels, Hoste

Crescendo of influence
(January–February 1885)

The last farewells were over, apart from a few local meetings, Reginald Radcliffe's tour, and a return to Oxford and Cambridge. Two days before Hudson Taylor crossed to France, the first signs of unusual excitement appeared in Edinburgh. Radcliffe, Studd and Stanley Smith had had small but packed meetings at Aberdeen, Perth and other towns in Scotland, with Landale, J. E. Mathieson the evangelist and Major-General Haig taking part in some. But on Sunday, January 18, more students than had ever been known to come together, 1,500 to 2,000 of them, filled the Synod Hall. Not China or consecration to Christ but 'Christ crucified' was each speaker's theme this time. Half the audience stayed on afterwards and on Monday a stream of students came for personal conversations with the team. 'Wonderful times. It is the Lord,' Stanley Smith told Jennie Taylor.

In the Glasgow area the story of many conversions and surrenders to the Lordship of Christ was repeated. They made Archibald Orr Ewing's home their base until the Friday when they returned to Edinburgh, to find 'all the signs of true religious revival'. The men converted the previous Sunday were helping their friends to yield to Christ. The last meeting excelled the others, with professors and students in tears, three or four hundred staying to ask 'how to be saved', and Christian professors and students going from man to man to show them the answer.[720] After that they went to Leeds, Manchester, Rochdale, and finally Liverpool again. And the same experience repeated, with 'huge' after-meetings, but for all social classes. People came to hear leading athletes, but God himself met them. And these rich young men learned lessons too,

> finding out so much about ... the poor in ... the great towns has increased my horror at the luxurious way I have been living [Studd wrote to his mother]; so many suits and clothes of all sorts, whilst thousands are starving and perishing of cold, so all

must be sold when I come home if they have not been so before.[721]

The night train from Liverpool brought them back to London in time for the 'final' meeting on January 30 at the Eccleston Hall, with all the Seven present. Many had to be turned away. Even before that the YMCA's leaders had been thinking ambitiously. The Cambridge party were due to leave Britain on Wednesday, February 4. Benjamin B. and John Stevenson had 'moved heaven and earth' to arrange meetings far them in Bristol on the 1st, Cambridge on the 2nd and Oxford on the 3rd. If their departure could be postponed just one day, the YMCA would take the great Exeter Hall for one supreme 'last night' meeting.[722]

After the long separation from October 1881 to March 1883, Hudson and Jennie Taylor dreaded parting again for a year at the least. But it had to be. This was the young men's hour, and he himself was needed in China. Dixon Hoste saw him as humbly 'slipping away' without stealing any thunder on their field-day, or diluting the impact of the young upon the young. He left on January 20, apparently by cab from the door of 6 Pyrland Road. 'After you left,' Jennie told him, 'I went in for a minute (with the children) and back to the study. Dear Amelia came in and cuddled me up for a little while.' Each parting could so easily be the last. Then on to business. The YMCA had made their urgent propositions. Both she and Benjamin at first thought it unwise, but he consulted the P&O. The Seven could join their ship at Brindisi, as Hudson was doing, without additional cost.[723] George Williams of Messrs Hitchcock, Williams at St Paul's Churchyard, founder of the YMCA, was 'not willing that we should be at any expense' for the Exeter Hall or emergency advertising of a meeting. So Benjamin went ahead. A letter was widely circulated, notifying everyone of the arrangements and asking for prayer that it would be what the Seven 'shall long remember with gratitude to God . . . (and) memorable for ever in the experience of many a young man as the time when he was led to decide for Christ'. Even that was to be a pale understatement of what transpired.

By January 30 some of the YMCA leaders 'hung fire . . . and wished to back out of it', until Benjamin removed all doubt with 'We shall go on whether you do or not.' Stevenson was backing him 'splendidly'. But in the thick of it all the Mission stalwart, A. G. Parrott, at home on leave, talked of resigning. Counter-attacks were as ever to be expected, but to lose Parrott would be deplorable. He stayed for a time on the London staff. Worse still, news came of Khartoum being captured by the Malidi on January 26, and General Gordon being left isolated by the dilatory progress of the relieving column. Was interest to be deflected from China as so often before?[724]

Between them Benjamin and John Stevenson were supervising all arrangements at Bristol, Cambridge and Oxford. Professor Babington the botanist would preside at Cambridge; Mrs Babington wanted Montagu Beauchamp to be their guest; J. H. Moulton, the classics scholar, regarded the phenomenon of these seven men forsaking all to follow Christ to China as 'a most remarkable thing in itself and in its influence upon the university'. The Guildhall would be too small, so an overflow meeting was being arranged for.

Hudson Taylor left the Bergers and Cannes on January 24. At Genoa a porter commissioned to collect his registered baggage returned as the train pulled out, saying he could not do it in time. Without his documents enforced idleness on the voyage would once again give him needed rest, but meant there would be a large backlog of work when the Seven arrived in China, bringing the vital boxes of papers and medicines. Instead, when he joined his ship at Suez he at once started teaching Chinese to the six men of his party. By February 4 they had learned three hundred characters. At Colombo, Singapore and Hong Kong he arranged meetings for the Seven when they arrived, giving them the option of coming on by a later ship if they judged that more time at Singapore would be profitable.

Studd and Smith made a quick dash to Bristol, where the crowd was too great for the Colston Hall, and were back at Cambridge the next day. There too 'every corner—floor, orchestra, gallery' of the Guildhall was crammed with people. Professor Babington led off as chairman, followed by 'Benjamin B.', Stevenson, Landale and then Stanley Smith on the love of Christ constraining them 'to go out to the world'. 'Unless we spread abroad the light, we will find in England . . . that we cannot hold our own with the powers of darkness'. Then each of the Seven testified to their allegiance to Jesus Christ as their Lord and Master: Beauchamp, tall and powerful, with a 'capacity to extract enjoyment from anything'; the soldiers erect and to the point but no orators; Studd's fire glowing through his quiet conviction—'God does not deal with you until you are wholly given up to Him' (but then he shows you that fame and wealth and self-centredness are trash compared with being given up to him); and finally the two theologians, Arthur Polhill-Turner and W. W. Cassels, no less straightforward, practical and profound.

The 'Cambridge Correspondent' of the *Record*, Handley Moule, judged it 'the most remarkable missionary meeting held within living memory at Cambridge', which was again to say a great deal. On the same issue a correspondent went deeper. Why had this Mission drawn to it man after man of this influential type? For one essential reason:

> The uncompromising spirituality and unworldliness of the programme of the Mission, responded to by hearts which have truly laid all at the LORD's feet, and whose delight is the most open confession of His name and its power upon themselves. I venture to pronounce it inconceivable, impossible, that such a meeting should have been held in connection with any missionary enterprise of mixed aims, or in which such great truths were ignored, or treated with hesitation, (or) did the work not demand of the workers very real and manifest self-sacrifice and acts of faith.[725]

After the tepid welcome to Oxford in November, it had required some faith for 'Benjamin B.' to book the Corn Exchange, with the city's greatest seating capacity. He need not have feared. 'With so many undergraduates present', even if fewer than at Cambridge, and enough townsmen to fill the place 'to overflowing', many standing, this meeting on February 3 also earned the comment 'of almost unparalleled interest'. Theodore Howard as chairman spoke admirably, after himself having been stirred at Cambridge the previous day.

'A blaze of publicity'
(February–March 1885)

Wednesday, February 4, saw the grand climax at London's Exeter Hall, in the meeting that might not have been. London's daily and weekly papers, including *The Times*, and religious periodicals, reported the occasion at length. Sheets of rain pouring down on the crowds who pressed into the hall deterred no one. When the great hall was full, with 'platform, area, galleries, every nook and corner . . . crowded', the lower hall filled and overflowed. 'Even then many were turned away at the doors.' Three thousand five hundred found places. The young men for whom the meeting had previously been intended were equalled in number by young women and people 'of all sections of the Church and grades of social life'. 'People of note and title had to get in anywhere and be thankful if they got in at all,' Benjamin wrote afterwards to Hudson Taylor.[726] 'Mr Denny, Mr Howard, Dr Barnardo . . . had to stand nearly all the time. It was almost impossible to reserve room on the platform for the speakers. Miss Waldegrave came beseeching a seat for Lady Beauchamp . . . Happily we could get her in beside her daughter'—at the organ. C. T. Studd's mother was there with Kynaston and his bride, Montagu's sister, and the Christian Polhill-Turner sisters had brought their reluctant mother. A large map of China formed the backdrop of the platform; beneath it were ranged forty Cambridge undergraduates dedicated to become missionaries, led by J. C. Farthing of Caius College, the future missionary bishop, who spoke as their representative.

George Williams (Sir George to be) led the 'platform party' out to their places, to a roar of cheers and clapping. After a spirited hymn he presented each of the Seven with a Chinese New Testament, gift of the Bible Society on whose committee he served. The CIM, he said, was the only society working overseas 'on an undenominational basis'. Benjamin briefly described the Mission and its principles, and introduced the Cambridge contingent. Robert Landale spoke as an Oxford graduate and law student who had already spent seven years in China and knew that it was 'no slight thing' to leave all and bury oneself in an often hostile land—not to be done on 'human enthusiasm' but only by those with hearts 'full of love to God'.

As at Cambridge, Stanley Smith then gave the main, spellbinding address. It cannot be read without conveying the atmosphere in that hall. Neither the apostles nor their successors today were charged with the 'milk and water of religion but the cream of the Gospel'. William Carey on leaving yet another meeting of colleagues in Britain to discuss 'the Gospel and the World', had protested, 'Are we going to separate again, and is *nothing* to be done? If David Livingstone could leap to life (again) what would he say? "Do not follow my body home to this cathedral, but follow where my heart lies . . . in Africa."' The five thousand would never have been fed if the apostles had served only the front rows again and again. Then seizing on the indignation of the hour, 'a greater than Gordon cries from Khartoum . . . the voice of Christ from the Cross of Calvary . . . "I thirst!" . . . He thirsts for the Chinese, for the Africans, for the Asiatics, and for the South Americans . . . Would you pass by that Christ? . . . There is "sin in the camp", the infidelity of Achan thwarting the victory of God's people, the triumph of the gospel.'

While Smith went down to the Lower Hall and Studd made his way up, Montagu Beauchamp called for many to put themselves at Christ's disposal. Dixon Hoste told how in the army he had been blind until Christ opened his eyes to see him and his command to 'Go! and preach the Gospel.' William Cassels saw the need for 'more heroism' in Christians. 'Oh, for shame, that He who gave His own life on the cross should still be crying for helpers.' Cecil Polhill-Turner, his resignation not yet gazetted, so still the serving officer of his crack cavalry regiment, simply told how his own life had been transformed and redirected. Arthur was three days from his twenty-third birthday. Leaving home to go to the unknown was not proving hard but 'like that of a bird when let out of a cage . . . very glorious'. J. C. Farthing spoke before Studd. After the Guildhall meeting, he said, 'I saw this: that we were to take up our cross and follow CHRIST; that there was to be no compromise, however small; that there was to be nothing between us and our Master; that we were to be wholly for CHRIST.'

C. T. Studd then told frankly about his conversion and slow progress and backsliding before his brother's near-fatal illness. 'I had formerly as much love for cricket as any man could have,' but after he yielded to Jesus Christ as Lord, 'my heart was no longer in the game.' He read what an atheist had written, 'If I were a thoroughly consistent Christian, my whole life should be given up to going about the world preaching the Gospel.' Then how he went to John McCarthy's farewell prayer meeting and knew that God was sending him to China. 'Choose who is to be your God!'—the true God or your own substitutes. Then obey Him.'

Two hours had passed. The Rev Hugh Price Hughes, billed as the final speaker, suggested to the chairman that he should not speak at all, but the audience were wanting more! He faced them with the need to 'submit to Christ', to offer themselves to God as a living sacrifice, declaring 'There is enough power in this meeting to stir . . . the whole world.' This very thing was beginning to happen. In the first missionary book she ever read, a young woman saw a report of this meeting and was 'drawn in spirit'

to the one who had 'counted as loss all that life as an officer of the Royal Artillery would have meant'. Amy Carmichael of South India went on to influence thousands in her lifetime. But she was only one so influenced.[727]

The 'boat train' left Victoria at 10.00 the next morning, February 5, the very day news of Gordon's death reached London. Sober Cassels, 'the old man of the party' a month short of twenty-six, had pasted red labels saying 'GOD FIRST' on each piece of his baggage. They travelled by Brindisi to Alexandria and by the desert train to join the *Kaisar-i-hind* at Suez.[728] On board and sharing their second class accommodation ('fit only for servants and dogs', it had been said, but at a twenty-five per cent discount to the CIM for many years), they found a drunken, hard-swearing sea captain of an Indian ship, already notorious among passengers and crew for his behaviour. Hoste at once got talking with him and was soon reading the Bible—'all rot'—and discussing it with him. Another of the party took a turn a few days later.

Alone in his cabin that night the captain cried to God to forgive and save him. He soon revealed how much he knew. 'He seemed to be a full grown Christian at once,' telling the ship's company and passengers, 'It's so simple; it's only trusting.' After that several of the crew and other second-class passengers were converted and joined the Seven for daily worship. Changing ship at Colombo, and after meetings there and at Penang, Singapore and Hong Kong (where they also visited the barracks in each place) they were met at Shanghai on March 18 by a Chinese they did not at first recognize, Hudson Taylor. He had arrived on March 3.

The teeming city crowds made the work ahead of them seem overwhelming, but for the present more meetings for foreigners had been announced, for all nationalities and types; for cricket and rowing club athletes; in the Royal Asiatic Society and in the Lyceum Theatre. Not even standing room could be found after the first day's meetings. The *Shanghai*

Mercury gave full and sympathetic reports. But the community was shaken from any complacency when at the largest meeting of all the port chaplain, the Rev F. R. Smith, incumbent of the cathedral church, came forward after Charlie Studd had spoken, and said that if he had died in the night he would have been a lost soul. He had never before understood the difference between being 'a Christian' and clergyman by duty and his own effort, and being made one by the Saviour in response to real confession and faith in him. After a miserable night he had consulted a young CMS missionary, Heywood Horsburgh, on an early morning walk, and had been helped to commit his soul to Christ. Some would ridicule him, but he implored all who were in the position he had been in to put it right with God as he had just done.[729]

The Seven's final weeks in Britain had been too full to allow much time with their families, to their mothers' distress. Mrs Studd had offered to pay the costs if only her son could stay a day longer and give her a few hours of his company. What did outfits matter? was the men's attitude. They were going into Chinese dress at the end of the voyage. 'I am deeply grieved to trouble you,' Mrs Smith wrote to Jennie late in January, 'but Stanley . . . gives no thought to temporal affairs. (Please) write by return of post and tell me what is *absolutely* necessary for (his) outfit as . . . he fancies he needs nothing and has sold or given away all . . . Also kindly tell us the *name of the vessel*.' But after the last Exeter Hall meeting, her maternal flutters subsided. 'Never shall I forget; it was a glorious ending to their labours in this country.' And three days later she wrote again. The mothers and families were going to meet in Mrs Studd's large rooms weekly or fortnightly to pray for the men and for missions in general. Would Jennie or Amelia or both come and show them how to go about it?[730]

When the boat-train had steamed out of Victoria Station, the Pyrland Road family returned to a new welter of work. Letters to Hudson Taylor came first.

Exeter Hall last night—what shall I say? [Benjamin scribbled in his fast flowing hand.] Such a meeting! I question if a meeting of equal significance and spiritual fruitfulness has been held in that building during this generation. Its influence upon the course of Missions must be immense— incalculable. [He was not mistaken.] I am filled with gratitude ... It was a most magnificent success ... *The Times, Standard, Daily News,* etc., etc. all had good articles ... It seemed as if the influence for good of the CIM for the whole of its existence was focused in that one night's meeting. We cannot praise God enough ... That meeting will be the talk of England ... the Halls were given to us free.

Theodore Howard had written very warmly, but said he was too busy to do more than chair the council meetings, so Benjamin would have to carry the main weight of the work in Britain. In the circumstances that was sheer joy, except for the 'teething troubles'.

You will hardly believe how much the meeting has been noticed (in the Press). The CIM seems to many to have emerged all at once into a very blaze of publicity, and we may be sure that it will provoke much comment, some very friendly and some very otherwise (from denominational viewpoints). [And on February 20]: A writer in the *Cambridge Review* speaks of support to unattached missions as the disloyal weakening of the older missions. I trust what I have written [for the Press] will be useful to counteract such notions.[731]

Benjamin was printing an extra 22,000 copies of *China's Millions*, increased by another 10,000 a few days later, describing the meetings which 'would have been worth £10,000 to the cause of Missions had they cost so much'. But in fact donations stemming from the meetings themselves had more than paid for everything. At the later May meetings he reported that few copies remained of 50,000 and 'we must without delay print more'.

'The Cambridge party' (as they were still being called) had won a place in the minds of Christians which remains unique today. In 1899 Eugene Stock looked back and said 'The influence of such a band of men was irresistible . . . No such event had occurred before.' Archbishop Benson called it 'one of the good signs of the times'.[732] And Stock again: 'Although all English Societies, and preeminently the CMS felt the influence of the uprising of missionary zeal for which their outgoing was the signal, the China Inland Mission naturally felt it most. Its energetic Secretary . . . and his colleagues . . . were quite overwhelmed by the multitude of applications for service.'

1885–90: BUILD-UP FOR EXPANSION

The China the Seven reached
(1884–85)

The great empire of the Manchus was rotten at its heart and breaking up at its extremities. The Peking court in Ci Xi's hands had become more than ever a place of intrigue, extravagance and corruption, while foreign powers strengthened their grip on Manchuria, Korea, Burma and Indo-China. Ever since the eunuch Li Liangying had stolen the imperial seal for Ci Xi to thwart the Jehol plot (see 1, pp 513–14) and secured himself in her favour, he had feathered his own nest, becoming one of the wealthiest and most powerful men in the nation. Permitted to speak without first being spoken to by his imperial mistress, a privilege denied even to the Grand Secretary and the child emperor's father, he took to referring to her and to himself as 'Zamen—we two'.

Prince Kong detested him. But Ci Xi felt insecure while Prince Kong headed the Grand Council of Ministers. By a surprise decree in 1884 she had admitted that 'Our Country has not yet returned to its wonted stability, and its affairs are in a critical state . . . There is chaos in the Government and a feeling of insecurity amongst the people.' This understatement covered far more riotous unrest in the southern provinces and whispers of rebellion among the secret societies.[733] Addressing Prince Kong and his colleagues of the Grand Council, on their knees with downcast eyes before her Peacock Throne in the great Audience Chamber, she declared that he and two others were forthwith deprived of office and fortunate not to be decapitated. Not until ten years later was he recalled, when she could not manage without him. She forcibly married the boy emperor to a cousin whom he hated. This daughter of Ci Xi's younger brother became her spy in his closest circle. And the Pearl Concubine whom he loved met with a 'fate even more horrible' than Alude's (see p 238).

Into this situation the indispensable statesman Li Hongzhang was brought again, charged with the protection of China from attack on her sea coasts. As viceroy of Zhili he had already ordered six gunboats from Europe, but they were laughable without trained commanders and crews. His Sino-Japanese Convention (signed on April 18 exactly one month after the Cambridge Seven landed at Shanghai) could only postpone attack by Japan, rapidly modernizing. The surrender of suzerain rights in Annam and Burma (1885–86) proclaimed to the world the weakness of China, offering too great a temptation at a time of foreign imperialism. France's ambitions in East Asia demanded a countermove by Britain, and the annexation of Upper Burma in 1886 was the logical step.

When Britain's hero-envoy to Peking, Sir Harry Parkes, died at his post on March 22, 1885, Sir Robert Hart was invited to succeed him. 'While his (Sir Robert's) entire loyalty to the Chinese government was never doubted, his guiding hand in the British legation had worked for the good both of China and of England.'[734] But who could succeed Hart as Inspector General of the Chinese Customs? He trusted his own brother James, efficient and popular, to maintain the standards of integrity. And after an attempt by the Chinese government to install W. A. P. Martin, an educator without the essential administrative experience, James Hart was appointed. Martin instead was honoured with the rank of Mandarin, Third Class, for his work as President of the Tong Wen Guan.[735] For the brother of the British minister to hold such a high rank in the Chinese Civil Service was too much for Li Hongzhang, always with an eye to the main chance, and Hart's irreconcilable rival. He manoeuvred to have James Hart replaced by the German Gustav Detring, 'a man of brilliant intellect and great diplomatic ability' who had been Li's own right-hand man since the Chefoo Convention of 1876. With Detring owing allegiance to Li 'of the itchy palm', the integrity of the Imperial Maritime Customs would soon have passed beyond his control. Sir Robert therefore resigned his position as Her Majesty's envoy in August and resumed duty as Inspector General to the satisfaction of all, including Germany, for Detring had never been as co-operative as his own countrymen wished.

The close link between France and Roman Catholicism in China, the French 'protectorate', naturally led to hostility in Guangdong against missionaries and Chinese Christians. Thousands of refugees fled to Hong Kong and Macao. In Yunnan, Guizhou, Sichuan, Shaanxi and Shanxi officials became hostile and placards threatening extermination appeared on city walls. Only after peace with France was concluded in September 1885 and copies of the imperial edicts of toleration (of 1884) were prominently displayed, did calm return. Protestants could not expect to be exempt. But when in the glum mood of the 1884–85 United States Depression a mob in Rock Springs, Wyoming, attacked innocent Chinese residents, killing nineteen, wounding many and driving hundreds from the town, violent protest in China could not be halted by mere compensation to the victims.

Catholic priests were flooding into China. The 250 in 1870 had become 488 by 1885. All, whatever their nationality, still carried French and Chinese passports. The towers of the Beitang, the North Cathedral at Peking, still overlooked the imperial palace in defiance of Ci Xi's repeated requests for the Lazarists to yield the site.

In exchange for land further away and the construction costs of a new building, it was at last incorporated in the palace gardens in 1888. As a diplomatic gesture, Pére Armand David's remarkable natural history collection was simultaneously conveyed to the government.

Further afield, the birth of the Indian National Congress gave evidence of new stirrings which in little more than sixty years' time would win independence for the subcontinent again. Karl Marx had died in 1883 but Engels completed the second volume of *Das Kapital* in 1885 (and the third in 1894), promoting the idea of class struggle by violence to bring to workers the full reward of their labour. Oblivious of the dawning of the political polarisation between 'east' and 'west', let alone of a Marxist day in China, Gladstone was still preoccupied with the intractable Irish Question. On October 10, 1884, King Mtesa of Uganda had died and in January 1885 his son Mwanga had begun the torture of Christians by sword and fire. Bishop Hannington and all but four of his fifty companions were massacred by Mwanga's orders on October 29, 1885. More deaths followed, from violence and disease. The faint hearts as usual cried, 'Abandon the attempt!' Mackay, all alone, wrote: 'Are

2.56 Prince Kong, chief minister and senior guardian of the throne

you joking?' Hand Africa over to Mwanga, to slave traders, gun-runners and gin merchants? 'They make no talk of "giving up" *their* respective missions!'[736] The church in China and worldwide took note. God did not always deliver his servants from the sword.

The Mission the Seven had joined
(1885)

Doubled in size during the past three years by the addition of the Seventy, the membership of the China Inland Mission stood at one hundred and fifty when the Cambridge party reached Shanghai. By the end of the year it was nearing two hundred. Unrest might interrupt but did not prevent progress. *China's Millions* carried reports of other missions' personnel and work, the CMS, the LMS, the Presbyterians and Baptists, side by side with the CIM's. Seldom in the news, the rank and file missionaries worked faithfully on in their allotted spheres. Preaching night and morning in their 'street chapels', visiting in homes or receiving guests, much as in the early days at Ningbo and Hangzhou, or tramping doggedly through the provinces 'scattering seed', they allowed themselves to be seen, the harmless 'exporters to virtue'.

Steady teaching of the Christians led to some going out to sell books or as 'helpers' to work with evangelists or missionaries in outposts, or even on the road as carriers. Growing experience and proof of having a gift of preaching or teaching made them 'fellow-workers in the Chinese church' and missionaries to distant regions. Wang Lae-djün had become, by natural growth of the Hangzhou church, the superintendent-pastor of a wide network of local churches planted and fostered by himself and his helpers. His wise relationship with the other missions in Hangzhou often brought them to seek his advice. Others were, like him, glad of the missionaries' greater knowledge of the Bible, but well able to care for the churches in their absence.

The Broumtons had seen proclamations promising protection of foreigners, and set out from Guiyang to Chongqing when James Broumton fell ill. Nevertheless on the way they were repeatedly robbed on the road, and in a wayside inn where they took refuge were stripped of all but their underclothes and left destitute; they hid in a loft there for a week before officials sent them on under escort.

Henry Soltau, in lower Burma with his wife and child, had learned of an attack on Bhamo in early December by hundreds of Chinese and Kachin rebels who had put the town to the torch. He had set off at once by steam-launch and arrived in time to rescue the American missionaries and Christians, under rifle fire. The Kachin rebels begged him as a friend to stay and support them in negotiations with the Burmese but to take sides politically was unthinkable. Bhamo was retaken in March. So came, in his words, 'this terrible ending to the first volume of Bhamo history. May the second be brighter.' The CIM returned there in 1887 but not the Soltaus.[737]

Hudson Taylor's report from China to the Annual Meeting in London was written while the Seven were still in Shanghai, almost daily addressing packed audiences.[738] They 'have more thoroughly affected Shanghai than any series of meetings that have ever been held', one report read. The editor of the *Courier* and his wife were among those converted, and scores of others in the Lyceum Theatre, the Masonic Hall and at special receptions for athletes. John McCarthy had already dispersed the accumulation of missionaries at the coast, waiting for more peaceful conditions upcountry. So the news was of parties of them pressing up to the north-west, and others going to Guiyang, Kunming and Dali, in the far south-west, from which two cities the first baptisms had at last been reported. George Parker had secured premises in Lanzhou, the capital of Gansu, and Riley in Chengdu, the Sichuan capital. Progress under persecution made Hanzhong a promising place for one party of the Cambridge men to start in, and Shanxi for a second group of them. Henan, one of the toughest provinces to crack, had at last allowed Sambrook to settle at

Zhoujiakou with two others, but not for long. Soon they were to be driven out and like Henry Taylor before him, Sambrook dropped out of the battle utterly broken in spirit.

Meanwhile the older churches in Zhejiang, Anhui and Jiangxi had struggled on through 'periods of excitement', a euphemism for persecution and riot. One highlight in Zhejiang had been response in 'revival' proportions to aggressive evangelism by the CMS. It was even possible to write of scope for more and more women in the areas of China already opened up. But Hunan remained impenetrable. With their base, at Shashi on the Yangzi in Hubei, Adam Dorward, Henry Dick, Thomas James and Chinese colleagues were quietly holding an outpost at Jinshi across the Hunan border, and making surreptitious journeys into the province. But even the freedom to travel in turbulent Hunan, which Dorward had earlier known, was for the present being denied to them.

Ever since he himself landed on March 3, Hudson Taylor had been swamped with work that could not wait to be done, including one hundred and twenty letters to be answered without delay.[739] A missionary charged with conducting the Mission's business in Shanghai had rented premises in his own name and after defecting, to run them as a private boarding house, was claiming them for himself. Hudson Taylor found two other houses in the Yuan Ming Yuan Buildings 'a stone's throw from' the British consulate. Their simplicity and down-to-earth practicality met with the Seven's approval. They had not come looking for luxury. He designated No 5 for offices and No 6 as a home for transients, ready in time for the next influx of newcomers. Within a few weeks, on May 4, he cabled for thirty more men to be sent from Britain, and twenty-nine set sail. J. E. Cardwell, often disaffected, had resigned but found life outside the Mission less than rosy. So he swallowed his pride at Hudson Taylor's suggestion, rejoined and took charge of business affairs, with John

McCarthy staying at Shanghai to handle Mission accounts and remittances.

There were now so many more missionaries to provide with accommodation at Shanghai, and so much coming-and-going between China and Europe, the coast and the interior, often in ill-health and needing special care, that serious thought had to be given to acquiring more suitable permanent quarters. To rent them would be a constant heavy drain on resources. To buy a site and build would be immensely costly, involving a leap of faith. Yet from this time Hudson Taylor kept it in view. His vision of the Mission's expansion and extension throughout China was itself enlarging beyond what he could yet share with others and far exceeding anything yet seen in the missionary world anywhere. At Colombo on his way out he had met and consulted the explorer Ney Elias (see pp 229, 233), serving as British political agent at Kashgar, about Turkestan and Tibet. The evangelisation of the whole empire would need hundreds. His mental picture of the premises needed would have alarmed even his closest colleagues. But he was level-headed. Two years later he telegraphed £1,500 from Britain to be put on deposit for a chosen site on Wusong Road to be levelled and built up above flood level, ready for ambitious development.[740]

His plan for the Cambridge men had been that all seven should pioneer the great province of Sichuan, apart from the river region between the already occupied cities of Chengdu and Chongqing on the Min River and the Yangzi (see maps 2.48 & 2.59: pp 376 & 480 respectively). Rich and teeming with millions of industrious people, Sichuan extended 600 miles westwards from the gorges near Yichang to the Tibetan marches, and 500 miles 'as the crow flies' from the mountains south of the Han River plain and Hanzhong to the southernmost loop of the Jin He, the River of Gold, dividing it from Yunnan. Each man was nominally an Anglican, even if only Cassels and Arthur Polhill-Turner favoured planting the Anglican Church on Chinese soil.[741] The principle of arranging for missionaries of the same denominational outlook to work together pointed to their forming a strong team in this strategic region.

But discretion required a careful approach. Seven athletic young men, among them two of undisguisedly military bearing, could arouse misplaced suspicion. So Hudson Taylor split them into two groups of three, for the present keeping Montagu Beauchamp to travel with him (as Lady Beauchamp had requested).[742] He proposed to go himself on a preliminary reconnaissance of Sichuan. C. T. Studd and the Polhills he sent up the Yangzi in Chinese clothes, with John McCarthy as escort-interpreter, and Montagu for the experience as far as Anqing. As Griffith John's guests at Hankou and by his arrangement, they addressed audiences including consuls, customs officials and merchants on three successive nights, for their message was Griffith John's own—'the power of the Holy Spirit daily renewed for Christian service'. '(We) greatly astonished the resident missionaries,' the Polhill brothers commented enigmatically. From there they ascended the swollen Han River rapids, with Dr and Mrs William Wilson in another boat, three Etonians on 'a continuous picnic', taking until mid-July to reach Hanzhong. At first their river days were filled by studying Chinese with a language teacher, relieved by walking on the trackers' towpath and swimming in the river. Plagued by an invasion of rats, they remembered the Leicester donor's Stilton cheeses and proved their guess right by presenting them to the Wilsons, for the rats changed boats.

Stanley Smith, Hoste and Cassels were sent by ship via Yantai to Tianjin, and on through Peking to Shanxi, there to learn Chinese and join in the work of which David Hill's convert Hsi (known as Xi Liaozhih or 'Shengmo') was becoming the remarkable leader. This would give the foreign communities in Tianjin and Peking an opportunity to hear them. A few days before sailing with them, J. J. Coulthard told Hudson Taylor that he had 'found almost by accident his own love for Maria

to be reciprocated'. Might they become engaged? Yes, he replied, delighted, but they must wait three years until she reached twenty-one before marrying. So he found a substitute escort for the Cambridge men in David Thompson of western Sichuan.

The immediate effect of their visit to Yantai was the drawing together of the different missions in the community for united communion services, previously neglected. And after they had left Peking all missions were meeting daily to pray for 'the baptism of the Holy Ghost on our own hearts' and for 'the outpouring of the Spirit on China'. Twenty-five missionaries and others signed a joint letter, sent to missions everywhere, saying what the newcomers had done for them and inviting them to adopt the same prayers.[743] By then the Cambridge men had gone on overland, enjoying the physical exercise and 'roughing it'. The commander of a Chinese cavalry regiment at Taiyuan invited them to a meal. And everywhere they were well received as they travelled on to Linfen (Pingyang), Hsi's home area in south Shanxi, meeting their American counterparts, the men of Oberlin College, at Taigu.

The pressure of demands upon Hudson Taylor at the coast, keeping him at his desk until midnight day after day, forced him to forsake his Sichuan journey. So he sent F. W. Baller and Montagu Beauchamp to join the others in Shanxi, and in response to urgent letters from Chefoo himself went there immediately to talk with some members affected by the 'Shanxi spirit'. Although Timothy Richard's own colleagues in the BMS had rejected his theses as 'another gospel', among those whom he had convinced these few members of the CIM were propagating his views.[744]

At the end of May Hudson Taylor was back in Shanghai, wearied by the difficulties he had faced and late night consultations, when word began to come of problems with the Cambridge men. He had hoped that Baller, an experienced, capable missionary but dry at heart, would absorb the spirit of his companions. Instead, he wrote, he was repelled by their extreme piety. Stanley

Smith and Hoste in his opinion were damaging their health by excessive prayer and fasting.

News from the Hanzhong party was more disturbing. C. T. Studd and the Polhill brothers had thought language study a laborious substitute for what they saw to be the biblical way of acquiring a foreign tongue. On the slow journey up the Han River they had put away their books and 'given themselves to prayer' for a Pentecostal gift of speech in Chinese. If anyone should have received it, surely men who had forsaken all and followed Christ could expect it as a mark of God's approval. Arrived eventually at Hanzhong, they persuaded two of the young missionary women there to do the same. But before October ended they saw their mistake, knuckled down to study and in time became fluent. 'How many and subtle are the devices of Satan,' Hudson Taylor wrote, 'to keep the Chinese ignorant of the gospel.' 'If I could put the Chinese language into your brains by one wave of the hand I would not do it,' he took to saying to new missionaries. Unadapted foreign thought and idiom merely translated into Chinese could do more harm than good. Months of submission to a Chinese scholar while watching and listening to evangelists and experienced missionaries taught wisdom as well as language.[745]

Within the same period in Shanxi the other Cambridge men were carrying on simple conversations and telling the gospel in memorised sentences. Stanley Smith, the orator who 'could hold the Sunday throng at the Achilles Statue in Hyde Park' swept ahead of the others. Once he could speak freely he held his Chinese audiences in the same way, and over the years, Cecil Polhill recorded, 'thousands have believed through his preaching'.[746]

Dixon Hoste in his periodic letters to Hudson Taylor mentioned 'some rather rough assaults by the "prince of the kingdom of China (meaning Satan)" who now that we are here, does all that he can to keep our lives from really getting mixed up with that of the Chinese.' No one complained that Baller kept too tight a rein on them, but later protests from language students at Anqing that he was by far too authoritarian for mature men to tolerate may explain Hoste's veiled wording. Discord among missionaries, and keeping them out of touch with the Chinese were two of Satan's favourite devices. The genuineness of all that Hoste wrote impressed Hudson Taylor. Nothing he said was for effect but revealed the true man. He chose to spend several months each year living in the villages or market towns with an evangelist, preaching at country fairs far from fellow-foreigners. He enjoyed having his 'utter rawness rubbed off', while seeing the need of constant 'forbearance and willingness to be the inferior' if the cultural gulf between Westerner and Chinese was to be bridged. 'Little acts of rudeness and contempt' for the alien by passers-by were a salutary lesson in humility. Less than two years after Harold Schofield died praying for his place to be taken by like-minded men, they were there. And soon Hsi Shengmo was to find in Dixon Hoste the wise adviser he as a Christian beginner most needed.[747]

A trap for the leaders (1885–86)

The Cambridge Seven had departed at a high point not only of the CIM but of all missions. No send-off had ever been so stirring, and no heart-searching so deep or widespread among Christians. 'In one short week, the China Inland Mission has been suddenly lifted into unusual and unexpected prominence and even popularity . . . The hour of success is often the time of danger . . . a snare and not a blessing.' Benjamin Broomhall's statement had its echo in many forms. John C. Thompson, a graduate of Edinburgh, called it 'a movement perhaps more wonderful than ever had place in the history of university students . . . The work is spreading itself in all its depth and reality throughout the whole country.' Thirty-five men applied for training to the Edinburgh Medical Missionary Society alone.[748]

In the remarkable *History of the Church Missionary Society*, 1885, '86 and '87 were named 'Three Memorable Years'. At the invitation of the YMCA another great 'memorable meeting for men' was held at the Exeter Hall on March 24, 1885. Parties of men from the universities, including fifty from Oxford and Cambridge, others from the Islington and Highbury Theological colleges, and three hundred from the City, packed the hall and overflowed into King's College. 'Ladies were banished to the west gallery,' but 1885 saw the foreshadowings of CMS women's work. Offers of service from men began to multiply. After the Seven's meetings thirty-one more students offered themselves to the CMS. By 1893 offers had reached one hundred and forty, making Handley Moule implore the Christian Union not to forget the needs of the United Kingdom. In October 1885 the largest valedictory service within living memory was held. And the CIM's own annual meetings in May were 'unequalled for blessing by any we ever had'. Gone were the days when an unknown 'small independent body of men' had been written off in those words by the great friend of the downtrodden, Lord Shaftesbury. Whenever he could he presided now at CIM meetings, saying 'I *like* this Mission.' But in 1885 Theodore Howard had to deputise for him at the May meetings, and in mid-October the London Council noted his death, at eighty-four.

Not only were 50,000 copies of *China's Millions* with the story of the Seven too few to meet the demand, but when Benjamin republished it in book form with photographs, maps and recent news of the Seven, amplified to 250 pages by an anthology of articles from many leading churchmen and public figures of the day, 10,000 were sold within a few months. The second edition had to be followed by a third in 1890 making 20,000 in all. First called A *Missionary Band: a Record of Missionary Consecration*, it was renamed *The Evangelisation of the World*, with sections on Africa and India as well as China. Queen Victoria accepted a copy of the gilt-edged edition, and others circulated by Sir George Williams profoundly affected young men in the YMCAs of Britain and the United States.

Robert Speer publicly stated that, apart from the Bible no books had so influenced his life of dedication to the cause of student missionary volunteers as Blaikie's *Personal Life of Livingstone* and *The Evangelisation of the World*. Robert P. Wilder, John R. Mott and other leaders of the student movements paid tribute to its impact in both continents and on their own lives.[749] But 'the time of danger' and the 'snare' lay not only in temptations for the Seven in the heart of China to despair and to question the rightness of what they had done, but in assaults on the leading men of the Mission.

For ten years Benjamin had been the chief and almost the sole executive administrator of the CIM in Britain. Others had played their considerable part as honorary director, treasurer and advisers, and had borne the ultimate responsibility in channelling funds and approved reinforcements to China. But Benjamin had carried the burden of correspondence, of public relations, of organizing annual and farewell meetings throughout the country, and directing the activities of missionaries on home leave. He had managed the office in Pyrland Road with its missionary assistants and employed staff, edited *China's Millions* in Hudson Taylor's name, using copy sent from China, and guided those who offered to go as missionaries from tentative enquiry and initial interviews through to formal application and appearance before the council. Although Amelia ran the home with its changing population of candidates and missionaries, in transit or residence for varying periods of time, Benjamin had the oversight and presided at meals and meetings. He was in his element. But danger lay in the rapid growth of the Mission. It was no longer possible for one man to carry so much.

Before leaving the country, Hudson Taylor had arranged for some responsibilities to be delegated to experienced members of the Mission detained at home by their own ill-health or their families'. C. G. Moore became Deputation Secretary, Charles Fishe the Financial Secretary (or cashier-accountant),

Cardwell, Benjamin's personal assistant, and Robert Landale (followed by Jennie Taylor) edited *China's Millions*, while the Auxiliary Council of Ladies interviewed women candidates; this meant that Benjamin was freer to exploit his *métier* of public relations. Revealed through his management of the Cambridge Seven's whirlwind tour of the country, this gift had become of unique value to the Mission.

In his early days Benjamin had been secretary to the Anti-Slavery Association and being naturally gregarious had a wide circle of influential friends. An 'alert and discerning observer of the trend of things . . . he had the gift of the effective word, the helpful suggestion, that brought him into touch . . . with a large number of England's leading men', especially in later years. Like his father, both Anglican and Methodist at heart, and regularly taking the periodicals of the leading churches, he was eirenic in his attitude to all. 'Unperturbed in spirit, never hasting and never resting, he continued at his desk regularly until midnight and sometimes beyond.' He travelled extensively and opened the way for the Mission's representatives to be welcomed to speak about China.[750]

Letter-writing was one of Benjamin Broomhall's greatest gifts, always in his own flowing hand and as warmly to the donors of small amounts as of larger sums. Very often it was the working man's donation or the widow's letter that he cited in *China's Millions* or from the platform. But it was 'the astonishing energy and practical wisdom with which he directed the burst of missionary zeal' at the time of the Cambridge Seven, that most impressed Eugene Stock and John Stevenson. This energy Benjamin now applied to the task in hand—and fell into a trap for the unwary, attempting too much.

In China, Hudson Taylor was giving himself without reserve until he too fell prey to the same unsuspected danger. By October he was commenting to Jennie that he needed to hear more often and more fully from London. Forty new missionaries, accepted from among many more offers, went out to China during the year. Others were in the pipeline. Advance information about them and plans for their dispatch made arrangements for their reception at Shanghai and upcountry so much easier. But between Benjamin and Cardwell in the pressure of work and the dependence of plans upon the funds coming in, details of who would sail and when tended to be held back. Even uncertain probabilities, qualified by 'funds permitting' would have been preferable to silence, Hudson Taylor pointed out. In response to his plea this phrase was adopted, and is still a current cliché in the Mission.

His own strength and tolerance were being undermined by bouts of his old enemy, dysentery. And he was pining again for Jennie. He and Benjamin had been good friends since boyhood, accustomed to forthright speaking of their minds. Warm friendship within the family circle did not prevent them from holding different views on some practical issues. Where letters to others would be more carefully worded, they tended to be outspoken between themselves. It only needed the stress of work and circumstances to make ill-chosen words give rise to misunderstandings, or silence to appear negligence. After the exhausting heat of summer Hudson Taylor felt aggrieved and wrote to Jennie that Theodore Howard and Benjamin were disregarding him, starving him of information. In a sense it was true, but explicable. Expansion and popularity were new, uncharted waters.

A young Canadian named Jonathan Goforth, one of the future great missionaries to China, wrote from Knox College, Toronto, to Hudson Taylor saying he had written to London in 1882 asking to be sent as one of the Seventy but had had no reply. 'He found out, later, that his letter had gone astray. Nothing daunted he wrote again,' his biographer explained. And Hudson Taylor advised him to consult his own church before joining the CIM. When his fellow-students at Knox learned that their own Presbyterian Church of Canada were unwilling to add China to their undertakings and declined to send him, they roused the college alumni and raised the funds to support him. Goforth himself bought hundreds of copies of *China's Spiritual Need and Claims* and distributed them to the ministers of his church. The church relented and he established a successful mission in Henan.[751] Meanwhile at the Niagara Conference of 1885 Goforth's zealous advocacy of China's claim on the church, with 'the face of an angel (and) the voice of an archangel', won to the cause a young American businessman, Henry W. Frost, of whom a great deal more was to be heard.

By honouring the responsibility of the young Goforth to his own denomination, rather than welcoming him to the CIM, Hudson Taylor had won a faithful friend, and the Canadian Presbyterian Church in 1888 sought his advice when starting their mission in Henan.[752] Years later, in 1911, Jonathan Goforth, a leader of the great Manchurian revival movement, approached the CIM again with the hope of at last becoming a member. He had been the first North American applicant to the CIM. But in 1885 a young medical graduate wrote from Philadelphia, came over to London to meet the council, and on April 21 left Britain with Archibald Orr Ewing and George Graham Brown for China. Dr J. C. Stewart set up his pioneer medical work at Guihuacheng on the Mongolian border of north Shanxi, the city strongly recommended by James Cameron.

Organizing for advance (1882–86)

With expansion of the CIM in hand, the main purpose of Hudson Taylor's return to China in 1885 was to organise the Mission to cope with growing numbers. Since 1882 and earlier, he had been experimenting with ways of sharing his load with others, and we need to go back to those days to recapture the context. He had appointed Dalziel as business manager in Shanghai, Coulthard as financial and general secretary in Wuchang for the western and south-western provinces and Parrott as 'corresponding secretary' to relieve him of purely business letters and the less personal and confidential correspondence. But still his own work multiplied as more and more missionaries consulted him and looked for personal attention. No longer could he be available to all or travel as widely to encourage the lonely and to deal with their problems.[753]

But the matter had developed a new angle. As loud as the clamour for him to delegate his duties there had come a growing protest that the deputies were coming between him and the rank and file. 'Any delegation of Mr Taylor's authority was apt to be regarded with misgivings if not opposed through misunderstanding . . . Much more of difficulty lay in the way of associating others with himself in these responsibilities than ever he anticipated.' No less than a constitutional crisis was brewing which came close to wrecking the Mission. His deputies suffered in the process by being grudgingly treated as favoured civil servants, until he issued a communiqué to all members: regional conferences would be held for mutual encouragement and discussion of difficulties and ideas. The Mission was a fellowship of equals, some voluntarily serving the others, from himself as their leader to the local secretaries and housekeepers. 'For love of the brethren', of the Chinese and the Lord himself, they were gladly sacrificing the pleasure of field work in a place of their own, to be servants of the rest. The Home Council were in no way different as a serving, not a ruling body, under a Director whom they 'voluntarily agreed to accept'.

For the time being he had said nothing about appointing a leader in each region to give direction to the work being done and backbone to those whose energies might flag in isolation and discouragement. In some areas each man had tended to do as he saw fit. Drift instead of direction characterised their work. The whole Mission could sink into the same state. Regional leaders were the natural answer. They could meet with him from time to time to compare experience and ideas, he himself would be kept in touch and they could agree on action to be jointly taken. He would benefit from their advice and they from his insights.[754] So ran his thoughts. That this sound plan could be the reef on which the CIM would face shipwreck never entered his mind.

At his second meeting with the London Council in 1883 (on April 17, after reaching Britain) he had outlined this plan for supervision and accountability throughout China. Experienced senior missionaries would consult together in provincial or regional councils under the chairmanship of the appointed leader or superintendent. And these regional leaders would meet together from time to time with him or his deputy directing the whole work in China. With the London Council's approval he had then written, on August 24, 1883, to all members of the Mission, proposing the appointment of a superintendent approved by his colleagues, if necessary for each main region, and a China Council made up of the Director and superintendents. He invited comment and opinion, saying:

> It is important to secure that no contingency shall alter the character of the Mission or throw us off those lines which God has so signally owned and blessed from the commencement. But our home arrangement of assisting the Director by a Council may be introduced into the China work ... No new principle will be introduced, yet our work will be rendered capable of indefinite expansion, while maintaining its original character.[755]

He personally favoured allowing each able missionary to develop his or her own work in their own way, in consultation with each other. Regional leaders and councils should not hamper initiative. And this was when he secured the London Council's agreement that when missionaries conferred about their work, 'the sisters be recognised as equals'. At the time, the concept was welcomed. The problem was, who were the godly and competent men fitted to superintend others? And who could step into his shoes in China if he should fall ill or die? Some good men had shortcomings.

Again and again over the years he had tried to train one after another, only to be disappointed. Each had his limitations. Others, very promising young men, needed time and experience and training. By learning the ropes as his assistants they could free him occasionally to go inland, or he could send them as his representatives.

In 1879 he had written to Benjamin on the role of leaders:

> The all-important thing is to improve the character of the work; deepen the piety, devotion and success of the workers; remove stones of stumbling if possible; oil the wheels when they stick; amend whatever is defective and supplement as far as may be what is lacking. This is no easy matter when suitable men are wanting or only in the course of formation. That I may be used of God, at least in some measure, to bring these about is my hope.[756]

Conspicuous, perhaps, in his evaluation is the absence of any reference to intelligence, initiative, energy or authority. These were only the equipment for being effective in applying the fundamental qualities he named. Whether in a team leader or a General Director, inappropriate use of the confidence accorded by his colleagues, whether by autocratic ways or unwise action, would soon result in his replacement. Hudson Taylor saw many fall by the wayside through such failings, men of whom he had been hopeful.

With his return to China in the spring of 1885 Hudson Taylor knew what he wanted if he was to convert vision into reality. A few key men were recognizable as well qualified to be leaders. After years of being too taciturn to win the confidence of his colleagues, John Stevenson (who always had the ability) had become 'a new man'. At the Keswick Convention, 1885, he had learned to submit himself to the will of God and be 'filled by the Spirit'. Welling up with 'the joy of the Lord', his strong lead was welcomed at home in Britain as it would be no less in China. He could be brought at once to Hudson Taylor's side and given a share in the administration. He arranged for his wife and adolescent family to stay in Scotland, and set out for Shanghai.

After the burst of generosity to the CIM early in the year, donors were tightening their belts and remembering the needs of other continents. Low receipts reaching China meant Hudson Taylor having to be on hand at the coast to send out monthly remittances of small amounts when quarterly allocations could not be made. The sooner a reliable man could be found to relieve him of this task alone, the better. John McCarthy, as senior as Stevenson, was keeping the accounts but lacked the ability to assess the requirements of the widely scattered mission. James Meadows, who had come out to Ningbo in 1862, was a successful pastor but uneducated and half-hearted in his loyalty to Hudson Taylor. One man had the ability and devotion to be a godly, sympathetic and efficient treasurer. Strong confidence in God was the first essential. But James Broumton's place at Guiyang would be difficult to fill.[757]

Hudson Taylor invited him to Shanghai and went over with him all that was involved in the job. At his finger-tips he would need to keep particulars of all Mission statistics, of each missionary and his growing family, his work, his Chinese colleagues, his rental of premises, the wages of employed teachers and workmen, his routine travel costs, running expenses of schools for Chinese children, and the fluctuating exchange rates in different parts of the vast country. They did the work together for a few months, and early in 1886 Hudson Taylor appointed him treasurer, the first in China. John McCarthy handed over the simple account books he kept, for them to audit, meticulously to the last cent, and at midnight, May 1, Broumton began the work he sustained for seventeen years. He left by steamer before dawn and set up his office at Wuchang, to be as nearly as possible at the geographical centre of the Mission. In February 1903 his assistant W. Hayward took over.

One example of the kind of problem Broumton could face was handled by Hudson Taylor in June 1885. A few inexperienced newcomers, he discovered, were in difficulties through irresponsible use of funds. Some were laying in so many stores before setting off on journeys to the back of beyond that they exceeded their credit at Mission business centres—in effect borrowing from their more conscientious colleagues. Some had so many coolie-loads or mule-packs as to invite robbery and to involve them in excessive costs. Thoughtlessly, two women heading for Kunming bought kerosene storm-lanterns. They then needed heavy drums of fuel, to be carried hundreds of miles on men's backs. Vegetable oil and charcoal were in use and available throughout China. Two others set out for Gansu like mandarins with sixteen mule-loads and two sedan chairs. They would learn. In June, Hudson Taylor introduced a simple device: CIM credit notes. 'In issuing these Notes we deposit in the Bank the silver they represent. Members of the Mission purchasing them must do so with ready money.' Orders from upcountry or between mission stations would in future be the equivalent of cash transactions. And he drew up advice on preparations for travelling and equipping remote bases. Most necessities could be bought locally. Forty pounds-weight of baggage, half a mule load, was a good standard to aim for. The smooth running of a complex organisation was greatly helped by a uniform way of doing things, so he began to outline some of these in printed leaflets or letters.[758]

With funds so low, reinforcements were delayed in coming out from Europe, and with each postponement Hudson Taylor's hope faded of quickly completing his arrangements and returning to Britain. At the end of June he wrote, 'The state of funds is serious. The LORD send help!' But shortages taught new lessons in economy of resources. The numerous boarding schools for Chinese children, many of them from Christian families, were costly to run and denied the children the knowledge of farming and domestic duties they would acquire at home. He arranged for them to spend the long winters at school and the summer months back in their villages. It was a major improvement, and the Christian children passed on the gospel to their families.

He had hoped to complete his enlistment of superintendents and to set up a China Council by the end of the year, but consultations also took longer than expected. Great distances had to be travelled in unsettled, dangerous times. Then what had appeared to be a setback proved to be an advantage. The more Hudson Taylor delegated his duties and responsibilities, the more whispers of protest began to reach him from old-timers. Who were these younger men to come between them and him? 'There was a good deal said that was unpleasant and bad feelings aroused,' James Meadows was to recall. But it was true only of the few, and indignantly denied in some provinces. If the process had been less gradual, the outcry might have been stronger.

The arrival of John Stevenson on December 24, 1885, restored balance. He brought with him six new men and the first two members of the Bible Christian Mission, Fanstone and Thorne, bound for Yunnan. Hudson Taylor sent Stevenson to visit two inveterate trouble spots in Zhejiang, and to Shaanxi and Shanxi to meet as many missionaries as possible. By April 1886 when he announced in careful words, 'Mr Stevenson . . . has undertaken to act as my deputy in districts which I cannot personally visit; and generally in matters requiring attention during my absence from China,' the appointment was popular. On the twentieth anniversary of the sailing of the *Lammermuir*, May 26, Stevenson wrote from Hanzhong, in conference with sixteen missionaries, including the Polhill-Turners, 'We had the full ride last night, and found it hard to break up such a glory-time . . . I think you would not have slept much for delight . . . The love and confidence the brothers and sisters lavish on me makes me feel humiliated (by) such a rich token of approval.'[759]

Formal recognition as 'Deputy China Director' followed naturally. The Chinese Christians at Hanzhong impressed him deeply, some of them with most decided convictions and a dauntless courage and enterprise for the Lord. 'I never was so hopeful as I am today with regard to the gospel in this land . . . I am amazed and gratified at the splendid material which we have here for the purpose [of evangelising northern and western Sichuan].'

By then Hudson Taylor had settled the question of whom to appoint as leaders in most provinces, with marked wisdom in some instances, and in others with unreserved admiration of the men available. For Zhejiang, with its rebellious Jackson and George Stott of pre-*Lammermuir* vintage, he named James Meadows, himself rebellious against wearing Chinese dress, with gentle James Williamson to mollify him. Responsibility as superintendent could bring Meadows to personal compliance with the 'Principles and Practice'. Faithful John McCarthy undertook supervision of Jiangxi and Jiangsu, where the chief women's work and women's training home were located. And James Cameron took Shandong, with Chefoo as his main responsibility. For Anhui he had William Cooper, a quiet, saintly but physically powerful and mature man who had come to China as recently as 1881 but was already recognised as exceptionally gifted. The church and the men's training home at Anqing were put under his guidance, but more significantly, the task of opening up the whole province by J. L. Nevius's methods. Nevius had published in the *Chinese Recorder* his system for promoting indigenous church growth and government, by 'self-reliance from the beginning', with no more foreign subsidies for Chinese preachers.[760] Frederick Baller had proved himself as a pioneer and linguist. After helping Hoste, Cassels and Stanley Smith to find their feet in Shanxi, Baller returned to supervise the central provinces of Hubei and Henan, and to prepare a Mandarin primer to simplify language study. Dorward was the unquestioned choice for the defiant provinces of Hunan and Guangxi. Easton on his return from furlough joined them as superintendent in Shaanxi and Gansu, and George Clarke for the north, in Shanxi and

Zhili.[761] No one was yet available for the south-western provinces, so John Stevenson himself took the oversight of Sichuan, Yunnan and Guizhou.

The fact that nothing was made of this important administrative development in *China's Millions* or at annual meetings of the Mission, is the measure of its deliberately unobtrusive beginning. The subservience of mere scaffolding to the building being erected, the church in China, was the simile John Stevenson used in his first general letter as deputy director.[762] The founder of the Mission whom all members had chosen to follow had asked these respected men to help him by sharing his burden. No thought of undermining his authority entered their heads.

Send more (1885–87)

One of the first impressions Hudson Taylor had received on reaching China in March 1885 was of the progress in his absence. No less clear was the cry from place after place for help. In spite of the Sino-French hostilities, the scope for preaching the gospel exceeded all that the thin line of pioneers could do. As soon as the funds permitted (on May 4, 1885) Hudson Taylor had cabled to London for thirty more men to be sent without delay. And in August, while attending the mortally ill Miss Murray, principal of the women's language school at Yangzhou, he planned and set in motion an enlargement of the premises there for the influx of women he also foresaw approaching. By November it was the men's training home accommodation at Anqing being reviewed in terms of an 'Institute'. And to friends of the CIM he wrote that newcomers were 'absorbed at once, leaving us as hungry as before for more workers. Our brethren in nearly every province are urgent in their cries for reinforcements; our sisters, were they to come out in ten times the number' would all find more than enough to do. If the veterans were losing their buoyancy, the energy of younger men and women was needed. Those pleading for help saw their own need as more urgent than elsewhere. What could not be

made public until later was the fact that more and more young women were going inland, deep into pioneering situations. 'Keep it quiet,' Hudson Taylor reminded those involved, 'until success or otherwise appears.'[763] He had in mind another development as adventurous as any the women had yet undertaken, the staffing of a large region almost entirely by women.

By the anniversary, May 26, 1886, forty new missionaries had gone to China in 1885 and a further nine in 1886 of the 119 who had asked to be sent. To the London staff this represented the correspondence and interviews with one man and one woman for each working day of the year so far. The full membership of the CIM had risen to 188, with 114 Chinese colleagues supported by the Mission. The total income of £20,221 in 1885 was almost £2,000 more than that of 1884, but it had not kept pace with the costs, which included providing passages to and from China, for the correspondingly increasing number of tired missionaries needing home leave. When the chairman of the Annual Meeting, George Williams of the YMCA, commented innocently, 'Are we right in allowing those who have the charge of this Mission to have an amount of anxiety like that?' he showed unfamiliarity with CIM principles. To them 'shortage' was testing or restraint from God but would never reach inadequacy for the objects God initiated. By the next annual meeting there were 215 members and 10 associate members, and of 184 applicants in the first five months of the year, 23 had already been accepted.[764]

The assessment of candidates for suitability to be CIM missionaries in China involved factors differing from selection for the denominational societies. For them it was usually for a thorough training for ordination and a pastoral or educational role overseas. For the CIM, in addition to general qualifications, sincere acceptance of the Mission's unusual principles and practical requirements was essential. Faith to trust God for the means to live, not in dependence on the Mission, could not be measured or vouched for by referees. Readiness to go inland dressed as a Chinese and deferring marriage while adapting to the climate and people could be sincerely intended and yet prove mistaken when faced with reality.[765] A sorrowing widow, convinced of her call from God to be a missionary, on reaching Shanghai could not face what was entailed. Sympathizing deeply, Hudson Taylor saw that grief had clouded her judgment. She was trying to put sorrow behind her. He kept her in Shanghai and, to his joy, before long his friend of many years, William Muirhead of the LMS, a widower whose love for the CIM often brought him round to visit them, asked her to marry him.

The qualifications for being an effective missionary were more and more shown to be not natural ability or education or the qualities commonly sought by selection boards, but primarily of a spiritual nature. When thanking Lord Radstock for two hampers of vegetables from his garden in August 1878, Hudson Taylor had written, 'Would not a man, called of God, go whether with us or not? . . . I would have worked my way to China as a common sailor, had no other way opened—I dare not have accepted man's conclusion when I knew God's mind.' If individuals were in any doubt, how could the CIM settle it for them? Only in so far as membership of this Mission was concerned. The two of them enjoyed close comradeship in this way. Lord Radstock wished he could in some way be a part of the CIM himself. 'I think you would get more spiritual power in the sending out of missionaries,' he replied from Stockholm, 'if in some way they could be sent more by the Church and not only by the committee . . . If all your believing helpers were not only subscribers but spiritually members, our power would be increased tenfold.' On this they were of one mind with each other and with Griffith John; the supreme qualification would always be daily constant dependence on the Holy Spirit for spiritual vitality and power. Yet in the end even an ideal personality would only stand the physical conditions in China if combined with the right physique. Hudson Taylor urged upon Benjamin and

the Home Director that they must be firm with unsuitable candidates. 'We know—they don't!' Few knew; fewer could guess what lay ahead. The accumulating wisdom and experience of the Mission was a factor to be respected.

Progress in China (1885–86)

Mere numbers and real estate were no measures of progress. What missionaries achieved and how they themselves developed as examples to immature Christians provided a truer indication of progress. Members of the Seventy had used their voyage out to point crews and passengers to Christ, as converted officers and men told later travellers. In spite of unsettled conditions due to China's war with France, seven men of the Seventy had gone to the north-west, including two to occupy Lanzhou, the capital of Gansu, where George Parker had at last succeeded in renting premises. From Shanghai to Lanzhou was 2,500 miles. Three were to go further, right up into Ningxia, a Muslim and Mongolian area. Even bare rooms in a rowdy inn seemed luxury after months of gruelling travel. Parker himself had Kashgar in far distant Turkestan (later Xinjiang) in view, as far distant again as he already was from the coast. To encourage his Chinese wife, Minnie Shao, as stalwart a pioneer as he, came the news that her mother in Yangzhou had been baptised.[766]

Two more men had reached Guiyang only to find the province too disturbed for any travelling to be possible; and another two, soon to be followed by two more, reached Dali, freeing George Clarke to bring his orphaned child to Shanghai. The first baptisms had taken place at Dali and Kunming, where the lamp they lit burns on today after years of attempts to snuff it out. But when F. A. Steven attempted to go westwards to Bhamo he excited strong suspicions of his being a spy and was glad to escape arrest. Bhamo had to remain unoccupied. In Chengdu, the capital of Sichuan, J. H. Riley had strengthened the Mission's foothold with his wife, the brave Jane Kidd of Guiyang, and her young companion Fanny Stroud. But tragedy was soon to strike them.

The intransigent province of Henan had once again let A. W. Sambrook break his homeless travelling from place to place by renting premises in Zhoujiakou (Chouchiakou, now Zhoukouzhen), on the south-eastern waterway to the Grand Canal and Yangzi River. Two new, untried companions had barely joined him when yet again they were driven out—the last straw for Sambrook's battered mind. As with Henry Taylor ten years earlier, the cumulative effect of having his devotion constantly scorned and rejected broke Sambrook's spirit and he had to be taken home to Britain as a sad casualty. But after the chief antagonist appealed for help to save a member of his family from attempted suicide, Zhoujiakou became the first permanent mission centre in Henan, followed in 1886 by Sheqidian (Shekitien), with the beginnings of a church in each. In the documents that have survived no explanation has been found of the fact that Hudson Taylor subsequently sent his own relatives, among others, to these two hard-won cities: J. J. Coulthard and Herbert Taylor, Maria Taylor and Herbert's wife, Geraldine Guinness and Howard Taylor, and in 1894 Dixon Hoste.[767]

In all the CIM's work during the year 1885 more than two hundred baptisms were reported, still slow progress but made in the face of opposition and persecution. Hudson Taylor in October called it 'war to the knife', 'a hand-to-hand conflict with the powers of darkness'. After a year in China he wrote of a total of 1,300 communicants throughout the Mission. Immense patience was needed, but with every advance the tempo of results was increasing.[768]

In the two parts of Shaanxi, separated by mountains, conditions were as different as could be. In the Hanzhong plain the church was expanding, with six self-supporting voluntary preachers and lively congregations. In the Xi'an plain the only possible way to work was still to keep moving from one place to another, but covering the same territory again and again. An influential Hunanese family as relentlessly as ever prevented Christians from settling in the capital, Xi'an.[769]

The province of Hunan remained more stubbornly invincible, except by a Chinese evangelist quietly working at Jinshi (Tsinshi) not far across the border. Adam Dorward had made Shashi on the Yangzi his base, travelling inconspicuously by boat into the north-western corner of the province, until a Spanish priest suffered the anger of the people at Lizhou and further access was forfeited. Henry Dick, one of the Seventy who joined Dorward, and less of a marked man, penetrated as far as Hongjiang and Changde, with a converted Buddhist priest as his companion, preaching the gospel and selling books. Making history in May 1886, they even entered Changsha, the provincial capital, to the consternation of the authorities. A dreaded, hated foreigner had not been repulsed by the guards at the gate! When Henry Dick adopted a new tactic and paid a courtesy visit to the *yamen*, they expelled him. To angry cries from the crowds of 'Beat the foreigner!' he and the evangelist were hustled back to their boat and a gunboat saw them well away. The conquest of Hunan still had years to wait for God's time.[770]

Guangxi continued almost as difficult to enter. A. A. Fulton of the American Presbyterian Mission (North) and his sister, a doctor of medicine, succeeded for a while to occupy Guiping in the eastern half, but they too were expelled. As long as other missions wished to attempt Guangxi,[771] Hudson Taylor held back his men, always bearing someone in mind for the task.

In Zhejiang the CMS were witnessing a remarkable turning to God in the region of Chuqi in the Hangzhou area. Two hundred people turning to Christ in about twenty-five villages, within a few months, was a rare phenomenon, the kind of movement all missionaries were praying for. Fujian, where J. R. Wolfe had served the embryo church alone after the death or retirement of five colleagues, was outstanding in a different way: the believers in 120 towns and villages were spreading the gospel through 70 preaching chapels, against bitter opposition and with one martyrdom. Four ordained ministers, 107 catechists and a theological college were strengthening the foundations of the church.

Towards the end of June 1885, Hudson Taylor himself made a long pastoral journey overland, with a motley party of companions on their way to their locations. He himself and his secretary Lewis were to visit Hangzhou to help Wang Lae-djün with problems in the church. John McCarthy was escorting some women up the Qiantang River to Qü Xian. Maria Taylor, caring for George Clarke's motherless infant son while he visited Shanxi, was in the party too. They travelled by canal boat to Hangzhou and on up the Qiantang to Yanzhou (to be distinguished from Yangzhou) where their various ways parted (see map 2.57: p 457). In mid-July, while McCarthy's boats went on upstream to Qü Xian, Hudson Taylor's party branched westwards up the Xin'an River to She Xian (Huicheng) in Anhui. Often when the currents were strong and rapids dangerous, the passengers would go ashore and walk along the trackers' towpath. On one such occasion Maria and her father had just crossed a headland where to trip would have meant a fall of many feet to the rocks below, when she slipped and went over the edge. At that point she fell only a few feet to a terrace and was unharmed. But the shock made Hudson Taylor ill. (The story of these months is punctuated by mishaps which added to the difficulties, as when the rickshaw he was in tipped backwards so that he fell head first on to the road.) During the long cross-country journey to Anqing, after a detour northwards to Ningguo, Maria went down with malaria and delirium. But he had seen enough of her potential as a missionary to take bold measures with her not long afterwards, sending her, though not yet twenty-one, to a pioneer outpost.

The church at Anqing, scene of the Meadowses' and James Williamson's early tribulations (see p 112) had become mature and reliable. Together with George King and William Cooper, Hudson Taylor ordained elders and discussed with them the need for sound future development on the principles which he had worked out with J. L. Nevius in 1879 (pp 167, 178, 346).[773] With their work still uncompleted, a telegram from Yangzhou summoned him without explanation to come at once. Emergencies at Yangzhou he knew could take unpleasant forms, so he asked the redoubtable Adam Dorward, just arrived from Shashi, to go with him. This gave them hours of consultation on the way, about Hunan and reorganisation of the Mission. The crisis was not riot but that the invaluable principal of the training home, Marianne Murray, was at death's door with dysentery. He was still on call as a doctor. After taking her and Maria to Chefoo, he returned in mid-November to Anqing and launched the Anhui church on the Nevius system for purely Chinese control, with William Cooper as their adviser. In conference with the missionaries and language students at Anqing he went over the 'Principles and Practice' which they had signed in Britain, to make sure all understood them well, and gave a series of talks which he subsequently published serially in *China's Millions* and eventually in book form as *A Retrospect*.

In mid-December Hudson Taylor was back at Hangzhou to visit Jinhua with Wang Lae-djün. The Taylors' action in leaving Hangzhou in 1868 to pioneer Yangzhou and the Yangzi valley had been fully vindicated. An indigenous church movement had grown up without dependence on foreign oversight. Lae-djün's pastoral oversight extended a 'hundred and fifty miles and more, over several churches with their own pastors. The country churches were going through severe harassment and Hudson Taylor's presence was timely. While he was at New Lane (Xinkailong), sleeping on the floor in what had been Jennie's room (see see ill 1.60: 1, p 749), two persecuted Christians were brought to him. One, a Dr Zong, had been rescued from enemies after they had cut off his ears, hoisted him up by his wrists, tortured, beaten and all but killed him for his refusal to deny Christ.[774] From there Hudson Taylor went on to Shaoxing to consult with Meadows and Williamson, reaching Shanghai on December 23, the day before John Stevenson landed.

The Guangxin dream comes true[775]
(1886)

Whenever Hudson Taylor was away from his Shanghai office for long, or arrived at the place he had named for correspondence to be addressed to, he faced mountains of mail. A letter of February 24, 1886, tells of his having been back to Yangzhou for a month (while Miss Murray and a language student were so ill again as to need a doctor near at hand). Desk work followed him, but on his return to Shanghai he took five hours to read half the letters and reports held over for him. He then slept from nine until midnight and returned to finish reading the rest before starting on his replies.

John Stevenson's return had raised Hudson Taylor's hopes of getting back to Britain by the end of the year, but first he had to work Stevenson in and be sure he was accepted as his deputy. While Stevenson made his long journey to Hanzhong and on through Shaanxi to Shanxi where the two of them planned to meet again, Hudson Taylor had an expedition of his own to make. Only Broumton taking over the Mission finances in China, with Baller back at Wuchang for the present to support him, set Hudson Taylor free to travel. He had a major development in mind and wished to re-examine the territory in Jiangxi which he had been through in 1880–81. This time John McCarthy and Herbert were with him in one boat, and convalescent Marianne Murray, her sister and two young women Jeanie Gray of the Seventy and Mary Williams in another. Leaving Shanghai on May 4 and following the canal route he had used so often in the past thirty years since 1855, they travelled fast, to join the Qiantang River again at Hangzhou, where McCarthy left them.

While the others went ahead to Qü Xian, Hudson Taylor had a detour to Jinhua to make on business (see p 454). The missionary he went to meet, Robert Grierson, years afterwards threw a pleasant

light on the mundane when he recalled that on arrival Hudson Taylor said he had something to talk about in private. Grierson took him into an inner room. To hold the door open Grierson had attached a string from the door to a bookshelf on the wall. In closing the door behind him Hudson Taylor pulled the bookshelf down 'on his devoted head', and in answer to Grierson's profuse apologies replied, 'There, you see the trouble that comes from interfering with another man's arrangements.' Even at Jinhua he was catching up on correspondence when he wrote, 'The carrots go ahead however fast the donkey runs. The work however is looking up nearly everywhere.'

At Qü Xian, Kate Mackintosh, also of the Seventy, took Mary Williams's place in the party, and the women pressed on to Yushan in Jiangxi with Herbert Taylor to look after them. Hudson Taylor, joined by David Thompson (see p 443) caught them up on May 24, (when Stevenson's conference was at 'full tide' in Hanzhong and the Polhill brothers joined the Mission). At once they saw that Herbert had made good use of his circumstances. As he explained to his brother Howard: in November 1885 he had been called to help with a case of opium poisoning (a suicide attempt) on which Jeanie Gray was also working, and promptly fell in love with her. But how to do any more about it in the segregated life they led drove him to despair. His father, ostensibly seeing how run down he was and in need of a holiday, had enlisted his help on this journey. An accomplice or not, he was delighted when at the journey's end they became engaged. Herbert was twenty-five and she twenty-three, 'the best of her bunch in health, character and progress in Chinese'.[776]

Nine years had passed since Hudson Taylor had visited the Douthwaites at Qü Xian with Miss Elizabeth Wilson (in 1877), and met the redoubtable Captain Yü of Yüshan and the earliest believers in the area. In 1860 Captain Yü had heard the rudiments of a distorted gospel from Taiping rebels, and without deeper knowledge had become a devout Buddhist in a sect that, like the Taipings, denounced idol worship. Hearing Wang Lae-djün and Douthwaite preaching the gospel at Jinhua fifteen years later, Yü had believed and in 1876 had been baptised by Lae-djün. Members of his old sect had lived near to and across the provincial border, in Jiangxi, and Yü went at once to share his discovery with them, bringing some back to Qü Xian with him. 'For forty years I have been seeking the Truth,' one said to Douthwaite, 'and now I have found it!' Another man in the Yüshan region not only believed but soon had a houseful of fellow-worshippers, at the village of Dayang, sitting on baskets, inverted buckets, anything they could find, to hear the preachers who visited them.

Two brief references will indicate what lay behind the steady growth and deep roots of the Qü Xian and Yüshan churches. When Hudson Taylor had sent Arthur Douthwaite and his bride to Qü Xian on their first assignment, he had given them this advice:

> Spend a month there, or perhaps ten days might be long enough at first. In that way you would soon see the interest deepened I think. On going with Mrs Douthwaite be sure to give it out that you are only going to stay a few days, then no one will take fright and try to *drive* you away, or when you have left, spread a report that you *had* been frightened away. I should be glad if eventually you were able to live there and take permanent oversight of the work ... in process of time occupying all the *xian* [or county] cities of these districts and extending into Jiangxi province. This would be the work of years ... Read the Word with much prayer with (your Chinese fellow-workers). Hold much holy communion with our Lord; then, fresh from His presence, minister Him to them ... Tell them what you are finding there. You will not be kept long sowing thus before you are rejoicing over the first fruits.

Douthwaite had followed this advice and the Christians 'spread over the wall' into Jiangxi sooner than expected. Speaking at a conference of evangelists and church elders arranged by Wang Lae-djün for the region between Hangzhou and Qü Xian, Douthwaite gave them these guiding 'Rules' to help them to develop:

1. Each was to write a comment on the daily passage of Scripture he read, sending a copy to Douthwaite, and also

2. copies of each prepared sermon,

3. a monthly record and statement of places visited, meetings held and books sold, and

4. a monthly essay on a given subject for Douthwaite's comment.[777]

Not surprisingly, by 1880 when Hudson Taylor visited Qü Xian and Yüshan again, a maturing church was sending evangelists further afield into Jiangxi, and planting daughter churches. They needed missionary help but who could go? At the time of his 'bombshell' he was launching unmarried women into the remotest provinces—sending Miss Wilson up the Han River to pioneer Hanzhong and Gansu (see p 367). Then the key event took place in 1885. An evangelist and his wife invited Agnes Gibson, of the Seventy, a girl of only twenty who had recently moved to Qü Xian, to come and stay with them at Changshan, between Qü Xian and Yüshan. As a result, when Hudson Taylor's party arrived in May 1886, the Chinese women who for years had resisted their husbands' conversion were as much in evidence as Christians as the men folk. They asked for a woman to be sent to live permanently among them.

As he travelled on through Jiangxi, in place after place Hudson Taylor saw how well received the missionary women were. Only one conclusion could be drawn. His firm belief since Maria (Dyer) in Ningbo and Jennie at Hangzhou had proved the point that women had at least as valuable a part to play as men, must now be demonstrated on a large scale to be valid. Quietly at first, to prevent an outcry, but justified in good time by results, they would go a hundred, two hundred miles beyond established mission centres and become part of the family in Christian Chinese homes.

He arranged for Jeanie Gray and Kate Mackintosh to return and live at Yüshan in the care of a trusted Christian couple. Nothing could have been safer or, as it proved, more satisfactory. That they could not take charge, as men might do, was pure asset. But they could teach, advise and encourage the Christians as well as any man. Within a year forty-two more were baptised, and at Yüshan the congregation grew from thirty to one hundred and eight. At one city after another down the Guangxin River a chain of churches developed, served by missionary women only, under the fatherly supervision of John McCarthy for the first five years. Mary Williams joined Kate Mackintosh in Yüshan when Jeanie Gray went to be married; Agnes Gibson and F. M. Tapscott, not yet twenty, went to Yanshan (Hekou) and Guixi lower down the Guangxin River, and Herbert and Jeanie Gray after their marriage took charge of the base at Dagutang on the Poyang Lake. By 1890 women were in Yangkou, Guangfeng, Yiyang and Ganren as well as the three original locations. At the same time a team of men led by Archibald Orr Ewing was opening up the south-western part of the province, first worked by J. E. Cardwell (1871–73) along the Gan River, the imperial route to Canton taken by Lord Amhurst and Robert Morrison (see 1, p 56). Thirty years later (in 1920) the church in this Guangxin region, still staffed by Chinese church leaders and missionary women in ten centres and sixty sub-centres, had over 2,200 communicant members and many more 'enquirers' and Christians preparing for baptism.

Hudson Taylor and his party crossed the Poyang Lake to Dagutang (now Xingzi) in early June 1886, while John Stevenson was plodding over the mountains from Hanzhong to Xi'an, and the Polhills were penetrating Sichuan to rent premises at Langzhong (Paoning), and Henry Dick was heading back from Changsha, capital of Hunan, to Shashi and Dorward again. News that John

Stevenson's Glasgow friend Archibald Orr Ewing and others were expected at Shanghai any day led Hudson Taylor to go straight there without visiting any Yangzi centres. How right he was in this decision became immediately apparent.

Wusong Road and Newington Green (1886–90)

The enlarged training homes at Yangzhou and Anqing were ready none too soon. But the new Mission premises near the Shanghai consulate were already inadequate and enquiries were progressing about a site on the Wusong Road in less fashionable Hongkou (Hongkew). Hudson Taylor arrived at Shanghai on June 14, to be told that in his absence others had been bidding for the site and the option granted to the CIM would expire that very day. T. W. Pigott of Shanxi and his wife had offered to cover the cost until the money was available, but no donation had been received. Because the site was so suitable, Hudson Taylor prayed at the noon prayer meeting for the seemingly impossible, that the needed amount should be given in time for him to take up the option.[778] That

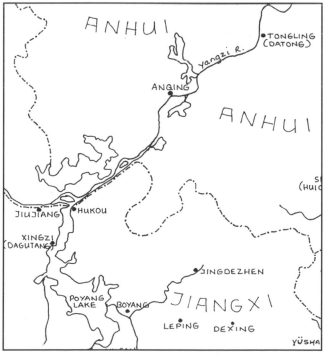

2.57 Jiangxi: the Guangxin River women's field

afternoon Archibald Orr Ewing, just arrived from Britain, on hearing of the site offered a first £1,500 as a gift. It was enough. On the strength of this double assurance the deal was struck. On June 15, Hudson Taylor wrote to Jennie, 'I have today signed the contract for about 2 acres of building and garden ground in Shanghai—price £2486.9.2.'

Archibald Orr Ewing's interest in China had been aroused in 1884 by John McCarthy and fanned by C. T. Studd and Stanley Smith. But at the Keswick Convention in 1885 Orr Ewing had made his decision, and Stevenson wrote in September:

> This dear fellow has finally surrendered himself to God for China and the CIM. He is very wealthy and has a most prosperous business. He has asked his partners to set him free ... and they have agreed ... He is ready to ... devote a large portion of his wealth to China. He feels he must spend a good deal of money yearly at the Vale of Leven where it was made ... His going will create a great stir in Glasgow.[779]

Orr Ewing was twenty-eight and unmarried. After a farewell meeting of leading businessmen in Glasgow he left Britain in April 1886 at his own expense, with his friend George Graham Brown and others. But his timely arrival at Shanghai only marked the beginning of his part in the Wusong Road developments. To steal a look into the future, China and the CIM in action so impressed him that he formally joined the Mission and when his business affairs in Scotland were wound up, he contributed not only the full cost of the site, but also of the extensive buildings erected on it. He served as an influential leader in China until 1911 and on the Council for the British Isles until his death on May 11, 1930.

The Pyrland Road houses had also long since become too crowded for comfort. Permission to build an extension had been refused, and Benjamin had suggested buying a house and land for building on a site available round the corner flanking Newington Green. Negotiations were begun and by July 19, 1887, a contract was agreed.

The great expansion of the CIM had begun. Numbering 163 members in March 1885, there were 409 on January 1, 1890, 621 by the end of March 1895, and 811 on January 1, 1900. So this provision came none too soon. The extensive buildings at Newington Green were completed only in 1894.[780]

Two days after Orr Ewing's arrival he was in Chinese clothes and together with Hudson Taylor, Herbert and Lewis the secretary was on a ship bound for Tianjin and Taiyuan. At long last, after many thwarted efforts to reach Shanxi Hudson Taylor was this time to succeed. Passing through Baoding in Zhili (the only place between the coast and Taiyuan with a resident missionary, worked by the American Board), they were in Huolo (Huailu) on June 29, preparing to 'exchange our jolting carts for swinging mule litters' to scale the mountains into Shanxi. On that day Stevenson reached Linfen (Pingyang) from Hanzhong, appalled by the devastation still remaining from the great famine of 1878–79. Judging that he was too late to reach Taiyuan for the planned conference of missionaries, he stayed to give the Linfen church a feast of teaching, and spent long, never-to-be-forgotten hours with Hsi Shengmo. But Hudson Taylor, Orr Ewing and the others arrived at Taiyuan to find smallpox dictating their timetable and the conference postponed.[781]

Shanxi and Hsi 'Shengmo'[782] (1885–86)

The strong church in Shanxi today owes much to its mission origins. After David Hill left Shanxi in 1879 to return to Hankou, following the famine, J. J. Turner and S. B. Drake had stayed on at Linfen (Pingyang), the chief city of south Shanxi (seat of the emperors Yao and Shun before the time of Abraham). Hsi Shengmo, the converted Confucian scholar had sometimes looked to them for help, but largely by giving himself to prayer and by force of character he broke free from his ten-year addiction to opium. What he recognised as a spiritual battle against evil forces he had won by the power of God. So he adopted the name 'Shengmo', conqueror of demons, defiantly, not arrogantly. When his wife ridiculed and opposed him and herself became convulsively demon-possessed, his neighbours challenged him to justify his boast and prove his faith. He fasted and prayed for three days and nights, laid his hands on her and in the name of Jesus commanded the evil spirit to leave her. She was cured and declared herself a believer.

From then on she worked with him in shepherding the Christian villagers and in running a medicine shop and preaching hall. He claimed that God taught him how to compound medicines with which to help other addicts to break free, and his pills became famous—the life-giving pill, the life-sustaining pill and the health-restoring pill, he called them. But prayer and exhortation to trust in Jesus played a greater part. Opposition to him became stronger. When the literati failed to make him recant they prevailed upon the corrupt literary chancellor of the province to disgrace Hsi by depriving him of his degree. He refused to pay bribes or take his case to law, but Drake laid the facts before the provincial governor who saw that justice was done. Hsi's degree and honours were restored.

Vast acres of wheat land in Shanxi had been given over to the opium poppy, and 'eleven out of every ten' in the province were said to smoke or swallow the cursed 'mud'. With opium so easy to obtain, suicide also became commonplace. When village elders pleaded with the landed gentry and magistrates to eradicate the curse, they did nothing. It was their chief source of wealth. And they too were addicts. From small beginnings with one or two 'opium refuges', Hsi extended his cures to village after village and then town after town. The leader of a vegetarian sect, named Fan, grief-stricken when two sons were killed by wolves, turned to Christ, and when Drake left the district Fan took over his dispensary and opium refuge, using Hsi's herbal drugs.

Hsi and Fan were therefore respected and appealed to by growing numbers of addicts wishing to be cured. In Fan's small village fifty or sixty converted ex-opium smokers worshipped together. In 1884 there were eight or ten refuges, and Christians in each place. Hsi longed to open another at the city of Hochou (now Huo Xian), but all his available money was committed to existing work. One day his wife presented him with all her jewellery—rings, ear-rings and hair ornaments—the prised symbol of social standing, saying, 'I can do without these. Let Hochou have the gospel.' Their work of a lifetime deserved all they possessed.[783]

Then in June 1885 the four 'Cambridge men' arrived—Stanley Smith, Cassels, Hoste and Beauchamp, tongue-tied in the Chinese language, but good men of striking personality. Frederick Baller, their escort, impressed Hsi by his fluency and scholarly knowledge of the Chinese classics. 'Scholars, merchants and farmers, young men and old, thronged the courtyard to watch the new arrivals and listen to Mr Baller's eloquent Chinese. 'When it grows dark,' they exclaimed with astonishment, 'not one in a hundred would suppose he is a foreigner.'

Hsi's 'keen, commanding eyes', sharp features and masterly ways no less won the admiration of the five men. He impressed them by his profound understanding and ability to expound the Bible. Although relatively untaught by missionaries, for his home was fifteen miles from Linfen, he constantly studied it, 'comparing Scripture with Scripture'. Visiting his home they heard him preach to a mixed crowd of Christians and unbelievers on the story of Paul's shipwreck, used allegorically, and took notes of the points he made. Each point he clothed in vivid colloquial, dramatically describing the ocean and sea-going ships, of which these mountain dwellers knew nothing. Frederick Baller who had heard Griffith John and William Muirhead was to write of one of Hsi's sermons, 'The whole exposition was equal to any I have heard from a foreign missionary.'[784] The people respected Hsi and recognised in him an authority greater than his social and literary standing merited.

As for the newcomers, by dressing, living and behaving as well as they were able like Chinese scholars, cultivating the appropriate gait and manners, the men were quickly accepted among the people of Linfen, and made good progress in the language. During the first three months Baller prospected with an evangelist and found three other cities with a nucleus of Christians who would welcome the presence of a missionary. Cassels and Beauchamp he placed in Xi Man (Sichou), near Daning in the western mountains, three or four days' travel away from Linfen. By then 'Cassels could understand more of what Chinese said to them, but Beauchamp was better at making himself understood!' And again, 'My soul was among lions,' Cassels confessed. The scorn over his dumbness, the desperate sense of a life wasted in a backwater, the fierce temptation to give up and go home, were no less than attacks by the devil.[785] Hoste chose to be alone among Chinese, and Baller committed him to the care of Christians at Quwo in the southern plain. Later he was joined by W. Hope Gill of Cambridge. Stanley Smith was making the fastest progress; Baller kept him at Linfen as William Key,

the only other missionary in the area, was little more advanced and Baller himself was soon to return to the Yangzi. Outstanding as a linguist, he was to take charge of the Anqing training home, and to write his *Mandarin Primer.* C. T. Studd came up from Hanzhong in the autumn and, joining his good friend Stanley Smith, soon made up for time lost from language study.

Years before, a copy of Mark's Gospel had found its way into a temple outside the west gate of Daning. The early seed sown by Cameron, Parrott, Pigott and the Bible Society colporteurs was germinating. Puzzled by it, the leading Buddhist priest of the county, Zhang Zhiben, asked a scholar named Qü to examine it with him. Deeply impressed, they burned incense first to the book and then to Jesus and the twelve disciples. Somehow they obtained a New Testament and before long 'began to worship the one true God and His Son Jesus Christ'. Zhang was beaten unconscious by the order of an official who had been his friend, and Qü was three times fearfully flogged in public for refusing to join in idolatrous ceremonies. Then at last they heard of Christians at Linfen and made the three-day journey to find them. A few days among kindred spirits gave them the reassurance they needed, and on their return they at once began to preach the gospel openly. At Xiaoyi, five days' journey to the north towards Taiyuan, eight families destroyed their idols and turned to Christ, the beginning of another church. With our knowledge of the Boxer rising in 1900 these early beginnings have a poignancy and significance beyond most.

Meeting Cassels at Xi Xian, Zhang took him to Daning in February 1886, and introduced him to Qü and twenty-two families of Christians. He decided to stay, leaving Beauchamp with the Christians at Xi Xian. Each shared persecution with the Chinese when a hostile mandarin was appointed, but not because of ostentatious foreignness—the only foreign things Cassels had with him were his English Bible, a pen and a pencil, and the only daytime space he could call his own were the two square feet where he sat sharing the *kang* in a little cave-house with his companions and visitors.

They were at a church conference in Linfen with new Christians from Xi Xian and Daning when word came of accusations against them. Cassels, for example, had destroyed an idol in the Daning temple! He and 'Monty' at once returned to face the music, arriving at dusk to find his own makeshift home barred against him. They stayed together for three weeks until convinced that the persecution of the Christians had ceased for the present, largely because of their presence.

At the conference seventy more believers were baptised, nearly doubling the membership of the Church in south Shanxi. And Hsi Shengmo took note that significant numbers of them came from the congregations that had the help of the young missionaries. The cheerful, animated personality of Stanley Smith so attracted Hsi that he asked him to help in opening a new opium refuge at the city of Hongtong, a few miles from his colleague Fan's home. Smith was to live unobtrusively in a village outside the city, quietly making himself known until premises were found in the city itself. With enough accommodation for twenty or thirty addicts and a large guest-hall for use as a chapel, physical and spiritual healing could proceed side by side. Before long ideal premises were rented. 'SPS' moved in, joined in May by Dixon Hoste at Hsi's request, while Hsi himself came often to supervise the refuge. So. began a blissful period of progress with the friendship between Chinese and foreigners steadily deepening. Hoste's aphorism, 'Study without preaching would be stifling,' typified their approach to the language and the job they had come to do.

The Shanxi conferences[786]
(July–August 1886)

When Hudson Taylor and his companions arrived at Taiyuan on Saturday, July 3, they found the CIM missionaries all gathered for a week's conference with them, and the BMS and Bible Society staff in Taiyuan ready to attend. Timothy Richard was away

in Britain trying unsuccessfully to get the BMS to take up his educational policy. Apart from the men from south Shanxi, the CIM in Taiyuan at the time consisted of Dr and Mrs Edwards, Hope Gill, Hudson Broomhall and his sister Gertrude, and five women including Maria Taylor. Unable to be present were six from the far north: George Clarke, remarried to Agnes Lancaster, and two men at Guihuacheng; and two more at Baotou on the Mongolian border. But Adamson of the Bible Society (B&FBS) had smallpox, and C. T. Studd and Montagu Beauchamp were nursing him.

On July 5, 6 and 7, therefore, instead of the planned consultation, Hudson Taylor gave expositions on 'The all-sufficiency of Christ for personal life and for all the exigencies of service'. Then he himself fell ill with acute dysentery, and further meetings were deferred until the 12th, 13th and 14th. 'The one thing the work needs here is a head or captain,' he wrote to Jennie on the 8th, 'not too strong on the one hand nor a weakling on the other.' (Pigott, absent in Britain, was too forceful, and Edwards too accommodating.) The one man all would welcome as their leader was Benjamin Bagnall, already thirteen years in China but under the Bible Society. And as he had already negotiated his transfer to the CIM, Hudson Taylor formally admitted him. Orr Ewing's journal also read: 'Joined the Mission, Saturday July 17, 1886 . . . Its attraction to myself was and is that it is nearest the lines of Scripture of any work I am acquainted with.'[787]

In the course of the disjointed conference Hudson Taylor, as his custom was, took many illustrations from his own experience to apply the lessons he was drawing from Scripture, and Beauchamp, using Stanley Smith's and others' notes, afterwards compiled the small book *Days of Blessing* often referred to in mission literature.

The conference over and Adamson recovering, three parties set off for the south, taking two weeks to reach Hongtong, where a conference of Chinese Christians was to follow. Key, Lewis and Stanley Smith went ahead; Cassels and Hoste headed south-west for Xi Xian and Daning to bring Christians from that region; and Hudson Taylor, Herbert, Studd, Beauchamp and Dr Edwards started south on July 21. Heavy rain flooded the Fen River and prevented the western party from reaching Hongtong in time. Hudson Taylor's party struggled in the rain through quagmires and over landslides which even he 'in the saddle' found exhausting, doing thirty miles at a stretch.

He wrote of 'glorious conferences' at Hongtong and Linfen, the first on August 1. The rooms round the inner courtyard somehow provided sleeping space for a hundred men as well as the missionaries, on the kangs, on planks, on doors and on rushes on the floor. And Christian women filled the rooms round the outer courtyard. By day the premises somehow held three hundred, for the curious public could not be excluded. On a platform between the two courtyards Hudson Taylor glowed with happiness over such a sight in one of the 'nine unevangelised provinces', and spoke on Christ's words 'My peace', 'My joy', and 'My glory'.[788]

For Hsi Shengmo the opportunity to preach the gospel to the unconverted was too good to miss. That evening John Stevenson based his own remarks on 'The Kingdom of God is not in words, but in power', and threw open the meeting to any who wished to testify to God's dealings with them. The first on his feet was the dynamic Hsi Shengmo. He told how in his youth the Confucian classics had failed to allay his fear of death. He turned to Daoism and found it as unsatisfying. By then he was practicing as a barrister, but falling ill he took to opium for relief. For eighteen months he grew worse and, expecting him to die, his friends dressed him in his grave-clothes. But in spite of the famine he recovered, except for his addiction. Then he heard of the essay competition run by David Hill and won the prize. But he did not dare to go and claim it.

I had heard many reports that foreigners could bewitch people, and I feared to fall under their influence ... I feared bewitchment, but I feared to lose the thirty taels. [So he took the risk and came face to face with David Hill.] One glance, one word, it was enough. As stars fade before the rising sun, so did 'his presence dissipate the idle rumours I had heard. All trace of my fear was gone ... I beheld his kindly eye and remembered the words of Mencius, 'If a man's heart is not right his eyes bespeak it.' I was in the presence of a true man ... Mr Hill led me to the gate, God caused me to enter, Jesus led me on. I remember weeping as I read how He died for me. Trusting Him I ceased to doubt.

One after another the Christians told their own story of how they had come to faith in Christ, and Hudson Taylor enjoyed every minute. His own role, unsought and unquestioned by any at the time or afterwards, was *de facto* that of a chief pastor, a bishop over other pastors and evangelists. The denominational churches did not challenge it; the general conferences of missions tacitly recognised it, for no title or comment was necessary; and three hundred Chinese and foreign preachers of the gospel looked to him as their leader. The new churches of Shanxi contained men and women of God already playing the part of pastors, elders and deacons. On the second day of the conference Hudson Taylor and his south Shanxi colleagues ordained them to serve the various local churches. Hsi Shengmo he ordained to a general charge as 'watcher over and feeder of the sheep of God' in the extensive area he already served under the prompting of the Holy Spirit. 'He is indefatigable in visiting the sick (and) helping those in any trouble,' Hoste wrote. Hsi was in fact the pastor-in-chief, acknowledged by all to be their leader with the necessary authority. But he had been a Christian less than ten years, so a free hand without the dignity of a title as supervisor was the wisest course.[789] After the baptism of fifty-six men and women and a communion service, they scattered to their farms, for it was harvest time.

The missionaries and leading Chinese went on to Linfen for a second conference, this time with the Xi Xian and Daning

Christians, and Hoste and Cassels. Mr Qü of Daning told his story of conversion and flogging, ending with the words, 'The official now wants to take away my degree, but I count it as nothing. Jesus has a greater glory in store for me.' Holding a degree he could not legally be flogged. But what (corrupt) mandarin 'could stop his enemies from beating him'? He too was ordained a pastor before the conference ended.

Ahead lay the long journey from Linfen to Hanzhong but first Pastor Hsi invited Hudson Taylor, Stevenson, Dr Edwards and Stanley Smith to his home for the weekend, while Beauchamp, Studd and Herbert Taylor went on to Quwo and returned to visit the churches with Hsi and Stevenson, on his way via Taiyuan to Tianjin and Shanghai.

At Daning, while Hsi and Qü the two literary graduates preached the gospel on the main street of the city, where Qü had been flogged, John Stevenson examined new candidates for baptism. There and at Qü's village twelve miles away, nineteen attested believers were baptised in the river. 'When, it was clearly pointed out that their profession would involve them in persecution and even death . . . and it was up to them whether . . . they would still continue to be Christians, they eagerly said, "Rather let life go than Christ."' Fourteen years later Shanxi became the scene of the most appalling massacres of Christians. One of these men was among the first to suffer.[790]

'A little man to sort of steer' (1886–87)

Cassels had already been in Shanxi longer than intended. He wanted to reach the unevangelised regions of eastern Sichuan and to pioneer a new church on Anglican principles. It troubled him to be where the established practices (of baptism, communion and ordination) were so different. He discussed it with John Stevenson after the Hongtong ordinations, but who if not the missionaries were to perform them? Two missionary couples were to be married soon, and as a minister of the Established Church his presence,

all assumed, could spare them the long, taxing journey to the coast and back. He reluctantly agreed to wait while Beauchamp and Studd accompanied Hudson Taylor to Hanzhong and (John Stevenson hoped) through Sichuan. Hoste and Stanley Smith chose to stay where they were needed and welcome in a thriving church.

Ironically, when the marriages were reported to the Registrar at Somerset House, London, their validity was questioned and registration refused by the Bishop of London also. It took William Sharp, the lawyer on the London Council, and 'learned counsel' until May 1887 to get the British Government to agree that marriages by Cassels in the interior of China without the presence of a consular official were indeed valid. But not until January 28, 1890, could the London Council finally minute the fact that the Foreign Secretary, Lord Salisbury, had assured William Sharp that he would instruct the consular service in China to recognise such marriages. The complexities of an expanding society were unavoidable. When the time came for Cassels to leave Daning in early November 1886, he could hardly tear himself away. The people were in tears. But after he reached Sichuan where he was the only licensed minister within hundreds of miles, he quickly earned his nickname, 'the Travelling Joiner'.[791]

Pastor Hsi was praying that Dixon Hoste would be appointed to Hongtong but in the autumn it was Stanley Smith who invited him to come. The way he put it, Hoste confessed, 'ruffled (me) in my spirit'. 'SPS' let it be known that he would be the leader and take decisions. Then how about asking the directors for a younger colleague? Hoste replied, aware of the 'loss of face' involved! But 'the Spirit of God probed me.' To be unwilling would mean 'parting company with the Lord Jesus Christ, who dwells with the humble ones, those who willingly go down.' So he went. And marvelled at the spiritual power in Stanley Smith. 'He was full of the Spirit . . . The more he was willing to let Pastor Hsi keep his natural position, the more God seemed to bless him.'

In the spring of 1887 they held another, greater conference at Hongtong with 300 attending and 216 being baptised at one time. But among seasoned missionaries apprehension and criticism were outspoken. Either some had been kept waiting too long, or some had been baptised too hastily, or this was a small 'mass movement', until then unknown in China. Time gave the answer. Five years later, 135 had remained faithful, 50 had backslidden mostly to opium, 20 were difficult to trace, 7 had transferred to other churches, and four had died. Fewer than 20 had returned to idolatry.[792]

Hoste and Stanley Smith went up to Taiyuan to study Chinese for some weeks without interruption, leaving Pastor Hsi to use their rooms at Hongtong. To a few disaffected Christians this was the last straw. Good man though Hsi was, his weak points were a quick temper and a suspicious mind, both liable to alienate those who suffered as a result. Careful as Hudson Taylor had been not to make Hsi look superior to the others, jealousy of Hsi's natural authority was ready to be voiced. That he should occupy the missionaries' quarters looked like arrogance. And Hsi spoke unwisely about it. While they were away, his colleague in the opium refuge work turned violently against him. The young church, swollen by the addition of new members, was split in two, some loyal to Hsi, some 'swayed by the vitriolic fury of Fan and his adherents'.

This Satanic attack continued for several months, followed by years of trouble. Fan and an angry crowd invaded the Mission premises, Fan armed with a sword, his temper out of control. More sober men restrained him. But they drove Hsi out of the place shouting, 'Down to Pingyang!' and took him as a prisoner before Benjamin Bagnall, by then leader of the Mission in Shanxi. Surrounded by raving, angry men, 'Hsi's perfect calmness and self-control' impressed Bagnall, but for hours he could make no headway. Hsi was in mortal danger, with Fan rushing at him time and again with his sword upraised. Bagnall 'felt as if in hell', in the devil's presence. He secretly arranged for a horse to be brought, and at a critical moment himself seized Fan for long enough to let Hsi mount and gallop away.

The immediate crisis was over, but fierce opposition continued. Fan disrupted Hsi's refuges and opened rival ones of his own, close to Hsi's, selling his medicines more cheaply. He accused Hsi of every evil for which the slightest pretext could be found, and hired disreputable men to spread lies about him. A plausible young man gained access to the Hongtong refuge and administered drugs to a patient of high social standing, who died. Pastor Hsi feared all the consequences falling on his own head. He prayed and fasted before showing himself—and found not only the patient's family in a conciliatory frame of mind, but he young man who had been arrested admitting his responsibility.[793]

When Dixon Hoste returned from Taiyuan, on hearing what had happened (Stanley Smith having gone to the coast), his loyalty to Hsi made him also the butt of animosity. What should they do? Strong disciplinary action in the divided church would certainly exacerbate the trouble. They decided to ask God to vindicate the truth and demonstrate to all the rights and wrongs of the matter. Hsi turned the other cheek and gave himself to praying and working on quietly as he had opportunity. Gradually men and women returned to him. As the months passed Fan began to alienate his followers by misconduct and inefficiency, while Hsi's patient, prayerful spirit restored confidence in him. After one of his sessions of prayer he became convinced that the end was in sight. He let it be widely known that within three months the spurious refuges would all fail and close. Fan's 'whole movement sank into disrepute' and before the three months were over the last one was dissolved. This factor alone brought back many who had been deceived, and Hsi's position as the leading pastor was confirmed.

The relationship between Hoste and Hsi had through this bitter experience undergone a change. Never an easy colleague, Pastor Hsi required unfailing humility and understanding in any missionary who was to stay with him. Hoste stayed for ten years, until Hsi died. But others including Bagnall became embroiled in open ill-feeling and antagonism to Hsi in which Hudson Taylor eventually had to intervene, giving Hoste the difficult task of superintending the district. Hoste wrote:

(Hsi) was rather an extreme case, because all the circumstances were extreme. Here was a man of exceptional force of character and organizing power, and whose education and position gave him weight, a man of exceptionally deep spiritual life. He had never had missionary supervision ... It was our place to recognise him in (this) position. Not to become his helpers ... one of his lieutenants; that you cannot be. The missionary should ... recognise to the full Hsi's God-given position ... not be blind to his limitations but ... remedy (them) ... win his love and confidence ... You will need grace with him and he ... with you ... We just grew together.[794]

Even before the Fan episode, Stanley Smith had proposed tackling the city of Lungan (or Lu'an, now Changzhi), seventy-five miles east of Linfen. On his return to Shanxi he began work there, adding Lucheng, a few miles to the north, later on. But Hoste had recognised the whole 'church' in south Shanxi as being indigenous, the fruit of vibrant spiritual life in the Chinese themselves. 'I do feel that I can only be of any use by being where the Master would have me; and that one might only go and do a lot of mischief by pushing into work which the Lord wanted to do through (the Chinese).'[795]

Stanley Smith had had a very different approach to Pastor Hsi and Hongtong.

He was the missionary in charge; I was just helping him at first, [Hoste wrote]. While he is a man of great vigour and great momentum, he isn't the man to run a big thing; he hasn't got that sort of mind. (His bright, cheery, genial, winning way was so necessary in order to warm up the people and restore them to a measure of love and confidence in a foreigner.) ... He is such a sweet-tempered man ... he wouldn't want to drive anybody, but he plunged

along [he acted precipitately] and Pastor Hsi looked rather grim, but still he loved and appreciated him ... The Spirit of God seemed sometimes just to fill the place when he was preaching ... He is a stroke [the pace-setter in the university boats] rather than a cox. It was a cox that was wanted, because Pastor Hsi was perfectly well able to stroke the boat ... What you want is a little man to sort of steer [while Pastor Hsi did the work].

I thoroughly saw, right from the beginning, that the man [Hsi] was a bishop (as the other church leaders recognised in time) and Mr Taylor had made him a bishop ... Hsi got gentler and mellower as the years went by.

Through this experience, Dixon Hoste's wisdom and spirituality became deepened, and the rightness of his attitude and policy could not but be noted by those who watched him. John Stevenson and Hudson Taylor recognised in him another outstanding leader in the making. In his thinking he was in fact far ahead of the average missionary of his day. Two missionary generations were to pass before a determined attempt was made on a large scale in China to apply these principles (of establishing indigenous leadership), enunciated by the SPCK in the early eighteenth century; by Charles Gutzlaff in 1849–50; re-echoed by Henry Venn with qualifications in 1851; by William Burns; by the English Presbyterian George Smith before 1878, and by John Livingston Nevius in greater detail in 1864, 1880 and 1885–86; as well as by Hudson Taylor from 1870 onwards (see note 795). By the twentieth century, when Roland Allen, Dr Thomas Cochrane and others through their publications brought the missionary world back to these first principles, the difficulty of extricating missions from the webs of alien methods and apparatus they had spun for themselves, and of freeing the Chinese church from dependence on foreign funds and initiatives had become almost insuperable. The drastic surgery of Mao's revolution was needed to effect emancipation.

In August 1887 John Stevenson returned to Shanxi, to put before Pastor Hsi the suggestion that his opium refuges should be greatly increased in number, not only in Shanxi but in neighbouring provinces as well. Archibald Orr Ewing wished to provide the funds for renting premises if Hsi would choose the places, run the refuges, find and train the staffs, and supervise the evangelism. Coming at a time when opposition to him was at its height, Hsi was encouraged. Fan and his faction were a threat only in south Shanxi. Reassured by Stevenson, whom Hsi admired, he accepted the challenge. Orr Ewing's nickname among Shanxi Christians was 'Mr Glory-face', an affectionate play on his Chinese surname Yong (Glory) and the light in his eye.

They began together in the Pingyao plain, south of Taiyuan, and opened eight refuges. Opium smokers in Wenxi, a hundred miles south of Hongtong, pleaded with Hsi to open a refuge for them. Five refuges resulted, extending from Puzhou in the sharp angle of the Yellow River (Huang He) in the south-west, to Jincheng (then known as Tsechou) (see map 2.32: p 281), in the south-east of Shanxi. Across the great river in Henan five more were opened, and one at Nanho, over the Zhili border. But perhaps most gratifying were the two refuges in Shaanxi, at Xi'an the capital, and at Weinan on the Wei River halfway between Xi'an and Puzhou at the Yellow River crossing. Because of the danger and difficulty he expected to meet with, Hsi undertook the Xi'an venture himself. On the way there he made the acquaintance of a Muslim military mandarin, a general, who hearing that Hsi practiced medicine and opium cures, helped him to find premises and as an addict put himself in Hsi's hands. His cure led other mandarins to come for treatment, and a grateful old gentleman whose sons had been cured, presented the refuge with an honorific tablet for the guest-hall praising its promoters.

After years of resistance to attempts by missionaries and Christian Chinese to gain a footing in Xi'an, opposition ended. The Hunanese ringleader was out-influenced, and when a Swedish missionary made another attempt he was successful.[796]

After Pastor Hsi's death on February 19, 1896, the refuge work went on, combining spiritual and medical means to secure the release of opium-slaves from the devil and the drug he used. In 1906 Albert Lutley of the CIM stated that since its inception 'probably not less' than 303,000 men and women had been treated, and 'probably more than 1,000 converts have been admitted to the Church by baptism, who first became interested in the gospel through these refuges.'[797]

Sichuan 'claimed' (1886–87)

Beauchamp and Studd were on their way to Hanzhong with Hudson Taylor. Cassels was soon to follow. Already, well before 'the full tide' conference with John Stevenson of May 25–31, 1886, Cecil and Arthur Polhill-Turner had made their first pioneering journey into Sichuan, 'the size of three Englands' with only Chongqing and Chengdu occupied by Protestant missionaries. With months of sound language learning behind them, and eleven months' experience in China to their credit, they had set out from Hanzhong with Chinese companions on Cecil's twenty-sixth birthday, February 23. Seven days on foot brought them to Bazhong (then Pachou) where they preached and sold books for

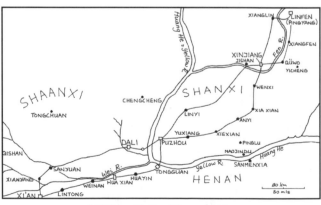

2.58 The Linfen-Xi'an corridor

three days before moving on to Langzhong (Paoning), four days' walk away. Eventually, both cities were to become strong points of the church in eastern Sichuan. Bazhong was to become Arthur Polhill's home for ten years, and Langzhong Cassel's base and the heart of the Anglican field, but only after months of opposition and frustration.

From Langzhong they tramped westwards for eight days to Chengdu and for two weeks saw how Samuel Clarke (unrelated to George) worked in and around 'this magnificent city'. The Clarkes had just lost their colleagues J. H. Riley and his wife Jane Kidd (see pp 385–86, 469) in tragic circumstances. Returning to Langzhong with its mulberry orchards and hilltop pagoda above the Jialing River, the Polhill brothers put up in an inn and 'worked' the city for a month. Finally they tramped the 150 miles back to Hanzhong and the May Conference with John Stevenson, fully convinced that they were on the right course and should formally join the CIM. 'We had in God's name claimed Sichuan, and thrown down the gauntlet to Satan,' they declared with the zest of youth and inexperience. Time would show what defying Satan could cost.[798]

Eighteen years had passed since Griffith John and Alexander Wylie had prospected the province of Sichuan in 1868 by travelling from Hankou through Chongqing, Chengdu and Hanzhong (see pp 89, 204). And nine years since John McCarthy had crossed in 1877 from Wanxian to Nanchong (Shunking) and down to Chongqing. A house had been rented in that year, and using Chongqing as their base, Cameron, Nicoll, Easton, Parker, Riley, Samuel Clarke and Baller had made wide evangelistic journeys. Mollman of the Bible Society and the American Presbyterian Leaman had joined them from time to time. 1881 had seen the arrival of the American Methodist Episcopal missionaries at Chongqing, and the occupation of Chengdu by the CIM. By comparison, it was as if London and Glasgow had been 'occupied' in Britain, the rest of the British Isles remaining almost untouched. The Xichang region beyond the high mountain ranges in the far south-west, could be thought of as Devon and Cornwall. Two more Englands filling the North Sea beyond the east coast of Britain would then represent East Sichuan. Langzhong, halfway between Chongqing and Hanzhong, was strategically placed, from which to penetrate and develop the evangelisation of this great eastern half of Sichuan. 'Occupation' was so far only a foothold from which to begin.

Stevenson had gone north to the Shanxi conferences after writing to Hudson Taylor that Cecil Polhill had donated the rental of one or more premises at Langzhong and was preparing to return there. 'God has opened first this station (Hanzhong) to give us the means of opening northern and eastern Sichuan.' In Uganda at this very time thirty-two Christians were being burned alive on one great pyre but in China there was liberty of movement and careful progress was meeting only mild resistance.

On June 7 (as Hudson Taylor reached Dagutang on his Guangxin River journey), Edward Pearse, Mr Ho (the first Hanzhong believer), a teacher named Liang and Cecil Polhill set out from Hanzhong again for Langzhong. The city when they arrived was full of examination candidates with the usual high flash-point of emotions. After a week they judged it best to leave Ho and Liang to look for a place to rent while they themselves went on to Chongqing and back, preaching and selling portions of the Bible on the way. As they entered Chongqing on July 3, they saw the American Episcopal Mission's new building in a commanding position on a hilltop, in the process of being wrecked. And on their way to find the CIM they were told the house had been demolished, and were cautioned to hire sedan chairs in which to keep out of sight. The place was standing but ransacked, and the thirty foreigners in Chongqing were said to be under protection at the magistrate's *yamen*. Everyone had lost everything he possessed. The Catholic cathedral and other buildings had been razed to the ground. Mr Bourne, the British Resident, had to be muffled up and hustled through the mob in the guise of a prisoner under arrest, and with all the Roman Catholics, was at the governor's *yamen*.

Pearse and Cecil Polhill were taken and held with the others in cramped quarters. There news reached them from Hudson Taylor of the seventy-two baptisms at Hongtong and Linfen. After two weeks the magistrate sent all but George Nicoll down the Yangzi at midnight, forbidding Pearse and Cecil Polhill to return to Langzhong. Nicoll had begged permission to stay, on the ground that he was responsible for the Mission's obligations to local Chinese. Lest the fugitives be attacked on the way, the magistrate personally escorted them through the streets to small, unpretentious boats.

All except Pearse and Polhill reached Yichang in safety. These two had made clandestine arrangements to have their own boat, and two ponies in another, so that after passing the major city of Wanxian they could pay the boatmen off and strike northwards across deep country to Hanzhong. J. J. Coulthard had once made this crossing by small roads with poor inns, and reported rough going. Five weeks after starting overland they were back again at Hanzhong feeling well initiated into the province. Hudson Taylor, Beauchamp, Studd and Herbert Taylor arrived from Shanxi a few days later, after an even more rigorous journey.

'The shock troops' of missions (August–November 1886)

Montagu Beauchamp carried clear recollections for many years of the August journey he made with Hudson Taylor from Shanxi to Hanzhong.

> Mr Taylor, feeling the heat so intensely, gave up all hope of continuing that journey beyond Pingyang unless he could travel by night; but after a very small amount of (it) C. T. Studd and Lewis fell out [and followed by day], Herbert Taylor dragged on, but Mr Taylor on a mule and myself on foot pushed on by night and reached Hanchung some two days before the

others, though Herbert Taylor was only a day behind us.[799]

Crossing the Yellow River, 'running high and very dangerous', they nearly came to grief. In an overloaded ferry-boat with carts, mules and passengers closely packed together, they began to roll in the strong current as they were swept miles downstream. Three or four mules toppled overboard, which saved the situation; and they reached the other side.

> A remarkable thing about Mr Taylor was his power of endurance, and his ability to sleep in the daytime, at any time ... No matter what the surroundings (he) was always the same man with the same spirit with food, without food, with rest, without it ... I would often carry him through the rivers which were all in flood [crossing strong streams waist-deep Beauchamp would have Hudson Taylor on his shoulders and a Chinese each side to steady them]. Still he would not be hindered—we would push on ... With so much rain we often got soaked through. One thing Mr Taylor never left behind was his medicine chest.

> Night travelling is one of the hardest experiences I have ever had, because I could not sleep by day. When I did manage to sleep, I would find Mr Taylor looking after me, rigging up a mosquito net to keep the flies off. While walking at night I have been so sleepy ... I have fallen right down. Mr Taylor rode but I preferred to walk. (He carried two pillows, one for the shoulder, the other for the thigh) and we each had a plaid ... We often used to lie down on the roadside.

At other times when they spent a night in an inn and Beauchamp woke to feed the mules before daylight, he would see Hudson Taylor reading his Bible by candlelight. 'He used to sing as we went along.' In this way they covered 2,500 Chinese *li* (about 888 miles), to reach Hanzhong on September 7, and the inevitable accumulation of letters. There he learned of the Chongqing riot and faced the choice between risking prolonged delay if he crossed Sichuan, or cutting his travels short. Reluctantly he accepted the inevitable, but first held a Shanxi-type conference with the Chinese and missionaries. 'I remember Mr Taylor saying,' Beauchamp wrote, 'we were not out in China just to settle down to girls' schools. The ladies must be up and out and amongst the women.'

Hudson Taylor's travel log noted that after a day of fasting and prayer for Sichuan on the 14th, Beauchamp and Cecil Polhilll set off for Chengdu on the 17th, and Studd with Arthur Polhill on the 18th, for East Sichuan, 'The shock troops' of Protestant missions in China, the CIM, were living up to their growing reputation, with Hudson Taylor their 'general' firmly in the front line.[800] He stayed two days to help Dr William Wilson with some major operations before taking Edward Pearse's little daughter down the Han River rapids with him to Wuchang on October 14. 'But for (the Chongqing riots) I should have been on my way to Sichuan ere now,' he told Stevenson. Once again his greatly hoped for tour of the province had been thwarted. He could not afford to be immobilised as Pearse and Cecil Polhill had been for weeks on end. Instead he called the China Council of newly appointed provincial superintendents to meet at Anqing in November.[801]

John Stevenson had said that the Wilsons were all they should be as missionaries and colleagues. The Chinese of Hanzhong greatly admired the doctor's ability to make his own medicines from herbs and minerals bought in the city. But his electrical equipment, a 'galvanic battery', an electro-magnet, electric bell and telegraph, 'all made in this house by native workmen, to my direction', amazed them. When the chief mandarin's father had been given up by the best local doctors as beyond cure, he had recovered under Wilson's treatment. The mandarin arrived one day with an honorific signboard in black enamel with large gold characters extolling the virtues of the doctor's skills and hospital. When the formalities of the presentation were over, Wilson demonstrated his instruments and equipment until, with the ice broken and friendship established, the high dignitary was trying in vain to pick a copper coin out of a bowl of electrified water. Prejudice died hard, but responded to medicine and friendliness. Hanzhong was a success. After only seven years since the Kings (the first missionaries) had moved in, a thriving church of ninety communicants and many more under instruction had only one Christian worker, the teacher, paid by the Mission. All others were serving voluntarily while retaining their previous occupations or assisting the evangelists at ten outlying chapels.

After visiting Griffith John, David Hill and Consul Gardner at Hankou, Hudson Taylor pressed on to Shanghai, in time to meet the eighty-one-year-old George Müller on a brief visit to China. After consulate formalities at Zhenjiang he conducted Herbert's wedding at Yangzhou, the scene of their escape from the riot eighteen years before, and on November 11 was on his way up the Yangzi again, taking bride and groom, Maria and a group of other young women to Dagutang en route for the Guangxin River experiment. He then returned to Anqing in time to meet his China Council.

Two years in China packed with achievement and advance had also, from the moment of his arrival on March 3, 1885, been one of the most painful periods of his life;[802] but he had had no premonition of peril to the very existence of the Mission. News of illnesses and deaths inexorably added to the pain. That two of the Seventy should have died within a few weeks of each other in 1885 was distressing, but the sequence of sorrows following the birth of twins to the Rileys in Chengdu moved Hudson Taylor to the depths. On October 12 Jane (Kidd) died of puerperal fever, and their colleague Fanny Stroud (aged twenty-seven) took charge of the three children. But soon Riley himself became ill, with symptoms which made others fear he would not recover, seeing double and being unable to stand unsupported. He asked Fanny Stroud to bring the children and servants and travel with him down the Yangzi to Shanghai. Before they reached Yichang he was having convulsions, fit after fit in one day. The consul, Mr Gregory, gave up his own rooms in the consulate to them, but Riley 'needed nursing as only a wife could nurse, and so Miss Stroud and he concluded to be married at once'. The ceremony was performed at his bedside, and they went on to Shanghai. 'I never saw such a wreck as Mr Riley is,' Hudson Taylor said. Six weeks later, on April 19, 1886, Riley died in a convulsion, but on June 5 Hudson Taylor was still full of the pathos and nobility of the situation when he wrote to Jennie: '(Fanny Stroud's marriage) is about the noblest thing I have ever come across in my life. (Of his) recovery the doctor gave her no hope; just to nurse him to the grave and care as mother for the three children . . . is what few would have done . . . She had none of the joys but all the anxieties, toils and sorrows of a wife.'[803]

His own heartaches could be intense. Separation from Jennie often seemed intolerable. Before leaving home he had written an editorial for *China's Millions* saying that costly sacrifice was God's chosen way, for 'though he was rich, yet for your sake he became poor', and 'He emptied Himself'.[804] 'It is crucifixion.' 'Sometimes I feel as if it was killing me, wearing me out.' 'Love to the dear Chicks. I feel as if my heart would break with longing. Let it break. And yours too, darling, if JESUS is glorified.'[805] But the end was in sight.

The 'Book of Arrangements'
(November 1886)

Saturday, November 13, 1886, was historic in the CIM as the day on which the General Director and the Deputy China Director and Superintendents whom he had appointed, met for the first time as the China Council, at Anqing. Only half the superintendents were present, McCarthy, Baller, Dorward and William Cooper. Meadows was not well enough to come. George Clarke and Benjamin Bagnall, James Cameron and George Easton were either on furlough or too far away to make the long journey on this occasion.[806] The meeting marked the climax of two years of thought and consultation, first with the London Council and by degrees with the individuals who agreed to be provincial superintendents. Their business was to achieve harmonious cooperation, by defining the practices which had been evolved by common consent over the years, and what are now called job descriptions of the various types of missionary. It was therefore to be largely administrative, much of it the dry mechanics of organisation; but clarification of the wording of the 'Principles and Practice', and a new proposition put forward by John Stevenson were to be considered. What follows may look tedious, but to the surprise of all who took part, within a few weeks it had become dynamite.

The Mission had grown to 187 missionary members, and the practical outworking of the 'P and P' needed to be down in black and white if all were to understand and apply it uniformly. Some leaflets already existed. A simple concise handbook was the obvious means to that end. It was to sum up all that the council agreed together. With it no one in any remote location need be in doubt about how to act, or lose time and energy consulting others about the commoner subjects, while the leaders would be left free to advise in unusual circumstances. Within the general framework the rank and file would be no less at liberty to show initiative. Most of it was obvious: instructive only to the uninitiated, and a restraint only on the individualist. To members of the London Council it would be a window on the obscure administrative domain of the directors in China. It was to be a little book of agreed 'arrangements' rather than rules and regulations. For supporters Hudson Taylor wrote an account of the council's meetings, in *China's Millions*. Neither he nor John Stevenson had any inkling of danger ahead. The Mission still works on the same pattern, with its periodically updated *Manual* and its graded language study requirements.[807]

'Several days' were first spent in prayer, with fasting on alternate days, for the tentacles of the Mission were stretching further and further into previously unworked regions, and more and more members were dependent upon each other's support in what was primarily a spiritual undertaking. Seventy-seven were experienced seniors, but no fewer than one hundred and ten were young and more vulnerable. When the council's agenda was tackled, the first subject to be dealt with was language study, their chief tool. John Stevenson had given this a great deal of thought and drafted a course in eight stages. Frederick Baller was formally charged with writing his *Mandarin Primer* and with establishing the Anqing Training Institute, with Robert Landale's help. The council itself was defined as existing 'to assist the Director and his Deputy with its counsel and cooperation in all such matters of gravity as the Director or his Deputy may feel it useful to lay before them'. That it was to be an advisory council and not executive was unquestioned, as the Minute read: 'That the said Council shall stand in the same relationship to the Director and his Deputy with reference to all the affairs of the Mission in China that the Home Council holds with reference to the affairs of the Mission at home.' Administration by directors and superintendents was not to be despotic but in Hudson Taylor's wordss, such as '*always leads the ruler to the Cross, and saves the ruled at the expense of the ruler* . . . Let us all drink into this spirit, then lording on the one hand and bondage on the other will alike be impossible.' He himself knew, all too well, the suffering entailed.

Clarification of the 'P and P' began on the 17th and ended the next day. Some statements as they stood were open to misunderstanding and needed to be rephrased. And the reorganisation of the Mission needed to be incorporated. Instructions for all members in their different capacities, as beginners, women, secretaries, travellers, superintendents and so on, occupied them from November 19 to 23. On the 25th they agreed that large reinforcements should come to China soon, one hundred within one year, and that

Hudson Taylor should return to Britain as soon as possible to promote this.[808] If this was the will of God, as they believed it was, the funds would be forthcoming.

Some difficult problems were discussed and solutions found. The fact that a body of such highly respected men agreed with Hudson Taylor in calling a halt to the actions of some individuals made protests less likely to be strong. For example, friends, sisters, servants or governesses were not in future to be brought to China without prior correspondence and written approval by the China Director (that is, by Hudson Taylor or John Stevenson, whichever was currently in China). This ill-advised practice had become an embarrassment to colleagues, and the mobility or efficiency of a missionary could be severely limited by his ill-assorted household. A carefully worded paragraph about Chinese dress and customs, how to avoid offending the prejudices of the people, and about demanding supposed rights from the mandarins, all based on hard earned experience, led into a thornier subject which had to be firmly stated. The habitual use of CIM premises by travellers and members of very different societies had raised serious issues, even to the withholding of passports. High-handed treatment of the Chinese provoked resentment. Friends of missionaries could not be governed by CIM procedures, but neglect of these had led to violence, not always one-sided. In particular, the display of firearms directly contravened the Mission's principles: 'It is therefore to be understood that none of our missionaries resident in the interior are at liberty to invite their friends for residence or prolonged stay in the premises of the Mission without the written permission of the Superintendent . . . These remarks do not apply to hospitality to travellers passing through.'

Recognizing that considerable economies could be made in the course of time by using telegraphic code words to convey whole sentences, a system known as 'Unicode' was already in use by some business houses. Now a CIM equivalent was to be prepared. Its convenience and versatility, eventually using numerals, resulted in its being adopted not only by the CIM but by secular organisations as well.[809]

Within two weeks the council dispersed, Hudson Taylor, and John Stevenson going to Dagutang to draft the 'Book of Arrangements'. They planned to distribute it in the form of a printer's page proof for comment by the London Council and absent superintendents, before eventually promulgating it. But the practical decisions it embodied were for immediate application. No thought occurred to them that this logical step in the Mission's development would provoke years of disharmony and be the reef on which the CIM could have come to grief.

The 'rich young ruler' (1886–87)

Going back to where we left them in September 1886, Montagu Beauchamp and Cecil Polhill were heading for Chengdu, and Studd with Arthur Polhill for eastern Sichuan. With less than two years' experience in China they were still novices, but their directors had given them a free rein to show their mettle. In each case the journey shaped their lives. To pick up the threads: Arthur made Bazhou (Pachow) his sphere for ten years. Cecil found his niche in the Tibetan marches and embarked on romantic, dangerous adventures. C. T. Studd and a companion daringly went on down to Chongqing in November, and amazed the British Resident by appearing alive and unharmed at his beleaguered consulate (or quarters provided by the magistrate), despite continuing anti-foreign unrest. Mr Bourne invited Studd to stay with him, and they were together when Montagu Beauchamp arrived.[810] He was taken into the magistrate's *yamen* and protected as an unwilling guest until Bourne and Studd persuaded him for his own 'health' to leave by junk down the Yangzi. Between them they saw enough to be convinced that the mainly anti-Catholic rioting had the tacit approval of the viceroy.

So Beauchamp rejoined Hudson Taylor at Dagutang while he was working on the 'Book of Arrangements'. When the time came for them to go on down to Shanghai, Beauchamp witnessed a typical example of Hudson Taylor's spirit. When carriers engaged to take his baggage to the ship arrived to collect it they demanded twice as much in payment as they had agreed on. Hudson Taylor would not yield, unpacked his luggage and wrote letters until after three hours the carriers came to terms. 'The battle was won for the benefit of all others, though to (his own) inconvenience.' He missed his steamer and did not get to Shanghai for Christmas, but the carriers would be less likely to take advantage of other travellers.

Rumour had it that the CIM had benefitted immensely from the wealth of its rich young men. There was truth in it but by no means on the scale alleged not only in Britain. *China's Millions* had to carry a formal denial that the Mission had large investments and sources to tap. The fact was that during C. T. Studd's two months in Chongqing (November–December 1886) official statements reached him of the fortune he had inherited on attaining the age of twenty-five on December 2 the previous year. He had given the matter prolonged thought and even before leaving London had consulted Hudson Taylor. There was no doubt in Hudson Taylor's mind that a life of sacrifice, poured out for Christ and China, made the words of Jesus 'Lay not up . . . treasures on earth' applicable to men like Studd.

'CT' had begun the process of self-denial even before associating himself with the CIM, and had gone further than the others in simplicity of living. He was ascetic to the point of choosing a bench rather than a seat with a back, 'a man who never spared himself, and took no care whatever of his health. Had he not married . . . it is doubtful whether he would have lived as long as he did,' the Polhill brothers wrote.[811] In Chongqing he was reading a 'harmony of the gospels' and came to Christ's words to the rich young ruler a few days before the letters arrived from his solicitor and banker. To him the will of God was stated in black and white. But the Resident refused to sign the papers 'CT' drew up granting power of attorney to his representatives in Britain. 'At the end of two weeks I took it back and he signed it and off the stuff went.' His inheritance was approximately £29,000 (at that time) and he decided to distribute £25,000 first. On January 13, 1887, he sent off four cheques of £5,000 each and five of £1,000 each, investing them in God's bank, he said, at 'a hundredfold', 10,000 per cent: £5,000 each to George Müller for his orphans and foreign missions; to D. L. Moody; to George Holland for God's poor in London; and to the Salvation Army in India—it paid for fifty new officers to be sent out. £1,000 each went to Annie Macpherson, General Booth, Archibald Brown and Dr Barnardo for their work in London's East End, and for similar use to Miss Ellen Smyly in Dublin.

Here we abandon chronological restraints to deal further with this subject of the CIM's 'rich young men'. Montagu Beauchamp kept his own secret for many years. He lived a peripatetic life in the hard school of doing what was required of him, first by assisting Hudson Taylor; then in making a long preaching colportage on foot through Henan to Shanxi and back to Sichuan, and another to Gansu, finally choosing to concentrate on Sichuan. Already more knowledgeable and widely experienced than the relatively static missionaries he found himself amongst, and at first unordained but in an Anglican field, he chafed under the ecclesiastical restrictions imposed upon him. He was known far and wide, speaking Chinese 'fluently and correctly', and often mistaken for a Chinese. Never at a loss how to act or to meet a difficult situation, he was also an attractive, able preacher, unflagging in his work and his praying. The consul at Wanxian paid him the tribute of saying that Beauchamp was so devoted to the Chinese people that he was 'at the beck and call of any coolie'.[812]

Many years later (May 10 but no year given) when he was asked, 'Has the reference to Montagu Beauchamp's having inherited and renounced a quarter of a million been verified?' he replied to Frank Houghton (later Bishop and the CIM's fourth General Director but at the time editor in London): 'Mr Taylor was the only living person who knew of my renunciation of my family estate of a quarter of a million; and he advised me to do so and to remain in China.' That was all. But he was never so well heeled. The audited accounts of the CIM contain no record of a large gift, for he never had it to give. Sir Montagu's father, the 4th baronet, had died in 1874 and the eldest son, Sir Reginald, having no male heir would have bequeathed Langley Park and all that went with it to Montagu—on conditions that he returned home to administer it. For Christ's sake and for China he renounced this possibility. After twenty-five years Montagu was in England when the First World War broke out. He served in the Mediterranean Expeditionary Force as Principal Chaplain, and in North Russia. His second brother, Sir Horace, the 6th baronet, and Montagu's eldest son were both killed at Suvla Bay, Salonika, on August 12th, 1915, and Sir Montagu succeeded to the baronetcy without the fortune. Inheritance mattered little. The cost of discipleship involved greater things.

C. T. Studd's brother had been reading for the Bar, intent on being a barrister, but illness dogged him until his doctors recommended a voyage to Australia. When 'CT' invited George to visit him in China on the way home, 'GB' booked his passage to Shanghai and arrived in May, determined to make his visit brief and to avoid becoming embarrassed by the hot gospel atmosphere of the CIM. In fact, he was to confess, he was 'running away from God'. He had chosen to be the staid and sober kind of Christian, not Charlie's type. On arriving at Shanghai he booked his passage to Japan and created a sensation when he played Studd-quality cricket at the Club.[813] But at the CIM the contrast in atmosphere disturbed him. He envied the peacefulness and contentment of everyone, whatever the news or disturbances. He asked for an explanation. 'Capitulate to Jesus and trust Him for everything', he was told. Worse still, revival meetings were soon to begin. He determined to escape to Japan. But his craving for a heart and mind at peace decided him to acquire it at any price. 'I surrendered to the Lord Jesus, trusting that He would make my will His own.' At a public meeting with cricketers present from the club he described what had happened, cancelled his passage and stayed to face the music.

There was a girl from Northern Ireland at the Mission, Priscilla Stewart, so natural in speaking about Jesus that she was attracting people to him day after day. Charlie was smitten. She went on her way to Dagutang but he pursued her with letters and by October 3 they were engaged. When the final figures of his inheritance were known, he gave away what remained from his distribution, 'mainly to the CIM' but retaining £3,400. When he presented this to his bride before their marriage in January 1888, she said 'Charlie, what did the Lord tell the rich young man to do?' 'Sell all.' 'Well then, we will start clear with the Lord at our wedding.' They sold out and gave the £3,400 to the Salvation Army, before starting work together at Lungan in south Shanxi.

In July 1887 'GB', 'CT' and Archibald Orr Ewing travelled together to Shanxi—in time to play their part in an outbreak of typhus or typhoid (seldom clearly distinguished in those days). 'CT' went down with it first, nursed by 'GB' and Stanley Smith. Then 'CT' nursed Stanley Smith through it. A young missionary, J. H. Sturman, recovered from 'typhus' but died while convalescing at Chefoo. In January W. L. Elliston died of typhoid. After his years as a schoolmaster at Chefoo, he had undertaken to 'open' Huolu in Zhili. At Taiyuan smallpox had taken the life of Dr and Mrs Edwards' infant son, but both parents survived 'typhoid'. In caring for them Archibald Orr Ewing and Dr Stewart each caught it and were nursed

by the BMS missionaries and Adamson of the Bible Society. But W. E. Terry of the CIM succumbed. Only the foundations of the Schofield Memorial Hospital had so far been laid. The cost of discipleship was not measured in monetary terms, as the growing list of widows testified.[814]

A hundred or two (November 1886)

How the idea arose of calling for one hundred new missionaries before the end of 1887 is not known for certain. Hudson Taylor made no mention of it when he was in Shanxi, and when it was put to him he was at first reluctant to adopt it. But on September 16, 1886, John Stevenson wrote to Jennie Taylor from Taiyuan (following his triumphal visits to the churches of south Shanxi): 'We are fully expecting at least 100 *fresh* labourers to arrive in China in 1887. 1 am happy to think that God is very likely to rebuke our small faith by sending many more than the (hundred) . . . The field is opening up most wonderfully.'[815]

Manuscript sources are few, but thirty years later, when the Howard Taylors were writing the second volume of their father's biography, John Stevenson was still in harness as China Director and often consulted by them. Their account of the Hundred is still in print. He had been in the company of four of the Cambridge Seven since Hudson Taylor left Shanxi, and was himself euphoric after what he had seen at Hanzhong. Speaking subsequently of those days, he said: 'I was just thinking and praying about it. We all had visions at that time, and Mr Taylor used to say I was going too fast.' 'We are fully expecting 100' suggests that the others shared his hopes.

John Stevenson reached Shanghai on Monday, October 25, two days after Hudson Taylor (and on the day the aged George Müller visited the CIM in their humble quarters). With such a thought so sharply present in Stevenson's mind it is unlikely that he would not have mentioned it. And with so much on Hudson Taylor's mind, 'going too fast' may have been his reaction, because one hundred was more than half the total strength of the CIM. But his mind was open. Then at Anqing when Stevenson raised the subject, the China Council prayed and fasted over it. If for no other reason a larger Mission would give wider scope for matching colleagues with each other—quite apart from matrimonial choices. On the last day but one, November 25, instead of himself writing to the Mission for the 'end of year day of prayer', Hudson Taylor deputed Stevenson to write. He noted that twenty-two new members had arrived in China during 1886 and went on: 'Our needs are, however, so great that this increase has appeared as nothing, and I would suggest that definite prayer for no less than one hundred new workers during 1887 be offered on our fast day, and also that it may be a subject of daily prayer afterwards.'[816]

Writing to Jennie two days later, Hudson Taylor himself said, 'We are praying for one hundred new missionaries in 1887. The Lord help in the selection and provide the means.' When they reached Dagutang and were working on the 'Book of Arrangements', the complexities of administration lay harshly before them. Already Hudson Taylor was carrying as heavy a burden as he thought he could bear, and from London evidence was mounting that the staff were no less hard pressed. For one hundred suitable men and women to be corresponded with, assessed, prepared and dispatched within one year would increase the strain immeasurably. 'Yes,' John Stevenson contended, 'but with needs so great, how can we ask for less?' Deploying them would present no problem. Far more could be placed, with China so wide open. The expense was another matter, but if this was 'of God', the funds would come in.

Walking up and down as he dictated letters to Lewis his secretary, Hudson Taylor repeated what he had written to Jennie. 'A hundred new missionaries in 1887.' John Stevenson saw Lewis look up incredulously. So did Hudson Taylor, and a surge of certainty seemed to come over him. 'After that, he went beyond me altogether. [Stevenson recalled]. Never shall I forget the conviction with which he said: "If you

showed me a photograph of the whole hundred taken in China, I could not be more sure than I am now."'

This whole incident once more belies the claim sometimes heard, that Hudson Taylor was an autocrat. No evidence in the sources supports that epithet, even in the extreme circumstances he was approaching.

They cabled to London, 'Banded prayer next year hundred new workers send soon as possible,' and Hudson Taylor wrote to Jennie:

> We are ready for receiving fifty, say, of the hundred at once ... The LORD did great things for us when He gave us Stanley Smith's party. He is able to do more. Let us honour Him with great expectations. [And to an inner circle] Some of us are hoping that His 'exceedingly abundantly' may mean fifty or sixty more missionaries besides the hundred for whom we are asking.[817]

It would cost fully £5,500 (equivalent to £200,000 today?) just to equip and send a hundred to China. If the bulk of this were to come in the usual small donations, the letters of thanks would alone need additional staff. The year 1886 was ending at a high point.

They wound up affairs at Dagutang and returned to Shanghai. On December 29, before two days instead of one of fasting and prayer, at last he could write, 'My darling, my own darling! I have wired tonight. Leaving on January 6th. I (am) almost wild with joy.' After he sailed, an enigmatic note from Stevenson followed him. 'Let me apologise for teasing you so much before you left.'[818]

In the two years, Hudson Taylor had travelled in nine provinces and covered as many miles in territory new to him as any member of the Mission. The scale of expansion which the China Inland Mission had entered upon was unprecedented among Protestant missions anywhere in the world and the prototype of the twentieth century international phenomenon. Many were to play their substantial part in the mobilizing of 'the Hundred', but although others had initiated it, the task of publicizing the appeal and arousing the church to take it up, in the event fell to Hudson Taylor more than anyone. He was to work so hard that Jennie feared for his life and pleaded with him to slow down. Nothing, no one, could stop him. Once convinced, he believed he was doing the will of God.

There was ice on the decks when he sailed from Shanghai on January 6, 1887, with the companions he might have chosen had he been given the choice—Adam Dorward and William Cooper, escorting Mary Ann Nicoll.[819] Dorward had been nine years in China and owed it to his mother to visit her. But in September the Yellow River burst its banks and flooded parts of Henan. To them his duty was clear. Dorward left Britain again on October 6, returned to China and travelled a thousand miles, mostly on foot, taking relief to the devastated area.[820] Cooper was to marry in London a girl who had gone to China in 1881, the same year as he himself.

At Marseilles Hudson Taylor parted from the others to spend a few days with William Berger at Cannes. From there Hudson Taylor wired to Jennie, 'Leave Nice midnight meet Hudson Paris Wednesday midnight old hotel near Gare (du) Nord', their usual trysting place. So they reached London together.

Division of the period after 1875 into separate books is artificial. Dictated only by convenience in handling what proved to be too much for one last volume without mutilation, it ends Part VI, 'Assault on the Nine', in full flight on several themes.

The nine provinces have yielded to the assault with the sole exception of Hunan. Even Taiwan, Manchuria and Mongolia have pioneers of other societies at work. Only Tibet and Turkestan remain, not untouched but unworked beyond the fringes.

'Occupation' as a first objective has been followed by 'consolidation' in the establishment of local churches, the nucleus of expansion. 'Reinforcement' of the pioneers with colleagues, and strengthening their lines of communication by the occupation of intervening cities have prepared the way for systematic evangelism of each area. The shock troops dig in.

Hudson Taylor's health at times has been failing. Satanic hostility, never absent, has taken new forms, 'deceiving if possible even the elect'. Portents of 'trouble ahead' suggest the withdrawal of the protecting hand of God. Disease has taken many. The dynasty is crumbling; violence is threatening. The saga, unbroken, is building up to its climax, and its thrilling sequel.

Part VII's triumphant affirmation, '*It is not death to die! It's glorious!*' takes us through the massacres and Hudson Taylor's death, the Revolutions of 1911 and Mao Zedong, to the end of the 'open century' and beyond.

Part VII

IT IS NOT DEATH TO DIE

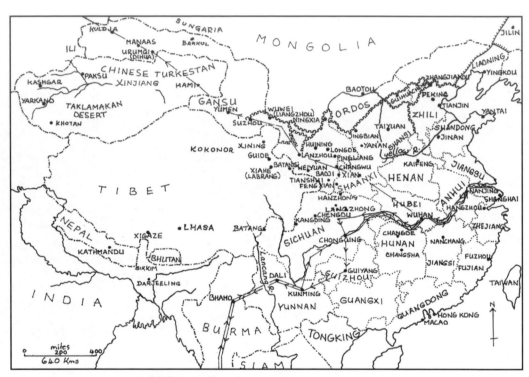

2.59 Extremeties of the empire: the longest journeys

Preface to Part VII

The exclamation 'It is not death to die!' came from an eye-witness at the bedside of a dying Chinese. Briefly regaining consciousness, this Christian seemed to have been to the very 'door of heaven'. Inexpressibly happy, she said. 'I have seen the Lord! I have seen heaven! . . . I wish you could come There is *nothing to fear.*' Whether seen in reality or not was immaterial, the truth is that death is a gateway, a transition in the eternal life already being enjoyed (see p 396).

In this last volume, thousands of Christians suffer and die at the murderous hands of the so-called 'Boxers'. Scores of missionaries and their children are among them, some already known to us from the preceding books. The CIM loses more than any other mission. But Bunyan's imagery proved true in the experience of the victims. The last river was deep and cold, but those crossing it knew that death was only physical. The welcome beyond already looked glorious. The empress dowager's great gamble failed, as more recent attempts to stifle the gospel have also failed. The living proof of martyr-seed being sown in China's good soil is the still-expanding church today. Imprisonment and death go so far but seldom far enough to stop its progress. As for Hudson Taylor, his passing marked a triumph of its own, at Changsha, capital of Hunan, the last province to allow the gospel to take root.

The previous part showed how obedience to God's direction, and determination 'not to try but to do it', brought success within ten or fifteen years. The far corners of the Chinese empire were penetrated and partly 'occupied' for Christ by the planting of his Church. Christian literature was widely distributed, sooner or later to germinate in people's minds. Not all the individuals introduced to the reader can be followed through the story. In the late nineteenth century, rank and family,

sport and education brought the spotlight to bear on the Cambridge Seven. So what became of them and of others who showed great promise needs to be included. And a few more must be singled out from the hundreds, even thousands, who joined them. When Hudson Taylor died, many believed his mission would disintegrate like 'a rope of sand'. But the work was God's, so it lived on and flourished, and 'he being dead still speaks'.

Inseparable from all the excitement and activity is the dark skein of Satan's attacks on the Mission: on its weaker members, its most valued ones, and its leaders. Good men and women faltered and failed, fell ill and died, or were murdered in their prime. Time and again Hudson Taylor recognised in his writings the essentially spiritual battle and the devilish enemy they faced. 'Your enemy the devil' was the apostle Peter's phrase (1 Peter 5.8). 'For we are not unaware of his schemes,' St Paul agreed (2 Corinthians 2.1), and, 'The weapons we fight with are not the weapons of the world' (2 Corinthians 10.4). 'Let Satan rage—God reigns,' Hudson Taylor repeated defiantly as the survival of the Mission was threatened by internal discord and disruption. How close he came to that disaster this book reveals. Beaten down, almost to surrender, it was not how he felt but how he acted that speaks most loudly.

Earlier biographies had to respect the feelings of people still alive. More than fifty years later the facts can be told, as a lesson on how 'your enemy the devil . . . like a roaring lion' looks for victims to attack and new 'devices' to employ. Failing on the spiritual front in Hudson Taylor's day, Satan turned to physical annihilation and failed again. Mass expulsions in our own day proved to be the best thing that could have happened to the Chinese church. How Hudson Taylor handled strong challenges not only to his leadership but to the founding principles of the CIM deserves attention: how he made his point without being dictatorial or alienating the colleagues whose convictions differed from his own.

Part VI ended with his return to Britain to face his critics, to justify the Mission's manual of instructions called the 'Book of Arrangements' which was to become such 'dynamite'; and in the face of distrust and impasse to find and send to China the hundred reinforcements needed. Part VII is also the story of reconciliation and unthinkable expansion, ending the solely British phase of the CIM, and making it international and seven times the size it was; 188 on May 26, 1886; 265 in December 1887; and 1,368 in 1934.

Tempted as we always are to include more narrative of a personal nature, of striking conversions and the testimony of new Christians, each has to be judged by the yardstick of relevance to the life and influence of Hudson Taylor and to the broad history of the church in China. To discerning readers, among them many familiar with China and the Chinese, the 'mass of detail' in these 'dull annals' is an ant-hill of industry, alive with significance.

AJB

Acknowledgments to Part VII

My special thanks to Donald Coggan for his kind benediction on my swansong.

I admire the patience of Hodder's David Wavre with my slow progress and his generosity in allowing so many pages; of my wide family in enduring a decade of my preoccupation with work, of my wife in typing thousands of pages of notes and draft manuscripts in her spare time, of Molly Robertson in so cheerfully turning seven much edited typescripts into immaculate copy; of Val Connolly in transforming a long succession of rough maps and engravings into their attractive final form; and of my faithful critics and advisers, Jane Lenon and Howard Peskett in particular, for keeping going to the last gasp.

Mrs W. P. K. Findlay gave me valuable insights into her great-uncle Dr A. W. Douthwaite's notable life in China. To thank her by establishing that he was probably the first Protestant missionary to work in Korea and survive, gives me great pleasure.

I am indebted, too, to Dr Charles A. Curwen of the School of Oriental and African Studies, and to Mr P. D. Coates, HBM consular service (retired), for help in tracing 'General' Mesny.

Frequent enquiries, 'When is the next book due?' have put me in debt to kind readers worldwide. The knowledge that some are in East Asia (not content to wait for the translation now being made) has spurred me on. Much more source material than for the earlier books, and limited time, if not space, have forced me to be more selective. I am sorry we have come to the end.

AJB

2.60 The 15,000 miles Hudson Taylor travelled

21

'Your Enemy the Devil' (1886–90)

"Your enemy the devil prowls around like a roaring lion looking for someone to devour."
1 Peter 5.8 (NIV)

PROLOGUE: THE ACCUSER

A mission in decline? (1886–87)

The 'bombshell' scattering the pioneers to China's farthest points had succeeded. The 'shock troops' had dug in, consolidating local churches to be 'the nucleus of expansion'. But trouble ahead loomed ominously at the heart of the empire and the Mission.

The nearer he came to Britain, the more apprehensive Hudson Taylor felt. Throughout the past year, 1886, the strain on his relationship with his London colleagues had increased. Ever since William Berger had resigned in March 1872, none of the arrangements for replacing him as the Mission's administrator in Britain had worked smoothly. The honorary director, secretaries and treasurer had found the demands upon their time too many. Communication between London and China had been inadequate, not from neglect but by preoccupation. At heart they were with him, but in practice they fell far short. The steps he had taken before returning to China in early 1885 had been enough to ensure a regular flow of information and funds as recruits and donations reached London. But inexperience, a mounting workload and personal shortcomings had too often left him in the dark. Again and again his ingenuity had been strained to the limit to allocate such irregular transmissions of money as were forwarded to him. To arrive and take a hand in these matters would bring him personal relief and lift the burden from the shoulders of his deputy in China, John Stevenson. 'The Lord will provide' involved being 'diligent in business'.

More distressing was the disapproval by the council in London of his own handling of affairs in China. Restraining strong-willed men in unwise actions, and weaker men from abandoning their principles under influences to compromise or to enter salaried employment, had been difficult enough. When 'London' listened to their complaints and sided with them, his leadership had been undermined. The 'father of lies' had maligned him personally.

On arrival in China the year before, Hudson Taylor had been greeted with the news that George Stott and Jackson, whose homes had been burned down during the Sino-French hostilities in the south, had claimed and received greater reparations than the consul considered right. Arising from this, their relationship with their colleagues and with Hudson Taylor and John Stevenson had become strained. No one was willing to work with them.

When the bookshelf fell on Hudson Taylor's head at Jinhua (see p 455), his business with the even-tempered Robert Grierson had been to ask him to put himself under Stott's heavy hand knowing full well what to expect. For Stott ruled his little kingdom with a rod of iron. Grace (Ciggie), his doughty wife, knew how to get on with him. Remarkably, the Chinese Christians, in gratitude for the gospel, accepted his powerful paternalistic regimen and thrived. At a time of tension the church paradoxically grew and spread. (Today's strong church at Wenzhou dates from those beginnings.) He resented Hudson Taylor's 'interference' and complained to 'London', threatening to resign. There was nothing for it but to let him go and, at last, Josiah Jackson too—in some ways a successful missionary but also a thorn in the side for twenty years.

After Hudson Taylor had written many letters and made several journeys to Wenzhou and Ningbo, E. C. Lord offered to be a go-between and found a formula which George Stott and his directors would accept. But Stott was taken very ill, went home and ended his last, extremely painful days at Cannes through the kindness of the Bergers. 'We witnessed the King of Terrors doing his worst,' an old friend wrote. He (Stott) was fighting for breath and 'strong pains were tearing at the vitals . . . But not for one moment did he falter, saying "It is only the poor body that is suffering; the soul is happy." How truly death is a vanquished enemy.'[821]

George King, honoured for his early pioneering in Shaanxi, and twice bereaved, had once again lost his foothold in Xi'an. He was tired and depressed and sent in his resignation. If he had had the funds, he would have gone home. Hudson Taylor talked him out of wild ideas and recognised the low Mission income at this time as truly 'providential' in restraining him. Griffith John wrote to Hudson Taylor agreeing that King was a sick man, needing not discipline but the warm, brotherly yet firm letters he was receiving from his leader.[822]

At a time when instability in several young missionaries was causing serious administrative problems, Hudson Taylor wrote to Stevenson with advice from his own experience of deploying personnel: solitary ones are 'apt to run dry spiritually if left too long alone'; Christian fellowship is health-giving; rather than put two good workers together, put each one with a weaker one whom he or she could lead and train. 'When a dear brother is too wise to take other counsel and too unwise to do without it, what can you do but regret the pain he causes to himself and the hindrance his non-success makes to the efforts of others?' He suggested one or two restless members of the Cambridge Seven might find their feet in a demanding situation on the Tibetan or Mongolian borders—'I think you will in that way prevent their

unsettledness from damaging others.' To one vacillating colleague he wrote, 'Pray about this and do what you think right', expressing his firm belief that God who said 'I will guide you' and had given sound faculties of wisdom and judgment to his people, would direct them through those abilities, if genuinely submitted to him. And to another, the advice to 'spend the night praying about it, and in the morning tell me your decision'.[823]

Annie Taylor he saw as strong, determined, an individualist, so bad at harmonious relationships with colleagues that she would have to be returned to Britain or stretched to her own limits. No one wanted to have her with them, so she was sent to the Gansu-Tibetan border (Qinghai) and in due course almost single-handedly came closer to Lhasa than any expedition, secular or religious, with their accoutrements, had yet succeeded (see p 559).

Others were so congenial or conciliatory that they needed to be protected from harmful influences they might not recognize. Schofield's successor, Dr Edwards, and even Archibald Orr Ewing were such delightful gentlemen that Hudson Taylor feared for them. 'Orr Ewing is too good and unsuspicious a man' to be wisely left in contact with Timothy Richard, when he returned to Shanxi. The Chefoo community of teachers and convalescing missionaries were a different kettle of fish, bickering 'like children' needing parental intervention, he confided to Jennie. The squabbling between some missionaries could make him feel 'frantic'. At the same time he could truthfully say that there had never been so much love in the CIM, the good compensating for the deplorable. As for the ineptitude of others—two men who wrote proposing marriage to unsuspecting women, in the same letter asking the recipient, if she declined the offer, to be go-between in approaching one of two or three others!

Disgruntled, unsettled and 'touchy' (JHT's word), some members of the Mission could be tolerated as natural variations from the contented, hard-working majority. But 'W. is such a nuisance', Hudson Taylor wrote, and of another inveterate slanderer and fabricator of lies, 'I don't know what to do to get rid of him.' Another, a veteran, 'with all his faults is one of our best workers'. One or two who took their complaints to other societies created a more painful problem. The first he knew of it in two exceptional instances was finding the name of the missionary in another mission's list of members. The courtesies were almost always observed between administrators, and most knew from experience that turncoats tended to bring trouble with them.

Physically remote from Hudson Taylor, the London Council had been undergoing a gradual change in its viewpoint unknown to him. The basic principle on which the CIM had been founded, that its leadership and control must be in China, had paled in the light of contemporary practice by other missions, merchant houses and the government. All paid the piper and called the tune from the homeland in Europe or America. Complaints to the London Council against the directors in China were taken as valid, without proper verification. In China the facts were known and understood. Men at a distance, with no personal knowledge of China or of the circumstances, could not adjudicate. Yet it was right that the London staff and council should be intimately concerned for the men and women they had prepared and sent to China. Correspondence on these issues had worsened rather than resolved the differences between London and Hudson Taylor. Only his return to Britain held any hope of agreement.

When he broke his journey to visit William Berger at Cannes he found little to reassure him. Cannes was full of visitors escaping the British winter, and social obligations prevented unhurried consultation about the things most on the two men's minds. William Berger approved of the call for the Hundred. The success of 'the eighteen' in the nine provinces had won him over. But he had blunt

things to say about the practical 'Book of Arrangements' and repeated them in a letter after his guest had gone. It was as Hudson Taylor feared. The controversy had spread beyond the staff and council to referees and supporters. The dissident missionaries' side of the story had been given a sympathetic hearing by the Home Director, Theodore Howard, the General Secretary, Benjamin Broomhall, and the lawyer, William Sharp, in particular.

Benjamin's propensity had for long been to champion the underdog.[824] In December 1886 he had cabled the good news of a doctor, two schoolmasters and two potential headmistresses sailing for Chefoo, and wrote, 'As to the hundred desired we shall rejoice if a hundred of the right type are forthcoming', but in the mail Hudson Taylor received at Marseilles or Cannes were ominous signs of deep trouble in store for him. Joe Coulthard, addressing Hudson Taylor as 'my dear Papa' on the strength of his engagement to Maria, warned of serious discontent in 'some parts'. A small China Council, it was being said, 'much younger in every way than those who have been over twenty years in the Mission', had laid down arbitrary rules for over two hundred others. In fact its part had been advisory, and the decisions were the General Director's, but after cosy personal relationships since *Lammermuir* days, any reorganisation was understandably distasteful to a few of that vintage.[825]

For London to question the composition and actions of the China Council they had supported Hudson Taylor in setting up, was far more serious. Law had replaced the grace and love demonstrated by Hudson Taylor, they contended. 'Now the Mission is growing so large we don't want it to be a big machine, but what it has been in the past—a family, only a larger one.' These words could have been written by Hudson Taylor himself or by any one of the China Council. But protests against change were as predictable as teething troubles from the rapid influx of novices.

Benjamin's letter harked back to April 1886 when Hudson Taylor had responded in 'strong words' to London's intervention in George Stott's quarrel with his leaders.[826] They must have an early conversation, he said, and come to an understanding if they were to work harmoniously as both desired. 'I do not think our separation would be for the good of the work.' Far from it. Confidence in the Mission would be shaken. But was feeling as strong as that? In John Stevenson's view, Benjamin was the best asset the CIM had after Hudson Taylor himself. As the chief executive in Britain, since 1877 when there were fifty-two CIM missionaries in all, he had played the major part in sending out most of the two hundred or so since added. All the dealings between their supporting churches and the Mission had been with the Secretary, whom they had come to value. Discord between Hudson Taylor and the London Council, especially his boyhood friend and brother-in-law at the heart of the Mission, could be most damaging. Separation could be lethal. The issue had become constitutional. The London Council as a whole, in objecting to the revision of the 'Principles and Practice' and the introduction of 'rule' in the 'Book of Arrangements', were claiming a say in both.

This was how things stood when he and Jennie met in Paris and crossed the Channel together, comparing notes on their agonising two-year separation from each other. To their delight his welcome home was as warm as ever. No one was in a hurry to air grievances.

1887: THE YEAR OF THE HUNDRED

'Expansiveness' (February–August 1887)

The boldness' of the call for a hundred new members within a year had fired the imagination of the Christian public. Hudson Taylor's homecoming to share in their selection and despatch to China smacked of the spirit they associated with 'the eighteen' in 1875 and the Cambridge Seven in 1885. The characteristic, very human slump in interest a few months after the Seven left Britain, had been offset by continuing enthusiasm in the universities and colleges. The potential was still there, and the evangelical churches welcomed the return of a focal point in Hudson Taylor and his dynamism.

As soon as his Shanghai cable of December 29, ('Coming'), arrived, Benjamin had publicised the fact, and invitations for Hudson Taylor to speak at conferences and preach at churches began to pour in. Only the first week after his arrival seems to have been kept free for him to find his feet. On February 25, after personal conversations with Theodore Howard and Benjamin, he could tell John Stevenson, 'The Lord *reigns*—let us grasp that great truth—a gospel indeed! . . . Our action (in China) has not met with unmixed approval, but when all is better understood I hope it will be satisfactorily resolved.' Four days later they were in the thick of a 'United Conference of Foreign Missions' at Leicester. With Benjamin as chairman, Hudson Taylor spoke twice on March 1, in the evening on 'The Baptism of the Spirit and the World for Christ'. The following succession of meetings around the British isles arranged by Benjamin was 'intense', such as Hudson Taylor enjoyed.

More requests for him were coming in than could be met. 'Enough work for two months had to be crowded into one.'[827] After conducting William Cooper's wedding and then a big meeting in the Mildmay Conference Hall on March 3, and another at the Eccleston Hall, he went up to Glasgow. Sixty candidates, more women than men, were waiting in Scotland to be interviewed. He saw forty at Glasgow, approved of thirty and received a promise of £2,500 towards their passages. One young man he told to go and meet the party about to sail to China as the best way to crystallise his thinking. And he wrote to Jennie, 'I told him *you* would give him a bed or sofa till Mrs B. has room for him . . . We shall not get the 100 if we do not strain our resources somewhat.' Amelia, still with five children under twenty, the youngest aged twelve, had her house constantly filled with people coming and going.

At Edinburgh where there were twenty more applicants, Jennie wrote, 'even his head has begun to swim.' Audiences of 1,600 or 1,700 in the United Presbyterian Synod Hall and more than 2,500 in St Cuthbert's Church heard him, supported by George Clarke, the lumberjack pioneer of Dali and the Mongolian border, on leave and a good speaker. One hundred and twenty stood to declare themselves at God's disposal, to go anywhere or to stay. But at Glasgow the meeting of the anti-opium society he took part in was a fiasco, with 'more speakers than hearers'. This cause was at its lowest ebb.

Month after month this travelling and speaking went on and during the whole year he wrote or dictated on average thirteen or fourteen letters each day. He believed in giving himself to the hilt and resting when he could keep going no longer. By March 17 he had not yet had a free half hour with some of his own children. Howard, his second son, had become a Member of the Royal College of Surgeons on January 20, and went on to achieve a first-class degree and graduate honours. Charles Edward, the fourth son, was preparing to enter Cambridge University with Benjamin's son, Marshall. And Hudson Taylor had been free for only one session of the Council, on March 23, between meetings in Scotland, London and Scotland again.

Objections to the revision of the 'Principles and Practice' had been voiced at that session, and Hudson Taylor had replied, but with so much urgent business affecting the Hundred, the subject had not been pursued. Enough had been said to betray the strength of feeling that existed. William Sharp apologised afterwards for having 'spoken more with salt than with grace', and offered to resign as Hudson Taylor had evidently not agreed with his (Sharp's) convinced opinion. The incessant travelling to meetings and selection of the Hundred with all that both involved went ahead while under the surface he was conscious of threats to the very existence

of the Mission.[828] Beyond the inner circle, however, an explosive force seemed to characterise this extraordinary society, abroad as much as in Britain.

Whatever the pace at home, events in China and John Stevenson's success as deputy director stayed at the front of Hudson Taylor's thinking. His long business letters could not but give Stevenson the sense of companionship in his duties. As far as he was able at a distance, Hudson Taylor commented on the matters reported or referred to him, and took up issues Stevenson might not be alive to.[829] His constant reference to the word of God for assurance and guidance matched his deputy's own attitude to his responsibilities. Feasting 'in the presence of my enemies' (Psalm 23.5) was Hudson Taylor's continuing theme. Let Satan rage and scheme: 'God reigns and fills our cup till it runs over. I have unbroken rest in (that) assurance.' He continued with specific instructions: move Orr Ewing away from Shanxi for the present; keep engaged couples' eyes on the sound reasons for delaying marriage until acclimatised, able to speak Chinese and able to do useful work; do not hesitate to pass the onus of decision on to me if faced with determined insistence; encourage the missionary whose son has been committed to prison for embezzlement.

Pastor Hsi was in the wrong to treat Stanley Smith as he did, but had apologised; consider visiting Shanxi again—'No part of the work is more important. If the Seven should go wrong or things go wrong between them and others, the result might be very serious and they are very young men and liable to young men's mistakes.' Studd needs careful handling. As an independent associate, not a member of the CIM, he was going his own way and failing to keep in touch, which associates all agreed to do.[830] 'I think (Beauchamp) chafes a little at the thought of being a layman under Cassels.'

'Pigott has mortally offended Hsi and cannot return to Shanxi; could he develop the part of Zhili between Baoding and the mountain route to Taiyuan? I am so thankful . . . that as far as you know the spirit of unity and harmony is growing everywhere.' Go ahead with getting Chinese clothes made for the hundred soon to be on their way. The women at Shashi are incomparably superior to the men as evangelists: 'Cannot you . . . get possession of that useful (Buddhist) machine that grinds men into women and vice versa? It would add wonderfully to your efficiency as Director.' So it went on in letter after letter, showing a detailed grasp of affairs and a light touch, even to details of buildings being erected at Yangzhou and Anqing. Physically he might be ageing, but mentally and spiritually he was as strong as ever.

From Aberdeen on April 13 he wrote at length to the *Christian* in support of some correspondents who had advocated the very principles he and John Nevius were emphasising.[831]

If the young church in other lands were to stand on its own feet, foreign funds should not be used to support or employ them directly, the effect of doing so was too often to diminish their influence. A man preaching the gospel in his own spare time impressed his hearers and was benefitted himself. But the fact that he received money from foreigners created prejudice against him and what he said. It induced inferior men to attempt hypocritically to be taken on. Independent, voluntary preachers and church workers welcomed teaching and advice and were respected wherever they went. The apostle Paul's example at Ephesus should be followed, remembering the Lord's words, 'I will build my church' (Matthew 16.18).

The Jubilee of Queen Victoria was being celebrated and in a climate of rejoicing Hudson Taylor could say in his 21st *Lammermuir* anniversary letter, 'The prospects (in China) were never so bright as today.' Enthusiastic audiences heard him speak confidently at the annual meetings of the Hundred being given (not only 'forthcoming') during the year.

> If ... my brother-in-law ... had sent me out a printed list of one hundred accepted candidates, it would not have added to

our confidence one whit ... We began the matter aright with God and we are quite sure we shall end aright ... Whether God (send) more than the literal hundred, or whether by stirring up other branches of the Church to send many hundreds—which I would greatly prefer—or whether by awakening a missionary interest all over the Church, and blessing the whole world through it, I do not know ... but sure I am that God will do it handsomely.[832]

In his words we again recognise a note of prophecy, as if he had known that before the year was out the great snowball would start rolling which made the CIM international, the Student Volunteer Missionary Union (SVMU) the force it became, and brought a host of other societies into existence.

Funds were coming in dramatically to send and support the Hundred of whom fifty had already been accepted and thirty had reached China. As always at annual meetings, receipts and estimates were reported without hesitation or elaboration. A visiting speaker said he was impressed by 'the expansiveness of the China Inland Mission', so involved with God that there seemed to be no limit to the number who could be sent to China and provided for.

As far back as April 1886, Hudson Taylor's vision of expansion and extension of the Mission had included the provision of business premises and residences in the major ports, at Tianjin, Wuchang or Hankou and the Yangzi ports of call, including the language schools. As John Stevenson remembered it in later years, Hudson Taylor had been slow to adopt the concept of central headquarters in Shanghai. But his memory was at fault, for while Stevenson was travelling, Hudson Taylor had bought the large site on Wusong Road and was working steadily towards developing it, with a residence capable of taking seventy in transit, offices, a small hospital and a shipping and supplies warehouse.

From Aberdeen on April 14, 1887, he telegraphed the £1,500 to Stevenson for raising the site above Shanghai's seasonal flood level, in spite of the immediate need of funds for Yangzhou, Anqing, London and the Hundred. He was ahead in his thinking and leadership. Archibald Orr Ewing's £2,500 was received on August 5, and preparations in Shanghai continued, but architectural planning of the actual buildings had to wait (while the raised earth settled) until Hudson Taylor returned to China in 1888; then construction began in 1889. What John Stevenson remembered was Hudson Taylor's urging that while he was away, Stevenson should make Zhenjiang his base, close to the language school at Yangzhou and away from the cloying influences of Shanghai on Lewis, his secretary, and the many impressionable young missionaries passing through the port, for the accommodation at Yuan Ming Yuan Road was inadequate.[833]

As the numbers of men and women asking in Britain to be included in the Hundred increased, it became clear that a second hundred would be given. They could not sail within the year 1887, but accommodation in Pyrland Road would continue to be taxed to the limit for months to come. To meet this situation the Pigotts authorised the transfer of their legacy from Shanghai to London, requiring only that the deeds of property purchased in the name of the CIM 'you will hold to my order as an equitable security for the money'.[834] Negotiations for Inglesby House, a gentleman's residence overlooking Newington Green, ended in July with the acceptance of the Mission's offer of £2,800 for the house and grounds, and the pressure was relieved. After general use for a time, Inglesby House became the men candidates' training home.[835]

At the same time another experiment began. Several members of the CIM had taken medical courses under Mission sponsorship and from having four doctors in China in 1886 the number rose to seven in 1887. Then a house was leased in Cambridge for seven years as lodgings for candidates whom further education would make more useful. By the time of the annual meetings in 1888 more than

six hundred men and women had offered to go to China, and even with Inglesby House much more space was needed: 'more office room, more storage rooms, more packing rooms, more bedrooms . . . and classrooms [to allow candidates to meet and mix with experienced missionaries coming and going]. The new missionary goes not from lodgings but from a home. The older missionary returning for rest and change . . . feels he is not calling at an office, but coming to a home.'

So plans for building a headquarters residence and office block on the Newington Green site had to begin. 'Expansiveness' entailed far more than people and money.[836]

The travellers (1886–89)

The merry-go-round in Britain could not obscure the advancing process of expansion in China too. While the rush to be in the Hundred was astounding those who witnessed its progress, a new aspect of the unconventional CIM was taking shape. Not content with reaching the far boundaries of the vast region that had challenged them so recently, some pioneers had raised their sights to the outlying dependencies. Strong, silent, glamorous Tibet beckoned some. Sullen, rebellious, Muslim Turkestan and the nomad millions of Mongols stretching from Manchuria to historic Sungaria of the Golden Hordes challenged others.

On the international scene the constant manoeuvring of Russia on her eastern and southern borders threatened her neighbours. But with the British Empire having extended further still, China was not so much Russia's competitor or antagonist as Britain, and both had their eyes on Tibet. Both, therefore, kept watchful representatives in Kashgar, gleaning information on the other's movements. Travellers from both, and from other European countries, explored the approaches to Tibet, the vast deserts of the 'Xinjiang' to be, and the southern mountains. Lhasa was the lodestone: to reach Lhasa, the goal of explorers and Christian missionaries alike. To leave the word of God in the monasteries, and to preach the gospel at the heart of Lamaism inspired some, as the sheer romance and danger drew others.

Two-thirds of the Tibetan tableland lie at 15,000 feet or more, with some passes at 20,000 feet. Lhasa stands at 12,000 feet. The highest mountain ranges on earth wall in Tibet on the south, west and north. Water boils at a temperature tolerable to the hand. The borders of Tibet have always been ill-defined, varying with political fluctuations or the vicissitudes of armed power, especially on the lower eastern flank where Chinese and tribal claims were strongest. 'True Tibet', if its ethnographic extent can be so labelled, extends into the politically determined regions of Qinghai, Gansu, Sichuan, Yunnan and Ladakh. Sir Charles Bell's 'Greater Tibet' is a reasonable term for it. Until the tenth century, warring Tibetans penetrated western China, the Turfan oases and Samarkand.

The Government of India was naturally most concerned with the southern border and in the convention with China signed at Peking on July 24, 1886, following the annexation of Upper Burma, Britain agreed 'not to press unduly the opening of Tibet'.[837] Consequently, the expedition of the Financial Secretary of Bengal, Colman Macaulay, agreed by the Chefoo Convention in 1876, was called off. He was to have proceeded from Darjeeling up the Chumbi Valley through Sikkim with three hundred Indian troops, but was confronted by Tibetan troops within sight of Darjeeling.

Meanwhile, in China, George Parker and his Chinese wife Minnie had established themselves outside Lanzhou, the capital of Gansu. It took the determined young individualist Annie Royle Taylor to secure the first foothold inside the city and from there to lay her plans for taking the gospel to Tibet.[838] On January 27, 1887, Hudson Taylor told Stevenson that the Parkers proposed moving five hundred miles further west to Suzhou (now Jiuquan) in March with a minimum of baggage. From there George alone was to go six hundred miles even deeper into Xinjiang to Urumqi

(Dihua), the heart of Chinese Turkestan, to prepare a place for his family to follow in the spring of 1888. They would be more than thirty-five day stages from the nearest other member of the Mission. During 1888–89 he was to travel among the Turki Uigurs south of Aksu, almost to Kashgar (see map 2.59: p 480), and northwards among the Mongols beyond Lake Barkul. On this venture he would come close to the Russian border.

By April, Hudson Taylor was coordinating a new turn of events. But it must be kept secret, he warned Stevenson, lest the authorities raise objections. An enterprising clergyman, the Rev Dr Henry Lansdell, DD, FRGS, one-time vicar of St Stephen's, Eltham, in southeast London, who had already been to Bokhara and Samarkand, was planning another expedition and wanted the CIM's cooperation. He proposed to go to Yarkand investigating routes into Tibet, and then if possible to go in and find southern routes out to India. Parker would be glad to join him, Hudson Taylor said. How about Cameron? The American Bible Society was to supply a consignment of selected Christian books in appropriate languages, which Stevenson was to freight to Lanzhou. Before long he could expect Dr Lansdell to be in touch with him at Shanghai. After getting travel passes from the Zongli Yamen, Lansdell would meet Parker and others upcountry.

On June 17, Hudson Taylor wrote again. The philanthropist Robert Arthington (almost a millionaire, who 'lived like the poorest of the poor' that he might promote the propagation of the gospel worldwide) had sent £200 for the CIM to take the gospel to Turkestan and Mongolia.[839] Parker's and Lansdell's journey came into this category. Hudson Taylor and another donor had each added £100, but Lansdell's own efforts to raise £600 more for the three-year enterprise were meeting with little success. The American Bible Society gave him a glowing testimony and voted $500 a year for three years to be applied by Dr Gulick, their Shanghai agent, 'for the exploration of Central Asia and Tibet, with a view of promoting the circulation of the Scriptures in that part of the world'.[840]

At this point the Episcopal Church of America offered Dr Lansdell a bishopric, which he declined. But in October when he visited Hudson Taylor he still lacked the essential funds. They left it that he would cable Stevenson to make definite arrangements with Parker or to release him from any obligation.[841]

At last, on Christmas Eve 1887, Hudson Taylor wrote that he was meeting Henry Lansdell again. 'Tibet seems retiring further and further in the distance, but all else seems promising.' The American Bible Society were contributing £1,000, and George Parker went ahead with his brave venture to take the word of God into Turkestan. At the May meetings in 1889 Parker's successful arrival at Gulja (Kuldja, the Chinese Yining) on the Sino-Russian (Alma Ata) border beyond Urumqi was reported (see map 2.59: p 480)—two decades before George Hunter in 1908 and three and a half decades before Eva and Francesca French and Mildred Cable ('The Trio') in 1923 followed in his footsteps. The epic journeys by Colonel Mark Bell VC and Lieutenant (at the time) Francis Edward Younghusband took place in 1887. Sven Hedin, Sir Aurel Stein and others followed in the late nineteenth and early twentieth centuries with Sir Eric Teichmann among contemporaries of the Trio.[842]

Dr Lansdell's story diverged after that from the CIM's. In the winter of 1888–89 he proposed to Archbishop Benson of Canterbury that as an Anglican lama he should carry a message from the Grand Lama of the West to the Grand Lama of the East. The archbishop responded dispassionately with the note, 'This is to certify that the Reverend Henry Lansdell, Doctor of Divinity and Fellow of the Royal Geographical Society' was undertaking a journey with 'no political, military or commercial objects' and asked for special facilities for him to visit Lhasa. Not to be outdone, and with far better understanding of the Asian mind, Lansdell mounted the document, signature and seal on yellow silk, rolled up as a scroll within a satin-lined red morocco case and cylinder of tin. But reaching Leh, the Ladakhi capital, in November 1888, he could find no one prepared to risk almost certain death simply for carrying the scroll to the Dalai Lama. At Kalimpong and Kathmandu he was similarly frustrated, so he went on to Peking. A Christian gentleman, lacking the wisdom of a serpent, he frankly stated his intentions. On March 21, 1888, two thousand British, Indian troops had clashed with nine hundred Tibetans on Sikkim territory. The British minister in Peking warned him, 'It would be out of the question to ask the Chinese for a passport to Tibet.' His attempt would worsen Anglo-Tibetan relations. Patriotically, Lansdell withdrew. Inadequate funds seems to have brought his attempts to an end.

The man who was eventually to enter Lhasa, but at the head of the British-Indian troops in 1904–05, Lieutenant Younghusband.[843] Leaving Peking on April 4, 1887, and Kalgan on the 10th, he passed through the Great Wall and reached Guihuacheng (Hohhot) on the 17th, to traverse China from east to west by a route never in recent centuries taken by a European. In his book, *The Heart of a Continent*, he told appreciatively of his welcome by George and Agnes Clarke at Guihuacheng:

> I met with that warm reception which is characteristic of missionaries ... The zeal and energy which this mission shows is marvellous. There is an excellent rule that, for a year or two after coming to China, the recruits need not belong permanently to the Mission; but if they find that they are not suited for the work, can return to England. The wisdom of this rule anyone can readily understand.

George Clarke was indefatigable in his search for a camel-owner willing to go with so small a party as Younghusband's instead of waiting for the next monthly trade caravan, and succeeded. A contract to reach Hami in sixty days was drawn up and they parted. In his assessments towards the end of his great travelogue, Younghusband wrote:

My sympathies are entirely with the missionaries, and having seen the noble men I have met within the far interior of China [Catholic and Protestant] and realised the sacrifices they have made, I say that the hearts of all ... Christian nations ought to go out to encouraging and helping them.

Little effect may have been produced in so short a time as a couple of centuries upon ... the most stationary and unimpressionable race in the world. But that was to be expected. In the first two centuries after Christ only the most infinitesimal effect had been produced upon Europe.

As Lieutenant-Colonel Sir Francis Younghusband (President of the Royal Geographical Society, 1919–22), he was to support and to honour the intrepid 'Trio' forty years later.[844]

George Parker confined his attention to the great north-west, and later in life to the Muslims of Henan. But Annie Taylor and Cecil Polhill-Turner, whose first aim was to take the gospel to Tibetans and only to Lhasa if the way should open, in 1887 chose the two frontier cities of Taozhou and Xining as their respective springboards.

Touch and go (March–November 1887)

After the 'more salt than grace' meeting of the London Council in March, Hudson Taylor was touring Scotland until mid-April and northern England until the end of the month. On his return to London the change of atmosphere could not but strike him. After the warmth of affection he had been receiving, even courtesy from friends was chilling. In his absence the Council had considered resigning over the 'P and P and little book of arrangements'. The influence of two or three had swayed the less discerning members. When grasping the nettle could have been disastrous he evaded it carefully. A busy month of May culminated in the annual meetings, and he could only say to John Stevenson, 'Things may go awkwardly . . . and the project of the 100 be brought to grief . . . (Yet) never

was God's help more manifest or more marvellous than this year, and all will yet be well.' In William Sharp he had a restive lawyer, prone to taking independent action when what was wanted was professional advice; or to jump to conclusions, as over the current issue of the 'P and P' and 'Book of Arrangements'.[845]

To hear of 'the spirit of unity and harmony growing everywhere' in the Mission in China brought immense relief, for it seemed all Satan's strength was set on breaking it up in Britain. Nothing was more necessary to such a mission as unity and harmony. Fortunately in July the Council was pressed for time, meeting three times a week to interview and decide about candidates, while Hudson Taylor travelled from the south coast to the far north. Briefly back in London to meet the Council on July 19, he wearily confessed to Stevenson that he was not only 'utterly used up' and 'tempted to wish that my turn had come, but He giveth power to the faint'. Subversion was always more sapping to the spirit than overt opposition. Off again on the 22nd to Keswick, Ireland, Wales and the south-west, he gasped, 'Well, praise the Lord. He helps me through day by day and fills one's heart with blessing and one's mouth with praise.'

Great changes had taken place at the Keswick Convention. Instead of missionary interests being excluded or a tent being grudgingly made available for a missionary meeting without the presence of any Convention speaker as in the previous years, the church's obedience in spreading the gospel to the wide world had been recognised as fundamental to consecration and spiritual health. Listed for the first time with Evan Hopkins, F. B. Meyer and Handley Moule (newly convinced by the 'Keswick message') was Hudson Taylor. His presence there had two incidental by-products. Lord and Lady Tankerville, seeing his weariness, offered him and his family the use of a cottage and a servant near Chillingham Castle, their home.[846] And Graham Wilmot Brooke, 'a young man of extraordinary capacity and great spiritual fervour', who had been trying since making contact with General Gordon in 1881 'to reach the heart of Mohammedan Africa', probably consulted Hudson Taylor at Keswick, for he sailed again for Africa as leader of a small team, gratefully armed with a copy of the 'Book of Arrangements', about which they had corresponded.[847]

A short holiday at Hastings and Hudson Taylor was off to Belfast. Normally calm, efficient Jennie was getting worried but had to content herself with writing, 'My own treasure . . . I am so glad to have had you yesterday.' A few days earlier she had written, 'Do, as a duty, get all the rest you can . . . Do rest before it is too late. It will not pay to kill yourself, even to get the 100.' He took to telling her in his frequent notes, barely legible from the vibration of the trains, how much rest he was getting day by day, and giving advice on the editing and lay-out of *China's Millions*. But it was that spirit of his which resulted in half of one of his audiences flocking to the station to see him on his way. The occasional critic might speak of his talent for 'making friends and influencing people' as a 'propagandist flair', but those who knew him saw it in the light of a man 'filled with the Spirit' and unable to contain the exuberance of concern for God's glory and China's salvation. A committee of clergymen and aldermen at Bolton, announcing his meetings by handbill, said: 'This mission was founded by the simple but courageous faith of the Rev Hudson Taylor, whose whole life has been a living exhibition of the wonderful works of the Lord. This visit is not for the purpose of soliciting funds, nor in the sole interests of the China Inland Mission.'[848]

By then his policy of meeting members of the London Council individually was beginning to pay dividends. William Sharp was friendly, and on August 5 it was possible to write, 'Things have nearly come round, as to our Home Council, and with a little patience all will be well. God has worked for us, or all would have been broken up' And on the 19th, 'If I were to doubt, you would not have the 100 missionaries, and the glory of God and good of China demand that we

make this our first work this year.' Although personal relationships were cordial again, the flashpoint of opinion was still critical. Benjamin was in Wales and Somerset arranging more and more meetings, farewells to the Hundred as well as for Hudson Taylor. William Berger expressed his warmth in a long public letter of support and by sending £500 from time to time, but again added his own protests about the 'Arrangements'.[849]

By September the Mission's membership list had reached 235, including five Bible Christian Mission associates. And by mid-October eighty-nine had been accepted and were preparing to go. Many more were 'under consideration'. One of Grattan Guinness's tutors, a Mr Barfield, joined the staff to train them, as a step towards a CIM training institute.[850]

The London staff were all exhausted, Hudson Taylor told John Stevenson (in the same letter as he suggested that Bhamo would have to be handed over to another mission if two good men could not be found to go there) that 'our excitable brethren in Shansi' must be handled carefully;[851] and that if Baller and Landale handled the mature language students at Anqing too autocratically they must be diverted to the academic work that suited them better. When on November 1 the Council accepted another three missionaries, that brought the total for the year so far to 102, with as many more in the pipeline. What was God doing to the CIM?

Frost's 'bog of blasted hopes' (October–December 1887)

The London staff and Hudson Taylor were working themselves to the bone, but were also seeing the outcome of it. Sunday, October 30, saw him addressing four services at Liverpool and walking seven miles between them. The next day the 'Great Social Gathering' in Lincoln, at which he was the attraction, began at 7.30 p.m. Every day of the week had its quota, in Doncaster, at Wakefield, and at Leeds by the invitation of a committee comprising Anglican, Congregational, Wesleyan,

Baptist, Primitive Methodist and Quaker 'Friends'. His themes attracted all kinds and he needed little time for preparation for (as he explained to curious enquirers) he spoke from his heart, drawing upon his early morning feasting on God's word: 'Our Lord's delight in the consecration of His people'; 'The evangelisation of the world'; or simply commenting phrase by phrase through a passage of Scripture. A meeting at St Stephen's parish church in Leeds led to its vicar, the Rev E. O. Williams, MA, of Trinity College, Oxford, offering to join William Cassels in Sichuan. He and his family sailed on December 13, 1888.

Audiences might be drawn by the hyperbole of organisers, as in Dublin where he was billed as 'MD, FRCS', but the stocky little man with his low fatherly voice might as well have been standing among them as on a platform, and once heard he needed no more advertisement. It was at Glasgow that he had the temerity on December 11 to speak on the 23rd Psalm and the Song of Songs to packed congregations in the United Presbyterian Church and the Town Hall with many turned away. In the words of the Provost, John Colville, whose guest Hudson Taylor was that weekend, the congregation listened 'with ears and eyes and mouths'.[852] And in the evening 'after a wonderful exposition of Zephaniah 3', Hudson Taylor's new personal secretary, S. F. Whitehouse, wrote, 'Mr T. . . . hadn't finished till close on 9.00, but you could have heard any ordinary clock tick most of the time . . . Not a few of us were moved to tears.'

Hudson himself told Jennie, 'Hundreds are daily finding blessing through our meetings. We are not separated for nothing.' From Doncaster, where he was with John N. Forman, a young graduate of Princeton University, he wrote, 'Yesterday I caught myself thinking: By this time next week I shall be on my way home. I shall be with my Jennie! You see what it is to have too little to think of !' But he would only be passing through London. At Limerick, after Dublin with Forman, Pigott and J. J. Luce, he was in bed with a bad cold, leaving

Forman to go ahead to Belfast. When he wrote to Stevenson he was feeling irritable, saying, 'The dentists are a bore', after crossing out 'a nuisance', followed by page upon page of administrative business.

> Nothing is clearer to me than that obtaining a hundred this year we have obtained a second hundred; to send them out and sustain them will require another £10,000 additional income, and in times like these it is a tremendous rise from a little over £20,000 to £40,000. One is so glad that God has Himself asked us the question—'Is anything too hard for the Lord?' But ... if we get less prayerful about funds we shall soon get sorely tried about funds.

> Every day I feel more and more thankful to God for giving you to us and for giving you such general acceptance. No human prescience or wisdom is sufficient for your position, but so long as you continue to seek His guidance in every matter and in the midst of the pressure of work take time to be holy and take time to pray for the workers, the LORD will continue to use and own and bless you.

'A second hundred'? He could not have endured the knowledge of what would in fact happen.

The Glasgow Foreign Mission Students Union (General Secretary, John Torrance) made him their Honorary President. It was the same in Belfast, where on December 5 he shared meetings with John Forman. After the 'galleries, aisles and pulpit stairs were packed', crowds could not get in. 'Some twenty students . . . fine young fellows' came on Forman's advice to talk with Hudson Taylor. Forman had come to Britain from the States as one of the early leaders of the new Student Volunteer Movement (SVM), which originated in 1886 during D. L. Moody's conference for students at Mount Hermon, Massachusetts. Robert P. Wilder, the son of a retired missionary to India, there enrolled one hundred kindred spirits to form the SVM. They adopted the watchword, 'The evangelisation of the world in this generation', a strong echo of Wilder's father and the General Missionary Conference of

1877 in Shanghai.[853] As Bishop Stephen Neill said in his *History of Christian Missions* (page 394):

> The slogan was based on an unexceptional theological principle— that each generation of Christians bears responsibility for the contemporary generation of non-Christians in the world, and that it is the business of each such generation of Christians to see to it, as far as lies within its power, that the gospel is clearly preached to every single non-Christian in the same generation.

The SVM burgeoned rapidly, with thousands signing the pledge, 'It is my purpose, if God permit, to become a foreign missionary.' Robert Wilder was travelling in 1887 through the colleges and universities of North America recruiting volunteers, while John Forman was in Britain. John R. Mott, one of the founder members, became the chairman of SVM in 1888, and Robert E. Speer the travelling secretary. Speer attributed his awakening to the responsibility for taking the gospel to the world to a reading of the CIM's *The Evangelisation of the World*.

While John Forman was travelling with Hudson Taylor to Oxford, Cambridge, Dublin and other major cities, urging upon university students the message of the SVM, another young American, Henry Weston Frost, was making his first approach to the CIM. In his college room as an undergraduate at Princeton, the son of an admiral had been casually showing Frost an old revolver his father had carried in the Civil War, assuming it to be unloaded. It had gone off, narrowly missing Henry Frost's head. 'Too moved for words', neither had spoken, but to Frost 'came the conviction that his life had been saved for a purpose'.[854]

Then one day when he was twenty-seven and married, he heard Jonathan Goforth declaiming the need of the unevangelised world for a Saviour, and on leaving the meeting was arrested by the attractive appearance of a book on display, larger and more decorative than most. He bought it, *A Missionary Band*, the first edition of *The Evangelisation of the World*, and read about the Seven and the Mission to China. Kynaston Studd told him more. But in 1886 he attended a conference at Niagara-on-the-Lake and heard Dr A. T. Pierson's arraignment of the disobedience of the church in relation to Christ's command 'Go into all the world and preach the gospel' (Mark 16.15). And at last, in 1887, Frost wrote to consult the CIM in London and even filled in an application form. His health was not good, and his wife was caring for an invalid father, so they were advised 'to wait upon God for further guidance'. But 'China's claim' weighed on him and he began to think, if he and his wife could not go themselves, could the CIM not open a branch in America to send young North Americans as it was sending young Britons to China? After profound thought and prayer he decided he would go and make this proposition in person to Hudson Taylor.

He sailed from New York on November 12 and on arriving in Glasgow met John Forman. 'I found that he too had been praying for something of the same kind for a long time, and that Mr Wilder, his companion [in the States], has also had the matter laid on his heart.' But he reached London to find Hudson Taylor away on his travels. Frost was taken into Amelia's family home and then moved into lodgings to wait for Hudson Taylor. The comings and goings of the Hundred, the 'simplicity, earnestness, comprehensiveness and spirituality (of the daily prayer meeting) beyond anything I had ever known' impressed him. But with the warmth of Hudson Taylor's welcoming letter and then on December 27 with his handshake and first remarks in his 'low, kindly voice. I had, then and there, what amounted to a revelation—first of a man and then of his God . . . From that moment my heart was fully his . . . and also in a new and deeper sense, his Lord's. [And afterwards] Mr Taylor had seemed to encourage the hope that the Mission would be extended to America.'[855]

By the evening when they met beside a glowing coal fire in the office, Hudson

Taylor had learned from Benjamin how strongly he opposed the 'transfer of a British organisation to American soil'. American missions would not welcome it, Benjamin thought, and too much would be involved when the CIM was already doubling its size. So Hudson told Frost frankly that 'he could not see the leading of the Lord'. Frost could not know that deep rifts were already threatening the structure, even the existence of the Mission. It was the wrong moment to introduce a revolutionary new development without unity of mind in the administration. A purely American society on the lines of the CIM might be the better way.

Frost was shattered, tempted to despair, in 'a veritable bog of blasted hopes'. He returned to America three days later, after seeing the last of the Hundred sail away, asking himself how he could ever again be sure of the guidance of God. In due time he realised that he need not have been so shaken. Everything was under God's control. What Hudson Taylor did promise when they said goodbye was that he would be willing to speak at Niagara-on-the-Lake and Moody's Northfield Conference on his way back to China, if invited by the conveners.

If 'the leading of the Lord' was not clearly discernible in December 1887, it was steadily unfolding. Other signposts were in sight. While Henry Frost was waiting in London for Hudson Taylor to return, a tall young Swedish pastor, Josef F. Holmgren, was writing on December 10 from Stockholm. So his letter was before Hudson Taylor at the same time as Henry Frost's proposition. He was not unknown to the CIM. In the first week of September 1883, in the office of the *Christian* in Paternoster Row under the shadow of St Paul's Cathedral, Hudson Taylor had been 'kind and courteous' to the muscular young stranger from Orebro, and they met once or twice more at Mildmay.[856]

A year later Holmgren subscribed to *China's Millions* and launched his own Swedish magazine on missions in all lands. By May 1887 he had translated parts of *China's Spiritual Need and Claims* and formed a committee in Stockholm, where by then he was pastor of a leading church, to assist an outstanding young gentleman, Erik Folke, who had gone independently to China and was in touch with John Stevenson. Folke had proposed joining the CIM under Hudson Taylor's leadership, but with financial support from Sweden. Now Josef Holmgren was suggesting that they form 'the Swedish branch of the China Inland Mission'. Would Hudson Taylor come over to discuss it? 'I could arrange meetings for you in the chief towns of Sweden and the people would flock to hear you by thousands. (A week in Stockholm and three weeks for other cities would be needed.) If you can't come, please write an appeal to the Swedish people.'

With Henry Frost's proposal of a North American branch of the Mission running into rough water, Hudson Taylor replied to Holmgren also offering alternative ways of cooperating. Swedish missionaries could become full members of the CIM (through London as Dr Stewart of Philadelphia had done) or associates (as several individuals and the Bible Christians were doing). Folke chose the system of association and his committee agreed, as the Swedish churches would find it more attractive and the name Swedish Mission in China had already been adopted. In China individual associates were all but members of the CIM, adhering to its principles and practice, while in their homelands the organisations were independent of each other.[857]

If Hudson Taylor had not already caught sight of the Delectable Mountains of a new international wave of response to the Great Commission, he must have glimpsed its possibility and been open to it in his first interview with Henry Frost. It mattered little to him whether more and more men and women went to China in the CIM or in association with it or with other societies, so long as they preached the same gospel with the same love for the Chinese. So if Benjamin's answer to Frost's proposition was the right one, the result would be just as satisfactory. He valued

Benjamin's judgment and could understand his reluctance to expand the Mission yet further into uncharted channels at such a time. Insularity was a pardonable outcome of having no experience of foreign travel.

In his own field of public relations, Benjamin inspired confidence. When the father of the girl betrothed to Herbert Norris refused to permit her to go to China, Hudson Taylor told Stevenson, 'I do not know any man in the world who is more likely to help . . . than my good brother-in-law.' When there was a move to change the name of *China's Millions*, Benjamin's insight and diplomacy saved the day for Jennie's inspiration. The overtones of the title, encapsulating Hudson Taylor's supreme message in *China's Spiritual Need and Claims*, were established assets not to be thrown away.[858] His success as the executive secretary had been due more to his flair and drive than to system and efficiency. He was genial but masterly, usually getting from his colleagues what was needed. So when he differed in opinion from Hudson Taylor both needed great grace.

The year of the Hundred with its excessive pressures had shown that changes were needed, not only in premises. The staff could not cope with a second hundred unless reinforced with competent men. The right ones were at that moment learning in the hard school, China. But after the Second World Missionary Conference in London in 1888,[859] the greatest achievement of Benjamin's life was to germinate and thrive in parallel with his commitment to the Mission—he was to play the major role for the CIM in ending the scandal of Britain's opium production and trade.

Prospects 'never so bright' (1887)

To John Stevenson, who was at the helm after Hudson Taylor had gone home in January 1887, everything seemed promising.[860] The Hundred would soon be coming in successive waves to fill the new language schools and go on into the provinces. The men and women of the big influx of 1885, led by the Cambridge Seven,

were progressing well enough to make their mark wherever they went—T. E. S. Botham constantly on the road in Shanxi; Thomas James with Dorward and Dick on the Hunan border; Grierson at Wenzhou. The veteran Edward Pearse was travelling extensively and continuously in Sichuan and Shaanxi, and occupied the city of Chengdu in the Hanzhong plain (see map 2.31, p 279). But yet again the anti-foreign Hunanese in Xi'an drove out the latest arrival, Charles F. Hogg.

In Shanxi Stanley Smith had left Hongtong to pioneer Lu'an and Jincheng (Tsechow), and over the border into Henan. Charlie and Priscilla Studd had joined him. Together they alarmed Hudson Taylor by adopting Salvation Army methods, marching through the streets with drums and gongs before preaching the gospel. 'A reckless SA band might easily drive us all out of any province in China . . . (and) Stanley Smith will not bear too much stimulus with safety.' As for the independent associate, CT—we must do all we can to knit him more closely to us for his own sake. We can do better without him than he can without us.'[861] The personal charisma that had given these two men the leading role in Britain needed the stability of Cassels and Hoste to make them successful in China. Marked progress in George Clarke's Guihuacheng district on the Mongolian border kept pace with the expanding church under Pastor Hsi in the south, though not as spectacularly.

'The formidable men' of Henan resisted the gospel still, but at Zhoujiakou, J. J. Coulthard baptised nine, to form the first Protestant Church in the province. Maria Taylor, at Dagutang in March, held an audience of women for half an hour while they listened with 'quite breathless attention'. Later she moved to Guiqi among the woman pioneers of the Guangxin River, more good preparation for Henan after her marriage in 1888 to Joe Coulthard.[862]

Annie Royle Taylor launched out from Lanzhou in July to live among Tibetans at Taozhou and master their language. Before the year was out her Tibetan serving man, Pontso, a native of Lhasa, was a true believer. Her sights then were on going with him to his home. He stayed with her for nearly twenty years. Cecil Polhill made Xining (now in Qinghai) his base for learning Tibetan.[863]

Yunnan was still excited by the French war in the south and Britain's annexation of Upper Burma, but the diplomatic settlement of July 1886 had opened the way for F. A. Stevenson to cross the border into Bhamo on his second attempt. Stevenson even wrote hopefully of a 'highway' being opened between Bhamo and Dali (by which he meant a mule trail). In Guizhou the unrest continued. George Andrew and Thomas Windsor were unable to obtain passes to travel outside Guiyang. But while Adam Dorward was away in Britain, Henry Dick made his daring visit to Changsha. Even if no foothold could be gained, the populace would slowly become more accustomed to having foreigners coming and going.

Any rejoicings in the sailings from Britain of party after party of the Hundred were tempered with sadness, especially for Hudson Taylor, when in September the news came from Ningbo that Dr E. C. Lord and his wife had died of cholera on September 17 and 15 respectively. Commissioned as US Consul in Ningbo, by Abraham Lincoln himself, Edward Lord had combined consular and missionary service for nineteen years and earned the marked respect of the mandarins. Two of his household staff had been with him for thirty-two years, as well as his cook for nineteen and his 'outside man' for seventeen—a tribute to his personality. He had been in Ningbo himself since 1847, a veteran before Hudson Taylor arrived as a youth. The CIM in Zhejiang had always had free access to his home and advice, and the church at large would miss his strong influence. The year also saw the death of Alexander Wylie, the apostle of Christian literature in China; of Dr Douthwaite's wife in Chefoo; of John Challice, the treasurer in London; and of George Stott. The fleeting brevity of life on earth was seldom far from Hudson Taylor's thoughts. A work to be done must be done 'now'.[864]

Since the arrival of the *Lammermuir* party in China in 1866, the Protestant missionary community in China had increased by 500, apart from wives. The CIM had spread into fourteen provinces previously unoccupied by any Protestant mission and had put down roots in sixty-four base cities and as many additional advanced posts, with 110 chapels, 66 organised churches, twelve ordained and forty-nine lay preachers and others making a total of 132 Chinese colleagues. The Mission had seven working doctors, three hospitals and sixteen opium refuges, apart from Pastor Hsi's. Douthwaite and Cameron ran the Chefoo hospital until Cameron returned to Chongqing; Edwards and Stewart carried on the work Schofield had begun in Taiyuan; Pruen and Herbert Parry in Chengdu won a welcome where preachers had been unable to stay. Pruen then moved to Guiyang to ease the pressure on Andrew and Windsor. Henry Soltau had resigned, but Frank Trench and Horace Randle were nearing graduation at Edinburgh.

F. W. Baller completed his *Mandarin Primer* and sent a consignment home to Britain in the care of J. E. Cardwell. But Cardwell suffered shipwreck, escaping only with his life. In China the *Primer* earned high praise among the sinologues, including Griffith John, the leading missionary author in Chinese. John's dream of the LMS opening work in Sichuan at last came true with the despatch of Wallace Wilson and an evangelist from Hankou to Chongqing.[865]

Twenty-two years after the little *Lammermuir* party battled through typhoons to attempt 'the impossible', the arrival of the Hundred in one year brought the strength of the CIM to 225 in May and 265 at the end of 1887. When the *Chinese Recorder* tabulated the statistics of Protestant missions in China for December 1887, the American Presbyterian Mission (North) had ninety-eight, two other missions seventy, one sixty-six, one fifty-three and thirty-two other societies each had fewer than fifty, making a total of 1,040, including wives. The CIM's annual income had increased from under £3,000 in 1866 to £33,000 in 1887, an increase of £10,000 over the previous year.

In retrospect, even the periods of scarcity had been an asset, for the lesson they clearly taught was that less was needed than had been thought necessary. The great gap between the foreigners' standard of living and the Chinese Christians' had been narrowed; adaptation had been accelerated; and undreamed-of expansion on a more cost-effective budget had become possible.

The Lord's provision for his own work could literally be 'taken for granted' in response to trust and obedience, but the true indicator of success lay in the three thousand and more baptisms through the CIM and the churches these Christians formed.

If at the beginning of the year the prospects had been 'never so bright', even by mid-October John Stevenson felt justified in claiming, 'the work is advancing all along the line'.[866]

1888: To become international?

After the Hundred (1888)

Among the scores of men and women offering to follow the Hundred to China or enquiring about the CIM were many most attractive candidates. In 1888, fifty-three were sent out, and forty-one the following year. On February 6, 1888, the council interviewed a superlative young Cambridge 'first' named G. L. Pilkington. Because there was 'a kind of feeling at Cambridge', to quote Eugene Stock, 'that the CMS was stiff, inelastic, old-fashioned, lacking in spiritual fervour . . . Pilkington offered himself to the China Inland Mission'.[867] But, without explanation in the council's minutes, he was deferred. His father was urging him to wait two years before taking action, and at the end of that time he offered to go to Africa in the CMS. The Master of Pembroke saw in him 'a Hannington or a Gordon'. Eugene Stock typically wrote in his *History of the CMS*, 'It was like Hudson Taylor's unfailing generosity to say to a CMS Secretary [Stock himself?] "The Lord give you many more such men."' Pilkington and Wilmot Brooke (see pp 494–95) were accepted by the CMS at the same committee meeting, on December 3, 1889, and the Exeter Hall was filled to overflowing on January 20 for a great valedictory meeting addressed by the African Bishop Crowther, with Dr A. T. Pierson taking part. China, Africa it was all one 'harvest field'. 'Mackay of Uganda' was lying ill at the time, and died within three weeks. The CIM mourned with the CMS.

In the first CIM party to sail, on January 26, was Geraldine (Grattan) Guinness, followed later by Edith, the third of Benjamin's and Amelia's family to go; by H. N. Lachlan MA, a barrister who quickly made his mark; by E. O. Williams of Leeds, the vicar, and his family; by the Barclay sisters Priscilla and Florence; and, among more than can be named, by E. J. Cooper, the architect's assistant who became the gifted architect-builder of the CIM. For accepting Florence Barclay 'an inexperienced child' on his own responsibility, and at short notice (except that he had known her family for years and Florence herself as she grew up) Hudson Taylor was rebuked by William Sharp of the Council.[868] She had become a professing Christian only a few weeks previously! He had no qualms; she did well as a missionary and married Montagu Beauchamp.

The incessant round of meetings continued to keep Hudson Taylor stretched to his limit, in the north and west country, until he exchanged them for a similar treadmill in Cannes, with scarcely a moment his own—in Alsace-Lorraine, Mentone, San Remo, Geneva, Lausanne, Vevey, Montreux and Neuchatel, from March 9 to April 7. If suggestions of North American and Scandinavian extensions of the Mission had occupied his thoughts, no hint of Switzerland's following suit appears in his correspondence at this time. That came later.

The annual meetings in May were the highlight, before he fulfilled his promise to Henry Frost by sailing to North America in June. His report on the year 1887, published in *China's Millions*, began on the note, 'What a FATHER we have to depend on!' He had sent more than the Hundred prayed for, and not only the extra £10,000 needed but an increase of income from £22,000 to more than £33,700.[869] Not only so, instead of an overwhelming flood of small donations involving many letters of thanks, God had moved major donors to send eleven gifts ranging from £500 to £2,500 to a total of £10,000. And CIM members had reached 294, with 132 Chinese colleagues. All but one of the unevangelised interior provinces now had resident missionaries, with only Hunan still defying all attempts.

When 'China's Sorrow', the Huang He (literally, Yellow River), had overflowed and washed away its banks again, the Mission had sent relief (through Dorward and others) and would continue to do so as famine followed the devastation. Dorward, after his long relief operation, returned to Shashi and quietly occupied the little town of Shishou a few miles from the Hunan border. From Shishou, inconspicuously reached by river, Hunan was to be penetrated from time to time.

The CMS had an unusual member in J. Heywood Horsburgh. While William Cassels's conviction deepened that Anglican Church principles and government were compatible with the CIM, Horsburgh's contentment in eastern China diminished.[870] He visited Sichuan in May 1888 with Arthur Polhill-Turner and conceived a plan to bring in a team of CMS missionaries dedicated to living and working 'on lines of unusual simplicity', even by CIM standards. His graphic letters to Britain created a stir upon which he built with 'persuasive earnestness' when he returned home in 1890.

The Committee of the CMS sanctioned his scheme and he set about recruiting his party. To meet resistance to his appeal he wrote a booklet, *Do Not Say*, of which

Eugene Stock wrote that it 'has perhaps been used of God to touch more hearts and to send more men and women into the Mission Field . . . than any modern publication'. That the CMS should sponsor independent action like that of Wilmot Brooke in Africa, Barclay Buxton in Japan and Heywood Horsburgh in China dispelled the undeserved reputation for fustiness it had acquired. Horsburgh wrote, 'Risks, sacrifices, the stretching of nerves, muscles, faith all to the very limit, are the stuff of conquest . . . Is the Christian warfare the only one in which it is wrong to run any risk?'[871]

In Shanxi, Pastor Hsi had weathered the storm of Fan's attack on the opium refuges (see p 464), and his mind was expanding in the warmth of John Stevenson's and Orr Ewing's encouragement to extend his opium refuges not only in his own but in neighbouring provinces also. He could never forget that he had been an addict, burning away his health and wealth in that sickly sweet smoke. The shame and suffering, the enslavement of his nation, of his emperor and imperial court, viceroys, governors and magistrates, fired his determination to do all he could to free all who would accept his help, and to complete their liberation by binding them to Christ.[872] But while Western nations forced opium incessantly upon China there was nothing he could do to stop the flood. Missions protested while merchants made much of their opportunities and governments supported them by imposing favourable trade agreements. But missions and even the anti-opium societies were half-hearted after decades of failure to stem the tide. In June 1888 the CIM was to supply the missing impetus in a way that Hudson Taylor himself took time to recognize.

An opium war declared (1888)

Those of us who have lived under the curse of opium know the enormity of its evil. To see, too late, the wreck of skin and bones who was once a mandarin, scholar or merchant was to know the long story of debt, of decimation of heirlooms and household effects, and the break-up of family and hopes. Dirt, disease and despair turned the cultured townsman and contented village elder into a scheming rogue and common thief. To walk or ride mile after mile through territory given over to the opium poppy where good crops once thrived; to see the magistrate with his armed escort collecting his dues for turning a blind eye; to meet bowls of black opium syrup on market stalls as both a commodity and currency in place of legal tender; to watch a mother feed opium to a child to keep it quiet; to hear children crying not only for the food their parents could no longer afford, but crying for opium; to know that men were selling their wives and daughters to buy more of the drug; to find one person teaching another to smoke it, simply to pass the time of day; to march the would-be opium suicide up and down, hour after hour, administering emetics and stimulants, and slapping his face, anything to keep him going while his overdose wore off—was all reality, yet no more than a microcosm of the vast scale on which this curse existed. Some, forced by pain to find relief in opium for lack of other treatment, had become dependent on it, but welcomed cure. True medicinal opium formed a minute fraction of the ship-loads being imported.

Missionaries could not travel without being guided, rowed, carried and accommodated by opium addicts, or robbed by opium fiends. To fall asleep after a long, hard day's travel, to the tune of the animals munching and the opium pipes sizzling in the close atmosphere of hay and sweat and opium fumes, was the upcountry traveller's common experience.

Every CIM missionary in this history was familiar with it and powerless to do much to help. Palliatives were futile. Treatment refuges (the best way of all) succeeded only when the patient was determined to be freed, or received new life through faith in Jesus Christ. Prevention would only be possible when the Chinese government made opium unobtainable. And that could only happen when foreign nations stopped the iniquitous traffic in opium from abroad,

when Britain ceased to base the revenue of her Indian empire on its production and sale to China (see 1, pp 369, 447, 848 n 496).[873]

From its inception, *China's Millions* had highlighted the opium scandal, with frequent articles and letters from CIM missionaries and staff.[874] Readers had a clear impression of social and personal conditions in a China plagued by opium. Chinese woodcuts reminiscent of William Hogarth's 'Rake's Progress' accompanied a long series of articles in 1878–79 by S. Mander on the history and effects of the traffic. Editorials by Hudson Taylor and Benjamin, and articles from other periodicals, reported what was being done or said at anti-opium conferences. An appeal by the Society of Friends against the opium trade, and a report of the Anti-Opium Conference at Mildmay in April 1881 were given space, with Lord Shaftesbury's denunciation of this 'greatest of modern abominations'. In April 1882, Hudson Taylor wrote strongly in condemnation of Britain's guilt and responsibility:

> Nothing is more clear than that the Chinese had both the right, the power, and the will to stamp out the use of opium in China at the time when they first came into collision with the power of England. We are fully convinced that but for England they would then have accomplished this; and hence we feel that England is morally responsible for every ounce of opium now produced in China, as well as for that imported from abroad. She wishes to make the importation of Indian opium unprofitable, for England's profession of Christian principles she too fully believes to be hollow and insincere.

After a united meeting of the societies on March 15, 1882, on 'The Truth about Opium-Smoking', Hodder and Stoughton published Benjamin Broomhall's booklet of the same title, amplifying the Exeter Hall addresses and exposing the lies of the pro-opium lobby.[875] And in 1883 *China's Millions* ran an illustrated series by Julius Jeffrey, FRCS, on the production of opium in India, all going to debauch the Chinese.

The *Chinese Recorder* spoke up strongly, and Sir Robert Hart's data, cited from the Chinese Imperial Maritime Customs, substantiated the contentions.[876] The total export trade of China in 1879 had been $100 million, but the opium imported from abroad totalled 100,000 chests of 1,000 million Chinese pounds weight (13⅓ million British pounds or 6 million kg). An equal amount of opium was by then being grown in China. The cost to Chinese consumers of 12 million kg weight of the drug was £25 million, but the value of wages in China was only one half of the value in Britain. So British people should regard this cost to Chinese consumers as £50 million, with opium imports exceeding China's total export trade of one hundred million dollars by twenty million dollars—as he expressed it.

A mandarin fellow-passenger told Hudson Taylor with conviction that Britain's plot was clearly to seize China by means of opium. Sir Robert's statement, with a sigh, that in his region of north China alone, of five viceroys three were opium smokers, indicated the extent to which the alleged plot was succeeding. And Benjamin's daughter, Gertrude, witnessed this penetration when a viceroy's daughter came to stay with her in Taiyuan to overcome her addiction. She became an active Christian.

In 1884 the *Church Missionary Intelligencer* published a paper by Dr R. N. Cust, an Indian Civil Service official, who from being a supporter of missions became a notorious critic of them. His arguments represented the attitude of the opposition:

> The missionary should not meddle in politics, or in culture of the soil, or in commerce. Nor should he be tempted ... to try his prentice-hand at ruling men ... (He is) in a false position when he attempts to hold the reins of Civil Government ... When he goes out of his way to deal with such tangled questions as a gigantic commerce betwixt two such great nations as India and China, he fails in his object, being unable to measure the surrounding forces ... Let him leave Caesar's business to Caesar, and keep his mind on the affairs of God.[877]

Dr Cust was answered as he deserved by the CMS and others, but he had demonstrated the probability that the British government in India would not change its ways without strong coercion from outside. The immense task of turning the British Indian economy away from opium and on to other sources of revenue could only be decided and enforced by the national will in Parliament at Westminster. The whole issue of the degradation of China, the imposition of the hated drug upon China, the opium economy of India and its perpetuation by successive governments in Whitehall was too vast to be undermined by spasmodic criticism or protest at any level. Sustained pressure to mould the minds of the nation had become imperative. Moral indignation must drive members of Parliament to support strong measures calling upon the government of the day to find those substitute sources of revenue for India. Only long sustained pressure would ensure measure after measure reaching the statute-book until all opium production and trade under British patronage came to an end.

But it would be a long haul first to change the ingrained attitudes of thousands who thought as R. N. Cust did. They were to be found even in the councils and committees of missionary societies, and to be met in specious statements such as Sir George Birdwood's that 'opium was not only innocuous but positively beneficial to the Chinese'.[878] The third International Missionary Conference held at the Exeter Hall in London, June 9–20, 1888, under the presidency of the Earl of Aberdeen, not only provided a glaring demonstration of this truth that national indignation must be aroused, but inadvertently launched the movement which did as much as any to win success in the end.

'National Righteousness' at stake[879]
(1888)

Two men approached the International Missionary Conference of 1888 with determination not to let the occasion pass without strong action being taken to end the opium scandal fully and finally. Such meetings of minds and organisations could only be arranged at intervals of ten or twenty years. Their potential was unique. If they spoke with one voice even governments would listen.

Dr James Laidlaw Maxwell, the English Presbyterian pioneer and first Protestant missionary to Taiwan, had figured prominently as an eye-witness speaker in the anti-opium cause. Benjamin Broomhall, on the executive committee of the Society for the Suppression of the Opium Trade and as secretary to the China Inland Mission, using *China's Millions* to make his voice heard, shared James Maxwell's indignation and resolve. In 1881 he had been nominated to join a deputation to Mr Gladstone, and reporting on the agreement protecting opium he declared, 'We ought never to cease our protest until the Indian Government ceases to manufacture or to encourage the manufacture of opium for sale in China.'[880] His biographer son wrote:

> The sufferings of humanity (and) his strong sense of justice made him the passionate denouncer of the iniquitous opium traffic and the fearless advocate of national righteousness ... (Parliamentary) blue books and papers (were) accumulated for his anti-opium crusade ... He trembled lest the judgments of God might fall upon his beloved country because of the wrong she had done to China.

These two men on the executive committee of the international conference urged their fellow-conveners from several leading societies to allocate time for debating this major obstacle to the gospel among a quarter of the world's population. But the abundance of subjects claiming the attention of the conference blinded the committee's eyes to the value of the potent instrument in their hands. 'They were told that the subject did not properly belong to a Missionary Conference, that it touched on politics, that there were different opinions on the evil of the opium habit, that the raising of such a question would cause trouble.'[881]

So thorny a subject might antagonise the government and endanger harmony among missions! For decades the same cavils had paralysed all attempts to coerce governments into halting the traffic. W. A. P. Martin had written a book in 1856 describing the effects of opium abuse and of current trade and legislation. For his pains his colleagues had reported him to his mission board for wasting his time. He had replied: 'The missionaries are the only ones to speak out—the merchants are involved and the officials are fearful. [And again] If the early missionaries had done more in pointing out the enormity of the opium evil, a curse might have been averted from China and a mountainous obstacle out of the way of Christian missions.'[882]

Thirty years had passed and the enormity of the crime had correspondingly increased. When the majority on the executive committee decided that no action should be taken, Maxwell and Benjamin appealed to the General Committee. The appeal was upheld, even though to provide for it the conference had to be extended by an additional day.

Delegates numbering 1,579 assembled from fifty-seven American societies, eighteen Continental societies and fifty-three British societies (eleven from the colonies). The Third Lambeth Conference of Anglican bishops (worldwide) was to take place three weeks later, but only one English bishop took part in this International Missionary Conference and few clergymen. The Christian public also appeared to think it was not for them. Exeter Hall could have held many more. Good addresses by outstanding men followed one on the heels of another, the American delegates of whom A. T. Pierson was one, were 'quite in the front for ability, culture and eloquence'. Hudson Taylor found accommodation in the Strand nearby, and as one among many speakers waited his turn. Eugene Stock was there, conscious of 'a sense, not exactly of failure, but of incompleteness, in the minds of many.'

Maxwell and Benjamin saw it in stronger terms. As it transpired, their session was to be the grand finale of the conference. But instead of having the whole time with an incisive single topic, three were to be run together: opium in China, drink in Africa, and licensed vice in India. Undeterred, they made capital out of this triad of targets. Sir Stevenson Arthur Blackwood, KCB, presiding, delivered a powerful opening speech that called for both protest and action. Each subject was then taken up separately, adding to instead of detracting from the others, with a resolution on each being moved by the main speaker. In an address full of proof and testimony to the evils of opium-smoking and Britain's culpability for imposing the scourge upon China, Hudson Taylor moved:

> That this Conference, representing most of the Protestant Missionary Societies of the Christian World desires to put on record its sense of the incalculable evils, physical, moral and social, which continue to be wrought in China through the opium trade—a trade which has strongly prejudiced the people of China against all Missionary efforts.
>
> That it deeply deplores the position occupied by Great Britain, through its Indian administration, in the manufacture of the drug and in the promotion of a trade which is one huge ministry to vice.
>
> That it recognizes clearly that nothing short of the entire suppression of the trade, so far as in the power of the Government to suppress it, can meet the claims of the case.
>
> And that it now makes its earnest appeal to the Christians of Great Britain and Ireland to plead earnestly with God, and to give themselves no rest, until this great evil is entirely removed. And, further, that copies of this resolution be forwarded to the Prime Minister and the Secretary of State for India.[883]

This was the first step, Hudson Taylor continued to mobilise Christians to ceaseless involvement 'until this great evil is entirely removed'. Christians were influential in Victorian Britain. Direct political activism was to follow. 'It is with sin that we have to wage war, it is against sin that we have to protest . . . The power of

Satan must be seen behind the actions of government and individuals . . . But the Son of God was manifested to destroy the devil and his work.'

This was part of the spiritual objective of missions. While the result of eighty years of Protestant evangelism in China was a church of 32,000 communicant members, eighty years of opium traffic had enslaved 150 millions of opium addicts and their families.

Dr Maxwell reinforced Hudson Taylor's plea, saying,

> There is the British House of Commons to be reached; and before that there is the conscience of England to be reached; and still before that, and most important of all, there is the heart of the Christian Church in England to be touched ... Of late years there has crept over Christians in this country a very strange and terrible apathy in dealing with this opium trade ... We have not got this matter inside our hearts as a burden upon our souls (of our great guilt) before God ... I am sometimes amazed at myself, at the want of feeling concerning the terribleness of this evil among the Chinese ... In this hall tonight there is a constituency large enough, if set on fire by the Spirit of God on this subject, to begin to move England from end to end.

Among the 'specially animated debates' of the conference, the one on the opium resolution was outstanding. Dr Cust 'faced an almost unanimously hostile audience'.[884] The resolution was 'unanimously adopted by the meeting' and they moved on to the other two subjects. But the conference committee had the final word. They declared themselves reluctant to recognise the resolution as representative of the conference as a whole. No appeal against this judgment was possible.

James Maxwell and Benjamin Broomhall were indignant. It was as they had feared. The resolution would languish as so many others on the subject had, year after year, decade after decade. They felt driven to independent action. They would undertake themselves to carry the message to the nation through an alliance of Christians 'for the severance of the connection of the British Empire with the opium traffic'.

Hudson Taylor sailed from Liverpool three days later, with a daunting program of engagements ahead of him in the States and Canada. On the same day, June 23, Jennie wrote to him, saying that Benjamin was 'full of a Christian Union against opium and a paper to be called *National Righteousness*'. Like the Society for the Suppression of the Opium Trade, which they intended to complement not to rival, their motto was to be 'Righteousness exalteth a nation, but sin is a reproach to any people' (Proverbs 14.34 AV). 'Union' was a current term. Trades Unions were in the news. 'Christians United' might today carry the same thrust. With a minimum of entangling, time-consuming organisation, and not even a 'constitution' to be debated and defined, Christians would work together and pray together until its purpose was achieved. Benjamin, with his already wide contacts through Britain would be the publicist, and edit the periodical, *National Righteousness*, in his own time. James Maxwell, as secretary, would handle the resulting correspondence, although founder and director since 1878 of the Medical Missionary Association (of London).[885]

Sir Stevenson Arthur Blackwood agreed to be president, with J. Bevan Braithwaite as chairman and James E. Mathicson of Mildmay completing the committee. An annual subscription of one shilling was to cover costs. 'As the Opium Question must ultimately be settled in the House of Commons it is intended to form Committees in the principal towns of the kingdom' to arrange public meetings and 'prepare for speedy and decisive action'— political pressure groups. Inside the cover of Volume l, Number 1, was the statement: 'The Christian Union was formed on Tuesday, June 26, 1888. Already the membership exceeds sixteen hundred.'[886]

A major achievement by the CIM for China was to be accomplished outside China.

It was Mr Broomhall's keen perception of the secret of the weakness of the anti-opium movement in the ignorance and apathy of the Churches, that lay behind this new effort [Dr Maxwell wrote]. There could be no hope of victory until the Churches had been thoroughly aroused ... (He) had a peculiar gift for incisive and tactful names, and ... National Righteousness as it began its course among the thousands and ten thousands of clergy and ministers and influential Christian laymen ... was nothing less than a summons to the Christian mind of the country.

So Benjamin added this work to the already oppressive burden of selecting and sending 'the second hundred' to China. And to organising the CIM's endless succession of farewell, annual and deputation meetings he added more to awaken the conscience of Britain through the church. Yet none of these provided enough expression of his most effective gift, which Maxwell again described.

He loved to bring men together in large social conferences. His breakfast gatherings, first in the Exeter Hall and later in the Hotel Cecil and other places, were a real strength to the movement. They brought together leading men in the Churches and members of Parliament and influential laymen, over this one subject. ... Nor did he neglect the House of Commons. He steadily strove to bring the influence of National Righteousness to bear on its members. The magazine was always so strikingly got up, its point so clear, its information so trustworthy, and the urgency of its morals so definite ... the cumulative effect of its messages had, there is no room to doubt, a powerful effect in moulding legislative opinion.

Benjamin was to continue this campaign until it succeeded when he was on his death-bed in 1911, twenty-three years later. Inescapably he earned from the apathetic the label of 'extreme and rabid'. Although his policy was to avoid 'red rag' publicity, he advocated: 'We must be as pungent as we can. We have no need to go cap in hand humbly to Ministers . . . or any other official. We must demand, and press our demand.' So persuasion on a large scale was to be sustained interminably. 'Even a quarter of a million copies of Dr (Handley) Moule's speech is little more than a drop in the bucket to arouse England . . . I propose to circulate a quarter of a million and 20,000 of Holcombe's book.' His tremendous energy and ability to work until midnight and later, day after day, were matched by as great a gift. 'In the goodness of God I have been saved through many years from yielding to discouragement for five minutes, and yet there are times when one feels weary.'

Hudson Taylor himself had attacked the opium scandal without remission for years already and continued to do so, but always as a complement of his great obsession, the gospel to the whole of China as soon as possible. His surviving documents contain few references to this side of Benjamin's work, but he played his part. Opium refuges could only save the scores, body and soul, while hundreds more became addicted. Benjamin had seen through to the heart of the evil. Prevention must overtake cure. Far from being a distraction from the main task, the eradication of this blot on the face of Christianity in China was a major prerequisite to the acceptance of the gospel. Hudson Taylor agreed. But to some extent Benjamin's commitment to the crusade undermined their mutual confidence and contributed to disharmony between them on matters of Mission policy. At the same time developments arising from Hudson Taylor's whirlwind preaching tour in the States and Canada looked in London even more like a red herring—the avoidable distraction of establishing the CIM in North America.

A journey in the dark
(June–October 1888)

Henry Frost's visit to Britain, the 'veritable bog of blasted hopes', within a few weeks showed firm ground for optimism. Unknown to any of those involved, that visit had already marked an epoch in the life of Hudson Taylor and the history of the CIM. At home again, Frost looked for invitations

to bring Hudson Taylor to the States. Dr W. J. Erdman, convener of the 'Believers Bible Study Conference' at Niagara-on-the-Lake, near to the Falls, responded at once and wrote to Hudson Taylor. Dr A. T. Pierson, the great expositor, and editor of the *Missionary Review of the World*, wrote to him (before the international conference), 'No man on earth whom I have not seen in the flesh has so much of my heart's best love as you. I am in profound sympathy with your aims, methods, mission and spirit.' Would he come at least for a short visit? But D. L. Moody, who already knew Hudson Taylor, failed to reply to Frost's suggestion that he should invite him to his summer conference for students at Northfield, Mount Hermon. For before Henry Frost's letter reached him he had already asked his brother-in-law Fleming H. Revell, on a visit to Britain, to deliver an invitation to him.[887] Frost had done his part and a welcome was clear. Hudson Taylor could only fulfil his promise.

Reginald Radcliffe, the fiery evangelist with whom Hudson Taylor had had so much to do in 1884 and whose stentorian voice had taken up the cause of the evangelisation of the world, had been

2.61 *The 1888 visit to the USA and Canada*

invited too. They met at Liverpool and sailed on Saturday, June 23, by the SS *Etruria*. Hudson Taylor, his personal secretary S. F. Whitehouse, Howard Taylor (free for a few weeks before taking up appointments as house-surgeon and house-physician at the London Hospital) travelled 'semi-steerage' by 'intermediate class', and

Mr and Mrs Radcliffe less austerely; but the ship's captain asked Hudson Taylor to conduct the Sunday service in the first-class saloon. Neither could know what lay ahead.

Annie Macpherson had written from Canada, where large numbers of her East End orphans had settled, 'I believe there are more brave and well-educated men waiting for your loved China in the Canadian colleges than in any other part of the globe.' But, Hudson Taylor was to write, 'Mr Radcliffe had remarked to me, and I to him, more than once as we were crossing the ocean together, that we felt we did not know what God was taking us to America for, though we felt that we were following His leading.'

An expansive movement among students had begun in North America as in Britain, interweaving British and American strands to direct tens of thousands of men and women into the service of God overseas and at home.[888]

In the States and Canada the American inter-collegiate YMCA was gaining strength in the 1870s and two members, Luther Wishard and Charles K. Ober, saw in D. L. Moody's Northfield conferences the right medium for rapid growth.

Northfield in Massachusetts on the Connecticut River that separates Vermont from New Hampshire, was Moody's lifetime home, his birthplace and retreat between strenuous campaigns and missions. In the rolling countryside along the river he created school campuses, one for girls and in 1881 at beautiful Mount Hermon one for boys. A training school for young Christians also grew up at Mount Hermon. During vacations he used them for conferences. The first Northfield Convocation (variously called Bible Conference or Christian Workers' Conference) in 1880 for anyone 'hungering for intimate fellowship with God and power to do His work', drew three hundred.[889]

Moody's second mission to Britain, 1881–84 (see pp 416–20), directly resulted in a conquest at Cambridge, the conversion of the Studds' father and some of the Cambridge Seven, and the surrender of others' lives to the service of Christ. Moody returned to his responsibilities at Northfield and Chicago, while the student world in Britain caught fire from the Seven. The fire then leapt the Atlantic to America. When J. E. Kynaston Studd went over in place of Stanley Smith, the third Northfield Conference, of August 1885, was ripe for A. T. Pierson's bombshell. Moody had allotted August 11 to 'prayer for worldwide missions'. A thousand Christians heard Pierson call at this 'hour for advance' for an appeal to the entire church to unite in planning a worldwide campaign to take the gospel to every living soul in the shortest possible time. Kynaston Studd was one of the signatories to the appeal, and Moody called for a vote of acclamation to ratify it. The ecumenical International Missionary Conference of June 1887 in London had been the outcome.

Luther Wishard was there at Northfield, and Studd toured the colleges with him. At Cornell, John R. Mott, a law student, was converted through 'JEK'. Big things were happening. Moody was still chary of close dealings with students, but Wishard knew his honest, bluff directness of speech and athletic friendliness counted for more than an academic education. 'He brought religion out of the clouds.' So Luther Wishard prevailed on him to invite not only YMCA leaders for a summer camp in 1886 but two hundred and fifty students, for 'Bible' morning and evening, with hours of baseball and swimming every afternoon.

Robert P. Wilder was among them, another of the great names of the student contribution to world mission. In 1883 Robert Wilder and four other students, in binding themselves together as the Princeton Foreign Missionary Society, had signed a declaration: 'We are willing and desirous, God permitting, to become Foreign Missionaries.' He and his sister Grace covenanted together to pray for a thousand volunteers from North American universities, and at Northfield brought together the twenty-three who were already committed, to pray for more. While swimming in the Connecticut River he urged Mott to become a missionary. He prevailed on Moody to give A. T. Pierson the session in which he spoke on 'the evangelisation of the world in this generation', the theme that had its germ in the 1877 Shanghai Conference (see p 296) and anticipated the Student Volunteer Missionary Union's great watchword. Three weeks later he asked Moody to allow nine students from overseas and a North American Indian to address the conference. That so-called 'meeting of the Ten Missions' made history. In the shade of the Mount Hermon trees, the natural trysting place with God, student upon student made his covenant, and one hundred signed a declaration of willingness to go 'into all the world'.

The Student Volunteer Movement (SVM) had been born. From it came the Student Volunteer Missionary Union (SVMU) in 1896 when the same watchword was adopted. Charles Ober recorded the part the CIM played in its inception: 'The story . . . of the Cambridge band, particularly the account of the visit of a deputation of these students to other British universities, with their missionary message, made a profound impression on us. *Here really was the germ thought of the Student Volunteer Movement.*'[890] Robert Wilder and John Forman toured the universities, and in 1887 Forman crossed over to the British Isles and found himself welcomed to visit the universities with Hudson Taylor. The Northfield Conferences had become annual events, the students' conference preceding the general conference for the Christian public. Every year several hundreds signed the Volunteers' declaration and within the fifty years 1889–1939 'more than 25,000 university graduates—the great majority being North American—(entered) that service.'[891] But the upheaval of the First World War contributed to changes in the nature of the SVM and its product the Student Christian Movement (SCM), while the Inter-Varsity (Christian) Fellowship (IVF in UK, IVCF in North America) with Robert Wilder's strong encouragement perpetuated the original aims and principles.

By 1888 the Northfield Conferences and many like them in other parts of North America were drawing Christians in their thousands 'to wait upon God and learn from Him'. Bible teachers from Britain and the continent of Europe were in demand, as were North Americans in the British Isles. Reginald Radcliffe's prophetic cry at Perth in 1877 (see p 296) was seen to be less immoderate than some had thought: 'Let us pray God to gift 2,500 women at a stroke and 2,500 men at a stroke, and . . . to scatter them to the ends of the earth.' North America was more ready for his and Hudson Taylor's visit than they realised. As for the CIM, it was about to 'leap over (yet another) wall'.

'A very serious matter'[892] (July 1888)

Henry Frost was on the wharf at New York when the *Etruria* tied up on July 1. He took them to his father's affluent home at 80 Madison Avenue. Descended from a family which had endowed the foundation of St John's College, Cambridge, and then helped to found Harvard University, the Frosts had thrived in the New World. Henry's father was a civil engineer and became a railroad owner-manager. He had a country home at Attica, near Buffalo in New York State, where he and Henry had installed the town's gas and water supplies. And he gave Henry and his wife another fine house nearby.

The five raw British guests were given a royal welcome at Madison Avenue and had their first lesson in adaptation to America. As the English custom was, on retiring to bed all put their footwear outside the bedroom door to be cleaned by the household servants. Henry and his father discovered and worked on them late at night. But Hudson Taylor found out what had happened, bought polish and brushes, and tongue in cheek daily cleaned the Radcliffes' shoes while they were with him.

They travelled the next day to Moody's Mount Hermon campus at Northfield Mass., to join the hundreds of students from ninety different colleges in their conference. D. L. Moody himself met them 'in the middle of the night' and took them to his home. From then, July 2, for two weeks they were at the disposal of the students, with an interval of two days, July 10–12, to address the Bridgeton, New Jersey, conference. George Studd was there, with ten or twelve British and Continental students. Moody's notice of the 'College students' summer school and encampment for Bible Study' had read, 'Special attention will be given to athletics and to systematic recreation . . . Delegates should come fully equipped for bathing, tennis, baseball, football, hill climbing and other outdoor exercise. They should also bring their own reference Bibles and a good supply of notebooks.'

'Mr Radcliffe thundered forth impassioned utterances of missionary obligation,' Henry Frost recalled, 'and after them earthquakes; as Mr Taylor spoke there was the still, small voice . . . the voice that was longest remembered.' They wanted more and asked for extra sessions taken from recreation time. It was not, however, 'the words only . . . it was the life of the man'. John Forman years later told Robert Wilder, 'One of the greatest blessings of my life came to me through, not from, the Rev J. Hudson Taylor.' Wilder knew exactly what he meant, for 'that was how we all felt'. Writing of return visits to Madison Avenue and to the Frosts' country homes at Attica, Henry said, 'His Bible readings at morning prayers upon the Song of Solomon were thrilling and transforming . . . they left us, not only at the feet of the Lord; but also at his.'[893] At Northfield 'he not only made the needs of the mission field very real, he showed us the possibilities of the Christian life . . . His sympathy and naturalness attracted men to him.'

Howard Taylor also made a strong impression when he testified that he was preparing to go to China. And the death of a student by drowning concentrated the minds of others. Two weeks later Hudson Taylor received a letter saying, 'I am one of the Student Volunteers for Foreign Missions . . . Can you kindly tell ·me . . . the possibility of a student from

America obtaining an appointment in your Mission?' It was signed by Samuel M. Zwemer, future apostle to the Muslims of the Middle East.[894] By then Hudson Taylor had received one of the great revelations of his life.

From Northfield he and the Radcliffes, Howard Taylor, George Studd and Robert Wilder, strongly drawn to them, went on to 'a little gathering of perhaps 400' at Niagara-on-the-Lake, a quiet town on the southern shore of Lake Ontario, twenty miles from the twin cities of Niagara Falls. The abundance of ministers of various denominations in both Canada and the States led Howard to write of 'Collegians at Northfield and parsons at Niagara'. There Hudson Taylor received two unexpected letters.

One, from Bridgeton, where he had spent only one day on a flying visit, was a copy of a letter addressed to fellow-missionaries, saying that 'the Union', a new interdenominational approach to the conference there, had put Foreign Missions on a new footing. 'People who have never believed in Foreign Missions are declaring their interest; people who had spoken against the coming of the Union express great satisfaction with it; some say that it has been the greatest religious event that Bridgeton has ever known . . . the sales of Hudson Taylor's books also were phenomenal for this community.'

The other came from Clifton Springs, also dated July 18, and signed by twenty-one church leaders, including William Dean, DD, the veteran of fifty years in Bangkok and China. 'To the Rev J. Hudson Taylor; the Hon. Reginald Radcliffe and Mr (George) Studd' inviting them to fit Clifton Springs into their itinerary. This too was to make history.

At Niagara, Hudson Taylor spoke at only two meetings, 'on the subject of Missions', but characteristically made little mention of the CIM or even of China, in view of the general nature of the conference. Henry Frost, himself an organising secretary of the conference, learned afterwards that a young woman had come dreading the thought of being told about China and would have backed out if her train ticket had not been bought. 'Instead of hearing much about China,' he wrote, 'she heard a great deal about the Lord Jesus, and it ended in her offering for China . . . There is no difficulty about getting blessing when souls deal directly with the great Blesser.'[895]

But D. L. Moody had prevailed upon Hudson Taylor to give him a long weekend, July 21–24, at his and other churches in Chicago, and he left Niagara with Howard on July 20. The year before Moody founded his Bible Institute in 1889, Reginald Radcliffe and Robert Wilder stayed at Northfield, and the Friday evening session was given to them. 'And how they did speak!' Henry Frost recorded. 'Mr Radcliffe's utterance was a polemic and Robert Wilder's a plea', for worldwide evangelism. Neither was speaking for the CIM, but an extraordinary response gradually developed in the conference. Wilder used as an illustration the case of 'a lady he knew who worked twenty-four hours a day'. 'She herself worked twelve hours, and then had a representative in India who worked the other twelve while she slept.'

Someone then asked Reginald Radcliffe, 'How much it would take to support a missionary for a year in connection with the China Inland Mission?' and he, 'British to the end', replied 'Fifty pounds', leaving it to the American to multiply the amount by five.

The conference committee had decided that the annual collection should be given to the CIM, 'with the suggestion that it should be used for North American workers in connection with the Mission'. But Dr Stewart in Shanxi was the only one, and he was self-supporting. Henry Frost as a conference secretary in touch with Hudson Taylor found to his surprise that more than $500 had been contributed. But the next morning 'a spirit of enthusiasm' came over the large meeting, and Dr W. J. Erdman, the chairman, allowed all the informality the audience wanted. One person and then another stood up to say he intended 'to work twenty-four hours a day for missions'.

A group of ten young women called Henry Frost outside to ask whether they could combine by giving twenty-five dollars each. Their offer stirred the audience and 'other contributions were set on foot'. Then someone suggested that another 'offering' be taken up. 'There are big hearts and heavy purses in America,' Mrs Radcliffe wrote to Jennie, 'but like the old country, men are bound by preconceived notions.'

Unintentionally, by the nature of the CIM and his own personality, Hudson Taylor was breaking through those prejudices and moving those big hearts. When Henry Frost in his hotel room added up 'the spoils', as he put it, he had enough given or pledged for eight non-existent missionaries and 'I suddenly found myself an informal treasurer of the China Inland Mission. After all it looked very much as if the leading I had followed in going to England was no *ignis fatuus*.' Mr Radcliffe had underestimated the costs, if travel and housing were included, but the response was clear enough. Frost was elated.[896]

Hudson Taylor was on the station platform when Frost's train from Niagara pulled in at midnight. As soon as they reached his bedroom in the Frost parents' house Henry could keep the news to himself no longer. 'Mr Taylor usually had a responsive face . . . But this time his face fell . . . For once I was deeply disappointed in him.' He said, 'I think we had better pray.' They knelt beside his bed and he 'began to ask God what it all meant'. They stood up again and he asked gravely, Was the money to be used for North Americans? Yes, that was requested. '"This is serious," was all he said, more to himself than to me.' He 'had had an immediate perception of the meaning of what had taken place. Previously, he had refused to extend the Mission to North America. Was God forcing him to reverse that decision?' Incidental donations handed to him since his arrival in America he had been transmitting to London. But this was another matter.

'He said afterwards, "To have had missionaries and no money would not have caused me any anxiety; but to have money and no missionaries was a very serious matter."' If he appealed for North Americans, 'which so far he had carefully refrained from doing the Mission would be established on this side of the ocean . . . His only concern at any time was to discover the Lord's will.' They parted at about one o'clock, and Hudson Taylor wrote to Jennie calculating more realistically than Reginald Radcliffe had done, 'The means for a year's support of 5 or 6 new missionaries is given or promised, and great issues are likely to result from our visit.' He was weighing the alternatives: to return the donations given by a conference (now scattered) for a specific purpose, or to acknowledge the inescapable and apply them as requested. He was coming round to seeing the unfolding events as the hand of God.[897]

A North American '*Lammermuir* party' (August–October 1888)

Not far from New York was the seaside resort of Ocean Grove, NJ, an Episcopal Church 'camp meeting' where conventions were conducted all through the summer. Chalets and tents housed 20,000 to 30,000 at the height of the season. From July 28 to August 1, Hudson Taylor gave daily addresses—'last night three or four thousand people, perhaps more,' and 'Howard spoke last night on the beach. I suppose there were 10,000 people present.' 'I think we must have an American branch of the Mission,' he wrote from there to John Stevenson. 'Do not be surprised if I should bring reinforcements with me.' The way the funds had come in surely indicated that actual men and women would soon materialize. It looked as if 'God was really working' to send Americans and Canadians to China. But he knew of no one to entrust with their selection or preparation. Even Henry Frost he had known very briefly so far. He must handle it himself. 'I never felt more timid about anything in my life', even 'frightened', he was to comment a year later. But after consulting Moody and other mature Christians his uncertainty vanished.[898]

Then on to Northfield again for Moody's third general conference, August 1–9, where Hudson Taylor grasped the nettle. Leaving arrangements for managing affairs in North America to be settled later, and believing that God would provide for all whom God took to China, he appealed for men and women to go. 'It is trying, to live in a crowd,' he groaned to Jennie, 'I am so sought after that I can scarcely cross the hall without being stopped.' Three of Moody's Northfield students approached him, from churches as far afield as Pittsfield, Mass., near the east coast; Detroit, Michigan, between Chicago and Toronto; and St Paul, Minnesota, three hundred miles north-west of Chicago. And Samuel Zwemer's letter (see p 511) of August 2 came from Chicago.

As Hudson Taylor's meetings progressed through August and September, Canadians also applied to him until he had assessed and accepted seventeen or eighteen out of forty-two who offered themselves. He decided to take six of the mature men and eight women with him to China in October, and to Henry Frost's alarm told him 'he would have to do the best (he) could with the rest'. But Hudson Taylor's own difficulties increased, in that he had more money than he could use.

D. L. Moody undertook to provide the outfit and passage money of the first, Edith Lucas, who offered to go at short notice, and her church at St Paul promised her support. A relative of the late Sir Moses Montefiore and the Rothschilds and well educated, she had been cast off by her family when she became a Christian, and was working for Moody as a trained nurse. The second had been at Northfield for four years; her father said he had savings enough to support her for one year if not longer, and would not hear of others paying for his daughter while he had the means. The third, Susie Parker, was given permission by her parents to go, in her father's words, 'I have nothing too precious for my Lord Jesus.'[899]

Henry Frost had to stay at home with his own father, who had been taken ill, but donations kept coming to him. When eight volunteers had been accepted, the original Niagara Conference fund was still untouched. Enough for fifteen was received. Cautiously Frost asked Hudson Taylor again, 'Will it not be well to establish a branch here? I have much to say to you.' He would need help and advice, and knew good men whom he believed would be willing to join him. But while Hudson Taylor could write, 'I feel sure that the Lord has sent me here . . . We shall get a few missionaries at once I hope,' he also wrote (to Jennie) 'Others will go to England and come out in the usual way [meaning first generation immigrants whose parents were in Britain. Edith Lucas's mother was in London and Jeanie Munro's in Scotland] and I hope the day will come when BB will come over and form a branch of our work here. It might soon become a very important part of the mission.' Whether he had in mind at this moment a branch under the only existing 'Home Council', the one in Britain, or a branch of the Mission in general, with a second Home Council, is not clear.

A letter came from William Berger at this stage with another gift of £500. Someone had written to ask him, was it true that the CIM had come to an end; that Mr Taylor had gone to America? Far from it. What struck John Stevenson when Hudson Taylor reached Shanghai in October was that his ideas had taken wings. The influence of Northfield and American big-thinking and doing had expanded Hudson Taylor's concept of what the Mission could become.[900]

After the Northfield Conference, things began to move more rapidly. Besides his prearranged speaking engagements, he now had to visit the new missionaries' home churches. At Clifton Springs the welcome by William Dean and his fellow-ministers could not have been warmer. In place after place he was melted by 'such a wealth of love'. 'It is not uniformity that we want but really manifested heart unity,' he wrote. From August 14–29 he was at ten towns and cities in Canada.[901] Howard Taylor was usually with him (until he left Detroit for England on the 29th, addressing meetings on the way). But Reginald Radcliffe and George

Studd came and went, sometimes together, sometimes apart, to meet the demand for meetings.

Interviewing five or six candidates took a whole morning. The secretary of the Hamilton YMCA told him that the Hamilton Christian Associations were praying that seven of their number would go to China. Four young women and two from Hamilton sailed with Hudson Taylor in October, and Rough, the secretary, went via Europe. 'Some dozen of our circle ultimately landed in China.' A local newspaper was impressed but baffled, saying, 'The venerable gentleman concluded a long, most interesting address, by informing the audience that the members of the China Inland Mission depended upon chance providences for a scanty subsistence.' Back at Toronto he preached four times on Sunday, 26th, and was in Chicago, 500 miles away, with Radcliffe and George Studd by the 30th. The demands on his stamina were unrelenting. Reading the mail accumulated there took until 2 a.m., but answering it adequately proved impossible. 'Such a nice long one from BB. I wish I could repay it.' But there were more candidates to be seen, and on Sunday, September 2, he walked sixteen miles and preached twice.

In the auditorium of the YMCA, Hudson Taylor finished speaking and, sensing the mood of the audience, D. L. Moody called for the ushers to take up a collection. Hudson Taylor intervened, but the opportunity was too good for Moody to let slip. Might he explain, Hudson Taylor asked? He thanked Moody and the meeting for their generous impulse. But the CIM never took collections lest money be diverted from the older missions. If anyone after supporting their own boards wished to help the CIM they could always write. When the Moody Bible Institute was inaugurated a year later, a Christian merchant revealed that he left Hudson Taylor's meeting glad that the $50 note he was going to donate still lay safely in his wallet. But his conscience troubled him until the next morning he sent a cheque for $500.[902]

In a sleeping-car on the way to

Minneapolis and St Paul, four or five hundred miles beyond Chicago, Hudson Taylor wrote, 'I think I shall get 8 or 10 associates [that is, fully supported and independent but working by CIM practices and under CIM direction]. How often I have wished for BB to give counsel about some of the candidates. I believe had he been here we might have had double the number and full support for them.' If Hudson Taylor underestimated his own judgment and influence, it was because 'the people have need to be understood, more than the Canadians, who are more like ourselves'. But he was undeterred. The British 'Bible Christians' in associate relationship with the CIM were on a different footing. They belonged to the Bible Christian Mission, as Erik Folke represented the Swedish Mission in China. There was no such organisation in North America, and none of these men and women was financially independent.

After St Paul they made a great detour south to Kansas city and St Louis, before returning via other places to the Frosts' Attica home. The scale of development of the CIM was clearly in his mind. By then the Mission had 216 members in China, with fifty more due from Britain 'this season', and a growing number winding up their personal affairs and outfitting in North America. In comparison, he showed Jennie in a letter from the train near Kansas city, American missionaries in China currently totalled 234 while British and Continental numbered 235. The CIM would reach 300 before long[903] (see map 2.61: p 508).

The party to travel with him to China were already assembling at Attica. The Frosts (Henry, his wife and parents) put their homes at their disposal and set no limit. They could overflow if necessary into lodgings and hotels. More farewell meetings for the travellers and their families and churches were to be held at Lockport, Hamilton, Guelph, Toronto and Montreal, where they would board the transcontinental train to Vancouver.

Accepting the substance of two accounts which diverge in detail, we have an example of the composure that Hudson Taylor's American friends remembered long afterwards. A Mr Joshua S. Helmer of Lockport had undertaken the arrangements for the party to board the Toronto train early one morning. But a delay in the carriage(s) coming to take them to the station left too little time for all handling of the baggage to be finished before the train moved off. To Mr Helme's great distress 'the whole company' were left standing on the platform. He turned to make abject apologies to Hudson Taylor, for no later train would get them to their destination for their farewell meeting. Instead he found him 'as calm and possessed as if the train were still waiting', and saying that the Lord could still get them there if it was his will. While they were still speaking, an unscheduled excursion train drew in. It connected with another and they arrived on time.

In the other account Hudson Taylor (with no companions mentioned) was alleged to say, 'My Father manages the trains and I'll be there.' He took a train in the opposite direction although the possible connection involved catching a train which normally left the junction ten minutes before he could arrive—and caught it. But hearsay notoriously gathers myth.[904]

The last days, in Canada[905] (September–October 1888)

The climax was in sight. Large-hearted America had swept them on from one great welcome to another. The crescendo continued. Remarkable meetings, 'which I have certainly never seen exceeded anywhere' followed closely on each other at Hamilton, Guelph and Toronto when the six men and eight women forgathered with Hudson Taylor and his secretary, Whitehouse. On Sunday, September 23, Hudson Taylor spoke in 'three or four of the principal churches' and Reginald Radcliffe elsewhere, before the final meeting in the new YMCA hall. All the approaches were so packed that the speakers could not reach the doors. A circuitous route brought them somehow to

2.62 The first North American party, with Radcliffes and Hudson Taylor; Henry Frost is behind Mrs Radcliffe

the platform. Standing people packed all aisles after the seats were filled. And when a second hall was full, 'vast numbers were unable even to enter the building'. The meeting lasted from 8.00 until almost 11.00 p.m. with 'no slackening of the pressure', 'close attention' and 'deep emotion'; 'meetings such as no one present would ever forget', the papers reported.

Each of the fourteen (all but two from Ontario) told how God had led them to 'give themselves for China'. Monday and Tuesday they spent with their families and friends, making final preparations, while Hudson Taylor discussed arrangements with Frost and others before leaving for Montreal to rejoin them at North Bay on the transcontinental railroad. After a communion service in Knox Church, at 9.00 p.m. on Tuesday night, the fourteen went to the Union Station, where a crowd of between five hundred and a thousand congregated to see them off. The station 'trembled with farewell songs', and when they had steamed out the YMCA men walked four abreast and singing through the main streets back to the Association hall.[906]

In his factual account of those days, Henry Frost went on to tell of how Hudson Taylor and he spent that Monday afternoon. Alfred Sandham, of the Christian Institute, Toronto, had agreed to interview and assess a continuing stream of Canadian volunteers, while Henry Frost was to deal

with Americans—twenty-eight and almost daily increasing. (As Benjamin could not come to take over, Hudson Taylor felt duty-bound to make provision of some sort.) The three of them were together in the Institute building, working out how to proceed after Hudson Taylor had gone. He explained that permanent arrangements would follow consultation with the China and London Councils, but a tentative auxiliary council was desirable for Sandham and Frost to consult. They were of one mind, and soon agreed that Dr H. M. Parsons of Knox Church, William Gooderham with 'philanthropic' connections, and J. D. Nasmith, a business man, should be approached. As they talked there was a knock at the door and Dr Parsons came in. He consented to act with Frost and Sandham and the conversation continued until interrupted by another knock. J. D. Nasmith appeared, and Hudson Taylor was able personally to invite him to join the others. At this Dr Parsons began to talk about prophecy. But when William Gooderham arrived as unexpectedly,

> his presence was almost like an apparition ... it was so startling ... It seemed to border on the miraculous (for) not one of the three knew that Mr Taylor was in the Institute, that all were seeking Mr Sandham and that two of the three had not been in the building for several months past. Thus gathered together by the Spirit of the Lord, we had, on Monday, September 24th, 1888, what was practically the first Council meeting of the Mission held in North America.[907]

Eight others were added soon afterwards.

In the train to Montreal Henry Frost read a Knox College magazine article, 'Hudson Taylor in Toronto'—a diatribe which made him hot with indignation. Lest Hudson Taylor see it, he slipped it under a pile of papers beside him. But Hudson Taylor had been told about it. He asked for it and read it 'from start to finish'.

Hudson Taylor is rather disappointing. I had in my mind an idea of what (great missionaries) should look like ... He being professedly one of the greatest missionaries of modern times must be such as they. But he is not ... A stranger would never notice him on the street ... except, perhaps, to say that he is a good-natured looking little Englishman. Nor is his voice in the least degree majestic ... He displays little oratorical power ... He elicits little applause ... launches no thunderbolts ... Even our own Goforth used to plead more eloquently for China's millions, and apparently with more effect ... It is quite possible that were Mr Taylor, under another name, to preach as a candidate in our Ontario vacancies there are those who would begrudge him his probationer's pay.

For some moments Hudson Taylor sat lost in thought. Then he smiled at Henry Frost and said, 'That is a very just criticism, for it is all true. I have often thought that God made me little in order that He might show what a great God He is.' They turned into their sleeping berths, but Frost,

> lay there in the darkness, the train rushing along at the rate of forty miles an hour ... thinking, thinking ... about the saint in the berth beneath me ... It is not hard for a little man to try to be great; but it is very hard for a great man to try to be little. Mr Taylor, however ... had entered into that humility which is alone found in the spirit of the lowly Nazarene.[908]

They parted at Montreal station, and Frost returned to Attica, dreading the task he had taken up, until welcomed home by 'someone therein who thinks—however great the hallucination—that you are something'. He had said to Hudson Taylor, 'But I don't know anything about dealing with candidates,' and the reply 'distressingly simple, characteristic of the man, but not exactly practical' had been, 'Quite true, but the Lord will help you.' That was before the episode at the Institute taught him new values. When Henry Frost went ahead trusting the Lord to direct him, he quickly knew the advice was 'exactly practical'.

Hudson Taylor and his party boarded SS *Batavia* at Vancouver and sailed on October 5 straight into rough seas. In the three busy months since July 1 when he landed at New York, he had received 824 letters and dealt with most of them. Knowing too well that China would confront him with stresses of its own, he used the voyage to finish his correspondence and accounts and to update *China's Spiritual Need and Claims*. The respite ended at Yokohama, where the mail awaiting him contained the first blow in an onslaught unrelenting until he sailed again for Britain six months later. But he seems to have been oblivious of the worst dangers ahead.[909]

Six nightmare months (November 1888–April 1889)

Trouble at the Chefoo schools through loss of staff and indiscipline among the teenage boys had ended with a new headmaster's arrival in 1884. Everyone liked Herbert L. Norris, and standards quickly rose under his direction. Results in the examinations were recognised in universities at home. Frank McCarthy, John's son, joined him, a future headmaster in the making. All was going well until early September 1888 when a 'miserable-looking dog entered the boys' schoolroom, and rushed in turn at several of the boys'. They dodged it by leaping on to their desks and it ran next to a bedroom where others were preparing for bed. Herbert Norris heard the commotion, pursued and cornered it. 'It flew at him and bit his finger', but lest it harm the boys he delayed getting the wound cauterised until the dog had been killed. On September 24 Norris fell ill, and died of hydrophobia three days later. The mail at Yokohama gave Hudson Taylor the news.[910]

But that was not all. Adam Dorward was dead. Adam Dorward of all people—'the apostle of Hunan'—such an exceptional man in personality, achievement and sheer saintliness, and one of the new China Council. A year before, in October 1887, he had cut short his home leave to take relief funds to the flood and famine areas of north Henan. Then back to Shashi, his springboard for Hunan. Of his Chinese companions and himself, he had said, '(Again and again) we have come to a city, by foot or native boat, and have entered it not knowing whether we should leave it alive or not.' From Changde, deep in Hunan, he had written in August, 'I feel as if I would be willing to do almost anything that would be honouring to God, and undergo any hardship, if only I could get

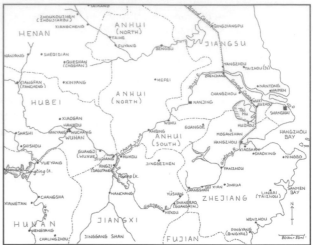

2.63 The Yangzi Valley provinces and ports

footing in Changde, and see men and women turning to God.'

The same mail as brought to his mother the news of his death brought also a long letter from Adam. Thomas James in their advanced post at Shishou was expecting a riot. The town was placarded with incitements to destroy the mission house. And in Shashi cholera was rampant. Men were falling down and dying in the streets. Would Dorward come and help to quell the disturbance? But Adam told her, 'You need not be in any way anxious on my account. I am just as much in the Lord's keeping here as I would be if I were at home . . . (He) can easily command that no evil befall me . . . But if the Lord should will otherwise still all *will be well* . . . Praise God that I am again honoured to go to the front of the battle! . . . May our confidence be in God alone.'

Hardly had he reached Shishou than he fell ill with dysentery. A very sick man was no use so, lest he add to Thomas James's difficulties, Dorward returned home. Three times James faced death from spears and from being drowned by the mob, and escaped only when a tropical deluge scattered them. But Dorward, all alone, suffered a perforated intestine and was dying of peritonitis when another colleague found him. They buried him at Yichang, the consul, customs officials and merchants honouring him at the graveside.[911]

That two such outstanding men should be taken was a counterblow from Satan, but allowed by God 'lest we get puffed up', Hudson Taylor wrote to Jennie. 'I feel almost overwhelmed . . . feel like a "weaned child"—I want to be alone with God. May He . . . make us all holy—more fit for His service, here or there. The Lord reigneth! . . . He can make no mistakes.' But there was no privacy on board ship, and he had sixty other letters to answer and the ship's services to take.

John Stevenson met them at Shanghai on October 30 and the two directors paced the wharf together with immediate problems to be solved. Unexpected arrivals from the interior, sick missionaries and others in transit, left little room in the Yuan Ming Yuan buildings for the large party. They went straight to the shipping office and booked passages on the Yangzi river steamer for the next evening. Quick transformations into Chinese clothes, and they were all away again. At Zhenjiang Hudson Taylor handed the women over to John McCarthy's care, and went on upstream to Anqing with the men, returning with Arthur Eason ill with typhoid.

From November 10 to 14 he buried himself in conference 'far into the night' with Stevenson and McCarthy at Yangzhou, not neglecting to give long, highly practical Bible discourses and talks about the 'Principles and Practice' to the language students preparing to go upcountry. As arrangements stood, business and transit quarters in Shanghai, Broumton's finance department at Wuchang, and the directors' offices at Zhenjiang were a good working system not to be jettisoned lightly. The objections to centralisation in Shanghai still held. Not for nothing had Shanghai earned its reputation as a sink of iniquity. And social distractions even in the large inter-mission community could consume precious time and blunt the edge of concentration on the job to be done.

Hudson Taylor was loth also to yield to the advantages of closer teamwork in a compact headquarters. But these crises of inadequate accommodation were becoming more frequent; the Wusong Road site was paid for and ready, and the cost of the first two big buildings had been promised by Archibald Orr Ewing. Continuing expansion of the Mission must be expected. The American potential promised that. 'I saw how Northfield had impressed him,' John Stevenson recalled. 'He was in an impressionable state of mind, open to new developments, and was *looking forward* . . . Everything seemed possible.' If he had known more he would have said 'Niagara' instead of Northfield, for there the matter had been taken out of Hudson Taylor's hands. 'This work really originated at the Niagara Believers' Meetings,' he had said in his article for the *Christian* and A. T. Pierson's *Missionary Review*.[912]

The choice was made. While John Stevenson carried on the routine administration, Hudson Taylor would take over the problem cases, the discouraged and disgruntled people and those who wished to resign and go home, good men like Henry Dick and Charles Hogg among them. And he with the businessman David Cranston's help (see p 209) would plan the new premises before calling in the architects and engineers. As it turned out, a flood of tribulations descended upon him, and creative planning became the relaxation that he needed. He designed two large buildings which by their very appearance and convenience gave future missionaries a sense of friendliness and home while providing all the facilities required (see ill. 2.67: p 540).

All kinds of trouble came his way. Another missionary died of typhus at Jinhua. The consuls declined to accept as valid Stanley Smith's marriage in Shanxi to Sophie Reuters, a Norwegian citizen, and they had to come to Shanghai and repeat the ceremony. 'Anti-CIM' feeling had developed among CIM missionaries in Chefoo through one or two influential malcontents. Far worse, hardly had John

Stevenson's daughter Mary arrived at Shanghai to help her father than she went out of her mind. 'Our house has been a hospital. It is now a lunatic asylum too.' Then word came that William Cooper, the member of the China Council whom Hudson Taylor valued more highly than all, had become desperately ill on the way out from Britain and might not live beyond Hong Kong. He recovered. But for weeks on end Hudson Taylor had Mary and other patients to care for while overburdened with office work. In the room next to his, Mary raved and tore her clothes and sheets in ribbons, anything she could lay hands on, taking several people to hold her in her most maniacal moments.[913]

Hudson Taylor took another house[914] and moved in with his patients, to spare the Mission home. But how could he work or sleep with Mary the other side of a thin wall? 'While the spiritual tone of the Mission is much higher than ever before the trials and conflicts are very great,' he told Jennie. 'The constant tension of sorrow and trial are enough to break one's heart. But I know the Lord's ways are all right and I would not have them otherwise. "Even so, Father," if our hearts do break or minds give way.' He faced it as an onslaught from the devil.

A few days later it was even worse. One emotionally disturbed was being sent home. Another far up the Han River was reported by telegram to be 'demented'. But Mary might die. Stevenson was looking ten years older. Then lovely, beautiful Maggie McKee of the Hundred, 'one of our brightest and most promising flowers,' was smothered with 'black smallpox' and dead in six days. 'I do not know,' said John Stevenson, 'what we would have done without Mr Taylor, but oh! the look on his face at that time.'[915]

A missionary couple had brought a nursemaid from England with them, dismissed her and left her in Shanghai to be sent home. But she too fell ill with typhoid. They never forgave Hudson Taylor for rebuking them.

Henan was in the forefront of the news.[916] After reaching twenty-one and marrying Joe Coulthard, Maria had gone with him to Zhoujiakou, the first woman missionary in the province. Simply by visiting one home after another she had personally explained the essentials of the gospel to 1,500 women. In November Herbert Taylor took his wife and child and Geraldine Guinness, a beginner, to Sheqidian. The river level being too low for boats, they had to endure hard, primitive overland travel all the way. But the Huang He (Yellow River) floods and resulting famine in the north still called for funds, and missionaries to distribute them. The need in other provinces was even greater, and funds donated for the CIM to use were shared with the Baptists and Presbyterians in Shandong where a million and a half were homeless and starving. Not until May 1889 were the breaks in the Yellow River banks closed, sixteen months after they were breached.[917]

The 'Canadian men' gave unmixed comfort to the hard-pressed directors. 'I wish we had a hundred such men.' The more they understood the Mission's principles the more they approved. Conferring with Stevenson, McCarthy and Marcus Wood (in charge of the Anqing training school, newly appointed a superintendent and a member of the China Council), they said they wanted to become full members, not only associates. Hudson Taylor saw no reason for excluding them. During 1888, five men of the CIM had died, two had resigned, and three might have to leave, but twelve new men had come to China. The Canadians were pure gain. They, not mission politics, settled the issue. North Americans were as much the CIM as anyone. He designated them to difficult Henan.

The women's special sphere on the Guangxin River (see pp 455–57) was the natural place for the girls of the party when their time came. Meanwhile, less than twenty miles from their Yangzhou training school, a riot broke out at Zhenjiang. Miss C. L. Williams[918] reported to Hudson Taylor, 'We stayed in the house until the flag was taken and the consul's house burning, and then we were taken . . . to the steamer . . . until the morning.' (They returned to feed the schoolchildren, but then had to withdraw again.) 'The mob was very great and they threw large stones and pieces of rock at us.' When the mob began setting fire to the mission house, Chinese soldiers drove them away. 'And after Chinese, American and British gunboats anchored offshore . . . we soon had everything in order again.'

Only his letters to Jennie once more revealed how painfully he was feeling their separation from each other. Far from it becoming easier with time, he confessed, 'I feel sometimes, dearie, as if the charm and even power of life were taken out of me by these long absences from you . . . Hope deferred makes the heart sick . . . but I cannot shake it off.' 'Longing removes the power of thought. The cross does not get more comfortable, does it?'[919] He had good reason for wanting to be able to talk with her as he could with no one else, not even John Stevenson, about new trouble with the London Council and Benjamin. Jennie as co-editor of *China's Millions*, was relieving him of almost all but editorials and annual reports. Correspondence went to and fro about an article by Montagu Beauchamp to which some readers had objected.[920] Taking a month or six weeks in each direction, it demonstrated the difficulty of coordinating the overseas and home sides of the Mission. But it exacerbated the feeling stirred up when Hudson Taylor formed the 'tentative auxiliary council' in Toronto without consulting London. He had kept them informed, but had not sought their approval. What was the status of the London Council?

No crisis after all (1888–89)

Rough water is found where strong currents meet. For the time being the contention over the 'Book of Arrangements' and 'P and P' had been set aside. But when Hudson Taylor left even a tentative auxiliary council in Toronto without formally consulting London, he met strong resistance. Dixon Hoste in later years made the comment: 'It

would have been little short of a miracle if the brethren at home had not raised difficulties and objections. It was a new thing (the ugly duckling!)—would excite suspicion, objections . . . It is the fate of all inventors, every man who is leading ahead. People don't understand what he is after; don't grasp his thought.'[921]

Not one other missionary society was international. Even the denominational missions and Bible societies were nationally distinct and independent. Hudson Taylor was making a new contribution to the high politics of missions as he had by initiating the principle of control over the field of action by men on the field. So when London heard of a North American council they reacted adversely. 'The question will be,' wrote Theodore Howard, 'whether it should be a Branch of the Home work . . . or work independently under the same lines and in fellowship and sympathy, but not under the same direction as the CIM.' A sibling 'home' department in the same family, autonomous in relation to London but equal in status under the General Director, seems not to have occurred to 'London'.

At first Benjamin was pleased with Hudson's letters and his discovery of such fine material ready to proceed at once to China. Then doubts appeared. 'Anything of the nature of an American branch' could bring 'disappointment if not utter failure', simply through inherent national differences of outlook and method. By the end of October, with all the labour of running 'about seventy meetings', including some in parts of Britain where China and the CIM were previously unknown, it looked foolhardy to Benjamin to take incalculable risks by expanding across the Atlantic. So he advised, first exploit the half-tapped reservoir, 'the richest mine' of Britain!

A month later Jennie wrote, 'Benj. and the Council are very dissatisfied . . . It would be far wiser to get them (the North Americans) to run a mission and help all we can. I hope it will be so for I think he is right.' By then the strain of having too much to do and too many callers who stayed too long was making Benjamin impatient; and in a Shanghai under deep snow the stresses and broken nights were having the same effect on Hudson. Where in writing to anyone else they would have been more careful, between old friends hurried notes and ill-considered wording left wrong impressions. He wrote to Hudson, 'I am deeply distressed', and 'the interests of the CIM will be imperilled', it would be 'suicidal' to go international. Hudson replied, 'Without a visit to America you cannot fully understand.' But rather than have a hand in what he saw with such misgivings, Benjamin wrote 'If you are resolved upon it I shall not offer opposition . . . I do not desire contention— I would rather retire altogether.'[922]

By February the new famine in China was adding a hundred letters a day to the burden on the CIM in London. Reports in the papers were conflicting with the facts observed by missionaries, and Benjamin was having to tread carefully. He declined an invitation to join the Lord Mayor's Famine Committee after Hudson told Jennie 'the money from the Lord Mayor's Fund is most of it going into the hands of the (mandarins) . . . The (Shanghai Famine Relief) Committee dare not publish here some of the bogus reports got up for the occasion.'

With no time in which to think dispassionately, 'this American question' loomed all the larger as a potential threat to the Mission. Strong supporters and members of the council were warning against it, he wrote, naming James Mathieson of Mildmay, George Williams of the YMCA and Robert Scott of the *Christian*, a major donor. Another said Hudson Taylor had been 'carried away by (his) reception in America'. So he, Benjamin, wished to dissociate himself from this 'peril to the work'. And then, ominously because ambiguously, 'I must ask you to accept my resignation if you have resolved to carry out this American plan.' Henry Frost understood him to mean, 'I shall have to resign if it comes to that', as Benjamin intended to convey, but Hudson Taylor in

the Shanghai nightmare read it as a firm declaration of intent.

In August, John Stevenson had written to Benjamin, 'It is often a wonder to me to see the unity and harmony that exists in the CIM', that strong differences of opinion could be held without hostility. Harmony and unity were coming under greater strain at the heart of the Mission. Looking back on these days, John Stevenson said, 'There had been so much success and such rapid extension. We were going forward with full sail set before a favourable wind and ballast was needed, but we did not realise it.'

Hudson Taylor's difficulty lay in his sincere submission of everything to God, and conviction that God would 'direct his steps'. This was how God had dealt with him for nearly forty years. 'I know God guided in the formation of the [Toronto] council' sounded arrogant to some who did not know him well. But to Stevenson his was 'a life that stands looking into, looking behind . . . Of course he was liable to the weaknesses of human nature. But I have watched it very closely under all conditions.' Hudson Taylor felt he had no choice. 'To hesitate would be disobedience in me,' he confessed to Jennie. 'I am not praying now that he (BB) may stay, but that he may "be filled with the knowledge of God's will" and that (our) love may be deepened.' And then the disclosure of how far his thoughts had progressed: 'this Canadian Council is His will—and others like it He will give us unless I am greatly mistaken.' So it turned out. The first approaches from Australia came during 1889 and from Germany in 1890 and 1891.

In March 1889 the future was still veiled. Plainly he must get home to London, clear up the confusion, and be ready to appoint someone to succeed Benjamin if he could not be persuaded to stay. He himself felt it deeply and saw it all as a spiritual battle, a diabolical counter-attack. 'Satan is simply raging—he sees his kingdom attacked all over the land—and the conflict is awful.'[923]

Mary Stevenson was quieter when he wrote to ask Jennie to meet him in Paris as usual. But he was keyed up, under strain, hurrying through his letters before catching the midnight river steamer to Hankou to go over the accounts with Broumton. Henry Frost had kept some prospective missionaries back from sailing, while the standing of the 'auxiliary' was under debate, and two men had turned to other missions. Were North Americans to be referred to London, he asked Hudson Taylor? What should he do?

> If you have any godly men fit for the work, don't keep them back; [Hudson Taylor replied] and if you have any suitable women and a suitable escort ... don't keep them back. The Lord Himself, whose they are, will care for them. The support of our missionaries is not dependent upon the existence of the China Inland Mission, but on the Word of the living God. [And on March 14, with plans to leave by German mail steamer in April] I am more than ever convinced that it is the will of God that our International Auxiliary (in North America) should exist and flourish.[924]

China and the work of God came first. Administrative niceties were subsidiary. But Hudson Taylor was already talking of an international CIM. 'These brave words were followed by a braver action,' Frost wrote. Hudson Taylor characteristically went to meet his opponents in person. And 'without further reference to the London Secretary or Council' Henry Frost sent off two more young women of whom Hudson Taylor had approved. Then he wrote, and his 'full explanations' to Benjamin 'were received in a most gracious spirit'.

Perhaps the gap was narrower than they thought. But the word was getting around that all was not well, and Hudson Taylor was alarmed. A frank explanation struck him as the best way to account for his abrupt return to Europe, and he hastily wrote a 'strictly private' letter to all members of the Mission. All too soon he was to regret it. Stress carries a red flag. Too often it leads to false moves.

The opening words betrayed his ruffled spirit. 'My dear Friends, A serious complication, involving very grave issues requires my immediate return to England.'

After referring to events leading up to the time of writing, March 25, he described with undisguised feeling the steps leading to Benjamin's 'intention if (an auxiliary) were formed, of resigning his position as Secretary'. In normal circumstances he chose his words carefully. In this letter he laid bare the reasons why he himself was 'greatly distressed', going into far greater detail than the young majority of the Mission needed to know. He was writing, he said, to correct misunderstandings, and emphasised that the China Council agreed the 'Toronto auxiliary' should be retained. It was so unlike him. It must have been plain to the discerning reader that this injudicious letter was written under exceptional strain.[925] So although it brought him candid rebukes from his friends, the warmth of their welcome surprised him when he got back to England.

He completed his work on the accounts and remittances with Broumton, spent a few days at Anqing in conference with William Cooper at the training school, returned to Shanghai for three days with the China Council, completed his work with David Cranston on the Wusong Road building plans and contracts[926] and sailed as planned, on April 12. Even on the steam launch going out to the liner he was dictating final messages. On board he wrote to John Stevenson whom he had just left—it would be good to appoint a peripatetic midwife for the confinements due in the north-west.

> Deal with and through our superintendents so as to make and keep them loyal and satisfied ... And yet it will not do to lose the advantage of direct communication with the missionaries ourselves ... Make (the superintendents) feel you are carrying out their views and wishes ... We need each brother to recognise a helper in the one immediately over him, not a master, and all to feel they have this in you and me. [And, nearing Aden] Pray much for me: it is so solemn to feel one may go to war against the enemies of the Lord as Samson did, unconscious that the Lord has left one, to win defeat and captivity and blindness.

May the Lord keep me and keep you very near to Himself.[927]

Did he fear that he had acted without the Lord's approval? Theodore Howard wrote to greet him at Marseilles, opening his heart, like the true friend he was:

> Your letter (to the Mission) ... came on me like a thunder clap. (The American issue had never been discussed at a Council meeting. And he himself could form no opinion without the relevant facts, though he considered Benjamin's arguments 'very weighty'.) He (Mr B.) did not think of taking any action ... during your absence ... (or) contemplate retirement (before) the matter had been fully gone into. (How could Hudson Taylor treat it as a fait accompli and 'publish it abroad' without first doing all in his power to avert 'a most fatal and disastrous mistake'!) I have no doubt that some modus vivendi can be found ... It is quite as certain ... that God has given you a most invaluable helper in Mr B. ... as it is that He has given you an auxiliary council in America ... God only knows the wholehearted devotion of Mr B. to the work; wise, loving, careful, he binds it together, and keeps it together in such a way as no other man could do it. (He was 'over-pressed', and 'somewhat hasty' in expressing his views, but) you cannot, you must not think of losing (him) the best helper God has given you. (Everyone shared this opinion, he went on. As for North America, Theodore Howard could not understand why the North American Council should not be independent of the CIM but affiliated like the Bible Christians. But) I shrink from the thought of setting up my judgment against that of a man of God at whose feet I willingly sit, and reverence almost with awe, but I would be unfaithful to my deepest convictions had I written otherwise.[928]

William Sharp wrote in similar vein. Both Hudson Taylor and Mr B. had been too precipitate. 'Things have been written on both sides that should not have been written or even said, and we must all forget them, and unitedly press forward.'

After a night at William Berger's hospitable home at Cannes, Hudson Taylor went on to meet Jennie in Paris. But more plain speaking followed him from his faithful old friend. Hudson Taylor's attitude towards divine guidance was questionable and dangerous, he suggested: 'a spirit of infatuation, claiming for yourself, shall I say it, divine and infallible guidance in the matter of the auxiliary'. As for personal relationships, William Berger continued, 'It takes two to make a quarrel . . . You are to all intents married to Mr B. and cannot be divorced.' So he must not think of separating, but must find that *modus vivendi*.

Richard Hill went further. If Mr B. was to be lost, he himself would resign as well. Charles Fishe was brief and to the point, 'No one will *hear* of BB going. Some *modus vivendi* must be found. It would be disaster for the Mission. It is *details* that need adjusting.'

'I reached England on May 21st (my birthday) and found the stone already rolled away,' Hudson Taylor reported to John Stevenson. Strong currents were as nothing where Christian love existed. Two evenings with Benjamin and the next day with the London Council giving an account of his tour in the States and Canada, and the clouds dispersed. At last they understood. Discussion of permanent arrangements was deferred until after the annual meeting. On June 18 it all ended amicably with the London Council accepting lock, stock and barrel Hudson Taylor's outline of the arrangements and status of the North American Council. Its duties were to be the same as the London Council's. It was to deal directly with the directors in China, not through London. Its funds would be distinct and its missionaries on the same footing as those from Britain. And they would be directed in China, not from America. What was left of the 'mare's nest'?

Benjamin had accepted the majority view. By common consent the *modus vivendi* was to be as Hudson Taylor had intended. He told John Stevenson, 'The Council have been very cordial . . . and I do not think BB will think again of leaving us.' Better arrangements have been introduced in the offices,' relieving the pressure on BB, and better still, on July 4, he could say of the disagreements over the 'P and P', 'All now cordially accepted' and being referred to the China Council for approval. A delightful letter was to be carried by Hudson Taylor 'from the London Council to the American Council . . . I do not think things have been so cordial for years.'[929]

Sound lessons had been learned—the inherent dangers in correspondence; the value of face to face courtesy and prayer together; the dangers of physical and mental exhaustion when matters of moment were under debate; and the truth that 'reckless words pierce like a sword' but 'love covers a multitude of sins.' If only that had been the end of disharmony. But 'the accuser of the brethren' (Rev 12.10) had more mischief in mind.

The emperor takes over (1889–92)

Culturally aware Chinese never forgot that the Manchus were aliens, and that Ci Xi was empress dowager of the Da Qing, of the Manchu dynasty rather than of the Chinese people. Ceaseless domestic intrigues and jockeying for influence among the imperial families and 'bannermen' were alien to the Han Chinese, whose secret societies dreamed of a Chinese dynasty restored. In the meantime, Chinese serving in the highest ranks of government consciously waited for the dynasty to crumble. Some, such as Li Hongzhang, were faithful to the ruling power. In 1884, Ci Xi's edict about the critical state of affairs had admitted, 'There is chaos in the Government and a feeling of insecurity among the people.' As the last decade of the nineteenth century was reached, many saw the end approaching. Ill-omens multiplied and the rumblings of deep unrest began to break the surface, recognizably disguised as anti-foreign action, but designed to shake the dragon throne. It lacked only a clear demonstration of the rulers' weakness to hasten the inexorable slide towards dissolution.

Ci Xi and her chosen courtiers clung tenaciously to the ancient ways, while the enlightened longed to emulate Japan's

2.64 Ci Xi, empress dowager, in 1903

metamorphosis into a modern state with a new constitution, a constitutional monarchy, a Chamber of Peers and elected Diet (and religious liberty at last). The Guang Xü emperor had come of age in 1887, but Ci Xi had not relinquished her command. Delicate as a child, nervous and retiring, with an air of great gentleness and intelligence, but always taught to regard Ci Xi's word as law, the emperor waited until he was nineteen before assuming power, declaring the regency (of 1881–89) ended. Ci Xi had hated him with 'a terrible, relentless hatred' since he spurned the bride she had foisted upon him. She retired to the Palace of Tranquil Old Age, fully intending to wield power as before. He could play the emperor in minor matters while still in duty bound to *ketou* to her as the most senior in the dynastic hierarchy.

She rebuilt the Summer Palace, burned out by the French and Lord Elgin's troops in 1860, using funds from the imperial treasury allocated to the navy Li Hongzhang had been commissioned to build up. No empress in the history of China was so pampered and luxuriously served by her attendant eunuchs. Li Lianying, her chief eunuch, said of her when her prayers to the Buddha appeared to end a great drought, 'It is as though she were Buddha

2.65 The Guang Xü emperor before the coup

desire that all shall work together to make this great work a success.[931]

Guang Xü's reforms had begun, but even Li Hongzhang had qualms. He had employed foreign civil engineers to close the Yellow River dikes, and had become financially involved in the railway projects. When the Tianjin railway was declared open, a palace gate had been burned down. What if a new Yellow River flood or a fire in the palace took place? Instead, the Temple of Heaven, jewel of Peking, went up in flames. The circular pavilion in three tiers, roofed with azure tiles of the finest porcelain clay, under which the dragon throne itself was placed when the emperor worshipped Heaven, had 'illuminated the whole sky' in its agony.[932] A shudder ran throughout China. The omen was conclusive. The emperor was doomed. But a great deal was to happen and Guang Xü was to live another nineteen years before Ci Xi's final act of premeditated evil fulfilled the prediction. For a while he had the cultured friendship and instruction of Zeng Guofan's remarkable son, 'Marquis' Zeng, Chinese minister to France, Russia and then the Court of St James, before becoming a member of the Zongli Yamen.

Viceroy Zhang Zhitong opened an imperial iron-foundry at Hanyang (across the Han River from Hankou), as Li had opened his shipyard, naval college, engineering works in Shanghai and Tianjin, and cotton mills. The old issue of *fengshui* again proved amenable to the profit motive. And the emperor went so far as to declare himself friendly towards foreigners, and ready to receive foreign envoys in audience. 'The modem movement' in China had begun. He kept his word on March 5,1891.

Whether or not there were direct links or causes, May and June of the same year were to see anti-foreign riots in several places in Jiangsu and along the Yangzi Valley, and at Nanjing, Wuhu, Wuxüe and Hanyang, and at Yichang in September 1891 and November 1892. On June 5, 1981, a Wesleyan missionary named Argent and a customs officer, Green, were murdered apparently without reason. J. K. Fairbank explained: 'There is evidence that the

herself.' The court were amused and quickly the habit spread through China of good humouredly referring to her as 'Old Buddha'.[930]

Guang Xü had listened to people of liberal views, and knew that modernisation was China's only hope. The great famine had shown the urgent need of rapid means of bulk transport. A demonstration railway line from the Dagu forts to Tianjin had been followed by Zhang Zhitong's proposal, endorsed by Li Hongzhang, that Peking and Hankou be linked by a strategic direct line. Guang Xü gave them his support and appointed Zhang Zhitong viceroy of Hubei, Hunan and Anhui. He held this vital post for eighteen years, 1889–1907, the key to the opening of Hunan to foreigners, and to the safety of the Yangzi valley in the terrors of 1900. Zhang, the beneficent governor of Shanxi in the great 1877–79 famine (see pp 326–338), had taken up Timothy Richard's far-seeing advice. On August 27,1889, the emperor signed an edict:

> The Sovereign is of the opinion, that to make a country powerful railways are essential, but recognising that at the outset the people will have doubts and suspicions, orders the governors and viceroys of Zhili, Henan and Hubei to issue explanatory proclamations, exhorting and commanding them to throw no impediments in the way. It is the Imperial

Yangtze Valley riots of 1891 were fomented in part by disgruntled secret society members whose aim was not to do injury to Christians, but to bring down the dynasty by forcing it into conflict with the Western powers.'[933]

At the same time vigilant Chinese were all too aware of the circle of steel and fire surrounding their country and pressing ever closer—France and Britain in the South, Japan in the east and Russia in the north and west. The Trans-Caspian railway to Bokhara and Samarkand facilitated fresh encroachments on Chinese Turkestan; and the Trans-Siberian railway was under construction, with a southward line through Alma Ata, a blatant strategic threat to China, however necessary to Russia's southern states. A resurgence of vile accusations from Hunan moved the emperor to prohibit all anti-foreign publications, by an edict on May 21, 1892. Significantly, Hudson Taylor with his ear to the ground, in constantly close relations with Chinese, referred from time to time to the 'eve of revolution', the possible imminence of an outright rebellion.

Henry W. Frost, man of faith
(July–December 1889)

With the London Council apparently satisfied, and a genial letter of greeting to the North American Council in Hudson Taylor's pocket, the time had come to put matters over there on to a secure footing. Throughout June he had had a ceaseless succession of business and speaking engagements and a good friend in Liverpool, Stephen Menzies, undertook to book his Atlantic passage for him. When Cunard told Menzies that intermediate-class cabins could not be reserved, he returned Hudson Taylor's cheque, claiming the privilege of himself meeting the cost of 'cabin-class' accommodation. So instead of tight-packed austerity between decks Hudson Taylor found himself travelling first class (July 6–14) and arrived rested and ready for thirty-four days of non-stop work, his prime purpose being to meet the provisional council and work out

permanent arrangements for Canada and the States. He also addressed forty meetings in eighteen different places, most of them those he had been to in 1888. Travelling the long distances between cities afforded time for correspondence.[934]

The timing of his visit coincided roughly with that of the year before. From New York, met by Henry Frost's father, he travelled to Attica for three days' consultation with Henry. Then together to the conference at Niagara-on-the-Lake where the members of the provisional council assembled to meet him. The most urgent matter was quickly resolved. A joint council for Canada and the United States was formally instituted, and the decision taken to base the Mission in Toronto.[935] A full-time secretary-treasurer was needed to handle the growing business affairs of the Mission in North America, and Henry Weston Frost's suitability for the post no one doubted. But it would mean his leaving Attica with his wife and three children, and moving to Toronto, in rented quarters with no fixed salary. Nor would they have a buoyant organisation behind them. In effect, in North America they themselves would to a large extent be the China Inland Mission, looking to God alone for the funds and wisdom, judgment in selecting and training candidates, and ability to submit the right matters to the council for advice. Until then, 'First in business life and then [after becoming an evangelist] through my father, all our wants had been supplied.' Now Hudson Taylor could only give him $250 towards the expense of moving to Toronto, and the few small sums he had in hand. Otherwise he would have 'only the Lord.' to look to, for his father and brother had fallen upon hard times—bought out of their railroad business by an unscrupulous takeover. The means of livelihood could no longer come from them. And most North American missionaries were individually supported by their churches. No comforting 'general fund' could be drawn upon, least of all from London. Henry Frost and his wife faced a supreme test of faith.[936]

A week after Niagara, at Clifton Springs the audience contained leaders of several denominational missions, when he spoke on the same subject. It gave them the opportunity to ask him in depth about the CIM and his principles. Their missions were sending abroad few unordained men, except medicals, and most of what they knew about the CIM was hearsay. 'Dr Clark of the American Board, Dr Ellinwood of the American Presbyterian Mission, Dr Reed of the American Episcopal Mission (and others) were all there. . . .They all expressed themselves as greatly relieved of misapprehensions and left I believe in real sympathy—an object worth the whole journey.'[937]

In August, Hudson Taylor and Frost met members of the council in long morning and afternoon business sessions at Toronto. Frost then returned home to Attica while Hudson Taylor spent a long weekend at Moody's Northfield Conference, and met Susie Parker's parents again, none of them yet knowing that she had died of 'malignant fever' (or 'typhoid') at Guiqi in Jiangxi. The news was on its way. When it reached them her father said, 'It is still true. Nothing is too precious for my Lord Jesus'—even if their one remaining child were to take Susie's place. The good work must go on. Moody offered his 'Northfield Hotel' during the winter as a training home for CIM candidates with a month of teaching on the Bible to be given by himself and Dr Pierson.

In Attica, Henry Frost and his wife were contemplating another revolution in their way of life. One day a heavy plaster ceiling in their home had fallen, harming no one but revealing the danger if other ceilings were as insecure. They had replaced them all, adding to the attractions of their home. Faced with leaving it, they happened to be praying in separate rooms when the words of Haggai 1.4 came to her with startling relevance, 'Is it a time for you, O ye, to dwell in your ceiled houses, and this house lies waste?' She took her Bible and laid it open on Henry's lap. 'From that moment . . . there was never a doubt in her heart or in

mine.' For the sake of God's spiritual house in China they made the decision to leave Attica and take what God might give them in Toronto, as soon as Hudson Taylor had gone back to Britain.

During the month together Hudson Taylor and Frost had interviewed and accepted five men for China, and received donations for the Mission amounting to about $4,700, the Niagara Conference contributing even more generously than in the previous year. A gift of $1,000 to Hudson Taylor personally he also handed over to Henry.[938] William Gooderham made available the top storey of his Christian Institute in Toronto for offices, and 30 Shuter Street was rented as a home for the Frosts and candidates coming for interviews or preparing to leave for China. So began the saga described in the Howard Taylors' biography of Henry Frost, and in David Michell's history of the Mission in North America.

Fifty million families?
(September–October 1889)

The imperial edict on railways was promulgated on August 27 (three days after Hudson Taylor landed again at Liverpool). The news of it and the razing of the Temple of Heaven was common property in September. The events of this autumn and winter and Hudson Taylor's vision for the future were therefore against the backdrop of new liberal trends in China, and of the ominous warnings of trouble to come. The whole scale of his thinking had undergone a change.

Writing to Jennie as he left England on July 6 he had said:

Darling, I do want our whole life to be an ascending plane—not resting in anything we have learned or felt or attained, but a pressing on and up ...

What would a Sovereign think of a proposal to add one hundred soldiers in the course of a year to his army of invasion in a country like China? We must get on to a higher plane of thought altogether, and of prayer, if we are to ... deal in any sensible way with the world's crying need.[939]

'Expect great things from God. Attempt great things for God' were Carey's words in 1792, a century before. Bolder thinking was needed. He felt 'in his bones' the stirrings of new developments. His immediate concern was to have the right men and women for each and every department of the Mission in the homelands and China.

'An enduement of power' in place of shallow consecration would be effective against 'the one, united, combined front of the flesh, the world and the devil.' Even the rapid growth of the CIM had come to seem paltry against the immensity of China and her spiritual need, and of the world. The last thing he wanted was a great unwieldy, bureaucratic CIM. But if all the societies increased their numbers and dedication, their common goal would be attainable. The untapped potential in America had fired his imagination again. After his return home his thoughts continued on this trend.

In 1888, Howard Taylor had relieved his father of the tiring and time-consuming petty affairs of travelling—packing, searching timetables, buying tickets, finding the way, or food and drink. They had grown together as never before, to Hudson Taylor's deep joy. Howard had just ended his year of medical and surgical appointments, and was taking three months to travel and work with his father before tackling the highest postgraduate examinations. So they gave September and October to England and Scotland, and November to Scandinavia.[940]

During his absence from the country, Hudson Taylor had heard from the ageing William Berger of his intention to give £4,000 to set up a superannuation fund 'for decayed, aged and retired CIM missionaries, and to give us £3,000, life interest to us, and then to our children equally divided'.[941] His old friend was thinking constantly of how to help the Mission before his own life ended. Nor could he forget the hardships and long separations suffered by the Taylor children. He wrote from experience of successful management of his manufacturing firm suggesting principles and practical details which could be applied

to the CIM: sufficient office space, sufficient staff and well-defined division of labour; reward according to responsibility and capability; 9.30 a.m. to 5.30 p.m. with an hour off at midday as the extreme demand on his employees; overtime compensated by early release on another day; everything 'to secure a real interest and pleasure in work'; heads of department not doing what a junior could do; promotion whenever possible, to encourage all to do their best, the right complement of the CIM's austerity and self-denial.

Then he went on: Hudson Taylor should provide for the CIM to continue if he himself should 'be taken'. It was time for the Mission to be incorporated by deed poll, with clearly stated procedures for appointing his successor if one had not by then been chosen. Aware that disharmony had arisen largely through overwork in China and London, Hudson Taylor was open to advice, and found to his delight that Benjamin and the London Council were 'equally prepared to go any length with me in reorganisation'. The only difficulty lay in finding the right people.

His letters to John Stevenson reflected the issues each was facing. Cecil Polhill-Turner must be given his head soon or he would be lost altogether. He was champing at the bit to get closer to Tibet. Annie Taylor had been home on leave and was in India for six or twelve months to find a way to Lhasa, starting from Darjeeling. A rash of threatened resignations and misdemeanours led him to advise, 'Go and talk with them if you can. If not, send for them to come and talk with you. Let them *see* that you do not lack sympathy, that you are with them in their troubles. It is a far greater triumph for Christ to put a man right than to get rid of him.' Rather than accept resignations easily, persuade them to wait until Hudson Taylor returned. 'Though we cannot scold people right, we may often love them into right.'[942] Recognise spiritual warfare and win a way through by spiritual means. Time and again the myth of Hudson Taylor being authoritarian is shown as in this context to be hollow. Their use of a popular code for long-distance cables ('Unicode') appears increasingly: 'amabilis': 'assistance is urgently required' was often used.

He formed a 'Ladies Council' which met for the first time on September 23, 1889, to help with the assessment of women for China. Recognising the close involvement of the wives of council members, the first to be appointed were Mrs Theodore Howard, Mrs Sharp, Jennie and Amelia.[943] Henrietta Soltau was asked to serve as secretary for women candidates, and then to run a women's training home. While he was in Glasgow, September 21–30, he formed an auxiliary council for Scotland under Provost John Colville, to handle all Scottish candidates. This was the occasion of the well-known story of J. Elder Cumming's train journey with Hudson Taylor.

> I ventured to say that he must often have felt the wonderful honour that God had put upon him as the founder of the Mission ... He turned to me, and with a voice trembling with suppressed feeling said he sometimes thought that God must have looked ... to find someone weak enough to do such a work, so that none of the glory could go to the man himself ...

> In (another) long railway journey he was very silent, but at the close he said to a companion ... that he was constantly occupied and had no time to rest. His companion said, 'Come now, you have had two or three hours now without anything to do.' 'I do not know what you call rest [Hudson Taylor answered] ... Since I entered this carriage I have prayed by name for every missionary in the CIM ... some hundreds.[944]

He and his son Howard were back for a London Council meeting on October 2, to discuss the duration of a term of service overseas before home leave would be justified. Acknowledging exceptional circumstances of ill-health and obligations to parents, Hudson Taylor considered ten years a reasonable span for the physically fit. 'While the rule is ten years for those in good health, not a few have returned within six or eight years, and some earlier.' Reason not rigidity governed the issue. To a mother

he explained, 'If each missionary came home at the end of ten years and spent one year in England . . . more than one-fifth of the whole sum available for the support of missionaries would be spent on furlough and the passages to and fro. In point of fact the actual expense is much greater . . . and donors might with reason complain were it increased.'[945]

On Sunday, October 6, they were in Hastings, spending Jennie's forty-sixth birthday with her father Joseph (Wm) Faulding. Hudson Taylor was mulling over the subject for his editorial in the December issue of *China's Millions*—that 'higher plane' of thought than even one hundred new missionaries a year for China's multiplying millions. A nagging question troubled him. The Lord's 'Great Commission' and last command, 'Go into all the world, and preach the gospel to every creature' was plain enough, but 'What did our Lord *really mean* by His command?' The CIM had enlarged from 91 members in 1880 to over 300, reaching an ever-increasing number of cities with a corresponding increase in the number of believing Chinese. But of China's 250 millions (at the most conservative estimate since recent holocausts), how many had heard 'the gospel' even once, or ever would?

In 1877 the General Missionary Conference in Shanghai had called for 'the Christian Church to evangelise China in the present generation', even in the present century. Half the time had gone and not one hundredth of the population had been given the gospel. In A. T. Pierson's words, Christ's command had 'laid the responsibility on the Church of each successive generation to give the gospel to each individual living in its own period'. Not to Christianise the nation or to convert everyone, but 'to give them the gospel', the gospel that the apostles preached, 'that Christ died for our sins according to the Scriptures, that he was buried, that he was raised on the third day' and that 'By this gospel you are saved' (1 Cor 15.1–4). Jesus said it, so he meant it. It could be done. But how? Hudson Taylor asked himself.

At last he understood. There was no mystery. Difficulty lay only in regarding Jesus' words as unreasonable. They were not. 'There is no impossibility in our Lord's command. Obey! Do it! It is mathematically practicable.'

Consider, as an oversimplified example to illustrate the fact, that the average family in China, a nation of families, numbered five. Then the nation would consist of roughly fifty million families. And 'a large proportion of Chinese live in courts or quadrangles containing from four to ten families each'. Over a period of three years (roughly a thousand days) a thousand evangelists could on average present the gospel each day to ten or twenty such homes or their equivalents on the streets and marketplaces. And much more could be achieved over a period of five or ten years. It was already being done on a small scale. So in the decade remaining of the nineteenth century, and allowing for other demands on time, missionaries and Chinese Christians together could at least give the whole nation an opportunity to hear the gospel put simply but intelligibly to them.

But was there the will to do what could be done, allowing for the fact that many existing missionaries were committed to established institutions and could not be released? To supplement those familiar with China and the language who could concentrate on evangelism, it would not be too much for Europe to send five hundred more—only one hundred from each main denomination with their thousands of ordained men and more thousands of lay men and women. They would soon be replaced. Scandinavia and the continent had made a beginning. Britain had risen to the challenge several times already and would do so again, North America was already responding with thousands of college students pledging themselves to be missionaries 'if God opened the way'. This was realism, not a pipe dream.

What then should be done?

1. Christ's answer was firstly, pray that he would send them out;

2. 'United, simultaneous action by the whole body' of Christians would bring the fullest results;

3. Intelligent cooperation, comity, in deploying across the whole of China would avoid any region's being neglected and duplication in others, already a serious problem;

4. 'Christly giving' by churches and individuals in support of their missions, in the sense of Christ's example, emptying himself, working and suffering to achieve what he came to earth to do; 5. immediate action: pray for '1,000 evangelists for China' without loss of time.

This article, 'Every Creature', and two more in succeeding issues of the *Millions* were published as a booklet, *To Every Creature*, to be distributed far beyond the 20,000 circulation of *China's Millions*. It quickly sold out and was reprinted. Churches and societies of all kinds would read this opening salvo of what developed into a continuous campaign. Objections were raised, of course, and in reply he cited example after example of conversions through one hearing or reading of the gospel, sometimes from posters left on village walls. But that was not the point. He proposed 'seed sowing'; reaping would follow: 'some thirty, some a hundredfold' depending on where the seed fell. 'If one offer of the gospel is insufficient, what shall we think of *none*?' But responsible evangelism was what he had in mind, the preachers spending time in a locality, available to build on impressions made, and if possible returning time and again. A valuable by-product of itineration was thorough knowledge of the country, with a view to the best choice of where eventually to base more settled work.[946]

As one of the senior veterans in China, Hudson Taylor had been invited to give the keynote address at the Third General Missionary Conference at Shanghai in May. He knew now what he would say. J. K. Fairbank wrote of 'Taylor's organisation taking the lead' in the missionary cause from early on, even before the Chefoo Convention of 1876. It had fallen to their lot again.

The first associate missions
(1887–1915)

A spate of new missionary societies springing up in Europe around this time owed their origins in part to Hudson Taylor's personal influence and in part to his articles and booklet, *To Every Creature.* The Swedish American, Fredrik Franson, played a big part, did so by taking up and pressing home this message among Scandinavians especially. A call from the Shanghai conference of missionary societies in 1890 served to add impetus to what had already begun.

Louise Desgraz of the *Lammermuir* party, a Swiss, was the first full member of the CIM from Continental Europe; and the first individual associate was Erik Folke of the Swedish Mission in China. But the first associate mission, the Bible Christian Mission, who paved the way in 1884, created such a good impression that Hudson Taylor had no qualms about cooperating with any other society which could accept the CIM's 'Principles and Practice' as the basis for association, and himself as their director in China. The Church Army enquired about associate status, but went no further. And the Quaker 'Friends' sent their first missionary to China in 1883 under the CIM's wing in Sichuan, but without formal connections. Each associate mission sprang from spiritual movements of the kind familiar to Hudson Taylor, being concerned to foster a closer personal relationship between each individual Christian and the Lord, 'the deepening of spiritual life'.

The Bible Christian Mission had strong roots. In 1815 the Anglican curate of Shebbear in North Devon brought together Christians, regardless of denomination, to learn from the Bible how to please God. But those who formed the Bible Christian Society in a Shebbear kitchen were predominantly Wesleyan Methodists.[947] In May 1884 some of them attended an undenominational conference for the enrichment of spiritual life at Newport, Isle of Wight. As it happened, most of the speakers and participants were Anglicans, but Hudson Taylor was given two sessions to speak on China's millions. 'With a map before him on a scale that almost extended to the width of the wall . . . he passed from province to province of the Empire with the facility of long familiarity, and with a wealth of graphic detail such as no other European living could probably have given.'

The Bible Christians had begun in 1821 to send missionaries to Canada, Australia and New Zealand. What they heard and learned by questioning Hudson Taylor convinced them that they could send and support men in China also. When he and Benjamin B. attended their annual conference at Hoxton (near Pyrland Road), on August 4, 1884, he 'fanned the missionary enthusiasm of the Conference to white heat'. They agreed with Hudson Taylor that 'the apostolic plan was not to raise ways and means, but to go, and do the work'. Two young ministers, Samuel Thomas Thorne and Thomas Grills Vanstone, were 'set apart' for Yunnan province on Hudson Taylor's recommendation. There were Methodists of the CIM already at Chongqing, Guiyang and Kunming. But the whole north-eastern region of Yunnan between Guizhou and the upper reaches of the Yangzi River had no one, from Kunming through Dongchuan and Zhaotong as far as the Sichuan border near Yibin.

As well as Chinese, hundreds of thousands of aboriginal tribesmen, Miao (Hmong) and Nosu, peopled the hills. No one had yet taken the gospel to them. Across the provincial border with Guizhou they extended in millions to where the CIM were preaching to them in the region of Guiyang and Anshun. And across the Yangzi, the Jinjiang, at least a million more 'wild, independent, Nosu' inhabited the Daliangshan.[948]

The Bideford conference 'subscribed £700 in a few minutes' to send Thorne and Vanstone off on November 4, 1884, with John Stevenson, Hope Gill and others of the CIM. 'And I shall be the next,' a Shebbear man in London, Samuel Pollard, wrote to his parents. Francis John Dymond then offered to go with him, and in 1886 they were commissioned together—two of the most outstanding missionaries to China. They sailed with three of the CIM Hundred on January 27, 1887, and were taught Chinese under Frederick Baller at the Anqing language school. Baller was impressed. He watched them closely and declared them 'good pioneers'.

A model relationship existed between the Bible Christian Mission and the CIM. Vanstone and Thorne, Pollard and Dymond fitted in ideally. Sam Pollard had 'the heart of a troubadour and carolled gaily as he walked the highway of life . . . buoyant, full of initiative and enterprise'. Dymond and Pollard 'incited and braced each other, faced death together, nursed each other through sickness, and one [eventually] buried the other'. They were wrecked on the way up the Yangzi gorges. 'More than once that all-devouring Tiger River has almost captured me.' They were posted to Zhaotong but alternated with Thorne and Vanstone at Kunming as part of the CIM team, working the cities between. 'What a lot of light these people received (from Confucius); but what little influence it has had on their hearts,' Pollard wrote.

Dymond went down with smallpox, nursed by Pollard. When death seemed close they took the Lord's Supper together, but Pollard wept and Dymond finished saying the words for him. Far from friends, not knowing how to arrange for a grave, Pollard faced a nightmare experience. But Dymond recovered, married one of the first women pioneers to Yunnan, and became the father-in-law of J. O. Fraser, apostle of the ethnic Lisu. Again and again, first Thorne and Vanstone and then other Bible Christians as they joined the first four fell ill with malaria. John Carter died of dysentery in 1890, Thorne of malaria in 1891. Pollard went to help and himself contracted malaria, running a high fever on his way to marry Emily Hainge, another of the CIM Hundred. On their return from Sichuan (December 4, 1891) they made Zhaotong their base. The sight of 'the Mountains of the *Manzi* (wild men)' made him long 'to spend a month among them'.

Twelve years later, in November 1903, a Nosu chief took him in, but only for a week or ten days.[949] Instead the subjugated Nosu and Miao of the Yunnan-Guizhou border hills captured his affections. From July 1904 a 'mass movement' with its centre at 'Stone Gateway' (Shimenkan) occupied all his energies, and (Frank) Dymond buried him there in 1915.

Dymond wrote to Hudson Taylor on September 5, 1890, 'You have so won our hearts that I think we feel more CIM than anything else.' He proposed to make his base at one city after another, itinerating for one or two months at a stretch and returning to base for two weeks—precisely what Hudson Taylor was advocating and admired in Benjamin Ririe at Jiading in West Sichuan, and Botham on the Shaanxi plains. To his regret, the Bible Christian Mission's leaders later changed their policy and withdrew from association with the CIM, but the model of marriage between two missions set a pattern for future developments.

By then Scandinavian, German and other associate missions were finding their feet in several provinces. Associate members of the CIM were as much part of the CIM as were the full members. Their superintendents became members of the China Council. Their contribution to the life of the CIM made it what it became. Twentieth-century members saw almost no distinction, feeling as much one with the multinational associates as with the full members from the same European and North American countries. The difference lay only in the 'sending societies' they belonged to. But at this level it was Hudson Taylor and John Stevenson who suffered the vicissitudes of a growing variety of associate missions.

The European associate missions (1889–99)

In the eventful years that lay ahead, and the Boxer nightmare especially, the Continental arm of the CIM was to play a major part. An all-too-short outline of its origins must replace the full chapter it deserves, but later pages will put flesh on these bare bones.

Two years passed after Hudson Taylor's consultations with Josef Holmgren of Orebro and Stockholm about the Swedish Mission in China. Erik Folke of Uppsala University made a good beginning at the Anqing language school and then in Shanxi, and three others joined him in the far south-western Yuncheng region of the province. In Sweden the committee wanted closer ties with Hudson Taylor and the CIM, and invited him to Stockholm. So on November 1,1889, he and his son Howard crossed the North Sea to Gothenburg and a welcome in Sweden that outshone all he had ever experienced. They addressed two thousand people at a meeting the same day, with Josef Holmgren as their interpreter, and found wherever they went throughout the month that audiences numbering 'two to five thousand daily' were to be expected. They spoke at Helsingborg, Copenhagen and Malmo at the southern tip of Sweden before separating. While Howard went to Lund and spoke five times at Linkoping, Hudson Taylor went via Tranas and Norrkoping to rejoin him at Linkoping.

Howard had crowned his postgraduate studies with three high honours and the launching on October 15, 1889, at a Missionary Convention with C. H. Spurgeon in the chair, of the 'Students Foreign Missionary Union'. More than 1,500 students attended, and 152 signed the pledge, 'It is my earnest hope, if God permit, to engage in foreign missionary work.'[950] The first name in the book of members reads, 'Taylor, F. Howard, MD, MRCP, FRCS (England), the London Hospital'.

Then father and son together worked through ten more towns including Jonkoping on the way to Stockholm. At fifty-seven, Hudson Taylor no longer enjoyed the vigour he had once had, and soon felt weary, but everywhere the enthusiasm bore him along. His insistence on not being lionised, on travelling third class and carrying his own suitcase, left a deep impression.[951]

An audience of 3,500 in Stockholm and a private Bible reading (on 1 Kings 10) with Queen Sophia[952] and four of her ladies-in-waiting at the palace were the highlights of three days in conference with the committee of the Swedish Mission in China. Working point by point through the 'Principles and Practice' of the CIM, discussing their meaning and implications—not least the wisdom of delaying marriage for two years of adaptation to China—an historic decision was reached. Instead of Folke and his

2.66 Frederik Franson, Swedish evangelist and founder of missions

companions being individually associate members of the CIM in China, the Swedish Mission itself was to be an Associate Mission in alliance with the CIM as a whole. Within the next five years one hundred Swedish men and women offered and twenty-one were judged suitable to go in this mission alone.

After the friendly informality of the hour with the queen came another drawing-room meeting 'with the nurses (all titled ladies) at the Queen's Hospital'. Father and son could hardly tear themselves away to catch the train to Uppsala for a weekend of appointments, before going on to 'Christiania' (as Oslo was still called) for the rest of the week. Even before reaching Norway, Hudson Taylor estimated that in twenty-four towns and cities they had addressed fifty thousand—'probably over 60,000'. Only three meetings, including the hospital's, had been in English.

In 1879 Reginald Radcliffe had awakened Norwegian interest in foreign missions. A leading businessman, named Rasmussen, and his family at Kristiansand on the southern tip of Norway came to be closely linked with the CIM.[953] Four years later, in 1883, the Swedish evangelist, Fredrik Franson (1852–1908), when travelling widely in Europe addressed meetings in the Rasmussen home. Two or three of the daughters eventually became missionaries in China, but their governess, Sophie Reuter (who married Stanley Smith), and a housemaid, Anna Jakobsen, whom we shall meet as a Hunan pioneer, went to England in 1884 and sailed on November 18, 1885, as full members of the CIM. Two years later a committee was formed to help Norwegian missionaries already in China and to send others. The chairman and treasurer of this Norwegian Mission in China[954] was Captain Hans Guldberg, a riding-master.

From Christiania, Hudson Taylor and Howard went south to Kristiansand for five meetings arranged by the Rasmussens, but formal association of the Norwegian Mission (as such) with the CIM appears to have followed some years later. In effect, although not in name, these Scandinavian missions became 'branches' of the CIM. Their members shared all the facilities and benefits of full members. In contrast, the British, North American and later the Australasian councils were established in consultation with Hudson Taylor as integral parts of the CIM.

Fredrik Franson had studied D. L. Moody's methods since 1875 and spent six years in evangelism in the States, but with a growing concern for the wider world he had then returned to Europe, 'more to harvest than to sow. Tens of thousands in Sweden heard him preach and thousands came to personal faith in Christ'. After four years

in Scandinavia he moved on to Germany, Switzerland, France and Italy.

At Barmen he found Christians whose hearts were already 'aflame' with concern for China, and his own 'burning message on China's need' so fanned the flames that a Deutsche-China-Allianz Mission was proposed. When the December issue of *China's Millions* arrived, and Hudson Taylor's booklet, *To Every Creature*, calling for a thousand new missionaries, they wrote to the London Council asking whether the German China Alliance could enter into the same relationship with the CIM as the Swedish and Norwegian Missions in China had established.[955] Fredrik Franson and his Swedish fellow-evangelist Emmanuel Olsson, who hoped to be one of the Thousand, went over to England to discuss plans with the London Council on June 2, 1890, and were promised all possible help. A third associate mission of the CIM was the outcome, and its first three missionaries, led by Olsson, of the Swedish Holiness Union, set foot in China on December 3, 1890.

They joined the CIM team at Baotou on the Mongolian Yellow River border of Shanxi (now deep in Inner Mongolia). When Hudson Taylor visited Sweden again in 1896, the Swedish Holiness Union accepted responsibility for the region between the two arms of the Great Wall.[956] Like a snowball gathering momentum, China was receiving a succession of fine evangelists.

Thoroughly international (1890–1951)

Once the willingness of the CIM to foster like-minded but inexperienced missions became known, leaders in other European countries approached Hudson Taylor. Fredrik Franson returned to the States on September 7, 1890, and announced a brief course of teaching on evangelism at Brooklyn in mid-October. In it he commended Hudson Taylor's concept of a thousand evangelists for China, and of the fifty attending the course about twenty volunteered to go at short notice, as members of an 'expedition' to leave at the end of January 1891. More eleven-day courses followed at Chicago, Minneapolis and Omaha, and he published an article on November 25 setting out his ideas for an Alliance Mission of Scandinavians from America. The title, '*China's Millions*', and the aim, 'to concentrate on the evangelisation of China within three years', under Hudson Taylor's leadership while responsible to the church sending them, were loosely based on Hudson Taylor's original article.

Thirty-five were chosen to leave on January 17 as the first expedition, and fifteen more to follow on the 29th. Further courses followed during 1891, and twelve more men and women went to China on February 14, 1892. Other expeditions went to Japan, the Himalayas, South Africa and elsewhere, all under what Franson named The Scandinavian Alliance Mission, afterwards known as The Evangelical Alliance Mission (TEAM), an associate mission of the CIM until 1951 when China closed its gates to foreigners again.[957]

When Franson arrived at New York in September 1890, he met A. B. Simpson, who had started an International Alliance Mission in 1881. (It became the Christian and Missionary Alliance—C&MA, 1897.) Franson offered to find two hundred recruits for this society and returned to Scandinavia for the purpose. By the spring of 1893, forty-five had arrived in China in two parties (unconnected with the CIM). Sixteen more members of the International Missionary Alliance joined them in 1894, and eventually extended their field from Kalgan to Ningxia. The area was vast, but the overlapping of new societies without comity agreements or experienced missionaries to guide them led inevitably to difficulties, exacerbated by the failure of funds to reach some of the late arrivals. With hard-earned experience, however, a strong and effective mission developed.

Seven other European associate missions come into the picture here; for their roots can be traced to this period, although some matured later. In 1891 a German pastor, H. Koerper, read Hudson Taylor's *Retrospect,* and spoke on his life and work at a Student Volunteer Conference at Frankfurt in 1892. This led to Hudson Taylor himself being invited to the 1893 conference and another at Blankenburg (the German 'Keswick') in 1896. As a result on June 27, 1896, some of these German friends were present at the CIM Saturday prayer meeting in London when Hudson Taylor arrived unannounced from China and quietly took a seat at the back. The emotional welcome he was given when his presence became known so confirmed the visitors in their impressions of the CIM that the Liebenzell Mission was constituted in 1897 as 'an integral part' or 'branch' of the CIM. It became an associate mission in 1906, when members were also sent to the Caroline Islands of the Pacific.[958]

The grand old man, C. F. Spittler, who had supplied the impetus in the founding of the Basel Missionary Society (*c* 1815), also established the Pilgrim Mission in 1840 at St Chrischona outside Basel (see 1, pp 591–92).[959] By 1915 it had about eighty of its own evangelists and had provided about nine hundred missionaries worldwide. The first formal link with the CIM was in 1895, when a Pilgrim missionary went to China as the first full member. Two years later (February 1897) Hudson Taylor was travelling from Cannes to Hamburg via Nice and Basel when, through not knowing that his connection at Basel was from a different station, he missed his train and found he had six hours to spare. He went up to St Chrischona on its hilltop and made himself known. The 'poverty and simplicity' observed on principle by St Chrischona and the CIM became a natural bond to strengthen ties between the two societies.[960]

One by one these associate missions multiplied until the inescapable transmutation of the CIM into an international society was seen to have come only just in time. The experience of a mature organisation was essential to the reception and initiation of the scores of raw evangelists, the Thousand, so soon to arrive in China. The 'incurable idiot' of just twenty years before (see p 102) had made his point.

22

The Adversary (1889–95)

1889–90: THE ULTIMATE AUTHORITY?

Turbulence in China (1889–90)

The steady advance of missions in China often fortified Hudson Taylor when events close at hand were unsettling. He basked in the knowledge that whatever the risks and setbacks, the grousing or failure of the very few, the main body of missionaries battled on steadily. As father of the mission family it was for him to step in where necessary. Some excelled, showing initiative, courage and qualities of leadership and faithfulness to God and the Mission. Ones and twos failed to learn enough Chinese, or in a strange and often trying environment showed traits of personality unrecognised at home, and had to be sent back. Most disappointing were those who 'did run well' and out of pride or under harmful influences became hostile or power-seekers. A few lone wolves worked well without colleagues, but in company left a trail of injured feelings. The correspondence between the directors and superintendents all too often carried 'ballast' of this kind.

It belongs to a true picture of the Mission, as does an insight from one of Hudson Taylor's letters to his wife. On September 1, 1885, when it was still exhaustingly hot at 90 °F after a long summer, he told her about one of the usually most saintly older men: 'Harsh, rude, censorious, (he) has nearly lost all the influence for good he had at first.' Hudson Taylor recognised that all too easily he himself could go the same way. The extreme heat was soul-searing, he said, like being parted from her. But this was offset by more examples of staunch devotion to the work in hand.

While Hudson Taylor was in Scandinavia, George and Minnie Parker were nearing the end of their year-long journey of evangelism and Bible selling from Lanzhou to Gulja (Kuldja) on the Russian border. They arrived in Britain on March 11, 1890, six days before Hudson Taylor left for China, but sixteen years before the second George Hunter followed in their footsteps to Urumqi, twenty-four years before Percy Mather and thirty-three years before Eva and Francesca French and Mildred Cable.[961]

'Minnie' Parker (Shao Mianzi, the Yangzhou schoolgirl) spoke in excellent English at the London annual meetings in May 1890. Two travelling CIM evangelists, T. H. King and Lund, were ejected from Henan. 'Henan is Henan still' their leader commented, not surprised. In Shaanxi, Thomas Botham continued his itinerant life, to city, town and village one after another, unable to rent premises to which he could bring a wife. His fiancée, Ellen Barclay, waited at Tianshui, across the Gansu border, until at last an innkeeper offered Botham three small rooms. He told her, 'The place won't do for you,' but she chose to join him whether on the road or in a shanty. So they married in 1889 and together continued his travelling life. Models of faithful perseverance, they demonstrated the soundness of Hudson Taylor's contention that China's families could be given the gospel systematically by persistence in going to them.[962]

Annie Taylor, the lone wolf, was a true missionary. Unlike Cecil Polhill and his wife (no less first-rate) who chose to win Tibetans for Christ and see them take the gospel to Lhasa, she looked for ways to reach the heart of Tibet in that forbidden city. After reconnoitring in the Qinghai region from her base at Luqü (Taozhou) in Gansu, she returned briefly to Britain and prospected Darjeeling as an approach to Tibet and Lhasa through Sikkim. The

British threat meant strong Tibetan forces barring the way, so she went back to Gansu and laid new plans.[963]

But all was not plain sailing throughout China. As long as the anti-foreign, anti-Christian viceroy remained in Sichuan it was unsafe to travel about. The British consul asked missionaries to restrict their movements as much as possible. George Nicoll was an exception. He could go out to the 'Lolos' (as the Nosu were derisively called) on the wild fringes of the Daliangshan. Hunan, far from relaxing its xenophobia, was republishing its scurrilous anti-Christian pamphlets, and Thomas James was in two minds about holding on year after year as Adam Dorward had done. He wanted to marry Fanny (Stroud) Riley in Sichuan (see p 469). The city of Luzhou (Luhsien) had suffered a devastating fire with over a thousand lives lost. Should they or should they not look for a foothold there? He consulted Hudson Taylor about whether to leave Hunan (Shashi and Shishou) with no one to take his place and start again in riot-prone Sichuan? He had to decide for himself, he was told—settle it with God. James vacillated, wanted more advice. Then it was that Hudson Taylor advised him to spend a night in prayer, responsive to God's will, and in the morning do what he believed to be right.[964]

In Shanxi, always turbulent, new problems called for John Stevenson's intervention. But he was on sensitive ground. Stanley Smith was doing excellent work, training five evangelists by teaching and fieldwork with them, but he and Charlie Studd, two volatile men, as feared were not being good for each other. Call Stanley away for a time, Hudson Taylor suggested. Let him teach and inspire language students at Anqing. Worse still, the Shanxi superintendent, Benjamin Bagnall, and Pastor Hsi had clashed, and afterwards Hsi had been attacked by his Chinese opponents. 'I wish Bagnall could see,' Hudson Taylor wrote, with deep knowledge of Chinese thinking, 'that this attack upon Mr Hsi is to no small extent a backhanded attack upon him (Bagnall).' No course was open but to commission Bagnall to open up a new area, as superintendent of the Shunde-Huolu area in Zhili, and to give T. W. Pigott the oversight of part of Shanxi.[965]

'We have had official commendation in government bluebooks for settling our difficulties without (appealing to) consular officials,' Hudson Taylor wrote to Stevenson. 'Do all you can to keep aggrieved men like Lund from trying to redress their wrongs in the old controversial ways. Go if you can, but if not, send for dissatisfied men to talk with you. Show sympathy and bring them round as friends. And (with the old 'Shanxi spirit' stirring again) try to get things settled before the Shanghai conferences in May or "no small trouble" could erupt during them.'

Discord at the top (1889–90)

A completely new threat to harmony had raised its head. The strong-willed senior missionary who had dismissed his family servant and expected the Mission to send her home to Britain, began lobbying for appointments in the CIM to be 'elective'. This challenge to the 'Principles and Practice' was contrary to the very genius of the CIM, Hudson Taylor immediately saw. In fact no missionary society chose its leaders in that way. The family of the CIM had been built up from the beginning on the principle of cooperation with its founder. Were self-opinionated men to stand like politicians for election by colleagues who scarcely knew them? Another senior refused to recognise the China Council unless he himself had a place on it. A deplorable new spirit had arisen.

But worse was to come. Although, or because, he was responsible to John Stevenson as Hudson Taylor's deputy, the campaigner for elections wrote to the London Council objecting to changes in the 'P and P' and to the restrictions in the 'Book of Arrangements' which affected him. Bringing a servant to China was one. Instead of referring him back to John Stevenson or consulting Hudson Taylor, Theodore Howard and some Council members took up his complaints by challenging the China Council's action. From this small beginning the status of councils, not least of the London Council, became a major issue. The seeds of a constitutional controversy had been sown, and not until five years later was peace fully restored. When it was, genuine misunderstandings were again seen to lie behind strong differences of opinion. But the damage had been done.[966]

The controversy held many lessons for the Mission, and its relevance today justifies its inclusion in this record. Most remarkable, perhaps, was the maintenance of personal friendships and affection when strong words and even rudeness threatened them.

One clause in the handbook touched off a debate on the right of Hudson Taylor and the administration in China to reject probationers or dismiss serious offenders without the approval of the men who sent them. In effect, it raised the question: Was London to have the last word? The 'Principles and Practice' and 'Book of Arrangements' themselves then became the chief bone of contention. The London Council believed they were witnessing an authoritarian departure from the comfortable family relationship between Hudson Taylor and the missionaries that had satisfied all for twenty-five years. The fact that the Mission had quadrupled in size seemed to be forgotten. The sustained pressure on Hudson Taylor to delegate his duties was lost sight of. These new challenges to his leadership emphasised the need for agreement on the essential principles, and after that the logical next step must be a handbook applying the principles to practical situations—a 'book of arrangements'. Most frontline missionaries had welcomed it, but the well-meaning men in London were too far from the scene to understand.

The rumble of distant thunder reverberates through letters of this period: references to the 'Book of Arrangements' as 'a law of the Medes and Persians'; to another 'crisis' of Hudson Taylor's

making; to some fearing a 'smash up' with 'deplorable injury to the work and sad humiliation' for him if he did not retract his new regulations; 'too much management, too much policy'.

After returning to London, Hudson Taylor had told John Stevenson he did not think the 'crisis' as great as some feared. 'I was surprised and very thankful at the real earnest desire manifested (by the Council) to leave my conviction of the proper lines for the Mission uninterfered with. . . . But Satan is certainly very busy.' Each daring advance seemed to be met by Satanic disruption. A tragic sequence of illnesses and deaths once again darkened the year; but what he feared more, as the General Missionary Conference at Shanghai approached, was the disgrace of disagreements between major societies and individual missionaries being thrashed out in public. Instead of doing good, such a conference could do inestimable harm. Crises in China and Britain at the same time might be more than he and the CIM could weather.

Intending to leave for Shanghai by the next mail steamer after his son, Howard, sailed with the Ballers, Hudson Taylor had to change his plan. William Berger's advice about a deed of incorporation of the Mission to provide for the General Director's death had been followed, but the deed had not been completed; reorganisation of the London offices had been delayed by Charles Fishe having pneumonia; and John Stevenson's two sons in Scotland had become dangerously ill. Hudson Taylor himself kept in touch with the surgeons, went up to Edinburgh to make arrangements personally, and kept their father informed. But the delay resulted in tentative acceptance in London of a clarified 'P and P'. Finally, on March 6, he cabled in economy code to Shanghai: 'Sons better. Sailing 23rd.'

Hudson Taylor had been described as having 'a big head on broad shoulders'. That he had a big head in more senses than one, and a big heart, all but a few in the Mission would have agreed. But he needed a broad back while the discord among his leading colleagues lasted.[967]

For the time being he was free to return to China. On March 17, 1890, he agonisingly tore himself away from Jennie again and from the family, was seen off at the station by Benjamin, spent three days in Cannes in conference with William Berger, and on the 23rd joined his ship at Marseilles.

Wusong Road and the General Conference (March–May 1890)

Travel by coal-burning steamer had few of the pleasures of the sea which Hudson Taylor had so much enjoyed. Smelly, smutty, crowded and crude third-class accommodation had to be endured. Noisy, rough fellow-passengers, loud-mouthed and drunken, had led him to comment, 'P&O is no line for our sisters to travel by—or for luggage', often damaged. The French mailboat was no better and his only English-speaking fellow-passenger was a Scottish manual labourer. But years of the rough and tumble of life had taught him how to make his own cocoon of silence. He prepared his keynote address for the General Missionary Conference, and read the newly published *Life of Bishop Hannington*, the martyr of Uganda. 'Our travelling is child's play compared with his.' Sitting in the half-shade of an umbrella on the seashore at Colombo, streaming with perspiration, he thanked Jennie for her prayers for him.

> Spiritual blessing ... is the one thing I want and need and must have. Given this and I have no fears; without it nothing else will (avail) ... May God forgive all that is wrong in me and in our mission ... Unwillingness to be separated from you ... has brought me under a cloud ... but I have left you unwillingly, instead of joyfully ... I do want to be whole-hearted in God's service. [And on July 12] My solitary life must continue as far as I can see *indefinitely*! ... However heart-breaking it may be. We are His, His *slaves*.[968]

When he had sailed away from Shanghai just a year before (April 12, 1889) the

2.67 Wusong Road, Shanghai: one of the three CIM buildings

plans and contract were complete for the new Mission headquarters on the Wusong Road site. On February 18, 1890, the first occupants had moved in. So when Hudson Taylor landed on April 27 it was to Wusong Road that he was taken. Everything was as he and David Cranston had designed it, down to the details of doors and windows, stair-treads and risers. On two sides of a large grassy quadrangle with a Chinese pavilion or summer-house in the centre, the gift of the building contractor, stood the Mission home and the office block, with a meeting hall seating two hundred. The home in particular had a charm that made it pleasant to live in. It was a resounding success.

With a series of conferences due to begin on May 1, about sixty CIM missionaries had arrived already. They thronged to greet him. The inscription at the entrance read, 'To the glory of God and the furtherance of His Kingdom in China'. 'I feel glad,' Hudson Taylor commented, 'that the CIM was not even mentioned.'

Instead of finding John Stevenson in good health with a strong hold on the administration, he found him hoping to hand over his responsibilities. While Hudson Taylor's horizon had broadened markedly during his year away, Stevenson still thought in the old terms of himself as a deputy rather than as the China Director. They agreed that he would continue routine administration while Hudson Taylor took over liaison with other missions and the major problems, the threatened resignations and dissidents. In few days' time he would be able to put his concept of a thousand more missionaries to the appraisal of the assembled societies.[969]

A new factor had arisen since he left home. His international commitments were about to embrace the Australasian colonies. Letters to him and to the London Council told of several potential members of the Mission waiting at Melbourne to be interviewed. Would he sanction the formation of a provisional council, and come himself to confer with them? Two days after he himself reached Shanghai, a young ordained Anglican arrived from Australia at his own expense, and asked to be admitted. This was the spirit Hudson Taylor liked—conviction followed by action. C. H. Parsons had brought a letter of commendation from his vicar, H. B. Macartney, the potential chairman of an Australian council. Without delay Hudson Taylor welcomed Charles Parsons into the CIM and cabled to Melbourne, 'Sanction committee'.[970]

On April 30 the new meeting hall at Wusong Road was inaugurated, with a full house of two hundred including his good friends of many years, William Muirhead, Joseph Edkins, Alexander Williamson, John Nevius and others. On that day the CIM had 382 members in China at 89 stations, a far cry from the much criticised *Lammermuir* party of 1866. The visionary enlargement of the Mission's Shanghai premises had come only just in time. Every corner was filled. Some old-timers like Charles Judd, from his quiet city of Ninghai in Shandong, were amazed. What had happened to Hudson Taylor, the exponent and protagonist of simplicity and the Chinese way of life? Immediately they saw that simplicity and adequacy were compatible. 'The sanest man I ever knew,' was one man's description of his leader.

The Wusong Road premises were to be stretched to their limit time and again in the coming months, and in the years ahead. The last decade of the century had begun on a prophetic note. The next was to begin with this haven crammed with refugees from the Boxer holocaust. Each decade was

to see it filled to capacity in emergencies. There were 'only thirty-one bedrooms available for those not on the permanent staff; but to the missionary accustomed to Chinese inns, a bed on the floor—and he generally carries his own bedding—in the hall, office or attics, is gratefully welcomed when others cannot be had.' At the time of the revolution which ended the Manchu dynasty, 1,333 passed through the home between September 1911 and October 1912.[971]

No danger existed of the 'Shanxi spirit' sweeping the General Missionary Conference of May 7–20, but a strong possibility of disharmony drove Hudson Taylor to call for six days of 'consecration' and waiting on God, from May 1–6, before the conference began. As many from other societies joined with the CIM, meetings in the new hall saw 180 to 240 daily taking part. Many were to recognise the success of a resolution in Parliament on May 3, a step towards ending the opium traffic, as being linked with this week of prayer for China.[972] On the last day Archibald Orr Ewing and Mary Scott (Robert Scott's daughter) were married at the cathedral. And the next day Howard Taylor and Geraldine Guinness became engaged.

The major conference began with a short session of prayer followed by Hudson Taylor's hour-long keynote address. None doubted the nature of what he would have to say, but the mood of the 430 delegates (226 men and 204 women) gave him wings. Almost exactly one-third of the entire Protestant missionary staff in China were present.[973] The simplicity of his subject and presentation, the feeding of the four thousand, and its application as a parable to the theme of 'the gospel to every creature' may have misled some who looked for an academic or philosophical address. But if they were disappointed, its clarity captivated the rest—a multitude to feed, a few to feed them, systematic cooperation, a lesson in comity and the stuff of life reached all.

Then his application to China: 'It would only want twenty-five (evangelists) to be associated with each society, to give us 1,000 additional workers.' A thousand more and every Chinese family could, as he showed mathematically, be given the chance of an intelligent hearing of the gospel before the turn of the century. His points went home: obedience required; obedience possible; obedience imperative—so that the resolution based upon his exposition became one of the historic features of the conference. 'The 1,000 idea is spreading,' he wrote home to Jennie.

To anticipate the conclusions of the conference, three appeals to the worldwide Church resulted from the twelve days of deliberation:

1. to send out as many hundreds of messengers of the gospel as could be secured;

2. that the best kinds of laymen and women including educationists and medical personnel should supplement the ordained ones—a revolutionary step for some societies; and

3. an appeal for '1,000 men within 5 years of this time'.

From England Hudson Taylor had written to John Stevenson, 'I do not propose making any definite attempt on account of the CIM before the conferences . . . If all (missions) will take it up so much the better. If not, we shall see if any will, or whether we must do it alone.' A thousand more in the CIM? It came to that. But the conference had risen to the occasion. Now it remained to see what mission boards and committees would do.[974]

The Third General Missionary Conference,[975] Shanghai
(May 7–20, 1890)

Two inter-mission conferences had previously been held, in August 1843 in Hong Kong, and in 1877 at Shanghai (see 1, p120 & 2, pp 293–97 also 1, p 120). At that time, 1877, the total number of Protestant missionaries in China was fewer than those who met together in 1890. Only two Chinese delegates were included. The English language was used, and the role of Chinese church leaders had not yet progressed to one of influence on the policy of missions.[976] The third conference

(in the Lyceum Theatre) was more wide-ranging and ambitious. Its official report ran to eighty pages of close print. But, as the election of John Nevius and David Hill as chairmen indicated, a wish prevailed for a high spiritual tone throughout. They managed to preserve it.

As a practical business forum it worked methodically through a long agenda of semi-technical subjects covering all aspects of missionary work—social, biblical, evangelistic, educational, medical, and related political and cultural tics, some highly debatable. Y. K. Yen, a Chinese minister of the Protestant Episcopal Church, urged missionaries to 'adopt a Chinese mode of life', and that 'none should be brought out who were overbearing in manner'. Hudson Taylor had been asked for a second paper on 'The Missionary', the physical, mental and spiritual qualifications he and she should have. Others spoke on the 'Evils of the Use of Opium' and 'The Value of Opium Refuges', self-support of the churches, and the role of women. One decision taken by the conference was greeted with the doxology ('three notes too high'): instead of having several versions of the Bible in circulation, agreement was reached that 'a version of the Scriptures uniform for all China' should be prepared, to be supplemented by three levels of Wenli, and regional dialect versions. That this was 'the crowning work of the conference' reflects the disorder that previously existed.

The resolution to appeal for a thousand men in five years, prepared by an elected committee, was also carried unanimously. A memorial to the emperor at first favoured by the conference was finally discarded for fear of its motives being misconstrued and resulting in the persecution of Chinese Christians. David Hill advocated the far-reaching enlistment of unordained men and women, stressing that the evangelisation of the world is the work of the whole church, not of a separated order among Christians. In this he complemented Hudson Taylor's own proposition to the conference, and a committee was appointed to frame an appeal to the worldwide church. It called for 'a largely increased force' of both ordained and unordained men. When asked if the work in China could not be done by Chinese Christians, Hudson Taylor gave it as his opinion that the ideal could not yet be realised. Were not all missions already encouraging Chinese of the right type to be evangelists? The report of a committee on Unity and Division in the Field (Comity) presented through Hudson Taylor as its spokesman, was also received with 'splendid warmth of unanimity'.

But on the subject of 'ancestral worship', strong divergence of views became apparent. The minority school of thought represented by Timothy Richard, W. A. P. Martin, Gilbert Reid and a few others, had been vocal for twenty years. This was their prime opportunity. The grey area of uncertainty about what was purely cultural, to be preserved and emulated, and what was part of pagan religious practice contradictory to Christian truth, needed to be discussed and clarified. The differences of opinion lay in the interpretation of common Chinese beliefs and observances. If Christians were to reject the idolatrous and to worship the true God alone, the distinction needed to be drawn between veneration, in the sense of deep respect to the point of awe and reverence, on the one hand, and outright worship, whether as adoration of the divine or appeasement of menacing spirits, on the other hand. The main difficulty lay in great variations among the Chinese themselves. The mandarin might hold an intellectual, agnostic or sceptical view of temple worship and ancestor worship in the home. Or he might in every way be like the common man, devoid of philosophical reservations, fearing and worshipping the spirits of the unseen world. Ancestor worship is, in fact, by common agreement, the basic religion of the Chinese.

So intricate a subject cannot be adequately treated in biography with the limitations of this one, but because unfactual statements about the Shanghai conferences of 1877 and 1890 have been made, we must briefly consider what 'ancestor' and 'ancestral' worship involved.[977] Following two papers on the topic, 'How far should Christians be required to abandon native customs?' by the American Episcopal, F. Ohlinger, and the American Presbyterian, H. V. Noyes, one from W. A. P. Martin (who had arrived in China in 1850) was read by his supporter, Gilbert Reid. His title, 'The Worship of Ancestors—a plea for toleration', summarised his case much as he aired it in 1877 (see pp 389–91, and note his train of thought). If this great obstacle to the conversion of the nation were to be removed, he argued, it must either be swept away wholesale, which was unthinkable, or be met by adaptations, as stepping-stones towards a satisfying conclusion. The effect of strengthening family bonds and moral restraints was to be admired in the rites. The cohesive social and ethical values of the ancient customs could not be destroyed without disastrous effects. Therefore the physical practices must be examined.

Martin admitted that the system of ancestral rites was tainted by 'a large admixture of superstition and idolatry' through 'invocations and offerings which implied that the deceased were tutelary deities'.[978] He agreed that 'anything that can fairly be construed as idolatry', the offerings and invocations, could not be countenanced. But, he claimed, these were accretions which could be eliminated. The rites could be made compatible with Christianity. The 'announcements' to ancestors could be so worded as to express affection without petition. Martin then ventured onto more dangerous ground. Bowing and kneeling, even the *ketou* were marks of respect and not idolatrous in some contexts, even if they were in others. Nor were salutations addressed to the departed, as much a Western custom as Chinese.

Here eyebrows were raised in the conference. Glaring differences lay between the Chinese status quo, idolatrous worship addressed to the dead, and poetic expression in the West. Martin's concern to honour the best in Chinese tradition, and to bridge the chasm between the Chinese and Christian positions, appeared to blind him to reality. The sympathy of the conference was forfeited. If he had incorporated into his address the emphases of the debate after the turn of the twentieth century, namely to discover Christian ways of showing respect for ancestors, without any vestige of worship or appeasement, a strongly positive note might have forestalled the controversy that erupted.

The next paper by a Dr Gilbert on 'The Attitude of Christianity towards Ancestral Worship' was greeted with great applause, showing the conservative mood of the conference. The scholar E. Faber, DD, of the Rhenish Mission (in China since 1865), chairman of the executive committee on the Wenli version of the Bible, and other committees, then summarised the main features of 'Ancestral Worship' to demonstrate its complete incompatibility with Christian truth, and William Muirhead (1847) protested that 'toleration of ancestral worship would be most injurious to the Christian Church'. Matthew Yates (1847) said that 'toleration of idolatry is treason to Christianity'. That a label of chief opponent to Martin has been attached to Hudson Taylor is clearly undeserved.

Some told of Chinese who said that relaxation to allow of worshipping their ancestors would see many, including mandarins, 'entering the Church'. What kind of 'Christians' they would be was another matter. But in Dr Martin's defence Timothy Richard (1869) reminded the conference that he was not asking for toleration of what was idolatrous. He had distinctly said that whatever was idolatrous 'cannot for a moment be entertained'. What Martin wanted was 'toleration of such rites in ancestral reverence as are not idolatrous'. For example, Richard suggested, the spring festival of *qing ming* 'so nearly coincided in time with Easter, that it afforded a very suitable opportunity to dwell on immortality and the resurrection of the dead'.

At least a positive note had been sounded, but it offered a substitute and

did not exemplify 'toleration of such rites in ancestral reverence'. Gilbert Reid then defended Martin by saying that he was seeking a *via media* for those who adhere to reverence but not to idolatry. 'Make the worship of Christ the foundation, and the Chinese would not worship ancestors as they worship God.' Put in these terms the problem looked more like one of lucid communication than of conflicting opinions. But was this in fact Martin's 'plea', or wishful thinking? Would the introduction of Christ into Chinese ancestral rites displace the misdirected worship of ancestors or legitimise the worship of both together? Few agreed that a solution lay in this direction.

The allotted time was up and Hudson Taylor (1854) who so far had listened without taking part, wanted the time extended. Frank Whitehouse, Hudson Taylor's personal secretary, in his own report of the conference, 'Items of Interest', wrote that Hudson Taylor had suggested that 'a rising vote of dissent' should be put to the conference. But an aroused audience had reacted spontaneously, pre-empting a formal motion, 'and there was something like a scene'. The official report reads, however: 'Without making a motion to that effect (he) asked those who dissented from the conclusion of Dr Martin's paper to rise. Most of the audience then rose, upon which one of the preceding speakers [Timothy Richard or Gilbert Reid] protested that this was not a fair way to treat such a subject.' It was agreed to return to the discussion in the evening. The action most in keeping with Hudson Taylor's personality would then have been to make an apology if he had acted unconstitutionally or unfairly. That he did not do so, but allowed Whitehouse's factual statement, supports the contention that he was misunderstood and chose not to justify himself.

When the subject was reopened in the evening the interlude had given time for reflection. Y. K. Yen rose to explain the notions underlying the use of ancestral tablets. He said he would not have in his house even a picture of his parents. Non-

Christians would assume that they were worshipped. When resolution and counter-resolution were proposed, the veteran Alexander Williamson (1855) warned that any hasty declaration by the conference could be misconstrued and rouse the angry opposition of all classes of Chinese. Any negative crusade against ancestor worship would be a disastrous mistake. The conference agreed. J. L. Gibson (1874), the Shantou (Swatow) Presbyterian, then stressed the fact that *fear*, not veneration or worship, was 'the real essence' of the rite. The gospel of deliverance from the power and bondage of demons was 'a great gift' which Chinese would learn to recognize.

Still the delegates had not had enough. The next morning C. W. Mateer (1863), the American Presbyterian of Shandong, proposed a resolution of dissent from his fellow-Presbyterian W. A. P. Martin's conclusions, and Hudson Taylor supported it with an amendment to end the debate. The resolution was 'carried by a large majority', 'almost unanimously', 'affirming the belief of the conference "that idolatry is an essential constituent of ancestor worship" and dissenting from the view that missionaries "should refrain from any interference with the native mode of honouring ancestors"'.[979]

Most missionaries could give examples of how Chinese when they put their faith in Christ Jesus knew 'instinctively', by the prompting of the Holy Spirit, that ancestor worship would have no place in their lives. Many destroyed the tablets and paraphernalia of worship. Some openly burned them with the family idols.[980]

The unresolved problem remained. How could Christians honour their ancestors in a Chinese way (for the Chinese certainly excelled in remembering and celebrating their debt to their forebears), keeping permanent records and yet avoiding all appearance of idolatry? But apart from the brief disturbance in the 1890 conference until time was allowed for talking the matter through, a spirit of harmony prevailed. Significantly, *Christian Alternatives to Ancestor Practices*, in referring to J. L. Nevius's

influence in Korea, says: 'The clear-cut break of the Korean Church from ancestor worship had become one of the important factors for the rapid growth of the Korean Church.' After the Boxer rising a new debate developed in the *Chinese Recorder*, in which W. A. P. Martin repeated his old contentions, and replies concentrated on finding Christian substitutes for ancestor worship. And late in the twentieth century the debate has been revived.[981]

Growing pains (May 1890)

At the height of the general conference a photograph of the delegates was to be taken. All who could foregathered at the photographer's where a bamboo scaffolding with 'cat-walks' had been erected. To discerning men it looked precarious, but Chinese scaffolding traditionally served its purpose well. Rank upon rank, of about 300 missionary men and women found a place on it. Hudson Taylor climbed to perch 'eighteen or twenty feet' from the ground and at one end of the back row. Suddenly the whole structure began to sag and disintegrate. People, planks and bamboo poles fell on top of those below. 'With some 200 ladies falling, there was not a shriek.' An uncanny silence followed as those pinned down waited for those above them in the heap to climb off first. William Rudland saw Hudson Taylor high up on the one corner that remained intact. He helped him down and (in the heat of May) worked to free others until he himself fainted. A Dr Wright, who also helped, said, 'Hudson Taylor . . . was as calm as if he were waiting for a wedding.' Mrs Jenkins of Shaoxing had a collar-bone and two ribs fractured. Not one other person suffered more than cuts and bruises. The photograph was taken four days later.[982]

But 'all the starch seems gone and I feel weak and weary,' Hudson Taylor told Jennie, in the same breath as, 'There is a great spirit of love and unanimity.' Annie Dunn, another recently arrived language student, was dying of 'black smallpox', her fiancé at her bedside in Zhenjiang. Vaccination was still an unperfected technique.[983] One of the Canadians of the first party had 'galloping consumption' and died on May 23, two days after another of the same group died on returning to the States. Arthur Polhill had typhoid, far away in Sichuan. An accumulation of anxieties again left Hudson Taylor drained of strength.

On May 16, the CIM was at home to the whole missionary community with a buffet reception on the lawns surrounding the pavilion at Wusong Road. The tall office block, with its spiral, iron, external staircase, and the inviting Mission home were open for inspection. Photographs of the reception and of the wrecked scaffolding were reproduced in *China's Millions*, 1890—the first to replace engravings. Hudson Taylor was too unwell to join the guests. But they 'accorded (him) generous recognition as a leading influence among missions in China', and the necessity of having such extensive premises reflected the degree to which the Mission had progressed.[984]

On his fifty-eighth birthday, May 21, the eighty-three members of the Mission still in Shanghai presented him with an illuminated address and $480 for his personal use. He felt he should not accept it—unless it could be used for travelling 'in the Colonies'. The address read, 'We desire (to express) our unshaken conviction that those principles on which you were led to found this Mission, and on which it has grown to its present extent and usefulness, are of God.' He was to leave in July with Montagu Beauchamp as his companion. Montagu had handed him a note the previous day expressing gratitude for his influence and enclosing £100. Before they left, H. N. Lachlan also sent a gift of fifty-two taels towards his expenses, and Orr Ewing £1,000 for the Mission. Criticism of the 'Principles and Practice' and 'Arrangements' had become public knowledge, and his loyal friends wished to demonstrate their support.

Sunday, May 25, they kept as a day of fasting and prayer for the CIM conference beginning the next day. Outstanding among speakers in the 'consecration' meetings before the General Conference and again on this day was Dixon Hoste. His words were taken down in shorthand.

> We must get to know God in secret—alone in the desert. (Like Joseph in the dungeon and David as a shepherd and a hunted man, we must expect testing and trial as a matter between God and each of us individually.) It does seem to me that true spirituality lies in this—utter dependence on God for everything ... We shall dread to ... do anything in our own wisdom ... If a man can only get down before God and get His plan of work for him, individually, that is what will make him irresistible. It does not matter whether (he) is a strong man or a weak one.

Hoste was exceptional and Hudson Taylor had his eye on him. He had written giving Hoste advice he could not accept, but afterwards received this letter: 'More than a year ago you wrote . . . As you know, I replied that I did not see my way to doing so . . . I felt free to keep my own opinions. I wish to say that experience has since then caused me to change my views . . . I thank you for your advice and your constant forbearance.' A man with this personality, honesty, humility, saintliness and strength would with experience one day prove his worth. Regular reports of his work with Pastor Hsi already showed his wisdom.

The informal CIM conference was incidental to the General Conference and not representative of the Mission, so decisions were not taken. But frank discussion of the 'Principles' and 'Arrangements' threw strong light on some weaknesses in administration, especially in Britain. Consultation before the appointment of superintendents was a good thing, but 'democratic election' and committee rule failed to win support. Hudson Taylor himself was convinced that the biblical pattern was godly leadership, and progress was too often hampered by committees.[985] He prized initiative and evidence of considerate leadership. As for itinerant evangelism of the kind necessary to take the gospel to 'every creature', Hudson Taylor said:

This work will not be done without crucifixion—without consecration that is prepared at any cost to carry out the Master's commands ... Given that, I believe it will be done. (But only) the operation of the Holy Ghost (would make it produce results). A man's conversion is, I believe, a regenerative change produced by (Him)—it is not an influence produced by man on the mind of his fellow-man ... If the Lord sends Paul to plant, He will certainly send Apollos to water.

The greatest practical obstacle to the CIM welcoming a large share of the thousand evangelists was paradoxically its need of administrative staff in China and Britain, and of businessmen and doctors. The sheer labour of getting large numbers equipped and transported to their spheres of work had demonstrated the shortcomings of unskilled staff.[986] A thoroughly efficient machine had become his own administrative priority. He could see some young men showing promise of this nature—Graham Brown, Marcus Wood, Hayward, Hardman and Amelia's son, Hudson, among them. Not yet free to come to China was another of Orr Ewing's friends, Walter B. Sloan, a Keswick Convention figure who would be one of God's best gifts to the Mission.

As soon as the conference ended, the China Council met for six hours daily, straining to eliminate features of the 'Book of Arrangements' which could give offence, while retaining essentials. In this they met resistance from one of their own number, the proponent of elections to whom Hudson Taylor had given a district to superintend. No regulations had been introduced that were not a definition of essentials to harmony in the Mission, yet this superintendent now wished for autonomy in his own region. And more: 'If he should retire from the Mission at any time he wished to take the work with him. The Council could not entertain that thought for a moment.' Not only so, but he intended to recruit his own colleagues, independently of the Mission. As he could not have his own way, he chose to resign.

(C. T. Studd followed his example soon afterwards.) The China Council then completed its work with agreement to make separate administrative offices for shipping and postal services at Shanghai as each had become so heavy.[987]

From mid-June until mid-July Hudson Taylor visited the Yangzi River stations and Yantai again, designating language school students to their inland appointments, 'trouble-shooting' and discussing finance with Broumton at Wuchang. One of the bitterest tribulations was Mary Stevenson's relapse into 'mania' again. Her brothers in Scotland had recovered, but the strain of work and sorrow were telling on their father. With his staff in Shanghai reorganised and strengthened, however, he agreed to carry on.

At midnight on Saturday, July 19, Hudson Taylor, Montagu Beauchamp and Frank Whitehouse, the secretary, embarked for Hong Kong to await their ship to Australia.

The second 'branch', Australia (July–December 1890)

The hidden history of God at work in the world admits of a clearing of the mist from time to time. The evangelist whose text, 'My son, give me thine heart' (Proverbs 23.26), first stirred the twelve-year-old Hudson Taylor to respond to God, was Henry Reed (see 1, p 127).[988] In later years he moved to Australia and made his home at Mount Pleasant, near Launceston, Tasmania. From time to time after, Hudson Taylor thanked him for his influence and they kept in touch, and after her husband died, Mrs Reed sent donations to the Mission. It is probable that when George Nicoll spent four years in Australia to recover his health, 1885–89, he had close links with the family. The eldest daughter, Mary (Maggie to the inner circle), was in England when she offered in 1887 to be one of the Hundred. She sailed to China as a self-supporting associate on January 26, 1888, with Grattan Guinness's daughter, Geraldine, but ill-health forced her out in 1889—out of China, but not of the Mission.

She became an indefatigable ambassador to the Australian churches. Incidentally, Geraldine's brother, Harry, newly qualified as a doctor, escorted his younger brother and sister (Whitfield and Lucy) to stay with Mrs Reed in Tasmania, fell in love with Maggie's sister, Annie, and took her home to England—the mother-to-be of future members of the CIM and other notables.[989] So their connection with the CIM was strong over many years. Moreover, George Soltau was their minister at Launceston.

In Melbourne four ministers had begun in 1889 to pray together for China, knowing nothing of Mary Reed having joined the CIM, until she was invalided home. H. B. Macartney and his curate, C. H. Parsons, were Anglicans, W. Lockhart Morton, a Presbyterian, Alfred Bird, a Baptist. Correspondence with Hudson Taylor through his friend Philip Kitchen led to Charles Parsons arriving at Shanghai in April 1890 and their consulting together about developments in Australia. Mary Reed was also writing of other potential missionaries and asking if they could not proceed to China as associates rather than go through the formalities in England. But H. B. Macartney proposed a council of the CIM, and Mary wrote at length to Hudson Taylor about it and her own activities.[990]

Strong prejudice against the Chinese, stemming from their immigration in large numbers, bringing opium, had diminished as Australians were given unbiased information about China. Soon there were crowded meetings. After Charles Parsons left for China, Mary Reed was all the more in demand as a speaker. Then Hudson Taylor was invited to come. George Soltau, one-time member of the London Council, had written to Theodore Howard proposing an Australasian Council, and in April a London minute noted that this was beyond London's brief. It was for Hudson Taylor to decide. The cable he sent on May 21, 'Sanction committee', raises a question, however, for he used words carefully. It would have been most like him to authorise a committee to assess the waiting candidates, but to delay the formation of a

council at Melbourne until he had met and consulted with Macartney and his friends in person. Perhaps an intermediate letter had not reached them. They took the cable at full value and called a meeting for the very next day, May 22, at which an Australasian Council was constituted with Macartney as chairman, Alfred Bird as honorary secretary and Philip Kitchen, treasurer. With a flying start the applications of eight candidates were considered. Within five years fifty, and in a decade a total of 101 missionaries had sailed from Australia and New Zealand.

Before he became Archbishop of Sydney, Marcus Loane, already a member of the Sydney Council for ten years, wrote *The Story of the China Inland Mission in Australia and New Zealand, 1890–1964,* to commemorate the centenary of the Mission and the sailing of the *Lammermuir.* Taking nothing for granted, Hudson Taylor and his companions (still in Chinese clothes) went to a Chinese hotel in Hong Kong until John Burdon, his companion on the Chongming Island adventure (see 1, pp 298–302), insisted that he always make his, the bishop's residence, his home when passing through.

Hudson Taylor had reached the dregs of endurance of seemingly interminable separations from Jennie and the children. In his polyglot Bible, Jacob's prayer is marked (Genesis 32.11 undated) 'Deliver me, I pray . . . lest he will come and smite me, and the mother with the children.' It would seem that Hudson Taylor had Satan's assaults in mind. His son, Charles Edward, a Cambridge undergraduate, was 'far from God' and having a bad influence at home.[991] Millie Duncan, their adopted daughter, was engaged and going to Canada and then India. Ernest and Amy were fifteen and fourteen. They needed Jennie. But so did he. 'Ask for me more patience and more joy in the will of God, in respect of our separation. Sometimes I feel as if I cannot bear it, and this is not right, is it? And people say, "Oh you are so much accustomed to it, it is nothing to you!" Do you think you could rightly join me on my return to China, darling?'

He was needed in London, too. The Council were challenging him again on their rights. But he feared lest John Stevenson break down completely, and must relieve him. Did that mean another year apart from Jennie? 'God has given us a costly sacrifice to offer to Him, an alabaster box to break at His feet.' If it was right he was willing; but like Lewis, his previous secretary, Whitehouse's shortcomings were making Hudson wish he could always count on Jennie's efficiency and discretion instead. Then, two days later, Yes, it was right. Make preparations, hand over *China's Millions* to Charles Fishe. 'I think that we must not separate as we have done,' again and again over twenty years. Yet on September 9, this solution created a new fear: 'It would be altogether heartbreaking if any harm came to our dear children through my selfishness in taking you away. To die, alone, would be better than that! God guides.' God did, and all was well.[992]

The ship to Australia had only first-class and steerage decks, so steerage it had to be, with rough Portuguese sailors as companions. But also a good friend in the cabin steward he had had on the voyage from Vancouver in 1888. They passed close to Mindoro Mindanao and Celebes, and berthed at the primitive Port Darwin on August 12, still in cool Chinese clothes, keeping their Western suits uncrumpled for Australia. Wrecks on previously uncharted reefs were etched into their memories of this voyage. Typically they found the Methodist manse and spent Sunday ashore, preaching and addressing an ad hoc meeting. But the young minister, F. E. Finch, warned them not to be too hopeful of finding missionary recruits in Australia, nor money. Trade was bad and the Chinese despised, he said.

Back at the ship they found their cabin empty. They had been moved up to the first class as the captain's guests. The steerage accommodation was all needed for Chinese labourers coming aboard, he explained. 'We saw no sign of any Chinese,' Beauchamp wrote. Then Thursday Island where 'Monty' went ashore to post letters

and recognised the broad back of Professor Drummond of Edinburgh, of all people, on his way to China. Of course he had to be the guest of the CIM at Wusong Road.[993]

Australia was gripped by strikes, enough to disrupt their planned travels, but August 26–September 1 at Sydney gave scope for meetings, the students glad to hear one of the Cambridge Seven.[994] Then on by ship to Melbourne and the first session with the new council on September 3. Interviewing candidates, addressing crowded meetings, shaking the hand of John G. Paton apostle of the cannibal islands—their days were full. Hudson Taylor's thoughtfulness for others, not least the domestic servants, impressed his host, H. B. Macartney. In Tasmania from September 15–24 it was the same. 'Money poured in', a ballroom reception was held at Government House, and men and women offered to go to China. Mary Reed became a full member of the Mission, and her mother handed Hudson Taylor a gift to pay Jennie's fare to China and to America if they should want to go there. George Soltau and his wife delighted in seeing him again and to be shown how to recognise the right type of candidate: 'How quietly he led us on to see the needs so that we suggested the rules that must be made and the provisions by the Council.' They collected as many Chinese as they could to hear him. George Soltau was walking arm in arm with him in Launceston when Hudson Taylor stopped, turned to him and said, 'There should be only one circumstance in our lives and that circumstance is God'—a memorable two weeks.[995]

Back to Ballarat, Adelaide, 'the city of churches', for twelve days, with meetings daily and Bible expositions four days running. Then Melbourne again, and the pace maintained. Three thousand young people in the Academy of Music; forty ministers from 10.00 a.m. to 5.00 p.m.; fifty-eight more candidates to interview; they were well into October and 'very busy', with Hudson Taylor troubled by neuralgia. This was when he suggested to the council that they pray for a hundred missionaries in ten years, one tenth of a thousand.

2.68 The first Australasian party, with Montagu Beauchamp behind and to Hudson Taylor's right

flood of sixty candidates. The coal strike forced the ship to coal at Newcastle, and gave time for a visit to Ipswich, rejoining the ship at Brisbane.

After meetings at Brisbane from November 13–20, they at last sailed away from Australia on the 20th. By then the party had the measure of the CIM and their director and were calling him their 'dear Father'. On December 3 they reached Darwin. Hudson Taylor took his companions to near the manse and went on alone. When the door was opened he said to Fitch, 'How many cups have you?' 'Why?' Fitch asked. 'And to (his) amazement we filed in thirteen strong.'[997] Again they sailed through the Torres Strait, where Hudson Taylor collected plants on an uninhabited island. He cared for them on board ship and planted them at Wusong Road. Then through the Philippines, close to Panay and Mindoro, and reached Hong Kong on the 13th.

Jennie and her party had arrived and gone on. If she had stayed, her note explained, his duty to his Australia party would have meant the two of them having little time together. She knew him too well. But the next ship to Shanghai had only first-class accommodation. He waited until the 18th to bring his companions with him. Some scraps of paper tell more about him and his influence on them than the contents at first suggest—letters of thanks to the captains of both Australian ships, and from the party for so much kindness on board. He told Maria in a letter how restful the voyage had been and how well he was. But the mail waiting for him at Hong Kong had its bitter vein, from William Sharp about the London Council, and from the Shanghai veteran claiming a seat on the China Council. When others advised a firm rebuff, Hudson Taylor said, 'He is an old man now. Be kind to him,' and kind they were. Over tea with the council men he was benign—his wife had driven him to write![998]

At last on December 21 they reached Shanghai and Wusong Road. Reunited, until her death in his old age, Hudson and Jennie never had to part again.

New Zealand wanted him to come, and Sir William Fox, 'long interested in the CIM', invited him to be his guest. But he had to be back at Shanghai to tackle the London Council's problems before the year ended; and a party of four men and eight women (including Mary Reed) was ready to travel with him. He could give them daily training and a start on learning Chinese.[996] Three thousand came to bid them farewell at Melbourne Town Hall on October 27, and on the 31st they left for Sydney. The formal photograph shows strong, intelligent young men and women and in the back row the magnificent figure of the eminent oarsman, Montagu Beauchamp. Jennie and a party of new missionaries had left Britain the day before.

On November 1, John Southey, an English clergyman of Ipswich, near Brisbane, wrote to say that after an illness he had come to Australia in 1880 on his doctor's advice. Riding ten or twelve miles between each of three services every Sunday, he had remained in good health. But he was thirty-four with a wife and three children. Might he go to China? Hudson Taylor, Montagu Beauchamp and the Australian twelve sailed from Sydney on November 10, leaving Whitehouse to help the council at Melbourne to cope with a

Franson's flood (1890–93)

Erik Folke of Uppsala University had arrived in China at his own expense in March 1887. Because he had gone there, his friend Josef Holmgren and two others had formed the committee to support him, which naturally came to be called 'The Swedish Mission in China', as there was no other. Folke consulted John Stevenson at Shanghai and their friendly relationship from the first was reflected in the agreements reached between his friends in Sweden and Hudson Taylor. Folke adopted Puzhou and the south-western tip of Shanxi as his sphere, surveyed by Turner and James in 1876, and found a foothold at Yuncheng. Before long his industry and gifts as a pioneer and leader of men led to his extending his territory to include thirty-eight counties in Shanxi, Shaanxi and Henan. After twenty-five years, his mission had developed twelve central bases for fifty-four missionaries, a thousand Christians and a training school for evangelists. All was in such close association with the CIM in China as to be virtually part of it, working on the same lines.[999]

While Hudson Taylor was preparing for his Australia journey, Fredrik Franson had met the London Council (June 2, 1890) and been assured of help for the Barmen mission, the 'German China Alliance', before going back to America, to inspire the Scandinavian churches with his message of 'the gospel to every creature' and his axiom 'from each church a missionary'. Within three and a half months the first thirty-five volunteers had their support guaranteed by the churches who sent them, and Franson was given $5,000 in addition for general expenses. The first to arrive at Shanghai from the Swedish churches in the States, on October 28, 1890, was followed by a married couple. Then, two months after the Australians reached Shanghai with Hudson Taylor, the incredible happened. Word had come that Fredrik Franson was sending a party of twenty-five Swedes and Norwegians

towards the Thousand, but no more was known. On the morning of February 17, 1891, two blond young men were seen approaching the Mission home and said they were the vanguard.[1000] 'How many are you?' asked Stevenson, wondering how to accommodate them, for the house was full and several parties from other countries were expected. 'Thirty-five,' they answered, 'and ten more next week.' Never before in the history of Protestant missions in China had so many come at one time. All were taken in.

The letter they brought from Fredrik Franson was as cheerful as it was unbusinesslike, a true reflection of the man himself, and as much a surprise as the advent of so many unannounced. 'The intention of this Mission is to be associated with the China Inland Mission, just as Mr Folke (of the Swedish Mission in China) and Mr Olsson (with the German China Alliance) are . . . Hoping you will extend the same fraternal feelings of sympathy to our present party.'[1001] Hudson Taylor had 'a very warm view of (Franson); a most remarkable man of God, worthy of the utmost honour',[1002] and of the seventeen men and eighteen women of good quality, trained as evangelists, and ready to take conditions as they found them. The house was filled with music, singing to their guitars; and as the language schools were already full (with sixty at Yangzhou), the Swedes had to stay in Shanghai. On the day of their arrival they were set to work learning Chinese and improving their English, until arrangements could be made to distribute them upcountry.

From October 19 to December 25, 1890, nine parties had reached Shanghai from Europe, Canada and Australia, numbering fifty-three in all. From January 1 to April 12, 1891, seven parties from Europe, the United States, Canada and Australia were received (including John Southey, his family and seven women) adding seventy-eight more novices. In a period of little over three weeks sixty-six had arrived: Franson's thirty-five on February 17, nine from England on February 21, four from Canada with Henry Frost on February 26, and fifteen instead of ten in Franson's second batch on March 10. Without the new premises the Mission could not have coped. In six months, before a year had elapsed since the General Conference's appeal, 131 men and women (members and associates) were added to the CIM. The stalwart lady-in-charge of the home was the Scottish landowner, Miss Williamson, thoroughly competent and in command of the seventy-five new arrivals she had at one point in her care. A rising bell sounded at 6.00 a.m. followed by breakfast at 7.30 and prayers at table. After the midday meal at 12.30 they sang a hymn and prayed for China. Tea at 3.30 p.m. made a break in language study and family prayers again followed the evening meal at 7.00 p.m.

Franson's men and women told Geraldine Guinness (in Shanghai to write the first volume of her *Story of the CIM*) that they had come 'with no certainty as to where or how they might be received' in China. Twenty-six men were sent under escort to Shanxi to be divided up between a dozen locations, and seven to Qü Xian in Zhejiang; and eighteen women to Dagutang on the Poyang Lake, followed by eight more of the second party. A field in Shaanxi and Gansu was allotted to them in 1894 and the Zhejiang seven joined the rest after Hudson Taylor had made another of his epic journeys.[1003] A. B. Simpson's International Alliance Mission had by then sent the forty-five Scandinavians recruited for him by Franson after dispatching his own fifty to China. They also arrived in two parties on February 15 and 23, 1893.

The godly Fredrik Franson little knew what difficulties he created for the young men and women he dispatched to the unknown, or for the already hard pressed veterans who received and supervised them in China, but these scores of zealous pioneers gave many years of good work. When Hudson Taylor drew A. B. Simpson's attention to the problems which Franson's flood created, he intervened. A thousand new missionaries in five years could readily be received, taught to speak Chinese and set to work in an orderly way, each mission taking its share of responsibility with due regard for the existing circumstances.

It happened that John Stevenson was taking his 'poor, afflicted Mary' home to Scotland, sailing on March 7 (the day Stanley Smith's wife died); that James Broumton had typhoid and his wife a life-threatening liver abscess; and that Hudson Taylor with his own work to do was the only one available with the necessary experience to take over the administration from Stevenson, and the financial responsibilities of Broumton when funds were uncomfortably low. Yet the overcrowding and coming and going made any work well-nigh impossible at times—all at a period of renewed attack on his own and his colleagues' integrity.[1004]

The 'father of lies' and 'accuser of our brethren' (1890–94)

Frequent references to Satan in the correspondence at this time show how convinced the writers were that the CIM was under his concerted attack. Every major advance seemed to be answered by major onslaughts, often taking the form of false accusations. Dr A. P. Happer, the veteran (1884) American Presbyterian of Canton, twice wrote to Hudson Taylor for the facts, that he might refute rumours in circulation.[1005] One of his letters arrived while the China Council was in session, so Hudson Taylor consulted the leading men of the Mission. His reply was a window on otherwise seldom mentioned subjects, for 'when gossip has distorted facts, and misunderstanding and misrepresentation have gone on indefinitely, the mischief done is often past recall': 'You mention "the matter of written instructions to (our) missionaries . . . not to associate with other missionaries". Such instructions have never been given . . . . None of (the Council) has ever given, or seen, or heard of, such instructions.'

Dr Happer had been told that members of the CIM were prevailed upon to become

Baptists. 'The statements you have heard of proselytism are entirely false and ungrounded.' The only possible source might be in the fact that the Mission Secretary in London often gave a book of Spurgeon's sermons to missionaries leaving for China. But he himself was both Methodist and Anglican in sympathy! Many joined the CIM because in it they would be free to immerse. A recent example was an Anglican clergyman from Australia. 'Though a Baptist myself,' Hudson Taylor continued, 'as the head of a pan-denominational mission I have for twenty years refused (to give) instruction on this point . . . We have six organised Presbyterian churches (in North Anhui and Zhejiang) . . . four Episcopal stations (in Sichuan), four Methodist stations (in Yunnan).'[1006]

The safety of women upcountry caused him no anxiety:

> They feel as much at home as they would in England, and are quite as safe—I think more safe—from annoyance and insults. The (Chinese) pastor or evangelist and his wife take great care of them ... My own daughter before her marriage was three months (without a foreign companion), as happy as the day was long, and too busy to be lonely. I have never heard of any insult even, much less assault, on any lady worker inland; more care is needed in a place like Shanghai or Hankou. The ladies 'walk with God', and the beauty of holiness ... gives them a dignity before which lewdness cannot live ... They are really entrusted to the care of our Lord Himself and He is faithful to the trust.

Far more painful were letters from a member of the London Council. On the strength of hearsay and without verification, an honoured veteran was being accused and condemned at a distance for alleged indiscretions with young women of the Yangzhou language school.[1007] Hudson Taylor knew the circumstances too well to allow of a moment's doubt about his good friend. Since he had arrived twenty-five years before, he had been all that had been hoped of him. Full enquiry showed there was no substance to the rumours. Colleagues had only good to say of him. Anything ill-judged in what gave rise to complaint was outweighed by the indiscretion of someone writing to a member of the London Council instead of to the directors in China, and of 'London' in minuting their discussion and conclusions.

Far worse, it precipitated another constitutional crisis. The London Council began to take a strong hand in 'Field' affairs. One member wrote saying it was time to consider whether someone indiscreet was wise enough and had the gravity enough for the post of superintendent. He should be removed from the China Council. The Home Director had also acquired the wholly false impression of his personality, 'that (he) "loves power and the exercise of it"'. But, Hudson Taylor replied, 'Few men care less about it than he does.' Because false impressions developed all too easily in correspondence, he went on, 'Is it possible for you to come out and look into things with me?' It was not.[1008] His reminder that the directors in China were in a better position to know and act in such a matter was curtly answered by William Sharp with, 'Your letter manifests such marked absence of trust . . . in your Home Council', whereas the trouble lay in 'your wrong ideas and your China Council's'. And this was followed by the misconception, 'Your chief contention for several years past has been that we as a Council should be entirely cut off from the missionaries once they have sailed for China.' Far from it. Missionaries and directors in China were troubled that so few friendly letters came from London.

For the London Council to intervene in administrative and disciplinary action from a distance was a very different matter. These bones of contention were evidence of underlying attitudes and more misconceptions. The status of the London Council and a supposed threat to it from the new China Council quickly emerged as the main issue. Confidence in Hudson Taylor could not be extended to 'a few of the brethren' comprising the

China Council. 'You have a Council here (in London) *nominally* to advise you', but it should be recognised as having administrative power. 'It would appear . . . that your view of unity or unanimity is accordance by all concerned in your own view.' So he, Sharp, 'could wish you were led to leave the Mission to get on by itself while you took up more largely the expounding of Scripture and stirring up of the Churches'.

Instead of Hudson Taylor, let London run the Mission? The 'Principles and Practice' appeared to have been forgotten, and the role of other councils overlooked. How would the Mission recover from such a rift, in such a spirit? Never before had such propositions been advanced, or Hudson Taylor's leadership been challenged. From its inception the London Council had been advisory, and Hudson Taylor had taken pains to explain and give reasons when his judgment differed from theirs. But the 'Principles' pre-dated the Council, and he must maintain them, whoever might object. All members had agreed with the 'P and P' in joining the Mission. The full manuscript sources show adamant insistence by London in exercising power which it had never had nor wanted until 1891.[1009]

Strong-willed men confronted each other, but the crux was not whose will would prevail but which view was right? As for the allegations, Hudson Taylor protested to Theodore Howard, 'He thought (the Council) would wish to reconsider their action in the matter, with further information already sent to England: "I trust you will be led to cancel the minute."' They did.[1010] The slandered veteran agreed to pioneer Guangxi, if moving away for a time would clear the air. But 'that sorrowful persecution of a beloved servant of God' continued until Henry Frost invited him to help him in North America 'for six months or a year'. He went, in December 1891. Then other pretexts for raising the status of the London Council were found. The 'accuser of the brethren' had had a heyday.

'Not against flesh and blood' (1891–94)

Following the General Conference in Shanghai, criticisms appeared in the *Chinese Recorder* under the heading 'Chinese Dress in the Shanghai Conference'. The writer quoted rumours 'that one half of those who enter China under its (the CIM's) auspices, return within two years, either to their homeland on earth or to the home above', and, 'that the average term of service for the whole body is only three and a half years'. Hudson Taylor wrote at once to give the facts. 'I find that 539 persons have been connected with the China Inland Mission . . . during the last 26 years.' Instead of one half (270) only forty-four left China within two years—twenty-one by death, five by illness, four resigned, five were asked to withdraw, and nine for marriage or family claims. Of 373 full members, not probationers, twenty died after an average of eight and a half years' service; twelve were invalided home after six and a half years on average, twenty-one retired, nine were asked to leave, eighteen left to marry or for family claims and four were transferred to the home staff. These eighty-six served for six years one month on average; not three and a half. Not included in those categories were 287 full members, about to complete an average of seven years' service the inevitable result of the recent rapid increase in numbers. The first fifty members of the CIM completed seventeen years on average, and of them sixteen averaged twenty-four and three-quarter years. 'We are led to conclude that our Mission is, by God's blessing, one of the healthiest in China.'[1011]

In July 1891 the *North China Daily News* published a letter from a Yichang resident accusing CIM women and men of travelling 'huddled together' in the same boat without chaperones and 'promiscuously travelling in company overland, apeing Chinese dress and manners' as a disguise, but ignorantly breaking their customs. Hudson Taylor wrote on his copy, '*Untrue*. Their man-servant was a quiet disciple, and the boat-woman who acted as their servant, there is some hope was converted and helped them to preach.' From the Chinese point of view they were fully chaperoned. The Chongqing correspondent of the *Daily News* 'spoke up warmly' on the 20th, saying he had known every party of missionaries making the journey up the gorges for the past eight years (so was he a customs officer?) and had 'never known of anything improper in their travelling arrangements'. The only exception to single women travelling in the care of a missionary couple had been the one instance—wrongly criticised because no male missionary was with them. Dr James Cameron joined in. As women on their own, the travellers had had less trouble than experienced men often met with from unfriendly people.[1012]

'The accuser' had not finished. His next barb was from the China secretary of another mission in August 1891 to James Meadows, the senior CIM superintendent in Zhejiang. Apparently overlooking Hudson Taylor's rebuttal in the *Chinese Recorder*, this writer questioned 'the very great loss of missionaries . . . year by year' in the CIM—'a grave defect in the management of the Mission.' Hudson Taylor replied that the single women who had 'disappeared' from the Mission's lists were those who had married. Excluding associates for whose selection and medical condition the CIM was not responsible (although Dr Howard Taylor and others were constantly on call for anyone in need), the losses in the first two years compared favourably with other missions. Those with conscientious objections to vaccination came to China at great risk to themselves and affected the calculation. (But because of the danger to others who had to nurse smallpox cases, no more unvaccinated people were sent by the CIM from about this time.)[1013]

An unusually tragic sequence of harrowing deaths had recently wracked the emotions of mission leaders, friends and families. Soon after the General Conference the veteran Presbyterian, Alexander Williamson, died suddenly. In November 1890, James Meadows's wife, Elizabeth (Rose), succumbed when nine foreigners and eight Chinese were ill with influenza in

the same house. Travelling back to Sichuan from the coast, Arthur Polhill and his wife found too late that a Chinese passenger on the same boat had 'typhus'. Arthur himself contracted it and nearly died. And on March 7, 1891, Stanley Smith's wife of three years (Sophie Reuter, of Kristiansand) died of typhus (or typhoid). In September Miss E. Tanner, a new missionary, fell off the Ningbo city wall, sustained a compound fracture and osteomyelitis, and later died after amputation. Returning from Yantai with George Andrew and his son, Hudson Taylor's ship barely survived a typhoon which smashed to wreckage another ship accompanying them. On October 3, Thomas Thorne of the Bible Christians died of typhus. 'Black smallpox' took its toll of some, dysentery of others. Most missions shared the suffering. For Hudson Taylor, Frederick Gough's death in Ningbo and C. H. Spurgeon's in London, on February 5, 1892, removed two more strong human props.[1014]

The CIM had become several times larger than any other society in China and correspondingly conspicuous. Misconceptions were understandable. If the CIM was named more often than other missions, surely its care of its personnel must be at fault. After deaths at Yangzhou from smallpox and malignant malaria, even the Zhenjiang (Chinkiang) acting consul complained of neglect. How strange, Hudson Taylor commented to him, for 'all Chinkiang' had depended on CIM doctors. Dr Cox had his hospital there, close to Yangzhou, and Howard Taylor, MD, FRCS, 'paid special attention' to the language schools. But still the deaths followed one upon another.

None of these events surprised those who saw the missionary adventure as a conflict 'not against flesh and blood but against principalities, against powers, against the rulers of the darkness of this world, against spiritual wickedness in high places', from which the people of God were not immune. In his New Year editorial for January 1892, Hudson Taylor remarked that 'almost every little church, and almost every station has had its trials'.[1015] But it was not one-sided. Baptisms were being reported from the worst affected places, and the gospel was being taken to the remotest regions—even to the gates of Lhasa.

The glamour of Tibet (1816–94)

Ever since an Englishman named Manning met the Dalai Lama in Lhasa in 1816, the magnetism of this city and its Bodala (Potala) Palace has drawn others. In the secular dress of lamas the Abbé Huc and Joseph Gabet travelled in 1846 with a Tibetan dignitary and his two-thousand-strong escort, and were well received by the Dalai Lama and Tibetan regent (see 1, p 129).[1016] Asked as Christian lamas to write something in their own language, Huc wrote, 'What does it profit a man if he conquers the whole world but loses his own soul?' Translated into Tibetan, these words of Christ impressed his hosts. Huc and Gabet would gladly have lived out their lives in Lhasa, but the unfriendly Chinese resident or ambassador had them expelled.

Repeated attempts by the Société des Missions Etrangères de Paris to cross the border were thwarted, until a firm foothold on the threshold at Batang and unlimited patience became their policy. We saw how Henry Lansdell with his message from the Archbishop of Canterbury in November 1888 failed to penetrate beyond Leh in Ladakh. The American William Woodville Rockhill was trying at the time to find companions for an attempt on Lhasa, with no greater success.

A comparison of dates showed the CIM pioneers in the perspective of efforts to cross Tibet and to reach Lhasa. They took their time. Annie Royle Taylor arrived in China in early November 1884. After language study and an introduction to conditions inland, she went to Gansu and rented a house in Lanzhou before any foreign man was tolerated in the city. But Tibet was her goal, she insisted, not China. Because she was an individualist and needed scope, she was given a free rein and learned lessons the painful way. But nothing could stop her.

By the summer of 1888 she had done her prospecting and found a springboard at Taozhou (now Luqū) on the Gansu-Qinghai border of ethnological 'Greater Tibet'. There she learned Tibetan, made contacts and prepared to take the big plunge. She returned to Britain in 1889 and on the way back to China spent six months at Darjeeling investigating the possibility of entering Tibet through Sikkim. In June 1890 Hudson Taylor wrote of 'dear Annie Taylor (having) a very hard time of it', but she persevered and set out from Taozhou on September 2, 1892, for Lhasa. In Peter Hopkirk's *Trespassers on the Roof of the World*[1017] is this tribute to Annie Taylor: 'Unshakable courage and absolute faith shine forth from every page of her battered journal.'

Cecil Polhill-Turner[1018] continued his language study in Chengdu with Samuel Clarke's help, and then joined the Laughtons at Xining, a hundred miles west of Lanzhou and inside the Eastern Tibetan region of Ando, included in Qinghai on modern maps. A life in and out of the saddle suited the one-time dragoon. He married Eleanor Marsden in 1888 and together they learned Tibetan from an old man who had travelled with Huc and Gabet. For a time they lived at 'Tankar', the last Chinese town before Lake Kokonor, and found the monks of the great Kumbum monastery friendly. Better still, the abbot Pancheda of Maying monastery, four days' travel from Xining, listened earnestly to the gospel, showed that he understood its implications and was 'convinced but not converted'. He also taught Cecil Polhill more Tibetan. They then took a house at 'Wachia' right among Tibetans sixty miles south of Xining, and succeeded in planting a church at Guide, fifteen miles nearer to Xining. But they had no thought of settling down.

During this period, in 1890–91 a Frenchman, Bonvalot, and Prince Henry of Orleans penetrated Tibet from the north, but were turned away from Lhasa when only ninety-five miles remained to be covered. They were permitted to travel eastwards to leave Tibet at Batang. Two Britons, Captain (later Major-General Sir) Hamilton Bower and Surgeon-Captain W. G. Thorold, entered western Tibet on July 3, 1891, only to be thwarted like everyone else. They regained Chinese territory in January 1892. But all bare statements convey nothing of the privations and dangers to life involved in every journey on 'the roof of the world'.

In 1891 the Polhills handed over the Xining region to H. French Ridley of the CIM, soon to make history in the Muslim rebellion, and joining a caravan of seventy Muslim merchants travelled to the important Labrang monastery (at Xiahe, see map 2.31: p 279). Labrang with its four or five thousand monks ruled over 108 similar monasteries. From there they returned to Gansu, to find Annie Taylor living in the main Chinese inn at Taozhou, before her attempt on Lhasa. In the Taozhou-Choni region the Polhills worked for a month, everywhere well received, before returning to Lanzhou and beginning another chapter of their lives. A. B. Simpson's C&MA Scandinavians then began in 1892 to take responsibility for the nucleus of Christian Chinese and Tibetans in the Taozhou-Choni area.

Already a distinct pattern is recognizable in the approach by the CIM to Tibet. Lhasa remained Annie Taylor's goal, but steady evangelism and thorough adaptation to the people and their ways was allowed to take even years before the big venture. The aim was to reach people, not places, the hearts of Tibetans wherever they might be. The heart of Lamaism might be Annie Taylor's ambitious goal, but Cecil Polhill's sense of commission was to preach Christ to Tibetans and have them carry the truth to others, eventually to Lhasa itself.

To digress for a moment, the complete freedom they had to develop their work in their own way, with Hudson Taylor's strong support and no interference, was also recognizable in Thomas Botham's incessant itineration on the Shaanxi plains and Benjamin Ririe's in West Sichuan, just as Dixon Hoste's choice of playing second string to Hsi Shengmo had his blessing. Dr

Arthur Douthwaite, building up a strong hospital practice at Yantai, also appreciated this policy, as did Dr William Wilson at Hanzhong.

> There is as much liberty in the CIM as any man could reasonably desire [Douthwaite wrote to his father-in-law, one of the Groves family of Bristol]. After he has given proof of ability to learn the language and has had five years experience under his seniors, he may choose his own sphere of permanent work and carry on that work in his own way as the Lord may lead him.[1019]

In November 1891, Cecil Polhill left his wife and boys at Tianshui and after visiting his brother, Arthur, at Bazhou and Cassels at Langzhong reconnoitred the mountainous region of Sichuan, south of Gansu and bordering the Tibetan marches with their semi-Tibetan and fully-Tibetan ethnic divisions.[1020] Montagu Beauchamp accompanied Cecil for part of the way, and a Christian ex-soldier, Wang Cuan-yi (Wang Ts'uan-i), volunteered to join him, unpaid.[1021]

They found the people of the remote frontier post, Songpan, to be friendly and pleased to meet a Westerner speaking Chinese and Tibetan. So while Wang stayed, Polhill rode across wild country with a government courier and the obligatory escort of soldiers as protection against robbers, making for Tianshui. At a monastery on his route the abbot assembled all his monks to hear the gospel and exhorted them to ponder what they heard and to do what their consciences might dictate. Cecil Polhill declined the escort of armed monks offered by the abbot, but welcomed the companionship of unarmed monks. They overtook a party of merchants who had been attacked, and one killed, on the day Polhill would have gone that way had the abbot not been so hospitable.

In March 1892 he set out again with his wife and sons, overland by pack train from Tianshui to Guangyuan in twelve days by safer roads, and from there westwards to Songpan in twenty-two days. Home was a room with two Chinese beds, two chairs and a small table, beside a yard often filled with yak. The Tibetans treated Cecil as one of their own monks, and for two and a half months all went well. Then drought drove the Chinese to pin the blame on someone.[1022]

On July 29, 1892, he, his wife, Wang the soldier and another Christian named Zhang were bound, beaten by the mob, stripped to the waist (Eleanor included) and led out of the walled town to cries of 'Throw them in the river!' 'Stone them!' 'Tie them up in the sun till rain falls!' No Tibetan or Muslim joined in. A military official rescued them and took them to the magistrate's *yamen*. But the mob had to be placated. For several hours the victims were left with arms tightly bound. Then Wang and Zhang were asked if they were willing to be flogged in lieu of the foreigners. They agreed, were beaten with sticks until raw and put in cangues. The Polhills were then freed and the two men shared a room with them until at last they were all allowed to leave and travel painfully to the plains.

On August 13 they found some missionaries on holiday at a hill temple, and at last had their injuries treated and wholesome food to restore them to strength. They then travelled through Guanxian to Chengdu, at the height of plague. Hundreds of coffins were piled up waiting for burial. After eight years in China, home leave followed, and Cecil Polhill urged that the CIM should expand to the extremities of China. Songpan was reoccupied by young men of the CIM and Heywood Horsburgh's CMS team.

The heroes of the Songpan riot had been Wang and Zhang, showing courage 'beyond the call of duty'. Zhang afterwards said, 'I couldn't help smiling . . . when we were being marched through the town with wrists tied—smiling that we were in a very small way like our Master, Jesus Christ.' In 1923 a mature Christian gentleman told a missionary that he had witnessed the events at Songpan and decided he must become a Christian. Wang and Zhang returned to East Sichuan and were known as exemplary evangelists in the Langzhong (Paoning) church.[1023]

Before the Polhills left for home in November 1892, Annie Taylor was ready to cross Tibet to Lhasa, one thousand miles 'as the crow flies', with Pontso, the Tibetan she had won for Christ. In addition to two men to manage her sixteen saddle and pack horses, for her tents and provisions she took on a Chinese, who used the Tibetan name Noga, and his Tibetan wife. Annie herself dressed and lived as a Tibetan, shaving her head like a Tibetan nun or 'Annia'.[1024]

They left Taozhou, near Kumbum, on September 2, 1892, and four months later, January 3, 1893, were closer to Lhasa than any foreigner since Huc and Gabet in 1846, only three marches away. By then bandits had harassed them, killed most of their animals and taken a tent and their changes of clothing. One man had died and the other forsook them. Noga turned on her, demanding money with threats to denounce her to the Lhasa authorities. Yet she kept a daily diary, never complained in it, and gamely made a Christmas pudding with the currants and black sugar, flour and suet she had brought with her. At that high altitude the centre remained uncooked. But Noga rode ahead and betrayed her. She was arrested. For bringing an alien with him Pontso was in danger of execution, and she of death if they forced her to travel out alone. A battle of wits with the help of God seemed her only hope. High-spirited, she demanded justice, argued that in their reduced condition they could not travel further than Lhasa. And when they insisted that she return to China, she argued until she was on friendly terms with them and had an escort, horses, clothing, bedding and food provided.

On January 22, 1893, they left Lhasa territory, on a journey through Batang even more harrowing than the first when she was her own master. Kangding was reached on April 12, and they passed through Chongqing on May 6, to arrive at Shanghai on May 20. The *North China Daily News* carried some of the facts, but another report had them choicely garbled to complete a journey from Darjeeling to Chongqing via Tibet. After all that,

Pontso deserved the voyage via Canada to reach Britain on July 1.[1025] (He looked as intelligent and at home in Western dress in London and Keswick group photographs as in his homeland.)

Annie Taylor's story was far from over. Within eight months she had floated the Tibetan Pioneer Mission with a London committee led by William Sharp, and left again for Kalimpong with a party of fourteen missionaries. They sailed on February 23, 1894, and on March 1 the Anglo-Chinese Convention on Burma and Tibet settled the confrontation. The way was open for them to approach Tibet through Sikkim. But before the end of the year they were in serious trouble.

A former French naval officer, Jules Dutreuil de Rhins, who was exploring the Karakoram and Kunlun mountain ranges, started for Lhasa on September 3, 1893. After four months he was only six days' march from Lhasa when he and his party were halted. They refused to be forced back and argued for fifty days before accepting the inevitable. At last on January 20, 1894, they too began the long trek out, only to lose de Rhins who died on the way. Sven Anders Hedin's remarkable travels also began in 1893 when this Swedish geographer of twenty-eight penetrated Chinese Turkestan from Tashkent and Bokhara, to enter north-western Tibet, two years before his Taklamakan desert journey.

The last five years of the century had a further dramatic saga in store.

'The eve of rebellion?' (1891–94)

If 1891 began with a flourish as floods of American-Scandinavians and Europeans arrived in China, the year continued packed with excitement of a different kind. The *Chinese Recorder*, mirror of the general community of Protestant missions, took note that the CIM had blossomed suddenly into international colours. Fifteen nationalities could be named, including Dutch, Finnish, German, Norwegian, Russian, Swedish and Swiss newcomers. As soon as they and others from the Australian colonies, Canada and the States could be dispersed from Shanghai they were sent on.

In April, twenty-nine of the thirty-one North Americans of Henry Frost's branch of the CIM met with Hudson Taylor and Frost (April 14–21) and unanimously voted in favour of becoming full members of the Mission. They wished their own funds from home to be merged with the general fund.[1026] They then scattered to their stations and Henry Frost toured their districts with the bereaved Stanley Smith as escort, beginning with Zhejiang and the Guangxin River region of Jiangxi. Hudson Taylor himself started up the Yangzi River to visit the language schools at Yangzhou, Anqing and Dagutang.

While he was at Yangzhou on May 6 the Catholic 'foundling hospital' was again the focus of a riot. Crowds collected threatening violence, but 'the magistrate acted promptly and with 400 soldiers dispersed the mob'. At Anqing the main Catholic orphanage building was burned to the ground and as much property destroyed as possible. The CIM premises were untouched. Foul accusations of what was being done with children were in circulation again, originating in Hunan as usual.[1027] Hudson Taylor paid a courtesy call on the Yangzhou magistrate and after four days went on up the Yangzi to the seat of trouble at Anqing. Returning on the 12th, his boat stood offshore at Wuhu for twelve hours, while the RC cathedral was burned down, waiting to evacuate foreign refugees from the riot.

On June 5 a Methodist missionary named Argent was on the wharf at Wuxüe (Wusueh, now Guangji, see map 2.63: p 518) in Hubei when a rumour spread that children were being taken downstream for immoral purposes. A mob attacked and killed him and a customs officer, Green, who went to his help. The authorities protected the two men's wives until a ship took them to safety. Some missionary refugees who reached Shanghai from Nanjing and Suzhou were welcomed at Wusong Road. But by the 8th Shanghai itself was in danger from the high feeling in the Chinese city. All missionary women and children were taken into the Settlement; troops protected the Jesuit headquarters at Siccawei; and Chinese guards were posted around the Wusong Road property. The night of Saturday, June 13, was 'crisis night', when an attack on the Settlement was expected. Tension reached its peak when a screaming child could not be quietened. It was impossible to know what this wave of rioting through the Yangzi valley would lead to. They could but wait and see. 'A good spirit' prevailed among the refugees at Wusong Road, and Hudson Taylor glazed the verandah of his room as a conservatory for the tropical plants he had collected in the Torres Strait. The climbers were beginning to clothe the pillars of the building itself.

Word then came from Jiujiang that the consul was advising the removal of the CIM women from Dagutang on the Poyang Lake. 'I wired back asking them to stop where they were, until Mr McCarthy should arrive. He left immediately for Jiujiang.' But on receiving the consul's letter the women had felt bound to leave Dagutang at once, reaching Jiujiang safely by boat. No riot developed, but the soldiers sent to guard their premises broke in and helped themselves. 'Even the foreigners (at Jiujiang) cannot scrape together enough reason for being scared just now,' McCarthy reported. 'They were beginning in the city, but it was all over in five minutes. The officials are all on the alert. We praised the Lord, (but) even the Lord's servants get into the current of unbelief.' He calmly took the women back to Dagutang.[1028]

Hudson Taylor wrote to warn Theodore Howard that while organised riots were indeed taking place, alarming newspaper reports should be read with reserve. Missionaries' relatives who enquired anxiously could be reassured. The riots were against Catholic property, not lives. In the *Cambridge History of China*, John King Fairbank stated:

> There is evidence that the Yangtze Valley riots of 1891 were fomented in part by disgruntled secret society members whose aim was not to do injury to Christians, but to bring down the dynasty by forcing it into conflict with the Western powers ... Conversely, the authorities themselves, in some instances, intentionally associated themselves with extreme anti-foreign stands ... because this was the only way to prevent popular anti-foreign feeling from being turned against them.[1029]

What mattered to Hudson Taylor was that the CIM should set an example of calmness from 'trust in the Living God, who is able to protect . . . and will do so unless for His own wise purposes He sees His own glory will be more advanced by their suffering.' At McCarthy's suggestion he wrote a general letter to all the Mission on 'The Attitude of Missionaries in Times of Danger'. Often in the past he had spoken and written on this subject, but the majority of those he was now responsible for were young and inexperienced.

First of all, he pointed out, the biblical injunction 'not to speak evil of dignitaries' applied to Chinese officials. Second, national pride had no place in the matter: missionaries were not representatives of foreign powers, but in China solely to preach Christ. Third, there were three good reasons for not leaving their posts from fear, but only if forced out: they were under God's protection; they were given an opportunity to set an example, encouraging the Christians to be brave; and the influence of their calmness would be great. 'A holy joy in God is far better protection than a revolver,' he assured them. Expounding Acts 9 one day in June at Shanghai, he said, 'The Lord did not say to Saul, "How hard for those you are, persecuting," but "How hard it is for you." How easy it would be for God to change the aspect of affairs (for us). We must pray for those who persecute us.'[1030]

Charles Fishe, following Jennie Taylor as sub-editor of *China's Millions* in London, took the same line in his editorial. The policy of the *Millions* was to exclude political matter, and not to follow the press, but to wait for facts and opinions from Hudson Taylor. Even *The Times* had exaggerated the news by giving space to rumours. Anyway, 'the wave of outrage . . . has probably spent its force.' Canton, historically notorious for its xenophobic outbreaks, had remained quiet, a sign that the Yangzi Valley riots were local in significance. A report which reached Hudson Taylor that the Shashi house had been burned down proved untrue. The 'looting' by soldiers at Dagutang turned out to be no more than a raid on the pantry. An imperial proclamation had quieted the people to the extent that they were prepared for missionaries to rent premises again. And the official *Peking Gazette* reminded the nation of the famine relief done by missionaries with 'a cheerful readiness to do good', so that they 'deserve high commendation'.

Even so, disturbances continued, though not on the scale of June 1891.[1031] Petite Kate Mackintosh, writing from Yushan at the head of the Guangxin River where six Swedish girls were learning Chinese, showed the right spirit: 'A good deal of rumour (has been circulating) since the riots, but we go on quietly as usual.' Most who lived far from any human protection other than the *yamen* might afford shared her faith. (She married H. N. Lachlan, the barrister, later in the year.)

Hangzhou was threatened; the Catholics at Chongqing had some trouble; Yichang and Shashi simmered in the summer heat, and when the riot erupted in September all foreign property in Yichang was destroyed. At Wenzhou people screamed and hid when a foreign warship without warning turned on its apocalyptic searchlights, a new and terrifying phenomenon. The atmosphere was tense.[1032] Hudson Taylor was badly needed in London, but the possibility that China was 'on the eve of rebellion', and an urgent need for him to visit some places in the interior made it impossible to go home. Torrential rains in October damped the ardour of rioters, and 1892 ended with relatively little disturbance.

An order on March 25 for the arrest of Zhou Han, the Hunanese author of scurrilous pamphlets and posters, may have had some effect. One edition of 'Death to the Devil's Religion', the most notorious pamphlet, of eight hundred thousand copies, had been distributed without charge.[1033] At Chengdu in Shaanxi accusations that the missionaries were poisoning wells provoked a riot. The premises were wrecked and plundered, but all except one Chinese Christian escaped injury by hiding in a neighbour's house. The magistrates did not deny the rumours, but announced that Henan men were the culprits, so peace returned. The Songpan riot appeared to have been genuinely due to superstition. Another major riot at Yichang on November 26 ushered in more violence in 1893. And at Jiangjin between Chongqing and Luzhou, two CIM women and one of the associate Friends' Mission had to escape over the roof to a neighbour's house when their own was broken into.[1034]

Then on July 1, 1893, at Songbu near Macheng, sixty miles north-east of Hankou, the two Swedish missionaries were killed in the street. Strong suspicions of official instigation were strengthened by the refusal of any compensation. Their death seemed to the Shanghai Missionary Association, a forum of different societies, to be a knell, the withdrawal of God's protection. They issued an appeal for fasting and prayer. 'Something of a crisis seems approaching . . . signs of the times . . . to be up and calling upon our God to stay the hands of His and our enemies.'[1035] Chinese and foreigners felt tension in the air, an intangible feeling of threat on the political, international and missionary fronts. J. A. Wylie, a Presbyterian, was murdered by Manchu soldiers in Manchuria in 1894, and in June of that year events began to move inexorably towards the fateful Sino-Japanese war. With a Mission membership of 560 (apart from home-staff) in his care, and hundreds of Chinese, Hudson Taylor was bearing heavy responsibility. But far outweighing the physical dangers was a resurgence of the spiritual battle in the guise of yet more conflict of opinion between the London Council and the General Director.

Heading for the rocks, a reminder (1886–93)

Violence and even massacre have strengthened rather than weakened the China Inland Mission on many occasions in the course its existence. Tightening its belt at times of low income has done it good, focusing its attention on the One who provides because it is his own work. What shook the Mission to its foundations in the last decade of the nineteenth century was the controversy over the 'Principles and Practice'. The seven-year challenge to parts of the 'P and P' and to Hudson Taylor's leadership coincided not only with attack from other quarters but, as we have seen, with several major developments—the numerical and territorial expansion, extension to America, Europe and Australasia, and the essential reorganisation in China. Yet, as he pointed out, the lessons learned did more to shape and settle the Mission than any points at issue did to weaken it—a fact to bear in mind as the story unfolds. An outline of what transpired is essential to this history.

From November 1886, tension persisted between him and London until July 1893. We remember that when the far-seeing action of the first China Council at Anqing in October 1886 came to the knowledge of the London Council they were up in arms. Led by Hudson Taylor, the China Council had called for the Hundred reinforcements and submitted for comment their draft revision of the 'Principles and Practice' and the highly practical little 'Book of Arrangements' (see pp 470–72). It is difficult to see why the Home Director and London Council forgot that before he returned to China, Hudson Taylor had gone through the 'P and P' with them and this revision was only the expression of what had been agreed. And the reorganisation of the Mission to cater for its expanding membership and ever more complicated make-up had been with London's encouragement and even insistence. What appeared to gall them was that they had been left out of the implementation. In fact they had not.

From its inception the Mission had by definition existed specifically 'to assist' Hudson Taylor in his work of evangelising China. This fact of history was fundamental to an understanding of the ethos of the CIM. When the sheer volume of work outstripped his time and strength, he had repeatedly been pressed to delegate duties to others. Eventually suitable colleagues had emerged to share responsibility and he had gradually installed Stevenson as his deputy director, Broumton as treasurer in China, and provincial superintendents to care for and guide the multiplying missionaries in their regions. That they should meet as a China Council to consult together, unify their policies and actions in the 'field', and speak with one voice, was the logical outcome.

Two understandable but discordant reactions touched off the resistance to this progress that came close to wrecking the Mission. In China some senior members who had enjoyed years of the free and easy family relationship in the early mission resented having others, even younger men, set over them. Deplorably, in Britain also the China Council was seen as a rival and, as argument developed, it became clear that the London Council saw itself as the chief council of the CIM and other councils as subordinate.

Few of these attitudes were apparent at first. Hudson Taylor was nonplussed. Urged to delegate he found his delegation of duties met with the cry, 'We want to deal with you personally.' Told to organize, and carrying out what London had agreed was necessary, he saw the London Council claiming rights and authority it had disclaimed in the past. The voluminous correspondence and recollections show beyond question that far from an authoritarian Hudson Taylor forcing his 'dictates' on 'nonentities', an embattled leader was having to defend the basic principles on which he had founded the Mission, and was being prevailed upon to withdraw concessions which he himself had introduced.

Objections to a North American

branch of the Mission claimed priority over affairs in China during 1888–89, but strong criticism by the London Council of the 'Principles and Practice' soon overshadowed that issue. With every courtesy they told Hudson Taylor, 'The Council wish you to be assured that there is no desire to interfere with the conduct of the work in China. They have never done so; on the contrary they have on various occasions of difficulty given you moral support.'[1036] This endorsed what Theodore Howard had written (see p 554), denying the notion that members could appeal to London against the directors in China. Yet when complaints came from China, the council had taken them up instead of referring them back.

Objections to the 'Book of Arrangements' as 'a law of the Medes and Persians' (see p 539) were made in a different spirit. It was only a manual to guide missionaries in the field, with a few rulings on unacceptable practices. The conference of CIM missionaries in May 1890 had found little in the documents to question. A field handbook was welcomed as useful. Yet in the light of London's comments, Hudson Taylor and the China Council again reviewed both the 'P and P' and the 'Arrangements'. Another proof-edition with wide margins was printed and circulated for yet more comment and correspondence, to be revised again after eight months or a year. Three and a half years had already passed since these papers had first been drafted. It was high time for them to be made official. The 'Principles and Practice' concerned the whole Mission, including Home departments, but practical 'Arrangements' for China were outside the London Council's sphere. Even so, courtesy copies again went to them and London returned month after month to discussing them, finding objections where those in China could see none. On January 6, 1891, they adopted a new tone. The Council minutes referred to their discussion as being 'final'. Attitudes were hardening. But a redeeming feature was that the sections of the 'Arrangements' with which they had no quarrel were already in use.

In the autumn of 1891 feelings ran high in London on their demands for the last word in some field matters. 'The supreme question is that of final headship,' Hudson Taylor wrote to Stevenson, 'but great gentleness and patience will be needed to make the reasonableness of this clear to all, and it is equally clear to me that it can only be vested in China.'[1037] London had little idea of how much they would become involved if their demand was conceded, or how impossible it would be to debate personnel problems by long-distance correspondence. Hudson Taylor could see no solution other than the status quo—the foundation principle of running field affairs on the field—and the China Council agreed with him. Still London saw the China Council as a departure from the principle of government in China by Hudson Taylor himself.

John Stevenson was still in Britain when Hudson Taylor wrote desperately from Shanghai on July 31, 1891.

> While I let you know in confidence that my mind is made up, I do not wish to bring pressure on the Home Council ... Do your best to get them individually to see (that they cannot take power by force), but do not put our refusal of it in the form of an ultimatum. Should I and certain other members of the (China) Council conclude on retiring, we will endeavour to do so in such a form as shall do least harm to a work dear to us all. Those of us who retire may form another mission for the purpose of preaching the gospel. But surely God will avert the danger as He has so many others.

[And on August 28 to Theodore Howard, swayed by persuasive arguments]

You very clearly stated the position in your draft of your letter of February 6, 1890: 'We were never supposed or intended to have and never have had any authority over the work in China; we never interfered ... we have been a Council of advice and consultation, not for government, as regards the China work ... Nor would it ever have been admitted that we were in any sense a Council to which missionaries in China could appeal from any decision of the China Directors or China Council.'

... Do not I beseech you for Christ's sake rend the Mission asunder by claiming what you yourself have repeatedly affirmed was never intended and would never be agreed to.[1038]

The new international nature of the Mission confirmed and reinforced the wisdom of the original principle. The work in China being done by so diverse a team from different nations, different denominations, different social and educational backgrounds, must be unified in China. London's arm could only reach British members. Together Hudson Taylor and the China Council set out in detail their 'Reasons' (as the document came to be called) for insisting on jurisdiction over affairs in China being exercised solely in China.

> To fuse the whole into one united body of workers is a matter of the utmost moment. Everything tending to keep up a feeling of distinctness and separation is to be avoided ... Either we must be equally free to deal with them all, or if necessary to decline to deal further with any one of them, or the harmony, the unity, and the welfare of the work will be sacrificed. 'No man can serve two masters.' The introduction of the proposed principle [of London having the last word] would in practice not only lead many to become disaffected, but to feel and say, 'We come from such and such a body; we owe allegiance to them, not to you.' A task already sufficiently difficult would be made ten times more so.[1039]

Well might he have added that a right of appeal to London against the word of the General Director would be fatal to the Mission's existence.

This internal crisis reached its height when the 'eve of rebellion' unrest in China was at its worst and the wave of criticisms in the press increased the strain on Hudson Taylor. In London, however, the Council were busy drafting and adopting a letter on 'the Council's relation to missionaries in the field', which ended as an ultimatum such as

Hudson Taylor had never before seen and never used.[1040]

Impossible ultimatum (1890-92)

The letter which Theodore Howard, as Home Director, signed on October 22, 1891, 'on behalf of the Home Council', was intended to establish the relationship of the London Council to the administration in China. In challenging the existence and powers of the China Council they argued that for the London Council to adopt Hudson Taylor's view 'would be a serious departure from the lines of the Mission hitherto prevailing'. The Christian public would trust Hudson Taylor's judgment in administrative matters, but not the China Council's. His devolution of any administrative powers to it was unacceptable. The decision on dismissals must be entirely his own. It was a vote of no confidence in the China Council—and in John Stevenson, although no one had objected when he was made Hudson Taylor's deputy in China. The 1886 revision of the 'P and P', they protested, had been the work of 'the small section (of the Mission) engaged in the actual revision'. That they were Hudson Taylor's chosen provincial leaders made no difference. Then followed an ambiguity rather than a concession—the London Council must at least have 'the right to make representations to the China Council'. It continued: 'This letter intimates as kindly but as firmly as possible the final (and I may say unanimous) decision of the Council in this matter, and we await your agreement, by wire or otherwise before proceeding with the revision of the Book of Arrangements.'[1041]

This letter reached Shanghai on November 30. Archibald Orr Ewing and Walter B. Sloan had arrived on the 4th, with Orr Ewing unsettled by close friendship with the Council in London, his wife being the treasurer, Robert Scott's, daughter. When Hudson Taylor talked it all out with him as a member of the China Council, Orr Ewing saw the impossibility of conceding London's demands. That same day, December 4, Hudson Taylor wrote his 'eve of rebellion' letter to Stevenson, about the political state of China, and the next day replied to the London Council—the persuasive letter of a friend, with no hint of defiance or coercion, or of claiming God as his ally against his opponents, as had been suggested.

Shanghai, December 5, 1891

To the Members of the London Council

Dear and valued Friends,

I am in receipt of Mr Howard's letter on behalf of the Home Council dated October 22nd and adopted by yourselves. I am greatly distressed and perplexed by it. I feel you do not apprehend the situation nor at all understand the gravity of the position you seek to establish; for I know your love for me personally and your desire to help me, and I know also your deep and abiding interest in this work of God on behalf of which you have spent so much time and thought. I feel that we have reached perhaps the gravest crisis that the Mission has yet passed through, and am very glad that our annual day of united fasting and prayer is so near at hand and will precede the next meeting of our Council here, when your letter must be considered. I have not at present any light modifying the conclusions we have already communicated to you. I dare not for peace's sake be untrue to my convictions, for if we forfeit the favour of GOD we have nothing to stand upon. You have not funds to support 500 missionaries; you cannot protect them against an insurrection or in riot; you cannot come out here and administer the affairs of the Mission; we must walk before God. I am sure you are agreed with me in this. For the present the only thing I can see is quietly to wait upon God. The wire we have just received of £170 to £270 of general funds [a drop in the bucket] is an instance of how vain it would be to trust in British resources instead of in the living God; but while we walk with Him we can rest in his faithfulness.

Yours gratefully and affectionately in Christ,

J. H. Taylor[1042]

On December 14 Hudson Taylor wrote at length to John Stevenson as his spokesman in London. It had at last dawned on him that the London Council had from the beginning taken the offending 'P and P' and 'Book of Arrangements' as *faits accomplis* imposed upon them, whereas both had been (and still were) 'proposed, not promulgated'. He took them up point by point to clarify the facts, becoming clouded by months of discussion, and again urged Stevenson to arrange to meet the Council members one by one for calm conversations. But, as Jennie's diary reveals, he himself was prostrate from the accumulation of strains upon him. In a letter to Mrs Howard she said the strain was too much for him. She feared for his life.

Meanwhile, in the crowded Wusong Road premises a series of public meetings was being held, with Geraldine Guinness a leading speaker, 'filled with the Spirit'. Night after night people were being converted. When HMS *Caroline* arrived at Shanghai there were no professing Christians on board. By January 6, after services at Wusong Road and on the ship, an officer and twenty men were claiming to have been converted and eager to learn more. At the same time 'the enemy' seemed to be out to 'harass and distress' missionaries on all fronts, Hudson Taylor told Theodore Howard. 'When any member of the Mission may double or quadruple his income' by transferring to another society or going into business, it was not surprising that some were tempted, especially if it meant that they need no longer wait two years before getting married. Others succumbed, disheartened, and returned home.

The toll of illnesses continued unabated. One whole family died of 'high fever'. Benjamin and Amelia in London were going through severe 'testing' at this very time through three of their family in China contracting nearly fatal typhoid or typhus—Edith, Hudson, and Marshall after he nursed Hudson. But almost daily conversions continued into March through Geraldine's and others' preaching.[1043] Jennie Taylor herself was riding the waves with her spirit strong. 'Now is the time to ask great things for China' from the Lord God 'who rideth on the heavens for thy help,' she told Marianne Murray, still in charge at Yangzhou.

In February John Stevenson left Britain for Shanghai and arrived on March 14. He found Hudson Taylor almost worn out with work which it was impossible to delegate. In mid-April he was prostrate again, giddy and helpless, preparing to face the music in London, but appalled by the prospect, so imminent did complete shipwreck of the Mission appear to be. The China Council in session addressed a letter to him identifying themselves with his view of the crisis, particularly as it concerned 'exclusion from the Mission' and dismissals.[1044]

> We value exceedingly the services rendered ... by the Home Councils, and especially ... for so many years by members of the London Council. But we fully agree with you ... It is manifestly impossible for those in the Home lands to know as fully as can be known here the character and influence, the competence or incompetence, of our fellow-workers ... [Ten signatures were appended.]

Loyal support encouraged him, yet while Hudson Taylor's spirit remained unbowed, stresses of this kind continued to undermine his physical endurance. He knew full well that his long-standing friends on the London Council were under forceful persuasion by the lawyer's scrutinising mind and the secretary's strong will, for reams of argument came in the mail to him also. Even Theodore Howard as director was too kindly a man to stand up to the pressure. So once again the best hope of a settlement was to go home and talk it out, however difficult it might be. It was like mounting the tumbrel. He and Jennie sailed on May 10 to Canada, for he had learned to value Henry Frost's wise opinions.

This crucial period had begun with London's intervention in support of individuals at odds with the administration in China, and objections to the 'Book of Arrangements'. Both were 'field' not 'home' matters. But when individual candidates sent to China by the London Council were sent home at the end of their probationary two years, only for strong reasons of unsuitability, London claimed the right not only of a voice, but the deciding voice in the action. One or two cases of disciplinary dismissal after all possible had been attempted to avert it were also challenged by the 'Home' council. With the basic principle of management under attack, great courage and wisdom were needed.

'Unanimity of decision' (1892–93)

An ill-ventilated cabin, 'gastritis' and neuralgia this time made the voyage an ordeal for Hudson Taylor, normally a good sailor. They had to break the journey across Canada at several points in an attempt to regain strength before meeting the North American Council. The 'esteem and love' in which he was held in Canada and the States made a few addresses and attendance at the Niagara Conference inescapable, but Henry Frost persuaded him to stay for a complete rest before crossing to Britain. They cabled to Benjamin, who replied reassuringly, 'run no risks'. So it was July 26 and the summer recess before they reached Liverpool.

The Keswick Convention had started and interest in missions had grown since he had first shown the inseparability of 'sanctification' and 'obedience to the Great Commission'. He took the chair and addressed an anti-opium meeting on August 1. They were in Keswick when word came that Mrs Robert Howard, Theodore's mother and Hudson Taylor's dear friend since 1850, had died. He and Benjamin were asked to conduct the funeral, so he travelled overnight and met the Council members 'at the grave' on August 2. Instead of tension, the mood was 'chastened'. Conversations with Theodore Howard, Benjamin and Robert Scott individually raised his hopes.[1045] Staying with the Grattan Guinnesses at Cliff House, he wrote, 'Eyes are upon us just now, and there are those who think that as the Council have been appointed by me, they are really nonentities and just carry out my or our plans and are not allowed to use their own discretion . . . We must be careful that this contention is not a true one.' A Council meeting on September 6, 1892—'a prayerful, happy one', at which he was 'cordially welcomed'—avoided thorny subjects, keeping them for the following week. Then, on the 13th from 2.30–9.00 p.m. they grasped the nettle. The meeting was 'harmonious throughout; and light seems to have been given as to how to meet the difficulty.'[1046]

So far, so good. Hudson Taylor explained to John Stevenson, 'the Council do not now wish to claim the power to adjudicate in dismissals or even to veto, but that in ordinary cases of inefficiency where there is no urgency they might have the statement of the case with a view to either concurrence or suggestion . . . they will then accept our conclusion . . . it being fully understood that there is no appeal from one Council to another.' The formal minutes stated that the council 'had no desire to be a Court of Appeal', but was given the right to have its representations carefully considered by the China Council. The thunder-clouds had vanished in an anticlimax. All seemed settled.

Another letter to Stevenson, packed with business detail, showed in October how firmly Hudson Taylor still had his finger on the Mission's pulse. He pointed out that estimates for building the new Chefoo boys' school were unreasonably lavish, and commented knowledgeably about one problem after another. 'Hitherto the Chinese government have known that we have never published anything against them,' was his observation on protests about the Songpan riots. But a passing reference to the London Council hinted at more trouble ahead. 'There is a nice spirit shown in our meetings; the point that was the difficulty seemed almost settled when a larger one cropped up involving . . . the reconstruction of the Home work.' As he had not yet discussed reorganisation with Benjamin, the secretary, he deferred making it a matter of debate. But Theodore Howard later explained to him that deep feelings were involved. They were still very far from a peaceful solution of problems in London. There was even more talk of the issues thought to be settled, and of an impending 'break-up'. Benjamin might resign. It would have wide repercussions.[1047]

This possibility gave Hudson Taylor an inspiration. If they lost 'BB', would not Walter Sloan be the ideal successor? Or better still the ideal colleague to halve Benjamin's load, freeing him for his major role, and his anti-opium campaign. 'It would infuse new life . . . and restore and increase confidence.' But how was Benjamin to be offered this idea? Discussion in Council of the need of reorganisation was producing heated exchanges. 'Everyone is very tired and the strain is great.' Hudson Taylor was in Scotland for meetings when 'a trying letter (came) from Mr Howard showing they think my objections to Mr Broomhall's ways are bad temper; they had decided not to meet again until we are reconciled'.

'I wrote to Mr Howard explaining (our) difficulties were not anything personal but official, and that if we in China had difficulties we met them with a day of fasting and prayer.' The suggestion was welcomed and the Ladies' Council joined the London Council 'for prayer only . . . a very good meeting'.

Part of the problem was Benjamin's increasing deafness, so Hudson Taylor set out his proposition in writing: 'The work is increasing and likely to increase; an infusion of vigorous young life is essential to continuous success . . . Would a partnership in the work be desirable or practicable, do you think?'[1048] To Jennie's relief Benjamin was 'in a good spirit', for 'Mr T. will not be able to bear the strain much longer.' To keep John Stevenson informed, Hudson Taylor wrote again in November, 'Matters here are approaching a crisis.' A cable calling for Walter Sloan was more likely than not. As an economy the code words 'VIOLA RUSTICE' would mean 'Sloan marry at once and come as soon as practicable.' If Benjamin decided to resign, the unpredictable effect could be catastrophic, others retiring with him and confidence in the Mission plummeting. Then a timely new factor appeared. Henry Frost and two of his council were coming over for consultations with Hudson Taylor about administrative changes in America. If they were to spend a few days at Pyrland Road, it would give the London staff and Council an opportunity to see what 'men of rare qualifications' they were, and Frost's wisdom could be drawn upon.[1049]

So it proved. Henry Frost, Joshua S. Helmer and J. D. Nasmith arrived on January 4, 1893, and on the 17th met the London Council. As Henry Frost had expected, his companions impressed and delighted the Council, who confided frankly in the visitors. Even the old wounds about the North American Council were reopened. Frost played a major role in finding a way out of the quagmire, and, where Hudson Taylor and the London Council were 'so weary of strife, jealousy (and) division', Frost's fresh mind saw light. Bold changes in organisation would benefit everyone. Hudson Taylor even wrote to Stevenson of 'the Mission-to-be', a phoenix from the ashes. He waited until Walter Sloan was suggested by William Sharp, as the right man to work with Benjamin, and the Council acclaimed the inspiration. W. B. Sloan's business ability and exceptional personality as a Christian made him no ordinary colleague.

On January 20, Hudson Taylor was still uncertain of what the outcome in the Council would be, but wrote to prepare Sloan for the cable as soon as everything was settled. Someone was needed 'to pull things together', with a place on the Council. Would Sloan take over management of all the routine office work in London, 'as head and not hands' of all departments, superintending other members of staff and missionaries on furlough in Britain, and handling all correspondence 'except such as Mr B. (as senior secretary) selected to deal with himself? Benjamin would advise and help to maintain continuity, and concentrate on his forte, public relations.[1050]

The CMS were also going through a long-drawn-out period of 'Controversies Within and Attacks from Without'—as Eugene Stock called his chapter 87 (1882–95), for 'the adversary' was a lion at large. And a serious clash between the CIM and CMS in Zhejiang on details of comity was occupying the attention of both societies' leaders. An unwise CIM missionary had complained to the consul about a Church Mission evangelist poaching converts with the archdeacon's encouragement! Pettiness as disgraceful as it was ludicrous. 'Salisbury Square' could no more intervene in the bishop's affairs in China than Benjamin could in John Stevenson's.

After the letter went off to Walter Sloan, events moved fast. On the 25th Hudson Taylor sent the cable and Sloan replied that he and his fiancée, a sister of Graham Brown, had felt it coming and were glad to comply. By February 17, difficulties were 'melting away' and there was 'a general feeling of relief and thankfulness'. (The same letter to Stevenson said that a 'Keswick missionary', Amy Wilson Carmichael, had not been accepted as a candidate, on grounds of health and temperament, but was to sail with a CIM party to join Barclay Buxton in Japan. The same Amy Carmichael was to become the 'Amma' of Dohnovur, a lifelong friend of the CIM.)

By February 27, Hudson Taylor could see that unimportant concessions would secure agreement on the fundamental principles, and on March 3 he outlined to John Stevenson the decisions reached. He was redrafting parts of the 'Principles and Practice' to incorporate them, and after approval by the London Council the way should be clear for making it final. After four more years of disagreement, Theodore Howard, William Sharp and Benjamin B., the most vocal objectors, had come to realise how great a gap existed between their understanding of conditions in China and the considerable expertise of the field leaders. Then they accepted the wisdom of the ultimate control being in the hands of those on the spot, and the status of the London Council as being advisory to the

Directors and representative of the Mission to the public at home.

'It brings to an end difficulties that are tearing the Mission to pieces,' Hudson Taylor continued; 'it settles the question of where the seat of power is, and with the consent of the London Council dismisses all question of their being a seat of power; it does not interfere with any working arrangements.' Once again peace reigned. All councils were to meet and act as before, but only to advise directors and not to be executive. In this he was conceding a major preference; preparing for his own death or retirement he had intended councils to have executive functions as an extension of his own management of affairs, until London took the bit between its teeth. In future the directors with authority would be responsible for decisions and action. Paradoxically, what had been challenged as autocratic was to become permanent by the insistence of the London Council itself. 'One sees more and more that we must get the officers from God and leave them to do their work unfettered . . . The first thing is to get love and confidence fully re-established . . . It seems to me that practically this solution leaves the working of the Mission just where it was.'[1051]

As for the 'Book of Arrangements' 'which frightens a great many people', its abandonment as a handbook was 'the only price of peace'. It would be broken up and used in separate sections for the guidance of each grade of missionary— hints for candidates, instructions for newly arrived missionaries, and so on. 'We are gaining what I felt was so essential—non-interference with the China administration.' Already it had led to the resignation of nearly thirty missionaries, unsettled by the controversy.

Henry Frost had been the catalyst of success. Years later he explained to Dixon Hoste:

> I found that the London Director and Council were strongly tending to the thought that they had and should have a pre-eminent place, as related to all the other Directors and Councils of the Mission ... (As) it had a definite bearing upon our work in North America ... I could not pass over the subject ... for manifestly, if the London Director and Council were supreme, then they were over us and we were under them, an arrangement to which we were not willing to agree. After much consultation, Mr Taylor took the position that all Assistant Directors and Councils, as related to the General Director, were and should be wholly and unconditionally on a par ... The 'seat of authority' is in the person of the General Director. If he is in China it is there; but if he is in some other country, it is there. In other words, the seat of authority is no more connected with the China Council than with any other Council.[1052]

Dixon Hoste's forthright comment on the whole sad upheaval was, 'Any idiot can wreck a train,' but it took consummate skill to steer a way through years of disputation and ultimata with the survival of the Mission at stake. In November 1892 when civil rebellion threatened in China and the London crisis was at its 'gravest', Hudson Taylor's editorial for the coming January 1893 issue of *China's Millions* reflected the depths of distress he could envisage. 'When the Apostle was nearing shipwreck his heart relied on the truth . . . "Whose I am and whom I serve." When all else fails, "THOU REMAINEST".'

By the end of February cordial understanding had been restored and an administrative principle of 'unanimity' had been recognised: the Deed of Constitution had stated it in March 1890, surprisingly, but in faith as, 'It is intended that as a rule the principle of unanimity shall continue to prevail in the management of the Mission,' and the China Council in July 1891 had declared their contentment with nothing less than 'unanimity' between themselves and London in reaching conclusions.[1053] But how could men with conflicting opinions attain unanimity? The answer lay in respect for each other's views, and willingness to accept them under the influence of the Holy Spirit. Therefore any impasse was an indication for 'waiting upon God'. Doing so led to a more satisfactory conclusion than by a majority decision against a reluctant minority.

The deliberations in London had demonstrated again the godliness and practicability of this concept of 'unanimity of decision'. But that willingness in the presence of God often brought unanimity of conviction also. With the painful differences settled, the Council moved on to deciding which architectural plans to adopt for the Newington Green headquarters building. Completed plans for offices, meeting hall, thirty bedrooms and public rooms were before the Council on May 2, 1893. Robert Scott and Benjamin, who preferred an alternative design, agreed that work should start on that chosen by the rest. Scott gave £500 and offered £2,000 on loan towards it. He had intended them for the scheme he favoured. The loan was declined, but an offer of £3,000 by a Miss Josephine Smith was accepted on the assurance that it was already left to the CIM in her will. Work therefore began on the first 120 feet of the foundations, the final forty feet of the building to be added later.[1054]

Walter Sloan and his bride arrived on March 25 and on the 28th he advised at a Council meeting that the creation of small provincial or regional councils in China would be regretted. For members to advise and not be decisive, might make difficulties for the missionaries and their superintendents. So here, too, Hudson Taylor accepted the choice of leadership by chosen individuals rather than by committees. (That he imposed it on the Mission is another myth.)

The completed revision of the 'P and P' was sent to Shanghai on May 16 and accepted by the China Council on July 7. W. B. Sloan was installed as Secretary, and Benjamin as General Secretary gave the annual report at the May meetings. With demands on his time reduced, he had more to devote to the abolition of the opium trade, from then on his major preoccupation. In June, Hudson Taylor announced the appointment of Henry Frost as Home Director in North America, and by November was anticipating 'a forward movement'. A new era had begun.[1055]

1890–95: 'GOD REIGNS'

'Successful crime', the opium trade (1888–94)

This is the 'triumph of successful crime', said an American diplomat to the Bishop of Victoria in Hong Kong in 1858 when the Treaty of Tientsin ended the first phase of the second opium war. 'We force them by treaty to take it from us,' Sir Rutherford Alcock admitted. 'The Chinese had both the *right, the power and the will, to stamp out the use* of *opium in China* at the time when they first came into collision with the power of England,' Hudson Taylor wrote. 'England is morally responsible for every ounce of opium now produced in China, as well as that imported from abroad.'[1056]

The launch of the activist Christian Union and its magazine *National Righteousness* in 1888 saw the propaganda against the opium trade multiplied from then on. Information about the trade and evidence of its evils were presented, with calls for the conscience of Britain to awaken. The government must be shamed into finding alternative revenue for India.

On May 3, 1889, the first resolution for the extinction of the trade was presented to Parliament and the names of those members who voted for it were listed in *National Righteousness*. A British-Indian newspaper estimated that if only one hundred or so votes for each parliamentary candidate in an election were swayed by the issue, the effect would be significant. Sixty thousand copies of the magazine reviewing the history of the opium wars, with photographs of Chinese killed in the fighting, and in January 1891 a letter bearing the facsimile signatures of leading Christians of fifteen denominations in the country was sent to 45,000 ministers. Another letter went to each member of both Houses of Parliament, with a statement about the opium trade.

A few weeks later a National Christian Anti-opium Convention was held, March 9–11, fully reported in *National Righteousness*. Highly respected witnesses from China spoke in session after session. Two Members of Parliament told of what was being done. A new resolution was to be presented in the Commons on April 10, 1891.[1057] A Committee of Urgency was set up. And one incisive resolution after another was unanimously adopted, including Benjamin's that the Guang Xü emperor should be assured that action for the abolition of the traffic was being pursued by Christians in England. Li Hongzhang had more than once requested this.[1058]

Publicity of one kind and another in time would move the most reluctant government in Whitehall. Sessions of two or two and a half hours for prayer alone, with no one called upon to take part, saw 'no awkward pauses (as) prayer flowed solemnly on'. 'The remarkable success of the Convention, the place Sir Joseph Pease obtained (in Parliament) for his resolution, the startling outburst of public feeling throughout the country, and the great moral victory in the House of Commons' were answers to prayer, Benjamin's editorial claimed. The resolution, carried by 160 votes to 130, had declared the opium trade to be 'morally indefensible'. 'The moral effect of this vote was unspeakably great; it startled both the British Government and the Government of India, and at once lifted the question from despised fanaticism to the level of the foremost questions of the day.'[1059]

It was followed by a memorial to Lord Salisbury, Prime Minister, signed by 1,500 Wesleyan ministers and 271,680 church members urging the abolition of the growth and manufacture of opium in India. And another signed by more than five thousand medical men in the United Kingdom declared that in India, as in Britain, opium should be classed as a poison and its manufacture and sale be prohibited except for medicinal purposes.

China's Millions joined in the action. George Andrew wrote about the prevalence of suicide by opium overdosage, and Minnie Parker (Shao Mianzi) told how her affluent family had been reduced to penury by the curse of opium. News of Pastor Hsi's refuges was given from time to time. And a report of the annual meeting of the CIM in May 1891 included a resolution that the people of Britain should 'bear some (fiscal) sacrifice in order to secure the immediate cessation of our Indian opium trade', unanimously adopted. In the March 1892 issue came a call to daily prayer for no less than,

> (i) The total and immediate prohibition of the growth and manufacture of Opium in our Indian Empire, except for medicinal purposes.

> (ii) The sale of Opium in India under such restrictions as shall ensure for the people of India safeguards against its improper use, similar to those provided for the protection of the people of Great Britain.

The alarm of the pro-opium lobby was heard in solemn claims that opium was no more harmful than the mildest tobacco and had no social ill-effects. Evidence to the contrary was already well publicised. And the press resorted to familiar kinds of criticism: 'The injurious results of the traffic are declared by the all competent authorities to be grossly exaggerated, if *they are not purely imaginary.*' ('Only an opium smoker could have said that,' a Chinese commented on hearing such a remark.) Other remarks included: 'the 160 geese who formed the majority (in Parliament)'; 'this scratch majority represents (those) still outside the walls of lunatic asylums'; 'It seems probable that the cackling of geese will destroy the British Empire'; The House of Commons has been caught sleeping', by 'fussy sentimentalists', 'intolerant faddists' and 'fanatics'.[1060]

As a general election approached in 1892, politicians began to adopt cautious attitudes to the subject. In a speech at Penicuik, near Edinburgh (where there was strong feeling on the opium issue), Mr Gladstone himself referred to bloodshed and shame in our former history. The evil may be put down at last, but think of the human misery and sin that have been engendered in the interval caused by delay ... Subject to the obligations of good faith, I shall ... forward any measure within the bounds of reason for (bringing the trade), if it can be done, altogether to an end.

As the incoming Prime Minister at the age of eighty-one he included in his cabinet seven ministers who had voted in favour of the anti-opium resolution, among them the two future premiers H. H. Asquith and Henry Campbell-Bannerman. 'What will Mr Gladstone do?' Benjamin asked in a heavy caption. The prospects looked promising.

Another Anti-Opium Convention was convened on October 6, at which Hudson Taylor, Marcus Wood and Geraldine Guinness made major speeches. And on December 17, Benjamin addressed a letter to Mr Gladstone enclosing a copy of *National Righteousness* which reported the Penicuik speech and the convention. 'You may now do a work for which millions will remember your name with gratitude.' The Prime Minister's reply showed how the politician's mind worked. He would 'always act in the spirit of his words (at Penicuik)', but would have to 'consult the Department more immediately concerned'. 'Mr Gladstone's letter is not satisfactory,' Benjamin's next editorial ran, in the February 1893 issue. 'He does not need to be told what are the prerogatives of a Prime Minister of England; nor is he the man to accept meekly the dictum of a Department.' The Penicuik speech had been specious electioneering. A leading article in the *Daily News* declared, 'The conscience of the British people will one day be fully roused on this point. The traffic will go, and, in half a dozen years after it has gone, we shall be wondering why it was ever regarded as the mainstay of Indian finance.'

A government Blue Book on opium in India and Burma was presented to Parliament on February 9, 1892 and *National Righteousness* quoted eight testimonies by ranking officials to the 'unmitigated evil', 'an absolute poison', 'a vice which we have introduced'. 'It could have been called, "The Strong Condemnation of the Opium Traffic by the Indian Government."' Yet it had no noticeable effect. 'Officials are blinded, the nation is not,' Mrs Grattan Guinness declared. When the Decennial Missionary Conference at Bombay of seven hundred missionaries from 36 societies withdrew a resolution against regulated vice, already adopted by an overwhelming majority, and refused resolutions against the abuse of alcohol and opium, the April 1893 *National Righteousness* devoted every line of the issue to the scandal, and a protest meeting took place in London.[1061]

June 30 was named for a new resolution on opium to be presented to Parliament. The motion took the wording of the successful April 10, 1891, resolution as its premise, and urged action without further delay. But an amendment independently introduced to specify action, called for a Royal Commission on ways and means of implementing it. Poor politics, this false step gave Gladstone a way out. What could have been 'the death blow of the Opium trade' supported by the strong body of anti-opium opinion among government ministers, became by Gladstone's own intervention a delaying tactic and a denial of the 'morally indefensible' nature of the trade. In a subtle amendment he advocated a Royal Commission on the whole complex subject. This time, while 105 members voted against Gladstone and for action to end the trade, 184 supported the aged Prime Minister. 'We forget our conscience. We barter our souls under a narcotic deadlier than the poppy,' a London evening paper protested. After this fiasco the 1894 annual meeting of the CIM gave the opium question a leading place with an address by Yen Yungking, the Chinese Christian minister.[1062]

The terms of the Royal Commission focused attention on opium consumption in India (never a major factor) rather than the effects of the trade with China. But the tendentious and specious proceedings and report of the Royal Commission scandalised the Christian public who knew the facts. Eugene Stock indignantly recorded what happened. The Commissioners examined witnesses in Britain and India, but not one member of the Commission went to China.

> Some grave complaints were made of the manner in which the Indian evidence was collected. (Only four of forty-four missionaries consulted in India) were in the smallest degree favourable to the use of opium; yet three of this four were quoted in the Report, and not one of the forty-one. (Only documentary evidence from China was considered, and only five and a half pages out of ninety-seven dealt with China at all.) There was a similar selection in the Report of one side of this evidence. A weighty memorial signed by seventeen missionaries of over twenty-five years' standing (including Burdon, Mottle, Muirhead, Griffith John, Mackenzie and Hudson Taylor) was entirely ignored; and while it was acknowledged that 'by the majority of the missionaries of every community in China the use of opium is strongly condemned', the only quotations were from three who claimed to 'take a less decided view'. (The Report is therefore) utterly inadequate and misleading.[1063]

Arnold Foster, whom we met as an organiser of relief in the great famine of 1877–79 published 'An Examination and an Appeal' in the format of a Parliamentary Blue Book with a preface signed by the Archbishop of Canterbury and 144 other distinguished men. The Society for the Suppression of the Opium Trade, the Christian Union and *National Righteousness* continued their campaign. But Gladstone's Royal Commission had set back their hopes of final success by a full decade. Wilberforce had freed the slaves in British colonial territories. But sixty years later Parliament remained deaf to demands that Britain's part in the evil of enslavement to opium, affecting millions, should be brought to an end.

Back to normal, a quick glance (1890–94)

A sharp drop in income was the natural result of whispers about the CIM circulating in Britain. For some years the Mission had been riding the crests; but no longer: £48,662 in 1889 and £29,932 in 1890 had dropped to £24,496 before recovering to £32,178 in 1893. But in North America and China receipts had risen in the two lean years, so that progress was 'restrained, not hindered'. The Hundred had brought the Mission to 225 strong by the end of 1887, and all who had stayed the pace had five years or more of the language and experience, enough to make them mature 'senior missionaries'. Between then and May 1893 more than three hundred had been added, beyond those lost by death or retirement. The troughs and setbacks, riots and fatal illnesses had been localised, while the main body of the Mission and of missionaries in general had steadily progressed.[1064]

In spite of anti-foreign excitement, seven new CIM work centres had been established, and 637 baptisms in 107 organised churches had increased the number of Chinese communicants to 3,637. The year 1893 saw 821 more baptisms take place in 134 churches, but baptism candidates and enquirers 'numbered thousands'. Hudson Taylor's report in May 1894 took particular delight in noting that the indigenous Hangzhou Church under his old friend Wang Lae-djün, and the circuit of churches which he supervised within a radius of a hundred miles, was not only independent of foreign funds and supervision, but had made a gift of $1,000 to Hudson Taylor. The gross income of the Mission had exceeded the previous year's by £6,000.

During his year and a half in Britain (July 26, 1892 to February 14, 1894), Hudson Taylor again travelled widely, in Scotland, Ireland and much of England. He owed it to the growing army of supporters to whom he personified the Mission. Confidence was quickly restored. But the impression gained from reading his voluminous correspondence is of the effect of the ceaseless battering he had endured for several years. The warm, relaxed, affectionate letters characteristic of him had become terse and to the point. He admitted to being no longer confident of remembering conversations accurately and had to keep more detailed memoranda. He felt older than his true age of sixty and could not stand the pace without sometimes having to sit while he addressed a meeting. Yet he drove himself on, until Jennie pleaded with him not to kill himself by overdoing it. She kept the news of James Cameron's death from cholera from him until he returned home from Ireland and had rested. But he rebuked her for her anxiety about him, 'so unlike you'.[1065] His long and frequent letters to John Stevenson showed no sign of any diminished grasp of administrative detail. He was a man for detail to the end. James Williamson (of the *Lammermuir*), speaking in 1895 of working with Hudson Taylor on the China Council, said:

> I was remarkably struck ... that (his) mental power and grasp ... his ability to take in all the details of the work ... and his Christ like personal sympathy with every worker in all their varied circumstances ... remained as strong as ever.

In April 1893, after welcoming Walter Sloan from China, Hudson Taylor visited the associate mission centres of Barmen, Cassel and Frankfurt with his daughter Amy. An award she had won for a paper on political economy covered her costs. And at this time also, Millie Duncan came of age, married and went to India. In August he returned with Jennie to Frankfurt, Heidelberg and Barmen, consolidating the Mission's bonds with the associate missions (August 9–21). His concerns had become more far-flung than ever before. The Australasian council minuted the need of a representative in New Zealand, and he was planning to go there as soon as possible to make arrangements.

Two hundred children of the CIM needed to be provided with schooling at Chefoo; and the sons and daughters of merchants, consuls and customs officials and of other missions swelled the number. The rapid growth of the mission also meant expanding the Chefoo sanatorium for convalescents. A good site was bought for a new school and playing-fields for one hundred boys, and Hudson Taylor was considering a proposal for financing its erection. His Liverpool friend, Menzies, offered to raise the funds through a limited liability company of a few friends, and to build the school for the CIM to rent very cheaply. After going into all that was involved, Hudson Taylor declined the generous offer. If for any reason the premises were to pass into other hands, the CIM could have a large body of close neighbours on its own territory, but not of its own choice. Influences on the children took priority over money. The outbreak of the Sino-Japanese war kept matters in abeyance, but when peace was restored Archibald Orr Ewing one day quietly offered to bear the whole cost of £5,000 in three installments, as he had also donated a third building at Wusong Road.[1066]

The Rijnhardt hornets' nest (1893–94)

Problems seldom came singly. In 1893 a new disciplinary crisis startled John Stevenson and soon involved Hudson Taylor. Some Americans had begun to arrive in Shanghai, hoping to join the CIM without first approaching the North American 'Home' Council. Among them was a Dutchman named Petrus Rijnhardt (variously referred to in correspondence and tales of his exploits as Peter Reynhart or by similar names). His bizarre story was to involve the CIM for several years. He created a good impression, so Stevenson consulted Toronto. As a pastor in Canada gave him a good testimonial, the North American Council recommended that he be admitted on probation. Rijnhardt went to language school and on to Lanzhou in Gansu.[1067] There he became engaged to Annie Slater of Carlisle, who with her friend Rose Basnett was a colleague of the Laughtons at Wuwei (Liangzhou), far off on the Great Silk Road towards Turkestan.

Meanwhile enquiries had been made in Holland where Rijnhardt had been a Salvation Army officer. From the information supplied there could be no doubt that he was a consummate impostor. Rijnhardt was called to the coast, faced with the evidence and dismissed. Annie and her friend could not believe what they were told. In great distress they resigned and followed him to the States. But by then his record of a dissolute life in Canada had also been exposed. In 1894 he married an American doctor with private means and they went to the Gansu-Qinghai border independently.

Meanwhile, during 1891–92, Robert P. Wilder followed in John Forman's footsteps, touring the British universities and reaping hundreds of student volunteers for service overseas. The Students' Foreign Missionary Union, started by Howard Taylor, had suffered from poor leadership since he went abroad, but now it merged with Wilder's Student Volunteer Missionary Union and the watchword 'The evangelisation of the world in this generation' was adopted— again showing strong roots in China.[1068] On November 22, 1893, John R. Mott wrote inviting Hudson Taylor to speak at the second International Student Convention at Detroit, Michigan, February 28–March 4, 1894, an opportunity for the starting of a great advance movement for missions.

> Our chief and only burden is that it may be a markedly spiritual Convention ... and we have faith to believe that you would be a great channel of spiritual blessing to this Continent and through it to the world ... You will have an opportunity to touch the leading representatives of every missionary agency of Canada and the United States ...
>
> We also very much want Miss Geraldine Guinness to be present. She has a wonderful hold on the students of America through her writings.

This fitted in well with plans to return to China via North America. Once again Hudson Taylor paid a farewell visit to William Berger at Cannes (each time it could be the last in their long friendship) and was back in London for the Mission's farewell meetings. The Exeter Hall was still crowded at 11.40 p.m. Mrs Grattan Guinness's life was 'hanging in the balance',

but Geraldine was preparing to travel with the Taylors to the States and China. She had been working on her *Story of the China Inland Mission* since early 1891, postponing her marriage. At last the second volume was finished and Howard was to be in Shanghai for their wedding when she arrived.

They joined their ship at Liverpool on February 14, and there Hudson Taylor signed the 'China Inland Mission Declaration of Trust', the completed legal document describing the structure of the Mission with its 'councils of advice' and 'arrangements for the control and management of the present and future properties and funds of the Mission'. He as General Director and the Home Director in the United Kingdom were 'advised and assisted in the work of the Mission in the United Kingdom by a body known as the "London Council".' Provision for his death and the procedures to be followed were clearly laid down. They sailed that day and reached New York on February 23, to be received by A. B. Simpson, and to meet a group of his International Alliance Mission students about to sail for Hong Kong to evangelise Guangxi.[1069]

Six of the principal addresses at the student convention had been allocated to Hudson Taylor, and the students benefitted by 'as much blessing as they were prepared to receive'. After CIM meetings at Toronto and an interview with Rijnhardt, Hudson Taylor went to Iowa to meet Rijnhardt's pastor, and on to Omaha to confront Rijnhardt in person again. Defiant and threatening, he vowed to wreck the CIM. Annie Slater had been saved from a shameless scoundrel. But the story had a sequel.

The Taylors and Geraldine travelled on, via Chicago for meetings, to San Francisco, and sailed for Shanghai, arriving (he for the ninth time) on April 17 'for a brief visit'. It lasted two years. He found the China Council in session facing a new upheaval. The Scandinavians of Fredrik Franson's and A. B. Simpson's Alliance Missions were in difficulties and the consul for Scandinavian affairs had called for urgently needed advice and persuasion.[1070]

John Nevius strikes gold (1890–93)

John and Helen Nevius had arrived in China in mid-February 1854, two weeks before Hudson Taylor. Their unbroken friendship through forty years had seen Helen recover from tuberculosis, but Maria Taylor die. In Shandong from 1861 John had worked out his 'methods' for planting Chinese churches untrammelled by foreign domination or sapped by dependence on foreign funds. Loyal to his Presbyterian colleagues, and in due time moderator of the northern synod, he had suffered from inability to convince the body of them that his methods held the key to success. He and Hudson Taylor had often compared notes on the subject. John Wesley had worked on similar principles, based on his own itineration. Nevius patiently worked on, making Yantai his base and travelling out to teach and advise the scattered congregations. (The bone-shaking torture of riding crude wheelbarrows led him to modify one with springs, and to sell one to Hudson Taylor.) Arising from discussions with intellectual friends, consuls, merchants and missionaries, who met from time to time to sharpen each other's wits, he also made a study of demon possession and wrote the tome, *Demon Possession in China* (see 1, p 573).[1071]

In 1890 his opportunity came. Presbyterian missionaries in Korea where the church was in its infancy invited him to come and expound his principles. His greatest success sprang from that brief visit to Seoul, for the missionaries and Christians adopted what came to be called the 'Nevius plan'. The Korean church attributes its dramatic growth largely to his influence, and China's 'Three Self' concept for the church owes its origin in part to the papers Nevius published.

The first principle was that the Bible should be taught systematically and thoroughly to all Christians, with periods of intensive study each year. Going away to distant institutions should be exceptional. Second, while each one continued in his or her own way of life and occupation, providing his own livelihood, he should witness actively for Christ in his own area—'self-propagation'. Third, each group of believers should choose its own leaders. Only if they as a congregation could afford to support a full-time evangelist or pastor would chosen individuals stop earning their own living. The methods, buildings and equipment used would also be governed by what the church could afford—'self-government' and 'self-support'. Fourth, a thoroughly Korean form of church activity, architecture and worship should be preserved. This high aim succumbed all too soon to foreign influence, due also to the highly independent nature of the Korean personality but a truly indigenous church developed. The first baptisms in 1886 resulted by 1894 in a church of 236 communicant members, and of

2.69 Manchuria, Korea and Shandong

thirty thousand by 1910, in spite of the Sino-Japanese war and of Japanese domination and suspicion. Today the Protestant Church in South Korea alone numbers millions.[1072]

But on October 19, 1893, John Nevius was preparing his mule litter for another tour of the Yantai circuit of country churches, when Dr Arthur Douthwaite rode across from his Chefoo hospital to see him. Nevius had been suffering from a 'weak heart' and his wife was anxious about him. One of his mules attacked Douthwaite's horse, giving Douthwaite a kick which reduced him to crutches for several days. But Nevius pelted the mule with stones, drove it off and helped Douthwaite indoors. They were sitting together when suddenly John Nevius slumped forward and died in spite of all the doctor did for him.[1073]

'Forward', too fast (1890–94)

Although Hudson Taylor declared after the General Conference appeal for one thousand men in five years, that the CIM would take no special measures to increase its numbers, by March 1893 they were coming too fast. In his enthusiasm Fredrik Franson was sending them as soon as they responded to his fluent appeals, but without enough preparations for receiving them in China. Those who came in the CIM's associate missions were treated as new members of the CIM. Others unconnected with the CIM no less needed help as they went straight out to the provinces. They had no language, experience or organisation to introduce them to a totally new life, so they were welcomed by the missionaries already established in Shanxi, on the Mongolian border, and in Shaanxi. Associates generally adhered to the CIM 'Principles and Practice'. Others did as they judged best, unaware of how strange their foreignness was to the Chinese. And some had beliefs and practices different enough from the CIM's to make cooperation difficult.

Emmanuel Olsson of the Swedish Holiness Union and his wife had agreed to act as leaders of those sent by A. B. Simpson's International Alliance Mission (Christian and Missionary Alliance from 1897), but were inundated. The first group arrived on February 15, 1893, and sixteen more followed a week later. When arrangements for the transmission of their funds broke down, they were dependent on the help of other missions and their consul. Hudson Taylor had seen trouble coming and advised Stevenson to steer clear of 'a full share of blame with very small power to help', but it was a matter of friends in need. For one thing, the CIM had decided not to accept anyone who refused on 'faith healing' principles or other grounds to be vaccinated, because of the danger to those who nursed them when they caught smallpox. Within five months of landing in China, five of the Scandinavian women had the disease.

But more serious factors made close cooperation difficult. In K. S. Latourette's words, 'As a rule the Alliance representatives had only a scanty education and attempted, with but imperfect adaptation to the Chinese environment, to reproduce the revivalism to which they usually owed their own religious experience. (But they) lived courageous and self-denying lives.' When the British ambassador, N. O'Conor, asked the foreign minister, Lord Rosebery, to alert the Swedish government to the dangers arising from the young Scandinavians' unwise actions, calling them CIM missionaries, it was time to act positively.[1074]

'Forward' and 'forward movement' were catch-phrases of the day in military and journalistic jargon. They found a place in Christian language not at first as a title but as a trend. While constitutional crises racked the Mission, any organised advance was unlikely, but on November 10, 1893, Hudson Taylor told John Stevenson, 'I propose organising a thorough campaign for the Mission such as has not yet been attempted.' They might be ready for it by May 1894. Some missions were responding well to the 1890 appeal for one thousand men, but women were outnumbering the men in volunteering. A month later, Hudson Taylor wrote, 'We are being encouraged as to our forward movement.'

A gift or promise of £1,600 towards advance had been received, 'receipts in 1893 exceeded those in 1892 by £7,500', and without special effort sixty-three new missionaries were sent from Britain. '(God) always prospers us when we go forward, does He not?' 'Several good men' were accepted in Britain during December, and Australia had 'five young men ready to sail', but low income was making the Melbourne council hesitate to send them. 'Send them as soon as you have the passage money available,' Hudson Taylor advised. 'If they are good men it would not be a great matter if for a time we had to help them' with funds from Britain and the States. This practice of pooling funds pleased everyone, and came into general use.[1075]

On arrival at Shanghai Hudson Taylor found John Stevenson utterly swamped with work and worn out although he had the very capable William Cooper and George Andrew to assist him. Stevenson was capable of more than most men, but although Hudson Taylor exhorted him to treat Cooper as a 'junior partner', he found it difficult to delegate to others. Cooper needed specific responsibilities of his own. And the whole mission needed to know what was happening. Hudson Taylor sent out a general letter saying that eight or nine years before, when the CIM had grown to two hundred strong, 'increasing dissatisfaction was felt because I was unable single-handed to meet the requirements of the work', so John Stevenson had been appointed Deputy Director and the council of superintendents had been created. However, by the year 1893 that two hundred had become six hundred, three times as many, so William Cooper, as Assistant Deputy Director (in line to wear Stevenson's mantle), would handle all administrative correspondence except what was addressed to Stevenson or Hudson Taylor and marked 'Private'. In addition, after seventeen years on the London staff, Charles Fishe was moving to Shanghai again. Stevenson, Cooper, Fishe and Broumton, the treasurer, were to be a Standing Council of Advice when the rest of the China Council

scattered to the provinces. With hindsight and the accumulated documents, the evidence seems clear that at thirty-four, with twelve years' experience in China, the physically powerful but gentle William Cooper had won Hudson Taylor's profound confidence and was being groomed for leadership at the highest levels.[1076] Anxiety over John Stevenson's state of health may have been a factor, for Jennie wrote, 'Your life and health are very precious.'

While most of the Mission were hard at work, progressing steadily, pockets of restlessness convinced Hudson Taylor that only a personal visit to Shaanxi and Shanxi would restore order. Dangerous individualism was threatening not only the Scandinavians but the future of the whole Mission. The Minister, O'Conor, appeared to be associating the CIM with whatever irregularities were being reported to him. And the CIM missionaries in Shanxi were themselves at sixes and sevens, with Stanley Smith and C. T. Studd deep in their own difficulties. When Lord Rosebery wrote 'kindly and courteously' but firmly, Hudson Taylor informed Stevenson:

> Remembering that we have now a Roman Catholic ambassador at Peking is very important, the main point being that the Foreign Office will sustain any consul in refusing passports to British missionaries if they are convinced that the (Chinese) authority cannot restrain the people from rioting. Now, nothing is easier for the (mandarins) than to pretend that they cannot restrain the people whom they have incited to riot, and many of our consuls ... may be very easily convinced of the impossibility of restraining a riotous population.

Missionaries should be reminded of the last article of the 'P and P' enjoining them to avoid dealings with the magistrates and consuls.[1077] Soon after reaching China, Hudson Taylor had received a friendly letter from the consul for Sweden and Norway asking for advice. A German newspaper at Shanghai had reported that 'twenty unmarried unprotected females' of Scandinavian missions were in danger in the far north of Shanxi without male missionaries to help them. Hudson Taylor wrote to reassure him and offered to intervene, but had his misgivings. A women's language school near Shanghai was a very different matter from congregating young women together at Guihuacheng near the Mongolian border.

Unfortunately the worst possible time of year was approaching. At the height of summer a long overland journey to Shanxi invited the dangers of heat stroke, dysentery, typhoid, malaria, and quick tempers in places where the populace were unfriendly. But the journey was unavoidable. Hudson Taylor and Jennie decided they must go, fully aware that it might cost them their lives. 'If the Lord has further work for us to do He will bring us safely through, and I think He will do so, but should it prove otherwise we ought to lay down our lives for the brethren.'[1078] Howard and Geraldine were married at the cathedral on April 24 and after they had left on a canal-boat honeymoon to Hangzhou, his parents prepared for their own journey.

Meanwhile a conference of twenty-one Scandinavians had been held at Qüwu in south Shanxi. All were connected in some way with Fredrik Franson, though in different missions. They were novices of less than five years in China and unrepresentative of many more who were not present. But this had not deterred them from passing resolutions of intention to move *en bloc* into Shaanxi, where the Scandinavian Alliance Mission from America and the original CIM pioneers were already deployed. They did not realise that by an influx of so many of them the resistant province would become dangerously overloaded with foreigners.

On hearing of their decision, Hudson Taylor addressed a pointed general letter to the Scandinavian and China Alliance missionaries and others acting with them, whether CIM associates or not, reminding them that they had been received and sent on their way by the CIM, who felt entitled to show concern for them. 'We cannot consider these resolutions as binding on

2.70 F. Howard Taylor and M. Geraldine Taylor, née Guinness

those of your Mission who were not present; and even with regard to those who were there, it is probable that the full bearing of the steps they are proposing is scarcely realised by them.' He went on to show that from lack of experience and advice some had fallen into grave mistakes from which those accepting guidance had been saved.

The Swedish government were considering recalling all its nationals to the coast and cancelling their passports. They and other European governments were 'making very minute enquiries and watching our proceedings very jealously'. To renounce consular control and help could land them in serious difficulties, financially and otherwise. And to cut themselves off from the CIM could be no less hazardous. The CIM were glad to help, whether they were associates or not, 'but anything like a rush into a large number of unoccupied centres (in Shaanxi) might be attended not only with riot and danger (murder) to the missionaries concerned, but also to those who are now safely and usefully settled in centres already open'. Footholds in Henan and Shaanxi had been gained only after years of perseverance and hardship. Thomas Botham had even written of danger from too many foreigners being already in Shaanxi, where he had been 'fleeing in circles' for years: 'We hope never to see a very large staff of foreign workers on the (Xi'an) plain. I think there may be too many missionaries in a place. I should not like to see foreign pastors of all the Chinese churches any more than I should like to see Russian pastors of all English churches.'[1079]

Botham and his colleague, Bland, would give seasoned advice on opening new work where they judged it to be safe.

Association 'cannot be one-sided'. Accepting help should be answered by consultation and cooperation. 'We must insist that in all future arrangements Lady Associates be located with or near to married missionaries, or in suitable stations occupied by ladies only, not with single men.' He then outlined the arrangements adopted by the CIM to restrain irresponsible moving around or leaving a place of work without approval by provincial leaders. So urgent was this matter that he was cancelling engagements in America and Britain and starting at once for Xi'an and then Shanxi in spite of the risks to health and life itself. 'I affectionately urge on all . . . to make no change and to begin no new movements until we can meet.' Scandinavian Alliance missionaries in Zhejiang and Jiangxi were also asked 'whether it is their purpose to maintain their connection with the China Inland Mission or to retire from it in the event of any . . . concluding to form a separate mission.'

It looked as if wholesale recruitment had got out of hand. The response to this forthright letter could be a watershed between successful cooperation and disaster.

To Shaanxi and Shanxi
(May–September 1894)

On the international front, dangerous developments were afoot. Anglo-Russian friction had arisen in protest against Russia's growing influence over China. The trans-Siberian railway began its Manchurian extensions after the inauguration on May 17, 1891, and the imperial edict of June 1893. But the power of Japan was becoming a greater threat as she rapidly modernised her armed forces and began sabre-rattling over Korea.

Korea lay uncomfortably between China and Japan, defensively significant to both. Historically China was the suzerain power, allowing Korea her independence while guaranteeing her against external aggression and internal disorder. This dual policy of non-interference and protection kept Korea as a buffer state.

China's suzerainty over the Ryukyu Islands, Annam, Siam and Burma had been whittled away. Only Korea remained. Her affairs were in the hands of Li Hongzhang and the Resident at Seoul, Yüan Shikai. But China's weakness meant that her only defence against Japan's progressive undermining of stability in Korea lay in treaties with the Western powers. At the same time Japan's best hope of being seen by the West as an equal power lay in military domination of China.

So provocation followed provocation in spite of the Tianjin Convention of 1885 between China and Japan.

The empress dowager had siphoned off huge allocations for strengthening the navy, to rebuild the Summer Palace. But as a sign of imperial favour when Li reached seventy years of age, the highest honour possible in the empire, the three-eyed peacock feather, was again bestowed on him in March 1894, the only Han Chinese ever to receive it (see 1, p 825).[1080] In June, Japan landed twelve thousand men in Korea, engineered a *coup d'état* at Seoul and made demands to which China responded by also shifting troops to Korea.

This was how things stood in May as Hudson Taylor travelled at the worst possible time of year. By then he was deep in the hinterland of Henan and Shaanxi, toiling painfully towards Xi'an. He, Jennie and their son-in-law, Joe Coulthard, had set out from Shanghai in mid-May, up the Yangzi to Hankou, calling on the missionaries at each port.[1081] While they were still there Howard and Geraldine arrived, alarmed to hear that Howard's parents were intending to travel in such heat. It was too late to change plans. They had cabled ahead to call conferences at four cities. 'Then let us come, too,' Howard pleaded. So the family party of five left Hankou by houseboat on May 22, changing to wheelbarrows on the 24th. Zhoujiakou was reached on June 2, Xiangcheng on the 6th in springless carts, and Tongguan on the 22nd, jolted incessantly and well-nigh intolerably, sometimes in dust and temperatures of over 100 °F in the shade, and sometimes in pouring rain. The armed confrontation in Korea had begun, but as yet no fighting.

Geraldine had started the journey ambitiously, keeping a diary.

> June 13. 6 a.m. This is indeed a moment of misery. We are sitting waiting in our carts in this filthy inn-yard, all ready to start— as we have been for an hour—while the rain pours steadily down and the carters are obdurate. For several nights ... we have slept but little (bed bugs). Outside in the courtyard half a dozen fiery mules were fighting and braying all night long. There being only one room, Mother and I occupied it; Father, Howard and Joe slept in the carts outside.

After that she could manage no more than mere notes. On June 14 a river barring their way was impassable and they had to return to a primitive type of inn. 'June 14. Dreadful-looking people—no inn—place dangerous. Had to return.'

'June 15. Quite an exciting moment! We are in the act of crossing a swollen river . . . One cart (overturned and was) washed away before our eyes (so) we felt it wiser to cross by ferry.' . . . 'Our rough, rough journey' ended at Xi'an on June 26.

Since the Hunanese family's opposition in Xi'an (see p 466) had been ended by friendly officials, houses for women missionaries had been secured in the west suburb and for others in the city itself. It seemed miraculous that now even a conference of foreigners could be held safely in what had for years been such a danger spot. Twelve Scandinavians of the first thirty-five, and four full members of the CIM (Easton, Bland, Steven and another) had gathered for conference with Hudson Taylor. Four days' travel to the west, Thomas Botham was nursing his wife, at death's door with high fever. Howard set off for

Fengxiang to help them, and found her recovering.

In Shaanxi there were none of the serious problems that awaited Hudson Taylor in Shanxi. He was impressed by the progress these Alliance missionaries had made in adaptation to China and by the success of their work. 'Very few of our men after three years in China are as competent as they have become, or as careful . . . Their plans for independent work seem so matured . . . they are looked on with much favour and get on well and wisely with the officials.' It was more a matter of organising cooperation in keeping with the 'P and P'.

By July 2, satisfactory arrangements had been made. One of the Scandinavians, Henriksen, was to be recognised as 'Senior Missionary Associate' working with Botham as Assistant Superintendent of the whole province of Shaanxi. Bland was to help Botham, and Botham would be responsible to G. F. Easton as superintendent of Gansu and Shaanxi. The complexity of this organisation reflected the great distances and growing numbers of missionaries involved. Others of their own Scandinavian Alliance, from Shanxi, Zhejiang and Jiangxi, would be found suitable locations to occupy, but in no hurry. Real difficulties had been created for the single women by the two year marriage rule, so Hudson Taylor simply waived it in the case of Scandinavians, putting the good of the cause before normal practice. This capacity for being master of the rules he made, instead of being mastered by them, stands out as one of Hudson Taylor's strong characteristics.[1082]

On July 4 they set off by cart again, back to Tongguan and over the Yellow River on the 7th, making for Yuncheng, Erik Folke's base for the Swedish Mission in China. Conditions had been gruelling. A pocket thermometer in the shade of a covered cart registered 110 °F. Outside it was considerably higher. When Howard Taylor caught them up his father was 'very seriously ill (with) cerebral congestion' although most of his head had been shaved. He recovered with treatment. After that they travelled by night to Qüwu for a third conference, this time with some of the restless Swedes. (An absence of records suggests 'the less said the better'.) Then on to Linfen (Pingyang) to be met on the road by Hsi Shengmo and Dixon Hoste.

The Linfen conference of thirty-five missionaries including eleven more Scandinavians and sessions for church members, lasted eight days (July 17–24). Personal consultation again secured agreement over where the Swedes could be safely deployed. And to general rejoicing Dixon Hoste and Gertrude Broomhall became engaged. After doing well in Shanxi as a missionary and in Britain and North America as a public speaker, she had only recently returned. (They travelled with the Taylors to Tianjin and were married at the consulate on September 6, 1894—a partnership in what they could not have dreamed would come their way.)

From Linfen onwards the Scandinavian problems became overshadowed by CIM disorder. Travelling from city to city for meetings with Chinese Christians and missionaries who could not get to the conferences, Hudson Taylor found a disgraceful state of affairs. Two factions, for and against Hsi Shengmo, lived in a permanent state of friction which their unbiased colleagues could not overcome. At Taiyuan this 'dread of Hsi' was compounded by a recurrence of the 'Shanxi spirit'—the 'Christianised Confucianism' being offered in place of (rather than as a means of presenting) the gospel. Recognising a degree of spirituality in Confucian classics, the minds of some lost sight of the uniqueness of Christ and therefore of Christianity. In Latourette's assessment, 'as Timothy Richard pointed out, there were two ways of regarding the Gospel: as a means of saving the soul of each individual, and as a means of saving a nation through the collective efforts of regenerated souls'.[1083]

At a more mundane level, distancing themselves from the heart of the CIM, some members showed the spirit of compromise in being 'loose on the dress question'. All too many of the CIM and Scandinavians in Shanxi were copying other missions and some who had resigned from the CIM, in compromising between Chinese and foreign dress, wearing a Chinese gown, but leather boots, pith helmet and no queue, a clownish hotch-potch scorned by the Chinese. The two doctors, some senior missionaries and Stanley Smith were among them.

SPS's vacillating loyalty to Mission principles and even to his beliefs had been one of the factors determining Hudson Taylor's return to China. They had already met (at Yokohama) and talked it over. This time Hudson Taylor wrote to William Cooper, 'It would be far better for him to retire from us and make his own arrangements with Studd' if both wished to work together. The doctors might resign anyway.

Two decisions faced Hudson Taylor. If he failed to nip this defection in the bud it would spread. 'Chinese dress' meant correct Chinese dress and deportment, unreluctant adaptation winning Chinese approval. That included the conventional hair style. Harmony and cooperation as a Mission team necessitated mutual respect and the end of dissension. He advocated courtesy to the Chinese by ceasing the charade of neither one proper dress nor the other, and won the compliance of most. Then with them he worked out a division of Shanxi into separate areas under different superintendents. To southern Shanxi, Hsi's region, he appointed Hsi's faithful companion Dixon Hoste. And to the central region one who would be pleased to have no more dealings with Hsi. To rally Dr Edwards, he offered him a seat on the China Council. By the time Hudson Taylor left Shanxi all knew that proper observance of the 'P and P' was a condition of membership of the CIM. Some were weighing whether or not to accept or to reject it. The debate among missionaries of all societies, for and against Chinese dress, was still very much alive, and the grass outside the CIM fence looked greener. Opinions differed within the ranks of a mission, opinions often strongly held. The CMS failed to reach agreement and 'Salisbury House' left it to individuals to do as they saw fit.[1084]

All through July the possibility of war between China and Japan over Korea had been degenerating towards probability. The *daotai* of Shanghai informed the consuls on the 23rd that he intended to block the entrance to the Huangpu River at the cost of strangling half of China's coastal trade. To prevent this, the British representative in Tokyo secured an undertaking by Japan to 'regard Shanghai as outside the sphere of its warlike operation', but Canton, Fuzhou, Ningbo and other ports constructed barriers. War would drastically affect missions, however far from the war zone. If Hudson Taylor knew what was developing, he disregarded it. Rumour and alarm were never far from the surface. Finally the sinking of the Chinese troopship *Kowshing* on July 25 (while they were at Hsi Shengmo's home) marked the start of major hostilities. But it was ill-health that brought the Taylors' journey to an untimely end.

Unable to check the enteritis they had developed on their hard journey, they decided to head for Shanghai while the way was open. After the council meetings in September, Hudson Taylor himself would come back, as the surest way of resolving the Shanxi disorder. So on August 16 they left Taiyuan, reached Shouyang in two days and stayed with the council member who had resigned to do things in his own way. They were Christian enough not to harbour resentment over strong deviations of policy. Four more days' travel brought them over the mountains to Huolu (Hwailu) and they reached Tianjin on September 4 with no worse mishaps than Jennie and Geraldine being ducked in the Sha River and, near Tianjin, 'a narrow escape, boat sunk in passing bridge'. But Jennie's dysentery became dangerously worse and on September 5, after the Hoste's wedding, they quickly took her on board a ship leaving at 1.00 a.m. for Shanghai, through

the Bo Hai Strait and disputed waters between Shandong and Korea.

To Shanxi alone
(September–December 1894)

Three weeks later, the council meetings over, Hudson Taylor sailed north again (September 25) looking 'very aged and tired' to reach Tianjin on October 2. Before leaving Shanghai he had written to Walter B. Sloan in London, 'Now the war has broken out, I am not sure that I ought to leave China . . . The authorities are diligently trying to protect the missionaries . . . but the greatest danger would arise from rebellion, should the secret societies think the government was so seriously embarrassed as to give them a good chance of success.'

After consulting other missions in Shanghai about the prospects, since by then the Chinese had been driven out of Korea and fighting had reached beyond the Yalu River (see map 2.69, p 576) he started inland on October 5 with one employee companion.[1085] Some sixty Japanese warships were reported at the mouth of the Gulf of Zhili and likely to blockade it. 'All seem to think . . . the dynasty unlikely to survive the shock.' He was carrying one thousand taels' worth of gold leaf and as much again in silver lest his communications be cut and a long enforced overland journey to the south become unavoidable. A letter to his daughter, Amy, reflects the fears at Tianjin.

> It may be that in a few days the war may shut the door by which I have entered; and some think ... there may be a time of dangerous anarchy before order can be restored ... I only know one thing, the LORD reigneth and under His reign all things work together for good to them that love God. This will be so if I am alive ... to return to you in peace ... But it will equally be so should this note be the last you receive from me.

Joe Coulthard, Howard and Geraldine were back in Henan, perhaps in great need of prayer when she received it, he said. He believed that revolution might break out any day and the lives of all foreigners, his own no less than others, would be in jeopardy. He sent it via Jennie who added a postscript: 'It is a time of strain . . . but God is over all and nothing can happen to us that has not first been sanctioned by Him who is Love.' In the event they had six more years before that protection was withdrawn.[1086]

This time he had no son or daughter-in-law to see to his comfort. He bargained with muleteers, rose at 3.00 a.m. to see that they fed their animals in time for an early start each day, and had to find accommodation and food for himself. 'I confess I do not like crossing the (treacherous) rivers and pools . . . Part of this journey has been a time of great spiritual conflict, but the Lord has greatly helped me.' He was feeling too old and drained of energy for such travelling. And the purpose of this journey, to reinforce discipline among the still recalcitrant missionaries, could hardly be more distasteful. But he knew the power of personal friendship and frankness.

At Baoding, Huolu and Shunde some were growing their queues again; not all. One had been impressed by seeing how pleased the Chinese were and how much notice had been taken of its absence. They were far from indifferent to the question, as some missionaries believed. At Shunde he found C. T. Studd and his wife 'in a beautiful spirit', on their way home to Britain. His asthma made it useless for 'CT' to stay longer. He hoped to return, but insisted on presenting to the Mission the fine large premises he had personally bought at Lu'an (Lungan, now Changzhi). 'I told him that dear SPS had so impulsively taken up views contrary to the platform of the Mission; that had he not . . . (retracted) all he had written on the subject, his continuance in the Mission would not have been possible. . . . Some sudden impulsive step' might yet sever the links.[1087]

Going on by mule litter across 'a sea of mountains—solid waves', taxed his endurance. Often in the dry beds of mountain torrents broken up by large boulders, flash floods from distant cloudbursts posed a threat. At Lu'an he spent a day with Stanley Smith, vacillating again, but as charming as ever. He doctored and bandaged the injured leg of an enemy of the Christians, and later heard that he had become 'almost a friend'. Then on in snow, with icicles forming on his litter and the man-servant he had employed ill with typhoid and having to be carried. Through one mission centre after another, finding loyal compliance by most missionaries, but obduracy from others, he reached Taiyuan from the south. There he wrote, '(Edwards) agrees, thank God', to live by the 'P and P'.

The Hostes, back at Hongtong, had had a royal welcome from the church. A large banner of blue with gold characters for 'With one heart serving the Lord' greeted them, as well as flowery furniture and bright curtains. Pastor and Mrs Hsi presented them with a warm quilt covered with crimson silk, the bridal colour. At a church gathering of four hundred with Hudson Taylor, sixty-nine were baptised and several deacons appointed. This was the true Shanxi. 'I left Taiyuan glad this time, a load removed. Nearly all I hoped for is accomplished.' 'Had I not been able to visit (Shanxi) and (Shaanxi) we should have lost a good many workers.'

But the war news was bad. Mukden fallen to the Japanese; the Taiyuan authorities were afraid they would be the next, to become a bastion against reinforcement from the west before the kill at Peking. Rumours abounded: Yantai bombarded, Zhang Zhitong a reformer, assassinated on the emperor's orders. Both proved untrue. Using a Chinese atlas he followed the Japanese advance through Manchuria. On November 20 he learned that two thousand Chinese troops were behind him. He must keep ahead or food and shelter would be hard to come by. Then a boat from Baoding to Tianjin through freezing temperatures and icy winds, not knowing whether the way was clear or Tianjin still free. It was. But all ships were full with people fleeing south. He reached Shanghai on December 4, having been on the move almost incessantly for seven months.

War with Japan[1088] (May 1894–1895)

The sinking of the troopship *Kowshing* on July 25, 1894, led to both China and Japan declaring war on August 1. But while the main Chinese army formed along the Yalu River, an advanced force at Pyongyang, halfway to Seoul, was routed by an overpowering Japanese army of 80,000. China's appeal for intervention by the Western nations had met with no success. The Korean royal family were seized and Korea declared war on China. Then on September 17 the decisive naval engagement of Haiyang Dao took place off the mouth of the Yalu. The Japanese established their control of the seas, and the remains of the Chinese fleet took shelter at Lüda (Dalian, Dairen, Port Arthur) and then at Weihaiwei on the Shandong coast east of Yantai.

Blame for the outbreak of war and this defeat were unjustly laid at the door of Li Hongzhang. Deprived on December 26 of his viceroyalty and two most prized decorations, the 'yellow jacket' and his three-eyed peacock feathers, he retained his unenviable responsibilities. And, after ten years 'in the wilderness', Prince Kong was recalled to head the government and 'piece together the smashed cup'. By the end of September Korea had been cleared of Chinese troops, and the Japanese crossed the Yalu River into Manchuria on October 24. On the same day they landed above Lüda and by November 6 were investing the port, to the intense alarm of Peking, for it was just across the gulf from Tianjin. The wealthy began to transport their riches and womenfolk by the Grand Canal to the safety of the south.

The empress dowager's sixtieth birthday on November 7 (the 10th day of the 10th moon) passed almost uncelebrated, but the foreign envoys were received with ceremony and the British and American ministers presented her on behalf of China's ten thousand Christian women with an ornate Wenli New Testament measuring 13 by 10 inches. Bound in solid silver covers embossed with golden characters for 'Holy Classic of Salvation', it lay in a silver casket.

Not long afterwards the young emperor sent a palace eunuch to the Bible Society asking for a copy of the Old and New Testaments for himself. The Old Buddha's birthday was also her opportunity to recall Yong Lu from punitive disgrace and once again to put him in command of the palace garrison.[1089]

When China had made a second appeal for foreign help, Britain could arouse no interest from the other powers, but Prince Kong tried again. This time the envoys asked Japan whether mediation would be acceptable. Not until China sued for peace, she answered. Overtures were then made through the American envoy for peace based on the independence of Korea and a negotiated war indemnity. These also failed. The Peking court petulantly meted out punishments to the unfortunate commanding officers and replaced Li Hongzhang as viceroy of Zhili.[1090]

So ended the year, but not the war. The Japanese army continued to advance until on March 5, 1895, they held Yingkou (Niuchuang). No natural line of defence remained before Peking except at Shanhaiguan, the last barrier of mountains where the Great Wall runs down into the sea. Capture of the pass would open the way to both Peking and Tianjin. Manchuria east of the Liao River was theirs, the region of Liaodong, dynastic home of the Qing. Across the strait they bombarded Penglai (Dengzhou) west of Yantai, three times in January, and landed twenty thousand troops and ten thousand transport coolies east of Yantai at Rongcheng Bay on the tip of the peninsula, only thirty miles beyond Weihaiwei. The remains of the Chinese fleet anchored in the harbour at Weihaiwei were mauled by gunfire and torpedoes. So the Chinese admiral and other commanding officers committed suicide to save themselves from decapitation and their families from death and confiscation of their estates. Rumours of Yantai being bombarded on November 14 were unfounded.

Meanwhile, more confused attempts to negotiate peace came to nothing,

2.71 Li Hongzhang in 1896

and on February 19, 1895, the Peking court had no recourse but to restore to the incomparable Li Hongzhang all his honours before appointing him ambassador extraordinary to negotiate with Japan. With his son, Li Jingfang, two other emissaries and a suite of 135 attendants he met the Japanese delegation at Shimnoseki in south-western Honshu on March 20 and requested an armistice. Only on surrender of Shanhaiguan, Tianjin, the port of Dagu at the river mouth and the railway between these places, the Japanese arrogantly replied. On March 24 they met to discuss terms for peace and Li was told that an expedition was on its way to occupy Taiwan. Would Japan's aggression stop at nothing?

On his way back in his sedan chair Li was shot at by a Japanese fanatic, the bullet embedding itself in the cheekbone below his left eye. Fuming with rage he quietly walked from the chair to his room and for seventeen days negotiated through his son. International feeling was outraged and Japan humiliated. The emperor expressed his regrets and his nation their

sympathy. They granted an armistice, reduced their demands, abandoned claims to exceptional privileges, and signed the Treaty of Shimonoseki on April 17. What war and diplomacy had failed to achieve, the venerable Li Hongzhang's personal suffering secured.

The terms, nevertheless, were harsh and humiliating for China: complete independence for Korea; cession of the large Liaodong region of Manchuria, of Taiwan and the Pescadores; an indemnity of two hundred million taels; more treaty ports and inland waterways to be opened to commerce; and Weihaiwei to be held until ratification was complete. But Russia, France and Germany jointly 'recommended' that all the Manchurian territory be returned to China. The Russian Mediterranean squadron was on its way, and by the time the exchange of ratifications was made at Yantai on May 8, the warships of many nations, including twenty or more flying the Russian ensign, had congregated there. Japan signed a subsidiary treaty on November 8, accepting an additional eighty million taels in lieu of Liaodong, which brought the total indemnity to about £40 million sterling, provided by loans from Russia, France, Britain and Germany, all secured by customs revenues.

On April 7, 1895, Sir Robert Hart wrote to his colleague E. B. Drew, 'Japan wants to lead the East in war, in commerce and in manufactures, and next century will be a hard one for the West.' Taiwan quickly fell to the expeditionary force after an abortive attempt to declare Taiwan a republic, when Britain and then France (close to war with each other over Siam) rejected a request from Taiwan to make the island a protectorate. 'The wires burned with telegrams.' The stakes were too high.[1091] The only authentic flag of the Taiwan republic to survive was in the possession of H. B. Morse himself, customs officer at Danshui.

Alicia Bewicke Little wrote of the Chinese people being crushed and fearful and of some viceroys and governors baying for Li Hongzhang's blood. But for

Ci Xi. he would have been beheaded, she maintained.

Hudson Taylor had not needed to use his emergency gold-leaf. He had left Baoding for Tianjin the day after the port of Uda (Port Arthur) was taken. Sailing from Dagu on the last day of November, his ship made straight for Shanghai, through the war zone, not calling in at Yantai. So he was back at Wusong Road when he wrote to Walter Sloan on December 6 of hopes of peace, but: 'There will be a time of danger while the troops are being disbanded. And if . . . they are defrauded of pay and given no means of returning home . . . the additional danger of rebellion or bands of banditti.' Two weeks later he wrote again of hoping to get up to Yantai where morale was understandably low, but he had heard of isolated missionaries in south-west China talking of resignation through sheer loneliness. If he took two years visiting all mission centres it could be time well spent, conditions permitting. 'Nothing but great urgency would justify my leaving China at present.' He himself was not well, but both Broumton and Stevenson were seriously ill again, so for the present he was anchored at Shanghai.

At Yantai the anxiety was justifiable when the two ports to east and west of them came under attack. The harbour was barricaded and plans made to evacuate all foreigners. Dr Douthwaite quickly prepared his hospital under the Red Cross, and insisted that it was to receive the wounded whether Chinese or Japanese. His good relationship with the amazed Chinese general made it possible to convince him that the hospital could be neutral territory. But his point was never put to the test. Desperately injured men dragged themselves through the snow from Weihaiwei to reach Chefoo frost-bitten. Every bed was soon filled, and untrained missionaries assisted him in his surgical operations.[1092] The schools had consular instructions to be prepared to leave at short notice, each child with his or her own bundle. When word came that a body of five hundred famished Chinese stragglers were retreating towards the schools, the consul warned the Mission to be prepared for looting. But they straggled past, to be received by the mandarins.

The armistice restored calm and the ratification of the treaty at Yantai, with the bay filled with warships, brought new excitement. Cholera broke out in the city and on the ships. Yet the school escaped. Without warning the general and his staff arrived one day at Douthwaite's hospital on horseback, a brass band playing and soldiers bearing a large honorific tablet which they set up with great ceremony. When the foundations of the big new school were being laid, a company of soldiers brought eight hundred 'loads' of quarried rock as a gift. And when the Douthwaite family left Chefoo, the general and a whole regiment paraded at the hospital. As Dr Douthwaite came out they dropped on their knees while a speech of thanks was made for all he had done for them. And he was escorted with a guard of honour to the harbour. Not content with that, the emperor awarded him (and ten other missionary doctors involved in the war) with the Order of the Double Dragon.

Hosea Ballou Morse, eyewitness of some of these events, particularly in Taiwan, made the comment, 'Unable to make headway against the Japanese, (the Chinese) hit hard at the missionaries.' In every month of 1895 the American legation at Peking had occasion to report on the dangerous position in which American missionaries were placed. Zhou Han, the evil genius in Hunan, surfaced again with more diatribes against foreigners in general and missionaries in particular.[1093] This time the blood of missionaries was to be shed as had not happened for generations.

23

'The Sleep and the Awakening' (1895–1905)

1895–97: CHINA IN CONVULSION

Rebellion in the air (1895–97)

A new maritime nation had appeared almost overnight. In less than twenty years Japan had modernised sufficiently to rank with any Western nation on the Oriental high seas. With a two thousand mile coastline to defend, China's nucleus of a navy lay in fragments. Counting on intervention by the powers to curb Japan's aggression, China had been disillusioned. Her government had scorned Japan, made little effort to match her growing strength, and had been forced to her knees by a navy built on the British pattern and an army modelled on the French and Germans. Finding herself 'in a state of utter helplessness', China (or at least her thinkers) saw more aggression and dismemberment as her likely fate. Stunned shock gave place to anger. All knew that the obscurantist rulers at Peking were to blame. But, above all, they were most ready to find scapegoats and to crush criticism at source.

Hosea Ballou Morse, as a customs official at Danshui (Taiwan) when the Japanese walked in, felt the pulse of the nation. Until humiliation opened the nation's eyes, 'a few thousands at most' of China's intelligentsia could see that modernisation in the Western mould was their only hope. Once defeat became not fear but a fact, 'many myriads in number burned with indignation and looked for reform', while others turned on the only foreigners within reach, the missionaries.

'Marquis' Zeng, the ambassador to Paris, to St Petersburg, and to London had written in 1887 urging reform in his book, *The Sleep and the Awakening*. In 1894 the Western-trained doctor, Sun Yatsen, first graduate (in 1892) of the Hong Kong College of Medicine, at twenty-five formed a cell of the revolutionary Golaohui

secret society at Canton. Before the start of the Sino-Japanese war he obtained the signatures of many educated Cantonese to a memorial to the throne on modernisation. In October 1895 he organised an armed raid from Hong Kong on Canton. It failed, and he fled to America and then London, organising revolt wherever he could. The Manchu secret service tracked him down, and in October 1896 kidnapped him in London. They held him prisoner at the Chinese legation until Lord Salisbury secured his release at the request of Dr James Cantlie, Sun Yatsen's professor in Hong Kong. For seventeen years (1895–1912) he was hunted with a huge price on his head, ready to be tortured and killed if only the Manchus could be ousted and replaced by a democratic republic.[1094]

The other outstanding angry young man was Kang Yuwei, also a Cantonese of Guangdong. Not a revolutionary but a reformer, his goal was to convert the literati, the mandarins and the throne to 'the wisdom and the necessity of reorganisation of the machinery of government', as a constitutional monarchy. His books were widely read and in calling him 'the modern sage of China' admirers were saying he was 'a second Confucius'. In April 1895, he presented a memorial to the throne signed by over a thousand *qüren* (MA degree men) urging non-ratification of the treaty of Shimonoseki.[1095] Both these young men were destined to share in the reshaping of the nation, but the spontaneous movement was widespread and growing stronger. Zhang Zhitong accepted the presidency of the Reform Association of China while viceroy of Nanjing before returning to Wuchang and being succeeded by Liu Kunyi.[1096] The Hanlin Reform Club of Peking included some of China's elite. From all over China viceroys, governors and military commanders deluged the empire with memorials in favour of rejecting the treaty and continuing the war.[1097] But this reforming spirit still clung chiefly to the coastal cities and along the Yangzi.

> (The people's) pride has been wounded [Hudson Taylor wrote to all 630 of his missionaries]; their respect for their own rulers lessened; rebellion is in the air, turbulence and unrest are found everywhere ... Rioting in (Sichuan) has been followed by riots against Christians (in Wenzhou and its neighbouring city of Bingyae), by the terrible massacre of missionaries in (Fujian), the attack on Fatshan near Canton, and by a tendency to revenge on Christians the losses from drought or flood or from other national or local disasters ... The Secret Societies may seize the opportunity to try to overthrow the Government altogether, when anarchy with all its horrors might be the result.

> [Calling for a day of 'waiting upon God' he continued] The counsel we have given in times past, as far as possible to remain at one's post strengthening the faith of (Chinese) Christians by our own restful trust in the Lord, we still recommend ... The (Chinese) know that we possess no firearms, but rely on the living God alone for our protection ... It behoves us ... not to yield to the spirit of unrest ... If filled with the Spirit we shall also be filled with love, joy and peace ... Come what may, we are on the winning side.[1098]

The Mission that faced the ultimate test five years later had been gradually prepared for it.

'Why *do* the heathen rage?' he asked Walter Sloan, not knowing from day to day what the next telegram would report. Why China raged soon filled the headlines. The journalist Alexander Michie wrote, 'China was defeated amid the applause of Europe and the whole world'—mistakenly glad in thinking that the inflexible empress dowager and her court could no longer live in the past and must face up to international realities. Mistaken, for nothing would change Ci Xi, but also because Japan and 'the lawless West' had

already earned and would go on earning China's hatred as they 'sliced the melon'.

Convulsions widespread (1895)

Hudson Taylor's letter was no over-reaction to events. In this year of 1895 alarm followed alarm. January saw the Japanese invasion of Shandong, and February the fall of Weihaiwei and surrender of the Chinese fleet. Chefoo lay in the path of extreme danger. In March a fracas between rival Muslim sects in the Gansu-Qinghai border regions was turning into full-scale rebellion with the defeat of a Chinese force sent to quell them. City after city, even Lanzhou, was reportedly in rebel hands. Nothing was heard of several missionaries, presumably engulfed (see pp 595–97). April brought news of the assassination attempt on Li Hongzhang, and then of peace at such a price that anger flared after tears of mortification. In May, Liu Pingzhang, the viceroy of Sichuan, fomented riots in his own province, affecting the CIM at his capital of Chengdu, at Leshan (Jiading), Yibin and Ya'an in the south, and (in June) at Langzhong (Panning) in the north. But when 'the great province became a hotbed of mob violence with the suddenness of a tropical thunderstorm . . . more than sixty foreigners [sixty-one in fact] were driven out. [Their] work was completely broken up. [But] several tens of thousands of Christians (largely Roman Catholics) suffered, many being killed.'[1099]

Xining in Gansu was under threat of siege, and the Ridleys sent out word that they were staying to help if they could. Grim persecution of the Christians broke out at Pingyang (Bingyae) halfway between Wenzhou and the Fujian border.

By mid-July the homes and possessions of twenty-one families had been destroyed. Fifty-nine refugees fled to the mission house and chapel. A murderous attack on Dr D. Z. Sheffield of the American Board at Tongzhou (now Tong Xian in Zhili) left him nearly dead with thirty-four severe wounds. But it was not all one-sided. A Wenzhou Christian commented, 'In the New Testament all the best people went to prison.'[1100] From Hanzhong, just north of Sichuan, came news of 'unmistakable signs of a great harvest' throughout the district. People came crowding simply to hear the gospel.

Then on August 1, the restraining hand of God was withdrawn and the worst massacre of missionaries in China since the mid-eighteenth century (see 1, p 28) took place in Fujian. The Xining siege was at its worst in the autumn and through December, until it was raised in January 1896. October brought news of ten CIM missionaries and Chinese at Wenzhou dead from cholera. In his review of the year Hudson Taylor only called 1895 'the most trying (year) experienced by (Protestant) missionaries in China'. The meaning of 'riot' to individual missionaries has been made clear in the earlier books of this series, but the Sichuan riots of 1895 taught new lessons and influenced the attitudes of the viceroys and governors of China, even if Ci Xi and her closest confidantes were unmoved.

Sichuan riots (April–July 1895)

The CIM had eleven 'stations' in Sichuan. In the absence of Dr Herbert Parry from Chengdu, his wife and two single women and the J. G. Cormacks were there, with Joshua Vale of Yibin on a short visit, when rioting broke out. James Cormack's letter home gave the facts, amplifying his note 'written when we did not know if we should be alive the following morning'.[1101]

In April a woman under treatment by Dr Hare of the Canadian Methodist Mission died, and the husband imprisoned the doctor, accusing him of murder. When a crowd gathered and set upon him, Dr Hare escaped and ran for his life. Vile stories about him were then circulated in the city. Again and again the magistrates were appealed to, but took no action to calm the people. On May 28, the Canadian Hospital was surrounded and stoned. To impress the mob Dr Kilborne shattered the top of the door with a rifle shot and when the attackers retreated the missionaries escaped to a nearby army camp. Driven away from

there, they hid in darkness on the city wall for several hours and then made their way to the CIM.

As soon as Joshua Vale heard of the rioting he too sent a messenger to the magistrates asking for protection for all mission premises in Chengdu. They did nothing. That night and through May 29, the Canadian hospital, chapel and all other premises were looted, wrecked and burned. Canadians from another part of the city also came to the CIM for refuge. But the rioters followed them. By 10.00 p.m. the Cormacks, Vale and Jackson of the CMS and seven Canadians, with seven children, knew their best hope was to escape. Four succeeded, hidden in curtained sedan chairs. The Cormacks were to follow. 'The mob set up an awful yelling', but *yamen* 'runners' cleared a way for them. As the mob burst into the premises and began wrecking, the five remaining adults and three children escaped over the back wall and were hidden by neighbours, 'huddled all together on one bed, the curtains drawn'. The din of destruction continued until 'not even a whole tile was left on the premises, everything being levelled to the ground and all that could be stolen carried off.'

The American Board's premises and six Catholic places were also looted and burned. For a week eighteen Protestant missionaries, eleven children and two Catholic priests were concealed in the nearest *yamen*. All had lost everything. The local magistrate treated them well, 'but higher officials have done so little as to appear to be accomplices'.

At Leshan, known then as Jiading, the Riries and Joshua Vale's fiancée, Annie Bridgewater of the CIM, had been joined by the Canadian Methodist doctors Hart and Hare and an American Baptist missionary when students and others arrived from Chengdu and began rabble rousing. Posters calling for mobs to beat the foreigners on June 5 were torn down by brave Chinese friends, but the damage had been done.

Ben Ririe went over to the Canadian Mission to see for himself. He was well known and respected in the city. As people came out with loot he calmly told them to put it in the lobby, and they obeyed. When the magistrate arrived with soldiers he returned home, to find a mob of several thousands preparing to break in. He learned that neighbours had helped the women over the garden wall to hide so he rejoined them. The city prefect arrived, 'got knocked about a bit', and could only withdraw, leaving the house to be looted.[1102]

After midnight they made their way to the *yamen*, and were treated as guests for three months. Housed in a beautiful cottage and garden built for the magistrate's son, and sent all their meals, 'very nicely done up', they were visited by 'the great man of the city' and urged to stay. 'Many asked us, if we went, to come back again . . . Our love for the people here grew as we saw how anxious they were for us . . . We are all of one mind, "don't go till we have to". We are . . . far better off than our Master who had nowhere to lay His head.' 'We were able to show the people that we can "take joyfully the spoiling of our goods". I never knew I had so many friends in (Leshan) until yesterday.'

This experience became full of lessons for the Riries and for the Mission when the full story appeared in *China's Millions*. Love for the Chinese and contentment with whatever affected them themselves spoke more loudly than any preaching when the testing came. They learned that the inflammatory posters had said that they were not to be touched because they had no firearms, as others had. Heywood Horsburgh of the CMS also learned at Chengdu that the rioters there had been told to leave the CIM untouched—until they gave sanctuary to the armed missionaries. Horsburgh's own calm and good humour seemed to influence the rioters so that they did not go beyond petty pillage at his place.[1103] Mrs Ririe told her parents that she saw the riots as Satan's show of anger for their 'working in his camp', and as good preparation for 'greater trials than this'. 'What we do feel (aggrieved over) is that such accusations as eating children and other vile sins too bad to mention should be put down to the name of Jesus' followers.'

Three CIM women in Qionglai near Chengdu at the time of the riots were not only taken into the *yamen*, but were 'saved from a riot by the headman of a secret rebel society . . . The very men who helped to smash the RC mission to pieces took (the women's) things to the *yamen* for them.'[1104]

At Guan Xian, Guangyuan, Yibin, Luzhou, Wanxian and other cities, the mandarins did 'all in their power' to protect the missionaries and their homes, but half-heartedly at Langzhong. And at Chongqing summary execution was promised to anyone who incited to riot or even spread wild stories.[1105] A clear picture was emerging of the general situation. Much seemed to depend on the attitude of individual officials, with little encouragement from their seniors to protect the foreigners. The relative value of firearms and friendliness left no room for doubt. And as striking as the danger was the unrealised presence everywhere of many who had become truly friendly to the missionary.

Considered conclusions (autumn 1895)

After most of the dust had settled, Hudson Taylor summed up his impressions in a letter congratulating the Riries for their good spirit and wise behaviour:

> I am convinced that missionaries who are going in for forcible claims and demands for punishment are, as you say, missing a grand opportunity for witnessing ... I doubt whether twenty years will make up for the practical misrepresentation of Christ which this action amounts to.

> It seems that the consul has made a great mistake in blaming you. You have acted according to the principles of your mission, which principles have received the official commendation of consul, consul-general, ambassadors, and have received at least the tacit approval of the Foreign Office ... they have published commendation of the action ... in the Blue Books ... I should be thankful to believe that none of our missionaries under any circumstances would be induced to take any steps to seek the punishment of those who may

have wronged them ... Christ's commands to us are unmistakable—'Resist not' and 'Resent not'. If obedience to Christ leads to martyrdom, even, it is none-the-less our privilege and duty.

I am very sorry for the under-officials who have been kind and done all they could for us and others. To treat them as if they were offenders is to make enemies and not friends ... Express (to the magistrate) our gratitude and belief that the riots were as truly his misfortune as our own.[1106]

John Stevenson had returned home to Britain, and Hudson Taylor at Yantai was very frail. William Cooper was at Shanghai in the administrative 'hot seat' when Hudson Taylor wrote: 'I would advise that a statement rather than a claim of losses be given to the consul . . . If the Emperor has ordered that losses be made good, then there seems no reason to refuse it.' But already the Leshan mandarins had given the Riries (unasked) 1,000 taels to repair their house, and 1,000 taels for personal losses.[1107] However, some CIM Sichuan missionaries had written about the 'glaring neglect of the officials'. 'Plenty of others have written and spoken of that, and it is not the CIM role.' He also wrote to the editor of the *Chinese Recorder*:

It is a serious question in my mind whether our work suffers most or gains by (asking) the interference of our government in such cases as Chengtu and Kucheng. It is true that pecuniary compensation may be obtained, and the missionaries reinstated ... but what of the effect of all this ... Are such appeals even good policy? ... Is it not that the missionary, if more dreaded, is also more disliked ... and that his converts also are more hated? ...

A former American Minister to China says, 'The theory of any body of men and women coming ... to a strange land and enduring hardships for the good of the people was something that no Chinese intellect could comprehend, not even the intellect of Li Hung-chang. There must be some ulterior purpose. And he would insist on associating the gospel with the sword, and see in the devoted persons who ... preached Christ, the men who had battered down the Taku forts [Dagu,1860] and forced opium upon China.' Must not the effect of appeals necessarily strengthen the belief of the literati that missions are a political agency designed, together with opium, to facilitate the absorption of China by foreign Powers? ...

A Chinese official must also necessarily look upon a foreign resident as a source of danger and difficulty. He never becomes a source of emolument, but he may become a cause of loss or ruin ... If a mandarin can keep us out, it must appear to him good policy to do so ...

The effect of appealing on the (Chinese) Christians: is it not to lead them to lean upon man rather than upon God? ... The teaching of Scripture on the matter (leaves) no uncertainties. 'Christ also suffered for us, leaving us an example.' I submit that our Saviour's command, 'Be ye wise as serpents and harmless as doves' distinctly forbids the carrying or use of firearms or other deadly weapons for self-protection, if it is not intended to use them, then to display them is to act a lie ... The Holy Spirit ... distinctly teaches us (1 Peter 4) to do good; to suffer for it; and to take it patiently ... No riot takes place without His permission; no persecution is beyond His control. 'The weapons of our warfare are not carnal'.

We have the example of St Paul in making known to the local governor a threatened danger and, therefore, have warrant for obtaining the friendly help of local officials ... (and) in pleading his Roman citizenship, 1. to prove that he had been punished wrongfully at Philippi; 2. to prevent his being wrongfully beaten at Jerusalem; 3. for the protection of his life by appealing to Caesar; but in none of these cases did he demand the punishment of the wrongdoers. Should we fail, however, to secure the friendly help and protection of the Mandarin we still have God to depend upon; and may count on grace to enable us to bear whatever He permits.[1108]

The Sichuan viceroy's order that telegraphic communication between Chengdu, Chongqing and Shanghai should be stopped, quickly gave rise to wild rumours of 'a fearful massacre of all missionaries . . .

The China Inland Mission premises at Paoning [ie Langzhong] are said to be destroyed and its members hunted about like wild beasts.'[1109] It was not true. Anxiety in the homelands led some to ask for more news. Hudson Taylor's laconic answer, among many matters connected with routine administration of several hundreds of members' affairs, was simply, 'Had any missionary been murdered I would have wired.'

On the British government's insistence, Viceroy Liu Pingzhang, of whose complicity there was no doubt, was degraded and transferred.[1110] But widespread unrest continued and the consuls forbade foreign women to return to Sichuan. News of the sufferings of Chinese Christians tended not to be reported to the same extent. *The Times* of September 5, 1891, said, 'Men, women and children are murdered by scores, their little property is destroyed, and hundreds of them are refugees from mob violence.' The same was true of 1895. In contrast, Joshua Vale on returning to Chengdu found himself feted by the mandarins.[1111] Light and shade chased each other across the face of China. But the massacre at Kucheng threw black shadow over everything else.

'Kucheng massacre'
(March–August 1895)

In almost ninety years of Protestant missions in China no atrocities like those in the Indian mutiny and in Africa had befallen the missionaries. Ones and twos had lost their lives by violence and many had narrowly escaped. In 1891 Dr John Rigg of the CMS in Fujian had been thrown into a cesspit and barely escaped alive. Two women missionaries had night-soil poured over them. Anything could happen in Fujian, where the expanding Church had thrived on frequent persecution. The Kucheng district (known now as Gutian, but honoured for all time as Kucheng) had a flourishing work of the CMS under Robert Stewart and his wife, and of ten single women of the CEZMS and two of the Victoria (Australia) Church Mission Association. All were under Stewart's

supervision. Like the CIM women on the Guangxin River they lived in Chinese style, 'going in and out among the (Chinese) women'. Eugene Stock's account of what happened on August 1 needs little amplification.[1112]

In March 1895 a religious sect of so-called 'Vegetarians' in rebellion against the authorities posed a danger to foreigners at Kucheng, eighty miles north-west of Fuzhou. On the consul's advice the women and the Stewart children withdrew to Fuzhou until the threat had receded in June. Twelve miles from Kucheng the mountain village of Huasang at two thousand feet offered relief from the great heat of summer. The missionaries had two small bungalows and met for conference coinciding with the Keswick Convention in the last week of July. In the final communion service on July 31 they all repeated together the words,

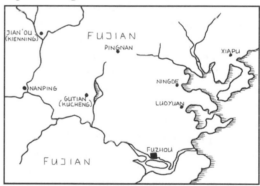

2.72 *Fujian, showing Kucheng and Kienning*

> Here we offer and present unto Thee, O Lord,
>
> ourselves, our souls and bodies,
>
> to be a reasonable, holy, and lively sacrifice unto Thee.

Early the next morning before some of the party were dressed, about eighty of the sect descended upon them and in a few minutes nine missionaries were dead, two small children fatally wounded, a fifth CEZ lady left for dead, and both houses in flames. The children's nurse, Lena Yellop, 'died covering the baby from the brutal blows', but two older children, one also wounded, escaped with two little brothers and the year-old baby from the burning house and fled to a nearby dwelling. Miss Codrington, 'terribly wounded, disfigured and mutilated', joined them there.[1113] A doctor called from Kucheng arrived the same evening, and the following afternoon the Kucheng magistrate with a hundred soldiers, by which time the attackers were far away. The Stewarts' ashes and the remains of the dead woman were taken to the city and sent downriver to Fuzhou with the wounded. One child died on the way, and a second a day or two later.

Wherever the news arrived, a sense of horror seized the secular and Christian worlds. Cries for vengeance from Hong Kong were rejected by the CMS and CEZMS. Instead the Exeter Hall in London was crowded on August 13 with sympathising friends from fellow-societies. Theodore Howard and William Cassels, whose appointment as Anglican bishop in Western China had just been announced at Keswick, took part.[1114] 'Not one bitter word was uttered; nothing but sympathy with the bereaved, pity for the misguided murderers, thanksgiving for the holy lives of the martyrs, fervent desires for the evangelisation of China.'

J. W. Marshall, father of one of the victims, preached to his congregation at St John's, Blackheath, on the words, 'Not unto death, but for the glory of God, that the Son of God might be glorified thereby.' The widowed mother of two Saunders sisters, trained nurses who died together, took her bereavement as an honour from God. She determined to go to Kucheng as a missionary, to see for herself 'a memorial of precious living stones', Chinese converted through their sacrifice—and did so. No clearer demonstration of forgiveness, love and heroism could have been given. 'Within a few months of the massacre there were more Chinese inquiring about Christ in the province of (Fujian)—in the Kucheng district itself—than ever before.'

D. MacGillivray, in *A Century of Protestant Missions in China*, 1907, concluded his account with the words, 'Thousands of converts have come from this blood of

the martyrs.' Not a hundred years later the truth was hundreds of thousands. On August 28, 1895, the remaining CEZMS missionaries issued a joint letter saying that for each of their four dead colleagues they were asking God for ten to replace them, forty in all.[1116] Early in 1897, Miss Codrington herself returned to Kucheng, no less to the amazement of the Chinese, and stayed to become the senior missionary of the CEZMS.

'Throughout the foreign communities of China great excitement prevailed, since it was felt that the lives of no foreigners were any longer secure.'[1117] Lord Salisbury's protest to the Chinese government resulted in the execution of some of the murderers, but when he asked the CMS and CEZMS what compensation he should demand, they told him they would accept none. Neither society wished to appear vindictive or to let compensation for wrecked property be regarded as indemnity for lives lost. The Zongli Yamen told Sir Claude Macdonald (O'Conor's successor as British minister at Peking) that this 'high-minded attitude commanded (their) profound respect and esteem'.

Hudson Taylor's encouragement to the CIM 'to remain at one's post' and 'rely on the living God alone for protection . . . not to yield to the spirit of unrest' was written in the shadow of this seeming tragedy; and it seems from letter after letter as the decade advanced, with a deepening premonition of a greater price to be paid for the soul of China.

Muslim rebellion and Xining siege[1118] (1895–96)

Eighteen years had passed since Yakub Beg died suddenly at Kashgar on May 1, 1877, and the great general, Zuo Zongtang, captured the city. His army was known to have halted to sow and reap a harvest on which to live, still far from Kashgaria. When they crossed the awesome Tianshan range by the almost unknown passes (used earlier by Colonel Nikolai Prjevalski), suddenly to appear before the walls of Aksu, they achieved complete surprise. The Muslim rebellion in the north-west had ended with the loss of millions of lives. In the affected part of Gansu only a tenth of the Chinese population was said to have survived, and one in three Muslims. For his part in Zuo Zongtang's campaign, William Mesny had been promoted to what he called in English 'Brevet-Lieutenant General'.[1119]

Muslims were widely spread throughout China, but congregated in some regions. Hezhou (now Hezuo) in Gansu was the home of thousands of 'Salars' and the seat of Arabic-speaking scholars. In 1875 it had been the scene of an uprising, savagely suppressed. Xining, sixty miles east of the Qinghai Hu (Lake Kokonor), lay in a narrow valley at eight thousand feet, reached by two mountain passes from Lanzhou, another hundred miles to the east. A fine city with high, strong walls, it was the home of twenty to thirty thousand Han Chinese, who had expanded into a large west suburb. In the east suburb ten thousand nominally Muslim families, very

lax in their religious observances, carried on the major trade in Tibetan and Mongolian wool. They dispatched it by camel train through Ningxia to Tianjin, or by raft to Lanzhou and beyond when melting snows fed the Huang He (Yellow River). Chinese and Muslims lived contentedly side by side with Tibetans, Mongols and aboriginal communities until early 1895.

The long tentacles of 'the octopus mission' had reached Xining in 1885 when George Parker and W. F. Laughton first lived there in an inn, until able to lease a home of their own. The Cecil Polhills took over from them for three years while travelling and learning Tibetan, and then were followed by James C. Hall. H. French Ridley had spent three years at Ningxia before he married and took his wife to Xining. Every day Hall and Ridley preached in open places along the streets of the city and suburbs or in a shop front to standing audiences of 100 to 150 friendly people. But none showed deep interest in the gospel.

For 250 years there had been two sects of Muslim Salars in Gansu, originating from Samarkand and related to the Turki-speaking Uighurs of Hami. At the time of the 1785 uprising at Hezhou they were either Shiite, known as Red Caps, or Sunni Muslims, called White Caps. But at Xining the wealthier, more powerful Muslims were called Black Caps. Strict Muslim missionaries from Turkey and Arabia had concentrated on the Black Caps for nearly a decade, until friction between them and the lax White Caps resulted. But all alike were waiting for the Chinese empire to become embroiled in a foreign war to avenge the holocaust of the 1870s.

The Sino-Japanese war was the signal. Hostilities began when the Salars wiped out a small city garrison. The Chinese responded energetically. Ninety miles from Xining, only three days in the saddle, ten thousand Salars were routed early in 1890. Their defeat roused Muslims of all sects, and the cold-blooded slaughter of nine hundred old White Caps and women and children infuriated them further. Reports reached the coast that the Silk

2.73 *Zuo Zongtang, conqueror of Kashgar and viceroy of Jiangsu, Jianxi and Anhui*

Road was impassable, Liangzhou cut off and Lanzhou fallen. This was untrue. But throughout Gansu the missionaries were isolated and Shaanxi expected to be involved. 'Take any action you may deem necessary,' Hudson Taylor instructed G. F. Easton, the superintendent. George W. Hunter, apostle of Urumqi in later years, but already winning his spurs in Gansu, was away from home in Hezhou when the city fell to rebels. Many believed that if it had continued, the revolt would have swept across China to Peking.

From February the Chinese of Xining were asking the Ridleys and Hall to stay, saying they 'felt safe' with them there. So they went on preaching until July 23, while the Muslim rebels came closer and closer, destroying everything and everyone in their way. From the city wall Ridley watched village after village in the surrounding countryside go up in flames. July 24 was the day of decision. Floods of refugees filled the city; excitement became intense. The Ridleys had money enough and at first could have left, but felt sure it was God's will for them to stay—even though refugee children and babies 'terribly hacked about' made them fear for their own six-month-old infant. After that the roads became impassable. Every night four thousand men on the city walls kept watch for attackers.

It was no time for preaching, but what else could the missionaries do? After four days a beggar pleaded with them to go to the Confucian temple and see the state of the refugees crowded there. They found the temple filled with lacerated women and children who had been thrown into flaming buildings yet had somehow escaped, terribly burned. An indescribable stench kept ghoulish onlookers at a distance, their noses in their sleeves, doing nothing to help.

Without medical training the Ridleys set to work, dressing the burns and wounds with cotton wool soaked in vegetable cooking oil, until darkness fell. The officials learned what they were doing and asked them to continue the next day. The city governor sent barley gruel for the patients. Day after day from morning to night they went from temple to temple and to public buildings, sewing up sword cuts with silk thread and dressing burns, using what native medicines they could buy, sulphur, alum and borax, and 350 feet of calico for bandages. Smallpox and diphtheria broke out and took the lives of almost every child. In the first three weeks they treated 250 diphtheria patients. Soon it was nearly one thousand. Ridley himself nearly died of diphtheria. The dead were simply thrown into the streets. Yet the Muslim suburb remained apparently loyal and the city gates stayed open until a small city under siege only twenty miles away fell to the rebels and three thousand Chinese were butchered.

Then suddenly, on Sunday evening, September 1, when Xining was packed with fifty thousand people, the suburb joined the rebellion. Hundreds of wounded again thronged the Ridleys, brought on stretchers or carried on men's backs. Mrs Ridley stayed alone in the house with her child, treating those who came to her, while Hall and her husband went out to work on their two thousand patients. One day she 'cut out' three bullets before they returned, using a pocket knife. Some people changed the name tablet on their house from Good News Hall to Save Life Hall.

After an ambush and night attack on September 21, it looked as if Xining was lost. But a large Chinese force was on its way from Lanzhou and the Muslims turned to intercept them. Hudson Taylor (Jennie wrote) would lie awake praying about Xining. Then a telegram from Redfern in Lanzhou reported that the siege had been lifted. 'Xining open—letters arrived here— all well—no cause for apprehension—we are able to remit.' Ridley's sangfroid and Redfern's misunderstanding at Lanzhou together misled the directors. Ridley's messages had been carried at night by army couriers using circuitous mountain tracks. In fact the worst period was beginning. Redfern himself died of typhus on February 6, 1896. From September to January the relieving force were hemmed in among the mountains without sufficient food or clothing. Another force from Shanxi took more than four months to reach them. Supplies were captured on the way to them. A thousand men, half the force, were lost before General Tong Fuxiang's loyal Muslim cavalry from the eastern provinces, under a General Ho, broke through to the survivors and with them reached Xining on January 14, 1896. It seems also, from our documents, that at this point General Sun, Dr Douthwaite's Yantai friend, came on the scene and befriended the missionaries.

Until then the mandarins of Xining[1120] had prevented the city people from slaughtering the Muslims in the suburb. At last the demoralised populace rebelled and turned on their rulers. The general had to rescue them, 'half dead'. But when a mounted Salar attack was made in February on defenceless Chinese, the troops and city people retaliated together. Thousands were slaughtered in the Muslim suburb amid horrendous scenes of cannibalism, and thousands of Muslim prisoners were beheaded daily in batches of fifty or more until October 1896. The toll of dead amounted to forty thousand Chinese, of whom ten thousand were soldiers and forty thousand Muslims, including ten thousand who died of exposure among the twenty thousand who retreated westwards towards Kashgar.

For more than five months the Ridleys had no contact with the outer world and for nine months received no supplies. In April 1896 Mrs Ridley went out to Lanzhou for a few months, but returned to Xining in October 1896, this time to clothe and feed Muslim survivors through the winter, for all were reduced to beggary. The Ridleys themselves could barely find enough to live on until the governor discovered their sacrificial existence and supplied them with sacks of flour until they left, 'saying we had done so much for the people he could not take money from us'. The wife of another official insisted that Mrs Ridley go to her house for a meal from time to time.

After two years, February 1895 to January 1897, it was all over. 'All the country now opened up to us—everywhere we go we find a warm welcome . . . "What, don't you know me?" they asked. "You saved my life in the rebellion!"' But the whole area had been devastated with hardly a house standing. Not in twenty years could it be restored to normality.

Tibetan Pioneer Mission[1121] (1895–1904)

Annie Taylor and her Tibetan Pioneer Mission were in trouble before the end of 1894, unfortunately, trouble of her own making. Her colleagues rejected her leadership and she herself went up to Gnatong at 12,350 feet on the Sikkim Tibetan border, with Pontso her Tibetan servant for company. 'We are the last but on the way to Tibet,' she wrote, not far from a military outpost of huts within a stockade. Tibetans from all parts of Tibet came there to trade, and she spent her days among them. A Danish member of their team had died of typhoid, but Pontso, ill at the same time, recovered. Bonfires had to be lit to thaw the ground so that the grave could be dug. Instead of men she asked William Sharp to send women pioneers, saying:

> The Tibetans respect women and do not even in time of war attack them. The political parties of India and Tibet are not so likely to look with suspicion on women missionaries ... They must be ready to endure all kinds of privation; to roll themselves up in blankets and sleep out in the snow; to live at times on barley flour alone ... to live as much like the Tibetans as possible.

By January 25, 1895, William Sharp was writing to ask if Hudson Taylor would take the Pioneer Mission team into the CIM. They had signed the same 'P and P' as the CIM when joining Annie Taylor. And in April he asked him to visit Kalimpong to meet the team. The tensions in China were too great for Hudson Taylor to be away, so Cecil Polhill-Turner went instead, until October. The men impressed him. He suggested bringing them to China if the way to Lhasa did not open by the end of the year. By June 6, Annie Taylor had moved sixteen miles further in, to Yadong in the Chombi valley inside Tibet, welcomed by the Chinese officials to open a medicine shop. Her courage could not be questioned.

At long last the Sichuan riots had simmered down, the Kucheng massacre alarm had proved to be localised and not the first of widespread attacks, and Tong Fuxiang's troops had put down the Muslim revolt at Xining. Writing to John Stevenson in Britain, Hudson Taylor said on January 18, 1896, '(Xining) is safe, thank God.'[1122] And in a note to Gansu in mid-October he showed how he felt for the front line missionary. 'You have lived in our hearts daily, almost hourly, and when awake through the night . . . may He preserve you in safety at this time of peril.' That same day he and Jennie boarded a ship to Calcutta. Robert Wilder and John R. Mott had asked him to speak at student volunteer conferences in Indian cities, so before going up to Darjeeling he took part at Benares, Agra and elsewhere. News of Redfern's death in raving delirium followed him. As he daily prayed for all his long list of missionaries, he knew the dangers nearly all were facing, and the difficulties from inflation following the war. 'If we do all that we can and ought, we can leave the results with (God)' he wrote to Walter Sloan as they neared Calcutta. While he was there, on February 19, Hsi Shengmo died after a long illness, and David Hill of typhus on April 18.

In Darjeeling Hudson Taylor shared Cecil Polhill's impression of the Pioneer Mission team. They showed great potential. Some chose to stay in India—six were to come soon to China—the Polhills and a young family would follow later. In China they were to be known as the Tibetan Mission Band, an associate mission of the CIM under Cecil Polhill's leadership.[1123] The Taylors sailed away again on March 10 and were in Shanghai to receive the six men, Soutter, Neave, Moyes, Amundsen, Johansen and Sorensen, and to send them up to Hankou *en route* for Sichuan. The Anqing language school had lost its principal, H. N. Lachlan, by a sudden stroke.[1124] 'We are utterly perplexed to know where to get anyone to take his place,'

Hudson Taylor confessed. When the Cecil Polhills arrived they lived in one of the forty large Tibetan inns at Kangding until they were able to rent a house and bring the team to Kangding as their base. From there the gospel in print and by word of mouth was sent, they believed, to widely scattered parts of Tibet from which the many traders came.

Tibetan sequels[1125] (1895–1905)

The lure of Lhasa continued to induce men and women to undergo the hardships of Tibetan travel. In January 1895 as the Salar rebellion began and Annie Taylor occupied Gnatong, a Berkshire landowner, St George Littledale and his wife set out from Kashgar for the same goal. Like everyone else they failed, but were only forty-nine miles from Lhasa when they were turned back and began the painful exodus to Ladakh. Henry Savage Landor entered Tibet on July 13, 1897. But the strange drama of Petrus Rijnhardt again breaks upon the Gansu and Tibetan scene at this time.

He married the Canadian doctor in 1894 and with her returned to Gansu. They were at Kumbum, where William Rockhill had lived for a month in the guise of a pilgrim, not far from Xining, when the Salar rebellion reached them, and the epidemic of smallpox and diphtheria. Fearing for their safety, the abbot of the great monastery invited them to move in, and there they stayed through 'the months of terror', learning Tibetan. With the return to peace they transferred to Danka (Tankar) on the Tibetan caravan route to Lhasa, and on May 20, 1898, set out in Tibetan dress with three servants, five saddle ponies, twelve pack animals carrying provisions for two years (with more they had sent ahead), and their son Charles whose first birthday fell on June 30. The hillsides were ablaze with flowers and 'we all sang for very joy', Susie Rijnhardt wrote.

But soon two of their men deserted, the five ponies were stolen, Charles died 'inexplicably' in Petrus's arms, and two hundred miles from Lhasa they were intercepted and told to return. With persuasion the outpost guards allowed them to make for the Tashi Gompa monastery on the headwaters of the Lancang Jiang (Mekong River), known there as the Za Qü (Tsa-ch'u). But on the way they were attacked and robbed. Across the river lay a Tibetan camp and Petrus waded in to parley with them. Then Susie saw him turn and start back. He rounded a big boulder—and was never seen again. When Susie gave up waiting and set off eastwards she saw that on the near side, not far up, lay another Tibetan encampment. She could only surmise that this was the robbers' lair and that Petrus had been killed or drowned. Whether she knew of his past history, we are not told. For two months she struggled on, to turn up at Kangding in November 1898, emaciated and frostbitten, to be nursed back to health by the Cecil Polhills.

The story must be ended without elaboration. Polhill, William Soutter and another, William Upcraft, travelled out over the 15,000 to 16,000 feet passes crossed by James Cameron in 1877 and by Susie Rijnhardt more recently, to visit Batang. Later on, Soutter went again, fell ill with typhoid on the way, and Susie went to look after him. He died and was buried 'in full view of the glorious, dazzling, snow clad Mount Nenda'. Susie eventually remarried and returned in 1903 to Kangding in the Foreign Christian Missionary Society, but died three weeks after giving birth to another son. A colleague, Dr A. L. Shelton, established work at Batang, but years later was killed by robbers.[1126]

Major H. R. Davies, author of *Yunnan, 1891–1900*, a notable traveller, turned up at Kangding on June 20, 1900, with two friends on their way from Yunnan via Litang to the coast. Who should he find living quietly in this out of the way place but Cecil Polhill? They had been at Eton together.[1127]

In another category of traveller, a Japanese physician, Ekai Kawaguchi, entered Lhasa on March 21, 1901, purporting to be Chinese. No missionary attempted it again, but the gospel was given to Tibetans in the Moravian field of Ladakh, on the Sikkim frontier, through the work of the Scandinavian Alliance Mission and Annie Taylor, and along the border with Xinjiang, Gansu and Sichuan over the years, through the CIM and C&MA. Small numbers of Tibetans came to faith in Christ.

In 1902 Russia's annexations, an unending story, led Lord Curzon to fear her intentions towards Tibet and India. On August 11, 1902, the British minister in Peking reported signs of an agreement whereby Russia would give China protection against other powers in exchange for her predominance in Tibet. Curzon briefed Francis Younghusband in May 1903 on what was to be a secret mission, but loud protests from Russia and China against his first moves drove the British government to strong, overt measures. Promoted to the rank of lieutenant-colonel with one thousand soldiers, ten thousand carriers, seven thousand mules, four thousand yaks, six camels, two maxim guns and four field guns, Younghusband entered Tibet through Gnatong and Yatong on 'one of the most contentious episodes in British imperial history'.[1128] The gallant Tibetans would only negotiate outside Tibetan territory, so Younghusband attacked and seven hundred Tibetans died at Guru on the way from Phari, at fifteen thousand feet the highest town in the world, and more in the Battle of Karo Pass at sixteen thousand feet, the highest recorded battle.

The Dalai Lama withdrew from Lhasa leaving no one to negotiate. So, after fruitlessly waiting, Younghusband himself left Lhasa on September 23, 1904 (and was knighted for his achievement), but civilian residents remained on friendly terms with Tibetan authorities, until they too withdrew in 1905. No proof of a Russian involvement with Tibet ever justified the invasion. But at the time high-handedness towards China seemed to be justified after what had happened in 1900 to the legations in Peking and numerous British subjects throughout the Chinese Empire.

'My head, my head' (1895–98)

A chronology of this post-war period is packed with more detail than most. The only way to present it intelligibly is to separate the main components of a kaleidoscopic jumble. Hudson Taylor's part in each story emerges incidentally, leaving an impression of a leader who has at last devolved the routine running of the CIM upon others while keeping his hand on everything. Standing back from detail he is sensitive to the mood of China and faint with apprehension of what he sees approaching. Yet, because the main task is still far from done, he believes that it must continue, 'if the Lord tarry'—however great the blood-price to be paid. We are left with a medley of matters which touched him intimately.

In April 1895 he and Jennie set off together to visit the main mission centres on the Yangzi, but she had to be left at Yangzhou with infection of a foot (erysipelas). His notes to her spoke often of being 'fit but feeble', or of resting and sleeping on the river steamer instead of working. He felt the need of 'the True Solomon's wisdom' for many hard decisions as he planned for the growing complexity of the mission. If missionaries' children could stay at Chefoo while their parents went on leave to their homelands, costs would be lower and furloughs more frequent, as urged by some advisers. So a 'preparatory' school for younger children was the answer.[1129]

On his 63rd birthday, May 21, 1895, he was feeling years older mentally and physically, but wishing he could write 'a little sketch of the Mission', a 'chatty, readable book' on China and progress so far towards her evangelisation. He complimented Lindsay, the current sub-editor of the *Millions*, on a job well done and suggested that he put together the materials for such a book. When Lindsay fell ill, Hudson Taylor completed his own account, *After Thirty Years*,[1130] as a factual, statistical statement of policy and fulfilment, to supplement Geraldine Guinness's 'chatty, readable' *Story of the CIM*. Conscious of a duty to report to donors and to keep the church informed, because the will to contribute funds always existed, he wrote for thinking Christians. And he corresponded at length with Walter Sloan instead of with Theodore Howard and Benjamin. For Howard had enough on his hands and Benjamin had formally retired in January after reaching sixty-six..

On March 8 the Mission's offices moved from Pyrland Road to the new building at Newington Green, but Benjamin stayed on at No 2 to pursue his anti-opium campaign until he died in 1911. Hudson Taylor wrote of 'our home', 8 Pyrland Road, having been sold for £570, a loss of £130—since the area had gone down in 'respectability' as the advancing tide of building engulfed it.

When John Stevenson was due to leave China to arrange for his family in Scotland he found it hard to go, for both Hudson Taylor and William Cooper were in precarious health. But he left on May 11, 1895. The news of Sichuan was 'not reassuring' and Hudson Taylor was painfully concerned for the missionaries in Gansu as the Muslim rebellion escalated. By mid-July he and Jennie were at Chefoo, both unfit for work, he hardly able to sit up. Henry Frost, visiting China to convalesce, was also seriously ill again. Many references to Hudson Taylor's head being unable to take more strain, or to neuralgia, stop short of a diagnosis in medical terms, unless as warnings of a threatened stroke (see 1, p 91).[1131] When they intended to return to Shanghai, the cholera epidemic in Chefoo decided them to stay there, if only as a comfort to others. In this condition he dictated his general letter about 'rebellion in the air', calling for a day of prayer for China. 'On all hands there are evidences of a great internal upheaval,' he said, listing the major examples.[1132]

But Chefoo always did him good. A month in the magic of 'Chefoo air' saw him

2.74 Benjamin Broomhall, CIM General Secretary, UK, 1878–95

'at his best', alert and competent, finding staff for the schools and planning the new Boys', Girls', and Preparatory School buildings, with F. J. Cooper, the architect's assistant before joining the Mission. They were at the same time planning the sanatorium and an isolation block. In mid-August 1895 workmen began on the schools, and the foundations were in by mid-September.[1133]

After his return from Barclay Buxton's convention in Kobe, September 10–18, the Riries' fine spirit through the Leshan (Jiading) riot confirmed his belief that the Mission would rise to any occasion. 'If obedience to Christ leads to martyrdom even, it is none the less our privilege and duty,' he wrote. The foreign powers were uneasy about China's instability and kept naval vessels on the move from port to port to 'show the flag'. Then cholera struck at Wenzhou in October 1895 and the Taylors took the first possible steamer, to be with the shocked survivors. Nine Chinese and three missionaries had died in the CIM premises, leaving Bella Menzies bereft of her husband and child. 'How to shepherd the six or seven hundred Christians at Wenzhou and Pingyang (Bingyae) we do not know,' they wrote. 'The dialect is spoken nowhere else.' Charles Fishe went down for a month to do what he could, followed by the Coulthards. Again it was his own family whom he sent to the danger spots.[1134]

'The most trying (year) that has ever been experienced by missionaries in China' came to an end with fifteen of the CIM dead from disease but not one from violence. And 1896 began with trouble from two familiar quarters rearing its head again. As Hudson Taylor was leaving for India on January 18, 1896, to help the disintegrating Tibetan Pioneer Mission, he asked Dixon Hoste to represent him in arranging for the CIM to hand over all its commitments in Taiyuan to Dr Edwards and the 'Shouyang Mission'.[1135] Once that was done, the most urgent need was to return to Europe, to straighten out an accumulation of problems with associate missions.

The CIM was still in the throes of transition, of persuading the older members to accept the authority of leaders other than Hudson Taylor himself.[1136] As for Dixon Hoste, the ten years spent with Hsi Shengmo while he supervised fifteen to twenty local churches with four ordained pastors, had done much to fit him for the years ahead as a leader of a mission to Chinese. Hsi's own tribute was, 'In all matters connected with Church or Refuges, Mr Hoste and I have united in prayer and consultation . . . We mutually help one another, without any distinction of native or foreigner, because the Lord has made us one.' Hsi's death on February 19, 1896, released Hoste to go on home leave, the last of the Cambridge Seven to do so.

Radical resolution of the chronic Shanxi problems led Hudson Taylor to observe, 'Come what may, we ought to have unity and peace among ourselves.' The same thought had decided him, when he regained his own health and China was quieter, to return to Europe while John Stevenson was still there. He needed to work out with the continental associate missions some kind of uniformity in place of their existing diversity, 'to unite many bands into one CIM'.[1137] If uniformity could not be reached, it would be better for each to go their own way, as the Bible Christians were doing. Where difficulties arose from one godly man's inefficiency as an administrator, a new appointment would be enough. Uniformity need not mean rigidity, he demonstrated repeatedly, for when circumstances differed he responded with flexibility. But there was strength in all sharing the same principles and basic practices.

For two months William Cooper would have to carry the burden of supreme leadership alone in China, but Hudson Taylor had full confidence in him. He did everything well and made no mistakes. The appreciation was mutual. 'Thank you for giving me the privilege,' Cooper wrote, 'of reading so many of your letters.' One particular feature of Hudson Taylor's letters won his correspondents' hearts, his familiarity with their children's names and progress. His caring betrayed his faithfulness in praying for them. This alone contributed largely to making the CIM a family.

That the skill in letter-writing which Cooper referred to was infectious had become apparent in Jennie's letters, too. Years as her husband's amanuensis for confidential letters led her to her own style becoming almost indistinguishable from his. Keeping other directors informed while he was away from home, and in spiritual counselling Jennie performed a valued service. Geraldine's sister Lucy Guinness wrote, 'I wish I were like her.'[1138] Jennie also kept a close watch on the many births to young families, to be sure of writing and of remittances being adjusted to include them. Children of CIM missionaries by then exceeded two hundred in number, and by May 1895 several had become full members in their own right: Herbert, Howard and Maria Taylor, Gertrude, Hudson, Marshall and Edith Broomhall, three of James Meadows' daughters, others of the Rudland,

Fishe, Baller and Williamson families, and more preparing to join in. Ernest Hudson Taylor, by then a chartered accountant, arrived in China on February 9, 1898, the fourth Taylor to join his parents.[1139]

On May 2, 1896, the Taylors and Dixon Hoste sailed from Shanghai with the Eastons (free to leave the north-west once the Muslim rebellion was over), with the widowed Mrs Redfern of Lanzhou and her children, and several others. They arrived in London on June 17. Hoste left them at Colombo to visit relatives, and barely survived a severe fever contracted there. Convalescing in Scotland, he then fell ill with typhoid and needed months of rest. Gertrude, his wife, was to visit Australia for a tour of meetings to speak about China, so Dixon joined her there before returning to China to become superintendent of Henan.[1140]

This was Hudson Taylor's nineteenth voyage and tenth period in Britain. Uneventful journeys could never be taken for granted. In June 1897 the SS *Aden* was lost with the lives of four CMS and other missionaries on board. Two CIM travellers had tried and failed to get berths on the ship. In October the Ballers survived a fire on their ship, and a month later the SS *Kaiser-i-Hind* with a CIM party was nearly lost in a typhoon in the South China Sea.[1141] Hudson Taylor's party were travelling at the time when every available berth was filled by people returning home for Queen Victoria's Diamond Jubilee celebrations. Hot, airless cabins and incessant noise and crowding on deck and in the saloons made it barely tolerable.

Too late for the annual May meetings he sent a written report of 'in many respects the most remarkable year we have ever experienced', of deliverances outweighing the setbacks. Growth and expansion of the Mission's work had continued in spite of all the upheavals. At the end of 1895, communicant Christians in churches served by the CIM had risen in number to 5,208 and mission centres to 135 with 126 substations. Organised churches had increased in the year from 149 to 155, with

461 paid and unpaid Chinese cooperating with 641 CIM missionaries. By May 1896 the number had become 672, and a year later 720, with income keeping pace in every home country.

On August 17, 1896, before visiting Germany, he began with another profitable tour of Norway and Sweden. The associate missions' leaders welcomed the invitation to become more closely knit to the CIM, agreeing to adhere to the same 'Principles and Practice', and Erik Folke of South Shanxi was made an associate superintendent with a seat on the China Council meeting each October.[1142]

Two weeks after Hudson Taylor's return on September 10, John Stevenson sailed for China, again leaving his wife and family at home. Hudson Taylor sent him on his way with a note of sympathy and thankfulness that with William Cooper and Walter Sloan the four of them enjoyed strong links of confidence and love.[1143] Stevenson, however, soon showed that he had been under heavy stress and was not really well enough to shoulder the burdens of his directorship in China. Before long he was at odds with Cooper, and Hudson Taylor was exhorting him to treat Cooper as 'a junior partner', not an inferior.

Through the autumn of 1896 an incessant round of speaking engagements kept Hudson Taylor on the move, working at full pressure, while news of one after another desperately ill or dead, kept coming to him. 'Headache and neuralgia' dogged him until in 1897 it became too much.

What of 'the Thousand'? (1895–99)

Five years had passed since the Shanghai Conference and the appeal for one thousand men within five years, and also for women. Hudson Taylor as the originator of the call, and chairman of the permanent committee, in May 1895 issued a report.[1144] Forty-five societies had sent a total of 1,153 reinforcements during the five years. Of these 672 were women (167 wives and 505 unmarried) but only 481 men. Of the 1,296 Protestant missionaries in China in

May 1890, only 589 had been men. The number had not even been doubled, and 'not a few' had died or retired from China in the same period. So not half the goal of one thousand men had been reached. Nothing was to be gained by claiming success or satisfaction. The report therefore ended, 'Will not the Church arise and take immediate and adequate action to meet the pressing needs of this vast land?' The church of every land should be active in sending its best young men and women to the far corners of the earth—young, if they were to learn new languages and adapt to new conditions.

In May 1890 the CIM had 383 members, and in May 1895 had more than 620. By the end of 1899 the CMS had added 'more than Eight Hundred names . . . to the roll' of their members in Africa, India and China. Ninety-three went to China between 1895 and 1899. Those close to the need were right to ask for large reinforcements, and societies whose leaders took it up had no lack of offers to go. But some mission boards, committees and churches in distant homelands seemed too remote and deaf. They needed more than an appeal.

What the historians have noticed was not an expansion of evangelism 'to every creature', though an effort was made, but a rapid expansion of 'Christianity' in China, which continued well into the twentieth century after the spiritually productive interruption by the Boxer rising.[1145] K. S. Latourette saw in this period a parting of the ways between orthodox missions and institutional societies, though many of the theologically orthodox societies did have ambitious schools, hospitals and presses. After twenty years, St John's College in Shanghai was teaching theology in English, with the whole range of Western learning in that language open to the graduates. By 1895, 143 Protestant doctors were running seventy mission hospitals and training 170 medical students, as well as serving opium refuges and widely distributed clinics. Well-meaning attempts to avoid overlapping succeeded to some extent, some missions being careful to consult with others before moving into already occupied districts and cities. Others saw room enough for all and a duty to present their own particular emphases, where exponents of different views of doctrine and church government were already established. Institutional societies and liberal, and foreign ways came more and more to share the field with the evangelists intent on first planting a spiritual church.

Good relations between the CIM and the Anglican Church took a new turn in 1895. Nominally the bishop of Anglican missionaries and churches in West China, George Moule had found it impossible to go two thousand miles to fulfil his duties in Sichuan. His crook, he told Cassels, was not long enough to reach so far. Heywood Horsburgh and his CMS team in West Sichuan, and W. W. Cassels, E. O. Williams, Charles Parsons and the CIM in the eastern half were witnessing a Chinese church enlarging on the Anglican pattern, but without a bishop. The CMS conceived the perfect answer. Without altering in any way Cassels's position as the CIM superintendent, informally advising the CMS team, his consecration as Bishop in West China would meet the ecclesiastical needs as well.[1146] With Hudson Taylor's approval, consultations in London and in China by John Stevenson with George Moule, resulted in Cassels becoming a full member of both missions. On the CMS payroll, he could continue as a member of the CIM China Council with his home and office at Langzhong. The Archbishop of Canterbury agreed.

Cassels and Beauchamp were sharing the missionary platform at the Keswick Convention with Amy Carmichael and Dr Herbert Lankester, Medical Secretary of the CMS, when the appointment was announced. Supporters of both the CMS and CIM approved, but each society received protests against association with the other body, of which the protester could not approve.[1147] The consecration by Archbishop Benson took place on October 18, 1895, in Westminster Abbey, and the Cassels family sailed for China a week later.

A close neighbour during their furlough in England had been the mother of Elsie Marshall, one of the CEZMS missionaries murdered at Kucheng (Gutian) (see map 2.72, p 593). The Sichuan riots were barely over, the siege of Xining was at its worst. The 'progressive' phase of the work in Sichuan was merging into the phase of 'opposition'. The charge William Cassels had accepted at the age of thirty-seven was no sinecure.[1148]

Hunan at last[1149] (1895–98)

Hunan and Guangxi were never far from Hudson Taylor's thoughts. Moving forward meant taking the gospel to those deprived of it. From the time of the Yangzi valley riots of 1891 until early 1896, Hunan seemed inaccessible. Whoever undertook to attempt the evangelisation of Guangxi became diverted by one thing or another. Even Shashi, Dorward's base with its nucleus of Christians, had to be worked as an outpost from Wuchang. Shishou on the Hunan border could only be visited from time to time, although a dozen believers were waiting to be taught. With Zhang Zhitong's return as viceroy, and a friendly governor of Hunan who set himself to eliminate public prejudice against foreigners, the prospects were brighter than they had ever been.

Early in 1890 a Presbyterian minister in the CIM, George Hunter (unrelated to George W. Hunter of Xinjiang), came to China with Hunan as his objective, but the death of the Chefoo schoolmasters Norris and Elliston created an urgent need which Hunter was asked to fill. In 1895 when Frank McCarthy, John's son, arrived to begin his outstanding thirty-five year headship (March 1895–summer 1930), George Hunter was free to begin. He took his family to Yichang and began travelling over Adam Dorward's old trails to Jinshi and Changde with his evangelist companions. He found the people friendly, wanting to know more about the outer world and Western progress.[1150] In September 1897, Dorward's friend the evangelist Yao succeeded in obtaining a deed of rental at Changde and T. A. P. Clinton moved in. A month later two men of the C&MA, Chaplin and Brown, gained a foothold at the other side of the city. By the end of 1899 a church of thirty-five members with six preaching chapels had grown out of the Changde root. But in March 1900 George Hunter had his baggage on a boat, ready to start from Changde, when he fell ill with a high fever and died within a few days.[1151] Even at the turn of the century the price of opening Hunan was to be high.

By 1898 several missions were approaching the province from different directions. Griffith John appealed for men to work in Hunan; the LMS established outposts in the Hengzhou region and openly baptised converts. The CMS tried to enter from Guilin in the south. And when the appearance of electric lighting in the governor's residence betokened a change in attitude to new ideas, B. Alexander of the C&MA tried again and again to get a footing in the capital city, Changsha.[1152] But lasting success came to Chinese missionaries from Hsi Shengmo's church in Shanxi and his opium refuge strategy, and to Anna Jakobsen, the one-time housemaid of Kristiansand, Norway.

She had come to China in 1885 with Sophie Reuter (Stanley Smith's wife), and spent nearly ten years at Huo Xian (Hochow) in Shanxi. Longing to tackle Hunan, the province that defied Adam Dorward and all the men who had attempted to occupy it, she knew that being unmarried was a major obstacle. Early in 1893 she became engaged to marry an evangelist named Cheng Xiaoyu, believing that here lay the key to acceptance in the hostile province. She had not considered the repercussions upon other single girls in the Mission. John Stevenson and Hudson Taylor persuaded her to think again, and for five years she followed their advice.

In the summer of 1896, however, she moved from Shanxi to Jiangxi to join A. E. Thor and his wife, intent on going into Hunan. Hsi Shengmo's friend, the evangelist Ren, who had also been concerned about Hunan, went ahead to rent premises, and started an opium refuge at the village of Chenghuang on the Hunan border. When Anna Jakobsen arrived, Hunanese women thronged to see her. One invited her to visit the wife of an ex-official who wished to break free from his opium addiction. Through him she found accommodation at Shengguanshi, near Chalingzhou, on the main route from Jiangxi into south-eastern Hunan, and quietly moved in. Here, too, she was well received.[1153] After three months she handed over to Ren and two other Christians from Pastor Hsi's area, and herself returned to Shanxi. This time she was determined to marry, to the alarm of John Stevenson and the superintendents, not through prejudice against inter-racial marriage—Minnie Parker had shown how successful that could be—but for fear of how her example would affect scores, even hundreds, of unmarried women missionaries, especially in the Guangxin River region of Jiangxi. So far they had been a phenomenon apart—no Chinese had looked on them as eligible for marriage. A Cheng-Jakobsen marriage could expose all the single girls to unwelcome attention by unsuitable men, if not to danger.

From England, Hudson Taylor wrote to Stevenson, 'Mr Hoste told me that there was a great danger of her heading a party of (Chinese) and together breaking away from the Mission—that good woman as she is, she is becoming a source of danger since the death of Pastor Hsi.' Since single women in the CIM first went into the interior of China, criticism had been strong in secular and missionary publications. Even one case of such a marriage going wrong could justify the pointing of accusing fingers at the Mission. Parents in the homelands might feel justified in refusing to allow their daughters to join the CIM if it did not protect them from reduction to a position as subservient daughters-in-law in unsympathetic families.

Anna Jakobsen was unmoved by their persuasion and by the fact that most missionaries in Shanxi were firmly opposed, for an ordained member of an American society agreed to perform the ceremony.

Hudson Taylor tried from a distance to dissuade him. Letters and even telegrams had no effect. A few CIM colleagues stood by her, weakly claiming afterwards that their motive was sympathy rather than approval. And as no church was open to them, the ceremony took place in a photographer's shop. The consul responsible for Norwegian affairs declined to recognise the marriage, and the American consul denied the right of the missionary to perform the ceremony. She had rejected all advice and had chosen to marry out of the CIM. What became of her subsequently is not apparent, but the work she and her Chinese colleagues had started in Hunan went on from strength to strength. The only clue lies in a note to 'A. Jakobsen Cheng' asking them not to complicate the lives of sister missionaries by returning to Jiangxi.[1154]

Towards the end of 1897 when A. E. Thor visited the city of Chalingzhou, he found a congregation of thirty, another solid result o f the evangelists' efforts. Months later, on October 26, 1898, Frank A. Keller moved into new premises in the city. Keller was an outstanding young German American physician, a travelling secretary of the Student Volunteer Movement in the States before joining the CIM. Friendly mandarins sent policemen to every shop in the city to say that the foreigner must be well treated, ensuring peace for a few months. But threats by the literati to kill Keller's landlord and destroy his medicine shop began to circulate. Keller's companion, a teacher named Li who had become a Christian through teaching the missionaries, proved to be like the devoted colleague who said to George Hunter, 'If you mean business, if you're going to preach and are ready to endure hardness, I will go with you', not otherwise. Together Li and Keller went through the 'house-warming' the mandarins could not prevent.[1155]

Big gifts bring problems (1895–97)

The instability of China made nonsense of any plans for organised expansion and advance. But there was still plenty of scope. The country was wide open. George Andrew walked 2,432 miles in Yunnan, Guizhou and Sichuan in the course of his service as superintendent, without being molested. The Burma frontier agreement made Tengyue a trade centre, a good base between Dali and Bhamo for work among the many border tribes (see map 2.59, p 480). Sam Pollard at Zhaotong and James R. Adam at Anshan could scarcely cope with the opportunities among the Miao of Yunnan and Guizhou. In spite of Montagu Beauchamp's indefatigable evangelism, large areas of Sichuan remained untouched. Hudson Taylor was thinking in terms of 'Spirit-filled Chinese' to reach 'this generation' and of twenty men of the Botham and Ririe type, wholly given up to evangelism. Many worked steadily but not intensively as they did. They should devote five years to this work, without thought of marriage for five years at least. Jiangxi offered the greatest promise, and in Archibald Orr Ewing had the right leader for five new districts with training centres in each for Chinese evangelists.[1156]

In 1895 Hudson Taylor had completed his reorganisation of the London staff. With Walter B. Sloan as Hon. Senior Secretary, after Benjamin's retirement; Miss Williamson of Shanghai in charge of accommodation at Newington Green; Graham Brown in Scotland; Marcus Wood in London for the male candidates and Henrietta Soltau for the women; and with William Cooper as Assistant Deputy Director in China helped by C. T. Fishe, 'Never before were we so well prepared for definite advance.' His emphasis on maintaining the pressure where it was possible received what he regarded as strong confirmation in two forms. In the three years 1894–96 the CIM received 221 reinforcements without special effort[1157] and 1897 began with forty more asking to be sent. Among all these were a few of whom he had great hopes. At the same time several large gifts and legacies were made conditional upon advance in specified directions.

Back in April 1891 when John Stevenson arrived in Scotland to care for his ailing family, he had met a Mr Gregg[1158] who took a close interest in China. This first link in a chain of events had immense consequences, for through Mr Gregg's contacts with a friend in England, he also became interested. This friend, J. T. Morton, had made a small fortune as a wholesale provisions merchant, and kept a yacht on which he wintered at Mediterranean ports, returning to Britain for the summer. At Dartmouth he met James Williamson, veteran of the *Lammermuir*, and questioned him about the CIM. As a result J. T. Morton began to send books and later ordered the despatch of crates of canned groceries to many CIM centres in China, in time for the Ridleys to survive the Xining siege by careful rationing of his bounty.

On June 15, 1895, J. T. Morton wrote to Hudson Taylor from 107–109 Leadenhall Street. If 'more extensively establishing schools in the different stations of the CIM (is in line with CIM's policy) it will give me great pleasure to assist you with pecuniary help. (Also) in training adult Chinese converts to act as evangelists, teachers and pastors,' he would like 'to help to initiate work of this kind where it does not at present exist'.[1159] Three months later a pencilled note from the philanthropist Robert Arthington read, 'You will receive within a few days a sum of money left by my sister for the China Inland Mission. I should like to see the whole of the aborigines of China embraced in a comprehensive well-arranged plan for evangelisation.'[1160]

Specification of how donations were to be used created its own problems. Their use depended on the availability of suitably experienced missionaries, and care needed to be taken to avoid weakening the indigenous church by encouraging dependence on foreign aid. Hudson Taylor advised that rather than ask individual missionaries to correspond with Mr Morton about his allocation of funds, it should all be done through John Stevenson as China Director. J. T. Morton fortunately agreed and the missionaries simply reported to him on progress. In October he sent £5 for each station, requesting individual reports. Difficulties increased. The directors needed to know whether the money was being wisely used, and asked for copies or summaries of the reports. As money given for 'the work', not for personal use, it had to be accounted for, as with all mission expenses.

In forwarding Mr Morton's lump sum to China, Walter Sloan commented, not ungratefully, 'It does seem a pity when we so sorely need money for the very carrying on of the work, that a large sum like this should be . . . a difficulty in the hands of workers who do not know how to utilise it.' For months on end donations had been minimal for 'general' purposes. 'What lesson should we be learning?' William Cooper asked Sloan. 'May we have the grace and wisdom to learn (it) quickly.' Perhaps the chief lesson was for the church at home to trust the experts overseas to apply funds wisely where advance could best be made. Somehow enough always arrived, often from unusual directions, and 'straitness' (as they called the thin times) taught the Mission that living 'off the land' instead of dependence on stores from the coast was not only salutary but more economical by far.

Writing to William Cooper in August 1896 about the Morton money, Hudson Taylor stressed that Chinese schools should be opened only where the missionaries could commit them to really suitable Chinese teachers and not themselves be side-tracked by new responsibilities from evangelism and teaching of believers. 'I have further pointed out (to Mr Morton) the inadvisability of doing for (Chinese) Christians anything that they are able to do themselves, and that it is much better to make help given stimulate them to help themselves, and to assist them in doing so.' J. T. Morton quickly saw that the men on the scene were best placed to judge how to apportion the money, and accepted Hudson Taylor's advice.[1161]

Meanwhile he was following the CIM's affairs with greater interest. Realising that epidemics of infectious disease in the Chefoo schools could become dangerous, he offered to pay for a site and buildings for an isolation block and sanatorium. On November 20 Hudson Taylor wrote to tell John Stevenson that Mr Morton was intending to make a substantial donation towards the new girls' school and building. Work on it had been halted when the building account ran dry, and in studying the accounts Hudson Taylor had pointed out that one of the missionaries in charge was consistently overspending. Some lessons in bargaining with contractors were needed. His letters were precise as to facts and figures, clear as to meaning, and careful to avoid misunderstanding between John Stevenson and William Cooper.

By June 1897 the pace had proved too fast and his strength unequal to demands. 'Great weakness and prostration' following 'mumps' and 'neuralgia' were preventing work altogether. Walter Sloan called it 'serious collapse from overwork'. Whatever it was, he recovered in time to face the stresses of September.[1162] On December 18 the difficulty was over. J. T. Morton sent £400 and work resumed. The boys' school was a separate project, financed by Orr Ewing, but Mr Morton wanted a hand in that too. His donation was received in February 1897. E. J. Cooper, the architect, reported to Hudson Taylor on September 1, 1896, that the roofs were going on and the final west wing being started. All work was being done 'in accordance with your desires, namely "*substantial* and characteristic (of the CIM, that is); at the same time *economical*."'

J. T. Morton's involvement became deeper month by month. On March 12, 1897, he instructed William Cooper to 'give me timely advice when you require additional money' for the sanatorium.[1163] Plenty of surrounding land should be provided 'for seclusion and relaxation', at his expense. And on May 5 he suggested twelve houses with gardens for missionary families convalescing or on short leave at Chefoo. Each letter pressed William Cooper to get on without delay, not realising that in China urgency put up prices and apparently endless patience saved large sums. By June 11, Hudson Taylor told Stevenson that he had been given *carte blanche* to buy up whatever land was necessary at Chefoo to allow the whole area to become one property. And after recovery from his serious illness and convalescence at Davos, he wrote that on September 1 the sum of £10,000 had come from J. T. Morton, without restrictions on how it was to be used.

The Morton legacy (1897–98)

Mr Morton's health was in a precarious state. If he died within a year, Hudson Taylor pointed out to Stevenson, at least £1,000 would be returnable as 'legacy duty'. In fact he died the day after sending the cheque. The Taylors left Davos on September 22 and two weeks later he wrote again. 'The death of Mr Morton considerably alters the position of things regarding expenses at Chefoo.' He had bequeathed his fortune of over £700,000 in equal amounts to four societies, the CIM, the Waldensian Church, the Moravian Mission, the Aged Pilgrims Friends Society, and further sums to others.[1164] But inexplicably his will left his wife and one of his sons and his employees 'hampered'.

Hudson Taylor was asked to hurry home from Stockholm, where the Swedish Mission in China were facing crucial decisions. Mr Morton's son was preparing to challenge the will in court.

In a letter of October 29, 1897, to John Stevenson, Hudson Taylor revealed how his own thoughts were shaping. The possibility of an income of £10,000 annually from the legacy for 'forward movement' struck him not only as an answer to prayer, but as an emergency. The Mission was unready, even unworthy of it. 'We are sorely needing fresh life infused into every part of our work; without this, (the legacy) may prove the greatest misfortune we have had for a long time; while inapplicable to general fund, it might lead (other) donors to withhold (their gifts), thinking we were rich.'

But also a misfortune if it led the Mission to neglect its dependence on God alone. Hudson Taylor planned to come out to

China to discuss 'a well-concerted plan for definite evangelistic extension'. He intended inviting Dr A. T. Pierson and Mr Inwood of Keswick to tour China to 'stir up the Christians to evangelise their own people'. 'Spirit-filled' Chinese were China's best hope, but Pierson and Inwood would also gain from the experience, 'so that when they returned to Europe and America they may set the Churches on fire'.

In his editorial in *China's Millions* for December 1897, under the title 'This Generation of the Chinese', he reiterated George King's strong appeal for Shaanxi, applying it to the whole of China. When King wrote in 1883 he was alone at Xi'an and Easton alone at Hanzhong. Since then the two outposts had become twenty and the two missionaries, seventy-seven. From there being no Chinese church at all in the province, a church of five hundred Christians had developed. This progress must continue.

In *China's Millions* of February 1898, Hudson Taylor wrote again, plainly stating the facts of the Morton legacy—'a share of the residue of his estate', an unknown amount, to be released by the trustees as not more than one-tenth in any one year, and to be used only in China (not even for related expenses in Britain or for sending missionaries out). Before the needed evangelists could be sent, however, the greatest need was for revival among the eighty thousand Protestant communicants in China and the missionaries already there. 'We may be quite sure that the spirit of evil will also be active.' The opposition since the appeal for the Thousand has been 'as never before'. A new advance such as this legacy seemed to justify could be expected to meet with the same response, so all should pray 'that in every way Satan's power may be curbed'.

Writing to Walter Sloan and William Sharp on January 29, 1898, Hudson Taylor expressed his opinion, 'that the question (of Mr Morton's legacy) is one of principle and not of expediency'. He knew his family's and his firm's circumstances when in good mental health he made his will,

and once the Mission received a donation it ought to be used for the purposes specified. It placed the CIM in a difficult position, in which to accept a legal judgment would be quite different from arbitrarily dividing the bequest made for evangelism and educational work in China because of claims upon it. 'The loss of the whole legacy [in court] would not be so great an evil as the loss of a conscience void of offence.'

So the matter went to court and the CIM was awarded £187,500 in trust. Although contested until March 1899, payment began in September 1898 and, continued until 1916 when the last sum of £250 was disbursed. At that point the 'Borden legacy' began to come in. Not only so, but word came in August 1898 of yet another will leaving £20,000 to the CIM.[1165]

Before any of this money became available in China there were months of painfully low transmissions from the homelands. With the Mission growing all the time, in May 1896, for the sixth month in succession, less than £1,000 came from Britain. To be unable to respond to estimates of expenditure from all 'stations' 'is a great strain' on the China directors and treasurer, William Cooper admitted, 'but Jehovah Jireh! (the Lord will provide) we will not fear'. When £1,400 arrived in December he wrote, 'the Lord be praised. He is faithful!'

Funds were forwarded when they became available, and belts were tightened and prayer became more realistic when, as sometimes happened, the message was, 'Sorry, but we have nothing to send you this month.' In some way or other 'the Lord will provide' has always stood the test. Large sums for special objects remained untouched, in keeping with the principle reiterated by Hudson Taylor: 'Nothing could be more contrary to the wishes of Mr Morton than to use his legacy as practically part of the general fund. Through years of correspondence with him I have never known him to propose giving one pound to that fund . . . God clearly gave us this money for a Forward Movement.'[1166]

The 'Forward Movement' seemed on course for ultimate fulfilment, but restraints of one kind and another, and premonitions of approaching distress appeared more and more likely to the Mission's leaders as China's own agony deepened.

'On a volcano' (1896–98)

At the annual meeting in May 1897, Hudson Taylor spoke of the growing number of Chinese church members, doubled in the last seven years to reach eighty thousand; and immediately went on to quote one of the Kucheng martyrs.

> 'What have we to face in China? God and the devil!' She speaks of what a solemn thing it is to be brought face to face with the great enemy of souls, and to know all the time that you are sitting, as it were, over a volcano which, apart from God's restraining power, may burst-forth at any moment ... God withdrew the restraint, and she and her fellow-workers were honoured with the crown of martyrdom ... While we are meeting here, it may be, some ... in some part of China are in extreme danger.[1167]

So far, still, in the thirty years of the Mission's history not one CIM life had been lost by violence. Daring policies and deep penetration into remotest China had been justified. But recently one mission and another had seen God's restraints removed. Hudson Taylor saw no reason why the CIM should be an exception. Writing from Frankfurt for his daughter Amy's twenty-first birthday, he thankfully observed that during her lifetime the only death in their family had been of one grandchild.

After the May meetings he was unwell for two months and confessed to John Stevenson he was finding the incessant demands on his strength more than he could bear. He ought to 'get away' and hoped to visit North America and China on the way to Australia and New Zealand. *China's Millions* reported 'quite a serious breakdown in his health', asking readers to spare him unnecessary business. Jennie took him to Switzerland where he relaxed and soon recovered.[1168]

But there at Davos he received a letter from William Sharp, the lawyer, urging him to name his own successor and to replace John Stevenson. Stevenson, he alleged, was alienating more and more members by unfeeling harshness in his administration. Sharp, it seemed, still had an ear for the disaffected. Then a cable brought news of Jennie's sister Nellie Fishe's death from 'heat apoplexy', leaving Charlie with five motherless children in China and five older ones in Britain. Maria (Taylor) Coulthard wrote on the same day to say that her year-old baby had died of dysentery at Wenzhou.

But in Stockholm a serious difference of opinion had arisen in the central committee of the Swedish Mission in China, and Hudson Taylor hurried over for two days' consultation. A baroness whose daughter wanted to join the Mission insisted on her being allowed to marry before going to China, and opinion differed sharply in the committee on whether the two year marriage rule should be relaxed. Some thought their circumstances exceptional in view of her social status. So serious was the rift that the survival of the Swedish Mission was at stake, but to Hudson Taylor the case was clear. To make an exception to the rule on this ground alone would not be keeping faith with others who had been held to it. What was needed was a friendly search with the couple for a way out that did not involve compromising principle. Together they found it. They could marry and go out independently to join Erik Folke as associates. Only actual membership of the Swedish Mission would be sacrificed. In China they would be no less part of 'the family' of the CIM. To have guided the committee back to agreement was a greater achievement than finding the solution.

From Stockholm he crossed the North Sea to Edinburgh to keep some appointments, and to his surprise found Jennie waiting for him at Mrs Kalley's (see p 415). She had news to break to him. Maria herself had died of dysentery shortly after her baby.

By November he could delay his return to China no longer. John Stevenson's apparent inability to work with William Cooper demanded his presence. Satan 'like a roaring lion' seemed insatiable in seeking whom next to devour. But William Berger was unlikely to live much longer, so Hudson Taylor paid a quick visit to Cannes (November 12–17) to say goodbye. After an express return journey his train back from Paris to Boulogne was travelling slowly from the town to the pier when it became derailed and his carriage thrown on its side. He was extricated with difficulty, but unhurt, and a week later (November 24) sailed with Jennie, Miss Hanbury (the hymn writer?) and Henrietta Soltau for New York.[1169]

Henrietta recollected that on this journey; all the way to China, he spent hours talking with fellow-passengers, for he was always an evangelist. But at other times he sat for hours deep in thought, and when he spoke 'Forward Movement' seemed to preoccupy him. Litigation over the Morton legacy would only affect the ultimate amount. The central fact remained unaltered: God had provided a massive sum for advance when advance seemed thwarted by few men of the right kind being available, and by China appearing at flash-point. What was God saying? That setbacks were secondary, delays immaterial and the devil's counter-blows to be parried or endured? How did the fulfilment of his dream of twenty years fit in with the opening of the Burma frontier, a British Commercial Resident and two CIM missionaries established at Tengyue and the Arthington bequest for the evangelisation of the aboriginal 'tribes'? (After J. R. Adam's successes among the Guizhou Miao, Hudson Taylor had thrown his arms around his neck and thanked him when they met in Scotland.)

With a succession of encouraging developments, the time looked ripe for advance. A Chinese Imperial Post had been created by Imperial decree. With an Anglo-German loan for China's reconstruction; with the Yangzi River open to foreign shipping as far as Chongqing, and steam-launches attempting to ascend the rapids in the gorges;[1170] with an agreement signed with Russia for a Chinese eastern railway in Manchuria; with Belgium contracting to build a Peking-Hankou railway; and with the French demanding the right to engineer a Tongking-Kunming line—in a word with China opening up for freer, faster access and communication—the call for missions to move forward sounded loud and clear. Except for the volcano.

What did Li Hongzhang's humiliation mean, after his return from Europe? Representing the empress at the coronation of the young Tsar, and honoured also in Germany, France and Britain, he had arrived back in 'remarkable vitality and spirits', only to be accused of 'trespassing' in the grounds of the Summer Palace, and fined a year's salary (37,000 taels) by Ci Xi, allegedly for remarking in her presence on the beauty of the Tsarina.[1171] During his absence from the country the emperor's mother had died in suspicious circumstances, the finger of accusation pointing once again at Ci Xi. What would this capricious woman be up to next? What threat to China's security lay in Russia's railways (even if called Chinese) with wide swathes of territory and their inhabitants each side under Russian control? And in French, Belgian and other lines to the very heart of China? The danger of China's dismemberment by Western nations struck Hudson Taylor as being a greater threat to the spread of the gospel than any opposition by the Chinese. At a stroke the Roman Catholic nations, or for political reasons the British, in control of a 'sphere of influence' could ban or hobble missionary activity as they were doing in their colonial territories elsewhere.

Even before the Taylors' journey started, the process soon known as 'slicing the melon' had begun. On November 1, 1897, two German Catholic missionaries of the Society of the Divine Word were murdered in Shandong. In retaliation a German force seized the port of Qingdao (Tsingtao) at the mouth of Jiaozhou Bay on the 14th, and to legalise their action, on March 6 wrested a ninety-nine year lease of the city and environs of Jiaozhou (Kiaochow) and Qingdao, and obtained exclusive railway and mining rights in Shandong province.[1172] On December 18, the day that the Taylors left San Francisco to cross the Pacific Ocean, Kaiser Wilhelm II informed Chancellor von Billow: 'Hundreds of thousands of Chinese will quiver when they feel the iron fist of Germany heavy on their necks.' Bombast as it was, the speech made history and branded 'the lawless West' in the eyes of the world. At a time of her own choice China would wreak revenge.

Only a year before, twenty leaders of Protestant missions in China had submitted a memorial to the Zongli Yamen for presentation to the emperor, asking for an edict banning slander against Christianity and reaffirming religious liberty. 'Instead of falling behind to rank among small nations,' they urged, '*China should rank among the greatest in the world*.' Hudson Taylor had joined his long-standing friends and younger men in signing it: Muirhead,

Burdon, Griffith John, David Hill, Young J. Allen, Timothy Richard and Gilbert Reid among them. After Timothy Richard had been granted interviews with the Zongli Yamen and with some ministers individually, he reported that: 'If these had their way there would be an end to our trouble at once. Indeed there was a general feeling for a few days among the mandarins and scholars of Peking that the memorial was approved of by the emperor, and that an edict would be issued within a few days.'[1173]

Unfortunately the Manchus were not of the same mind. 'They seemed to have made up their minds that Christians are all a bad lot.' So no more was heard of the gesture. After the volcano erupted the sinister hand of the empress dowager could be recognised behind the fate of the memorial. In days to come friendship unsoured by treachery and bloodshed would succeed where words were impotent. But the mailed fists of nominally Christian nations would first make the word of all Christians seem untrustworthy.

1898–1900: THE REFORMERS

Reform and reaction (1898–99)

'The abasement of China . . . produced a profound effect on the educated classes' of China. Blind refusal to learn its lessons characterised the empress dowager and her coterie of mostly aged advisers. Enlightenment of the more open-minded, predominantly younger men, but not exclusively, set them on a course of reform. While Sun Yatsen and the impatient activists took to armed protest and attempts to seize power as revolutionaries, Kang Yuwei, 'the Erasmus of the reform movement', opted for constitutional reformation. Only a republic would satisfy Sun, but Kang worked for reform of government and nation brought about by the emperor himself. Kang's published studies of *The Reform of Japan* and the *The Reform of Russia* (by Peter the Great) illustrated his aim, 'a republic with a nominal hereditary ruler', a constitutional monarchy.[1174] The obscurants

were to drive both into exile with a price on their heads.

By early 1898 there were few of the younger mandarins or literati who did not favour reform to some extent. Their attitude towards foreigners showed a marked change, which in places off the beaten commercial tracks benefitted missionaries more than merchants, for 'missionaries were the largest and most widely dispersed body (of foreigners) in China'.[1175] Even the younger members of the Manchu nobility were infected. Every major city had its Manchu garrison quarter, and provincial capitals their powerful enclaves (like the British in India). On April 18, 1898, the *North China Herald* reported the presentation 'by a prince of the blood' of a memorial signed by 1,200 officials and recent *chinshi* (doctorate) graduates, protesting against the government's weak stand against the grabbing Russians in

Manchuria and Germans in Shandong, 'slicing the melon' of the motherland. Even in Peking an outspoken weekly called *Chinese Progress* could count on selling 10,000 copies, and became a daily.

The Imperial Grand Tutor, Weng Tongho, had access to the young Guang Xü emperor and the support of most Chinese government ministers in his patronage of reformers. Prince Qün, the emperor's father, had died in 1891, and Prince Kong died in May 1898, or the sorry events of 1898 to 1900 might never have happened. Li Hongzhang, on the Grand Council, but consigned to the political wilderness, had little influence except from the distant viceroyalty of revolutionary Canton to which he was posted.[1176]

Early in June 1898, Weng Tongho commended Kang Yuwei to the thirty-year-old emperor, who began to read his books, was immediately impressed, gave him official rank, and summoned him to an audience on June 14. Guang Xü's 'introduction to Western learning, under the indirect supervision of W. A. P. Martin, had been going on for some years'. He had been 'enormously impressed' by Timothy Richard's translation of Dr J. K. Mackenzie's 'hymn to the conquests of science and the dogma of progress': *History of the Nineteenth Century*. A million bona fide and pirated copies were in circulation.[1177] Already on June 11, Guang Xü had issued a decree that reform was necessary, but when another on June 13 deprived Weng Tongho of rank and dignities and ordered him home to his native place, the hand of Ci Xi cast its sinister shadow. Another edict commanded all high officials on appointment to appear before her as well as the emperor. And yet another made her old friend Yong Lu viceroy of Zhili and commander of China's best army. After the first decree the wily Old Buddha had scented the wind, had reacted immediately and was ready for more.

At this point in June 1898, Zhang Zhitong, the enlightened viceroy of Hunan and Hubei, produced a literary masterpiece entitled *Learn, an Exhortation to Learning*. Of this also a million copies were soon sold and read throughout the empire. From a platform of admiration of the Confucian precepts and the Qing dynasty, and rejection of republicanism which would encourage insubordination and destroy social stability, he advocated learning from the successful nations. 'Chinese learning for the essential principles; Western learning for the practical application', summed up his argument. So retain the classics and add science. 'Learn' how little Japan became strong. 'Learn' how weak nations—India, Burma, Korea—fell into the hands of the strong. 'Learn' how other nations govern themselves and grow in strength. Send students abroad to 'learn'. Multiply schools at home. Translate books, tolerate all religions, build railways, maintain powerful armed forces. Much of what he advocated has its echo in our own day.[1178]

The Hunanese quickly took 'a leading part in the march of thoughts'. From heading the anti-Christian movement by means of the outrageous Zhou Han publication, *Death to the Devil's Religion*, Hunan became for a time more peaceful than the rest of China. The Society for the Diffusion of Christian and General Knowledge (SDK) with Timothy Richard as secretary, could not keep up with the demand for books. At Changsha a new College of Reform had been established in 1897 and the SDK was asked to nominate a president for it. The sales of Bibles doubled, and foreign and Chinese scholars poured out translations and digests of Western books of learning. The contribution of missionaries became recognised as crucial to this awakening and development.

Timothy Richard, Young J. Allen and Gilbert Reid, through his 'Mission among the Higher Classes in China', enjoyed their heyday.

Timothy Richard had been secretary of the SDK since 1891. Every book of any value was also being pirated extensively, and 'the Chinese names of men like Timothy Richard and Young J. Allen were on people's lips throughout the country'. Kang Yuwei himself told a reporter in 1898 that 'he owed his conversion to reform chiefly to the writings of Richard and Allen.'[1179] Through the SDK's *Review of the Times,* Richard and Allen made their influence felt increasingly. Young J. Allen's keen analytic mind, his ready wit and forceful expression were matched by his striking appearance. Born to be a statesman, he had devoted his talents to the service of missions. By his faithful marshalling of the facts month by month, and his emphasis on the essential weaknesses of China, he aroused public opinion, especially among the official classes, to a realisation that China must either advance or be destroyed.

In a different key, Western dress and rejection of the 'queue' (imposed upon the Han Chinese by their Manchu conquerors) were adopted by the daring. Zhenjiang had its foreign restaurant with knives, forks and spoons. (Singapore led the way with the first automobile, a Benz, in 1898, but Shanghai did not follow, with an Oldsmobile, until 1902.)[1180]

When Hudson Taylor and his companions arrived at Shanghai on January 15, 1898, he quickly detected the new climate. China was seething with conflicting currents. A ferment of new ideas and new activity by both the Chinese and the foreign powers spelt instability, the seedbed of disaster. The daily newspapers reflected the anxiety of the foreign community. Blind avarice led nation to follow nation in stealing advantage from China's weakness.

'Non-alienation' of the Yangzi Valley was agreed on February 11 and of Fujian on April 26, but a Sino-German convention about Jiaozhou and Qingdao on March 6 and a Sino-Russian convention on March 27, confirming the cession of Port Arthur to Russia, took more slices from the melon. A French claim to a lease of the Bay of Guangzhouwan close to Tongking (Vietnam), and a spate of contracts to build railways, carried the tentacles of foreign power further into China's heartland. A Franco-Russian scheme to link Manchuria with Tongking by a joint railway project, like a sword thrust through the heart of China, came to nothing when the other powers called a halt. An American contract

to build a Canton-Hankou line was signed on April 14, and for a British Shanghai-Nanjing line on May 13. Russia secured a contract for a line into Shanxi, and Britain to mine Shanxi's mineral wealth. On July 1 Britain leased Weihaiwei as an answer to Russia's Port Arthur and Germany's Qingdao, and on July 6, Russia concluded another agreement for railway extensions through Manchuria to Port Arthur. Britain disclaimed Shandong and Russia disclaimed Korea, but on June 9 a Sino-British convention extended the leased territories of Hong Kong. More was to follow.

April saw the Spanish-American war over Cuba spread to east Asia, when Admiral Dewey sailed into Manila Bay at 5.00 a.m. on May 1, 1898, and destroyed the Spanish fleet. British colporteurs from Hong Kong had been garotted by the Spanish for taking Bibles into the Philippines. The Philippines were made vulnerable to occupation by any European power, but seemed unready for self-government. So the Americans stayed in control of Manila and Manila Bay. A brief war of independence ended with annexation on February 6, 1899, when the USA promised to hand over government after fifty years of preparation. In the event this took place after the liberation by General MacArthur at the end of the Second World War. The United States had become a colonial power with colonies in the Philippines, in the Pacific at Guam and Hawaii, and in Cuba and Puerto Rico. Suddenly the whole archipelago was free from the medieval grip of Rome and Protestant missionaries moved in. Agonising China saw her own autonomy at risk.

Sir Robert Hart's exemplary management of the Chinese Imperial Customs had so benefitted the nation that at long last the collection of *likin* taxes on internal movements of merchandise was also entrusted to him. Revolt against this innovation almost broke out at Hankou (at a time when Hudson Taylor was there) for private pockets inevitably suffered by the curtailment of corruption. In Sichuan, on the other hand, revolt did erupt and was not finally suppressed until a year later. The

Sichuan riots of 1886 had been attributed by the Chinese authorities to the expanding real estate and secular power of the Roman Catholics, and, as J. K. Fairbank put it, 'the arrogant, even unscrupulous behaviour . . . of converts', especially 'the grip on the local economy' some had gained.[1181] During an attack on the leading Chinese Catholic's home in Chongqing a rioter was killed and the French consul failed to prevent the Catholic being executed.

At about the same time a wealthy Chinese, who became known as Yü Manzi, lost a lawsuit against a Catholic owing, it was believed, to intervention by a foreign priest. Yü's son raised a force and attacked the Catholics, but was caught and executed. Yü then became 'the implacable enemy of all Catholics'. By 1898 he had several thousands of men destroying Church property and making 'over twenty thousand Christians' homeless, according to Lord Charles Beresford in his book *The Break-up of China*. The brash manner of young Lord Charles's visit to China and the crudity of statements in his widely circulated book further incensed the nation against foreigners. Protestant Christians suffered persecution and annoyances, but were not the primary objects of attack as the Yü Manzi revolt continued into 1899.[1182]

The dismemberment of China with regions coming under the rule of foreign powers, while a possibility in the early stages after the Sino-Japanese war, could not materialise because of jealousy and rivalry between those powers, and their preoccupation with commitments elsewhere in the world. But more dramatic events were about to startle everyone.

'The hundred days', too much too soon (June–October 1898)

Between June 11 and September 20, 1898, the youthful enthusiasm of the emperor and the inexperience of the political philosopher, Kang Yuwei, together resulted in a rickety pyramid of seventy-three reforms. Edicts of increasing weight, each sound in itself and necessary to progress, poured out of the palace. But 'the pyramid stood on its apex' and fell in ruins. As Sir Robert Hart wrote to H. B. Morse when it was all over, 'They simply killed Progress with kindness—they stuffed it . . . with food enough in three months for three times as many years.'[1183]

For instance, a decree ordered the Zongli Yamen to encourage art, science and agriculture; another urged speed in constructing the Peking-Hankou railway; another reformed the examination system. The Manchu Bannermen were ordered to adopt Western arms and drill. July saw commands for every province to have its agricultural college, and every city its modern schools and colleges. Inventors and authors were to be encouraged, and protected by patent and copyright laws. Courts of law were to be reformed and merchants to be assisted. In August an Imperial university was established at Peking by decree with the seventy-one-year-old W. A. P. Martin as head of the faculty under a Chinese chancellor and others, and he was honoured by elevation to the second civil rank with a red cap button as worn by viceroys. If disaster had not followed 'it is very likely that Richard would have been invited (on Kang Yuwei's recommendation) to join the inner circle of imperial advisers'.[1184]

On and on the edicts flowed until at the end of August they struck at corruption and began to hurt. Sinecure boards at Peking and duplicate governorships were abolished, as were Salt and Grain Commissioners in provinces which produced no salt and sent no tribute of grain. In the first two weeks of September military conscription was begun, with abolition of the antiquated but honoured 'Green Banner' army. Uncultivated land attached to military garrisons was to be thrown open to the people, and the right granted to all subjects to memorialise the throne. Manchus were permitted to take up trade or a profession which many understood (correctly it may be) as a threat to their idle lives. And annual publication of budgets, receipts and expenditure threatened the age-long corruption throughout the palace and people. For his reactionary attitude and perhaps because of his loyalty to Ci Xi, Li Hongzhang was dismissed from the Zongli Yamen on September 7 and for resisting the right to submit closed memorials to the emperor, high-ranking officials of the Ministry of Rites (including a relative of Ci Xi's) were replaced by reformers.

Reaction by the diehard conservatives became inevitable. They urged Ci Xi to resume power. The emperor decided to strike first. But during 'The Hundred Days' China's ferment broke out in rioting and rebellion, often unconnected with the emperor's reforms beyond the fact that the nation's weakness and a spate of reformation literature were the talk of the teashops. Railways were being extended urgently, without adequate negotiation to avoid disturbing the *fengshui*. A rising in Guangxi quickly gained ground, and continued unquelled for five years. And in Sichuan, Yü Manzi captured two Catholic priests and held one, M. Fleury, for six or seven months. 'Catholic villages were plundered and no priest was safe.' A local uprising had become rebellion against the government.[1185]

Through the autumn and winter, anti-Catholic outbreaks in other provinces took a grimmer form. Riots in Hainan, Shashi, Songbu and Yangzhou heralded the return of the notorious Hunanese Zhou Hun, urging the slaughter of Chinese converts. In Guangdong a priest and thirteen Chinese were killed, while in Hubei a Franciscan priest 'was tortured and beheaded after eight neophytes had been done to death before his eyes'.[1186] Imperial decrees on January 15, July 12 and October 6, 1898, ordered special protection for Christians, but the mandarins' power to prevent outrages depended on local compliance. Too many riots took place to be given prominence in the papers. *China's Millions* recorded those that affected the CIM, with stories of great heroism by Chinese Christians.[1187] Property was looted and destroyed at Changshu in Jiangxi, and at Nanchong (Shunking) in Sichuan.

At Changshu a friendly magistrate was stoned for protecting the missionaries and an unfriendly one who refused to help nevertheless had his own *yamen* destroyed.

As Hudson Taylor explained in *China's Millions,* most of this rioting was in protest against the transfer of inland customs duty (*likin* tax) to foreign administrators. 'Thousands will lose their squeezes and don't like it.' He himself wrote, 'There were riots at Huzhou the day before I arrived. Three men were beheaded . . . You will have learned that (Ningbo, Shaoxing and Wenzhou) have also had riots', from crop failure. Two weeks later he explained that he could not leave headquarters while anything might happen. 'There is serious rebellion in (Guangdong) and . . . nearly half (Guangxi) is in the hands of rebels. The authorities seem powerless to deal with it and France may take the opportunity to do something' by seizing territory. He himself was in better health than for the last three years, but Maria's brother, Samuel Dyer, the Bible Society secretary in China, was dying of high fever.

Part of the trouble was that officials aware of great changes taking place at Peking were feathering their own nests as fast as they could, and the prestige of the Manchus had sunk to danger point. One riot was entirely by disgruntled soldiers on the rampage. Disintegration of the nation seemed a possibility. Drought had struck central China, and famine conditions existed in a broad swathe from Qingjiangpu in Jiangsu to Laohekou on the Han River in Hubei province. George King, newly qualified as a doctor and back in China, undertook the Mission's relief work.[1188]

The Hundred Days came to a dramatic end when Old Buddha decided it should. By then the merchants wanted stability under which to trade; the *laobeixing* ('old hundred names', the proletariat) simply wanted to be left alone; the gentry clung to time-honoured customs, and officials resented interference with their privileges and profits; Manchus saw their ascendancy threatened and the court felt the foundations of the throne shaking. With reformers in one position of power after another, Ci Xi had begun to fear for her life.

'The core of the matter' (1898)

To run your eye down a chronology of this period is to see its confusion in perspective. France's move towards the Sudan, quietly checked by Britain, may explain to some extent the fact that France did not slice off part of southern China while it could in 1898. Britain's preoccupation with the Mahdi, ending in his defeat at Omdurman on September 2 (with Winston Churchill taking part), distracted her from the tempting fruits in China. Sir Claude Macdonald, the minister at Peking, an evangelical Christian, preferred to arrange financial loans to help China's reconstruction. The eclipse of the sun on China's New Year's Day foreboded calamity, a fatalistic thought in the minds of prince and pauper. For Hudson Taylor, holding the reins in Shanghai, it was the year of tension, of danger in Sichuan from Yü Manzi, of the Jakobsen marriage affair, of litigation over the Morton legacy, of Hunan opening fast, of Rijnhardt back in Tibet, and of the very first death by violence in the CIM. The year of the Hundred Days also became the year of the unscrupulous Ci Xi's return to power.

Hudson Taylor's articles in *China's Millions* were as ever the barometer of his thinking. As 'ROCK FOUNDATIONS' reaffirmed the sure ground of truth on which the Mission stood, so it also revealed his sense of approaching trial. Destitution, even death, might be the price to be paid, but 'I will never leave you nor forsake you,' remained God's immutable promise. With that foundation, the *raison d'être* of the China Inland Mission, 'the core of the matter' for which huge legacies had been given was 'forward movement'. Four installments in *China's Millions* kept attention on the subject. Suitable men were slow in offering to give five years to intensive evangelism, but a sensational start was made in Jiangxi under Archibald Orr Ewing's leadership. The owner of a house in Nanchang, Jiangxi, who merely agreed

to sell land to Orr Ewing, received one thousand blows as punishment. Thomas Botham and the Scandinavians P. E. Henriksen and G. A. Carlsson continued their systematic ploughing and sowing of the Shaanxi plains. The pioneers out on the fringes of Gansu, Ningxia, Tibet, Yunnan, Guizhou among the Miao, and at last in Hunan, pressed boldly on. George Andrew went to Guizhou as leader of the dispirited team. Month after month the *Millions* repeated that Xinjiang (Sinkiang) remained 'almost untouched'. George W. Hunter of Xinjiang had arrived in China, and Eva French also, but their own Xinjiang adventures were still years away.[1189]

'The core of the matter', however, was not territorial advance or the dispersal of teams; to Hudson Taylor 'not by might, nor by power but by My Spirit' said it all. Missionaries of all societies needed help in maintaining their spiritual tone, dulled by drudgery or overstrain; help in opening their hearts to be 'filled with the Spirit'. Some had lowered their standards through pride of achievement. The colleagues of an individualistic veteran at Taizhou were waiting impatiently for him to go on home leave so that they could spring-clean the whole mission in the region. Hudson Taylor questioned whether one-third or a half of the people he had baptised were true believers. Only by bringing such men back to humility before God would their work become more than 'wood, hay and stubble'. He asked the Keswick Council to send speakers, 'missionaries to missionaries', and Dr and Mrs Inwood arrived in October to spend months in conferences for members of all societies and foreign communities in the north, south, east and west of China. But since 1894 a more complicated problem had troubled Hudson Taylor. Increasingly he felt that God, by withholding 'general' funds month after month, and the best kind of men to take the gospel to 'every creature', was saying to 'Joshua': 'There is sin in the camp', something to put right.[1190]

'Special support' (1894-98)

A system of 'special support' existed, whereby the friends and home churches of some missionaries agreed together to provide their missionary representatives with regular amounts of money. 'Independent' (self-supported) members of the Mission also had their sources of supplies separate from the funds distributed to other members. No one took exception to the system, for all alike were trusting God for everything they might need, not least for health and protection. But big fluctuations in exchange rates sometimes resulted in those receiving 'special support' ending up with far more in Chinese currency. In January 1894 a difference of forty per cent occurred, affecting Australians more than others.

Another anomaly lay in the fact that overheads (in the form of premises, repairs, travelling expenses, training homes, business departments and Chinese employees) were met from 'general funds' to the benefit of all alike, although 'special support' missionaries' funds were not drawn upon. On May 11, 1894, Hudson Taylor wrote to all concerned: 'Specially supported missionaries are asked to give thought to this subject while all may give thanks that while Mission income has decreased from home sources the change in exchange rates has greatly benefitted the situation in China.'[1191]

By 1896, when copper was becoming scarce in China and copper coins were being smelted down, the inflationary effect necessitated larger remittances to missionaries at a time when receipts were low. In July 1898 the China Council faced the fact that while the estimated 'apparent need' of the Mission in China amounted to £1,500 each month, for three months running only £500 had been transmitted each month from the United Kingdom. Belt-tightening and solemn reviews of expenditure saw them through, and a £2,000 legacy (unknown to them as yet) was coming in August. 'If we do all we can and ought, we can leave the results with (God),' Hudson Taylor remarked.

But beyond asking God to guide and provide, what lessons should they be learning? Both the China Council and London Council agreed that dependence by some missionaries on 'special support' was undermining their dependence on God, apart from their supporters. The time had come to consult both 'special support' donors and missionaries and to propose a change. The risk of losing some of each kind would have to be accepted, in the interests of unity in China and true adherence to the 'Principles'.[1192]

During 1898, when so many tensions took time and thought for the well-being of the widely scattered Mission, Hudson Taylor and the China Council grasped the nettle, obtained the approval of the London and North American Councils, and issued a carefully drafted letter to all members. In it they explained all that was involved and asked for 'hearty concurrence' in its solution.

Any fears proved unjustified. Letters poured in from 'special support' donors and recipients, so that by June 1899 Jennie wrote of 'great joy and thanksgiving' over acceptance of the proposals by all affected. Over the years of continued expansion, with nine associate missions and international developments, the Mission had tended to become fragmented. A need 'to unite as one mission, not separate bands' had become paramount. 'Unity involves diversity', Hudson Taylor said, 'the diverse members of one body animated by one spirit . . . heart unity, not uniformity.'[1193] This unity and trust in God's faithfulness proved to be the cement. The fault had been remedied and the CIM made ready, it seemed, to move forward when peace returned.

'After you die' (1898-1900)

Another issue on Hudson Taylor's mind during these fateful months in the summer of 1898 had been raised by William Sharp in June. 'For the future well-being of the work Mr Stevenson must on no account be entrusted with the principal oversight in China. I doubt if the Mission would hold together for six months after you were gone.'[1194] Sharp's judgment was not always reliable, and this looked like a return to the fault of tales told in London by individuals from China being taken at face value, or of Stevenson's part in earlier controversies having delayed effects. The worst about Stevenson seemed to be brusqueness and sometimes indecision, according to some. No one could work harder or keep his finger more efficiently on a myriad matters at once. Paltry shortcomings mattered little in comparison when big men were scarce. In later years they were to accuse Dixon Hoste of indecision, but both men were imperturbable, waiting until they could see the target clearly before pulling the trigger.

But Hudson Taylor had to take seriously the question of his own successor. Sharp went on, 'I am a good deal struck with Mr Cooper's apparent fitness for dealing wisely and well with whatever may come before him . . . He has qualities evidently suited to the position you have given him.' Here they were of one mind without doubt. If Hudson Taylor were to die, 'who should take the initiative?' The only one Sharp could think of as General Director was Henry Frost, first-rate, but frail and lacking experience as a working member in China. Sharp's letters on this theme continued periodically through 1899 and into 1900. Stevenson 'must know that he is not liked,' and, 'If you *could* work in someone else—say Mr Hoste—it would probably be more agreeable to Mr Stevenson than if Mr Cooper were there . . . You know how willing (Cooper) is for anything—he would gladly go . . . if it would save friction or Mr S.'s feelings.' William Sharp was not surprised to learn from Hudson Taylor that John Stevenson 'commands esteem outside the Mission'. But after Hudson Taylor appointed William Cooper to deputise for him as 'Visiting China Director', to travel extensively trouble-shooting and encouraging the frontline missionaries, Sharp continued to criticise Stevenson. The matter, he said, must be dealt with. Dixon Hoste had 'very valuable qualities

for leadership'. He and Cooper would work well together.

Taking note and replying non-committedly to the importunate lawyer, Hudson Taylor kept his own counsel. Whether he had a written deposition, a directive set aside for the event of his death, will never be known, but the evidence points to the probability that at this stage he had William Cooper and after him Dixon Hoste at least in mind. He showed no anxiety about the possibility of being taken unprepared, and had more serious matters to attend to. The ferment in China was taking a dangerous new turn. Young Guang Xü and Old Buddha were to strike simultaneously.

Plot, coup and counter-reformation (July–September 1898)

While the emperor 'devoured (the Bible) with avidity' (according to Charlotte Haldane)[1195] and poured out his reforming decrees, 'a constant procession of petitioners' besought Ci Xi to intervene and rescue them from the iconoclasts. Egged on by the young progressives, Guang Xü and his mentor, Kang Yuwei, became bolder, striking not only at the evils of weak and corrupt government but at their roots. This could not but excite the hostility of powerful men. Promoting modern military training and examinations in place of horsemanship and archery, brain instead of brawn, angered the old brigade. The venom of reform was stupefying not only the younger literati but the highest in the land.

While Liu Kunyi, viceroy of Nanjing, kept his distance from trouble, Zhang Zhitong dared to add to his doctrine of 'Learn' the accusation that the old conservatives were 'stuck in the mud of antiquity'.[1196] Yong Lu went so far as to recommend for appointment a young reformer radical enough later to be executed. Even Old Buddha scandalised the purists by approving an edict declaring that on October 29 the emperor and she would 'travel by fire-carriage on the iron-road to (Tianjin)' (to quote Morse's literalism) to review the modern 'model army'.

But Ci Xi was too astute to be deceived. This thing could end in the taming of the Manchu tiger or even in the republicanism for which Sun Yatsen was on the run. She knew she had two loyal supporters in Li Hongzhang and Yong Lu. Li's dismissal from the Zongli Yamen had ostensibly been because he was too friendly to Britain and too weak in ceding Liaotong to Russia. He approved of modernisation, but opposed sweeping reform and belonged finally to Ci Xi's faction. On September 8, Sir Claude Macdonald reported to Lord Salisbury, 'Li Hung-chang has recently shown himself markedly antagonistic to our interests.' Yong Lu was not only viceroy of Zhili at the gateway of Imperial China, Tianjin, but commander-in-chief of the whole northern army. In 1895 Yüan Shikai, ex-Resident at Seoul, had been appointed civil commandant of the crack foreign-trained Tingwu division of five thousand troops. Yong Lu's elevation to the viceroyalty and army command therefore made him Yuan Shikai's direct superior. Yuan was in his prime, and Yong Lu already in his late sixties.[1197]

The rising head of steam behind the reform movement had already made it apparently an irresistible force. Domination of the antiquated Manchu system had become only a matter of time. But while the immovable object of the empress dowager's will-power remained, a cataclysmic collision was inevitable. Both decide to pre-empt the issue. Control of the model army would settle it. Constitutionally the emperor, but actually the retired dowager held the key of loyalty. Yong Lu would obey Ci Xi's orders. Yüan Shikai favoured reform. Where did his loyalty lie? All her life Ci Xi had used time to her own advantage, while always ready to strike. She patiently played her reforming nephew's game, intending to consult Yong Lu privately on October 29 when they ventured to ride the fire-carriage to Tianjin.[1198]

Guang Xü feared that at any moment she might veto his reforms and restrict his freedom. He decided to act. Whether on his own initiative or Kang Yuwei's advice he took the only course open to him and sent for Yüan Shikai, who 'convinced him of his zeal for reform'. He then gave him the brevet rank of vice-president of a ministry with responsibility for organising the army, making Yong Lu's northern army command subservient. Finally, on September 20 at a second audience, the emperor gave him a decree investing him with Yong Lu's offices of viceroy of Zhili and direct command of the northern army, and secret orders: he was to have Yong Lu decapitated and at once to bring the army to Peking, to surround and imprison the empress dowager in her Summer Palace, and to arrest the leading reactionaries.[1199]

Between the two audiences Ci Xi had told Guang Xü to arrest Kang Yuwei for slandering her, but instead he warned Kang to flee for his life, armed with an imperial order to establish the official Gazette in Shanghai. Kang at once went into hiding and consulted Timothy Richard, asking him to enlist the support of the British and American envoys. Richard was later rebuked by Sir Claude Macdonald for interfering in affairs of state, but at this crucial moment he and other envoys and Sir Robert Hart

2.75 Yong Lu, viceroy of Zhili and guardian of the throne

were absent from Peking and unable to help.

It so happened that Kang Yuwei and Yüan Shikai with his fateful orders travelled on September 20 by the same train to Tianjin. And Kang, preceded by telegrams to arrest him, after several narrow escapes in which British ships and officials protected him, reached Shanghai and later Europe in safety, with a price of one hundred thousand taels on his head.[1200]

According to Yüan Shikai (in 1911 when his own reputation was at stake), as soon as he met Yong Lu at his *yamen* at Tianjin, Yong Lu said, 'You have come for my head!' claiming that he had already been told of Guang Xü's orders. Either he was bluffing to delude Yüan Shikai, or palace eunuchs had moved to save Ci Xi. But in 1898 the common knowledge believed by the foreign envoys, the reformers and 'generally by historians' after investigation, was very different. By it he reached Tianjin before noon and at once reminded Yong Lu that they were blood-brothers by a pact unknown to the emperor. Because of it he could not carry out his orders and instead revealed the whole plot. Yong Lu left immediately for Peking and the Summer Palace. Ci Xi called in her trusted advisers and with a full plan of counteraction decided, Yong Lu returned to Tianjin the same night. As commanded by the emperor the model army moved on Peking, but to surround the Forbidden City instead of Ci Xi in the Summer Palace.[1201]

On the morning of September 22 the emperor was to give audience to Marquis Ito, a Japanese statesman, but was himself summoned by Ci Xi. 'Like a rabbit mesmerised by a snake' he cowered before her; 'his whole body trembled . . . and his powers of speech left him.' She forced him to sign a decree reinstating her as Regent and confined him to prison on a promontory jutting into the Winter Palace lake, the laughing-stock of lesser eunuchs. 'The Emperor being ill, the Empress Dowager has resumed the Regency' (for the third time) the world was told. This gave rise to considerable anxiety, since it seemed to suggest that with her aid 'Guang Xü would very soon mount the Dragon and go to join his ancestors.'

The real enemy, foreign devils (September–December 1898)

Li Hongzhang was still China's most astute statesman. This trifling with emperors angered him. And Viceroy Liu Kunyi bravely broke his silence to protest in a memorial against it. But Zhang Zhitong quickly played safe by urging action against the culprits. The British and other ministers left no doubt in the minds of the Zongli Yamen that they would take strong action if the emperor's life were endangered, for several navies immediately headed northward—another factor in his survival and possibly in the fate of the legations eighteen months later. Liang Oichao, editor of *Chinese Progress*, escaped by a hair's breadth to Japan, together with a few other leading reformers, but six of the most notable were executed. Others suffered the even harder sentence of exile to the deserts. Yong Lu was elevated to 'a position of power unprecedented in the history of the dynasty', and a decree on September 26 swept away many of the reforms, restored the sinecures and anachronisms, including the hoary sword-brandishing military examinations, but retained some of the educational measures.

As soon as she had suspected what was afoot Ci Xi had sent for the 'coarse old rough-neck' Tong Fuxiang and his twelve thousand Muslim cavalry from Gansu, and thousands more troops from other frontiers to congregate near the capital. The uniform answer from Tong's men when asked where they were going was 'to drive the Germans at Jiaozhou into the sea'.[1202] From then on, the unsettled state of the empire owed as much to this fact as to the palace intrigues. The riots of the spring and summer were followed by more at Canton on October 25, by the first CIM death from violence in November, and by attacks at Yizhou, Shandong, on a German and three Americans. In December two Catholic missionaries were murdered at Yizhou and their missions destroyed.[1203]

But for miles around Peking itself the chief danger to foreigners lay in the teeming presence of the 'turbulent soldiery', of whom the most unbridled were Tong Fuxiang's horsemen, the savagery of the Xining siege fresh in their memories. When some of them attacked members of the American and British legations on September 30, the foreign envoys all sent for their marines to guard them. The approaching winter made early action imperative. In deep winter the frozen sea and land routes could make protection impossible. But on October 23, Tong's men again attacked some engineers and British legation personnel, without being disciplined. The attitude of troops and rowdies became so menacing that the envoys jointly demanded the removal of the Gansu troops to a distance. This placed the court and government in a dilemma, for while unruly troops were present in force the dynasty itself was at risk. Probably by filling the pockets of Tong and his generals, Morse thought, they withdrew a mere eighty miles eastwards, only to bring terror to the foreign residents of Tongzhou.

In late December 1898 a Tongzhou correspondent of a Shanghai paper summed it up with blood-curdling restraint. Tong Fuxiang's cavalry rode, he said,

> At a slow trot, in compact companies of fifty; with waving silk banners and fluttering scarlet cloaks and long red-tufted lances quivering in their hands like reeds ... so conscious of their strength and their power to crush foreigners, when the word is given, that they look on them more with pitying contempt than with active dislike ...

> Something unusual is under way; and if the Empress Dowager has undertaken the overturning of the whole Imperial policy towards foreigners, she has taken good care to gather troops enough to ensure the success of her policy, however ruthless. Everywhere, in both city and county, we hear the same tale, that all foreigners are to be killed or driven out, and that our day is close at hand. These remarks are seldom made to us personally ... but the ears of native helpers and converts are

filled with them ... The feeling of unrest ... merely includes the dispassionate though agreeable conviction that our lives are drawing to a close.[1204]

'Killed for the present'
(October 1898–99)

The Hundred Days were over; the reform movement looked dead. Its resurrection seemed to its sympathisers an impossible dream. But not to its promoters. Spurred on by the offers of blood-money, the hunters of Sun Yatsen, Kang Yuwei and Liang Qichao stayed hot on their trails. Uncowed they continued to work for the reformation

2.76 The Cassels' home in Langzhong, Sichuan

and were rewarded for their courage only twelve years later. Far from being 'a Manchu family quarrel', as undiscerning foreigners chose to say, the clash between progressives and obscurants had exposed a major rift, a geological fault in the political bedrock of the nation. The old Manchus, in the ascendancy again for a few brief years, made audacity their policy. A show of strength, a scorn of aliens quickly became their attitude while they used them to press forward the modernisations of which they did approve. On October 10, 1898, in the heat of change, an Anglo-Chinese loan contract for railroad development in north China was signed. As late as December 2, 1899, a Franco-Belgian east-west railway across Henan received approval.[1205] Seen from the side of imperialism, deep cuts in the melon were still being made, with areas of influence and exploitation in vogue until the American 'open door' policy, welcomed by

Britain, restored the sanity of unrestricted competition.

The remarkable world traveller and author, Isabella Bird (1831–1904), (married at 50 to a Dr John Bishop (1881–86) but widowed) arrived at Shanghai in January 1896 as the guest of Hudson Taylor and the CIM at Wusong Road and travelled for most of the year through Sichuan to the Tibetan marches and back.[1206] Ascending the Yangzi gorges and crossing Sichuan from Wanxian through Langzhong, she braved the terrors of crowds shouting 'Kill the foreigner' as well as the dangers of rapids and mountain tracks and Tibetan passes in the snow. Her firm conviction, supported by many good photographs, that China was far from breaking up or decaying, as Lord Charles Beresford declared, she based on observation of the strong personalities and industrious lives of the people. She could see that China's economy was growing strongly and that humiliation at the hands of Japan and the West had been a spur to revival. Reaction took time to penetrate the empire. At Langzhong as the Cassels' guest she saw the need of a hospital and forthwith bought and presented to the Mission a Chinese mansion, in memory of her sister. The Henrietta Bird Memorial Hospital went from strength to strength until the end of the 'open century', and afterwards developed into a medical college at Nanchong (Skunking).

Writing on October 24, 1898, from Guangyuan near the Sichuan–Shaanxi border, Montagu Beauchamp said of the reform movement, 'In fact there is a widespread rumour that the Emperor has believed, and ordered the temples to be turned into schools. [The truth was that the edict merely ordered that schools be opened in temples.] Let me quote a FACT. We have proclamations in this city, coming from the Central Government, declaring that he ancient teaching of Confucius is out of date, and therefore Western learning must be taught in all schools, if China is to hold her own with other powers.' His own comment was, 'All this will attract more attention than ever to the Gospel.'[1207]

The effect on foreign missions, Catholic and Protestant, took many forms, related to wide differences in their activities. The Roman Catholics largely stood aloof from the reform movement, although it had been the early Catholics at Peking who used Western science as an effective key to the heart of the empire. Instead, in 1899 they took a different sensational leap into notoriety with startling consequences as we shall see. Western learning could be obtained almost solely in Protestant institutions while the universities and schools projected by Guang Xü's edicts were in preparation.

In 1897 the Methodist Free Church at Wenzhou was teaching English in its high school, and at Hangzhou the American Presbyterian high school became a college. The Canadian Mission Press was established in Sichuan in 1897, and the West China Religious Tract Society in 1889 as a product of the inter-mission conference at Chongqing convened by Hudson Taylor. The Presbyterian missions in Manchuria had more appeals for evangelists and teachers than could be responded to, yet church membership rose from under eight thousand in 1896 to almost twenty thousand in 1899. In Fujian a similar expansion took place, and in 1898 the CIM reported 1,029 baptisms, with the number in Shaanxi increased threefold and in Henan, another resistant province, by sixty per cent.

After John R. Mott's visit to China, student groups connected with the YMCA grew rapidly. Germany's occupation of Jiaozhou (Kiaochow now Jiao Xian) led to three societies moving into the area, a short-sighted action which again stamped Christianity indelibly with the brand-mark of imperialism.[1208] The favours shown to the reforming missionaries, and the subsequent demonstration of their success, went far towards substantiating the divergence between what J. K. Fairbank has called the evangelical and the 'secular' missionary. 'Professionalisation' of missions (especially in medicine and education) 'increasingly divorced from evangelical aims', resulted in about four hundred higher level institutions in the next eight years.[1209]

On March 16, 1899, a growing trend in Catholic practice received imperial approval by the issue of a rescript on the access by Catholic missionaries to mandarins. Since 1860 the Catholic hierarchy in China had assumed official status by imitating the mandarins in dress and appearances in public. Official cap buttons, formal sedan chairs preceded by a formal 'thousand name umbrella', even the firing of cannon on their arrival at a town, and the issue of proclamations in the official form, had all appropriated to themselves the honours and dignities of officials. By the March rescript recognising these practices the Peking government was seen to wish to deal directly with the Church instead of through the French protectorate. Bishops were to have access to viceroys and governors and to rank with them, leading priests with *daotai's* and priests with prefects and magistrates. The move miscarried terribly, unless Ci Xi's deep scheming anticipated the resentment which 'an empire within the empire' would stir up against the church. 'Extra-territorial' rights already accorded foreigners greater freedom from the arm of the Chinese law than even the literate of China enjoyed (see 1, pp 113–14, 117).

When the *North China Daily News* of May 19 pointed out that under the 'most favoured nation' clause Protestants automatically enjoyed the same privileges as Catholics, Arnold Foster (see pp 327, 329) addressed the editor in terms of this lapse by the Chinese government (in yielding to French pressure) as 'one of the gravest importance to the future of China as a nation, and also to the future of Christian Missions'. He spoke of 'the danger to the peace and well-being of the Chinese people; danger to the interests of all foreigners living in China and . . . danger to the very life of the Christian Church'. He quoted Sir Rutherford Alcock in *The Times* of September 13, 1886, in which he denounced the whole system of priestly interference in the political affairs of China. To it he attributed 'the perennial hostility

towards Christianity and its teachers in every form, which now pervades the whole nation.' When the Chinese government made a determined stand against Catholic pretensions, Sir Rutherford said, 'It is in the interest of religion and of all foreign nations that they (the Chinese) should not fail.' Arnold Foster found it easy to imagine that the shrewd Chinese were trying to play off Catholics against Protestants as two rival religions, and France against the Protestant nations. Refusal of the same privileges would expose Protestant Christians and missionaries to persecution by pagan and Catholic alike, but it was vital that political status should be rejected if the purity of the Chinese church was not to be compromised.

From the first, Protestant rejection of the actions and privileges was almost unanimous, though some were slow to understand.[1210] In September 1899 the Anglican bishops in conference protested against growing Catholic interference in provincial and local government and courts of law. But the damage had been done. Nationwide resentment already threatened the safety of Catholics and Protestants alike.

The CIM's first martyr (November 1898)

Yü Manzi's rampaging in Sichuan led the consuls in Chongqing to send foreign women downriver to safety, but by November 1898 all seemed quiet. The Hudson Taylors set off up the Yangzi on November 15 with the Charles Inwoods of Keswick for conferences in Hankou and Chongqing. On the 18th a *North China Daily News* 'Extra' carried a telegram from Chongqing,

> MURDER OF MISSIONARIES. Mr W. S. Fleming, a China Inland missionary, and a native evangelist were murdered on 4 inst. at Panghai. (Guizhou). (The Kueifu RC mission, Sichuan, was all burned down two days after the new viceroy passed.)

London papers quoted it on the 21st. After thirty-three years of courting danger, the CIM had lost its first member in this way.

A young Scotsman who had settled in Australia after five years at sea, Fleming had been in China since 1885, and at Panghai only a month (see map 2.72: p 593). He and two 'Black Miao' evangelists both named Pan were starting on a two-week journey together to Miao villages when they ran into trouble. Roving bands of robbers and rebels, said to be encouraged by Yü Manzi's success against foreigners, were pillaging the countryside. Fleming decided to return to Guiyang, but had ridden only ten miles on November 4 when armed men attacked them. Seeing one of his companions, Pan Shoushan, wounded, Fleming dismounted to help him, instead of escaping, and both were cut down by a cavalry sword. The other evangelist made good his escape and took the news to Guiyang.

Local mandarins fabricated a report that Fleming had been supplying the Miao with weapons, but after full investigation the verdict was reached: 'There is no doubt that the murder had been arranged by the leading men of the district.' Whatever the facts, confused and contradictory accounts could not conceal the truth that this was one of the earliest instances of deliberate violence against foreigners following the counter-reformation coup at Peking. When the consul proceeded to claim an indemnity, Hudson Taylor intervened, writing to W. B. Sloan in London,

> We hear that the Consul here had kindly thought to help Mr Fleming's parents by claiming for them £2,500 ... (Could you) use your influence with them not to accept this money as ... the effect on the Chinese will be bad; in the Kucheng massacres the CMS refused all blood-money. To the Chinese it will seem as if the parents were quite satisfied to sell their son. It is a pity to encourage the idea that the lives of missionaries can be paid for.[1211]

By December the lull had ended and 'unsettlement all over China' was causing greater anxiety than ever. The counter-reformation had gathered strength and ominous things were happening. When Alicia Bewicke Little quoted the Tongzhou correspondent's words, 'Our lives are drawing to a close' she added, 'We all read it, and some of us thought a good deal.'

24
The Boxer Madness (1898–1900)

The rise of the Boxers (1898–1900)

'The times are too ticklish to go in for adventures . . . caution and discretion are everywhere necessary,' wrote Sir Robert Hart to his commissioner, Hosea Ballou Morse, on October 24, 1898.[1212] Beneficial regulations for the control by the customs service of steamers on inland waters were resulting in greatly increased traffic. Cargo ships and launches towing trains of Chinese lighters were ruining the age-old sailing junk trade as railways were stealing the livelihood of carters and muleteers. In March 1899 the anger of the junk men, already incensed by the crop failure in central China, erupted at Zhenjiang and Yangzhou in anti-foreign incendiarism and rioting. Hunan, to the surprise of all who had known the bitter spirit of the province in the past, agreed to the opening of Yueyang (Yochow), at the entrance to the Dongting Lake system from the Yangzi, as a trading port (see map 2.20: p 204). As titular commissioner of customs at Hankou in 1899, Morse was responsible for establishing good relations with the gentry of the province. In this he had the backing of Zhang Zhitong and the wisdom and long experience of Griffith John to help him. Morse quoted John as saying as late as May 23, 1900, 'that the complete transformation of the Hunanese into friendliness still continued'. In comparison with the rest of China, Hunan was peaceful, but only relatively.

Risings in the famine-stricken areas of northern Jiangsu and Anhui and in western Hubei had their echoes south of the Yangzi. On January 20, 1899, W. J. Hunnex, his wife and three children were attacked at Nanyang, the capital of Jiangxi. Travelling past the city on a little boat, they suddenly 'saw boats full of excited men and women closing in on all sides . . . A number of women, who seemed beside themselves with passion, crowded on to our boat, and kneeling down knocked their heads (on the deck) before us, at the same time screaming violently and demanding that we should give up the four *dead children* whom we had stolen and were taking away.' The sight of foreigners had started a rumour. It had swelled into a battle-cry and instantly drew the crowds, crying 'Kill the child-stealers.' Their extreme danger ended as suddenly. Providentially rescued by missionaries of another society who were nearby in a larger boat, and by river police, they got away unharmed.[1213]

In June and August Zhejiang, Fujian and Yunnan saw dangerous unrest. Sam Pollard was told that his name was on a hit-list of victims when the time became ripe. At Jian'ou (Kienning) in northern Fujian the CMS premises were burned and a Christian killed, three missionaries barely escaping with their lives.[1214]

After Dr Keller's 'house-warming' at Chaling in Hunan in March 1899, and insistence that his landlord should be compensated in full while he himself would take nothing, he struck up a warm friendship with the magistrate's son, Han Xiaoye. In May he was called to attend Han's wife, in obstructed labour for three days, and saved not only hers but their child's life, too. During June he had narrow escapes at Hengshan and Hengzhou, west of Chaling, where LMS and Catholic premises were destroyed and three Italian priests killed, mutilated and burned. But he was at Xiangtan, south of the provincial capital, Changsha, where 'great crowds followed me . . . two miles to the ferry. Shouts of "Beat!" and "Kill!" filled the air and some of the mob began to strike me. God raised up a friend for me; a man of evident power sprang to my side, shouted to the mob "Don't strike him; he is leaving; isn't that enough for you?" . . . This man stayed by me all the way to the ferry, constantly holding back the crowd.'

Returning to Chaling he and a colleague were told of a rumour being circulated that an imperial decree to kill all foreigners was on its way. Han Xiaoye was deputising for his father the magistrate and kept armed patrols on the streets to nip trouble in the bud. But a force of men from Hengzhou came through the city saying they were on the way to the coast to kill foreign devils. 'Why don't you kill (them here)? We have killed them all at Hengzhou, they are being killed all over China . . . Take us to their hall and we will do the job for you.'[1215]

Han tried to persuade the men to leave Chaling, and took Dr Keller and his companion into his own residence, but he himself 'looked pale and worn (and) could not eat'. A copy of a decree from the empress dowager had in fact been received by the anti-foreign element at Chaling, and he expected the *yamen* to be destroyed and his father and himself to be killed. Keller at once insisted on leaving, so Han enlisted friendly members of the Golaohui secret society to escort them to the Yangzi, starting at midnight. 'An almost uninterrupted tirade of threats and curses' accompanied them, but Keller reached Shanghai safely on August 31. Instead of his feeling relief, the extreme test of nerve had angered and embittered him. He arrived determined to demand compensation, whatever Hudson Taylor might say.

The fact emerged later on that in Jiangxi and Hunan the Roman Catholics were being identified with the Taipings who had stormed through the provinces fifty years earlier (see 1, p 202). In October the prefect at Changsha promised Edward Pearse to reinstate Keller at Chaling, and on December 6 he reoccupied his house, destroyed in June but rebuilt for him. Perhaps most notable in these events was the friendliness of the mandarins, from the viceroy to the junior magistrate, whatever the temper of the rabble rousers.

The history of events at Hengzhou also deserves more attention. In 1892 a native of Changsha named Peng, 'from being the wildest and worst of characters, had been transformed' after his conversion through Christians baptised by Griffith John. 'So remarkable was his conversion . . . that one of the leading publishers of the vile pamphlets of 1891 came to Hankou expressly to . . . learn what (had) produced the change in (Peng).' In 1897 Griffith John found twenty to thirty believers at Hengzhou asking for baptism, and left Peng to teach them, with the result that by 1899 out of hundreds of adherents 192 were baptised. But a year later they and their chapels became the target of renewed attack during the Boxer madness.[1216]

Meanwhile, in Sichuan, Yü Manzi's fortunes had waxed and waned. From malice towards Roman Catholics his aim had become the expulsion or destruction of all foreigners. But on January 20, 1899, he was forced to release M. Fleury and surrendered to strong government forces. Spared the executioner's sword, he was even given parole. H. B. Morse, after long acquaintance with corruption, inferred that 'silver bullets played as great a part in the suppression as lead'. During a lull before Yü Manzi renewed his attacks, the eighty members of the inter-mission conference at Chongqing (to which we shall return) were able to disperse again to their homes. Then the uprising was renewed and spread widely with a big riot at Nanchong (Shunking) after Yü Manzi was re-arrested.[1217]

The influence of Yü Manzi spread to neighbouring provinces and communities (engulfing Fleming and Pan) and extended to the Muslims of Gansu and Xinjiang who called for a *jehad*, to Hubei via the Golaohui, and to Shaanxi where 'a great conspiracy to exterminate foreigners' was reported. Riots and destruction in too many places to be named sometimes enveloped CIM missionaries. At Yangzhou secret meetings of the Golaohui and Dadaohui ('the Great Swords') planned rebellion against the Manchus, sensing that the opportunity had come to destroy the Qing and re-establish a Han Chinese dynasty. A clash between Russian Cossacks and Chinese in Manchuria resulted in ninety-four killed and 123 wounded. Russia had to pay full compensation, but too late. The hatred stirred up by this massacre took a greater toll. 'In every province in the empire there had been unrest, riot or rebellion through the whole of 1899 and continuing into 1900; mission stations had been attacked in every province, and railway engineers in Yunnan and (Shandong), the only classes of foreigners who were not ordinarily in the shelter of the treaty ports.'

High-handed action by Germany, and demands by Italy for a mid-China anchorage at Sanmen Bay in Zhejiang (see map 2.63: p 518) on the same terms as Qingdao, buttressed by four 14,000-ton cruisers with 110 guns, drove the Peking government to put the armed forces on a war footing. Italy backed down, but preparations continued throughout the year 1899, accompanied by hate-filled yet justifiable edicts from the dowager empress against alien intrusions. 'The various powers cast upon us looks of tiger-like ferocity . . . It behoves all our

2.77 A Boxer recruit at drill, from a drawing by Savage Landor

Viceroys, Governors and Commanders-in-chief . . . to unite together and act . . . so as to present a combined front to the enemy.' Foreign aggression and imperial reaction, therefore, fuelled the spreading anti-foreign feelings while to the superstitious, drought and famine showed Heaven's displeasure at China's tolerance of such treatment. Ci Xi appointed Kangyi, as rabid a Manchu reactionary as existed in all China, to raise large sums of money for her coffers. With Gilbert and Sullivan holding the London stage, Kangyi became known by the press as the 'Lord High Extortioner'. Passed down from superior to inferior, his demands hit the common taxpayers most severely and intensified their resentments.

In Shandong tensions rose to snapping point after three German engineers were attacked by villagers and in retaliation German soldiers razed their villages and took five of the gentry as hostages. Military 'exercises' were mounted as a demonstration to the Germans. Yüan Shikai with 5,500 men, Tong Fuxiang with 9,000 Gansu veterans, and 7,500 others marched into Shandong, but returned to Zhili within a month. Anger and frustration at the foreigner largely out of reach could only be vented upon Christian villagers. A secret society or association of societies calling itself the Yihochuan came to the notice of the *North China Herald* in September 1899. Including the Dadaohui or Great Swords and many criminals and riff-raff, it had ostensibly been formed for the promotion of boxing and gymnastics.[1218] Mystic rites of initiation and training made them invulnerable, they believed, to bullet, spear or sword.

'*Yi-ho-chuan*' could be understood as 'Association for Justice and Harmony' (a euphemism) or as 'Fist of Patriotic Union', the truer sense, for after May 26, 1899, when the association had come into being, their banners carried four characters: '*Fan Qing Mie Yang*', meaning 'Overthrow the Qing; exterminate the foreigner'. Newspaper reporters then introduced the word 'Boxers', for the first time in print, but there was nothing flippant about the

Boxers' intentions. Chinese officials and gentry aided and shielded the Boxers, and a military mandarin who arrested some was himself assassinated. Troops sent to control them were withdrawn on the orders of Ci Xi's henchman Yü Xian, the governor of Shandong since March, and their commander was dismissed although he was Yüan Shikai's brother.

In October a tell-tale and sinister change in the slogan to 'Uphold the dynasty; exterminate foreigners', betrayed collusion at the highest levels, the espousal of the Boxers for the palace's own ends. By the turn of the year the Boxer movement had spread far into Zhili. The new factor of alliance between anti-foreign officialdom and the Boxer movement looked convincingly like a device 'to prevent popular, anti-foreign feeling from being turned against them'. Certainly Ci Xi increasingly took their part and used them as her tools, perhaps with the foresight to think that if they were not destroyed in the approaching hostilities, she could complete the process herself when it suited her.[1219]

On December 31, 1899, a twenty-four-year-old Anglican (SPG) missionary in Shandong, S. M. Brooks was attacked by a band of men wearing red headcloths and with red girdles—the symbol of the Boxers soon to be feared far and wide. When he broke away mounted men chased and beheaded him.[1220] The first Boxer martyr had fallen.

To Chongqing in spite of Yü Manzi (1898–99)

Looking back to 1898, the strain on Hudson Taylor of political tensions from the time of his arrival in China on January 15, 1898, until he left for Australia on September 25, 1899, a year and nine months later, led him to develop his 'leisure interests'. When sapped by the heat or an excess of demands on his time and strength, he would go up to Chefoo or to one of the new hill resorts of Guling or Moganshan near Shanghai. For the first time he mentioned in a letter that they were boiling their drinking water as a precaution against disease. At Chefoo

he enjoyed conferring with E. J. Cooper, building the schools and sanatorium. Jennie Taylor wrote that when he was doing this he was at his best in health and spirits. A note records his instructions for insulating ceilings with sawdust covered by two inches depth of sand as a fire precaution. Another asks for all his photographic equipment to be sent, and again of talking photography with a nephew. He planned to buy a quarter-plate lens. Others mention his veranda greenhouse and tropical plants at Shanghai. When John Stevenson drove himself too hard, Hudson Taylor wrote urging him to get regular exercise and fresh air, implying that he did so himself.[1221]

But nothing suited Hudson Taylor better than travelling, away from the pressure and out among the Chinese he loved. When Yang Cunling brought his son to meet Hudson Taylor on the river-boat at Wuhu it was an emotional moment. Children always attracted him, and a prayer and patriarchal blessing would have been most natural in their relationship. 'To watch the head of the Mission entertain (Chinese) friends with simple, unaffected and expert politeness was an example', the missionary at Ningguo wrote. Much more so his brothers in Christ.

In an unusually agitated letter to John Stevenson, Jennie complained that Hudson had gone up the Yangzi to Jiujiang and Jiangxi without a Chinese or missionary companion, knowing full well that dysentery or hostile people could endanger his life. Her distress was misplaced. He had soon found someone to travel with him.

His accountant son, Ernest, volunteered to be a 'forward movement' pioneer, and joined Dr F. H. Judd at the newly occupied Jiangxi city of Shangrao (known then as Raochow). For nine months Howard Taylor had been acting as superintendent in Henan while suffering from intractable dysentery. When he asked to be replaced and freed to get proper treatment, his father confessed that he had no one available to take over. He urged Howard to stay on, for 'we ought to lay down our lives for the brethren'. Then he invited Dixon Hoste, at last in better health, to become superintendent in Henan instead of Shanxi.[1222]

Returning by canal boat through Hangzhou and his 'old haunts' of forty years before, Hudson Taylor claimed to be in better health than at any time in the last three years. But only a few months later he was at Guling again, febrile and bewildered, troubled about the spiritual morale of the Mission being in decline at a time of deepening crisis in China. 'A fiery trial' might be what would do most good. Like Griffith John, certain that effort, zeal and organisation achieved little without 'a close walk with God', he was doing all he could to help members reach and live by conviction of this truth. 'Not by might, nor by power, but by My Spirit, says the Lord of Hosts.' And Henrietta Soltau was being so successful as a missionary to missionaries that he persuaded her to extend her time in China. It would be better to close the women candidates' department in London than to lose opportunities to help those who 'are not spiritually equal to the harass and strain of the present crisis in China.' Other missions were sharing in the benefits her visit brought.[1223]

As Dr A. T. Pierson could not come, the Keswick Convention council took up Hudson Taylor's request and not only sent Charles Inwood and his wife to China but other representatives as a 'Keswick mission to missionaries' in other continents as well. Societies in Shanghai and the south and north of China welcomed the Inwoods to conduct conferences for them, and on November 15, 1898, the Hudson Taylors and Inwoods started up the Yangzi to the far west. Wherever they held meetings the gratitude of widely differing types of missionary showed how timely and appropriate their teaching was. The 'perilous, long and difficult journey' up the Yangzi rapids brought them to Chongqing on January 7, 1899.[1224]

There the inter-mission conference Hudson Taylor had convened drew up to eighty missionaries of seven Protestant societies from Guizhou, Sichuan and Yunnan, and members of the business and customs community. After a week of meetings (January 16–21) they asked for a second week. Many more were prevented from attending by the dangerous conditions in Sichuan. Out of it came not only spiritual renewal but a comity agreement on the division of Sichuan to avoid duplication of effort, a standing inter-mission 'committee on polity', and the West China Religious Tract Society, a monthly *West China Missionary News*, and a condemnation of the opium traffic 'by a rising vote'.

Before the conference ended, news came of Yü Manzi's first surrender, and on January 24 Charles Parsons set out for Langzhong (Paoning), expecting William Cassels to follow with the Hudson Taylors a week later. Parsons had come through unscathed when 'dragged and driven' out of Nanchong, and when rescued by the magistrate from a riot at Langzhong in 1895 (see map 2.72: p 593). But this time he came closer to losing his life. The prefect at Chongqing had sent four unarmed soldiers to escort him and a Chinese Christian by boat up the Dialing River. But on the way they were attacked by about two hundred men commanded by an adopted son of Yü Manzi. The Christian bravely defended Parsons, warding off the spears until wounded himself, so Parsons jumped into the river from which he was hauled by a government patrol and defended until dark. He arrived back at Chongqing still wet but none the worse for his experience. A week later he and Cassels tried again, hidden in a boat, and reached Langzhong safely. But the Taylors again had to abandon as untimely their long-deferred plan to visit the Sichuan stations.

Hudson Taylor had missed conference sessions through illness, and before the end of January developed 'influenza'. By February 10 he was 'more ill (with bronchitis) than Jennie had ever known him'. News and correspondence were kept from him. They were still in Chongqing on March 1, but back in Shanghai on April 6. He saw the Inwoods off to Britain on May 24 and went up to Chefoo, but incapacitating headaches and then dysentery limited the work he could do. Instead, Jennie carried his heavy load of correspondence. Typically she advised a fraught mother, 'Try praising because it is His way.' But the truth had become plain to them that at sixty-seven, looking and feeling much older, his active days were coming to an end.[1225]

Cooper's worth (1898–1900)

In 1898 when William Cooper was run over and seriously injured while away in Britain, Hudson Taylor had written to Walter Sloan, 'The Lord preserve his precious life.' And in March 1899 while William Cooper was conducting meetings in Canada at Hudson Taylor's request, 'his life is of priceless value to the Mission, far more so than my own.' Is the inference that Hudson Taylor wished Cooper to be known in North America before promoting him further as a leader or the leader of the CIM?[1226]

A few weeks earlier, in January 1899, William Sharp and the London Council had again raised the matter of John Stevenson's alleged unpopularity. Sharp went so far as to draft the wording of a letter for Hudson Taylor to send to Stevenson, asking him to retire. 'There is perhaps one other course . . . to place the responsibility of the matter on the London Council, who are in a better and more independent position for doing what is best for the Mission than anyone else'. The lesson of years of disharmony seemed forgotten.

Yet again, William Sharp and, so it turned out, Theodore Howard and the London Council failed to understand their role in the management of the CIM. W. B. Sloan, 'a rock of strength', and Marcus Wood were 'quite admirable' in Britain, and William Cooper had the full confidence of the council in London, but, as Theodore Howard wrote to Hudson Taylor in September over the signatures of Sharp and Richard Hill as representing the Council: '(we) expect that you will not leave China (for Australia) without . . . Mr Stevenson retiring altogether from the post (of China Director). In Mr Cooper you have a tried man, loved, trusted and honoured by all his brethren and well qualified for the work.

With him should be associated as his second in command a man of somewhat similar gifts, and proved ability, and one perhaps, who has had a fuller educational training'— Dixon Hoste.[1227] In the minds of some men the succession seemed clear.

Hudson Taylor kept his own counsel, but although London's pressure verged on the unconstitutional, their thinking resembled his own—except for their unrelenting rejection of the faithful, wise and selfless John Stevenson.

With the thermometer at 95 °F the China Council met in July. Then the Taylors retreated to Moganshan. Although capable of less work, his grip on practical matters still showed no sign of diminishing and without question he knew what he was doing about a successor. But the time was of ripe to declare it. John Stevenson was 'open to God', had 'had a blessing' through Charles Inwood and was too valuable to lose. Hudson Taylor was content to watch developments. During these hot summer days the Hunan riots were taking place and Dr Keller was being hounded through Jiangxi, to reach Shanghai indignant and set on laying the matter before the consul-general. If the mission would not allow him to do so, he would resign and handle it himself. John Stevenson persuaded him to wait for Hudson Taylor.

> During our first interview [Keller recalled] Mr Taylor did not even refer to the subject. He discussed the work in general and asked my advice about the use of certain drugs, and when the dinner bell rang ... asked me to call again at 3.00 o'clock. I felt guilty at taking up so much of his time and (at 3.00) said, 'Mr Taylor, I see the whole matter differently and am prepared to act as you may direct.' 'Thank God!' exclaimed Mr Taylor. This experience was a turning point in my life; it taught me how even strongly formed purposes can be changed, and how men's hearts can be influenced by prayer alone.[1228]

By Dr Keller declining reparation in any form, while ensuring that his Chaling landlord was fully compensated, a lasting friendship with the city prefect was formed, to prove valuable when the Boxer madness flared.

Miracle in Toronto (1899)

While missionaries and the church in China were being tested and disciplined in many ways, the home countries were not immune. Since the beginnings in North America nine years before, the Toronto premises of the CIM had become inadequate for all that had developed. One hundred and thirty Canadian and American missionaries had been sent to China, apart from the Scandinavian associates. A move had to be made, and freehold ownership would avoid the constant drain of rental payments. But Henry Frost's bank balance was laughable. The ideal would be a large residence he had long known on the other side of the road, if ever it was for sale. Meanwhile, the CIM's landlord had raised the rent. Frost and his council prayed for a solution and in China Hudson Taylor prayed with them.

On the morning of January 9, 1899, the eighty-four-year-old William Berger dressed and came downstairs, sank on to a sofa and died.[1229] By his will he left £1,000 to Hudson Taylor which he immediately passed on to Henry Frost—the largest single donation so far to come Frost's way. The next morning a 'FOR SALE' sign appeared on the property he thought suitable. Frost hurried to tell his colleague, Joshua S. Helmer, and together they prayed that the place might become theirs. They then called on the owner, a Mr Somerville, who showed them round. It was as they thought, perfect in every way, with coach-house and stables which could become offices and a new billiard room large enough for meetings.

Mr Somerville knew nothing of the CIM, but when Henry Frost explained, he reduced the price to $13,000 and agreed to accept $5,000 in down payment. Hudson Taylor's £1,000 from William Berger was equivalent to $4,850. The balance of $8,000 they declined to secure by mortgage, on the Mission principle of not entering into debt of any kind. Instead Frost offered 'a unique proposition', that several well-known Council members would serve as trustees to pass on any sums received, acting for the CIM and for Mrs Somerville and her heirs. On payment being completed within thirty years, without financial obligation during that time, the deeds would be transferred to the Mission! To their surprise Mr Somerville signed a legal agreement on those extraordinary terms. Within ten days $2,000 more were paid, and the total sum within a year. What had cost the owner $23,000 he gave with all its carpets and fittings for $13,000. They called it Berger House. But 'Somerville House' would have been justified.[1230]

Countdown to 1900 (1898–1900)

On September 11, 1899, Hudson Taylor wrote to Walter Sloan, 'The state of things in China is very serious just now—might I not say throughout the world China weakened by insurrections within and torn to pieces by Romish intrigues will be powerless before any foreign power or powers who may attack her when England's hands are tied.' [The Boer War began on October 10.] And on September 23, two days before sailing to Australia, 'I am very sorry to leave China at this time; to miss Mr William Cooper and Bishop Cassels . . . but I feel it is now or never; for I cannot rush through all the work that urgently needs to be done in Australasia and be at New York for the (Ecumenical) Conference if I further delay.'[1231]

The loss of William Berger, a faithful friend of many years, could not but move Hudson Taylor deeply, but during these months his grief was renewed again and again. The death of eight or nine members of the Mission (leaving 816 on May 25, 1899) compared very 'satisfactorily' with the losses suffered by other societies and with public health figures in the West. But the death of George Müller at ninety-two on March 10, 1898, after seven decades of Christian service, and Arthur Douthwaite's distress after his second wife died, were only the beginning. James Adam of Guizhou had lost his wife from toxaemia, and in May 1898 was shattered by the death in convulsions of his second wife from the same cause. In the same month the Scandinavian Alliance lost both their leaders in Shaanxi, Henriksen and Carlsson, from typhus. During the 'Hundred' Days' of reform and the start of the Yü Manzi rebellion, Hudson Taylor's brother-in-law; Samuel Dyer, the Bible Society representative, died in Shanghai and two more old friends in England: Montagu Beauchamp's mother and Mrs. Grattan Guinness, Geraldine's mother, on November 3. In Australia his saintly old friend Philip Kitchen, treasurer of the Melbourne Council, died in October of pneumonia. On October 22 the 'indispensable' Thomas Botham died of typhus at Lanzhou, and on November 4 W. S. Fleming was murdered at Panghai. William Soutter, of the Tibetan Pioneer Band, died on the Tibetan heights in December.

It was almost as if Hudson Taylor like Job was being inured to such news in preparation for worse. Frequently one or another, and sometimes several missionaries together were fighting for their lives with typhoid or typhus, some of Hudson Taylor's own family among them. In 1899 four valuable leaders returned to China after home leave. E. O. Williams died of typhoid in July, within six weeks of reaching Sichuan; Dr Douthwaite himself of dysentery on October 6; and George Hunter of Hunan of malaria on March 12, 1900. William Cooper was to be the fourth. For D. L. Moody 'Heaven opened' on December 22, 1899.[1231]

In the explosive atmosphere of those days, sad news had to be absorbed with the excitements—the frequent riots and escapes, the coups and counter-coups—and with the flood of good news constantly coming of the eight hundred missionaries and seven hundred Chinese colleagues in nearly two hundred centres. Archibald Orr Ewing reported two hundred baptisms in Jiangxi, with eight hundred to one thousand promising candidates under instruction. In Shanxi, a church conference at Linfen (Pingyang) under Pastor Hsi's successor Elder Si, showed every sign of Christian maturity and readiness to face greater persecution if it were to come. Si's own example of maturity had echoed Hsi's under attack by his rival, Fan. An influential man, jealous of Si's preferrment by the churches, opposed him bitterly. But when this enemy died, Si took his widow and three children under his own protection. In China as a whole sixty Protestant societies with 2,400 members reported a total of eighty-five thousand communicants. While CIM's 'forward movement' suffered from 'money but few men', the Church in China had begun to burgeon.[1233]

Montagu Beauchamp, pioneer evangelist par excellence in East Sichuan, was facing a personal parting of the ways which many Anglicans have faced since his day. While his contemporaries in other provinces were drawing men and women to Christ and forming them into congregations, local churches under elders, deacons and pastors, Montagu being an unordained Anglican could neither baptise nor conduct a communion service. New Christians had to wait for an ordained man to visit them from elsewhere, and for William Cassels as bishop to confirm them. The system was a drag on the Sichuan church. Hudson Taylor sympathised, but could suggest only two alternatives, to be ordained and stay in East Sichuan or to accept responsibility for an entirely pioneer field outside the Church of England area. The far south-western corner of Sichuan still had no evangelist. With a base at Xichang (Ningyuan) he would have the whole Ranchang Valley as far as the River of Golden Sand (the Yangzi in the south) and the wild minority peoples in the mountains on each side, the Yi (or Nosu) in the Daliangshan and the Xifan, Naxi and Moso towards the Tibetan border. Beauchamp chose East Sichuan and was famed as a prophetic and proverbial figure for decades to come. Xichang and the mountains had to wait until after the Second World War.

In the volcanic cauldron of China as 1899 ended anything could happen. No record has been found of any discussion or decision to continue in the hope of a return of peace as Peking regained control and prestige, or to withdraw (the women first) from any threatened region. 'Stay on if you can, and by your calm confidence in God set an example', seemed the right advice as it had always been. Henry Frost had put the Mission's united conviction into words when he declared in 1898,

> It is more than a possibility that not a few of our fellow-workers might be called to lay down their lives ... Leave GOD out of account, and fear must possess and overwhelm us. Bring GOD into account and there is perfect peace ... Satan is mighty, but GOD is almighty. Not one thing can man do which GOD does not allow to be done ... Would He be less strong to keep in the hour of death than He has been in the days of life? ... What is to be done for this generation (of Chinese) needs to be done at once, in spite of all danger. Let the cost be what it may, we must press quickly forward ... Face to face then, with whatever the future has for us as a Mission ... and because of threatenings, we ask the LORD's followers to go to those who threaten ... since the very wickedness of their threatenings is the revelation of their need of CHRIST. We pray, therefore, for men and women whose lives have been cast by the SPIRIT into martyr-mould.[1234]

A year later, when Hudson Taylor went to Australia, the threat had not diminished, but the church had grown in strength and maturity. When rioters at Hekou on the Guangxin River destroyed and pillaged the Catholic and CIM premises, September 20–28, 1899, 'all the mandarins came' and took the women missionaries safely to the *yamen*; and the people of Hekou, indignant that outsiders had committed the outrage, rebuilt their home and welcomed them back.

'The great miscalculation'[1235] (1900)

An omen of disaster for the nation had occurred in the year of the hundred days of reform, a solar eclipse. Passing over Lhasa and Inner Mongolia, its deep shadow had devoured five-sixths of the sun even at Peking, to feed the brooding fears of palace and people. Coming like a harbinger of doom before the fateful conjunction of an eighth intercalary month with the *gengzi* year of the lunar calendar, an event last seen in AD 1680, the two ill-omens together promised calamity for dynasty and people alike. Ci Xi, the evil genius as shrewd as she was superstitious, chose to manipulate the omens to reassert the dominance of the Qing over both rebels and aggressors. The secret societies set on restoring a Ming dynasty also took their opportunity to ferment civil convulsion. The food shortages from two years of drought across Hubei and North Anhui confirmed the omens and fired anger against the government and foreigners.

To deflect the anti-dynastic aims of the Golaohui and Yihochuan, Ci Xi chose to ride the tiger by aiding and abetting them against the hated barbarians. Proverbially, getting off a tiger becomes more dangerous than staying on. Memorials against the deposition of the emperor, and begging him not to abdicate were flooding in. Li Hongzhang, Liu Kunyi and Zhang Zhitong joined in the protests. But even as a prisoner Guang Xü remained a threat to Ci Xi and her faction. To eliminate him by death would bring trouble from Western nations, especially Britain, as much as from the great majority of younger officials and literati who admired him. When he was reported to be ill (like other victims before him), Sir Claude Macdonald warned that he must not 'die'. A French physician was allowed to examine him. Instead a decree in Guang Xü's name declared on January 24, 1900, that as he did not belong to the direct line of succession and had no heir, not only should a legal heir be appointed, but Pu Jün, the son of Prince Tuan, had already been selected as Prince Imperial. Confronted by Ci Xi with a decree of abdication, Guang Xü was unwilling to sign it, until impelled by her menacing eyes and steely will to do so. Then with a blanched face he sank on to his chair, 'dyed his robe and the carpet with his life's blood from a burst blood vessel', and was carried weeping all the way back to his prison.[1236]

After the murder of S. M. Brooks in Shandong, those responsible were tried by a Chinese court and sentenced to death. But Sir Claude reported to London that the governor of Shandong, Yü Xian himself, was the real culprit. While he and an ambiguous edict from the dowager empress encouraged the Boxers, no one could restore order. The American envoy, Major E. H. Conger, demanded Yü Xian's recall, and Yüan Shikai took his place. But Ci Xi received Yü Xian in audience 'with all the marks of favour'. When Yüan Shikai tried to suppress the Boxer trainbands he quickly learned to change his tune, by obstruction from Peking. The envoys of Britain, America, Germany, France and Italy then read the signs clearly and advised their respective governments that a joint naval demonstration was needed in the Gulf of Bohai, off Tianjin. It began on March 13. Ominously, three days later Yü Xian was appointed Governor of Shanxi. The envoys protested, but another two-faced edict against 'bad elements' in the Golaohui and Boxers successfully placated them and they withdrew the warships. Yü Xian arrived at Tai Yüan on April 20, and Boxers began drilling in broad daylight, while posters declared, 'The Boxers' leader is a royal person.'[1237]

Through the early months of 1900 tension increased all over China. Two British members of the Burma boundary commission were killed, and in Yunnan the message circulating through the bazaars and street restaurants was 'sharpen your weapons for the coming struggle', against the French in particular and their railway from Tongking. A Catholic missionary was wounded in clashes at Taizhou in Zhejiang, and reports of Ci Xi's ruthless ally, Prince Tuan, having sent eight thousand armed men to stiffen the Boxers in Zhili, gained credence.[1238] The old statesman in Li Hongzhang despaired as he saw the way things were going. 'I have exhausted every reasonable resource of speech or writing,' he wrote in his diary. In one interview with Ci Xi 'he urged her to crush the Boxers. "In an instant she was alive with wrath and angry words, and I immediately withdrew." '[1239]

Although German railway engineers were attacked in Shandong, a German newspaper in Shanghai ridiculed alarmist reports as 'wild tales'. An extension of the French concession at Shanghai then desecrated the ancient cemetery in defiance of Chinese sentiment and beliefs, inviting retaliation sooner or later. Anti-foreign feeling had not been so high in Peking since the French and British looted and burned the Summer Palace in 1860.

A member of the family of Zeng Guofan and 'Marquis' Zeng strongly warned in a despatch to the *North China Herald* that a blood bath was imminent.[1240] A scheme had been worked out, he revealed, to crush all foreigners and take back all leased and ceded territory. Behind it was an all-Manchu 'Army of Avengers' of ten thousand under Prince Tuan, 'a vicious and violent man'; thirteen thousand under Kangyi, 'Lord High Extortioner'; and fifty thousand under Prince Qing, an old adversary of Yong Lu. To his credit Yong Lu had remained loyal to Guang Xü and urged the viceroy of Zhejiang and Fujian not to act on Ci Xi's edict to enlist and train bands of criminal types to exterminate foreigners. In the north, Tong Fuxiang's Muslim horde and the Boxers were to be used as expendable tools against the foreigners, whether armed or unarmed. Bunkers were being built in the palace and the Eunuch Guard being armed. 'All Chinese of the upper classes know this, and those who count foreigners among their friends have warned them, but have . . . been more laughed at . . . than thanked.'[1241] 'Wolf, wolf!' had rung in their ears for decades. The Boxers, this correspondent said, had increased tenfold since the new year, even in Peking and Manchuria. Indoctrination teams were touring the provinces enlisting and training Boxers to drive the invaders from their strongholds, and to kill foreigners scattered in the interior. Chinese Christians were to be the first attacked, leaving the missionaries unprotected.

Still the ministers of the various legations held their hand, not advising their nationals to withdraw to the coast, or to leave the ports or Peking. Retreat would be to play into the hands of their enemies. Sir Robert Hart, who knew China and the Chinese as well as any foreigner, wrote in retrospect, 'Those of us who regarded the movement as likely to become serious . . . put off the time of action to September; our calculations were wrong.' Others believed that the calculations were right, that the scheming dowager empress intended wholesale action throughout the empire in the ill-starred intercalary month (September), wreaking havoc upon the foreigners and turning ill-omen into victory for the Qing. While Britain celebrated the relief of Mafeking on May 17, more and more acts of violence were taking place in China. On May 20, Monseigneur Favier, the bishop in Peking and well informed, also warned that the explosion was nearer than the optimists believed.

The Boxers were impatient, chafing to begin. Before Ci Xi was ready, they precipitated the holocaust.

Before New York, Australia and New Zealand
(September 1899–March 1900)

Nearly ten years had passed since Hudson Taylor's first visit to Australia in 1890. The one hundred missionaries within ten years, which he had urged the Melbourne Council to pray for and send to China, had been exceeded in September 1899. Four hundred had offered to go. The eighty-nine sent from Australia and twelve from New Zealand had already lost two by high fever and W. S. Fleming by violence in Guizhou. A fourth was dying as the Taylors set sail from Shanghai on September 25, 1899, to fulfil his long-promised return visit.

Since his arrival at Shanghai on January 15, 1898, for his tenth extended period in China, Hudson Taylor had carried the heavy end of the administrative burden and all its major stresses. While John Stevenson handled the routine administration, no light task, the hammer blows had fallen to

Hudson Taylor's lot. Through the Hundred Days of reform and the crises of Ci Xi's coup, the Yü Manzi rebellion, Fleming's murder, the death of leading missionaries, many riots and the ominous movements of troops and Boxers in the north, he had been largely single-handed. Dissension in the mission, 'Special Support' negotiations and the Morton legacy litigation, with his frequent illnesses and much travelling had taken their toll. William Cooper had left on March 29, 1898 for Britain, and after recovering from his accident had spent two months in Canada. He did not reach Shanghai again until October 21, 1899, the day on which the name 'Boxers' first appeared in print.

Hudson Taylor's approaching keynote address at the great Ecumenical Conference of Foreign Missions in New York, in April 1900, was the fixed point upon which all his movements had to hinge. To allow for two months in Australia and two in New Zealand, a thousand miles distant from each other, and then the long ocean journey to North America, had meant leaving China on September 25.

The moment for this uprooting had seemed woefully inappropriate. The volcano threatened to erupt. The anti-foreign fever was being fostered from the palace. Further afield, after years of skirmishing the Boer War had started in earnest. The United States had proposed the 'Open Door for China': a policy of fair-trading between the nations in place of spheres of influence and the competitive land-grabbing that had started. But Russia was believed to be waiting only for Britain's hands to be tied before extending her grip on Manchuria.[1242]

Ci Xi's tragic prisoner, the Guang Xü emperor, had 'begged permission' on September 4 to abdicate; Yü Xian and the Boxers, far from being in disgrace for attacks in Shandong and the murder of S. M. Brooks, were flaunting their welcome to Peking and appointment to Shanxi with chilling elation. At the heart of the CIM, the influential Stanley Smith's disruptive espousal of the eccentric 'bowie sect' and 'universal restoration' in place of the 'annihilation' theory he had previously favoured, had led Hudson Taylor to call him to Shanghai for a frank discussion. Dixon Hoste (back from his long recuperation in Australia) was 'answering him well', but 'SPS' this time was adamant. He chose to leave China rather than to adhere to the Mission's principles. C. T. Studd's intractable asthma had decided him not to return. Instead he took his wife and four beautiful daughters to Ootacamond in India, to serve as pastor of the community church.

John Stevenson had been left in charge at Shanghai, with dark clouds looming on a close horizon, but William Cooper's return in October would allow some sharing of the strain. Loth to go, Hudson Taylor had been sure that 'duty called', as he explained in an open letter to the Mission after meeting for five days with the China Council, September 11–15. Duty to God, to be doing his will, mattered supremely. 'Pray that we may be kept near to God, walking with him, with the eye kept single and the heart pure and simple in these dangerous days . . . Satan will try to unsettle us and subvert us, and the weak will go to the wall.' Had he delayed his departure it would quickly have been far harder to get away. As it was, Jennie (or more often 'Jenny' now)[1243] seems to have sensed a finality in their going. She had become a mother figure to the predominantly youthful members of the mission, but in writing from the ship to all her 'sisters' to say goodbye, without any other hint of premonition, the tone of her letter was one of farewell for the last time.

The voyage was what they needed, and Hudson Taylor was 'at his best' off the Australian coast, taking photographs and developing them himself. They hoped to visit each colony in turn, were met by John Southey at Brisbane and stayed with a niece. At Sydney they received a 'very cordial' welcome from Archbishop Saumarez Smith, and Hudson Taylor spoke at meetings almost every day. Then on November 11 they boarded a ship to Melbourne.[1244]

Meeting the Melbourne Council was his chief purpose, but a hundred ministers came to hear him on November 17, two hundred friends of the Mission attended the Saturday prayer meeting and on the 22nd he addressed fifteen hundred. In ten days he gave twelve addresses. And both John Southey and the Howard Taylors who were accompanying him took his place on other occasions. Correspondence kept him in touch with China. He replied to Stevenson that it was urgent for William Cooper to visit Chefoo and Shanxi if four or five resignations were to be prevented.

In Britain, although Robert Scott was the London treasurer and R. C. Morgan a member of the council, their popular 'weekly', the *Christian*, strongly criticised the principle of what they called 'faith missions'. (The misnomer was to take root, emphasising 'faith' instead of God's faithfulness.) This time William Sharp replied for the CIM, rightly saying that its members were 'an association of missionaries' who themselves chose to live in daily dependence on God's promised provision, and did not want the kind of 'assured support' which the editor anonymously advocated under the pseudonym Quartus.

After ten days at Adelaide where he was 'brisk and well, for him', and two at Ballarat, with Jennie also speaking with 'power' at her own meetings, they sailed from Melbourne to Tasmania on December 22. 'Almost daily meetings' and the inexorable round of social events, as in every place, brought them to the end of the year and the voyage to New Zealand. Still accompanied by John Southey and the Howard Taylors, they sailed from Hobart on January 5 1900, bound for Invercargill, on the southernmost tip of New Zealand.

China was never far from their thoughts or public speaking. On Christmas Day Hudson Taylor had remarked, 'How many men we have lost this year and last!' And on December 30 Jennie wrote apprehensively, 'One wonders what next year may bring.' Her fears were justified the very next day, when S. M. Brooks's murder heralded the coming storm. And on board ship Hudson

Taylor, writing again to Amy on January 6, said they might have to return direct to China 'if any very serious complication arose there'. 'One cannot tell what this sad African war may lead to. I have no light beyond New York.' But they would probably be in England by July. 'Till the Lord gives us His light I must not fix anything for myself, or may lose His light and guidance.'[1245] The way ahead was no clearer on January 30 when they had spent three hard-working weeks in the South Island. From Christchurch he wrote again, 'We cannot at present make plans and have no light beyond New York.'

In China the ill-omened *gengzi* year was about to begin, with the evil powers about to have their heyday. (January 24 was the fateful day on which Guang Xü was forced to abdicate, and Pu Jün, son of the extreme Prince Tuan, was by decree appointed Heir Apparent, Prince Imperial.) But Hudson Taylor's sense of Satan, having more rein to harass the Church, to which he had referred in his farewell letter to the Mission, turned his thoughts increasingly to the truth that whatever God might permit, 'power belongeth unto God'. During 1899 forty-seven new members had brought the CIM to a total of 811 members, many of whom were comparatively young and inexperienced. To carry anxiety for them would be too much to bear. To be the servant, the instrument of God their Lord and Father, was altogether another matter. Satan could not go beyond the limit set for him by the One who held the power.

To Hudson Taylor's disappointment, John Stevenson, outstandingly efficient in other ways, was failing again to let William Cooper share his responsibilities 'as a partner'. So Hudson Taylor wrote on January 8 to announce at the next meeting of the China Council his appointment of Cooper 'as Visiting China Director in place of his former appointment as Assistant Deputy Director'. And to Cooper himself, 'I am convinced that you need to visit and know the whole mission', especially in Shanxi. 'In visiting feel you have full power as China Director to do whatever is

necessary, but as far as it is possible let it be felt that you and John Whiteford Stevenson are one as two wise parents are one in managing their children.'[1246] If practicable, Cooper should return from Shanxi via Shaanxi, Gansu and Sichuan, as Hudson Taylor had hoped to do, but if not, through Henan.

In the event, even this arrangement did not satisfy members of the London Council. William Sharp wrote on March 10, urging again that William Cooper and Dixon Hoste should actually replace John Stevenson. But events were transpiring which made the experience and ability of Stevenson irreplaceable. God had other plans for both Cooper and Hoste.

An equally busy month in the North Island, with a visit to the hot lakes as guests of the government, brought them to March 20, their date of departure to San Francisco. New Zealand's position close to the international date line on longitude 180°E and W, meant that they sailed on the first of two days called March 20. Plague at Honolulu prevented their going ashore, and they landed at San Francisco on April 5.

In China tension had mounted increasingly. Wholesale initiation ceremonies and drilling were daily adding to the Boxers' strength. The worst anti-foreign feeling in Peking since 1860, made the foreign community and Chinese Christians fear for their lives. In mid-April eight thousand followers of Prince Tuan, evil genius with Ci Xi, joined the Boxers. And on April 20 when Yü Xian arrived at Taiyuan and set Boxers on to enrolling new members, he began collecting church membership lists. The empress dowager's ambiguous edict of April 17 blaming 'bad elements' in the Boxer movement was being interpreted as intended as approval of the majority of Boxers.

William Cooper and John Stevenson himself were anxious about Stevenson's health, so although Cooper was on his way to Shanxi, he meant to return early to Shanghai and to complete his long journey to the west at a later date. From Baoding on April 6 he proceeded to south Shanxi.

The Ecumenical Conference of Foreign Missions in New York was to run from April 23 to May 1, so the Taylors travelled first to Los Angeles for three days of meetings arranged by George Studd, and on to the Moody Bible Institute at Chicago, preaching in what had been Moody's church. More meetings followed at Cleveland, and they reached New York on April 20. A letter from the President of the Union Theological Seminary, Charles Cuthbert Hall, welcomed Hudson Taylor. 'I beg to ask that you will preach or deliver an address in the Chapel of the Seminary on Sunday afternoon, April 29 . . . The work of the China Inland Mission is dear to our hearts'

New York and beyond (April–June 1900)

'The immense Carnegie Hall', seating 3,500, was filled to capacity with large simultaneous overflow meetings to accommodate the enthusiastic public who joined the 1,845 official delegates. Of these 779 were missionaries of 108 societies, including the Hudson Taylors, Howard Taylors, Henry Frost, Walter B. Sloan, George Graham Brown and six other members of the CIM. The President of the United States and the Governor of New York State 'attended to welcome the conference on its assembling', thereby attesting its significance.

Initially a two-hour session was exclusively devoted to prayer. The published subject of Hudson Taylor's opening address was 'The Source of Power for Foreign Missionary Work', and the impact of his address made itself felt from his first words. 'Power belongeth unto GOD.' The futility of attempting to take the gospel to the whole world, apart from being the channels of that power, must govern all consideration of methods, personnel and message.[1247]

Thirty-two years later Henry Frost wrote:

I am still meeting men and women who declare that Hudson Taylor's address that morning radically changed their lives. [And again] The impressions produced by Mr Taylor were nothing less than phenomenal ... There at the front of the platform, (he) stands a moment in silent prayer ... As he

begins to speak his voice takes on a kindly, companionate quality. A hush which can be felt falls on the vast audience ... When Mr Taylor finished, there was almost an audible sigh of spiritual relief, so many of his hearers realising that they understood as never before the will and way of God.

A New York minister who attended the Adams Chapel service at the Union Seminary wrote to Howard Taylor after his father's death:

As I listened to Mr Taylor I kept constantly comparing the idea of sainthood expressed in the paintings (of the four evangelists) above his head with the living man who addressed us. (These thoughts) gave rise to a sermon on 'The Reality of Saintliness in Daily Life', which I have repeated a number of times since. Mr Taylor was, I believe, one of the noblest and greatest leaders whom God has given to the Church in our times.

In addition, Hudson Taylor preached twice on the same day at the Central Presbyterian Church, after attending 'as many of the conference meetings as his strength would allow.'

In view of Oberlin College having its representatives in Shanxi alongside the CIM,

The whole tenor of an address by Dr J. H. Barrows, its President, on 'The Right Attitude of Christianity toward the non-Christian Faiths' met with general approval. He pointed out that these other religions were entitled to be dealt with in a kind and respectful spirit, but that there simply could be no compromise whatever between faiths which were merely the products of the human heart reaching out in its darkness after God, and this Gospel of redemption, which had come to men as the only revelation from heaven.

Such an answer to the liberalism colouring the statements of some missionaries in China and from such a source was timely. To Henry Frost the conference was 'one of the major events in the history of the Christian Church', and certainly its widespread influence placed it in the same rank as the great Edinburgh Conference of 1910, but in a different way.[1248]

The Howard Taylors were to give the following winter months to the Student Volunteer Movement in universities and colleges throughout North America, so on May 1 they sailed for Britain, leaving his parents in the care of Henry Frost. They spoke at Princeton on May 2 and 3, and reached Toronto on the 5th for meetings of the CIM Council, saw Berger House, and fulfilled more preaching engagements. For the frail old man, the pace was too great.

Walter Sloan had addressed the Ecumenical Conference on 'The basis of admission to Church membership, and Church Discipline', in which he had referred to the problem of polygamy. After Sloan's return to Britain, Hudson Taylor was challenged on the subject, and on May 16 wrote 'a weighty letter' in reply. His conclusion as it concerned China, he said, was the same as the official view of the Moravian Church: 'that while no Christian could be allowed to contract a polygamous marriage, a heathen who had two wives, when converted could not, without great injustice and scandal, be called to put away either of them, as this would put an innocent woman in an impossible position, and render the children illegitimate.'[1249]

In the evening of the same day, May 5, after consultation with Henry Frost they took the night train to Boston. A restless journey and the usual sociabilities before going on to a public meeting soon after arrival left Hudson Taylor more fatigued than others realised. Dr A. T. Pierson had come on ahead of them and shared the platform with him. As Hudson Taylor was speaking, his doctor son, Howard, later wrote, 'he lost his train of thought, I think,' and A. T. Pierson 'immediately came to the rescue', taking over the meeting from him. Pierson added that he repeated the same phrase several times. Geraldine Howard Taylor, not present, conjectured, 'Recovering from the threatened stroke, Mr Taylor continued his journey'. But no mention has been made of any other signs or symptoms, so the word 'stroke' was hardly justified.[1250]

He was advised to 'knock off work altogether for a time', and did no more public speaking, but attended a communion service at Germantown, probably on May 29. 'In all my twenty-five years' ministry I never saw anyone so moved at the mention of the love of God, and in receiving the emblems of our Lord's body and blood as your dear father was that morning,' D. M. Stearns recalled.

They cut short their time in America and booked a passage to leave a month sooner than previously planned, while a very humble Henry Frost took Hudson Taylor's place at his engagements. On May 29 they travelled to Northfield to visit D. L. Moody's widow and on June 5 went to Pittsfield, after working on a paper to be read for Hudson Taylor. From there to Boston again to join their ship. They sailed for Liverpool, on June 9 and reached London on the 19th.

Eleven societies met at the Exeter Hall on the 20th to pray for China in crisis, but whether the Taylors were present is not clear. They spent the weekend of the 24th with Jenny's father at Tenterden. But the laconic entry in her diary the next day read, 'News serious'. Ci Xi's wolves had been unleashed. The legations at Peking were already under attack. Atrocities were multiplying. After a family consultation in London on July 2, they decided that the peace and seclusion of Switzerland would give Hudson Taylor the best hope of recovery. He himself wrote on July 6 to John Stevenson, 'If my head were in a condition to do mental work I should certainly have been on my way back to China before now. We are just preparing to go to Davos as that seems the quickest way of getting fit for work.' They arrived there on the 10th.

News from inland China travelled slowly, taking weeks to reach Shanghai. Even in late July cables from John Stevenson still told of danger, but as far as was known all were still safe. This was far from the terrible truth. Massacres had, in fact, been taking place since early June. Special concern for William Cooper was mentioned in letters, but Hudson Taylor had no inkling of how serious the situation had become. He even suggested that a hospital should be opened in Henan at the first possible opportunity, to break down prejudice.

Long after it was all over, the true story was still being pieced together. Eyewitnesses were difficult to find and slow to relive their bitter experiences. As always, the firsthand statements are best, within the limitations of exhaustion, of euphoria after deliverances from death, or of ability to express what remained all too vivid in their minds.[1251]

Martyred Missionaries of the China Inland Mission was in print well before the teams of mission representatives returned inland to learn what lay behind terse telegrams listing all too many names and ending 'murdered'. The *Chinese Recorder* carried only what came to its editor.[1252]

If the Christian world was staggered by the extent of suffering permitted by an omnipotent God, how much of what was known could be endured by the sick old man who loved his CIM family as dearly as his own children? Until the worst was over they kept it from him; but in the early days few had any concept of the horrifying truth; or that Cooper's headless body lay where it fell on July 1, outside the Baoding city wall.

May-July 1900: The wolves unleashed

'Alarms and excursions'
(May–June, 1900)

The leader and human inspiration of the CIM had been set aside incapacitated at the moment of supreme crisis. John Stevenson never lost the sense of horror as, virtually alone at the CIM headquarters in Shanghai, he bore the battering of desperate reports from place after place in China. In one way or another he was responsible for the welfare of eight hundred men and women, hundreds of children, and many more Chinese Christians under threat of persecution and death. Looking for the help or advice he often could not give, they tried to maintain contact with him and each other, until uprooted and overwhelmed, many fleeing for their lives, destitute or tortured they suffered until the end. As the reports came in, weeks or even months after the events, Jenny Taylor in her strength kept from her husband all that she judged to be unbearable. Told bit by bit what was happening, he reached the limits of endurance and had to be spared any more. 'I cannot think, I cannot pray, but I can trust,' he said at the height of the inferno. Like Job and like the victims in China he clung to the faithfulness of God, saying, 'Though he slay me, yet will I trust in him' (Job 13.15 AV).

We pick up the threads of 'the great miscalculation' in May 1900, when the unthinkable took the foreign community by surprise and the empress dowager championed the Boxers. 'Had the crisis not been precipitated before the plans of the Chinese Government had been completed . . . in all probability few foreigners would have escaped to tell the sad story.'[1253] Of eighty-nine missionaries of the CIM and other societies in the province of Shanxi at the time, forty-seven were known to have been killed by October, and their children with them. On this scale what would the toll have been throughout China, had brave viceroys, governors and court officials not risked decapitation and worse to negate the edicts of the evil Ci Xi? In the view of contemporary writers, 'nothing can be gained by the narration of harrowing details'. But in our day full knowledge of the facts is deemed necessary to true understanding. In most cases death came quickly, but the protracted sufferings of others carry their own timeless message.

Events had led inexorably to this calamity. On her return to Britain after her eight-thousand-mile journey in China and 'outer Tibet', Mrs Isabella Bird Bishop observed, in a paper read to the Church Congress at Newcastle: 'Everywhere an increasing hostility to foreigners was apparent.'[1254]

The seizure of Qingdao Bay and Jiao Xian (Kiaochow) by the Germans, and the policy it engendered of land-grabbing by other powers, had roused a storm of anger against foreigners. The empress dowager was fully justified in saying in her edict of November 1899, when she called upon all her officials and armies to resist any further attempts to invade Chinese soil, 'There are certain things to which this empire can never consent. Let no one think of making peace.' The author of *Martyred Missionaries of the CIM*, himself in Shanxi when Tong Fuxiang's horde of Muslim cavalry were passing through the province towards Peking, was invariably told in answer to his questions, 'We are going to drive the Germans out of Kiaochow!'

Wherever the Roman Catholic Church acted on the edict of March 15, 1899, granting official rank to each order in the priestly hierarchy, anti-Catholic feeling and resistance were aroused. When the rains failed and famine threatened, the desecration of graves, and disregard of *fengshui* were blamed. Between Peking and Baoding where the Boxers were recruiting and drilling, the flash-point of violence was particularly low as May progressed, while in Shanxi the newly-arrived governor, Yü Xian, was waiting for no one.

Towards mid-May armed Boxers raided three Roman Catholic villages near Baoding, the capital of provincial Zhili, eighty miles south-west of Peking and Tianjin (see map 1.34: 1, 491), 'killing and

2.78 William Cooper and David Barratt leaving Linfen, 1900

burning alive some seventy' converts. On May 17, Sir Claude Macdonald, British minister, reported sixty-one killed in three villages. Two days later, halfway between Baoding and Peking, two largely Protestant Christian villages in Laishui county and the LMS chapel at Gongcun were attacked and destroyed (see map 2.81: p 656). In the carnage the pastor perished heroically.[1255]

Meanwhile William Cooper had passed through Baoding to Shanxi, visiting Taiyuan and 'a large number of stations' before meeting thirty-two missionaries of the 'south-central region' in conference at Linfen (Pingyang) on May 17. William Cooper had already detected the oncoming of the storm, when reports began coming in that Elder Si of Hongtong, had been attacked and severely wounded. Yü Xian, the provincial governor, had sent mounted Boxers from Shandong through the length and breadth of Shanxi to recruit and drill reinforcements in three categories: to fight for the empire—these were sent to Peking; to fight for the gods—these were to attack Christians and missionaries; and to fight for their homes—'defending' their own villages, even against destitute refugees on the run.[1256]

The Hongtong Boxers had announced on May 14 at a public parade that they would begin by killing Elder Si, and at once went to his home, plundered it and gave Si a fatal sword thrust through his side. Dr Millar Wilson rode out to his village home at once, but Si suffered for months before dying. His assailants went next to Linfen where the missionaries were congregated. William Cooper therefore spoke on Hebrews 13, verses 5–6: 'I will never leave thee, nor forsake thee. So that we may boldly say, The Lord is my helper, and I will not fear what man shall do unto me.'

When the Boxers took no action he moved on to Lu'an (now Changzhi), Yuwu and Lucheng, and again this was his theme in speaking to Chinese Christians and missionaries alike. It was likely that all would be called upon to suffer for Christ, and in sharing the lot of the Chinese, the foreign missionaries could set an example of fortitude and peace of heart. The first attack on Lu'an came two weeks later.[1257]

He had intended to follow Hudson Taylor's wish, as Cooper regarded it, and to return to the south through Henan. But John Stevenson needed him without delay. So he made instead for Baoding, to go by sea from Tianjin to Shanghai. He walked straight into trouble. The attack on Si had coincided with the attacks on the Christian villages between Baoding and Peking. And a week later the Boxers plundered Pastor Hsi's home, declaring that they had come by imperial orders through General Tong Fuxiang to exterminate foreigners. They severely beat Pastor Hsi's wife and old mother, and distributed the family's possessions among hundreds of onlookers. When the Boxers had gone, some people returned the loot to the family.

During the last days of May, the railway and telegraph lines had been cut between Baoding and Peking and between Peking and Tianjin. When thirty Belgian, Greek and Italian engineers fought their way through to Tianjin, 'for three days fighting all day long, closing round and at last carrying their women folk', in their final extremity they were rescued by sixty mounted volunteers who rode out to meet them. Nine of the original party were missing, and only nine remained unwounded.[1258]

When William Cooper reached Benjamin Bagnall's home at Baoding all appeared quiet and some Boxers said they bore no ill-will towards Protestant missionaries. But to continue towards the coast was impossible. Two SPG missionaries, Harry Y. Norman and Charles Robinson, had repeatedly warned the consul at Tianjin that Boxers were massing near Yongqing, and urged the Christians to escape to safety. While any were in danger they themselves refused to leave. On June 1 they were attacked. When they took refuge in the magistrate's *yamen*, the Boxers demanded that they be handed over. The magistrate let them escape through a backdoor and they sought asylum in a Confucian temple, but were turned away and caught. Robinson

was killed instantly, but after a brief evasion Norman was carried off and murdered in cold blood the next day.[1259]

The gravity of the situation at last impressed the allied envoys and on June 4 an appeal was sent to Europe for adequate protection. It would take weeks to come. At any point in May or early June all foreigners in Peking could have been wiped out, but until the Boxers forced her hand Ci Xi had more far-reaching intentions. As she and her prisoner, the emperor, returned from the Summer Palace, she issued her decree justifying the Boxers' action, and the increased activity around the capital at once flared into riot and the massacre of eight Chinese Christians at Tong Xian. The fuse had been lit. The last trains from Peking to the coast pulled out; a dangerously vulnerable party of fifteen Tong Xian missionaries at last braved the fifteen miles to the safety of the capital; the missionary communities in the city rapidly congregated for greater safety; those in the Methodist Episcopal Mission premises formed committees including one for defence; and Sir Claude Macdonald, a seasoned soldier, requested a relief force of British marines from Tianjin without delay.

By then (the weekend of June 9 when Hudson Taylor was leaving Boston for Britain) the forced exodus of missionaries from their homes in many provinces had begun. A 'rain procession' at Lu'an, trying to break the drought, attacked the mission premises on June 6, doing little damage, but prompting A. E. Glover to take his pregnant wife to the coast while he thought he could. Such was their isolation from reliable news. They started north on June 9, in mule litters, on a journey which was to cost them a thousand miles of suffering, death and deliverance. By the time they reached the Martin Griffiths at Shunde, the countryside of Zhili was seething. After eleven days in hiding, there remained no choice but to return to Lu'an and try a southern route through Henan. Only 'ten miles from (Shunde) we were stoned and captured and given over to death'. But 'a thousand miles of miracle' had begun.[1260] The Martin

Griffiths also set out separately for Lucheng, but failed to arrive. For months there was no news of them.

Massacre and mayhem[1261]
(June 10–24, 1900)

Two fateful weeks began on June 10 with the final severance of the telegraphic link between Peking and the outer world. The last letter out was dated July 14, and the last from Tianjin reached the Peking legations on the 18th. Ill-founded optimism in the cushioned diplomatic circle suffered a sequence of shocks as the Boxers burned the grandstand at the race-course only six miles from the city walls on the 9th and the legation hill resort the next day. Also on the 10th the extremist Prince Tuan was appointed President of the Zongli Yamen. Within hours of receiving the requisition from Peking for more marines, Admiral Sir Edward Seymour set out from Tianjin with a quickly mustered defence force of 2,000 men of various nationalities. Expecting them to arrive the next day, or at least by the 12th, a number of legation diplomats rode out to welcome them; but the resistance Seymour had encountered was too strong and no reinforcements arrived. Instead, to the diplomats' alarm, Chancellor Sugiyama, secretary of the Japanese legation, returning to the city was dragged from his carriage by Tartar cavalry and clubbed to death.[1262]

The 13th became more fateful still: an imperial decree commanded the viceroy of Zhili and the commanders of the northern army to 'resist any further foreign reinforcements and to stop the Allied force from coming to Peking'. Admiral Seymour had reached Langfang (see map 2.81: p 656), only forty miles from the capital, but as fast as his men repaired a sabotaged stretch of railway line, Boxers wrecked another. Food, drink and fuel supplies dwindled and the relief force was encircled. Fighting to retreat, and twice suffering costly defeat, they had not yet regained Tianjin when the empress dowager's worst edict, of June 24, stunned the world.

She, the Boxers and irregular armed bands each ran wild in their own way. Demonic hordes of fanatics, criminals, drought-starved peasants and ill-disciplined troops, all wild with bloodlust and a passion for plunder, stormed into Peking brandishing whatever weapons they could lay hands on. Most horrific were their flaming torches, seeking out and destroying every foreign house and all Chinese property in any way connected with foreigners. Starting with a Methodist Mission chapel, the flames engulfed the most prosperous quarters, not sparing innocent Chinese whose homes and businesses happened to stand alongside the objects of hatred. Even Sir Robert Hart's Imperial Maritime Customs Inspectorate, the Chinese

2.79 Outline plan of Beijing (Peking)

Imperial Bank, and postal and college premises suffered the fate of the French and other European legations. The Greek Orthodox Church, the Roman Catholic East Cathedral the LMS and American Board establishments went up in flames.[1263]

None suffered more than the Chinese Christians and their families. Without distinction between Catholic and Protestant converts and adherents, all were hunted and if caught were tortured and killed. Crowding into the churches or cowering at home they were burned alive. Any who escaped, often wounded and burnt, were rounded up and thrown back into the flames. All who could barricade themselves in defendable buildings did so. The Beitang (the North Cathedral), packed with three thousand refugees, was 'held by forty-three French and Italian marines and some five hundred converts armed with spears and a few rifles' for two long months. In the Methodist Episcopal Mission the committees of defence and 'general comfort' prepared to be attacked.[1264]

On June 14, a group of Frenchmen dramatically rescued the Catholic priests, nuns and Sisters of Charity from the South Cathedral before it was put to the torch. And on the 15th rescue parties from the American, Russian, British and German legations searched for Chinese Christians in the southern quarter. They found 'women and children hacked to pieces, men trussed like fowls, with noses and ears cut off and eyes gouged out. Chinese Christians (accompanying the rescuers) ran about in the labyrinth of streets calling upon the Christians to come out from their hiding places . . . Boxers were even now caught red-handed at their bloody work.' Some refugees succeeded in reaching the remaining legations and were taken in.

On the following day the *Times* correspondent, Dr G. E. Morrison, with an international troop of thirty-five marines under the Japanese military attaché, Colonel Shiba, searched the east city. Morrison's report (of October 15, 1900) described how cries reached them from a Daoist temple used by the Boxers for their occult rites. Forcing their way in, the patrol found Christians bound hand and foot, waiting to be tortured and executed. Shockingly mutilated bodies lay still warm and bleeding, sacrificed as part of the Boxers' frenzied ritual.[1265]

The Chinese city of Tianjin, close to the foreign business settlement, similarly fell into the Boxers' hands, and all Christian premises were destroyed. On the 16th the settlement itself came under gunfire. D. J. Mills of the CIM took his wife and children to Dagu at the river mouth, and returned at once by armoured train to attend the wounded throughout the week-long assault from all sides. 'Bullets . . . entered every window and shells damaged the CIM house', but neighbouring fires were contained and the settlement held out until relieved.

When the Dagu forts fired on allied ships offshore, the admirals demanded their surrender, and at dawn on the 17th took them by assault, before pressing on to the relief of Tianjin. Lord Elgin's feat of 1860 had been repeated. Ci Xi was furious, and Prince Tuan seized his opportunity to sway her opinion from following Yong Lu's counsel of moderation to one of belligerence. At a meeting of the Imperial Council, Tuan presented her with a forged ultimatum purporting to be from the allied envoys. Its crudity should have condemned it as spurious, for it demanded that the emperor be restored to power, with a proper place of residence, that all revenues should be collected by the foreign envoys and all China's military affairs should be under their control. So outrageous a document—for she 'never for a moment suspected its authenticity'—left her with no alternative but to do as Prince Tuan intended. She sent three of her ministers to challenge the envoys to haul down their flags and leave China under safe escort. Far from having hostile intentions, Sir Claude Macdonald pointed out, the Allied forces were bent on restraining the excesses daily devastating the capital, Tianjin and other cities. Unmoved, Ci Xi ordered the envoys out of Peking within twenty-four hours.

And they were prepared to comply, until suspicions of perfidy were confirmed. Prince Tuan had offered 'five hundred taels for every dead foreigner'.[1266]

Meanwhile unrest in the provinces was taking conflicting forms. On June 14 Boxers arrived at Datong between the two arms of the Great Wall in northern Shanxi, an outpost of the CIM (see map 2.80: p 652). Stewart and Kate McKee and their two children, Charles and Florence I'Anson and three children, Margaret Smith and Maria Aspden were stationed there. They could but wait and pray as the Boxers drilled and recruited. It was too late to escape even to Mongolia.[1267]

Away to the east in Manchuria, Boxer agitation and attacks on Christians had been building up, held in check by the viceroy but encouraged by his Manchu deputy. Their private power struggle ended on June 19 when the viceroy, recognising that his rival was in direct touch with the Peking court, quietly capitulated by gently urging good Boxers to keep the peace. Further and further afield the prospects for foreigners and Christians were daily becoming worse.[1268]

Between Datong and Guihuacheng on the Mongolian border, Soping was a centre for the Swedish Holiness Union, the associate mission of the CIM. Each year they and their colleagues in other cities met in conference on June 24. In 1900 the ten members were joined by two C&MA couples and their children, and Chinese delegates from each local church. As soon as they set out for Soping, mobs wrecked and burned their homes at Hunyuan and Zuoyun, driving the Christians into the flames. So, as at Baoding and Datong, the fourteen missionaries, two children and 'many' Chinese Christians at Soping were cut off, unable to find any way to escape.[1269]

The point of no return
(June 20–24, 1900)

On June 20 a secret meeting of the Manchu Grand Council formally decided at 5.00 a.m. on outright war. But for their characteristic inertia, they could have annihilated the scattered foreign community within hours. Instead the hardening of their attitudes became apparent. When the envoys requested an interview they were snubbed, and some serious incidents at last convinced them that decisive action must be taken immediately for the protection of all under threat.

Against his colleagues' advice, Baron von Ketteler, head of the German legation and 'a very passionate and excitable man', set out at 8.00 a.m. with his secretary, Herr Cordes, and an escort of marines for the Zongli Yamen. Meeting an apparently friendly squad of Manchu soldiers, von Ketteler sent his escort back and proceeded with the Manchus. Cordes, bringing up the rear, saw one of them take aim and fire point-blank at von Ketteler from behind. The baron was killed, and soon afterwards Cordes himself was severely wounded in both thighs. He managed to escape to where he could be rescued. A strange rumour had already been circulating at Tianjin for a week, that Baron von Ketteler had been killed.[1270] No explanation was found.

The alarm spread rapidly and foreigners of all kinds poured into the strongly walled legation with their Chinese dependants. At the same time the Catholic Beitang (Cathedral) entered a true state of siege. And two thousand other Chinese Christians, whom Sir Claude Macdonald described as 'survivors of a massacre intended to be complete', crowded precariously into unsuitable premises elsewhere. The dozen or so buildings of the British legation were crammed to capacity, but seeing how vulnerable the two thousand Chinese were, Dr Morrison of the *Times* and Professor Francis Huberty James, of the 1878 CIM famine relief team, succeeded in persuading the allied envoys to allow them also into the precariously defended legation. They negotiated with a Prince Su to guard and preserve his adjoining palace if he would allow the refugees to occupy it, and courageously led them through the streets to its relative safety. There Japanese marines and other volunteers manned the perimeters. Into the confined space under siege the troops of Tong Fuxiang began at 4.00 p.m. to pour shells and rifle fire in 'a fusillade which was generally constant and furious, at times interrupted by periods of quiet'. They had a vantage point on the city wall, so a daring sortie under full observation had to be mounted to drive them off.

From the first the Christians made themselves indispensable, doing the manual labour of digging, carrying and sandbagging the defences, and driving mine shafts under the attackers' positions. But seeing how heavily the odds were weighted against them, some took their own lives, among them the father of Wang Mingdao, a month before his son was born. The child's grandmother prophetically named him Tiezi, 'Iron'.[1271] Apart from 'some thousand of Chinese converts', the lives of 473 foreign civilians were at stake—245 men, 149 women and 179 children. International jealousies made coordination difficult, but with the experienced soldier Sir Claude Macdonald as commander, 451 guards fortified and held the legation against almost incessant attack for eight long weeks. A missionary was put in charge of fortification and another of 'general comfort'.[1272] At the end they were highly commended for their outstanding success. After Sir Claude, the most distinguished of the military men, and most admired by the defenders, was the Japanese attaché, Colonel Shiba, 'reckless in courage, unceasing in his vigilance, and fertile in plans'.

On June 22 a proclamation offered fifty taels for any foreign man taken alive, forty taels for a woman and thirty taels for a foreign child. This incentive was later found to have contributed to the sufferings of many missionaries in Shanxi and Zhili in the ensuing weeks.[1273] Much of what is known of events in Peking, in court and government circles, has come from the personal diary of the Manchu aristocrat Jingshan, a high government official who himself had a hundred Boxers billeted at his mansion.

The 'primary devils', he wrote, were barricaded in the legation, but on June 24 the 'secondary devils' (Chinese friendly to foreigners) received the full force of Manchu anger and Boxer bloodlust. By decree, Prince Chuang and Kangyi together were given command of the Boxers, and Prince Chuang presided over the execution outside his palace of 'many hundreds of Chinese Christians'. 'There was no mercy shown . . . innocent people perished with (those called) guilty.' A week later another batch of 'over nine hundred people were summarily executed' outside his gates. The empress dowager congratulated and rewarded the Boxers for their gruesome work. Then, on June 29, a tiny note from Sir Robert Hart dated June 24, probably sewn into the clothing of a daring courier, was received by the Allied commanders at Tianjin: 'Besieged in British Legation. Situation desperate. MAKE HASTE.'[1274]

For the 'primary devils' outside the partial protection of the legation defences, June 24 had become the blackest day of all. The empress dowager issued a secret decree 'of savage ferocity'. No copies survived to be held as proof of her guilt, but reliable evidence in time emerged to implicate her incontrovertibly. On July 4, Jingshan recorded that 'ten days ago' she had sent Yü Xian, governor of Shanxi, a secret decree: 'Slay all foreigners wherever you find them; even though prepared to leave your province they must be slain.'[1275] Of Protestant missionaries alone there were eighty-seven in Shanxi, but also many Catholics. In Henan a friendly official in the military mandarin's *yamen* confidentially handed to a CIM missionary a copy of a decree 'in the appalling and unexampled words':

> Yang ren bi sha, yang ren tui hui ji sha: Foreigners must be killed, even if they withdraw (or escape) they must still (or instantly) be killed.

A. H. Smith in his book, *China in Convulsion*, wrote that warning of the edict was

> brought to missionaries and others by friends in the *yamen*s, friendly telegraph operators and by officials—some of them

of high rank—in at least three provinces and in numerous places hundreds of miles apart, almost simultaneously. Twice at least the original despatch was seen by foreigners.

The fact that people and places were not named in these contemporary reports testifies to their veracity; for Ci Xi remained the tyrant even in defeat, afterwards taking revenge on some whom she learned had thwarted her commands. The supreme heroes were two of her own ministers in Peking, Yüan Zhang and Xü Jingcheng,[1276] who intercepted the decree about to be telegraphed and changed the word *sha* (kill) to *bao* (protect). Other, unaltered, copies dispatched by courier were received and 'obeyed ferociously and without hesitation'.

But enlightened viceroys and governors took their stand on the amended imperial decree they received by telegram, and later rejected 'unsubstantiated reports of a different intention'. Outstanding among them was one of whom the *North China Herald* later carried this account. On receiving the command by courier, he defied the empress dowager's madness even without benefit of Yüan Zhang's alterations.

> The interim Manchu Governor of (Shaanxi), Tuan Fang, has so protected the lives and property of some eighty foreigners that ... it is owing to his care that they are now alive. When the Edicts of the 20th to the 25th of June, that gave imperial sanction to the murder of foreigners, reached (Xi'an), that humane governor was so distressed that he wept in the presence of other high officials, and could neither eat nor sleep for some time. He immediately suppressed these drastic Edicts, and issued stringent orders that at any cost and all hazards order was to be maintained.

In so doing he condemned himself to execution, but before long found he had the support of powerful viceroys who shared his own convictions. He beheaded Boxer ringleaders, replaced inflammatory posters with his own counter-proclamations, sent cavalry at the gallop to protect a Swedish

missionary, and his own bodyguard to escort others travelling to the safety of Viceroy Zhang Zhitong's protection at Wuhan.[1277] Altogether he was credited with saving the lives of two hundred foreign residents and their families, and others passing through his jurisdiction.

The viceroys intervene[1278]
(27 June–July 1900)

The admirals at Dagu were in a quandary. By June 20 nothing had been heard 'from Peking since June 10, from the Seymour force since June 14, or from (Tianjin) since June 16'. They notified their respective governments that they were assuming responsibility to safeguard their national interests, and all received official approval. Reliable word of Baron von Ketteler's murder and the start of the legation siege did not reach them until a week after the strange rumour about him had been in circulation. They acted on the known facts of—mayhem in the capital, Seymour's predicament at Langfang and the Boxer holocaust in the Chinese city of Tianjin, threatening the adjoining foreign settlements. On June 20 (the day of the Grand Council's decision on war), therefore, to reassure the Chinese government and people they jointly announced their intentions. They would use force only to rescue their fellow-countrymen from Boxers or any others who threatened them or resisted the rescue attempt.

Several viceroys were already predisposed to welcome such a declaration, and the Chinese ambassadors to Western courts shared their views. Li Hongzhang had been appointed to Canton ostensibly to control the reformers, but largely to remove him from Zhili. The belief became general that had he remained at Tianjin, the Boxer rising would have been stamped out. On June 21 he informed the Chinese envoys that if the Western governments did not consider themselves at war with China he himself would go north, take steps to suppress the Boxers, and then negotiate with the powers for a settlement. The response was mixed and Li did not go.

The Yangzi basin viceroys, Zhang Zhitong at Wuhan and Liu Kunyi at Nanjing, regarded the secret societies as a menace sworn to the subversion of the Manchu dynasty, and therefore to be resisted. Early in June, Liu had ordered the execution of apprehended members of the Dadaohui (the Great Swords), and on June 16 with the support of the governors of Jiangxi, Anhui and Shandong memorialised the throne by telegram begging the empress dowager to recognise the Yihochuan (the Boxers) as revolutionary, not patriotic. To ride this tiger was to invite disaster. But the Boxers and their powerful patrons had already forced her hand.

When the admirals' declaration reached him, Zhang Zhitong, the classical scholar, issued a proclamation in poetic wenli 'Obey decrees; arrest rebels; keep the peace; rumour mongers and disturbers of churches will be executed.' The diarist Jingshan noted that Liu Kunyi's refusal to send troops to help Ci Xi massacre helpless foreigners had 'excited her wrath'. Liu's neutrality towards reform during the Hundred Days now contrasted strongly with his 'sturdy resistance to reaction'. Four-fifths of the empire's officials were Han Chinese loyal to the dynasty, who in the current crisis suspected the empress and insisted on their loyalty to the emperor, still nominally on the throne, as well as to her.

On July 3 the viceroys together proposed to the Chinese envoys that agreement be negotiated guaranteeing 'protection in accordance with the treaties to the lives and property of people of all nationalities within their respective jurisdiction', in exchange for the foreign powers agreeing not to send foreign forces into the interior of Jiangxi, Zhejiang or the Yangzi valley, whatever might transpire in the erupting north. Visions of the dismemberment of China in retaliation for widespread atrocities against foreigners clearly prompted the proposal, but the adoption of America's 'open door' policy had already halted the race to carve up China into acquisitive spheres of influence. The powers agreed, the two viceroys Zhang Zhitong and Liu Kunyi issued proclamations to the nation,[1279] and Li Hongzhang accepted the pact in principle, agreeing 'no longer to recognise the Peking government'—to quote Consul Warren to Lord Salisbury on June 29. Yüan Shikai telegraphed from Shandong, 'My views are the same as those of the viceroys.' And Tuan Fang, the brave governor of Shaanxi, was found to have adopted the same course of action independently. In this way, 'all the high officials in the southern and central provinces had allied themselves with the foreign powers, on the basis of the declaration that this was an insurrection and not a foreign war, and that the powers sought no acquisition of territory.'

In the remoter provinces of Guizhou, Yunnan, Sichuan and Gansu, hesitation due to poor communications delayed conformity with the rest, but with persuasion they too left the Boxer 'rising' to fulminate only in the provinces north of the Huang He (Yellow River). Henan and Zhejiang proved to be the tragic exceptions Such facts were not public property. As 'the great flight' of many hundreds of foreigners from the interior of China to the coast proceeded, it was in ignorance of what fate lay ahead of them. Only the bitter experience of fear and differing degrees of suffering would enlighten them.[1280]

Crescendo of horror (June 21–26, 1900)

On the day after the Peking siege began and the court declared war (June 21), Ci Xi issued an apologia in the name of the Guang Xü emperor, in defence of her action. Foreign encroachments and insults to the gods in return for extreme kindness by China had evoked indignation and riot by patriotic people, she claimed. The nation of four hundred millions was united in choosing to fight rather than to be eternally disgraced. Hundreds of thousands of patriotic volunteers (the Boxers) had taken up arms, even children carrying spears 'to vindicate the dignity of our country'. She could only approve, deviously saying nothing of the armed forces already driving

Admiral Seymour back to Tianjin and battering at the frail walls of the legation enclave. Those 'patriots' were unthinkingly setting fire to the ancient Hanlin Academy adjacent to the legation, intent only on igniting the legation buildings. The timeless Hanlin library, filled with immeasurably precious manuscripts, went up in flames leaving the legation buildings intact.[1281]

Shandong province under Yüan Shikai had remained relatively peaceful since S. M. Brooks's murder. But with events in neighbouring Zhili becoming desperate, all Shandong missionaries fled to the protection of the ports, those from the provincial capital Jinan to Yantai and from Wei Man to Qingdao. F. H. Chalfont held off an attack at Wei Man single-handed with a revolver until the mission premises were ablaze, and then escorted his colleagues to safety. The missionary community as a whole was divided between those who were prepared to use firearms in self-defence and those who would not in any circumstances.[1282] With their exodus, fearful persecution of the Shandong Church broke out. Faced with the torture and death of many members at Qingzhou, two pastors publicly recanted in the name of all Christians in their congregations, saying afterwards, 'The sin was ours and ours alone' and 'I decided to take on myself the shame and the sin', 'so that old and young would be spared the terrors of a massacre'.

At the same time, June 21–25, in Manchuria the viceroy was keeping secret the anti-foreign edicts, to allow time for foreigners to escape. Russian railway engineers took the Mukden (now Shenyang) women, children and younger missionaries to safety at Yingkou (Niuchuang), and when the streets everywhere resounded with the unearthly shouts of the Boxers, 'Slay!' and 'Burn!' the Christians insisted that the three male missionaries who had stayed behind should escape while they could.[1283]

Five members of the American Board fleeing from Zhangjiakou (Kalgan) and three Swedish families who had joined them in Mongolia found the magistrate at

Harausa unfriendly. He ordered them to leave at once, saying that a force of Boxers was only ten miles away. What were they to do? The fearsome Gobi Desert lay between them and Siberian Russia (see map 2.59: p 480). It happened that the British consul at Shanghai had planned a journey, now impossible for him, and a caravan of twenty camels, six camel carts and nineteen horses was available. They decided to take the plunge. Then, before they started, four more Swedes arrived. One of the women had been 'almost clubbed to death' and one of the men 'presented a frightful spectacle, covered with blood and dust'.[1284] Together the twenty-two refugees set off to cross the desert northwards making for Urga (Ulan Bator) and the Russian border at Kiakhta. Bandits, dry water-holes and Boxers would endanger their lives until they were in Russia—a journey of fifty days.

By June 24 all hope of a peaceful conference of the Swedish missions in Soping had vanished. When threatening placards appeared on the walls in the city and hostile crowds chanted, 'All foreign property has been destroyed in other cities; burn this place down!' two of the Swedish men went to consult the friendly magistrate. He confessed he was powerless, but urged them all to take refuge at his *yamen*. He would send them safely to Zhangjiakou (Kalgan) when he could. As soon as the missionaries moved out, however, their premises were put to the torch and all the Christians, employees and friendly neighbours were herded into the inferno and burned to death. In the commotion a doorkeeper named Wang Lanbu fainted and somehow escaped the fate of the others. When discovered he was flogged and left for dead, but before daylight recovered enough to go into hiding. Eventually he made his way to Tianjin, gathering information about the atrocities in place after place from which the conference delegates had come.

From the massacre by fire the mob went to the *yamen* and demanded that the foreigners be handed over to them. To win time the magistrate had five of the men shackled, and announced that all would be sent to Peking 'for execution'. At first this seemed to satisfy the ringleaders. But when an escort of soldiers took them out through the city gates on the morning of June 29, all sixteen were ferociously dragged from their carts and stoned to death.[1285] One of the children was literally 'torn asunder by the violence of the mob'. In the mêlée two of the young men broke free, only to be caught, killed and their bodies burnt; but all the rest were decapitated before being burnt, and their heads displayed on the city walls. On the same day the Christians at Yingzhou were burnt alive.

Three engineers prospecting for new railway routes had travelled unhindered from Canton through Hunan and Guizhou to Sichuan and Gansu before heading east to Tianjin. On June 24, their raft on the Yellow River was wrecked and one, John Birch, was drowned. Another, Harry Matheson, somehow made his way alone to Tianjin. But Captain Watts-Jones, RE, the leader, continued on to Ningxia and 'was later subjected to a lingering death by torture'.[1286]

In Zhili, Shanxi and Manchuria the Boxers systematically called upon Christians to recant and deny the faith, and afterwards often killed those who complied. But some magistrates whose own lives depended on placation of the Boxers, especially under the authority of Yü Xian, 'the Butcher of Shanxi' (see p 672), attempted to avoid confrontation and to protect the people under their jurisdiction. They made recantation appear as innocuous as possible. A mere formality, representative recantation by one or two pastors on behalf of a community, as in Shandong, or simply signature to a document undertaking 'no longer to practise the foreign religion' would secure freedom from action against them. Many convinced themselves that Christianity was no more a foreign religion than Buddhism or Islam, and took refuge in the play on words. Proclamations then announced that they 'had returned to their position as Chinese subjects'.[1287]

The subtlety of such wording often made the temptation to comply more than unlettered countrymen could resist. One devoted old Christian afterwards told with chuckles of delight how he had hoodwinked the Boxers with the greatest of ease. But if many hundreds, thousands, saved themselves and their families from atrocious suffering, as many (if unsubstantiated generalisations are to be accepted) chose to suffer and die rather than to yield at all. Often 'adherents' not yet accepted as true believers or baptised, proved as staunch as mature Christians when confronted by a terrible death. Large numbers of Catholics and Protestants so proving their fidelity were honoured after the holocaust ended, but the records at best were incomplete. Those who not only died 'as partakers of Christ's sufferings' but would not leave their foreign friends in the last extremity have a place of their own in the history of Christian martyrs. R. C. Forsyth gave example after example, of men, women and children who died by the sword rather than deny their Lord, and missionary survivors had many stories to tell of Chinese companions who would not leave them. 'Liu Mingjin, a chapel-keeper, was bound to a pillar in the temple (but) kept preaching to his persecutors . . . One of the Boxers in a rage cried, "You still preach do you?" and slit his mouth from ear to ear.' A 'Bible-woman' named Wu was taken to the same temple, bound to a pillar and flogged, without uttering a cry. The flesh was burned off all her face, and her hands and feet were cut off before she was taken out, hacked to pieces and burned. The appalling sufferings of many missionary men, women and children even compared favourably with what their Chinese brothers and sisters endured.[1288]

'Escape!' but how? (June 26–30, 1900)

June 26 was the day the southern and central viceroys promised protection within their jurisdiction. The north was beyond their power and given up to obeying Ci Xi's every whim. On that day also Dr Millar Wilson, suffering he believed from 'peritonitis', rejoined his wife and son

Alexander in Taiyuan. And on the same day the mission at Pingyao (forming an arc with Taigu, Jiexiu, Xiaoyi, Fengzhou (now Fenyang) and Yongning south-west of Taiyuan) was attacked and looted.[1289] A. R. Saunders at once took his wife and four children, Alfred Jennings and a single woman named Guthrie under official escort to the supposed safety of the provincial capital. None of them yet knew that on the 24th the empress dowager's command to kill had been received and relayed on the 25th by Yü Xian to his officials in each county as 'withdraw protection from all foreigners'. Boxers would do the rest.

Only seven miles from Taiyuan, Saunders and his companions met a Christian who told them that the Schofield Memorial Hospital and the Shouyang Mission premises in Taiyuan had been burned down. Several thousands of people were surrounding them and in spite of a military guard round the house were preparing to raze it to the ground with its occupants that same night.

Saunders decided to head south again and make for Lucheng, miles away to the south-east. Their escort deserted them, and after three attacks by Boxers, Saunders succeeded in 'buying' the protection of the officer in charge of the imperial couriers' stables for the rest of the way. But tension was building up to a riot in Lucheng itself when they arrived there eight days later.

The destruction of the Schofield Hospital and mission premises on June 27 had been without warning. Dr and Mrs A. E. Lovitt, G. W. Stokes and his wife, and James Simpson and his wife forced their way through the crowd and, although separated, all succeeded eventually in reaching G. B. Farthing's house. But Edith Coombs, a nurse, seeing the hospital on fire returned to rescue a child patient. On leaving the building she was 'struck on the head with a piece of iron' and, according to Dr Millar Wilson quoting an eye witness, was stoned to death before being thrown back into the burning house.[1290] Attempts by Farthing to get protection by the authorities failed so blatantly that their connivance had to be assumed. From this time the city gates were kept closed to prevent any foreigner or Christian from leaving. On June 28, young Dr Lovitt, formerly of the London Hospital and Mildmay Mission Hospital, wrote, 'We cannot but hope for deliverance (hope dies hard) and our God is well able . . . even to save us . . . There is not much time. We are ready.'

The six young women[1291] who had moved to Jiexiu, as a quiet country town less likely to see disturbances, had been there only three weeks when news of the riot at Pingyao precipitated an attack on the mission house. Annie Eldred had gone to stay with the A. P. Lundgrens at Fenzhou (Fenyang), but the five others, led by Eva French, escaped to the *yamen*. The friendly mandarin told them he was forbidden to protect them, but sent them concealed in carts with an escort to Linfen. For this he was later cashiered by Ci Xi on her flight to Xi'an. On the way, at Hongtong on

2.80 The killing fields in gruesome Shanxi

June 30, unruly crowds tried to break down the doors of the house they were in, so Eva French, showing the courage and initiative that made her a great apostle of the Gobi Desert in later years, as she wrote, 'called for a cart and went myself to the *yamen*'. Again the mandarin proved as friendly as the one at Jiexiu, told her about the fire and Miss Coombs's murder at Taiyuan, and that their only hope lay in escaping to Hankou. He told the church elder who accompanied her that he would have to recant and worship idols, and shortly before midnight sent carts to take them on to Linfen.

Not content with all her inflammatory edicts, the empress dowager promulgated yet another on June 28, 'praising the Boxers and commanding all viceroys and governors to support the rising'. As it happened, on that same day the viceroys and governors of the southern and central provinces declared Ci Xi's extremist adviser, Prince Tuan, a rebel and united to resist him. Her goading was unnecessary in the north where destruction and slaughter were already out of hand, and futile in the rest of China where restraint was being applied. In the two provinces of Zhejiang and Henan neither course met with absolute compliance. Before July was out, Zhejiang was to taste supreme tragedy, but as early as June 29 the first exodus from Henan began.[1292]

The Canadian Presbyterians had been advised by the British consul at Tianjin to withdraw from Zhangde (now Anyang) [close to the Henan-Zhili border and across the Taihang mountains from Lu'an (now Changzhi)] and to make their way north-eastwards to Jinan, capital of Shandong. From there they could travel concealed in canal boats to the coast and be picked up by steamer. Two doctors and their families, with one single lady, had already succeeded in this. But when they applied to the prefect for an escort he refused to do anything for them. They therefore cited the treaties, saying, 'The foreign powers have seized Dagu and a settlement of this trouble must come.' At this he changed his tune, but only

to allow them to travel southwards, deeper into Henan (see map 2.84: p 662).

A large party of them left Anyang on June 28. Jonathan Goforth and his family, four or five other families and three single men were stoned on one occasion, but crossed the Yellow River (the Huang He) safely, and on July 1 met three armed British railway engineers of the Peking Syndicate with an official Chinese escort.[1293] All stayed together and made good progress until ten miles from Nanyang. There they learned of danger ahead. The engineers took the Slimmon and Mitchell families with them to obtain escorts for the rest of the party, and reached Nanyang safely. But here also the prefect refused protection on the pretext that China was at war with Britain. Risking attack, the Goforth, Mackenzie and Leslie families with three single men, McIntosh, Douw and Pike, came on without a proper escort and reached Nanyang late on July 7. Then their real troubles began.[1294]

Cornered, with nowhere to go (June 27–July 8, 1900)

The county town of Shouyang lies eighty miles east of Taiyuan, about halfway to the Guguan Pass. When T. W. Pigott withdrew from the CIM and by agreement with Hudson Taylor continued to work at Shouyang and Taiyuan, he retained a young tutor, John Robinson, for his son, Wellesley, and a governess, Mary Duval, welcoming other children to be educated with him. Two Oberlin missionaries of the American Board named Atwater entrusted their two daughters to them, and they were in Shouyang on June 29 when desperate events began.[1295]

The Shouyang magistrate informed the Pigotts that by order of Peking through Yü Xian, the provincial governor, protection was being withdrawn from foreigners. He offered to escort them to the county border, but could do no more. While they were considering what to do, word came of the destruction of the hospital and the murder of Edith Coombs in Taiyuan on the 27th. Immediately they began preparing to escape.

It happened that a Christian from the country was visiting them at the time. He invited them to go out to his home in an isolated hamlet of ten families in loess cave-dwellings. Darkness had fallen by the time they all arrived there. But the next morning word of their coming quickly spread and a stream of curious villagers flocked to see them, openly discussing what the Boxers were doing elsewhere. As soon as they had left Shouyang, a crowd led by a renegade church member plundered their home, carrying away even the doors and windows. And two days later some Christians were killed only a few miles from the hamlet. At once a crowd collected and began to pillage the Pigotts' few possessions and the home they were staying in. They therefore returned to Shouyang.

At midnight, when they reached the magistrate's *yamen*, asking for sanctuary, they found that his attitude had hardened. They were all put in the guard house and soon afterwards sent to Taiyuan with Pigott and Robinson in handcuffs, all together in a large uncovered farm cart, escorted by fifty soldiers. At roadside halts for watering the animals, Pigott and Robinson preached to the crowds that surrounded them, and heard people say, 'They are going to be killed for preaching, and yet go on doing so.' In the evening of July 8, two hundred more horse and foot soldiers met them about three miles from Taiyuan and took them, not to join the other foreigners as they requested, but to the common gaol.

Forty-five miles north of Taiyuan, at Xinzhou on the Datong and Soping road, was a BMS mission centre staffed by Herbert and Mrs Dixon, William and Clara McCurrach, Bessie Renaut and Sidney Ennals.[1296] On June 29 when they heard that the Schofield Memorial hospital had been destroyed, visitors from Taiyuan, Thomas Underwood and his wife, were with them. News of the Soping massacre had not yet reached them. Immediately they all decided to flee.

They left Xinzhou unhindered, in two carts and a mule litter, with two riding horses, but had covered only ten miles when a messenger caught up with them. They were wanted by the Xinzhou magistrate. They pressed on all the faster, to the cave-dwelling of a Christian 'at the head of a narrow valley with high, steep sides on either side'. After two weeks their hiding place was discovered by men who had been out searching for them, and the friendly villagers on whom they had depended for food and water had to go into hiding themselves. As the missionaries were known to possess firearms, in an easily defended defile, no attempt was made to capture them until soldiers came out from Xinzhou. They put up a brief resistance but were outnumbered and Dixon surrendered. The whole party were then thrown into the common gaol in Xinzhou, among all the filth, stench and vermin for which such places were notorious, especially in the heat of high summer.

The Chinese who had left Xinzhou with them were the first to suffer. Ho Cungui, one of the first to become a Christian in that area, also became the first martyr. Caught by young Boxers when looking for an escape route for the missionaries, he was beaten with a thousand strokes on the magistrate's orders and thrown into prison in manacles and the stocks. Another Christian prisoner cared for him until he died on the fourth day. Two others, An Xügan and Zhang Lingwang, a boy of sixteen, had stayed with the party until supplies ran low, when they were persuaded to return home. But on the way they were taken by Boxers, interrogated, hacked to death and burned, young Zhang refusing to leave his friend when offered the chance.[1297]

In a strong account by F. C. H. Dreyer of events with which he was concerned around the time of his successful escape to Hankou, is the passage:

We destroyed all (Chinese) and foreign Church registers, collection books, lists of children, Chinese letters, etc., and reminded others to do so lest they fall into the hands of the Boxers ... having been told that the Boxers at (Xiaoyi) got the names of many Christians from a silk banner which had been presented to the ladies and hung on the chapel wall.[1298]

News from Xiaoyi had been minimal, as after the massacre no one was left to pass it on. But on September 19 a letter to Erik Folke from the shadowy figure known to the CIM as 'CCH' lest he be caught and punished, contained the words, 'At (Xiaoyi) the two ladies and many of the Christians have been killed, and many have had to flee. Their houses have all been destroyed.' Eventually a Christian teacher named Wang Yinggui, who narrowly escaped the slaughter referred to, told the full story; but even the *Last Letters* of December 1901 could only say (mistakenly) that they had died on June 30.

On June 28 a messenger had brought news of rioting and plunder at Pingyao and Fenzhou and on his way to inform Emily Whitchurch and Edith Searell had thoughtlessly spoken about it in the town. A hostile crowd quickly gathered at the mission door, battering at it while the two women and loyal Chinese inside prayed together, and a leading Christian, He Xiaofu, climbed over the back wall, ran to the *yamen* and rang the great bell kept for life-threatening emergencies. The magistrate hurried to the mission, found nothing in his opinion to justify the appeal and punished He Xiaofu for raising a false alarm. He told the local constable to guard the door. But when he had gone, the rioters returned, smashed the heavy gate and began stoning the missionaries.

This time the magistrate took the threat more seriously and told them to leave Xiaoyi, saying he could not protect them. Again his control of the rioters was short-lived. Early the next morning, June 29, they forced their way in and battered the two women to death as they knelt together to pray. They then 'stripped, exposed and defiled' their dead bodies and piled all their possessions in the courtyard to be carried off.

The magistrate sent two cheap coffins such as were used for pauper criminals, and the two disfigured bodies were deposited in the chapel. Then began the witch hunt for all Christians in Xiaoyi, and the looting and destruction of their homes and property.[1299]

The Baoding massacre
(June 25–July 1, 1900)

A fortnight had passed since William Cooper joined the Bagnalls at Baoding in Zhili. As late as June 25 he managed to send a telegram to John Stevenson in Shanghai, saying it was still impossible to travel, but he thought there was no cause for anxiety. A month later Stevenson cabled to London, 'Authentic information has been received that all missionaries have been murdered in (Baoding). We apprehend the worst for Mr and Mrs Bagnall and Mr William Cooper.'

Letters were subsequently found in the viceroy's *yamen* at Tianjin saying that Europeans and Americans had been massacred at Baoding on June 30 and July 1. The facts were known to the highest mandarins, but treated as unimportant, a mere incident in the nationwide extermination that had been planned.

To the outer world, events even in the previous provincial capital of Zhili remained unconfirmed and indistinct, and not surprisingly at Wusong Road. John Stevenson lived until August 15, 1918, but never lost the sense of horror that he suffered day after day as the responsible leader in China during the Boxer rising and for months afterwards, until everyone was accounted for.

Not until May 1901 did the *Chinese Recorder* print such meagre information as had been obtained, and the *Last Letters and Further Records of Martyred Missionaries* published in December 1901 had little to add. But gradually the truth was pieced together from eye-witnesses and from the victims' last messages. J. Walter Lowrie of the American Presbyterian Mission at Baoding happened to be away when the Boxers cut the city off from the outside world. But after the Peking siege was lifted and an allied commission assumed control at Baoding, Lowrie served as an interpreter-adviser during the restoration of normal conditions there. His reconstruction of

2.81 Zhili, showing the scene of the sieges and sufferings of Norman, Robinson, the Greens and J. Gregg

events formed the basis of Robert Forsyth's narrative.[1300]

Of the normal Protestant community of thirty-two men, women and children at Baoding, only fifteen were present in June, 1900. At the American Presbyterian premises north of the city were Dr G. Y. Taylor, Dr and Mrs C. V. R. Hodge, and F. E. S. Simcox, his wife and three children. The Roman Catholics also had a fine church, residences and schools. And south of the city at the American Board were Horace T. Pitkin (his wife and son having returned to the States) and two single women, Mary S. Morrill and Annie A. Gould. The Bagnalls lived close by in charge of the CIM business office for relaying funds and supplies to the interior, and William Cooper was their guest.

When Ci Xi's edict of slaughter was made public some of the missions' employees fled, but many others stayed or returned and were slaughtered with their foreign friends. Among the Presbyterian Chinese Christians alone, thirty-five gave their lives in this way. Meng Jixian, first pastor of the American Board congregation, on learning of the missionaries' danger,

hurried to join them and commanded his son to make his way to safety, in order that he might carry on his father's work. On June 28, Meng Jixian was packing up books in the chapel when he was seized by Boxers, carried to the temple they were using, tortured and beheaded. The word 'tortured' sums up the appalling cruelties associated with their human sacrifices (see p 645). Daring Christians recovered his body from the ditch behind the temple. The nature of what to expect had become luridly plain to all. Educated gentlemen came and shed tears with Dr Taylor, but could do nothing to protect him. Fair-weather friends among the literati kept well clear, and officials known to have been friendly went into hiding to preserve their own lives. [1301]

As always, Boxers were joined by street rabble bent on plunder when they came to the north suburb on June 30, heaped stubble against the outer gate of the Presbyterian premises and quickly reduced it to ashes. Breaking in, they looted the missionaries' homes and set fire to them. Two faithful gatekeepers and other employees, with their women and children, were either killed or driven into the well to drown. The foreigners all took refuge in the Simcox home. Two armed with a rifle and shotgun tried to drive the mob back. They killed the leading Boxer, but the rest surged on. 'Mr Simcox was seen walking to and fro, hand in hand with his two little sons, as the flames enveloped them.' Dr Taylor from the window of his own room pleaded the many kindnesses they had all done as missionaries, but also died in the flames of his own house. His medical assistant, refusing to escape, was buried half alive in a shallow grave after being brutally wounded.

The American Board and CIM in the south suburb soon heard of the massacre and prepared to die. Horace Tracy Pitkin, given his life purpose at Moody's Northfield Conference and serving first as one of the best secretaries of the Student Volunteer Movement, wrote a note to his wife and gave a verbal message to a Chinese Christian. At Pitkin's request the Christian scaled a wall and escaped, eventually to deliver the message: 'Tell little Horace that his father's last wish was that when he is twenty-five years of age he should come to China as a missionary.' He did.

In pouring rain on the morning of July 1 the main gate of the American Board was broken open by the mob and imperial soldiers. Pitkin and the two ladies retreated to the chapel and, firing from its windows, he tried to defend them until his ammunition ran out. They then hid in an outhouse, but were soon found. With one sword stroke 'Mr Pitkin's head was severed from his body' and 'the ladies were rudely seized by the brutal mob'. In horror, Annie Gould sank limply to the ground. Her hands and feet were roped together and she was carried suspended from a pole between two men, like a pig being taken to market. Mary Morrill walked alongside, exhorting bystanders to prepare for the life to come by trusting in Jesus Christ, and even 'gave some silver to a poor creature in the crowd'. They were taken to the infamous Boxer headquarters in the temple.

Hearing the commotion at the American Board a few hundred yards away, William Cooper[1302] and the Bagnalls with their little daughter quickly collected up their money and valuables and decamped to the imperial military cantonment nearby, in the faint hope of a safe escort to Tianjin. Instead the colonel relieved them of all their valuables and handed them over to the provincial judge. He delivered them to the Boxers, and they were taken to join Mary Morrill and Annie Gould in the temple. A few hours later (hours of terror to any who could not face death with the Christian confidence and composure of these missionaries), the Boxers roped the hands of each one very tightly to his and her head and neck and to each other. With little Gladys Bagnall walking alongside, they led them out in single file to their execution.

At some point, probably as they walked to the south-east corner of the city wall, outside the city, Mary Morrill, aged thirty-six, tried to persuade the Boxers to be satisfied with taking her life and sparing the others. A young imperial soldier, aged twenty, heard what she said. Thirteen years later, at an evangelistic meeting in Peking, addressed by John R. Mott on a visit to China, Major Feng Yuxiang made a profession of faith in Christ.

> A forthright man of towering physique and great energy, he gave himself wholeheartedly to his new faith as he understood it. Feng rose rapidly in rank and in influence and by 1922 was a national figure ... He encouraged missionaries (especially Goforth) to preach to his troops. Thousands (of them) received baptism. Many of his officers were professing Christians ... In the army ... a daily religious meeting with Bible reading, prayer and hymns was usual. (General) Feng himself often preached to his soldiers.[1303]

As the Baoding victims stumbled to their execution, 'guns were fired and demonstrations (of sword play) made'. Intended to celebrate a Boxer triumph, they were more than that. They marked the triumph of life over death, for 'it is not death to die', and 'from the ground there blossoms red, life that shall endless be'. All were beheaded, Gladys after being thrust through with a sword. And after lying exposed overnight, all were buried in one grave.

What then of 'Cooper's worth'? Often sick and partly deaf since having typhoid, his character had seemed refined by hardship so that W. B. Sloan could quote a tribute to him: 'One of the very few blameless lives that I have ever come into contact with'.

2.82 Where William Cooper died, outside Baoding city wall

No hiding place (July 1900)

That another edict from the dowager empress should have been issued on July 2, ordering the expulsion of foreigners and persecution of Christians, was as perfidious as any of her actions during these days of the Boxer madness. The government was to be seen as expelling foreigners, with the implication of doing so for their protection. That they should be deliberately driven into the hands of Boxers and ruffians waiting for them outside city walls was left unsaid. The Boxers bore the guilt of massacring them.

All through Ci Xi's erratic career as emperor's concubine, regent, and dowager empress, she had practised the wily art of covering her traces, to safeguard the possibility that events could turn against her. She could always lay the blame on someone else. The Boxers were to do most of her butchery, but while using them she took care to refer on July 1 to 'wanton murder and robbery committed by persons feigning to belong to the Yihochuan'.

That on the next day she should appeal in the name of the emperor to the Western powers for help to restore order was duplicity in the extreme. The legations were under constant attack, yet her appeals attributed the 'upheavals' in China to dissension between 'Christians and the people of (Zhili) and Shandong'. The current hostilities she blamed on the seizure of the Dagu forts. But to each ruler the appeal was addressed in different terms, calculated to yield the best results. The concept of psychological warfare was not generally exploited at this phase of history, but Ci Xi's intelligence may be credited with measures to weaken resolve and delay counter-action.[1304]

It resembled the extraordinary events in the palace on June 25. Sixty Boxers, led by the extremist Prince Tuan and Prince Chuang, burst in, 'clamouring noisily for the emperor, "the foreigners' friend"'. An irate dowager empress confronted them, expostulating that she alone had the power to create or depose the emperor and for that matter the heir apparent, Prince Tuan's son, whom she had arbitrarily appointed.

In fury she ordered that 'in accordance with imperial commands to protect the foreign envoys' all fighting in Peking be stopped, and that Yong Lu should negotiate terms of peace at a bridge north of the British legation. When a legation representative under a white flag came to the bridge, however, he faced levelled rifles and withdrew. No communication from the government was delivered, but after a short interval 'the attack was renewed more furiously than before'.

Sir Robert Hart wondered whether the episode was to throw the defenders off their guard or to put some 'friendliness' on record for future use. Ci Xi, the court and government were at sixes and sevens. The 'furious sound of rifle-shot' against the legation defences was sometimes punctuated by 'the shell of old pieces'.

> During the two-month siege it was calculated that 2,900 shell fell within the legation area, but it was one of the miracles protecting the besieged that the shell fire was not more abundant or more accurate. Credit for this is given to (Yong Lu) ... He would not allow (his) artillery to be used 'so near to the imperial palace', and he refused point-blank to sanction the use of his reserve guns—beautiful new pieces, not yet even unpacked. [Yong Lu even dared to memorialise the Old Buddha, warning her that] the persons of envoys are always held inviolate within the territories of any civilised state and that 'This attack on the legations is worse than an outrage, it is a piece of stupidity which will be remembered against China for all time.'[1305]

This then was the climate at the seat of power when the foreigners widely scattered throughout the empire realised their danger and began to withdraw to the coast. In Manchuria parties of missionaries, merchants and engineers profited by the warnings given them and accepted the protection of Russian troops through many attacks and considerable hardships until evacuated to safety by railway and river steamer. But their property was destroyed. At Mukden (now Shenyang) on July 3 the Roman Catholic bishop, priests, sisters and hundreds of Christians were burned to death in their church. 'Three hundred Chinese Protestants were slaughtered, some with great cruely . . . A native sect, the 'Fasters' (*Tsaili*) joined the Boxers and the government in an orgy of extermination.'[1306]

Huolu and the Greens (July 1900)

On July 2 Charles Green and his wife and Jessie Gregg at Huolu in Zhili (near the entrance to the Guguan Pass) received the unsettling news of the Baoding massacres less than a hundred miles away. But that was not all. A riot had taken place at Shunde (now Xingtai) where their nearest CIM neighbours, the Griffiths, had lived, and the much feared Yü Xian was soon to arrive at Huolu with his Shanxi troops and Boxers.[1307]

A prolonged drought had ruined the previous autumn's harvest and prevented sowing in the spring. Placards then began to appear saying that there would be no rain until all foreigners were exterminated, but a friendly mandarin promised to protect the Greens. Most Christian Chinese in and around Huolu were the only Christians in their families and came increasingly under persecution. Night after night intruders disturbed the missionaries' sleep, until the mandarin posted guards round the premises. These facts, and rumours about the fate of foreigners elsewhere, became the talk of the town; and couriers employed by the various missions in Shanxi began to be intercepted and killed by Boxers when caught carrying foreign mail.

From June 30 rain fell for several days, enough to allow of sowing to avert famine. But on July 3, after news of the Baoding atrocities arrived, 'a shouting, howling mob' began to pelt the Greens' front door with stones. At once their landlord urged them to leave Huolu, lest his property be damaged. Hearing that mission property in Taiyuan had been destroyed and lives lost, they began to plan their escape. A few days earlier a temple-keeper had offered them a room on a nearby mountain, and they

decided to put themselves in his hands, but when?

Their city of Huolu was already in a ferment of excitement when a messenger arrived saying that after the CIM at Shunde had been rioted, the Martin Griffiths and R. M. Brown had gone into hiding; the Glovers trying to return to Lu'an had been robbed; and no magistrate would lift a finger to help any of them. Another messenger then came in. The Shouyang mission homes had been wrecked and the occupants taken away in chains (see p 654). The Greens and Jessie Gregg at once took a change of clothing, some bedding, essential food and cooking utensils, and left under cover of darkness for the temple.

As soon as they had gone, on July 5, their Huolu house was stripped by the landlord of anything he coveted, and thrown open to looters. They were homeless. And worse still, they were seen and the big village gong was sounded to call everyone to decide what to do. On the 8th, the local bully came and told the fugitives to leave at once or be driven away. They had nowhere to go to. But as soon as the bully had gone, the temple-keeper said, 'Don't be afraid; I have . . . a natural cave high up on the face of the mountain; plenty of room inside, but a very small entrance; few know of its existence.' 'Shouldering a giant's share of our things, he then led the way', each of them carrying a load up the difficult, stony pathway. At last a steep 300 foot climb away from the track and they crawled into their 'cool, new home'. The only patch of dry ground for three adults and the children aged five and two to lie down measured five feet by three. The children were already crying piteously for water, but the only available water would have to be fetched from the foot of the hill after dark; and other voices could be clearly heard across the valley on the opposite hillside. The children's crying would give them away.

Brave Chinese friends in two small groups began searching for them as soon as they learned that the temple was empty, and met a party of Yü Xian's Boxers who asked, 'Are you looking for the foreign devils, too?'

But the cave was well hidden. 'This was the first of our (nine) wonderful deliverances from death.' Meanwhile the temple-keeper had gone to tell the Huolu Christians where to find and supply them. He led one to the cave after nightfall. 'What a meeting! How we praised God together!'

Two days and nights 'chilled to the bone and huddled together' were enough in that cave. So they were glad when six friends arrived late on the third night and carried their children and belongings by moonlight to an isolated farmhouse, a mile from any village. They left them in the care of Farmer Gao, an influential man and his wife, with an alert watchdog and two small children whose voices would mask those of Vera and John. But by day the terraced hillsides were worked by labourers who came to draw water from the well alongside their room. They were to live under constant strain lest their presence be discovered. Even so, Charles Green managed to get a telegram sent from Huolu to Shanghai, giving Stevenson the first news of rioting at Taiyuan and a hint of their own dilemma. Their home in Huolu was being used to train twenty men and youths in Boxer mysticism and trances, to make them invulnerable to sword and bullet. Dysentery, abscesses or neuralgia were weakening each of the family.

Then to their distress word came of the Griffiths and R. M. Brown having turned up at Huolu almost destitute.

The mandarin at Shunde had sent them to Shanxi, but the Pingding mandarin, near Shouyang (see map 2.80: p 652), told them that Pigott was dead and it would be certain death to go any further west. Moneyless, they had had to walk the seventy miles back to Huolu, intending to return to Shunde, eighty more miles away. By then Mrs Griffith and her baby were too ill to go further, but, still without encountering Boxers, they struggled on as far as Zhengding, twenty miles to the east. The cathedral premises in Zhengding had been successfully defended against Boxer attacks and, almost uniquely, the brigadier commanding the imperial troops had decided to protect them, banning Boxers from entering the city. Hearing of the Griffiths' plight, the bishop invited them to move in. So from then onwards, through Christians who took their lives in their hands, the Greens near Huolu and Griffiths at Zhengding were able to keep in touch until suddenly Boxers searched the Greens' farmhouse.

July 1900: The great exodus

'Go south!' (July 1900)

Silence or vague rumours of what was happening in the north, by July were being replaced in the Yangzi valley by authentic reports of atrocities. The consuls were calling all their nationals to head for the coast or to leave the country by whatever route they could. From Yunnan they went south to Tongking (Vietnam); and from Guangxi and Guangdong, even from Canton, to Hong Kong and Macao. From Manchuria and Mongolia they made for Siberia, or eastwards to Vladivostok, or southwards to Yingkou (Niuchuang). From the Yangzi River provinces, including Sichuan, they passed through Chongqing, Yichang, Wuhan and the river ports, congregating in great numbers in Shanghai and being dispersed as soon as possible to Japan, to Singapore or their homelands.

Telegrams to Europe and America at first reporting only riots and tragedy, began increasingly to say 'friends safe', meaning the missionaries from places named.[1308] But soon among the lists of those who 'arrived safely, all well' were the names of others 'recovering' or 'murdered' or 'feared dead'. Week after week the whereabouts of many was unknown. Some found themselves guarded and escorted through hostile regions to the safety of territory under the enlightened viceroys. Others set out almost empty-handed only to be robbed of what little bedding, clothing, money and food they had with them. Destitute, wounded, cursed and pelted with stones like pariah dogs they stumbled, often barefoot and half naked, without covering from the sun, on and on for hundreds of miles, dramatically re-enacting the last few verses of Hebrews 11, a comfort to those who recalled them: 'They wandered in deserts, and in mountains, and in dens and caves of the earth. And these all, having obtained a good report through faith, received not the promise' (Heb 11.38–40 AV).

Their stories are scattered in fragments through old copies of *China's Millions*, newspapers and books long out of print. But they belong to the deathless history of the Church.

On July 6, Dr J. W. Hewett left Yuwu, north of Lu'an and Lucheng to consult E. J. Cooper (the architect) and A. R. Saunders, and found them at Lucheng threatened by hostile crowds. While he was away his colleague David Barratt was forced out of Yuwu, so Hewett returned there, hoping by his presence to delay the destruction of their property. Instead he found himself fleeing for his life from place to place for a month, never sleeping under the same roof for more than two or three nights, yet never more than ten miles from Yuwu. Neither he nor the Christians who harboured him could stand the strain, especially after a proclamation threatening death and destruction to any family taking him in, but a safe escort to the coast for any foreigner giving himself up. Having nowhere to turn, Hewett decided to risk consulting a friendly headman: he took Hewett to the police station.[1309]

An enlightened magistrate and chief secretary agreed with him that the proclamation was a trap and by their own admission spent sleepless nights working out some way of saving his life. They told him they would put him on trial, and he must go down on his knees and bow to the ground before the magistrate; pleading that he preferred to die in custody than to be turned loose, at the mercy of the merciless. He would then be sentenced to prison, shackled for all to see, and locked away, but must not be afraid; he would be unchained and kept out of sight until it was safe again to travel.

He did as he was told, and to his amazement was treated kindly even by the prison underlings, was sent extra food by the secretary's family, and was brought a few books by the village headman. The mandarin even sent for Hewett's clothes and language study books which he had left in the care of Christians, so that he could learn to write Chinese and amuse himself by sketching.

No one knew where he was. John Stevenson cabled as late as on September 6, 'Dr Hewett, no information', and on October 8, 'apprehend the worst for . . . Dr J. W. Hewett'. Not until November 1 was it safe for Hewett to report that he was heading for Hankou.

His case, like the Griffiths', was another remarkable exception. David Barratt and Alfred Woodroffe of Yoyang (between Hongtong and Yuwu), still in their twenties, both individually fled to the hills, not knowing where the other or Hewett was. Each succeeded in evading the Boxers, but, destitute, died from their privations during the summer months.[1310]

A few parties travelled to safety even from southern Shanxi, passing through hostile territory with documents and escorts

2.83 Hewett's prison yard, his sketch made with Chinese brush and ink

from high mandarins. Members of the Swedish Mission in China were the first to be favoured in this way, as citizens of a neutral nation. But Ci Xi later degraded the *daotai* responsible. It happened that a large sum of money had been committed to them shortly before they had to leave their base at Yuncheng. So they entrusted about £200 (thousands today) to an elder in the church (one of the first believers in Shanxi) for distribution to missionaries in distress.

With skill and daring this 'CCH' organised a secret cell of Christians who travelled through the mountains trying to keep in touch with those in hiding or making their way out of the province, and supplying their needs. Until long after the rising ended he continued to be referred to in the Mission correspondence and publications as 'CCH', lest Ci Xi should establish his identity and take revenge.[1311] The danger to his family became so great that after his home was looted he took them to Xi'an and directed the cell from there, himself making hazardous journeys back into Shanxi. In Xi'an the Scandinavian Alliance gave him £145 more, to use in the same way. Without his help several groups of fugitives could not have survived. The story of his undercover contact men should be researched and published. Ten pages are to be found in *Martyred Missionaries of the CIM*.

2.84 *The viae dolorosae of the fugitives from South Shanxi, Shaanxi and Henan*

Knowing that Christians were being hunted, tortured and killed, three of these men attempted to penetrate even into Taiyuan and the surrounding danger zones. Their search for information and for the one or two Christians in hiding who knew where each group of fugitives was hidden, and their circumstances, was in itself highly dangerous. Eva French eventually wrote: 'Elder Chang Chih-heng (Zhang Zhiheng) looked us up twice on the road as we were fleeing from Shanxi, and helped us and others with money'.

The acting-governor of Shaanxi, Tuan Fang, was making his province safer than Shanxi, Zhili, or Henan. So Shaanxi was the better place to make for. But several parties from Shanxi had to pass through Henan. Although out of Yü Xian's jurisdiction, some Henan mandarins were strongly anti-foreign and menacing to refugees within their grasp. None could know this when planning their routes. And the hard attitudes of Henan people that had broken the spirit of at least two early pioneers, made the long, agonising journeys of desperately sick men, women and children almost unendurable.

Three young women of the Swedish Mission in China (E. Anderson, S. Engsstrom and M. Pettersson) worked at Xin'an, south of the Yellow River, but included in the south Shanxi 'field' of their mission. To escape the great heat they were on holiday, living in cool cave-houses, but drawing large crowds of country folk. Alarmed that they were so conspicuous, the mandarin sent an escort and asked them to leave. On the way, via Xiangcheng (see map 2.84: p 662) they were threatened several times by Dadaohui (Great Sword Society) men and robbed of their few possessions, even to some of the clothing they were wearing. When one swordsman ordered M. Pettersson to kneel down for him to decapitate her, 'she smiled, put her hand on his shoulder and looking up into his face said, "We are not afraid to die, but first let us speak a few words to the men escorting us.'" Their assailants looked at one another, smiled and went away, saying, 'You cannot die because you are devils.' When they had gone, M. Pettersson fainted, 'lost her voice for the whole day' and had to be carried.

For days they hid in the fields or in haylofts, helped by some, betrayed by others, rescued by Christians and seen on their way, only to be sent back and threatened again. Walking twelve miles at night, twenty miles the next day, eight the following night and fifteen in pouring rain on muddy roads the second day, they eventually reached a *yamen* and asked for help. The kindly mandarin and another in the next city, 'provided us with a cart and would not let us start until we had had some food'. They also gave them some clothes and money and sent them on to Taihe in safe Anhui. This made the hardship and persecution they had gone through bearable. But while they were resting on the shore of a large lake, a ferocious hurricane suddenly wrecked the boat they were travelling by, drowned people in thirty other boats, and 'drenched and bruised us'. What would Satan be allowed to do next? 'We felt that we could not go through any more.'

At last they reached Qingjiangpu on the Grand Canal, where the Christians overwhelmed them with kindness and saw them on to a canal launch on the way to Shanghai. Their ordeal had lasted more than a month.

To the hills[1312] (July 1900)

The missionaries at Qüwu, south of Linfen, had very different experiences. Within a few days of the conference at which William Cooper had prepared the delegates for suffering, they found a marked change in the way people treated them. Duncan Kay was in charge at Qüwu and greatly loved by the Christians for miles around. As death-threats increased, he sent for his colleagues to come to the relative safety of the city. 'Here we remained,' one of them wrote, 'for five weeks in great suspense, expecting every minute to be called into the presence of the King.' When the mandarin said he could no longer protect them, they decided to separate into two parties and hide in the mountains until the danger passed. Duncan Kay, his wife and child and some Christians were to hide in the mountains of Jiangzhou while Graham McKie, Marion Chapman and Matilda Way and other Christians went to the Yichang range[1313] (see map 2.80: p 652).

McKie's party set off on the night of July 4, dressed in men's clothes, and by 4.00 a.m. had covered ten miles and had some sleep in a mud hut; when they heard that the Boxers were searching for them. Hiding by day they walked twenty miles into the mountains on the second night and lay low in a hay loft for six weeks, able only to speak in a whisper. A devoted youth named Yuan'er brought them food three times a day. By then, mid-August, their 'whereabouts seemed to have leaked out' and they decided to walk by night to Hankou, six hundred miles away. Only once between July 4 and October 21 did they venture out in open daylight.

Duncan Kay and his wife and child waited two more days before starting on the forty-mile journey to their chosen hiding place. Too great a distance to cover in the dark, it meant that they were seen and talked about. Their colleague in Linfen, F. C. H. Dreyer, even heard from the magistrate that their whereabouts was known. He also heard that 'CCH' had given Kay 200 taels and the promise of more should he need it. In such difficult days there were non-Christians prepared to house and feed people in exchange for payment. They could be relied on because once they sheltered those whom the governor was hunting, their own lives were at risk. But Duncan Kay was a marked man, hated by the Boxers for speaking against them. For two months he and his wife and child dodged from place to place before being caught.[1314]

A. R. Saunders and his family and colleagues, saved from 'the lions' mouth' at Taiyuan, had changed direction and travelled a hundred and fifty miles to

Lucheng, arriving on July 5 (see map 2.80: p 652). Even then they thought they might be the bearers of the first report from Taiyuan and wrote to tell William Cooper what they knew—Cooper who unknown to them had died on July 1. Saunders's own story was given in full in *The Times* of September 29, 1900, and in his booklet *A God of Deliverances*.[1315] After only one day to rest at Lucheng they were caught up in a riot, so at midnight all the missionaries in each place set out 'secretly' upon a nightmare journey towards Hankou, in their case seven hundred miles away.

2.85 *Hattie Rice and Mary Huston shortly before they fled*

The Lucheng party was large: the Saunders and their four children, with Alfred Jennings and Miss E. Guthrie, now joined E. J. Cooper, his wife and two children, and two single women, Mary Huston and Hattie Rice. They put their essential baggage on two donkeys and starting walking, carrying the small children. One donkey disappeared almost immediately and was not seen again. An opportunist had guessed their plight. Soon after daylight they hired more donkeys at a village, for the women to ride, but had gone only a mile or two when they met two hundred armed men and were robbed of all they had, even their clothes.

> Most of us were left with only a pair of Chinese trousers on, the upper part of our bodies and our heads being entirely unprotected from the awful burning of a July sun ... Although we were now almost naked, without either shoes or stockings, the people would not believe that we had no silver secreted about us, and we were beaten most unmercifully (to) bring some confession as to where the silver was (concealed). The people of one village would follow us to the boundary of the next, stoning us ... and beating us on the back and head ... from village to village ... Mr E. J. Cooper was dragged to the outside of (one) village by a rope and left by the roadside as dead. [They believed that if he died in the village his ghost would haunt it.] If we sat down anywhere to rest awhile we were stoned and beaten all the more,

and the only rest we got was under cover of darkness, (in) some lonely spot (when we) slept on the hard ground ...

> The first two days we had nothing to eat and no one who would even give us water to drink ... (In one village) we refused to go on (until) they at last gave us some bread and water ... When we had gone about two miles a man, altogether unknown to us, came up (and gave us) three dozen hard-boiled eggs, even at this unfriendly time in China ...

A magistrate gave them money to buy food, and provided a cart and escort for a few miles, but within a mile they were robbed and left without food or money. At another stage they were stripped of some of the scanty clothing they still had. Alex Saunders was left stark naked until a single remnant was handed to him. At another, more hostile village Hattie Rice could go no further. When the others were driven on with sticks and whips, Mary Huston doggedly stayed with her, saying they would come on more slowly. The others had no choice, being beaten till they moved.

Saunders and E. J. Cooper hoped the mandarins at Jincheng (Tsechou) would send a cart back to fetch the women; and they did, but too late. On July 13, Hattie was beaten to death at the roadside and as Mary Huston lay already terribly injured 'they even ran a horse and cart over her to break her spine'. When the mandarin returned her to the others at Wuzi, near the Yellow River she was alive, but had a head-wound exposing her brain.[1316]

The Glovers' 'thousand miles of miracle' (July 1–9, 1900)

Archibald Glover had been at Oxford and a colleague of Prebendary Webb-Peploe before joining Stanley Smith at Lu'an. Flora his wife and two children, Hedley and Hope, had joined him there in 1897. So they were relatively junior to Caroline Gates, a stalwart of fifteen years' experience in China.[1317] In June a Boxer placard had been posted on a city gate at Lucheng blaming Christians for the long drought and saying that the gods had come down to give supernatural powers to any who would exterminate Christians. It claimed that all foreign ships in Chinese waters had been destroyed and most foreigners had been driven into the sea. All good Chinese must join in completing this work. But when another 'rain procession' attack was threatened at Lu'an after the Glovers left for the coast, a friendly high mandarin had not only sent troops to protect the mission, but himself went with a civil magistrate and a military mandarin—the three highest officials in the city—to stand outside the house as thousands roaring hate streamed past. Inside, Caroline Gates and five Christians who would not leave her spent the day on their knees, at first praying and then praising God for his protection.

After the Glovers returned from their mauling at Shunde, and several other terrifying brushes with death the same magistrate sent word to Archibald Glover that he had orders to withdraw all protection from foreigners. Violence against foreign nationals was to be seen as part of a people movement with no demonstrable link with the government. Boxers had been training in the neighbourhood and were expected soon to start their gruesome work, so the mission's employees had been sent home and before the Glovers' return Caroline Gates had decided to escape to the hills. Two faithful Christians, Zhong Shengmin and Bao'er, had refused to leave her. They were going to take her to a mountain cave and care for her there.

The date for the foreigners' execution was fixed for the tenth day of the sixth moon. It was time to go. In his daily reading of Scripture Glover had come to Joshua 8 (AV). On the morning of July 5 his attention was caught by the words 'Flee before them . . . flee before them' (vv 5, 6) and 'See, I have commanded you' (v 8). And when the household met for family prayer, the Scripture for that day (about David in 2 Samuel 15.14 AV) read, 'Arise and let us flee . . . make speed to depart.' With it came the conviction to each of them that God's will was for them to lose no time in going. With difficulty they found two men willing to take them by mule-litter to Zhoujiakou, where they could find a boat

2.86 The Glover family before leaving on their '1,000 miles of miracle'

down the Huai River to safety. Had they reached Zhoujiakou (now Zhoukouzhen) they would probably have been killed, but sufferings almost worse than death were to save them from that.

Near midnight they lifted the sleeping children from their beds and carried them to the litters, hoping to put some distance between themselves and the city before daylight. But one delay followed another, deliberately, they were to discover. Armed men in league with the muleteers gave chase and soon they realised that they were no more than prisoners. After a little food at noon on July 6 they were denied anything except weeds for two days and nights. From then onwards, in fact for forty days and nights, they 'were never free from storm and tempest and the shadow of death'.

A detachment of Boxers arrived and Shengmin, hearing their conversation in an inn courtyard, came in, and said, 'We are all to be killed,' leant his head on Caroline

Gates's shoulder and wept that he had been unable to save them. Faced with death, Glover afterwards recalled, 'The peace of God took possession of our hearts', and even the children's terror was calmed as their mother taught them to say, 'I will trust and not be afraid.' They said goodbye to each other and 'rejoiced in the thought of so soon meeting the Lord'. Shengmin and Bao'er were free to escape and save their own lives, but refused to go.

A night of threats and taunting in a crowded inn room ended with a mock trial and an all too serious sentence of death. Taken in their mule litters 'in a kind of sacrificial procession' they ran the gauntlet between lines of spearmen who at a signal fell upon them and fought like wild beasts to pillage their few possessions. The strong litters were wrecked and their occupants 'seemed almost buried under a frantic mass of struggling humanity from which it seemed impossible that they should come out alive'. But the Boxers were nowhere to be seen, apparently bought off by the robbers, expecting a profitable haul. And their victims were uninjured.

At the next village a mob tore their clothes off them. Again they were physically unharmed. Bao'er gave Glover a pair of trousers, and 'someone in the crowd threw (him) a beggar's coat of filthy rags', himself appearing later in Glover's clothes.

Again they struggled on, surrounded by abusive crowds, yet still with the faithful Shengmin and Bao'er beside them. Told to take a certain road, but sensing from the steady beat of a gong that it led into a trap, they turned down a side path, and the whole crowd stopped dead in their tracks. No one followed. Glover did not know why, but suspected that as night had fallen fear of evil spirits near a graveyard could have been the explanation. In bright moonlight they met four Boxers who called others to help and 'fell savagely on them', stripping the women to the waist, but scorning the beggar's rags. When Glover chided them for being so shameless, they sullenly threw the women's clothing back and moved off

so deliberately as to suggest more ominous plans. The fugitives fled for their lives.

After escaping down a dry torrent-bed and sleeping until midnight in the graveyard, they tramped across open country and through undergrowth to hide in the hills nearby. More Boxers loudly searching for them passed close by, but on the bare top of one of the hills they found a depression deep enough to sit in, shivering with cold. When the sun rose, however, on Sunday, July 8, the heat became unbearable. Their thirst was intense and the children wailed, 'Water, water!' So Shengmin went down to find water. He failed to return. 'A great sense of loneliness came over us.' Their mouths became dry. Flora Glover showed signs of exhaustion, panting and gasping for breath, until by the end of her struggle she cried, 'Oh, God has forsaken us!' At once,

> God put into Miss Gates's mouth the most wonderful song of praise I have ever heard. Kneeling by (her) side and holding her hand, she poured forth passage after passage, promise after promise from the Scriptures exalting His name, declaring His faithfulness and proving His unchanging and unchangeable love sworn to us in the everlasting covenant and sealed to us in the blood of His own beloved Son. Never shall I forget the music of that heavenly utterance. Instantly the darkness was past and the light was shining again. The expression in my wife's face (was) of joy unspeakable ... Then together we repeated right through—with parched lips ... but with hearts that had tasted the wine of heaven—the beautiful hymn: 'How sweet the name of Jesus sounds in a believer's ear!'

Hotter and hotter the day became under the merciless sun, and still no sign of Shengmin. Bao'er had gone ahead and failing to find them again made his own way home. Then Caroline Gates fainted. They must get water. In the distance they could see a small stream shining in the sunlight. They stumbled down the hill and across ploughed fields and plunged into it, drinking on and on. From there to the burial ground again with cypresses to sleep under, and their sunburnt faces and bodies blistered and peeling.

A procession passed by and they were seen. To their amazement the sub-Prefect of Lu'an had come with *yamen* underlings and a cart to look for them and take them on towards Hankou. Shengmin failed to find them, so he too went home. The sub-Prefect ordered them to climb in, showing them a safe conduct pass and a bundle of clothing. So, taking the risk that he was lying and would deliver them to Boxers, they obeyed and were carried to the next town, Wangfang, and given a meal. 'Shall I ever forget the fragrance of the savoury pork dumplings set steaming hot before us!' After all that had happened it was still Sunday, July 8, only the third day since they left Lu'an. But the pork dumplings were deceptive.

Soon they discovered that Wangfang was full of Boxers, hundreds wearing their insignia. It was a trap. A guard was placed at the door of their room and great activity outside showed that preparations were being made for some event. A little old woman hobbled in on her bound feet and told them, 'They are piling wood all round you to burn you to death in this room. The Wangfang evangelist's wife is to die with you.' The room was then emptied of furniture, even the bed mat, confirming the old woman's message. So they cried to God who had delivered them time after time already.

Apart from the miraculous, their only hope seemed to lie in the fact that the sub-Prefect's mule was still tethered near the cart outside. Suddenly Glover saw a man untethering it. 'Now or never: come at once!' he cried, and together they dashed past the sentry and into the cart, taking the Boxers and the *yamen* escort by surprise. They were under the safe-pass and in the sub-Prefect's hands. He must hand them over or the Boxers must snatch them back. 'Burn them in the cart,' some suggested. But the mandarin had been worsted and (to save his own face) he 'mounted his horse, the soldiers tore at the mule's mouth and off we dashed pursued by hundreds of local

Boxers, shouting, "Death to the foreign devils!"'

Deposited for the night at an open theatre stage where homeless beggars slept, in the next town, they were told they were to be killed in the morning. All hope seemed again to have forsaken them, when four-year-old Hedley said, 'I think Jesus must have slept in a place like this when he had nowhere to go! We ought to be glad that we are like Jesus, oughtn't we?' Very well, they thought, if this was where their Father God allowed them to be, they would be content. But the official and escort were nowhere to be seen until noon the next day, when two mounted soldiers with drawn swords rode past them—their executioners, they were told. 'Thus our minds were directed perpetually to the thought of death.' Then the sub-Prefect reappeared, led them through the city gate and told them to mount two springless coal-carts of a type known as 'mountain tigers'. 'What else could this mean than that we were common felons riding to a felon's death?'

Glover protested that his pregnant wife could not endure such treatment, but without effect. They drove on, bumping and crashing from boulder to boulder over the pass, their escort telling onlookers that they were to be executed at Gaoping. Sure that this time they were going to their death, Glover suddenly thought of the words 'Mighty to save', describing Jesus. He ran forward to tell the others, and Flora reminded him that her hopes were pinned to Job's declaration, 'I shall not die, but live, and declare the works of the Lord.' In the shadow of death they feared no evil as they reached Gaoping—and kind treatment in the *yamen*.

The magistrate sent his son to reassure them and gave them money for clothes and the next day's travel. One *yamen* gentleman gave Glover a clean gown and removed his beggar rags. 'A beautiful supper' was served them and a supply of rice, bread and eggs for their journey. They thought they would soon be out of nightmare Shanxi and into a more peaceful Henan. But across the Yellow River half-a-dozen groups of refugees were in the same predicament, and in central Shanxi on that same day 'no fewer than fifty' missionary men, women and children, and unnumbered Chinese Christians, were being put to the sword.

Escape to Hankou![1318] (July 1900)

Two hours after the Canadian Presbyterians reached Nanyang on July 7, the innkeeper told them that seventy armed men were on the way to take the inn and everything in it. The Canadians sent word to the magistrate that they held him responsible for their safety, and prepared to defend themselves. Barricades of carts and household paraphernalia, and heaps of stones, were made ready. But he sent an escort and they set out the next morning through massed thousands of townsfolk and 'two bands of several hundreds armed with swords, spears and guns'. 'We had only three revolvers amongst us,' Jonathan Goforth wrote. 'The whole crowd came on us with a rush . . . We had to defend ourselves. I got nine wounds on my arms and hands, the only serious one being . . . at the back of the skull; I also got eight blows with clubs.' But they escaped, robbed of almost all their possessions, and pressed on southwards towards Fancheng (now Xiangfan). At a Muslim village 'the men said they would fight' for (them), but when the attack was renewed, the travellers fought alone. Dr Leslie had his revolver hand nearly severed by a sword cut, and a tendon of one knee cut through. Some cited Ci Xi's edict that all foreigners should be killed, and attacked them repeatedly until they reached the Han River at Fancheng. There the leading engineer in their party, Jamieson, sent a telegram to the viceroy, Zhang Zhitong. He sent two gunboats and soldiers to see them all safely to Wuhan, where two American consuls came out in a tug to meet them (see map 2.84: p 662).

Passing Sheqidian on July 7, the Canadians had sent a message to the CIM there, warning them to escape.[1319] Dr Whitfield Guinness, H. S. Conway, his wife and month-old baby and W. Wilson, a young single woman, wrote to the Nanyang mandarin for help, but the few soldiers who came to guard them soon melted away. When 'a vast crowd' assembled and began breaking through the main gate, the household climbed a wall and into the neighbour's loft. Their Chinese teacher, 'pale and nervous', said, 'Hide! It does not matter if you are killed, but I fear worse things may happen to you!' In the loft among all the dust and lumber they lay listening to 'the crash and falling of masonry and timber, (and) a crackling of flames', waiting for the child to cry and give away their hiding-place.

Time and again men came searching for them and each time their neighbour managed to deter them from searching the loft, and a second loft to which he moved them. As they lay in a dark corner for four days, men stacked straw and timber round the whole house, saying, 'We will burn them out and kill them if they run.' Whitfield Guinness wrote a letter to his parents on the back of some sermon notes, telling how they planned to escape. At last the neighbour could protect them no longer. He appeared at the trap-door and said, 'Fly! They have come with swords to kill you!' The debris of their own home remained the only place to flee to, and there they crouched under a blazing sun. A man came over the wall. It was impossible to avoid discovery. But he said, 'They have gone!'

Five days after the riot friendly Chinese disguised them and took them through the streets to large business premises where they were hidden in a strongroom and the chief merchant himself, armed with a gun, a sword and two daggers, 'a man of power', stood guard to protect them. Then one night their friends took them secretly to a small boat on the river and escorted them downstream, all together in one cabin for two weeks. Thirty days after their home had been destroyed, they reached Hankou.

C. M. Lack was alone at Sihua, an outpost of the Zhoujiakou mission, when a mob attacked it after dark on July 7.[1320] He and a Chinese companion fled to the *yamen*, and thirty soldiers were sent back with him. 'Reaching the place, the soldiers rushed in with a yell, and what a sight?' Everything of any value had been looted and the place was a shambles of discarded waste. As the crowd scattered, Lack and the evangelist slipped away and in spite of being trailed by four men 'armed with swords and guns', reached Zhoujiakou on Sunday, July 8, unharmed. There he had two days' respite before being rioted out again.

An Italian-born member of the CIM, Alfonso Argento, was the only missionary in the city of Guangzhou, 140 miles south of Zhoujiakou on that Sunday, July 8, when a mob armed with knives attacked the mission premises.[1321] The street was 'packed from one end to the other', and there was no other way of escape. Manhandled by a dense crush of attackers in the guest-hall, Argento struggled out of his Chinese gown by which they were holding him, dived to the ground and reached a corner where he crouched out of sight. As everything was being wrecked, a screen fell, partly covering him, until he could crawl under a table. The house was wrecked and broken timber was being piled in the centre of the main room and soaked with kerosene, when a man with a burning firebrand looking for more fuel saw Argento. 'With a rush they . . . dragged me from under the table and on to the pile of wood.' Others used benches to batter him. 'They poured kerosene on my clothes and set them on fire.' Neighbours tore off his burning jacket and dragged him outside by his hair. At this the rioters struck at his head with a pole and knocked him unconscious. When the mandarin came that night and found him lying in the street in a pool of blood, he had him moved into the ruined chapel. There, some Christians took turns to stay with him until he regained consciousness on the fourth day, Wednesday, July 11.

Hearing that plans to decapitate Argento were being discussed, the mandarin, in spite of threats against himself, had him put on a bamboo stretcher and carried the 140 miles to Zhoujiakou. 'Take him away,' he said, 'I don't want him to die here.' An escort of fifty foot-soldiers and twenty mounted men, all well armed and led on

the first day by the mandarin himself on horseback, protected him from repeated assaults on the way. But on Sunday, July 15, while the stretcher-bearers and escort were resting at an inn, he was left in the open for an hour at the mercy of 'thousands' who crowded round him, pulling his hair and knocking him about although he feigned death. Finally a local mandarin, only twenty-five miles from Zhoujiakou and friends, refused to let him go further and forced the cavalcade to return to his starting-point at Guangzhou. On the way, at place after place he was maltreated.

Hearing that he was lying abandoned in a *yamen* yard, a gentleman came and took him home, put him to bed and gave him three good meals each day for three days while it poured with rain. He even urged him to stay until he could send him safely to Hankou, but the choice was not the victim's to make. To the many visitors who came to sympathise with him, Argento explained the gospel. But finally the mandarin sent for him and sent him under escort to Guangzhou.

There again the mandarin left him in the *yamen* yard for four hours 'at the mercy of large crowds of enemies who abused me and mocked me, saying, "God has brought you safely back, has he? Your God cannot save you. Jesus is dead." They spat in my face . . . and others expressed themselves in the most vile way.' The magistrate's chief concern was to prevent Argento from being killed while in his custody. So after dark he sent him on towards Hankou, with an escort who abandoned him at the roadside. He stayed where he was until daylight and, walking on, took refuge at a little inn. When some thirty armed men came looking for him, the innkeeper denied having seen him. Argento was lying on the ground with his face to the wall and his arm over his head, and was not recognised although they stayed until first light before setting off again.

He continued his journey alone, later in the day, feeling too weak and despondent to do more than stagger painfully along. A man coming towards him stopped, looked closely at him, and went on. Then he stopped again, turned and said, 'Are you not Mr Ai?' Cautiously Argento answered, 'Who are you?' and was told 'Lo of Wulidian'. Then Argento remembered meeting him at Runan two years before, and said, Yes, he was Argento. At that the man shed tears and offered to take him all the way to Hankou.

As good as his word, Lo collected money, food and clothing from his home and for a week they travelled on together. Three times their 'lives were at stake', but they reached their journey's end on July 31; as Argento put it in another understatement, 'glad to have the dangers and sufferings over, and to be able to rest and get medical treatment'.

Heartless Henan was exacting a high price from its victims. Their experiences varied greatly and were still far from over.

Escapes through Anhui (July 1900)

C. Howard Bird, an Australian, had been away on a preaching trip for six or seven weeks when he returned to Xiangcheng on July 7 to find 'frightful reports' circulating, and his colleagues preparing to leave at short notice.[1322] Amid great excitement the townsfolk were making human effigies of dough and boiling them, to shouts of 'Boil the foreigners!' The engineers of the Peking Syndicate with their retinue and Canadian Presbyterians had already passed through, and the Christians were urging the Gracies and John Macfarlane (on a visit from Tasmania) to go north to Zhoujiakou or they would be killed. Howard Bird chose to stay with the Xiangcheng Christians if he could.

The others left early on July 8, but on arrival at Zhoujiakou found large crowds converging on the mission. Their mules were seized and led into an inn yard where hundreds surrounded them, shouting 'Kill the foreigners!' In this extremity they succeeded in persuading some officials to escort them a few miles south-eastwards towards Taihe in Anhui where they could hire a boat to take them by river to the Grand Canal. After several brushes with death they reached Zhenjiang on the Yangzi on August 4.

A general spirit of unrest had seized the country-folk, as in the worst regions of the drought. They began looting the granaries of the wealthy. Soon, they believed, they were going to need everything they could lay hands on to buy food. At Xiangcheng the evangelist and others came to Howard Bird with reports of foreigners being killed further south. He must escape while he could.[1323] He set off with one companion carrying some bedding, silver and small change. People were friendly but guessed from the absence of baggage that they were in trouble. After the first night they were told that all the foreigners at Zhoujiakou had been killed. It was untrue. But while Bird hid in the fields by a riverbank, his Chinese companion went to find a boat and took him to it. Bird hid under a mat covering but was discovered by an inquisitive youngster. The crowd that quickly gathered robbed him of everything but his trousers. *Yamen* underlings then dragged him down the street of the nearby town by his hair.

Desolate and helpless, Bird was befriended by an unknown Muslim who gave him food, hid him for two days and then hired another boat on which Bird hid below the deckboards all that night and the next day. And when they reached Zhoujiakou and learned that the Chinese Christians' homes had been pillaged and most were in hiding, the boatmen lured him ashore and left him destitute 'in a great city full of enemies'. A gatekeeper let him sleep in his hovel, and he left at dawn and trudged unharmed to the next city. But again the *yamen* would not move a finger to protect or help him. Still destitute, he wandered on until a passer-by directed him to a village where Christians took him in, gave him a tub of hot water and a meal; and made him lie down and rest. Two of them went on with him but only forty miles from Taihe they fell into the hands of robbers. 'Three great ruffian-looking fellows . . . led me to a field . . . produced three great swords and began swinging them about just above my head . . . I really thought my last moment had come. I just lifted my heart up to God. I had no fear, only joy that I should soon see Jesus. But it was not to be.'

That night, half a dozen or more of the gang encircled him and his friends and all settled down to sleep. Bird whispered to one of the Christians that he was going to escape. He crept away 'and then ran for dear life, not resting till I was some six or seven miles away'. Nor did he eat or rest properly until he had covered seventeen miles to the city of Shengiu and reached the *yamen*, not knowing what reception he would be given. His surprise at a kindly hearing was no greater than the officials' amazement at his story. They took him in, gave him a good breakfast and sent him on by cart under escort. At about 10.00 p.m. on July 24 they reached Taihe. 'The city gates were shut, but on sending in the mandarin's letter they were at once opened, and a great array of officials and soldiers with big lanterns ushered me into the city and escorted me to the (mission) house. What a welcome I had!'

One after another had almost reached Zhoujiakou from the north, south and west, only to find such danger that to go nearer would be foolhardy. So each party had bypassed the city, only sending messages to the two couples, two single men (Charles Lack and Robert Powell) and four single women trapped inside.[1324] The pro-Boxer mandarins in the main city of Chenzhou (now Huaiyang) and at Zhoujiakou itself prevaricated, while rumours spread that on July 24 first the Christians and then the foreigners were to be killed. On the 9th they refused to see Powell and in the hearing of a crowd said they could not protect them—an admission as good as a licence to kill.

Early the next morning the mission was attacked at its three entrances simultaneously, and all the missionaries had to climb over a high wall to take refuge in an unwilling neighbour's home. The mandarin then came with soldiers, but merely said to the mob, 'Take what you like but don't hurt the foreigners,' and

went away. So when their hiding place became known there was no alternative but to take the great risk of brazenly walking out into the crowd. They found them so busy carrying off all their belongings that with the help of some well-disposed onlookers they reached the *yamen* of the chief of police. To their delight Yan Dalao, a Hunanese, took their side and gave them his best room to use. But he said he could do no more than help to make arrangements for them to travel to Anhui. More than once he returned, unable to persuade boatmen to take the risk, and even wept with concern for his guests.

With reports of hundreds of men waiting to intercept them if they should leave the city, they succeeded in arranging for an escort of soldiers, but half of them decamped, afraid of the consequences. At that Yan Dalao said, 'If God does not help you now, we can do nothing.' They were all in the act of praying together when, outside, a shout announced the arrival of a force of soldiers from Huaiyang, the prefecture. And more were following behind them. The date was Friday, July 13. An order had been received, it was said, from the great Li Hongzhang on the 12th, that all foreigners were to be protected. But possibly it came from Liu Kunyi and Zhang Zhitong (see p 649).

Li had been reinstated on July 9 to the viceroyalty of Zhili and Senior Guardianship of the throne, and had left Canton for Hong Kong and Shanghai without delay. He had been honoured with the privilege of wearing on the official square on his chest back and front a five-clawed dragon, such as only the emperor wore on a circular plaque. The Western communities were unimpressed. They wished to keep him in the south to protect the Yangzi agreements. He did not resume his viceroyalty in Zhili until October 1.

Whatever the truth, the effect of a report that he had ordered the protection of foreigners everywhere had immediate effect when it was received and made public. But where telegraph lines were lacking, wilful delaying tactics appear to have been employed by anti-foreign officials in Henan, Zhejiang and, predictably, in Shanxi. Some parties escaping from Shanxi to Henan suffered no more physical injuries after July 16, but were shown undisguised hatred by the Chenzhou mandarin as long afterwards as the 22nd. After all that had happened, Shanghai was still in the dark, and John Stevenson could only send his first tentative crisis cables to the homelands on July 21 and 23.

'The butcher of Shanxi' (July 9, 1900)

If little mercy had been shown before Li Hongzhang intervened in the south, none at all could be expected from the military, the Boxers, the riff-raff or the anti-foreign mandarins in Governor Yü Xian's Shanxi. July 9 was the worst day of horror and the signal for atrocities continuing until September.

The twenty missionaries and children (called thirty in error) crowded together in G. B. Farthing's home in Taiyuan well knew the danger they were in. After the destruction of the old CIM premises (taken over and expanded by the Shouyang Mission) and the Schofield Memorial Hospital, the survivors had fled to the BMS. All were 'protected' by armed guards, but as it later proved, were themselves under house arrest.[1325] Dr Lovitt's words 'We cannot but hope for deliverance' were echoed by Millar Wilson in a note to

2.87 Yü Xian, 'the butcher of Shanxi'

F. C. H. Dreyer at Linfen: 'It's all fog, but I think, old chap, that we are on the edge of a volcano, and I fear Taiyuan is the inner edge. I'd rather be where you are.' In spite of this, after the hospital went up in flames, Wilson wrote asking for medicines and surgical instruments to be sent to him.

As early as June 21, G. B. Farthing had written to Herbert Dixon of the BMS in Xinzhou saying that the Taiyuan telegraph clerk had told him about Ci Xi's secret edict, that all foreigners were to be killed. 'If it is true, I am ready and do not fear; if such be God's will I can even rejoice to die.' Dixon's comment to an evangelist named Zhao had been, 'I feel just the same.'[1326]

Reports from the rest of the province added to their fears. Dreyer had heard of one thousand Boxers being expected 'to clear the province of Christians', and four hundred were soon at work. The Soping and Xiaoyi murders had been a foretaste. After a disturbance at Fenzhou (ten miles from Xiaoyi), the prefect and city magistrate took energetic action to control the attackers, and urged the missionaries to fire on them if in danger. At the time the A. P. Lundgrens and Annie Eldred of the CIM were staying with two Oberlin College couples of the American Board. When the edict arrived, withdrawing protection from foreigners, like other good men in authority this mandarin also wept. With such friends in office the missionaries were still hopeful when preparations for an escape came to nothing, and were still there in August. But in Taiyuan stories were being put about that missionaries were poisoning wells. The rumour was widespread, often to the effect that hired renegades and beggars did it for them. As a result many innocent people were being accused, tortured and killed.

Troops had been passing through Huolu, Zhili, for several days, going they said, 'to stop the Russians', when the Greens learned that Governor Yü Xian himself was expected. He and a regiment of soldiers had been summoned by Ci Xi. But a display of reluctance by the people of Taiyuan to let him go (a customary ploy possibly staged this time by Yü Xian himself) led to his deferring his departure long enough for him personally to direct the events of the next few days. He boasted of his subtlety when he claimed his reward from the dowager empress.

On July 3 all foreigners, Catholic and Protestant, were told to congregate 'for their protection' at the previous headquarters of the Railway Bureau alongside the magistrate's *yamen* in the Boar's Head Lane (Zhu Tou Xiang) near to the governor's *yamen*. After well-justified hesitation they moved in on the 6th. All mission property was immediately wrecked and ransacked by the mobs, another portent. There at the Bureau they were kept waiting in suspense for death that could come to them at any moment.[1327] The Catholic bishops, Gregory Grassi and Francis Fogolla, two foreign priests, the Sisters of Mary who ran five orphanages, and a lay brother were accompanied by Chinese priests, students for the priesthood and nine servants. The BMS was represented by G. B. Farthing and his wife, with three children, their governess E. M. Stewart, and Hudson Taylor's one-time personal secretary, Frank Whitehouse, and his wife. Dr and Mrs A. E. Lovitt and an infant, and the G. W. Stokes and J. Simpsons, were joined by Dr and Mrs Millar Wilson and their baby, Jane Stevens and Mildred Clarke of the CIM, and by Alexander Hoddle and the W. F. Beynons of the B&FBS with their three children. T. W. Pigott and his party had not yet arrived from Shouyang.

The first eye-witness account of events in Taiyuan came from Yong Zheng, a reliable Christian who escaped and carried the news to Dr J. A. Creasey Smith of Peking (see p 701). On July 8, Yong Zheng was in a village about three miles from the city of Taiyuan when he saw two carts containing the Pigotts and other Shouyang foreigners, John Robinson, Mary Duval and the Atwater girls, with an escort of seven or eight soldiers. After the main escort arrived, Pigott asked that they might be taken to join the others at the Bureau, but his party

were all thrown into the common prison for the night.

Governor Yü Xian had netted his victims. On the morning of July 9 he sent for them all to be brought to his *yamen* 'before being sent to the coast'. His motive may have been less cat and mouse than to ensure their coming quietly. Accounts of what followed are largely based on Yong Zheng's statement:

> The next day I was on the street near the Governor's *yamen*; I saw a big crowd and went to see what it was they were following. I found it was the foreign pastors and their wives and children and Roman Catholic priests and nuns and some Christians. I heard people say they were going to be killed, and I tried to get out of the crowd, but could not, so stayed and witnessed with my own eyes the killing of all the foreigners.

> [Forsyth added: They were all ranged in line outside the *yamen* entrance in the open space next to the street.] The whole number of men, women and children were then stripped to the waist like common criminals, and were made to wait in this degrading condition till the Governor came out to inspect them. [He asked their nationality, laughed scornfully at their answer, and at once gave the order for their decapitation.]

> The first to be led forth was Pastor Farthing. His wife clung to him, but he gently put her aside, and going in front of the soldiers, himself knelt down without saying a word, and his head was struck off by one blow of the executioner's knife.

> He was quickly followed by Pastors Hoddle and Beynon, Drs Lovitt and Wilson, all of whom were beheaded with one blow by the executioner. Then the Governor (Yü Xian) grew impatient and told his bodyguard, all of whom carried big beheading knives with long handles, to help to kill the others. Pastors Stokes, Simpson and Whitehouse were next killed, the last one by one blow only, the other two by several. When the men were finished, the ladies were taken. Mrs Farthing had hold of the hands of her children who clung to her, but the soldiers parted them, and with one blow beheaded their mother. The executioner

beheaded all the children and did it skillfully, needing only one blow; but the soldiers were clumsy, and some of the ladies suffered several cuts before death. Mrs Lovitt was wearing her spectacles and held the hand of her little boy even when she was killed. She spoke to the people, saying, as near as I remember: 'We all came to China to bring you the good news of salvation by Jesus Christ; we have done you no harm, only good; why do you treat us so?' A soldier took off her spectacles before beheading her, which needed two blows.

When the Protestants were killed, the Roman Catholics were led forward. The Bishop, an old man, with a long white beard, asked the Governor why he was doing this wicked deed. I did not hear the Governor give him any answer, but he drew his sword and cut the bishop across the face one heavy stroke; blood poured down his white beard, and he was beheaded.[1328] The priests and nuns quickly followed him in death.

Then Pastor Piggott and his party were led from the district gaol which is close by. He was still handcuffed; so was Mr Robinson. He preached to the people till the very last, when he was beheaded with one blow. Mr Robinson suffered death very calmly. Mrs Pigott held the hand of her son, even when she was beheaded, and he was killed immediately after her. The lady and two girls [Mary Duval and the Atwater girls] were killed also, quickly. In all on that one day forty-five foreign people were beheaded—thirty-three Protestants and twelve Roman Catholics. A number of native Christians were also killed; I did not see them all, but I was told there were thirteen ...

All were surprised at the firmness and quietness of the foreigners; none cried or made any noise, except two or three of the children.[1329]

Hosea Ballou Morse, using Forsyth and quoting Yong Zheng's accounts in the *Chinese Recorder*, emphasised that the order was carried out,

> first on the Protestants of Taiyuan, then on the Roman Catholics, then on the Protestants from Shouyang ... So perished

... under the eyes of the governor and by his orders, 34 British Protestants and 12 Roman Catholics—15 men, 20 women, and 11 children; in addition, the heads of six American missionaries killed at Taigu were, according to his own report to the Empress Dowager, sent to this governor, now 'infamous for ever'. [But the Taigu massacre happened three weeks later.]

Discrepancy exists between the eyewitness Yong Zheng's figures: forty-five foreign people (thirty-three Protestants), and Forsyth's summary, by name including Edith Coombs: 'Forty-six Europeans—thirty-four Protestants and twelve Roman Catholics ... besides Miss E. Coombs, who died on June 27.' But Forsyth's own summary in *China Martyrs* (p 140) includes Miss Coombs in his total of forty-six. Morse's total follows Forsyth's, omitting his observation that 'This made the full tally of fifty-one (not counting Miss Coombs) for which it was afterwards found (Yü Xian) had claimed a reward from the Empress Dowager in Peking.'[1330] What may well be the explanation was found in the diary of Jingshan, the Peking court official, on July 16: '(Yü Xian) has memorialised the throne, reporting that he cunningly entrapped all the foreigners, cast them into chains, and had every one of them decapitated in his *yamen*. Only one woman had escaped, after her breasts had been cut off, and she had hidden herself under the city wall; she was dead when they found her.'

This could also throw light on Yong Zheng's statement about some ladies receiving several sword cuts, although he was referring primarily to the soldiers' inferior ability.[1331]

Another enigma has no explanation or sequel: 'CCH' also wrote on July 26 to Eric Folke, 'I heard a rumour that in Taiyuan, on the 12th of the 6th moon (July 9) thirty-seven foreigners and thirty Chinese were massacred. I have heard the same report from five different *yamen*s. I cannot vouch whether this rumour is true or not.'[1332]

'CCH' left his family five days later on one of his mercy missions in Shanxi, learning all he could of what was happening to his fellow-Christians and missionary friends. On his return he wrote again, factually and precisely. He gave no hint of unverified rumour in saying, 'The Prefect of (Puzhou), returning from (Taiyuan) brought a foreign child; sex unknown. We do not know to whom the child belongs.' Such a report would certainly have been investigated when the uprising ended, and much would have been made of it if the child had been recovered. But on this there is silence.[1333]

Yong Zheng's report continued:

> The bodies of all were left where they fell till next morning, as it was evening before the work was finished. During the night they were stripped of clothing and other things, such as rings and watches. Next day they were removed to a place inside the great South Gate, except some of the heads, which were placed in cages on the gates of the city wall. On the 11th July the remains were temporarily buried outside the great South Gate, to the west side. On the 10th July there were also killed many Catholic Christians, I heard six, and during the next few days a few more Protestants were also killed.[1334]

Another source of information was an Evangelist Zhao, from Shandong, who had spent eighteen years at Xinzhou, north of Taiyuan. Because he was well known he lay low while a companion, Wang Xiyo, the son of a general, gathered information and reported to him. Trustworthy people who were not eye-witnesses supplied him with all that they learned. Understandably, their accounts differed in several respects from the other sources.

To deviate a little from the chronological presentation, during the months of July, August and September, 'CCH' collected the names of many Chinese Christians who had suffered and were suffering still for the faith, and reports of recantations. He revealed his own standing with officials and Christians alike, making references such as,

> I sent (Cao Qingho) to (Quwu, Linfen, Hongtong, Hezhou, Fenzhou and Taiyuan) to obtain information ... I also sent Lui San to ascertain ... the whereabouts and condition of the missionaries ... I have

sent men to tell the Christians to leave their homes and go into the country, and those near (Shaanxi) to cross over into that province ...

> Near Linfen the people rose up and got hold of all the (remaining) Christian men and women, with a knife cut a cross on their foreheads, and they afterwards tortured them before killing them, throwing their bodies into the Fen River ... The villagers then destroyed all their properties and homes ... My own home has been looted. I have in consequence taken my whole family to (Xi'an), barely escaping with our lives ... I write the letter with tears; and my family, after hearing the above news, were unable to eat for three days ... The persecutions of the Christians in Shanxi are indescribable ... The wives and daughters of the Christians have been shamefully treated and tortured.[1335]

Late in October Matilda Way wrote, after her eventual escape,

> Our hearts are filled with joy when we think of the faithfulness of the Christians at Taiyuan. The missionaries were beheaded first, and then the (Chinese) Christians [those brought for execution] had to kneel down and drink their blood, and as they knelt, were killed—not one denied Christ. The schoolgirls were taken to the *yamen* and the Governor said to them, 'You follow the foreigners'; they answered 'No, we follow Christ.' He then said, 'You read the foreigners' book'; to which they replied, 'No, we read God's Book.'

These schoolgirls were martyred with their fellow Christians in Taiyuan. After this butchery a new wave of persecution and bloodshed swept through Shanxi with the loss of many lives. Among the mature believers who refused to recant or pretend to do so, were children who would not be moved by threat or torture.

Miracles continued, and withheld (July 9–13, 1900)

The Glovers and Caroline Gates learned late of Yü Xian's order that all foreigners in Shanxi be sent to Taiyuan.

> Why, therefore, we were not sent north instead of south is a mystery, (but) we

were sent on under arrest with nothing but a criminal's passport and at the mercy of each magistrate ... We never knew when we left one city what awaited us in the next. More than once we were on the point of being sent back to Lu'an, and once it was all but decided to send us direct to Yü Xian himself. Of the nineteen yamens through which we passed, fourteen were so anti-foreign that it was a moot point with each whether we should be passed on, sent back or executed there and then.[1336]

After spending the night of that bitterest of days, July 9, sleeping the sleep of the exhausted on a stone platform, they were taken for thirty miles on the same springless coal-carts as far as Jincheng (Tsechou). At each market town they passed through, hostile crowds surrounding them discussed in their hearing how they were to die.

Foreign blood must be spilled by reason of the drought. But ... how much? Should all our party be put to death, or only one? ... A child or an adult? ... Finally (it was) decided to put the ladies to death on the spot ... The thought of having first to witness and then to survive the murder of my wife was insupportable ... But no one raised a hand against them.

They arrived there to be mobbed and threatened, but not injured, while the Roman Catholic mission was set on fire. All the next morning, crowds which 'seemed to spring from nowhere' as they continued the journey, chanted the Boxer song, 'Foreign blood must be spilled e'er the rain can fall.' Spiritism and the ancient fertility rites had reared their ugly heads in a wholesale submission to the powers of evil. Blistered and wailing from unrelieved exposure to the July sun, the children's misery even moved the callous escort to lend an old straw hat to shade them. But no allowances were made for Flora Glover's pregnancy, or dysentery.

Near Huaiging, close to the Yellow River, they were locked into a room with five stark naked, opium-smoking guards while a mob outside yelled for their execution to end the drought. As Glover listened, he remembered the words of Scripture, 'And

call upon me in the day of trouble: I will deliver thee, and thou shalt glorify me' (Ps 50.15 AV).

Accordingly, kneeling up on the bed we poured out our hearts before Him, in Chinese so that the gaolers might know exactly what we were doing and what we were asking ... Scarcely had we risen from our knees when ... down upon the howling mobs swept the sudden fury of a torrential flood of waters. In a few seconds the street was deserted and not a sound was heard but the ... rushing rains.

The effect upon our gaolers was immediate; something akin to awe took the place of their hard incredulity ... The rain fell in sheets ... all that day and far into the night.[1337]

The door was unlocked and an official came in, ordered the guards to kill their prisoners, and withdrew. Thereupon an attempt to stupefy them by poisonous fumes barely failed. In the morning the guards explained, 'These people have been praying to God, and we could do nothing against their prayers.' Instead they were taken on, past people too busy in their fields to pay attention to doomed prisoners. They crossed the Taihang mountain range and the Henan border—out of Yü Xian's jurisdiction—only to find the Dadaohui still active in Henan and more crowds as merciless as ever. But it was July 13, the day after Li Hongzhang's order had been circulated. It was also the day that Hattie Rice and Mary Huston were separated from the Saunders and E. J. Coopers, and fatally attacked near Jincheng, where the Glovers had just been spared.[1338]

The Datong six (June 24–July 12, 1900)

While the sieges at the Beitang cathedral and the legations in Peking kept their imprisoned thousands in constant danger, the consolation of being in it all together made their suffering in some ways more tolerable than for the isolated individuals and handfuls in the provinces. And terrible as were the long drawn-out sufferings of those trying to escape to the south through Henan, the terrors of being at the mercy of

Yü Xian's indoctrinated Boxers were more acute.

Away to the north of Shanxi, between the two arms of the Great Wall, the CIM had two couples and two women at Datong (see map 2.81: p 652) serving a thriving church. Charles and Florence I'Anson of Grattan Guinness's Harley College and Cambridgeshire, and Stewart and Kate McKee of Glasgow, had as colleagues two young women, Margaret Smith and Maria Aspden. Unconfirmed news of the massacre of six missionaries at Datong reached the coast early in 1901, but hope was slow to die that they might have escaped through Mongolia to Russian Siberia. Not until June 1901 did eyewitnesses arrive at Tianjin to tell the full story.[1339]

Boxers had appeared at Datong on June 14, 1900, and began drilling recruits in public. But eighteen new Christians had dared to be baptised four days later. The long-expected attack came on the 24th, and the missionaries, with three I'Anson children and four-year-old Alice McKee fled to the *yamen* under a hail of stones. The apparently friendly prefect took them in, and when they returned home a few days later for the birth of Kate's baby, he posted guards to protect them. Meanwhile, the atrocities at Soping, Zuoyun, Yingzhou and Henyuan had fed the lust for blood in the prefectural city.

Three days after the Taiyuan massacre, a minor official came to take their names, a cold-blooded act 'for the record' and rewards, and three hundred horse and foot soldiers surrounded the house to prevent their escape. All were killed by the sword and flung into the flames of their burning home. Thirty-two Chinese Christians met a similar death, including those newly baptised. When the Roman Catholics in Datong shared the same fate, the toll of victims rose to more than one hundred. When teams of investigators eventually arrived, eyewitness accounts confirmed the first hearsay reports

Daning and Hejin (July 12–16, 1900)

Enlightened mandarins somehow maintained the peace at Linfen in south-central Shanxi. But over the mountains to the west, semi-isolated on the western flank, were country churches in the cities of Xi Xian and Ji Xian (then known as Sichou and Chichou), and in the smaller towns of Daning and Hejin (spelled as Ho-tsin at that time). Daning and Xi Xian had been pioneered by Montagu Beauchamp and William Cassels in 1886 when the first church was formed (see pp 460ff). As late as July 7, John and Alice Young at Ji Xian and on July 8 the Nathan sisters, Edith and May, and Mary Heaysman at Daning wrote of feeling safe, unthreatened, and well cared for by local Christians. Four days later the news of Emily Whitchurch's and Edith Searell's brutal murders at Xiaoyi on June 20 reached them, and they fled to the hills with three trusty Christians (see p 463).[1340]

Not knowing whether her letter would ever reach her family, Edith Nathan wrote,

> My heart bleeds for the Christians ... They will have to suffer much ... Our hearts are sick and sad ... Truly these 'child Boxers' are devilish and a device of the devil. We in England know little of what the power of Satan can do over the mind of a child. God deliver us from a like fate ... I happened to say to (our dear old Pastor) 'We are pitiable!' He said, 'There is One to care for you better than all earthly magistrates.' (His face is full of light and brightness, not born of earth but from constantly looking into his Master's face.) Could you but see our Christians ... you would think as I do; it is quite worth while coming to such a pass, to find out how much they love us. Last night some of the men almost cried ... We know our times are in God's hands. Don't grieve as those without hope!

For a month they waited in a mountain farmhouse, tense and ready for the worst at any moment, yet often bored except when Christians met with them to pray or the approach of strangers forced them to scramble up the hillsides and hide. Still the Boxers did not come.

Roughly fifty miles to the south, Hejin was home and workplace to George and Bella McConnell, their son, and two young women, Annie King and Elizabeth Burton, still struggling to learn the language. John and Alice Young of Ji Xian were with them when warning of danger arrived. They decided to head for the Yellow River without delay. By crossing into Shaanxi or getting a boat down to Tongguan they could go on south, they hoped, to safety.

On July 16 a troop of mounted soldiers overtook them, saying they were from the *yamen*, presumably an escort. On reaching the riverbank they said they had not come to protect them but to murder them, unless they recanted. They refused. 'McConnell was then dragged from his mule and dispatched with a sword,' and his wife and child after him. Annie King embraced Elizabeth Burton and both died together in the same way. The Youngs were then killed in each other's arms and their attendant, Ke Tianxüan, also refusing to recant, 'met with a violent death'.[1341]

An unsigned letter from a Hejin Christian to another later said, 'Men's hearts are shaking with fear. We cannot rest, night or day. All Christians and inquirers are being persecuted.' On July 22 May Nathan wrote her last letter to her mother:

> Edith met me and said, 'All the Young's party are killed.' I said, 'What?' in high falsetto. It was such a shock. I wanted to cry, but the pastor said 'Don't', so I sat as in a dream while he read out the letter ... All of them young, married a little over a year ... and oh, such a death! It makes one shudder—hacked at with knives, I suppose ... I don't want to die, and such a death, but if it comes, well ...

> Many will say, 'Why did she go? wasted life.' Darling, No. Trust God does His very best, and never makes mistakes ... Dear, it may be the deliverances will come through death, and His hands will receive ... the incorruptible, glorified spirit ... Now we are called to endure, perhaps, extreme bodily suffering. But, darlings, death is but the gate of life, we shall see His face, and, darling Mother, I'll wait and long for you there! ... Now is the hour and power of

darkness ... How long, O Lord, how long? ... It is rather like the hare being hunted by the hounds. Stones (for pillows) are not soft.

[The pastor, Zhang Zhiben, wrote to their families]:

> On (August 12) Yang Dequn was killed ... After he was dead the three ladies were seized (beloved sisters, alas, alas) dragged to a temple outside the city (of Darting) where it was difficult either to stand, sit or lie down, hungry and thirsty, with no one to look after them, and surrounded by a gang of evil men. At early dawn on the morning of (August 13) the three were killed ... News of the victories of the foreigners reached us during the second intercalary eighth moon (September 24–October 22). On (November 1) the Daning magistrate and gentry placed the corpses in coffins and deposited them in a temple in the western suburbs ...

> Happily I was seized a few days later (August 21) with my son. The edict of the Governor Li, who succeeded Yü Xian, which saved our lives, came to the yamen on (August 20 or 21).

The Linfen refugees (July 2–16, 1900)

When the Swedish Mission in China were issued with safeconduct passes early in July and all left the Yuncheng district under escort, F. C. H. Dreyer and his wife were in charge of Linfen, with the Hoskyn sisters. Albert Lutley, his wife and two children and their colleagues, E. Gauntlett and Edith Higgs, were with them from Hongtong; and Eva French's party of young women (see pp 652–53) had also arrived on July 2 from Jiexiu. Both Lutley, the most senior, and Eva French had high qualities of leadership, but he was ill with high fever and she naturally deferred to the missionary in charge. All fourteen looked to Dreyer to deal with the authorities and prepare for whatever action they would have to take. He showed himself well able to do this.[1342]

It happened that one of Elder Si's attackers and five Boxers had been imprisoned in the stocks at Linfen for a major robbery: On their capture a large crowd of townsfolk had ridiculed them, shouting 'Hello! We thought you could ride the clouds! That you were invulnerable!' After Yü Xian intervened to free them, 'the mandarin sent word that Linfen was full of wild rumours', and ordered the missionaries all to leave, promising an escort for a few days' stages. But for the wisdom and courage of Dreyer, Lutley and Eva French all might have joined the sad procession of destitute victims southwards through Henan. They knew nothing of that yet, simply that a mere 'road pass' could land them in deeper trouble. So they refused to yield until an official pass (a *wenshu*) of the highest status was issued by the highest officials to ensure their safe conduct all the way to Hankou. From that time their doors were guarded and no troublesome crowds molested them.

When the Roman Catholics hired 'athletes' to escort them to Hankou, the officials urged Dreyer to join them. Again he refused on the ground of propriety, for his party were mostly unmarried women. China should protect them. Then came the news of the murder of Emily Whitchurch and Edith Searell at Xiaoyi, and of the difficulties the Days and McKie were in among the hills beyond Quwu, the Nathan sisters at Darting and McConnell's party at Hejin. Woodroffe, too, alone on the run, sent a message that he would like to join them, if only to die with them. But he could not get into the city. News of the Taiyuan massacre on July 9 only reached them on July 20 when they were travelling towards Xi'an, but the officials knew earlier and put pressure on them to go. Impossible, Dreyer answered. With ten women, two children and Lutley so ill, they could neither hide nor divide up into smaller parties. They must be openly escorted under official protection. At that the mandarins told the guards on their gates that they could disperse, an open invitation to plunderers, but Dreyer 'gave the (guards) a few (good) reasons in the shape of copper cash' for staying until his negotiations with the prefect ended.

Boxers had been drilling and boy and girl recruits learning to become possessed, 'foaming at the mouth and lying . . . as in a trance' until given orders. There was no time to be lost.

On July 14 the officials became insistent that they leave and agreed to all their demands: to supply a document giving all fourteen safe conduct, and an escort to Hankou. They agreed to pay the cost of passage, but could not find carters willing to go the whole way. So in their anxiety to avoid responsibility for imminent bloodshed in the city, they decided to provide 'government carts' instead. A mob was said to be waiting outside the south gate already, and an attack was to be made the next day, so a midnight start was agreed.[1343]

Four Christians set off with them (Sang Sifu, a well-known courier, Liu Baolin, a Hongtong deacon, and two young men, Go Wangde of Xi Xian and Li Wenhuan of Linfen), brave men determined to do all they could to help, well knowing that they made themselves the objects of bitter hatred. Within 'three hundred paces' one was violently knocked off a cart, another was flogged at the city gate and all four were reviled as 'secondary devils' and 'false foreign devils'. Go Wangde and Li Wenhuan when prevented from leaving Linfen climbed over the city wall before daybreak and rejoined the party ten miles away. On the first day, Dreyer and Eva French were dragged out of the carts by their hair (evidence that they were at the front, shielding others further in), robbed and threatened with swords at the neck, to say where their silver was concealed. Enemy underlings had planned it in advance, but could do no more.

'The remainder of the journey was less adventurous (though) frequently the Lord allowed us to get almost to the point of despair . . . with apparently no possible way of escape.' The intense heat in tightly curtained carts, so that they 'could scarcely breathe', resulted in nearly everyone becoming ill, 'and several were in so critical a condition that we almost despaired of

2.88 Sang Sifu, hero companion of the Dreyer-French party

their reaching the coast alive'. The Lutleys' two girls died.

After the adventure ended, Dreyer paid tribute to some mandarins and,

> men of all ranks who sympathised and showed us kindness. Even (at Linfen) there were those who would have helped us if they had dared. One man of position and influence told us he had been ill with rage at the utter stupidity of his Government. 'While you,' he said, 'are the ones to suffer now, the tables will be turned, and China's turn of suffering will come within a very few months.'

He promised to do all he could in secret to help them. Their escape in such favourable conditions, with effective safe-passes, could well have been his doing.

Eva French cited another mandarin in a city they passed through, who came to sympathise with them and afterwards sent them seventy eggs and a basket of apples. Another sent the sick man, Lutley, two bottles of stout, cans of condensed milk and marmalade and four packets of cakes. Such kindnesses were shown at great personal risk. But the chief credit belonged to the four Christians, Sang, Liu, Go and Li who stayed doggedly with the party, finding them food and shelter, and speaking up for them in threatening situations.

The Qü Xian tragedy[1344]
(July 21–24, 1900)

A bitter bungle by the governor of Zhejiang was to cost the lives of the county magistrate of Qü Xian, of thirty of his family and followers, and of two CIM families and four single women. These eight adults and three children and an uncertain number of Chinese Christians paid the price of the governor's irresolution.

Widespread unrest had resulted in armed 'marauders' congregating near the provincial borders, traditionally the regions of loose control and ease of escape by criminals from one jurisdiction to another. Ostensibly to protect Qü Xian against these banditti, the literati raised a militia who quickly became an even greater danger to both citizens and missionaries. Encouraged by the county magistrate, however, David Baird Thompson and his wife and colleagues stayed where they were.

When the provincial governor, Liu Shutang, received the dowager empress's original edict to kill, he already knew of the altered version adopted by the viceroys, and reinforced by their own orders to protect foreigners. So he vacillated, until his Manchu provincial judge prevailed on him to publish the edict. The Nanjing viceroy, Liu Kunyi, at once reprimanded and threatened the governor, so he countermanded his own proclamation, but too late. The militia and 'brutal soldiery' had lost no time. They seized the magistrate and all his household, dragged them to the prefect's *yamen* and in his presence murdered all thirty-one of them. On the same day, July 21, a mob encouraged by the military mandarin, who should have protected the mission, broke in and plundered it, even removing bricks from its walls. The evangelist Chen Tianfu escaped and appealed at the *daotai's yamen* for help, but was rebuffed. David Thompson had received a head injury in the riot, so his wife Agnes and Josephine Desmond tried again, only to find the county magistrate being beheaded in the *yamen* court.

Under the treaties the mandarins were duty bound to give asylum and to defend foreigners in trouble. There was nowhere else to go. David Thompson, therefore, took his wife and children and Josephine Desmond back to the *yamen*, the highest to which they could appeal. The door was closed against them. At this signal the mob seized Thompson, dragged him into the street and 'stabbed him to death with knives and tridents'. They then stabbed his two sons before their mother's eyes, and finally the two women.

Etta Manchester and Edith Sherwood lived elsewhere in the city, and both were severely wounded in an attack on them the same day. Neighbours hid them in a temple until they were discovered on the 24th. Pushed and dragged through the streets to the Roman Catholic chapel they, too, were stabbed to death and their bodies flung into the chapel.[1345] As the militia and people had been declaring that all Christians were to be killed, Chen Tianfu, the evangelist, and his family went into hiding.

At Changshan, near the border thirty miles to the west, the danger had seemed even greater, so on the friendly mandarin's advice George and Etta Ward and Emma Thirgood left home on July 21 to join the Thompsons in Qü Xian. The women and the Wards' child with his *amah* travelled by boat, while Ward and two Chinese companions followed overland. When they reached the city at daybreak on the 22nd and found it barred against them, they rightly hired another boat to take them downstream to Hangzhou. As they were loading their goods on board in full view of six Chinese gunboats with their officers and men, soldiers arrived, killed both mother and child at the breast with one sword-thrust and beheaded Etta Ward with the next. Emma Thirgood sank to her knees in prayer and also met her end.

The marauders had entered Changshan after the women left, and George Ward had escaped on foot with the local evangelist and Mao Liyuan, an 'inquirer'. Five miles short of Qü Xian a mocking crowd surrounded them and clubbed them to death, except for the evangelist, who feigned death and crawled away under

cover of darkness to report events to James Meadows at Shaoxing.

Across the provincial border, only 25 miles from Changshan, in the Jiangxi town of Yüshan (of great historic interest to the CIM, see pp 178, 427, 455–57),[1346] Kate Lachlan had returned to the work she was doing before her marriage and bereavement. As Kate Mackintosh she had pioneered the first stages of the Guangxin River experiment, and in 1900 was the senior missionary to seven junior women. When 'the marauders' became more and more powerful, many Chinese families left Yushan, among them a solicitous mandarin, Zhang Laoye. 'He told us we were in a twofold danger from the Empress Dowager's edict and the rebels, but we felt it best to remain.' Still he urged them to escape at any time to his large house in Guangxin (now Shangrao) twenty miles downriver.

On July 24 Yushan became agitated by news of the murders at Qü Xian, and although many people protested against what had happened, both Zhang Laoye and the mandarins in office at Yushan and Guangxin feared for the women and repeatedly offered to escort them to safety. Again they chose to stay, till one day 'we quietly left the city (with) a good escort' and eventually reached Jiujiang.

At this very time the Martin Griffiths, reduced to destitution, were being taken in by the Catholic bishop at Zhengding, Zhili, under the brigadier's protection. And Alfonso Argento destitute and wounded was being befriended by the stranger Lo. Others, in Shanxi, were vainly trying to evade capture, and party after party was in desperate straits crossing Henan.

'From prison to prison'
(July 15–October 25, 1900)

One of the most poignant episodes in the whole sad saga of the Boxer rising belongs to this period. From Caroline Gates's careful narrative, sparing of emotion, and Archibald Glover's expressive detail, as if the vivid memory were etched indelibly on his mind; from A. R. Saunders's restrained letter to *The Times* and E. J. Cooper's terse notes, and letter to his mother; and from C. F. H. Dreyer's factual report, a picture of incredible suffering emerges. But the suffering is borne with such Christian fortitude that an impression is given of more than acceptance of the lash permitted in God's wisdom. A vein of gladness in being 'partakers of the sufferings of Christ,' runs perceptibly through each page, even through the death of those dearest to them. This is the miracle, as much as that of deliverance from death time and again.[1347]

'Friday, July 13, was the eighth day of our second flight from Lu'an and the week seemed like a year, so much had been crowded into it of misery and suspense,' Glover wrote.[1348] Flora Glover and Caroline Gates and the children were in a disintegrating mule litter, and Archibald Glover had to choose between the agony of riding on an unpadded wooden saddle-frame or walking in calico socks and one cloth shoe, or barefoot. Although out of Shanxi and in Henan, their persecution by evil mobs continued hour after hour. While the escort rested, their prisoners out in the glaring sun could neither rest nor persuade anyone to get them food or water. 'The children kept sobbing with hunger, terror, sores and utter weariness. My wife, overcome by her great fatigue . . . fell heavily sideways and struck her head violently.' And when they moved on towards the river they had to flounder through quagmires until they reached Huaiqing—and a great surprise. Treated as criminals they were made to cross the city on foot behind the prefect's sedan chair. To 'follow the chair' was defamation akin to condemnation. But he did it in self-defence. He took them to a good inn, good food and free access to a privy (an open cesspit but such luxury) and to a water butt, a chance to wash. Glover's mention of such things revealed the depth of degradation in which they (and all such victims) had been forced to exist. Mats on the ground to sleep on and bricks for pillows completed the hospitality.

As if physical suffering were not enough, at Wuzhi mental torture was added. They were told by a young mandarin flaunting his authority that all foreigners had fled from Hankou and Shanghai and none was left in the whole of China. But the mandarin's wife gave the children some cast-off clothing and, asking many questions about the gospel, gave them the opportunity they welcomed to tell her about Jesus. Cruelty and kindness alternating were almost harder to bear than sustained hardship. On Sunday, July 15, they again faced death—at the hands of their escort. Then after hours of menacing the hapless family, the men thought better of it and allowed their prey to cross the Yellow River to Zhengzhou—the seat of a rabid mandarin.

Progress became more settled then, but for eleven days they travelled about thirty miles each day by agonising cart and barrow, always treated as prisoners. Their route was to take them due southwards through Zhengzhou and Queshan (Choshan). It seemed as if officials cared for nothing more than to get rid of them, each callously passing them on to the next city. The suffocating crowds and animosity continued, flaming at times into terrifying vehemence. At other times kindnesses almost too much to bear reduced them to tears. The prefect at Zhengzhou

> stormed and raved, hurling invective and anathaema with an exhaustless energy that could only be of the devil ... Wheeling suddenly upon me, he said or rather shrieked into my face: 'You devils ought to have your heads off ... there is an Imperial Edict out for your destruction', and with

the edge of his hand (he) chopped and sawed my neck so violently that it felt tender for hours afterwards.[1349]

A week later this same mandarin treated the Saunders-Cooper party to the same performance.

Lodged in a guard-room or 'in a cell immediately adjoining that occupied by convicts', in the darkness they knew the nature of their unlit, filthy quarters by the clanking of fetters and the stench of excreta on the ground where they must sleep. Yet *yamen* ladies sometimes sent for the children, Hope and Hedley, and treated them generously with gifts of 'sweetmeats', clothing or a wadded quilt to lie on. At last, on July 26, they reached Xinyang, near the Hubei border, and were delivered to the *yamen*.

A young official greeted them in English and led the way to an inner courtyard where they were received so kindly by other officials that it 'quite broke me down'. A barber was called and gave Glover his first shave for three weeks. Housed in a temple within the *yamen* grounds, among the idols and without a stick of furniture, they were kept hidden from public view for eight days of as blissful a rest as sleeping on 'mother earth' allowed. Soldiers were on the march to join in the defence of Peking against the foreign allies, they were told. It would be too dangerous to travel on. The third day saw a large parcel delivered to them, containing five complete sets of brand-new clothing. At last they could discard their verminous beggars' rags except to use them as pillows. Sunday worship for the first and only time on their long journey lifted their spirits to be ready for anything. But the shock they received on the fourth day was unimaginable.[1350]

They crossed the Yellow River, but the magistrate on the south side spurned them and forced them back to Wuzhi saying their pass was invalid. There they found Mary Huston, sent on by the Jincheng magistrate. To her, alone and dreadfully injured, with Hattie her companion dead, their arrival was a breath of heaven.

Together they were all taken to the river again and discarded on the north bank with no travel passes. So the ferries could not take them. At last on the third day a semi-official courier boat took them across and, a week behind the Glovers, they walked the thirteen miles to Zhengzhou. At the *yamen* the viceroys' directive to protect foreigners had just arrived. So the same wild mandarin who 'chopped and sawed' at Glover's neck could go no further. Resentfully, he abused them, saying, 'An edict has come today ordering that all foreigners be sent under escort to Hankou. Had you come here yesterday I would have had you all killed!' Treating them as common criminals he had the whole party of men, women and children thrown all together into the revolting gaol, separated from the chained prisoners only by wooden bars.

Night after night, as they continued the journey, they received the same treatment. By day they trundled on, grimly enduring the torture of their comfortless carts or barrows. Then, prosaically, Saunders wrote, 'We reached (Xinyang) on Monday, July 30, were treated well and clothes were given us . . . It was here, too, that we overtook Mr and Mrs Glover, two children, and Miss Gates, who . . . had met with similar treatment to ourselves.' Glover's account of their arrival told what Saunders left out.

> Shall I ever forget the sight? Slowly and painfully they were descending from the carts—three men, four women and five children in their rags, emaciation and utter woebegoneness, more like apparitions than beings of flesh and blood ... the Lucheng-Pingyao party, recognizable still though so pitiably changed ... My dear wife ran to (Margaret Cooper) and with a tender embrace led her gently in. She just lifted her eyes and smiled wearily as she greeted me, 'Oh, how nice to see somebody clean!' Next came her husband, his arms around a litter of loose dirty straw [anything to soften the carts and hard ground], then the Rev A. R. Saunders and Mr Jennings in like manner—followed by Mrs Saunders, Miss Huston and Miss Guthrie, leading or carrying the children, though scarcely able to support their own weight.

Truly it was 'a time to weep' Stretching themselves on the ground as we had done five days before, (they) gave thanks to God ... for rest after weeks of torture. But oh, the sadness of that sight! The earth floor of the room was covered, every yard of it, with sick and wounded ... Mrs Cooper's (rags and tatters) revealing gangrened sun-wounds about the breasts, and with ulcerous sores where the cruel (coal-carts) had galled her limbs, (and) the pains of dysentery. By the incense table was stretched Miss Huston with a broken jaw, a gaping scalp wound that laid bare the brain, flesh wounds in either forearm deep to the bone, and her whole body a mass of contusions—the work of the Boxers. Next to her was Mrs Saunders terribly reduced by dysentery; and near the door Miss Guthrie, apparently in the last stage of the same disease. The children, who in their painful distress looked the personification of misery, to which their moans and sobs bore continual witness ... were all in the throes of dysentery; and ... in the agony of undressed sun-wounds. Jessie Saunders and Edith Cooper perhaps suffered the most. Their arms from the shoulder to the elbow were gangrenous sores, alive with maggots.[1351]

Two of the party, Hattie Rice and the Saunders' baby, had already died and been buried. When Mary Huston had recovered consciousness during the night after their lynching at Jincheng, and found her own and Hattie's faces plastered with a mask of mud, she knew they had both been declared dead. Realising it was true of Hattie, she had warded off the hungry dogs, 'waiting for her own expected end', until the *yamen* people sent her on southwards to die somewhere else. Even as she rested among friends in that temple room, 'a haunted, hunted look' betrayed her thoughts. She spoke little except to her friend Caroline Gates, the only one not physically ill. Outside the room, 'under the fierce heat . . . the latrine just below the window (the only provision for seventeen people of whom nine and soon twelve had dysentery) had become a fetid mass of reeking corruption; while within, wounds and bruises and putrefying sores fouled the atmosphere.'

When Miss Guthrie lay apparently dying, she asked Archie Glover 'to pray over her "the prayer of faith" and from that time she received strength to recover'. They gave their 'pest-house' the name 'Christ's Hospital', though water was almost their only remedy, and washing each other's putrid clothes and bodies their main service. From watching the uncomplaining fortitude of its patients, suffering as much from their memories as from their pain, Glover 'saw a new meaning in the words, "The noble army of martyrs praise Thee." . . . The ministry of mutual cleansing was beautiful to see.'

At last, on August 3, the Glovers' ninth day and the Lucheng party's fourth at Xinyang, they were sent on by 'cruel wheelbarrow' with Flora Glover (within days of her confinement) and Margaret Cooper in stretcher chairs. A discarded pair of trousers, stuffed tight with the filthy straw, made a serviceable bolster, and two quilts softened 'the excruciating pain' of riding 'the long file of barrows with their screeching wheels and dislocating boards'. All were surprised, however, when little Jessie Saunders quietly died at an inn that night—put out in the street by the landlord, for fear of her homeless spirit, and buried on a hillside at sunrise.

They ran into an unexpected column of troops who cried, 'Army and Boxers are one' and were only kept from killing them by the courage of the party's escorts With the army officers' support, Mary Huston and Caroline Gates were roughly manhandled, and a spear levelled at Hope Glover reduced her to a 'terror that now settled upon (her)'. At Yingshan an LMS evangelist named Lo greeted them, took them all in and did all he could for them, refusing to leave them until he had delivered them to a hospital in Hankou. But a hundred miles from their destination Margaret Cooper died, on August 6, and on the 11th Mary Huston died at sunset. 'More than once (on Sunday, August 12) I thought my wife was dying,' Archibald Glover confessed, but they reached the LMS church at Xiaogan and received from the Christians 'a foretaste of the love of heaven'. Sent on by boat and nearing the end of their journey, 'the old dreadful yell went up, of curses for the foreign devils, and they pelted us until we were out of reach'.

At last on August 14 they arrived safely in Hankou and under medical care. Only Caroline Gates was thought fit to go on to Shanghai, but no sooner had she started than she succumbed to a terrible reaction . . . with critical nervous prostration'. Ceaseless tears could not wash away the memory of such weeks in which she had been a tower of strength. Brainerd, the Coopers' youngest, died on the 17th; Flora Glover's baby was born the next day, their fourth day in Hankou, and died on the 10th day; Hedley Glover nearly died in fever, and Hope could only scream. But by mid-September the Glovers were well enough to go by ship to Shanghai.

Flora's last letter to her parents said little about their sufferings, but instead 'it is better to dwell on the *glory* side', and then, '*my heart longs to return to Lu'an as soon as possible.*' Reduced to the point of having no resistance to disease, she died on October 25 of what they called 'peritonitis', aged only twenty-eight, 'the last of the martyrs of 1900 to pass from the cross to the crown'.

In those months, August through October, the agony for many others was prolonged, in their shared experience illuminating the hymns of Heaven

Who shall separate us from the love of Christ? Shall trouble or hardship or persecution or famine or nakedness or danger or sword? As it is written,

'For your sake we face death all day long; we are considered as sheep to be slaughtered.'
No, in all these things we are more than conquerors through him who loved us (Rom 8.35–7 NIV).

These are they who have come out of the great tribulation
Therefore, they are before the throne of God and serve him day and night
Never again will they hunger; never again will they thirst. The sun will not beat upon them, nor any scorching heat.

For the Lamb at the centre of the throne will be their shepherd; he will lead them to springs of living water.
And God will wipe away every tear from their eyes (Revelation 7.14–17 NIV).

The Oberlin martyrs and others
(July–August 1900)

Good mandarins in Shanxi had a hopeless task: By retaining office they could control to some extent the savagery of the madness at large. By helping the hunted they could endanger not only their own lives but those of their families and friends. That some protected the missionaries for as long as they did, and secretly advised and helped their sympathisers, such as 'CCH' and his 'wanted' men, stands to their great credit. That as close to Taiyuan as Taigu and Fenyang (Fenzhou) the Oberlin College members of the American Board could stay in their homes until July and even August, is remarkable.

On July 30, another day to be remembered, the five American Board and twenty-two C&MA Swedish refugees from Zhangjiakou reached Urga (see map 2.59: p 480) after thirty-eight days crossing the Gobi Desert from south to north. The Russian consul-general welcomed them hospitably, but with the news that ten thousand Mongols were gathering for a festival and two thousand Mongol soldiers in the area might be hostile. He was waiting for three hundred and fifty Cossacks for his own protection, and urged the travellers if they valued their safety to leave as soon as possible. They met the Cossacks on their second day out, reached Kiakhta on August 13, and St Petersburg on September 18.[1352]

July 30 had been the day the woebegone Saunders-Cooper party joined the Glovers at Xinyang, that Argento was nearing Hankou with his God-given companion 'angel', Lo, and in Shanxi and Zhili several groups of refugees were hiding in the hills. The Nathan sisters and Mary Heaysman of Daning were still in the care of Christians, and somewhere in the same mountains the CIM team from Xi Xian (Sichou), William and Helen Peat and their two little girls aged seven and three, with Edith Dobson, a hospital nurse, and Georgiana Hurn, only two years in China, were hiding in a remote natural cave. Three hundred Boxers, furious that they had slipped the noose, destroyed their home and were searching the hills for them. 'Are we to be saved—a remnant for the glory of God?' Peat wrote in his last letters to his mother, 'or are we to be taken . . . ?' Then two days later, 'The soldiers are just on us, and I have only time to say "Goodbye". We shall soon be with Christ, which is far better for us. We can only now be sorry for you who are left behind.'

And Helen: 'At the last moment I say, "Goodbye!" Our Father is with us and we go to Him', while 'Georgie' Hurn wrote, 'After this time of trial China will be a very different land . . . God ruleth over all, and He must have some wise purpose in allowing all this to come to pass . . . It would be nicer to be taken and be with so many who have laid down their lives; but for (your) sake and for the sake of the many heathen who are still without Christ, one would like to stay . . . We have heard that the people are coming, so we are going to our Heavenly Home.'

Instead they were dragged before the magistrate and 'regarded as the off-scouring of the earth; they were refused protection; and were sent in the usual squalor from city to city'. Some officials tried to befriend them and send them to Hankou, 'but after weeks of weary wandering and imprisonment, they were attacked by two Boxers fifteen miles south of (Qüwu) . . . and all the party were put to death on August 30'.[1353] No more is known.

While friendly mandarins were able to protect the Oberlin missionaries they carried on their work, but from July 16, after news of the Taiyuan massacre on July 9 reached them, hope faded. Yet they stayed where they were, safer with friends than among strangers. At Taigu eight Chinese Christians stood by them, waiting for the end.[1354] It came on July 31 when the yells of a mob, 'Kill! Kill!' became louder and louder, and the gates were broken in.

Elder Liu was seen calmly sitting in the courtyard when he was attacked and killed. The missionaries, D. H. Clapp and his wife, Francis Davis, George Williams, Rowena Bird and Mary Partridge, retreated with some of the Chinese to a flat roof from which they fired on the three hundred Boxers and soldiers sent against them. 'But their ammunition soon gave out, and they were easily overpowered and beheaded. The heads of them all were sent in a basket to Taiyuan to the governor. Their bodies were thrown into the flames of the burning houses, and were speedily reduced to ashes.' Now Yü Xian felt ready to go up to Peking for Ci Xi's congratulations. His personal tally of missionary heads had reached fifty-one.

The Oberlin missionaries at Fenyang (Fenzhou), Ernest and Elizabeth Atwater with two daughters, and Charles Price with his wife and one girl, had been on good terms with their prefect and magistrates, and knew they would continue to be protected. When other cities became unsafe, and Emily Whitchurch and Edith Searell were murdered at Xiaoyi, only ten miles from Fenyang, the Prices invited their CIM friends, the A. P. Lundgrens of Jiexiu and a newcomer, Annie Eldred, to come and stay with them. Nowhere else offered even a hint of the protection they enjoyed. At this point Eva French and her companions in Jiexiu had decided to join the Dreyers at Linfen. From city after city the tragic trail of fleeing missionaries was clinging precariously to life or falling to the Boxers' swords. For two weeks after the tragedy at Taigu, no change took place at Fenyang, but hope of escaping alive forsook the seven missionaries. 'Lizzie' Atwater wrote to her brothers and sisters:

> I have tried to gather courage to write ... [about the massacre at Taiyuan, when her stepdaughters had been beheaded, and the second massacre at Taigu]. We have tried to get away to the hills, but the plans do not work ... The people know we are condemned ... I long for a sight of your dear faces, but I fear we shall not meet on earth ... I was very restless and excited while there seemed a chance of life, but

God has taken away that feeling, and now I just pray for grace to meet the terrible end bravely ... My little (unborn) baby will go with me ... Dear ones, live near to God and cling less closely to earth. There is no other way in which we can receive that Peace from God which passeth understanding. My married life, two precious years, has been so very full of happiness. We will die together ... If we escape now it will be a miracle.

Ten days later, on August 13, the friendly prefect died. Only fifty miles from Taiyuan, he was quickly replaced by an anti-foreign mandarin. At once he demanded of the subordinate magistrates, Why had the Americans not been driven out? He flogged the dispenser at the mission clinic with three hundred blows and sent him to collect the foreigners' firearms, two pistols and two shotguns or rifles. 'Lizzie' Atwater's confinement was expected very soon, but the prefect had no mercy. They must 'leave for the coast' the next day.

A young Chinese schoolmaster from Zhili, Fei Qihao (Fei Ch'ihao), educated by missionaries of the American Board at Tong Xian, near Peking, and speaking English, had faithfully stayed with them.[1355] On August 15 he accompanied their carts on horseback through thousands of ghoulish spectators crowding to see them go. But when he saw that he himself was attracting unwelcome attention from the soldiers escorting them, he joined the Atwaters on their cart. His suspicions had been aroused. Talk of the coast was a ruse.

They had covered thirty-seven miles and were approaching a small market town when one of the soldiers said to Fei, 'Escape for your life! We are about to kill the foreigners!' He jumped down and ran. But ahead were twenty more soldiers. They robbed him of almost everything he had, but let him go. Then as the travellers reached them an official gave the signal and all seven missionaries and the three children were killed with swords and bayonets, stripped of their clothing and (on the insistence of the villagers) buried in a nearby pit. Every last member of

the American Board in Shanxi had been slaughtered—five men, five women and five children, and nearly half the Chinese Christians associated with them.

Fei Qihao was destitute and uncertain what to do. His decision to escape from Shanxi as soon as he could and take the news to Tianjin brought the first authentic reports of these events to the outer world. There is also a strong probability that he played a significant role in saving the life of Charles H. S. Green of the CIM. And of interest to missions is the link Fei had with the Kong family, descendants of Confucius. On Fei Qihao's flight from Fenyang, he visited a teacher named Kong at Taigu, a well-to-do country gentleman, who tried to persuade Fei to 'leave the foreigners, come back and worship (his) own gods'. Kong had a nephew also at the Tong Xian College of the American Board, who like Fei 'refused to apostatise and escaped after great perils'. This Kong Xiangxi (K'ung Hsiang-hsi) later graduated from Oberlin College, became principal of the Oberlin school in Shanxi and later a prominent member of the Guomindang to the end of the 'open century'.[1356]

The 'Peking sieges' lifted
(June–August 1900)

Since mid-June the foreign communities of both Beijing and Tianjin had been held at gun-point. Worse still, China had the power to overrun the legations and the foreign settlement at Tianjin. The Chinese city of Tianjin was already in Boxer hands, and the settlements were being shelled. After being fired on from the Dagu forts, the allied ships offshore landed marines, who took the forts on June 17 and advanced to the relief of Tianjin. At once the Chinese attacks on the settlements were intensified on three sides.[1357]

At Beijing the British legation and Prince Su's adjoining palace were packed with Chinese and foreign refugees, under shellfire from June 20 and hopelessly undermanned. Should Tong Fuxiang set his Gansu army and the Boxers on to swamping them with attacking waves, they would soon be overrun. In this extremity Sir Robert Hart sent his cryptic message, 'Situation desperate, MAKE HASTE!' by secret courier on June 24. By then about eight thousand marines from Dagu had relieved the Tianjin settlements, and Russian troops had rescued Admiral Seymour's retreating force in its last stand at Xigu. On June 27 the Chinese eastern arsenal of Tianjin and on July 9 the western arsenal fell to determined Allied assaults. Ten thousand Russian, German, Japanese, American, French and British men captured the walled city of Tianjin after a costly all-day battle on July 14. As a direct result threats to Yantai and Shanghai receded.[1358] The Boxers, and after them imperial troops, had already 'slaughtered, burned and plundered freely' in the old city. Now the foreigners took their turn, smashing fine porcelains and shipping tons of silver ingots abroad. On one day alone, 1,400,000 taels in silver were landed at a Japanese port. 'Military raids were made in all directions and . . . it is certain that the three shortest of the Ten Commandments were constantly violated on an extensive scale.' On July 14 some Russian shipping on the Amur River had been fired on, and the next day a Chinese battery bombarded the Russian settlement of Blagoveshchensk. For this the Russians exacted a terrible revenge. The corpses of many thousands of Chinese men, women and children floated down the Amur. In Beijing after the siege the worst excesses were attributed to the Russians. Certainly China had few reasons to love the foreigner.

Defeat weakened the Chinese commander Yu Lu's resolve, but any prospect of the Allies breaking through the massing forces between Tianjin and Beijing depended on strong reinforcement from overseas. On the Dagu-Tianjin front their combined strength totalled fourteen thousand, of which ten thousand were Russians and Japanese. The Russian admiral judged '20,000 to 30,000 men' to be required for the relief of Beijing, in addition to twenty thousand guarding communications. But the council of admirals set the figure at 'at least 60,000'

apart from the guards. The international cable still ended at Shanghai, and internal telegraphy was unreliable. Ships took three days at least to reach Tianjin, so the capitals of the West were always slow to receive up-to-date news, and slow to respond. The relief of the legations looked impossible.

Meanwhile, in Beijing, three almost inexplicable truces gave some respite to the legation thousands in their bunkers:[1359] the first on the day after the infamous edict to kill (June 24) when the *North China Herald* reported 'an imperial decree on June 25 ordering that the foreign envoys in Peking be protected at all costs', and firing stopped at one point while carts laden with vegetables and melons (not even poisoned) were delivered by order of Ci Xi to the severely rationed inmates. Such 'double dealing' was unfathomable to any who did not know Ci Xi's wiles.

A month after Yüan Zhang and Xü Jingcheng heroically changed her telegram 'Kill' to 'Protect', they were savagely executed. 'This morning my son Enming witnessed their death,' Jingshan wrote in his diary. They were cut in half and beheaded.[1360]

Each brief respite was followed by renewed attacks but, Sir Robert Hart commented, 'that somebody intervened for our semi-protection seems probable; attacks . . . were never pushed home, but always ceased just as we feared they must succeed . . . probably (due to) a wise man who knew what the destruction of the legations would cost empire and dynasty'. Yong Lu was thought to be that man.[1361]

Weeks were passing as the Allied governments faced the practical difficulties of distance and other commitments (the British in South Africa and the Americans in the Philippines). The estimate of needed troops then rose to eighty thousand. Only Japan could provide unlimited thousands, and decided to increase her expeditionary force to twenty thousand. America sent seven thousand from Manila and British Indian troops reinforced the two thousand already in north China.[1362] Delay was becoming crucial. As missionary refugees had found, Chinese troops were on the march from distant provinces to defend the capital. Even the British commander at Tianjin who advocated a daring advance, with Lord Salisbury's support, thought a relief column of twenty-five thousand essential. 'Fear that a reverse would imperil the lives and fortunes of all foreigners in north China,' prolonged the delay. Such was the lack of 'intelligence'. Every single foreigner in North China was already in direst peril or dead. An urgent message from Major E. H. Conger, the United States envoy, then succeeded in showing that action had become more urgent than full preparation. And the arrival of the American General Chaffee gave timely support to the British General Gaselee. Together they persuaded the other nations' reluctant generals (whose men formed two-thirds of the whole) to advance on August 4.

By an extraordinary stroke of mischief or mishap, a report found its way into the *North China Herald* on July 18, claiming that the Director-General of Telegraphs at Shanghai had received a telegram from Yüan Shikai announcing the massacre of all occupants of the Beijing legation: 'No one left alive.' And the Chinese servant of a foreigner escaped from Beijing was quoted as confirming the report. 'The startling news had already been telegraphed to all parts of the world' when the director-general, too late, denied having received such a telegram. Charlotte Haldane in *The Last Great Empress of China* attributed the 'story of the so-called Peking massacre' to the Shanghai correspondent of the *Daily Mail,* who picked up sensational fiction from the vernacular newspapers and embellished them from his own imagination. Whatever its origins, *The Times* of July 17 carried two-column obituaries of Sir Robert Hart, Sir Claude Macdonald and Dr G. E. Morrison, and a solemn memorial service was ordered at St Paul's Cathedral for July 23. Only 'the urgent remonstrances of Mr J. D. Campbell' of the Imperial Maritime Customs secured its postponement. Then a small boy disguised as a beggar was let down from the Beijing city wall and carried confirmation of the survival of the legations to the Allies.

Meanwhile the Zongli Yamen received an enquiry from the Chinese ambassador in Washington, Wu Dingfang, as to the situation of the beleaguered United States envoy, Major E. H. Conger. They cabled Conger's coded reply that he had been besieged for a month, supplies of food and ammunition were low, and 'quick relief only can prevent general massacre'. The other envoys were denied the right of sending messages in code and instructed to state *en clair* that all was well with them. The Beijing government then told Wu Dingfang that all the allied envoys were safe and well, provisions were being supplied to them, relations were 'most friendly', and the envoys were to go to Tianjin for negotiations. But Major Conger's statement that to leave the legation would be 'certain death' convinced the powers that the need for action had become more urgent than preparations. 'A storm of shot and shell, and . . . all the privations and dangers of a siege' resumed on July 29.

The siege of the Beitang cathedral continued uninterrupted and at Xian Xian, a hundred miles south of Beijing, thirty thousand other Catholic converts, of whom twelve thousand were armed, were successfully defending themselves. But twenty miles closer, at Hejian, over a thousand were slaughtered by troops accompanying the fanatical Li Pingheng (previously governor of Shandong) to Beijing.

In the legation, as the ammunition stock fell lower and lower, ears were straining to hear the sound of an approaching army from Tianjin—even before the capture of Tianjin city. But at last, on August 4, the field force of sixteen thousand moved out, the Russians and French Annamese as a right wing following the east bank of the river, and the Japanese, British (mostly Indian) and Americans as the left wing on the west bank. Beitang fell on the 5th and Yangcun (now Wuqing) on the 6th and the viceroy of Zhili in command, Yu Lu, shot himself in shame on the 8th. The column reached Tong Xian on the 12th. With the enemy only fifteen miles from the capital, the court prepared to flee (see map 2.81: p 656).

By imperial decree Li Hongzhang was appointed plenipotentiary to negotiate with the powers and tried by diplomacy to halt the allies at Tong Xian, without success. Behind the advancing allies swarms of disorganised Chinese soldiery and Boxers were scattering. But a nation faced with defeat could resort to desperate acts. 'At Shanghai and along the (Yangzi River) much apprehension was felt.' A thousand volunteers stood ready to defend the Shanghai Settlement, backed by fifteen to twenty warships.[1363] Three thousand Indian troops were sent from Hong Kong to defend Shanghai, reaching Wusong on the 12th, and each allied power sent detachments to join them.

At Beijing 'the night of August 13–14 was marked by the most furious and persistent assault that the legations had experienced', but the 14th dawned with the Allies only five or six miles from the city walls. Coordination between the Allied troops broke down as the Russians, disregarding agreed strategy, attacked and took the Dongbian Gate (see map 2.79: p 644). Some Americans then cleared the top of the Tartar city wall and unfurled the Stars and Stripes. South of the British legation, however, was a water-gate under the wall of the Tartar city, through which secret couriers had succeeded in passing from time to time. Sir Claude Macdonald now sent a cipher message to advise General Gaselee of this easy access to the city. At 3.00 p.m. on August 14, Sikh troops were the first to enter.

Inside the legations the defenders faced incessant firing from the Chinese lines, in spite of a torrential downpour of rain,

> Lead was simply poured into us ... We thought (they) were preparing to assault. Suddenly (a Japanese) called out, 'Listen! Do you hear the machine-gun outside the Hatamen? The relief force is outside the city.' We laughed, we joked ... Soon after tiffin (lunch) ... Konavaloff rushed in with

a shout—'The relief force is in! The Sikhs are in the legation! Listen to the shouting.' Men, women and children, everyone out on the lawn, cheering, yelling, crying, mad with excitement and delight, and there coming in, line after line, waving their turbans and cheering, real, live, big, burly Indian troops ... I rushed up to the first one I saw; I clapped him on the back; I shook his hand; I yelled, I cheered ... I was at last saved![1364]

For eight weeks one thousand foreigners, accustomed to great comfort, and three thousand Chinese had survived on rationed rice and occasional horseflesh; 458 marines and seventy-five volunteers had suffered, seventy-six killed and 179 wounded, 255 casualties in all, but very few among non-combatants. No child had been hit, and the only woman to be injured received her wound after the liberation. The next day Psalm 124 verse 7 was cabled to the outer world: 'The snare is broken and we are escaped.'

Also on August 15, General Chaffee and the American troops cleared Chinese troops from the imperial city, from which they still threatened the legations. Forcing gate after gate into the Forbidden City they reached the last before the imperial palace when they were stopped by an imperious intervention by the Russian general. His troops and the Japanese were burning and sacking the Tartar city, where a heavy pall of black smoke rose from the huge conflagration, but he insisted on having a hand in the richest prize.

The Roman Catholic Beitang was crowded with three thousand Chinese converts. About five hundred of them under forty-three marines had been armed with improvised spears and a few rifles, and the attacks had been 'more furious than on the legations'. Rations were five ounces of food per head from August 1 and three ounces from August 8. Altogether four hundred Chinese and eleven French marines were killed before their siege was at last lifted on the 16th.

Confusion reigned in the Court from August 12 as Ci Xi weighed Yong Lu's advice to stay and 'prove her innocence' by executing guilty Manchus, against Prince Tuan's and Kang Yi's persuasion to flee. But on August 15 she and her hostage, the emperor, both in peasant clothing, left secretly in a common cart for the Summer Palace of Yüanmingyüan. 'Mistress of the situation to the last', before leaving she ordered the emperor's favourite concubine to be thrown down a well and drowned. A body of troops escorted them from the Summer Palace to Zhangjiakou (Kalgan) from where she was to travel southwards to Taiyuan on the way to Xi'an.

After the sieges
(August 15–October 1900)
Five days after the relief of the legations, a service of thanksgiving was held on Sunday, August 19, addressed by A. H. Smith of the American Board. Under the title 'The Hand of God in the Siege of Peking,' he reviewed ten remarkable aspects of the experiences they had been through:

1. The fact that the foreign community was not annihilated before the first marine guards arrived;

2. the guards' arrival just before all access was made impossible;

3. the immunity from attack on widely scattered groups coming through the city to the legations;

4. the Methodists' success (under semi-siege for twelve days before moving to the legations) in working out ways and means of defence and survival, and in training personnel who were ready when the move was made;

5. the late addition of the two thousand Chinese Christians and of the palace of Prince Su, both of which factors became essential to survival;

6. the discovery of 'mountains' of wheat, rice, corn and much else in shops within the periphery of the defended area, of an exceptional number of mules and ponies in the stables, of ample water in eight wells, and more than enough coal and timber;

7. apparently inexhaustible sources of clothing, curtains and calico for about fifty thousand sandbags, and even a smithy and raw material for the armourers to use;

8. the restraining hand of God on the attackers, who seemed afraid of coming to close grips with the defenders—shelling ceased just as the right range was found, and between a million and a million and a half rifle rounds fired into the legation killed and wounded so few;

9. many diseases, including typhoid and smallpox, occurred while overcrowding was excessive; yet no epidemic developed;

10. while the attackers seemed confused and irresolute, in spite of rivalries and jealousy between nations, defenders and defended enjoyed 'a spirit of unity rare to see' with Greek, Roman Catholic and Protestant Christians fraternising as never before.[1365]

But Christian unity and thanksgiving were only small glimmers of light in an otherwise sombre situation. Unbridled sacking of Beijing by the victorious troops followed the city's occupation, and continued for a week or two until a semblance of control was gradually restored. By making strong representations to the commanding officers, Moir Duncan of the BMS was able to save the Beijing mansion of Tuan Fang, the enlightened Manchu governor of Shaanxi, from destruction. The shameless rape of Tianjin was exceeded at Beijing; 'the troops were out of hand and looked on Peking and all it contained, persons and property, as prize of war, subject to their will'. During those days 'countless thousands of women put an end to their lives (and) many thousands of men were killed in a wild orgy of slaughter'.[1366] The common people had suffered similar treatment, first from the Boxers, then from the soldiers, and finally from foreigners 'with a sordidness more despicable than the madness of the Boxers'. The dowager empress had brought it all on her people and herself, but the bloodlust of baying mobs and vicious Boxers had been matched by their victims' 'rescuers'. Quickly the parts of the city occupied by certain of the allies were drained of Chinese, fleeing into other parts policed by the more civilised conquerors, among whom the Japanese had a good record.

The Forbidden City was not occupied until the German Field-Marshal von Waldersee set up his headquarters in the emperor's palace in October. But on August 28 detachments of foreign troops marched through the sacred courtyards, and the envoys and senior officers 'inspected the imperial throne rooms and chambers'. China had been humiliated to the depths, and the Western powers rode roughshod over the devastated capital and countryside. Where only eight hundred French Annamese and no Germans had had a part in the victory, by September 10 the *North China Herald* reported two thousand Germans and 1,500 French troops in occupation of segments of Beijing assigned to them. The fact that the German envoy had been murdered was enough for the other powers to grant Germany a predominating influence in dealing with the Boxer revolt. On the day after news of Baron von Ketteler's murder reached Germany, the German emperor had ordered the formation and despatch of 'an expeditionary force' of seven thousand, in the words, 'When you meet the foe you will defeat him. No quarter will be given, no prisoners will be taken.' Citing Attila the Hun, he declared 'that no Chinese will ever again even dare to look askance at a German'.

But where some cooperation had existed in lifting the sieges, the allies were at sixes and sevens from then on. In exchange for a free hand in Manchuria, Russia entered into negotiations with Li Hongzhang to secure the withdrawal of foreign troops from the capital and restoration of Chinese control in conquered territory.[1367] Britain and America refused to go along with the scheme, and Sir Claude Macdonald reported to Lord Salisbury on September 7 his opinion that 'a general massacre of Christian converts and of all Chinese who have shown themselves friendly to foreigners would most certainly ensue if all foreign troops were to leave now.' The glaring mistake of such a withdrawal as had happened in 1860 and on other occasions (interpreted by the Chinese as inability to hold what had been captured) must not be repeated. The allied powers then welcomed 'so distinguished and experienced' a soldier as Count von Waldersee to head the international forces in north China. In this capacity of commander-in-chief he set up his headquarters in the imperial palace and began punitive operations into the surrounding countryside.

Retreating Boxers and demoralised troops were heavily defeated by Yüan Shikai's Shandong troops, and on August 28 the siege of Xian Xian was relieved from Baoding by the guilty, and now devious, acting-viceroy of Zhili, pending Li Hongzhang's return. But the organised imperial armies retreated south-west to Baoding and Shanxi, and north-west to Zhangjiakou '(Kalgan), from where Tong Fuxiang and his Gansu Muslims accompanied the court via Taiyuan to Xi'an. The countryside surrounding the capital for hundreds of miles was still being terrorised by those marauding Boxers and disorderly soldiers. So although essential control of communications between the coast and Beijing was maintained by foreign troops, missionaries who had so recently been besieged needed courage to go out to the relief of Christians in distress. Armed foreign escorts who went with them levied fines in the most culpable places, to provide food for destitute Christians who would have starved in the approaching winter.

As soon as troops could be spared from the cities, punitive expeditions destroyed Boxer centres and pockets of resistance, to restore a free flow of market produce and provisioning of the cities. The coastal forts at Shanhaiguan, Qingwangdao and Beitang (near Dagu) were occupied, and on October 8, one thousand French troops marched south to relieve the Catholics holding out in several places against the Boxers. Another French column relieved those being protected at Zhengding by the friendly brigadier, and another column from Xian Xian entered Baoding unopposed on October 13 to find the Greens and Jessie Gregg being held prisoner.

An international column of 3,500 from Beijing and four thousand from Tianjin also reached Baoding on October 18, and formed a tribunal to investigate the murder of foreigners on June 30 and July 1. As a result, the acting-viceroy, the Tartar-General and the camp commandant who had refused sanctuary to the CIM and Presbyterian missionaries on July 1, were executed. The city gates and a corner of the wall were blown up and the Boxer temples demolished. Heavy fines were exacted for the relief of survivors in distress, and 3,200 Germans and French remained in the city for the winter. J. Walter Lowrie, the American Presbyterian who happened to be away from Baoding when disaster struck, and returned as interpreter-adviser to one of the generals with the international column, by his influence was credited with saving hundreds of Chinese from the vengeance of the vindictive expedition.[1368]

Territorial ambitions and land-grabbing by the occupying powers risked clashes between them, with scheming Russia the chief menace to harmony, but pacification of the country continued. Between December 12, 1900, and the end of April 1901, forty-six expeditions, thirty-five of them German, were sent out. One of the first by German troops reached the Guguan Pass, signalling a panic evacuation of Taiyuan by officials and wealthy gentry. In Beijing itself, by the irony of an imperial decree, various princes, dukes and leading officials were deprived of rank and office and committed to trial, while the evil genius of massacre and mayhem no longer in disguise went her way to the ancient inland capital, Xi'an, meting out punishments as she went.

At Taiyuan she 'lingered for a short time' and left her imperial clansman, Yü Xian, 'infamous for ever', in office as governor. In his *yamen* courtyard he demonstrated to her how the foreigners had been beheaded.[1369] She arrived at Xi'an on October 28, and not surprisingly 'every act of administration ordered from (Xi'an) only served to accentuate the continuance of anti-foreign and pro-Manchu tendencies of the court'.

The allies protested at her worst moves, such as the appointment of the notoriously anti-foreign governor of Henan to be governor of Hebei with his seat at Wuchang, a threat to the wise viceroy Zhang Zhitong. She countermanded the appointment, but it was believed that Tong Fuxiang, the tiger she had chosen to ride and could not dismount, was dominating her. When under pressure from the Allies an imperial decree condemned the barbarous princes Tuan and Chuang to imprisonment for life and Yü Xian to banishment, Tong Fuxiang's punishment was 'reserved for consideration'. His fifteen thousand battle-hardened men were there with him. As a ruse, Yü Xian was reported dead by suicide while he left Shanxi, but the subterfuge was transparent and the Allies insisted on his execution. A new decree ordering the death penalty was put into effect at Lanzhou, but by having his throat cut instead of decapitation. 'By a stroke of superlative hypocrisy Her Majesty ordered that all her pro-Boxer Decrees and Edicts be expunged from the records of the Qing Dynasty.'

Negotiations to bring the court back to Beijing began almost as soon as they escaped in August, and intensified when the influence of 'pernicious advisers' made diplomatic progress difficult. But the heavy-handed occupation of Baoding and execution of its rulers frightened the imperial court into keeping its distance at Xi'an until October 1901. Beijing, Tianjin and the province of Zhili were therefore under the command of the official plenipotentiaries, Li Hongzhang and Prince Qing, joined by the two Yangzi viceroys, Liu Kunyi and Zhang Zhitong, in negotiating reparations. On August 25 they made a proclamation that all killing must stop. But it took weeks to take effect. The rest of the empire remained nominally under Ci Xi's control. All too slowly the Boxers and bloodthirsty soldiery learned that their licence to kill had expired. Numberless Christians and helpless missionaries were yet to succumb.[1370]

The Shanxi toll continues
(August–September 1900)

On August 22 'CCH' wrote again to Erik Folke reporting on his activities. His businesslike letters cannot disguise his anguish and anxiety. 'The hiding-place of Mr and Mrs Duncan Kay of Qüwu has become known. Some local rebels, pretending to be Boxers, captured him and are holding him to ransom. Elder Shang Guan and the evangelist have had to flee . . . therefore we have no means of communication with Mr Kay.' Nor was there any word from the Kays after the end of July, but he was seen alive on August 17. Then only the news that they and their child were 'cruelly put to death on September 15'.

'CCH' also wrote that on August 7, Yü Xian had 'issued a proclamation ordering the people in every town and village to practice the Boxer arts, and now all are practising. The persecutions of the native Christians in Shanxi are indescribable.'[1371] Two days later, on August 9, the Baptist missionaries imprisoned at Xinzhou north of Taiyuan were told they were to be taken to the coast, and a guard of ten soldiers sent by Yü Xian took them out of the city in four carts. As they reached the gates they were set upon, stripped of their clothing and immediately killed by blows to their heads with swords. For some days their bodies lay unburied outside the city until their friend, the literary chancellor, hired men to wrap them in mats and bury them at the foot of the city wall.[1372] Yü Xian then set out, on August 11, for Beijing, and entered the experiences of the Greens and Jessie Gregg.

When the flight of missionaries from Zhangjiakou (Kalgan) and Guihuacheng across the Gobi Desert took place, two former members of the C&MA, Mr and Mrs Helleberg, and 'a new colleague named Wahlstedt' succeeded in covering two hundred miles before being murdered by Manchu soldiers. At Guihuacheng itself seventeen adults and twelve children of the C&MA delayed their escape across the Gobi until one member's confinement was over. As they travelled they were robbed repeatedly even of clothing, and accepted the invitation of four Catholic priests to join them. But C. L. Lundberg wrote that Boxers and soldiers were coming: 'Tell our friends we live and die for the Lord . . . The way He chooses for me is best, may His will be done. Excuse my writing; my hand is shivering.' And on August 22, 'the soldiers have arrived, and will today attack our place. The Catholics are preparing to defend themselves, but it is vain. We do not like to die with weapons in our hands; if it be the Lord's will, let them take our lives.' Emil Olsson, the leader, and Lundberg escaped, but were caught and beheaded. 'The whole place was burned and the missionaries perished.[1373] Out of thirty-eight members of the C&MA in the whole of China, twenty-one and fourteen children died in the Boxer rising.

One of the Scandinavian missions to Mongolia known as the Scandinavian Alliance Mission of Chicago consisted of three men and three single women devoted to rough pioneering from Mongol tents with no settled home until after several years.[1374] On September 1, Boxers murdered D. W. Stenberg and the three women at Dallat Hosso near the Yellow River in the Ordos desert region, and C. J. Suberten or twelve days later, but N. J. Friedstrom escaped.

In the same Ordos area the Roman Catholic Bishop Hamer 'after a valiant resistance, was captured, his fingers and toes were cut off, and he was taken from village to village until death ended his sufferings'. Elsewhere in the same region two priests were executed and their heads exposed. And in another place three were burned to death in a church. Four thousand more Catholics survived the siege of one mission centre, and fifteen Catholic missionaries escaped across the desert to Siberia, taking forty-two days. Altogether nine Catholic missionaries and three thousand converts were killed, and many died of privation in Mongolian territory alone.[1375]

F. C. H. Dreyer's party had been driven to despair by hostile people, and almost suffocated in their closed carts by the time they reached Zhengzhou in north Henan on August 3. The first of the Lutleys' two daughters, Mary, died that evening, and the second, Edith, on the Henan-Hubei border on the 20th. Each night they were all thrust into the same foul prisons as the Glovers' and Saunders' parties had occupied, and heard tall stories of their plight. But even then a sense of humour did not forsake them. Noisy crowds blocked doors and windows in their eagerness to see the 'foreign devils', denying the prisoners the fresh air they desperately needed. 'It was most comical seeing them holding their noses and yet breathing through their mouths the bad and poisonous smells which they thought emanated from us.'[1376]

Because of the dangers in Henan, 'CCH' shed tears when the *daotai* of Tongguan forced them to take the Henan route instead of through safer Shaanxi. Yet the same official's commissioner congratulated them on safe travel so far, and at other cities, including Queshan (Choshan), they were given generous supplies. LMS and Methodist Christians in Hubei did all they could for them, as for the earlier parties to pass through, and on August 28 they reached Hankou. After Erik Folke's Swedish Mission, theirs were the lightest sufferings of those who escaped from Shanxi. The experiences of the Greens and Jessie Gregg and of the Ogrens were to be many times more heart-rending.

Caught! The Greens and Jessie Gregg[1377] (August 1900)

Charles Green, his wife and children and Jessie Gregg had been sheltered in the isolated farmhouse for three weeks when the Boxers suddenly searched the place. Farmer Gao had heard whispers among the villagers that the fugitives' presence was suspected, but instead of sending them away, for the sake of his own family, he tried to hide them more securely. He dug a tunnel through the loess cliff behind his home, to link it with two derelict caves where they could hide. The very small tunnel entrance was easily hidden behind household chattels. But a Chinese Christian

named Geng came to invite them to move to his home forty miles away, and an invitation had also come from the Catholic bishop in Zhengding to join the Griffiths there.

On the morning of Thursday, August 9, while they were half-dressed and discussing which offer to accept, the alarm was raised. Men were approaching. They all crawled through into the cave, joined by Geng, and Gao's wife hid the tunnel entrance as the Boxers arrived. There was 'a tramping of many feet' and 'a banging of utensils, then a shout of triumph!' To the minds of each adult came the words, 'Thou art worthy!' but the children's cries '"Are they going to kill us now?" pierced deeper than any Boxer's knife . . . We could only tell them that very soon we should be with Jesus.'

Charles Green crawled along the tunnel to plead for the women and children, and as he emerged a Boxer fired a shotgun from close range. 'By the dull heavy thud on my head I knew I was wounded, and was conscious of falling through the entrance, then rising to my feet I seemed to spin round two or three times (and) leaned against the wall for support.' He staggered from room to room, blood streaming down his face, and as the Boxers outside tried to fire at Green again, Geng crawled out and escaped. Green then rejoined the others and together they decided to surrender. As they came out of the house into the courtyard, men on each side of the doorway brandished 'their huge ghastly swords' and laid them on their necks while they robbed them of everything they possessed except what they were wearing—and a pocket Bible which they handed back to Jessie Gregg, saying, 'If you read that you can get to heaven.' Seeing the children's distress, they said they would not kill any of them. They then led them off in procession to the city, each under a sword, with the firearms bringing up the rear. Enormous crowds lined the streets, many showing real sympathy. When Jessie Gregg saw the tear-stained face of their own house-help, she called out, 'We are not afraid; God is with us!'

They were taken to the wreck of their own home in Huolu, and when the men began to whet their swords it looked as if their hour had come. But the Boxers left for their daily ritual and a policeman friend of the family said, 'Don't be afraid; the mandarin will be here directly.' A hand passed a pot of water to them through a broken window. They were not alone. The mandarin arrived with an escort of two hundred soldiers, and thousands lined the streets as the prisoners, 'too faint and giddy to care', were taken on foot all the way to the *yamen.*

The mandarin told them he would send them to safety at Zhengding or Baoding, and had them lodged in the *yamen* temple. At last the women could examine Charles Green's gunshot wounds. Because of his crouching position as he crawled out of the farmhouse tunnel, not only had his head but his 'face, shoulders, arms and back had taken their share of No 1 shot.' As blood, hair, and clothing were now firmly clotted, they decided to leave it to be dealt with properly at Zhengding. But bricks for pillows and the pain and stiffness made sleep impossible.

Early in the morning Mrs Liu, the house-help, came to the *yamen*, even though told they had been executed singing hymns! She took the children in her arms and embraced their mother and Jessie Gregg, oblivious of the onlookers. 'Her calm, strong faith in God and loving, helpful words . . . enabled us to share St Paul's joy over his converts, "I am filled with comfort; I am exceeding joyful in all our tribulation."' A soldier escort took them to Zhengding, but the Baoding Boxers, wearing Green's clothing and carrying bundles of booty, followed, always within reach of them. At the sight of the Boxers, the Zhengding mandarins were adamant that neither they nor their prisoners could enter the city; the wounded man would have to wait for treatment.

This time the Boxers' bundles and weapons were piled on the prisoners' cart as they headed for infamous Baoding only six weeks after the massacres. The provincial governor had more recently declared by proclamation that all foreign teachers of religion were devilish deceivers, and all Christians must recant or be killed. They covered fifteen miles by midnight and twenty-three more by daylight, but after an hour and a half's rest and only some millet gruel and bread rolls to eat, were sent on another twenty-mile stage. Their road took them through Boxer territory where every Catholic had been killed. 'It seemed so improbable that we should be allowed to pass through alive, but our hearts were kept lifted up to God . . . that He might be glorified in us, whether by life or by death.'

At Ding Xian they were put into the *yamen* prison for a few hours, with ten or more chained prisoners in a cage at one end, and given some food. But at 3.00 p.m. they started off again on another twenty-three-mile stage, much of it up to the axles in mud and water. This time the ten Boxers were outnumbered by *yamen* soldiers and officials, and the journey took until midnight again, when they reached another prison.

After travelling for forty hours with little food, and no sleep for three nights and days, nothing could keep them awake. In the morning a subtle change of attitudes towards them raised their hopes. They had their first wash since Huolu, and the prison warder told them that the emperor had ordered the protection of missionaries. ('Missionaries and merchants have nothing to do with the war.') It was August 12. The allied expeditionary force had reached Tong Xian, fifteen miles from Beijing, and the government was protecting its own interests. Another forty miles of jolting in a springless cart brought them to Baoding at daylight, 'understanding as never before how Jesus must have felt as He went up to Jerusalem for the last time'.

Suddenly, before they realised what was happening, the women and children were taken to the women's lock-up, and Charles Green found himself alone 'in a filthy yard among some twenty prisoners in various stages of dirt and wretchedness'. His exhaustion overcame him, and he lay on the ground and wept at being separated at such a moment, so that they could not die together. But after half an hour he was taken out again—to find them refreshed and combed, by the kindness of the women's warder. The magistrate, however, refused to receive them and was bent on sending them back to where they had come from.

> A fast increasing and excited mob was surging about the cart, and a number of the city Boxers appeared with their guns and great swords, and took up their position all around us ... The heat became intense, and we sat like that for at least two hours ... I heard the spokesman of our (original) Boxer party say, 'There will be trouble here very shortly.' To that man, under God, we undoubtedly owe our lives on this the third wonderful deliverance from death. He had gone to the mandarin and pleaded for us, showing him that we should certainly be killed as soon as we got out of the city, even if we were allowed that far.

The mandarin relented and they were returned to their prison quarters. Charles Green was then taken before him and treated kindly. The current troubles were Britain's fault, he said, but as Green and the others had come to Baoding they would be protected, and as a favour Green was allowed to rejoin his family. At last with a broken penknife and a needle they began cleaning his wounds, and removing the lead shot. Most were embedded too deeply.

Miracles one after another[1378]
(August–September 1900)

On August 14, when the legations were relieved and the imperial court were preparing to become fugitives themselves, the Greens and Jessie Gregg were told they were to be sent by boat to Tianjin. Two carts came to take them to the riverside and they were given cash for travelling expenses. But four or five local Boxers with drawn swords and eight of their first Boxer escort joined them on the boat, with no representative of the mandarins. What could this mean? Three miles out, the local Boxers left them, and by sunrise the boat had covered thirty

miles. Perhaps they were going to Tianjin after all. They tied up at the riverbank and the two leading Boxers went ashore.

> My wife cried, 'Oh, Charlie, something is wrong; do ask the others what it is.' I spoke to one of them, but he only wrung his hands and said, 'This is terrible! terrible!' Then the two men returned, and the leader said, 'It is all a lie about you being taken to Tianjin. It is impossible to get there. The river is held by Boxers at several points ... Our orders from the Governor were to bring you so far down the river, and then kill you.' As he spoke he pointed to his long ugly knife, which I had seen him sharpening ... Then he went on, 'We don't intend to commit such a sin; we have no quarrel with you; but you must leave the boat now and make the best of it for yourselves.'

They were advised to hide in the tall reeds until the evening and then go to Anxin (then called Hsin-an), the city they had passed, and see what the mandarin would do for them. 'We were simply stunned as if in a dream.' They took what food and bedding they could carry, and were soon among the reeds and undergrowth. Either to think or pray was too difficult. For a fourth time they had escaped death as by a miracle.

> Our God had delivered us from a cruel death, touching even the hearts of these Boxers for us ... All the way from (Huolu) we had maintained a quiet, respectful demeanour towards them, and they played with the children ... Tears came into the eyes of the spokesman when, on stepping from the boat with John in my arms, I turned and, putting my hands together in the Chinese manner, thanked him.

Most of the day among the reeds they spent praying, holding their breath at the sound of footsteps on a nearby path. Charles asked 'what the Lord was saying' to his wife. 'Delivering thee from the people . . . unto whom I now send thee,' she replied. And Jessie Gregg? 'I have been waiting all day for a little bird to bring us a letter,' was her surprising answer. [I, AJB, cannot write this without a vivid sense of our friend Jessie Gregg's personality; it is so typical of her, like an old-time prophet with a sixth sense.] They laughed at the time, but their troubles were far from over. A boy saw them and, 'with a scared face gave me a wide berth. I must have been an object with dirty, bloodstained undercoat and trousers, no gown, worn-out shoes, unshaved, wounded face and dishevelled hair of six months' growth . . . No wonder he was frightened.'

Boxers came searching for them, 'shooting off guns into the reeds', but went away again. Then a thunderstorm drenched them and chilled them to the bone. 'O Lord, was there ever a more helpless, hopeless, desolate band of Thy little ones?' Green added to his narrative. They were still half dressed as they had been when surprised by the Boxers at the farm. They decided to do the right thing and go to the *yamen* in the city. On the way they came to a cottage, asked for help, and were told to wait while a man with a boat was called. This looked promising.

> Suddenly we were startled by an unearthly sound ... With a slash of a drawn sword the reed curtain at the door was dashed down, and we were again face to face with a crowd of fierce Boxers ... I was seized by the hair, dragged to the ground, and was conscious of blow after blow (and) then of being trampled on by many feet as others rushed over me to seize my wife and Miss Gregg. I remember a pang as I heard the heart-rending shrieks of the children, and then a sweet calm filled my soul as I committed my spirit to God ... We have each been able to testify that this was the calmest moment in our lives ... never doubting that we should immediately be killed.

> Now we were dragged outside and thrown down in the mud, then bound hand and foot. Suddenly I missed the cries of the children and was glad that (they) were spared more of these terrible sights. Miss Gregg was hauled by the hair into a kneeling position, and her head pressed down on to a stone (incense table). One cried: 'Who will strike?' But other voices overruling cried: 'No, take them all to headquarters first.' As we lay there bound in the mud, one and another struck us heavily again and again with the backs of

swords or the handles of spears ... As blow after blow fell on (Miss Gregg) no sound escaped her lips, only a long, deep sigh.

> [The command was given to carry them off.] The handles of two spears were put under my left arm, two men taking the ends on their shoulders, and I was taken off hanging between them by one arm, with hands tied to my feet behind me ... about a quarter of a mile (in) excruciating pain ... My wife (similarly suspended) by both hands and feet, (Miss Gregg) by one arm and one leg. (The children were tied hands and feet, John carried and Vera made to walk.)

The Boxers would not believe their story, convincing themselves that they had captured Roman Catholics from the nearby mission who had shot two of their number. But they moved Mrs Green's head out of a pool of dirty water and eased Jessie Gregg's thongs at Charles's request. Lying there on the wet ground (and later in the Boxers' temple building), still trussed like fowls, they said, 'For Jesus' sake' and prayed together. For three or four days they were held, bound more reasonably and cross-examined, until Charles Green's 'mouthful of Huolu dialect' and 'two wives and children' convinced the Boxers that they spoke the truth. At last their ropes were removed.

From the 16th to the 18th they were on show to curious crowds of hundreds of Boxers 'carrying their ghastly weapons, and by their looks thirsting for our blood,' while messengers went to Baoding to discuss their fate. On their return with the news that the governor was angry when told that the foreigners were still alive, and had ordered their execution, a consultation of civilian Boxers, superior to the armed gangs, was held in the temple. These literati and tradesmen (playing the part, it transpired) decided to hold them until it was safe to send them on to Tianjin. In explanation they said that Charles Green must have 'accumulated so much merit that heaven itself had intervened on our behalf (to save us again and again)'.

Don't be afraid for
Chinese robbers nearly all
have been killed by both
Chinese + foreign soldiers
Peking + Tientsin belong to
European now I will go to
Tientsin + tell your armies
to protect you

You may tear it into pieces when
you have seen

2.89 *The 'little crumpled tuft of paper', Fei Qihao's (?) message of hope to the Greens and J. Gregg*

Two meals a day of the coarsest food became their next hardship. Dysentery struck the children and Mrs Green, but their bedding and the little Bible were again returned to them, and occasional gifts of cash by sympathisers provided odds and ends more suitable to eat. After a week they were allowed to wash themselves and their verminous clothes.

Then, early one afternoon, Charles Green was fanning the sleeping women and children to keep the flies away, and looking through the open latticework of the door at their slumbering guard and a solitary sightseer. A 'little crumpled tuft of paper' fell though the lattice to the floor at his feet—an act of contempt, Green thought, and went on fanning. The young man had moved off, but stopped, came back, and pointed at the floor. Green unrolled the paper and read in English, 'Don't be afraid . . . Peking and Tientsin belong to Europeans. Now I will go to Tientsin and tell your armies to protect you. You may tear it into pieces when you have seen.' 'Looking up I motioned my thanks, and my unknown friend left hurriedly . . . I was so excited that I woke the ladies to show them. Miss Gregg at once claimed it as the "little bird" letter she had looked for . . . and kept it.'

Three weeks passed. Then on Monday, September 3, a large hostile company of Boxers arrived, and for two hours crowded into the prison to see them. 'One thrust the muzzle of his gun into my wife's face and said . . . they were "going to begin business today"'. They declared that they were coming to kill them. But 'the whole town and neighbourhood were in an uproar about us'—determined to protect them! Leading gentry were negotiating with the Boxers, and plans being made to hide the foreigners and hold the city against any attack. They were moved into a little storage room, 'overrun with rats and vermin', while shouting and much excitement went on outside. The Boxers were told they had been sent down river, and a 'monster meeting' succeeded in persuading them to call off an attack. But the prisoners in the storeroom had been overlooked.

> Sick, ill, tired, cold, hungry and uncertain, the black pall of despair was settling down on my soul ... [Charles Green wrote]. With tears I implored my wife and Miss Gregg to pray for me, when suddenly there was quiet and music in my heart. I listened to catch the tune (and) sang,

> > Praise the Saviour, ye who know Him,
> > Who can tell how much we owe Him?
> > Gladly let us render to Him
> > All we have and are.

> As the Lord's own peace flowed again into our hearts, we did not try to keep back the tears that would come.

At last they were brought food and told that the British consul had heard of their plight at Anxin, and demanded a safe escort for them to Tianjin. But the countryside was full of Boxers, so they were to be taken back to Baoding at once. They called this their seventh deliverance from death, but heard later of others unknown to them at the time. Just after they were taken from Huolu to Zhengding, Yü Xian himself had arrived at Huolu and made minute inquiries about them. The fact that they were in Boxer hands already was probably what saved them from his further attention. And while they were being kindly treated in the women's prison at Baoding, ruthless Boxers had only been prevented by a strong guard from breaking in and killing them. As in God's words to the ocean (in Job 38.11 AV), 'Hitherto shalt thou come, but no further: and here shall thy proud waves be stayed,' they recognised that evil men with the worst intentions could go no further than God allowed.

Fei Qihao to their rescue[1379]
(August–October 1900)

On the day that the Oberlin staff at Fenyang were massacred, August 15, the young schoolteacher, Fei Qihao, made his escape to Pingyao. But as he prayed about what he should do, as a destitute fugitive without friends, he became convinced he should return to Fenyang at all costs.

After dark he arrived and crept by a back street to the home of a Christian courier, on the point of fleeing. They left together and went to a poor Christian who out of his poverty gave Fei an old garment and some cash. Fei then made his way to Taigu where an old gentleman of the Kong family gave him more clothing and cash. Going on to Yuci, he was told of the Boxers having killed one hundred church members in July. Doing thirty miles a day, and amazed that he was given the strength for it, he crossed the mountains and arrived at Huolu, hoping to find someone at the CIM. Instead he found Yu Xian and two thousand soldiers in the city, and the missionaries already taken as prisoners to Zhengding. So Fei Qihao pressed on.

'Every day as he passed between (Huolu) and (Baoding) he met countless hordes of (Tong Fuxiang's) troops . . . escaping after their defeat. They marched along, looting all the way, but poor Fei in his destitution had nothing to fear.' At Zhengding he went to the cathedral and found 'a bishop, three priests, five foreign sisters, five railroad people and others; in all nineteen foreigners', including the Martin Griffiths and H. M. Brown of the CIM. Five couriers had been killed near there so they did not ask Fei to carry letters, but sent an oral message to the consuls.

Again he travelled thirty miles and stowed, away in a railway freight-car until near Baoding. There he joined a boatful of defeated soldiers and Boxers, and an old man looking for his soldier son. With him he lay low when they encountered boatloads of Boxers, still with their swords and red sashes. Day after day the rain poured down, and in the misery of being wet and cold he inadvertently said aloud in English, 'Oh, dear, dear!' but no one noticed it. In Mrs A. H. Smith's account there is no mention of his passing through Anxin, on the direct route between Baoding and Tianjin, or of seeing the Greens; but when she questioned him he had not yet seen the consul. He was a discreet young man.

He reached Tianjin on August 30, only fifteen days since leaving Fenyang. Passing French soldiers, Russians, Sikhs and Japanese, he made himself known to an American who took him to his captain. Fei produced a little rag given him by C. W. Price, the Fenyang martyr, on which were the words 'What this man says *is true!*'[1380] He was interrogated at length, and at midnight, worn out, was taken three miles further to face a British officer. The officer told him to go and get some sleep. Given a bed of clean sheets and blankets, Fei 'felt as if he was in heaven'. The next day he had interviews, one with Mrs Smith of the *Tientsin Times* and others, and one with the British consul for an hour. Finally he went to the American Board college where he had been educated. At the sight of his rags and dirt and long hair some shed tears. But what news of the 'Oberlin Band' he had to bring to them!

Only then could he start hunting for his wife and family. He found his village home a heap of rubble and a solitary man alarmed by his arrival began to run. Instinctively Fei called out his brother's name. The man stopped and turned towards him. They wept and wept together. Their parents were dead and what was left of their family had scattered. Their elder brother had become a Boxer, the rest had fled in abject terror of the frightful Hindu soldiery, 'who took the men as carriers and outraged the women, old and young indiscriminately'.[1381] Large bodies of Boxers were in the neighbourhood. They had to flee, first to Tong Xian and then, with Sikhs who beat him, to Beijing. As they entered the city he saw E. G. Tewkesbury, his friend and tutor, and A. H. Smith. His wife was rescued and brought to him, and his adventure had ended.

The timing of Fei Qihao's journey and of the Greens' movements, as well as the contents of the crumpled note and the behaviour of the one who brought it, leave little if any doubt that Fei Qihao was the one who told the consul about the prisoners at Anxin.[1382]

The report Fei brought of the massacres in Shanxi was, according to Robert Forsyth, the first to reach his mission in Tianjin and, it seems, the first accepted by the consuls.[1383] When the news was telegraphed to England, Queen Victoria instructed Lord Salisbury to write, on September 20, 1900, to the Emperor of China in protest. (This suggests that the account by Yong Zheng of the Taiyuan massacre (see p 673) was literally 'the first eye-witness account', not the first report.)

Another Christian who arrived at Beijing on September 19 from the horrors in Shanxi was Wang Lanbu, the door-keeper at Soping who escaped after being flogged and left as dead on June 24. His own mother and his little daughter had been burned alive at Yingzhou and he had taken two months to complete the journey. But of all his hardships, one of the most distressing was being robbed of what little money he had left by European soldiers after his arrival. His report on the atrocities in the northern cities, near the Mongolian border, was substantially confirmed by another, Zhang Rufeng, when he reached Tianjin on October 19.

When bad weather prevented the boat conveying the Greens from Anxin to Baoding from arriving when expected, the now anxious officials sent two boatloads of soldiers to search for them. They all reached the city together on September 7. A high-ranking commissioner who came to meet them asked how the consul knew they were at Anxin, and it was easy enough

to say that a complete stranger on his way to Tianjin had told them he would report their plight. How Baoding had changed! Apart from soldiers, the streets were empty and many shops were closed. A rumour that foreign troops were on the way had panicked many who stood to lose by staying. The viciously anti-foreign mandarins were trying to play safe, ending the siege of Xian Xian and protecting the Greens on the one hand and still harbouring Boxers on the other. They feared for their own future.

Once again their prisoners were taken to the women's lock-up, but a marked change in their treatment began. Cheap bedding was provided. The mandarins' own barber attended them. The 15th of the eighth moon, a feast day, saw them provided with a good meal from the mandarin's own kitchen and gifts for the children. Their rags were removed, and clean new clothing, even though the cheapest, was provided. The next day they were taken to clean rooms in a *yamen*, with a courtyard and garden for their own use, a cook and four soldiers under an official exclusively to guard and serve them. Eventually they learned that on September 7 at John Stevenson's request the consul-general in Shanghai had called on Li Hongzhang to draw his attention to their conditions. Three Christians were allowed to visit them, and told them the harrowing truth about the Baoding massacres of June 30 and July 1. At the acting-governor's expense Charles Green broke the silence of four months with a telegram to Shanghai, and towards the end of the third week received a letter from the Tianjin consul. But they had not yet been given their liberty.

Here Charles Green's account ended, for he fell ill. His wife and Jessie Gregg were mournfully discussing their situation when Vera looked up at them and said, 'Auntie, the Lord looseth the prisoners', and went on playing—the words that had encouraged them during their long anxiety at Anxin. For weeks Vera and others of them at different times had been suffering from painful dysentery: On October 8 her pain increased and at 4.00 a.m. on the 10th she died.

> We did not sorrow as those who had no hope [Mrs Green wrote], for we know that those who sleep in Jesus, God will bring with Him ... Her bright loving ways had touched the hearts of people and led them to spare us; her life was laid down for Jesus' sake and for China

> Each day found (Charles) decidedly weaker. We heard rumours of French troops approaching, which filled us with hope and thankfulness, but we could not understand why the officials left us so much alone these days.

On October 13 the French entered Baoding, but not until the 16th did the colonel hear that there were English prisoners in the *yamen*. He sent an ambulance to bring them to his camp, although the mandarins told him that they did not want to go to the coast. In fact they had been holding them as hostages for use in negotiating with the allies. Then on the 19th other allied troops arrived from Beijing, General Gaselee came to see them, and transferred them to the British field hospital under an army surgeon. 'With grateful adoration too deep for words, we praised God.'

Then Martin Griffiths and H. M. Brown arrived from Zhengding on the 21st, after twelve weeks' protection by the Zhengding brigadier, and on the 23rd all were taken in the care of the doctor by boat to the coast. At Anxin Surgeon-Major Thompson invited the leading townsman, a Mr Zhao, who had

2.90 The C. H. S. Greens and Jessie Gregg, all safe in Shanghai

befriended the prisoners, to come aboard, and took the names of others instrumental in saving their lives. He then gave Mr Zhao a document promising them rewards, and addressed a crowd on the river-bank. Ten days later at a public meeting the British commander from Baoding thanked the whole town, gave $100 to each of the leading men, and a Union Jack for them to display if troops of any nationality should trouble them. The names of Farmer Gao, who had sheltered the fugitives for a month, and the temple-keeper who first hid them were also given to the authorities at Tianjin for reward in due time.

But Charles Green had typhoid fever, contracted in the *yamen*. On the way downriver he became delirious and was still unconscious when they reached Tianjin on October 27. He recovered consciousness two days later. 'So many had been called to lay down their lives,' they wrote. Why then had they been spared? They had no answer, but 'often turned to Acts 12', where they read, 'Herod . . . killed James . . . and proceeded . . . to take Peter' (vv 2–3 AV), but God brought Peter out of the prison.

Vera was buried at Tianjin. Then Mrs Green and little John became critically ill. A month later the rivers and northern seas were about to freeze and be closed to shipping for three months. So they decided that even in their condition it would be best to go south. The Russian general in charge of the railways provided an ambulance car; Jardine Matheson and Company put a steam launch at their disposal and gave them privileges on board their ship; and on the tenth day they were welcomed at Wusong Road, Shanghai. Dr F. H. Judd, one of the first Chefoo schoolboys then removed the remaining shot from Green's arms, head and face, and on January 5, 1901, they sailed for Europe. 'But thanks be to God, who in Christ always leads us in triumph, and through us spreads the fragrance of the knowledge of him everywhere' (2 Corinthians 2.14, RSV).

Alfred and Olivia Ogren[1384]
(July 13–August 1900)

A wealth of impressive writing about the Boxer rising has somehow obscured Olivia Ogren's inspired record of her own and her husband's experiences. It ends this summary on the note that scores of others sounded, yet with a potency of its own. This twentieth-century fulfilment of the words of Jesus in Matthew 10 makes them as relevant today as to the listening disciples and to the despairing fugitives of the Boxer nightmare.

> I am sending you out like sheep among wolves ... On my account you will be brought before governors and kings as witnesses to them ... But when they arrest you, do not worry about what to say or how to say it for it will not be you speaking, but the Spirit of your Father speaking through you ... All men will hate you because of me, but he who stands firm to the end will be saved ... When you are persecuted in one place, flee to another ... Do not be afraid of those who can kill the body but cannot kill the soul ...
>
> Whoever loses his life for my sake will find it (Matt 10.16–39 NIV).

In a word, 'We are more than conquerors through Him who loved us', for 'It is not death to die!'

Alfred and Olivia Ogren were a young couple from Jonkoping in Sweden, but full members of the CIM. After six years in north Shanxi, they had pioneered Yongning (now Zhongyang) in 1899—across the high Luliang range from Fenyang, and about five days' travel from Taiyuan (see map 2.80: p 652). The 'bold and independent' people of Yongning had been 'well disposed' towards them, until drought and threatened famine revived their superstitions and made them look for scapegoats. Even then the magistrate secretly asked the Ogrens to pray to the God of heaven and earth for rain. In May 1900 strangers with Shandong accents arrived, and awe-struck countrymen saw how they, the Boxers, could kindle fire from magic buttons of celluloid. Rumours multiplied, and one that foreigners were poisoning wells was seen to be true when the water in a well near the Ogrens turned red.

On July 5 word came of the murder on June 29 of the ladies at Xiaoyi, only fifty miles away. The friendly magistrate told the Ogrens to escape while they could, supplied them at midnight with one hundred taels of silver; and took charge of their premises. They had already cut and disguised a secret exit through the big back door of their garden. Before daylight on July 13 they and the evangelist mounted a mule litter to take them under guard the twenty-five miles to the Yellow River. There they were confronted by people armed with clubs and openly hostile, blaming them for the drought. But the local official helped them to hire a small boat to Tongguan in Shaanxi, three hundred miles to the south. Because of the strong current and rapids, boats only travelled downstream and were sold on arrival. But hiring one, and a change of escort, were expensive, so that they had to send to Yongning for more money. The *yamen* secretary himself brought it four days later, with 'a cordial letter of recommendation by our friendly mandarin'.

Halfway to Tongguan they came to three miles of impassable rapids where a porterage had to be made, and heard of the massacre of the McConnell's and Youngs on the river-bank not far away. No testimonial could help them against such ferocity. An old ex-mandarin, who proved to be a friend of the Yongning magistrate, invited them to his home in Shaanxi and protected them from a troop of Linfen soldiers who suddenly appeared with orders to drive them away. But soon after they started towards the old man's home they 'saw men skulking among the rocks ahead' who leapt out at them brandishing weapons and began rifling their baggage. One with a great sword 'began whetting it with the strange Boxer movements, shouting "Kill" at the same time. We thought our last hour had come, and expected that soon our dead bodies would be hurled into the rushing river.' But they were spared and crossed into

Shaanxi before another squad of soldiers arrived on the Shanxi bank to arrest them.

After two days of weary tramping over the hills, carrying their infant Samuel, they reached the old man's village, only to be turned away by the villagers and robbed again by two gangs of men. They found shelter in a small cave deep in the mountains, but starvation drove them back. Alfred Ogren's 'awful agony from hunger' distressed his wife, but he said, 'It is no matter what we suffer for Jesus' sake,' and, 'I rejoice that through these sufferings the Church will be awakened into new life. The field is being watered with blood; what a harvest there will be!'

The Boxers had offered a hundred taels for every foreign head, and the villagers had to hold back a villainous young man among them who raved like a madman and rushed at the Ogrens with raised sword. But they were not given food. What could they do? Not knowing that Governor Tuan Fang had made Shaanxi a safer province, they decided to walk back to Yongning and the kind mandarin. Without money and with only the infant's coverlet and pillow, a saucepan and some flour on which to feed the child, the clothes they wore, a Bible and a pair of scissors to offer to a ferryman, they could not buy food. But Jesus had said, 'So do not worry, saying, "What shall we eat?" or "What shall we drink?" your heavenly Father knows that you need them' (Matthew 6.31–2 NIV). 'However it be, I felt that to die of starvation for Jesus who died for me was easy.'

Following bypaths and scrambling up and down hills they came upon people who treated them kindly, so that they had at least one meal a day and a roof over their heads at night. An old man took them by the hand to ford a big river, and led them to his home. But after another long day on foot, two rogues searched them, emptied the feathers from Samuel's little pillow and burned them, and took the Bible. 'The vehemence with which I declared I could not and would not part with that Holy Book' made him hand it back. The rogues forced the ferryman to take them all over the Yellow River and delivered them to the Boxers on the Shanxi side. While Alfred was being questioned, a crowd surrounded Olivia and with a sardonic grin a man put his head on one side and remarked, 'The Daning missionaries have gone back to heaven.'

The Boxers then marched them fifteen miles to their leader in a temple, and Alfred was taken in while Olivia and Samuel sat in the outer courtyard. She recalled,

> I could hear (him) pleading, telling them who we were ... when he was quickly interrupted by a loud shrieking voice. Then came the sound of the sharpening of swords, followed by a weird moaning, as of someone being tortured. My feelings were indescribable. I could only pray God to cut short my husband's sufferings, and fill his heart with peace, and give me grace to meet my lot without fear. [She did not know that the Boxers were only going through their weird ritual but in preparation for his execution.]

> (Again she heard her husband pleading.) Again he was interrupted, and again came the same moaning as before. Then all was silent! My husband was killed, and I was left alone with my helpless babe.

It was dark and she was six months pregnant. But she tried to escape. The original two rogues saw her, and dragged her behind a wall saying,

> 'The General is coming, and he can't abide the sight of a woman.' There was a great firing of guns and shouting, and the whole crowd came out of the temple yard carrying, as I supposed, my husband's corpse. (As they approached) I thought, 'It is my turn now' though I wished to rise, I could not. A man ... taking my hand led me down to the side of the river. At some distance ... I saw lanterns and heard a great uproar ... After a long while some men came along and said my husband had run away. It seemed strange to me ... as I thought him dead.

Olivia alone[1385]
(August 1900–February 1901)

They locked Olivia in a tomb-vault for the night with only a bowl of water, but brought her some rice in the morning and led her away. Suddenly they cried out, 'Hide! the big man is coming!' So she hid, but when she peered out; even the two men had gone. 'So I was alone with my little Samuel. Yet not alone. Oh no! Had He not said so distinctly to me, "Fear not, I am with thee"?' Bravely she set off walking to Daning where the Peats were said to be in prison, 'for to be with friends in prison was better than this awful freedom'. 'At times Boxers pretended to be about to kill me; at other times some women would come round me and give me food.' She tried to wade across a river with Samuel in her arms and was being carried away, when strong men pulled her up the bank, only to jeer at her 'widowhood'. Wet through, she settled down as she was, to sleep in the open, but long after dark two other men led her to a cave and left her 'with a 'God bless you'.' They were Christians, but they could do no more.

Before daybreak she started towards Daning again, only to be caught by Boxers. A village headman rescued her, gave her food and a pair of socks, and sent two men to escort her to the Daning *yamen*. 'The Boxers stamped and jumped in the frenzy of their rage', but she was safely put in the common prison. The Peats had passed through two days previously, before being murdered near Qüwu.

In the morning the warder passed some bread and half a watermelon to Olivia through a hole in the iron-clad door of the prison yard, and told her to say her child was a girl, as all males were to be killed. But when asked she told the truth. So in the afternoon when the door was opened and she was ordered, 'Bring out the boy!', 'terror seized me as if I had been struck by a thunderbolt'. She was made to kneel before the magistrate and sternly questioned about her husband, who, he said, was still alive. She did not believe him, thinking he could not admit to the murder in his county. But gradually he began to speak more kindly as if pitying her. Afterwards, the county secretary's wife told her she had offered a reward for finding Alfred and bringing him in. Then Olivia was led back to prison.

The bed was alive with vermin so she lay on the ground outside. For days one of her eyes had been badly inflamed, painful and swollen. She could not sleep. At daybreak she was dozing off and thought she heard Alfred's voice. She leapt up. 'Again that longed for, tender-voice, "Olivia! Oh, Olivia!" But it came from the hole in the prison door.' She ran to the door and looked out. 'His clothes hung in tatters and his head was bound up with a piece of some garment . . . I could see Boxers running wildly about in the *yamen* yard.' Someone opened the prison door and took them both to where she could dress his wounds. She washed the blood from his shirt and tore it in strips as bandages. 'What a sight! A great piece of the scalp hung loosely down; one ear was crushed and swollen; his neck bore two sword gashes; near the shoulder were two spear cuts, one very deep; and all his back was red and swollen from beating.'

Crowds flocked to stare at them until the evening. Then they had quiet enough for him to tell his story.

In the temple the Boxer 'general' had had him bound with his hands behind his back, and everyone had kicked and beaten him. Then they led him to the riverside, to kill him, they said.

> They forced me down on my knees and set upon me from all sides, but as their weapons clashed one on another they did not kill me. Loss of blood made me feel faint, but I was so happy! ... I felt no pain ... heaven seemed open, and one step would take me there.
>
> Then came to me suddenly ... the thought of my wife and child ... I leapt from the midst of the crowd (of thirty or forty men) into the (deep) water. I managed to get out on the other side, and with my hands still bound behind my back, started to run ... barefoot over the rocks. Under cover of darkness I got out of sight, (and) after about fifteen miles I dared to stop and free my hands by rubbing the cords on a stone.

Heading again for Yongning, he lost his way several times and to his distress found himself back on the Daning road, until someone told him his wife was there.

Entering the city, he was seen by Boxers who gave chase, but he ran for his life and reached the *yamen*. They let him in, protected him, and took him to Olivia and Samuel.

Two days later, on August 30, in spite of their condition they were put on donkeys with unpadded pack-saddle frames and sent towards Linfen, escorted by an officer with four soldiers and four brutal Boxers. Riding was such agony that Alfred preferred to walk. But at Pu Xian, halfway to Linfen, they were sent back to Daning. The Linfen officials had refused to have them.

Prison at Daning was a relief. But privations too much for Samuel to bear reduced him to 'a limp little body too weak to cry'; Olivia's second eye began to swell painfully, and she could only sit and endure. Alfred became delirious with fever, struggling to escape his terrors, so that he had to be tied to the verminous bed.

'God only knows the horror and misery of those hours,' Olivia wrote. 'After that awful night' each of them recovered slowly. But when Olivia shared her scanty ration with her child and husband, they punished her by stopping her own rice and milk supply.

'Harder than all weariness were the filth and vermin. The very sight brought scalding tears to my eyes.' But that no one could prevent her from escaping to 'the God of all comfort' consoled her. A *yamen* 'gentleman', knowing that the other prisoners abused the Ogrens for their quiet faith in God, even in such circumstances, asked if they still prayed. 'At my simple assurance of the peace of those who have the comfort of God's loving presence, he seemed much impressed and listened respectfully.' And with Alfred able to talk rationally again, they thanked God for the training he was giving them, and its effect on the official.

'After a month of misery and untellable sufferings' until October 4, they were taken to Linfen. ('CCH', who knew as much as anyone, on September 19 still had no idea of what had happened to the Ogrens.)[1386] But four miles short of the city they heard

that the empress dowager and retinue were passing, *en route* to Xi'an. They had to lie low, and the week in a temple on the coarsest of food left Alfred very weak. But on October 12 the politeness of their reception of Linfen and the news that some missionaries had escaped, distracted them from their own extremity.

Olivia failed at first to realise that Alfred was dying. On the 14th,

> a terrible fear seized me ... Oh, how I cried out to God in the anguish of my soul! ... No human words are full enough of sadness to tell my awful loneliness. No tears were bitter enough ... A storm of grief overwhelmed me, until God gave me comfort ... To my heart came the words (of Jesus) outside the gates of Nain, 'Weep not!'

A young Christian widow kept her company in the *yamen*. Her husband had been the Linfen mission courier, imprisoned by the magistrate in an attempt to protect him. But the Boxers had dragged him out and beheaded him. His head, along with those of many other Christians, had been nailed to the city wall, until she was released from prison and took it down. Her own physical sufferings had been relatively light. Some Christians had been maimed for life. One old man had been strung up by his thumbs for half a day. Others were scarred by the cross, cut into their foreheads. Terrible as the sufferings of missionaries had been, they were a fraction of the anguish the Christians had endured. But peace and security were returning.

Before Alfred Ogren died they heard that four Roman priests had held the Boxers at bay in Hongtong and survived; and Graham McKie with the two young women, Marion Chapman and Matilda Way were still hiding in the hills near Qüwu. At midnight on August 19 (five days after the end of the Peking siege) they had started walking with six Christians towards Hankou, six hundred miles away. Captured and released again, they lived in caves for six more weeks, evading the Boxers, and in a loft above two children with smallpox, until on October 1 they were taken safely back to Qüwu. For five months they had not taken off their clothes. But when the Linfen magistrate sent soldiers to bring them to him, 'the (Qüwu) Christians wept bitterly when (they) left'. Even in October no one could ever be sure what might happen.

So Olivia Ogren 'had the glad surprise' on October 24 of being joined by Graham McKie and the two girls. 'I could not speak as I pressed their hands.' They were with her when her baby was born on December 6, and on the long journey to Hankou (from January 6 to February 16, 1901) under the protection of two officers, sixteen mounted and two foot soldiers. Dr J. W. Hewett, in spite of his long imprisonment, had arrived there on November 6, three and a half months sooner.

Olivia ended the story of her sufferings with the words, 'After all that the Lord has given me to bear I can yet say from my heart—"Bless the Lord, O my soul, and all that is within me, bless His Holy Name."'

She and her companions had been the last of all the fugitives to reach the comfort and security of the outer world again. Mutual admiration of each other's qualities through the long weeks of suffering and danger had soon developed into love, and led to the marriage of Graham McKie and Marion Chapman. In a euphoric narrative, Matilda Way wrote of the Linfen Christians,

> Nearly all have a large cross on their forehead, inflicted by the Boxers ... I rejoice to think of the glorious harvest yet to come. I heard that the Taigu Christians had met for worship, and the Boxers had come and killed them all but two my first twelve months in China have been full of a wonderful experience ... I am hoping to have a rest, and return to my work in Shanxi.

She did, with Eva French.

25

A New China (1900–1950)

Directors' dilemma (1900–01)

There was nothing new to Hudson Taylor or the China Inland Mission in being forced, helpless, to their knees. The division of labour at Shanghai between John Stevenson and William Cooper that satisfied both had defied solution until Hudson Taylor took decisive action. His gift, of seeing through the brushwood of confusion to recognise the jungle trail to open fields beyond, had shown him a way out. So Cooper, as an equal partner with Stevenson in responsibility in China, was to have supplied the personal touch, the sympathy and understanding that the dour Scotsman did not lack but found hard to show. As travelling director, Cooper was to get close to the men and women of the outback, see their circumstances, listen to them, sense their spiritual morale, and give them advice and support.

The darkening thunder clouds of early 1900 had intensified the need for consultation between the leaders and with the rank and file. So William Cooper had gone north to Shanxi and Zhili, and Dixon Hoste, superintendent in Henan, was called to Shanghai to share Stevenson's load. He dealt with the day-to-day matters, the visitors with little concept of the pressure of such work, and missionaries with grievances or problems they wished to discuss at length. What needed to be referred to Stevenson he presented concisely, with his recommendations. The system worked well. Stevenson welcomed and valued him. Both kept in touch with Hudson Taylor, fully occupied with international commitments, who frankly stated his opinions but left decisive action to the men in China.[1387]

The correspondence during these years reveals their loyalty and affection, and that of Frost, Sloan and Marcus Wood among others. James Meadows's recollections of Hudson Taylor's 'affectionate reverence (for God) which made the godliness of the good man stand out conspicuously', in a marked degree expressed these outstanding men's own attitude to their human leader. It is not only apparent in their letters but expressly stated in their own words.

Although prostrated by the Boxer dispatches, Hudson Taylor still exerted strong leadership, and the Mission welcomed it. Physical and mental fatigue, culminating in the 'lapse of memory' at Boston, had cut short the General Director's active life and brought him home to Britain just as alarming news of developments in north China plunged Stevenson and Hoste into the crisis without precedent in the mission's experience. But Hudson Taylor's retreat to the comparative calm of Switzerland had been expressly for him to recover his vitality as quickly as possible.[1388]

In the States, in London and increasingly in Switzerland concern for William Cooper's safety found expression in letters that could only generalise while factual detail was unknown and newspapers for lack of information were fictitiously sensational. John Stevenson warned the home country directors to believe nothing until he could confirm it.[1389] The fabricated 'massacre in the legations' soon justified his caution. For some weeks no foreign casualties had been reported, except in the north. But unrest everywhere in China, with riots erupting in place after place, had been enough to lead the consuls to call for a general evacuation of all foreigners from the interior. Soon the safety of the treaty ports came into question and additional allied troops and warships came for their protection. Volunteer defence forces were formed, and tension in the international settlements increased.

After long delays, reliable news of the atrocities in Zhili and Shanxi began coming in and was relayed by cable to the homelands of the missionaries most affected. In and around Beijing hundreds of Christians were savagely slaughtered. The legation siege began. William Cooper was trapped, then unable to communicate with Stevenson, and finally reported dead. Four weeks after the massacre of all missionaries in Baoding, it was only possible to say that 'the worst' was feared for them. William Cooper's death was not confirmed until October 29. Emily Whitchurch of England and Edith Searell of New Zealand were brutally bludgeoned to death on June 30. Word of it took a month to reach Shanghai and was the first to be cabled home.

Gradually the truth emerged, with strong implications that much more was happening of which little if anything was yet known. The cables received in Britain revealed the difficulties that Stevenson and Hoste faced in Shanghai. No more missionaries were to be sent out, and for some in the interior it would be more dangerous to travel than to stay where they were.[1390] Available funds had been distributed to all members and associates as soon as the crisis was recognised, but transmission to some soon became impossible. How could adequate help be given to any, let alone to so many in dire straits?

Not until September 8 did reports from Chinese sources tell of the Taiyuan massacre of July 9, but (revealing a black hole of ignorance of almost all that was going on) it was September 17 before Stevenson could relay Charles Green's telegram from macabre Baoding that he, his family and Jessie Gregg were relatively safe in the *yamen* after repeated brushes with death. Anxious relatives waiting to be put out of insufferable suspense learned on October 8 that the Duncan Kays, Graham McKie and the Misses Chapman and Way had met their death on August 30, only to learn four days later by another cable that the report affecting McKie, Chapman and Way had been contradicted.

The Foreign Office cooperated closely with the societies in Britain, as the consuls and (after the siege was lifted) the minister in Beijing worked confidently with the missions in China, passing on such information as each received. In this way Stevenson cabled on November 26 that Alfred Ogren had been killed, but Graham McKie and the two young women and Olivia Ogren were safe in 'Taiyuan'—a synonym for horror. The Foreign Office passed the same report to the CIM in London. But in fact they were in Linfen. That more misinformation did not complicate affairs at such a time was remarkable.

R. Logan Jack, an explorer crossing China 'from Shanghai to the Irrawadi', illustrated the problems faced by Stevenson and most missionaries in remote places. On June 6 at Xicharig (Ningyuan, in Sichuan) the prefect told him about the Boxers, but not until July 29 did 'a bombshell (fall) into our camp'—a telegram from Chongqing dated June 30, 'Go to Burma. Europeans and consuls ready to leave Chongqing at a moment's notice . . . Probable that all foreigners at Pekin have been killed.' And a July 27 telegram received on August 10 said, 'Foreign Office London instructions (to) remove all British subjects from China.' Other messages to 'keep west' told Logan Jack of Lieutenant Watts-Jones's fate in Ningxia. The same advice reached the Cecil Polhills at Kangding, but the children had measles and could not travel. Eventually the family travelled to Chongqing and all the way down the Yangzi to safety.

As news reached London it was relayed to Hudson Taylor at Davos. Having set himself to rest and regain strength he was taking graded exercise and enjoying his hobby of photography, developing and printing his own exposures. By June 9 he was 'gaining ground', and did what he could as General Director to advise John Stevenson. As he would do all in his power to help the missionaries and Chinese church, how much more would their 'heavenly father do in His love and wisdom and power!' On July 16 he wrote to say that as refugee missionaries arrived in Shanghai they should be sent to Japan, Singapore or home.[1391] The lavish Morton legacy was for evangelism and education, but 'in an emergency it would be quite justifiable to use any of (it) for travel expenses'. It could be replaced later on. Money on deposit in the banks was at risk of looting, even in Shanghai, and better put to use. Transmissions from Britain of Morton funds would be restricted until required for use.

Then on July 27, after hearing of the Whitchurch-Searell murders 'and doubtless Chinese Christians with them', and unconfirmed news of a massacre at Taiyuan, he wrote and wired advising the withdrawal of all women from the interior. The Chefoo schools could go in a body direct to Japan. War at Tianjin might make all the provincial viceroys act against foreigners, all banks freeze their funds and all means of transmitting money be closed. The time was ripe to 'make free distribution' rather than have large sums blocked and unusable. 'All willing to take the risk of travelling should be allowed to come to Shanghai . . . Chinese Christians would probably be safer if the missionaries were absent.'

To Marcus Wood at Newington Green he suggested 'an early day for united fasting and prayer', preferably with all societies joining in. 'The advance on Peking might mean the death of thousands of missionaries' if the viceroys withdrew their protection. '(Benjamin B.) might be able to get the Archbishop to act promptly in the matter', to make it a national observance. 'Though all human power seems so unavailing, it is still true that the LORD reigneth.'

A long 'unnerving telegram' came from London on July 31. It must have been the one about Taiyuan, the Glovers, Greens, Henan escape attempts and finally 'the worst' for the Bagnalls and William Cooper. Jenny had it in her hand and was going to break its contents gradually to Hudson, but 'he came across my path and so had to know of it'. 'Where will the end be?' he asked, alive to the horrific consequences of unchecked anti-foreign action. He reeled, and Jenny feared lest shock after shock should be too much for him. Writing the next morning to Marcus Wood she said, '(He) felt as if he must get out or he would go crazy, so Amy (their daughter) and he went up a mountain.' And to John Stevenson: 'We are suffering with you all so much that I don't think we could feel more.'

That anyone could have taken a photograph of him at such a time is puzzling, but gives us an insight into his sufferings (see 1, p 838). Someone wrote on one copy, 'Tho' he slay me, yet will I trust in him' (cf Job 13.15).[1392] He felt he should be in China where the decisions had to be taken, but knew that in his state of health he would be more in the way than useful. So as the reports came in, long after the events, Jenny told him only what he could endure.

The ubiquitous Howard and Geraldine Taylor came over from London to support Howard's parents for two weeks, but found them coping with the crisis. Made aware that the strain on John Stevenson could prove too much, and that his own condition was precarious, Hudson Taylor had come to the conclusion that a successor must be worked in without delay. A letter to Shanghai could take too long. He cabled to Stevenson that morning, 'expressing sympathy and concern for him' and appointing Dixon Hoste 'to act as General Director . . . during my incapacity . . . so that the responsibility may be shared'.

He then wrote lucidly to Theodore Howard as director in London, saying in confidence what he had done. Announcement of the move could follow when it had been accepted by all councils. 'Cooper is probably gone and Stevenson alone with all this burden of responsibility. It seems to take all my strength away and to defer indefinitely my being able to go out and help.' Cameron, Dorward, Hunter, Lachlan—so many outstanding men of whom he had had high hopes had died. But Hoste was in Shanghai, and difficult though it was to bypass John Stevenson, the nettle had to be grasped.

Stevenson was invaluable as senior administrator, the managing director in China, but lacked essential qualities required of a General Director, the international leader and inspiration of the Mission. Sooner or later he would have to face the fact and accept a younger man in office over him. Hoste's personality and ability had impressed him. Now the time had come for Hoste to be more than merely his assistant. As William Cooper had already found, Stevenson was not good at working in partnership as equals. He had to be told candidly of Hoste's promotion, and be trusted to weather the blow. Acting for Hudson Taylor would work Hoste gradually into the saddle and ease the transition for John Stevenson. If Cooper should return from the dead, as it would seem if somehow he survived, the way would still be open for reconsideration of who should become General Director. So 'after much thought and prayer' the cable had been sent. Hudson Taylor concluded to Theodore Howard, 'What a blessing to know that God is king above the water floods and that nothing can be done without His permission,' and ended 'Yours in deep sorrow'.

The graphic events of those days failed to close his mind to other things. The CIM had come dramatically into the limelight again, and the public would be looking for information. 'People will read about China now especially and the Mission needs an increase of funds (perhaps £50,000 or £100,000) which will not be obtained without seed being sown.' America and the Colonies were asking for Geraldine's books, *In the Far East* and *The Story* of *the China Inland Mission* to be reprinted. The sanity of his balance between dependence on 'God alone' for all the Mission's immense and recurring needs, while recognising that people respond to knowledge of the facts, impressed his friends and colleagues. His shoulders were broad enough to bear any charge of 'money-raising'. It took more than reprinting books to raise so many thousands of pounds over and above the forty thousand normally required.

But the tragic news continued to come in, and the stress of work, however slight, was making Hudson Taylor giddy and exhausted. Jenny 'after prayer concluded to act on Dr (J. L.) Maxwell's advice and keep all letters from (Hudson) except those I feel will help and not hinder his health', for 'his heart's action was impaired and power of walking almost left him'.

In Shanghai the nightmare of those days and weeks seared and scarred John Stevenson as he read reports and lived through the imagined plight of those unaccounted for. He never lost the sense of horror.[1393] Yet somehow Jenny remained optimistic. 'Some may be in hiding who have been reported murdered.'

Reluctant successor
(August 1900–March 1901)

Hudson Taylor's cable on August 6, 1900, struck both John Stevenson and Dixon Hoste between the eyes. Neither had any inkling of such a possibility. Hoste would not be forty until July 23, 1901. After the initial shock and two days of thinking and praying about it, he wrote declining the 'appointment by telegram'. His letters to Hudson Taylor and Stevenson, and their replies, kept the issue unresolved until the end of the year, during which time the China Council and Home Directors were consulted. The correspondence illuminates the personalities concerned.[1394]

Hudson Taylor needed to appoint as his potential successor one whose wisdom, ability and acceptance by his colleagues were beyond doubt. Above all he had looked for the man who 'walked with God', one to whom God would make known his will. He had found these qualities in both William Cooper and Dixon Hoste. On August 8, Hoste wrote that in July Stevenson had spoken appreciatively to him and wished him to stay and help with his advice 'as he might ask for it during the present difficult times'. Because of his respect for Stevenson he was glad to do so, acting as a go-between, he said, and doing all in his power to strengthen Stevenson's position. When all was eventually settled, Archibald

2.91 Dixon Edward Hoste, successor to Hudson Taylor

Orr Ewing wrote candidly, 'I fear if some such step as this were not taken, soon the love and harmony in the Mission would have been seriously affected; numbers have spoken to me of the very unsatisfactory way in which their matters had been dealt with.' But Dixon Hoste had come to a different conclusion.

> Effects of an opposite and very grave character, which both Mr Stevenson and myself agree in thinking most likely (would) follow such an appointment ... It would have the effect of weakening and, to a certain extent discrediting Mr Stevenson ... without inspiring confidence. (Stevenson had done well in his direction of affairs in the crisis, members of the China Council were agreed.) ... My appointment to act now on your behalf (during your present incapacity) would come as a complete surprise, and is one to which they would not agree, and ... would be calculated to weaken and even produce disruption in the Mission ... PS. I have not touched on the point of my own unfitness, mental and physical ...

John Stevenson also wrote, '(Mr Hoste's) help at the Council meetings was most valuable and I thank God for his prayerful sympathy and advice. I consult him very

freely.' But on September 20 Hudson Taylor replied to Stevenson confidently and forthrightly as usual,

> I have been most grateful to recognise how God has helped you in this unparalleled crisis, and have (wanted) to take some of the grave responsibility off your shoulders and also off my own. I felt that I had a responsibility which I was unable, here and in my state of health, to bear, while my known previous judgment as to remaining quietly in the stations in times of difficulty might hamper you, hence my two telegrams. [The final authority should not be distant from the scene of action:]

> You have correctly read my wire as to the wording, but it left your position the same as it has so long been; it was not my wish to put Mr Hoste into it. My own health is precarious, and the terrible news from China caused my strength to fail so fast that I felt it was urgent to appoint someone to take my place provisionally. I knew your esteem for Mr Hoste, and that if I were removed he would be accepted in London, America and Australia, and that no one else would be so accepted. I knew ... that he would be the last one to take advantage of his position to weaken yours. Everyone has recognised the indefatigable, self-denying service that you have so long rendered the whole Mission ... but not a few ... have feared that it would break up unless some change were introduced by which the members ... could be bound to it by a uniform expression of sympathy that you are unable to show. I thought my appointment of Mr Hoste would help in this way, and also that acting with you in Shanghai he would be gaining in the necessary experience for becoming General Director at my death. (To leave the appointment of a successor to be made by others would not be for the good of the Mission or Stevenson's own comfort.)

> Another thought in my mind ... was the fear that you might break down under the long, heavy strain, and that then no one would be empowered to act ... I made the appointment temporary, for I feel that all such important appointments should be so in the beginning, and in doing so I did not abdicate my own position.

I am remaining here (in Davos) feeling quite unfit to return to England.[1395]

Frail and under strain Hudson Taylor might be, but still fully in command.

Crossing that letter came one from Dixon Hoste protesting his strong feeling not only of being unworthy and unequal to the demands of acting for Hudson Taylor but unfit. It troubled him to go against his wish and so 'to grieve or disappoint' him, but he was glad of the telegram, as

> It may serve as an indication to Mr S. of your mind, which it may be well for (him) to accustom his mind to assimilate. I think it came as a great surprise and even shock ... to him. [Hoste expressed his deep sympathy for Hudson Taylor in the 'avalanche of suffering' being reported constantly to him.] A telegram (received) last night tells of the Home-going to Christ of eleven more dear ones from Xi Xian, Daning and Yoyang. I feel Shansi is honoured, and my heart beats for her more than ever, and the fears come too, as I think of so many friends of early manhood, gone in blood and tears.[1396]

Henry Frost responded characteristically to Jenny on being told of Hudson Taylor's action:

> The choice seems to me, as far as I can judge, an eminently suitable one ... I say all this with deep sadness. My love is fixed presently on Mr Taylor, and it is hard to have any person come between himself and myself ... Please let me urge once more, however, that Mr Taylor may not give up his office, and that no person may be asked, so long as he lives, to be more than an assistant to him ...

> As telegram after telegram reaches us reporting the deaths of our loved ones, and as letter after letter comes to hand describing the terrible suffering ... it seems sometimes as if the heart could hold no more, and at all times the mystery of God's providence comes upon one in almost overwhelming force. But ... 'perfect love worketh no ill' ... I never dreamed that God would allow us to pass through such bitter sorrow. But it is all right. Our Father is teaching us new lessons regarding our privileges, for He has written: 'For unto

you it is granted (as a privilege) in the behalf of Christ, not only to believe on Him but also to suffer for His sake.'

Then Dixon Hoste went down with typhoid, so often lethal, and a month later Gertie, his wife, told Hudson Taylor that although it had been a mild attack, 'the old trouble of clots in the veins has developed'. 'November 5: Both arms and legs are affected, so he is quite helpless . . . I think so often of you, dearest Uncle, and plead your need of help when I ask God to spare my beloved Dick.' The risk of the thrombosis spreading and of emboli (clots) breaking loose kept them on a knife-edge of danger. Her prayers were answered in his complete recovery, but even more in his helpless dependence on night and day nursing being a parable to him and shaping his thinking about the future. On November 14 'Dick' dictated to her a long letter for Hudson Taylor.

> I was in the Lord's hands ... and I now feel that I should, when restored to health, take steps to carry into effect your wishes; and in the event of Mr Stevenson or others of importance demurring, leave the possibility ... upon them ... (I) hope the Lord may yet raise you up more speedily than anticipated, and render the necessity of my appointment void ... I could conceive of no higher honour and privilege than being your helper, much more your representative or successor.

> [November 23] I need the strong love of Christ to constrain me to spend and be spent for others ... The thrombosis in the forearms has disappeared and so far as Dr Judd can perceive, in the upper arm also. (In) my legs ... the clots remain. My present purpose is, when I get up again, to tell dear Mr Stevenson that in the light of your letters I feel it my duty to accept the appointment. But that I equally feel his heartfelt acceptance and happy concurrence in it is a necessity.

On December 15, for the sake of clarity, Hoste put his conclusions in writing for John Stevenson also. 'I feel I ought to accept the appointment; if, however, you do not see your way to agreeing . . . I shall feel free from responsibility.' But Stevenson told him 'of his decision to agree'.

> It ... cost him a great deal, and I have been not a little impressed with the eminently Christian spirit and largeness of mind which he has displayed ... I ... shall endeavour to act upon your words as to my appointment not being intended to supersede Mr Stevenson in his present position Pending your promulgation the matter is being kept quiet.

> [December 26] Dear Mr Stevenson called me into his office a few days ago and, with tears in his eyes, told me that the Lord had given him not only peace about it but joy in the assurance that it was of God and would be for blessing. I think Cassels was specially a help to him.

Then on March 22, 1901, John Stevenson released an open letter from Hudson Taylor to the whole Mission in China, presenting in full Hudson Taylor's decision made known on January 24,

> to appoint Mr D. E. Hoste to act as General Director during my present incapacity through ill-health; of course this appointment does not in any way supersede Mr Stevenson in his position or work, but will supply him with the help which I would gladly afford him myself did health permit ... Matters that might otherwise need to be referred to me can be dealt with without delay in China, by Mr Hoste, and I shall not have the mental strain of feeling that I am not adequately attending to my part of the work. A few months' freedom from responsibility may be God's means of restoring me to ... permit of my once more visiting you.[1397]

The China Council, with Henry Frost and Walter B. Sloan also present, 'unanimously and most cordially concurred' in the appointment. Frost and Sloan had come specifically to spend a few months among the hundreds of refugee missionaries filling the Wusong Road premises and several additional rented houses in Shanghai. The potential danger of crowded conditions and emotional reaction against severe hardships and personal losses being exploited by the old enemy Satan, needed to be faced decisively. These two men were singularly gifted as counsellors and public speakers, Sloan in expository preaching on 'victorious Christian living', and Frost, by choice on this occasion, in systematic teaching of Biblical theology.[1398] Their presence proved timely for Hoste and Stevenson also. Hoste wrote of feeling bereft when they had to return home.

A discreet note from Orr Ewing to Hudson Taylor said, 'There is no one in our midst so well fitted to take the position—a great many who were hoping that Mr W. Cooper would take a more prominent part in the work, were terribly disappointed when the Lord saw fit to take him home.' And on April 4, 'this decision has cost Mr Stevenson days of prayer . . . I am deeply thankful (for) the manifest grace of God seen in (him). He has throughout shown himself to great advantage; he could scarcely have been in a more trying position.' Even then, at the public meeting in Shanghai to announce Dixon Hoste's appointment, it was emphasised that it was 'a temporary measure' to hasten the recovery of Hudson Taylor.[1399]

The trauma of this harrowing predicament had fallen on each man during and because of 'the avalanche of suffering' through which so many of the rank and file were passing. The end of the killings was the start of an almost equally heartbreaking phase of recovery.

How many died? (1900–01)

The *Chinese Recorder*, a mirror of events and opinion, vaguely reflected the uncertainties of early 1900. Among the social and academic contents to be expected came an article on the Society for the Diffusion of Christian and General Knowledge; a comparison of methods leading to the goal of Christianity in China; the difficulties of Protestant Chinese Christians opposed by 'non-Christian and Roman Catholic power', moral and political; and then the first rumblings of the Boxer storm. The bones of the reformer Kang Yuwei's ancestors were reported exhumed and destroyed on Ci Xi's orders; S. M. Brooks's severed head was 'offered to the wayside god' by his murderers; the Beijing *coup d'état* and proclamation of Pu Jün (Pu Chun), son of the vicious Prince Tuan, as heir to the late emperor Tong Zhi, left the imprisoned Guang Xü out of account; a price of one hundred thousand taels was placed on the heads of the reformers Kang Yuwei and Liang Jichao (Liang Chi-ch'ao) dead or alive; the walls of Beijing were placarded with denunciations of the Boxers while the two-faced court was encouraging them and the Manchu nobility joined the 'Boxer Association'.

Then at last came an editorial on the Boxers, on the murder of Norman and Robinson, on Prince Tuan adopting 'all the pomp and authority of an emperor' and, suddenly, that the consuls in Shanghai had assumed the role of acting-ministers of their respective countries. The main organ of Protestant missions in China was groping for the facts.

A list was given of missionaries under siege and of others 'safe' because absent for one reason or another from their homes in Beijing, Baoding and elsewhere. The friendly ex-*daotai* of Shanghai, promoted to be the governor of Sichuan, was doing all he could to protect foreigners in his province. The consuls had great confidence in him, but the people were unpredictable and the viceroy, Gui Zhun, a Manchu reactionary, was persuaded with difficulty by the provincial treasurer, Zhou Fu, to suppress the imperial edicts. According to Professor W. E. Soothill, the viceroy thrust the edicts 'into the privacy of his high boot', denying their existence to his anti-foreign officials.[1400] And then in the September issue, still haphazard, Psalm 2 appeared in full, 'The Imperial Decree': 'Why do the heathen rage . . . ?' followed by a spate of horror stories from the Canadians of Henan; of the relief of the legations; from A. R. Saunders; George Parker on how he was shown the edict to kill and then given a running start to safety only just ahead of his pursuers.

Between the news of more than thirty allied men of war at Shanghai to defend the foreign settlements and an account of the Peking siege, came an article by Dixon Hoste on the future of Chinese church-missionary relations, with 'Possible Changes and Developments in the Native Churches arising out of the Present Crisis'.[1401] His long-sustained reputation as a thinker and statesman had begun; the point of his essay: that the upheavals and sufferings of the Church had thrown up God-given leaders who should be respected and not hampered by the returning missionaries. To go back expecting to take control again would be perverse. Foreign missionaries should return prepared to work with and under the Chinese church. Ten years with the powerful man of God, Hsi Shengmo, had proved to Hoste how it could be done as equals, neither subservient to the other, yet control belonging to the Chinese.

Teams of investigators would soon be going out, looking for survivors, distributing relief, and re-establishing shattered congregations. The opportunity for doing it on right principles could so easily be lost. Readers would not miss the significance of a related article from Korea, clearly demonstrating that J. L. Nevius's influence had launched the Korean church on its successful course of self-government, self-support and self-propagation.[1402]

On September 7, 1900, four hundred missionaries of twenty societies, many of them refugees, meeting in Shanghai, appealed to their home governments to make a lasting settlement for the good of the Chinese people, restoring the Guang Xü emperor to the throne, punishing the guilty and safeguarding the church, without alienating officials or citizens by demands too heavy to be borne without resentment. The debate on reparation and indemnities had begun.[1403]

China's Millions for the first few months of 1900 had little to say about the Boxer menace beyond noting a 'critical state of affairs'. Too little was known for certain. General news was in the papers. Long, long lists of missionaries and their locations carried the occasional note 'Absent'—on home leave. The Christian perspective was maintained by reminders that 'unto you it is given in the behalf of Christ, not only to believe in him, but also to suffer' (Phil 1.29); 'that Christ shall be magnified in (my body), whether it be by life, or by death' (Phil 1.20 AV). And prayer was asked for those fleeing the country, with no hint of the horrors that cliché implied, until at last in October and November it became possible to publish authentic martyr and refugee news.

An editorial, urgent and deeply understanding, insisted, 'that there must be no cry for vengeance. Let us not forget the provocation that China has had.' It lamented 'the incessant and almost incredibly ignorant talk about partitioning China', and the opium trade. 'We have sown the wind; can we wonder if we reap the whirlwind?' The Western nations were not less to blame than the Manchus and their Chinese subjects.

News from Shanxi came piecemeal—the Xiaoyi ladies dead, and many (named) whose whereabouts or fate remained unknown even so late in the year. All twenty-eight Henan missionaries were reported alive and safe after varying experiences. A policy of understatement seemed preferred. The secular press supplied more than enough exaggeration and fiction. Then the 'latest telegrams' arrived. September 17: the Greens and Jessie Gregg safely in the care of the provincial judge—one of the last episodes, but here among the first to be publicised; September 20: the Youngs and McConnell's killed; September 21: the Swedish Mission in China, none missing, arrived safely, all well—among the first to reach safety, but only now confirmed. So it continued, with hundreds, thousands of relatives waiting to know the worst or at least to end the suspense. The circumstances were without precedent.[1404]

Calculations followed, some right and some mistaken. At first a tentative report that 'no fewer than eighteen were massacred' filled all with alarm. Soon more telegrams dwarfed such figures. The November *China's Millions* reported the CIM death-toll to have reached fifteen adults and fourteen children, but 'Hewett safe'—the doctor hidden incommunicado in an inner gaol for his own safety. With the restoration of calm and civil order, although the guilty imperial court was still at Xi'an, 'final figures' began to appear in print. John Stevenson's 'official list of killed and missing to 29th September' (submitted to the British Consul General on September 15 and amended to date for publication as a supplement to the *Shanghai Mercury*), gave a total of fifty-five adults and twenty-two children dead in Shanxi alone, and thirteen adults and four children in Zhili. The total for Shandong, Shanxi, Zhili and Zhejiang had reached seventy-seven adults and twenty-nine children.

But no less sombre was his tally of quite as many 'missing and unaccounted for'. In Shanxi forty-three adults and eight children of all missions, added to those in Zhili and Scandinavians on the Mongolian border, brought the total of missing persons to eighty adults and twenty-seven children. The scale of horror had become unspeakable, as descriptions by Glover, Saunders, Argento, Bird and others followed one after another. Eventually the list of missionary martyrs numbered 135 adults and 53 children, 188 in all, of whom 159 were in Shanxi.

Most poignant, perhaps, of all the appalling results of the Boxer rising was the plight of the orphans, away at school in Chefoo or the homelands, and the smaller societies wiped out of existence or left with one or two missionaries absent on furlough. Ten members of the Swedish Holiness Union were killed, leaving one man. The Scandinavian Alliance Mongolian Mission were annihilated with one exception. The Swedish Mongolian Mission died to a man. The Baptist Missionary Society in Shanxi suffered the same fate so that two retired missionaries returned to replace them. Of what had been the Shouyang Mission all died with the exception of Dr and Mrs E. H. Edwards, in Britain at the time. And the Christian and Missionary Alliance of its total force of thirty-eight in China lost twenty-one and fourteen children, its whole strength in the north. By contrast, with deaths from 'natural causes' the CIM lost sixty-three members in 1900, ending the year with 745 alive if not all well.

A rash of speculation (1900–01)

When the siege in Beijing ended, the onslaught in Shanxi became more ferocious than ever. But when Li Hongzhang's command to stop the killing reached throughout the province and sympathetic officials replaced the vicious and weak ones, the general reaction among survivors at the coast was less of relief than a long, deep sigh, from a sense of having barely escaped. On all sides people were saying, What if the wind of change had veered so very little against the foreign community in China? The intended holocaust in every province and every city, in Shanghai and Canton as much as in Hankou and Chongqing, would have cost thousands of lives. Every one of those half-naked fugitives would have died. What if the courage of the southern and central China viceroys and governors had failed, if they had literally safeguarded their own necks, obeying the inhuman empress dowager instead of anticipating the world's outcry and retaliation? What if Yong Lu had not played his secret game of keeping the modern artillery in its crates and restraining Tong Fuxiang's attacks on the legations? What if they had fallen, as could have happened at many points of time? Thousands of defenders and defended would have died at a stroke. What if the Boxers had not struck at the hottest time of year, when many were away on holiday at the coast, but after they returned? Or conversely, what if the consuls and envoys had judged differently and ordered an early evacuation of the interior, instead of being caught out by incredulous speculation on the ill-omened inter-calary month? Such conjecture deepened gratitude to God.

The spirit of reform among the literati of China was already so advanced and widespread that even if Ci Xi and her reactionaries had had it their own way, they would only have won a delay in the inevitable reformations. Most were elderly and their cause would die with them. Had the missionaries been ordered out by their consuls or directors, the Christians would have had to face the same attack alone. The example set by missionaries old and young—and of their children to no small degree—would have been denied to the church. Then why did some try to escape? Because the time came when their presence could do no further good, and their Christian friends exhorted them to hide or flee. In this a precedent was set, to be followed when the nation turned its fury on the Manchus in 1911, and civil war found its scapegoats and suspects in the late 1920s and 1940s.

The Boxer rising had been an imperial fiasco. The intended holocaust had in its very concept been a display of Manchu weakness. Ci Xi's failures sprang from the wisdom and sanity of the provincial rulers; their loyalty to the throne, nation and people exceeding loyalty to the fallible Old Buddha. Superstition accounted for much of the origins and nature of the rising. Some Christians were chopped into small pieces and scattered on running water—to ensure their failure to rise again, as they claimed they would.[1405] But the seed sown in agony was to reap a harvest beyond expectation. Hudson Taylor's preface in October 1901 to *Last Letters and Further Records of Martyred Missionaries of the CIM* drew the parallel of Christ's deliverance from death being through death. 'He asked life of thee, and thou gavest it him, even length of days for ever and ever' (Ps 21.4 AV). The martyrs' prayers were answered in God's own way. 'As for God, his way is perfect.' As one wrote, 'If my Lord offered me my choice . . . I would prefer what He chose for me.'

At home again in England, A. R. Saunders addressed the crowded 'Meeting in Memory of the Martyred Missionaries' on February 12, 1901, at which several survivors of the rising spoke. Using St Paul's declaration as his own, Saunders said:

'We would not ... leave you ignorant of our trouble which came to us in Asia, that we were pressed out of measure above strength, insomuch that we despaired even of life. But we had the sentence of death in ourselves, that we should not trust in ourselves but in God which raiseth the dead, who delivered us from so great a death, and doth deliver.'

Such words as these were a comfort to us many a time on that long journey from Shansi to Hankow ... We could not tell why GOD should permit such suffering. We could not see how GOD could in any way get glory to His name by such humiliation of His servants. But we rest in the blessed assurance that it was GOD's way. He makes no mistake ... We think of those dear friends who are now in the presence of our LORD JESUS CHRIST ... Perhaps thousands have seen their triumphant death, which yet is not death to the child of God.[1406]

The miscarriage of Ci Xi's plans was among the factors considered miraculous by observers of the whole grisly affair. No less remarkable and 'attributable to an exceptional intervention by God' was the consistent exhibition of his grace in the courage of the martyrs, Chinese and foreign. That they could experience peace of heart and mind, show consideration for others at the extremity of their own ordeals, and calmly preach the gospel until the moment of death, had an immeasurable influence on the Church and on pagan observers.

The nation swung within months from indifference or opposition to curiosity and outright admiration. Sir Robert Hart allowed the elation of deliverance to prompt his prophecy of China becoming a Christian nation within fifty years. Inevitable reforms went hand in hand with openness to foreigners and receptiveness to their recommendations, technological and religious. A new China was being born. But before the dying and the crying had ended, the foreign nations were planning punishment, reparations, indemnities and territorial domination—and the reinstatement of Ci Xi, instead of the Guang Xü emperor as the missions urged.

Reprisals or statesmanship? (1900–01)

After all that had happened, settlement of the tensions between China and 'the powers' claimed priority. New envoys took the place of those who had been through the Peking siege, and the representatives of China who had tried to fill the gap left by the flight of the court, Li Hongzhang and Prince Qing, attempted to open negotiations in August and September, 1900. Li, the 'grand old man' of China, who had carried the main burden of statesmanship ever since the Taiping rebellion, confided his grief to his diary:

Oh, if my hand were not so weak and my cause so much weaker! The Court is in hiding and the people are distracted. There is no government and chaos reigns. I fear the task before me is too great for my strength of body, though I would do one more thing before I call the earthly battle over. I would have the foreigners believe in us once more; and not deprive China of her national life; and I would like to bring 'Old Buddha' back to the palace, and ask her if she had learned her lesson.

At first they failed. The allies were reluctant to recognise their credentials. And the Germans insisted on the surrender for punishment of those 'whose guilt in instigating or committing the crimes there is no room for doubt'. These could be named, but most had fled. And proof could not be established within months. To nail responsibility where it belonged, on Ci Xi herself, could prove impossible. Not that the envoys would attempt it. Like Nelson, they chose to turn the blind eye of diplomacy in her favour and to dictate her tacit exoneration and reinstatement, while using her to punish the instruments of her own infamy.[1407]

The American government held that no punitive measures could be as effective as 'punishment of the responsible authors by the supreme imperial authority itself'. But negotiations dependent on prior punishment by sovereign or government might be deferred interminably. Negotiation would therefore have to go ahead and include punishments in its terms. Surprisingly, an imperial decree of September 25 removed this difficulty by ordering the trial and sentencing of some leading Manchus. But were they the right ones and were their sentences severe enough? Coordination of action by the erstwhile allies became confused as the Germans took punitive strikes into their own hands; Russia proceeded to absorb Manchuria and grab control at Tianjin; and Britain, for diplomatic reasons affecting German military supplies to the Boers, concluded an Anglo-German agreement on October 16.

After some indecision the foreign powers matched the imperial court's manoeuvering to minimise its concessions to their demands. On October 15, Li Hongzhang approached the powers with an admission of China's culpability for attacking the legations contrary to international law, and her liability to indemnify the injured parties, and proposed that hostilities should cease. Guilt and liability were the premiss of negotiation, so this attempt 'fell still-born'.[1408] On December 24 the envoys telegraphed a joint note to Xi'an, embodying 'irrevocable decisions', which Ci Xi accepted by wire two days later, followed by an acceptance in writing for each power, sealed with the imperial seal. Penalties acceptable to them were ordered by imperial decrees in February 1901; and for the next eight months the envoys sought agreement among themselves on the final Peace Protocol signed on September 7, 1901. Meanwhile, the Germans were prevented with difficulty from pressing their military advantage to 'operations on a large scale', understood to have Xi'an as their objective.

An imperial prince of the first rank, young Prince Qün, had already gone to Germany to express China's regrets for the murder of Baron von Ketteler, and another went to Japan for that of Chancellor Sugiyama. Punishment of the provincial literati taxed the envoys' ingenuity, for they were less readily identified than the mandarins had been for execution, exile, imprisonment or cashiering. To satisfy the foreigners an imperial edict on August 19 decreed what Ci Xi in her cunning way may well have recognised as counter-productive, 'the suspension of official examinations for five years in all cities where foreigners were massacred or submitted to cruel treatment', six in Manchuria, twelve in Zhili, twenty-two in Shanxi, two in Henan and one in each of Zhejiang, Hunan and Shaanxi. Suspension of official examinations meant closure of the door to the most sought-after careers for thousands of innocent and often progressive scholars. For those five years the most intelligent and educated young men were penalised for the guilt of a minority of others. Their deep resentment was understandable. Missionaries returning upcountry frequently encountered it, and while sympathising could do nothing to help them.

But the imposition of indemnities outstripped in folly the discrimination against the literati. At first the American envoy wisely urged a demand for 'a lump sum within China's ability to pay', perhaps three hundred million taels (£140–50 million).[1409] The claims of each power could then be scaled down to realistic figures. The fire-breathing envoys led by Germany saw no need to be considerate of China, and 'the urgent need of Britain to maintain her entente with Germany' forced her hand. China's annual budget showed 'reported receipts' as approximately 100 million tacls which could be increased to 118 million by recovering from the tax collectors and their mandarin patrons the sums they habitually diverted.

Although an aggregate of claims by the powers amounted to 450 million taels, an imperial decree on May 29, 1901, accepted this demand. Again, did Ci Xi see the foreigner bearing the brunt of criticism for such coercion? Payment would be slow. With interest at four per cent the total sum payable by 1940 would exceed 982 million taels—with a legacy of resentment calculated to pay bitter dividends long before that.[1410]

With two exceptions the atrocities had been limited to the north-eastern provinces, but additional taxation would weigh heavily on every province. The innocent, including many who had protected the victims, would suffer resentfully for the guilty, and blame the foreigner. Statesmanship had been forgotten in the lust for retribution. Britain and Japan submitted only moderate claims. But the United States provided the notable exception, declining any more than $25 million, and in 1908 remitting part of this indemnity in favour of education in China. Neither did these indemnities take into account the huge quantities of bullion seized at Beijing and Tianjin.

Other articles in the protocol provided the right to maintain legation guards in the capital of the empire, and greatly expanded legation territories. The coastal forts were to be demolished and the route from the coast to Beijing kept open. China had reached a stage of national degradation so low that she retained few of the attributes of a sovereign and independent state.[1411]

When Li Hongzhang signed the Peace Protocol on September 7 his days were already numbered. He died on November 7 in his seventy-ninth year. Strong, able, unscrupulous and immensely wealthy from acquisitions during forty years of high office, his wisdom and service to the empire deserved 'the highest posthumous honours ever accorded to a Chinese subject of the Manchus'.

The greater of the two Yangzi viceroys, Liu Kunyi of Nanjing, died on October 6, 1902, and the legendary Manchu bannerman, Yong Lu, on April 11, 1903. 'The service of the state was left to be carried on by lesser men.' Zhang Zhitong returned to the viceroyalty of Nanjing, and Yüan Shikai replaced Li Hongzhang as viceroy at Tianjin. With the signing of the Peace Protocol and the withdrawal of foreign troops, apart from legation guards, Ci Xi felt able to return to the palace in Beijing. 'An early return was imperative if the dynasty was to be preserved.'[1412] The court left Xi'an on October 6, 1901, but halted at Kaifeng until December 14. So Li Hongzhang failed to see the Old Buddha again. She was at Kaifeng when he died.

Statesmanship had conspicuously failed. The supreme opportunity to distinguish between the true villains and the true China, and to mete out true justice for each, had been lost. 'Behind the destruction which followed in (the Boxers') train there was a small Manchu clique, and not the Chinese nation.' The *Chinese Recorder* drew the hypothetical comparison of Finland dominating Russia for three hundred years.[1413] But the Western powers in their own interests chose to label the dowager empress the victim of the clique and of the Boxers. For the sake of even temporary stability and the advantages it would bring them, they left the emperor and China's reform at her mercy. The evil genius returned to the palace with the emperor still under her heel. And the impositions of 1901 played their own part in subsequent anti-foreign nationalistic movements, including the banishment of all but a few foreigners at the close of the 'open century'.

The missions debate indemnities (1900–01)

Not only the world powers saw China's instability as their opportunity for expansion and profit. Church and missions foresaw a change of attitude towards them and their teaching. Both had suffered severe losses and faced determined efforts by the secular powers to obtain substantial reparations for them. But these were being made at the same time as they claimed for the destruction of legations and the cost of naval and military operations. In spite of a new rift between France and the Vatican, the French worked strongly to reinstate the Catholic Church. The Tianjin Notre-Dame des Victoires, rebuilt after the massacre of 1870 (see pp 125–26, 142), again lay in ruins, as did the four cathedrals at Beijing and many provincial churches.

Imperious behaviour in making local settlements reinforced the resentment against foreigners in general. A different attitude could have served to distinguish Christian from secular standards, Church from State, with lasting benefit. But, as the

North China Herald reported of reparations at Taiyuan,

> The Roman Catholic ... claims are not so easy to settle. As their cathedral was destroyed, they demanded that one of the public buildings should be given them either the Governor's *yamen* (at the outer gate of which the massacre took place) or a large college (called the Provincial College). The Governor said he was unable to give away public property, and eventually they (declared that) they would go and occupy the college, and if they were opposed and there was trouble, they would hold the local officials responsible [in accordance with the peace protocol] ... The authorities induced the resident staff and students to leave (and the Catholics moved in).[1414]

By March they promised to withdraw within two months, reduced their claims to two and a quarter million taels and gave up their demand for two named market towns to be surrendered to them. It had become imperative that Protestant and Catholic Christianity should be recognised as distinct from each other. Again and again missionaries on the run had saved their lives and those of their companions by convincing their tormentors that they were neither engineers nor Roman Catholic priests. Their defence was convincing. The anti-foreign anger of the people had been as much as anything against the assumption of official rank and intervention in judicial processes. In the matter of indemnities the Protestant Church adhered to biblical principles, distinct from current secular and Roman attitudes.[1415]

The efforts of the new envoys to press claims on behalf of the hard-hit missions met with a varying response from the different Protestant societies. Not all approved of being part of the pretext for teaching the Chinese government a lesson. Some tried to disassociate themselves from aspects of the foreign governments' actions, and from being linked with the Roman Catholics under the general term 'missionaries'. On September 7, 1900, the four hundred missionaries of twenty societies assembled in Shanghai appealed to their home governments to recognise Ci Xi's responsibility for the Boxer rising, which she had 'instigated, ordered and encouraged', and to work for China's benefit in the eventual settlement of differences. 'No settlement can be satisfactory or permanent which does not aim to secure the real good of the Chinese people and the rightful interests of all foreigners resident in China.' Therefore any settlement should aim at the restoration of the Guang Xü emperor to the throne, protection of missionaries in their legitimate work and residence, protection of law-abiding Christians from persecution, just punishment of the murderers, and adequate proclamation throughout China of the historical facts.[1416]

Compensation for losses of life or property did not come under debate until November, in a series of articles in the *Chinese Recorder*. Bishop George Motile recognised the basic right to require of the Chinese government full compensation for both loss of life and of property, but held that it would be good policy not to press such claims. 'Blood money' could not be accepted for the life of a Christian martyr. The LMS found in later years that reparations did more harm than good, and renounced all claims after a fresh outbreak of troubles.[1417]

Each mission came to its own conclusions. The American Board submitted no claim for damaged mission property, but actively requisitioned land and fined guilty Chinese on behalf of the Christians of Tong Xian. In twenty-three villages, 166 Christians had been killed and 184 homes been destroyed. The fines were used to relieve distress; ninety-six acres of land and small plots for cemeteries were confiscated; and the guilty were made to rebuild nineteen chapels.[1418]

In spite of all the sufferings of foreign missionaries, far more Chinese Christians had suffered and to a far greater degree. In this, too, each mission followed its own judgment in presenting its claims, in every case through their foreign governments. But the American societies made a united presentation of their claims to the Department of State. The governments 'included in their demands indemnities for societies, individuals and Chinese who had suffered in person or in property in consequence of their being in the service of foreigners'.[1419] 'In consequence the indemnity paid to Chinese Christians (did injury) by sowing the seeds of a mercenary spirit.'[1420]

'A military presence' at the funeral at Baoding compounded the confusion in Chinese minds. French and German military bands playing hymns after punitive action against the city had no justifiable place in the settlement of such rifts between two races. But at the reburial of Chinese Christians at Tong Xian, the voluntary presence of a Chinese army commander and 1,500 troops clearly expressed regret and apology.[1421] While some took advantage of the presence of foreign troops (as at

2.92 The Baoding martyrs' memorial procession, photographed by Dr E. H. Edwards

Tong Xian) to obtain just compensation for Christians and missionaries alike, others took trouble to prove their independence from foreign secular influence, and worked as far as possible through the Chinese authorities.

J. W. Lowrie, an American Presbyterian of Baoding, and Dr E. H. Edwards, sole survivor of the Shouyang missionaries, had searched without success for remains of the Presbyterians who had died in their burning premises to the north of the city. But in the south suburb where they looked for graves of the American Board and CIM martyrs, they found on February 22 what was left

in shallow pits outside the city wall. 'These remains had been much disturbed and were seemingly indistinguishable' when the first punitive expeditions had uncovered them, Dr Edwards wrote. 'We found only the skeleton of one headless body, recognised by some garments . . . as that of Miss Gould . . . In the same pit were seven heads, six foreign and one Chinese . . . all recognised by some distinguishing mark. Most of the coffins will contain only a skull.'[1422]

Memorial services on March 23 and 24 were attended by Chinese officials and representatives of each society, including H. M. Brown of Shunde for the CIM. The coffins of eight foreigners and 'nearly twenty' Chinese Christians, representing forty-two martyred for their faith, stood in a pavilion beside a cross surmounted by a crown and the inscription 'Le bet ku jia' ('They carried the cross of suffering with joy'). After the service in Chinese the coffins were all borne in procession through the streets to the site chosen for a cemetery, and buried in one long line of graves.[1423]

In Shanxi an unusual development paved the way for exceptionally satisfactory solutions to be found. The enlightened governor, Ceng Chunxüan (Ts'eng Ch'un-hsüan),[1424] who replaced the 'butcher' Yü Xian, in his admiration of Timothy Richard consulted Li Hongzhang and with his approval invited Richard to Shanxi. In April 1901, Li Hongzhang and Prince Qing asked the British minister to enlist Richard's help in settling all the complex cases facing the governor in Taiyuan, and Richard hurried north from Shanghai. At Tianjin, Li conferred with him for an hour and a half. They were no strangers to each other. Often during Timothy Richard's periods in Tianjin and Beijing and at other times, they had had occasion to meet. Viceroy Zhang Zhitong very possibly had spoken favourably of Richard's work and advice in Taiyuan. An old friend named Zhou Fu, *daotai* of Zhili, future governor of Shandong and viceroy at Nanjing and Canton, also joined in the interview.

Richard was ideally placed to influence the leading officials in north China after the Boxer rising. In May he telegraphed on behalf of Governor Ceng to invite representatives of the main Protestant societies to join them in settling the most numerous and widespread incidents of the Boxer holocaust. And the governor set aside two hundred thousand taels to be divided between Catholics and Protestants. A party of eight representatives was quickly formed. On June 26 they set out from Baoding (three months after the funeral) under an escort sent by the governor to bring them safely to Taiyuan.[1425]

By choice nothing for the CIM
(1900–01)

Every one of the Mission's eight hundred members was personally affected by the upheavals of 1900. Least disturbed were the Nicholls of Dali in far western Yunnan. (Pioneers among the minority peoples of the province, they are to be distinguished from the George Nicolls of Sichuan.) They scarcely heard of the Boxer rising until it was all over and carried on their work throughout the crisis. A drastic drop in British donations to the CIM appeared to have a scarcely credible explanation: The Boer War and Peking siege held the headlines, and had not missionary work all but ceased? But a single large gift of £5,000 and more from other sources compensated for the shortage, so that members received almost as much as usual.[1426]

Most were uprooted from their homes and possessions and spent a year first on difficult journeys and then in crowded refugee conditions. Hundreds came and went from Shanghai, but most stayed. Many were distressed and needing comfort and special care. But morale was high, and with time on their hands they spent it in consultation together and in preparation for their return to work. The Mission's leaders had to listen and advise on an endless stream of personal problems. Provincial superintendents, refugees themselves, absorbed most of this, but much came to John Stevenson and Dixon Hoste,

crushed by the awfulness of the Boxer tragedy and their responsibilities. The year 1900 was the hardest in the Mission's history. Disorganised, it had to face an uncertain future. After providing for the flood of fugitives arriving at the river ports and Shanghai, the directors began planning reorganisation and return to the interior. Their task increased as missionaries who had been on leave in their homelands began to come back to China, bringing new members who had offered to take the martyrs' places. In the words of Johann Ludwig Krapf on the death of his wife in East Africa in 1844, 'The victories of the Church are gained by stepping over the graves of her members.'[1427]

Dixon Hoste's appointment by Hudson Taylor 'to act as General Director' had come at the peak of the crisis. The announcement to the CIM on March 22, 1901, and to the public on the 26th, came only a few weeks before the governor of Shanxi's surprise call for help in resolving the reparation problems of his province. No one was better fitted to go than Hoste himself. Ten years as a colleague of Hsi Shengmo had won for him the confidence of the Shanxi Church. Scores, hundreds of the persecuted and martyred Christians were personally known to him. Archibald Orr Ewing, waiting for Jiangxi to reopen to his team in exile, was ideal as a companion, to stay on and implement decisions after Hoste had to return.

In November 1900, Stevenson had spoken of soon filling up the houses at the treaty ports, among them the language schools and Zhenjiang. And on January 30, Hoste told the Taylors that re-occupation of cities in the Yangzi valley was proceeding.[1428] Shanxi, Shaanxi and Gansu would 'present considerable dangers and difficulties'. But by April he was able to give the whole mission lists of missionaries returning to Sichuan, Guizhou, Yunnan, Zhejiang, Anhui and Jiangxi. In Jiangsu all but one centre was already occupied, and soon the Guangxin River team would be on their way back. After little more than a year from the outbreak of the Boxer rising and five months since the last death, the work of the Mission had been re-established in most of the empire. The most resistant places opened up soon afterwards. Shanxi remained one of the most sensitive provinces.

Some funds were available, but in each location throughout China great wisdom and tact were needed in dealing with officials, landlords of premises left vacant for so long, and local Christians who had handled all affairs of the churches in the missionaries' absence. Mission income from all sources in 1900 had been 2,780 taels lower than in the previous year, while travelling and rentals in China had cost 3,504 taels more. At the same time passages by sea had cost 22,833 taels, an increase of nearly ten thousand taels. Return to the interior and rebuilding wrecked premises would inflate expenses. So the talk of indemnities was highly relevant.

The elderly, indecisive governor of Zhejiang whose vacillations had cost the lives of the eight missionaries at Qü Xian, had been the first to raise the matter of reparations with the CIM. Sensing the approach of a tidal wave of similar circumstances, John Stevenson and the China Council referred the subject to Hudson Taylor for his opinion on the principles. And Dixon Hoste wrote (on a river steamer between Yichang and Hankou on January 30, 1901, personally investigating the security of those regions) saying he thought official recognition and reinstatement of each station to be desirable, but he personally would be prepared to forgo it. In Chinese eyes the important matter of 'face' was involved. After degradation and expulsion the process ought to be publicly reversed. What did Hudson Taylor think? He replied, through Marcus Wood, secretary in London (and, it may be assumed, to each homeland), advising that the CIM should

CLAIM FOR NOTHING, but to accept, where offered, compensation for destroyed Mission premises and property, as I feel we hold these on trust for God's work.

For private property, we must leave each missionary free to accept or decline, through the Mission only.

For injury or loss of life, to refuse all compensation.

The Mission, likewise, should be responsible for the orphan children of Missionaries.

For native Christians ... I think we should do what God enables us to help them, and to care for bereaved relatives.

Compensation to Christians was regarded as a separate matter between the Chinese government and its own subjects. They were not 'in the service of foreigners' or under the 'protection' of the Mission, although everything possible would be done to help them.[1429]

In a fuller letter to Shanghai, Hudson Taylor pointed out that to claim compensation for loss of life, injury or loss of property, whether private or belonging to the Mission, would contravene Article 15 of the 'Principles and Practice', which stipulated: no appeal and no demands. Accepting compensation offered by the Chinese would be left for each individual to decide in view of circumstances in their own locality, but in Hudson Taylor's opinion it would as a rule be wiser not even to accept compensation lest its acceptance have a harmful influence on the Christians. In February this was all conveyed to each member and associate of the CIM, and the first part to the consuls and Sir Ernest Satow, British Minister at Beijing.

Relatives of some members of the CIM had applied direct to the Foreign Office 'making long claims for compensation for lives (lost)'. So the London Council had in December conveyed to Lord Lansdowne the wish 'that this Mission should be entirely disassociated from all claims for life, or bodily injury, that may be put forward by (relatives or friends)' of members.

When unvarnished news of the atrocities committed by allied troops in and around Beijing reached Hudson Taylor he was appalled and protested to Theodore Howard about the atrocities being seen by

China as perpetrated by 'Christian' nations. The contrast between nominal and true Christianity must be stressed, or hatred of foreigners and Christianity would be intensified.

> It (is) imperative that we should dissociate ourselves as missionaries as far as possible from government action. I have ... advised Mr Stevenson to inform the consul-general that as a Mission we will not accept any money compensation. Thousands of Chinese as innocent as our missionaries seem to have been ruined and robbed of their all, and large numbers slain, through the action of the allies, for which China will not be compensated ... It therefore seems better to me now that we should trust in God to enable us to rehabilitate our stations when the time comes to reopen them. Though it will mean many thousands of pounds to restore all that was destroyed, He is able to provide.[1430]

His change of mind, Hoste pointed out, was in part attributable to his rapid ageing.

Ten days later Jenny told Marcus Wood that Hudson was 'at his best just now', and in June they were in Britain meeting family, friends and survivors of the rising. There was nothing in his change of mind to apologise for. He had accepted advice, and his conclusion was lucid, deliberate and progressive, in the fighting spirit most characteristic of him. A money-conscious nation like the Chinese could be counted on to recognise such a clear-cut distinction between the motives of the secular powers and those of missionaries 'as witnesses to Christ and the Gospel'. It would show 'the meekness and gentleness of Christ'. And so it proved. At the end of February the CIM formally decided 'not only not to enter any claim against the Chinese Government, but to refrain from accepting compensation even if offered'. There was no need to publicise the fact, for the reasons could not very well be given without giving offence. Provincial superintendents passed the word on, acting on this policy, and D. E. Hoste applied it meticulously in Shanxi, with startling results.

Back to Taiyuan (June–July 1901)

After the relief of the Peking legations and the return to Baoding, with their secular overtones, the official welcome back to Shanxi stands supreme. The spontaneous action of Governor Ceng Chunxüan in inviting Timothy Richard and other mission representatives to negotiate with him in person required no little courage. The scale of public ceremonies and the generosity of his proclamations and memorial tablets are as much a historical highlight as they made him a marked man. His liberal attitudes and wisdom are honoured in this triumphal story of the return and reinstatement of Christian missions and the church. Heavy indemnities were expected and justified in law, and he was intent on fair settlements for each atrocious action of his predecessor, Yü Xian, but he was to meet with surprise after surprise.

It was right that D. E. Hoste, Acting General Director, and Archibald Orr Ewing, with their intimate knowledge of Shanxi, should lead the party of investigators, for major decisions lay ahead. Erik Folke's colleague in the Swedish Mission from south Shanxi, C. H. Tjader, went with them to represent the associate missions. And Hudson Taylor's accountant son, Ernest, won commendation for his role as Hoste's assistant. Large sums of money were to be involved. They left Shanghai on June 1 with no more arranged than 'a respectful welcome' and safe conduct assured by the governor, and the request made to him for an official funeral for the martyrs as at Baoding. At Beijing, Hoste and Orr Ewing had an hour's consultation with the minister, Sir Ernest Satow, who showed 'an intelligent interest in missions', but remained unyielding about single women returning to 'the interior'. They were joined by Moir Duncan and Dr Creasey Smith of the BMS, by Dr E. H. Edwards, sole survivor of the Shouyang missionaries, and by Dr Atwood of the American Board, who were to enquire into the annihilation of their missions in the province; and by Major Pereira of the Grenadier Guards 'travelling for pleasure' but perhaps an

2.93 Pastor Qü in his MA robes

official observer. A government 'deputy' was appointed to make all arrangements for them on their long journey.[1431]

Starting by train on June 22, via Baoding where they hired mule litters, they received 'a very cool reception' at Huolu on the 29th by the same mandarin as had put the Greens into the Boxers' hands. But when the investigators responded by declining to pay their respects to him, and their sponsorship by high-ranking officials dawned on him, he sent local gentry to apologize. When their long cavalcade set out for Taiyuan, he came with a full deputation of officials and gentry to see them off. Heavy new fortification of the Guguan Pass showed that strong resistance would have been offered if the Germans had attempted to break through into Shanxi. Hoste's party, however, was received by an escort from the governor and at every resting-place a feast was ready at the official inn. Outside each city the magistrate met them ceremoniously, and when they left

made his bow after accompanying them for a respectful distance along the way.[1432]

At Shouyang on July 4, Pastor Qü, Elder Xü and Elder Si (Hsi Shengmo's brother-in-law, still suffering from the sword thrust from which he was to die) met them to plan their movements in the province. Rain for three days preventing travel gave them more time to hear about the sufferings of the church and missionaries. The magistrate of Shouyang, who had collaborated with the Boxers in sending Pigott and his family and friends to die at Taiyuan, had nominally been banished by imperial edict, but was there in the same capacity as before. Men who had so recently been commended by the empress dowager could not be deposed in a hurry—unless named in the Protocol.

Thirty miles from Taiyuan outriders enquired when the travellers would arrive at the city. Ten miles further on the trumpeters of Governor Ceng's own bodyguard 'blared out their welcome and unfurled their standards'. Ten miles from the city fresh cavalry joined the escort, and after two more miles mounted police saluted them. Three miles from Taiyuan they were transferred from their litters to official passenger carts and taken to the great South Gate where 'an immense crowd' was waiting. Among them stood many delighted Christians, their faces showing 'clear traces of their sufferings'.

A *daotai* of the Foreign Office (Shen Dunhe, who had spent a year at Cambridge) and high mandarins and civil dignitaries of Taiyuan received them with refreshments in a pavilion before they were conducted into the city. At the official quarters they were to occupy, the Provincial Treasurer, Provincial Judge, the Tartar General, City Prefect and other mandarins welcomed them 'with all politeness and cordiality', repeatedly expressing their regrets for the events of 1900. This was not the obsequious deference of guilty men, but a dignified admission by reasonable gentlemen that the emperor's representatives must redress the excesses of that year. Without design, it happened to be July 9, the exact anniversary of the massacre by Yü Xian. And, providentially, a heavy rain fell shortly after their arrival, for this was regarded by the common people as a favourable omen. With timely rain they could sow their grain and reap before the hard winter.

The governor himself had sent formal documents to greet the deputation at Huolu, but on the day of their arrival was 'laid up with a rather serious illness'. He had talked with Elder Xü PüYuan a few days earlier, and before that had spontaneously offered and distributed forty thousand taels to Christian victims of the persecution who were in danger of starving.[1433] On the 10th (through a representative) he gave 'a very elaborate dinner served in a large, beautifully carpeted hall'. Then, after two more days of courtesy calls and returning the compliments, formal discussion of compensation and rehabilitation of Christians and missions began. Meanwhile fifteen or twenty leading Christians were waiting for Hoste and his companions to be free from official obligations to work on church affairs. After ten days Hoste wrote to Hudson Taylor,

> Shansi has been convulsed from end to end, first by the Boxer movement, and then latterly by the fear of foreign invasion. There was a general stampede (of guilty officials) from this city. Numbers of the more prominent Boxers have been put to death, or committed suicide; many more are in hiding.

> [And a few days later:] It has been a time of great strain both in the quantity and the kind of work ... Satan was let loose in Shansi last summer, and it is sober fact to say that for two or three months it was like hell on earth. The sufferings of the Christians have been frightful, and it is almost overwhelming to hear them at firsthand, and to be living in this place where so many were massacred. Never before have I felt so utterly unequal to the responsibilities on me ... One great comfort is that some of the (Church) Elders have developed much since I last saw them, notably (Xü Puyüan). His powers as an administrator are remarkable, and all the others, including Pastor (Qü), seem gladly to recognise him as the moving spirit.

Very capable, and stronger than Si, [Xü, showed] a robustness and capacity for responsibility.

The pastors and other elders of the church in the CIM districts of Shanxi had unanimously asked him to take the lead.[1434]

'The most painful experience' (July–August 1901)

The Foreign Office *daotai* had already chosen a good site for a walled cemetery, on a hillside overlooking the city and plain, and had had the missionary victims of the massacre buried there. No official funeral could be held, but official gestures were adequate. In the centre of the burial ground stood an attractive hexagonal tiled pavilion with flower gardens on each side; and each grave was marked with a cross on a stone pedestal.

On July 18, sedan chairs with four bearers for each came for the missions' representatives, and at the Prefect's *yamen* mandarins of the highest rank received

2.94 Elder Xü Puyüan and attendant in Beijing to consult about destitute Shanxi Christians

them. With nineteen tall banners of red satin bearing the Chinese and foreign victims' names, surmounted by a canopy, and with many wreaths from the governor and leading officials and literati, all then went to the governor's *yamen*. On the site of the massacre outside the main gate a temporary pavilion had been erected, and there Dr Edwards conducted a brief service.

A procession then formed, to march through the crowd-lined streets and out through the East Gate to the cemetery. Men with gongs led the way. Behind them came the mandarins, followed by the wreaths, two hundred infantry and fifty cavalry, the foreign deputation in sedan chairs, Chinese Christians, the scarlet banners and more soldiers. At the cemetery a mandarin read out an address in classical wenli by Governor Ceng. The mandarins then returned to the city and Dixon Hoste conducted a Christian memorial service. Among the Chinese government's undertakings was the promise to erect a granite memorial tablet in honour of the Taiyuan martyrs. A few years later it fell to the lot of Amelia's youngest son to see it fulfilled at the rebuilt hospital.[1435] In every city and town where missionaries had been martyred this pattern of public apology and commemoration was followed during the next two months.

Most of the Christians had accepted the governor's offer of compensation for their losses, waiting for the deputation's advice on how to proceed. The governor and Foreign Office *daotai* therefore asked Hoste's help in organising the collection of particulars and distribution of indemnities. 'We drew up a list of trustworthy men in each district'—such was the confidence of the missionaries and Church leaders, Qü, Xü and Si, in their integrity. Each claim was to be investigated and confirmed locally and then by the elders. Finally all claims were to be submitted to the governor. But to the mandarins it was inconceivable that claimants would submit accurate calculations and that their representatives would not inflate the figures to their own advantage. The wheels of the empire ran

on that principle. To get the right amount, ask for more and expect a reduction. From Taigu on August 8, Hoste wrote to Stevenson:

> The (*daotai*) wished to take twenty or thirty per cent from whatever was claimed, but to this I demurred, as I felt that compliance was virtually admitting that the Christians were exorbitant in their estimate. The Christians were not making charge for the loss of their crops, nor for the loss of time or expenses of travelling in connection with their flight ... Precautions are being taken against possible exorbitant claims ... The (*daotai*) looked rather blue when I declined his proposition ... On our return (to Taiyuan) we (the CIM) shall present a carefully made-out estimate, and then tell him that we do not want any of it, and I shall endeavour to explain the grounds for this action.[1436]

The team of investigators then split up and toured the province to learn all they could and to consult with church leaders in each place. Finally a letter addressed to all churches linked with the CIM set out the standard of action to be taken. 'The Lord's honour and not simply our own affairs' should be safeguarded.

> Christians who have had relatives murdered and are willing that they should have laid down their lives for the Lord's sake, and do not wish to report the case to the official, will be following the best course ... Those who have been wounded and are maimed or disabled, but who have property and are able to support themselves, and are willing to forgive their enemies and therefore do not wish to report the matter to the Official, will do well. (Others should follow the normal process of law for 'the action of the temporal Government in vindication of law and order is also recognised as being of God') ... There must be no carelessness or overstating, lest by your falseness the Lord's name be dishonoured before your enemies; and the Official and the Church will then have nothing to do with your affairs ...

The matter of recantation posed another problem for missionaries and church elders to face together.

The ground we have taken is that anyone recanting places himself by his own act outside the Church, and it remains for those concerned to consider the question of his readmission. We find that there have been great varieties in the degree and manner of recantation. In many cases certificates were received from the Mandarin as a temporary expedient for averting extreme penalties while the storm lasted. Many Local Officials shrank from carrying into effect the sanguinary orders of the Governor (Yü Xian) and hit upon this device (to) tide over the difficulty. Other cases (present) varying degrees of conformity to idolatry. You can understand how extremely difficult our position is ... by any want of sympathy and love, nothing could be easier than to quench the smoking flax and simply drive the poor, disheartened, suffering Christians to despair ... Not to deal clearly and decidedly with the matter would mean the end of all discipline and Church order in the future.[1437]

Paul himself had exhorted the Corinthian Church, 'you ought to forgive and comfort him [a repentant believer], so that he will not be overwhelmed by excessive sorrow. I urge you, therefore, to reaffirm your love for him' (2 Corinthians 2.7–8 NIV).

Hearing in place after place the grim details of torture and maiming, terror and coercion, shame and bitter grief over denying Christ, Dixon Hoste endured what he called 'the most painful experience of my life'. After Taiyuan, Taigu and Pingyao, he and Ernest Taylor toured the eastern cities of Lucheng, Lu'an and Hongtong, while Orr Ewing took the western route and Tjader went to Yuncheng in the south.[1438] Meeting at Qüwu they returned up the central plain through Linfen to Taiyuan again. Nowhere could they spend as much time as the Christians wished. There was always more to be said and done. They had to move on. A veiled report about one missionary woman's body having been sexually abused, to the deep distress of relatives, they carefully investigated and found to be untrue. Even in such circumstances the Boxers had shown restraint far exceeding that of some foreign soldiers.

Chinese deacons were to take relief funds to Datong and the northern region pending the arrival of more missionaries, as soon as John Stevenson could send them. Shen Daotai of the Foreign Office was pressing for not only men but women to return. Only the minister's and consuls' restrictions kept them back. Cassels had taken his wife home to Langzhong, to Sir Ernest Satow's alarm and Hudson Taylor's concern. But more women and children were being held in the oven of Chongqing at greater risk from illness than from harm in their country homes. To change the envoy's mind, Hoste visited him and wrote persuasively, citing Shen Daotai's assurances until given a free hand again. By the end of 1901 all refugees had left Shanghai and either returned to their work or home on leave. Very few 'stations' were still closed.[1439]

The Shanxi Church were more than ready for the help and comfort of missionaries, not least those who had been their friends before the crisis. Eva French and Matilda Way soon won permission to wait on the doorstep at Huolu, ready to re-enter Shanxi. Hoste hoped that when experienced missionaries returned they would do nothing to take control or exercise too strong an influence over less mature Christians—'not that we lord it over your faith, but we work with you for your joy' (2 Corinthians 1.24 NIV). 'The former basis of full independence', assisted by missionaries, led to a stronger church than joint leadership and responsibility by Chinese and missionaries together.[1440]

Governor Ceng and Timothy Richard (June–October 1901)

With his summons to help the governor of Shanxi, Timothy Richard's great opportunity had come. Reparations should include the establishment in Shanxi of the university he had dreamed of for years. When he discussed with Dixon Hoste in Shanghai the formation of an inter-mission team to settle indemnities in

Shanxi, Hoste told him the CIM's decision to accept no compensation for lives lost, bodily injury or loss of property. Applying indemnities to even as good an object as setting up a university would have the CIM's approval, but could not be in the Mission's name. Money obtained by taxation and fines could rightly compensate Chinese victims in the normal process of law, or be devoted, at Richard's instigation, to a Chinese institution for modern education in the province, but must not be levied to indemnify the CIM. So great a crime against her own people as well as foreigners could not be ignored by China's government. A university built by the government with funds declared to have been declined for the best motives by injured parties could only benefit the country by dispelling ignorance and prejudice, while acknowledging official liability.

Timothy Richard proposed to Governor Ceng and the emperor's plenipotentiaries (led by Li Hongzhang) that a fine of half a million taels (about £100,000 at that time) spread over ten years should be imposed and used for educating the province's ablest young men in Western learning. China's hope lay in a new generation alive to a progressive world. 'Fifty thousand taels a year for ten years would be a trifling sum for so large a province' to spend on the cream of its own people—especially while the classical examinations were in abeyance under the Peace Protocol. The plenipotentiaries at once approved the plan and put all administration of the funds, appointment of university staff and choice of curriculum into Richard's hands for ten years. But the implied insult to the governor and a strong party of officials at Taiyuan soured his relationship with them. They also resented the emphasis on Western learning, and launched a rival college of Chinese classics.

Richard's diplomacy was put to the test. After long negotiation they adopted the compromise that both disciplines should be combined in a secular university, and harmony was restored. Moir Duncan was installed as Principal and taught

comparative religion, while Christian activities were carried on as an extra-curricular optional alternative.[1441]

When D. E. Hoste submitted a statement of the CIM's losses to Shen Daotai and Governor Ceng, and added that no compensation would be claimed or even accepted by the CIM or the associate missions for whom he could speak, they were incredulous. He explained the Christian thinking behind this decision and suggested that a statement by the governor to be hung in each newly-erected chapel, would be enough. The result was extraordinary—a proclamation by the governor on October 11, 1901, placarded wherever the CIM had worked and suffered, throughout Shanxi. It 'went a long way to re-establish friendly feelings when the missionaries returned' and went further than years of preaching to acquaint the educated and uneducated with 'the teaching and spirit of Jesus'. In the proclamation the name of Jesus was honoured each time it was used, by being raised above the next (vertical) line.

> The Mission, in rebuilding these Churches with its own funds, aims in so doing to fulfil the command of the SAVIOUR OF THE WORLD, that all men should love their neighbours as themselves, and is unwilling to lay any heavy pecuniary burden on the traders or on the poor. I, the Governor, find ... that the chief work of the Christian religion is in all places to exhort men to live virtuously. From the time of their entrance into China, Christian missionaries have given medicine gratuitously to the sick and distributed money in times of famine ... They regard other men as they do themselves, and make no difference between this country and that. Yet we Chinese ... have treated them not with generous kindness, but with injustice and contempt, for which we ought to feel ashamed ... contrasting the way in which we have been treated by the missionaries with our treatment of them, how can anyone who has the least regard for right and reason not feel ashamed of this behaviour? ... JESUS, in his instructions, inculcates forbearance and forgiveness, and all desire for revenge is discouraged. Mr Hoste is able to carry out

these principles to the full; this mode of action deserves the fullest approval. How strangely singular it is that we Chinese, followers of the Confucian religion, should not appreciate right actions, which recall the words and the discourses of Confucius, where he says, 'Men should respond with kindness to another's kind actions.'

I charge you all, gentry, scholars, army, and people, those of you who are fathers to exhort your sons, and those who are elder sons, to exhort your younger brothers, to bear in mind the example of Pastor Hoste, who is able to forbear and forgive as taught by JESUS to do, and, at the same time, to exemplify the words of Confucius ... Let us never again see the fierce contention of last year ... to enforce this on all persons, soldiers or people, is the aim of this special proclamation, which let all take knowledge of and obey.[1442]

The governor also allocated another ten thousand taels to the relief of Christians.

Dixon Hoste returned to Shanghai, leaving Archibald Orr Ewing, Tjäder and Ernest Taylor to help the churches to return to normal life, and missionary replacements to find their feet in Shanxi. Geraldine's brother, Dr Whitfield Guinness, was one of these. But not until late 1902 did the foreign governments allow single women to re-enter the province, when the Greens returned to Huolu and released Eva French and Matilda Way to do so. Floods of new and returning missionaries were by then filling the Shanghai premises and dispersing 'over the bodies of the slain' (in Ludwig von Krapf's phrase) to every corner of China.

The *Chinese Recorder* carried long lists of arrivals from each continent, to reinforce each mission. In September 1901 it also quoted from the close of Tertullian's 'Apology' before pagan judges: 'The Christian blood you spill is like seed you sow, it springs from the earth again and fructifies the more'—conventionally reduced to the familiar words, 'The blood of the martyrs is the seed of the Church.'[1443] The martyr T. W. Pigott had written in May 1896:

When I first reached this province there was not one baptised Christian here. Now there are many hundreds ... and a large number of stations where thousands are brought under Christian influence. How shall we look on the investment of our lives and labour here, even from the near standpoint of one hundred years hence? ... The work pressed home now will make all the difference a few years hence.[1444]

Only four years later he laid down his life, and the church in Shanxi went on from strength to strength. How shall we look on the investment of our lives and labour one hundred years later?

Return of the 'fat puss' (1901–08)

If Ci Xi's sharp mind, sharp tongue and sharp claws were the essence of her strong personality, 'a certain cosiness' also characterised her. Her love of flowers, of silks, of porcelain and jade, of carpets, of decorum and of opera were as much part of her. The lap of luxury and her innate cruelty earned her the epithet 'fat puss'. She could make emperor, prince and minister tremble, and fussed over domestic detail as well as 'any thrifty housewife'.[1445]

After the court's arrival at Xi'an on October 28, 1900 she quickly amassed gifts, tribute and her own replacements for lost antiquities and furniture from her Peking palaces. Operatic performances by three large troupes amused her; she fed well while the people were close to starving; and with generous make-up she looked twenty-five years younger than her true age. The Guang Xü emperor, meanwhile, took responsibility for the disasters of 1900 and looked worn and unhappy, anxious and sad, 'one of the most pathetic figures in history'.[1446]

She could afford to wait until the Peace Protocol was signed on September 7, 1901, and foreign forces withdrew from Beijing before the advance guard of her court set out for the capital on October 6. Her advisers had impressed on her the importance to the stability of the empire and dynasty of an early return, but she alone would decide how and when. That decision rested upon her astrologers' notions. She and her entourage followed on October 20. But at Kaifeng, another ancient capital, she delayed to celebrate her 66th birthday on November 14 with more theatricals, and chose the auspicious 7th of January, 1902, to re-enter Beijing.

The loyal old statesman, Li Hongzhang, died on November 7 in his seventy-ninth year, hoping she had learned her lesson. She had his name engraved with the greatest of China's statesmen in the Temple of Faithful Ministers where it would be venerated, and elevated him posthumously

to marquess of the first rank.[1447] Too late to change appreciably, she saw that China must adapt to a fast-changing world, and carried her Imperial Council with her. But the most they could attain was a few relatively futile measures dictated by the old aim of preserving Manchu domination in China. An imperial decree from Kaifeng established state education in Western learning, and banished her puppet Heir Apparent, Pu Jün, a rampant young lecher, to join his father, the disgraced minister Prince Tuan in exile. In his place she named Pu Lun, a grandson of the Dao Guang emperor. But to cover the traces of her guilt she honoured the Pearl Concubine posthumously for 'committing suicide in loyalty to the Empress Dowager and Emperor when unable to catch up with the court on their departure'! Ci Xi had not changed.

More genuinely she conferred on Sir Robert Hart the distinction of Junior Guardian of the Heir Apparent for his advice and assistance in the peace negotiations—having unleashed the wolves against him only eighteen months earlier. His home and library, and the lifetime's diaries of an intimate observer of the Chinese scene, had gone up in flames, searing his spirit inconsolably. The honour was poor consolation for the underlying wish to exterminate him with all other foreigners. Elevation in 1908 to the brevet title of President of a Ministry added little comfort in the year when he received doctorates from Oxford and Dublin universities and the freedom of the Cities of London and Belfast and Borough of Taunton to add to his baronetcy and high honours from thirteen other nations.[1448]

Li Hongzhang was only one of Ci Xi's influential men to die. Kang Yi died during his flight from the capital, on his way to join her. As for Yong Lu, during his last two years he was in effect the prime minister and ruler of the empire, for if he disapproved of any action she might take, she would reverse it. The news of his death moved her deeply. Since their youth Yong Lu had remained her dashing hero (see p 247), and in his prime and maturity had closely resembled Li Hongzhang in astute wisdom. As soon as possible after the fall of Beijing he had rejoined her. Without him and Liu Kunyi she was left with two irresolute men to look to, Prince Qing and the scholar viceroy Zhang Zhitong—and the ambitious Yüan Shikai replacing Li Hongzhang as viceroy of Zhili, elder statesman and leading member of the Imperial Council.

The anti-foreign clique of Manchus and swashbucklers had finally been shaken off when she left Xi'an: Tong Fuxiang to banishment in the north-west, and Yü Xian to have his throat cut at Lanzhou.[1449] She was free to pursue a policy of 'benign affability' towards her conquerors. The foreign governments had taken the grotesque position of pretending that their troops were helping the Chinese government to put down an insurrection, even while their armies were routing Chinese generals and capturing Chinese cities. Instead of reinstating the emperor and curbing Ci Xi as press and missions urged with one voice from long experience in China, the reverse had become the diplomats' choice.[1450]

Her message sent ahead from Kaifeng welcomed the foreigners to watch her arrival at the Tartar City and the ministers to be received in the Central Throne Hall in the palace as soon as she arrived.

She and the emperor crossed the Yellow River in a specially constructed dragon boat, resplendent in gilt and lacquer. From Zhengding they completed the long journey by that once diabolical fire-carriage, the train. Luxuriously furnished compartments decorated with imperial silks for the emperor and dowager empress made the return triumphant. Foreign onlookers on a high balcony at the great gate into the Tartar City watched as the procession approached and 'finally the Imperial palanquins (of yellow silk flashing with gold) advanced at an almost incredible speed between two lines of kneeling soldiers.' They 'seemed to move as fast as Tartar cavalry'.

At the gate they stopped for simple rites of home-coming and the emperor and dowager empress alighted—the emperor 'sad, silent and self-contained'. The rites over, the Old Buddha looked up to the balcony, raised her small hands together under her chin and made a few little bows, to a burst of applause. 'All was forgiven and forgotten!—by the magic of Old Buddha's gesture. Something told us that the return of the court to Peking marked a turning point in history.' The sacrifice of a few anti-foreign notables and a purr from the 'fat puss' and all was affability for seven more years. Parties for the diplomats' womenfolk, photography, even sittings for an American portraitist, and then back to normality, as nearly as could be, with many familiar faces missing. 'A corrupt and cankered Court had been preserved at the expense of the nation . . . There does not appear to be much hope for China now,' wrote Alicia Bewicke Little, ending her biography of Li Hongzhang.

A turning point in the history of China it certainly was. But Ci Xi's *coup d'état* against Guang Xü had been 'the bomb that destroyed the dynasty'. No empire could hold together with its emperor a captive, its reigning family disrupted by repeated disregard of the true line of descent, and flouting of tradition. 'Like any convict on parole, obliged daily to visit the police', Guang Xü still had daily to perform the ritual *ketou* of obeisance to Ci Xi until he died.

Changing China, changing world (1902–08)

The Victorian era ended with the queen's death on January 22, 1901, and the ascension of the sixty-year-old Edward VII. Her Diamond Jubilee in 1897 had been marked by 'a vast military thanksgiving parade in London, with proud contingents from every continent (and) the little old lady in black . . . driving (in an open carriage) through dense, cheering crowds' to St Paul's Cathedral. Her sense of vocation had found expression in new moral standards for her nation. But colonialism in the guise of moral obligation had reached its peak, and her successive governments had been deaf and blind to the national conscience about Britain's opium curse on China. King Edward's brief hedonistic reign and achievement of the *entente cordiale* in Europe then supplied a new climate for relations with China, cooperation in her strong drive against opium in ports, cultivation and consumption, and for the missionary movement.

Yehonala (Yehe Nara), who became Ci Xi, born on November 3, 1835, and an empress for decades, outlived Victoria by seven years, long enough to see the changes she had fought to prevent. Her own change of mind (not belief) on reform began in January 1901 when she solicited advice from her ministers, viceroys and envoys abroad. Self-seeking and 'precedent', die-hard conservatism, had brought the nation close to ruin, she confessed, and modernisation had so far proceeded to no greater extent than the 'skin and hair', the superficial aspect of Western technology. How should China become rich and powerful again? Memorialists led by Liu Kunyi and Zhang Zhitong had quickly responded, but with nothing new. No new solution existed. Foreign study and travel would make up for deficient education at home; that outworn education must be reformed to include Western learning alongside the Chinese classics. Corruption, sinecures, the official sale of appointments and fatuous military examinations based on physical prowess must all be eliminated.[1451]

It was all so clearly true, though it had provoked a dynastic crisis and *coup d'état* in 1898. This time Ci Xi declared, 'There is no other way out', much as she hated it. But the changes must be gradual. Zhang Zhitong detected duplicity, 'a noisy demonstration without substance', compounded by the appointment of incapable Manchus to implement the changes and ensure slow progress. But other startling edicts in Ci Xi's name took all by surprise: 'the customs and beliefs of Manchus and Chinese are now alike'—so after 250 years of the Qing dynasty's strict prohibition, intermarriage was to be permitted; the cruel custom of foot-binding (by which Chinese (never Manchu) girls' feet were tightly bandaged from infancy, to turn all but the big toe under the instep) was denounced; and selected Manchu clansmen were to be educated abroad. The Imperial University of Peking was re-established with a Chinese chancellor and W. A. P. Martin as president of the foreign faculty—a phoenix from the Boxer bonfire.

Timothy Richard's University of Shanxi became a resounding success, a state institution under foreign control, but a model for other provinces. His dream of such a college or university in each provincial capital was slow in coming to fruition. Neither funds nor faculties of sufficient calibre could be mustered at short notice. The Russo-Japanese war of 1904–05 brought progress to a halt. But the portentous exhibition of a small newly-modernised Asian country crushing the mighty Russian forces on land and sea drove the Chinese nation to acquire the knowledge that made it possible.

From undisputed military possession by Russia of the whole of Manchuria at the dawn of 1902, and a Russo-Chinese Convention, signed on April 8 providing for Chinese authority to be re-established in stages, Russian dominance was challenged by Japan in the autumn of 1903. Russia in Manchuria threatened Japan's hold on Korea, and also Japan's intended expansion of trade with Manchuria. On February 8, 1904, Japan broke off diplomatic relations with Russia and war broke out—to decide who should dominate the three Manchurian provinces of the Chinese empire, the home of the Manchu rulers of the subject Chinese millions! So low had the Qing dynasty sunk. Russia was worsted on land and sea. The Russian Baltic fleet reached the war zone on May 27, 1905, and was practically annihilated by Admiral Togo's fleet in the Sea of Japan the next day.

China had declared her neutrality, and the foreign powers obtained from Japan and Russia an undertaking not to cross the Zhili border, lest the Beijing court and government panic and take to 'the Imperial Chariot' again. On June 8, 1905, President Theodore Roosevelt urged both nations to talk peace, and the Treaty of Portsmouth, New Hampshire, was signed on September 5. Manchuria was to be evacuated by both powers and taken over by China, except for the Liaodong peninsula and ports which Japan was to lease. Chinese sovereignty and an 'open door' to other nations were recognised. No indemnities were claimed, and Japan returned to Russia the northern half of Sakhalin Island. Japan had settled the old score from 1894 when a Russian general menacingly laid his sword across the Sino-Japanese treaty at Yantai, and forbade its ratification.

Japan's victory 'electrified' China.[1452] A new sense of nationality seized reform-minded Chinese. Thousands of Chinese students in Japan, hundreds in America and scores in Europe reacted strongly. In China itself 'student agitations swept the country, and the government took action.' Young China imposed its will on old China, and a new commercial, cultural and educational 'invasion' of China by Japanese began.

Before this, sporadic anti-foreign outbreaks had punctuated the relative peace following the Boxer rising—relative because demobilised troops and outlaws resorted to widespread brigandage. A neo-Boxer movement in Sichuan cost the lives of 1,000 Catholics and posed a serious threat from 1902–04. Yet Cassels called for thirty more missionaries; the requests for their teaching were more than could be met. On August 15, 1902, a mob, not politically motivated, murdered two young men of the CIM, J. R. Bruce of Australia and R. H. Lowis of Britain, at Chenzhou in Hunan. A cholera epidemic had been attributed to the medicines they dispensed. But a strong gunboat reaction by the British led to a fine of £10,000 being exacted and offered to the CIM, who declined it.[1453]

The two most obdurate provinces, Henan and Hunan, had in fact opened up after the Boxer fever ended. An editorial in the *Chinese Recorder* celebrated 'a hearty welcome (to missionaries) almost without exception' by both officials and people throughout the empire, so that 'a positive danger' had arisen 'that soon there (would be) more difficulty in keeping people out of the Church than getting them in'.[1454] Popularity and false motives went hand in hand. The refugees from Henan were received back with deference and apologies. Howard Bird and Alfonso Argento met wide-eyed astonishment. Everyone 'knew' they had been 'killed'. In 1905 Bird learned that at 'the place (Xiao Yao) where I was set upon and robbed of all my clothing . . . there is quite a little band of Christians and nearly fifty enquirers . . . They (repeatedly) say that my sufferings were the beginnings of their interest in the gospel. One man is the opium sot in whose room I hid . . . now broken off opium.' Robert Powell of Zhoujiakou waited until the dowager empress had left Kaifeng and then with considerable courage 'occupied' the city, the first to do so since Henry M. Taylor made his risky reconnaissances in 1875 (see pp 264, 269, 281).[1455]

An official had said to Griffith John, 'When Peking wants Hunan opened it will open.' The appointment of the right governor was the key. In May 1901 Governor Yü Liansan lent his steam launch to Griffith John, and everywhere on the way to Hengzhou and back to Wuhan he and his LMS companions were received 'with every demonstration of respect' and friendship. 'The old opposition is dead, the city (of Changsha) is open . . . We met with nothing but civility.' The highest mandarins asked the LMS to move in.[1456] Also, in May 1901, Dr F. A. Keller of the CIM moved from Chaling to Changsha and with the authorities' help ('they have been extremely kind') was installed in good premises on June 11, the start of his celebrated hospital. But in November 1902 inflammatory proclamations by a provincial commissioner led to several hundred volunteering to rid the province of foreigners again. Change involved instability. When Ci Xi ordered the arrest of reformers in Beijing and one was 'most brutally beaten to death' in 1903, she revived terror such as they had suffered during the *coup d'état* in 1898. Reactionary violence lurked wherever progress was to be found.[1457]

The Spectator hailed the Christian survival of the Boxer holocaust, and the reasonable approach to compensate, as 'a pure cause nobly vindicated'. But 'blind prejudice, lies and rumours' about missionaries calling for vindication of their wrongs were aired in the world press. The *Chinese Recorder* replied with the proverb, 'A lie will go round the world while truth is putting its boots on', expressing missionary concern that false accusation, like anti-foreign indoctrination, was not easily reversed. The end of the Boxer outbreak was not the end of the story. The greatest change in the CIM's experience and another test of resolution, unlike the Boxer years but potentially disastrous, was approaching.

In Switzerland, building strength to return (1900–02)

For the first year in Switzerland Hudson Taylor kept the one aim before him, to get fit enough to return to China. He was only sixty-eight and had more fight in him. The pace of life had overstrained him. Incessant responsibility, travel, public speaking and the tidal wave in China mounted to terrifying heights. But rest and exercise had often done wonders before. He knew how to shelve the stresses and relax with the glory of mountains and Alpine meadows, botany and photography, walking-stick and ice-axe as his companions.[1458] When the Boxer wave broke over the men, women and little children he loved, Chinese and missionary, the agony of heart had been as much as he and Jenny could endure. The poetry of Geraldine Howard Taylor's chapter on this period gives what she observed through being with them while completing her biography of Hsi Shengmo. Escape to the mountainside, to come home tired out, kept him sane and soon would give him strength to get back, he hoped. If only to weep with those who wept, his presence might help to bring the Mission through.

So for the first six months they stayed at Davos-Dorf in eastern Switzerland, where the calm climate and relatively constant sunshine had made it a popular health resort. By January 1901 the nightmare in China was over and the Mission was reoccupying 'safe' territory. Hudson Taylor was little better in health, but they were cold in Davos and William Berger's widow was ill at Cannes, so they went to be near her for three months, and to see the C. H. S. Greens, convalescing from their Boxer ordeal and typhoid. By April Hudson Taylor had recovered so far as to visit Britain, and met survivors of the grim death marches through Shanxi and Henan.

While in England, they received a letter from Lord Northampton, President of the Bible Society (the sixth marquess who with the Marquess of Aberdeen bought 'Gordon's Calvary' and garden tomb), offering to make Hudson Taylor a vice-president, as 'an expression of our sympathy with the China Inland Mission and our admiration of its Founder and Director'. He accepted gratefully. They visited Jenny's father, eighty-four and in retirement at Tenterden in Kent, who showed them his considerable geological collection, a lifetime's hobby. Then briefly to Germany and back to Geneva on May 23.

While Dixon Hoste and his team were in Shanxi, W. B. Sloan and Henry Frost came to Geneva for two weeks of intensive consultation about Mission affairs. Hudson Taylor thought highly of both men and they found him still mentally well able to advise on complex and thorny subjects. Geneva in July became too hot for comfort and the Taylors moved across the lake to Chamonix on the French side and to the hamlet of Trelechant at the head of the valley, below Mont Blanc. A letter of August 13 tells of his walking and climbing again, still intent on recouping strength to get back to China. Amelia, his beloved sister, and her surgeon son came to stay with them in September, and Ben borrowed Hudson Taylor's well-worn ice-axe to visit the glacier with a guide.

Bought in July, it had already seen good use. On August 15 Hudson had 'startled' Jenny by saying, 'I must have had a slight stroke', for one side of his body was 'weak', but a fall when his foot slipped on pine needles might explain it, they decided.[1459]

When Amelia left, they returned to Geneva for six weeks of 'the greatest mental effort of recent years', ploughing through 'voluminous pages' from Stanley Smith, and from Handley Moule, Bishop of Durham, refuting Smith's views on 'conditional immortality' and 'final restoration of unbelievers'. The Evangelical world had become less dogmatic about interpretations of biblical statements on this subject, and in August Hudson Taylor remarked to William Sharp that if the CIM were being organised in 1901 instead of 1865, the clause in the 'P and P' on 'the eternal punishment of the lost' might have been worded differently. It was not that his own attitude had changed, but that 'the Mission having been formed as it is, should not now be altered, our workers having joined it on this basis'. It would also be unfair to donors who supported the Mission with this understanding.

The historic principle of the CIM, unity on theological fundamentals and mutual tolerance of different views on lesser issues, made harmony and cooperation possible while wide variation existed along denominational and eschatological lines. Stanley Smith wrote, 'I admit that final restoration is not *clearly revealed* in Scripture, hence I cannot preach it. Any hope I may privately hold concerning it, is based on premises which are open to question.' On this undertaking Smith's return to China in the CIM was agreed by the London Council.[1460]

Geneva proved restless, and wanting peace and quiet they retreated to Chateau d'Oex for the three months of November 6 until mid February, deliberately not settling anywhere. During part of January and February 1902, Hudson Taylor was 'at his best', but after another visit to London with full days and jolting vehicles, he became 'very exhausted and feeble' (the word they used for 'frail') with a recurrence of pain

in his spine. Returning by gentle stages to Switzerland, they stayed for three weeks at Vevey and Veytaux , before moving to Geneva until early July. In May his extreme frailty often made Jenny 'very concerned' and for four months he depended on a 'Bath chair' (cap??) whenever he left the house. May 21 was his seventieth birthday. But weak or strong he was still General Director of an expansive international society. They faced the sad truth that his active days were over; he could never return to China as Director, if at all. He must act without delay to provide for his decease.[1461]

Painful transition
(June–December 1902)

The frailty that threatened to end Hudson Taylor's life was poor preparation for winding up his part in Mission affairs and handing over to others. Jenny wrote of 'both head and legs so powerless'. But his capacity for bracing himself to face the inescapable came to his rescue again. Before he could relax he must steer the transference of his responsibility to Dixon Hoste through several stages. First, a contingency measure in case of his own early death. By the end of June he had provisionally appointed Hoste to succeed him in that event, 'subject to the approval of the various Councils', and had begun consultations about the substantive appointment.[1462] The time had also come for Walter B. Sloan to be recognised as assistant or associate Home Director with Theodore Howard. And agreement needed to be reached on procedures for the appointment of future general directors, should any die or be incapacitated before naming their successor constitutionally. This had then to be legally incorporated in Mission documents. And the scintillating, much-loved but frequently trouble-prone Stanley Smith's relationship with the CIM had to be clarified once and for all. On arrival in China he had returned to expounding his views in terms of a 'larger hope' disrupting the community at Chefoo.

With an indefinitely prolonged period of ill-health ahead of them, the time had come for the Taylors to make a more settled home somewhere. The difficulty of access by jolting coach excluded Chateau d'Oex, so they took rooms in the Pension La Paisible at Chevalleyres above Vevey, which they could reach by boat from Geneva. The *pension* suited them ideally. Facing south across the lake, with a 'glorious outlook over the Savoy Alps and up the Rhone Valley', their rooms had the added boon of a glazed veranda such as they loved, idyllic for an invalid. The proprietors, M et Mme Bonjour, did all they could for their comfort, sending their meals up to them. They quickly became good friends. So this was home for the next two years.

Within a week of their settling in, news came of the Mission treasurer James Broumton's wife having died at Chefoo. A raging epidemic of cholera was spreading from port to port up the China coast and Yangzi River. Danger of infection threatened all exposed to it. A few days later a letter came from Walter Sloan, whose brother-in-law, in business in Swatow, had just died of cholera. But he had 'appalling news' to give them. 'Be alone before you read on,' he told Jenny. In the Boys' School at Chefoo, Amelia's grandson, Gershom, the only son of Hudson Broomhall and 'so promising', had fallen ill with what was thought to be ptomaine poisoning, and died within four hours. They buried him beside Mrs Broumton. Nine others then died in quick succession on the same day, and three later. Charles Fishe's son, Howard (Jenny's nephew); Duncan Kay's son, Stewart; Dr Parry's son, Herbert; and Gray-Owen's two sons, Hugh and Norman, at one blow—these all belonged to the CIM family. Worse still in one respect, the remaining seven had been committed to the Mission's care by other societies, by imperial customs officers and by merchant homes.

'Even in this . . . calamity (God) is putting to the proof our confidence in His love and faithfulness,' Sloan wrote. Hudson Broomhall acknowledged the Chefoo news by telegram: 'God makes no mistakes', and in a letter echoed Hudson Taylor on the death of his daughter, Grace, in 1867 (see 1, p 815): '"Who plucked this flower?"

said the gardener. "The Master", was the answer. And the gardener held his peace.' (On the first anniversary of Gershom's death another son was born to them.) There happened to be a ringleader of disorder in the school who escaped when the others died. Driven to think deeply by his brush with death, he turned to Christ. This, too, softened the blow. A full consular investigation soon established with the help of bacteriologists in Shanghai that cholera, a cause regarded as less avoidable even with utmost care, not food poisoning, had been to blame.[1463]

When case after case of typhoid fever in the mission followed the cholera, Hudson Taylor urged Stevenson to insist that missionaries eat or drink no uncooked food of any kind. 'All our people ought to know this.' He was still reading widely.

A letter from the saintly Francis Coillard of the Upper Zambesi came as strong comfort to Hudson Taylor.

> From the very beginning of all the trouble and calamities in China, I have suffered with you as much as the human heart is able, we ourselves here passing at the same time through deep affliction ... Your sorrows, your bereavements are ours, they are the sorrows and bereavements of the Church ... They will, by the example of those modern martyrs, stimulate a spirit of truer and more joyous consecration.[1464]

When Stanley Smith had agreed that his views on 'eternal punishment', 'conditional immortality' and 'the final restoration of all' were philosophical and could not be shown positively to be taught by Scripture, he had undertaken to keep them to himself. As long as he vacillated, doubting his own arguments, and did not confuse Chinese Christians or colleagues, endless patience and persuasion in dealing with him, a lovable friend for seventeen years, seemed the right policy. The apostle's advice 'Accept him whose faith is weak, without passing judgment on disputable matters' (Rom 14.1 NIV) had its relevance to SPS. But when he wrote 'declaring himself a positive believer in the final restoration of all', he distanced himself from the CIM and the 'Principles and Practice' he had signed. Hudson Taylor still hoped against hope to bring him back to biblical realities, but Dixon Hoste and the China Council were less sanguine. He was doing too much damage. Another missionary had resigned over the issue.

Worse still, Henry Frost was 'greatly distressed' that 'SPS' had gone back to China with strong reservations. And Walter Sloan shared his objections. Howard and Geraldine in America as travelling speakers for the Student Volunteer Movement for a year already, wrote urgently to Hudson Taylor. In America and Canada, the CIM would be condemned even for leniency towards Stanley Smith. If he remained in the Mission, Frost himself might feel it necessary to resign from his position as Home Director, but as quietly and inconspicuously as possible. The issue was becoming one of disruption of the Mission rather than one of Smith's beliefs.[1465]

Howard and Geraldine Taylor were fulfilling their undertaking for the SVM with outstanding success, Frost reported. And the CIM was benefiting greatly. Could they be spared for another year to continue the good work? But behind the scenes their role as mediators was no less valuable. The 'extreme gravity' of this confused situation justified their staying, and merited Hoste travelling halfway round the world to meet with Frost and the North American Council before travelling on to Switzerland. His coming would give Hudson Taylor the opportunity he needed to go over a hundred and one other mission matters with him before responsibility for them descended on his shoulders.

In October 1902, Henry Frost visited the *pension* for two weeks of conversations with Hudson Taylor. Much as he admired Dixon Hoste, his devotion to Hudson Taylor still made the thought of his proposed retirement difficult to accept. Robert Wilder and his sister Grace, the initiators of the SVM, were in Switzerland for their health and, joined by his mother, wife and children, moved into La Paisible during

Frost's visit, until they left for Norway in April 1903.

In the company of these two outstanding men, Hudson Taylor's state of health improved, until writing to point out to Stanley Smith that he could no longer remain in the Mission. Then Hudson Taylor relapsed, but rallied to continue four days of consultations with Hoste and Sloan together and nine more with Dixon alone. In January he had written to 'Dick': 'Dear Stanley maybe led but cannot be driven . . . ought not to be driven.' In the end even 'mild and inoffensive' dealings with him had failed.

The business with Hoste and Sloan then covered a wide range of other matters. Formal appointment of Dixon Hoste as General Director in place of Hudson Taylor came first. The American Council had been impressed with Hoste as 'a man of God and a person of unusual intelligence and gifts'. And he himself could see that the time had come, when the consultations sapped Hudson Taylor's strength so that he was 'pretty well done up, with bad headache'. While Dixon plied him with questions, the old man, physically ten years older than his age, paced slowly up and down the room, sharing his wisdom and experience with his Elisha.

On November 11, Walter Sloan returned to London to become Assistant Home Director.[1466] And on November 17, before Hoste headed back to China on the 20th, Hudson Taylor gave notice to Theodore Howard of his intention to declare Hoste General Director as soon as he received confirmation from the Council. All were unanimous in welcoming him, and on January 1, 1903, Hoste's appointment and Hudson Taylor's retirement became official. At the Anniversary meetings in May the announcement was made generally public; Hudson Taylor was to be known as Founder and Consulting Director. On November 21, 1902, he wrote at length to Theodore Howard, giving his 'mature thoughts on the future conduct of the Mission', almost a last will and testament. A few quotations will show its nature, and his mental ability.

The CIM is not a Church, nor a section of the general Church, but a voluntary union of members of various denominations, agreeing to band themselves together to obey the Saviour's last command in respect to China; holding in common the same fundamental truths, accepting the directorship rule of the Mission, and receiving where needful such ministration as God may make possible from its funds …

In my judgment the Holy Scriptures do not hold out any hope for those who die impenitent …

If the Directors and Members of our Councils are godly and wise men, walking in the spirit of unity and love, they will not lack divine guidance in important matters, and at critical times; but should another spirit prevail, no rules could save the Mission, nor would it be worth saving. The CIM must be a living body in fellowship with God or it will be no further use and cannot continue.[1467]

He was frail but not decrepit. Even so, Hoste found oversights in the letter to correct. The load off his shoulders, the strain of hard mental work over, and news of single women at last re-entering Shanxi in October coming as a bouquet of joy to him, Hudson Taylor was 'quite at his best again' by Christmas. On New Year's Day, 1903, Jenny wrote to their adopted daughter, 'Millie' (Duncan), 'He finished reading his Bible through in a year for the 40th time yesterday.'

The new 'GD' (1903)

His duty done, and a man of such qualities wearing his mantle, Hudson Taylor regained strength. A succession of visitors to Chevalleyres continued through the year, among them Sister Eva of Friedenshort,[1468] and from time to time he and Jenny made short journeys, together to Thun and the Bernese Oberland, and separately to Zermatt or to see the invalid Mrs Berger in Geneva. Stanley Smith pressed for his case to be reconsidered, but all councils of the Mission were united in seeing no merit in reopening the matter. That the controversy

continued at all, with Henry Frost pressing his unwilling colleagues for a more explicit mission 'Basis of Faith', was enough.[1469]

On July 6, Hudson Taylor wrote reminding Frost that God did not allow David to build the temple 'because he was a man of war'. The time and energy spent on disagreement could lead to disaster and would be better used positively. To Hudson Taylor another aspect of the matter applied, as it had often done with others in the past, though he did not raise it with Frost— they joined the Mission on its existing constitutional basis and should not try to change it.

Dixon Hoste had taken firm hold of his leadership, modifying Hudson Taylor's proposed measures for appointing directors, and encouraging the missionaries to launch out confidently in their work, whatever the past history or present opposition. He invited the two outstanding men at the 'Home' end, Frost and Sloan, to come and resolve the so far intractable dispute together with the China Council. (John Southey, their equivalent in Australia, had not yet become Home Director.) At first when they met in February 1904, it looked as if a disastrous mistake had been made in laying all cards on the table. Failure could polarise opinion irreparably. Dixon Hoste wrote forlornly to Hudson Taylor that at one point he had prayed, 'Lord, I admit all my blunders and folly and sins, but that is just the reason why I count on Thee to undertake the matter.' Then on the third day the whole picture changed. Henry Frost's account to Hudson Taylor revealed his own amazement: 'It looked for a time as if agreement would be impossible and that disruption must follow. (Then) we found ourselves seeing eye to eye and the danger passed. We fell on our knees to praise the Lord, and rose to sing the doxology. Now we feel we can give ourselves anew to our work . . . as never in the past.'

The truth was that Dixon Hoste as Chairman had shown the God-given skill and wisdom that impressed Governor Ceng in Shanxi and were to become a byword in the missionary and secular community in China. He had no easy task. One of his first duties had been to dismiss a provincial secretary for embezzling large sums of mission money. He was not to be prosecuted if he packed up and left immediately.

In contrast, an author-traveller named W. E. Geil, after crossing China to Burma wrote to Stevenson,

> Never have I seen the people's money made to go so far as under your wise administration. My own accounts without exception were promptly, politely, properly attended to. In an age of commerce and high-pressure commercial enterprises ... it is good to find equally wise methods applied to the gifts of the Church ... Among the CIM workers (I was impressed) by a spiritual atmosphere saturated with ... kindness and commonsense ... Your missionaries receive very small pay, but ... never has salary been mentioned, but the ready reply has come, 'It is sufficient.' God bless the self-effacing missionaries of Inland China.[1470]

With all districts reoccupied since the return of the imperial court to Beijing, ample funds coming in, and good news of progress, Hoste had thoughts of renewing the advance interrupted by the Boxers. Between May 1902 and May 1903, 132 members had returned and 57 new reinforcements arrived, 189 in all. But the potential for many more suggested putting the subject to the church at large. The first step was to bring the existing Mission to its knees before God. Walter Sloan and Henry Frost, already well known and admired, were the right men to lead them in conference after conference 'for the deepening of spiritual life' at convenient centres.

The Chinese church was growing strong. The number of members in the whole of China at the end of 1902 was about one hundred thousand, with two hundred and fifty thousand adherents not yet baptised. Within four weeks, three hundred carefully vetted baptisms had been reported, and in 1903 a total of 1,688, nearly seven hundred more than in 1902, had included some distinguished literati. One was the son of a literary Chancellor. In Shanxi,

250 repentant former members had been reinstated, and 150 families in Pastor Hsi's district had professed faith in Christ and destroyed their idols. One of the poignant instances of reinstatement after recanting had been none other than Elder Si before his death on July 2, 1902. Still suffering from his sword wound and weeping on his bed over the sufferings of the Christians and their missionaries, in 1900 he had been menaced again and shrank from the pain. But his recantation had been a lie. He cringed in shame. When pitied and forgiven by his fellow-Christians, he had besought them to stop calling him 'Elder', he was so unworthy. But they insisted, and cared for him until he died. One congregation had managed to continue worship throughout the rising. Others as late as 1903 were still too terrified to begin again. In the Hongtong area the Christians built a chapel seating one thousand, and at Yuwu eight hundred attended a church conference.[1471] The greater danger had become the admission of false applicants.

In Sichuan a unique development highlighted the change for good in the political climate. Governor Ceng, who had dealt so strongly with Yü Xian's Boxers in Shanxi, executing their leaders, was promoted to Viceroy of Sichuan, to stamp out the neo-Boxer outbreak there.[1472] When his son immolated himself beside his mother's coffin, an imperial commendation and monument eulogised his filial piety— such was the underlying ambience of a nation grasping uncertainly at reform. But when the missionaries in Sichuan presented the new viceroy at Chengdu with an address of welcome, he replied,

> ... I earnestly hope that this insurrection may be speedily suppressed, and that both the people and the Church may enjoy tranquillity.
>
> Regarding my management of affairs in Shanxi, it was entirely owing to the fact that all the leaders of your Church were truly able to act according to the precept of the Save-the-World religion, 'Love men as thyself.' Therefore, the honour should be divided between us

I earnestly hope that ... there may be between us (also) mutual confidence and sincerity.[1473]

After only eight months, during which the neo-Boxers were recruiting members and a thousand Roman Catholic Chinese and twenty Protestants were killed, he was promoted to Guangzhou (Canton). Again the Protestant community in Chengdu wished him well, presenting him with a replica of the New Testament given to the empress dowager in 1894. He answered,

> ... my talents are few and I am not worthy of your praise. I have barely suppressed the disaffected, and have but roughly pacified the country. Besides this I have scarcely made a beginning to all the reforms that are necessary ...
>
> Chinese and foreigners are coming more and more into cordial relations, and the country enjoys a lasting peace. This fills me with joy and hopefulness ... My hope is that the teachers of (British and American Missions) will spread the Gospel more widely than ever, that hatred may be banished and misunderstanding dispelled, (creating) boundless happiness for my people of China ... My thoughts will be with you ...
>
> May the Gospel prosper!

The Literary Chancellor of Shaanxi in addressing five hundred Chinese graduates declared that missionaries had come to China to do good, and stories to the contrary should not be believed. Urging them to cultivate the acquaintance of Protestant missionaries, whom he complimented on their Christian literature and on not intervening in litigation to gain 'advantage for their converts', he said, 'If you wish to enter the Protestant Church you are at liberty to do so.' That one who had obtained the highest degree in the Empire, and occupied such a position, should speak so fearlessly and favourably of Christianity was unheard of. The graduates could hardly believe their ears. China was changing dramatically and fast.

Instability was also in evidence. To replace Governor Ceng in Shanxi, the friendly governor of Hunan, Yu Liansan, who had lent Griffith John his steam launch in 1901, was appointed to Taiyuan. But because Bruce and Lowis had been murdered in Hunan (prompting strong-arm action by the British in sending a gunboat), the foreign envoys objected. Yu Liansan's appointment was withdrawn. But Shanxi was to enjoy years of peace and prosperity under the 'model governor', Yan Xishan (Yen Hsi-span, see p 763).

Dixon Hoste knew well enough when he accepted the directorship that it was no bed of roses. In the thirty-three years he was to serve as General Director, the CIM was to grow to 1,360 members, and the Qing

2.95 Yan Xishan, 'model' governor of Shanxi in the new Republic (note the Western-style uniform with full mandarin-style sleeves)

dynasty was to founder, while revolution and massacre of the Manchus were to bring back the fears of 1900. In republican China warlords were to fly at each other's throats, militant nationalism was to be directed against foreigners again, and the emergence of communism in China and of

Japan's imperial ambition were to herald the greatest upheavals yet.

Late in July 1903, Jenny was found to have an abdominal tumour. She had been losing strength for ten months. When a surgeon on the North American Council, who was visiting Switzerland, came at Howard Taylor's request to see her, examination under chloroform showed the tumour to be inoperable. Somehow she and Hudson Taylor understood that it 'would not need to be removed', and no one disillusioned them. She remained free from pain well into 1904. Howard expected 'obstruction' and a slow agonising end to her life, but not until nine hours before she died on July 30, 1904, did she suffer greatly, and then from respiratory distress.

In these circumstances the past mattered little. Jubilee celebrations would have been incongruous. Neither September 19, 1903, the fiftieth anniversary of Hudson Taylor's sailing from Liverpool on the *Dumfries*, nor March 1, 1904, the anniversary of his reaching Shanghai, deserved to be celebrated, except in a jubilee number of *China's Millions*. 'If I had a thousand lives, China should have them', had been fulfilled as he had never dreamed when he first wrote the words. More than 1,300 men and women had joined the CIM, and unnumbered others had gone to China in other societies through his urging; 1904 was also the centenary year of the British and Foreign Bible Society. But with Jenny so ill these milestones were barely noticed.[1474]

To be within reach of medical help the Taylors moved to Lausanne for the winter, but were back in their *pension* home when news came of eighty-five-year-old Joseph Faulding's death on March 25, 1904.[1475] From April, Jenny was on liquids only and by June her diary was recording 'bad days'. On July 16 she told Geraldine, 'I only live by the day now', but continued making entries and on the 25th wrote her last letter. The next two days' diary entries were simply 'Tired all day.' A French friend who called to see her commented on her 'tranquil serenity'. Asked if she thought about the joys of heaven ahead of her, she answered characteristically, 'The Bible says more about Him than it does about heaven. No, I do not often think of heaven. He is here with me, and He is enough.'[1476] Another friend wrote to Grace Wilder of Jenny's forgetting herself to the last, 'always bright and patient, enquiring about one's health, et cetera'.

On the 29th she dictated goodbye letters to members of her family and friends, and towards midnight 'began to sink rapidly'. Fully conscious until the last quarter hour, she said repeatedly for Hudson's sake, 'No pain, no pain.' But her difficulty in breathing increased. 'For about two hours at daybreak (her 'fight for air') was so terrible that she begged (him) to pray the end might come quickly.' Afterwards he confessed that this was the hardest prayer to pray, but as he himself was suffering intensely with her he found words to ask the Lord 'to take her from me to Himself'. Again 'Never did I feel more gratitude than when my prayer . . . was answered within five minutes.'

'Death' had come, but, 'precious in the sight of the Lord is the death of his saints' (Psalm 116.15). 'She is not dead, but entered into life,' Theodore Howard wrote, 'not death but life immortal', for only her mortal body had ceased to live. Bunyan's imagery of the passing of Christiana over the last 'river' expressed Jenny's strong faith, and her family's. 'Behold, all the banks beyond the river were full of horses and chariots, which were come . . . to accompany her to the City Gate. So she . . . entered in.'

In private, Hudson Taylor was 'heartbroken and desolate that the dear person was out of reach', but at the funeral services, while others wept, he rejoiced that Jenny had 'entered into the joy of her Lord', and was composed. At the cemetery he shook hands with everyone and thanked them for coming. She had chosen the place for her grave, near the creeper-clad church tower of La Chiesaz at St Legier, in a beautiful position looking out over woods, hills and the mountains of Savoy across Lake Geneva. After Howard and

Geraldine had taken him up the Rhone Valley for a brief change of environment, he often visited 'the sacred spot in the little churchyard, sacred until the Resurrection morning'. And, all stresses ended, he steadily regained his health.

'O greatly beloved', back to China (February–June 1905)

Returning strength revived in Hudson Taylor his hope of visiting China again, and 'the Mission leaders' freed Howard and Geraldine to travel with him. The Hostes were due in Europe before long, so he planned to reach Shanghai before they left. The old zest had returned and he 'set his heart on a visit to Changsha, the capital of Hunan'.[1477] For decades Hunan had been 'the most violently anti-foreign province', and after it Henan. But conditions had greatly changed since the Boxer year. He could sail up the Yangzi in April, visit Henan by train in May and Changsha by ship, and be back at Shanghai by mid-June.

They crossed the Atlantic on the 24,000-ton White Star Line SS *Baltic*, one of the biggest ships afloat, sailing on February 15. On the way they heard news of Russia's defeat by the Japanese at Mukden, quickly followed by the loss of her fleet. The voyage from San Francisco on May 18 via Honolulu to Japan and through the 'inland sea' brought them to Wusong on April 17. The long calm journey had been a tonic to him.

A tender took them up the Huangpu River to Shanghai, as a pilot boat had taken him fifty-two years before. Then, his 'heart felt as tho' it would burst from its place'. This time all the sights, sounds and smells were familiar, charged with memories. Then, he did not know a soul in China. Now John Stevenson and friends without number thronged to welcome him at the Wusong Road mission home and offices he had planned and built. The China Council was in session, and photographs had to be taken of all together, and of Hudson Taylor with the two most senior members, Meadows and Stevenson—historic photographs, for the Council had decided in 1904 that the wearing of Chinese clothes in the ports

should be optional. In 1907 the motion was extended to other cities with large foreign communities.[1478] In an open letter thanking all who had written to welcome him, he said, as if thinking of hard times in the past and the unknown ahead, or perhaps of God's patience with his own shortcomings and unfulfilled aims: 'He does not expect or require anything in us that He is not willing and able to impart.' And again, in the simple terms he had come to use in his old age, he wrote: 'We cannot do much, but we can do a little, and God can do a great deal.' The greatness of God, his growing realisation.

At Zhenjiang he visited the graves of Maria and his children in the little cemetery among the hills, 'where he had always hoped that he might some day rest himself', and spent Easter Sunday at Yangzhou, scene of the first great riot in 1868. Speaking to young missionaries at Zhenjiang, soon to scatter inland, he said,

> You do not know what lies before you. I give you one word of advice: Walk with the Lord! Count on Him, enjoy Him ... He will not disappoint you—[echoing words he had used about two years before] 'For forty years I have made it the chief business of my life to cultivate a personal acquaintance with the Lord Jesus Christ ... No (trifling) with self-indulgence or sin— and there is no reason why the Holy Spirit should not be outpoured.'

On a new, fast-river steamer they made the journey to Hankou, and in Griffith John's home the two veterans again sang hymn after hymn together as they had often done since 1855. Fifty-one years had passed since they had cut their milk-teeth together as newcomers to Shanghai.

W. A. P. Martin came over from Wuchang on April 29 to welcome his colleague of Ningbo days, and historic photographs of the three veterans mark the occasion.[1479] The weather had been exceptionally cool, and all three were wearing overcoats. Hudson Taylor looked well. Martin had arrived in China in 1850, Hudson Taylor in 1854 and Griffith John in 1855. Joseph Edkins had reached Shanghai in 1848, but news of his death in Shanghai on April 23 came while his three good friends were together—the Joseph-Edkins with whom Hudson Taylor had made his first inland journey, and 'who had forgotten more about China than most of us ever knew', the learned A. H. Smith was to write. W. A. P. Martin, so highly honoured by China, had returned in 1902 from America, to confer with Viceroy Zhang Zhitong, about establishing a University of Wuchang. But after nearly three years as President, during much of which time Zhang was absent at Nanjing and Beijing by imperial command, 'the University existed only on paper', so Martin returned to Beijing.[1480]

The heat of summer was approaching. On May 1, Hudson Taylor, Howard and Geraldine boarded the Belgian train on the Hankow-Beijing line, and six hours later (instead of weeks of heat, dust and jolting by springless cart and wheelbarrow as in days gone by) they thundered in a cloud of smoke through a long tunnel into Henan.

At Xiangcheng, where Charles Bird had suffered so appallingly, at Zhoujiakou and the Howard Taylors' old home at Chenzhou, they met and worshipped with survivors of the Boxer atrocities and with others newly Christian. And at Taikang (another city 'opened' by the Howard Taylors) they met Bird and Ford, working as if they had never been the victims of such hatred and superstition. At place after place the venerable old man with his long white beard was feted and honoured. Scarlet satin banners with golden Chinese characters hailed him as 'Benefactor of Inland China' and 'O Greatly Beloved!' Red bunting draped the pavilions and platforms erected to refresh him. Someone tucked a copy of *Punch*, the satirical magazine, into a basket of food for him, and amazed bystanders cried, 'See, what an example to us! The venerable teacher must be at least a hundred and there he is still storing his mind with wisdom.' To Howard it seemed that 'happier days there could hardly be on earth!'

Back at the railroad and joined by Jane of Sandeberg, whom Hudson Taylor had

2.96 *Three veterans in Hankou, April 1905: W. A. P. Martin, Griffith John and Hudson Taylor*

known as the child of his first hosts in Sweden, they reached Hankou on Friday May 26, the thirty-ninth anniversary of the sailing of the *Lammermuir*. After travelling for three and a half weeks he needed to recuperate for a few days. So Griffith John, W. A. P. Martin and the leaders of several missions, the Methodist Episcopal Bishop Roots, Arnold Foster of the LMS and others came to see him at the CIM the next day, and more photographs were taken in the garden. Griffith John in particular seemed drawn to his old friend. Their attachment had always been at a deeply spiritual level, and but for his mission's insistence on a different strategy, he also would have been a trail-blazer. In the event he had become a model of the effective, city-based church planter and author of powerful Christian literature in immaculate Chinese. Of Hudson Taylor he wrote, 'I never felt more attached to him than I did . . . before he started for Changsha. I was longing to see him again on his way to Shanghai and home.'

The Japanese ship on which the Taylors were hoping to travel cheaply, ran aground, and reluctantly they had to go by 'saloon class' on the largest steamer to Changsha, with the whole accommodation to themselves. Always ready to help lovers hindered by unfavourable circumstances, Hudson Taylor invited Jane of Sandeberg and Geraldine's doctor brother, Whitfield, to travel with them. Within two days and still on board, they were engaged.

Since Charles Judd's first attempt in 1875 to gain a foothold in Hunan, and Adam Dorward's journey with Yang Cunling, his ex-soldier friend, in 1879, many persistent efforts had been made and suffering endured, until Dr Keller succeeded at Chaling. Until eight years previously not one Protestant missionary was resident in Hunan. In 1905 there were 111 of thirteen societies, and many Chinese colleagues, working from seventeen central stations. For Hudson Taylor to stand on Hunan soil and set foot in CIM premises in the last but one citadel of China to yield to the gospel, marked in a sense the Browning moment of his life. Hunan was the last province, and Kaifeng the last capital to be occupied. Simeon's prayer might well have been his own, 'Now let your servant depart in peace.'

'And all the trumpets sounded'
(June 1905)

On Friday, June 2, the first full day in Changsha, Hudson Taylor climbed without difficulty to the upper storey of the pavilion on the highest stretch of the Changsha city walls. It commanded extensive views of the great Xiang River valley and surrounding hills, and in the city the handsome temples and mansions of the rich and powerful. The governor had offered to present a site of several acres to Dr Frank Keller for a hospital, so they went to inspect it. In the afternoon the Imperial Customs superintendent and his wife invited the visitors to their home. Hudson Taylor was feeling the humid heat and had not been sleeping well, but when Chinese Christians from several Hunan churches came to meet him the next morning he addressed them in the Mission chapel—another high point, his son thought, of his father's missionary career.[1481]

He would not start a journey or even travel on the Lord's day if it could be avoided, but if the steamer captain would postpone leaving until early Monday morning, he would walk to the jetty on Sunday evening, though it would take him an hour. Otherwise he would wait for the next Thursday boat. No answer came to a telegram asking the shipping company to authorise the delay. Storm damage had cut the wires. What could they do? At this point Hudson Taylor said that he had 'always been accustomed to think that circumstances must be made to bend to the requirements of God's law, and not God's law to our convenience'. The ship's captain agreed on his own authority to wait; and an hour or two later the company's wire came through authorising the delay.

A reception for all missionaries in Changsha and his friends from Customs was planned for 4.00 p.m. on Saturday, so as he was tired he spent a quiet day, reading in a long-chair. At four he came downstairs looking fresh and well in a newly-laundered suit of Shandong silk, and chatted with the thirty or more guests from six societies over tea in the garden. Dr Keller enjoyed seeing the pure joy on Hudson Taylor's face. Then informal photographs were taken, and no one appears to have noticed that Hudson Taylor was exhausted. A photograph caught him looking drawn and supporting his head on his hand. As soon as most had gone he went up to his room, and a Dr Barrie joined him. In conversation, 'I remarked that the distinction between small and great things frequently came into my mind . . . at times of prayer After a pause . . . he said, "There is nothing small and there is nothing great; only God is great, and we should trust Him fully."' A lifetime of proving this truth had shown him that a half-sovereign in a glove (see 1, p 185) or an empire opening to the gospel against the wishes of its rulers, were neither here nor there, only God's will and God's action.

He did not feel ready for another meal, and decided to retire early for the night. Howard brought him a tray of 'good things' and prepared to read to him while

Geraldine encouraged him to eat a little. Howard went for something missing from the tray, and Geraldine stayed chatting. She was in mid-sentence when Hudson Taylor 'turned his head on the pillow and drew a quick breath'. She disregarded it until he caught his breath again, 'gasping'. Then she saw he was not conscious. She called out, and Howard and Dr Keller came, in time to see him draw his last breath. 'No cry, no word, no choking or distress.' In *Daily Light* for that evening was the verse, 'And Enoch walked with God . . . and God took him' (Gen 5.24 AV). It seemed more like translation than dying, and to the stricken son came the words, "My father, my father! the chariots of Israel and the horsemen thereof!"'[1482]

The Chinese Christians of Changsha insisted on buying the best coffin they could find, lining it beautifully, though this was normally the son's duty, and on paying for it to be taken to the ship. They gathered round his bed to say goodbye, and one old woman whispered, 'Tens of thousands of angels have welcomed him.' At Hankou, Griffith John grieved as for a brother. 'I was longing to see him again . . . What a wonderful life your father's life has been! What a work God has enabled him to do! . . . Eternity alone can show how much China owes to Hudson Taylor.'

The Yangzi ship's captain flew his flag at half-mast. Flowers and wreaths were brought aboard at every river station, till the coffin was hidden. John Stevenson met the boat at Zhenjiang, and Dixon Hoste came up from Shanghai to conduct the funeral and commit the loved body to the ground beside Howard's mother, sister and brothers, Grace, Samuel and Noel, 'in sure and certain hope of a glorious resurrection'.

After the 'Liberation' of China in 1949 the little cemetery largely disappeared beneath industrial buildings, but in 1988 Hudson Taylor's great grandson made a discovery. The former British Consulate, scene of many episodes in this history, had become a museum. There, preserved, were the monument stones, the inscriptions all intact.[1483] Only his 'dust' lay buried. His true monument is still alive and growing.

There at Zhenjiang, after the funeral, Geraldine wrote to Theodore Howard, 'Surely this is not death! He is gone from us. We know it . . . But life it is that has come suddenly into our midst, not death. He was caught away from us; he did not seem to die . . . We look up rather than into the grave, and cry instinctively—"My father, my father!—the chariots of Israel and the horsemen thereof!"' No one really mourned. The passing of Hudson Taylor was 'promotion to higher service'. No cortege but a simple Chinese procession of Chinese Christians and family and friends had been enough. The 'sound of trumpets' was on 'the other side'.

'More like translation than dying,' echoed Bunyan's concept of crossing the last river. When Valiant-for-Truth's turn came, Bunyan put into his mouth the immortal words spoken in effect by every valiant contender for the truth to follow him.

> My sword I give to him who shall succeed me in my pilgrimage, and my courage and skill to him that can get it.
>
> My marks and scars I carry with me to be a witness for me that I have fought his battles, who now will be my rewarder ...
>
> 'Death, where is thy sting?' 'Grave, where is thy victory?' So he passed over, and all the trumpets sounded for him on the other side. 'IT IS NOT DEATH TO DIE!'

In memoriam, the tributes agree (1905)

Although the primary purpose of this biography is to bring as much as possible out of the archives, our summary has now to be even more selective, especially of tributes. Two days after the coffin bearing all that remained of Hudson Taylor to await the resurrection was trans-shipped at Hankou, the missionary community together honoured him with 'spontaneous and informal' tributes. It was not a time for criticism. Arnold Foster spoke of his having stimulated the zeal and exertions of all missions in China. W. A. P. Martin, who recorded the occasion, recalled that in his *Cycle of Cathay* he had dubbed Hudson Taylor 'the Loyola of Protestant Missions in China'. And added that like Martin Luther he needed no honorific title. It was enough to know them by the names their mothers used. Griffith John remembered how a Shanghai missionary had denounced Hudson Taylor's enterprise as extravagant when seventy men and women were about to be sent inland. 'How many have you now?' John asked the Hankou secretary. 'Eight hundred,' he replied. 'Faith and prayer gave Hudson Taylor power with God,' John continued. 'Firmness and love procured him a moral sway over the hearts of men.'[1484]

A memorial article in *China's Millions* for July 1905 agreed. That over a million pounds sterling should have been contributed to the Mission without solicitation was only one indication. A column in *The Guardian* newspaper 'stated with striking precision the object and aim of Mr Taylor in his lifework: "He had but one aim—to preach CHRIST to China by any means that came to hand . . . There was nothing so real to him as the individual soul, and GOD in CHRIST for its salvation." Above all things his life exemplified the power of prayer; the value of faith in God . . . in a manner the simplest and most natural.' A member of the Society of Friends (the Quakers), remarked, 'I regard his life as one of God's best gifts to humanity . . . not to China only, but in as real a sense to the Church of Christ in all lands.'

At a CIM memorial service in Shanghai, the Mission could be allowed some hero worship, but most tried to be objective. Dixon Hoste struck a note which he and others frequently repeated,

> (Hudson Taylor's) complete concentration on the fulfilment of his divinely-appointed trust and calling. He laid aside every weight (yet) he was no ascetic, putting (aside) pleasures for the sake of doing without them, (but) to live in the world as Christ lived ... We can witness to his beautiful character ... the sources of his influence

lay in his humility, love and sympathy. He never suggested that others should go into difficulty and danger while he remained in ease and safety. He led the way. And always with a contagion of love.

Griffith John knew him well enough to give an off-the-cuff biographical review.

> He loved the Chinese with a Christ like love ... He lived for China and he died for China ... Today the Mission (has) 200 central stations, 450 outstations (with) since its foundation a total of nearly 20,000 baptisms ... It was ridiculed as the offspring of ignorance and religious frenzy; it is now universally respected as a grand civilising as well as evangelising agency ...

> It was impossible to come into close contact with Mr Taylor without feeling that he was not an ordinary man and that as a Christian he towered far above most men ... God and His love, Christ and His Cross, the Gospel as God's one remedy for China and the whole world, were realities to him. His trust in God was implicit ... He lived in Christ and Christ lived in him ...

> His heart was full of love ... His love for the Chinese was manifest to all, and they knew it. His influence over men, and especially the members of his own Mission, was very remarkable (due) in great measure to his kindliness of heart, his humility and self-denial. He was the servant of all ...

> Then he was a man of consummate commonsense ... It was emphatically so ... He knew how ... to bring the best out of them ... God had given him this work to do, and he did it. 'This one thing, I do.'

On June 13 a memorial service in London at the Mildmay Conference Hall so closely connected with Hudson Taylor and the CIM drew representatives of many societies, not only to honour the Founder's memory but 'to re-examine the foundations of the work and . . . to rise with the assurance that the foundations are of God and stand secure'.

Excerpts by definition omit much else. Theodore Howard did not hesitate to draw the parallel of the apostle Paul in his many journeys, perils, sufferings, privations and 'the care of all the churches'. On Hudson Taylor's last journey in Henan the Christians of Taikang came out to meet him, only to learn that he was too weak to come further. At once they knelt in the road and prayed, 'What have we done, Lord, that our great archbishop who brought Thy gospel to inland China, should come so many miles, and stop just one day short of our city?' He came. Of his practical competence Theodore Howard wrote much as Griffith John had spoken: 'Hudson Taylor was gifted with remarkable powers of organisation. He paid the greatest attention to detail. He was extremely particular that the funds of the Mission should be dealt with in the most economical way, and that the accounts should be kept with scrupulous exactness . . . His humility, his tenderness, and his sympathy endeared him to all.'

J. E. Mathieson, who had followed William Pennefather as director of the Mildmay Centre, introduced himself as 'a neighbour and friend of dear Mr Taylor'.

> You must remember [he said] that the great provinces of China are as big as many of our European kingdoms. With a pointer in his hand and a large map of China on the wall, he would take us from province to province and city to city, and name ... the cities, towns or stations in which the China Inland Mission was working; and not only so, but name by name he would mention every missionary in every part of those vast provinces all over China [for he constantly prayed for each and for their children] ... Because Hudson Taylor remained lowly in his own eyes, God was able to take that beloved man up and to make him a prince

Eugene Stock, 'only one of the three Secretaries of the Church Missionary Society on the platform', took up Bishop Cassels's prayer of praise to 'the Lord and not men'. '"He that exalted the humble and meek"—describes exactly what the Lord has done with Hudson Taylor.' On the Monday the newspapers had announced his death, and 'the first eulogy', published on Wednesday in *The Guardian*, had been written by a High Church bishop—'in praise of the Lord for His grace in the man'. Eugene Stock continued:

I have tried to think which of (the great missionary pioneers) our dear friend was like ... John Eliot ... Carey and Duff, Morrison and William Burns ... and Gilmour ... John Williams ... and Allen Gardiner ... Moffat and Krapf and Livingstone ... some of them, as the world would say, much greater than our dear friend; but I do not find one among them exactly like him, and I am much mistaken if we shall not in the course of years ... begin to see that Hudson Taylor was sanctioned, enabled and permitted by the Lord to do a work, not less than any of them, if, indeed, one might not say greater in some respects ... He did a mighty work for China, and he did a mighty work for the Church at home ... He was a man who saw visions, but ... they were not fulfiled quickly ... Ten years passed before more than two provinces had been occupied. But the day came ... He braved the criticisms of the smoking-rooms of Shanghai, and let the women go ... into the interior ... What a work the women have done and we owe it to the China Inland Mission which set the example! ...

It was not for the China Inland Mission that Hudson Taylor pled. I have heard him plead many times. It was China, and not China only but the world. It was just as much joy to him when men went to Africa or to Japan, or to India ... Persia ... South America or the islands of the sea ... (George) Pilkington had first intended to join the China Inland Mission, and yet without any hesitation whatever ... dear Taylor would say to me, 'The Lord send you many more such men.'

R. Wardlaw Thompson's tribute, as secretary of the LMS, was from one who had only met Hudson Taylor on public occasions.

I felt that the oldest Protestant missionary society in China ought not to be backward in expressing to the largest and most remarkable missionary organisation in that country, its sympathy on ... the loss of ... a great missionary, a great leader of missions, and in a very profound sense a prince in the Church of Christ ... The name and influence of Hudson Taylor have steadily grown and spread, even among men who have ... criticised (his) methods severely. All great men must be criticised ... They had to recognise the wonderful work God permitted him to do.

Doctor Harry Guinness, brother of Geraldine and Whitfield, and honorary director of the Regions Beyond Missionary Union, recalled visiting the Taylors in Switzerland. 'I noticed that in his prayers he was always praying for South America.' His friends, Dr and Mrs Kalley of Edinburgh, had long since won his support for their venture, 'Help for Brazil'. And Walter Sloan, who had known Hudson Taylor intimately for many years, referred to 'perhaps the most wonderful thing we have in the Mission . . . that family feeling that exists . . . Essentially one thing originated it. It was that large measure of God-given sympathy that Mr Hudson Taylor was able to afford every one of the workers with whom he came into contact.'

Walter Sloan then quoted from the story, fresh from the hand of Elder Cumming himself, of his conversation with Hudson Taylor in the train (see p 530), and added:

> God must have looked (for) someone weak enough to do such a work ... and said, 'This man is weak enough. He will do.' Those of us who knew Mr Taylor most intimately, know that that was the genuine expression of the feeling and the thought of his heart, as he came into the presence of GOD concerning this work.

> Mr Taylor ... in Chinese dress, came down to the side of a river in China one evening when the light was beginning to fade, intending to cross, and he hailed (a) boatman ... A (Chinese gentleman), dressed in silk, when the boat came near ... not seeing that Mr Hudson Taylor was a foreigner ... struck him a great blow on the side of the head and knocked him over into the mud. I heard Mr Taylor say himself how the feeling came to him ... to smite that man, and how God immediately stopped him ... The man went to get into the boat, but the boatman said, 'No, I came across at the call of that foreigner.' The (gentleman) said, 'What! You a foreigner; and ... you did not strike me back?' ... Mr Taylor stepped into the boat and replied, 'Come in and I will take you where you want to go.' On the way ... he

> (told him) the gospel of salvation which had made him ... treat in this way (one) who had struck him.[1485]

An 'Appreciation' by John Stevenson carried weight after all they had gone through together.

> His meekness and lowliness of mind, which were so characteristic, made him pre-eminently gracious, gentle, and courteous in his bearing to all ...

> Besides his long seasons of private devotion in the stillness of the night or early morning 'Pray without ceasing' was his constant habit in considering any question or difficulty that came up in the course of the day ... His courageous stepping out in faith and definite committing of himself for this stupendous undertaking marks the beginning of a distinct epoch in Church history ... [And again:] No thoughtful person can seriously contemplate the history of the China Inland Mission ... without being impressed with the statesmanlike tact and wisdom ... in all the arrangements.

The variety of sources with one voice testified to the same truths. But what would be said after months or years had passed? The historian A. H. Smith of the American Board wrote in 1907, 'His name will never be forgotten as long as Christianity lasts.'[1486] Now we have a wider and perhaps deeper perspective. After Hudson Taylor's death a meditation in his hand was found, dated 1874, when he was forty-two. It puts the praise into perspective, where it belongs, to God. In the period when he and the 'adolescent' CIM were at their lowest ebb, in Eugene Stock's words, 'pathetic in the extreme'; when Hudson Taylor was bedridden and apparently forgotten by many of his friends; when the Church's interest in China seemed non-existent; he had many lonely hours in which to think and pray. He opened a window on his soul, on the true Hudson Taylor who wanted to be like Christ, cost what it might.

> If God has called you to be really like Jesus in all your spirit, He will draw you into a life of crucifixion and humility, and put on you such demands of obedience

that He will not allow you to follow other Christians; and in many ways He will seem to let other good people do things that He will not let you do. Other Christians and ministers who seem very religious and useful may push themselves, pull wires and work schemes to carry out their schemes, but you cannot do it; and if you attempt it, you will meet with such failure and rebuke from the Lord as to make you sorely penitent. Others may brag on themselves, on their work, on their success, on their writings, but the Holy Spirit will not allow you to do any such thing; and if you begin it, He will lead you into some deep mortification that will make you despise yourself and all your good works.

Others may be allowed to succeed in making money, but it is likely God will keep you poor, because He wants you to have something far better than gold, and that is a helpless dependence on Him, that He may have the privilege (the right) of supplying your needs day by day out of an unseen treasury. The Lord will let others be honoured and put forward, and keep you hidden away in obscurity, because He wants some choice fragrant fruit for His coming glory which can only be produced in the shade. He will let others do a work for Him and get the credit for it, but He will let you work and toil on without knowing how much you are doing; and then to make

your work still more precious, He will let others get the credit for the work you have done, and this will make your reward ten times greater when Jesus comes.

The Holy Spirit will put a strict watch over you, with a jealous love, and will rebuke you for little words and feelings or for wasting your time, over which other Christians never seem distressed. So make up your mind that God is an infinite Sovereign, and has a right to do as He pleases with His own, and He may not explain to you a thousand things which may puzzle your reason in His dealings with you. He will take you at your word and if you absolutely sell yourself to be His slave, He will wrap you up in a jealous love and let other people say and do many things which He will not let you say or do.

Settle it for ever that you are to deal directly with the Holy Spirit, and that He is to have the privilege of tying your tongue, or chaining your hand, or closing your eyes, in ways that He does not deal with others. Now when you are so possessed with the Living God, that you are in your secret heart pleased and delighted over the peculiar, personal, private, jealous guardianship of the Holy Spirit over your life, you will have found the vestibule of Heaven.[1487]

1906–12: TWILIGHT OF THE QING

Flood tide of reform (1906–08)

A few quiet years remained to Ci Xi and Guang Xü, but very few. Reform movements were gaining strength and deepening gloom was descending on the centuries-old dynasty (1644–1912). Ci Xi could 'see in the dark', but the best Manchu leaders left to her could not. On her return to Beijing she had soon replaced the abundance of priceless *objets d'art* with which she liked to be surrounded. 'The wanton destruction of irreplaceable works of art, in (the) search for the Empress's hidden treasure' angered her still, but the gold plate, jewels and bullion bricked in at the bottom of a well had not been discovered. After her death the value was assessed as 99 million taels of

silver and 1,200,000 taels of gold (about £22 million sterling in 1900) apart from wealth in kind.[1488]

After the Russo-Japanese treaty signed at Portsmouth, USA, a boycott of American trade expressed the resentment of the people, especially of Canton and San Francisco over restrictions on immigration into the States, and Americans were murdered in Guangdong. But Anglo-Chinese agreements in 1906–07 provoked little resentment.

A new expression of nationality took the form of moral protest against the evil of opium smoking. The student generation 'imposed its will on old China', and the court seized its opportunity to assert itself. Thousands of Chinese students who flocked to Japan saw the benefits of an absolute ban on opium and attributed Japan's dramatic ascendancy to immunity from its curse. And hundreds of thousands who had been under foreign influence in mission schools and colleges since the Boxer Protocol shared in the protest.

A strong, even daring, imperial decree of November 21, 1906, ordered that all land planted with the opium poppy be converted to grain within ten years, that smoking by government officials cease, and that negotiations bring to an end the import of foreign opium within ten years. All such opium was shipped from British ports.

The timing at last was appropriate. The conscience of Britain had at last awoken. In December 1906 the British government agreed to restrict Indian exports by one tenth each year; an international convention (called by the United States and chaired by Bishop Brent of the Philippines) in 1909 resolved to limit smuggling and overt shipping of opium by other powers. When China reduced her production more radically than planned, Britain agreed at another convention on May 8, 1911, to end all imports by 1917; and in January 1912 another international convention at The Hague agreed on all controls needed to suppress production, trade and smuggling of opium. Opium smokers abandoned the habit by millions, but millions more found means to gratify their addiction. The price in loss of revenue was borne by China and Britain.

In two articles in *The Times*, Dr G. E. Morrison, the Peking correspondent, pointed out that three things 'had made it practically impossible for the British Government to continue . . . the gradual process (towards the abolition of the opium trade) by an annual ten per cent reduction': (i) the resolution passed at the Edinburgh Conference of 1910 (in response to Benjamin B.'s strong pressure); (ii) the Day of National Humiliation and Prayer arranged for October 24, 1910; and (iii) the resolutions passed by the Chinese National Assembly. When Benjamin on his deathbed was shown *The Times* and the words, 'The

agreement means the extinction of the opium trade within at least two years', he gathered up his strength and said with an effort, 'A great victory. Thank God I have lived to see it.' He died on May 29, 1911. On May 7, 1913, 'the British Government announced, "We are in the satisfactory position of saying that the (opium) traffic is dead."' This admission that it had been 'traffic' rather than trade would have given the old warrior added satisfaction.[1489]

The long, long campaign for 'national righteousness' to stop Britain's guilty trade had at last achieved its aims. Parliament had twice pronounced the opium trade 'morally indefensible', without taking action. So belated steps to end it by gradual stages had left no room for pride. Until the cultivation of the poppy was suppressed, Christian farmers had a losing battle on their hands. The income from sowing grain was far less than that from opium; and the birds of vast areas converged on grain fields to feed. When revolution weakened and removed government control, the country reverted to growing opium.

Desperate to regain its hold on the nation, the Manchu government introduced reforms designed to strengthen its own position. Railways were extended in all directions; Western education was encouraged, and selected Manchus were sent overseas to study science, including political science. *The Times* of April 15 and 16, 1908, reported the cancellation of the imperial rescript of 1899 which granted official rank to Roman Catholic priests, a heavy blow and 'loss of face' to forty-six bishops and over a thousand priests.

Diehards of the old school had to be placated. In spite of her edicts, Ci Xi herself remained one of them. Manchu interests had to be protected if the dynasty was to survive.[1490] And conservative attitudes among the literati and *laobeixing*, the Old Hundred Names (a term for all the people), had to be conciliated. On December 30, 1906, an imperial decree raised 'the sage Confucius from the level of the Sun and Moon, to which the high ministers of state paid worship, to the level of Heaven and

Earth, to which the Emperor alone made ceremonial offerings'. And a college was established at his birthplace to perpetuate his teaching. When a move was made in 1914 to recognise Confucianism as the national religion, Protestants, Catholics and representatives of other faiths saw to its rejection. Japan sent strong Buddhist representations and funds to restore temples and teach Buddhism. The strong tide in favour of Christianity after the Boxer attacks had powerful opposition to contend with.

Constitutional reform, however, became the decisive current in the floodtide of change. Constitutional government became the goal of thinking Chinese, literati, governors and viceroys. Liang Qichao, in exile, advocated the sovereignty of the people, with liberty and equality, but with a constitutional monarchy, at any rate at first. Zhang Zhitong still favoured retention of the dynasty, reformed. But Sun Yatsen stood squarely for revolution and a republic, and ridiculed Liang Qichao. Ci Xi was forced to resist him by favouring moves towards a constitutional monarchy—the crime for which she had been holding the Guang Xü emperor captive for years. The Japanese model looked preferable to Western concepts of monarchy.[1491]

On September 1, 1906, she approved proposals made by an imperial commission, but typically specified no date for their promulgation. They would centralise government in favour of the Manchus, and curb the power of the predominantly Chinese viceroys. She formed a new Ministry of the Army, by which Yüan Shikai lost four of the six divisions in his foreign-trained Beiyang (Northern) army. And in August 1907 she transferred Zhang Zhitong, and Yüan Shikai, the two most powerful viceroys, to Beijing as Grand Councillors under her own eye. In September she enacted a National Assembly of Ministers.

Pressure for a constitution became so strong, with young Manchus supporting it, that Ci Xi drew up an Outline of Constitution in August 1908 by which an elected parliament would advise the emperor in whom legislative, executive and judicial power would reside in perpetuity. Provincial Assemblies were to be organised and inaugurated in 1908–10, and in 1910–11 a National Assembly. Implementation of government from 1911–15 and abolition of the distinction between Manchus and Chinese in 1915–16 would then bring in parliamentary rule by two houses. By then the nation should be educated in constitutional government subordinate to the throne. At seventy-three (in 1907) she appeared to believe she would live to see the new constitution implemented.

But the first declaration in her published draft fuelled the fires of revolution: 'The Great Qing dynasty shall rule over the Great Qing empire for ever, and be honoured through all ages!' Her reform began at the apex of the pyramid and left the broad base of the nation's millions almost where they were, without equal justice, protection from tax extortion, or from officials (not least herself) diverting huge sums into their own coffers. But by then she had only three months to live.

One hundred years since Robert Morrison (1907)

'And so, Mr Morrison, you really expect that you will make an impression on the idolatry of the great Chinese Empire?' 'No, Sir,' he replied. 'I expect God will' (see 1, p 45). Robert Morrison landed at Canton on September 4, 1807, and died on August 1, 1843, with a bare dozen converts to his name. 'The unsectarian unity of Morrison, Elijah Bridgman and others was not achieved. Each mission and each denomination started its own work. Even the two Anglican Church societies, American and British, went their own ways. "Unfriendly and wasteful competition" caused confusion in the minds of the Chinese, but "by no means as much as might be supposed."' (see 1, p 134). The first General Inter-Mission Conference met at Hong Kong in August 1843 and initiated the translation of the Bible into literary Chinese. 'Despise not the day of small things!'

By 1905 the Protestant missionary community in China had risen to 3,445 with 178,000 communicants; and five years later to 5,144 with 15,500 Chinese colleagues and two hundred thousand communicants. The (wrongly named) 'Third' General Inter-Mission Conference of 1907 (after those in 1877 and 1890, discounting 1843) drew a total attendance of five hundred delegates and 670 others, including representatives of home boards. Convened for 1900 it had been postponed on account of the Boxer upheavals. But while Shanghai was filled with missionary refugees an informal conference had been held in 1901. More than twice as large as in 1890, the 1907 conference was still a forum of foreign missionaries with only six or seven Chinese delegates present. The Chinese church remained fragmented by the denominational differences of the west.[1492]

The conference also reflected a growing concern with organisation and education, in the name of the gospel but overshadowing it. Cooperation between the missions and the Chinese churches included plans for turning over the control of the Church to the Chinese—beginning with the union of churches of similar ecclesiastical order. The slogan 'China for the Chinese' was being heard, and a committee to consider the formation of a Chinese National Missionary Society was proposed. Again the old arguments for toleration of ancestral rites, including worship, were advanced. The conference held that the ultimate judge of the issue and what substitutes could be introduced must be the Chinese church. But they agreed as before that 'the Worship of Ancestors is incompatible with an enlightened and spiritual conception of the Christian Faith. Reverence for parents and affectionate remembrance of the dead' must be encouraged, but not worship. This time Hudson Taylor was beyond the reach of criticism.

On the proposition by Dr Thomas Cochrane, the conference recommended a Christian Federation of China composed of Chinese and missionary delegates in each province and meeting at national

level at least once in every five years. This quickly led to developments such as the adoption of the goal of 'One Protestant Christian Church for West China'. But how were Anglicans, Baptists, Methodists, Presbyterians and others to agree on modes of baptism and admission to Holy Communion? Delay in the implementation of the 1907 agreement became permanent when three years later the continuation committee of the World Missionary Conference at Edinburgh superseded it. A common name 'to manifest the unity that already exists among all faithful Christians in China', the 'Christian Church in China', came into use.[1493]

The 1907 Inter-Mission Conference also gave Richard a platform. John King Fairbank remarked in his volume on the Late Qing (*Cambridge History of China*, vol. 10), 'The Chinese names of men like Timothy Richard and Young J. Allen were on people's lips throughout the country. And had the *coup d'état* of September 1898 not taken place, it is very likely that Richard would have been invited (on Kang Yuwei's recommendation) to join the inner circle of imperial advisers.' W. A. P. Martin, and Gilbert Reid by his 'Mission among the Higher Classes of China', focused their attention on the scholar-gentry of the empire and met with 'massive unresponsiveness' to the spiritual message of Christianity. 'The message (they) finally succeeded in conveying to Chinese of prominence turned out to be secular rather than religious in content.'[1494]

Fairbanks's essay on 'The professionalisation of missionary work' focuses on the difficulty the CIM faced after the turn of the century, with the hunger of educated Chinese for western learning and science. Schools, colleges and medical institutions had been used in the nineteenth century as adjuncts to the Christian gospel of Christ. But muting of this message to accommodate the objections of some students and officials, and its exclusion from the curriculum as in Richard's University of Shanxi (although permitted on the premises 'out of hours'), led to its gradual neglect and replacement. 'A significant shift towards professionalisation' developed as the subject and the missionaries themselves 'became increasingly divorced from evangelical aims'. Medical missionaries were beginning 'to plan for the health of the entire Empire', and for many the creation of a healthy China was starting to assume as much importance as the creation of a Christian China. The means of presenting the gospel was replacing the gospel itself. The CIM, among many missions, rejected this trend in the face of growing criticism and earned the label of 'uncooperative'.

That phrase 'the creation of a Christian China' summed up the shift in emphasis. 'Christian nations' had waged war on China, forced opium on China, wreaked vengeance on China. The concept of 'Christianising' the nation had seductively misled missionary thinking away from Christian truth. Timothy Richard maintained in the *Chinese Recorder*[1495] that the gospel could be seen in two ways, as a means of saving the souls of individuals, or 'as a means of saving a nation through the collective efforts of regenerated souls'. But his understanding and use of the words 'souls', 'saving', 'regenerated' and 'conversion' no longer meant to him what they meant when he heard them in the Second Evangelical Awakening, nor what they still meant to most missionaries in China.

So much is heard of Timothy Richard that a paragraph by way of illustration is not out of place. At the Shanghai Conference in February 1901 he gave a long discourse on 'How a Few Men may make a Million Converts'. Because one soul is more valuable than the whole world and many were open to adopting a new religion, he reasoned, while the Student Volunteer Movement was aiming at no less than 'the evangelisation of the world in this generation', an acceptable gospel offered in an acceptable form could see millions accepting it. Change mission methods and change the appearance of the gospel. So he summarised the leading religions of the world to show features they had in common. One of them, Christianity, he subdivided. Early Christianity 'had higher ideals than Judaism' and other religions. 'By making God universal instead of merely national, by substituting faith for old ritual and higher ethics for lower, by mystic union with God and consequent immortality, Christianity was an advance on other religions.' But 'Reformed Christianity', still higher than early Christianity, he claimed, was conquering the world by substituting individual liberty of conscience for papal authority, by improved education, by letting the people have more voice in government, 'by enlightened uplifting of all nations and races'—still with no mention of Christ. The religions of the world must be studied, for 'the power of the Holy Spirit is believed in by them all. Not that they use our phraseology, but they have the same ideas.'

'When (the missionary) has given an outline of the material, social, intellectual, and religious advantages and has persevered till they thoroughly understand, then the conversion of China will be accomplished as suddenly as the explosion of a mine . . . Why should we follow antiquated methods of mission work when the new produces results a thousand times better?' Richard asked. The gulf between him and orthodox missions had become unbridgeable: a gulf of his own making. 'A thousand times better' in his view could only refer to the hunger for education and reform, for 'uplift'.

Without any wish to be at odds with any others in the missionary community, the orthodox societies and individuals by continuing the 'foolishness' of preaching 'Christ crucified' with profound effect, found themselves accused of schism and failure to cooperate in the 'better, wiser' way. 'Mass conversion', 'conversion by the million', through persuasion and the intellect should come first, they were told. 'Conversion' of individuals would follow in great numbers. Education, reform, progress, literature, health, good servants of the gospel if rightly used, became all important to 'progressive' colleagues. Christianising and 'uplifting' China became the gospel substitutes for 'the glorious gospel of the grace of God' in Christ, and 'the offence of the cross'.

Nearly seventeen thousand Protestant schools in 1890 had become nearly fifty-eight thousand by 1906, four hundred of them higher level institutions. In the interests of consolidating local churches, the CIM also multiplied its Christian schools, purposely restricting their size. Propagating the gospel of reconciliation with God through the death of Christ could not but result in social reform.

Kang Yuwei and Liang Qichao became Richard's true friends, and only the violent collapse of Guang Xü's reforms during the Hundred Days kept Richard from the inner sanctums of the empire. But Kang Yuwei himself went no further than to adopt a Christianised Confucianism, and later tried to make Confucianism the national religion. The Christianity that he and others embraced was largely nominal. As secretary of the Society for the Diffusion of Christian and General Knowledge (SDK), later the Christian Literature Society (CLS), Richard poured out material for publication faster than his printers could produce it. But (as J. K. Fairbank points out) in the first decade of the twentieth century national reforms sped away from missionary influence, 'the Chinese quickly discovering that they could reject God and still have progress'.[1496]

As we have seen in earlier volumes, the 'indigenous principles' of self-government, self-support and self-propagation had for long been discussed by missionaries, and practised with varying degrees of success by those who grasped the meaning of them. John McCarthy at Hangzhou (see pp 154–55, 177–78) and Dixon Hoste with Hsi Shengmo in Shanxi (see pp 465, 469 & note 760) had clung to Hudson Taylor's guidelines, while all too many doubted the maturity of their Chinese colleagues and fellow-Christians and kept control of them, sometimes with a heavy hand. Church members welcomed both kinds of care, patronage and financial props as much as liberty with responsibility. Then drastic removal of foreign supervision during the

Boxer period taught many churches to stand on their own feet, and Hoste tried hard to inculcate a preference in them and returning missionaries for Chinese autonomy with missionary help. As every community has its leading members, so the church no less reveals its potential if given the chance. In many regions he failed. In some he succeeded. In most of China the missions returned to preside with loving condescension over Christians who only lacked the opportunity to mature in action.

The CIM, 'a rope of sand' (1905–12)

The epithet 'a rope of sand' was applied to evangelical Christianity in the nineteenth century to express its intellectual weakness. 'Thank God it is so,' Henry Venn would say; 'so is the seashore,' able to withstand the buffeting of waves. When Hudson Taylor, the moving spirit of the CIM, began to fail, some recalled the phrase and spoke of the Mission's approaching disintegration.[1497] In Griffith John's words, 'It was predicted that the retirement of its founder from active control would be the death of the Mission; but the Mission has never shown greater stability, vitality and force. To this Hudson Taylor replied, "If it be of God it will last; if it be 'my work' the sooner it goes the better."'

The gradual relinquishment of control to a deputy who proved himself while acting for the General Director was the first explanation of survival. The readiness of the founder to stand by his principle that control in China must be exerted by directors in China, and to trust his deputies, was the second. The humility he had shown, continued by D. E. Hoste in leading from the front rather than imposing control on the Mission from a base, ensured a smooth transition.

Hoste's letters to the rank and file, finding encouragement from the limitation of massacres to three provinces, rather than harping on the sufferings endured, inspired his colleagues. He led and they followed, though he remarked to Hudson Taylor at first that a 'GD' seemed to be the Mission's 'whipping boy'. A godly, strong man, he looked beyond the disaster of 1900. That was over. A new, changing China offered unprecedented promise as a field for evangelism, and he grasped it. His policy from the start became advance, expansion, with consolidation of churches already founded. Pioneering of remote regions continued, especially among the minority 'tribes' of West China, with striking success. But the original strategy of starting in the chief cities and spreading from them to smaller cities, towns and villages was pressed home. While mission centres increased in number, their outposts multiplied. Instead of travelling in circles looking for a welcome, missionaries met with more invitations than they could accept. W. W. Cassels on a one thousand-mile itinerary through eleven counties of East Sichuan found 'a great movement towards Christianity'. In twenty to thirty different places he found any number from a handful to one or two hundred wanting to 'enter the church'. This proven strategy had to be followed against the current of the 'modern' alternative policy.

Those who speak and write of conflict between Timothy Richard and Hudson Taylor over Richard's philosophies too often show confusion over the chronology and only partial knowledge of the facts. Their spoken disagreement ended in 1890, and Hudson Taylor retired at the turn of the century. Stevenson and Hoste had to answer the new reasoning. They did it not by debate but by the largest society in China quietly treating it as contrary to divine revelation, and continuing to work effectively as before. In this they had the unquestioning support of the church in the sending continents, with steadily increasing numbers of reinforcements, of mission stations, organised churches, Chinese church workers and believers baptised. By the beginning of 1908 members of the CIM exceeded nine hundred, and one thousand by 1912. Communicants numbered more than nineteen thousand in 1908 and four years later over twenty-six thousand.[1498] By 1905 the annual total of baptisms recorded by the CIM had risen from hundreds to thousands, seven hundred in 1895, 2,500 in 1905 and 2,800 in 1908, and rose to 4,500 and five thousand in 1913 and 1914. The 'rope of sand' was never more than a figment of imagination.

At the Shanghai Missionary Conference of 1907 a resolution was unanimously adopted calling for united prayer that God would raise up men with special evangelistic gifts whom he could use in reviving the life of the churches, and in gathering in the tens of thousands who already had some knowledge of the gospel. A great spiritual awakening was in progress in Korea. After the conference Jonathan Goforth travelled through Korea to Manchuria 'spreading the flame of revival' there also. And in 1908–09 Albert Lutley and Wang Qitai, an evangelist, preached in Shanxi a call to repentance, confession, forgiveness and response to the sufferings of Christ, very quietly, without demonstration or excitement. From there they carried it to Shaanxi and then Sichuan. Everywhere the sense of God's personal presence was frequently so real that the whole congregation would fall on their knees with their faces to the ground in prayer and confession. The wave of 'revival' continued to sweep from province to province until in 1911 public meetings became impracticable when the empire became convulsed by armed revolution.

The legacy of Hudson Taylor's resolute 'contending for the faith that was once for all entrusted to the saints' (Jude 3 RSV), continued by the Mission, paid rich dividends decade after decade. No vocal opposition to the exponents of 'another gospel' was needed. Persistence in preaching 'Christ crucified' and in well-doing ensured a harvest as great as could be gathered and conserved at the time, and contributed to the ultimate millions of believers in China today.

The CIM also undertook social service on a wide scale. In 1907, only thirty years after the appalling drought and famine in North China which took the lives of between nine and twenty millions, abnormal rains and flooding devastated an area as large as England in Jiangsu, Anhui and Henan. Relief committees raised large sums of money, and to allay the fears of the viceroy, Tuan Fang, Protestant missionaries promised not to claim indemnities for lives lost in distributing relief. Instead of providing money for the starving refugees to buy food, a policy of supplying flour in payment for work was adopted.

Ten or more members of the CIM among others took part. The report of one, O. Burgess, assisted by a woman recorder, graphically described his achievements at Qingjiangpu. Using 1,500 men they first filled up a three-acre swamp to a depth of eight feet to make dry land. They then surrounded an area of inundated houses with a raised road linked to a highway and continued through the city, isolating lakes of water later to be drained dry. Meanwhile three thousand more men dug out ten miles of river bed and a new canal, to drain away the flood water. They enclosed the city with a raised road and nine connecting roads, some of which they paved with stone, widened and deepened all main drains, and made ramps over the city walls for the thousands of men carrying earth into the city. Four large and nine smaller stone and timber bridges and a stone canal lock completed the major work. By the end Burgess was controlling eleven thousand workmen in addition to his three thousand to four thousand mud carriers. 'Men, miles and mud' filled his memories of those months. His assistant recovered from typhoid fever, but Dr J. E. Williams of the CIM, Dr J. Lynch, the Zhenjiang port doctor, and two American Presbyterians gave their lives.[1499]

Care of the whole person, not only the soul, took different forms. Hospitals, opium refuges and leprosaria began to play a greater part.

The medical arm of missions
(1807–1912)

Even amateur knowledge of Western medical methods gave unskilled missionaries the means for helping the sick. Many instances in these books have shown in passing how it was put to good use. The Ridleys' extraordinary success with locally bought materials at Xining during the Muslim rebellion (pp 596–97) had its humbler counterpart through the years wherever missionaries were at work. But the development of medical missions was slow in coming, largely because medical men and women were slow in venturing out to China. Ten medical missionaries in China of all missions in 1874, forty years after Peter Parker, and nineteen in 1881, was the pace of the CIM's experience too. If enough of the right type of doctor had joined the Mission, great progress would have been made (see pp 410–11). But of all societies, sixteen hospitals in 1876 and sixty-one in 1889, with forty-four dispensaries, gave the measure of how ambitiously those who did come aimed high with little equipment. Motivation was consistently Christian, and orthodox biblical teaching was given in parallel with treatment. Relief of physical suffering and disarming prejudice were accompanied by the gospel for patients' spiritual needs.[1500]

Hudson Taylor's two years' apprenticeship at the London Hospital had made him enough of a doctor to be able to take over William Parker's hospital in Ningbo (see 1, pp 474–76) and perform amputations, but even after graduating as a member of the Royal College of Surgeons in 1862 and forming his own mission with a score or more of colleagues, all medical care of them and of his own family devolved upon him. In the 1870s came a transition period in which two or three doctors shared the responsibilities with him. Then Harold Schofield arrived in China in June 1880, followed by William Wilson and E. H. Edwards in 1882, and several experienced missionaries took short courses and qualified as doctors, Douthwaite, Cameron, George King and George Parker among them.

We can only speculate on what Harold Schofield might have achieved at Taiyuan, had he not died of typhus. And, for that matter, Howard Taylor with his high qualifications in medicine and surgery if severe deafness had not handicapped him increasingly after his missionary career began, and if Hudson Taylor had not recognised that Geraldine's value as an author far outweighed whatever service she might have given in an inland city. The part they played in the Student Volunteer Movement and in non-medical roles probably outweighed in effect what they would have been able to do medically.

Dr Millar Wilson, the Taiyuan martyr, had opened another hospital at Linfen at his own expense. Dr William Wilson developed one at Hanzhong in south Shaanxi and later at Yibin (Suifu) in Sichuan. After Kaifeng reluctantly opened its gates to missionaries (the very last provincial capital to do so) Drs Whitfield Guinness and Sydney Carr began medical work there in 1902. The only Jewish colony in China was to be found in Kaifeng, and a Chinese Jewess became their first patient. In 1891 the rising star of China, Yüan Shikai, a Henan man, called Dr Howard Taylor to attend his mother, dying of cancer. In recognition of his services no less than Li Hongzhang presented Howard Taylor with an honorific tablet; and as a result he occupied the city of Chenzhou (see p 671) in 1895.[1501]

The Henrietta Bird Memorial Hospital began work at Langzhong Sichuan in 1903 and the CIM opened another hospital at Taizhou, Zhejiang, in 1904. In Changsha, Drs Keller and Barrie began their influential hospital on the site bought with the viceroy's gift (see p 746). Other hospitals on a smaller scale were opened by Dr F. H. Judd at Shangrao (Guangxin), Jiangxi, by Dr W. L. Pruen at Chengdu and Guiyang, by Dr E. S. Fish at Anshun for the aboriginal Miao people, at Lu'an in Shanxi, at Zhenjiang by Dr G. A. Cox, and at Dali, Yunnan, originally by Dr W. T. Clark. The Borden Memorial Hospital and leprosaria followed at Lanzhou, Gansu, in memory of William W. Borden who died in Cairo while studying Arabic in preparation for work among the Muslims in north-west China.

By 1906 the CIM had seven hospitals, thirty-seven dispensaries and 101 opium refuges. As action progressed against opium production and smoking, refuges decreased in number, but in, 1912 there were still fifty-seven in action. Three years later there were ten CIM hospitals, sixty-eight dispensaries and fifty refuges (and, incidentally, 135 boarding-schools with 4,295 students and 237 day schools with 5,412 pupils). Medical work by other missions expanded more rapidly. Of 3,445 Protestant missionaries in China in 1905, 301 were doctors of medicine, of whom 94 were women, in 166 hospitals and 241 dispensaries. The (British) Baptist Missionary Society sent Dr H. Stanley Jenkins to Xi'an in 1904 and Andrew Young in 1905. Dr Cecil Robertson joined them, and these three were in Xi'an during the fighting and massacres of Manchus and missionaries in 1911. Young was in Britain in 1912 when Jenkins and Robertson died of typhus, so he returned at once to replace them.

The medical profession as a whole did not recognise the overriding importance of primary health care and preventive medicine until another seventy or eighty years had passed. So the emphasis remained on curative medicine and surgery. Even Western medicine was still a young science when the cataclysmic changes of 1908–12 once again threw China and missions into turmoil.

Death of a grand dowager (1908–12)

When the emperor died on November 14, 1908, and Ci Xi on the 15th, suspicion of foul play was inevitable. Accounts of what happened in the palace varied with their sources. *The Times'* own correspondent in Beijing attributed the dowager empress's death, immediately following the emperor's, to foul play against her. 'The more natural explanation' appeared to the historian Hosea Ballou Morse to be action in keeping with her character during her long reign. Realising that her own death was approaching, and unwilling that Guang Xü should outlive her, to guide the destinies of 'her' empire at so critical a time, 'she took the steps necessary to avert the calamity'.

Charlotte Haldane in *The Last Great Empress of China* gave first a more lenient account and then the inside story from the diary of Der Ling, Ci Xi's longstanding lady-in-waiting on whom Charlotte Haldane constantly drew for inside information. Der Ling was the daughter of a Manchu nobleman and a secret Christian, partly educated in France. She claimed to have received the confidence of Ci Xi and on occasion of Guang Xü also. Charlotte Haldane frequently used her statements because of 'the ring of truth' in them. In 1908 Der Ling was no longer at court, but stated that the details had been given her by a former principal eunuch.[1502] Sudden deaths and palace intrigues were always carefully covered by plausible versions of what took place, and the royal deaths were no exception.

In August 1907 when Ci Xi was seventy-two she suffered a slight stroke, affecting her face, but 'her mind and tongue remained as sharp as ever'. The emperor, a prisoner since 1898, was deeply depressed and ailing, but not seriously ill. 'I feel in my heart that I shall outlive the Old Buddha,' he indiscreetly wrote in his diary. But Ci Xi told the chief eunuch, Li Lianying, that the emperor's illness was incurable. In that world of fantasy, this had a clear meaning. As he became weaker she relaxed some of the restrictions she had imposed on him, no longer requiring the long ritual obeisance on his knees in her presence.

In 1908 his condition deteriorated considerably. She was well enough to celebrate her seventy-third birthday picnicking on the palace lake, but bouts of dysentery were dragging her down. On November 10, Guang Xü's condition degenerated further and she summoned Prince Qing to attend her appointment of the emperor's successor.

For a third time she violated dynastic law. She summoned the Grand Council, ascended the throne and 'spoke with all her wonted vehemence and lucidity'. Again overriding the Council's views and the rightful succession she named Yong Lu's grandson, Pu Yi, the two-year-old son of the young Prince Qün by Yong Lu's daughter, as heir apparent in place of Pu Lun. The

child was doomed to become the last tragic occupant of the dragon throne. Finally on November 14 when the thirty-eight-year-old Guang Xü lay dying, Ci Xi came to see him and showed no emotion unless of relief. When she herself died the next day, it became 'very widely believed' that she had committed or caused to be committed the murder of yet another emperor before taking her own life.

Der Ling's account was explicit, based on details given her by Zhang De, the former assistant to the chief eunuch, Li Lianying. When the chief eunuch had heard of Guang Xü's belief that he would outlive Ci Xi and be able to avenge himself on his enemies, not least his eunuch jailers, he told Ci Xi, 'It would be beneficial to all concerned were His Majesty to die before Old Buddha.' At once she understood and replied, 'His Majesty is desperately ill . . . Those preparing his medicines have perhaps been careless. Hereafter, Li, you will personally administer them to Guang Xü.' She had given him the licence he had intended. Systematically he poisoned his prisoner. Der Ling wrote that Guang Xü died in agony after being dressed in burial clothes while still conscious.

Edicts announced the child emperor's reign title as Xüan Tong, and he was placed on the Dragon Throne with Ci Xi's own status in future to be Empress Grand Dowager, retaining final authority over all others. On November 15 she fainted at her midday meal and after recovering summoned the Grand Council. In their presence she declared that she was dying, and transferred all power to Prince Qün as regent, 'subject only to my instructions', thereby retaining supreme power to the last moment. She dictated a long, lucid justification of herself and her lifetime of misdeeds, and died at 3.00 p.m.

Death of a dynasty (1908–12)

The Mongol Yüan dynasty had lasted only eighty-nine years, and the Qing dynasty 268 (by 1912). After the decadence of the late Ming empire, the early Manchus, Kang Xi, Yong Zhang and Qian Long, did well.

But by 1800 'the sun had begun to set and the moon to wane', as the proverb put it. Domestic rebellion and foreign invasion to which decadent rulers could not adapt, doomed the dynasty to extinction. While Meiji Japan initiated far-reaching reform and became a modern state, Qing China in the lifetime of Ci Xi disintegrated and foundered.[1503]

The whole Protestant missionary enterprise in China had been set in a climate of turmoil. From Morrison in the Canton 'factory' to the martyrs and fugitives of 1900, the penetration of China by the gospel had been precarious or hazardous at best. Opium wars, Taiping and Muslim rebellions, Tianjin and other massacres had found Manchu rule either inadequate or conniving in persecution. But the Chinese people recognised Manchu inflexibility and Manchu weakness as the chief cause of China's vulnerability—and at last, China's hope for the future. Only an oversimplified epitome of a long, confused melee is possible here.

Kang Yuwei's campaign for progressive, constitutional reform, and Sun Yatsen's avowed revolutionary campaign for the overthrow of the dynasty, germinated in good soil. When the Manchus, after the dowager empress's death, tried to strengthen their own position against the ethnic Chinese, they sealed their own fate. No Chinese in the empire held a higher place than Yüan Shikai as Senior Guardian of the Heir Apparent and member of the Grand Council concurrently with Zhang Zhitong—until on January 2, 1909, the regent, Prince Qün, ordered him to resign and return to his home province of Henan. (Zhang Zhitong died on October 5 the same year.)[1504] Wealthy and astute, Yüan knew he had alienated the reformers by betraying the reforming emperor in 1898, and the reactionaries by opposing the Boxers. He saw the approaching end of the dynasty and had the grandest personal ambitions. So he bided his time until the reformers needed him to fulfil their aims.

Ci Xi had set her constitutional reforms in motion, designed to gratify reformers while consolidating Manchu power. The provincial assemblies met in October 1909, 'little more than debating societies'. But collectively they demanded that the national parliament should be convened within two years, only to be rebuffed by a decree of January 10, 1910. The first national assembly opened at Beijing on October 3, 1910, and it also demanded that the first parliament be summoned early, with the Grand Council responsible to it! No inspired Ci Xi remained to wave the magic wand, and Prince Qün, the regent, in his early thirties had no experience behind him.

On May 8, 1911, an imperial decree went so far as to abolish the Grand Council and two others, creating a Cabinet and Privy Council in their place, with old Prince Qing, president of the defunct Grand Council, as prime minister. This cosmetic move, under 'a decrepit, irresolute, wily, corrupt and inefficient old man', was transparently doomed to failure. The national assembly was called for October 1911, but on October 10 armed rebellion broke out at Wuchang, spreading to Hankou and Hanyang. Risings in other principal cities of the empire succeeded with little fighting in central and southern China.[1505]

But in some of the provincial capitals with large Manchu garrisons and Manchu quarters occupying many acres, resistance led to massacre. At Xi'an rebellion was interpreted as licence to rob, burn and kill.

> The massacre of Manchus in the city lasted five days. Even though they fell on their knees and begged for mercy, they were slain, excepting some of the women and children ... Others roamed about till they died of hunger. Not reckoning those who jumped into wells or were buried alive in underground passages, there was ... a funeral expense for 21,000 corpses, many of them being Chinese. Even at the lowest estimate, 15,000 Manchus lost their lives, these five days ... The rich were robbed without mercy. The highest Chinese official in the city had to pay a million taels to be permitted to live.

Mutinying soldiers were mostly to blame.[1506]

E. R. Beckman of the Scandinavian Alliance Mission of North America escaped with his youngest daughter when his wife and two other girls of eight and thirteen were massacred in Xi'an. With them died one other missionary schoolteacher and four children between ten and fifteen years of age. 'They passed through severe suffering. Their (stoned and) pierced bodies were found buried in a field.' An instructor at the Military Academy at Xi'an, C. T. Wang, escorted the survivors to Hankou, and other missionaries escaped unharmed from Xi'an and other Shaanxi cities, although 'robbers' in thousands were bent on attacking them. C. T. Wang reported to 'His Excellency the President of the United Provinces of China' and the Vice-Minister of Foreign Affairs wrote personally to E. R. Beckman in July 1912.

Ten years later the Xi'an Manchu quarter still lay devastated. Looking out from my home at the Jenkins-Robertson Memorial Hospital, separated only by a high wall from the ruins, I (AJB) could see the great city wall away on the other side and everywhere between, a battlefield. No house appeared to stand higher than a few feet, and every yard of earth had been deeply dug, probably in the search for valuables. Skulls and bleached bones still littered the ground, a lasting image of the frenzy of 1911.

The court recalled Yüan Shikai, giving him sweeping powers to save the dynasty. He retained command in the north and retook Hankou, but too late. Kang Yuwei's brand of reform, favouring a constitutional monarchy, had been made hollow by Manchu rejection of parliamentary sovereignty, and Sun Yatsen's followers took control of the revolution. On February 12, 1912, 'the emperor' abdicated and the court retreated to the palace refuge in Jehol, last used in 1860 (see 1, p 513 and ill. 1.34: 1, p 491). The empire and dynasty had fallen apart.

Rise of a republic[1507] (1896–1912)

'Sun Yatsen', the name by which the West knows the architect of the revolution, was secondary to his personal name, Sun Wen. Chinese use his revolutionary name, Sun Zhongshan (Sun Chungshan). After his kidnapping and release in London in 1896 (see p 588), he stayed in Europe studying social and political developments, and enunciated his Three People's Principles, the famous San Min Zhu Yi: Nationalism or National Consciousness; Democracy, or People's Rights; and Socialism or People's Livelihood, which he liked to compare with Abraham Lincoln's 'of the people, by the people, and for the people'. When he returned in 1897 to Japan and was joined in exile by his rivals Kang Yuwei and Liang Qichao—refugees from the coup that ended the Hundred Days of reform—his attempts to find common ground failed. His republican aims and their Emperor-Protection Society clashed 'like water and fire'. So he turned to plotting armed action, with little effect. But when an independent uprising at Wuhan in 1900 was disclosed prematurely, Sun came to be seen as no longer an outlaw but a patriot.

In 1905 he organised a revolutionary party, the Tong Men Hui, which adopted his Three Principles. As a rallying-point it received strong support from literati and progressive army officers in all provinces, and risings multiplied between 1906 and 1911. A major attempt to take Guangzhou (Canton) failed in April 1911, but six months later success came at the Wuhan conurbation of three cities. Great unrest followed the nationalisation of railways in which many had invested savings. On August 24, 1911, more than ten thousand demonstrators clashed with troops in Chengdu, Sichuan, and fighting between the government and people of Sichuan intensified. The two issues, the railway controversy and outright revolution, 'fused into one'.

As the Sichuan imbroglio became more serious, part of the Hubei 'New Army' was sent to maintain order, leaving Wuchang vulnerable. On October 9 the accidental explosion of a bomb betrayed the existence of secret arsenals, and rebel army units attacked the offices of the governor-general and army commander, controlling the city on the 10th. The former chairman of the Hubei provincial assembly then urged other provinces by telegram to declare independence of the Qing court and persuaded the foreign consuls in Hankou to maintain strict neutrality. Within six weeks 'fifteen provinces, or two-thirds of all China seceded from the Qing dynasty'. Shanghai was lost to the revolution early in November, and Nanjing on December 4, 1911.

Sun was in Denver, Colorado, when he read a newspaper report of the Wuchang revolt. He suppressed his desire to hurry back to China, and embarked on ambitious but successful diplomacy with Britain and France to check aid to the Manchus and prepare for recognition of a new government. He reached Shanghai on Christmas Day and on December 29 was elected provisional president of the Republic of China. His government-to-be 'adopted the solar calendar in place of the lunar one and named January 1, 1912, as the first day of the republic'.

When the helpless Qing court turned to Yüan Shikai, he named his own terms, four measures to please the revolutionaries and two to make him the most powerful man in China. The regent capitulated. The Qing cabinet was replaced by a 'responsible' one, and control of the army and navy and adequate funds passed to Yuan. Shanxi seceded on October 29, Prince Qün resigned as regent and Prince Qing as prime minister. Yüan Shikai replaced him, and showed his power by recapturing Hankou and later Hanyang. But two divisional commanders and Yan Xishan (Yen Hsi-shah), the revolutionary leader of Shanxi, prepared to march on Beijing to prevent Yuan's return. He foiled the attempt, formed his cabinet, ensured military control of the capital and began negotiations with the revolutionaries. Only the presidency would satisfy him. He threatened to fight for a constitutional monarchy. But when the Qing diplomats

abroad on January 3, 1912, urged the abdication of the emperor, Yuan told the revolutionary Nanjing government that he 'would induce the voluntary abdication of the Qing throne' if the presidency were offered to him.

To avoid civil war Sun stepped down, adroitly telling Yuan that he had accepted the honour of provisional president until Yuan could replace him. But he used the news media to make Yuan's appointment conditional upon declaration of his support for the republic, and provisional election by parliament. Yuan obtained the court's compliance, with Nanjing's offer 'to treat the deposed Qing emperor with the same courtesy as a foreign sovereign', to let him use the Summer Palace, and give him four million taels annually. These 'generous' concessions were later modified. The abdication was made public on February 12, 1912, 'and with that . . . the last of China's twenty-five dynasties came to an end'.

But that was not the end of the Ci Xi story. Her funeral a year later was the costliest in living memory. And her mausoleum, containing rich treasure, was so strong that dynamite was used by titled looters in July 1920 to break it open. The imperial remains were hacked in pieces and scattered, and the loot found its way to the markets of the world. After she died the fragile Qing dynasty had survived for only three years. And the tragic figure of Pu Yi, 'Henry Pu-yi' as he became, drifted from place to place, patronised by changing masters.

Yüan 'sows the dragon's teeth'[1508]
(1912–16)

The Hudson Taylor story has been told. But has it? In 1989, a long lifetime since his death, we find him again the butt of hostile criticism. Why? Called a blackguard, an enemy of China 'masquerading as a servant of God', the real Hudson Taylor does not fit the description. No one has ever been a truer friend or given his life, health and family more entirely for China's millions. So, if the allegations are to be understood, we must add a sweeping bird's eye view of China, the CIM and the Chinese church after the Revolution of 1911–12 and under the People's Republic.

In 1912 the doomed dynasty had foundered, but the 'rope of sand' had held. The national banner of hope, in horizontal bands of red, yellow, blue, white and black (for the five constituent elements of the nation), waved over the new Republic of China. Christianity seemed to stand for progress, and a spirit of enquiry was abroad. But the tables had turned and Christians, not least the missionaries in their rebuilt premises, had become cities of refuge for hunted Manchus.

Protestant Christians were being brought into local, provincial and national government. Vice-president Li Yüanhong, fresh from capturing Nanjing, said: 'China would not be aroused today as it is, were it not for the missionaries.' And Huang Xing, one of the leading republican generals, replied to Bishop J. W. Bashford of the American Methodist Episcopal Church:

> Christianity is far more widespread than you realize. Its ideals have largely pervaded China ... it brings a knowledge of Western political freedom, and ... inculcates everywhere a doctrine of universal love and peace. These ideals appeal to the Chinese; they largely caused the Revolution and they largely determined its peaceful character.[1509]

Amazingly, April 27, 1913, was set aside by the ruling cabinet as a day of prayer when Christians worldwide were asked to pray for China and the government. Services were held throughout China and in many churches in Europe and America.[1510] The grounds of the historic Altar of Heaven were opened for evangelistic services where formerly the emperor prostrated himself on behalf of the nation. Although a minority in the population of China, by the time of the revolution 'an elite of educated, alert (men of) integrity and resolution' were ready to take responsibility. The expectations of all missions in China had become greater than they had ever been. And it was no dream.

Looking back to Robert Morrison, risking death simply for learning the language, we marvel at what was achieved in a brief century. During the first half of it China was a closed land. But history moved on inexorably, from anti-barbarian dynasty to pro-Western republic. Within two years the result proved to be hollow. The first enthusiasm waned in 1914, reaction set in, reaching full force after 1922, and republican China became fragmented. In this debacle the church faced even more difficult times than at any time during the dying dynasty.

The story of the CIM through the twentieth century has been graphically presented by Leslie T. Lyall in *A Passion for the Impossible*. Even a summary would be out of place here. The 'open century' merges with the heyday of missions and ends with the eclipse which looked to some like the end of both church and mission in China. Far from the Revolution of 1911 or the Second Revolution of 1916, forty years of upheaval ended in greater turmoil than even the Second World War. For missions the 'open century' ended in 1950. For the church, the Body of Christ in China, another valley of the shadow of death proved yet again the seedbed for new life, growth and maturity.

But another glance at the perspective of the few decades under the Republic may broaden our vision and understanding. For it reveals a nation groping for self-government and stability, and missions polarised in their day of opportunity by dissension over motives and methods. Four decades of greater political instability under fumbling politicians and revolutionaries, and of personal insecurity during years of civil war and brigandage, still saw greater expansion and progress than under the dynasty. Most painful and regrettable was the divergence and distrust between the two schools of thought, the theologically mutable and the conservative orthodox who continued under criticism and pressure, unchanged in loyalty to the unchanging gospel. Mutual respect, friendship and comity to avoid overlap and competition were constantly sought, but compromise on irreducible essentials was unthinkable. Bishop Stephen Neill understood the dilemma when he wrote in his *History of Christian Missions* (page 431):

> Scores of Christian schools could record that every single student had been baptised before leaving school. This rising Chinese Christianity ... was little interested in the question of personal salvation. Not 'How can I be saved?' but 'How can China live anew?'—this was the burning question. It had little to do with the Churches. Most of these young people ... had a very real loyalty to Christ and to His message (but) what they stood for was 'the Christian movement in China'.

The two currents of missionary emphasis were like oil and water.

The first phase of the Republic lasted from 1912 until 1916, typical of revolutions in which thought and energy had concentrated on taking power, but relatively little on applying it to government. A middle-class intellectuals' revolt had largely left the peasant proletariat out of their reckoning. The people wanted peace. A medley of strong men, reformers and generals jostled for influence and power, and each failed through personal inadequacies, inexperience or selfish ambitions.

Yüan Shikai, last of the great viceroys, secretly inserted in the imperial rescript of abdication a clause to show that he personally derived the provisional presidency of the Republic from the Qing emperor. After forty-five days in that office, Sun Yatsen resigned in Yüan's favour, and Yüan's inauguration took place on March 10, 1912.

After some hesitancy the provisional parliament made Nanjing the capital, but Yüan stayed at Beijing. From the Wuchang rising on October 10, 1911, the 'Double Tenth', to the establishment of the Republic on January 1, 1912, only eighty-three days had elapsed. But to Sun's grief few showed concern for reconstruction and the welfare of the people. His three-stage plans for reconstruction were ignored, and the way was paved for two attempts to restore the monarchy and for the chaos of rivalry between warlords.[1511]

As provisional president, Yüan Shikai at once made a travesty of the Republic. 'He stamped out the tender shoot of democracy' and in less than a year rescinded the constitution. He appointed his own henchmen to the ministry of foreign affairs, internal affairs, war and navy. By turning on his charm, Yüan disarmed potential opponents. Only minor ministries went to the architects of revolution. Sun Yatsen and Huang Xing, 'the Napoleon of the Chinese Revolution', were made directors of a national railway system. The cabinet had become Yüan's puppet.

But by December the revolutionary Tong Men Hui and four satellite parties had amalgamated as the Guomindang, the Nationalist Party (KMT: Kuo Min Tang), which won a landslide victory in the parliamentary elections. A chain of assassinations followed, leaving Yüan Shikai heavily under suspicion. When troops surrounded the parliament in session and Yüan dismissed Nationalist provincial governors, six southern provinces declared independence. Yüan crushed this Second Revolution within two months and left his generals in control of the Yangzi area—as little more than warlords.

Yüan's personal ambitions knew no limits after that. With a crowd of ill-disguised men of military bearing in mufti surrounding the parliament building and shouting, 'Elect the president we want or do not expect to leave!' Yüan on the third ballot became substantive president. He dissolved the Nationalist Party, revoked the credentials of 358 members of parliament, and eighty more later, and contrived to become 'legally' the lifelong president, ruling without a cabinet and with the right to appoint his own successor. 'On December 23, 1914, (he) performed at the Altar of Heaven the immemorial rites which have been the sole prerogative of the emperor. The journey from his palace to the temple grounds was made in an armoured motor-car!'

So by 1915 he was ready to be made emperor. He accepted Japan's infamous Twenty-one Demands which would have robbed China of all remaining freedom, and secured the publication of an article by the president of Johns Hopkins University favouring a monarchy in China on the lines of the constitutional monarchy of Japan. Yüan himself remained conspicuously aloof, denying any wish to be made emperor. But a 'representative assembly' of his choosing approved the reintroduction of a monarchy and petitioned Yüan to accept the nomination. He 'reluctantly' acceded on December 15 and the next day decreed that his reign would begin on January 1, 1916. He had misjudged the nation.

Sun Yatsen had fled to Japan after the Second Revolution and in 1914 organised a Chinese Revolutionary Party to fight Yüan and his betrayal of the Republic. In exile he worked on the implementation of his Three Principles, the San Min Zhu Yi. War began with the capture of a government naval vessel; an ultimatum was delivered to Yüan; an anti-monarchist army came into being in Yunnan; and on December 25 the province declared its independence. Guizhou and Guangxi followed suit; in Shandong another anti-monarchist army was formed; and two of Yüan's strongest

generals declined to lead armies against his opponents. Yüan's dream evaporated.

Trying to revive a cabinet he watched helplessly as five more provinces declared independence and prominent citizens of nineteen provinces also refused any longer to recognise him as president. Such utter loss of face was insufferable. 'Overcome with shame, anxiety and grief, Yüan suddenly died (of uraemia) on June 6, 1916, at the age of fifty-six.' But he had 'sown the dragon's teeth', the seeds of warlordism—power to him who seizes it. Vice-President Li Yüanhong took over the presidency, and the 1912 constitution was restored.[1512]

Ill winds blow some good[1513] (1912–16)

A bias in favour of Christianity at a time of such fluctuation added momentum to church and missions. All factions had this attitude in common. Sun Yatsen to his dying day professed to be a sincere believing Christian.

The CIM had passed the membership mark of one thousand including associate members, with 2,500 Chinese colleagues in 1,200 centres and secondary schools largely for the children of Christians. Many missions frowned on sending Chinese students abroad to study theology. Too many who went chose not to return or came home unable to readapt to the conditions they found. So small theological and academically lower training colleges sprang up in China.[1514] The CIM saw the identical problem in taking potential church leaders out of their natural environment and making scholars of them in an age of politically militant students. And, too readily, zeal to equip themselves for service in the church became blunted by academic study. The genius of training men and women 'on the job', by systematic teaching and example as had been practised by the pioneers for decades, was capable of unlimited expansion.

Acknowledging the good work being done by Christian universities and theological colleges, the CIM chose to retain the method used by Jesus with his disciples, Paul with his companions and

Hudson Taylor, Dorward and many others with their Wang Lae-djüns and Yang Cunlings.

Educationists looked for academically trained Chinese in the churches connected with the CIM and many like-minded missions, and saw few. But the majority of missions, among them the CIM, saw the institution-trained clergy, pastors and evangelists preaching over the heads of their hearers or lacking 'heart knowledge' of basic Christian truth.

A strong letter to the *Chinese Recorder* from an American Southern Baptist, 'an ardent educationist', stressed that huge sums of mission money were going into secular education, that the colleges were not producing evangelists and ministers but businessmen and government officials, cultured but not Christian graduates. The Chinese church could not take over the colleges and were pauperised by dependence on foreign funds. It must be shown by missionary example that preaching the gospel is the primary object of the missionary's calling, and familiarity with the Word of God the first tool to be mastered.[1515]

The orthodox societies deliberately equipped peasant leaders for peasant churches and educated men and women for the type of town and city churches they were to serve. 'Bible Institutes' produced men and women by the hundred, well fitted for their particular work. This policy was misunderstood by critics, but has stood the test of time and adversity. The survival of the church in China through years of attempts to exterminate it is attributable to its grass-root leadership with the encouragement of the few heroic intellectuals. Dr Frank Keller's 'Biola' travelling Bible school,[1516] in boats on the Hunan waterways, studying while they evangelised, had its counterparts in several provinces.

These early years of the Republic also saw undreamed-of access to Chinese schools, colleges and army camps. The experience of Arthur R. Saunders, the tortured fugitive of 1900, at Yangzhou is an example. Fifteen thousand troops under General Xü Baoshan were stationed in and near the city, potential recipients of many thousands of pamphlets and New Testaments. Saunders consulted a junior officer and was summoned to an interview with the general. 'Preach to them too!' Xü told the astounded Saunders, and appointed his brother, the military governor of the city, to accompany him from camp to camp. 'We were received with military honours at each camp, and (had) personal conversation with the regimental officers.' The officers themselves then distributed the booklets to the men and Saunders preached for half an hour. General Xü gave Saunders a pass to admit him to any camp at any time. It bore the general's seal and the words, 'A deputy of Jesus to preach the Gospel'. A month later General Xü invited him to preach every Sunday to his officers and afterwards to the troops, saying, 'Get the officers and you've got the men.' The first year of such work ended on April 27, 1913, the day of prayer called by the government in Beijing.[1517]

During the next decade, and often afterwards in the other parts of China, missionaries had similar experiences. Between the eruptions of violence, calm periods permitted exceptional freedom for the church to expand in strength and influence. But by 1916 the First World War had been raging for two years, and the spectacle of so-called Christian nations at each other's throats disillusioned China. Meanwhile a renaissance of Confucianism and Buddhism, abetted by Japan, returned the nation to its previous religious imbalance.

A decade of warlords[1518] (1916–1926)

Yüan Shikai had at least maintained some order. After his death and Li Yuanhong's assumption of the presidency; chaos and disorder engulfed the nation. Li was a soldier, the captor of Nanjing, but not a statesman. His premier, Tuan, declared war on Germany without consulting parliament or president, so he dismissed him. In Tuan's support the encircling provinces of Zhili, Shandong, Shanxi and Shaanxi and others declared their independence and prepared to march on Beijing. So President Li called on the swashbuckling military governor of Anhui, Zhang Xŭn, to come to his rescue, and on his insistence dissolved parliament. Zhang Xŭn then threw off restraint, and restored the ex-emperor Pu Yi to the throne, on July 1, 1917. On the 12th, Zhang himself was driven out with his twenty thousand troops, so ending the hapless Pu Yi's brief 'reign'.

Such disregard of the Constitution of 1912, as much by the president as others, led Sun Yatsen to launch a Constitution Protection Movement under a military government at Canton in August 1917, while Premier Tuan again took control in the north. By declaring war on Germany again, Tuan naively secured a loan from Japan in August 1918 'to sustain the war effort', and sent troops to curb Sun Yatsen's 'revolt'. But clashes within Tuan's own political 'cliques', as they were called, sabotaged his campaign and brought about his fall. In the process, the former bandit, Zhang Zuolin (Chang Tso-lin), came into prominence in 1922 holding Manchuria against the Beijing regime. And another warlord, Wu Peifu, emerged in support of the in-and-out of office President Li.

By 1923, disgusted with politics in the north, public morale hit rock bottom. The only hope lay in the south. But in 1918 southern warlords had again driven Sun Yatsen in deep frustration to Shanghai. Frustrated but not despairing, he reorganised his Revolutionary Party and revived the name Chinese Nationalist Party (Zhongguo Guomindang). By skilful manoeuvres he regained power at Canton, and formally established a republican government on April 2, 1921, only to be thwarted by a turncoat who forced him once again to escape by warship to Shanghai. His Constitution Protection Movement had so far proved abortive.

During 1923 and 1924 fierce in-fighting between the warlords of several provinces compounded the chaos. When Wu Peifu, commanding a Zhili army of 170,000 men, went north to confront Zhang Zuolin who

was already advancing on Beijing, the Christian general Feng Yüxiang occupied Beijing with his own 'National People's Army' on October 23, 1924. He forced the usurping president (Cao Kun) out of office, reorganised the cabinet, and with others invited Sun Yatsen to Beijing to discuss peace and reunification.[1519]

Sun had cancer and his strength was failing, but he arrived on December 31, 1924, to a spontaneous welcome by a crowd of one hundred thousand. Within three weeks his condition worsened and he died on March 12, 1925, a disappointed man, apparently unaware of his high place in history. The Republic had brought the nation more suffering from lawlessness and war than misrule by the Manchus. But he was soon to be honoured as Father of the Revolution and the inspiration of opposing factions for decades to come. His embalmed body was buried at Nanjing four years later, and he was canonised as Lenin had been.

Within the Nationalist Party a small group of men (Sun among them) had begun studying the Russian Revolution of 1917 and Marxist-Leninism. The First World War had shaken his faith in Western democracy, and he looked to Russia for advice and example. A delegation under Mikhail Borodin came to Canton at his request, and helped him in the reorganisation of his Guomindang on the Comintern model. Sun had also established a military academy with German instructors on the island of Whampoa in the Canton river, under young General Jiang Jiaishi—to be known to the world as Chiang Kaishek. Sun and Chiang had married the beautiful Soong sisters, Chungling and Mayling, daughters of a Methodist minister, and were close allies. In 1926, after Sun's death, Chiang embarked on his 'northern expedition' which, after an historic rift with the communist party, was to break the power of the northern generals. After fifteen more years he was to preside with Churchill, Roosevelt and Stalin at the overthrow of Hitler and Tojo. Then the tide of success was to turn.

K. S. Latourette's droll comment on missionary life under the warlords, that it was 'an extra-hazardous occupation', was an understatement.[1520] Among many deaths from disease the CIM suffered the loss by typhus of W. W. Cassels and his wife in 1925, a major blow. Until 1926, being a foreigner still conferred some protection in some circumstances; but the kidnapping and murder of missionaries by bandits or unruly troops or looting mobs occurred all too often. The shooting of demonstrating Chinese students by Shanghai police on May 30, 1925, intensified nationwide agitation. And the inept shelling of Wanxian in Sichuan by a British gunboat aggravated the indignation.

'China for the Chinese' increasingly became the spirit of the church as well. Foreign prestige slumped dramatically. The consuls called upon their nationals to withdraw to the coast, and by the end of 1926 fully half the large missionary force had complied. Two hundred CIM centres remained staffed and active, and in some regions more Christian 'literature' was sold than previously. New believers with the courage to be baptised in 1925 numbered 4,577. The National Christian Council of China was formed in 1922, and in 1927 the Church of Christ in China, a minority organisation with the strongest influence. Membership 'on the basis of a simple confession of faith in Jesus Christ as revealed in the Scriptures' satisfied some and left the interpretation of the words too wide open to reassure others. Neither the Anglican nor Lutheran churches became members.[1521] Nor did the churches connected with the CIM. But the new tide of xenophobia was rising.

The Two Hundred (1927–32)

For Christians in China, whether foreign or Chinese, 1927 was most alarming, 'the hour of apparent disaster'. Always an embarrassment and anxiety to their consuls, whose responsibility was to avoid international incidents and to maintain prestige, missionaries had a predilection for trouble. Newspapers called them 'troublemakers'. A London daily ran the headline 'Millions Wasted in China. Missionaries' Dreams Shattered', and another stated, 'Hardly a trace remains in China today of all those vast missionary enterprises to which so much money has been subscribed by the British and American public'—journalists' fantasy.

In fact attacks increased and at Nanjing several foreigners were killed, missionaries among them. So the American and British ministers urgently ordered the wholesale evacuation of all in the interior. Memories of 1900 were still too fresh. At least nine-tenths complied. Of 8,300 Protestant missionaries, nearly four thousand left China for furlough, two thousand never to return. Two-thirds of those remaining congregated in eight port cities with no foreseeable prospect of returning to work. Less than 1,500 remained inland. Of the CIM's 1,185, over 213, mostly Continental associates, were free to stay upcountry and did so. Many of the rest believed that to stay would have been less dangerous than to leave their friends and travel. One father and child were shot dead on the way from Guizhou and the young mother wounded and held hostage with other companions. But if they had stayed, the persecution of Christians, 'running dogs of imperialism', would probably have been worse.

Schools, hospitals and homes were destroyed, others were taken over by troops for billets. Dr Whitfield Guinness died of typhus. And the magnificent Dr George King Jr, tall, powerful, gifted and popular, after organising the evacuation of the Gansu missionaries by five rafts on the Huang He (Yellow River) from Lanzhou to the railhead at Baotou on the Mongolian border, was swept away by strong currents and drowned. In the crucible of suffering, the church in China had been brought closer to destruction than in 1900. But again God knew what he was doing. A stronger church emerged.

Contrary to Latourette's mistaken understanding of the CIM's strategy, church-planting and church-building were basic policy from the beginning. Frank

Houghton, a future General Director, wrote in 1932:

Hudson Taylor's intention from the very first was to establish self-governing and self-supporting churches, but gradually there had been 'a tendency . . . to look upon the indigenisation of the Chinese church as a goal to be aimed at rather than as the foundation of all our policy as a Mission . . . If the Chinese leaders, whose development had been inevitably arrested by the very competence . . . of their foreign-friends, were enabled . . . to demonstrate that (God) had indeed given gifts to His Church, then the evacuation would prove to be a blessing in disguise.'

So it proved. The uprooting from preoccupations, and the involuntary crowding together at the coast also led the CIM to pray and consider the future in a series of conferences. Had the work of consolidating the expanding churches led to neglect of 'preaching Christ where His name is not known'? Hudson Taylor's catchword, 'Always advancing', was recalled. Xinjiang had received no missionary reinforcements for twenty years. Unevangelised regions still abounded. Walled cities stood waiting. Tibet, Mongolia, the aboriginal 'tribes' were hardly touched. We might be 'an army of contemptibles', but was this not the time to get ready to advance again?

Dixon Hoste, 'a quiet man (and) most of all a prayerful man and therefore a wise man' was calmly directing operations with the 1,185 missionaries and over four thousand Chinese colleagues. He called for a careful calculation of how many new recruits could be deployed as soon as the way opened. The sum total of 199 led him to express the China Council's conclusion as 'some two hundred new workers are required within two years'.

Three missionaries were murdered in Jiangxi just before the appeal for the Two Hundred was made known. And in the same week as the General Director was writing, hopes of the reunification of the country were shattered by the outbreak of a major civil war. Within a few months eight foreigners were murdered, thirty were held to ransom, five in Henan alone. Many more were robbed or captured briefly. Yet 1,200 or more men and women approached the Mission with a view to going to China.

The first party sailed in 1929 when the evacuees were returning inland, 185 by November 1931 when peace was restored in many regions, and the last of 203 on the last day of the year. Among them were six doctors.[1522] Others became gifted evangelists and Bible teachers. Fourteen became superintendents, one the Mission treasurer from 1941–71, and another the Deputy China Director and Overseas Director in South-East Asia. A price had to be paid. Some died in their first year, others before they could achieve much. And Hudson Taylor's 'bombshell' policy was followed—the Two Hundred were deployed with little language or experience, to learn the hard way in pioneer conditions. Some found it too hard. Others thrived on it.

In 1932 Dixon Hoste at the age of seventy-one laid down his directorship. The China to which the Two Hundred came was still a sad travesty of the true China. Opium growing had become widespread again, an anodyne for the intolerable distresses of the tormented populace. The 'wars of the ricebowls' had left them hungry. To pay their troops the warlords taxed the people, and when they could mulch no more, the disbanded soldiers 'lived off the land'. China had sunk into an abyss of misery.

The advent of Mao (1927–36)

As the revolutionary troops of Sun Yatsen entered Changsha in 1911, a young man of eighteen stood watching. Mao Zedong joined the army for a year before becoming a student. He read widely and by 1920 was a committed Marxist. The first secret congress of the Chinese Communist Party founded on July 1, 1921, four years after Lenin came to power, saw Mao present. Its policy of infiltration had already begun. Mao joined Chiang Kaishek and Zhou Enlai (Chou En-lai) with Sun Yatsen's Nationalists at Canton, and with his fellow-communists began to dominate the Guomindang

(KMT). In 1926 he took part in the Northern Expedition of Chiang Kaishek's five hundred thousand-strong army to quell the warlords and unify the nation. But after the pacification of Hunan and the fall of the three cities destined to comprise Wuhan, the Communists with the help of three or four KMT generals they had won over, challenged Chiang's leadership. The irreparable rift between them and the Nationalists took place, and a life-and-death struggle began.[1523]

During 1927 Stalin's influence was strongly felt in China, and revolutionaries went to be trained at a Sun Yatsen University in Moscow. Several uprisings in south China showed the nature of things to come. After one setback Mao found a haven in the Jinggangshan (Ching Kang Shan), a remote mountain range in Jiangxi close to the Hunan border, and in 1928 was joined by Zhu De (Chi Teh) and others. While Chiang completed his northern expedition, the Communists created a strong base and set up a Soviet of Jiangxi peasants organised for revolution and guerrilla tactics against Chiang's Nationalist garrisons (see map 2.97: p 552).

Chiang Kaishek recognised this as his greatest obstacle to the unification of China, and embarked on a policy of 'encirclement and extermination'. In the north he had broken the power of Zhang Zuolin, last of the warlords, and on August 4, 1928, transferred the capital from Beijing to Nanjing, in keeping with the 1912 Constitution. All restrictions on missionaries' travel in the interior were removed. On October 22, 1930, when Christianity was still despised as an alien religion, Chiang astounded China and the world by being publicly baptised. He never denied the faith, and his funeral in Taiwan in 1976 testified strongly to his Christian convictions.

In 1931 and 1932 a Japanese invasion of Manchuria (when Pu Yi was made puppet emperor of 'Manchuguo'), with a second front attack on Shanghai, gave enough respite from Nationalist pressure for the Communists to score some successes. Other Soviets were formed in south-western Fujian and in Hunan between Changsha and Yichang. But a truce with Japan allowed Chiang to return for his campaign against them with seven hundred thousand men in October. 1933. Encircled and deprived of necessities, the Communists had to break out or be overcome. But ideological power struggles within their own ranks threatened their survival, until they embarked on their historic 'Long March' on October 15, 1934. Pounded by the Guomindang, they outdistanced the Nationalists, trained for positional warfare, and crossing into Guizhou they reached Zunyi (Tsunyi) in January 1935.

Mao's personal struggle had been against Chiang Kaishek, but also against the Communist Party (CCP) politburo. His guerrilla tactics using rapid mobile units to confuse the enemy and 'pick them off one at a time' had been singularly successful, but until the break-out he was virtually under arrest by his political opponents. Their military 'adviser', in command as 'Li Te', was a German Communist named Otto Braun. The Long March officially began with eighty-five thousand soldiers, fifteen thousand civilian officials and the wives of thirty-five high leaders, but heavy losses had been sustained. In vehement speeches at Zunyi, Mao nailed responsibility for the debacle on Braun and the extremist politburo, won the argument and became head of the CCP and Secretariat.

Mao eliminated 'Li Te' and his own rivals, chose north Shaanxi as the strategic destination of the thousands now under his command (another Soviet base had been established there), and set off for the wild regions of far western Sichuan. In July 1935, a veteran of the party, Zhang Guotao, challenged Mao's choice of destination and led a column of his own towards the Tibetan borderlands and possibly Xinjiang. All endured extreme hardships on the march northwards through the mountainous border regions and Gansu until finally eight thousand survivors under Mao reached Wuqi, north-west of Yan'an (see map 2.97: p 552). In October, they joined the local Red Army corps of seven thousand. Other columns arrived later, including Zhang Guotao's, to bring the total strength under the undisputed leader Mao Zedong to thirty thousand. On the Long March they had tramped and fought over six thousand miles. They captured Yan'an and moved their headquarters there a year later, in December 1936.

The CIM on the Long March[1524]

(1934–35)

Marxist-Leninist doctrines carried to extremes caused intense suffering to the people of China. Even Mao Zedong resisted the liquidation of landlords, large and small, and redistribution of land to the very poor only, excluding any better off. China's Bolshevik politburo meted out death and destruction wherever they took power. Mao favoured levelling down the more prosperous peasants and small landlords, but only to equality with the upgraded poor. The politburo alienated millions by their atrocities. In Jiangxi alone one hundred thousand homes were destroyed, 150,000 so-called 'bad elements' were exterminated, and one and a half million refugees fled to other provinces. Changsha was sacked and the CIM's Bible Training Institute became the Communists' temporary headquarters. Henry S. Ferguson, a CIM flood-relief worker, was put on show in place after place as a hated imperialist, for weeks indomitably preaching Christ until executed. Sichuan suffered similarly in 1933.

Two of the Two Hundred, John and Betty Stam, were taken prisoner at Jingde (Tsingteh) in south Anhui on December 6, 1934, by a sudden advance of thousands of Communists. Condemned to die as 'imperialist spies', they wrote, 'We praise God, peace is in our hearts . . . May God be glorified whether by life or death.' A Chinese who pleaded for their two-month-old baby to be spared, received the retort, 'Your life for hers,' and was killed where he stood. On the morning of December 7, John and Betty Stam were stripped of their outer clothes, tightly bound and led out barefoot to be executed. A Christian medicine seller pleaded on his knees for them and shared their fate. John was beheaded first. Betty quivered, fell on her knees beside him and the great sword flashed again.

Their calmness throughout, and the look of joy seen on John's face afterwards impressed bystanders. The baby and the headless bodies were found by an evangelist thirty hours later.[1525]

At Jiuzhou (Kiuchow) in Guizhou five more members of the CIM and two children had been captured on October 1 and 2. Alfred Bosshardt, of Switzerland, and Rose, his English wife, Arnolis Hayman, an Australian, Rhoda his wife, and two children, and Grace Emblen were 'tried' and a ransom of Mex $700,000 demanded. The women and children were an encumbrance to an army on the march, and were released, but Grace Emblen only when exhausted by a week of forced marches. The men were held captive and repeatedly threatened with death. They could not be silenced. Hermann Becker of the Liebenzeller Mission, a German CIM associate, had been on friendly terms with Ho Long,

2.97 Hayman and Bosshardt's routes: caught up in the Long March

one of the Communist leaders, and acted as go-between to raise the ransom money. And three Chinese named Chai, Yang and Ho, who doggedly persisted as messengers in finding and pinning access to the 'Red' leaders, won the praise of the Communists for their courage. They took their lives in their hands each time.

For over a year, while still together, Hayman and Bosshardt trekked north-eastwards into Hunan at Sangzhi (Sangchih). There they parted company. When Arnolis Hayman was released on November 18, 1935, after 413 days' captivity, Bosshardt said, 'Pray that I may recklessly preach Christ.' He was taken by a different route all the way back and on through mountainous Guizhou to Dading and Bijie before heading south into Yunnan. Not until Easter Day, 1936, five months later, after 560 days as a prisoner, was Alfred Bosshardt also set free near Kunming, with dangerously advanced beri-beri.

They had shared the exciting life of their captors, under Xiao Ke (Hsiao K'eh), the twenty-five-year-old 'general'. Always on the go, harried by the Nationalists, suffering scarcity and privation, and brutally flogged when they tried to escape, they won the Communists' admiration and sympathy by their cheerfulness and transparent love not only for each other as Christians but for their captors. Fifty years later, in 1985 when Xiao Ke, head of the Peking Military Academy and the last surviving general of the Long March, was in Paris, he read in a newspaper about Alfred Bosshardt and asked his embassy to make inquiries. He was put in touch with the ninety-two-year-old veteran, and gratefully ordered that Alfred Bosshardt's inspired account of their experiences (dictated from his sick-bed in Kunming and published by Hodder and Stoughton in 1936) be translated into Chinese. Devoid of rancour, *The Restraining Hand* is a timeless classic of missionary literature to be read and re-read.[1526]

Too many missionaries suffered at the hands of the ubiquitous Communists before and during those years for the full story even to be summarised here. Russian

2.98 The Bosshardts before the Long March

influence and outright intrusion into Xinjiang, making the area an economic satellite, provided a strong rearguard to Mao's forces in north Shaanxi, and directly threatened the CIM's distant pioneers. In 1935 'the intrepid Trio', itinerant pioneers of the Gobi Desert oases and Xinjiang from June 11, 1923 to August, 1936, were arrested and held prisoner for months. These women were inseparable: Eva French of the Boxer rising in Shanxi, the leader of the three, Francesca French, Eva's younger sister, and Mildred Cable, the youngest, the author and platform figure, called 'our star' by the others.[1527]

From Huzhou in Shanxi to Suzhou in Gansu took fifty days' travel; from Suzhou to Urumqi (Dihua) thirty-six days; from Suzhou to Chuguchak sixty-two days, from Suzhou to Kashgar ninety-six days (see map 2.59: p 480). They covered the Suzhou-Urumqi route four times and the oasis area six times. Their books about their own decades in the Gobi Desert, and biographies of George Hunter[1528] and Percy Mather of Urumqi (Dihua) are classics of exploration and adventure, as well as of missionary pioneering in Central Asia between Gansu, Kashgar and Chuguchak, far, very far from fellow-Christians and colleagues. Eva was sixty-seven when they were forced out of Central Asia. They picnicked on her birthday in the open Gobi, on a precious jar of meat paste and 'the last lick of Chuguchak honey'.

Seven of the Two Hundred had crossed the Mongolian Gobi by Ford truck to Hami with Hunter in 1932—a journey plotted for them by the great explorer Sven Hedin. They joined Percy Mather on November 12, in time to be with him through the next Muslim uprising.[1529] When the storm burst upon them in January, ten thousand Kazakhs and Turkis attacked Urumqi, and the nine missionaries were overwhelmed with more wounded and typhus-ridden patients than could be handled. Worn out by incessant work, Mather and Emil Fishbacher, the only doctor, had no stamina to resist typhus when it claimed their lives.

The loss of Percy Mather stabbed George Hunter with greater pain than all his other experiences. 'When I knew that he must die I gave one loud cry to God for mercy, but then . . . I stilled my heart to accept His decrees.' Even so, in his loneliness he sometimes called aloud for his friend. When the Russians took control, the young men were told to leave Xinjiang,

2.99 George Hunter in Urumqi before the KGB took control

and Hunter's greatest ordeal began. He was held prisoner by the Russians for eighteen months, deprived for one year of a Bible, and tortured by the NKVD, the Soviet secret police (1934–43), before being deported by plane to Lanzhou. [I write with feeling, for after his torture and deportation I saw him as a patient at our hospital in Lanzhou.] A shattered old man, he set off for the Xinjiang border again to re-enter when he could, but died a few weeks later among Chinese Christians at Ganzhou (now Zhangye) on December 20, 1946.

Decade of war and opportunity
(1936–46)

About fifteen years of the 'open century' remained; years in which Roman Catholic and Protestant foreigners could snatch opportunities to continue their work, wars and rumours of wars permitting. Their success in this period is another epic of resilience. Unrelenting civil war between the Nationalists and Communists continued, while a New Life Movement to heal and strengthen the tortured nation was pursued. The firm policy of 'Generalissimo' Chiang Kaishek and the KMT, to break the power of the Communists, consolidate the nation, and then, but only then, to lead a unified China against the Japanese aggressors, called first for a determined offensive against the Yan'an strongholds. A north-western army was to attack from Gansu and a north-eastern army from Shaanxi and Shanxi, under the 'Young Marshal' Zhang Xüeliang (Chang Hsuehliang), son of the old warlord Zhang Zuolin.

The rise of the German Nazis, Italian Fascists and Japanese militarists had alarmed the Soviet Comintern. National Communist parties were urged to form alliances with other anti-Fascists against the common enemy. To be free to fight the Japanese, Mao needed a firm assurance of safety from the KMT. He launched a propaganda campaign with persuasive slogans: 'Chinese must not fight Chinese', 'War with Japan, not Communists', and popular pressure mounted. Mao's men infiltrated the two KMT armies and led the generals to favour a 'United Front'. On December 3, 1936, Chiang flew to Xi'an to restore morale, and on the 12th was put under arrest by Zhang Xüeliang and mutinous troops. They demanded among other things an end to civil strife, the release of political prisoners, the right of assembly and freedom to organise a people's patriotic movement. Asked what he required for his captivity he replied, 'A Bible only.'

The world was stunned; Chiang was needed to fight the Japanese. And faced with mounting Fascism in Europe, Moscow needed friendship with China to preserve stability with Japan, and could not stand aside while the Nationalists avenged themselves against Zhang Xüeliang and Mao. 'Chou En-lai emerged from behind the mountains to offer mediation.' From 'anti-Chiang, anti-Japan' the Communist party line changed overnight to 'Ally with Chiang against Japan'. A repentant 'Young Marshal' flew back to Nanjing with Chiang, on Christmas Day, to be spared all punishment except house arrest. And the Nationalist campaign against the Communists was called off, though the blockade of northern Shaanxi continued. The United Front against Japan consisted of two distinct and uncooperative parts, Communist in the north and Nationalist elsewhere. But while civil war ceased under the truce, subversion increased on a large scale. Communist cells in Nationalist China multiplied, and Nationalist morale declined.

By 1937 Japan's ambitions overflowed from Manchuguo. Control of the five northern provinces, isolation of China from Russia, domination of China's policies at home and abroad, and an East Asian Hegemony and New Order embracing all of south-east Asia were only beginning. After the Marco Polo Bridge incident at Beijing, when a Japanese soldier was killed, Japan's army swarmed over north China. Then Shanghai was occupied and Nanjing taken with the massacre of forty thousand and bestial excesses against survivors. Wuhan fell in October 1938 and Yichang at the

mouth of the Yangzi gorges soon afterwards. Japanese control extended one or two hundred miles each side of the river.

Chiang Kaishek made Chongqing his wartime capital and spurned peace offensives, fighting where he could. But all ports were seized and the necessities for war prevented from reaching the west except by the French railway from Vietnam to Kunming, by air from Burma and by the hastily made 'Burma Road'. Missionaries surreptitiously left Japanese territory and crossed the Yellow River floods to reach 'Free China'. One convoy of cars and trucks driven by new missionaries travelled north from Haiphong in Vietnam to Chongqing, taking the octogenarian Sir Montagu Beauchamp with them. He died at Langzhong on October 26, 1939.[1530]

There were times when China trembled on the brink of collapse. After Japan had attacked the US Pacific Navy at Pearl Harbour, Hawaii, on December 7, 1941, bringing America into the Second World War, the seemingly unstoppable Japanese war machine swept over south-east Asia, occupied Burma, and pressed south to the gates of Australia before being halted. Backward, underdeveloped west China received forty to sixty million refugees, among whom were tens of thousands of migrating high school and university students and staff from the east trekking thousands of miles on foot, as well as thousands of displaced Christians carrying the gospel with them.

Industrial equipment hastily dismantled before the advancing Japanese was reassembled, and unexploited sources tapped to provide essentials. The survival of China and containment of the Japanese verged on the miraculous. Unbridled currency inflation was somehow adapted to. At its worst the populace resorted calmly to barter. But widespread profiteering and corruption undermined the sincere efforts of the government. Mail not carried by air over 'The Hump' from India came through Tibet by yak, taking three months. The postage on one home letter cost me Mex. $23,500 in local currency, but a year after the Japanese surrender inflation stood at three to four thousand times the pre-war figures.

By 1944 and the end of the Second World War the Communists had a governmental machine of nine hundred thousand including a well trained army of six hundred thousand which, with their plans well laid, they insisted on retaining. On August 8, 1945, after the Hiroshima bomb had been dropped on August 5, Russia declared war on Japan, one week before she surrendered to the victorious allies; and prevented the Chinese government from occupying Manchuria. But Mao's troops were freely allowed possession and established their new base. Henry Pu Yi was carried off to Russia for indoctrination, and sent back after five years 'almost crazy' with humiliation and anger. After ten more years of 're-education' he was made a gardener, but later engaged in historical research.[1531]

The membership of the CIM had climbed to 1,368 in 1934, and in spite of world recession in the 1930s, income at nearly £160,000 was higher than five years previously. Until 'Pearl Harbour' when Japan went to war with America and the European allies, foreign missions were free to take Chinese refugees into their premises and had endless scope for helping and comforting displaced people, receptive to the gospel. Plans for the CIM were all in terms of advance. Recorded baptisms in 1939 although incomplete were 9,364, but probably exceeded ten thousand in churches connected with the CIM alone. But under war conditions missionaries able to work fell to only seven hundred in Free China, leaving 250 in Japanese occupied China—and these were soon interned, unless from Axis or neutral nations.

In 1940 the General Director George Gibb's health failed and he appointed Frank Houghton, Bishop of Eastern Sichuan since January 1937, to succeed him. Hardly could a General Director have had a worse moment to take responsibility. Frank Houghton's complete tenure of office was to be in the most desperate of times. Before

the year was up emergency headquarters of the CIM were established at Chongqing. He redirected the CIM's emphasis to self-government, self-support and self-extension by the Chinese church where adherence to the policy had lapsed: 'not to try but to do it'. The Mission must always be auxiliary to the Church. The price in terms of his own health led to his having to hand over the leadership in 1951, without naming a successor.

Strong Chinese Christian leaders emerged to steady and strengthen the tormented churches, and disruption of remaining dependence on foreigners prepared the church nationwide for meeting the greater ordeal after 'Liberation' by the Communists. Leslie Lyall's biography of the great evangelist John Sung, and biographical sketches of Yang Shaotang, Wang Mingdao and of Ni Tuosheng should be read.[1532] But what of Andrew Gih, Jia Yuming and the rest? Before it is too late to collect first-hand information, someone must write an unbiased, documented history of the gallant church in China. During and after the war years zealous Christians were called to serve in the highest councils and ministries of Chiang Kaishek's government. Many outstanding Christians in commerce and education also deserve to have their contribution to the church recorded. But not only the leaders who have hit the headlines. The history of the now burgeoning Church among the minority peoples of China deserves to be chronicled, to the glory of God.

The first intensive work among the many ethnic groups of Hmong or Miao (the Chinese term) began in 1896, nineteen years after James Broumton led the first one to Christ in 1877 (see pp 367, 385). W. S. Fleming and his He Miao companion, the evangelist Pan Shoushan, were murdered in 1898. But by 1909 James R. Adam knew of thousands of believing Miao and Nosu (Yi) in Guizhou alone. The farthest away towards Yunnan he referred to Samuel Pollard at Zhaotong, and soon the ten thousand Christian Miao and Nosu (Yi)

2.100 John Sung, the great evangelist

of the Shimenkan (Stone Gateway) area were more than Pollard could shepherd adequately. Thousands more in the Gobu, Jiegou region (including 3,300 communicants) built themselves a chapel for a thousand to worship at a time. When Adam was killed by lightning at his own front door many superstitiously believed it to mean that he was secretly evil, punished by God, but the church stood firm.[1533]

Christians from the Zhaotong area migrated to the Wuding mountains north of Kunming, and there thousands more turned to Christ. Believing Miao at Sapushan and Yi at Salowu soon numbered thousands, the spontaneous product of testifying Christians among their own people. And yet more among the Lisu, Lahu and Gopu people near them. Arthur G. Nicholls and Gladstone Porteous of the CIM served them for decades, and G. E. Metcalf further west. Numbers have swelled in the intervening years. On a visit to China in 1988 I met three university students from one of these minority areas and asked, 'How many Christians are there in your region?' They looked surprised and answered, 'We don't know. We speak of how many are not Christians.'

Far off in western Yunnan another minority race, the Lisu, heard the gospel from James O. Fraser, a graduate engineer with a flair for music, and a genius for establishing a strong indigenous Church. Taken into Yunnan by John McCarthy (who ended his days serving in the province he had crossed on foot in 1877), J. O. Fraser arrived in 1910 and six years later began to see Lisu turning from animism to Christ in increasing numbers. Lisu Christians won other families by the hundred. By 1918 sixty thousand tested believers had been baptised. A team of effective missionaries was built up over the years.

John Kuhn, an Elisha, joined Fraser in 1928. A strong, well-taught, self-governing, self-supporting, and self-propagating church became the model for future church-planting ventures in other regions and other lands. But Fraser died of malignant malaria on September 25, 1938. He was only fifty-two. His dust lies on a hill overlooking Baoshan (see map 2.59: p 480), but the apostle lives on 'in the Glory' and in the hearts of the Lisu. They are designated a Christian community by the Communist government. The Lisu Church now spans the mountains from the Lancang Jiang (Mekong River) to the Irrawaddy in Burma. The Salween valley sides still resound with Christian singing.[1534]

In the autumn of 1944 the Japanese drove strongly westwards to threaten Guiyang and the Burma Road. Urgent evacuation of women and children and many men reduced the CIM to a few hundred in Yunnan, Sichuan and the north-west. Associates of neutral and Axis countries continued under difficulties in Japanese territory in eastern China and valiantly did all they could to ease the lot of fellow-missionaries in the crowded internment camps. But surrender in Europe on May 8, 1945, and then in the Pacific arena, was the signal for missionaries in hundreds to flock back to China. Six hundred filled the holds in tiers of canvas bunks on the SS *Marine Lynx*, a US Navy transport ship. A golden age appeared to lie before us. The signal was sent for new reinforcements to come and begin language study. No one realistically foresaw the sudden bursting of the dam that released a flood of conquering Communists upon the nation exhausted and demoralised by so many years of civil and global war.

The 'gates of brass' slam shut[1535] (1946–53)

With world war ended and China apparently on the way to recovery, the national government returned to Nanjing and the CIM's administration to Shanghai. The Japanese vacated the headquarters buildings and the CIM moved in, not dreaming that in only five years' time they would be occupied by Communists. Drought and famine affected tens of millions of Chinese at a time when the wheels of government and missions were least geared to relief of such distress. Teams of missionaries and Chinese Christians returned to comfort and help old friends. The indigenous movement known as the 'Little Flock', led by 'Watchman' Ni Tuosheng (Ni T'uo-sheng), flowered into new life, as did other Christian bodies with no foreign connection—not least the Jesus Family. They migrated in family groups to set up as Christian communities in devastated and remote regions.

Most remarkable and promising for the new China was the flame of spiritual life among China's students. In the 1940s it spread widely from west China to the eastern provinces vacated by the invaders. National conferences of Christian students, in Chongqing, Nanjing, Shanghai, faced the increasingly strident voice of Communism and its implications. 'Christ or Communism' had become the issue looming larger and larger before all Chinese Christians. Commitment to Christ posed no hypothetical risks but the decision to testify and suffer for him. Together with the YMCA, thoroughly infiltrated by Communist agents, the China InterVarsity Fellowship (CIVF) met attempts to take control and use it for political purposes. True spiritual life in an individual could not be feigned, and wolves in sheep's clothing

could be recognised. The influence of those true student Christians of the 1940s on the church in China is incalculable.

In 1948 a member of the Swedish Mission in Shanxi, Miss Lenell, and a church elder were taken before a 'people's tribunal', condemned and shot. If missionaries were to be vulnerable to that extent, hundreds were at risk. And what of the hundreds of thousands of church members? Should all the CIM be withdrawn, or each region be treated according to the threats against it? The northern provinces were in Mao's hands, though the KMT still held Beijing. In June Kaifeng, Henan, was threatened. Would the CIM hospital be safer than non-medical centres? It was handed over to a courageous Chinese doctor who offered to run it, and the missionaries were withdrawn before the city was 'liberated'. The Nationalists (KMT) seemed incapable of checking the advance.

A North China People's Government was declared on September 1, 1948. By Christmas the People's Liberation Army (PLA) had reached the Yangzi and by mid-March 1949 were massed and ready to cross. Nanjing fell on April 23 and on the 25th Chiang Kaishek and his government sailed for Taiwan, their cruiser laden with all the gold bullion in the Bank of China. British and American warships moved to the Yangzi estuary; HMS *Amethyst* made her dash under fire from the banks of the Yangzi. Beijing fell on May 5, the attack on Shanghai began ten days later and ended on the 25th. On October 1, 1949, the People's Democratic Republic of China was proclaimed at the Tian An Men, the Gate of Heavenly Peace, in Beijing.

Of all Protestant missions more than four thousand had remained in China (4,062), and as many Roman Catholics. Only 185 members of the CIM were advised to withdraw. The year ended with 737 and many children still in China, 119 in associate missions.

May 1950 showed the shape of things to come. A 'Christian Manifesto' was drawn up in Beijing by Zhou Enlai and pro-Communist or crypto-Communist members of Christian organisations, and on June 30 this was presented at a meeting of Christian leaders and missionaries summoned and addressed by high Communist government officials. Subsequently thousands of church members were enlisted to put their signatures to it. 'While China is putting its house in order,' Zhou Enlai said, 'it is undesirable for guests to be present.'

The meaning was clear. But 'fair words before the true face' of what Christianity in China was up against, meant that no expulsion order against foreigners would be issued; the church was to rid itself of all traces of 'missionary imperialism'. 'Love Country, Love Church' had become the priorities. [While my own colleagues, my family and I were under house arrest for several months with fixed bayonets at our doors, we were assured that we could stay as long as we liked.] The CIM perhaps naively felt innocent of the imperialist label. Neither foreign hands on the purse-strings nor control of the churches could be held against them. Any hope of being tolerated died a quick death. 'It became clear not only that the missionaries would be allowed to do nothing, but that their continued presence in the country would bring danger to their Chinese friends.'[1536] One by one the societies instructed their members to withdraw.

Two remarkable events connected with this period stand engraved in the history of the CIM. The first occurred in 1930, when the Wusong Road premises became inadequate for the expanding mission and the sale of the site and properties more than covered the erection of two large multi-storey buildings at Sinza Road. Residences, offices, hospital and public rooms met all needs when the move was made in 1931. Second, in 1950, at a time of greatly increased expenditure, the power-play between two strong Communist government organisations ended dramatically in one paying three years' rental in advance for the Sinza Road mission home—where it could have been commandeered.[1537] Enough cash suddenly in hand, restricted for to use in China, allowed all members of the CIM

still upcountry to travel out by any means available. And large Mission incomes in 1950 and 1951 covered the inflated costs of dispersal once they were out.

God's provision convinced the Mission's leaders that even the apparent end, not only of the 'open century', but of the existence of the China Inland Mission was no more than the end of a phase. More than fifty years later the transformed Mission continues to work on the unchanged principles—years of constant, adequate provision for work in a dozen other East Asian countries by over one thousand active members from twenty-seven nations, as well as hundreds of superannuated members, children of missionaries and longstanding salaried colleagues.

To those of us who worked in the remotest regions it seemed impossible that the Communist Party, so recently blockaded in the sterile north of Shaanxi, should take control of more than a limited area of north China. When their armies reached the Yangzi, they appeared to be overstretching their resources. Astounding organisation, training and control of newly enlisted or conscripted reinforcements, consolidated each achievement. A period of anarchy or numb waiting for the unknown descended after the KMT officials melted away into anonymity and began the hazardous process of working their way to the coast and beyond.

Then the 'liberation'. And after a few days or weeks of charm and public entertainment with acrobats and music the rapid tightening of *baojia* control, by which the responsible member of every ten units (individuals, families, factories, streets, towns and so on) answered for the acts or thoughts of those under him or her. No one could move without official authorisation. Regimentation, parades, mass meetings, or indoctrination, for accusations for denunciation and sentencing to imprisonment or firing squad were well underway before we left. Our colleagues' truck halted while eight were executed by the roadside. It then went on. Christian accusing Christian, congregations accusing their pastors, children their parents, madness erupted on a vast scale. A reign of terror began, soon to be exceeded when Mao unleashed the children of the Red Guards to smash, burn, assault and even to kill in the name of a 'cultural revolution'.

The role of China Director passed to Arnold Lea. What he could do for Mission members travelling out, or held for investigation, or committed to prison, was limited. But his long list of those still in China slowly dwindled. At the beginning of 1951 it held 627 names. By April, 371 and as June ended, 203; ninety in September, and thirty-three as the year ended. The sufferings of the last missionaries to leave, 'harassed, humiliated, reduced to penury, denied the necessities of life' and imprisoned, may be read in A *Passion for the Impossible, Green Leaf in Drought* and *China: The Reluctant Exodus.* On May 22, 1952, eight remained, and on January 1, 1953, four: Dr Rupert Clarke, Arthur Mathews and his wife and daughter. Clarke was accused of murder.

Harry Gould, a member of the CIM, had succeeded in finding employment in Butterfield and Swire, a foreign shipping firm still tolerated at Shanghai, and found ways to transmit funds inland. On March 24, Wilda Mathews and her child were escorted out, and on July 20 the two men. A few months later, the Goulds left Shanghai— one hundred years since Hudson Taylor first sailed off to China. A few men of other missions were kept in prison for several years. But not until April 1959 did Helen Willis, an elderly, independent lady missionary, follow them out, the very last Protestant missionary to go. Of all the CIM's many members involved in this great evacuation, not one life was lost, not one limb—or as one put it, 'not a hoof or a husband was left behind'. The gates had slammed shut on the brief 'open century'.

The people of China stand up
(1949–89)

A few broad strokes of the brush bring this epic up to date. The 'open century' ended with the exclusion of foreigners from China, with the exception of the chosen few. Slowly the gates slid ajar again for some who could help to fulfil the Communist Party's aims, and increasingly for tourists bringing foreign currency. But to Christian aid for the Chinese church they remained barred and bolted. The impact of Communism on individual Christians and their corporate life has been devastating for many and profound for all. Temporary relaxation has sometimes raised hopes, but Marxist dogma on religion underlies all government policy. The elimination of all religion is the strategic aim. The Christian Manifesto (see p 564) was designed to eject all missionaries, to shackle the church and to direct it towards ultimate extinction. At first appearing drastic but tolerable, it ushered in years of bitter persecution.

When Mao Zedong declared the inauguration of the People's Democratic Republic of China from the Gate of Heavenly Peace, the Tian An Men, on October 1, 1949, he made the historic statement, 'The Chinese people have stood up.' With the end of the Second World War China had become a 'new' nation. After all the oppression and exploitation of the Qing dynasty and by foreign aggressors for more than a century, the renunciation of extra-territorial rights and a new dignity in the family of nations justified Mao's words. He used them with a new defiance.

With the expulsion of the Nationalist government, the Communist Party's attention turned to consolidation of power throughout China. Anti-Communists of all kinds, 'counter-revolutionaries', Nationalist agents, other 'class enemies' and politically naive employers, landlords, and landowners, found themselves the victims of vindictive accusation meetings. The 'people' were drilled for hours and taught party songs and slogans. (To this day they ring in the ears of all of us who were threatened by them.) Massed audiences yelled in unison the verdicts and penalties, in self-defence. The predominant emotion of the largest nation on earth had become fear. In the first six months of 1951 between one and three million executions took place. Mao himself admitted to eight hundred thousand. A 'Three Anti-' campaign directed against corruption, waste and bureaucracy was followed by a 'Five Anti-' campaign against bribery, tax evasion, fraud, theft of government property and theft of state economic secrets. The net was flung wide. Mao's control was absolute. The year 1954 saw the adoption of a Constitution of the People's Republic of China, but in 1957 the independent judiciary was swept aside. Might was right.

The first five-year plan launched in 1953 led in 1955–56 to the regimentation of the nation in cooperatives of one hundred to three hundred families. Overconfident of support, the 'Great Helmsman' embarked on three great gambles. Each in turn miscarried tragically. By 1957 Mao judged that he could allow some freedom of expression—or set a trap for unwary opponents. Quoting from the classics he called on them to 'Let a hundred flowers bloom and a hundred schools of thought contend.' A storm of protest and accusation against the actions of Party and government poured in. Mao reacted with a 'rectification' campaign against what he called 'stinking intellectuals' and 'rightists'. Blind to the value of professionals, intellectuals, writers and students, he banished thousands to labour camps. For twenty years the services of the nation's most needed able men were lost.

Worse things lay ahead in the second decade. Dissatisfied with China's economic progress, Mao then took the 'Great Leap Forward' in which the millions, in his commitment to permanent revolution, were marshalled into communes, work brigades and production units. By 1962 eighty per cent of the people were in communes. The entrepreneurial genius of the Chinese people was fettered at a stroke. Great engineering feats were performed by mass labour. But by 1975 the gradual dissolution of communes had begun. Natural calamities combined with the repugnance of the people at being denied their individual or family independence to produce a disastrous famine. After Mao's death in 1976 the government acknowledged that twenty million had died of starvation. But meanwhile the campaign against students and intellectuals continued until by 1965 forty million had become farm labourers. Ironically their exile saved many of them from a worse fate. Mao's ideological dreams of a Communist Utopia of his own design lured him into his third and worst gamble.

In 1964 Mao abolished the United Front Works Department and everything under it, including the Religious Affairs Bureau and Three-Self Patriotic Movement. Then, on July 13, 1966, he closed all schools and called upon all children to serve the motherland as Red Guards.[1538] Himself wearing the uniform red armband, Mao addressed a succession of massed thousands, 114 million in nine rallies, on the vast parade ground at the Tian An Men. He commissioned them to rebel, to flout the law, to destroy the 'Four Olds'—old ideas, old customs, old culture and old habits. Inspired or hysterical, with the Little Red Book of 'The Thoughts of Chairman Mao' and the haunting chant 'The East is Red' to marshal them, millions ran wild. In a 'gigantic frenzy' nationwide they destroyed, tortured and killed, more viciously and more extensively than had the 'child devils' of the Boxer nightmare. According to Hu Yaobang, General Secretary of the Communist Party, they publicly humiliated and assaulted thirty million victims. Many were maimed for life, and 1,600 were executed. By October 1967 this so-called Cultural Revolution that vandalised the nation's treasure and best brains had appalled its originator. Mao used the army to call a halt, disbanded the Red Guards and sent eighteen million 'bourgeois' students, including Red Guards, to work on the farms. He substituted a new phase of 'Struggle, Criticism and Transformation'. During five years of madness and economic dislocation, the outer world had been cut off, in almost total ignorance of events in China, while a whole generation of young Chinese found themselves in 'the vacuum of a lost hope'.

As unpredictably, the third decade saw Mao and his doctrinaire 'leftists' yield to pressure from more liberal colleagues. There followed the relaxation of controls to allow an influx of tourists and specialists. Without them China would have taken decades to recover from her economic destitution. But defying the dangers, perhaps 280,000 Chinese fled the country between 1972 and 1978 to find sanctuary in Hong Kong. In 1976 the old hardliners received the blow from which they have not recovered. Zhou Enlai, the statesman and premier, died; then Zhu De, the veteran marshal of the army, and on September 9, Mao Zedong at the age of eighty-three. Mao's estranged wife Jiang Qing and her three extreme leftist collaborators in the 'Gang of Four' failed in an attempt to seize the initiative. They were arrested on October 26. Since then a left-right seesaw of political pressures has made the work of Deng Xiaoping's more liberal regime uncomfortable. But the Four Modernisations of agriculture, industry, science and defence have progressed, and the lot of Christians became not easy but easier than during the thirty years between 1950 and 1980.

The Chinese church stands up[1539] (1949–89)

Even before the foreign 'scaffolding' was removed, the Chinese church could see the shape of things to come, and prepared for repression. Communist spokesmen give the total number of Protestant Christians in China at 'Liberation' as seven hundred thousand. One million is probably a more realistic figure, even after nominal 'Christians' by attachment rather than by faith have been discounted. If not, the record of their multiplication is even more remarkable.

The reign of terror begun in 1951 against 'spies, counter-revolutionaries, landlords and capitalists', caught up many Christians among those brought to summary trial, pilloried, imprisoned, executed or driven to suicide. Congregations were coerced into denouncing their pastors, fellow-Christians and foreigners with whom they had been associated. Hudson Taylor, Timothy Richard and other notable missionaries were and still are made the objects of attack for 'spreading the poison of imperialist thought' and serving the purposes of imperialist aggression.

Chinese church leaders bore the brunt of denunciation. Ni Tuosheng, the influential leader of the 'Little Flock' Assemblies, was sentenced to fifteen years' imprisonment as a counter-revolutionary and died shortly after his release. Wang Mingdao of Beijing received a life sentence but was released in 1979, twenty-three years later. The government agency responsible for their elimination boasted that 'the counter-revolutionary rings headed by Ni and Wang had been smashed!'[1540]

Persecution increased until the Cultural Revolution erupted in 1966, when Christians dared not show recognition of each other in public. Church life was completely suppressed and Christian books of all kinds destroyed. Whispered prayer in secret with one or two others became the only Christian fellowship still possible. In Amoy, to take one instance,

> Every pastor was made to 'walk the street' with a dunce's hat on his head and a placard around his neck announcing his crimes ... One woman was beaten to death. Communist cadres and Red Guards ... forced (twenty YMCA and YWCA secretaries) to kneel in front of a pile of burning (Bibles, hymnals and other books) while a large crowd stood around ... As the flames radiated their heat towards them, the victims cried out in excruciating pain ... Tormented by their excessive burns, most of them ... committed suicide by jumping from high buildings.[1541]

Marxism is dedicated to the extinction of religion and superstition. Temporary tolerance of the religions of China, with freedom of religious belief, is part of the strategy for achieving the goal of extinction. Control of a social phenomenon too powerful for control by other means has proved to need a lighter rein than was at first applied. Suppression of Islam in China began to provoke armed risings, so thousands of mosques have been built at government expense and Islamic practice tolerated. Attempted suppression of the Christian Church was counter-productive. They did not suffer or die in vain. Persecution purified the Church from false and weak elements, and demonstrated its indestructibility and vitality. New believers were attracted to it, even from the ranks of the Party. As a result the million Protestant Christians have become five or more millions by reluctant government admission, and twenty or more million by conservative estimate from an abundance of testimony and evidence.

The strategy of the Chinese Communist Party (CCP) is public knowledge. It works through the government's United Front Work Department (UFWD), with units throughout China, to coordinate and unify all aspects of national life, in fulfilment of Party policy. The United Front works through the Religious Affairs Bureau (RAB) centrally and locally, by 'patriotic organisations' in each religion. In the case of Christianity, the official arm of the government began as the Three-Self Reform Church, but was never a church in structure or function. This was soon changed to Three-Self Patriotic Movement (TSPM), adapting in name the familiar 'indigenous principles' of self-governing, self-supporting and self-propagating churches. The Three-Self Movement, both centrally and wherever it is represented locally, is answerable to the Religious Affairs Bureau and as a government body calls upon the Public Security Bureau to enforce its will. In parallel with the administrative TSPM since 1980 is the China Christian Council (CCC). To it is delegated the pastoral aspects of the churches.

Launched in April 1951, the Three-Self Movement conducted a prototype 'accusation meeting' in Beijing and carried the method to Shanghai and throughout China. In 1955 it conducted a nation-wide accusation campaign against Wang Mingdao, who had become the leading

2.101 Wang Mingdao: preacher, author and survivor of imprisonment, 1956–79

evangelical preacher in Beijing. Its first chairman, Wu Yaozong (Y. T. Wu), until then the general secretary of the YMCA, was an avowed Marxist and committed Communist. He quickly wound up all other Protestant Christian organisations, to leave the TSPM the sole government-recognised representative, and in 1958 'consolidated' city churches in a form without denominational distinctions. In Beijing sixty-five were reduced to four, in Shanghai fifteen survived for a while out of two hundred. Rural churches had already been closed during the land reform period.

But the Three-Self Movement was also religious. In 1966 when Mao through the Red Guards and Cultural Revolution attacked religion in any and every form, even the government-sponsored Three-Self churches and personnel came under the same lash. Silence fell on the religious scene until 1972. Marxism seemed to have triumphed. 'The church is extinct,' the enemies and pessimists croaked. Believing that 'religion is the opiate that lulls the spirit of the people', and that 'all worship or veneration of supernatural forces can be called superstitions; religions are also superstitions but not all superstitions are religions', only the abolition of religion was acceptable to the purists. After the death of Mao and the return of Deng Xiaoping to power in 1978, a policy of uniting to heal the wounds of the Cultural Revolution revived the TSPM (moribund for fifteen years) to regulate the measure of religious freedom permitted.[1542]

Even in the first decade of severe repression, strong evidence of Christian survival occasionally emerged. In 1957 Christian students were meeting to pray and study the Bible together in nine universities. Wherever they scattered they went as leaders. Following the Great Leap Forward of 1958, the 1960s saw the number of Christians in the communes increase dramatically. Successful work units even came to be known with approval as 'Jesus Production Team No 1'. With the dangers of the Cultural Revolution removed, and Christians showing their colours again in 1978, the complete failure to extinguish the church became apparent. In contrast, it had grown stronger in numbers and spirit. Under suffering, faith and loyalty had been tested, spiritual maturity had deepened. A stronger, buoyant, indomitable church emerged. After the release from prison and labour camps of many undaunted Christians, new confidence became evident. 'Revival' took place in province after province, with every evidence of God's Holy Spirit using remarkable men and women to turn whole communities to Christ. The growing edge of the church was in this spontaneous expansion, unrelated to the regimented churches. To harness it became the government's priority.

On July 28, 1954, Wu Yaozong delivered a long report at a conference of the Three-Self Patriotic Movement (TSPM) in Beijing.[1543] After summarising the part played by missionaries in the early history of nineteenth century Sino-International relations he said:

> We have always thought that China Inland Mission founder Hudson Taylor was a warm-hearted evangelistic 'missionary'. But in 1888 at the London Centennial Missionary Conference he spoke greedily

of the mineral resources of China. He said, 'These resources can make western nations rich.' He was afraid that China would wake up; he approved the special privileges which the unequal treaties gave to the 'missionaries', saying, 'Now under the protection of these treaties we can take our passport in our hand and go comfortably by road or river boat into every province in China.' He wanted foreign 'missionaries' to take advantage of the opportunity, and through preaching the gospel to extend imperialistic aggression against China.

> It is just these mission boards and these 'missionaries' who for over a hundred years have controlled the personnel, government, finances ...

The Centennial Conference to which Wu Yaozong referred was the one we outlined at which Hudson Taylor and the CIM pleaded strongly for China and against Britain's opium traffic. The two-volume report of the conference[1544] gives Hudson Taylor's address verbatim. Referring to China he said:

> If you will think not only of the number of people who live there, but of their capacity, you will see that we have a mighty nation to deal with, who deserve, as has been well said, our best prayers and our best efforts. They are an intellectual people. Where is the government that has surpassed China in diplomacy? Where are the merchants that have exceeded the Chinese in their ability or in their success? ... Allow him to compete at our universities, and he will not only secure our academic degrees, but will take them with honours. This people is a great people, and they are capable of great things. The purposes of God with regard to them, moreover, must be great purposes ... We have seen the rise and the fading away in succession of Egypt, of Assyrian of Babylon, Persia, Greece, and Rome; but China is neither old nor effete; today she is a living nation, young and vigorous and full of power ...

> We all believe in the God of whom we have been hearing as the Creator of heaven and earth. Is it by accident that beneath the broad acres of China the greatest mineral wealth of the world has been stored? Had God no purpose in view in those immense

coalfields, which would supply the world with coal for two thousand years? Had God no purpose in view in giving China everything in the shape of mineral wealth which has made any country in the west to be great or prosperous? Surely, these things are not by accident. God surely has great purposes for China in the future ...

They are on the move. Telegraph lines now span the empire ... Railways are being surveyed for and prepared, and China is on the move ... China will soon be a factor in the world's history, if we mistake not the signs of the times ...

Now what has Christianity done for this great people? ... After eighty years of missionary labour we are thankful for thirty-two thousand communicants; after eighty years of commercial labour there are more than one hundred and fifty millions of opium smokers in China [corrected by Hudson Taylor to 'opium smokers and their families who are suffering directly from the evil'].

We have given China something besides the Gospel, something that is doing more harm in a week than the united efforts of all our Christian missionaries are doing in a year. Oh, the evils of opium! ... I entreat you to pray to the mighty God that He will bring this great evil to an end. Do we not owe China, then, by the wrong we have done her, and by her great needs, the Gospel? Now is the time of opportunity ... I need not tell you the whole country is open to us. Now by treaty-right, with passport in hand, we pass into every province with safety and comfort, travelling along the great highways and the rivers of China.

'God surely has great purposes for China in the future.' With transparent admiration and love for China Hudson Taylor was emphasising her greatness, with endless resources to make her greater still. He stressed the moral debt the West owed her, to give her the gospel. Only two explanations of Wu Yaozong's interpretation are possible. Either his understanding of the English language and of Hudson Taylor's meaning was too limited; or he deliberately distorted Hudson Taylor's words and fabricated others. Did Hudson Taylor speak 'greedily of the

mineral resources of China'? that 'these resources can make western nations rich'? Quite the reverse. China's vast resources were God's gift to China to make *her* rich and great. Quoting Marquis Zeng's *The Sleep and the Awakening*, Hudson Taylor praised China's awakening and openness in 1888 as her great opportunity to hear the gospel. Frequently found in the Hudson Taylor archives are references to Napoleon Bonaparte's alleged remark, 'China? There lies a sleeping giant. Let him sleep, for when he wakes he will move the world.'[1545]

Over the years others have used Wu's words and added to them, for their own purposes, accusing Hudson Taylor of a lifetime of deliberate fact-gathering for the consuls and merchants. Knowing as we do from so much evidence, that the CIM avoided dealings with both, such allegations could be amusing if they did not deceive the uninformed.

Wu Yaozong died in 1979 and was succeeded by Bishop Ding Guangxun (K. H. Ting), as chairman of the Three-Self Patriotic Movement, and of the China Christian Council.[1546] Following Deng Xiaoping's visit to the States and the resumption of diplomatic relations, it became safe again for about two years for Christians to meet in each other's homes. The Three-Self Movement gave expression to a new policy: to restore so-called religious 'liberty subject to control'; to return confiscated properties to so-called 'open churches' under the TSPM and CCC; and to unite all Christians under the TSPM and CCC. Christians who for good reasons chose not to register as individuals or congregations with these agencies became the objects of special attention. However, reassured by the prospect of freedom to worship together under government protection, many former pastors and church members of the best type registered in the 'open churches'. In spite of the 'Love Country, Love Church' emphasis and regular political indoctrination received, they see membership as the way forward. If regarded as a crescendo meaning 'Love Country, Love Church, Love Christ', the slogan is acceptable.

The record of the TSPM before the Cultural Revolution, and suspicion of its motives and fair words kept many more away. In large and small groups, depending on the presence or absence of leadership and teaching, they embrace the majority of Christians in China today. Some adopt church structures with pastors or elders and deacons, baptisms and communion services. Others, 'taught by the Holy Spirit' though lacking human leaders, cling together for prayer and singing, and Bible reading if they possess any Scriptures. Whether meeting in homes or outgrowing them and meeting in the open or in other buildings, they are 'independent', 'unregistered' congregations which have come to be called (often inappropriately) 'house churches'. Many number hundreds and, linked up with each other, thousands, whom the government (after seeing how repression backfires) rightly hesitates to regiment by force. International awareness and published concern for them are also known to contribute to their protection.

The presence of crypto-Communists in the Chinese church before 1951 is well documented. Li Chuwen, a notable Shanghai pastor, when about to be beaten by Red Guards, escaped by revealing that he was a party activist. In 1983 he was appointed Deputy Director of the New China News Agency in Hong Kong. Another elsewhere told them to read the proof in the United Front Work Department that he too was an infiltrator. A high-ranking official in the Religious Affairs Bureau has spoken frankly about members of the TSPM deputations to western countries. The favourable front presented to Archbishops and other church dignitaries and through the media has been designed to mislead. The Roman Catholic Church has its own story to tell. 'Religious liberty' as understood in the West is a very different matter from the frayed thread of 'liberty subject to control' conceded in China for political reasons. The *raison d'être* of the Three-Self Movement has been to 'rally all Chinese Christians under the leadership of the Chinese Communist Party and the People's Government'. And 'the CCC religious policy sets definite limits to the enjoyment of religious freedom beyond which believers step at their peril.' A leading member of those who maintain their independence asks, 'Should the Body of Christ be led by the atheistic Communist Party?' even if its leaders have been 'consecrated' as bishops?

From the earliest days political opponents accused missionaries of sinister and repulsive motives. But from the end of the warlord period until the present day, criticism and attack have been in terms of imperialism, spying, and fantasy. The inextricable involvement of missionaries with their aggressive governments has been recognised in each volume of this series. They still suffer the penalty of that involvement every time they are called the religious arm of the imperialists.

Accusations that Hudson Taylor and the CIM engaged in prospecting for coal and iron are only part of the modern propaganda by falsehoods. The recent misuse of quotations from CIM publications (such as *China's Millions*) and condemnation of the Mission's innocuous telegraphic economy code of 1907 are only examples of distortion of the facts for the same purpose. When Hudson Taylor protested to a consul that using force against China was futile but goodwill shown by famine relief gained friends, he was sincere. But his words have been manipulated to mean that aggressive intentions were better served by the relief of suffering. Hudson Taylor himself was described in lectures at the (TSPM) Nanjing Theological Seminary in which Bishop Ding Guangxun took part, as 'masquerading as a servant of God while actually representing colonial imperialistic foreign interests' and having 'a materialistic interest in the vast coal and mineral deposits of China' by which 'the capitalists can fill their mouths.'[1547]

In 1981 a book by Yan Changsheng on *Missionaries and Modern China*, published in Shanghai, said:

Besides doing missions, Hudson Taylor also aimed at offering intelligence information to the British aggressors, and exerting himself for British businessmen in the economic exploitation of inland China. Every CIM missionary carried a secret telegraphic code book, compiled by the CIM itself. Taylor collected information wherever he went, and, using the secret code, he dispatched telegraphic messages to the CIM Shanghai office, whence the information was then transmitted to London. Some of the economic information was passed on to British merchants in Shanghai. These British merchants in coastal China regularly authorised the inland missionaries to sell commodities and investigate the market. Thus the missionaries offered a great deal of help to the merchants (p 117 ff).

Another, in 1988, edited by Ma Chaogun, *Two Thousand Years of Christianity*, takes up the same falsehoods and amplifies them:

> The British missionary Hudson Taylor founded the China Inland Mission in 1865. He supplied the British forces, in their aggression in China, with enormous supplies of intelligence. Each CIM missionary had hidden beside him a secret telegraphic code book. Thus, at any time, they could use the code to send intelligence reports they had made, from all parts of our country to the CIM office in Shanghai for transmission to London (p 242).

Hunan's Zhou Han has equally imaginative successors. Certainly 'the father of lies' and 'accuser of the brethren' is as busy as ever. The facts are simple. Hudson Taylor founded the CIM in 1865. So neither he nor CIM missionaries worked in the theatres of either opium war, of 1840–42 or 1858–61. Even in 1900 only one young family was in Tianjin when Chinese troops and Boxers besieged it. 'Enormous supplies of intelligence' is pure fantasy. 'Each (or every) CIM missionary had hidden beside him (or carried) a secret telegraphic book . . . compiled by the CIM'? This too is wide of the mark. During Hudson Taylor's times the commercial economy code known as 'Unicode' was available for use by the

general public. '*Lammermuir*' and 'Inland' were adopted as telegraphic addresses from about 1904, but the CIM's own comprehensive code book was collated by J. J. Coulthard, T. G. Willett and Charles T. Fishe in 1907, after Hudson Taylor's death. He never used one, let alone to despatch information from wherever he went for transmission to London. Such allegations are unworthy of intelligent Chinese authors.

Revised and enlarged in 1929 by Frank Parry, as a private (copyright) mission handbook, it was used by many other missions and by businesses. Based on messages actually received and sent in the normal rise of things, it was in no way secret. Quite long sentences could be represented by a single word. '*Homuriyupu* with the help of the code book tables meant Mr and Mrs J. R. Sinton and children are leaving by Butterfield and Swire's Line on the 9th.' The 1929 edition weighed 1.5kg. Far from every missionary carrying one with him, a copy was kept for use at each Mission centre in cities and towns with a telegraphic office. They may be searched in vain for subversive or suspicious words or phrases such as secret agents would need; or, in the same way, any with economic, commercial, significance. An analysis of the contents clearly shows it to have been primarily for domestic and administrative communication, while making provision for reporting emergencies such as occurred all too frequently. It simply reduced the cost of telegrams to a fraction of what it would have been if spelled out in full. In wartime its use was of course banned.[1548]

If any answer to all these accusations is needed, it must be that the burden of proof lies on the accusers to substantiate their suppositions. Meanwhile it is significant that the attitude of foreign governments, consuls and merchants towards Hudson Taylor and the missionaries belies the allegations. In his lifetime and since, only a handful of honours for famine, earthquake, flood relief and social service have been awarded to individuals, but never anything at all to the alleged arch-offender himself. But the Chinese government before and since the

1911 Revolution did award high honours, though not to Hudson Taylor. No, in this 'spiritual warfare' the 'father of lies' fears the truth, while Hudson Taylor has since 1905 been far removed from all attempts to condemn him Attacks on him are attacks on what he taught.

This review has brought us to 1989, but the winds of change blow hot and cold. Bishop Ding in mid-February 1989 stated (in an interview with News Network International, Los Angeles) that the Three-Self Patriotic Movement was to be dissolved by the end of 1991. Since then much has happened, and the future is unpredictable. But while the weather vane may swing, 'GOD reigns!' and 'holds the key of all unknown.'

The sufferings and continuing difficulties of Christ's Church in China are by-products of its life, of the life of Christ in them. They may be 'a rope of sand' in vulnerability, but 'sand like the seashore' in withstanding the waves. Since Robert Morrison and William Milne rejoiced over the first Chinese to respond to their 'good news'; in not much more than a century and a half Protestant Christians alone have multiplied to many millions. On July 16, 1814, Morrison wrote in his journal (see 1, p 134): 'At a spring of water issuing from the foot of a lofty hill by the seaside, away from human observation, I baptised [Cai A-fu, the first convert after seven long years]. May he be the first fruits of a great harvest; one of the millions who shall believe and be saved.'

Nearly five thousand 'open churches' and thirty thousand registered 'meeting points' are now acknowledged to exist, while governmental concern is apparent over the innumerable but probably one hundred thousand or more independent, unregistered meeting points in the cities and countryside. Official figures represent the tip of the iceberg. The persecuted church in China had burgeoned to ten, twenty or more times its numerical size of one million when 'liberated' (in 'new-speak') at the close of the 'open century'. Where does it stand now?

The International Bulletin of Missionary Research's 'Annual Statistical Table on Global Mission' for 1987 (compiled by David B. Barrett, of the Church Missionary Society since 1956 and research officer for the Anglican Consultative Council and the Lambeth Conference since 1970, currently to the Foreign Mission Board, Southern Baptist Convention) commented:

> Suddenly, by 1986 China has become the fastest expanding nation for church growth ever. This year's surveys indicate that China has a total of at least 81,600 worship centres (churches, congregations, house groups) with 21,500,000 baptised adult believers, and a total Christian community of 52,152,000 Christians affiliated to churches, including children. Thirteen large cities have baptised church members numbering over 10 per cent of the population. House churches are now known to exist in virtually every one of China's 2,010 administrative counties. A vital evangelising church has come into existence almost everywhere throughout the nation.

If such spontaneous growth can take place under conditions of repression, what would full liberty result in? Given true freedom of belief and expression, what golden prospects will lie before China in a new 'open century' ahead! 'China evangelised by the Chinese!' And overseas? Already there is a strong body of Chinese Christians dedicated to worldwide evangelism.

The crown of life

From beginning to end this sketch of the church in China and Hudson Taylor's part in it have reflected the story of the New Testament Church. The seed must die to release its life. Scripture consistently rates the physical below the spiritual. 'Do not be afraid of those who kill the body but cannot kill the soul,' were the words of Jesus himself (Matthew 10.28 NIV). 'Blessed is the man who perseveres under trial, because when he has stood the test, he will receive the crown of life that God has promised to those who love him' (James 1.12 NIV). 'Be faithful, even to the point of death, and I will give you the crown of life' (Revelation 2.10 NIV).

When Hudson Taylor, the CIM and their fellow-Christians of all kinds treated life as on trust to be spent to the full, as part of continuing service for God in the life to come, its fruit 'the Church that will not die' sprang up. War, hatred, persecution, death, as incidentals formed the climate in which Christ's promise was fulfilled. 'I will build my church' (Matthew 16.18 NIV).

After Peter's strong defence, 'We must obey God rather than men!' (Acts 5.29 NIV) the advice of Gamaliel to the rulers enshrined another undying principle which China will do well to heed: 'I advise you: Leave these men alone! Let them go! For if their purpose or activity is of human origin, it will fail. But if it is from God, you will not be able to stop these men; You will only find yourselves fighting against God' (Acts 5.38–9 NIV).

Perhaps we are still near the beginning.

2.102 Hudson Taylor in 1904 at Jennie's graveside, near Vevey in Switzerland

Appendix: Chronology of the Boxer Crisis (1898-1901)

Place names appear in capitals, martyrs in bold, survivors in italic

'Herod killed James... and seized Peter... [but God] brought Peter out.' (Acts 12)

1898–99

Nov 4,1898	**Wm S. Fleming**, CIM; Pan Shoushan, killed by sword, GUIZHOU
May 26, 1899	Boxer Society formed, Shandong
June 14-25	Kienning, Fujian, riots; missionaries escape
Nov 1899	Ci Xi's edict: resist foreign aggression; Boxers dominate Shandong, enter Zhili
Dec 30, 1899	**S. M. Brooks**, SPG, Shandong, killed by sword, beheaded

1900

Jan 11	Ci Xi's edict supports Boxers
April 20	Yü Xian, governor, arr Taiyuan, trains Boxers
May 12-14	**61 RCs** massacred, ZHILI
May 14	**Elder Si**, Hongtong, sword thrust, dies Oct 1901
May 17	GONGCUN, Zhili, Prot. **Pastor** and **Christians** massacred
May 23	*Mother, wife of Hsi Shengmo* beaten, plundered, Shanxi
May 17-28	**Wm Cooper** at Shanxi conferences
May 29	30 railway **engineers** fight, 6 die from Baoding, Zhili, to Tianjin
May 31	Allied reinforcements arr Beijing

JUNE 1900

June 1	**C. Robinson**, SPG, YONGQING, Zhili, killed
June 2	**H. V. Norman**, SPG, YONGQING, killed
June 4	**Wm Cooper** dep Lu'an to Baoding
June 5	*Eva French* party to Jiexiu for safety
June 6	LU'AN riot; 5 **Christians** killed; *A. E. Glover*, **wife**, *two children*, and *C. Gates* attacked
June 7	Ci Xi's edict justifies Boxers
June 8	TONG XIAN **Christians** massacred; Beijing foreigners congregate for defence; cable US President, 'outlook hopeless'
June 9	*Tong Xian missionaries* to Beijing; *Glovers* dep Lu'an for Tianjin
c 9	(*Fei Qihao* report) 100+ **Christians** massacred at YÜCI, Shanxi
June 10	*5 Am Board* dep Zhangjiakhou to cros Gobi to Kiakhta
June 11	BEIJING Jap **Chancellor** killed
June 13	BEIJING massacre, 100s of **Christians**; Boxers burning, looting. *Glovers* arr Shunde c/o *Griffiths, Brown*; rioted

June 14	Boxers arr DATONG, N Shanxi;**McKees**, **I'Ansons**, **Aspden**, **M. E. Smith** cornered, doomed
June 14	BEIJING RC Beitang siege begins
June 15	**Wm Cooper** arr Baoding c/o **Bagnall family**
June 19	**Dr Millar Wilson** dep Linfen
June 19, 20	**Swedish Holiness Union** (CIM) dep HENYUAN, YINGZHOU, ZUOYÜN to SOPING; **Christians** massacred
June 20	BEIJING German **envoy** killed; legation siege begins; **Francis James** killed; massacre of **Christians**
June 21, 25	*Shandong missionaries* escape to coast; Christians persecuted
June 23	Tianjin settlement siege lifted
June 23	*Am Board 5* (June 10) joined by *17 C&MA*, *4 Swedes*, cross Gobi
June 23-25	Manchuria foreigners escape
JUNE 24	EDICT TO KILL all foreigners; Prince Chuang supervises massacre of 100s of **Christians**; edict to kill changed to PROTECT by Yüan Zhang, Xü Jincheng
June 24	**Lt Watts-Jones** wrecked, killed
June 25	Gov Yü Xian unleashes Boxers
June 26	**Millar Wilson** arr TAIYUAN; Zhang Zhitong promises to protect foreigners in Yangzi valley provinces
June 26	*A. R. Saunders* family, *A. Jenkins*, *E. Guthrie* rioted at Pingyao
June 27	*Saunders* party dep Pingyao, to Taiyuan, Lucheng, arr July 5 TAIYUAN, hospital destroyed, **E. A. Coombs** killed; 6 flee to BMS
June 27	Jiexiu riot, *Eva French* party escape 28th to Linfen
June 28-29	BAODING,Pastor **Meng Jixian** killed; XINZHOU BMS 8 cornered
June 28	*Jonathan Goforth*, *Canadians* dep Anyang, Henan; YINGZHOU **Christians** burnt alive
June 29	SOPING massacre of **10 Swedish**, **4 C&MA**; *Wang Lanbu* escapes SHOUYANG **Pigott family**, **Robinson**, **Atwater girls**, **Duval** flee to the hills
June 30	XIAOYI, **Whitchurch**, **Searell** killed Shunde riot, *Griffiths*, *Brown* escape BAODING North, **5 Am Presbys** killed, Mukden church, mission burnt

JULY 1900

July 1	BAODING South **Am Board 3** killed; CIM **Bagnall**, **wife**, **children**, and **Wm Cooper** all beheaded
July 2	New edict: expell foreigners, persecute Christians; *Eva Fench* party join *Dreyers*, *Lutleys* at Linfen
July 2	**Pigott party** return to Shou yang, Huolu, Zhili, *C. H. S. Green family*, *J. Gregg* hear of massacres, riots
July 2-3	Yücheng, S Shanxi, *Swedish mission* given safe passes; leave funds with 'CCH' undercover; dep Shanxi
July 3	*Glovers* arr Lu'an from Shunde; Mukden **RCs** massacred; *O'Neill*, Irish Presby, dep Fakumen with Russians

July 3	Huolu riot, *Greens, Gregg* to hills; Imperial govt appeals to foreign govts for help!
July 4	*Goforth Canadians* and *engineers* through Xiangcheng, Henan
July 4	Xin'an *3 Swedish ladies* dep to Anhui
July 4	QÜWU, Shanxi, 2 parties, **Duncan Kay family**; *Graham McKie, Way, Chapman* separately to hills
July 4	**Barratt, Woodroffe** to hills; *Gracies, Macfarlane* dep Xiangcheng; *C. H. Bird* stays; **Alfred**, *Olivia Ogren* hear of Xiaoyi murders
July 4	Yong Lu refuses artillery to Tong Fuxiang
July 5	*Saunders* party arr Lucheng
July 6	*Jennings, Guthrie,* join *E. J. Cooper,* **wife**, **Huston**, **Rice** party of 14 dep Lucheng, attacked
July 7	Lucheng, Lu'an riots; *Glover* family *C. Gates* dep LU'AN
July 7	Henan riots: Sheqidian, *W. Guinness* party, Sihua, *C. M. Lack* escapes; Nanyang, *Goforth* party attacked
July 8	First Shanghai-London crisis cables; *Glovers-Gates* destitute on hilltop; *A. Argento* escapes from Guangzhou, Henan; *Gracies, Macfarlane* rescued
July 8, 9	*Greens, Gregg* from temple to cave, *Argento* left for dead, Guangzhou
July 9	Sheqidian attack, *Guinness* party hide; arr Hankou 30 days later
July 9	TAIYUAN MASSACRE: **35 Protestant British**, **12 RC**, **about 30 Chinese** all beheaded
July 9	*Dreyer, Lutley, French* parties told to dep Linfin, insist on safe passes
July 9	Li Hongzhang reappointed viceroy of Zhili, orders protect foreigners
July 10	Zhoujiakhou riot; police chief protects 9 CIM homeless
July 11	*C. H. Bird* dep Xiancheng; *Glover, Gates* to die, pray for rain
July 12	DATONG CIM massacre: **McKee, I'Anson, Aspden, M. E. Smith, Nathan sister, Heaysman** escape from DANING to hills
July 13	*Saunders, Cooper* parties flogged, **Rice** killed. **Huston** terribly injured. Ogrens flee Yongning to Shaanxi
July 14	*Saunders, Cooper* parties dep Linfen; forced through hostile Henan
July 15	False news of Beijing legation massacre; Blagoveshchensk, Manchuria, massacre by Russians
July 15-17	HEJIN **McConnell, Young** party killed
July 16	*Saunders, Cooper* parties enter Henan
July 19	*Greens, Greggs* to isolated farm
July 21	QÜ XIAN, Zhejiang, massacre of **Thompsons, Desmond, Manchester, Sherwood, magistrate's family**
July 22	CHANGSHAN, Xhejiang, **Wards, Thirgood** escape to Qü Xian, killed. *Saunders, Cooper* parties arr Zhangzhou; rabid mandarin
July 24	*Argento* destitute meets Godsend, Lo
c July 25	*Griffiths, Brown* protected at Zhengding RC cathedral by brigadier

July 28	Yuan Zhang, Xǔ Jincheng (June 24) beheaded
July 30	*Saunders, Cooper* parties join *Glover, Gates* at Xinyang, S Henan; some near death. *Am Board, C&MA* Gobi party arr URGA
July 31	*Argento and Lo arr Hankou;* TAIGU, Shanxi, **Oberlin 6** and **8 Chinese** beheaded

AUGUST 1900

Aug 3	**Mary Lutley** dies at Zhangzhou; *Saunders, Cooper, Glovers, Gates* dep Xinyiang; **Jessie Saunders** dies
Aug 4	**Huston**, **Gates** manhandled by soldiers. Allied relief force starts to Beijing
Aug 5, 6	Battles at Beicang, Yangcun
Aug 5	*Dr Hewett* to police cell
Aug6/8	**Mrs E. J. Cooper** dies at Yingshan from injuries, 100 miles from Hankou
Aug 9	XINZHOU **BMS 8** massacred
Aug 9, 10	*Greens, Gregg* in farm cave, found, *Green* shot, all captured, taken to Huolu
Aug 11	**Mary Huston** dies
Aug 12	**Flora Glover** as if dying; LMS Christians' welcome
Aug 13	DANING, Shanxi, **Nathan sisters**, **Heaysman**, **Christians** killed. *Am Board, C&MA* party arr Kiakhta. *Greens, Gregg* in Baoding prison
Aug 14	BEIJING SIEGE lifted; *Saunders, Cooper, Glover* party arr Hankou; **Brainerd Cooper** dies; *Greens, Gregg* by boat past Anxin
Aug 15	Imperial court flee to Kalgan, Xi'an; FENYANG **Oberlin 4**, **Atwater family**, **CIM Lundgrens**, **Eldred killed**; *Fei Qihao* excapes to Tianjin
Aug 16	Beijing RC Beitang siege lifted
Aug 17	*Hewett* sentenced, imprisoned until November
Aug 18	**Glover baby** born; *Hedley Glover* dying, recovers
Aug 20	**Edith Lutley** dies
Aug 20, 21	Yüan Xian's successor orders stop killing
Aug 21	*Pastor Zhang and son* of Daning save by order to stop killing
Aug 21-24	**C&MA** desert fugitives killed
Aug 22	'CCH' reports on Shanxi killings
Aug 23-24	*J. Gregg's* 'little tuft of paper'
Aug 24	Li Hongzhang, Prince Qing appointed plenipotentiaries and
Aug 25	Issue orders to stop killings
Aug 28	**Glover baby** dies; *Dreyer, Lutley, French* party arr Hankou
Aug 28	**A.** &*O. Ogren* reunited
Aug 30	**Peats**, **Hurn**, **Dobson** killed

SEPTEMBER 1900

Sep 1	**Scandinavian Alliance** (Chicago) **4** killed in Ordos desert
Sep 3	*Greens, Gregg* danger from Boxers
Sep 5	*Greens, Gregg* by boat to Baoding prison; 8th to yamen, 6 weeks
Sep 8, 11, 16	Punitive expeditions by allies
Sep 15	**Duncan Kay family** and **Christians** killed near QÜWU
Sep 18	Germans demand punishments before negotiations
Sep 19	*Wang Lanbu* arr Beijing from Soping. 'CCH' reports **Barratt**, **Woodroffe** dead from privations
Sep 20	Li Hongzhang arr Tianjin, assumes viceroyalty Oct 1
Sep 24	Russians begin complete occupation of Manchuria
Sep 24–Oct 22	News of allies control reaches Shanxi Christians

OCTOBER 1900

	J. Walter Lowrie returns to Baoding, saves hundreds from allies' revenge
Oct 5	**Alfred**, *Olivia Ogren* dep Daning, wait one week while Ci Xi and court pass
Oct 10	**Vera Green** dies, *C. H. S. Green* has typhoid; *Dr Hewett* freed, to Hankou
Oct 13	French occupy Baoding
Oct 14	Ogrens arr Linfen
Oct 15	**Alfred Ogren** dies
Oct 16	*Greens, Gregg* to French camp
Oct 17	Germans set up allied HQ in Imperial palace; *Griffiths, Brown* dep Zhengding to Baoding
Oct 19	British force arr Baoding, visit *Greens, Gregg*
Oct 20	*Greens, Gregg* to field hospital
Oct 22	*Greens, Gregg, Griffiths, Brown* c/o army doctors by boat to Tianjin, arr 27th, Green delirious
Oct 24	*Olivia Ogren, McKie, Chapman, Way* together at Linfen
Oct 25	**Flora Glover** dies at Shanghai
Oct 29	*Green* conscious; gunshot pellets removed at Shanghai

NOVEMBER 1900

Nov 5	Guilty Baoding magistrates executed
Nov 6	*Dr Hewett* arr Hankou
Nov 13	Allied punitive expedition to Zhangjiakou (Kalgan)
Nov 26	Telegram: *McKie, Chapman, Way, O. Ogren, child* safe

DECEMBER 1900

Dec 6	Ogren baby born

JANUARY 1901

Jan 6	*Ogren, McKie* party dep Linfen with big escort

FEBRUARY 1901

Feb 16	*Ogren, McKie* party arr Hankou; 28th Shanghai
Feb 22	Yü Xian executed at Lanzhou. Dr E. H. Edwards investigation team exhume BAODING martyrs' remains

MARCH 1901

Mar 23, 24	Baoding funeral and memorial sevices
Mar 27	**J. Stonehouse**, LMS, shot by ex-Boxer outlaws

Afterword to the Series

When the first of these volumes appeared, I had the privilege of writing a 'Foreword to the Series'. That was in 1981. Now, eight years later, I am honoured to write a Postlude.

For twelve years Dr Broomhall has been beavering away at the archives. The result is seven volumes, of which this is the last—some three thousand pages of research.

Who would have guessed, even when he began his research, that when he ended it the Amity Press would have been set up in Nanjing, equipped to provide Bibles and New Testaments in Chinese for the People's Republic of China? Who would have dreamed that by 1986 China would have 'become the fastest expanding nation for church growth ever'? (David B. Barrett, Annual Statistical Table on Global Mission: 1987).

Hudson Taylor might have dared so to guess and so to dream, for he was a man of faith, and 'faith laughs at the impossible and cries, "It shall be done"'.

It is well that the Church should have these volumes available—to remind it of the centrality of its missionary outreach and the faithfulness of its God. If its sometimes deaf ears are opened by the reading of this extraordinary story, the author will be rewarded—his labour will not have been in vain.

Donald Coggan,
Winchester

Notes to Volume 2

Please note that resources listed in the Bibliography are referred to here only once with full bibliographic details; subsequent references use short titles: where only one title is listed by an author, only the author's name appears; where more than one title is listed, author name and a short title is used.

1 Fairbank, John King, *China Notes* (Division of Overseas Ministries, NCC/USA) Vol X1 No 4, 1973.
2 Cooper, T. T., *Travels of a Pioneer of Commerce in Pigtails and Petticoats or An Overland Journey from China towards China*, Arno 1967.
3 *The Chinese Recorder and Missionary Journal*, March 1869, p 240; *CIM Occasional Paper* 19, p 301; Foster, Arnold, *Christian Progress in China: Gleanings from the Writings and Speeches of Many Workers*, London 1889, p 126.
4 Morse, Hosea Ballou, *The International Relations of the Chinese Empire* (9 vols) 1910 [2386.c.17] II, p 226.
5 *Chinese Recorder*, Sept 1868, pp 77–82; Oct 1868.
6 Morse II, pp 224, 233 f.
7 Latourette, Kenneth Scott, *A History of Christian Missions in China*, SPCK 1929 [4763.g.4], pp 331, 337; Younghusband, Francis E., *The Heart of a Continent*, John Murray, London 1898, p 41; Medhurst, W. H., jr, *The Foreigner in Far Cathay*, Edward Stanton 1872 [010058. ee.35], pp 33–34.
8 Hosie, Alexander, *Three Years in Western China: a Narrative of Three Journeys*, Philip & Son, London 1890; Latourette, *History of Missions*, pp 310, 344, 361f.
9 Morse II, p 115.
10 Morse II, pp 140, 158–61; idem. III, Preface; Little, Bewicke Alicia, *Hung-chang: His Life and Times*, Cassell & Co. Ltd 1903, p 64.
11 *Chinese Recorder*, 1917 p 118; 1880 p 227; Martin, W. A. P., *A Cycle of Cathay*, 1896 [010056.g.7], pp 162, 181, 222, 233–34, 238.
12 Ibid.
13 Ibid.
14 Martin, pp 294, 297–98, 301, 316–17; Morse II, p 474.
15 Covell, Ralph, *Martin, Pioneer of Progress in China*, Wm B. Eerdmans Publishing Company 1978, p 192.
16 Little, pp 61–64; Morse II, pp 186, 188, 193, 195, 203, 228; Martin, p 377.
17 Pott, F. L. Hawks, *A Short History of Shanghai*, Kelly & Walsh 1928 [010056.aaa.46], p 106.
18 Qiantang: strictly the Fuchun river in this stretch.
19 OMFA 3421a; Anne and the baby, closer to the floor where carbon dioxide would be less concentrated, had not yet been seriously affected.
20 Woodcock, George, *The British in the Far East*, Weidenfeld & Nicholson 1969 (A Social History of the British Overseas), pp 215–16; in the 1830s the Canton community published Morrison's *Chinese Repository*, Jardine's *Canton Press*, Dent & Co's *Canton Gazette*, 1845, Hong Kong, *China Mail* launched, and in 1903, *South China Post*; 1850, Shanghai, *North China Herald*; 1864, *North China Daily News*; around that time also *Shanghai Evening Courier* and *Shanghai Recorder*. Existing chiefly to provide shipping and commercial information, the newspapers also voiced opinions which differed from the government's, put pressure on consuls, ministers and the British Foreign Office to be more aggressive towards China, and criticised the Imperial Maritime Customs (Robert Hart) for unwelcome impositions.
21 Taylor, J. Hudson, *After Thirty Years*, Morgan & Scott/CIM 1895, p 32, a change of magistrate could account for this.
22 OMFA F423, 'A Report of the Hangzhou Branch of the CIM', pp 5, 8.
23 OMFA 4115.31.
24 OMFA 3412h.
25 OMFA G126.1–6, 10.
26 Morse II, pp 224–25; Latourette, *History of Missions*, pp 568–69; Parliamentary Papers (Blue Books), *China* No 3, p 24; *Chinese Recorder*, August 1868, pp 65–68.
27 Morse II, p 225; Parliamentary Papers, *China* No 3, Sir R. Alcock to Admiral Sir H. Keppel, Aug 14, 1868.
28 Broomhall, Marshall, *The Chinese Empire: A General & Missionary Survey*, Morgan & Scott/CIM 1907 [4767.eeee.4], p 88.
29 Taylor, J. Hudson, 'A Brief Account of the Progress of the China Inland Missions', OMFA 3 Book 5, p 4.
30 Burns, Islay, *Memoir of the Reverend William Chalmers Burns*, London 1885; *Chinese Recorder* 8, p 208;. Broomhall, M., *Chinese Empire*, p 311; Latourette, *History of Missions*, p 396.
31 Stillbirths were perhaps due to the common medicinal use of laudanum, tincture of opium.
32 Broomhall, Marshall, *The Jubilee Story of the China Inland Mission*, Morgan & Scott/CIM 1915 [4763.g:4], p 55; Guinness, M. Geraldine, *The Story of the China Inland Mission*, Morgan & Scott, London 1893 (2 vols) I, p 357; Taylor, J. H., 'A Brief Account',

p 30; *Occasional Paper* 15, pp 191–92; Morse II, p 226.

33 Taylor, J. Hudson, 'Summary of the Operations of the CIM', OMFA 441.11, p 12.

34 Affidavit: OMFA G213; *China Mail*, Oct 19, 1868; Parliamentary Papers, *China* No 1, Sept 3, 1868, Medhurst to Alcock.

35 Morse II, pp 223, 226.

36 Parliamentary Papers, July 2, 1870.

37 *Occasional Paper* 15, pp 190–91.

38 OMFA 4126.39; 12 Book 11.178; G333.

39 OMFA 4115.37, 40.

40 *Chinese Recorder*, Jan 1870, pp 228–29.

41 *Occasional Paper* 15, pp 190–91, 210–12; No 16, p 234.

42 Parliamentary Papers 64, 1868–69, *China* No 2, pp 3, 19 and 247 (OMFA G213); *Occasional Paper* 15, pp 191–93.

43 Parliamentary Papers 64, *China* No 2, p 3 (OMFA G213).

44 Ibid., Chinese enclosure No 2.

45 Affidavit: OMFA 4131; G213; *Occasional Paper* 15, pp 191–210.

46 Parliamentary Papers 64, Chinese enclosure No 3 (OMFA G213).

47 Extracts translated from Le Kiangnan en 1869 (*Relation historique et descriptive par les missionaires de la Compagnie de Jesus en Chine*) (OMFA G212).

48 cf. Guinness, M. G., *Story* I, p 363.

49 OMFA 12 Book 11.180; G211b; G213: 'The members of the Mission present on the occasion of the outrage (were) Mr Taylor, Mr Duncan, Mr Reid and Mr Rudland, Mrs. Taylor and Mrs. Rudland, Miss Desgraz, Miss Blatchley and Mrs. Annie Bohannan. Children, four: Herbert Taylor aged 8, Frederick Taylor aged 6 , Samuel Taylor aged 4, Maria Taylor aged 2.'

50 *Occasional Paper* 12, pp 200–205; No 15 pp 198–200; OMFA 4123b, 4131, 4133d;12 Book 11.177–95.

51 Partial separation of the placenta.

52 Parliamentary Papers 1868–69 (OMFA G213); *Occasional Paper* 15, p 205.

53 Parliamentary Papers 64, enclosures 3, 5, 6.

54 OMFA 4131, Aug 24; *Occasional Paper* 16, p 209.

55 On hearing of what her son had gone through, William Rudland's mother, 'a woman of remarkable Christian character and faith', sent him a copy of Foxe's *Book of Martyrs*, as if to keep his thoughts in perspective.

56 *Chinese Recorder*, 1869, p 88.

57 Parliamentary Papers, *China* No 1, Aug 27, 1868.

58 *China's Millions*, June 1888, p 63; circulated in Shanghai, not denied by consuls or ministers.

59 Parliamentary Papers 64, pp 19, 247.

60 *North China Herald*, Sept 11, 1868.

61 Parliamentary Papers 64, Medhurst to Alcock, Sept 3; *Occasional Paper* 16, pp 221–22.

62 Ibid., pp 17–18.

63 Brawl: *cao-nao* (ts *'ao-nao*) instead of *chiang-an* (*ch'iang-an*).

64 Parliamentary Papers 64, No 3, enclosures 5, 4.

65 Ibid.

66 *North China Herald*, Sept 5, 19, 1868.

67 Parliamentary Papers 64, *China* No 2; *North China Herald*, Sept 19, 1868; *Occasional Paper* 16, pp 222–24; OMFA G214.

68 Parliamentary Papers 64, *China* No 2, enclosure 2, one among other misprints, names Mr for Mrs Taylor. Maria's bruises were still visible a full month later. As Medhurst reported to Sir Rutherford – the one-time military surgeon of the peninsula wars and lecturer in traumatic surgery at King's College Hospital – Mrs Taylor's injuries were 'of such a nature as to preclude personal inspection.' Her bruising was around her knee and hip. Miss Blatchely 'sustained a fracture of the outer prominence of the elbow joint', and 'Mr Reid assured me that he was unable to see clearly with the affected eye.' Rudland's hernia was unquestionable.

69 *The Times*, Dec 1, 1868, dispatch of Oct 13.

70 Parliamentary Papers 64, *China* No 2; *North China Herald*, Sept 5, 11, 19, 1868; *Occasional Paper* 16, pp 224–26; *The Times*, Dec 1, 1868, despatch of Oct 13.

71 OMFA 13 Book 8 (MS); H11.2-4 (typed).

72 *Chinese Recorder*, Aug 1869, p 58. In 1874 Jane McLean was still working in Shanghai, and JHT frequently spoke at meetings in her home.

73 OMFA 3322A14; HTCOC Book 4, pp 247–8.

74 OMFA 342.11a, b; 4118.57-8, 66,68; Wagner, Gillian, *Barnardo*, Eyre & Spottiswoode 1979; Wagner, Gillian, *Children of the Empire*, Weidenfeld and Nicolson 1982; Marchant, James and Mrs Barnardo, *Memoirs of the Late Dr Barnardo*, Hodder & Stoughton 1907.

75 OMFA 4115.37; 4118.58-9, 61.

76 Stock, Eugene, *The History of the Church Missionary Society 1899-1916* [4765.cc.28] (3 vols), II p 650.

77 Ibid., pp 397–98.

78 Ibid., p 584.

79 Among Hudson Taylor's many Anglican friends, perhaps most notable were Burdon, Cobbold, Gough, Hobson and Pennefather. The CIM was later to provide three bishops in China: W. W. Cassels, F. Houghton and K. G. Bevan.

80 Morse II, p 225; Latourette, *History of Missions*, p 469.

81 Parliamentary Papers 64: Adm. Keppel to Alcock, Feb 23, 1869.

82 Parliamentary Papers 64, *China* No 6,1869; Morse II, pp 230f.

83 *North China Herald*, Oct 13, 17, 31; Nov 14, 1868; *The Times*, Dec 1, 1868; Parliamentary Papers, *China* No 2, pp 43, 68–69; Alcock to

84 Lord Stanley, Oct 29,1868, and Medhurst to Alcock, Nov 13,1868, p 54; *Chinese Recorder*, Sept 1869, pp 104–6; *China Mail*, Nov 18, 1W, quoting *Shanghai Evening Courier*.

84 Michie, Alexander: *The Englishman in China, as illustrated in the Career of Sir Rutherford Alcock*, Wm Blackwood & Sons, 1900 edn [09057. d.3] (2 vols) II, pp 168f; *North China Herald*, Oct 13, 31, 1868.

85 Ibid.

86 *The Times*, Dec 1, 1868.

87 Little, p 53; cf *The Times*, Dec 29, dispatch of Nov 10.

88 *North China Herald*, Nov 22, Dec 2, Oct 27.

89 Parliamentary Papers, *China* No 2, pp 59, 69; *North China Daily News*, cited in *China Mail*, Dec 5,1868; *North China Herald*, Sept 29, 1868.

90 Parliamentary Papers 64, enclosure No 2; OMFA 12 Book 11.174.

91 *China's Millions*, June 1888, pp 63f.

92 Little, p 70.

93 On the day of reinstatement at Yangzhou, Nov 18, the Judds and Mary Bowyer left Hangzhou for Zhenjiang; J Meadows and family started from Ningbo a week later.

94 OMFA 6128; no reference to this in JHT papers.

95 Parliamentary Papers 64, *China* Nos 2, 7, 8, 1869; Morse II, pp 228–33.

96 Sharp Peak: Parliamentary Papers, *China* No 2, 1869: Consul Sinclair to Adm. Keppel, Jan 19, 1869.

97 Cockchafer: Parliamentary Papers, *China* No 7, 1869, Lieut. Kerr to Commodore O J Jones, Jan 21, Apr 19,1869, pp 1–34.

98 Parliamentary Papers, *China* No 8, 1869: *Affairs in China*, p 5; Morse II, p 233; *Occasional Paper* 19, pp 300–301.

99 OMFA 4133C.

100 Parliamentary Papers, *China* No 2, 1869, p 63.

101 *Chinese Recorder*, June 1869, pp 24–25; *The Times*, March 10, 1869.

102 *Chinese Recorder*, June 1869, p 25; Stock II, p 592.

103 *The Times*, March 10, 1869; *Chinese Recorder*, April, June 1869, p 258; Stock II, pp 591–92; *China's Millions*, June 1888, p 63; Spurgeon, C. H., *Sword and Trowel* (magazine), Jan 1869.

104 *Chinese Recorder*, April 1869, p 20;1875, p372.

105 Thompson, R. Wardlaw, *Griffith John: The Story of Fifty Years in China*, The Religious Tract Society 1907, pp 250, 231, 245.

106 Latourette, *History of Missions*, p 388.

107 OMFA 4221a.

108 OMFA 4224a, b, Feb 11, May 2, 1869.

109 *Chinese Recorder*, March 1869, p 77.

110 *Chinese Recorder*, Nov 1874, p 360.

111 *Chinese Recorder*, Jan 1870, pp 228–9.

112 OMFA 4241.74, Sept 5, 1869.

113 *Chinese Recorder*, Nov 1869, pp 172–73.

114 Taylor, J. Hudson, 'Summary of Operations of the CIM', OMFA 441.11, p 12.

115 *The Scotsman*, April 12,1869.

116 Pott, p 94.

117 Burdon: *Chinese Recorder*, Sept 1869, pp 97–98.

118 Thompson, R. W., *Griffith John*, pp 252, 259–60, 263–64, 267–68.

119 Parliamentary Papers 69, *China* No 9, 1870, pp 4–12.

120 *Chinese Recorder*, Sept 1869, pp 100–110.

121 Woodcock, p 102; Neill, Stephen C., *Colonialism and Christian Missions* (*Foundations of Christian Mission* Series), Lutterworth Press 1966, pp 147–49, citing Cohen, Paul A., *China and Christianity: The Missionary Movement and the Growth of Chinese Anti foreignism, 1860–70, passim*.

122 Stock II, pp 588–91.

123 Stott: *Occasional Paper* 18, p 284.

124 OMFA 4215; G331.

125 *Chinese Recorder*, July 1869, p 56; Aug 1869, p 80.

126 *Occasional Paper* 19, p 307; Morse II, p 234; *Chinese Recorder*, Oct 1869; p 142; Dec 1869, p 200; OMFA 4122e; 4221h; 4216; 4241.72; 4222h, i, j.

127 Morse II, p 234, citing Cordier, Henri, *Histoire des Relations de la Chine avec les Puissances Occidentales 1860*–1900, Ch'eng-Wen Publishing, 1966 (3 vols), I, pp 335, 341.

128 *Chinese Recorder*, Oct 1869, p 142; Dec 1869, p 200.

129 *Chinese Recorder*, May 1870, pp 32–4.

130 *The Exchanged Life*, a letter from JHT to his sister Amelia, published as a booklet under this title; reproduced in Taylor, Dr and Mrs F. Howard, *Hudson Taylor's Spiritual Secret*, CIM 1932, pp 110–16; also *Hudson Taylor and the China Inland Mission: The Growth of a Work of God*, CIM and RTS 1918 (2 vols) II, pp 168–83.

131 OMFA 4226a.

132 OMFA 4241.74; 4227a.

133 OMFA 4211b.

134 *Occasional Paper* 20, p 337; No 21, pp 360–61; OMFA 4216; 4212.

135 Morse II, p 234; *Chinese Recorder*, Dec 1869, p 207, citing *Shanghai Recorder* of Nov 13.

136 OMFA 13 Book 8 (JHT's MS manifold) p 33; typed, H12; 4241.79.

137 Latourette, *History of Missions*, p pp 20811; Parliamentary Papers, *China* No 1, 1871 and *Tientsin Massacre*, 1870.

138 OMFA 4241.83.

139 Taylor, J. H., 'Summary of Operations', p 14.

140 Parliamentary Papers, *China* No 1, 1869: Lord Clarendon to R. Alcock, Jan 14, 1869.

141 OMFA 13 Book 8 (manifold), H12 (typed) pp 57, 60–1.

142 Ibid., p 60, 4326a.

143 OMFA 5423.

144 Little, p 5.

145 Urakami: devastated by World War II atom bomb, RC victims.

146 Nevius, Helen S. C., *The Life of John Livingston Nevius*, Revell 1895 [4985.eee.5], p 287.

147 Morse II, pp 239–40, 242, 244–45, 251–52; Latourette, Kenneth Scott, *A History of the Expansion of Christianity 1800-1914*, Eyre and Spottiswoode [4533.ff.22] p 290; Stock II, pp 592–93; *Chinese Recorder*, Nov 1870, pp 150–53; Jan 1871, pp 208–11; Parliamentary Papers, *China* No 1, 1871 and *Tientsin Massacre*, 1870.

148 As for note 147; see also Latourette, *History of Missions*, p 388.

149 Taylor, J. H., 'Summary of Operations', p 17.

150 M. G. Hollingworth, A. K. Cunningham, F. M. Youd; *Chinese Recorder*, June 1870, p 15.

151 OMFA 4228.EB7; 4324f.

152 OMFA 4331a.

153 OMFA 4331b.

154 OMFA 13 Book 8 (manifold), 1412, p 116.

155 OMFA 4241.92.

156 OMFA 13 Book 8, H12, p 119.

157 OMFA 4241.93.

158 OMFA 4228.75.

159 OMFA 13 Book 8, H12, p 126.

160 Morse II, pp 246–48; *Chinese Recorder*, Nov 1870, p 150; Parliamentary Papers, July 3, 1870, p 45 and *China* No 1, 1871, p 366; Stock II, p 593; Moule, Arthur E., *The Story of the Cheh-Kiang Mission*, CMS 1879, p 137; Guinness, M. G., *Story* II, pp 79, 419; OMFA 4241.94; Beauchamp, Montagu H. P., *Days of Blessing in Inland China: An Account of Meetings held in the Province of Shan-si etc.*, Morgan & Scott 1890, pp 49–50.

161 OMFA 4228.EB8, 9; 4241.97; 43249; h; 4228.75; 4241.96; 13 Book 8, H12, pp 129, 131,136–37, 141,179; 4325c; G414, G428, G429e.

162 OMFA 13 Book 8, H12, p 179; 4325cii; 4228.97; 4324h; 4241.89.

163 Kidner, Derek, *Genesis (Tyndale Old Testament Commentary* Series), p 33, said of Abraham.

164 Morse II, pp 249, 255–57; *North China Herald*, July 29, Aug 11; *Shanghai Evening Courier*, July 22.

165 Latourette, *History of Missions*, p 351.

166 US Foreign Relations, 1870, p 371.

167 R. Hart to Commissioner E. B. Drew, Sept 9, 1870: 'The spirit of all their policy is to hedge – to say "No" to the foreigner in such a way as not to provoke him, and to say "Yes" in such a way as to advance the aims of anti-foreign China.' Morse II, p 256 n 85.

168 Parliamentary Papers, *Tientsin Massacre*, 1870: Wade to Lord Granville, pp 171–72. Sixteen years later, W. A. P. Martin wrote of a succession of such events (*A Cycle of Cathay*, p 445), 'Most of these massacres have conformed to the original type [that of the Tianjin massacre] in every particular

– beginning with tracts and placards as their exciting cause, followed by studied negligence on the part of mandarins (who always contrived to come too late when their aid was invoked), and finishing with an enquiry how many heads and how much money would satisfy the resulting claims.'

169 Parliamentary Papers, *Tientsin Massacre*, 1870: Medhurst to Wade, p 120; *Occasional Paper* 24, p 26.

170 Haldane, Charlotte, *The Last Great Empress of China*, Constable 1965, pp 67–69; Little, p 68.

171 OMFA 4228.101.

172 Morse II, p 255 fn.

173 Parliamentary Papers, *China* No 1, July 3, 1870: Wade to Lay; Morse II, pp 243, 257–58.

174 *North China Herald*, Feb 22,1871.

175 *Chinese Recorder*, Jan 1871, p 212; Morse II, pp 257–58, 261.

176 Morse II, p 261; Latourette, *History of Missions*, p 351.

177 Michie, *Englishman* II, p 244.

178 Parliamentary Papers, *China* No 1, 1870.

179 Parliamentary Papers, *China* No 1, 1870; OMFA 13 Book 8, H12, pp 170–72, 266; OMFA 4228.99.

180 OMFA 432. 10s, t, u.

181 OMFA 4332a; G426 typed; Latourette, *History of Missions*, p 388.

182 Croup: strident respiration from laryngeal obstruction; perhaps CET had whooping cough: UK death-rate in 1860, 42 per 1,000 cases in infants.

183 OMFA 13 Book 8 (manifold), H13 (typed) p 188; N8.255.

184 No textual justification has been found (by AJB) in any source material, for the supposition that JHT ever thought of taking his own life.

185 OMFA N8.267-90; *Monthly Gleaner* No 6, June 1871.

186 OMFA 13 Book 8, pp 209, 315, 320–21, 373; H13, pp 207, 210–11, 319; H14, p 252.

187 Broomhall, M., *Jubilee Story*, pp 73–74; Ward, A. W. (ed), *The Cambridge Modern History* (12 vols), XI: *The Growth of Nationalities*, p 814.

188 OMFA 4415a, c, d.

189 Taylor, J. H., 'Summary of Operations', p 30; H13.216; Parliamentary Papers, 1870–72.

190 Morse II, p 262; idem. III, pp 267, 270; Little, pp 65–68; Stock II, pp 595–600.

191 *Chinese Recorder*, Sept 1874, p 258.

192 Stock II, p 594.

193 T. Richard, see Latourette, *History of Missions*, p 378; *Chinese Recorder*, Sept–Oct 1877, p 380.

194 *Cycle of Cathay*, p 213; Nevius, pp 276, 287, 447.

195 Ibid.

196 Muirhead, see Broomhall, M., *Chinese Empire*, pp 87–88.

197 *Occasional Paper* 28, pp 151–52; Minutes of London Council, March 24,1873. Add Crombies and Emily Blatchley in UK, Taylors

198 and Rudlands travelling 32 in all, 6 years after founding of CIM in 1865 – apart from losses.

198 Parliamentary Papers, 1872; OMFA 4413a,b; 4414b,c; Stock II, p 593.

199 *Occasional Paper*s 20, 28, 32; *Monthly Gleaner*, 1871; OMFA H14-16; on Nevius, see *Chinese Recorder*, 1886–87 'Methods', March 1900 (Vol 31, No 3) p 109 (nota bene).

200 H14.224.

201 Guinness, Joy, Mrs Howard Taylor: *Her Web of Time*, CIM 1949, p 23.

202 OMFA H538; N8.54: not an anachronism; Henrietta Soltau's clear recollection is of 1872, not 1873 or 1874 when JHT was in China, until Nov 1874, and then immobilised on his back. June 1872, a trough in the waves, saw the venture of faith, culminating in the appeal for 'the eighteen', published in Jan 1875.

203 Council, see OMFA 4417d, e; *China's Millions*, 1909, pp 126–27; Minutes of London Council, Oct 1872.

204 *Chinese Recorder*, Sept–Oct, 1876, pp 344–47; July–Aug, 1874, p 233.

205 Haldane, p 79–84; Little, pp 85–94; Morse II, p 266; *Chambers Encyclopaedia* III, p 475.

206 Yule, Sir Henry, *The Book of Ser Marco Polo, the Venetian*, 1872 (2 vols), II, p 39.

207 Broomhall, Marshall, *Islam in China*, Marshall, Morgan & Scott/CIM 1910, pp 123–24.

208 OMFA 4533.28.

209 OMFA 4523.3.

210 OMFA 4514p, r (£1000 may be thought of as £20,000 today).

211 For Hudson Taylor's indigenous principles, see OMFA 4531.2, 5–6; 4512.8, 11; 4513f, g, h; also Gutzlaff (see *Shaping* 1, pp 144–45), Roland Allen, Nevius, etc.

212 OMFA 4531.6.

213 *Occasional Paper* 34, pp 96–101.

214 *Chinese Recorder*, Nov–Dec 1874, pp 372–73.

215 *Chinese Recorder*, Jan 1874, p 206.

216 Ibid.

217 OMFA Judd 2; London Council, July 27, 1873.

218 Wylie and John, see *Chinese Recorder*, Nov 1876, pp 418–26; Thompson, R. W., *Griffith John*, pp 226–8.

219 Chairman, Oct 5, 1875; appointed Home Director, Feb 1879.

220 Probably Dr E. P. Hardy, WMMS (1870–75) who replaced Dr F. Porter Smith (1864–70); *Chinese Recorder*, Nov–Dec, 1876, p 418.

221 In 1853 changed course from S of Shandong peninsula, Yellow Sea, to N. Gulf of Zhili (now Bo Hai).

222 Some entries give born Oct 6, but on her gravestone, October 7, 1843.

223 OMFA 4526.

224 Minutes of London Council, Oct 8, 1872.

225 Morse II, pp 271–77; Michie, *Englishman* II, p 255.

226 Unpublished MS by Mrs. W. P. K. Findlay.

227 *Occasional Paper* 39, pp 245–52, an edited version. Printed in *Occasional Paper* 37, pp 174, 193: 'If God graciously provide the men and the means (from £1500 to £1800 annually, in addition to our present outlay), we may very soon place a gospel light in each of these dark districts'—the kind of 'appeal' about which JHT was protesting?

228 OMFA 4513k, 1; 4532 Challice; 4531.23; 4512.

229 *Occasional Paper* 37, pp 197–98, tabulated in Broomhall, M., *Jubilee Story*, p 90.

230 *Occasional Paper* 37, pp 194–95.

231 OMFA 4513l.

232 Knowlton: 441.11; Taylor, J. H., 'Summary of Operations', pp 14–15.

233 Taylor, Dr and Mrs F. Howard, *Hudson Taylor* II, p 267; OMFA 4511Q, R, T; 4531.24.

234 Weir: OMFA H517Q.

235 Hongkew: The first CIM business centre, forerunner of the major organisation supplying up to 1300 CIM missionaries and others from Wusong Road and then Sinza Road, Shanghai.

236 Knowlton: *Chinese Recorder*, Nov–Dec 1874, p 360; Jan–Feb 1875, p 78.

237 Morse II, pp 283–87; Broomhall, Marshall, *John W. Stevenson: One of Christ's Stalwarts*, Morgan & Scott/CIM 1919 [4956.aa.33], pp 36–37; *Chinese Empire*, p 247; *Journal of the RGS* XL, 1870; Parliamentary Papers, 1876: correspondence respecting the Indian Expedition to Western China and the Murder of Mr Margary; *Chinese Recorder*, May 1875, p 234.

238 *Occasional Paper* 39, pp 238–45; H511.

239 *Chinese Recorder*, Nov 1874, p 371.

240 *Chinese Recorder*, Nov 1874, p 372; *Occasional Paper* 39, p 232.

241 A. Strittmatter and J. R. Hykes.

242 Map: Henrietta Soltau, H538; later on wall, H537.

243 The shares realised £400.

244 Appeal for 18: £4000 largely from Jennie's legacy; *The Christian*, Jan 21, 1875; Broomhall, M., *Jubilee Story*, p 100; OMFA H532a; *Occasional Paper* 39, p 230.

245 Morse II, pp 287–91; Parliamentary Papers: correspondence on attack on Expedition, 1876 and memorandum by Wade, July 1875; CIM London Council Minutes, Dec 14, 1874 (Sladen's colleagues not named).

246 *Chinese Recorder*, Jan 1876, p 79.

247 OMFA 511.10c.

248 Morse II, pp 279–81; Haldane, pp 82–94; Little, p 91.

249 *Chinese Recorder*, 1905, p 382.

250 March 27, 1875: Morse II, pp 279, 281, citing Bland, J. O. P. and E. Backhouse, *China under the Empress Dowager, being the History of the Life and Times of Tzu Hsi*, William Heinemann 1912, p 129.

251 Gill, William, *The River of Golden Sand: The Narrative of a Journey through China and Eastern Tibet to Burmah, with an Introductory Essay by Col Henry, Yule*, CB, RE, John Murray 1880 (2 vols), I, p 69, comment on Margary's journals.

252 FO Parliamentary Papers, *China*, 1875; Morse II, pp 290–97.

253 *Foreign Relations of the United States 1875*, p 318.

254 Morse II, p 293; Cordier, *Histoire*. Chonghou said of Wade's changes of mood: 'now this, now that–today Yes, tomorrow No; the rages, the sulks, and the outbursts in which he indulges leave us unaffected.' And on 24 Sept 1875 Wade himself wrote to Prince Kong, 'For my frequent loss of temper in argument, I put forward no excuse ... The Chinesegovernment leave me ... little option.'

255 Morse II, p 299.

256 On Jackson-Wade, see Latourette, *History of Missions*, p 353; OMFA 5117d, N9c pp 43, 59.

257 Latourette, *History of Missions*, pp 303–415; *Chinese Recorder* Jan 1875 pp 77, 80; Stock III, p 218.

258 *China's Millions*, p 64; Broomhall, M., *Chinese Empire*, p 28.

259 Veterans: *Chinese Recorder*, 1875, p 340.

260 *Chinese Recorder*, 1875, p 136; Stock III, p 35.

261 Stock III, p 244.

262 Neill, Stephen C., *A History of Christian Missions* (*Pelican History of the Church* 6), Penguin Books 1964, p 240.

263 Stock III, pp 24–26, 73, 805; OMFA N9c, 1875, pp 49–50; 5113k.

264 Ibid.

265 OMFA H52.11, JHT's own claim in letter to CIM: OMFA H526, JET to E. Turner.

266 Broomhall, M., *John W. Stevenson*, p 36; OMFA 51131.

267 *China's Millions*, July 1877, pp 94–5.

268 On conferences, see Stock III, pp 29–33; OMFA 5115ci.

269 Mark 11.22: not intended as translation; OMFA 8, Book 1: *After Thirty Years*; *China's Millions*, 1875, pp 19, 55.

270 OMFA 5118, 5119.

271 OMFA 8, Book 1, pp 8–9; *China's Millions*, 1875, p 31.

272 OMFA N9c, p 42; H537.

273 *China's Millions*, 1875, p 36; OMFA N9c, p 42; H537.

274 In 1875 Thomas Weir, Shanghai, arranged with the Castle Line for members of the CIM to be charged only £50 between the UK and Shanghai. The French Mail cost £46 third class from Marseilles; Holt's Blue Funnel Line charged £84; and the P&O nearly £100. The Castle Line concession lasted into the 1880s. A saving of £4 per head or £20 for a party of five in 1875 may be thought of today as £800, well worth saving. Economy mattered; comfort was secondary. When a missionary spoke disparagingly of the French Mail after travelling with his wife by another line, Hudson Taylor wrote to Jennie, 'It makes me feel angry.'

275 OMFA 5114ai, ii.

276 OMFA N9c p 49; 5114aii.

277 OMFA H417.

278 Guinness, M. G., *Story* II, p 130, citing S. Wells Williams.

279 *China's Millions*, 1875, July suppl., pp 1, 7–8, 61; Broomhall, M., *John W. Stevenson*, pp 35–45; OMFA 5118b, 5119, 52.10.

280 Tsiang Siao-vong (? Zhang Xiaofeng): *China's Millions*,1875, p 2.

281 OMFA H311, H53.12a; *China's Millions*, 1965 (Centenary issue), pp 93–94.

282 OMFA 5119, H515; 5115d.

283 OMFA H417. The legacy from Jennie's uncle in Australia had come under her control. 'The whole is the Lord's (to be) used for Him and ... not for private purposes,' she had said, and she had contributed £3500 (well over £100,000 today) already banked in Shanghai, for advance into the nine unoccupied provinces. To imagine that she encouraged him to shoulder the expense of the Pyrland Road property and Benjamin's help would be reasonable, though unsupported by specific evidence. Whatever the source, if God approved he would provide the means.

284 Pyrland Road property: factual evidence is scanty. On June 30, 1875, Hudson Taylor's father, James Taylor, resigned from the directorship of the Barnsley Permanent Building Society which he had founded, and managed since 1855. He and his wife retired to the south coast. On December 30 he resigned all control. To share in the support of Amelia and her children, he invested capital in five newly built houses in Pyrland Road and assigned to her the income from their rental. (At her death, 1918, Nos 38, 40, 42, 46, 48.) On April 6, 1876, the CIM Council of Management minuted that it proposed to buy five homes in Pyrland Road, letting out two or three to tenants until they were needed, 'and thus securing on advantageous terms permanent possession for the Mission'. On April 27 another minute read that the two houses in use (Nos 4 and 5) would be secured for the rent of one. 'As the proprietor was willing to leave £500 out of £700 (the price of each house) on permanent mortgage, the total sum required to secure the five houses would be only £1000'; this 'wise' arrangement was adopted. By 1987 the value of each house, long since in other hands, was more than £100,000. Yet another minute noted that the landlord had donated a sum to the Mission, the property was in the hands of trustees, and the mortgage could be paid off at any time. Such unusual circumstances and the acceptance of this mortgage arrangement strongly suggest that an exceptional donor was involved. Nothing in the records hints that Jennie's

legacy was used or that William Berger was the benefactor. Minutes of the London Council 1876, May, June 30, July 31. No 2 Pyrland Road was the home of Benjamin and Amelia for forty years.

285 OMFA 8513, Wm Sharp.

286 *China's Millions,* 1965 (Centenary Issue) pp 193–94, Easton reminiscences; OMFA H53.12a.

287 OMFA H539; OMFA 5112h, l; OMFA H532b; *China's Millions* 1875 p 69; Broomhall, M., *Jubilee Story,* p 103

288 The highest reaches of the Yangzi River were (and are) known as the Jinsha Jiang (the River of Golden Sand); the northward-flowing reach of the great loop, as far as the junction with the Min River (map p 260) was the Jin He (the River of Gold). Gill I, p 61, Col H. Yule's introduction re T. T. Cooper's route: Chengdu, Batang, Weixi, and back to Ya'an.

289 *Chinese Recorder,* 1876, p 422.

290 *Chinese Recorder,* 1876, pp 226–31. A Wylie, *Proceedings of the RGS* XIV, p 168; *Chinese Recorder,* 1877, p 385; Broomhall, M., *Chinese Empire,* p 28; *Chinese Recorder,*1876, p 422.

291 Object of the 'assault': Broomhall, M., *Jubilee Story,* April 1873, p 90; Plan of Operations: OMFA 4513f; JHT's 1872 Bible flyleaf.

292 Broomhall, M., *Jubilee Story,* p 104. Already in China: J. W, Stevenson, J. McCarthy, C. H. Judd, F. W. Baller, M. Henry Taylor, Edward Fishe. New volunteers: Henry Soltau, George King, James Cameron, George Nicoll, George Clarke, J. F. Broumton, G. F. Easton, Joshua J. Turner, Charles Budd, S. Adams, Edward Pearse, Francis James, George Parker, Horace Randle, Robert J. Landale. See also note 299 below.

293 See pp 234–35.

294 *He* means 'river'. From Zhoukouzhen (Chouchiakou) the Sha He flowing south-east into Anhui joined the Huai He, an unbroken waterway through the lakes and Grand Canal to the Yangzi at Zhenjiang. Southwards a fan of waterways, principally the Bai He and Tang He, feed into the Han River to join the Yangzi at Wuhan (Hankow) (map (first of the nine)p 54). North of the Yellow River, the Wei He flows north-eastwards for 400 miles to Tianjin. Overland travel could be 20–40 times as expensive as by water on these navigable rivers. Only in 1905 was a railway begun between the chief cities of Kaifeng and Luoyang (Loyang), crossing the Peking-Hankou railway at Zhengzhou (Chengchou), soon to equal them in size and importance. The Yellow River was not bridged until June 1905, opening the 750-mile Peking-Hankou line at long last.

295 J. McIntyre, United Presbyterian Church of Scotland, trying to reach Kaifeng from the north was turned back at the Yellow River in 1874. Henry Taylor's second journey, dep. Hankou Oct 24, 1875, returned Hankou

Jan 15, 1876, via Runan, Zhoukouzhen, Chenzhou, Guide, Kaifeng (Dec 10).

296 *China's Millions,* 1875, pp 2, 46, 60, 78; 1876, p 181; 1878, p 181.

297 Broomhall, M., *Chinese Empire,* pp 165–66. At one time six of the empire's seven viceroys were Hunanese. And General Zuo Zongtang's troops who quelled the Muslim rebellion in the north-west (see p 213) had a high proportion of Hunan men, many of whom settled in Gansu.

298 OMFA H539.

299 *China's Millions,* 1875, p 69; OMFA H532d. Francis James: Forsyth, Robert C., *The China Martyrs of 1900,* Religious Tract Society 1904, p 106. Several versions of the list of 'Eighteen' have been drawn up showing that this number was exceeded, as different factors have been taken into account, such as Robert Landale's private means delaying his formal membership of the Mission. He went to China in September 1876 and took part in strenuous pioneering. Of more than 60 applicants in 1875, 30 to 40 spent longer or shorter periods at Pyrland Road to learn what would be involved and to be assessed for suitability.

300 OMFA 5122b; the Misses Anna Crickmay, Celia Horne, Marie Huberty, Jessie Murray and Katherine Hughes.

301 *China's Millions,* 1875, p 76; 1876, p 160.

302 *China's Millions,* 1876, p 158.

303 *CMS Missionary Gleaner,* Nov 1874.

304 OMFA 5115a, Sept 26.

305 Ibid.

306 Possibly Yao Shangda. *Sifu* means 'master-craftsman'. *China's Millions,* 1877, pp 10–11,13–15, 30–31; 1875–76, p 225.

307 Ibid.

308 *China's Millions,* 1876, p 210; 1877, p 12.

309 *China's Millions,* 1882, p 94; 1877, pp 43, 76, 86–87; Guinness, M. G., *Story* II, p 100.

310 Ibid.

311 M. H. Taylor: OMFA 5122e.

312 Chefoo Convention: Morse II, pp 283–306; FO Parliamentary Papers: Murder of Mr Margary 1875–76 and further corr. re Mr Margary, 1876; Michie, *Englishman* II, pp 273–81; *RGS Supplementary Papers,* Vol 1, Part 1, pp 154–92; Parliamentary Papers Report, *China* No 3, 1878 and 1877 p 51, further corr. re Mr Margary; Parliamentary Papers, *China* No 3, 1876 and Aug 5, 1876; Little, pp 99–109; Morse II, pp 203, 314.

313 Gill I, pp 66–73, introduction by Col H Yule.

314 The man who had savagely ended the Yunnan Muslim rebellion.

315 Wen Xiang had died on May 26.

316 Little, pp 1, 6. Detring became Li's adviser for 20 years and briefly succeeded Robert Hart as Inspector-General when Hart became British Minister at Peking.

317 In *The Englishman in China* Alexander Michie said that Wade had 'found himself cornered'.

Certainly he 'was a chastened man' after all was over, and in H. B. Morse's words, 'the honours of the occasion were with Mr Hart.'

318 *China's Millions*, 1875, p 77; Stock III, p 225; Broomhall, Marshall, *Pioneer Work in Hunan by Adam Dorward and Other Missionaries of the China Inland Mission*, Morgan & Scott/CIM 1906, pp 3–4.

319 Stock III, pp 224–25.

320 Minutes of CIM London Council, Aug 1876; OMFA H42.14.

321 OMFA 5121, Oct 14; Beauchamp, p 80 (Conference Report).

322 OMFA 5121, Oct 25; 5122c, Oct 11; 5126; 5122d.

323 Duncan: OMFA 5121, Nov 8; *Chinese Recorder*, 1876, p 74; *China's Millions*, 1877, p 24.

324 *Chinese Recorder*, 1879, p 150; cf Alexander Stronach, Feb 6,1879; *China's Millions*, 1878, pp 135–36.

325 OMFA 5115p, E Wilson; I123: 'From 1876–80, Mr Taylor's advent, we used to say, was like a bombshell scattering us abroad.'

326 Broomhall, M., *John W. Stevenson*, p 46–49.

327 OMFA 5123a,b.

328 *China's Millions*, 1877, pp 47, 57, 92,104, 150.

329 *China's Millions*, 1877, pp 58,141.

330 OMFA 5122g, Jan 12.

331 OMFA 5122e; 5124, 5127; 1123; *China's Millions*, 1877, pp 64, 86–7.

332 OMFA 5115b; 5122g; 5124; 5127; *China's Millions*, 1877, pp 56, 70–72; *Chinese Recorder*, 1871, p 212.

333 Ibid.

334 OMFA 5115p.

335 At Zhenjiang, Nanjing, Wuhu, Datong, Anqing, Jiujiang.

336 OMFA 5122g; 5124 Jan 6;1877; Feb 2,16.

337 Ibid.

338 *China's Millions*, 1877, pp 154–56;1878 pp 80–82.

339 OMFA 5124.30; *China's Millions*, 1878, p 69.

340 Ibid.

341 The use of 'tribes' not in the strict sense of having a dominant 'tribal' leader but ethnic communities with distinct customs, dress and language, in three groups: 1. Mon Khmer including Akha, Miao, Yao; 2. Tibeto-Burman including Lisu, Moso, Nosu; 3. Shan, calling themselves Tai, and the Minjia. True independence of the 'tribes' ended with their subjugation by Kublai Khan in 1252, but the campaigns of a General Mang in AD 230–40 are remembered by a temple erected to his memory.

342 Guinness, M. G., *Story* II: Mesny played a significant part in quelling the Miao rebellion. J F Broumton wrote of Mesny's concern for the Miao people. There is no evidence that he was one of Charles Gordon's officers in the Ever-Victorious Army. Discretion led to his usually being referred to as 'Mr Mesny' but sometimes as 'General'

or 'Major-General', the equivalent rank he eventually reached. The use of 'Chiang Chün', a very high rank, was probably inappropriate. In his *Middle Kingdom* 1, Samuel Wells Williams renders Chiang Chün as 'commander-in-chief, major-general' as if taking 'major' to mean 'senior', in ignorance of Western military usage.

343 Latourette, *History of Missions*, p 362; Broomhall, M., *Jubilee Story* (1st Edn. 1915), p 111; *China's Millions*, 1877, p 85.

344 *China's Millions*, 1877, pp 49, 93.

345 *China's Millions*, 1883, pp 2, 3; OMFA 5122g.

346 Howell, George T., 'Yang Ts'uen-ling', *China's Millions*, 1878, pp 57–63, J. McCarthy to T. T. Cooper, Bhamo Resident.

347 *China's Millions*, 1877, pp 78–79; 1883, pp 2–3.

348 OMFA 5124.28; *China's Millions*, 1877, p 128.

349 OMFA 51228; *China's Millions*, 1877, pp 64, 74, 84; *Chinese Recorder*, 1877, pp 498–516 – fit for *Journal of the RGS*.

350 *China's Millions*, 1877, p 126; *Chinese Recorder*, 1877, pp 498–516.

351 OMFA 51228; *China's Millions*, 1877, p 85.

352 *China's Millions*, 1877, p 92 (anti-foreign literati).

353 *Chinese Recorder*, 1877, pp 512–16.

354 *China's Millions*, 1883, p 3.

355 Stock III, p 225.

356 *Shanghai Courier*, Dec 12,1876; *China's Millions*, 1877, p 43.

357 *China's Millions*, 1875, p 31.

358 OMFA 5124.14.15; *Chinese Recorder*, 1877, pp 98–9.

359 Ibid.

360 OMFA 5124.17; 511.

361 OMFA 5115a.

362 Also present at Wuchang conference: Horace Randle, E Wilson, Marie Huberty, Edward Pearse, Eliz. (Jane) Judd, Hudson Taylor; OMFA N10b33.

363 Judd wrote: 'Whenever there was a difficulty about opening a station Mr Taylor always called for a day of fasting and prayer, which rarely failed to remove the difficulty ... When difficulties arose and we could not get a footing, or were driven out, there was fasting and prayer for a day. Of course the fasting was optional. Some would go without breakfast and dinner, but Mr Taylor always fasted the whole day till the evening. He would take food then. It was not asceticism. He simply felt it was the scriptural and right thing to do, when waiting on God for anything special.' (Recollections).

364 G. John: *China's Millions*, 1877, p 143.

365 Records of the General Conference of the Protestant Missionaries in China, Shanghai, May 10–24,1877 (Shanghai 1878); *Chinese Recorder*, 1877, pp 239–50; *China's Millions*, 1877, pp 104–15,119–25, 137–40,147–48;156–8: pp 1879 p 83; OMFA 113. 1 1; Latourette,

History of Missions, p 413; OMFA 4500 J. L. Nevius et al. Sept 1874 proposal.

366 Attributed to A Koestler, paraphrasing Goethe (*Brit Med Journal*).

367 An accurate count impossible owing to irregular attendance and the presence of 15 associate members including some who had been missionaries previously or were otherwise involved (including Doctors McCartee and Macgowan, Charles Schmidt and merchants David Cranston and Thomas Weir). Fourteen members of CIM were present. Stock lists numbers.

368 Elected committees deliberated and reported on inter-mission comity; on Romanization of Chinese sounds; on an appeal to the Churches of the West to send more missionaries; on the production of Christian literature, periodicals and school books; on the term for `God'; on opium; on a document summarizing for the Chinese literati and officials the Protestant beliefs and practices; and on petitioning the Bible Societies of Europe and America to change their rules or constitutions to permit `a short preface, captions and brief unsectarian notes' to make their publications more acceptable and intelligible in China.

369 Denunciation of ancestor worship and idolatry by the early missionaries had been discarded and discouraged by most, including Hudson Taylor. See summary by M. T. Yates at 1877 Shanghai Conference; *Chinese Recorder*, 1877, pp 239–250, 489–98; *China's Millions*, 1875–76, pp 171, 190, 204, 218, 230; OMFA N10b.51.

370 The terms itinerate, itinerant, itinerancy, itinerary (Collins Dictionary) were widely used in the world of missions, all relating to travel from place to place: *Chinese Recorder*, 1875, pp 241–3. Early in the nineteenth century German missionaries of the CMS perplexed their bishop in Bengal, T. F. Middleton, whose restricted world of parish and parson offered no status to such people. 'I must either silence them or license them,' he wrote, but to what (non-existent) parish could they be licensed! Stock I, p 187.

371 *China's Millions*, 1877, p 109.

372 Covell, *Martin*, pp 123, 249–50; Hubbard, G. E., Director of Information, Royal Inst of International Affairs 1933–45 in *Chambers Encyclopaedia* III, p 451.

373 Covell, *Martin*, p 123; *China's Millions*, 1877, p 109.

374 Compare Reginald Heber (1783–1826), Bishop of Calcutta, hymn writer, 'who soon after his arrival in India wrote affectionately to Carey and Marshman in favour of the union of the Churches, "If a reunion of our churches could be effected, the harvest of the heathen would ere long be reaped." The Baptist brethren were personally touched but theologically unmoved.' Neill, *History*, p 268.

375 Wilder, R., *The Great Commission*, p 78; *The Christian*, quoted in *China's Millions*, 1877, p 121.

376 *Chinese Recorder*, 1877, pp 432–6.

377 No 7 Seward Road, with David Cranston as business manager.

378 Promoted to Commander and CBE, 1875.

379 Neill, *History*, pp 378–79, the Mission was 'eager and adventurous but without the needed staying power'. It was absorbed by the American Baptist Mission. True access to the interior, with a steamer on one thousand miles of navigable Congo and stations at one hundred mile intervals, fell to the English Baptists (BMS) in and after 1884.

380 Stock II, pp 94–104; Neill, *History*, p 384.

381 Padwick, Constance E., *Mackay of the Great Lakes*, London 1917. He died of fever in early 1890.

382 *Chinese Recorder*, 1878, pp 169–74; *China's Millions*, 1877, pp148–50; 1878, pp 7–8, 72.

383 *Chinese Recorder*, 1878, p 179 by G. W. Clarke; *China's Millions*, 1878, pp 14, 72; Guinness, M. G., *Story* II, p 204, so different that it smacks of hazy recollections.

384 *China's Millions*, 1878, p 72 says dep. Guiyang Sept 21, arr. Hankou Nov 7; *Chinese Recorder*, 1878, p 179 says dep. Guiyang Sept 24, arr. Wuchang Nov 1; this should probably read Yichang Nov 1, Wuchang Nov 7.

385 *RGS Supplementary Papers*, Vol 1 Part 1, 1882; Gill I, p 72. Col H. Yule's introduction.

386 Gill, I, pp 3, 15, 23, 159.

387 Ibid., p 262.

388 Ibid., pp 262, 277.

389 OMFA 1128: *Proceedings of the RGS*, August 1879, Vol 1 No 8, pp 489–509; paper read by J. McCarthy on April 28,1879; *China's Millions*, 1877, pp 135–36; Diary 1878, pp 3, 57–64 account for T. T. Cooper and Indian Government; *The Times*, 1879, p 76; 1883, p 2.

390 Namely a Christian capable of reading official documents, addressing mandarins correctly, advising the missionary on etiquette, and negotiating contracts with landlords or employees.

391 Cameron, not McCarthy or Judd, had been the first of CIM to enter Sichuan. If Baber had not cooperated with Gill and Mesny in their private venture to court danger in Xinjiang and Tibet, J McCarthy might well have been thwarted.

392 July 2 according to *China's Millions*, 1878, p 57; also pp 3, 103–5; OMFA 5124, cf. 1128; 51234 (itinerary and dates); 5123e, f, g.

393 Gill II, p 345.

394 Distances, see OMFA 51234; *China's Millions*, 1878, p 57.

395 OMFA 5124.

396 *China's Millions*, 1877, pp 131–2: Harveys dep. Rangoon July 8, wrecked July 18, Rangoon 31–Aug 17; Calcutta steamer Aug 25 to UK Oct 10.

397 OMFA 5123e,f; *China's Millions*, 1878, pp 57–64.

398 'Across China from Chinkiang to Bhamo,'
Jan–Aug 1877, by J. McCarthy, read at
evening meeting of the RGS, April 28, 1879;
OMFA I 128, *Proceedings of the RGS*, August
1879, Vol 1 No 8, pp 127, 489–509; map, p
544.

399 Ibid.

400 Gill did not mention Minya Gongga. Was
Nenda another name or another peak not
mentioned by others because lower than
Minya Gongga's 24,900 ft (7550 m)?

401 Mesny: played *micare digitis* (of old Rome;
morra in Italy), possibly acquired by China
from early contacts with the West. Yule, H.
in Gill II, p 203: 'With mounting excitement
and ever louder voices the players thrust
their hands in each other's direction with
upheld forgers, calling out words and
numbers fast and furiously until within half
a minute one or other had lost and had to
drain a cup of rice wine dry – except that
Mesny would take nothing stronger than tea.'

402 Garnier took an active part in the defence
of Paris, 1871, and then returned to China
hoping to reach Lhasa, but joined in the
Indo-China war, where he fell.

403 Gill I, pp 77–79. Yule cited Alexander
Williamson's 'excellent work' in *Journeys
in North China, Manchuria, etc*, London
1870, and Alexander Wylie's lecture in the
Proceedings of the RGS XIV, p 168.

404 Gill I, pp 17, 77, H. Yule's Introduction;
Journal of RGS XLVIII, p 57; *China's Millions*,
1879, p 76, citing *The Times*; a fascinating
description of the 'road over the high
plateau'.

405 *RGS Supplementary Papers*, Vol 1 Part 1, p 176.

406 Authors note: I travelled twice by this route,
and lived for nearly four years (1947–51)
in the Daliangshan. Many Nosu were my
height, 6 ft; a few were inches taller, but most
between 5 and 6 feet.

407 Yule, H. in Gill I, p 74, introduction by
Col H. Yule; Baber, Colborne: 'Travels and
Researches', *RGS Supplementary Papers*, Vol 1
Part 1, pp 118–24; *RGS* 1881 'Latest Edition',
Vol XXIV, quoted at length in translation
from the *Annales de la Propagation de la Foi*.

408 *Daliangshan* means 'great cool mountains'. As
a result of the different Chinese characters
for the same sound *liang* in the same tone,
the name Daliangshan is restricted in
some maps to the highest region, using the
character for 'ridge', and in others is applied
to the whole range with the character for
'cool' or 'cold'. The 'cap of liberty' refers to
the conical cap given to a Roman slave on
emancipation.

409 *China's Millions*, 1883, pp 1–5; OMFA
5124.28. By July 2, Hudson Taylor had heard
of this repossession of Yichang and the
occupation of Sichuan.

410 *Chinese Recorder*, 1878, p 89.

411 *China's Millions*, 1878, pp 75–77;1879, pp 65–
73, 97–104, 109–116; 1890, pp 67–70; 1883,

pp 1–5; OMFA 1221; Guinness, M. G., *Story*
II, pp 225–28.

412 *China's Millions*, 1879, p 98.

413 *China's Millions*, 1879, pp 109–16.

414 *Chinese Recorder*, 1878, pp 85–100; *China's
Millions*, 1878, pp 75, 77;1879, p 67;1880, pp
67–70.

415 Nosu (Lolo), see *China's Millions*, 1878, pp
75, 77.

416 Title based mostly on OMFA 5124.12, 17, 24–
5, 27, 29, 33; 5127; 5115b.

417 Mission Office moved to 351 North Soochow
Road, Hongkew from Seward Rd but
continued under David Cranston. *China's
Millions*, 1878, pp 15–27.

418 The railway, little more than a tramway
between Shanghai and Wusong, had been
completed in 1876 after four years of
haggling over *fengshui*. But before long a man
was killed on it, and on October 21, 1877, it
was handed over to the authorities to be torn
up until public attitudes changed. OMFA
5122h; Philippians 4.1.

419 OMFA 5124.36; 5127.

420 *China's Millions*, 1875, pp 19, 55ff.

421 *China's Millions*, 1877, p 43.

422 *China's Millions*, 1876, pp 82,168; 1877, pp
112,147–48; 1888, ff.

423 Mander, S. S.: *China's Millions*, 1878, pp 31–
32, 43, 65, 77, 129, 145, 153; Li Hongzhang,
Guo Songdao: *China's Millions*, 1878, pp 35,
154.

424 *Chinese Recorder*, 1878, p 157.

425 Morse II, pp 307–11; *China's Millions*, 1879,
pp 134–35.

426 *Chinese Recorder*, 1880, p 237; *China's Millions*,
1878, p 116, F. H. Balfour; British Library
11102.6.20, 'Illustrations, by a Native Artist'.

427 *Chinese Recorder*, 1880, p 357; Latourette,
Kenneth Scott, *These Sought a Country* (Drew
University Tipple Lectures 2–5, 1950);
Soothill, p 64; *China's Millions*, 1877, pp 120,
71, 156, 69.

428 OMFA 5127.

429 OMFA 5125a,b; *China's Millions*, 1878, p 30;
OMFA 5124.36, 37.

430 *China's Millions*, 1879, pp 134–39; Morse,
Trade and Administration, p 323; Parliamentary
Papers, *China* No 2, 1878: Report on the
Famine (R J Forrest).

431 Ibid.

432 Forrest report: *China's Millions*, 1879, pp 135–
36; *Shanghai Courier*, June 25, 1878.

433 Parliamentary Papers, *China* No 2, 1878, p11;
Morse II, p 309 note, May 24,1877; *China's
Millions*, 1878, p 71; 1879, p 148; 1879 p 137.

434 *China's Millions*, 1878, pp 114–16; *The Times*,
Jan 23,1878; Feb 19,1878.

435 *China's Millions*, 1878, pp 56,120. Inflation:
comparisons are misleading, values varying
by factors of 50 to 200, very approximately. If
£5000 is thought of as £250,000 to £500,000

the enormity of the opium outrage against China may be better realized.

436 *China's Millions,* 1878, pp 111,117,120,130–34, 156,178; 1879, p 138.

437 OMFA 5124, Feb 1878, 5134; *China's Millions,* 1878, p 72.

438 OMFA 5132; 5222x.

439 *China's Millions,* 1878, p 98.

440 OMFA 5138b.

441 *China's Millions,* 1878, pp 72, 79,111;114–27, 133–39, 147–48.

442 *China's Millions,* 1878, pp 115,136.

443 *China's Millions,* 1879, pp 1, 48,147–48;1878 pp 69–71.

444 Ibid.

445 *China's Millions,* 1879, pp 63,148, 219, 224. Until a suitable burial place could be found, in December, his coffin lay in a ruined temple used as a government mortuary outside Taiyuan. Governor Zeng offered 400 taels to take his remains to the States, and on this being declined, refunded the price of the land eventually bought as a cemetery.

446 Deaths: *China's Millions,* 1878, pp 122,134;1879 p 138; *London and China Telegraph,* July 13, 22,1878; *Shanghai Courier, Chinese Recorder,* 1878, pp 224, 232, 460; 1879, p 219.

447 Reported by HBM Consul R J Forest, *China's Millions,* 1878, p 122.

448 *China's Millions,* 1878, pp 116,157; 1879, p 19; OMFA 5135 (JET).

449 Orphans: *China's Millions,* 1878, p 157; 1879, p 19; OMFA 5135.

450 *Chinese Recorder,* 1878, p 389; *China's Millions,* 1878, pp 165,178.

451 *Chinese Recorder,* 1881, p 70 (JHT-AC); *China's Millions,* 1879, pp 19, 20.

452 Ibid.

453 *China's Millions,* 1879, pp 12, 19–22, 40, 50, 137, 148.

454 *China's Millions,* 1879, pp 138–39, 140; OMFA 5135.

455 OMFA 1131, 132; 513.10. In his reminiscences 30 years later, J. J. Coulthard, who travelled out with JHT, wrote of Jennie having dreamed that JHT was ill. She dep. Taiyuan Feb 3, arr. Shanghai March 5. From Baoding she wrote to him saying she would be better employed at Shanghai preparing to receive reinforcements than to stay at Taiyuan. She did not mention a dream, to him or to Amelia or Benjamin. JHT dep. London Feb 24, via Amsterdam and Cannes, and sailed from Marseilles, March 9; arr. Shanghai April 22, 1879.

456 Morse II, pp 309–10, 313; *China's Millions,* 1878, Preface, p 126; 1879, pp 79, 91–41879, p 137; *London and China Telegraph,* July 26.

457 *China's Millions,* 1878, pp 154–5.

458 British Library 112.6.20; *China's Millions,* 1878, p 124.

459 Morse II, p 313; Smith, Arthur H., *The Uplift*

of China, The Young People's Missionary Movement of America 1909, p 163.

460 Morse II, p 315.

461 *China's Millions,* 1881, pp 136–9.

462 Later Sir Walter Caine Hillier, KCMG, CB, Order of the Double Dragon; Adviser to the Chinese Foreign Office. *China's Millions,* 1880, pp 4–8, 20–24;1879 pp 133–39.

463 *Chinese Recorder,*1879, p 139;1880, pp 237ff, 241. Chinese official estimate: 20 million dead. Population of China: 300 million. $500,000 received by Protestant and Roman Catholic agencies, $189,000 by RCs from their own appeals. More than forty RC distributors were listed; but reports of their work were apparently not made public. Latourette only noted Moir Duncan's allegation that land and property were acquired at this time, and stated that six priests died in Zhili alone, and orphanages were crowded with homeless children. *Annales de la Propagation de la Foi,* Vol 50, pp 385ff, 392.

464 *China's Millions,* 1880, pp 78, 106.

465 *Chinese Recorder,* 1880, p 237. In addition to fundraising by the CIM in UK and China, relief by J. J. Turner, Francis James, J. E. Taylor, A. Crickmay, C. Home, F. W. Baller, M. H. Taylor, G. W. Clarke, A. G. Parrott, W. L. Elliston, S. B. Drake, J. Markwick. *China's Millions,* 1880, p 76.

466 Transcribed in *Chinese Recorder,* 1880, pp 260–69, 464.

467 Woodcock, p 106.

468 *China's Millions,* 1878, pp 85–99; OMFA 5134 JHT to L Desgraz, Feb 22.

469 Ibid.

470 OMFA 10.321 (1880).

471 Minutes of London Council, May 21, 1878 (May, June, August).

472 Minutes, Feb 26, 1878.

473 OMFA 5135, June 14.

474 OMFA 5135, 5134, 5135. His nephew BCB spoke of borrowing JHT's ice axe.

475 BB, Gen. Sec.: London Council Minute, Feb 5,1878.

476 No statement found, but safe to assume that he had inherited his father's position as director of the family chemical manufacturing enterprise.

477 Broomhall, Marshall, *Heirs Together: A Memoir of Benjamin & Amelia Broomhall,* Morgan & Scott/CIM 1918 [4908.e.6], p 97.

478 *Chinese Recorder,* 1879, pp 151ff; Stock II, pp 227–29; OMFA 5139.

479 Married T. A. P. Clinton.

480 OMFA N11a.95; 5138b; 5135.

481 OMFA 5139; *China's Millions,* 1879, p 52.

482 *Sword and Trowel,* May 1879.

483 OMFA 1127; Guinness, M. G., *Story* II, p 310.

484 OMFA 513.10.

485 Morse, Hosea Balou, *The Trade and*

Administration of the Chinese Empire, Longman, London 1908, p 247; Morse II, p 231.

486 Morsed II, pp 331–39.

487 Boulger, Demetrius C., *The Life of Sir Halliday Macartney K.C.M.G. Commander of Li Hung Chang's Trained Force in the Taeping Rebellion*, John Lane The Bodley Head 1908, p 347.

488 Ibid.

489 *China's Millions*, 1881, pp 45–50.

490 *Chinese Recorder*, 1876, p 383; 1881, p 139.

491 OMFA 5211.

492 OMFA 5211, 5212, 5214.

493 Passports: OMFA 1217, 5211, Nllb.41.

494 Houghton, Stanley et al., *Chefoo*, CIM/RTS 1931; *China's Millions*, 1883, pp 88–89;1880 p 76.

495 OMFA I319.

496 Arr. China with A. G. Parrott and S. B. Drake, early December 1878; most of 1879 at Linfen (Pingyang), Shanxi, through the worst, final stages of famine. Arr. Yantai Nov 20, 1880, married Annie Groom, Oct 25, 1882.

497 *Chinese Recorder*, 1879, p 304; OMFA 5222b.

498 Broomhall, M., *Chinese Empire*, p 27, quoting from E. Stock.

499 OMFA I217.

500 Latourette, *History of Missions*, p 374; idem., *History of Expansion* 6, p 323.

501 Latourette, *History of Missions*, p 364; Thompson, R. W., *Griffith John, passim.*

502 *Chinese Recorder*, 1880, p 49; OMFA 5221a.

503 OMFA 122.14b.

504 Divided yet again after Russell's death in 1879, the name 'North China' was transferred to the SPG diocese of Yantai, Tianjin and Peking, nominally including Shaanxi, and George Motile's diocese of Shanghai and Zhejiang, extending theoretically to Sichuan, was called 'Mid-China'.

505 Stock III, pp 318–20, 564, 774; *China's Millions*, 1880, p 28; 1883, p 28; 1878, p 42, welcome CIM. Hudson Taylor helped by assessing and sending him potential diocesan assistants and ordinands, explaining that his own objective was not to extend the CIM but the knowledge of Christ. He had already met candidates of whom he had thought 'just the man for Bishop Burdon', and two had joined the CMS. Burdon was holding out the prospect of ordination and recommendation to the CMS for those he trained, but Hudson Taylor advised caution, for 'secondary considerations may become primary almost unconsciously.' Let them come to help in his work for God, and if suitable would then be 'the more grateful if you are the one to first suggest CMS and ordination,' as a reward rather than a right mentioned in advance. Twenty-three years had passed since together they were manhandled on the island of Chongming (Shaping 1, pp 298–302).

506 *China's Millions*, 1883, pp 27–32, 41–44; where immigrants from Fujian were

507 establishing a foothold against violent opposition by the aboriginal people.

507 The merest sketch of his journeys can be given here, but his own summary of his journals well repays an interested reader. *China's Millions*, 1879, pp 14, 31–34; 1880, pp 27–33; 1883, pp 1–5, 27–32, 41–44, 58–60,126, 140–41,147–49, 160–62; 1884 pp 39–40, 46–49, 58–63,70–72.

508 'Spoor', cf. Job 13.27 NIV/NEB branded soles of feet.

509 Hosie, p 55.

510 Latourette, *History of Missions*, p 333 (331–37).

511 *China's Millions*, 1883, p 32.

512 CMS, LMS, Basel Mission, APM, American S. Bapt, Am. Episc. Church, English Presby. Mission, Berlin Mission, Rhenish Mission, Am. Board (ABCFM), Am. Reformed Mission; *Chinese Recorder*, 1869 list for comparison.

513 Probably A. G. Kerr MD of APM at Peter Parker's hospital; *China's Millions*, 1880, pp 27–33.

514 OMFA 5211, 5214.

515 *China's Millions*, 1880, pp 38–43,111–13,130–31, 133–36, 146. Cameron and Pigott: 1881, pp 17–19, 127; Cameron: 1882, pp 24, 37, 108–10, 154; Cameron: 1883 (map of Cameron's journeys), pp 2–5, 27–32, 41–44, 58–60, 140–41, 147–49, 160–62; 1884, pp 39–40, 46–49, 58–63, 70–72.

516 Latourette, *History of Missions*, pp 259, 396.

517 *China's Millions*, 1880, pp 38, 42–43; OMFA 5211.

518 *China's Millions*, 1880, p 41;1883 pp 58–60, 140–41.

519 *China's Millions*, 1880, pp 111–13, 130–31, 133–36;1881, pp 17–19.

520 The boundary lay between Changchun and Jilin, but now between Changtu and Changchun.

521 *China's Millions*, 1883, p 148.

522 Colportage, in *China's Millions*, 1880, pp 111–13, 135 TWP; 1883, p 160 JC.

523 OMFA 5224; *China's Millions*, 1883, pp 160–62 (July 27, 1880, twenty cities). 'Kalgan' is 'Halag' in Mongolian, mangled by transliteration.

524 OMFA 5224 July 27, 1880; Beauchamp, p 3.

525 Ibid.

526 OMFA 5221b Aug 23.

527 Map, in *China's Millions*, 1884, pp 39–46, 58.

528 *China's Millions*, 1884, pp 70–2.

529 *China's Millions*, 1883, p 126.

530 OMFA I214.

531 Ibid.

532 Williamson: *China's Millions*, 1876, pp 137–8.

533 OMFA 5224.

534 OMFA 10.321; I. 111 lists yearly totals in China, as against new arrivals; *China's Millions*, 1879, p 15.

535 Ibid.

536 Stock III, p 232. Value of women to indigenous Church: The Society for Promoting Female Education in the East had in 1875 seconded a member to run a girls' school for the CMS in Fuzhou. As Eugene Stock recorded, it was not the policy of the CMS to send women, or on the whole to use unordained men. A separate Church of England Zenana Missionary Society (CEZMS) was formed to provide for India's women, and a few members found their way to China, the first in 1881 (Latourette, *History of Missions*, p 369). Even F. F. Gough's daughter, fluent in Chinese and working as a missionary with her father and step-mother (Mary Jones) in Ningbo, after applying to the CMS was transferred to the CEZMS before returning to China. (However, she married J. C. Hoare of Ningbo.) In 1882 Bishop Burdon strongly advocated 'Medical Missions and Women's Work', with little effect (*CM Intelligencer*, Jan, Feb 1883). Miss Aldersey (in Shaping 1, parts I & II) had been exceptional, going independently to Ningbo in 1843, after Malaysia and Hong Kong. The example of American Protestant Episcopal Church and the American Methodist Episcopal Church in 1859 had been followed by the Presbyterians and Baptists in 1866 in sending a few single women to China. Stock III, p 227; *China's Millions*, 1877, pp 119–21.

537 Thompson, R. W., *Griffith John*, pp 310–11; 314–15.

538 Broomhall, M., *Chinese Empire*, p 203.

539 'A Daughter of Lausanne' (unpublished), OMFA 5211, Aug16, 23; *China's Millions*, 1881, p 35, Blakiston's sketch of gorges.

540 Latourette, *History of Missions*, p 390.

541 *China's Millions*, 1880 pp 76, 78.

542 *China's Millions*, 1880, p 78; see also Taylor, Dr and Mrs F. H., *Hudson Taylor* II, p 340; Guinness, M. G., *Story* II, p 325–28.

543 Clarke: *China's Millions*, 1880, pp 78,138. Others, see also Taylor, J. H., *After Thirty*, pp 11–20; Guinness, M. G., *Story*, chs 23, 24; idem., *Letter from China*, passim.

544 OMFA 5115b; 1123; 5221b June 25; 5225

545 'Only God': *China's Millions*, 1880, pp 125–26; 5223, March 6; 5225, March 20.

546 Ibid.

547 *China's Millions*, 1880, pp 107–9, 118, 137–38, 151–52 (Ballet); 1881, pp 125–26, 140 (Kidd and E McC); 1882, p 99.

548 Broumton, Trench: OMFA 5221a,b.

549 *China's Millions*, 1880, pp 74, 78, 91,116; 1881, pp 2, 8, 32–33; OMFA 5222b; 5223, March 6; 5115b, E. Wilson.

550 Han R. travel: OMFA 122, 12, A. L. Fausset remin.

551 *China's Millions*, 1878, pp 42, 111.

552 Ibid., p 78;1879, pp 35, 105, 143, 165;1880, pp 14–19.

553 *China's Millions*, 1880, pp 13–15, 43–44, 57–60.

554 OMFA 5232a; 5233b.

555 OMFA 5138d July 5,1878; 5215b.

556 *Chinese Recorder*, 1880, p 75; OMFA 5215b, Feb 25, 1880. In 1987, 78 Asian members from 10 countries.

557 *China's Millions*, 1880, pp 25, 90, 147;1881, pp 10, 33, 44; 1883, p 83.

558 *China's Millions*, 1883, pp 12,78–79.

559 OMFA 5314; *China's Millions*, 1882, p 104.

560 Latourette, *History of Missions*, p 391.

561 Yunnan: *China's Millions*, 1881, pp 6–7.

562 *China's Millions*, 1881, pp 98–9.

563 FO Parliamentary Papers, *China* No 3, 1880. (Conventionally only the consul's surname is given, but we excuse the anachronism by its use in the *Chinese Recorder* and Mission papers.) *China's Millions*, 1880, p 1.

564 *China's Millions*, 1880, p 118; Broomhall, M., *John W. Stevenson*; *China's Millions*, 1879, p 158; 1880, pp 26, 52, 92, 132; 1881, p 102; OMFA 5223.

565 *China's Millions*, 1881, p 103.

566 *China's Millions*, 1881, pp 101–6, 117–20, 140–41; Broomhall, M., *John W. Stevenson*, pp 52–53.

567 *China's Millions*, 1882, pp 27–28, 61,141; 1883 pp 90, 137, 158, 172; *J W Stevenson*, pp 53–56; *Proceedings of the RGS, 1880–81*: Soltau, Henry, 'A Journey from the Irrawaddy to the Yangtze', *Journal of the RGS* III, pp 493 and 'Notes on Yunnan', *Journal of the RGS* III, p 564, compiled by William Soltau from letters of H. Soltau.

568 Latourette, *History of Missions*, pp 246–53.

569 *China's Millions*, 1881, pp 69–72, 140.

570 *China's Millions*, 1880, pp 25, 34–36,124; 1881, p 98.

571 *China's Millions*, 1880, pp 124, 149; 1882, p 81.

572 *China's Millions*, 1882, pp 61,112; 1883, pp 38, 90.

573 *China's Millions*, 1881, pp 142, 145; 1882 pp 12, 22, 26, 28, 37, 53, 61; 1883, p 90; Colquhoun, Archibald R., *Across Chryse from Canton to Mandalay* II, Sampson Low, Marston, Searle & Rivington, London 1883 (2 vols), pp 183, 184–87, 247–63, 291; *China's Millions*, 1883, p 12, Eason between June 24 and July 1; Hosie, p 55.

574 Ibid.

575 Colquhoun II, pp 356–58.

576 Like *Lolo*, Miao-tzu was loosely used by Chinese for aboriginal people, including the Hmong or Miao. The translation occupies 30 pages in Colquhoun II, pp 364–94.

577 *China's Millions*, 1883, p 12.

578 *Chinese Recorder*, 1879, pp 379ff; *China's Millions*, 1878, p 74; 1880, pp 9–10, 122–23.

579 Broomhall, M., *Pioneer Work*, p 12; OMFA 5221a, 5224 Sept 22, Oct 13, 1880.

580 Broomhall, M., *Pioneer Work*, pp 12–14 and maps; *China's Millions*, 1881, pp 106–11.

581 Colportage: F. W. Baller said they were to deliver a consignment to Guiyang also. Oct 18 dep. Wuhan, Nov 16–29 Changde, Dec 25 Hongjiang. *China's Millions*, 1881, p 10. Jan 14,1881 dep. Hunan to Guiyang; Jan 17–21 and Feb 17–22 Chenyuan; March 2 Hongjiang again; April 1 Wuhan.

582 OMFA 5221a; *China's Millions*, 1880, p 132; 1881 pp 6, 98–99, 129–35, 143–45.

583 OMFA 5233c Apr 2, 5233g Apr 8, 1 22.10.

584 *China's Millions*, 1881, pp 121–22, 126; OMFA I228, 5231h.

585 Ibid.

586 Wuhan: *China's Millions*, 1881, p 122; OMFA 5231h,i,j,k,1; 5233f.

587 *China's Millions*, 1881, pp 129–35,143–45; Broomhall, M., *Pioneer Work*, p 14.

588 *China's Millions*, 1882, pp 6, 23; 1881, pp 143, 145.

589 Ibid.

590 Opium, see *China's Millions*, 1882, pp 23, 29, 33, 62, 80.

591 OMFA 122.10; *China's Millions*, 1882, p 80; 1883, pp 12, 38, 50, 72, 90.

592 Ibid.

593 *China's Millions*, 1882, p 6; Broomhall, M., *Pioneer Work*, pp 18–19.

594 Broomhall, M., *Pioneer Work*, p 24, 30; *China's Millions*, 1882, p 141; 1883, pp 72–75, 93–94,163–65.

595 Not reported in *Chinese Recorder* or G John biography. Thompson, R. W.: *Griffith John*, pp 339–346 describes mobbing at Xiangtan, 1880, but nothing about Longyang or mobbing in 1883. Broomhall, *Pioneer Work*, pp 26–27 incident not dated, nor references; *Chinese Recorder*, 1905, G. John jubilee: John Archibald tribute to 'numerous journeys made with Dr John, in perils oft'; *Chinese Recorder*, 1912, p 541, G. John obituary, no mention.

596 Broomhall, M., *Pioneer Work*, pp 26–27.

597 *Chinese Recorder*, 1880, pp 430–41.

598 *Chinese Recorder*, 1902, p 253, P. F. Price.

599 *Chinese Recorder*, 1903, p 199; 1904, pp 237–45; E. O. James, Prof. Of History and Philosophy of Religion, London Univ., *Chambers Encyclopaedia* I, p 404 and III, p 443.

600 Ibid.

601 Those versed in Chinese, *Chinese Recorder*, 1881, p 154.

602 Latourette, *History of Missions*, pp 378–80; idem., *These Sought*.

603 Soothill, William E., *Timothy Richard of China*, Seeley, Service & Co. Ltd, London 1924. Soothill appears to have hurried this biography into print without research into the facts. Anachronisms and mistakes of recollection impair it.

604 Soothill, pp 106, 111, 149.

.605 *China's Millions*, 1881, p 89; Barber, W. T. A., *David Hill: Missionary and Saint*, Charles H. Kelley, London 1903, p 207.

606 Mary Richard, in Soothill, pp 111–12.

607 OMFA 5223, 5224, 5228; 513.10; 1 22.14b; 4223 May 24, 1880; G. Clarke: OMFA 5212, Aug 20.

608 OMFA 5137, 5212 Aug 20, 5223, 5228, 5224 to Baynes, 5223 May 24, 1880.

609 OMFA 5231z; N12b.13.

610 Soothill, pp 156–57; Neill, Stephen C. et.al, *Concise Dictionary of the Christian World Mission*, United Society for Christian Literature, London 1971, p 526.

611 Ibid.

612 *China's Millions*, 1878, p 99; 1880, p 1: 'dysentery' from many causes struck all types of foreigners in China and killed many. To hazard a guess, Hudson Taylor's condition had a psychosomatic element: stresses were often linked directly with relapses; while his spirit rose to meet the situation his body protested. Infections accounted for most.

613 OMFA 5232i, dep. UK May 2, 1878.

614 OMFA 5231A, 5241f; N13a.11.

615 OMFA 5223.

616 James Taylor: OMFA 52321, m.

617 *China's Millions*, 1880, p 70.

618 *China's Millions*, 1882, pp 35–36.

619 *Chinese Recorder*, 1881, p 394; OMFA 5134. The CMS income was £207,508; the BMS received 'the largest income yet'; and the WMMS suffered a deficit of £38,000.

620 OMFA 511a, 5231A Shanghai ,Nov 14,1881, to JET; 5226; *China's Millions*, 1881, p 44; 1883, p 85.

621 Ibid.

622 OMFA 5223; 5231y.

623 Lifestyle, see OMFA 5221b.1; I226; 5231o, r; 5221b.

624 OMFA 5224, 5223; N12a.27.

625 OMFA 5231A, C, D; N9c. 61–62; 5124.1o; *China's Millions*, 1882, p 26.

626 OMFA 1228; 5134, 5244a; see also *China's Millions*, 1881, pp 84–6.

627 Ibid.

628 'Mon centre cèee, ma droite recule, situation excellente. J'attaque!' (Aston, *Biography of Foch*, 1923, ch 10).

629 OMFA 513.60, March 18,1879; I231, 232.

630 *China's Millions*, 1881, p 143; Judges 5.23

631 Seventy: *China's Millions*, 1888, p 111; 1883, p 53; 1885, p 4; OMFA I232.

632 OMFA I233.14.

633 Baptism: no reasons or discussion recorded. OMFA 5242a, 5241b.

634 OMFA 5242b; *China's Millions*, 1885, pp 4–9.

635 *China's Millions*, 1882, pp 85–87, 90–91.

636 Ibid.

637 *China's Millions*, 1881, pp 77–96.

638 *China's Millions*, 1883, p 112.

639 *China's Millions*, 1878, pp 86, 89.

640 OMFA 5233h.

[641] Pyrland Rd: OMFA 5231D, 5226, 5241C; *China's Millions*, 1881, p 157.

[642] *China's Millions*, 1883, pp 95–96.

[643] OMFA 5241b, n, C, H, I, J, N, T, X.

[644] Latourette, *History of Missions*, p 390; Taylor, Dr and Mrs f. Howard, *Hudson Taylor* II, pp 360–70 (362).

[645] OMFA 5241a, f, i, j, m, n, p, q, r, s, t, v.

[646] Anqing: OMFA 5241X, 5243c.

[647] Shanxi: OMFA 5241B, K, R–U.

[648] Tempted: OMFA 5241.1.

[649] *China's Millions*, 1885, p 9.

[650] OMFA 5241.2, 3.

[651] *China's Millions*, 1885, p 9; Broomhall, Marshall, *Archibald Orr Ewing, That Faithful and Wise Steward*, CIM 1930, p 50; *Jubilee Story*, pp 159–60; Taylor, Dr and Mrs F. H., *Hudson Taylor* II, pp 369–70.

[652] Latourette, *History of Missions,* p 354; 311–12, 325, 354, 470; idem., *History of Expansion,* p 251; Morse III, p 368.

[653] Stock III, p 233.

[654] Ibid., p 588.

[655] OMFA 5314 A,B,C; 5221a; *China's Millions*, 1880, pp 62, 132; *Chinese Recorder*, 1881, p 139; OMFA 5226 Nov 6,1879; July 14, 1880; Nov 14, 1880; Dec 23,1881; Memorials of the late Dr Harold Schofield by his Brother, Dr Alfred T. S. Schofield: *Memorials of R. Harold A. Schofield (Late of the China Inland Mission): First Medical Missionary to Shan-Si, China*, Hodder & Stoughton 1898.

[656] After winning a London matriculation bursary of £20 for two years (£1000 today?), he had gone to Owen's College, Manchester, where he won another £40 scholarship in Classics. From there he proceeded to London University, to graduate BA (1869) aged 18, and BSc (1872). In October he went up to Lincoln College, Oxford, with a residential exhibition of £60 per an. for four years, taking first class honours in Natural Science and holding an appointment in the Museum of Comparative Anatomy. During this time he won a prize of £25 in New Testament Greek open to the whole university. He also won the Burdett Coutts award in geology, £80 per an. for two years, and an entrance scholarship of £100 to St Bartholomew's Hospital, London. There he added the Foster Scholarship in Anatomy, the Junior and Senior Scholarships of £20 and £30, the Brackenbury Medical Scholarship, £32, and the Lawrence Scholarship, £30, and gold medal. At about this time he was awarded a Radcliffe Travelling Fellowship in Natural Science at Oxford, worth £200 per an. for three years. (OMFA 5314A, a note in Geraldine Howard Taylor's hand adds MD Lond. and MRCP Lond. to the list of his qualifications, but his obituary in *The Lancet* did not include these, and the London University denies the MD (Registrar, personal letter).

[657] Chinese dress: OMFA 5221a, 5223, 5224, 5226, 5227.

[658] Schofield, p 245; OMFA 5226, Dec 23, 1881; 5314B, Aug 24, 1883; 5314C.

[659] *Schofield*, p 247; *China's Millions*, 1882, 126–27;112; 133–34; 1884, p 4.

[660] *China's Millions*, 1883, pp 134, 155, 174–76, 240, 249; 1884, p 13, *Lancet* obituary; OMFA I 316a–d; 5314B, C; *Memorials* p 244.

[661] Schofield, p 249.

[662] W. Wilson: *China Medical Journal*, 1884–95; Pruen, Mrs, *The Provinces of Western China*, Holness and Allan 1906, pp 80ff.

[663] *China's Millions*, 1880, p 41; 1883, pp 58,124.

[664] OMFA 5225; *China's Millions*, 1882, pp 40–43.

[665] Korea: *China's Millions*, 1884, p 98; pp 25–6. Douthwaite 'circulated a considerable number of copies of the Word of God there.' Bishops Burdon, Moule and Scott proposed to the Archbishop of Canterbury an Anglican mission to Korea, which he referred to the CMS. In 1884 J. R. Wolfe visited Korea, and the Church in Fujian sent two Chinese preachers for two years.

[666] Mackenzie: OMFA 5226, Nov 14.

[667] OMFA 5322h Jan 22; July 16, 1883; 5313j.

[668] Radstock, OMFA 5313D, I.

[669] John 15.2 NIV.

[670] OMFA 5241X.

[671] OMFA I315a, b.

[672] OMFA 5312, Lady Tankerville donated a two-storey Scandinavian chalet to the CIM, erected at Bidborough, Kent, and still in constant use.

[673] OMFA 5313m; *China's Millions*, 1883, p 144; OMFA I32.10, 11; 5317.

[674] Rosa Minchin and Emily Whitchurch, OMFA I 313a; 5315b; Luce, I315; Sharp-BB, 5313E; N13b.36.

[675] *China's Millions*, May 1932, Centenary Number, Vol LVII No 5.

[676] OMFA 5317.

[677] OMFA 53131; *China's Millions*, 1885, p 52. JIIT reckoned 9+18+46=73; FHT reckoned 11+20+46–77. But Guinness, M. G., *Story*, p 415: 76 in three years, but four more dep. UK Jan 16,1885, ie ready before the end of 1884, making 80 at least without including those of the Cambridge Seven who would have gone in December. 10.321 lists 19+46; Broomhall, M., *Jubilee Story*, 9+18+46 in 1884, making 73. OMFA I32.16.

[678] Beauchamp, p 60; Mott: OMFA I32.14.

[679] Pollock, John C., *The Cambridge Seven, A Call to Christian Service*, Inter-Varsity Fellowship, from which I have drawn freely, pp 10, 124 (1985 Edn).

[680] Ibid.

[681] Pollock, John C., *Moody without Sankey, A New Biographical Portrait*, Hodder & Stoughton 1963 and *The Cambridge Seven* are essential reading.

682 Refers to university athletic distinctions: light blue for Cambridge, dark blue for Oxford.

683 Sir Thomas Beauchamp, Bt, died 1874.

684 See Norman P. Grubb, *C T Studd, Cricketer and Pioneer*, Religious Tract Society 1933; Pollock, *Cambridge Seven*; Polhill-Turners, Arthur and Cecil, "Two Etonians in China', unpublished, OMFA.

685 Stock III, p 284 note.

686 Lecturers, tutors, professors.

687 Polhill-Turner: the name Turner was assumed in satisfaction of a legacy and discarded later.

688 Hoste: when Queen Victoria bought Sandringham in 1861, the old house was demolished. Sir William Hoste, Baronet, GCB, KMT, at the head of four frigates defeated greatly superior combined French and Italian squadrons, March 13, 1811, and was severely wounded; married 3rd daughter of 2nd Earl of Oxford. Sir George Charles Hoste CB, married Mary, 3rd daughter of James Burkin Burroughes, Esq, of Burlingham Hall, Norfolk. OMFA I 317a.

689 OMFA I 317a, b; 131.13 Reminiscences.

690 D. E. Hoste: OMFA I 317b;1 Pet 4.11 AV, NIV; OMFA 5331a, b.

691 Beauchamp, p 65; Broomhall, Marshall, *W. W. Cassels, First Bishop in Western China*, CIM 1926, p 5.

692 Woodcock, p 107; Hoste: OMFA I 31.13; 5331c, d; 5423. D. E. Hoste signed P & P Sept 22, 1884.

693 Grubb, pp 32–41; Pollock, *Cambridge Seven*, pp 66–76; *China's Millions*, 1885, pp 36–7.

694 Beauchamp: OMFA I 315; I 317–19; 5135; see also Pollock, *Cambridge Seven*, Manuscript Sources, Bibliography. *China's Millions*, 1900, p 119.

695 OMFA I32.16.

696 OMFA 5324a; Broomhall, M., *Archibald O Ewing*, p 26.

697 Hogg and McMullen; OMFA 5323b. While at Belfast a friend wrote down for JHT the account of John Taylor's blow, 'Take that for Jesus Christ's sake (see *Shaping* 1, p 122).

698 Stock III, p 285; OMFA 5323c; N14a.9; I32.18.

699 OMFA I32.18.

700 Arthington in 1886 sent £200 for use in Chinese Turkestan; no earlier donations listed.

701 OMFA 5324c, e, g.

702 OMFA I 319; 5322Gii; 5322H, 5334a, b; I 313a, b; *China's Millions*, 1884, pp 154–57.

703 Ibid.

704 OMFA 5325b, 5323f.

705 OMFA 5322P.

706 OMFA 5334a–f, m.

707 OMFA 5325b, 53331; I318a.

708 OMFA 5334j.

709 OMFA 5313K; I32.15; 5313m.

710 OMFA 5322A, B, Q; N14a.20, 50.

711 Padwick, Constance E., *Henry Martyn: Confessor of the Faith,* Intervarsity Press 1953 edn, title of ch 15; C. T. Studd, *Daily Telegraph,* July 27, 1931, 'Death of great missionary'.

712 A printed card announcing Stanley Smith's Cambridge meetings named on the back as coming for the November meetings, Hudson Taylor; John McCarthy; R. J. Landale, MA, Exeter Coll, Oxford, seven years in China; W. W. Cassels BA, St John's Coll.; S. P. Smith, Trinity Coll.; and D. E. Hoste, late Royal Artillery, shortly to proceed to China. London Council Minutes, Nov 11, 1884; Miss A. Maxwell, N14a.44.

713 Stock III, pp 284, 184; OMFA 53341.

714 OMFA 5334q,s, g, v; Broomhall, M., *John W Stevenson*, p 60.

715 A suggestion that JHT's departure before the Seven showed an 'anti-intellectual' bias is clearly groundless.

716 Stark, noted Feb 10 minute of London Council. OMFA N14b.4, 6; 5422.

717 *China's Millions*, 1885, p 84; OMFA 5335a,c. At Liverpool the subject was to be 'The Evangelization of the World', to us familiar but in 1885 it smacked of originality. Jan 9 Liverpool; 10–12 Aberdeen; 13 Banff; 14 Huntley; 15 Montrose; 16 Perth; 17–19 Edinburgh; 20–23 Glasgow; 24–25 Newcastle. Hoping to add English towns including Sutherland, Leeds, L'pool or Manchester, Derby, Birmingham, Cardiff and Bristol.

718 OMFA 5332a, b.

719 Polhill: OMFA 5332d; Studd: OMFA 5333j, l, m; 5411 Jan 22, 1885.

720 OMFA 5334g, x; *The Christian*, Feb 19, 1885.

721 Grubb, pp 46–47.

722 OMFA 5336c; *China's Millions*, 1885, p 28.

723 Note signed by Chas Fishe stated £171 5s for five (before the P-Ts); OMFA 5336p; 1318c.

724 Gordon: OMFA 5411; Neill, *History*, p 388.

725 Handley Moule, quoted in *China's Millions*, 1885, p 28.

726 OMFA 5336c; Pollock, *Cambridge Seven*, p 111; *China's Millions*, 1885, pp 21–38.

727 Thompson, Phyllis, *D E Hoste, A Prince with God*, CIM 1947, p 36.

728 *China's Millions*, 1885, pp 72–75; OMFA I 318b, W. W. Cassels.

729 F. R. Smith: OMFA I318c; 5338b; *China's Millions*, 1885, p 76

730 OMFA 5336a, 5333e, f; N14b.13.

731 OMFA 5336c, d; 5332d; 5336e, f.

732 OMFA 5332e; 5336e; Stock III, pp 275, 284–85.

733 Broomhall, M., *Chinese Empire*, p 103.

734 Morse II, pp 368–71.

735 Covell, *Martin*, p 183.

736 Stock III, p 413.

737 *China's Millions*, 1885, pp 48–9.

738 Shanghai: *China's Millions*, 1885, pp 81–82; OMFA N14b.21.

739 OMFA 5338c, 5411, 5412i, v.

740 *China's Millions*, 1885, p 52; OMFA 5411, 6114.

741 Broomhall, M., *W W Cassels*, pp 52–53. Divided on grounds of discretion, and influence on regions visited. In 1902 the Polhill-Turners by deed poll reverted to using Polhill alone; by then in common use, so a pardonable anachronism in this history. Broomhall, M., *Jubilee Story*, p 206; *China's Millions*, 1885, pp 81–82, 105, 122; OMFA 5338, 5412e.

742 Ibid.

743 OMFA 5412k, 5422, 5412m, o, p.

744 Latourette, *These Sought*.

745 OMFA 5412s,u,N, 5423; *China's Millions*, 1899.32.

746 Polhill-Turners, p 21.

747 Hoste: OMFA 5423.

748 *China's Millions*, 1885, p 29; Stock III, p 323.

749 Broomhall, M., *Jubilee Story*, p 166 and footnote.

750 Broomhall, M., *Heirs Together*, pp 95 ff.

751 OMFA 5412i,v; 7121g; 1241; Neill, et al,. *Dictionary*, p 230; Goforth, Rosalind, *Goforth of China*, Marshall, Morgan & Scott 1937; McNab, John, *They Went Forth*, McLelland & Stewart Ltd 1933, pp 168–87.

752 OMFA 6113i.

753 *China's Millions*, 1888, p 137; OMFA 5242j; Taylor, Dr and Mrs F. H., *Hudson Taylor* II, p 293.

754 OMFA 5316; Taylor, Dr and Mrs F. H., *Hudson Taylor* II, p 375.

755 Ibid.

756 OMFA 5139.

757 Taylor, Dr and Mrs F. H., *Hudson Taylor* II, p 395; OMFA J 132.

758 OMFA 5425; 5412P,x, V, iii.

759 Broomhall, M., *John W Stevenson*, pp 61–63; OMFA 5433 letters.

760 *Chinese Recorder*, 1880, p 357 on Shandong Church, followed by 'Principles and Methods Applicable to Station Work', *Chinese Recorder*, 1881, p 131; *China's Millions*, 1886, pp 71, and Nevius's *Methods of Mission Work* (CIM); OMFA N14b.49, 55.

761 OMFA 14b.55; Bagnall took responsibility for S Shanxi later.

762 Broomhall, M., *John W Stevenson*, p 66.

763 *China's Millions*, 1885, p 44; OMFA 5431a Feb 4; N14b.49b, 57–8.

764 *China's Millions*, 1887, pp 132–34,147–48; OMFA 5431b.

765 OMFA 5137.

766 *China's Millions*, 1886, pp 3, 62; OMFA 6211, 5431c, 5444.

767 *China's Millions*, 1886, p 81; Broomhall, M., *Chinese Empire*, p 160.

768 *China's Millions*, 1886, p 3; OMFA 5412iii.

769 Broomhall, M., *Chinese Empire*, pp 198, 204–5.

770 Broomhall, M., *Pioneer Work*, pp 50–54, 57–59; *China's Millions*, 1886, p 157.

771 *China's Millions*, 1886, p 3.

772 *China's Millions*, 1885, p 135; OMFA 5412A, B, E, H, I, K.

773 *Chinese Recorder*, 1880, p 357;1881 p 131; *China's Millions*, 1883, pp 170–71; 'Missionary Methods in China' (reprint from *The Christian*), 1886, pp 71–72,118–21,133–36,142–46.

774 OMFA 5412V, Y; *China's Millions*, 1886, pp 41–44.

775 *China's Millions*, 1887, p 3, cf 1895 pp 154–56; OMFA 5431a, 5445a, b, e, 5444, 5445a.

776 OMFA 5445b, a.

777 OMFA I214; *China's Millions*, 1876, p 193 (Jan 5, 6, 1876); 1880, pp 25, 98.

778 OMFA 5431b, 5421a; I319.97.

779 Ibid.

780 OMFA J21.18; 8213; *China's Millions*, 1888, p 94.

781 OMFA 5431b, 5433.

782 Taylor, Mrs Howard, *Pastor Hsi* (biography) *passim*; Thompson, P., *D. E. Hoste*, *passim*; Broomhall, M., *Chinese Empire*, pp 198, 204–5, 209–23; *China's Millions*, 1881, pp 42, 48, 91; 1883, p 86; OMFA L21.12.

783 Taylor, Mrs Howard, *Hsi*, p 144.

784 Broomhall, Marshall, *F. W. Baller, A Master of the Pencil*, CIM 1923, p 25.

785 Broomhall, M., *W W Cassels*, pp 67–68; idem, *Chinese Empire*, pp 213–15.

786 Richard dep. Taiyuan October 18, 1887, to Shandong; Soothill, p 155; *China's Millions*, 1886, pp 81,160–65; Beauchamp, *passim*; Grubb, p 61.

787 Bagnall: OMFA 5431a; Orr Ewing: Broomhall, M., *Archibald O Ewing*, pp 40–41.

788 *China's Millions*, 1887, pp 4–11; OMFA 5431b.

789 *China's Millions*, 1886, p 138.

790 *China's Millions*, 1887, pp 1, 44–45.

791 OMFA 54316; Broomhall, M., *W W Cassels*; London Council Minutes, May 13, 1887; Jan 10, 1888; Jan 28, 1890.

792 *China's Millions*, 1887, pp 119, 122; 1892, p 89.

793 Thompson, P., *D. E. Hoste*, pp 56, 58; Taylor, Mrs H., *Pastor Hsi*, pp 197ff.

794 OMFA 5423, Sept 12, 1886; 5446.

795 On indigenous principles, see for example *Shaping* 1, p 25; Gutzlaff: *Shaping* 1, pp 144–45; Venn: *Shaping* 1, p 145 & Stock II, pp 411–17; Burns: *Shaping* 1, p; Nevius: *Shaping* 1, p 573; Hudson Taylor: *Shaping* 1, p 810 & *Shaping* 2, pp 147, 178, 187–88, 200.

796 *China's Millions*, 1884 p 89; OMFA J 425

797 Broomhall, M., *Chinese Empire*, p 213.

798 Polhill-Turners, pp 36, 40–44; OMFA 5433; *China's Millions*, 1886, pp 127–30.

799 OMFA 5431b, 10.331.

800 OMFA 5444, 5431b; Neill et al., *Dictionary*, p 106.

801 OMFA 5432;10.331; *China's Millions*, 1887, pp 17, 45.

802 OMFA 5431b, c; 5442,5444.

803 OMFA 54311; *China's Millions*, 1886, pp 17, 27,103.

804 OMFA 54121; *China's Millions*, 1885, p 13; 5412H, J.

805 OMFA 5431a.

806 OMFA 5441c; 5442; 5444; J 132b, c; Broomhall, M., *Jubilee Story*, pp 170–73; *China's Millions*, 1887, p 42, 109, 111; Taylor, Dr and Mrs F. H., *Hudson Taylor* II, p 735, 421.

807 Taylor, Dr and Mrs F. H., *Hudson Taylor* II, p 421 (source uncertain).

808 OMFA 5441.

809 OMFA 5433, 5432; chiefly concerned with matters of health, travel and business, it also provided for dealings with consuls, a fact misused to impugn the Mission as an agency of foreign governments. But the worst examples cited by critics were no more open to objection than 'Consul already requested Peking'; 'already obtained confidential intelligence'; 'according to intelligence received, state affairs indicated.' Perhaps ignorance of the fact that the word 'intelligence' was used in the nineteenth century as 'information' is now, accounts for the misunderstanding.

810 OMFA 5445d, Nov 26,1886, Beauchamp from Ching Li Yamen, Chongqing. Another source says Bourne also in the yamen. Bourne and Studd were is good spirits; 'they seemed to be reconciled to their fate of always being disappointed at any suggestion of going out.' 'The authorities have no guarantee of the good behaviour of the people as there has not been a soul punished for all the rioting which really seems to have been very serious.'

811 Polhill-Turners, p 30.

812 Polhill-Turners, p 46. Forty years later, 1939, when Sir Montagu returned to Sichuan, where he died, I (AJB) acted as his medical companion and driver by car and truck from Vietnam to Chongqing. An educated Chinese hearing him preach said to me, 'This is fascinating. He speaks the language of an old book.'

813 *China's Millions*, 1887, pp 125–6.

814 Typhus: *China's Millions*, 1888, pp 81, 115; 1892, p 90.

815 OMFA 5433; Guinness, M. G., *Story* II, pp 422–25; Broomhall, M., *Jubilee Story*, pp 172,175; idem., *J W Stevenson*, p 65.

816 Broomhall, M., *Jubilee Story*, pp 172–73; idem., *John W Stevenson*, p 67; OMFA 5431c, Nov 27, 1886.

817 OMFA 5431c Dec 10; 5445m Dec 18.

818 OMFA 6213a Jan 12.

819 P&O £25 to Marseilles: OMFA 6221, 6231.

820 Broomhall, M., *Pioneer Work*, p 62; OMFA 6231.

821 OMFA 5431a, 5412f, T, V; Stott, Grace, *Twenty-six Years of Missionary Work in China,*

Hodder & Stoughton, 1897, Apl 23, 1889; *China's Millions*, 1889, p 77.

822 OMFA N14b.33, 37,40–41, 46; 5412E, 5433.

823 T James: OMFA 6114, April 29,1887; 6211, Hunan or Sichuan.

824 Broomhall, M., *Heirs Together,* p 97; OMFA 5445d; he had been Secretary of the Anti-Slavery Association, was on the Committee of the Society for the Suppression of the Opium Trade, and a supporter of the campaigns against vice and other moral evils in Britain.

825 OMFA 5445d; 6111; J 251. Meadows: Feb 5, 1887. Those over 20 years in CIM were Meadows, Stevenson, Williamson, Rudland, Mary (Bowyer) Bailer, Louise (Desgraz) Tomalin, John McCarthy, the Cardwells and Charles Judds.

826 OMFA 5431a (letters not preserved); 6111 Feb 12; 6211.

827 OMFA 6224. In J 215 Stevenson was mistaken; BB made all the arrangements and held the fort while JHT travelled. JWS was in China.

828 OMFA 6111, Mar 24.

829 OMFA 6114, 6211; *China's Millions*, 1884, p 69.

830 *China's Millions*, 1884, p 69.

831 OMFA I319; *The Christian* Apl 21, 1887.

832 Broomhall, M., *Jubilee Story*, p 173; *China's Millions*, 1887, pp 88, 92.

833 OMFA 6114, 6211, 6212.

834 London Council Minutes, Sep 29, Oct 11, 1887.

835 Newington Green: payment completed Oct 4, 1887; adjoining house bought for £1,000, Feb 19, 1889. For the Monte Cristo property behind Inglesby House £8,550 was asked on May 13, 1890; negotiations continued into Aug 1891; building in preparation, Oct 1893, completed 1894.

836 *China's Millions*, 1888, p 94.

837 Morse II, p 372.

838 *China's Millions*, 1887, p 156.

839 Neill et al., *Dictionary*, p 35; OMFA 6211, 6113xi; *China's Millions*, 1896, p 38, Jas. Gilmour.

840 Lansdell: OMFA 6226, July 8, 1887. Central Asian Scriptures: see Broomhall, M., *Chinese Empire*, pp 410–18.

841 OMFA 6212 July 22, Oct 27; 6231 Oct 27; 6311xxiv Dec 24,1887; *China's Millions*, 1889, pp 87–96; K 412; Broomhall, M., *Chinese Empire*, p 296, G Hunter named Lansdell with Parker in Xinjiang, 1888.

842 Hopkirk, Peter, *Foreign Devils on the Silk Road: The Search for the Lost Cities and Treasure of Chinese Central Asia*, OUP 1984; idem., *Trespassers on the Roof of the World: the Race for Lhasa*, John Murray 1982; *China's Millions*, 1889, pp 87–96.

843 Younghusband, *The Heart*, 1896, pp 70–75.

844 The Trio, Eva and Francesca French and

Mildred Cable dep Shanxi to Xinjiang 1923; dep Xinjiang 1938.

845 OMFA 6114, 6211 June 3, 1887; 6212.

846 OMFA 6232.

847 See at length in Stock III, pp 362–63 and Index; OMFA 61130.

848 OMFA 6111 July, 12, 13, 1887.

849 OMFA 6113z; *China's Millions*, 1887, pp 92, 99.

850 OMFA 6212, Oct 14, 1887; 6223q, v.

851 Shanxi: OMFA 6212 Oct.

852 OMFA 6231 Oct 30, Dec 12.

853 OMFA 6231; 6113F, Q, xv.

854 Taylor, Dr and Mrs F. Howard, *By Faith: Henry W Frost and the China Inland Mission,* CIM 1938.

855 *China's Millions*, 1932, pp 99–90; Taylor, Dr and Mrs F. H., *By Faith*, pp 49ff; OMFA 6225; *China's Millions*, 1893, pp 45–46,59–61,73–75.

856 OMFA 7113a,d.e.f; N13b.31; Mildmay: Pyrland Road or conference centre.

857 OMFA 7133e,i,j.

858 OMFA 46211 June 17,1887; 6225j; 6212 Dec 22;1887.

859 Conferences: Liverpool 1860; London, 1888; New York, 1900; Edinburgh, 1910; Neill et al., *Dictionary.*

860 *China's Millions*, 1887, p 73, letter to CIM.

861 *China's Millions*, 1887, p 73; 1892, p 90; OMFA 6212.

862 Maria: *China's Millions*, 1887, p 79; Annie Royle Taylor: Ibid., p 156.

863 *China's Millions*, 1887, p 156.

864 *China's Millions*, 1888, p 95.

865 Latourette, *History of Missions*, p 364.

866 OMFA 6213.

867 Stock III, pp 361–64; *China's Millions*, 1889, p 87; 1890, p 101.

868 OMFA 6227a.

869 OMFA 6222, Engagement Calendar.

870 Cassels: Broomhall, M., *W W Cassels,* pp 143–8.

871 Stock III, pp 433, 577; Horsburgh, J. Heywood, *Do Not Say; or The Church's Excuse for Neglecting the Heathen,* Marshall 1908, p 36.

872 Taylor, Mrs Howard, *Pastor Hsi: Confucian Scholar and Christian,* CIM 1900, pp 213–24; *China's Millions*, 1888, p 44.

873 Opium wars: 1840, 1858–60; Thompson, R. W., *Griffith John,* p 287; *China's Millions*, 1877, pp 112,147–48; *Chinese Recorder,* 1876, p 422; Stock III, pp 233–34.

874 Examples in *China's Millions*, 1875, pp 77, 82,105; 1877 pp 39, 105; 1878, p 77; 1879, pp 35, 75, 94; 1880, pp 95, 100, 104; 1881, pp 6, 38–39, 62, 85, 90–91; 1882, pp 38, 49; 53, 574, 119–25; 1883, pp 6–7, 45, 118, 148 (see Indices).

875 *China's Millions*, 1882, p 39; extracts, 119–25. British Library ref: 8425-c75.

876 *Chinese Recorder,* 1881, p 418.

877 Stock III, pp 348, 688; *Church Missionary Intelligencer,* Dec 1884, p 279.

878 Stock III, pp 233–34.

879 Broomhall, Benjamin (ed): *National Righteousness,* Vol 1 Nos 1–13; Vol 2 No 26: 'The Truth about Opium Smoking'; Broomhall, M., *Heirs Together,* pp 95–114.

880 *China's Millions*, 1885, pp 63, 85, 89,102–3 (see note 874 above), by a duty of 90 taels = £30 per chest, free from inter-provincial *likin* tariff.

881 *National Righteousness,* Vol 2 No 26, Aug 1911.

882 Covell, *Martin*, p 62; Martin to American Board, May 22, 1856, and Nov 16,1859.

883 *National Righteousness,* Vol 1 No 1, Dec 1888, p 8.

884 Stock III, p 649.

885 *National Righteousness,* Vol 1, Dec 1888, pp 2–5.

886 A list of 'well-known names' followed: Dr Baedeker, Dr Barnardo, Andrew Bonar, George Cadbury, Rev C. C. Fenn (Gen Sec of CMS), Eugene Stock, Grattan Guinness, Evan Hopkins, Maj-Gen Hoste, Donald Matheson (one-time director of Jardine Matheson), Handley Moule, C. H. Spurgeon, and a sprinkling of titled supporters.

887 Taylor, Dr and Mrs F. H., *By Faith*, p 76; idem., *Hudson Taylor* II, p 439; Broomhall, M., *Jubilee Story*, p 184; *China's Millions*, 1893, p 46.

888 Student movements, see Johnson, Douglas, *Contending for the Faith: a History of the Evangelical Movement in Universities and Inter-Varsity Colleges,* IVP 1979, pp 32–65; Moule, Handley C. G., *Charles Simeon*, 1892 and IVF 1948 seq.

889 Pollock, *Moody*, p 186ff.

890 Taylor, Dr and Mrs F. H., *Hudson Taylor* II, p 442, footnote; Broomhall, Benjamin, *The Evangelisation of the World,* CIM 1889; Johnson, pp 61–62.

891 Volunteers, in Neill et al., *Dictionary*, pp 570–71.

892 Taylor, Dr and Mrs F. H., *By Faith*, pp 76–108; *China's Millions*, 1888, p 151; 1889, p113; 1893, pp 45–46; 59–61, 73–75; 1930 *passim*; Michell, D.: 'One Hundred Years of the CIM-OMF in North America, 1888–1988' (D Missiology thesis).

893 JHT expositions, see *China's Millions*, Centenary Edition, No 5, 1932; Taylor, Dr and Mrs F. H., *By Faith*, p 78.

894 Zwemer: OMFA 6321j.

895 Frost and Moody, in Taylor, Dr and Mrs F. H., *By Faith*, p 79; OMFA 6322b,c.

896 *China's Millions*, 1893, p 46; OMFA 6311j, k; J233b.

897 Taylor, Dr and Mrs F. H., *By Faith*, p 85; *China's Millions*, 1893, p 46; OMFA 6311j, k.

898 Selection: *China's Millions*, 1888, p 151; 1889, p 112; Broomhall, M., *Jubilee Story*, p 185; OMFA 6311k; J 412; Taylor, Dr and Mrs F. H., *Hudson Taylor* II, p 449.

899 *China's Millions*, 1889, p 112; 1893, p 46; Broomhall, M., *Jubilee Story*, p 185; OMFA 6322b, c; J 231.

900 OMFA 6311n; 6312 Aug 3; J313.

901 Canada: OMFA 6311o, 6321b, g, k; Broomhall, M., *Jubilee Story*, p 186; Taylor, Dr and Mrs F. H., *By Faith*, pp 95–96.

902 Chicago: OMFA 6311q, T, S; Taylor, Dr and Mrs F. H., *By Faith*, pp 93–94.

903 OMFA 6311n, s, u.

904 OMFA 6331. Two versions demonstrate unreliability of faulty memories: 1. Henry W. Frost, pp 89–90: Northfield, Aug 9 – Attica Sept 18; Clifton Springs, Aug 11–13; Rochester, Sept 15. 2. Howard Taylors, *Hudson Taylor* II (1918), pp 451–52 use the recollections of Christina K. Cameron of St Louis (6321w), a child at the time but told of the train incident by the Rev Dr Brookes, convener of the Niagara Conference. Either he or she seems to have mistaken the facts and expressed the principle as 'My Father manages the trains.' Henry Frost's eyewitness account by J. S. Helmer (6331) reads more convincingly and was used in the Howard Taylors' 1938 biography of Henry Frost.

905 *China's Millions*, 1888, p 152; 1889, p 113; 1893, 59; OMFA 6321n, u; 6322a, b, c; 6331; 6411c–w; 6412, 6413, 6414, J 231, J 234.

906 OMFA 6322.

907 Council: OMFA 6331.210-12; *China's Millions*, 1893, p 60.

908 OMFA 6331.213-15.

909 OMFA 6311c, w; 6413.

910 *China's Millions*, 1889, pp 3–4.

911 Dorward: *China's Millions*, 1889, pp 4; 5,117; Broomhall, M., *Pioneer Work*, pp 62–73; OMFA 6412, Dec 12.

912 OMFA 6322b; 6422 Feb 1; 6423 Jan 29.

913 Troubles: OMFA 6412, 6422, J 313.

914 Corner of Peking and Jiangxi Roads, Shanghai.

915 *China's Millions*, 1889, p 33; OMFA 6422.

916 *China's Millions*, 1889, p 22, Oct 21, 1888; OMFA 6413.

917 Floods: *China's Millions*, 1889, pp 25, 29; 33, 57–58, 70; OMFA 6412, Nov 28; 6414; 6422.

918 Distinguish from L. C. Williams, married Marcus Wood.

919 OMFA 6422, Feb 1, 1889. 'It is crucifixion, this constant separation,' was how he had put it in 1885.

920 Editor, *China's Millions*, Nov 1888, pp 139–41; OMFA 6312, Nov 17; 6411i, j.

921 OMFA J323–24.

922 OMFA 6411c, d, f, h, k, 1; J313, J322; 6414; 6422, Feb 22, Mar 1.

923 OMFA 6422, Feb 8, Mar 8, 15.

924 OMFA 6333, p 254.

925 OMFA J 322e; 6422 Mar 27, April 5.

926 OMFA 6425, £5000.

927 OMFA 7122, May 3.

928 OMFA 7123, May 7,16,19, 20.

929 OMFA 6225j; 7122 May 29, 31; 7123.

930 See Haldane, p 118.

931 Little, p 169 *passim*.

932 Temple of Heaven, in Little, pp 169, 177; not the open marble altar of sacrifice used for emperor's annual act of atonement.

933 Fairbank, John King, *The Cambridge History of China*, CUP 1978– multi-volume, 10, p 573.

934 *China's Millions*, 1889, p 143; OMFA 7124b, g.

935 Council for N America, see Broomhall, M., *Jubilee Story*, p 188 (list).

936 Taylor, Dr and Mrs F. H., *By Faith*, chapters 16, 17; *China's Millions*, 1893, p 73.

937 Niagara Conference: *China's Millions*, 1893, p 45; OMFA J 412, K 412; 7121g, j.

938 OMFA 7121k; 7124g.

939 OMFA 7121e.

940 OMFA 7132; J425.

941 London Council Minutes, April 1,1890; OMFA 7121k; 7123, June 5,1889; J F. H.425.5.

942 OMFA 7132 Sept 12, 24, Oct 4.

943 London Council Minutes, June 1889; OMFA 7132.

944 OMFA 7135d.

945 OMFA 7135A.

946 'To Every Creature', *China's Millions*, Feb 1890; Fairbank, *Cambridge History* 10, pp 555–57.

947 Associate Missions: Grist, W. A.: *Samuel Pollard, Pioneer Missionary in China*, Cassell & Co., Ltd (undated). Bible Christian Mission: in 1907 the Bible Christian Society joined New Connexion and Methodist Free Churches to form United Methodist Church. Pollard, Samuel, *Tight Corners in China*, Henry Books 1920, p 18.

948 1888, Anshun occupied by Thomas Windsor and James Adam.

949 Grist, pp 167–78.

950 Johnson, p 61.

951 *China's Millions*, 1890, p 2; 1895, pp 116–17; Broomhall, M., *Jubilee Story*, pp 194, 357–58; OMFA J425; 7133b, 7134, 8336a.

952 Queen Sophia, Stockholm: OMFA J411, J42.14; 7134, Nov 23, 26, 1889; 8336a–c.

953 The initiative of all JHT travels, America, Australasia, came from the countries visited, except to Basle in Switzerland, accidental. Broomhall, M., *Jubilee Story*, p 361 (1889 given in error); *China's Millions*, 1890, p 2; Torjesen, Edvard P., *Fredrik Franson: A Model for Worldwide Evangelism*, William Carey Library 1983.

954 Norwegian Mission in China, Oslo: known first as Norwegian China Committee, then as Christian Committee for the Norwegian Mission in China. 'The Christian Committee of the Norwegian Mission in China' (as it was called), which had invited him to Norway, had like its Swedish counterpart come into being in 1887.

955 Torjesen, pp 49, 65–86; *China's Millions*, 1891,

p 54; London Council Minutes, June 2, 24, 1890.

956 Broomhall, M., *Jubilee Story*, p 359.

957 Torjesen, *passim*.

958 OMFA 8334; Taylor, Dr and Mrs F. H., *Hudson Taylor* II, pp 519, 561 footnotes; Broomhall, M., *Jubilee Story*, pp 362–63.

959 Broomhall, M., *Jubilee Story*, p 364.

960 OMFA 8335; 8421; Broomhall, M., *Jubilee Story*, p 361.

961 Xinjiang pioneers, in Broomhall, M., *Jubilee Story*, p 288–90. Evangeline (Eva) French, Francesca French (1873–1960) and Mildred Cable (1877–1952). In China 'Eva' was 'The Trio's' leader. But Mildred Cable had gifts useful for public relations in the West, so they called her 'our star' and let her take the limelight as author and speaker (close friends of my family in China and Dorset).

962 *China's Millions*, 1890, pp 29, 150–51; OMFA 7142, J 425.

963 OMFA 7132.

964 OMFA 7124b, 7142.

965 OMFA 7132, 7142 Feb 14,1890.

966 The P and P and Arrangements had been referred to London and Mission members for discussion before being promulgated. The London Council mistakenly thought it a *fait accompli* and were indignant, while JHT assumed they understood. Incorporation: A 'Memorandum of Association of the China Inland Mission Corporation' acting as Trustee for CIM property, gave temporary cover until formal incorporation could be completed on Nov 25, 1890. But before he left home on March 17 he signed and sealed (on the 14th) a printed copy of a Deed of Constitution or description of the CIM comprising a minimal statement of faith and particulars of councils in Britain, China and North America with himself as 'Director in Chief' (OMFA 7142 Feb 3, 1890). C. T. Fishe became financial secretary to a finance committee; Marcus Wood was brought home from China to run a men's training home in Inglesby House; Henrietta Soltau opened a women's training home in Pyrland Road; Barton, the Harley House tutor, became assistant to Benjamin B, relieving him of much pressure; Robert Scott (of Marshall, Morgan and Scott) accepted the task of Treasurer; and Jenny Taylor continued as sub-editor of *China's Millions*. Because of the cramped quarters at Pyrland Rd, Benjamin proposed extending the property on Newington Green and erecting an adequate office and Mission Home building. It was completed in 1894 and occupied in 1895.

967 OMFA J425.

968 OMFA 7143, 7244 Apr 10, 14, 1890.

969 OMFA 7224 May 1.

970 OMFA 7231a, b; 7224 May 1.

971 Broomhall, M., *Jubilee Story*, pp 196–98; OMFA 7224, K 112. Shanghai premises: Nov 1873–Sept 1876, Broadway; 1876–78,

nil; April 1878–80, Suchow Creek until demolished; 1880–84, Seward Rd; 1885–90, Yüanmingyuan Buildings; Feb 1890–1930, Wusong Rd; 1930–42, 1945–51, Sinza Rd.

972 *National Righteousness*; OMFA K212; *China's Millions*, 1892, re April 10, 1890.

973 Protestant staff in China, 1890: 1295 men and women from 520 organised Chinese churches of which 94 were entirely self-supporting and 22 partially so. Missionaries: 589 men, 390 wives, 316 single women. Chinese: 209 ordained, 1,260 not ordained; 180 women. Hospitals: 61 treating a third of 1 million patients each year; among them the Schofield Memorial Hospital and Chapel at Taiyuan, begun in 1887. *China's Millions*, 1890, p 51.

974 OMFA J 112; 7142 Jan 17, 1890.

975 *Records of the General Conference of Protestant Missionaries in China 1890*, Shanghai, 1891; *China's Millions*, 1890, pp 108–11; *Report of the Missionary Conference, Shanghai, 1890*, 'Ancestors' pp 57–59, 61–65; Whitehouse, S. F., *Items of Interest: an informal record of the General Missionary Conference and subsequent CIM Conference, May 26–28, 1890*, CIM.

976 Latourette, *History of Missions*, p 414; *China's Millions*, 1890, pp 108–11.

977 Bong Rin Ro (ed.), *Christian Alternatives to Ancestor Practices*, Asian Theological Association 1985, considers a resurgence of unbiblical compromise and a sincere search for cultural observances honouring ancestors without contravening Biblical principles. This debate is complicated by mistaken understanding of the evangelical position and by unfactual statements on the history of the Shanghai conferences of 1877 and 1890, particularly about Hudson Taylor. He drew the limelight upon himself by *asking* for a standing vote but did not in fact play a leading role in the arguments. Phrases like 'as decreed by Hudson Taylor' are very wide of the mark, cf Minamiki, George S. J., *The Chinese Rites Controversy from its beginning to Modern Times*, Loyola University Press, 1985.

978 Covell, *Martin*, pp 249–50.

979 Latourette, *History of Missions*, p 414; *Conference Report*, p 65; Whitehouse, p 22.

980 Tablets, see eg *China's Millions*, 1882, p 110.

981 Bong Rin Ro; *Chinese Recorder*, 1901, pp 253–55; 1902, pp 117–19, 201 Martin, pp 253–55 Price, pp 258–70; 1903, p 199 Walker; 1904, pp 237–45, 301–308 Martin, pp 419–21 Wolfe; 1907, p 504 T. Richard, 'Conversion by the Million'; 1911, pp 408–11 Wei.

982 Whitehouse, pp 15, 21; *China's Millions*, 1890, pp 109,124 (photograph); OMFA 7143, 7224, 7222b; K112, 113.

983 OMFA 7224, May 13, 1890.

984 CIM expansions, in Fairbank, *Cambridge History* 10, p 555; OMFA K113.

985 Whitehouse, S.F., *Items of Interest*.

986 OMFA 7228, 7143; K113.

987 OMFA 7143, 7228 June 6, K113.

988 OMFA 7231a.

989 Reed sisters, see Guinness, Howard W., *Journey among Students*, Anglican Information Office 1978, pp 17–18.

990 Australian Council, see OMFA 7224, 7231a Feb 23, 1890; 7231b, May 19.

991 JHT's children: OMFA 7232.

992 OMFA 7232 July 24, 30.

993 OMFA 7231y, K; 7232.

994 OMFA 7231X; Broomhall, M., *Jubilee Story*, p 199.

995 OMFA 7231E, J; 7232 Sept 19,1890; 7233; *China's Millions*, p 3.

996 First Australians, see Loane, Marcus: *The Story of the China Inland Mission in Australia and New Zealand*, CIM/OMF 1965, pp 151–70, all members and particulars tabulated; *China's Millions*, 1891, p 14.

997 OMFA 72310.

998 OMFA 7232; 7351d; K311.

999 Latourette, *History of Missions*, pp 392–93; Broomhall, M., *Chinese Empire*, p 221; idem., *Jubilee Story*, pp 357–9.

1000 *China's Millions*, 1891, pp 63–64; Taylor, Dr and Mrs F. H., *Hudson Taylor* II, pp 499–502.

1001 Franson's letter, *China's Millions*, 1891, pp 81–82.

1002 OMFA M 321; 7143.

1003 Swedes, see OMFA K212, 213.

1004 OMFA 7441 Mar 24,1893; Latourette, *History of Missions*, p 392 (Continental Missions resulting from Hudson Taylor's influence listed).

1005 OMFA 7234 July 2, 3.

1006 See *Shaping* 1, p 508. His membership of the Westbourne Grove Baptist Chapel and brief links with the Baptist missionary Society reflect the personal choice of a most open-minded man.

1007 OMFA 7321b, Nov 27,1890; Feb 23,1891; K 113.

1008 Th. Howard, Sharp, see OMFA 7331 April 7; 7321b, d, e, f.

1009 OMFA 73211, Aug 28,1891.

1010 OMFA; K113, 213.

1011 *Chinese Recorder*, Dec 1890; Jan 1891.

1012 OMFA 7311 A, C; 7351l.

1013 *Chinese Recorder*, Jan 1891; OMFA 7312, K 11.10.

1014 On Saturday 26, 1892, in a Shanghai prayer meeting, Hudson Taylor prayed with unusual urgency and concern for D. L. Moody. It proved to be the day his ship the *Spree* came close to sinking in the Atlantic. OMFA 7311c; 7352; *China's Millions*, 1890, pp 146, 159;1891, p 77; Pollock, *Moody*, pp 241–3.

1015 *China's Millions*, 1892, pp 1, 2.

1016 Neill et al., *Dictionary*, p 261; Huc, Evariste Régis, *High Road in Tartary: The Story of a Celebrated Journey from Peking to Lhasa*, 1867 [10057.aa.39], pp 184–86; idem., *Travels in Tartary and Thibet*, Herbert Joseph 1937.

1017 OMFA 5433, 7132, 7143; Hopkirk, *Trespassers*.

1018 Polhill-Turners, pp 109–28.

1019 A. W. Douthwaite, Sept 25,1893; unpublished MS by his great-niece Mrs W. P. K. Findlay. (In my own experience in China and Mindoro, Philippines, 1947–64, the same held true.)

1020 Modern Chinese maps carry the political boundary between Sichuan and Xizang (Tibet proper) far to the west of the ethnic dividing line, but add to Qinghai at Gansu's expense. Xikang (Sikang) is no longer recognised, and the whole drainage area of the Yalong River is now in Sichuan. The new border follows the Jinsha Jiang, 'the River of Golden Sand', which is the upper stretch of the Yangzi River.

1021 Wang Cuan-yi also called Wang Zongyi (Wang Ts'uan-i and Wang Tsung-i); Polhill-Turners, pp 139–49.

1022 Polhill-Turners, pp 146–49; *China's Millions*, 1892, pp 163–65; 1895, p 78; 1898, p 5.

1023 Wang and Zhang, *China's Millions*, 1893, pp 105–7; 1894, pp 75–77, 80; J. G. Cormack, CIM; Knipe and another, CMS holding fort until Cecil Polhill returned.

1024 Hopkirk, *Trespassers*, pp 92–98; *China's Millions*, 1893, pp 103–104, 160.

1025 Annie R Taylor and Pontso, see OMFA 7441, 7442; *China's Millions*, 1893, p 112; 1894, pp 46–48; OMFA 8224a.

1026 OMFA 7331; K212, 213.

1027 OMFA 7331d; K212.

1028 *China's Millions*, 1891, pp 113, 156; 1896, p 84; OMFA 7331d, 7352e.

1029 Fairbank, *Cambridge History* 10, p 573.

1030 OMFA 7331d.

1031 *China's Millions*, 1891, pp 100, 141–42; OMFA 7331d, 7351k, m; 7352e, i; K212.

1032 OMFA 7311C, also Nov 26, 1892.

1033 Zhou Han pamphlets, see Broomhall, M., *Jubilee Story*, p 230; idem., *Chinese Empire*, p 175; *China's Millions*, 1893, pp 23, 39.

1034 *China's Millions*, 1893, p 105; OMFA 7441, 7442.

1035 *China's Millions*, 1893, p 148; OMFA 7442.

1036 Minutes, Mar 7,1889; OMFA 7141a, b, f, m; 7228 May 31, 1890.

1037 OMFA 7331d May 30,1891; K 214.

1038 JHT-Th. Howard: OMFA 7311A, B.

1039 OMFA 7311D; 7411a.

1040 OMFA 5431c; 6114, 6227, 6412 Dec 28, 1888; 7122, 7124b, 7132, 7141, 7227, 7228, 7311, 7321, 7331, 7341; 7342, 7343, 7352, 7361, 7362, 7363, 7411, 7412, 7414, 7442.

1041 Ultimatum: London Council Minutes, Oct 20, letter Oct 22, 1891; OMFA 7342a-e.

1042 OMFA 73521 Dec 5, 1891; 7342d.

1043 OMFA 7352j; 7363.

1044 *China's Millions*, 1892, p 96; OMFA 7361, 7363.

1045 OMFA 7412l, o, q, r, w; K 313.

1046 OMFA 7412A, B, C.

1047 OMFA 7412J, M, O, R.

1048 OMFA 7412O, R, S; 7441.

1049 Sloan and Frost, see OMFA 7412W; Codes: 7352o, 7437, 7411d.

1050 Amy Carmichael, Eva French: OMFA 7437; July 4, 1893.

1051 OMFA 7141b; 7441.

1052 OMFA 7442D.

1053 A twentieth-century term not found in the archives; OMFA 731IB; 7411a, b.

1054 OMFA 7422; London Council Minutes, Oct 31, 1893.

1055 Newington Green: OMFA 7437, 7441, 7442. Oct 4, 1887, payment for Inglesby House completed; Feb 19, 1889, house adjoining Inglesby purchased for £1000; June 14, 1889, discussion on buying a strip of land adjoining Inglesby House; June 21, 1889, and Dec 3, 1889, purchase of 'Monte Cristo' property again discussed; April 1, 1890, first mention of building; May 13, 1890, £8550 asked for Monte Cristo property; Feb 17, 1891, Monte Cristo auction on 27th; Aug 4, 1891, Monte Cristo negotiations continued; Oct 31, 1892, decision to proceed; Dec 1893 foundations in; Mar 8, 1894, Newington Green building occupied.

1056 *National Righteousness*, Vol 1 No 7, 1891.

1057 Stock III, p 575; *National Righteousness* Vol 1 No 7, April 1891, pp 1–48; Resolution: 'That this House is of opinion that the system by which the Indian opium revenue is raised is morally indefensible, and would urge upon the Indian Government that they should cease to grant licences for the cultivation of the poppy and sale of opium in British India, except to supply the legitimate demand for medical purposes, and they should at the same time take measures to arrest the transit of Malwa opium through British territory.'

1058 *National Righteousness*, Vol 1 No 13, Sept 1893, p 13.

1059 *China's Millions*, 1890, pp 86–88, 125; 1892, pp 41–42.

1060 OMFA K316; *National Righteousness*, 1899.

1061 *National Righteousness*, No 10 Feb 1893, pp 3–5; No 11 April 1893; Parliamentary Blue Books, Feb 9, 1892, C.6562; Stock III, p 506.

1062 *China's Millions*, 1894, pp 102–4,106.

1063 Stock III, pp 575–76; *China's Millions*, 1894, p 106 verbatim; 1899, p 21.

1064 *China's Millions*, 1893, p 115;1894 pp 91–92; Broomhall, Marshall, *Faith and Facts, as Illustrated in the History of the China Inland Mission*, CIM 1909, pp 75–77.

1065 OMFA 7412E; 7421b.

1066 *China's Millions*, 1893, p 9; OMFA K 13.11, 7433, 7434 C, 7441, 7442 D.

1067 Rijnhardt, see OMFA 7412o, p, F, G, L, W; 7442, 7443e–h; 8113. Has been called Dr Petrus Rijnhardt in error.

1068 Neill et al., *Dictionary*, p 571.

1069 OMFA 7442B Feb 14, 1894; 7443.

1070 OMFA 8111a.

1071 Smith, *The Uplift*, p 183; Nevius, *passim*.

1072 Neill et al., *Dictionary*, pp 326, 437; idem., *History*, pp 343–44; Latourette, *History of Expansion* 6, pp 308, 425.

1073 Unpublished MS by Mrs W. P. K. Findlay quoting Mrs Douthwaite (Connie Groves) October 22, 1893; Latourette, *History of Missions*, pp 367, 427, 430.

1074 OMFA 7441, Mar 24,1893; 7442; 8113 Apr 27, 1894; May 11, 1894; *China's Millions*, 1893, p 83; Latourette, *History of Missions*, p 399.

1075 OMFA 7442, Nov 10, Dec 9, 12, 1893.

1076 OMFA 7441, Mar 31, May 22, 1893; 8116d, May 22, 1893; 7442, Nov 17, 1893; 8116d, May 22, 1894.

1077 OMFA 7441, Mar 24,1893; 8111 a, Apr 24, 1894.

1078 OMFA 8113, May 11, 1894.

1079 OMFA 7351 Aug 25, 1891.

1080 Three-eyed peacock feather first given to Li Hongzhang after Nianfei campaign.

1081 Shaanxi-Shanxi, OMFA 8112, May; 8 Book 2, 3; *China's Millions*, 1894, pp 118–19,134–36,148–49, 155; 1895 pp 2–3,16–18, 33–34.

1082 OMFA 8115a, Sept 1894; 8112, July 16, 1894; 'the Sabbath is made for man, not man for the Sabbath.'

1083 Neill, *History*, pp 358–59 re India; Latourette, *History of Missions*, p 619; *Chinese Recorder*, 1901, p 124.

1084 OMFA 8112 Aug 24, 1894; 8113.

1085 OMFA 744213; 8114 Oct 5, 15, 1894; N17, pp 22–28.

1086 OMFA 10.351; 8114, 8115.

1087 OMFA 8114 Oct 18, 1894.

1088 Morse II, pp 27–39.

1089 *China's Millions*, 1897, pp 23, 38; 1895, p 22; Haldane, p 127.

1090 Later it was claimed that if Li Hongzhang had not been removed from Zhili the Boxer rising would not have taken place.

1091 Morse III, pp 49, 50 footnote 56; Little, *passim*.

1092 *China's Millions*, 1895, p 65, 152–53; 1897, pp 73,102–4; Judd, Frederik H., *The Chefusian*, 1987; Mrs W. P. K. Findlay MS; OMFA 8213 Aug 15, 1895.

1093 Morse III, p 54; *U S Foreign Relations*, 1895, pp 87–98; *North China Herald*, Oct 11, Nov 8, Dec 6, 1895.

1094 Sun Yatsen, see Morse III, pp 129–32, citing Cantlie, James, *Sun Yat Sen and the Awakening of China*, Revell 1912, p 63 seq.

1095 Morse III, p 131 seq; *North China Herald*, Dec 6,1895.

1096 Morse III, p 129.

1097 Little, p 247.

1098 OMFA 8223, Aug 30, 1895; 8213 June 1895.

1099 Smith, *The Uplift*, p.166; Little, p 12; *China's Millions*, 1896, p 1.

1100 *China's Millions*, 1895, p 103; 1896, pp 25, 98; OMFA 8213.

1101 *China's Millions*, 1895, p 53; OMFA 8223, May 30, June 4, 1895.

1102 OMFA 8212, June 12; 8223, June 5.

1103 Stock III, p 581; OMFA 8212, July 23.

1104 OMFA 8223, July 6, 1895.

1105 *China's Millions*, 1895, pp 93, 134; 1896, p 14; OMFA 8212, 8213.

1106 OMFA 8223, Oct 1895.

1107 Indemnities: OMFA 8212 Aug 19, 28, 1895

1108 OMFA 8221c Nov 17, 1895.

1109 Broomhall, M., *W W Cassels*, p 177; OMFA 8212 Aug 4.

1110 *China's Millions*, 1895, p 159; Little, pp 159, 201, 252; Stock III, p 582.

1111 *China's Millions*, 1896, p 48.

1112 Stock III, pp 582–87.

1113 MacGillivray, Donald, A., *Century of Protestant Missions in China*, Shanghai 1907 [4764. ff.11], p 54; both breasts severed.

1114 *China's Millions*, 1895, pp 129, 131, 159.

1115 *China's Millions*, 1896, p 6.

1116 Fujian Church, see MacGillivray, pp 51–54.

1117 Smith, *The Uplift*, p 165.

1118 *China's Millions*, 1895, p 144; 1896, pp 9, 65–66; 1898, pp 124, 145; 1897, p 89; 1899, pp 110–11; 1900, p 40; OMFA K424, 8 Book 5; 8233.

1119 Mesny, personal communications: P. D. Coates, one-time HBM Consular Service, China; Dr G. A. Curwen, School of Oriental and African Studies, Lond. Univ.; Hon. Librarian-Archivist, Société Jersiaise, Jersey.

1120 OMFA 8233; friend of Douthwaite.

1121 OMFA 8114, 8213, 8224a–f.

1122 *China's Millions*, 1896, pp 35, 75; OMFA 8232 Jan 18, 1896.

1123 OMFA 8231, 8232 Mar 1896; 8234; Polhill-Turners, pp 151 seq.

1124 OMFA 8231 Apr 1896; 8233.

1125 Hopkirk, *Trespassers*, pp 104, 137–48.

1126 Latourette, *History of Missions*, pp 579–80.

1127 Polhill-Turners, p 158.

1128 Hopkirk, *Trespassers*, pp 159–92.

1129 OMFA 8213; London Council Minutes; Sept 17,1895.

1130 OMFA 8 Book 1; 8221c, 8213.

1131 OMFA 8232.

1132 *China's Millions*, 1895, p 145; OMFA 8223.

1133 OMFA 8212 Aug 13, 28, 31, Nov 9.

1134 Cholera: OMFA 8221c, 8236; *China's Millions*, 1895, pp 130;150;173; 1896, pp 1, 2, 7; Wenzhou cholera: *China's Millions*, 1895, p 173; 1896, p 7; OMFA 8221c June 16, 1905; 8213 Oct 17.

1135 OMFA 8231, 8232, 8235.

1136 OMFA 8235 Jan 1896.

1137 OMFA 8231, 8233 Oct 1898.

1138 Lucy Guinness: 1900 married H. K. W. Kumni of North Africa Mission, co-founder of Sudan United Mission; OMFA 8312, 8323.

1139 *China's Millions*, 1897, p 1.

1140 Thompson, P., *D E Hoste*, pp 82–83; OMFA 8111b, 8233.

1141 *China's Millions*, 1898, pp 8,15; OMFA 8312, 8324.

1142 OMFA 7435,8312,8313,8331,8334,8336; *China's Millions*, 1896, p 134.

1143 OMFA 8312 Oct 1

1144 *China's Millions*, 1890, p 111;1895 pp 134,157–8.

1145 Latourette, *History of Missions*, pp 370, 567ff.

1146 Broomhall, M., *W W Cassels*, pp 146–47,177; OMFA 8212, 8213, 8222, J 313.

1147 OMFA 8213,8222; Stock III, p 476 (Dr A. C. Lankester), 310, 661 (Herbert Lankester), pp 695, 705 (physician to CMS).

1148 Broomhall, M., *Chinese Empire*, p 224.

1149 Broomhall, M., *Pioneer Work*, pp 72–80; *China's Millions*, 1891, p 91; 1892, p 158; 1898, p 104, 106.

1150 *China's Millions*, 1898, p 43; 1899, pp 53,101–2; OMFA 8411 Feb 1887.

1151 *China's Millions*, 1898, pp 104, 106; 1900, pp 18–28,87–88; OMFA 9221.

1152 *China's Millions*, 1898, p 26.

1153 OMFA 7441 Feb 3,1893; L 12.13; *China's Millions*, 1897, pp 55, 74, 96, 98–99, 104–6, 114–16; 1898, p 99; 1899, pp 53, 101–2,, 150.

1154 OMFA 8515a–d (7441).

1155 OMFA 8421; *China's Millions*, 1897, pp 5,7; Broomhall, M., *Pioneer Work*, pp 82–83.

1156 *China's Millions*, 1897, Dec; 1898 pp 69 editorial, 102–3.

1157 1894,71 added; 1895, 71; 1896, 79.

1158 Father of Dr Gregg of Manchuria.

1159 OMFA 8221c June 1895,8321, 8412; McKay, M. J., thesis, Aberdeen, (unpublished) 1981, p 240 seq.

1160 OMFA 8221c Sept 24,1895.

1161 OMFA 8312 Aug 11, 1896.

1162 OMFA 8312 Aug 11, Oct 13; 8422 June 11; 8414. 'Mumps': recurrent episodes with toothache, with frequent visits to dentist in 1896–97, suggest dental abscess.

1163 OMFA 8321 Mar 12,1897; particulars requested by donors to guide contributions were supplied (unsolicited): £10,000. OMFA 8321, 8412, 8422 Sept 2,16.

1164 OMFA 8412, J. W. Stevenson notes; Broomhall, M., *John W Stevenson*, p 72; *China's Millions*, 1898, p 24.

1165 J. T. Morton legacy: OMFA 8522 Jan 29,1898; L 213,122,128; London Council Minutes, Sept 20,1898; *China's Millions*, 1907, editorial notes. An annual income of £12,500 from J. T. Morton came to China at least until 1907, and in 1912 £14,000 of it were received for missionaries' needs, with 6,000 taels 'for permanent school buildings'. £2,000: This may have been the bequest later referred to as the 'Joy' legacy.

1166 OMFA 8322 May, June 5,1896; *China's Millions*, 1898, pp 151,156.

1167 *China's Millions*, 1897, p 96.

1168 *China's Millions* 1897 p 119; OMFA 8414, 8422.

1169 *China's Millions* 1898 pp 9, 53, 99; OMFA 8413, 8423.

1170 *China's Millions*, 1898, p 53 Reuter cable; first to reach Chongqing, Mar 8, 1898.

1171 Little, p 266; Haldane, p 124.

1172 Morse III, Chronology; Latourette, *History of Missions*, p 489.

1173 *China's Millions*, 1896, p 145. From time to time in the archives reference is made to a quotation alleged to be from Napoleon Bonaparte: 'China? There lies a sleeping giant. Let him sleep, for when he wakes he will move the world.' Used by John R. Mott in addressing invited guests in London 1902, and quoted in his report of his world tour as General Secretary of the World's Christian Students' Federation: *Strategic Points in the World's Conquest*. And by B. Broomhall as the title to an article in *China's Millions* in April 1902 anticipating the effect of Chinese evangelists worldwide. Cited in full by Robert Payne in *Mao Tse-tung*, p 275, Abelard-Schuman Ltd 1950 edn but omitted from the 1961 edn., see note 1545 below).

1174 Morse III, p 128; Fairbank, *Cambridge History* 10, p 586.

1175 Neill, *History*, p 339; Morse III, pp 132–33.

1176 Morse III, p 134.

1177 Fairbank, *Cambridge History* 10, pp 581, 587.

1178 Morse III, pp 128–37.

1179 Fairbank, *Cambridge History* 10, pp 559, 581–82, 587; *Chinese Recorder*, 1888, pp 358–64, 397–402, 465–72. Gilbert Reid (1857–1927). Soothill, p 183.

1180 Woodcock, p 183; Covell, *Martin*, pp 220–1; *China's Millions*, 1898, p 26.

1181 Fairbank, *Cambridge History* 10, pp 567–73 quoting Cohen, pp 568, 572.

1182 OMFA 8512, 8522 Nov 7; *China's Millions*, 1899, pp 12, 30, 97; Beresford, Lord Charles: *The Break-up of China*, pp 140–2.

1183 Morse III, pp 153, 155 (Oct 24, 1898), 157.

1184 Fairbank, *Cambridge History* 10, p 587; Soothill, p 238; Covell, *Martin*, p 185; Mandarin buttons: Morse III, p 87; Mines and Railways assent: Yong Lu to prepare naval academy and training ships.

1185 Morse III, p 151; Latourette, *History of Missions*, p 498; Broomhall, M., *Chinese Empire*, p 233; Sir C. Macdonald to Lord Salisbury, Parliamentary Papers 1, 1899.

1186 Latourette, *History of Missions*, p 498.

1187 *China's Millions*, 1898, pp 117, 136–37, 150–51; 155–56; OMFA 8522, May 16, 1898; 8521 July 1, 1898.

1188 *China's Millions*, 1898, pp 117, 151.

1189 OMFA 8523, 9111.

1190 OMFA 8116c, 8231, 8522, 9114, L2117, circular letter; L21.11; L222.

1191 OMFA 8116 May 11, 1894.

1192 OMFA 8116, 8231, 8522, L 2117, L 21.11, L 222, 'though a mistake was unwittingly made (when special support was welcomed), its recognition demands its correction (China Council, July 1898). It is therefore concluded ... that from 30th June, 1899, the system be discontinued (whereby) sums of money become the definite salary [donations] towards the support and share of expense of a missionary (will be pooled in the General Fund and distributed) on a uniform scale.'

1193 Unity, not uniformity: OMFA 851.12, 8522 Oct 10.

1194 OMFA 8513.

1195 Haldane, p 131.

1196 Morse III, pp 135, 137, 140–47.

1197 Foreign Office Parliamentary Papers, *China* No 1, 1899, p 240 Sept 8, 1898.

1198 Morse III, pp 141–47; Haldane, p 136.

1199 *North China Herald*, Oct 10,1898; Little, p 283; Soothill, pp 238–39; Morse III, p 145 fn.

1200 Morse III, p 146. Consul Brennan, Shanghai, met Kang at Wusong and had him transferred to P&O *ss Ballarat*.

1201 Coup, see Morse III, p 143; *North China Herald*, Oct 10,1898; Haldane, pp 145–47.

1202 Broomhall, Marshall, *Martyred Missionaries of the China Inland Mission, with a Record of the Perils and Sufferings of Some who Escaped*, Morgan & Scott/CIM 1901, p 4 footnote (1st edn p 6); Morse III, p 150.

1203 F O Parliamentary Papers, *China* No 1, 1899, p 336 and April 15–Dec 26, 1898; Latourette, *History of Missions*, p 501.

1204 Little, pp 289–90.

1205 Morse III, pp xxxv, 87.

1206 Isabella L. Bird (Mrs Bishop), *The Yangtze Valley and Beyond*, 1899, last of series: *Pacific Islands*, 1875; *Rocky Mts*, 1879; *Haokkaido, Japan*, 1880; *Malaya*, 1883; *Persia*, 1891; *Ladakh*, 1894; *Korea*, 1898; *China's Millions*, 1897, pp 90, 92; 1899, p 46.

1207 *China's Millions*, 1899, p 46.

1208 Latourette, *History of Missions*, pp 490–501.

1209 Fairbank, *Cambridge History* 10, pp 543–44, 574–81

1210 Catholic status, see Latourette, *History of Missions*, p 500 footnote.

1211 OMFA 8512, 8522, 9112a; *China's Millions*, 1899, pp 6, 22, 121; Broomhall, M., *Chinese Empire*, p 267.

1212 Morse III, p 157; *North China Herald*, June 6, 1900.

1213 *China's Millions*, 1899, p 65 seq.

1214 Latourette, *History of Missions*, p 501; Grist.

1215 Broomhall, M., *Pioneer Work*, pp 83–88; *China's Millions*, 1899, p 107; OMFA L 21.13.

1216 Hunan, see Broomhall, M., *Chinese Empire*, pp 183–4.

[1217] OMFA 9112x; *China's Millions*, 1899, pp 12, 30, 97; *North China Herald*, 1899, May 13, June 17, Aug 28, Sept 4, Oct 9, 23, Dec 4; Morse III, p 169, clashes in many provinces.

[1218] 'Boxers' – an imperial edict approved, transparently: 'When peaceful and law-abiding people practice their mechanical skill for the self-preservation of themselves, this is in accordance with the public spirited principle (enjoined by Mencius) of keeping mutual watch and giving mutual help.' Morse III:, pp 175 seq; Fairbank, *Cambridge History* 10, p 573.

[1219] Haldane, pp 178–80; Fairbank, *Cambridge History* 10, p 573; Hubbard, G. E., 'Royal Institute of International Affairs', *Chambers Encyclopedia* 3, pp 474–76.

[1220] *North China Herald*, Mar 21,1900.

[1221] OMFA 8517, 8522, 8523, 9113d.

[1222] OMFA 8514b, 8521, 8522, 8523, 10.351.

[1223] OMFA 8522, Oct 17, 1898.

[1224] Chongqing conference: OMFA 8517; 8523, 9111, 9112x; *China's Millions*, 1899, pp 71, 80,120; *Chinese Recorder*, 1899, pp 157–60; Latourette, *History of Missions*, p 496.

[1225] OMFA 9111x, 9112a.

[1226] OMFA 8522 Nov 3, 1898.

[1227] OMFA 9112b, Jan 11, Sept 8, 1899.

[1228] OMFA 9112x, L 21.13.

[1229] M. J. McKay thesis, Aberdeen, (unpublished): W. T. Berger's financial contributions to CIM totaled approx. £18,000; *China's Millions*, 1899, pp 18–20, 47.

[1230] OMFA 9114, 9212; Taylor, Dr and Mrs F. H., *By Faith*, pp 238–41.

[1231] OMFA 9112, Sept 11, 1899.

[1232] Pollock, *Moody*, p 270; *China's Millions*, p 87; OMFA 9221.

[1233] OMFA 9112; L 222; *China's Millions*, 1899, pp 108, 185.

[1234] *China's Millions*, 1898, pp 156–7.

[1235] Morse III, pp 177–91; Broomhall, M., *Jubilee Story*, pp 242–46; Haldane, pp 176–85; Little, pp 291–306; Forsyth, *passim*.

[1236] Little, p 296: eyewitness account by Chinese eunuch, *North China Herald*, Mar 14, 1900.

[1237] F O Parliamentary Papers, *China* No 3, 1900, Mar 29, p 12; Latourette, *History of Missions*, pp 501–26; *History of Expansion* 6, p 291.

[1238] *North China Herald*, April 11, 18,1900.

[1239] Broomhall, M., *Jubilee Story*, p 245.

[1240] *North China Herald*, May 8, 16, 1900.

[1241] Little, pp 304–306.

[1242] OMFA 9112a; L 222.

[1243] Jennie/Jenny – both spellings common, the latter used more often in later years by JHT.

[1244] OMFA L226, 9112a, 9121,10.351; Loane, *passim*.

[1245] OMFA 9211b, 10.351; 9115 Jan 30, 1900; Morse III, p 178.

[1246] OMFA N17.1900 p 2; 9215a.

[1247] OMFA 9212, 9213; D. M. Stearns, Aug

[1248] 6,1905; Taylor, Dr and Mrs F. H., *By Faith*, pp 242–43.

Ecumenical conference: *China's Millions*, 1900, p 115.

[1249] Polygamy: OMFA N17.1900 p 9, F. Howard Taylor report.

[1250] OMFA N17.1900 p 10; 9212 July 6.

[1251] Boxer rising: this is only a summary. Research is needed into the archives of each society in China at the time, and the many publications on the subject. Most narratives relate to localities with little attention to chronology. This one attempts to keep the perspective of chronology, at the cost of interrupted narratives.

[1252] Discrepancies, eg see Forsyth, pp 202–18 and *Chinese Recorder*, 1900, pp 458–63.

[1253] 'Great miscalculation', see Broomhall, M., *Martyred*, preface.

[1254] Ibid., pp 2, 3–10.

[1255] Morse III, p 191.

[1256] Forsyth, *passim*; Broomhall, M., *Martyred*, p 19.

[1257] Broomhall, M., *Martyred*, pp 77,103.

[1258] Engineers, see Little, p 306; Haldane, p 185; Morse III, p 199.

[1259] Forsyth, pp 13–18.

[1260] Glover A. E., *A Thousand Miles of Miracle in China*, CIM 1904, 20th edn 1944, abridged by L. T. Lyall 1957, *passim*.

[1261] Morse III, *passim*, see pp 231, 233 fn; Haldane; Broomhall, M., *Martyred*; Little.

[1262] Haldane, p 187. Haldane says killed June 12; Forsyth and Broomhall, 11th.

[1263] Morse III, pp 205 seq (Ch 8); Haldane, pp 188–89; Forsyth, p 101; Broomhall, M., *Martyred*, p 260.

[1264] Morse III, p 280; *Chinese Recorder*, 1900, p 475; Latourette, *History of Missions*, p 508; *History of Expansion* 6, pp 291–2.

[1265] Broomhall, M., *Martyred*, pp 259–60.

[1266] Haldane, p 190.

[1267] Broomhall, M., *Martyred*, pp 144, 297; idem., *Last Letters and Further Records of Martyred Missionaries of the China Inland Mission*, Morgan & Scott/CIM 1901, pp 51–61; Forsyth, p 77.

[1268] *Chinese Recorder*, 1901, p 423; Forsyth, p 298.

[1269] Broomhall, M., *Martyred*, p 144; Forsyth, R. C.: *China Martyrs*, p 79.

[1270] Forsyth, p 102; Haldane, p 194; Morse III, p 247.

[1271] Wang Mingdao, *A Stone Made Smooth*, Christian Mayflower Books 1981, p 2.

[1272] Morse III, p 225; F. D. Gamewell, E. G. Tewkesbury; Francis James; Forsyth, p 475.

[1273] Morse III, pp 238–39; Jingshan's Diary.

[1274] Morse III, p 263.

[1275] Ibid., III, pp 236–38; Jingshan's Diary, p 287; Broomhall, M., *Martyred*, p 9; Smith, Arthur H., *China in Convulsion*, 1901 (facsimile reprint, Irish University Press 1972) (2 vols) II, p 294.

1276 Yüan Zhang, Xŭ Jingcheng (Yuan Chang, Hsu Ching Ch'eng); Morse III: 238.

1277 Tuan Fang, see Broomhall, M., *Martyred*, pp 286–87; Forsyth, p 489.

1278 F O Parliamentary Papers, *China* No 3, 1900, p 67: Admiral Bruce to Admiralty; Morse III: 227–28, 231–32.

1279 *North China Herald*, July 11,1900; Morse III: 232; Consul Warren to Lord Salisbury, June 29, 1900, Parliamentary Papers, *China* No 3, 1900, p 85.

1280 Morse III, pp 265, 268; Little, p 308 – Alicia Bewicke Little was herself a refugee from Chongqing.

1281 *Chinese Recorder*, 1900, pp 512–5.

1282 Forsyth, pp 250–70.

1283 Ibid., pp 299–302.

1284 Ibid., pp 85–87; Broomhall, M., *Martyred*, p 144; *Chinese Recorder*, 1900, p 528; Latourette, *History of Expansion*, p 339. Swedes not identified; possibly C&MA, making their party seventeen; Mr and Mrs C. Blomberg, Mr and Mrs O. Forsberg and child, of C&MA, died with Swedish Holiness Union ten.

1285 Soping: named in Forsyth, p 79–80; Broomhall, M., *Martyred*, pp 144–9: Mr and Mrs S. A. Persson, Miss J. Lundell, E. Pettersson, N. Carleson, O. A. L. Larsson, S. McKee, Miss M. Aspden, Mr and Mrs C. S. I'Anson, Miss M. E. Smith.

1286 Morse III, p 242, citing '*North China Herald*, July 25, 1900 and private notes'.

1287 Forsyth, pp 346–82.

1288 Ibid., pp 346–82.

1289 Wilson and Saunders, see Broomhall, M., *Martyred*, pp 67–76, 107–8, 126, 130; Forsyth, pp 116–17.

1290 Broomhall, M., *Martyred*, pp 69–70,114–15, 126, 140; Forsyth, pp 33–34, 117, 430.

1291 Broomhall, M., *Martyred*, p 101: Eva French, Johnson, Gauntlett, Higgs, Rasmussen, Eldred; *China's Millions*, 1900, p 74.

1292 Broomhall, M., *Martyred*, p 147.

1293 Henan Canadians, see *Chinese Recorder*, 1900, pp 458–63; Forsyth, pp 202–18; Broomhall, *Martyred*, p 147.

1294 Another, Griffiths, mentioned later; *Chinese Recorder*, 1900, pp 458–63 adds yet another, T Craigie Hood; no list complete.

1295 Forsyth, pp 34–37, 428–29.

1296 Ibid., pp 43–64, 443–51; Broomhall, *Martyred*, p 145.

1297 Forsyth, p 45, July 25; Chinese Christians: pp 368–73.

1298 Broomhall, M., *Martyred*, pp 110,103–25.

1299 Ibid., pp 24, 26, 29,109, 268, 293, 295; *Last Letters*, pp 30, 34, 37, 66; Forsyth, pp 65–68.

1300 *Chinese Recorder*, 1901, pp 264–66; Forsyth, pp 25–26 (19–29), 412–24.

1301 *Chinese Recorder*, 1901, p 265; Latourette, *History of Expansion*, p 338; Presbyterians: Forsyth, pp 23–24.

1302 Broomhall, M., *Martyred*, pp 57, 77, 103, 112,

154–57, 293; *Last Letters*, pp 28,98; Forsyth, pp 25–26; Latourette, *History of Missions*, pp 777–79.

1303 Latourette, *History of Missions*, pp 777–79; Broomhall, Marshall, *Marshal Feng: A Good Soldier of Christ Jesus*, CIM/RTS 1923, pp 5–12.

1304 Morse III, p 248; Broomhall, M., *Martyred*, p 299.

1305 Ci Xi's perfidy, see Morse III, pp 246–47, citing Jingshan's diary, July 4, pp 284–88; July 7 p 288.

1306 *Chinese Recorder*, 1901, pp 423–35, general review; Morse III, p 242; Forsyth, pp 273–310, 489; Latourette, *History of Missions*, p 511; idem., *History of Expansion*, pp 292, 339.

1307 Green, C. H. S., *In Deaths Oft*, CIM 1901, *passim*; Broomhall, M., *Martyred*, pp 161–7. So recent were these events, that many of the individuals involved were personally known to large numbers of people still living.

1308 Broomhall, M., *Martyred*, pp 293–97.

1309 Broomhall, M., *Last Letters*, pp 89–93.

1310 Broomhall, M., *Martyred*. pp 25, 54, 116, 268, 297.

1311 Chang Chih-heng, see Broomhall, M., *Martyred*, pp 11–12, 262–63, 268–72; Swedish Mission, pp 17, 22–24, 230–35, 245, 263, 305.

1312 Broomhall, M., *Martyred*, p 265; idem., *Last Letters*, pp 27, 84, 86, 88; Forsyth, pp 134–47.

1313 M. E. Chapman, see *Loane*, p 28.

1314 Broomhall, M., *Martyred*, pp 110–12, 262–63; Forsyth, p 75.

1315 *The Times*, Sept 19, 1900; Saunders, Alexander R., *A God of Deliverances: The Story of the Marvellous Deliverances Through the Sovereign Power of God of a Party of Missionaries, When Compelled By the Boxer Rising to Flee from Shan-si, North China*', CIM/Morgan & Scott, *passim*; Broomhall, M., *Martyred*, pp 66–78, 82, 100, 115, 294; idem., *Last Letters*, p 89; Forsyth, pp 116–26.

1316 Broomhall, M., *Martyred*, pp 73–5.

1317 Glover, abridged 1957, *passim* (outstanding among all missionary literature); Broomhall, M., *Martyred*, pp 25, 64, 66, 75, 77–78, 81–88, 89–101, 293–94, 297; Forsyth, pp 127–33.

1318 Wuhan of today is the conurbation of Hankou, Wuchang and Hanyang. By 1900 Hankou was the commercial, consular and missionary centre (the name most used in literature of the period). Wuchang was a Chinese city, seat of mandarins; Hanyang, industrial. Retaining Hankou here avoids an anachronism.

1319 Broomhall, M., *Martyred*, pp 205–17, 254, 293–94; Forsyth, pp 219–27.

1320 Broomhall, M., *Martyred*, pp 205, 233–34.

1321 Ibid. pp 236–43, 276; Forsyth, pp 238–49.

1322 C. H. Bird with A. Gracie family, John Macfarlane (also as MacFarlane, McFarlane, M'Farlane); Loane, *passim*; Broomhall, *Martyred*, pp 205, 217–19, 245, 273.

1323 Broomhall, M., *Martyred*, pp 205, 231, 295; escape pp 244–50; Forsyth, pp 228–37.

1324 Mr and Mrs Shearer, two children; Mr and Mrs Robert Powell, Biggs; Charles M. Lack; Misses Kidman, E. L. Randall, Taylor, Bevin, in Broomhall, M., *Martyred*, pp 205, 225–29, 287.

1325 Broomhall, M., *Martyred*, pp 69, 107, 111, 114–16, 127, 140 list, 163, 261, 264; 266–67; Forsyth, p 40 list. BMS: G. B. Farthing, Mrs Farthing, children; Miss E. M. Stewart; S. F. Whitehouse, Mrs Whitehouse; Shouyang: T. W. Pigott, Mrs Pigott nee Kemp, child; Miss Duval, J. Robinson, Ernestine and Mary Atwater, children, ABCFM; Taiyuan: Dr A. E. Lovitt, Mrs Lovitt, child; G. W. Stokes, Mrs Stokes; J. Simpson, Mrs Simpson; Miss A. E. Coombs; independent, A. Hoddle; CIM: Dr W. Millar Wilson, Mrs Millar Wilson, child; Mrs J. Stevens, M. Clarke; B&FBS: W. F. Beynon, Mrs Beynon, 3 children. Previously CIM: Pigotts, Beynons, Hoddle, Simpsons, Stokes.

1326 *Chinese Recorder*, 1901, pp 132–37; Broomhall, M., *Martyred*, p 155; murders: p 265; Forsyth, p 32.

1327 Forsyth, pp 34, 37–40; *Chinese Recorder*, 1901, p 210; Broomhall, M., *Last Letters*, pp 21–24; Latourette, *History of Missions*, p 510.

1328 Bishop Fogolla, see Latourette, *History of Missions*, p 510, from RC sources: 'Yu Man himself dealt the aged Fogolla the first blow'—whether the facial wound or decapitation, not clarified.

1329 Taken from Yong Zheng's report as recorded by J. A. Creasey Smith; *Chinese Recorder*, 1901, pp 210–11; Morse III, p 241.

1330 Forsyth, pp 40–41.

1331 Morse III, p 241, citing Jingshan's diary, July 16, p 292: Woman referred to was a CIM missionary, unnamed.

1332 Broomhall, M., *Martyred*, pp 264–69. August 22 CCH added, 'Some say forty–two foreigners (and) one hundred (Chinese Christians)'. Hearsay, dates unspecified, perhaps not only Taiyuan. Yong Zheng more precise.

1333 Broomhall, M., *Martyred*, p 266, re CCH.

1334 *Chinese Recorder*, 1901, pp 211, 134 (132–37).

1335 Chinese martyrs, see Broomhall, M., *Martyred*, pp 264–66; idem., *Last Letters*, pp 27, 84, 86, 88; Forsyth, *passim*, pp 135, 346–82.

1336 Glover, 1957 edn, pp 123–24.

1337 Ibid. (1904 edn), pp 251–53; (1957 edn) pp 144–45.

1338 Ibid. (1904 edn), pp 335, 355; (1957 edn) pp 145–51; Broomhall, M., *Martyred*, pp 97–99.

1339 Broomhall, M., *Last Letters*, pp 27, 51–53, 36–37, (51–61); idem., *Martyred*, p 144; Forsyth, pp 77–78; Morse III, p 242; Latourette, *History of Missions*, p 514; *China's Millions*, 1902, pp 32–33.

1340 Broomhall, M., *Martyred*, pp 25, 47, 113–14; *Last Letters*, pp 34–42, 47; Pastor Qü or Zhang Zhiben.

1341 McConnell, Young, King, Burton, Nathan, see Broomhall, M., *Martyred*, pp 30, 113, 265, 309; *Last Letters*, pp 43–48; Forsyth, p 74. Report by Miss E. G. Ulff, Shaanxi, from Chinese sources. Nathan sisters, Heaysman, see *Last Letters*, pp 34–38.

1342 Broomhall, M., *Martyred*, pp 67,103–31, 294.

1343 A. Lutley, Mrs Lutley, 2 children; F. C. H. Dreyer, Mrs Dreyer; Misses E. Gauntlett, A. F. Hoskyn, A. Hoskyn, E. French, E. Higgs, E. C. Johnson, R. Palmer, K. Rasmussen (fourteen); Broomhall, M., *Martyred*, pp 66–67, lists: pp 117–22, 125, 272, 288.

1344 Broomhall, M., *Martyred*, pp 183–97, 276–77; idem., *Last Letters*, pp 9,10, 21–23; Forsyth, pp 90–97; Latourette K. S.: *History of Christian Missions*, pp 512, 516.

1345 Concerning Manchester and Sherwood accounts differ in details; I judge this sequence to be correct.

1346 Molly Robertson who typed the manuscripts of these seven volumes is Kate Lachlan's granddaughter.

1347 Broomhall, M., *Martyred*, pp 77–126.

1348 Glover, using 20th edition (1944), pp 268–313 and (abridged 1959 edn), pp 152–69.

1349 Ibid. (1944), pp 311–14.

1350 Ibid., pp 326–32; Broomhall, M., *Martyred*, p 100.

1351 Glover, pp 333–40. With medical knowledge they would probably have said 'purulent' or 'suppurating' instead of 'gangrenous'.

1352 Gobi party, in Forsyth, pp 88–89.

1353 Xi Xian six, in Broomhall, M., *Last Letters*, pp 29–33; Forsyth, R. C.: *China Martyrs*, pp 76–7.

1354 Forsyth, pp 68–69, 453–56.

1355 Ibid., pp 41, 383–98.

1356 Ibid., p 386; Latourette, *History of Expansion* 6, p 339.

1357 Morse III, pp 230 seq., Chronology.

1358 Ibid., 3.245; Decennial Reports 2.521; F O Parliamentary Papers, *China* No 3, 1900, p 101. Bullion: *Tokyo Press*, August 3, 1900; Savage-Landor, A Henry, *China and the Allies*, Charles Scribner's Sons 1901 (3 vols), I, p 201; Smith, *China* II, p 583.

1359 First truce on June 25 (day after edict to kill); second one on July 18–28; third one on August 3–4.

1360 Morse III, p 254; Broomhall, M., *Martyred*, p 9.

1361 Morse III, p 233 from Hart, R.: *These from the Land of Sinim*, p 39.

1362 Morse III, p 265; page 295 cites Jingshan diary.

1363 *Chinese Recorder*, Aug 1900, pp 434, 512–15; 1901 W. A. P. Martin, pp 83, 206–7. Beijing, see Morse III, pp 275–87.

1364 Morse III, pp 275–87, citing J. H. Macoun,

Imperial Customs Service; Psalm 124; *Chinese Recorder*, 1901, p 838.

1365 *Chinese Recorder*, 1901, pp 83–8.

1366 Morse III: 284; Jingshan diary, Aug 15, p 302; Weale, D. L. Putnam, *Indiscreet Letters from Peking*, Dodd Mead 1911, pp 227–301; Latourette, *History of Missions*, p 506. Japanese, see Morse III, p 285, R. Hart to E. B. Drew, Aug 18, 1900.

1367 Morse III, p 306; F O Parliamentary Papers, *China* No 1, 1901 p 128.

1368 Latourette, *History of Missions*, p 520.

1369 Haldane, pp 216, 222. Death of Yü Xian, eyewitness account: *China's Millions*, 1902, p 67.

1370 Forsyth, p 382.

1371 Broomhall, M., *Martyred*, p 267.

1372 *Chinese Recorder*, 1901, pp 134–36; Forsyth, pp 43–46, 49–64, 443–51.

1373 Forsyth, pp 82–84; Emit Olson (Superintendent), Mrs Olson, 3 children; Mr and Mrs C. Noven, 2 children; Mr and Mrs E. Anderson; 2 children; Mr and Mrs O. Bingmark, 2 children; Mr and Mrs M. Nystrom, 1 child; Mr and Mrs C. L. Lundberg, 2 children; Misses K. Hall, K. Orn, A. Gustasson, E. Erickson, A. E. Palm (12 couples, 12 children, 5 single ladies).

1374 Ibid., pp 80–81: D. W. Stenberg, C. J. Suber, N. J. Friedstrom, Misses Clara Anderson, Hilda Anderson, Hannah Lund.

1375 Latourette, *History of Missions*, p 511.

1376 Broomhall, M., *Martyred*, p 122; *Chinese Recorder*, 1900, pp 484–87, G. Parker report.

1377 Green, 1936 edn, pp 25–41; Broomhall, M., *Martyred*, pp 167–69,173, 300; Forsyth, pp 43–46.

1378 Green, 1936 edn, pp 42–61.

1379 Forsyth, pp 383–98.

1380 Ibid., p 390, footnote says 'written in blood': almost certainly a gloss, for until the last moment they thought they were being escorted to safety.

1381 Ibid., p 392.

1382 Greens, Gregg, 'little bird': Aug 9 captured; Aug 10 dep from Huolu to Zhengding; Aug 12 at Ding Xian; Aug 13 arr. Baoding; Aug 14 by boat past Anxin; Aug 15 in reed beds, captured; Aug 16–18 on show at Anxin; c Aug 23–24 'tuft of paper'; Sept 3 hostile Boxers arr Anxin; Sept 4 hidden in storeroom; Sept 5 told of consul demand for their protection; Sept 5 dep Anxin; Sept 7 art Baoding; c Sept 14 Greens' telegram to John Stevenson; c Sept 28 letter from consul and note from J. W. Lowrie; five to six weeks at Baoding as hostages till Oct 14; Oct 10 Vera died; C. H. S. Green ill; Oct 8 French expedition dep Tianjin; Oct 13 French enter Baoding; Oct 16 Greens to French camp; Oct 18 international column arr Baoding; Oct 19 Gen Gaselee visits Greens at yamen; Oct 20 to British military hospital; Oct 21 Griffiths and Brown arr Baoding; Oct 27 all arr Tianjin;

Nov 1 Vera buried at Tianjin; early Dec to Shanghai; Jan 5 1901 dep Shanghai to UK.

1383 Fei Quihai, see Forsyth, p 41. Wang Lanbu, in Broomhall, M., *Martyred*, pp 145–7

1384 Broomhall, M., *Last Letters*, pp 65–83.

1385 Ibid.

1386 Broomhall, M., *Martyred*, p 268.

1387 Hoste: OMFA 9215a; 9319 Nov 8,1900: *Monthly Notes* Apr 1; 9325.

1388 Sequence of residences: OMFA N18.1900; L 21.

1389 OMFA 9212; L 234.

1390 *China's Millions*, 1900, pp 122–23; OMFA 9319.

1391 OMFA 9214 a, b.

1392 JHT: OMFA 9214a, b.

1393 J. W. Stevenson: OMFA 9214a.

1394 OMFA 9215b.

1395 OMFA 92144.

1396 OMFA 9215b

1397 J. W. Stevenson and JHT: OMFA 9311

1398 *China's Millions*, 1901, p 100. W. B. Sloan, autumn 1900; H. W. Frost, winter 1900; both in China until April 22, 1901, sailed for Europe, shipwrecked.

1399 A. Orr Ewing: OMFA 9315 Mar 13,1901; 9319 Mar 26.

1400 Soothill, pp 251–52.

1401 *Chinese Recorder*, 1900, *passim*; *China's Millions*, 1901, p 163; OMFA L21.12.

1402 *Chinese Recorder*, 1900, p 384.

1403 Shanghai conference: *Chinese Recorder*, 1900, pp 529–30.

1404 Shanxi *news*: *China's Millions*, Oct 1900, pp 151–55.

1405 Smith, *The Uplift*, p 187.

1406 *China's Millions*, 1901, p 41.

1407 Morse III, pp 308, 320.

1408 Ibid., pp 339, 343–44.

1409 Ibid., 3.352, tables of international equivalents.

1410 Taylor, F. Howard, *These Forty Years, A Short History of the China Inland Mission*, CIM/ Pepper Publ. Co., Philadelphia 1903, p 433, quoting *North China Herald*; Broomhall, M., *Last Letters*, p 13; Latourette, *History of Missions*, pp 521–25; idem., *History of Expansion*, p 260.

1411 Morse III, pp 359, 262.

1412 Ibid.

1413 *Chinese Recorder*, 1901, p 382–83.

1414 Broomhall, M., *Last Letters*, p 13; *China's Millions*, 1902, p 38.

1415 Taylor, F. H., *These Forty*, pp 392–93.

1416 Shanghai conference: *Chinese Recorder*, 1900, pp 529–30.

1417 *Chinese Recorder*, 1900, pp 537–50, 617–19; Latourette, *History of Missions*, p 818.

1418 Morse III, p 314 footnote; General Chaffee to Minister Conger, Oct 1900.

1419 Latourette, *History of Missions*, p 523.

1420 *Chinese Recorder*, 1923, pp 257 seq.

1421 *China's Millions*, 1902, pp 38, 65.

1422 Forsyth, pp 26–29; Broomhall, M., *Last Letters*, pp 98–100.

1423 Ibid.

1424 Ceng Chunxŭan: son of viceroy of Yunnan, Guizhou 1875 (HTCOC 5.431; 6. *passim*); Li Hongzhang: Soothill, Index, pp 168, 188, 225; Zhou Fu: *Chinese Recorder*, 1901, p 312.

1425 Broomhall, M., *Last Letters*, p 100.

1426 OMFA 9221, 9316, 9319.

1427 Stock I, p 462.

1428 OMFA 932; N18 Nov 22,1900; Broomhall, M., *Last Letters*, p 104.

1429 OMFA 9311, L 243; Broomhall, M., *Jubilee Story*, p 257.

1430 OMFA 9313.

1431 Investigators: OMFA 9321 pp 91–99, 114 July 22; L 242, 245 July 12 to JHT.

1432 Mandarins: *China's Millions*, 1901, pp 143–44, 164.

1433 *China's Millions*, 1901, pp 145–46; OMFA 9322.

1434 Elder Xŭ Puyŭan: OMFA 932 pp 97–99 July 12; 9322 Oct 26; L 245, Hoste, July 22.

1435 Personal communication, BCB to AJB; Broomhall, M., *Last Letters*, p 14.

1436 Hoste, OMFA 932; L 245

1437 Ibid.

1438 Taylor, F. H., *These Forty*, p 425; OMFA 932 pp 116,118; *China's Millions*, 1902, p 53, A. Orr Ewing, colourful account.

1439 OMFA 9323, 9412.

1440 Taylor, F. H., *These Forty*, pp 4, 7–8; cf. *Chinese Recorder*, 1901, p 147; *China's Millions*, 1902, p 169; Indigenous: OMFA 9322 Oct 26.

1441 Shanxi University: Soothill, pp 253 seq.

1442 Gov Ceng's proclamation: *China's Millions*, 1902, pp 33, 36; Broomhall, M., *Jubilee Story*, pp 258–59; idem., *Last Letters*, p 14.

1443 *Chinese Recorder*, 1901, p 441.

1444 Broomhall, M., *Last Letters*, pp 15–16

1445 Little, p 317 seq.; Fleming, Peter, *The Siege of Peking*, Harper and Bros 1959; Haldane, p 229.

1446 Little, p 321.

1447 Little, p 329; Haldane, pp 231, 223; Soothill, p 272.

1448 Morse III, pp 362, 470, Appendix E.

1449 Haldane, p 220; *China's Millions*, 1902, p 153; Yong Lu, 1903 p 64; Y6 Xian, 1902 p 67.

1450 Little, pp 318, 331; Haldane, pp 231–35, 240.

1451 Hsü, Immanuel C. Y., *The Rise of Modern China*, OUP 2nd edn 1975, pp 499 seq.

1452 Morse III, pp 434, 436; *Chinese Recorder*, 1901, p 356.

1453 *China's Millions*, 1902, Oct p 131,138,141;1903, pp 93b,106;1904, p 136.

1454 *Chinese Recorder*, 1901, p 572; 1902, p 100, 147, 180; 1905, p 171.

1455 OMFA 9412.

1456 *Chinese Recorder*, 1901, p 314;* Thompson, R. W., *Griffith John, passim*.

1457 *China's Millions*, 1902, p 166; 1903, p 93.

1458 OMFA N18, p 5 footnote: box and half-plate stand cameras, Zeiss lens, darkroom, enlarging equipment; Taylor, Dr and Mrs F. H., *Hudson Taylor* II, ch. 40.

1459 Stroke? OMFA 9313 Aug 17; 9314, 9316; N18.1901 p 7, 8.

1460 OMFA 9421 Oct 19,1901; N18.1901 p 19.

1461 JHT retires: OMFA 9411; N18.1902 p 20.

1462 Thompson, P., *D E Hoste*, pp 96–102; OMFA 9413, June 25,1902; *China's Millions*, 1903, p 87 and monthly covers: May, JHT: General Director, DEH: Acting GD; June, JHT: Consulting Director, DEH: General Director: July–Aug JHT: Founder and Consulting Director, DEH: General Director.

1463 Chefoo deaths: OMFA 9423.

1464 OMFA 9423 Aug 14; Francis Coillard died May 29,1904.

1465 OMFA 9313 Oct 3,1901; 9314 Oct, 1901; 9318, 9413 July 19, Sept, Oct; 9421 S. P. Smith papers 1901; 9422 D. E. Hoste, 1912, on disruptive effect of such debates; London Council Minutes, especially oct, Dec 1902; OMFA L 244, N18.1901 p 19; N18.1902 p 14; N18.1902 Aug 8, pp24–26; N18.1902 Dec 27.

1466 *China's Millions*, 1903, p 36, by Theodore Howard's appointment.

1467 OMFA 9511a,b; N18.1903 pp 30–3.

1468 Sister Eva von Thiele-Winkler.

1469 China Council Minutes, April 1, 1903: OMFA N18.1903 p 11(10–15), 20; 9414 Sept 1902.

1470 OMFA N18.1903 pp 9–10.

1471 OMFA N18.1903 pp 12,96–111.

1472 Sichuan and S Henan.

1473 Gov.Ceng, Chengdu: *China's Millions*, 1903, 22, 93b, 154, 157; 1904, p 7.

1474 Wm Moseley had published in 1798 his *Memoir on the Importance and Practicability of Translating and Printing the Holy Scriptures in the Chinese Language*. Six years to the day later, on March 7, 1804, the Bible Society had been formed and turned its attention to doing what Dr Moseley urged. On Sept 19, 1853, the Bible Society resolved to print one million copies of the Chinese New Testament – the day young Hudson Taylor sailed from home for the first time.

1475 Oct 19, 1903–March 14, 1904.

1476 *China's Millions*, 1904, p 122; 1903, pp 117–22; Rev. 21.18, 21; Bunyan's *Pilgrim's Progress*.

1477 *China's Millions*, 1905, p 94.

1478 London Council Minutes Nov 24, 1904 p 236, Feb 5, 1907 and June 18, 1907, pp 112,115.

1479 OMFA N18.1905 gives May 29, but Taylor, Dr and Mrs F. H., *Hudson Taylor* II, p 608 says April 29. They met in Hankou on both days, photographs taken both times. *China's*

Millions, 1905, p 103; p 395 says May 24 in error.

1480 Covell, *Martin,* p 188.

1481 JHT's last day: *China's Millions,* 1905, pp 94,119–29.

1482 *Chinese Recorder,* 1905, p 373; OMFA N18.1905 p 19.

1483 Gravestone: 'Sacred to the Memory of the Rev J. Hudson Taylor, the revered Founder of the China Inland Mission, born May 21, 1832, died June 3, 1905. "A MAN IN CHRIST" 2 Cor. XII.2' and 'This Monument is Erected by the Missionaries of the China Inland Mission as a Mark of their Heartfelt Esteem and Love.' (Quote from 'I know a man in Christ Jesus who ... was caught up to the third heaven ... caught up to Paradise.')

1484 Tributes: *Chinese Recorder,* 1905, pp 379–86, 387–95, 423; W.A. P. Martin, p 24; *China's Millions,* 1905, pp 105, 106, 110, 131–34; OMFA N18.1905 p 17.

1485 *China's Millions,* 1905, pp 114–15. J. W. Stevenson: *China's Millions,* 1905, pp 118–19, 131–34.

1486 *Chinese Recorder,* 1907, p 419; *China's Millions,* 1905, pp 131–34.

1487 JHT meditation: OMFA H517.

1488 Ci Xi's treasure, in Haldane, p 238; Morse III, p 442 footnote; *North China Herald,* April 171909, citing Chinese press.

1489 Morse III, pp 437–39; Broomhall, M., *Heirs Together,* pp 134–35.

1490 Morse III, p 446.

1491 Ibid., 3.440–42; Hsü, pp 504–10.

1492 'China Centenary Missionary Conference Records'.

1493 Latourette, *History of Missions,* pp 665–70.

1494 Fairbank, *Cambridge History* 10, pp 559, 589; medical, pp 574–76.

1495 'Christianise': *Chinese Recorder,* 1901, pp 124–25; Latourette, *History of Missions,* p 619.

1496 Fairbank, *Cambridge History* 10, pp 581–89.

1497 Stock II, p 652; *China's Millions,* May 1932, Centenary Number, p 93.

1498 Broomhall, M., *Jubilee Story,* appendix 3, tables; Shanghai Resolution: idem., *Jubilee Story,* p 269.

1499 Broomhall, Marshall, *Present-Day Conditions in China: Notes Designed to Show the Moral and Spiritual Claims of the Chinese Empire,* CIM 1908, pp 35–41.

1500 Latourette, *History of Missions,* pp 268–69, 452–60; *Chinese Recorder,* 1875, p 342; 1878 p 115; 1882, p 308.

1501 Broomhall, M., *Jubilee Story,* p 298.

1502 Haldane, pp 113, 243, 280 seq.; Morse III, p 441; *The Times,* Nov 15, 1908.

1503 Hsü, pp 539–48.

1504 Morse III, p 442.

1505 *The Times,* May 17,1911

1506 *Beckman, E. R., *The Massacre at Sianfu,* 1913, pp 79, 100. C. T. Wang: (Wang Chang-tsuen, Wang Zhang-cun). Scandinavian

Alliance Mission of North America. Martyrs: Mrs Beckman, W. T. Vatne, Hilda Nelson (aet 15), Selma Beckman (13), Ruth Beckman (8), Oscar Bergstrom (13), Hulda Bergstrom (12), George Ahlstrand (10). C. T. Wang became Foreign Minister.

1507 Hsü, *passim;* Morse III, *passim; Chinese Recorder,* 1896–1912, *passim; China's Millions,* 1896–1912, *passim.*

1508 Hsü; *Chinese Recorder,* 'The Month' series; Latourette, *History of Missions in China;* Broomhall, M., *Jubilee Story;* Neill, *History.*

1509 Latourette, *History of Missions,* p 609; *China Mission Year Book,* 1913, p 95.

1510 *North China Herald,* May 3, 1913; Latourette, *History of Missions,* p 612; Broomhall, M., *Jubilee Story,* p 325.

1511 Hsü, p 374; Broomhall, M.: *Jubilee Story,* p 324.

1512 Hsü, pp 575–83; *Chinese Recorder,* 1908–13, The Month series.

1513 Latourette, *History of Missions,* pp 527–823; Broomhall, *Jubilee Story,* pp 322–27; Lyall, L. T., *A Passion for the Impossible,* Hodder and Stoughton 1965/OMF Books 1976, pp 81–87.

1514 Neill, *History,* p 338.

1515 *Chinese Recorder,* 1912, p 543–6.

1516 Biola: Bible Institute of Los Angeles.

1517 Broomhall, M., *Jubilee Story,* p 324.

1518 Lyall, *A Passion,* pp 85–95; Hsü, pp 584–88; Latourette, *History of Missions,* pp 687–704.

1519 Broomhall, M., *Marshal Feng.*

1520 Latourette, *History of Missions,* p 818.

1521 CCC, see Neill, *History,* p 551.

1522 Latourette, *History of Expansion* 6, p 329; Houghton, Frank, *The Two Hundred,* CIM 1931, Appendices: two hundred named.

1523 Hsü, pp 666–74.

1524 Bosshardt, R. A.: *The Restraining Hand: Captivity for Christ in China,* Hodder & Stouglhton 1936; Lyall, *A Passion,* pp 109–11.

1525 Taylor, Mrs Howard, *The Triumph of John and Betty Stam,* CIM 1935, pp 102–14; *China's Millions,* 1934–35, *passim.*

1526 Alfred Bosshardt: still living (in his 90s) at time of first publication of this book.

1527 Known firsthand, as friends of author's family.

1528 Distinguish from George Hunter of Hunan.

1529 Cable, Mildred and French, Francesca, *The Gobi Desert,* Hodder & Stoughton 1943, pp 232–57.

1530 As one of the doctors, I (AJB) was Sir Montagu's driver-attendant.

1531 Haldane, pp 274–75.

1532 Lyall, L. T., *John Sung: A Flame for God,* CIM 1954; idem., *Three of China's Mighty Men* OMF Books 1973: Yang Shao-tang; Nee Tuo-sheng; Wang Mingdao. *T'uo* is a watchman's rattle.

1533 Clarke, Samuel R., *Among the Tribes of South-West China,* CIM/Morgan & Scott 1905; Broomhall, M., *Jubilee Story,* pp 274–89; *China's Millions, passim.*

[1534] Taylor, Mrs Howard, *Behind the Ranges: A Biography of J. O. Fraser*, CIM; Crossman, Eileen, *Mountain Rain: A New Biography of James O Fraser*, OMF Books 1982; Lyall, *A Passion*, p 133; *China's Millions, passim*.

[1535] Psalm 107.16; Lyall, *A Passion*, pp 132 seq.; idem., *God Reigns in China*, Hodder & Stoughton 1985, pp 125 seq.

[1536] Neill, *History*, p 467; Lyall, L. T.: *God Reigns in China*, p 127.

[1537] Sinza Rd, see note 971 above; Thompson, Phyllis, *China: The Reluctant Exodus*, Hodder & Stoughton/OMF 1979, pp 55–72, 103.

[1538] Lyall, *God Reigns*, pp 140–47, 162–65.

[1539] See Adeney, D. A., *China: Christian Students Face the Revolution*, SU Book Centre Singapore 1973, *passim*; idem., *China: The Church's Long March*, Regal Books/OMF 1985, *passim*.

[1540] Lyall, L. T., *New Spring in China*, Hodder & Stoughton 1979, pp 168–69.

[1541] Ibid., p 148.

[1542] Chao, Jonathan: *China's Religious Policy: An Analysis*, Chinese church Research Center, Hong Kong, 1979.

[1543] China Christian Council, see Peter Morrison, 'Religious Policy in China and its implementation in the light of Document No 19', in Keston College, *Religion in the Communist World*, Autumn 1984; Y. T. Wu, in Neill, *Colonialism*, p 162: 'A few like Y. T. Wu were already enthusiastic Marxists.'

[1544] *Tian Feng*, Sept 5, 1954; *Documents of the Three Self Movement*, National Council of the Churches of Christ (USA, 1963) pp 85–95; *Report of the Centenary Conference on the Protestant Missions of the World* 1, ed. James Johnston, Conf. Secretary, pp 172–77.

[1545] Original source not traced; John R. Mott, to guests, 1902, Report of world tour as General Secretary of World's Christian Students' Federation: 'When China is moved it will change the face of the globe', see note 1173 above.

[1546] See note 1543 above.

[1547] On 'masquerading' see D. Randall, USA, in *Church World News*, Dec 9, 1983; cf. Wuhan Theological Seminary lecture notes, 1986. Coal: see remarks by von Richtofen and China's Marquis Zeng, see above, pp 282, 308.

[1548] *China Inland Mission Private Telegraph Code*, Methodist Publishing House, Shanghai, 1907; Tientsin Press, 1929; cf. *Marconi's Wireless Telegraph Code*, compiled by S. F. Cuthbertson.

Personalia: Non-Chinese

ABEEL, David: American Seamen's Friend Society, chaplain; 1830–33 Canton (Guangzhou), Bangkok; 1839–45 Am Board (ABCFM); 1842 Gulangsu Is., Amoy; initiated women's missionary socs. in UK, USA

ABERDEEN, Lady: widow of George John James Hamilton-Gordon, Lord Haddo, 5th earl (1816–64) son of Earl of Aberdeen (1784–1860) Prime Minister 1852–55; 5th earl and Lady A. influential evangelicals, supported CMS, T. J. Barnardo.

ADAM, James R: CIM arr China 1887, settled Anshun, Guizhou, 1888; 1889 began work among Miao minority people; baptisms 1898; 1903 met Gobu (Kopu) Miao, began Gobu church; killed by lightning in own home.

ADAMS, J.: surgeon, London Hospital; member of Council of Royal College of Surgeons.

AITCHISON, William: Am Board; 1854 Shanghai, Pinghu.

AITKEN, Canon W. M. Hay: curate to Wm Pennefather (qv) St Jude's, Mildmay; leading missioner of 1870s influenced by D L Moody 1875; an initiator of Keswick Movement, patterned on Mildmay Conferences.

ALABASTER, Challoner: HBM consul, Yantai, Shantou, Hankou.

ALCOCK, Sir John Rutherford (1809–97): MRCS at 21; 1832–37 Peninsular Wars, Dep. Director of Hospitals; 1835 partially paralysed; 1843 Diplomatic Service; 1846 HBM consul Fuzhou (Foochow), Amoy, Shanghai; 20 June 1862 knighted, KCB; HBM minister, Peking.

ALDERSEY, Miss Mary Ann (c 1800–64): 1824–5 learned Chinese from R. Morrison; 1832 Malacca (Melaka); Batavia (Jakarta); 1842 Hong Kong; 1843–59 Ningbo.

ALFORD, C. R.: 1864 Bishop of Victoria, Hong Kong; proposed a new C of E society for East Asia; 1874 resigned.

ALLEN, Clement F. R.: HBM consul, Zhenjiang; member, Col. Browne's 1875 expedition, Burma-Yunnan.

ALLEN, Young J.: Am Meth. Episc. (South); 1860 Shanghai; edited reform publications read by Chinese from peasants to emperor; 1868–74 *Church News, Globe News, Review of the Times*; 1882 founded Anglo-Chinese College; Shanghai; 1887 Member, Socy for the Diffusion of Christian and General Knowledge among the Chinese; consulted by reformers.

ALOPEN: Syrian Nestorian named in Nestorian monument; Xi'an (Sian) ; AD 635 arr China.

AMHERST, William Pitt: Lord Amherst, 1816 Peking embassy; 1823 Gov.-Gen. of India; first Burma war; 1826 earldom; d 1857.

ANDREW, George: CIM, dep UK 5 Jan, 1881; Guizhou (Supt.), Yunnan; 17 Oct, 1883 m J. Findlay.

ARCHIBALD, John: Bible Society agent, Hankou.

ARTHINGTON, Phoebe: sister of Robert; donor to CIM and Müller (qv).

ARTHINGTON, Robert (1823–1900): wealthy Quaker, lived frugally supporting missions; 'Arthington's millions' through Arthington Trust, half to BMS, two fifths to LMS, £2,000 to Free Church of Scotland Missionary Society, £100 to Müller's orphanage, sums to other institutions (incl. CIM) (ref. LMS archives).

ARTHUR, William (1819–1901): 1839 Methodist mission to India; 1858–60 CES Board; 1861–68,1871–88 Secy WMMS; 1866 Pres. Wesleyan Conference.

ASPDEN, Maria: CIM, arr China 6 Feb 1892 martyred at Datong, N Shanxi, 12 July 1900.

ATWATER, Ernest R: Oberlin College; wife d 1896; m Eliz. Graham 1898; daughters Ernestine and Mary killed at Taiyuan 9 July 1900; Celia, Bertha and one unborn all killed at Fenyang, 15 Aug 1900.

AVELINE, Mr: one-time missionary to Demarara (Br. Guyana); personal secy to Wm T. Berger (qv).

BABER, Edward Colborne (1843–90): 1872 vice-consul, Taiwan; 1876 interpreter to Hon. W. G. Grosvenor expedition; 1877 Commercial Resident, Chongqing; explorer; consul; Chinese Secretary of Legation, Peking; 1883 Medal of RGS; 1885–86 Consul-General, Korea; Resident, Bhamo; 16 June, 1890 died at Bhamo.

BABINGTON, Charles Cardale (1808–95): Prof. of Botany, Oxford Univ.; archaeologist.

BAGLEY, Paul: Am Meth. Episc. local preacher; 1865 independently, Peking, travelled to Sichuan-Tibet border.

BAGNALL, Benjamin: B&FBS, arr China 1873; Taiyuan; 1886, joined CIM; Supt. Shanxi, Zhili; 1894, Baoding, Zhili; 1 July 1900 killed by Boxers with wife and child.

BALFOUR, Maj-Gen. Sir George, CB: Capt. 1840 opium war; 1843–46 first consul Shanghai; 1865 nominated JHT for FRGS; knighted after 1865.

BALL, Richard: businessman, Taunton, Somerset; moving spirit in Chinese Association and Chinese Evangelisation Society (CES); editor, *Chinese Missionary Gleaner*; author, *Handbook of China*, 1854.

BALLER, Fredk William (1852–1922): linguist, sinologue; b 21 Nov 1852; one of H. Grattan Guinness' first Institute students; CIM, dep

UK 3 Sept 1873 with C. H. Judd, M. Hy
Taylor, M. Bowyer (*see* Part 4, Personalia);
arr Shanghai 5 Nov 1873; m M. Bowyer 17
Sept 1874; Supt. Anhui, Jiangsu, Hubei,
Henan; pioneer traveller; famine relief:
1876 with G. King to Shaanxi; 1878 with Mrs
Hudson Taylor, Misses Home, Crickmay to
Shanxi; 1880 took party through Hunan to
Guiyang; 1885, secretary, first China Council;
1887 began literary work, *Mandarin Primer*
(used by consular service), 1900 *Analytical
Chinese-English Dictionary*; translator, member
Union Mandarin Bible Revision Committee,
NT 1907, OT 1907–18 Beijing; 1915 Life
Governor of B&FBS; Vice-President Nat BS
of Scotland; Life Member Am BS; author in
Chinese of 18 books, pamphlets, millions in
circulation; April 1922 *Life of JHT* in Chinese;
widowed 1909; 23 Jan 1912 m H. B. Fleming;
1919 first furlough, after 21 years; d 12 Aug
1922.

BARCHET, Stephan Paul: German; 1865 Ningbo,
sent by JHT; later doctor of medicine.

BARCLAY, Florence: dtr of Robt Barclay, Reigate;
CIM dep UK 13 Dec 1880; 24 May 1892 m M.
Beauchamp (qv); d 2 May 1955.

BARING-GOULD, Rev A.: Wolverhampton;
assoc. with Hay Aitken (qv) missions.

BARING-GOULD, Rev B.: St Michael's,
Blackheath; 1882 CMS Assoc. Secy; 1894 to
Japan, China.

BARNARDO, Thomas John (4 July 1845–19 Sept
1905): 1862 converted; 1866 met JHT in
Dublin; April 1866 to London.

BARNES, Susan: 1866 met JHT, Limerick; CIM
Lammermuir party, Hangzhou, Shaoxing; 1868
resigned.

BARTON, Samuel: 1862 Missionary Secretary,
United Meth. Free Church.

BATES, Rev J.: CMS Islington College; 1867
Ningbo; 1884–89 B&FBS NT revision
committee; 1895 still active in China.

BAUSUM, J. G.: independent, Penang; 1845–46
m Maria Tarn Dyer, mother of Maria Jane.

BAUSUM, Mrs: 2nd wife of J. G. Bausum; mother
of Mary; 1856 Ningbo; 1861 m E. C. Lord
(qv).

BAUSUM, Mary: daughter: m Dr S. P. Barchet
(qv).

BAXTER, Robert Dudley (1827–75):
parliamentary lawyer in father's firm Baxter,
Rose & Norton, chief Conservative election
agents; cousin of C. R. Alford, Bishop of
Victoria, Hong Kong; CES Board; chairman
FES; declined nomination to stand for
parliament.

BEAUCHAMP, (Sir) Montagu (Bart.) (1860–
1939): son of Sir Thomas (qv); nephew of
Lord Radstock (qv); Cambridge Univ. oar;
one of the 'Camb. Seven'; 1885 to China;
made several journeys with JHT.

BEAUCHAMP, Sir Thomas Proctor-: 4th Bt of
Langley Park, Norfolk; m Hon. Caroline
Waldegrave, daughter of second Lord
Radstock (qv); supporter of JHT, CIM.

BELL, Henry: UMFC; Barnsley; close friend
of James Taylor (qv); confidant of James
Meadows (qv).

BELL, Capt. M.: Master of John Willis and Son
tea clippers; 1864 converted; 1866 voyage of
Lammermuir with JHT and CIM party.

BELL, Mary: Malvern, Glos.; 1866 CIM,
Lammermuir, Hangzhou, 1867 m W.
D. Rudland (qv); 1868 Yangzhou riot,
Zhenjiang; 1871 Taizhou; d Oct 23, 1874.

BENSON, Archbishop (1829–96):1877 Bp. of
Truro; 1882 Archbp. of Canterbury, after
Tait.

BERGER, William Thomas (*c* 1812–99): London
starch manufacturer; JHT's friend, supporter,
co-founder of China Inland Mission; first
Home Secy; benefactor.

BERGER, Mary: wife of WTB; (*c* 1812–Feb
16,1877)

BERGNE, Samuel Brodribb: Independent
minister, co-secy B&FBS, 1854–79.

BETTELHEIM, Dr B. J.: converted Jewish
physician; Loochoo Naval Mission to Ryukyu
Is. 1845–53.

BEVAN, Francis Augustus (1840–1919): son of
Robert Bevan (qv); donor to CIM; 1896 first
chairman of Barclays Bank.

BEVAN, Robert Cooper Lee (1809–90): a
founder of LCM; friend of CMS; first
chairman of YMCA; CES Gen. Committee.

BEWLEY, Henry (1814–76): Dublin printer,
built Merrion Hall, Brethren; supporter and
Referee of CIM.

BEYNON, W. T. and wife: CIM 1885; Shanxi;
1895 B&FBS; 9 July 1900 killed by Boxers.

BICKERSTETH, Robert: member of CES
committee; Bishop of Ripon.

BIRD, Charles: Gen. Secy Chinese Evangelisation
Society.

BIRD, C. Howard: CIM dep UK 9 Oct 1896;
Xiangcheng, Henan; 11 July 1900 escaped,
robbed, destitute, via Taihe, Anhui to
Zhenjiang.

BIRD, Rowena: Oberlin College, Am Board; b
31 July 1865; dep to China Sept 1890; Taigu,
Shanxi; 31 July 1900 killed by Boxers.

BISHOP, Isabella Bird (1831–1904):
independent traveller, author (*see*
Bibliography); 1881 m Dr John Bishop
who d1886; 1896 c/o JHT, CIM, Shanghai,
Sichuan, Tibetan marches; donated hospital
premises, Langzhong.

BISMARCK, Prince Otto Eduard Leopold von
(1815–98): leading German statesman;
1862–90 Foreign Affairs; 'Iron Chancellor';
PM of Prussia; 1865 Count, 1867 Prince;
defeated Austria, France; united Germany;
first chancellor of Reich; 1890 'old pilot
dropped'.

BLAKISTON, Capt.: adventurer; 1861 reached
Tibetan border.

BLATCHLEY, Emily (1845–74): 1865 Home and
Colonial Training Coll. grad.; 'right hand'
secy, governess to JHT, family; 1866 CIM,

Lammermuir, Hangzhou, 1868 Yangzhou, riot; March 1870 UK with three JHT children; 1870–74 London, guardian, secy; d July 25, 1874.

BLODGET, Henry, DD (1825–1903): Am Board; 1854 Shanghai; 1860 first Prot. to preach at Tianjin, Peking; 1864 translator, Peking 30 years.

BOGUE, Dr: principal Missionary Academy, Gosport, *c* 1805–20; friend of Dr Wm Moseley (qv); nominated R. Morrison, S. Dyer to LMS for China.

BOHANNAN, Annie: widowed sister of Mary Bell (qv); nurse to JHT children; 1868 m Edward Fishe (qv).

BONAR, Andrew: Scottish divine.

BONAR, Horatius (1808–89): Scottish divine, hymn writer.

BONHAM, Sir George: *c* 1856 HBM plenipotentiary, Hong Kong, after Bowring (qv).

BONHOURE, M/Mme: Paris Prot. Mission; 1861 Tianjin, Yantai, Mme died, M retired.

BOONE, William Jones Sr, MD, DD: Am Prot. Episcopal Church; 1837 Batavia; 1840 Macao; 1842 Gulangsu Is., Amoy, with Abeel; 1844 Bishop, Shanghai; d 1864.

BOOTH, Catherine (née Mumford) 1829–30: m Wm Booth (qv) June 16, 1855; Salv. Army.

BOOTH, Evangeline: b 1865 C'mas Day, to Wm and Catherine (qv); famed SA evangelist; US Natl. Commander SA; 1934–39 General, SA.

BOOTH, William (1829–1912): Methodist evangelist; June 16, 1855 m Catherine Mumford (qv) Methodist New Connexion; 1865 'found his destiny' in London's East End and with Catherine formed The Christian Mission; 7 Aug 1878 changed name and form to Salvation Army; son Bramwell, daughter Evangeline (qv) among successors as 'General'.

BORDEN, William Whiting: b 1 Nov 1887; descended from Normans 1066 and Col Wm Whiting, Yarmouth, UK; founder of Hartford, Conn. USA; 1905–09 Yale Univ; 1909–12 Princeton Seminary; spring 1910 CIM delegate to Edinburgh Conference; autumn CIM N Am Council declared his goal, Muslims of N W China; Dec 1912 dep USA to Cairo for Arabic studies; d April 1913, meningitis, aged 25; legacies, CIM $250,000; $100,000, $50,000, $25,000 to churches, Theol. Insts, missions; CIM residuary legatee; Borden Memorial Hospital, Lanzhou, Gansu.

BOSSHARDT, Rudolf Alfred: CIM; hero, with Amolis Hayman, of Communist 'Long March', 1935–36.

BOTHAM, Thomas Earlum S.; CIM dep UK 26 Aug 1885; pioneer in Shaanxi; Supt. Shaanxi, Gansu; China Council; 1889 m Ella A. Barclay; d 22 Oct 1898.

BOWRING, Sir John (1792–1872): HBM consul, Siam, Canton; 1854 plenipotentiary, last Supt. of Trade; sinologue.

BOWYER, Mary: 1865 Wm Pennefather's

training school; 1866 CIM, *Lammermuir*, Hangzhou; 1868 Nanjing; 1875 m F. W. Baller, CIM sinologue.

BRADLEY, Daniel Beach, MD: Am Board (ABCFM); 1840–49 Bangkok, physician to Thai royal family.

BRIDGMAN, Elijah Coleman, DD (1801–61): Am Board (ABCFM); 1830 Canton; 1832 first editor *Chinese Repository* with R. Morrison; 1843–44 US interpreter-negotiator; 1845–52 translator, Chinese Bible, Delegates' Committee, Shanghai.

BRIDGMAN, Mrs: 1845 Canton; 1847 Shanghai; 1864 Peking.

BROOKE, Graham Wilmot: CMS 3 Dec 1889; pioneer leader in W Africa and Sudan; d 5 March 1891.

BROOKS, S. M.: SPG, first martyr of Boxers, Shandong, 29 Dec 1900, aged 24.

BROOMHALL, A. Gertrude: eldest dtr of Benjamin (qv) and Amelia HT (qv); b 18 June, 1861; CIM dep UK 24 Sept ,1884; Shanxi; 7 Sept 1894 m D. E. Hoste (qv); 3 sons; d 12 April, 1944.

BROOMHALL, Benjamin (1829–1911): m Amelia Hudson Taylor; 1879–95 Gen. Secy China Inland Mission; editor, *National Righteousness*, organ of anti-opium trade campaign, to 1911 (*see* Maxwell).

BROOMHALL, Albert Hudson (1862–1934): eldest son of Benjamin (qv); b 31 Aug, 1862; CIM dep UK 24 Sept, 1884; Shanxi; m 14 May, 1890 Alice Amelia Miles; treasurer CIM, Shanghai; d 18 Aug, 1934.

BROOMHALL, Marshall: 2nd son of Benjamin (qv), MA Cantab.; author (*see* Bibliography); CIM dep UK Oct 1890; editor, Lond., d 24 Oct, 1937.

BROUMTON, James F.: brother of Eliz. Judd; one of 'the eighteen', dep UK 21 Oct, 1875; pioneer Guizhou; m 1881 Mrs Wm McCarthy (qv); 1886–1905, treasurer CIM Shanghai.

BROWN, George Graham (1863): Company secy; CIM dep UK 21 April, 1886; UK staff.

BROWNE, Col. Horace A.: Indian Army, leader of Br. expedition, Burma-Yunnan 1875, when A. Margary killed (qv).

BRUCE, Sir Frederick: brother of Lord Elgin (qv); 1858 envoy, rebuffed by emperor; 1859 repulsed at Dagu, Tianjin; 1860 first Br. Minister, Peking.

BRUNTON, John: first officer, *Lammermuir*.

BUDD, Charles: CIM, one of 'the eighteen' dep UK Nov 1875; pioneer Henan, Shaanxi; resigned 1879.

BUNSEN, Baron Chevalier: 1839 emissary of King Fredk Wm IV of Prussia to London; with Lord Ashley (Shaftesbury) worked for natl. home for Jews, toleration for Christians in Holy Land; warned King Fredk Wm of Gutzlaff's hyperbole; urged by king to arouse C of E to vigorous evangelisation of China; friend of Hy Venn; studied Chinese Lang.; helped Ld Shaftesbury create Bp. of Jerusalem.

BURDON, John Shaw (1829–1907): CMS; 1853 arr Shanghai; pioneer evangelist; m Burella Dyer (qv); 1862 Peking; 1874 3rd Bishop, Hong Kong; Bible translator.

BURGEVINE, H. A.: Am soldier of fortune; after F. T. Ward, commanded Ever-Victorious Army; later joined Taipings.

BURLINGAME, Anson (1820–70): barrister, Congressman, Methodist; 1861–67 US minister, Peking, appointed by Abraham Lincoln; ambassador-at-large for China.

BURNS, Prof. Islay, DD (Glas.): biographer of brother, Wm C. Burns (qv).

BURNS, William Chalmers (1815–68): first English Presby. to China; 1847 Hong Kong; Amoy; 1855 Shanghai; 1856 Swatow; 1863 Peking; d Niuchuang; translator of *Pilgrim's Progress*; close friend of JHT (qv).

BURTON, Eliz: CIM, to China Sept 1898; Hejin, Shanxi with McConnells (qv), A. King; 12 July 1900 left hiding, killed beside Yellow River 16 July 1900.

BUXTON, Sir Edward North, Bart., MP (1812–58): son of Sir Thomas Fowell Buxton, 1st baronet; CES Gen. Committee.

CABLE, A. Mildred (1877–1952): CIM 1901, Huozhou, Shanxi, with Evangeline and Francesca French (qv); youngest of 'The Trio'; qualified chemist; Shanxi 1901–23; 1923–36 Gansu, Xinjiang, Gobi Desert; author, public speaker, B&FBS (*see* Bibliography).

CAI YUAN (Ts'ai Yuan): a prince of Yi, conspirator with Prince Cheng (qv) and Su Shun (qv) to kill the heir presumptive's mother Yehonala (qv) and seize government as regents.

CALDER, Eliza: Arbroath, Aberdeen; 1866 m Lewis Nicol (qv), CIM, *Lammermuir*, Hangzhou; 1867 Xiaoshan, outrage; 1868 left CIM.

CALDWELL, John R.: Glasgow silk merchant, influenced by JHT; faithful CIM supporter.

CAMERON, James (1845–91): CIM, one of 'the eighteen'; dep UK 4 Aug 1875; pioneer traveller until end of 1881; 1884 supt. Shandong, later Sichuan; 1884 MD (USA); m Mrs Randall; 1886 China Council; d 14 Aug 1891.

CAMERON, Verney Lovett, Lieut. RN: led search for D. Livingstone (qv), March 1873; surveyed Lake Tanganyika, 1873–75; crossed Congo, W Coast Nov 1875; promoted Commander, CBE.

CANNING, 1st earl (1812–62): 1855 Gov-Gen. of India during mutiny; 1858 first viceroy; 1859 earldom.

CANNY, J. M.: merchant; French *chargé d'affaires*, consul Zhenjiang; friend of CIM.

CARDWELL, J. E.: CIM, 1867 Hangzhou; 1868 Taizhou, Zhejiang; Dec 30, 1869 Jiujiang, pioneered Jiangxi.

CAREY, William (1761–1834): founder of Baptist Miss. Soc.; 1793 India; 1800–30 Prof. of Oriental Languages, Calcutta.

CARLYLE, Thomas (1795–1881): historian, biographer.

CARMICHAEL, Amy Beatrice (Wilson) (1868–1951): first Keswick missionary, 1892; Japan, Ceylon, S India; founded Dohnavur Fellowship; author, crippled by arthritis from 1930s; lifelong friend of JHT, CIM.

CASWELL, Jessie: Am Board (ABCFM) Bangkok, tutor to Prince Mongkut.

CASSELS, William Wharton (1858–1925): b 11 March 1858; Repton; 1877–80 St John's College, Cambridge; Ridley Hall; ordained 1882; 'Camb. Seven' CIM dep UK 5 Feb, 1885; 1885–86 Shanxi; 1886 Supt. China Council; Sichuan; 4 Oct, 1887 m M. L. Legge; 18 Oct, 1895 consecrated Bishop in W China; d 7 Nov, 1925 (wife d 14 Nov).

CAVAN, Fredk John Wm Lambart, 8th earl of (1815–87); Lt. Col. 7th Dragoon Guards; CES Gen. Committee; supporter of CIM, Mildmay Conf., D. L. Moody; Welbeck St Brethren.

CHALLICE, John: director of six companies; deacon, Bryanston Hall, Portman Square; member, first CIM council; treasurer UK; d 1887.

CHALMERS, James (1841–1901): LMS; 1866 S. Pacific; 1877 New Guinea; murdered by cannibals 2 Jan 1901.

CHAPDELAINE, Auguste: Paris Mission (Société des Missions étrangéres de Paris); 1856 executed.

CHAPMAN, Robert Cleaver (1802–1902): High Court attorney; C of E; 1832 Strict Baptist minister; Brethren; 2nd Evang. Awakening evangelist; JHT's friend.

CHATER, Baptist: with Felix Carey, first Prot. missionary to Burma.

CHEETHAM, Charles: Foreign Missionary Sec., UMFC after R. Eckett.

CHOLMONDELEY, Wm Henry Hugh: 3rd marquis (1800–84); hereditary Grand Chamberlain of England; CMS Committee; 1872 CIM Referee.

CIGGIE, Grace: 1865 Glasgow recruit for Ningbo; 1870 m George Stott.

CLAPP, Dwight H.: b. 1 Nov 1841; Oberlin College; m 1884 Mary Jane b 1845; Am Board to Taigu, Shanxi; killed 31 July 1900.

CLARENDON, Earl of (1800–70): Foreign Secy to Lord Aberdeen 1853, Lord Palmerston 1855, Lord Russell 1865, Gladstone 1868.

CLARKE, Dr Andrew: renowned physician, London Hospital.

CLARKE, George W.; CIM, one of 'the eighteen', dep UK 4 Aug 1875; Dali, Yunnan; m F. Rossier 15 Sep 1870, (d 7 Oct 1883); 1886 Guihuacheng; Supt. N Shanxi, Zhili; China Council; m A. Lancaster, April 1886, (d 8 Aug 1892); m R. Gardiner 12 Oct 1893.

CLARKE, Mildred: CIM, Linfen, Shanxi; to Taiyuan June 1900; killed 9 July 1900.

CLARKE, Samuel R.: CIM dep UK 2 May 1878; Chengdu, Sichuan; m A. L. Fausset (qv);

1889 Guiyang; 1892 to Guizhou minority races.

CLELAND, J. F.: LMS, 1850 Hong Kong.

CLINTON, T. A. P.: CIM, first to obtain deeds to property in Hunan, Changde Sept 1897; occupied.

COBBOLD, R. H.: CMS, 1848–62, Ningbo; translator, Ningbo romanised vernacular NT.

COKE, Thomas: Oxford Univ.; Anglican clergyman; 1776–1813, Wesley's colleague; 1786 appealed for missions to New World; first bishop, Am Methodist Episc. Church; d 1813 on way to India.

COLLINGWOOD, R. G.: Oxford philosopher, expert on Roman Britain; grandson of Wm Collingwood (qv).

COLLINGWOOD, W. G.: biographer of Ruskin; son of Wm Collingwood (qv).

COLLINGWOOD, William (1819–1903): Fellow of Royal Watercolour Society; Oxford; 1839 Liverpool; C of E until Brethren; 1850 responded to C. Gutzlaff, supported CES; met JHT Sept 1853 and supported JHT/CIM.

COLLINS, W. H., MRCS: 1858 CMS Shanghai, 1863 Peking.

COLQUHOUN, Archibald R.: engineer, Indian govt.;1881 travelled E-W, Canton to Burma, advised by J. W. Stevenson (qv) and J. McCarthy (qv).

CONFUCIUS: *c* 551–479 BC; Chinese philosopher-sage.

CONGLETON, John Vesey Parnell, 2nd Baron (1805–83): Brethren, Teignmouth, London, Orchard St., Welbeck St.; travelled widely; donor to JHT/ CIM.

COOMBS, Edith A.: b 1862; BA (Oxon); CIM; Shouyang Mission Hospital, Taiyuan (Schofield Memorial); 27 June 1900 riot, tried to save Chinese child; stoned, killed.

COOPER, E. J.: CIM 1888, 'architect' of CIM buildings, Shanghai, Hankou, Chefoo schools, sanatorium, with JHT; m 1891 Margaret; Lucheng, Shanxi; 6 July 1900 dep; after great suffering arr Hankou 14 Aug; Margaret d injuries Aug 6, son Brainerd d Aug 14; author of lucid reports.

COOPER, T. T.: adventurer, Sichuan, Tibet; agent, Calcutta Chamber of Commerce; 1862 Rangoon; 1867 Shanghai; 4 Jan, 1868 dep Hankou; Kangding April 30; Tibet in Chinese clothes, forced back; 1871, author, *Travels of a Pioneer of Commerce*; proposed Yangzi-Bhamo (Irrawaddy) railway; Br. Resident, Bhamo; assassinated 24 April, 1878.

COOPER, William: YMCA secretary, Gourock; CIM dep UK 24 Nov 1880; Anqing Training Inst; Supt Anhui; China Council 1885; completed Maria (Dyer) Taylor's Romanised NT, published by BFBS 1888; m1887; Asst. China Director; Travelling Director; d 1 July, 1900.

CONGLETON, John Vesey Parnell, 2nd Baron, (1805–83): 1830–37 with A. N. Groves, Baghdad, m Iranian Christian widow of Shiraz; Brethren leader, Teignmouth,

London, Orchard St, Welbeck St; travelled widely; donor to JHT/ CIM.

CORDON, Henry: 1867 CIM, sent by Berger (qv); Hangzhou; 1868 Suzhou.

COULTHARD, J. J.: CIM dep UK 7 March 1879; personal secretary to JHT; Supt. Henan, 1888 m Maria Hudson Taylor (qv); China Council.

COX, Josiah: Wesleyan Meth. Miss Socy; 1852 Canton; 1862 Hankou; 1865 Jiujiang (Kiukiang); d 1906.

CRAIK, Henry: Presbyterian then Brethren; close colleague of Geo. Müller, Bethesda chapel, Bristol; 1863 author, *New Testament Church Order*.

CRANAGE, Dr J. Edward: Anglican; 1859 witnessed Welsh revival, conducted meetings at Wellington, Salop, to pray for revival, mass attendance.

CRANSTON, David: Shanghai merchant, Shanghai & Putong Foundry & Engineering Co.; Feb 1874 victim in Shanghai riot; friend of CIM; directed CIM HQ building developments.

CRICKMAY, Anna: CIM dep UK Oct 1876; with Mrs JHT to Shanxi famine 1878, Taiyuan; 1 Feb, 1881 m J. J. Turner (qv).

CROMBIE, George: Aberdeen farmer; 1865 JHT's second recruit, to Ningbo.

CULBERTSON, Dr M. S.: Am Presbyterian; 1850 Shanghai, co-translator of Delegates' Version, Chinese Bible (NT); with E. C. Bridgman (qv) of OT, 1852; d 1862, cholera.

DARWIN, Charles Robert (1809–82): 1835 voyage in *Beagle*; author 1859 *Origin of Species*; 1871 *Descent of Man*; FRS; buried in Westminster Abbey.

DAVIES, Evan: LMS Malaya; author, 1845, *China and her Spiritual Claims*; 1846 *Memoir of the Reverend Samuel Dyer*.

DAVIES, Major H. R.: prospected proposed Burma-Yunnan railway; travelled widely, Dali, Batang etc.

DAVIS, President Jefferson (1808–89): Confederate leader and president at start of Am Civil War.

DAVIS, Sir John Francis, Bart.: Chief, Hon. East India Co.; Canton; friend of R. Morrison; 1844 HBM plenipotentiary, after Pottinger (qv); Supt. of Trade, Hong Kong.

DEAN, William (1806–77): Am Baptist; 1834 and 1864 Bangkok; 1842 Hong Kong.

DELAMARRE, Abbé: Paris Mission; 1858–60 interpreter, French treaty; falsified Chinese version.

DE LA PORTE, Dr: French Prot. medical; 1847–57 Swatow, Double Island.

DE MERITENS: 1860 with Abbé Delamarre, interpreter for Baron Gros, Peking.

DE MOGES, Marquis: 1857–58 member of Gros embassy to Tianjin and Japan.

DE MONTAUBAN: 1860 French general with Baron Gros, Peking; plundered Summer Palace.

DENNISTON, J. M.: Presby. minister, London,

Torquay; associated with W. C. Burns revivals and JHT founding CIM; co-founder Foreign Evangelist Socy.

DENNY, W.: Scottish ship-owner; 1865 gave free passages to China to Barchet and Crombie (qv).

DENT, Thomas and Launcelot: high-living merchant ship-owners; chief rivals of Jardine, Matheson.

DERBY, J. N. (1800–82): barrister, ordained Anglican, resigned 1827; trilingual preacher; leader of Exclusive Brethren.

DERBY, Lord, 14th earl (1799–1869): Prime Minister in govts of 1852, 1858, 1866.

DESGODINS, Abbé Société des Missions étrangéres de Paris; 1855–58 several attempts to reach W. China through Tibet from Darjeeling; arr Batang June 1860; driven from Bonga; host to Mesny (qv), Gill (qv), Jas Cameron (qv).

DESGRAZ, Louise: Swiss governess to Wm Collingwood family, as a daughter; 1866 CIM, *Lammermuir*, Hangzhou; 1865 Yangzhou, riot; 1878 m E. Tomalin.

DESMOND, Josephine: RC, Irish American; b 1867; to Moody, Northfield, BTI Chicago; CIM 1898; Xiaoshan, Qü Xian, Zhejiang; killed 21 July 1900.

DE TOURNON, Charles Maillard (1668–1710): papal legate to China 1705; antagonised Kang Xi (Kuang Hsi) over Confucian rites.

DETRING, Gustav: German in Imperial Maritime Customs under R. Hart (qv); advised Li Hongzhang (qv), Chefoo Convention 1876; and for many years; 1885 briefly interim successor as Inspector General.

DEW, Capt. Roderick, RN: 1862 commander, Ningbo front, against Taipings.

DICK, Henry: CIM dep UK 29 Aug 1883; 1884 joined A. C. Dorward, Hunan pioneer; daring visit to Changsha.

DISRAELI, Benjamin (1804–81): 1st Earl of Beaconsfield; son of Isaac d'Israeli; statesman, social novelist; 1837 MP; 1868, 1874–80 Prime Minister, bought Suez Canal shares, friend of Queen Victoria, made her 'Empress of India'.

DIXON, Herbert: BMS 1881, 21 years; 5 years Congo; m 1884; Taiyuan, Shanxi 1885; Xinzhou; 29 June 1900 heard of Coombs murder (qv); 8 BMS fled to hills; captured 25 July; killed 9 Aug 1900.

DOBSON, Edith: CIM nurse, 1894; Chefoo with Dr Douthwaite (qv), Red Cross Hospital, Sino-Jap war 1894–95; to Xi Xian, Shanxi, with Peat family and A. Hurn (qv) 21 July 1900 to hill caves; 30 Aug 1900 killed near Qüwu.

DODD, Samuel: Am Presbyterian; 1561 Ningbo; 1865 married Crombie-Skinner (qv).

DOOLITTLE, Justus: Am Board; 1850 Fuzhou; 1862 Tianjin, editor *Chinese Recorder*.

DORWARD, Adam C.: Scottish manufacturer; Harley House under H. Grattan Guinness,

CIM dep UK 2 May 1878; entered Hunan 18 Oct 1880; Supt. Hunan, Guangzi; China Council; d 2 Oct 1888.

DOUGLAS, Carstairs, LL D (1830–77): English Presby. Mission; 1855 Amoy; introduced J. L. Maxwell (qv) to Formosa (Taiwan); knew JHT Shanghai, London.

DOUTHWAITE, Arthur Wm: Harley House 1874; CIM dep UK 26 Feb 1874; Zhejiang; 6 Feb 1875, m E. Doig; Qü Xian; 1882 Yantai; 1883–84 first Prot. missionary to Korea, distributed Scripture; 15 Oct 1890 m Groves; MD (USA) 1894 Order of Double Dragon for service in Sino-Jap war; d 5 Oct 1899.

DRAKE, S. B.: CIM dep UK 29 Oct, 1878; Shanxi famine relief; joined BMS.

DREYER, F. C. H.: CIM 1895; Qüwu, Linfen; 14 July 1900, Lutley (qv) ill, so Dreyer i/c party of 14 dep midnight, through hostile Henan; 28 Aug arr Hankou; author, report on Shanxi events.

DUDGEON, J. MD: 1863 LMS Peking.

DU HALDE, P. J. B.: author *The General History of China* (Ldn. 1736, 1741); *A Description of the Empire of China and Chinese Tartary ... Korea, Tibet*, etc, 2 vols (Ldn. 1741).

DUNCAN, George: Banff, Scotland, stonemason; 1865 CIM; 1866, *Lammermuir*, Hangzhou; 1867 Lanxi, Nanjing; 1868 Yanzhou riots m Catherine Brown; 1872 UK; 1873 d TB.

DUVAL, Mary: aged 42 offered to CMS; 1899 with Pigotts (qv) to Shouyang, Shanxi, to teach Pigott, Atwater children; killed 9 July 1900, Taiyuan.

DYER, Burella Hunter: b 31 May 1835; elder daughter of Samuel Dyer Sr; 1857 m J. S. Burdon; d 1858.

DYER, John: Secy, Royal Hosp. for Seamen, Greenwich; 1820 Chief Clerk to Admiralty.

DYER, Maria Jane: b 16 Jan 1837; younger daughter of S. Dyer Sr; 20 Jan 1858 m JHT, 5 sons, 3 daughters; d 23 July 1870, Zheniiang.

DYER, Maria Tarn: daughter of Wm Tarn Sr, director of LMS; 1827 m Samuel Dyer Sr; 1845/6 m J. G. Bausum; d 21 Oct 1846.

DYER, Samuel Sr (1804–43): son of John Dyer (qv); Cambridge law student; LMS; m Maria Tarn, daughter of LMS director; 1827 Penang; 1829–35 Malacca; 1835–43 Singapore; d Macao.

DYER, Samuel Jr: b 18 Jan 1833, son of Samuel and Maria Tarn Dyer (qv); 1877 agent of B&FBS, Shanghai, after Alex. Wylie.

DYMOND, Francis (Frank) John: Bible Christian Mission, dep UK 27 Jan 1887, with S. Pollard (qv); arr Shanghai, CIM associates, 14 March; 1888 Yunnan; daughter Roxie m J. O. Fraser (qv).

EASON, Arthur: CIM dep UK 5 Jan, 1881; 1882 pioneer, Guizhou, Yunnan; 1892 resigned to join Sal. Army.

EASTON, George F.: printer; CIM, one of 'the eighteen', dep UK 21 Oct, 1875; 29 Dec, 1876–77 pioneer Xi'an, Shaanxi; Jan

1877 Lanzhou; with G. Parker; Aug 1881
m Caroline Gardner; 1885 Supt. Gansu,
Shaanxi; China Council.

ECKETT, Robert: Foreign Missionary Secy,
UMFC; d 1862.

EDKINS, Joseph (1823–1905): LMS evangelist,
translator, philologist, expert in Chinese
religions, author, well known to Taiping
rulers; 1848–60 Shanghai; 1860–61
Shandong, Yantai, and Tianjin; 1861 Peking.

EDWARDS, Dr Ebenezer Henry: CIM dep UK
20 Aug 1882; Taiyuan, Shanxi; 1896 CIM
Taiyuan work transferred to Shouyang
Mission; m Florence Kemp, sister of Jessie
Pigott (qv); 1900 in UK; with J. W. Lowrie
(qv) found Baoding martyrs' remains; BMS;
with Moir Duncan, Creasey Smith (qv) and
CIM team to Taiyuan 1901, to negotiate
reparations; 1910 Order of the Double
Dragon.

EITEL, E. J., PhD: Basel Mission, S China, 1862–
65; 1865–78 LMS Peking; sinologue; Dec
1862 baptised first Peking Prot. Christian;
1878 *et seq* adviser to Hong Kong govt.

ELDRED, Annie: b 22 Dec 1871; CIM dep UK
Sept 1898, Linfen, Hongtong, Shanxi; 1900
from Jiexiu with A. P. Lundgrens (qv) to
Fenyang c/o Oberlin ABCFM; killed 15 Aug
1900.

ELGIN, Earl of, son of Thomas Bruce, 7th earl
(Elgin marbles): 1857 Indian mutiny; 1858
envoy, Treaty of Tientsin; treaty with Japan;
1860 second opium war, captured Peking,
burned Summer Palace, negotiated Peking
Convention.

ELIAS, Ney: explorer, studied new course of
Yellow River; member of Col. Browne's
1874–75 Burma-Yunnan expedition; British
Political Agent, Kashgar.

ELLISTON, W. L.: CIM dep UK 29 Oct, 1878
Shanxi; 1881 first headmaster Chefoo School;
27 Dec, 1884 m A. Groom; Shanxi; d 1887.

ELLIOT, Capt. Charles, RN: 1835 third Supt. of
Trade, Canton; 1836 Chief Supt.; confronted
Commissioner Lin (qv); 1840–41 political
chief in first phase of first opium war; HBM
plenipotentiary, negotiated Convention of
Chuanbi.

ELMSLIE, Dr W. J.: Scottish Presbyterian, CMS
Kashmir dep UK Sept 1864; May 1865
Srinigar; d 18 Nov, 1872. Biography led to H.
Schofield (qv) going to China.

ELPHINSTONE, J. T.: president, Select
Committee, East India Co., Canton; friend
of R. Morrison; later Member of Parliament.

ENNALS, Sydney W: b 1 Nov 1872; BMS dep
UK 11 Sept 1899; Shanxi; Xinzhou; killed 9
Aug 1900.

FARNHAM, J. M. W.: Presby.; 1860 Shanghai with
Wm Gamble (qv); friend of CIM.

FARTHING, George Bryant: b 19 Dec 1859;
BMS, dep UK 12 Sept 1886; m 23 Apr 1889,
Catherine Wright; Taiyuan, Shanxi; 9 July
1900, first Taiyuan martyr beheaded, with
wife, children Ruth (10), Guy (8), Eliz.(3).

FAULDING, Jane E. (1843–1904): m JHT 28
Nov 1871, 1 son, 1 daughter; 1877–78 led
CIM team, Shanxi famine relief, first Western
woman inland.

FAULDING, William F.: father of Jane E.
Faulding (qv).

FERGUSON, Henry S.: USA; 15 Feb 1895 arr
China with F. C. H. Dreyer (qv); Taihe,
Anhui; 1932 flood relief in Jiangxi; prisoner
of Bolsheviks, executed.

FISHBOURNE, Capt., RN: rescued Amoy
victims; strong supporter of missions and
anti-opium socy; later, evangelist.

FISHE, Colonel: Dublin; HEIC Madras Horse
Artillery (retd.); father of Edward and
Charles (qv).

FISHE, Charles Thomas: son of Col. Fishe;
Dublin (qv); influenced by H. G. Guinness
(qv), JHT; 1867 asst. to W. T. Berger (gv);
1868 CIM, Yangzhou; 1871 CIM China Secy;
1875 m Nellie Faulding (qv).

FISHE, Edward: elder son of Col. Fishe, Dublin
(qv); 1866 influenced by H. G. Guinness
(qv), JHT; 1867 to China independently;
attached to CIM; m Annie Bohannan (qv);
1868 Zhenjiang.

FITTACK, W. H.: HBM consul, 1867 Ningbo.

FLEMING, T.: 1860 CMS recruit taught by JHT;
Ningbo, Hangzhou; 1863 invalided home.

FLINT, James: East India Co. official; petitioned
Qian Long (Ch'ien Lung) emperor for
trading rights; imprisoned.

FOCH, Ferdinand (1851–1929): Marshal of
France; 1918 commander in chief of Allied
armies, World War I, Western front.

FOLKE, Erik: first individual associate of CIM;
Swedish Mission in China formed to support
him; initiated S Shanxi-Henan field; supt;
1900 led team to safety at Hankou.

FORD, Henry T.: CIM dep UK 28 Oct 1892;
Taikang, Henan; dep 11 July 1900 safely to
Zhenjiang.

FORMAN, John N: Princeton Univ; Trav. Secy
Student Volunteer Movement, USA; 1887 to
Britain, travelled with JHT, Scotland, Ireland,
England.

FORSYTH, Robt Coventry: BMS, Shandong;
author *The China Martyrs of 1900*.

FORREST, R. J.: 1860 HBM consular interpreter,
later consul, Ningbo and other places.

FORRESTER, Col.: 1861 second-in-command to
F. T. Ward, Ever-Victorious Army; captured
by Taipings at Qingpu; refused to succeed F.
T. Ward.

FORTUNE, Robert: Royal Hort. Socy botanist;
1843 arr China; explorations 1843–46, 1848–
51, 1853–56, 1861–62, disguised as a Tartar;
supplied India with tea plants.

FOSTER, Arnold: LMS; 1871 Hankou; 1887–89
Secy China Famine Relief Committee,
London; d 1919.

FOWLER, Sir Robert N., Bart. (1828–91): 1860
Treasurer Chinese Evang. Socy; 1871 MP,
supported Anti-Slavery Socy; 1880 MP for

City of London; 1983 Lord Mayor, re-elected 1885; July 1885 baronet; d 22 May, 1890.

FRANCKE, August Hermann: pietist, 1696 founded Orphan Houses, extensive by 19th century; prof. divinity, Halle Univ. Germany; d 1727.

FRANSON, Fredrik (1852–1908): Swedish evangelist, long resident USA; studied D. L. Moody's methods (qv); strongly influenced by JHT (qv) *To Every Creature*; sent many missionaries to China, India; influenced formation of several European associate missions of CIM.

FRASER, James O.: CIM, graduate engineer, musician; apostle to minority peoples of W Yunnan; 1918, 60,000 church members of strong indigenous church; CIM superintendent, China Council; d malignant malaria, 25 Sept 1938.

FRASER, John: Scottish missionary to Egypt; initiated movement resulting in Foreign Evangelist Society.

FRENCH, Evangeline (Eva) (1871–1961): CIM dep UK 1 Sep 95; Huzhou, Shanxi; leader of 'the Trio' with Francesca French and Mildred Cable (qv); 1923 to Xinjiang till 1936; d 1961, aged 90.

FRENCH, Francesca (1873–1961): CIM Shanxi (*see* Evangeline); member of 'the Trio'; d 3 weeks after Evangeline; co-author with Mildred Cable (qv).

FROST, Henry Weston (1858–??): 1876–79 Princeton; civil engineer; 1885 read *China's Spiritual Need and Claims* and *A Cambridge Band*; influenced by J. Goforth; 1887 London, met JHT; 1888 JHT to N Am; HWF Secy, 1889 secy, treasurer, N Am Council; 1893 Home Director.FULLER, W. R.: first United Meth. Free Ch. missionary to China; trained by JHT; 1864 Ningbo.

FULLER, Wm R.: first United Meth. Free Ch. missionary to China; trained by JHT; 1864 Ningbo; 1867 invalided to UK.

FULTON, A. A. and sister, M. D.: Am Presby. Mission (North); 1885 pioneers in Guangxi; expelled from Guiping.

GAINFORT, Mrs: Dublin; influenced students to join CIM.

GAMBLE, William: Am Presby. Mission Press; 1858 Ningbo; 1860 Shanghai; friend of JHT, CIM, received *Lammermuir* party.

GARDNER, Christopher T.: 1867 HBM consular interpreter., Ningbo; 1870 consul Zhenjiang; Yantai.

GARNIER, Lieut. Francis: 1868 French Yunnan expedition from Tongking; Jan 30 dep Dongchuan via Huili to Dali; forced back; 1871 defence of Paris; killed in Franco-Chinese war, Tongking.

GARIBALDI, Giuseppe (1807–82): with Mazzini and Cavour created united Italy; 1860 freed Sicily, took Naples; Victor Immanuel proclaimed King.

GATES, Caroline: CIM; dep UK 10 Mar 1887; Fancheng, Hubei; 1896 Lu'an, Shanxi;

intrepid companion of Glover family, *1,000 Miles of Miracle*, escape from Boxers.

GAULD, Dr Wm: Engl. Presby. Mission, *c* 1863 began med. work at Shantou (Swatow), largest in China for years; 1867 new hospital.

GENÄHR, Ferdinand: Rhenish (Barmen) Mission; 1847 Hong Kong, Guangdong (Kwangtung) under C. Gutzlaff; m R. Lechler's sister; one of the first Prot. missionaries to reside outside treaty ports; d 1864.

GENGHIS KHAN (1162–1227): Mongol conqueror of N China, W Russia, Central Asia, NW India to Adriatic; military genius.

GILL, Lieut. Wm J. Royal Engineers: 10 July 1877 dep Chengdu; Batang Aug 25; Dali Sept 27; Bhamo Nov 1; author *River of Golden Sand*; RGS medal; promoted Captain.

GILMOUR, James (1843–91): LMS Mongolia; May 1870 arr Peking; Kalgan; Kiahkta (Outer Mongolia); d typhus, Tianjin.

GLADSTONE, William Ewart (1809–98): three times prime minister, 1868–97.

GLOVER, Archibald E.: MA (Oxon.); curate to Preb. Webb-Peploe; CIM 1897; Lu'an, Shanxi with S. P. Smith (qv); 1900 escaped with family and C. Gates (qv); author, *1000 Miles of Miracle*; wife d 25 Oct 1900.

GOBLE, Jonathan: Am marine under Commodore Perry, to Japan as missionary; 1870 invented rickshaw.

GODDARD, Josiah: Am Baptist, Bangkok; 1848 Ningbo.

GOFORTH, Jonathan (1859–1936); Canadian Presby Church; applied to join CIM 1885, 1888, 1911; advised to stay with own Church; 1888 arr China; pioneer in Henan; Changde 1895; 1908 led great revival, Manchuria; 1900 escaped with family and party, Anyang (Changde) Henan to Hankou.

GOODRICH, Chauncey: Am Board; Zhangjiakou (Kalgan); m May 30, 1878, widowed Sep 3; Bible translator, Union Version with Mateer and Baller (qv); 1872 hymnbook with Blodget.

GORDON, Lt. Col. Charles George (1833–85): 1860 Tianjin, Peking campaign; 1862 Shanghai, commanding Ever-Victorious Army; 1864 Taiping Rebellion ended; honoured by emperor and Queen Victoria (CB); 1865–71 London; donor to JHT; 1880 adviser to Chinese govt.; 1883–85 Maj-Gen., Sudan.

GOSSE, Philip Henry (1810–88): naturalist, author; 1855–*66 Manual of Marine Zoology*; 1860–62 *Romance of Natural History*; through W. T. Berger joined Hackney Brethren; early donor to CIM.

GOSSE, Sir Edmund Wm (1845–1928): (aged 15–20 while JHT at Mile End); 1867–75 asst. librarian British Museum; poet and critic; 1904–10 librarian, House of Lords; author, histories of literature, and *Father and Son*, biographical.

GOUGH, Frederick Foster (DD): CMS 1849–62

Ningbo; 1862–69 London, Ningbo vernacular romanised NT revision with JHT; m Mary (d 1861);1866 m Mary Jones (Ann Maria) (qv); 1869 Ningbo.

GOUGH, Mary (Ellen): daughter of FFG.

GOUGH, Mrs Mary: first wife of FFG, d 1861.

GOULD, Annie Allender: b 18 Nov 1867; Am Board 1893; Baoding, Zhili; killed 1 July 1900.

GRANT, Hay Macdowell: laird of Arndilly; 1865 chairman Perth Conference.

GRANT, General Sir Hope: 1860 commander, land forces, under Lord Elgin.

GRANT, Gen. Ulysses Simpson (1822–85): commander in chief Union forces in Am civil war (1864–65); 1869–76 President USA.

GRANVILLE, Lord (1815–91): 2nd earl; 1851, 1870–74 Foreign Secretary (after Lord Clarendon), and 1880–85.

GRAY, Jeanie Isabella: b 31 March, 1863, Newton Stewart, Scotland; CIM dep UK 22 Oct, 1884; one of the Seventy; Guangxin River pioneer, Yüshan; 1 Nov, 1886 m Herbert H. Taylor (qv); Henan; d 15 Jan, 1937; grandmother of James Hudson Taylor III, CIM General Director, 1980; President of MSI Resource Center.

GREEN, C. H. S.: arr China 1891; to Zhili; Huolu; 1900 escaped Boxers with wife, children Vera, John and J. Gregg (qv); Vera died, buried at Tianjin; author *In Deaths Oft*; returned to Huolu Nov 1903.

GREEN, D. D.: Am Presby.; 1859 Ningbo; 1865 Hangzhou.

GREGG, Jessie G.: CIM, arr 1895; Huolu, Zhili; 1900 escaped with C. H. S. Green (qv) family; returned 1903.GRETTON, Henry: CMS 1867 Hangzhou, alone without Chinese companion after G. E. Moule dep; 1870 Shaoxing.GRANT, General Sir Hope: 1860 commander, land forces, under Lord Elgin.

GRIERSON, Robert: dep UK 4 Nov, 1885; Jinhua, Wenzhou, Zhejiang.

GROS, Baron: 1860 French plenipotentiary, second opium war, Peking treaty, plundered Summer Palace.

GROSVENOR, Hon. T. G.: led expedition with E. C. Baber (qv), A. Davenport after Margary (qv) murder; dep Hankou 5 Nov 1875; via Zhaotong, Kunming 6 March 1876; Bhamo 21 May 1876.

GROVES, Anthony Norris: (1795–1853); early exponent of 'faith principle'; brother-in-law of G. Müller; missionary to Baghdad; initiator of Brethren movement.

GUINNESS, G. Whitfield: son of H. Grattan G. (qv); BA, MB, B Ch; CIM 1897; Henan; 1900 led colleagues to safety at Hankou; Kaifeng Hospital; d typhus.

GUINNESS, Dr Harry: eldest son of H. Grattan Guinness (qv); principal, Harley College.

GUINNESS, H. Grattan, DD, FRAS: gentleman-evangelist, 1859 Ulster revival, drew thousands; JHT's friend from 1865;

founded East London Institute (Harley College), trained 1,330 for 40 societies of 30 denominations; initiated RBMU; greatly influenced Barnardo; author, astronomy, eschatology.

GUINNESS, M. Geraldine (1862–1949); daughter of H. Grattan Guinness (qv); m F. Howard Taylor (qv); author, biography of JHT.

GULICK, John T.: Am Board; 1865 first missionary to Kalgan; evangelism with wife in Mongolia; ill, moved to Japan.

GULICK, H.: Am Bible Society agent, 1876.

GUTZLAFF, Agnes: blind Chinese adopted by Mrs Gutzlaff; educated in UK; teacher in Ningbo under Miss Aldersey (qv).

GUTZLAFF, Charles (Karl Frederich August) (1803–51): 1826–28 Netherlands Miss. Socy, Batavia (Jakarta), Java; 1828 independent, Bangkok; 1829 m Miss Newell, Malacca, first single Prot. woman missionary to E Asia who d 1831; 1831–35 voyages up China coast; 1834 m Miss Warnstall d 1849; 1839 interpreter to British; 1840 and 1842 governor of Chusan Is.; 1842 interpreter-negotiator, Nanking Treaty; 1843–51 Chinese Secy to British govt Hong Kong; initiated Chinese Union, Chinese Associations and missions; 1850 m Miss Gabriel. For a list of European missions attributable to Charles Gutzlaff see volume 1, note 6.

HAIG, Maj-Gen. F. T.: active Christian in Indian army; 1881 served in CMS Godavari Mission; CMS committee; Eastern surveys; friend of CIM.

HALL, Capt. Basil, RN: 1816 voyage up China coast, Korea, Ryukyu Is.; author, *Narrative of a Voyage …*

HALL, Charles J.: 1857 CES missionary Ningbo; 1860 Shandong; d 1861.

HALL, H. H.: Am Meth. Episc. Mission; 1870 Jiujiang; 1873 Ruichang riot.

HALL, William: manufacturer of footwear; deacon, Bryanston Hall, Portman Square; 1872 member of first CIM London council.

HALL, William Nelthorpe; Methodist New Connexion; 1860 Shanghai; 1861 April Tianjin; 14 May 1878 d 'famine fever'.

HAMBERG, Theodore: Basel Mission; 1847 Hong Kong, under Gutzlaff (qv); with R. Lechler (qv) to Guangdong (Kwangtung) Hakkas; first Prot. missionaries to reside outside treaty ports; d 1854.

HANNINGTON, Bishop James; Oxford; 1882 CMS den. UK; 1884 first bishop, Eastern Equatorial Africa; 29 Oct 1885 murdered on Mwanga's orders; death roused 'the whole Church'; *Memoirs* inspired thousands; Hannington Hall, Oxford, counterpart of Henry Martin Hall, Cambridge.

HANSPACH, August: Chinese Evangelization Socy of Berlin (Berlin Missionary Socy for China); 1855 Hong Kong; 11 years extensive inland travel.

HAPPER, Andrew P., DD: Am Presby. 1844
Macao; 1847 Canton.

HARPER, Andrew P., DD: Am Presby. 1844–46
Macao (debarred from Canton); 1847
Canton; 1887 first president, Canton
Christian Coll.

HARDEY, Richard, brother of Robert Hardey:
early photographer, Hull; m Hannah Maria
Hudson, portrait artist.

HARDEY, Robert, brother of Richard Hardey:
surgeon, Hull Infirmary and medical college;
JHT his assistant.

HART, Sir Robert (1835–1911): b 20 Feb
1835;1854 consular interpreter, Ningbo;
1857 Canton; Nov 1862 Inspector-General,
Chinese Imperial Maritime Customs; 1865
Peking; 1864 3rd class mandarin; 1869 2nd
class; 1881 1st class; 1885 Peacock's Feather;
1889 1st class of 1st Order for 3 generations;
1901 Junior Guardian of the Heir Apparent;
1911 posthumous Senior Guardian; CMG,
1882 KCMG, 1889 GCMG; 1st Baronet
1893; 1885 succeeded Sir Harry Parkes as
Br. Minister, Peking; resigned to resume
IG; 1900 40-year diary and house burned by
Boxers; 1 May 1906 resigned, but Emeritus
IG until death.

HART, V. C.: Am Meth. Episc. Mission; 1866
Jiujiang, friend of CIM.

HARVEY, Thomas P.: master-butcher; 1866 med.
student with T. J. Barnardo, London Hosp.,
Mile End; 1869 China; 1872 Lond. Hosp.
graduated; 1876 Bhamo, Burma.

HAVELOCK, Maj-Gen. Sir Henry, KCB (1795–
1857): hero of Indian mutiny, Cawnpore,
Lucknow.

HEAYSMAN, Mary: b 29 July 1874; CIM dep
UK 1897; Daning, Shanxi with F. E., M. R.
Nathan; Boxer rising, 1900, July 12 fled to
hills, Aug 13 killed.

HEDIN, Sven: Swedish archaeologist, explorer;
studied under von Richtofen; 1894 aged
28, Tashkent to Kashgar; 1895 crossed
Taklamahan Desert; 1899–1902 explored
Tarim Basin.

HILL, David (1840–96): 1865 WMMS, Hankou
(independent means); 1878–80 with J. J.
Turner (qv) CIM, to Shanxi famine relief;
1879 means of conversion of 'Pastor Hsi'
(qv); Wusue; founded houses for aged, blind,
orphans; fought opium trade; started a
hospital; 1890 co-chairman with J. L. Nevius
General Missionary Conference, Shanghai; d
1896 aged 56, typhus from famine relief.

HILL, Richard Harris, FRIBA: civil engineer,
evangelist; helped build Mildmay Miss.
Hosp., CIM Newington Green; m Agnes,
daughter of Henry W. Soltau (qv); 1872 Hon.
Secy London CIM.

HILLIER, Sir Walter Caine, KCMG, CB: 1910
Order of the Double Dragon; HBM Consul;
China Famine Relief Committee, Tianjin;
surveyed famine areas; adviser to Chinese
Foreign Office.

HOBSON, Dr Benjamin: LMS; 1841 Macao; 1843
Hong Kong; 1846 Canton; 1856 Shanghai.

HOBSON, J.: CMS, chaplain to Br. community,
Shanghai; JHT's friend.

HODDLE, Alexander: Canada 10 years; YMCA
local secy UK; CIM 1889; Huolu, Baoding,
Zhili; Taiyuan, Shanxi, in Shouyang Mission,
then independent; 9 July 1900 killed by
Boxers.

HODGE; C. van R., MD Pennsylvania: Am Presby
Mission, Baoding, Zhili; killed 30 June 1900.

HODGE, Wm Bramwell: Meth. New Connexion;
1866 Tianjin; 1869 companion of Jas
Williamson, LMS; murdered.

HOGG, Charles F.: CIM dep UK 21 May, 1884;
pioneer in Shaanxi;1887 expelled from
Xi'an.

HOLLAND, Capt.: 1863 Gen. Staveley's chief-of-
staff; commanded E-V Army after F. T. Ward's
death (qv); defeated at Taicang.

HOLMES, J. L.: Am Southern Baptist; 1860
pioneer of Shandong, Yantai (Chefoo);
killed.

HOLMGREN, Josef: Swedish pastor, Orebro;
Sept 1883 met JHT in London; 1887
translated China's Spiritual Need & Claims;
pastor Stockholm, formed committee of
Swedish Mission in China to support Erik
Folke (qv).

HOLLINGWORTH, M. G.: Brit. merchant,
Jiujiang; friend of CIM; 1870 Jiujiang to
Fuzhou, Fujian, overland.

HOPE, Vice-Admiral Sir James: 1860–62, naval
commander-in-chief, China; 1861 negotiated
'year of truce' with Taipings; opened Yangzi
River to foreign shipping.

HOPKINS, Evan H. (1837–1919): 1874 met
American Pearsall Smith, 'Higher Christian
Life' conference, Oxford; 1875 with Canon
Battersby, G. R. Thornton, H. W. Webb-
Peploe at Keswick for embryo Keswick
Convention meetings; 1883 Cambridge
convention on Keswick lines; 1884 published
Law of Liberty in the Spiritual Life; 1886 joined
by Handley Moule (qv).

HORNE, Celia: CIM dep UK Oct, 1876;1878
Shanxi famine relief with J. E. Taylor (qv)
one of the first women to go deep inland.

HORNE, Mr: leading member of Brethren,
Clevedon, Bristol; confidant of JHT .

HORSBURGH, J. Heywood: CMS, contemporary
of Graham Brooke (qv), G. L. Pilkington
(qv), Barclay Buxton; 1883 to Zhejiang;
1890 wrote Do Not Say, great effect; 1891 led
team to W Sichuan; 1895 at Chengdu calm
humour quelled riot; retired.

HOSTE, Dixon Edward (1861–1946): b 23
July, 1861, son of Maj-Gen. D. E. Hoste, RA;
Clifton College and Royal Military Academy,
Woolwich; 1882 Lieut. R.A.; 1882, converted
at D. L. Moody meetings; 23 July 1883,
approached JHT; met Council Feb 1884,
accepted 7 Oct, 1884; 'Camb. Seven', dep
UK 5 Feb, 1885; Shanxi 1885–96 colleague of
Hsi Shengmo (qv); 1896 sick leave Australia;

Supt. Henan; China Council; 1900 assistant to J. W. Stevenson; Jan 1901 Acting GD; Nov 1902 General Director; 7 Sept 1894 m Amelia Gertrude Broomhall (qv); three sons; d 11 May, 1946.

HOSTE, William: brother of D. E. Hoste, Trinity Coll. and Ridley Hall, Cambridge; persuaded D. E. Hoste to hear Moody.

HOUGHTON, Frank: b 4 April, 1894, CIM dep UK 10 Nov, 1920; Sichuan; 1923 m. Dorothy Cassels, dtr of WWC;1926–36 editorial secretary, London; 25 Jan 1937 consecrated bishop, East Sichuan; 21 Oct, 1940 General Director; 1951–72 Consulting Director; d 25 Jan, 1972.

HOUGHTON, John: son of Richard (qv) Liverpool; Feb 1866 host to JHT; introduced to H. Grattan Guinness.

HOUGHTON, Richard: father of John (qv); 1866 as 'perfect stranger' read JHT's *China*, donated £650 (modern equiv. ?£13,000).

HOWARD, John Eliot (1807–83): quinologist, FRS, Fellow of Linnaean Socy; manufacturing chemist; early leader of Brethren, Tottenham; member of B&FBS committee and CES Board; JHT's close friend and supporter.

HOWARD, Luke: meteorologist, father of John Eliot and Robert.

HOWARD, Mrs Robert: wife of JEH's brother, Tottenham; intimate friend and supporter of JHT, Maria and JET from first acquaintance.

HOWARD, Robert: brother of John Eliot; also chemist, leader of Brethren, on Board of CES; supporter of JHT and CIM.

HOWARD, Theodore: b c 1840, son of Robert Howard (qv); Oct 1872 member of first Home Council of CIM; Oct 1875, Chairman; Feb 1879 Home Director; d 1915.

HOWELL, Alfred: Dent & Co, Japan; 1866 donor to CIM in approval of Chinese dress.

HUBERTY, Marie S.: Belgian, CIM dep UK Oct 1876; 1878 Shansi famine relief; Sept 1878 m Francis James (qv) who adopted her name.

HUC, Abbé Everiste Regis: travelled with Gabet 1844–46, Mongolia, Tibet; 1846 in Lhasa, deported; 1857 author, *Christianity in China, Tartary and Thibet*; d 1860.

HUDSON, Adoniram (1788–1850): Am Board, became Baptist; 1813 pioneer with wife in Burma.

HUDSON, Amelia (1808–81): mother of JHT; m James Taylor.

HUDSON, Benjamin Brook (c 1785–1865): maternal grandfather of JHT; Wesleyan Methodist minister; portrait artist; 3 sons, 4 daughters: Amelia, b 27 Jan 1808, d Nov 1881, m James Taylor; Mary, m Hudson, scholar, Barton-on-Humber; Joseph, Vicar of Dodworth, Barnsley; Hannah Maria, portrait artist, m Richard Hardey, photographer, brother of Robert Hardey, surgeon, Hull; James, artist, died aged 21; Sarah Ann, m Rev Edward King, C I M Australian Council; Benjamin, portrait artist, Soho and India.

HUDSON, Thomas & John: sons of Mary (née Hudson); JHT's cousins.

HUDSON, T. H.: General Baptist Mission; 1845 Ningbo; 1850–66 translated NT into *wenli* (literary Chinese).

HUTCHINSON, Sir Jonathan (1828–1913): 1859 general and ophthalmic surgeon, London Hospital; 1882 FRS; 1889 President RCS; Nov 1908 Knight Bachelor; benefactor of JHT.

HUGHES, Katherine: CIM dep UK Oct 1876; 1878 Shanxi famine relief; m Dr W. L. Pruen; Chengdu, Sichuan; Guiyang, Guizhou.

HUNTER, George: CIM Hunan; Scot. Presby.; 1889 headmaster Chefoo schools; 1895 Yichang, base for Hunan; d1900.

HUNTER, George W. (1861–1946): Scotsman; 1889 CIM Gansu, Xinjiang 1905, itinerating from Lanzhou; 1906 Urumqi as base; 1907 to Kashgar; 1914 P. Mather as colleague; Cable-French 'Trio' occasionally; prisoner of NKVD during Soviet occupation, tortured, expelled, d 20 Dec 1946.

HURN, Georgiana: b 6 July 1868; CIM, dep UK 3 Jan 1898; 21 July 1900 hid in hills with Peat family (qv) and E. Dobson (qv); killed 30 Aug 1900.

HUSTON, Mary E.: b 1866 Pennsylvania; CIM, 1895 to China; 6 July 1900 dep Lucheng, Shanxi, with E. J. Cooper family (qv), Hattie Rice (qv), and A. R. Saunders party (qv); 13 July 1900 savagely wounded, H. Rice killed; d 11 Aug 1900.

I'ANSON, Chas: Harley College; CIM dep UK 3 Nov 1887; wife Florence, children Arthur, Eva, Dora, all killed by Boxers 12 July 1900, Datong, Shanxi.

INNES, James: obstreperous ship's captain, Jardine, Matheson.

INNOCENT, John, (1829–1904): Methodist New Connexion evangelist; 1860 Shanghai; 1861 Tianjin with W. N. Hall (qv); 1864 visited Mongolia.

JACKSON, Charles: 1862–79 Anglican Secy of B&FBS with J Mee (qv); cf John Jackson B&FBS 1823–49.

JACKSON, Josiah A.: CIM dep UK 26 May 1866, *Lammermuir*; Zhejiang; 1873 m. (1) F. Wilson d1878; (2) 20 Sep, 1882, d July 1883; dep China; Aug 1884 left CIM; returned Shanghai, secular; d 1906.

JAMES, Francis Huberty: b June 1851; CIM, one of 'the eighteen', dep UK 1876; 1877–79 Shanxi famine relief; Sept 1878 m Marie S. Huberty, Belgian; 1881 to UK; 1883 BMS, Shandong, Qingzhou, Jinan; 1890 paper on Chinese secret sects, Shanghai General Conference; 1892 resigned from BMS; Europe and USA, 1895 Lowell lectureship, Boston, following Prof. Henry Drummond; 1897 Imperial Arsenal, Shanghai; 1898 Imperial Univ., Beijing 1900 with Dr Morrison rescued 2,000 Chinese Christians, protected by Br. legation forces; 20 June, 1900 reported beheaded on Yong Lu's (qv) orders.

JAMES, Thomas: CIM dep UK 15 Jan, 1885; April 1885 Hunan with Dorward (qv) and Dick (qv); Sichuan; m F. (Stroud) Riley (qv).

JARDINE, William: surgeon, merchant ship-owner; 1841 Member of Parliament; d 1843.

JENKINS, Horace: ABMU; 1860 Ningbo, joined Knowlton (qv), Kreyer (qv).

JOHN, Griffith (1831–1912): LMS; 1855 Shanghai; pioneer evangelist; 1861 Hankou; 1863 Wuchang; 1867 Hanyang.

JOHNSON, Stevens: Am Board, Bangkok; 1847 Fuzhou (Foochow).

JONES, Ann Maria (Mary): wife of John; 1863–66 with Hudson Taylors, London; 1866 m F. F. Gough; 1869 Ningbo; 1869–71 fostered Chas Edw. Taylor; d Nov 1877.

JONES, Hannah: CIM dep UK 16 Feb 1881;1882 Gansu; 1885 m W. E. Burnett.

JONES, John, CES: 1856–57 Ningbo; independent, 1857–63; early exponent of 'faith principle', influenced JHT; d 1863. II: 345-9, 351,359-75, 390-1, 421; III: 8, 21, 24, 28-9, 33-6, 40, 44-5, 47, 53, 57, 61, 63-6, 68, 70, 72, 76, 78-79, 85-6, 95-98, 107, 110-11, 121, 123, 129-33, 135-36, 154-56, 158-59, 161, 172, 175-77, 179, 185-88, 193-97, 207, 239-40; 249, 272-76, 278, 281-2, 298-99, 301, 308-13, 316, 318-19, 327, 329, 338, 405, 427, 371, 399, 415, 429; IV: 46, 57, 66, 76, 99, 112, 136, 159, 215, 407.

JONES, Mary: wife of John; 1863–66 with Hudson Taylors, London; 1866 m F. F. Gough. III: 41-42, 54, 56, 60, 80, 91, 128, 205, 331, 333-34, 337-39, 342, 365, 368, 375, 379, 418, 422; V: 139, 393; VI: 159, 232, 295 (Mrs Mary Jones (daughter) VI: 291, 295). See also John Jones, Frederick Gough.

JUDD, Charles H. Sr (1842–1919): 1867 CIM through influence of T. J. Barnardo; 1868 Yangzhou; 1869 Zhenjiang; 1872–73 UK; 1874 Wuchang, with JHT; 1875 with 'Yao' (qv) and 'Zhang' (qv) rented house at Yueyang (Yochow), Hunan, forced out; 1877 with J. F. Broumton via Hunan to Guiyang, Guizhou; Broumton settled, Judd via Chongqing to Wuchang; 1879 built at Yantai before school and sanatorium.

JUDSON, Adoniram (1788–1850): Am Board, became Baptist; 1813 pioneer with wife in Burma.

JUKES, Andrew: East India Co. officer; deacon, Anglican Church; c 1842 independent minister, Brethren congregation; 1866 built Church of St John the Evangelist, Hull.

KAY, Duncan: CIM dep UK 8 Oct 1884; Anhui; 1889 Qüwu, Shanxi; energetic evangelist, beloved by Chinese; 4 July 1900 fled to hills with wife, child; killed 15 Sept 1900.

KEESON, Dr: 1863 Secy Wesleyan Meth. Miss. Socy.

KENNAWAY, Sir John H., Bart.: son of first baronet; 1872 MP, anti-slave trade; 1887 President CMS; 1893 coined phrase 'Ask the Lord and tell His people'; 1897 Privy Council.

KENNEDY, Rev: Congregational minister, Stepney.

KERR, Charlotte: nurse; CIM dep UK 15 April 1880; 1881 pioneer Guiyang; later Shanxi, Shouyang Mission.

KERR, Dr John G., MD: Am Presby. Mission (North); 1854 Canton; trained 200 Chinese medical students; translated many medical books; performed 480,000 surgical operations; founded the Asylum for the Insane; d Canton 1901.

KIDD, Jane: CIM dep UK 26 Dec, 1878;1880 first unmarried Western woman into far western provs. of China; Feb 19–April 20, journey to Guiyang; Oct 1882 m J. H. Riley (qv); d 12 Oct, 1886.

KIDD, Samuel (1799–1848): LMS; 1824–32 Malacca; third after Morrison and Milne, before Dyer, Tomlin; Prof. of Chinese Language and Literature, University College, London.

KING, Annie: b 16 Mar 1870; CIM dep UK 22 Sept 1898; Hejin, Shanxi; killed 16 July 1900.

KING, George: CIM dep UK 15 May, 1875, aged 18; one of 'the eighteen', arr. Shanghai 14 July after shipwreck; pioneer, Shaanxi, Gansu, Henan; m (1) E. Snow (d Hanzhong 10 May, 1881); (2) Harriet Black; qualified physician.

KING, Dr George Edwin: son of G. King (qv) b 20 Nov 1887 on Han River; excelled at school; Edinburgh Med. Missionary Socy; Edin. Univ, graduated 1909 first class with distinctions; CIM dep UK 22 Nov 1910; Kaifeng with G. W. Guinness (qv), S. H. Kerr; March 1912 Linfen (Pingyang) Shanxi at Millar Wilson Memorial Hosp.; Feb 1914 arr Lanzhou, Gansu with P. Mather (qv) en route Urumqi; m 6 Feb 1915; had Dr Gao Jincheng as colleague, R. C. Parry; 1927 general evacuation by foreigners during nationalist movement; 5 June 1927 drowned in Yellow River.KINGDON, Edwin Frank: BMS recruit trained by JHT; 1864 Shandong, Yantai.

KING, Charles W.: Am merchant ship-owner, partner of D. W. C. Olyphant (qv).

KINGDON, Edwin F.: BMS recruit trained by JHT; 1864 Shandong, Yantai.

KINNAIRD, Hon. Arthur Fitzgerald, 10th Baron (1814–87): supported CMS, LCM, Barnardo. Son, of same name, 11th baron m niece of Hon. and Rev Baptist W. Noel (qv); she helped found Foreign Evangelisation Socy, 1871, and Zenana Bible and Medical Mission (now BMMF).

KLOEKERS, Hendrick Z.: Netherlands Chinese Evangelization Socy; 1855–58 Shanghai; 1862 BMS; 1862–65 Shandong, Yantai.

KNOWLTON, Miles Justice: ABMU; 1854 Ningbo; friend of JHT.

KOCH, Robert (1843–1910): German bacteriologist, discovered B. tuberculosis; cholera, and others.

KRAPF, Johann Ludwig (1810–81): missionary

linguist; 1836 sent by CMS to Ethiopia; 1844 Mombasa; 1853 to Europe.

KREYER, Carl T. ABMU: 1866 Hangzhou (Hangchow); lent his home to *Lammermuir* party.

KUBLAI KHAN: Mongol ruler, 1216–94; conquered Song (Sung) dynasty, founded Yuan (Yuan) dynasty; ruled all China, Central Asia, Persia, E Europe.

LACHLAN, H. N.: barrister; CIM dep UK 29 Nov 1888 aged 31; Guizhou, Yunnan, Chongqing; Principal, Anqing Training Inst. after Baller (qv); 29 Oct 1892 m Katherine Mackintosh (qv); dtr H. Evelyn m D. de B. Robertson, CIM architect; d 18 April 1896.

LAGRENE, M.: French envoy, 1843 treaty; negotiated edicts of toleration by Qi Ying (Ch'i Ying), for Prots. as well as RCs.

LANCASTER, Agnes: CIM dep UK 14 Nov, 1880; Shanxi famine relief; 1886 m G. W. Clarke (qv); Guihuacheng, Mongolian border; d 8 Aug, 1892. LANCE, Henry: 1864 minister in Devonshire twenty years; Berger Hall, Bromley-by-Bow.

LANDELS, Dr William (1823–99): minister Regent's Park Baptist Chapel.

LANCE, Henry: pastor, Berger Hall, Bromley-by-Bow (c 1865–70); trained first CIM candidates, later opposed JHT's principles, esp. Chinese dress.

LANDALE, Robert J.: MA Oxford Univ.; dep UK 1876, independent; joined CIM 1878; one of 'the eighteen'; pioneer in Hunan, Guizhou, Guangxi, Henan, Shanxi; associated with 'Camb. Seven'; 1881 m Mary Jones, step-dtr of F. F. Gough (qv); 19 Jan, 1882 widowed.

LANKESTER, Dr Herbert: consultant physician, 1892 CMS Medical Board, Hon. Secy; physician to all CMS members, 55 medical staff, 30 mission hospitals overseas.

LANSDELL, Dr Henry, DD, FRGS: traveller in Bokhara, Samarkand; attempts on Tibet supported by Am Bible Socy and JHT, with G. Parker (qv) foiled; may have reached Xinjiang, colportage with Parker.

LATOURETTE, Kenneth Scott: late Willis James and Sterling Prof. of Missions and Oriental History, Yale Univ.; author, *see* bibliography.

LAUGHTON, Richard Fredk, BMS: 1863 Shandong, Yantai.

LAY, George Tradescant: naturalist; 1836–39 agent for Bible Socy (B&FBS); 1840–42 interpreter, opium war; HBM consul, Canton, Fuzhou (Foochow), Amoy; co-founder of 'Medical Missionary Socy in China'; d 1845, Amoy.

LAY, Horatio: HBM consul, Fuzhou, Canton; 1866 first Inspector-General, Chinese Maritime Customs; negotiated 'Lay-Osborne fleet'; 1862 dismissed; succeeded by Robert Hart (qv).

LECHLER, Rudolf (1824–1908):: Basel Mission pioneer; 1847 Hong Kong Guangdong (Kwangtung) Hakkas, under Gutzlaff; with Hamberg (qv); 52 years in China, to 1899.

LEES, Jonathan: LMS; 1862 Tianjin, many years; 1869 pioneer visit to Shanxi; d 1902.

LEGGE, James, DD, LL D (1815–97): LMS; 1839–43 Anglo-Chinese College, Malacca; 1843–70 Anglo-Chinese College, Hong Kong; translator, Chinese classics; 1877–97, Prof. of Chinese, Oxford Univ.

LEISK, Mary Ann: aged 14 to Ningbo as protégé of M. A. Aldersey (qv); m W. A. Russell; d 1887.

LEWIS, William Garrett: Baptist minister, Westbourne Grove Ch., London; urged JHT to publish *China: Its Spiritual Need and Claims*.

LIGHT, Francis: captain of merchantman; 1786 occupied Penang Is., founded Georgetown.

LINCOLN, Pres. Abraham (1809–65): US anti-slavery congressman; 1861 President; 1863 Gettysburg speech; 'government of the people, by the people, for the people'; 1865 assassinated.

LINDSAY, Capt. Hugh Hamilton, RN: 1832, commanded ship *Lord Amherst*, on survey of China coast, Korea, with Gutzlaff (qv).

LINDSEY, Gen. Sir Alexander: 1865 host to JHT, Perth.

LISTER, Joseph, Lord, PC, OM, FRS; (1827–1912): father of asepsis and antisepsis, 1895–1900 Pres. Royal Socy.

LITTLE, Alicia Bewicke: author, *Li Hung-chang, His Life and Times*, 1903; wife of Archibald Little, British Legation official, Peking.

LIVINGSTONE, Dr David: (1813–73) Scotsman; Charing Cross Hospital 2 years; LMS Botswana; 1841–52 with Moffat, m. Mary Moffat; travelled through Bechuanaland, Kalahari Desert; 1849 found Lake Ngami; 1851 Zambesi River; 1852–56 major travels, Angola, W. coast; W-E to mouth of Zambesi 20 May, 1856; 1855 Victoria Falls; 1857 challenge at Cambridge; 1858–63 consul, led expedition Nyasaland; opened way for Church of Scotland and Universities' Mission; Tanganyika, Nyasaland (Malawi), Congo; 1859 Lake Malawi, 1866 search for source of Nile; 1871 met by H. M. Stanley (qv); 1871–73 Zambia; d 1 May, 1873; buried Westminster Abbey 18 April, 1874. Exposed slave trade; awakened Church to Africa and world mission.

LLOYD, E. R.: Anglican relative of Howards of Tottenham.

LOBSCHEID, Wilhelm: Rhenish (Barmen) Mission to China; Guangdong (Kwangtung); 1852 CES, resigned 1856; 1855 interpreter, Powhattan voyage to Japan.

LOCK, Sir Henry: 1860 private secretary to Lord Elgin (qv); with Parkes (qv) prisoner; historian of second opium war; 1889–95 Governor of the Cape, S Africa.

LOCKHART, William (1811–96): surgeon, FRCS; LMS; 1839 Macao; 1840 and 1843 Shanghai; 1840–41 Chusan with Gutzlaff, first British missionary Hong Kong; 1848 mobbed in 'Qingpu (Tsingpu) Outrage', Shanghai; 1861 first Prot. missionary in Peking.

LOMAX, Mr: Berger Starch Works executive; elder, Berger Hall, Bromley-by-Bow.

LORD, Edward Clifford, DD (1817–87): ABMU; 1847 first Am Baptist to Ningbo; 1853 NT Baptist version, with Dean and Goddard; 1863 independent Am Bapt. Mission, Ningbo; 1887 still there; appointed US consul by Abraham Lincoln; JHT's friend; d with wife, of cholera, 17 Sept, 1887.

LORD, Mrs: (1) d Jan 1860; (2) Jemima (Bausum) m 1861.

LOVE, Capt. John: laird of Knowes, father of Mrs J. L. Stevenson.

LOVITT, Arnold E: b 4 Feb 1869; London Hosp., Mildmay Mission Hosp; Shouyang Mission, 1897 Taiyuan, Shanxi, Schofield Memorial Hosp; killed 9 July 1900.

LOWE, Miss Clara M. S.: daughter of Lt-Gen. Sir Hudson Lowe (1769–1844) (Governor of St Helena, custodian of Napoleon Bonaparte); English tutor to Russian nobility; early friend of CIM; pension on acct. father.

LOWE, Lieut-Gen. Sir Hudson (1769–1844): 1814 knighted; 1815 Governor of St Helena, custodian of Napoleon; daughter, Clara M. S. Lowe.

LOWRIE, J. Walter: Am Presby Mission, Banding, Zhili; absent when Boxers struck; interpreter to allied force; saved 100s of Chinese from vengeance; with Dr E. H. Edwards (qv) found remains of Am Board, CIM and Chinese martyrs; arranged official burial and memorial honours.

LOWRIE, Reuben (Robert, in some sources): took brother's place; 1854 Shanghai.

LOWRIE, Walter: US senator, resigned to become Secy of Am Presby. Mission.

LOWRIE, Walter M. (William in some sources): son of senator; 1845 Am Presby.

Mission, Ningbo; 1847 drowned by pirates.

LUNDGREN, A. P.: b. Denmark 1870; to N Am 1887; dep USA 1891 Scand. China Alliance; 1898 full member CIM, Pingyao and Jiexiu, Shanxi; with Oberlin Am Board, Fenyang, killed by Boxers 15 Aug 1900.

LUSH, Lady: wife of Sir Robert (1807–81) (Lord Justice, CES Gen. Committee); attended Regent's Park Chapel; donor to CIM.

LYMAN, Henry: Am Board, Sumatra; 1834 killed with Samuel Munson by cannibal Bataks, Lake Toba.

MACARTNEY, Lord: 1793 embassy to Peking, failed.

MACARTNEY, Sir Samuel Halliday, MD (1833–1906): related to Lord Macartney, ambassador to China 1792–93; in Ever-Victorious Army under Burgevine; appointed by Li Hongzhang (qv), director Imperial Arsenal, Nanjing, 1865–75; 1877 Secy to Chinese Embassy, London, 30 years till Dec 1905, adviser to all Chinese ambassadors; 2nd degree mandarin, with Peacock's Feather; 1885 KCMG; m a Chinese; son, consul-general Kashgar.

MACGOWAN, Dr D. J.: Am Baptist physician; 1843 Ningbo.

MACKAY, George Leslie (1844–1901): first Canadian Presby. missionary to China; 1872 N Taiwan; 60 churches at his death; founded Taiwan Theol. College; 1894 Moderator of Can. Presby. Church.

MACKENZIE, Francis A.: philanthropist of Dingwall, Scotland; donor to CIM..

MACKENZIE, Dr John Kenneth; LMS 1875, Hankou, Tianjin; saved life of viceroy Li Hongzhang's wife; 1880 built hospital, trained doctors, sponsored by Li; 1882 to UK; d 1888; author, A History of the Nineteenth Century translated by T. Richard sold 1 million.

MACKINTOSH, Katherine B: CIM dep UK 22 Oct 1884; one of the Seventy; Guangxin River pioneer, Yushan; 29 Oct 1892 m H. N. Lachlan (qv); mother of H. B. (Anuei) Lachlan who m D. de B. Robertson, CIM architect.

MACKINTOSH, William: with J. Fraser (qv) initiator of FES; missionary to Cairo.

MACPHERSON, Miss Annie: mid-19th century schoolteacher, social reformer, evangelist; 'ragged schools'; organised emigration to Canada; firm friend of CIM; introduced W. D. Rudland (qv).

MAGEE, Dean of Cork, Dublin: Bishop of Peterborough; Archbishop of York; d 5 May 1891.

MAGELLAN, Ferdinand (c 1480–1521): Portuguese explorer; served Spain; via Cape Horn to Leyte, Philippines; killed, but expedition completed first voyage round world.

MAGRATH, Miss: CES missionary; 1857 arrived in Shanghai, Ningbo; soon independent, Hong Kong.

MAIN, Dr Duncan: 1881 CMS Hangzhou; developed a large hospital and medical school; 1892 leprosarium.

MANCHESTER, M. Etta: b 11 Nov 1871; dep US 12 Aug 1895; 1897 Qü Xian, Zhejiang; killed 24 July 1900.

MARA, John: United Meth. Free Ch.; trained by JHT; 1865 Ningbo.

MARGARY, Augustus Raymond: b1845; HBM consul Yantai; 1874 as interpreter to Col. Browne's Burma-Yunnan expedition, dep Shanghai 22 Aug, 1874, via Hunan, arr Bhamo 17 Jan, 1875; murdered 21 Feb at Manyün.

MARJORIBANKS, Charles, MP: ex-Chief, East India Company, Canton.

MARKHAM, Sir Clements R. (1830–1916): explorer, Arctic, S Am., Ethiopia, India; Secy and Pres. RGS (1893–1905).

MARKWICK, J.: CIM dep UK 7 March, 1878; Shaanxi famine relief rejected, but 1880 eyesight failed from privations.

MARSHALL, Thomas D.: minister, Bryanston Hall, Portman Square.

MARSHMAN, Joshua (1768–1837): 1799 with Carey, Serampore; 1811 completed Chinese NT; 1822–23 OT.

MARTIN, Samuel N. D.: older brother of W. A. P. Martin (qv); Am Presby. Mission; 1850 Ningbo, i/c boys' school founded by R. Q. Way (qv).

MARTIN, William Alexander Parsons, DD, LL D, (1827–1916): Am Presby. Mission; educationalist; 1850–60 Ningbo; 1862 Peking; 1869 president, Tongwen Imperial College; 57 years in China; book on Christian evidences had huge circulation, China, Japan.

MARTYN, Henry (1781–1812): 1801 Senior Wrangler, Fellow of St John's, Camb.; 1806 Calcutta; 1810 completed Hindustani (Urdu) NT; 1811 Shiraz, Persia; 1815–16 Martyn's Persian NT published.

MATEER, Calvin Wilson, DD (1836–1908): Am Presby.; 1862 Dengzhou, later Yantai, Shandong; founded Shandong Christian Univ.; author, *Mandarin Lessons*; opposed Nevius' methods; chairman, translation committee, Union Mandarin Version of Bible with Baller, Blodget, Nevius *et al.*

MATHER, Percy Cunningham: b 9 Dec 1882; applied to CIM Mar 10, 1908; CIM dep UK 10 Sept 1910; 1911 Anhui, 1914 to Xinjiang; 5 June 1914 joined G. Hunter (qv); 1928 to Kashgar; 1932 six of 'Two Hundred' arr Urumqi; Muslim rebellion Mather d typhus, 24 May 1933; Dr Emil Fishbacher 27 May (*see* Bibliography).

MATHESON, Donald: merchant partner, Jardine, Matheson; 1837 Hong Kong; converted, resigned 1849 over opium traffic; active in Presby. Missions; 1892 chairman, Socy for the Suppression of the Opium Trade.

MATHESON, James: heir to baronetcy; merchant ship-owner, partner of Jardine (qv); Member of Parliament.

MATHIESON, James E.: gentleman-evangelist in 19th century revivals; active in anti-opium campaign (*see* Maxwell).

MARX, Karl (1818–83): German Jew; Univs. of Bonn, Berlin, law, philosophy, history, economics; 1848 *Communist Manifesto*; 1849 lived 28 Dean St, Soho; 1864 helped found Comm. International; 1867–83, *Das Kapital.*

MAXWELL, James L. MD: b 1836; English Presby. Mission; 1863 Amoy; 1865, pioneer, Takao, Taiwan; 1885 founder, Medical Missionary Association (London); 1888 co-founder with B. Broomhall (qv), 'Christian Union for the Severance of the Connection of the British Empire with the Opium Traffic'.

McAULAY, Alexander (1818–90): Wesleyan minister, missionary; 1876 Pres. Wesleyan Conf., Gen. Secy Wes. Home Miss.; CIM Referee.

McCARTEE, Divie Bethune, MD (1820–1900): Am Presby.; 1844 Ningbo 28 years; 1845 organised first Prot. church on Chinese soil; 1851 extended work beyond treaty ports; 1853 m Juana Knight, first single Presby. woman to China; adopted Yu Meiying, orphaned daughter of pastor as own daughter, first Chinese woman doctor educated abroad, returned as missionary to China; 1861 met Taiping leaders, Nanjing, negotiated protection Am citizens, Chinese Christians; Dec 1861–April 1862 earliest Prot. miss. in Japan; his tract translated into Japanese was first Prot. lit. in Japan; 1862–5 Shandong, Yantai; 1864 Ningbo again; 1872 Japan with Chinese envoy negotiated release of coolie prisoners on *Maria Luz* (Macao-Peru), received gold medal; 1872–77 Prof. of law and natural science; Tokyo Univ;1877 secy. foreign affairs to Chinese legation, Japan; 1880 USA; 1889 Presby. Miss. again, Tokyo; good scholar in Greek, Chinese, Japanese; 1899 invalided USA; d 17 July, 1900 (*Chinese Recorder* 1902 Vol 33 p 497f).

McCARTHY, Frank: John's eldest; CIM dep UK 31 Dec 1886; 1 March 1887 Chefoo School staff under H. L. Norris (qv), promoted morale, discipline; 20 Oct 1893 m E. Webb; March 1895–1930, Principal, 'did more than any for the schools'.

McCARTHY, John: Dublin, member H. G. Guinness (qv) training class; Feb 1866 influenced by JHT; 1866 CIM; 1867 Hangzhou; 1877 Jan–Aug Hankou to Bhamo, Burma on foot; 1886–91 Supt. Jiangxi, Jiangsu (Guangxin River and Yangzhou language school); influential speaker UK, USA.

McCARTHY, William L.: Dublin, John's brother; with wife dep UK 7 March, 1879; died heatstroke; widow married J. F. Broumton, Jan 1881.

McCLATCHIE, Thomas: CMS; 1845 Shanghai with George Smith (qv).

McCONNELL, George: N Ireland, Dundee; CIM dep UK Jan 1890; Hejin, Shanxi; m Bella Dec 1894, son Kenneth; all killed by Boxers 16 July 1900.

McCURRACH, Wm Adam: b Aberdeen 30 Mar 1869; BMS, dep UK autumn 1896; wife Clara; to Xinzhou, Shanxi; 29 June 1900 cornered by Boxers; 9 Aug 1900, 8 BMS killed.

McGILVARY, Dr Daniel: 1858 arr Thailand, Am Presby. Mission; 1860 Chiang Mai, began medical work, schools.

McILVAINE, Jasper S.: Am Presby; 1868 arr China; 1872 Jinan, Shandong; 1877 famine relief; 1878 Jincheng, Shanxi, famine relief.

McINTYRE, J.: United Presby. Ch. of Scotland; 1874 forced back before reaching Kaifeng.

McKEE, Stewart and Kate: CIM, 10 years Datong, Shanxi; 24 June 1900 attacked by Boxers, wounded, fled to *yamen*; 27 June son born; 12 July killed; child Alice hid, killed 13 July.

McLEAN, Jane: Inverness 'Bible-woman'; 1866 Wm Pennefather's training school; CIM, *Lammermuir*; Hangzhou; 1867 engaged to

John Sell (qv); 1868 resigned, worked for LMS Shanghai.

McLEAN, Margaret: twin of Jane; 1867 CIM, Hangzhou, 1868 resigned, worked for LMS Shanghai.

MEADOWS, Elizabeth (née Rose): friend of Martha Meadows; d; 1866 CIM, *Lammermuir*, Ningbo, m Jas Meadows (qv); 1869 Nanjing, Anqing, riot.

MEADOWS, James J. (1835–1914): JHT's first recruit to Ningbo Mission, 1862, and CIM; wife Martha d Ningbo 1863; 1866 m Eliz. Rose (qv); 1868 began pioneering; 1869 Anqing.

MEADOWS, Thomas Taylor: heroic interpreter; HBM vice-consul, Ningbo; certified JHT's marriage.

MEARS, Mr: works manager, Berger's Starch Works, Bromley-by-Bow; helped CIM crating, freighting.

MEDHURST, Sir Walter Henry: son of W. H. Medhurst, DD; HBM consul, and ambassador, Peking.

MEDHURST, Walter Henry, DD (1796–1857): LMS printer; 1817–20 Malacca; 1820–21 Penang; 1822–43 Batavia, Java; 1826 toured Chinese settlements on Java coast; 1835 voyage of *Huron* up China coast; 1843 Shanghai, interpreter adviser to Br. consul G. Balfour (qv); 1845 inland journey in disguise; 1848 victim of 'Qingpu (Tsingpu) Outrage', Shanghai; translator, Delegates' Committee, 1852 Chinese Bible; doyen of Br. Community.

MEE, John: 1858–61 Anglican Secretary of B&FBS, with S. B. Bergne.

MELBOURNE, Viscount: Prime Minister, 1835–41; chief adviser to Queen Victoria.

MENGKU KHAN: Mongol ruler, grandson of Genghis Khan; tolerant of all religions, attended Nestorian worship.MERITENS, Baron de: with Abbé Delamarre (qv) interpreter to Baron Gros (qv) 1860.

MERITENS, Baron de: with Abbé Delamarre (qv) interpreter to Baron Gros (qv) 1860.

MERRY, Joseph: Cambridgeshire farmer; brother-in-law of Annie Macpherson (qv).

MESNY, William (1842–1919): Jersey, Channel Is.; arr China 1860; officer in Chinese army suppressed Miao rebellion; high rank in command Guiyang arsenal; with Gill (qv) travelled Chengdu, Batang, Dali, Bhamo; 1896 equiv. Brevet-Lt. Gen. under Zuo Zongtang in campaign to suppress Yakub Beg (qv), Kashgar.

MEYER, F. B. (1847–1929): Baptist minister York; Leicester; Regents Park Chapel, Lond.; Christ Church, Westminster; profilic writer; Keswick Council.

MEZZABARBA: 1720 papal legate after Mgr de Tournon; concessions on Chinese rites repudiated by Rome.

MILL, John Stuart (1806–73): Engl. philosopher; author, *On Liberty*; *The Subjection of Women*; *Principles of Political Economy*.

MILNE, John: Scottish divine; organiser; Perth Conf.; friend of Wm Burns, JHT.

MILNE, William, DD (1785–1822): 1813 Macao; 1815–22 Malacca; 1818 Anglo-Chinese College, Malacca; Hon. DD Glasgow; baptised Liang A-fa (qv); 1822 completed OT translation with R. Morrison.

MILNE, William C.: son of William and Rachel Milne; 1842 Chusan Is.; 1842–43 Ningbo; 1846 Shanghai; 1857 travelling secy, Chinese Evang. Socy.

MOFFAT, Robert (1795–1883): LMS; 1817 S Africa, 50 years; close friend of Matabele chief; 'apostle of Bechuanaland'; initiated Botswana Church; daughter married D. Livingstone.

MONTE CORVINO, John of: first RC priest to China; dep 1289, arr 1294; 1307 archbishop of Cambalac (Peking); d *c* 1328–33.

MOODY, Dwight Lyman (1837–99): 19th century's greatest evangelist; 1873–75 first Br. mission; 1882 Cambridge Univ. mission stimulated 'Camb. Seven'; 1886 first Northfield student conference gave impetus to Student Volunteer Movement.

MOORE, C. G.: CIM dep UK 24 Jan, 1878; UK staff.

MORGAN, Richard Cope (1827–1908): editor, *The Revival* (*The Christian*); chairman, Marshall, Morgan & Scott; co-founder, Foreign Evangelist Socy.

MORRILL, Mary S.: b 24 Mar 1864; Am Board, Baoding, Zhili; killed 1 July 1900; her calmness before execution impressed Feng Yüxiang (qv), future army marshal.

MORRISON, John Robert (1814–43): son of R. Morrison; aged 16 official translator, East India Co.; Canton; 1842 interpreter-negotiator to Sir H. Pottinger, Treaty of Nanking; 1843 Chinese Secy to Gov. of Hong Kong; chairman, first LMS and General Missions Conferences, Hong Kong.

MORRISON, Robert, DD, FRS (1782–1834); LMS; 1807 Macao, Canton; 1813 completed Chinese NT; 1814 first convert; 1816 interpreter-negotiator to Lord Amherst embassy; 1817 Hon. DD Glas.; 1819 completed OT with Milne (qv); 1822 completed Chinese dictionary; 1824 FRS etc.; 1834 interpreter to Lord Napier; d, Aug 1

MORSE, Hosea Ballou: Imperial Chinese Customs, Taiwan; commissioner Hankou; historian, author (*see* Bibliography).

MOSELEY, William, LL D: Congregational Minister; 1798 found in British Museum MS of RC Chinese translation of NT books; urged translation of whole NT; introduced R. Morrison to LMS and to Dr Bogue (qv).

MOTT, John Raleigh (1865–1955): b Iowa, USA; with 100 others signed first Student Volunteer Movement declaration, after being 'won for the cause of Christ at Cornell University by J. E. Kynaston Studd'; and influenced by Robert Wilder (qv), 1883; 1895 launched World Student Christian

Federation; Hon. Secy, later chairman; 1910 chairman, Edinburgh World Missionary Conference; widely travelled.

MOULE, Arthur Evans: CMS; 1861 Ningbo; 1876 Hangzhou (Hangchow); archdeacon.

MOULE, George Evans: CMS; 1858 Ningbo; 1864 Hangzhou (Hangchow); 1880 Bishop in mid-China.

MOULE, Henry: Anglican minister; father of Handley, Bishop of Durham; George (qv) Bishop in mid-China; and Arthur (qv) archdeacon, Ningbo.

MOULY, Mgr Joseph Martial, Lazarist: 1841 vicar-apostolic, Mongolia etc.; sent Abbé Huc and Gabet on Tibet journey; 1853 deported; 1856 vicar-apostolic N Zhili (Chihli) (Peking); 1861 obtained territorial concessions for RC Church.

MTESA, King of Uganda: visited by Speke, Grant, Stanley; invited CMS; sent envoys to Queen Victoria; d 10 Oct 1884.

MUIRHEAD, William, DD (1822–1900): LMS; evangelist, renowned preacher, translator; 1846–90 (53 years) at Shanghai; 1848 victim of 'Qingpu (Tsingpu) Outrage', Shanghai.

MÜLLER, George (1805–98): German-born; married sister of A. N. Groves (qv); 1832 read biography of A. H. Francke; 1835 founded Orphan Homes, Bristol, 2,000 children, financed 'by faith in God'.

MURRAY Sisters, Cecilia, Marianne: CIM dep UK 22 Oct, 1884; in charge Yangzhou language school.

MURRAY, Jessie: CIM dep UK Oct 1876; d 22 Dec, 1891.

MUNSON, Samuel: Am Board; 1834 with H. Lyman to Lake Toba Bataks, Sumatra; 1834 'killed and eaten'.

MWANGA, son of Mtesa: king, brutally persecuted Christians; had Bishop Hannington killed 29 Oct, 1885.

NAPIER, Lord: 1834, William IV's envoy to China; Chief Supt of Br. Trade; d 1834.

NAPOLEON I, Bonaparte (1769–1821): 1799 proclaimed himself First Consul of France; 1804 Emperor; 1805 virtually dictator of Europe; 1814 abdicated, sent to Elba; 1815 escaped; 18 June 1815 Waterloo; exiled to St Helena.

NAPOLEON III, Louis (1808–73): 1848 made Pres. of French Republic; 1852 *coup d'etat*, made Emperor; 1870 Franco-Prussian war wrecked second empire; died at Chislehurst, England.

NATHAN, Frances, Edith and May Rose: CIM; F. E. dep UK Sept 1894, M. R. dep Jan 1899; Daning, Shanxi; 12 July 1900 fled to hills with M. Heaysman (qv); killed 13 Aug 1900 by Boxers.NEILL, Stephen C.: b 31 Dec. 1899; Fellow of Trinity College, Cambridge; CMS missionary in S India; Anglican Bishop of Tinnevelly (120,000 members); co-negotiator of Church of South India; professor of missions.

NEATBY, Thomas, FRCS: boyhood friend of JHT;

assistant to James Taylor and Robert Hardey (qv); surgeon, St Bartholomew's hospital; biblical expositor.

NELSON, R., DD: Am Prot. Episc. Church; arr. Shanghai 1851;1870 translator, Shanghai colloquial NT; co-chairman Gen. Miss. Conf., Shanghai 1877.

NESTORIUS: bishop of Constantinople until Council of Ephesus, AD 431; d 451; Nestorianism extended to Syria, Persia, India; AD 635 to China (*see* Alopen); Nestorian monument erected 781, discovered 1625 near Xi'an (Sian).

NEUMANN, Robert: Berlin Miss. Socy for China; colleague of Gutzlaff; 1850–54 Hong Kong, Guangdong (Kwangtung).NEVIUS, John Livingston (1832–93): Am Presby. Mission; 1854 Ningbo; 1859 Hangzhou (Hangchow); 1860 Japan; 1861 Shandong (Shantung); Bible translator, author; 1890 Korea, exponent of 'indigenous church' policy.

NEWTON, B. W.: dominant leader of Plymouth Brethren, at first with Darby (qv); 'Bethesda controversy' was over views propounded by Newton.

NICOL, Lewis: blacksmith, Arbroath, Aberdeen; 1865 CIM candidate; 1866 m Eliza Calder (qv), *Lammermuir*, Hangzhou; 1867 Xiaoshan outrage; 1868 dismissed.

NICOLL, George: CIM, one of 'the eighteen', dep UK 4 Aug, 1875; Dec 1876 Yichang riot; May 1877 Sichuan, circled Daliangshan; 1879 m M. A. Howland; 1880–81 Chongqing; ill, Australia, N. Zealand.

NIGHTINGALE, Florence (1820–1910): pioneered hospital reforms; 1854–56 Crimea, 'lady with the lamp'.

NOEL, Rev and Hon. Baptist: Anglican clergyman; 1848 became Baptist; revivalist, 21 Sept 1859 drew 20,000 at Armagh.

NOMMENSON, Ludwig Ingwer: Rhenish (Barmen) Mission; 1862 pioneer of Bataks, Sumatra, after Lyman and Munson were martyred.

NORMAN, Henry V.: SPG; arr Yantai 1891; ordained 1892; 1897 with Chas Robinson (qv) to Yongqing, Zhili; 1 June 1900 escaped from Boxers, killed June 2.

NORRIS, Herbert L.: CIM dep UK 28 Jan 1885; headmaster Chefoo School; d rabies 27 Sept 1888.

NORRIS, Sir William: Chief Justice, High Court, Straits Settlements; friend of Dyers (qv).

NORTH, Brownlow: b 1809, grandson of bishop successively of Lichfield, Worcester, Winchester, whose brother, Lord North, was Prime Minister to George III; roué, converted aged 45, studied Bible and prayed for two months, then began as evangelist; Free Church of Scotland; drew thousands.

NOTMAN, Jean: recruit sent by JHT to Ningbo, 1864; assistant to Mrs Bausum (qv).

OLIPHANT, Laurance, MP (1829–88): novelist, traveler, secy RGS.

OLYPHANT, D. W. C.: Am Presby. merchant

ship-owner, partner of C. W. King; 1826 Canton, donated press and office for *Chinese Repository*; donated 51 trans-Pacific passages for missionaries; d 1851.

OGREN, P. Alfred: wife Olivia, son Samuel; Alfred b 1874, Jonkoping, Sweden; full members of CIM; 1893 Shanxi; 1899 Yongning; 1900 after terrible suffering Alfred d 15 Oct; baby born Dec 6; Olivia, Samuel, baby arr Hankou 16 Feb 1901.

ORR EWING, Archibald: b 1 Aug 1857; 4th of 7 brothers, heirs to uncle's fortune, nearly £500,000; litigation settled by law lords July 1885; 1880–81 toured China coast; 1882 Moody Mission in Glasgow, dedication to Christ; invited J. McCarthy; 6 April 1884 committed to China, 1885 with W. B. Sloan at Keswick commitment confirmed; CIM dep UK 21 April 1886; 17 July 1886 officially joined CIM after Shanxi conference; 4 years Shanxi; walked 50 miles daily on trek; 6 May 1890 m Mary Scott (of Morgan and Scott); 1891 Supt. Jiangxi 20 years; donor of Wusong Rd HO and Chefoo schools.

OSBORNE, Capt. Sherard: 1861 engaged by H. N. Lay (qv), commanded 'Lay-Osborne fleet' to China debacle.

PALMERSTON, Viscount (1784–1865): Tory Whig statesman, 1808–65; 1830–51 periodically Foreign Secy; 1855, 1859–65 Prime Minister.

PARKER, George: CIM, one of 'the eighteen', dep UK 5 April, 1876; Nov 8 with Easton (qv) dep Wuhan to Shaanxi, Gansu; Dec 20–24 Xi'an; 20 Jan, 1877 Lanzhou; 1878 forced out of Xi'an; worked Han River by boat; 1879 Chongqing, engaged to Shao Mianzi (qv); Sept–Oct, Gansu with Easton; 25 Feb, 1880 m Shao Mianzi; to Hanzhong and Gansu; 1882 Tibet border; 1887–89 Xinjiang with Lansdell (qv); 1905 G. Hunter of Urumqi reported evidence of Parker-Lansdell colportage found; 1891 doyen of CIM.

PARKER, H. M.: Am Prot. Episc; 1861 Shandong, Yantai; Oct killed with J. L. Holmes (qv).

PARKER, Dr John: brother of Dr Wm Parker; 1863 Ningbo, independent; 1865 United Presby. Ch. of Scotland, Ningbo.

PARKER, Dr Peter, MD: (1804–88); Am Board (ABCFM); 1834 Canton; first medical missionary in China (not first western physician); 1835 Ophthalmic Hospital; 1838 formed 'Medical Missionary Socy in China'; 1843–44, semi-skilled interpreter-negotiator for US treaty; 1850 General Hosp, Canton; several times US *chargé d'affaires* and minister.

PARKER, Dr William: CES 1854–61; Shanghai, Ningbo; wife (1) d 26 Aug 1859 of cholera; m wife (2) UK 1861; 1862 to Ningbo; d injuries 1 Feb 1863.   Parts II, III, IV, V.

PARKER, H. M.: Am Episc.; Shangdong (Shantung); 1861 martyred, Yantai (Chefoo).

PARKER, Mrs Wm: (1) d 26 Aug 1859 of cholera; (2) m 1861; 1862 with Dr Parker (qv) to Ningbo; widowed 1 Feb 1863.

PARKES, Sir Harry Smith (1828–85): cousin m C. Gutzlaff (qv); 1841 sister m Wm Lockhart (qv); 1841 Macao; 1842 asst. to J. R. Morrison (qv.); 21 July, 1842 with Sir H. Pottinger at assault on Zhenjiang, *aet.* 14; present at signing of Treaty of Nanking; 1842–43 Zhoushan (Chusan) Is. with Gutzlaff; 1843 Canton consular asst.; 1845 Fuzhou, interpreter with R. Alcock (qv); August 1846 Shanghai with Alcock; 1852–54 Canton; 1853 author Parl. Paper No. 263 on *Emigration* (Coolie Trade); concluded first Br. treaty with Siam for Sir John Bowring; 1856 vice-consul Canton; Oct, *Arrow* incident; 1858–60 Br. Commissioner, Canton; 1861 Hankou Feb–Apr with Adm. Sir Jas Hope; 20 May, 1862 KCB knighthood *aet.* 34; intimate friend of Col. Gordon; strongly opposed by *Li* Hongzhang (qv); 1865 Br. minister, Japan, 'won the most signal victory Br. diplomacy ever gained in the Far East' (Dickens, F. V.: *Life of Parkes*, II.44); 1871 UK; 1872–79 Japan; 1879–82 UK received KCMG, to Japan; 1883 Br. minister Peking, after Sir Thos Wade; 1883 treaty with Korea opened ports; d 22 March, 1885 'Peking fever'. (*Dicty of Nat. Biog.* Vol XV; H. B. Morse.)

PARNELL, J. V. (*see* CONGLETON)

PARROT, A. G.: CIM dep UK 29 Oct, 1878; pioneered western hill cities of Shanxi; JHT's 'corresponding secretary'; Nov 1881 Wuchang Conference call for 'the Seventy'; 21 Dec, 1882 m Annie M. Hayward.

PARRY, Dr Herbert: CIM; dep UK 24 Sept, 1884; Chengdu, Sichuan.

PARTRIDGE, Mary L: b New York 27 Mar 1865; Oberlin College, Am Board; arr China Oct 1893; Taigu, Shanxi; killed 31 July 1900.

PASTEUR, Louis (1822–95): French scientist; identified and designed measures against bacteria, applied by Lister (qv); developed immunisation against rabies, etc.

PATON, John Gibson (1824–1907): 1847–56 Glasgow city missionary; 1858 Tanna, New Hebrides; 1864 Moderator of Reformed Presby. Church; 1866–81 Aniwa, New Hebrides, S Pacific.

PATTESON, John Coleridge: 1861 1st bishop of Melanesia; 1871, killed.

PEARCY, George: Am Southern Bapt., Shanghai; cholera at Shanghai, nursed by JHT.

PEARSE, Edward S: CIM, one of 'the eighteen' dep UK 26 Jan 1876, m 18 Dec 1877 L. E. Goodman; 1879 Anhui pioneer; ubiquitous, 1886–87 Shaanxi, Sichuan; supt. Guangxin R iver region.

PEARSE, George: London stockbroker; CES foreign secy; co-founder Foreign Evangelist Socy; friend and adviser of JHT's; later missionary to N Africa, initiated N Africa Mission.

PEAT, Wm Graham: CIM, dep UK 1 Dec 1887, one of the Hundred; Pingyao, Shanxi; Mar 1891 m Helen Mackenzie; Xi Xian; 21 July 1900 fled to hill caves with children

Margretta, Mary, and Edith Dobson (qv) and 'Georgie' Hurn (qv); all killed 30 August.

PENNEFATHER, William (1816–73): vicar, Christ Church, Barnet; 1864 St Jude's Mildmay, N London; convener, Barnet and Mildmay conferences; deaconess school; hymn writer, friend of JHT.

PERBOYRE: Lazarist priest; 1836 Fujian, Wuchang; 1840 executed; 1846 his sister arr Hong Kong, Sisters of St Paul.

PETRIE, David: 1866 Shanghai; Jardine, Matheson agent; friendly to CIM.

PERRY, Commodore: 1853–54 Am treaty with Japan.

PIERCY, George: 1850 to China at own expense; 1851 Canton; 1853 adopted by Wesleyan Meth. Miss. Socy; joined by Josiah Cox (qv).

PIERSON, A. T., DD: New York evangelist, Bible teacher; friend of JHT; 1886 with Moody held student conference for SVM (newly founded); 1888 at Centenary Conf. of Prot. Missions, Lond.; 1896 chief speaker, SVMU Liverpool Conference.

PIGOTT, Thomas W.: CIM; Shanxi pioneer; m Kemp 16 July 1883; resigned.

PILKINGTON, George Lawrence: b 1864; converted through CICCU; 1887–88 offered to CIM; persuaded by his father to delay two years; 1889 to CMS; Master of Pembroke said: 'There is a Hannington or a Gordon in him'; to Uganda; shot 11 Dec 1897 aged 33, in mutiny.

PITKIN, Horace Tracy: b Philadelphia 28 Oct 1869; graduate, Yale 1892; Union Seminary 1896; m Oct 1896; to China Am Board Nov 1896; wife and son Horace to USA 1900; HTP killed by Boxers 1 July 1900.

PILLANS-SMITH, Helen: from 1866 longtime friend of CIM.

POLHILL-TURNER, Arthur Twistleton: 3rd son, Capt. F. C. Polhill, 6th Dragoon Guards; MP, JP, High Sheriff, Bedfordshire; 'Camb. Seven'; CIM dep UK 5 Feb, 1885; Hanzhong; Bazhong, Sichuan; ordained Anglican.

POLHILL-TURNER, Cecil Henry: 2nd son Capt. F. C. Polhill (see above); dep UK 5 Feb, 1885; Hanzhong; Xining, Gansu; Songpan, Sichuan; Darjeeling; Kangding, Sichuan.

POLLARD, Samuel: b 20 April 1864, Methodist, Bible Christian Church, Cornwall; 1885 with F. J. Dymond offered, 27 Jan 1887 dep UK, first associate mission of CIM; shipwrecked in Yangzi gorges; Chaotong, Yunnan, 1888; 1905 to minority peoples; devised Pollard script for Miao; d 15 Sept 1915.

POLO, Marco (1245–1324): son of Nicolo; 1275 Peking, served Kublai Khan; aet. 30 gov. of Yangzliou; official journeys of SW China, Burma, Indo-China, India; 1292 with Nicolo and Matteo escorted royal princess to Persia; to Venice; 1298 in war with Genoa, imprisoned, dictated travels.

POLO, Nicolo and Matteo: 1260 to China; 1267 welcomed by Kublai Khan; 1269 arr Venice with Khan's request to Pope for 100 wise men; 1271 to China with Marco (qv).

POLWARTH, Baron Walter Hugh Hepburne Scott (1838–): friend of JHT and CIM.

POTT, F. L. Hawks, DD: Am Prot. Episc.; president, St John's Univ., Shanghai; historian of Shanghai.

POTTER, Miss: CIM recruit, met JHT at Brighton, 25 June 1865.

POTTIER, Francois: founder 1756, West China mission of Socy des Missions étrangéres de Paris.

POTTINGER, Sir Henry: 1841 HBM plenipotentiary, Supt. of Trade, succeeded Capt. Charles Elliot; concluded first opium war; 1842 'diplomatic honeymoon' with Qi Ying (qv), negotiated Nanking Treaty.

PRESTON, John: Wesleyan Meth. Miss. Socy; 1855 Canton.

PRUEN, Dr W. L., LRCP, LRCS Edin.: CIM; dep UK 30 Nov, 1879; Chefoo, Chongqing, Chengdu; Guiyang; m K. Hughes; Shanxi; author, *The Provinces of Western China*.

PUGET, Col. John Henry: brother of Dowager Lady Radstock (qv); generous donor to CIM.

QUARTERMAN, J. W.: Am Presby.; 1847–57 Ningbo; smallpox, nursed by JHT; d 1857.

RADCLIFFE, Reginald: leading UK evangelist; 1860 initiated theatre services, Lond.; the first in Victoria Theatre, Lambeth, denounced as travesty of religious worship, even illegal; 24 Feb, 1860 defended in House of Lords 3-hour speech by Lord Shaftesbury describing the poor and common folk who flocked to hear Radcliffe; leading part in evangelical revival following 1858 US revival; devoted last active years to advocating worldwide evangelism, 'Consecration and the Evangelisation of the World ought to go together'; 1886–87 secured use of Keswick Convention tents for missionary use, JHT as speaker, 1887; travelled and preached in USA and Canada with JIIT, 1888.

RADSTOCK, Dowager Lady: mother of Lord Radstock (qv), Lady Beauchamp (qv), Hon. Miss Waldegrave (qv); Welbeck St Brethren; friend and supporter of JHT.

RADSTOCK, Lord, Hon. Granville Augustus Wm Waldegrave (1833–1913): 3rd Baron; converted at Crimean War; raised, commanded W. Middlesex Rifles for 6 years; evangelical Anglican evangelist in aristocratic Russian, E European society; closely associated with Brethren; friend of JHT and CIM; 1872 CIM Referee.

RAFFLES, Sir Thomas Stamford (1781–1826): 1805 Penang; 1811–16 lieut-gov., Java; 1817 knighted; 1817 *et seq* gov. of Sumatra; 1819 founded Singapore; 1820–24 gov. Singapore and Bencoolen, Sumatra.

RANDLE, Horace A.: CIM; one of 'the eighteen' dep UK 5 April, 1876, Jiangxi pioneer; qualified MD (USA).

RANKIN, Henry V.: Am Presby.; 1847 Ningbo; co-translator of Ningbo vernacular NT.

RANYARD, Mrs, (née Ellen White): means of conversion of M. S. Alexander, Prof. of Hebrew, Arabic, Bishop of Jerusalem; founded London Bible Women's Assn. and Ranyard Mission.

RAO, O. Paris Prot. Mission; 1861 Yantai, Tianjin.

REED, Henry: Tasmanian gentleman-evangelist, influenced JHT *aet.* 14; donated £20,000 to build Mildmay Conference hall; £5,000 to Wm Booth personal endowment.

REED, Hon. W. B.: US ambassador, Peking, 1858–60.

REID, Henry: 1867 CIM, Hangzhou; 1868 Yangzhou riot, eye injury; 1873 retired.

RENAUT, Bessie Campbell: b 1871; BMS, Xinzhou, Shanxi, with Dixons (qv); killed 9 Aug 1900.

RICCI, Matteo/Matthew (1552–1610): Socy of Jesus; 1582 Macao; 1585–89 Zhaoqing, Zhaozhou (Chaoch'ing, Chaochow); 1601 Peking; by 1605 had converts at Court and Hanlin Academy, 200 neophytes; enjoyed confidence of Kang Xi (Kaang Hsi); policies repudiated by papacy.

RICE, Hattie Jane: b USA 1858, 1888 heard JHT at Northfield, offered, sailed 1892; Lucheng, Shanxi with M. Huston (qv), E. J. Coopers (qv), 6 July 1900 Saunders (qv); Cooper party dep Lucheng, July 13 all flogged, HJR killed.

RICHARD, Timothy (1845–1919): missionary educationalist; 1859 convert of Welsh revival; offered services to JHT, referred to BMS; 1870 Shandong; 1876–79 famine relief, founded Univ. of Shanxi, Taiyuan and Christian Literature Socy; his policies akin to the techniques of Ricci (qv); adviser to emperor and Chinese govt; received two of the highest honours of the empire.

RICHTOFEN, Baron Ferdinand von (1833–1905): geologist, geographer, explorer; 1860; first East Asian expedition; 1875 Prof. of Geology, Bonn; 1882 Leipsig; 1896 Berlin; author, China, 5 vols and atlas; 1872 dep Chengdu to reach Dali, Kunming via Xichang (Ningyuan); forced back by troops on Da Xiang Ling; showed Ranchang valley to be Marco Polo's 'Caindu'.

RIDGEWAY, Joseph: CMS Assoc. Secy; editor CMS Intelligencer, Record, Gleaner; 1869 opposed C. R. Alford's proposed CMS Mission for China; d 1871.

RIDLEY, H. French: CIM, dep UK 2 Oct 1890; 1892 Guihuacheng; Xining, Gansu; 1895 Muslim rebellion, Xining siege till April 1896; Ridleys (untrained) did relief, medical work throughout, till Jan 1897.

RILEY, J. H.: dep UK 2 May, 1878; Sichuan pioneer, Chongqing, Chengdu; urged by G. Nicoll to take gospel to Nosu, Daliangshan; Oct 1882 m (1) J. Kidd (qv) d1886; (2) F. Stroud (qv) on own deathbed, d 19 April, 1886.

RIPON, Bishop of: (*see* Bickersteth).

RIRIE, Benjamin: CIM, 1887 arr China; 1889 Leshan, Sichuan; 1895 Sichuan riots; model evangelistic missionary.

ROBERTS, Issacher Jacocks (not RJR as in some sources): Am Bapt; 1833–67 Canton, Shanghai, 1837 Canton, taught Hong Xiu-quan (qv), Taiping leader; 1842 first missionary in Hong Kong, with J. L. Shuck.

ROBINSON, Charles: SPG; 1897 to Yongqing, Zhili; 1 June 1900 killed by Boxers.

ROBINSON, John: b 1 Sept 1875; BA Lond. Univ. 1896; YMCA secy; became Baptist; with T. W. Pigott (qv) to Taiyuan, Shanxi; Shouyang; 29 June–2 July, 1900 hiding in hills; in chains to Taiyuan, killed July 9.

ROSSIER, Fanny: Swiss; CIM; dep UK 2 May, 1878; 15 Sept, 1879 m G. W. Clarke; first woman to Yunnan, Dali; d 7 Oct, 1883.

RUDLAND, William D.: Eversden, Cambridgeshire blacksmith/farm mechanic; 1856 CIM; 1866 *Lammermuir*, Hangzhou; 1867 m Mary Bell (qv); 1868 printer, Yangzhou riot; 1869 Taizhou, Zhejiang many years; 1874 UK, wife died; translated (adapted) Taizhou vernacular romanised NT; 1878 m Miss Brealey, d cholera, 1878; later m Miss Knight; d 1913.

RUSSELL, Lord John (1792–1878): 1st earl; 1832 Reform Bill; 1846, 1865–66 Prime Minister.

RUSSELL, William Armstrong: CMS; 1847 Ningbo; 1872–79 first bishop in N China; d 1879.

RUTHERFORD, Samuel (1600–61): Scottish divine; prof. of divinity, St Andrews Univ.

RYLE, John Charles, DD: 1880–1900 Bp. of Liverpool; uncompromising Evangelical leader, writer, C. H. Spurgeon's 'best man in the Ch. of England'; author *Knots Untied, Holiness, Practical Religion.*

SAMBROOK, A. W.: CIM dep UK 12 Dec 1878; Henan; 1884 secured permanent footing, Zhoujiakou, after 8 years' frustration of M. H. Taylor, G. W. Clarke, others; but driven out, resigned.

SCARBOROUGH, W.: WMMS, 1865 Hankou with David Hill.

SCHALL von BELL, Johann Adam (1591–1666): Socy of Jesus; astronomer; 1622 Peking; 1645 president, Imperial Board of Astronomers; 'chaplain' to imperial palace.

SCHERESCHEWSKY, Samuel Isaac Joseph (1831–1906) (pron. *Sher-e-sheff-skie,* called 'Sherry'): Russian Lithuanian rabbi, converted; 1854 USA Gen. Theol. Seminary, NY; 1859 ordained Am Prot. Episc. Church by Bp. Wm Boone Sr; 1860 Shanghai; 1862–75 Peking, began Dicty of Mongolian; alone translated OT into Mandarin while committee trans. NT; 1865 with J. S. Burdon (qv) trans. Anglican Book of Com. Prayer; 1875 nominated bishop, declined; 1876 consecrated; 1878 founded St John's College, Shanghai, and St Mary's Hall for girls; 1879 *wenli* Prayer Book, Wuchang; 1881 paralysed limbs; speech, to Europe; 1883 resigned episc. office; 1886 USA, began OT revision—

impaired speech excluded Chinese help, typed with one finger, 8 hours daily—1888–95 easy *wenli* OT, NT romanised; 1895–7 Shanghai, romanised into Ch. character; 1897 Japan, to supervise printing; 1902 OT revision publ.; sole object 'to make plain the Word of God to the Chinese'; d Tokyo, Sept 15, 1906, *aet.* 75 in working chair, (*Chinese Recorder* 1906 Vol 37, p 615f).

SCHMIDT, Charles: 1864 officer of Ever-Victorious Army, converted through James Meadows (qv); became missionary in Suzhou; friend of JHT.

SCHOFIELD, Robert Harold Ainsworth: b 18 Jan 1851; 1869 grad. London Univ; 1870 Oxford; 1877 MA, BM Oxon; May 1878 FRCS Eng.; dep UK 7 April; 1880 with wife; Taiyuan, Shanxi; . typhus 1 Aug 1881.

SCOTT, Charles Perry: SPG; 1874 dep UK with Albert Capel; Yantai;1878–79 Shanxi famine relief; 1880 Bishop North China, Shandong, Zhili, taking over CMS (J. S. Burdon) work in Peking.

SCOTT, William: Dunedin, Edinburgh, manufacturer; staunch friend of CIM.

SEARELL, Edith: New Zealand; 1895 to China; musician, linguist, taught at Chefoo schools; May 1896 to Taiyuan, Shanxi; Xiaoyi with Emily Whitchurch (qv); 30 June 1900 killed together.

SELL, John Robert: Romford, Essex; 1866 CIM, *Lammermuir*, Hangzhou; 1867 engaged to Jane McLean (qv), Ningbo, d smallpox.

SEYMOUR, Admiral Sir Michael: commander-in-chief, East Asia; 1856 blockaded, bombarded, occupied Canton; deported viceroy, Ye Ming-sheng (qv).

SHAFTESBURY, Lord Anthony Ashley-Cooper (1801–85): 7th earl; evangelical philanthropist; legislated to relieve ill effects of industrial revolution.

SHARP, William: solicitor; 1883 CIM London Council, active member; patron, secretary, Tibetan Pioneer Mission.

SHEPHERD, William: one of Wesley's first seven travelling preachers; daughter (? grand-daughter) m John Taylor, JHT's grandfather.

SHUCK, J. Lewis: first Am Baptist in China proper; 1836 Macao; with I. J. Roberts (qv), first missionary in Hong Kong; member of Delegates' Committee, 1852 Bible.

SIMCOX, F. E. S.: b USA 30 Apr 1867; 1893 grad. Western Theol. Seminary; m June; dep US Sept 1893; children Paul (5) Francis (2) Margaret; Am Presby, Baoding, Zhili; all killed 30 June 1900,

SIMEON, Chas: b 24 Sept 1795; Kings Coll., Camb.; Fellow; ordained 1782–83; vicar Holy Trinity Church, Camb. 1782–1836 (54 years); d 13 Nov 1836; had profound influence on Henry Martyn (qv) among many.

SIMPSON, James: Aberdeen YMCA, wife YWCA; CIM, dep UK 15 Dec 1887; Taiyuan; Shanxi; joined Shouyang Mission; 27 June 1900 rioted out of Schofield Memorial Hosp; 9 July 1900 killed.

SIMPSON, Sir James Young, Bart., FRS (1811–70): Scottish surgeon, established chloroform anaesthesia; evangelical Christian.

SISSONS, Elizabeth: rejected JHT's proposals.

SKINNER, Anne: Cornwall fiancée of Geo. Crombie (qv); 1865 Ningbo; m Crombie; 1866 Fenghua; 1882 retired.

SLADEN, Col. E. B.: 1868 (Major) led Brit. expedition, Burma-Yunnan; resisted by Col. *Li* Zhenguo; promoted colonel; 1874–75 *Li* Zhenguo hospitable to Margary, warned Ney Elias (qv); 1875 a member of Sladen expedition visited CIM Lond. requesting missionaries.

SLOAN, Walter B.: company secretary, Keswick Convention speaker; CIM dep UK Sept 1891; became Gen. Secy CIM UK after B. Broomhall.

SMITH, Elizabeth: first CMS single woman to China; 1863 Fuzhou, 1864 Peking; 1869 not listed.

SMITH, George: CMS; China survey, 1844; 1846 returned with T. McClatchie (qv); 1849–64 first Bishop of Victoria, Hong Kong.

SMITH, Lieut. George Shergold: son of naval officer on anti-slave trade patrol who 1822 rescued Adji (Samuel Crowther), future bishop of the Niger; 1876 Shergold Smith led first CMS Uganda party including Alexander Mackay; 13 Dec, 1876 massacred.

SMITH, Margaret Eliz.: b Canada 1858; CIM dep 1896; Datong, Shanxi; killed 12 July 1900 with McKee family (qv).

SMITH, Pearsall: American exponent of the 'higher Christian life'; influenced originators of Keswick Movement.

SMITH, Stanley Peregrine: b 19 March 1861; youngest son of Henry Smith, FRCS; Repton and Trinity Coll., Camb.; 1882 BA; influenced by Granville Waldegrave (qv); capt. of Trinity boats, stroke of Camb. Univ. eight 1881; 'about the end of 1883' in touch with JHT; 1 April 1884 accepted by CIM Council; 5 Feb 1885 'Camb. Seven' dep UK; 1885 Shanxi; 1889 opened Lu'an, Lucheng; 1902 Jincheng (Tsechou); m (1) Sophie Reuter (Norwegian) who d 7 Mar 1891; (2) Feb 1893 Anna M. Lang.

SOLTAU, George: son of Henry W. (qv); Lamb and Flag Mission and schools, London; 1872 on first CIM London Council; Tasmania; Australian Council.

SOLTAU, Henrietta E.: daughter of H. W. Soltau (qv); 1873 London, asst. to Emily Blatchley; Tottenham home for children of missionaries; later, CIM Women's Training Home and Ladies' Council.

SOLTAU, Henry Jr: son of H. W. Soltau (qv); Aug 1872 Hon. Secy CIM, London with R. H. Hill (qv); 1875 to Bhamo, Burma with J. W. Stevenson (qv); 1880 with Stevenson first Westerners to cross China W-E, Burma,

Chongqing, Wuchang, Shanghai; qualified as doctor of medicine, to India.

SOLTAU, Henry W.: Chancery barrister, Plymouth and Exeter Brethren; sons George, Henry, daughters Henrietta, Agnes (m Richard Hill qv), all in CIM.

SOLTAU, Lucy: daughter of H. W. Soltau (qv); d young, 1873.

SOLTAU, William: son of H. W. Soltau (qv); 1875 Asst. Secy CIM, London, with R. H. Hill, B. Broomhall.

SOOTHILL, Prof. W. E.: United Meth. Free Church; 1888 translated Gospels, Acts into Wenzhou dialect, publ. 1894; 1901 NT completed, printed by CIM press; educator, author, biographer of T. Richard; Analects of Confucius in English; elected President, projected Wuhan Christian University; Prof. of Chinese, Oxford Univ. following Legge (qv) 1897.

SOUTHEY, John and wife: CIM dep Australia Mar 1891; Feb 1896 invalided to New Zealand; Dec 1896 to Melbourne, training new missionaries; 1898 Austr. Council; 1908 Home Director; 5 Jan 1900 with JHT, JET to NZ; 1914 home in NZ till d 6 Jan 1922.

SPEER, Robert E. (1867–1947): son of lawyer, member of Congress; 1889 graduated, Princeton; Student Volunteer Movement; 1886 travelling Sec, Board of Foreign Missions, Presbyterian Church of USA, senior Sec till 1937; Moderator; author.

SPITTLER, C. F. (and son): founded St Chrischona Pilgrim Mission; influenced formation of Foreign Evangelist Socy; many St Chrischona missionaries in CIM during 19th and 20th centuries.

SPURGEON, Charles Haddon (1834–92): renowned Baptist preacher, Metropolitan Tabernacle; lifelong friend of JHT.

STACEY, Miss: one-time Quaker, member of Brook Street chapel, Tottenham; long a friend of JHT.

STALLYBRASS, Thomas: Mongolian-speaking son of Edward Stallybrass, LMS missionary to Buriat Mongols, 1817–44 offered to CES.

STAM, John, Betty (née Eliz. Alden Scott): both Moody Bible Inst.; m 25 Oct 1932; Priscilla born Sept 1934; captured by Communists at Jingde (Tsingteh) 6 Dec 1934; killed Dec 7.

STANLEY, H. M. (1841–1904): Welshman; fought for Confederates in Am Civil War; 1867 correspondent of N Y Herald, sent to find Livingstone; 1871 found at Ujiji; with him explored northern end of Lake Tanganyika; founded Congo Free State (under Belgians); author; knighted, GCB.

STAUNTON, Sir George Thomas, Bart.: aged 15 to China; 1793 interpreter, East India Co. and Lord Macartney's embassy; Chief of East India Co., Canton; 1816 First Commissioner on Lord Amherst's embassy. STEIN, Sir Aurel (1862–1943): b Budapest; Brit. archaeologist, central Asia.

STAVELEY, Sir Charles: 1862 commander, British land forces, China.

STEVEN, F. A.: CIM; dep UK 1 Mar, 1883; Yunnan, Dali, Tengyue; crossed to Bhamo second attempt; CIM N Am and UK staff.

STEVENS, Edwin: Am Seamen's Friend Socy and Am Board (ABCFM); 1832–36 Canton; d 1836.

STEVENS, Jane: CIM dep UK Sept 1885; Shanxi, Huo Xian (Hochow) with Mildred Clarke (qv); 9 July 1900 killed at Taiyuan.

STEVENSON, John Whiteford (1844–1918): son of laird of Thriepwood, Renfrewshire; with G. Stott (qv) first of CIM after Crombie (qv); Oct 1865 dep UK; 1866–74 Ningbo, Shaoxing (Shaoxing); 1875–80 Burma; 1880 crossed China W-E 1,900 miles; 1885–1916 deputy director, CIM.

STEWART, Ellen Mary: b 11 May 1871; 1894 governess to E. H. Edwards (qv) children, BMS, Taiyuan, Shanxi; killed 9 July 1900.

STEWART, Dr J. C.: 1885 med. grad. Philadelphia, USA; to UK Council; CIM dep UK 21 April, 1886 with Orr Ewing, Graham Browne; Shanxi, Guihuacheng.

STEWART, Robt W.: graduate, Dublin; reading for Bar when converted through Evan Hopkins (qv); ordained 1876; CMS, Fuzhou 1878;1 Aug 1895 killed with 7 other colleagues and own children, Kuchang.

STOCK, Eugene (1836–1928): CMS UK staff; editor 21 Dec, 1875–11 Dec, 1906; historian, author The History of the Church Miss. Soc., Vols I–III; warm friend of CIM; d 7 Sep, 1928 aged 92.

STOKES, George W: b Dover 1863; printer; Harley House; CIM dep UK 1892; Shunde, Zhili; Taiyuan, Shanxi; 1897 m Margaret Whittaker, Shouyang Mission, nurse; both killed 9 July 1900.

STOTT, George: Aberdeenshire schoolmaster, one leg; 3 Oct 1865 dep UK; 1866 Ningbo; 1869–89 Wenzhou (Wenchow); d 1889.

STRONACH, Alexander: LMS; 1838–39 Singapore; 1839–44 Penang; 1844–46 Singapore; 1846 Amoy.

STRONACH, John: LMS, 1838–76, 30 years without furlough; 1838–44 Singapore; 1846 Amoy; Bible translator, Delegates' Committee, 1852; S. Dyer's friend.

STRONACH, W. G.: HBM consul; son of John Stronach (qv); m Catherine Duncan (née Brown), widow of George Duncan (qv); she died 31 Oct, 1877 leaving a daughter whom JHT adopted at her dying request.

STROUD, Fanny: CIM dep UK 25 Oct 1882; Chengdu, Sichuan, pioneer; cared for Jane Riley (née Kidd) (qv) children when she died; then nursed J. H. Riley (qv), married him on his deathbed; April 1886; later m Thos James, CIM 1885.

STUDD, Charles Thomas: 3rd son of Edward Studd, Tedworth House, Andover; b 2 Dec, 1860; Eton and Trinity Coll., Cambridge; 1884 BA; cricket 'blue' 4 years, captain

1883; CIM dep UK 5 Feb, 1885; Hanzhong, Shaanxi; Shanxi; Jan 1888 m Priscilla Livingstone Stewart (arr Shanghai 1887); Lu'an, Shanxi; sick leave, resigned; 1900–06, India; founded Heart of Africa Mission; d 16 July, 1931.

STUDD, George: 2nd son, Eton and Cambridge, cricketer, captain 1882; Nov 1883, seriously ill; 1887 visited Shanghai, Shanxi; pastor, Los Angeles, USA.

STUDD, Sir John Edward Kynaston, Bart.: eldest son; Eton and Cambridge cricketer, captain 1884; 1885 m Hilda Beauchamp; twice Lord Mayor of London, 1st baronet.

SZéCHéNYI, Count Béla: Central Asian explorer; 1882 met Easton (qv) at Xining, Stevenson, Soltau at Bhamo.

TAIT, Archibald Campbell (1811–82): headmaster of Rugby; 1856 Bishop of London; 1869 Archbishop of Canterbury.

TALMAGE, John van Nest, DD: American Board; Amoy 1847 (Dutch Reformed Church of America).

TAMERLANE (Timur-i-leng) (1335–1405): descendant of founder of Mogul dynasty, India; conquered Turkestan, Persia, Syria; a scourge; died preparing to invade China.

TANKERVILLE, Earl of (1810–): Chillingham Castle, Northumberland; friend of JHT and CIM.

TARN, Joseph: son of William Tarn Sr (qv), cousin of Maria Taylor.

TARN, William Jr: son of William Sr (qv); cousin of Maria Taylor; Secretary, RTS.

TARN, William Sr: brother of Samuel Dyer Sr's wife; director, LMS; guardian of Burella and Maria Dyer (qv).

TAYLOR, Amelia (1808–81): first daughter of Benjamin Brook Hudson; JHT's mother.

TAYLOR, Amelia Hudson (1835–1918): JHT's sister.

TAYLOR, Annie Royle: dtr of well-to-do Cheshire businessman; aged 28 sold valuables, took basic medical course as lady probationer; London Hospital; CIM dep UK 24 Sept, 1884 aiming for Tibet; Taozhou, Gansu-Qinghai border nr Kumbum, 2 Sept, 1892 dep Taozhou; 3 Jan, 1893 100 miles from Lhasa; expelled; 1893 to Darjeeling, India-Tibet border.

TAYLOR, Arthur: CES missionary, Hong Kong, 1853–55.

TAYLOR, Ernest Hamilton: 6th son of JHT, by JET, b 7 Jan, 1875; accountant, m E. Gauntlett; dep UK after 1900 Boxer rising, volunteered (with C. H. Judd) for Shanxi; 9 July, 1901 arr Taiyuan with D. E. Hoste, A. Orr Ewing (first anniversary of massacres).

TAYLOR, Frederick Howard (1862–1946): second son of JHT and Maria Jane Dyer; 1888 MD (Lond.); 1889 MRCP; FRCS (Eng.); m M. Geraldine Guinness; CIM missionary, biographer of JHT.

TAYLOR, George Yardley: b USA 18 May 1862;

1885 MD Univ. of Pennsylvania; 1888 Am Presby Mission, Beijing, Baoding; killed 30 June 1900.

TAYLOR, Grace Dyer: daughter of JHT and Maria (qv), b Ningbo July 31, 1859; *Jubilee*, *Lammermuir* voyages; d nr Hangzhou, Aug 23, 1867.

TAYLOR, Herbert Hudson: eldest son of JHT and Maria, b Bayswater, London, April 3, 1861; Jan 1881 CIM, to China; *c* 1886 m Jean Gray, CIM 1884; father of James Hudson Taylor II.

TAYLOR, James (1807–81): father of JHT; chemist; founded, managed Barnsley Permanent Building Society 1855–75; retired Dec 1875; m. 5 April 1831 Amelia Hudson, 3 sons, 2 daughters: James Hudson, William Shepherd, Amelia Hudson, Theodore, Louisa Shepherd.

TAYLOR, James Hudson (21 May 1832–3 June 1905, d at Changsha, Hunan): 1853 dep UK; 1 Mar 1854 arr Shanghai; 20 Jan 1858 m Maria Jane Dyer, 5 sons, 3 daughters: Grace Dyer (b Ningbo, 31 July 1859, d 23 August 1867), Herbert Hudson (b London, 3 April 1861, d 6 June 1960, m 1 November 1886, 9 children), Frederick Howard (b London, 25 November 1862, d 15 August 1946, m Geraldine Guinness, b 25 December 1862, d 6 June 1949), Samuel Dyer (b Barnsley, 24 June 1864, d 4 February 1870), Jane Dyer (b/d London, 7 December 1865), Charles Edward (b Yangzhou, 29 November 1868, d 13 July 1938), Noel (b Zhenjiang, 7 July 1870, d 20 July 1870); JHT 1857 with J. Jones (qv) began Ningbo Mission; June 1865 founded China Inland Mission; 28 Nov 1871 m Jane E. Faulding, 1 son, 1 daughter: Ernest Hamilton (b 7 January 1875), Amy (b 1876, d 3 July 1953).

TAYLOR, James Sr (1749–95): paternal great-grandfather of JHT; mason, Barnsley, Yorkshire; host to J. Wesley; m 1776 Elizabeth Johnson, 2 sons, 3 daughters.

TAYLOR, Jane (Jennie/Jenny) Elizabeth (née Faulding): b 7 Oct, 1843; 1865 assistant to JHT and Maria, London; 1866 CIM; *Lammermuir*; Hangzhou; m JHT 28 Nov, 1871; 1877–78 took Anna Crickmay (qv) and Celia Horne (qv) to Shanxi famine relief, Taiyuan; first women deep into interior; d 30 July, 1904.

TAYLOR, John (1778–1834): paternal grandfather of JHT; linen reed maker, 1799 m Mary Shepherd (*see* Wm Shepherd), 4 sons, 4 daughters.

TAYLOR, Louisa Shepherd: b 1840, second daughter of James Taylor (qv) and Amelia Hudson.

TAYLOR, Maria Hudson: daughter of JHT and MJT; b Hangzhou, Feb 3 1867; 1884 CIM to China *aet.* 17; m J. J. Coulthard (qv) d Sept 28, 1897.

TAYLOR, Maria Jane (née Dyer) (1837–70): daughter of Samuel Dyer (qv); wife of JHT;

mother of Grace, Herbert Hudson, Frederick Howard, Samuel, Jane, Maria, Charles, Noel.

TAYLOR, M. Geraldine (*see* Guinness).

TAYLOR, M. Henry: CIM dep UK 3 Sept 1873; first CIM pioneer Henan; met strong opposition, heartbroken, to Zhejiang; 1878 Henan famine relief rejected by mandarins; resigned.

TERTULLIAN: *c*160–*c* 220 AD; theologian of Carthage; his *Apology* before pagan judges, re 'blood of the martyrs'.

THIRGOOD, Emma Ann: CIM dep UK 28 Nov 1889; to Changshan, Zhejiang with G. F. Wards (qv); killed at Qü *Xian* 22 July 1900.

THOMAS, R. J.: LMS: 1865 distributed scripture for Nat. Bible Socy of Scotland for 2½ months on Korean coast; 1866 again, killed.

THOMPSON, David Baird: CIM dep UK 1880; 1885 m Agnes Dowman; Qü Xian, Zhejiang; both killed 21 July 1900.

TIDMAN, Dr Arthur: Foreign Secy, LMS; member CES General Committee.

TOMALIN, E.: CIM dep UK 12 Dec, 1878; 1882 m Louise Desgraz (qv), Shandong.

TOMLIN, Jacob: LMS; 1827 Malaya; 1828 Bangkok with Gutzlaff. TRENCH, Frank: independent, dep UK 19 May, 1878 with CIM; pioneer, Hunan, Guizhou, Yunnan; June 1884 medical course, Edin.; retired.

TRESTRAIL, Frederick: BMS Secretary with E. B. Underhill (qv).

TRUELOVE, Richard: 1865 recruit for Ningbo, failed to go.

TURNER, Joshua J.: CIM, one of 'the eighteen', dep UK Nov 1875; Oct 1876 to Jan 1877 Shanxi; famine relief, typhoid, Taiyuan; 1 Feb 1881 m A. Crickmay; in UK 1900; BMS to Taiyuan.

UNDERHILL, C. B.: Secy BMS; friend of JHT, nominated him for FRGS.

VALENTINE, Jarvis Downman: CMS recruit taught by JHT; 1864 Ningbo; 1870 Shaoxing; d 1889.

VALIGNANO, Allesandri (1537–1606): 1579 Jesuit Visitor to Japan.

van SOMMER, James: member, Hackney Brethren circle with W. T. Berger (qv) (brother-in-law) and Philip H. Gosse (qv); editor, *The Missionary Reporter*.

van SOMMER, John: brother of James.

VAUGHAN, Marianne: first fiancée of JHT.

VENIAMINOV, John (Innokenty) (1797–1879): Russian Orthodox pioneer, Aleutians, Kuriles, N Siberia, Manchuria, Japan; Metropolitan of Moscow; founded Orthodox Missionary Socy.

VENN, Henry 'the elder': vicar of Huddersfield, leading promoter of first evangelical revival; grandfather of Henry Venn 'Senior'.

VENN, Henry 'the younger': known as 'Senior' (1796–1873); son of John Venn, grandson of Henry 'the elder'; St John's, Holloway; 1841–73, Hon. Secy CMS; sent 498 clergy overseas.

VENN, Henry 'Junior': second son of Henry 'Senior'; *c*1869–72 Assoc. Secy CMS.

VENN, John: rector of Clapham, member of 18th century 'Eclectic Socy'; a founder, first chairman of CMS; father of Henry 'the younger' or 'Senior'; d 1813.

VERBIEST, Ferdinand (1617–88): Jesuit astronomer, Peking.

VIGEON, James and Mrs: 1865 recruits for Ningbo, prevented from going.

VOGEL, Karl: Kassel Miss. Assoc.; 1847 Hong Kong, Guangdong (Kwangtung); Gutzlaff's recruit.

WADE, Lieut. Thomas Francis: British forces, Ningbo, 1841; vice-consul Shanghai under Alcock; Battle of Muddy Flat; became sinologue; HBM minister, Peking; knighted.

WALDEGRAVE, Hon. Miss: daughter of Dowager Lady Radstock (qv); supported CIM.

WARD, George Fredk: CIM dep UK 1893; 1895 itinerating;1897 m Etta L. Fuller, b 1866, dep USA 1894; Changshan, Zhejiang; 22 July 1900 escaped to Qü Xian, killed.

WARD, Col. Frederick Townsend: Am. commander, Ever-Victorious Army; 1862 mortally wounded at Cixi (Tzeki), Ningbo.

WARD, Hon. John E.: 1859 US plenipotentiary; 1860 at capture and Convention of Peking.

WAY, R. Q.: Am. Presby.; 1844 Ningbo; brother-in-law of J. W. Quarterman (qv).

WEATHERLEY, Joseph: early CIM supporter; 1872 first chairman, CIM London Council, met in his home, 51 Gordon Sq.

WEIR, Thomas: Shanghai merchant, 1865 influenced by JHT Glasgow; long a friend; negotiated reduced fares by Castle Line, UK-China, effective many years.

WELTON, Dr W.: CMS; first medical, Fuzhou (Foochow).

WENTWORTH, Dr E.: Fuzhou missionary; 1858 appealed for missionaries and for comity partition of China between missions.

WHITCHURCH, Emily: of Downton, Salisbury; 1883 heard JHT; CIM 27 Feb 1884, dep UK as one of 'Seventy'; taught at Chefoo; 1887 to Xiaoyi, Shanxi; 30 June 1900 killed by Boxers.

WHITEFIELD, George (1714–70): at Oxford with J. and C. Wesley; Methodist until 1741, then independent; d in America.

WHITEHOUSE, Silvester Frank: b 14 Aug 1867; CIM dep UK 5 Oct 1888 with JHT as private secretary; 1892 Harley House; B&FBS 3 years colportage; 1893 m Legerton, CIM Chefoo; Spurgeon's College; July 1899 BMS; Taiyuan, Shanxi; 9 July 1900 both killed.

WHITING, Albert: Am Presby. Mission, Nanjing; joined David Hill, dep Shanghai (March 1878) to Shanxi famine relief; d 25 April, 'famine fever'.

WHITWORTH, John: architect friend of JHT from youth.

WILDER, Robert Parmelee (1863–1938): son of India missionary; 1886 grad. Princeton;

initiated SVM; 1886 promoted SVM at Moody's student conference; 1888 travelled for SVM to colleges, univs; 1889 to UK univs, after J. N. Forman (qv); Gen. Secy SVM; 1891–92 UK, SVMU; 1902 India, students; thereafter evangelist to students in UK, Europe; (1891–92 at Med. Miss. Ass. c/o Dr J. L. Maxwell, negotiated union of (FHT's) Students' Foreign Miss. Union with SVM, completed April 2–9,1892, with A. T. Polhill as trav. secy.).

WILLIAMS, E. O.: Trinity Coll. Oxford; vicar, St Stephen's, Leeds; CIM dep UK 13 Dec 1888; East Sichuan; d July 1899, typhoid.

WILLIAMS, Sir George (1821–95): of Hitchcock, Williams & Co., London; 1844 founded YMCA for employees; friend of CIM, of Lord Shaftesbury (first YMCA President); chairman, CIM meetings;1894 YMCA Jubilee, knighted.

WILLIAMS, Wells Samuel, DD (1812–84): Am Board, printer, scholar; 1833 Canton; 1847 author, *The Middle Kingdom*; 1851 succeeded E. C. Bridgman (qv) editor, *Chinese Repository*; interpreter to US legation, Peking; *chargé d'affaires* to 1876; Prof. of Chinese, Yale Univ.

WILLIAMSON, Alexander, LL D (1829–90): 1855 LMS Shanghai; 1863 National Bible Socy of Scotland, Shandong, Yantai; 1865 Peking, Mongolia, Manchuria; 1887 founded Christian Literature Socy.

WILLIAMSON, James: younger brother of Alexander W. (qv); 1863 LMS Tianjin; 1869 murdered.

WILLIAMSON, James: Arbroath, Aberdeen, carpenter; 1866 CIM, *Lammermuir*, Hangzhou, JHT's assistant pioneer; 1869 Anqing riot.

WILLIS, Capt John Jr: 'Jock' Willis, son of 'Old Stormy', clipper master and owner, known in London as 'White Hat' Willis; *Lammermuir*, *Cutty Sark*; favoured CIM.

WILLIS, Capt. John Sr: clipper master and owner; 'Old Stormy' of sea shanty 'Mr Stormalong'; founder of John Willis and Son.

WILSON, Eliz: Kendal; b 1830, niece of Miss Stacey (qv); CIM dep UK 26 Jan, 1876 (aged 46);1880 pioneer, Hanzhong, Shaanxi; Tianshui, Gansu.

WINDSOR, Thomas: CIM dep UK 27 Feb, 1884; Guiyang, Anshun.

WILSON, Eliz: Kendal; b 1830, niece of Miss Stacey (qv); CIM dep UK 26 Jan, 1876 (aged 46);1880 pioneer, Hanzhong, Shaanxi; Tianshui, Gansu.

WILSON, James: 1864 recruited by JHT; joined Presby. Mission Socy.

WILSON, Robert, MD: 1861 LMS, Hankou with Griffith John.

WILSON, Dr Wm: Oxford; nephew of Eliz. Wilson (qv); CIM dep UK 20 Aug, 1882; pioneer, rejected at Xi'an, welcomed at Hanzhong, Shaanxi, m Caroline Sarah Goodman.

WINDSOR, Thomas: CIM dep UK 27 Feb, 1884; Guiyang, Anshun.

WINNES, Ph.: Basel Mission; 1852 joined Theodore Hamberg (qv), Guangdong (Kwangtung) after R. Lechler died.

WOLFE, John R.: 1862 CMS, Fuzhou; 'missionary par excellence of Fukien'; 1864 began indigenous expansion of church by deploying catechists and visiting them; 1873–75 alone, missionary colleagues all ill or dead; church members, adherents, doubled 800 to 1,656 under persecution; 4,450 in 1882;1884 and 1886 visited Korea; 1884 Fujian Christians to Korea learned language, withdrew after two years; 1899 JRW still active in Fujian.

WYLIE, Alexander (1815–87): LMS; 1847 Shanghai, printer, Delegates' version of Bible; 1863 Bible Socy. (B&FBS); one of the greatest sinologues.

XAVIER, Francis (1506–52): Basque co-founder with Ignatius Loyola of Jesuit order; 1542 India; 1549 Japan; 1552 d Shangquan (Shangch'uan) Is., near Macao.

YAKUB BEG: Muslim conqueror, 1864 captured Kashgar, Yarkand; appointed ruler by Emir of Bokhara; added Urumqi, Turfan to his kingdom; 1872 independence recognised by Russia, GB, Turkey; honoured with title only used by caliphs of Baghdad; great Muslim revival predicted, with conquest of China; but 1876 Urumqi fell to Zuo Zongtang (Tso Tsung-t'ang) (qv); May 1877 Yakub Beg died suddenly; Dec 1877 Kashgar taken, kingdom ended.

YATES, Mathew T. (1819–88): Am S Baptist; 1847 Shanghai; sinologue, learned contributor to *Chinese Recorder*; Am vice-consul; translator, Shanghai vernacular NT; leading proponent of orthodox views on Ancestor Worship at Gen. Miss. Conf., May 1877.

YOUNG, John: Glasgow BTI; 1894 CIM; dep UK 1 Oct 1896; to Ji Xian (Chichou) Shanxi; 1 April 1849 m Sarah Alice Troyer, b USA 1871; CIM, Jan 1896 dep to China; 16 July 1900 both killed with McConnells.

YOUNG, Miss: sister of Mrs John Jones (qv).

YOUNGHUSBAND, Lt. Col. Sir Francis Edward: 1887 (Lieut.) across China and Turkestan by Mongolian route; 1889 wished to attempt Lhasa, politically untimely; 1902 Russian intentions re Tibet prompted Brit. armed expedition, 1,000 troops, 10,000 coolies, 7,000 mules entered Tibet 12 Dec 1903; 1904 led troops into Lhasa; 23 Sept 1904 dep Lhasa; 1919–22 Pres. R. G. Socy; 1936 founded World Congress of Faiths; as Pres. R. G. Socy supported, honoured 'Trio' (*see* Cable, French).

YULE, Col. Sir Henry, CB, RE: geographer, historian, author *Marco Polo*; Dec 1879 introduction (95 pp) to Gill (qv): *River of Golden Sand*.

ZWEMER, Samuel Marinus (1867–1952): b Michigan, USA; Reformed Church; July 1888 asked JHT how to join CIM; 1890 accompanied Thomas Valpy French, CMS Bp of Lahore (1825–90) to Muscat, Arabia; arr Feb 8; May 14 French died; Zwemer lived 60 more years; 1890 to Basrah, Bahrein; m CMS Australian; 1911 editor, *The Muslim World*; 1912 Cairo for Arabic Christian literature; 1917 to China, promoting mission to Muslims; 1929–37 Prof. of Christian Missions and History of Religions, Princeton Seminary; author of 37 books; co-author 12 more.

Personalia: Chinese, Manchu

ALUDE: Manchu; Tong Zhi emperor's choice as consort; niece of Chonghou (qv); granddaughter of Prince of Cheng; victim of Ci Xi's displeasure (qv); died in suspicious circumstances, 27 March 1875.

'CCH' (Chang Chih-heng, Zhang Zhiheng): trusted undercover cell leader during Boxer crisis; supplied and assisted persecuted Christians, missionaries.

CHENG CHUNXŪAN (Ts'eng Chun-hsüan): governor of Shanxi after Yü Xian (qv); viceroy of Sichuan 1902; of Canton, Guangdong-Guangxi 1903; made pro-missions proclamations.

CHIANG KAI-SHEK (Jiang Jiaishi) (1887–1975): chief Chinese leader 1925–49; president 1928–31,1943–49, Republic of China, Taiwan, 1950–75; 1926 Northern Expedition; 1930 baptised, married Soong Meiling; 1936 arrested by 'Young Marshal' Zhang Xüeliang (qv).

CHONGHOU: Manchu; 1870 Imperial Commissioner for Foreign Affairs, Tianjin; central figure at time of Tianjin massacre; 1879 envoy to Europe; saved from death sentence.

CHU (see Zhu).

CHUANG, Prince: bloodthirsty Manchu appointed 1900 by Ci Xi (qv) to command Boxers with Kangyi (qv); decapitated hundreds of Christians and friends of foreigners; himself executed on Ci Xi's orders.

CI AN: Empress Dowager, co-regent with Ci Xi (qv); died in suspicious circumstances 1881.

CI XI (1835–1908): Yehonala (Yehe Nara), (Ts'u Hsi); Manchu concubine Yi, mother of Tong Zhi emperor (qv); Empress Dowager, co-regent with Ci An; 1860–1908 supreme power in China, 22 Sept 1898 imprisoned emp. Guang Xü (qv) till death 1908; d 15 Nov 1908, day after Guang Xü.

FEI QIHAO: Christian educated by Am Board, Tong Xian, colleague of Oberlin teams, Taigu, Fenyang, Shanxi; survived massacre, escaped to Tianjin with first news; probable source of C. H. S. Green's (qv) 'little tuft of paper'; friend of Kong Xiangxi (qv).

FENG YÜXIANG: b circa 1880; soldier influenced by courage of Mary Morrill (qv) on way to execution; 1913 converted through John R. Mott; baptised in Am Episc Church; 1923 promoted field marshal; 23 Oct 1924 occupied Beijing, invited Sun Yatsen (qv) to assume presidency. Second to Chiang Kaishek, Nanjong, 1928.

GIH, Andrew: Post Office official fired by Paget Wilkes' preaching; formed Bethel Worldwide Evangelistic Band; joined by John Sung (qv).

GUANG: Bible Society colporteur, travelled June 1879–Dec 1882 with Jas Cameron, Manchuria, Shanxi, Shaanxi.

GUANG XÜ (Kuang Hsü) emperor: 1875, four-year-old puppet of Ci Xi (qv); son of Prince Chun, 7th son of Dao Guang emperor; 1889 assumed power; 1898 imprisoned after *coup d'etat* by Ci Xi, d 14 Nov 1908, day before Ci Xi, poisoned?

GUO SONGDAO: 1876 Chinese ambassador to France, Russia, Britain; arr London 21 Jan 1877, succeeded by Marquis Zeng (qv); spoke out in UK against opium traffic.

HO Xianseng (ie 'Mr'): Sichuanese teacher at Hanzhong, Shaanxi; first Hanzhong Prot. Christian; pioneer evangelist to his home town, Tongjiang, with Jas Cameron (qv); 1886 with Ed. Pearse and Cecil Polhill secured first foothold at Langzhong.

HONG XIU-QUAN (Hung Hsiu-ch'uan) (1813–64): Taiping Wang, leader of Taiping rebellion; 1837 visions and fantasies; 1844 began preaching; 1846 with Hong Ren (Hung Jen) (qv) taught by I. J. Roberts (qv); 1849 led Worshippers of Shangdi; 1851 began hostilities; 1852 assumed imperial title; *1853*–64 Nanking; 1853 advance to Tianjin halted; 1864 suicide.

HONG REN: cousin of Hong Xiu-quan; known as Gan Wang, Shield King; ex-evangelist.

HSI SHENGMO (Xi Liaozhi) (1830–96): Shanxi classical scholar, opium addict, converted 1879 through David Hill (qv); 1886 ordained as leading pastor, south Shanxi; established scores of opium refuges, Shanxi, Shaanxi, Henan, Zhili; secured influential foothold in anti-Christian Xi'an, Shaanxi; had D. E. Hoste (qv) as colleague 1886–96; d 19 Feb 1896.

HUANG KEZHONG: Christian with leprosy; key colleague of pioneers at Hanzhong, Shaanxi.

JIANG LIANGYONG: Hangzhou, Zhejiang, Christian; initiated Yuhang church who provided his financial support.

JIANG SUOLIANG (see ZHANG).

JIANG QING: actress wife of Mao Zedong (qv), later estranged; radical, one of the 'Gang of Four', arrested 26 Oct 1976.

JIANG XIAOFENG: evangelist at Shaoxing, Zhejiang; converted by seeing J. W. Stevenson often on his knees. (In Ningbo dialect Tsiang Si a-Yong, Pinyin probably ZHANG.)

JINGSHAN: Manchu diarist, source of inside information on Boxer rising.

JIA QING (Chia Ch'ing), (1796–1820): mediocre 5th emperor of Qing (Ch'ing) dynasty.

KANG XI (K'ang Hsi), (1622–1722): 2nd Qing (Ch'ing) dynasty emperor; for 60 years;

aged 7 dismissed his regents; one of China's strongest rulers; pro-Christian; 1692 Edict of Toleration; 1700 pro-Jesuit, anti-Rome.

KANG YI: Manchu nobleman, 'Lord High Extortioner' in Ci Xi's (qv) administration; with Prince Chuang (qv) i/c Boxers; died during flight to Xi'an.

KANG YUWEI: 'Erasmus of the Reform Movement', author of *The Reform of Japan, The Reform of Russia*; tutor to Guang Xŭ emp.; fugitive with price on his head till 1912; favoured constitutional monarchy. Xiucai, Bachelor; Qŭren, Master; Anshi, Doctor; Hanlin, Academician—the former two by provincial examination, the latter two at Peking.

KONG, Prince: son of Dao Guang emperor; brother of *Xian* Feng emperor and Prince Qŭn; survived Jehol plot; 1860 negotiated treaty with Allies at Peking; rank equivalent to Prime Minister; his own son rejected by Ci Xi and Prince Qŭn's made emperor; repeatedly degraded by Ci Xi; died 1898, 'a national calamity'.

KONG XIANGXI (K'ung Hsiang-hsi): descendant of Confucius; Oberlin College friend of Fei Qihao (qv); became a leading figure in Nationalist govt.

LIANG Xianseng ('Mr'): Christian teacher at Hanzhong, Shaanxi; occupied Langzhong, Sichuan, with Ho (qv), Pearse and C. Polhill.

LIANG QICHAO (Liang Ch'i-ch'ao): reformer in exile with Sun Yatsen (qv) in Japan since 'Hundred Days of Reform'.

LI HANZHANG (Li Hanchang): brother of Li Hongzhang (qv); viceroy of Hubei, Hunan.

LI HONGZHANG (Li Hung-Zhang) (1823– 1901): holder of the highest academic degrees, highest honours after defeat of Taiping rebels; enlightened liberal but failed in modernisation of China; 1895 forced to cede Taiwan to Japan; the Grand Old Man of China, leading statesman until death, 7 Nov 1901.

LIANG A-FA (1789–1855): Canton engraver-printer, 1815 to Malacca with W. Milne; 1819 Canton; colporteur; arrested, flogged; 1821 Malacca; 1828 Canton; 1834 arrested, escaped, betrayed, escaped; 1839 returned, tolerated by Lin Ze-xu (qv); first Prot. pastor; 1845 mobbed; d 1855.

LIANG A-DE (Liang A-teh): son of A-fa; translator to Lin Ze-xu (qv); interpreter for British, Nanking Treaty; Chinese Imperial Maritime Customs.

LI LIANYING: Chief Eunuch; unscrupulous tool of Ci Xi (qv).

LIN ZE-XU (Lin Tze hsu): gov-gen. of Hubei-Hunan; viceroy commissioner, Canton, to control opium traffic; 1839 strong-arm methods contributed to war, 1840–41; disgraced, exiled.

LIU KUNYI: viceroy of Nanjing (Jiangxi, Jiangsu, Anhui); with Zhang Zhitong (qv) defied Ci Xi's (qv) edicts to kill foreigners; preserved peace in Yangzi valley provinces, protected foreigners.

LO: Bible Society colporteur; 1880 crossed Hunan with Baller (qv), Evangelist Yao (qv), J. McCarthy (qv) and Jane Kidd (qv), to Guiyang, Guizhou.

MAO ZEDONG (Mao Tse-tung) (1893–1976): founding member of CCP (1921); with Sun Yatsen (qv) and Chiang Kaishek (qv) but separated 1926; formed soviet in Jiangxi 1931–34; led Long March 1935–36; inaugurated People's Republic of China 1949; chairman until 1959; CCP chairman until death; launched Cultural Revolution 1966; d 9 Sept 1976 aged 83.

MENG JIXIAN (Meng Chi-hsien): Boxer martyr; first pastor of Am Board congregation, Baoding, Zhili; tortured, beheaded 28 June 1900.

NI TUOSHENG (Ni T'uo-sheng): name means a watchman's warning (*tuo* = rattle), hence 'Watchman Nee'; b 4 Nov 1903;1928 originated church movement known as 'Little Flock'; prolific author; 1952 arrested, released April 1972; d 1 June, 1972.

PAN SHOUSHAN: He (Black) Miao evangelist, martyred with Wm S. Fleming, CIM, Panghai, Guizhou, 4 Nov 1898.

PU JŬN: Manchu noble, son of Prince Tuan (qv); made Heir Apparent by Ci Xi (qv) on forced abdication of Guang Xŭ (qv) emp; fled with Court from Beijing on 15 Aug 1900; a ne'er-do-well; deposed, banished Nov 1901.

PU LUN: Manchu noble elevated to Heir Apparent replacing Pu Jŭn (qv); deposed by Ci Xi (qv) in favour of Pu Yi (qv) just before death of Guang Xŭ emp (qv) and Ci Xi.

PU YI, HENRY (1906–67): last of Manchu Qing dynasty; named Heir Apparent aged 2 by Ci Xi (qv) circa 10 Nov 1908; grandson of Yong Lu (qv), son of Prince Qŭn (qv); known as Xŭan Tong emp.; 'abdicated' 12 Feb 1912; abortive restoration 1–12 July 1917; puppet emp. 'Kang De' (1934–35) of Japanese 'Manchuguo'; taken by Russians to Moscow for indoctrination, 're-educated' by CCP.

QIAN LONG (Ch'ien Lung) (1736–96): 4th emperor, Qing (Ch'ing) dynasty.

QING, Prince: Manchu, adversary of Yong Lu (qv); backed Boxers with 50,000 men; plenipotentiary with *Li* Hongzhang (qv) after Boxer rising; senior statesman of Grand Council after death of Ci Xi's (qv) best men, Prince Kong (qv), *Li* Hongzhang, Yong Lu; weak, vacillating; briefly first premier, May 1911, Republic of China.

QI SHAN (Ch'i Shan): 1840 gov. of Zhili (Chihli); viceroy of Canton after Lin Ze-xu (qv); cashiered, exiled, after Convention of Chuanbi (Ch'uanbi).

QIU A-GONG (Ch' u A-kung; Kew A-gang): Christian printer, Malacca, with Liang A-fa (qv).

QI YING: 1842 succeeded Qi Shan; initiated 'diplomatic honeymoon', negotiated

Nanking Treaty; gov. of Canton; issued edict of toleration.

QÜ (1) (Ch'ü): scholar of Daning, Shanxi, became Christian with Zhang Zhiben (qv) through studying Mark's Gospel; three times publicly flogged; pastor; survived Boxer rising; with Elder Xü (qv) negotiated with governor Ceng (qv) rehabilitation of persecuted Christians.

QÜ (2): Wuchang evangelist; to Guiyang through hostile Hunan with Broumton (qv), Yao Shangda (qv) and Sen Sifu.

QÜN, Prince (Ch'ün): Guang Xü emperor's brother; married Yong Lu's (qv) daughter; 4 Sept 1901 conveyed China's regrets to Potsdam for murder of German envoy Baron von Ketteler (qv); regent of his son Pu Yi (qv); d 1891.

REN CHENGYÜAN (also Ren Ziqing): b18 Feb 1852, ordained 24 June 1877, d 11 Feb 1929; descended from a Tang dynasty marquess; son-in-law of Wang Lae-djün (qv) co-pastor with him at Hangzhou, Zhejiang; testified to JHT's constant insistence on indigenous church principles (see Bibliography).

REN ZIQING (Pastor Ren): son-in-law of Wang Lae-djün (qv); co-pastor with him at Hangzhou, Zhejiang; fully supported by church members.

SANG Sifu; CIM Linfen, Shanxi, courier; heroic leading voluntary escort-attendant to Dreyer (qv) refugee party, 14 July–28 Aug 1900.

SEN Sifu (ie master craftsman): Broumton's colleague at Guiyang, 1877.

SHAO MIANZI: Yangzhou, Jiangsu, schoolgirl; 25 Feb 1880 married G. Parker; pioneer in Gansu, Xinjiang, Henan; finally doyenne of CIM after husband died 17 Aug 1931.

SHEN DENHE: Chinese Foreign Office *daotai*, trained at Cambridge, appointed to agree reparations for Shanxi foreigners, Christians, mission premises.

SI, Elder: of Hongtong, Shanxi; brother-in-law of Hsi Shengmo (qv); died 2 July 1902 from sword thrust 14 May 1900; with Qü and Xü (qv) and D. E. Hoste (qv) negotiator for church reparations.

SOONG family: father a Methodist minister; daughter Qingling (b 1890) m Sun Yatsen (qv), Meiling (b 1898) m Chiang Kaishek (qv); son, T. V. Soong, financier.

SU, Prince: agreed that 2,000 Christian fugitives occupy his palace adjoining foreign legations, Beijing; palace defended, protected, by Japanese marines, Col Shiba.

SUNG, John (Song Shangjie, Sung Shang-chieh) (1901–1944): of Fujian, Ph D, Ohio, joined Andrew Gih (qv), Bethel Band, 1928–34; independent missioner to all China, S E Asia.

SUN YATSEN (Sun Zhongshan) (1866–1925): Chinese statesman; 1891 first medical graduate, Hong Kong; 1905 founded China Revolutionary League, in Europe, Japan; 1911–12 founder and first president Republic of China; m descendant of Paul Xü (SOONG

QINGLING, dep. chairman Nat. People's Congress till d 1981). Dec 29, 1911 elected provisional president, Republic of China; 1914 organised Chinese Revolutionary Party to resist Yüan Shikai; 1924 invited by Feng Yüxiang and associates to Peking to re-establish the republic; died of cancer, March 12, 1925; 1929 buried in mausoleum at Nanjing.

SU VONG, Dr V. P.: Chinese Christian scientist at Nanjing imperial arsenal with Dr Halliday Macartney (qv); delegate to 1877 General Missionary Conference, Shanghai.

TONG FUXIANG: Muslim general i/c 15,000 Gansu Muslim cavalry; rallied to Ci Xi (qv) Beijing 1900; supported Boxers, commanded forces against legations; escorted exiled Court to Zhangjiakou (Kalgan), Xi'an; 'too powerful to punish'.

TONG ZHI, emperor: only son of Ci Xi (qv); 1861 acceded to throne aged five; rejected Ci Xi's choice of consort, chose Alude (qv); died of smallpox 3 Jan 1875 having reinstated Ci An (qv) and Ci Xi as regents; Ci Xi believed guilty of ordering his infection.

TUAN FANG: Manchu acting-governor, Shaanxi; without knowing of viceroys' support defied edicts to kill, saved lives of hundreds of foreigners, Christians; became a viceroy, supported reform, 1911 revolution.

TUAN QIRUI (T'uan Ch'i-jui): premier under Pres. Li Yüanhong, 1916; on his own responsibility declared war on Germany, 14 May 1917; dismissed; after abortive restoration of Pu Yi emp. (qv) July 1–12 1917, premier again; negotiated Japanese loan for WWI war effort and used it against Sun Yatsen (qv) and Constitution Protection Movement.

TUAN, Prince: Manchu 'evil genius'; ruthless ally of Ci Xi (qv); provided 8,000 men to reinforce Boxers; 10 June 1900 Pres. of Zongli Yamen; forged an ultimatum 'by foreign envoys', swayed Ci Xi to attack; Tuan offered 500 taels per dead foreigner; escaped from Beijing with Court; 25 Sept 1900 sent for trial.

WANG CUANYI (Wang Ts'uan-i or Tsung-i): Christian ex-soldier; evangelist with Cecil Polhill; volunteered to be flogged instead of Polhills; East Sichuan evangelist.

WANG LAE-DJÜN: Ningbo Mission convert; with JHT in London 1860–64, taught systematically, always practised indigenous church principles; pastor, Hangzhou, Zhejiang, until death, Sept 1901; daughter m Ren Chengyüan (qv).

WANG LANBU: doorkeeper for Swedish Mission, Soping, Shanxi; survived massacre, June 24 1900; took news to Tianjin, arr Oct 19.

WANG MINGDAO: 'man of iron', son of Dr Wang Dehao who took his own life during Beijing siege; born in Prince Su's (qv) palace, 25 July 1900; school name, Wang Yong-sheng; a preacher from age 22; edited *Spiritual Food*

Quarterly; 1950 attacked by TSPM leaders; arrested midnight 7 Aug 1954, wife also, imprisoned; 1970 labour camp, Datong, Shanxi; released May 1979.

WENG TONGHO: Imperial Grand Tutor to Guang Xü emp; 1889 commended Kang Yuwei (qv), reformer, so degraded by Ci Xi (qv).

WEN XIANG: Manchu; Grand Secretary of the Imperial Council; used delaying tactics with T. F. Wade, British minister; d 26 May, 1876.

WU, Colporteur: Bible Society; 1879 to Manchuria with James Cameron.

WU DINGFANG: Chinese ambassador to Washington; conveyed Major E. H. Conger's coded report of impending massacre, Peking; key to rescue.

XI (*see* Hsi).

XI LIAO-ZHU (Hsi Liao-chu, Hsi Sheng-mo) (1835–96): graduate (Xiucai) of Shanxi (Shansi); 1879 converted through David Hill; hymn writer, well-known as 'Pastor Hsi'.

XIAN FENG (Hsien Feng) (1851–61): 7th Qing (Ch'ing) dynasty emperor.

XÜ GUANG-QI (Hsü Kuang-ch'i, Paul Hsü): Ming dynasty official; convert of Matthew Ricci before 1610; 1850 his family home Xu Jia Wei (Siccawei) became Jesuit headquarters, near Shanghai.

XÜ JINGCHENG: with Yüan Zhang (qv) government minister; altered Ci Xi's (qv) edict telegrams from 'kill' to 'protect'; savagely executed.

XÜ PUYÜAN: leading Shanxi church elder; survived Boxer rising with Qü (qv) and Si (qv); met D. E. Hoste (qv) investigators; negotiated with Gov Ceng (qv) reparations for Christian Boxer victims, property.

YAO, Evangelist: 1880 crossed Hunan to Guizhou with Baller (qv), Trench (qv), Mrs Wm McCarthy (qv), J. Kidd (qv).

YAO SHANGDA, (possibly Yao Sifu): colporteur; 1877 crossed Hunan to Guiyang, Guizhou, with Judd (qv) and Broumton (qv); again with Judd Oct 1880; 1881 travelled with Adam Dorward.

YAO SIFU, (possibly Yao Shangda): Hunanese Christian converted in Jiangxi; accompanied missionaries; expelled from Yueyang, Hunan.

YAO Xianseng: Nanjing teacher; 1876 to Shanxi with J. J. Turner (qv), F. James (qv).

YANG CUNLING: (Yang Ts'un-ling) ex-soldier; evangelist; 1877 with J.McCarthy (qv) in Yichang riot; on foot Yichang to Bhamo and back; strong bond with JHT.

YANG SHAOTANG: son of one of the first Christians at Qüwu, Shanxi; born during persecutions of 1900; became Qüwu pastor; 1934 formed Ling Gong Tuan (Spiritual Action Team); 1948 China Bible Seminary, Shanghai.

YAN XISHAN (Yen Hsi-shah): 'model governor' of Shanxi after 1911–12 revolution; resisted Yüan Shikai's (qv) attempt to seize power, be emperor.

YE MING-SHENG (Yeh Ming-shen), imperial commissioner and viceroy, Canton; 1856–57 *Arrow* incident and Br. attack on Canton, captured, d Calcutta.

YEHONALA (*see* Ci Xi).

YONG LU: Manchu imperial bannerman related to Ci Xi (qv); counsellor to Tong Zhi emperor; 1875 protected Ci Xi in her coup; loyal even when disgraced; became Viceroy of Zhili, Senior Guardian of the Throne, but supported Ci Xi's (qv) coup 22 Sept 1898 deposing Guang Xü (qv); resisted 1900 attempts to exterminate foreigners; wisest statesman after *Li* Hongzhang (qv); d 11 April 1903.

YONG SAM-TEK: Chinese mandarin in London, 1805; taught Chinese to Morrison; later helped him in Canton.

YONG ZHENG: trustworthy Christian eyewitness, reported on N Shanxi Boxer events.

YÜ, Captain: 1860 heard part gospel from Taipings; 1875 converted through Wang Lae-djün (qv); carried gospel to Yüshan, Jiangxi—beginning of Guangxin River churches.

YUAN BAOHENG: 1878 High Commissioner for Famine Relief, Taiyuan, Shanxi; well disposed towards Richard (qv), Hill (qv), Whiting (qv) who died; himself died of 'famine fever'.

YÜAN SHIKAI: Chinese Resident, Seoul, 1894; governor of Shandong after Yü *Xian* (qv) viceroy of Zhili after *Li* Hongzhang (qv); negotiated abdication of last emperor, Pu Yi (qv), 1911–12; tried to seize power; President of new republic 10 March 1912; schemed to become emperor 1915; d 6 June 1916.

YÜAN ZHANG: with Xü Jingcheng (qv) heroically changed 'kill' edict telegrams to 'protect'; executed.

YÜ MANZI: anti-Catholic, anti-foreign, Sichuan outlaw, 1896–98.

YÜ XIAN: Gov of Shandong, encouraged Boxers' murder of foreigners; deposed but appointed Gov of Shanxi; recruited Boxers; 'Butcher of Shanxi', executed hundreds; himself executed on Ci Xi's orders.

ZEN YÜYING (Tsen): governor of Yunnan, savagely ended Muslim rebellion.

ZENG GUOCHUAN: brother of viceroy Zeng Guofan (qv); governor of Shanxi during Great Famine of 1878–79; welcomed relief teams.

ZENG, Marquis: son of viceroy Zeng Guofan; 1879 ambassador to France, Russia, Britain; 1880 negotiated favourable treaty with Russia over Ili after Chonghou (qv) debacle; author *The Sleep and the Awakening*.

ZENG GUOFAN (Tsang Kuo-fan) (1811–72): scholar, provincial governor; 1854 defeated Taipings; viceroy of the 'Two Jiangs' (Jiangxi, Jiangsu and Anhui), then of Zhili (Chihli); 1870 after Ma Xinyi assassination returned Nanjing; d. 11 March, 1872.

ZHANG (Chang): colporteur with LMS; 1875 with M. Henry Taylor to Henan; expelled from Queshan (Choshan); possibly the Zhang with Yao Shangda (qv), Judd (qv), Broumton (qv).

ZHANG SUOLIANG (also referred to as Jiang and Tsiang): pastor at Zhenjiang, Jiangsu; travelled with CIM pioneers.

ZHANG XIAOFENG (*see* JIANG).

ZHANG XÜELIANG (Chang Hsueh-Gang): son of Zhang Zuolin (qv); 'Young Marshal', arrested Chiang Kaishek (qv) Xi'an, 1936, precipitating joint action against Japan, expansion of Communism.

ZHANG ZHIBEN (Chang Chihpen): 1885–86 leading Buddhist priest; converted with Qü (qv) through reading Mark's Gospel; beaten unconscious by magistrate; church leader, Daning; Shanxi; survived Boxer rising; pastor.

ZHANG ZHITONG (Chang Chih-t'ung): Governor of Shanxi, 1882–84; viceroy of Guangxi-Guangdong, 1884–90; viceroy of Hunan-Hubei (Wuchang), 1890–1909 with interlude at Nanjing (Anhui); scholar, author, *Learn*; with other Yangzi valley and south and west China viceroys resisted Ci Xi's (qv) edicts, protected foreigners; reformer; co-plenipotentiary with *Li* Hongzhang (qv), Prince Qing (qv).

ZHANG ZUOLIN (Chang Tso-lin): northern warlord, father of 'Young Marshal' Zhang Xüeliang (qv); with Wu Peifu last of old power-seeking veterans; subdued by Chiang Kaishek, 1928, Northern Expedition.

ZHONG WANG (Chung Wang): Taiping 'Loyal Prince'; military strategist, commander in final successes, 1863–64, before defeat ending rebellion.

ZHOU ENLAI (Chou En-lai) (1898–1976): with Mao and Chiang Kaishek joined Sun Yatsen's Nationalists, Canton, (Guomindang); joined Mao in breakaway 1926 during Northern Expedition; 1936 with Zhang Xüeliang (qv) negotiated terms of Chiang Kaishek's release; foreign minister of People's Republic 1949–58; premier 1949–76.

ZHOU FU (Chou Fu): Provincial treasurer, Sichuan, persuaded viceroy Gui Zhen to suppress edicts to kill; *daotai* of Zhili; old friend of T. Richard (qv); governor of Shandong; viceroy of Jiangxi, Jiangsu, Anhui (Nanjing); of Guangdong, Guangxi (Canton); supported T. Richard's appointment to negotiate Shanxi reparations; 'of all Chinese officials he was the most lovable,' (T. Richard).

ZHU (Chu): Christian who travelled with M .Henry Taylor, expelled from Queshan (Choshan), Henan.

ZHU DE (Chu Teh) (1886–1976):1928 joined Mao in Jiangxi soviet; commander-in-chief, Red Army 1931, on Long March, 1935–36, to Yan'an, Shaanxi; leading politician, statesman of PRC (1959–76).

ZHU JIU-DAO (Chu Chiu-tao): Taiping rebel leader; planned anti-Manchu, pro-Ming revolt; joined Hong Xiu-quan (qv) to wage Taiping rebellion.

ZUO ZONGTANG (Tsuo Tsung-t'ang): one of China's greatest generals; quelled Muslim north-western rebellion ;1875 sowed and reaped harvest for troops, Hami; reached Kashgar 1876; quelled Yakub Beg (qv) forces; viceroy of Gansu-Shaanxi; and later of Nanjing.

Bibliography

Note: British Library references appear in square brackets.

ADENEY, David H. *China: Christian Students Face the Revolution.* SU Book Centre, Singapore 1973

—*China: The Church's Long March.* Regal Books/OMF Publishers, Singapore 1985

AITKEN, J. T. Fuller, H. W. C, and Johnson, D. *The Influence of Christians in Medicine.* Christian Medical Fellowship, London 1984

ATLAS of China. *Zhonghua Renmin Gongheguo Fen Sheng Dituji.* Ditu Chubanshe, Beijing (Chinese People's Republic Provincial Atlas)

BABER, E. Colborne. *Supplementary Papers of the Royal Geographical Society,* 'Travels and Researches in Western China'. John Murray, London 1882

—*Journal of the RGS* XLIX, 1884, pp 421 ff

BALL, Richard. *Handbook of China.* OMFA 11, 1854

B&FB Society. *Monthly Reporter,* Vols 1 & 2, 1858-88 [London III, pp. 926 ff.]

BARBER, W. T. A. *David Hill: Missionary and Saint.* Charles H. Kelley, London 1903

BARRETT, David B. See *International Bulletin of Missionary Research*

BEAUCHAMP, Montagu Harry Proctor. *Days of Blessing in Inland China: An Account of Meetings held in Shan-Si.* Morgan and Scott London 1890

BECKMAN, E. R. *The Massacre at Sianfu.* Personal 1913

BENTLEY-TAYLOR, David. *Java Saga: Christian Progress in Muslim Java (The Weathercock's Reward).* CIM/OMF Books 1967/1975

—*My Love must Wait.* Hodder & Stoughton

BERESFORD, C. W. D. *The Break-up of China, 1899.* [8022.dd.32]

BISHOP, Isabella Bird. *The Yangtze Valley and Beyond.* John Murray 1899 /Virago Press Ltd 1985

BONG RIN RO (ed). *Christian Alternatives to Ancestor Practice.* Asian Theological Association 1985

BOONE, M. Muriel. *The Seed of the Church in China.* St Andrew Press, Edinburgh 1973

BOSSHARDT, R. A. *The Restraining Hand: Captivity for Christ in China.* Hodder & Stoughton 1936

BOTHAM, Mrs Mark. *Two Pioneers: Thomas and Mark Botham.* CIM/RTS 1924

BREDON, Juliet, *Sir Robert Hart.* Hutchinson & Co 1909 [010817.de.10]

BRIDGMAN, Mrs E. J. G. *The Life and Labors of Elijah Coleman Bridgman.* 1864

BRIDGMAN, Elijah C. & Eliza J. G. *The Pioneer of American Missions in China.* 1864 [4985. aaa.27]

BRINE, Lindsay. *The Taiping Rebellion.* 1862 [9056.b.10]

BROOMHALL, Benjamin. *The Evangelisation of the World.* CIM 1889

BROOMHALL, Marshall. *Archibald Orr Ewing, That Faithful and Wise Steward.* China Inland Mission 1930

—*Faith and Facts, as Illustrated in the History of the China Inland Mission.* CIM 1909

—*F. W. Baller, A Master of the Pencil.* CIM 1923

—*Heirs Together: A Memoir of Benjamin & Amelia Broomhall.* Morgan & Scott/CIM 1918 [4908. e.6]

—*Islam in China.* Marshall, Morgan & Scott/CIM 1910

—*John W. Stevenson: One of Christ's Stalwarts.* Morgan & Scott/CIM 1919 [4956.aa.33]

—*Hudson Taylor: The Man who Dared.* Religious Tract Society/CIM [4907.aa.34]

—*Hudson Taylor: The Man who Believed God.* Hodder & Stoughton 1929 [4907.dd.21]

—*Last Letters and Further Records of Martyred Missionaries of the China Inland Mission.* Morgan & Scott/CIM 1901

—*Marshal Feng: A Good Soldier of Christ Jesus.* CIM/RTS 1923

—*Martyred Missionaries of the China Inland Mission, with a Record of the Perils and Sufferings of Some who Escaped.* Morgan & Scott/CIM 1901

—*Our Seal: The Witness of the CIM to the Faithfulness of God.* CIM/RTS 1933

—*Pioneer Work in Hunan by Adam Dorward and Other Missionaries of the China Inland Mission.* Morgan & Scott/CIM 1906

—*Present-Day Conditions in China: Notes Designed to Show the Moral and Spiritual Claims of the Chinese Empire.* CIM 1908

—*W. W. Cassels, First Bishop in Western China.* CIM 1926

—*Robert Morrison: A Master-builder.* CIM 1924 [4908.ee.24]

—*The Jubilee Story of the China Inland Mission.* Morgan & Scott/CIM 1915 [4763.g:4]

—*Hudson Taylor's Legacy.* Hodder & Stoughton 1931 [10823.a.16]

—*By Love Compelled: The Call of the China Inland Mission.* CIM 1947 (H & S 1936) [4768.a.34]

—*The Chinese Empire: A General & Missionary Survey.* Morgan & Scott/CIM 1907 [4767. eeee.4]

BROOMHALL, Marshall and F. A. KELLER. *Concerning Hunan and Changsha.* CIM 1910

BROWNE, Stanley G. et al. *Heralds of Health: The Saga of Christian Medical Initiatives.* Christian

Medical Fellowship 1985

BRYANT, Sir Arthur. *A Thousand Years of the British Monarchy.* Collins 1957

BURNS, Islay. *Memoir of the Reverend William Chalmers Burns.* London 1885

CABLE, Mildred and FRENCH, Francesca. *The Gobi Desert.* Hodder & Stoughton 1943 (ten reprints, and Landsborough Publications Ltd 1958 pocketbook)

—*Through Jade Gate and Central Asia.* Constable 1927

—*Something Happened.* Hodder & Stoughton 1933

—*A Desert Journal, Letters from Central Asia.* Constable 1934 (with Evangeline French)

—*The Making of a Pioneer: Percy Mather of Central Asia.* Hodder & Stoughton 1934

—*George Hunter: Apostle of Turkestan.* CIM 1948

—*Wall of Spears.* Lutterworth Press 1951

CARY-ELWES, Columba. *China and the Cross.* Longmans, Green & Co 1957 [4768.ccc.21]

Chinese Evangelization Society. REPORT 1853. OMFA (Archives of OMF)

CHEFOO MAGAZINE, THE. Organ of the Chefoo Schools Association, Vol 1 No 1, Christmas 1908, Vol 81 No 2 Christmas 1988

CHEFUSIAN, THE. Journal of the Chefoo Schools Association, Vol 79, No 2, December 1986

CHINA MAIL (Hong Kong). [British Library, Colindale]

CHINA'S MILLiONS. Magazine of the China Inland Mission 1875–1951

CHINESE RECORDER AND MISSIONARY JOURNAL. Vols 1–3, 5–12 (May 1868–May 1871), editor Justus Doolittle; Vol 5 bi-monthly Jan–Dec 1874 (after 2-year interlude)–Vol 12, 1881

CHINESE REPOSITORY, THE. Canton 1832–42

CLARKE Agnes L. *The Boy from Shoreditch.* OMF Books, Clipper Series

—*China's Man of the Book.* OMF Books (68 pp).

CLARKE, Samuel R. *Among the Tribes of South-West China.* CIM/Morgan & Scott 1905

CLARK-KENNEDY, A.E. *'The London' (Hospital)* (2 vols). [9059.df.15]

CMS, *CM Gleaner, Intelligencer, Register, Reports.* Church Missionary Society

COAD, F. Roy. *A History of the Brethren Movement.* The Paternoster Press 1968

COATES, P. D. *The China Consuls: British Consular Officers in China 1843–1943.* OUP (Hong Kong) 1988

COLE, R.A. *The Gospel according to St Mark,* Tyndale Commentary. The Tyndale Press 1961

COLLIER, Richard. *William Booth: The General Next to God.* Collins 1965 [X.100.1629]

COLLIS, Maurice Stewart. *Foreign Mud.* 1946 [9059.df.15]

COLQUHOUN, Archibald R., *Across Chryse, from Canton to Mandalay* (2 vols). Sampson Low, Marston, Searle & Rivington, London 1883; *Journal of the RGS* IV, p 713

CORDIER, Henri. *The Life of Alexander Wylie.* 1887 [10803.cc.4/6]

—*Histoire des Rélations de la Chine avec les Puissances Occidentales 1860–1900* (3 vols). Ch'eng-Wen Publishing, 1966

COVELL, Ralph. *Confucius, The Buddha and Christ, a History of the Gospel in Chinese.* Orbis Books 1986 (USA)

—*W. A. P. Martin, Pioneer of Progress in China.* Wm B. Eerdmans Publishing Company 1978

CROSSMAN, Eileen. *Mountain Rain: A New Biography of James O. Frase.,* OMF Books 1982

DAVIES, Evan. *China and her Spiritual Claims.* John Snow 1845 [1369.b.24]

—*Memoir of the Reverend Samuel Dyer.* John Snow 1846 [1372.c.20]

DAYS OF BLESSING in Inland China, being an Account of Meetings held in the Province of Shansi (compiled). Morgan & Scott 1887

DU BUSE, H.C. *The Dragon Image and Demon: The Three Religions of China.* A.C. Armstrong (USA) 1887

DYSON, Verne. *A Hong Kong Governor: Sir John Bowring.* Macao 1930 [010822.df.39]

EAMES, James Bromby. *The Englishman in China – as illustrated in the life of Sir Rutherford Alcock.* 1909 [09008.f.19]

EDGAR, J. Huston. *The Marches of the Mantze.* CIM 1908

FAIRBANK, John King. *Trade and Diplomacy on the China Coast* (2 vols). 1953 edn Cambridge, Massachusetts [Ac.2692.10]

—(ed). *The Cambridge History of China.* CUP 1978–, multi-volume.

FORBES, Archibald. *Chinese Gordon.* George Routledge & Sons 1884

FOREIGN OFFICE LIBRARY, Public Records Office. *A Century of Diplomatic Blue Books.* China FO/17

FOREIGN OFFICE LIBRARY China, FO/ 17, Public Records Office

FORSYTH, Robert C. *The China Martyrs of 1900.* Religious Tract Society 1904

FOSTER, John. *The Nestorian Tablet and Hymns.* SPCK

FULLERTON, W. Y. and WILSON, C. E. Report of the China Missions of the Baptist Missionary Society. BM House, London 1908

GLEANER, CES, *The Gleaner in the Missionary Field, The Chinese & General Missionary Gleaner, The Chinese Missionary Gleaner.* Chinese Evangelization Society 1850–60 OMFA

GILL, William. *The River of Golden Sand: The Narrative of a Journey through China and Eastern Tibet to Burmah, with an Introductory Essay by Col Henry Yule,* CB, RE (2 vols). John Murray 1880

GLOVER, A. E. *A Thousand Miles of Miracle in China.* CIM 1904, 20th edn 1944; abridged by L.T. Lyall 1957, reprinted 1962, 1965, 1971

GOFORTH, Rosalind. *Goforth of China.* Marshall, Morgan & Scott 1937

GREEN, C. H. S. *In Deaths Oft.* CIM 1901, reprinted 1912, 1923, 1936 (27,000 copies)

GRIST, W. A. *Samuel Pollard, Pioneer Missionary in China.* Cassell & Co., Ltd (undated)

GRUBB, Norman P. *C. T. Studd, Cricketer and Pioneer.* Religious Tract Society 1933

GROVES, Mrs. *Memoir of the late Anthony Norris Groves.* 2nd edn 1857

GUINNESS, Joy. *Mrs Howard Taylor: Her Web of Time.* CIM 1949

GUINNESS, M. Geraldine. *The Story of the China Inland Mission* (2 vols). Morgan & Scott, London 1893

GUTZLAFF, Charles. *A Journal of Three Voyages along the Coast of China in 1831, 1832 & 1833 with notices of Siam, Corea and the Loochoo Islands.* 1833 [1046.c.16]

—Report of Proceedings on a Voyage to the Northern Ports China (see LINDSAY, H.H.). 1833 [1046.c.15]

GUY'S HOSPITAL GAZETTE. Centenary Number

HACKNEY GAZETTE. North London: Historical Associations. 1928

HALDANE, Charlotte. *The Last Great Empress of China.* Constable 1965

HALL, Capt. Basil, RN. *Narrative of a Voyage to Java, China and the Great Loochoo Island.* Edward Moxen 1818 [982.1.16]; 1840 edn [G.15729]

HART, Sir Robert. *These from the Land of Sinim.* [8022.cc.48 / 010817.d.10]

HOLT, Edgar C. *The Opium Wars in China.* 1964 edn [X.709-581]

HOOK, Brian et al. *China's Three Thousand Years: The Modern History of China.* The Times Newspapers Limited 1973

HOPKIRK, Peter. *Foreign Devils on the Silk Road: The Search for the Lost Cities and Treasures of Chinese Central Asia.* Oxford University Press 1984

—*Trespassers on the Roof of the World: the Race for Lhasa.* John Murray 1982

HOSIE, Alexander. *Three Years in Western China: A Narrative of Three Journeys.* George Philip & Son, London 1890

HOUGHTON, Frank. *George King: Medical Evangelist.* CIM 1930

—*The Two Hundred.* CIM 1932

HOUGHTON, Stanley et al. *Chefoo.* CIM 1931

HUC, Evariste Régis, Abbé. *Christianity in China, Tartary and Thibet.* 1857 [2208.bb.8]

—*High Road in Tartary: The Story of a Celebrated Journey from Peking to Lhasa,* 1867 [10057.aa.39]

—*Travels in Tartary and Thibet.* Herbert Joseph 1937

HUGGETT, Frank E. *Victorian England as seen by PUNCH.* Sidgwick & Johnson 1978

HSÜ, Immanuel C. Y. *The Rise of Modern China.* (2nd Edn) OUP 1975

INTERNATIONAL BULLETIN OF MISSIONARY RESEARCH. Annual Statistical Table on Global Mission. 1987 (David B Barrett)

HUMBLE, Richard. *Marco Polo.* Weidenfeld and Nicolson 1975

JOHNSON, Douglas. *Contending for the Faith: a History of the Evangelical Movement in the Universities and Inter-Varsity College.* IVP 1979

JOHNSTON, James. *Report of the Centenary Conference on Protestant Missions.* London 1888 (BL 4766.ee.13)

JUDD, Frederik H. (ed). 'A History of the China Inland Mission School at Chefoo, China (1880-1942)'. *The Chefoo Schools Association Magazine* 79, no 2, December 1986, pp 3-39

KNOLLYS, Sir Henry. *Incidents in the China War, 1860* [9056.bb.19]

—*English Life in China.* 1885 [10058.e.31]

INGLIS, Brian. *The Opium War.* Hodder & Stoughton 1976 [09059.pp.30]

KUHN, Isobel. *Green Leaf in Drought: The Story of the Escape of the Last CIM Missionaries from Communist China* (Rupert Clarke, Arthur Mathews). CIM/OMF 1954

LATOURETTE, Kenneth Scott. *A History of Christian Missions in China.* SPCK 1929/Macmillan 1932 [4763.g.4]

—*A History of the Expansion of Christianity 1800–1914.* Eyre and Spottiswoode [4533.ff.22]

—*These Sought a Country* (Drew University Tipple Lectures, 1950). Edn Harper & Brothers [4807.e.25]

LEGGE, Helen E. *James Legge (1815-97).* Religious Tract Society 1905 [04429.1.37]

LEGGE, James. *The Famine in China.* 1878 edn [11102.b.20]

—*The Nestorian Monument* (Oxford University Lecture). 1888 edn [4532.ee.13 / 14]

LINDSAY, H. H. *Report to the Hon. East India Company on a Voyage to the Northern Ports of China 1832* (voyage of the Lord Amherst).

LINTON, E. Lynn. 'A Night in a Hospital' (from magazine *Belgravia*). 1879

LITTLE, Alicia Bewicke. *Li Hung-chang, His Life and Times.* Cassell & Co. Ltd 1903

LOANE, Marcus. *The Story of the China Inland Mission in Australia and New Zealand.* CIM/OMF 1965

LOCKHART, William. *The Medical Missionary in China.* 1861 edn [10058.d.16]

LUBBOCK, Basil. *The China Clippers.* 1914

LYALL, L. T. *John Sung, A Flame for God.* CIM 1954

—*Come Wind, Come Weather.* Hodder & Stoughton 1961

—*A Passion for the Impossible,* Hodder & Stoughton 1965; OMF Books 1976

—*Red Sky at Night.* Hodder & Stoughton 1969

—*Three of China's Mighty Men.* OMF Books 1973

—*New Spring in China.* Hodder & Stoughton 1979

—*God Reigns in China.* Hodder & Stoughton 1985

McCARTHY, John. 'Across China from Chinkiang to Bhamo'. *Proceedings of the Royal*

Geographical Society, Vol 1 Aug 1879, No 8, pp 127, 489 seq

MacGILLIVRAY, Donald. *A Century of Protestant Missions in China* (Centennial Conference Historical Volume). Shanghai 1907 [4764. ff.11]

MacGREGOR, David R. *The Tea Clippers: Sailing Ships of the Nineteenth Century.* London 1952

McGILVARY, Daniel. *A Half-Century among the Siamese and the Lao.* Fleming, Revell & Co. 1912

McNEUR, George Hunter. *Liang A-fa.* Oxford University Press China Agency 1934

MARTIN, W.A.P. *A Cycle of Cathay.* 1896 [010056. g.7]

MEDHURST, W.H., senior. *China: Its State and Prospects.* John Snow 1838 [571.g.10]

—*A Glance at the Interior of China in 1845.* Shanghai Mission Press 1849 [10055.c.25]

MEDHURST, Sir W.H., junior. *Curiosities of Street Literature in China.* 1871 [10057.aaa.16]

—*The Foreigner in Far Cathay.* Edward Stanton 1872 [010058.ee.35]

MICHIE, Alexander. *Missionaries in China.* Edward Stanford, 1891 edn [4767.ccc.10]

—*The Englishman in China: as illustrated in the Career of Sir Rutherford Alcock.* Wm Blackwood & Sons, 1900 edn (2 vols). [09057.d.3]

MINAMIKI, George S. J. *The China Rites Controversy from its Beginning to Modern Times.* Loyola University Press 1985

MORRIS, E. W. *The London Hospital.* Edward Arnold 1910

MORRISON, Mrs Robert. *Memoirs of Robert Morrison* (2 vols). Longmans 1839

MORSE, Hosea Ballou. *The International Relations of the Chinese Empire* (9 vols) Vols I–III. 1910 [2386.c.17]

—*The Trade and Administration of the Chinese Empire.* Longman, London 1908

MOULE, Arthur E. *The Story of the Cheh-Kiang Mission.* CMS 1879

—'Recollections of the Taiping Rebellion', lecture, Shanghai, Dec 1883. *Chinese Recorder* (?), 1884

MOULE, Handley C. G. *Charles Simeon.* 1892, first IVF Edn 1948

MÜLLER, George (ed. G.F. Bergin). *Autobiography: Narrative.* Jas Nisbet & Co. Ltd. 1905

NEATBY, Mrs Thomas. *The Life and Ministry of Thomas Neatby.* Pickering & Inglis

NEILL, Stephen C. *A History of Christian Missions* (*Pelican History of the Church* 6). Penguin Books 1964

—*Colonialism and Christian Missions* (*Foundations of Christian Mission* Series). Lutterworth Press, 1966

NEILL, Stephen C. et al. *Concise Dictionary of the Christian World Mission.* United Society for Christian Literature, London 1971

NEVIUS, Helen S. C. *The Life of John Livingston Nevius,* Revell 1895 [4985.eee.5]

NORTH CHINA DAILY NEWS (newspaper). [British Library, Colindale]

NORTH CHINA HERALD (newspaper). 1854 *et seq* [British Library, Colindale]

ORR, J. Edwin. *The Second Evangelical Awakening in Britain.* Marshall, Morgan & Scott 1949

OVERSEAS Missionary Fellowship Archives (OMFA)

PADWICK, Constance E. *Mackay of the Great Lakes.* London 1917

—*Henry Martyn: Confessor of the Faith.* Inter-Varsity Fellowship 1922

PARLEY, Peter. *China and the Chinese.* Simpkin Marshall 1843 [10058.a.26]

PARLIAMENTARY PAPERS: Foreign Office Blue Books. Official Publications Office

PARLIAMENTARY PAPERS 1831–32 Vols VII, X, XI, XXXVI, XLI (*see* Foreign Office 1840-60, Opium Wars), 1857 XLIII relating to the opium trade with China

PIERSON, A.T. *George Müller of Bristol.* Jas Nisbet & Co. Ltd. 1905

POLHILL-TURNERs, Arthur and Cecil. 'Two Etonians in China'. Unpublished manuscript, OMF archives

POLLOCK, John C. *The Cambridge Seven, A Call to Christian Service.* Inter-Varsity Fellowship 1955, Centenary Edition, Marshalls 1985

—*Hudson Taylor & Maria.* Hodder & Stoughton

—*Moody without Sankey, A New Biographical Portrait.* Hodder & Stoughton 1963

POLO, Marco. *The Book of Ser Marco Polo, The Venetian.* 1298, First printed edition 1477 (*see* YULE)

POTT, F. L. HAWKS. *A Short History of Shanghai.* Kelly & Walsh 1928 [010056.aaa.46]

PUNCH. *PUNCH Panorama 1845-65* (*see* HUGGETT, F.E.).

RATTENBURY, Harold B. *David Hilt, Friend of China.* Epworth Press 1949

REAVELY, Wm. *Reminiscences of the late Adam C. Dorward, Missionary to China.* 1904

ROWDON, H. H. *The Origins of the Brethren.* Pickering & Inglis 1967

ROYAL GEOGRAPHICAL SOCIETY. *Journal* IV, p 713 'The South China Borderlands', Colquhoun; Vol XLIX, pp 421 seq, Baber; Vol XLV III pp 57 seq, Gill; *Magazine* iii pp 493, 564; *Proceedings* X.485 'A Journey across Central Asia', Younghusband; *Supplementary Papers* Vol 1, Part 1, Baber: 'Travels and Researches in Western China'

SCHOFIELD, Alfred T. S. (ed). *Memorials of R. Harold A. Schofield (Late of the China Inland Mission): First Medical Missionary to Shan-Si.* China, Hodder & Stoughton 1898

SELLMAN, R. R. *An Outline Atlas of Eastern History.* Edward Arnold Ltd.

—*Sianfu: The Nestorian Tablet.* [WP.4683.49]

SMITH, Arthur H. *The Uplift of China.* The Young People's Missionary Movement of America, 1909

—*China in Convulsion* (2 vols). 1901 (facsimile reprint Irish University Press, 1972)

SOLTAU, Henry. 'A Journey from the Irrawaddy to the Yangtze', compiled by Wm Soltau from letters. *Journal of the RGS* III, pp 493, 564

SOOTHILL, William E. *Timothy Richard of China.* Seeley, Service & Co. Ltd, London 1924

STOTT, Grace. *Twenty-Six Years of Missionary Work in China.* Hodder & Stoughton 1897

STOCK, Eugene. *The History of the Church Missionary Society* Vols I–III, 1899–1916. [4765.cc.28]

TAYLOR, Dr and Mrs F. Howard. *By Faith; Henry W. Frost and the China Inland Mission.* CIM 1938

—*Hudson Taylor in Early Years: The Growth of a Soul.* CIM and RTS, 1911

—*Hudson Taylor and the China Inland Mission: The Growth of a Work of God* (2 vols). CIM and RTS 1918

—*Hudson Taylor's Spiritual Secret.* CIM, 1932

TAYLOR, Mrs Howard (see also Guinness, M. Geraldine). *Behind the Ranges: A Biography of J.O. Fraser.* CIM

—*Pastor Hsi: One of China's Scholars* (2 vols). CIM

—*Pastor Hsi, Confucian Scholar and Christian.* CIM 1900

—*The Triumph of John and Betty Stam.* CIM 1935

TAYLOR, F. Howard. *These Forty Years, A Short History of the China Inland Mission.* CIM/ Pepper Publ. Co., Philadelphia 1903

TAYLOR, J. Hudson. *China: Its Spiritual Need and Claims.* 1st–6th edns 1865 *et seq*, CIM; from 7th edn onwards it was called *China's Spiritual Need and Claims*, 7th edn 1887, CIM 8th edn 1890, CIM

—*A Retrospect.* 1875, CIM

—*After Thirty Years.* Morgan & Scott/CIM 1895

—'A Brief Account of the Progress of the China Inland Mission from May 1866 to May 1868', OMFA 3 Book 5

—'Summary of Operations of the CIM', OMFA 441.11

THOMAS, W. H. Griffith. *Principles of Theology.* The Church Book Room Press, London 1945

THOMPSON, Phyllis. *China: The Reluctant Exodus.* Hodder & Stoughton/OMF 1979

—*D. E. Hoste, A Prince with God.* CIM 1947

—*Proving God: Financial Experiences of the China Inland Mission.* CIM 1956

THOMPSON, R. Wardlaw. *Griffith John: The Story of Fifty Years in China.* The Religious Tract Society 1907

TORJESEN, Edvard P. *Fredrik Franson: A Model for Worldwide Evangelism.* William Carey Library 1983

WALEY, Arthur David. *The Opium War through Chinese Eyes.* London 1958 [09059.pp.30]

WANG, Mary. *The Chinese church that will not Die.* Hodder & Stoughton 1972

WEISE, J. 'The Early History and Development of the Berlin Missionary Work in South China'. *Chinese Recorder*, 1925, paper read at Canton Missionary Conference, 29 March 1924.

WHITEHOUSE, S. F. *Items of Interest: an informal record of the General Missionary Conference and subsequent CIM Conference, May 26–28, 1890.* CIM

WILLIAMS, Fredk Wells. *The Life and Letters of Samuel Wells Williams, LL D, Missionary, Diplomatist, Sinologue. G P*, Putman & Sons, New York and London 1889

WILLIAMS, Samuel Wells. *The Middle Kingdom.* 1847

—*History of China. Being the Historical Chapter from 'The Middle Kingdom'.* 1897

WANG MINGDAO. *A Stone Made Smooth.* Christian Mayflower Books 1981

WOODCOCK, George. *The British in the Far East* (A Social History of the British Overseas). Weidenfeld & Nicholson 1969

WURTZBURG, C. E. *Raffles of the Eastern Isles.* Hodder & Stoughton 1954

YOUNGHUSBAND, Francis. *The Heart of a Continent*, also abridged as *Among the Celestials.* John Murray, London 1898

—*Proceedings of the RGS* X, p 485: 'Journey Across Central Asia'.

YULE, Sir Henry. *The Book of Ser Marco Polo, the Venetian* (2 vols). 1878

—Introduction to Gill, W. *River of Golden Sand.*